American Jewish Year Book

The American Jewish Committee acknowledges with appreciation the foresight and wisdom of the founders of the Jewish Publication Society (of America) in the creation of the AMERICAN JEWISH YEAR BOOK in 1899, a work committed to providing a continuous record of developments in the U.S. and world Jewish communities. For over a century JPS has occupied a special place in American Jewish life, publishing and disseminating important, enduring works of scholarship and general interest on Jewish subjects.

The American Jewish Committee assumed responsibility for the compilation and editing of the YEAR BOOK in 1908. The Society served as its publisher until 1949; from 1950 through 1993, the Committee and the Society were co-publishers. In 1994 the Committee became the sole publisher of the YEAR BOOK.

American Jewish Year Book 2008

VOLUME 108

Editors
DAVID SINGER
LAWRENCE GROSSMAN

AMERICAN JEWISH COMMITTEE
NEW YORK

Hardcover Edition ISBN 978-0-87495-145-5
Trade Paperback ISBN 978-0-87495-146-2

Library of Congress Catalogue Number: 99–4040

PRINTED IN THE UNITED STATES OF AMERICA

Preface

The year 2008 marks six decades since the creation of the State of Israel. The YEAR BOOK marks this anniversary with a special article by Prof. Jack Wertheimer, "American Jews and Israel: A 60-Year Retrospective," which offers a sweeping and original analysis of how American Jewry has been affected by the reemergence of Jewish sovereignty in the ancient Jewish homeland.

In its regular articles, the volume covers the events of 2007. The YEAR BOOK's coverage of American Jewish life includes treatments of national affairs, Jewish communal affairs, and American Jewish population trends. The article on Israel and those about other Jewish communities around the world chronicle important events and trends. Updated demographic data are provided in the article on world Jewish population. Carefully compiled directories of national Jewish organizations, periodicals, and federations and welfare funds, as well as religious calendars and obituaries, round out the volume.

We gratefully acknowledge the assistance of our colleagues, Cyma M. Horowitz and Michele Anish, of the American Jewish Committee's Blaustein Library, and the contribution of Rachel Kaufman, our assistant, in preparing the index.

THE EDITORS

Contributors

TOBY AXELROD: Correspondent, Jewish Telegraphic Agency and *Jewish Chronicle* (London); Berlin, Germany.

ARNOLD DASHEFSKY: Doris and Simon Konover Chair of Jewish Studies, professor of sociology, and director, Center for Judaic Studies and Contemporary Jewish Life and Mandell L. Berman Institute-North American Jewish Data Bank, University of Connecticut.

SERGIO DELLAPERGOLA: Professor and head, Division of Jewish Demography and Statistics, Avraham Harman Institute of Contemporary Jewry, Hebrew University of Jerusalem, Israel; senior fellow, The Jewish People Policy Planning Institute.

BERNARD EDINGER: Former longtime international correspondent for Reuters; Paris, France.

ETHAN FELSON: Assistant director, Jewish Council for Public Affairs (JCPA); New York.

ELISE FRIEDMANN: Director of Anti-Semitism Research, CIDI, Center for Information and Documentation Israel; Amsterdam, Holland.

PAULINA GAMUS: Former minister of culture, senator, member of Congress, Venezuela; former vice president, Union of Jewish Associations in Venezuela; attorney, newspaper columnist; Caracas, Venezuela.

LAWRENCE GROSSMAN: Editor, AMERICAN JEWISH YEAR BOOK; associate director of research, American Jewish Committee.

RUTH ELLEN GRUBER: European-based American journalist and author, specialist in contemporary Jewish affairs; Morre, Italy.

MIRIAM L. KOCHAN: Freelance journalist and translator; Oxford, England.

LEV KRICHEVSKY: Bureau chief, Jewish Telegraphic Agency; Moscow, Russia.

COLIN L. RUBENSTEIN: Executive director, Australia/Israel and Jewish Affairs Council; honorary associate, Monash University; Melbourne, Australia.

GEORGES SCHNEK: President, Jewish Museum of Belgium; former president, Jewish Central Consistory of Belgium; emeritus professor of biochemistry, Free University of Brussels, Belgium.

MILTON SHAIN: Professor of Hebrew and Jewish studies, and director, Kaplan Centre for Jewish Studies and Research, University of Cape Town, South Africa.

HANAN SHER: Former senior editor, *The Jerusalem Report;* Jerusalem, Israel.

IRA M. SHESKIN: Associate professor of geography, and director, Jewish Demography Project of the Sue and Leonard Miller Center for Contemporary Judaic Studies, University of Miami.

MURRAY GORDON SILBERMAN: Adjunct professor, Austrian Diplomatic Academy, Vienna, Austria.

BRIGITTE SION: Former secretary general, CICAD, the Committee against anti-Semitism and Defamation; Geneva, Switzerland; assistant professor/faculty fellow, program in religion and School of Journalism, New York University.

HAROLD M. WALLER: Professor of political science, McGill University; director, Canadian Centre for Jewish Community Studies; Montreal, Canada.

JACK WERTHEIMER: Joseph and Martha Mendelson Professor of American Jewish History, Jewish Theological Seminary of America.

Contents

DIRECTORIES, LISTS, AND OBITUARIES

Special Article

American Jews and Israel: A 60-Year Retrospective*

By Jack Wertheimer

Ever since Israel's founding, American Jews have contended with the freighted symbolism and complex realities of the Jewish state. How could it be otherwise? After living for nearly two millennia as a minority, scattered across much of the globe and dependent upon the tolerance of host countries, Jews around the world have been confronted since 1948 with a radically novel situation: A Jewish state in the land of their ancestors, with a Jewish majority exercising sovereignty and considerable military might, not only conducting its life according to the rhythms of the Jewish calendar and in the revived Hebrew language, but also defining itself as the homeland of every Jew and as the defender of Jews around the world.

Israel's existence has proven especially challenging for American Jews. Citizens of the largest and most powerful democracy, Jews in the U.S. have felt a special responsibility to protect and aid Israel. Yet simultaneously, American Jews have also maintained undiminished allegiance and profound gratitude to their land of residence, whose ethos from its inception has been shaped by the belief that America is the new Promised Land.

The complexities began to dawn on some American Jews immediately upon Israel's creation in May 1948. Initially, the dominant question was how to think about Zionism once Israel had come into existence, an achievement that fulfilled the primary goal of the Zionist movement. Here is how the 27-year-old Rabbi Arthur Hertzberg framed the dilemma little more than a year later:

> What shall I do with my Zionism? I know that I am not alone with this problem, that it is now being much discussed. But I have yet to

*Several colleagues generously offered advice and assistance in the preparation of this essay. My thanks to Steven Bayme, Steven M. Cohen, Lawrence Grossman, Shaul Kelner, Eli Lederhendler, Alan Mintz, Ted Sasson, Boaz Tarsi, and Chaim I. Waxman.

> hear any suggestion that really hits the mark . . . . The experience of Israel, a nation in the making, is complex on the surface but in reality simple—it is the problem of getting on with the job . . . . The Diaspora has chosen to live on as such. How to make it live on creatively and how to maintain inner identity between it and Israel—these are the most important questions that face us today.[1]

Little wonder Hertzberg subtitled his article, "A Movement in Search of a Program."

Meanwhile, on the eastern shores of the Mediterranean, the political leadership of the new Jewish state was similarly struggling to find a way of reframing its relationship with American Jewry. The official Zionist ideology espoused by Israel's political elite "negated" the Diaspora, assuming that it was doomed to wither, and expected Diaspora communities to play a subordinate role to Israel in all Jewish affairs. Simultaneously, however, leaders of the newborn state were acutely aware of their dependence on American Jewish largess to help absorb immigrants and build Israel's infrastructure, and also hoped American Jews could influence their government to aid Israel. As a result, Israeli leaders issued contradictory messages to their American Jewish counterparts, sometimes pleading for more financial and political help and at other times berating them for not immigrating to Israel—in Zionist parlance, "making aliyah"—at so momentous a time in Jewish history, or at least sending their youth to the Jewish homeland.

Matters grew so tense that leaders of some American Jewish organizations insisted upon a formal agreement to clarify the proper relationship between the two sectors of the Jewish people.[2] In an orchestrated exchange of statements, David Ben-Gurion, Israel's first prime minister, and Jacob Blaustein, president of the American Jewish Committee, did just that in August 1950. They both agreed that American Jews would be "partners" with Israel, even as "the integrity of the two communities and their institutions" would be preserved. The primary role of American Jews was "to do their share in the rebuilding of Israel, which faces . . . enormous political, social and economic problems." American Jews would

---

[1]Arthur Hertzberg, "American Zionism at an Impasse," *Commentary* 8, October 1949, pp. 341, 345.

[2]The background to this historical clash and its resolution is traced in Zvi Ganin, *An Uneasy Relationship: American Jewish Leadership and Israel, 1948–57* (Syracuse, 2005), esp. chaps. 3–6.

provide philanthropic and political support. As for aliyah, Ben-Gurion swallowed his Zionist pride and limited himself to calling upon American Jews to offer "their technical knowledge, their unrivaled experience, their spirit of enterprise, their bold vision, their 'know-how,'" but immigrants would come to Israel only as "a matter of [their] own volition."[3]

While much attention has focused on Ben-Gurion's reduced expectations—particularly his backing away from calls for mass aliyah—the very demand by American Jewish leaders for such a statement of understanding signaled the highly unusual nature of the relationship between Israel and American Jewry. How often, after all, do citizens of one country ask the government of a foreign sovereign state to issue a public explanation of their relationship? Making the agreement even more noteworthy is the fact that the preponderant majority of Jews in the U.S. did not then, and still do not now, have any family members who had emigrated from modern Palestine/Israel. Blaustein, the AJC leader, was trying to work out an understanding between the Israeli government, on the one hand, and a population with no political or legal connection to the Jewish state, on the other, and the deal that emerged dramatized the extraordinary ties that would bind American Jews and Israel over the next six decades.[4]

Another aspect of this agreement also continues to resonate. When Israel was founded, some American Jewish leaders feared the charge of "dual loyalty." They therefore pressed Ben-Gurion to acknowledge explicitly that American Jews "have only one political attachment and that is to the United States of America," and to pledge not to "interfere in any way with the internal affairs of Jewish communities abroad." Ironically, the matter of interference would come to loom ever larger with the passage of time, in both communities. Israeli government officials and religious leaders have repeatedly pressured American Jewish groups to follow their

[3]"David Ben-Gurion and Jacob Blaustein: An Exchange of Views," *American Jewish Year Book* 53 (New York, 1952), pp. 564–68. At the time, AJC was the most prominent non-Zionist Jewish organization in the U.S. On the divisions between Zionist and non-Zionists leading up to the establishment of the Jewish state, see Menahem Kaufman, *An Ambiguous Partnership: Non-Zionists and Zionists in America, 1939–48* (Jerusalem, 1991).

[4]Charles S. Liebman, "Diaspora Influence on Israel: The Ben-Gurion–Blaustein 'Exchange' and Its Aftermath," *Jewish Social Studies* 36, July/October 1974, pp. 271, 276; Eli Lederhendler, "The Diaspora Factor in Israeli Life," in Anita Shapira, ed., *Israeli Identity in Transition* (Westport, Conn., 2004), p. 109.

lead on numerous issues, even as American Jews have increasingly intervened in internal Israeli affairs through their funding of political and social causes. What seemed a clear-cut taboo on mutual interference in the Ben-Gurion–Blaustein agreement has become ever more complex, as both parties try to maintain the fine and uncertain line between assistance and meddling.[5]

Indeed, many aspects of the relationship between Israel and American Jews have developed in unpredictable directions since the early years of statehood. The organized American Jewish community considerably expanded and deepened its involvement in funding Israeli ventures even as it engaged in a range of activities to lend political support to the Jewish state. Over time, what historian Zvi Ganin has called the "uneasy relationship" between American Jewish leaders and Israel has evolved into a partnership, albeit one sometimes marked by tensions and unpredictable turns. Through it all, the connection to Israel came to assume a far more prominent role in the public and private lives of American Jews, encompassing activities and preoccupations that no one could have anticipated in 1948.

This essay sketches in broad brushstrokes the multifaceted and rapidly changing nature of American Jewish engagement with Israel as it has evolved over the past six decades.[6] It begins with an often overlooked question—how pervasive is Israel in American Jewish religious, cultural, educational, and organizational life? This is followed by detailed discussion of how American Jews think and feel about Israel, the role Israel plays in Jewish public discourse and institutional life, and the debates it has engendered within American Jewish society, which have attracted much attention over the years because they serve as measures of strengthening or waning Jewish solidarity.

Two preliminary comments are in order. First, the period from

---

[5]Charles S. Liebman, *Pressure Without Sanctions: The Influence of World Jewry on Israeli Society* (Rutherford, N.J., 1977). A recent example is the investigation of Prime Minister Ehud Olmert for allegedly taking cash gifts from an American Jewish businessman, apparently the latest example of the common practice of American Jews bankrolling Israeli political groups and ideology-driven media operations. See Haviv Rettig, "PM Probe Embarrasses Diaspora," *Jerusalem Post,* July 18, 2008, http://www.jpost.com/servlet/Satellite?cid=1215331011991&pagename=JPost%2FJPArticle%2FShowFull

[6]The roughly 120,000 American Jews who have settled in Israel since 1948 are not included in this discussion.

1948 to the present has hardly been uniform. The Israeli reality encountered by American Jews shortly after the founding of the Jewish state has changed repeatedly in subsequent decades. American Jewish attitudes have shifted direction frequently in response to changing conditions on the ground in Israel and also within American Jewish society, and the focus of Israel-centered activities has varied from one decade to the next.

There seem to have been three watershed events that redirected American Jewish-Israeli relations since the creation of the state in 1948: the momentous transformation of Israel and its place in the world occasioned by the Six-Day War in 1967; the rise of right-wing governments in Israel and the outbreak of the first intifada in the 1977–87 decade; and the emergence of Israel as both a victim of terrorism and a thriving economic success in the early years of the twenty-first century, coinciding with a decline in the attachment of American Jews to Jewish causes and institutions. A booklength study of American Jewish responses to Israeli developments in chronological sequence would be highly desirable.[7] However given space constraints, this essay takes a thematic approach, necessarily telescoping some of the different time periods.

Second, no one knows with any degree of certainty how large a part of American Jewry is engaged with Israel. While survey research does provide some data about the percentages of American Jews who claim to have traveled there and say they feel a strong connection to Israel, it is far harder to quantify how often Israel is discussed around the dinner table or at social gatherings; how many American Jews check the Internet or their local press for the latest news from Israel; how often rabbis address the topic from the pulpit; and how commonly Israel arises in casual conversations between Jews and their friends, both Jewish and Gentile. Simply put, we do not know how frequently Israel impinges on the consciousness of the average Jew. Based upon the limited evidence available, researchers generally divide the American Jewish population into thirds: one third indifferent to Israel, another third moderately

---

[7]Melvin I. Urofsky's survey of the history of American Jewish-Israeli relations, *We Are One! American Jewry and Israel* (Garden City, N.Y., 1978), only goes through the mid-1970s.

connected, and the final third actively engaged.[8] We shall have occasion to assess the validity of this tripartite division.

ISRAEL IN AMERICAN JEWISH LIFE

Historian Marc Lee Raphael has noted "an axiom among some of those who study American Judaism, especially sociologists, that Israel was a minor component in the religious life of American Jewry in the 1950s and the (early) 1960s, and that only with the Six-Day War of 1967 did Israel become a major component." Raphael has his doubts. After quoting two historians who wrote that before 1967 "analysts of American Jewish life . . . had little to say" about Israel and the Holocaust, Raphael suggests: "They may be right with respect to 'analysts,' but they certainly are wrong in the area of the synagogue."[9] While Israel perhaps did not loom large until 1967 in the ways American Jews constructed their identities, during the first decades of statehood Israel gradually penetrated into the lives and institutions of American Jews.[10] The impact of Israel on American Jewish life was a steadily evolving process. An important foundation was laid even before the creation of the state, and the first decades of statehood witnessed a significant expansion of religious, educational, and cultural engagement, with even more extensive contacts developing after 1967.

Religion

"It is justified to speak about a Zionized American Jewry represented in large measure by its religious movements," observed Israeli historian Evyatar Friesel.[11] Throughout Israel's history, the

---

[8]Steven M. Cohen and Charles S. Liebman, "Israel and American Jewry in the Twenty-First Century: A Search for New Relationships," in Allon Gal and Alfred Gottschalk, eds., *Beyond Survival and Philanthropy: American Jewry and Israel* (Cincinnati, 2000), p. 18. For a more recent estimate that reduces the "most engaged" sector to 20–25 percent of American Jews, see Shaul Kelner, "The Impact of Israel Experience Programs on Israel's Symbolic Meaning," *Contemporary Jewry* 24, 2003–04, p. 126.

[9]Marc Lee Raphael, *Judaism in America* (New York, 2003), p. 129.

[10]For a detailed demonstration of Israeli influences see Emily Alice Katz, "That Land Is Our Land: Israel in American Jewish Culture, 1948–67" (Ph.D. diss., Jewish Theological Seminary, 2008).

[11]Quoted by David Ellenson, "Envisioning Israel in the Liturgies of North American Liberal Judaism," in Allon Gal, ed., *Envisioning Israel: The Changing Ideals and Images of North American Jews* (Jerusalem, 1996), p. 147.

American Jewish religious movements have played a critical role within the organized Jewish community as promoters of Israel and as educators about the importance of Israel. These efforts were no doubt driven by elites within the movements, primarily rabbis, but in time their work trickled down to the masses of Jews who attended their synagogues and schools.

Prior to the establishment of the state, each of the Jewish denominations defined and redefined its posture in regard to Zionism. In its "classical" phase, the Reform movement rejected any national component to Jewish identity or hope for the restoration of Jews to Zion. But in the years immediately preceding the outbreak of World War II, the Reform rabbinate, grasping the necessity for a Jewish haven for refugees in Palestine, developed a more neutral approach, and by the time the state was established Reform officially threw its support behind Israel, even as some holdout rabbis and lay leaders joined the American Council for Judaism, created in 1942, to express their anti-Zionism.[12] The Conservative movement, by contrast, was led since its inception early in the twentieth century by cultural Zionists, who regarded Zionism as a movement for revitalizing Jewish life in the land of Israel *and* the Diaspora.[13] As early as 1917, the United Synagogue of America, the congregational body of the movement, "join[ed] with the Zionists throughout the world in voicing the claim to a legally recognized and internationally secured homeland for the Jewish people in Palestine."[14] American Orthodox Jews were divided between a minority that opposed Zionism as a religiously invalid refusal to wait for the Messiah, and the Mizrachi movement, founded in Russia in 1902, that espoused an Orthodox religious interpretation of Zionism.[15]

Once the state was established, the religious movements accom-

---

[12]On the council, see Thomas A. Kolsky, *Jews Against Zionism: The American Council for Judaism, 1942–48* (Philadelphia, 1990).

[13]Naomi W. Cohen, "Diaspora plus Palestine, Religion plus Nationalism," in Jack Wertheimer, ed., *Tradition Renewed: A History of the Jewish Theological Seminary of America* (New York, 1997), vol. II, pp. 115–76.

[14]Neil Gillman, *Conservative Judaism: The New Century* (New York, 1993), p. 173. Mordecai Kaplan, the founder of Reconstructionism, who remained active in the Conservative movement until the founding of the Reconstructionist Rabbinical College in 1948, placed Jewish peoplehood at the center of his ideology, and both he and his supporters were staunch cultural Zionists.

[15]Mizrachi stands for the Hebrew phrase *mercaz ruhani,* meaning spiritual home.

modated to the new circumstances. Orthodox institutions were at a great advantage because religious life in Israel was, and has remained, officially Orthodox. From the earliest years of the Jewish state, American Orthodox groups forged bonds with Israeli counterparts. Already in the 1950s it was not unusual for Israeli religious leaders traveling to the U.S. on fund-raising and goodwill tours to visit only Orthodox or secular institutions, and for American Orthodox groups to raise money for favored Israeli Orthodox causes, mainly by appealing to adults, but also by enlisting school-age children to collect small sums of money.[16]

Jewish day schools, which in the 1950s were almost exclusively Orthodox, recruited teachers from Israel. This not only brought students into contact with individuals who pronounced Hebrew with an Israeli/Sephardi inflection, but also, since these teachers spoke little English, immersed them in classes conducted entirely in Hebrew. After the Six-Day War, the frequency of travel by American Orthodox Jews to Israel increased dramatically. The Orthodox were the most likely Jews to go there for vacation or to celebrate the Jewish holidays, and young Jews—as will be explained in greater detail below—began to spend a year of more studying in Israeli yeshivas. Such activities strengthened what Israeli sociologist Menahem Friedman has called "the Orthodox global village,"[17] with Israel at its center.

The decades that followed Israel's establishment coincided with the heyday of Modern Orthodoxy, which was dedicated to greater openness to the wider world and Jews of other persuasions. Under the leadership of its preeminent rabbinic leader, Rabbi Joseph B. Soloveitchik, Modern Orthodoxy and its central educational institution, Yeshiva University, embraced Israel. Soloveitchik was pivotal in a number of ways. First and most important, he rejected his own family tradition and the views of many other major Orthodox immigrant rabbis who maintained a non-Zionist position. After World War II, Soloveitchik identified as a Zionist, serving as honorary president of American Mizrachi and cultivating con-

---

[16]I personally recall the principal of my day school urging students during the 1950s to sell raffle tickets and in other ways to raise funds for a particular Israeli yeshiva.

[17]Cited by Chaim I. Waxman, "If I Forget Thee, O Jerusalem . . . : The Impact of Israel on American Orthodox Jewry," in Waxman, ed., *Religious Zionism Post Disengagement: Future Directions* (Orthodox Forum Series; New York and Jersey City, 2008), p. 432, n. 30.

tacts with non-Orthodox Zionists. Pointing out that Soloveitchik published several essays in the Hebrew-language journal *Hadoar,* Lawrence Grossman notes, "That the leading American halakhist would publish in a 'secular' Zionist organ says much about the nature of Religious Zionism in that era." Moreover, Soloveitchik's own thinking was capacious, emphasizing the common bond all Jews, secular and religious, shared by virtue of their collective "covenant of fate."[18] American Mizrachi, which paralleled the Orthodox political party of the same name in Israel (later called the National Religious Party, NRP), also developed a women's branch (there are today two of them, Amit and Emunah) and the youth movement Bnei Akiva that runs a camping network oriented toward preparing Orthodox youth for settlement in Israel.[19]

American Orthodoxy's non-Zionist wing found institutional expression in Agudath Israel, established in Europe before World War I by East European and German Orthodox rabbis opposed to Zionism. Buoyed by the influx of Holocaust-era refugees to America—some of whom, like the Satmar Hasidic sect, viewed even Agudath Israel as insufficiently militant in the battle against Zionism—the non-Zionist Orthodox sector came to embrace and speak for much of the Haredi and Hasidic population of the U.S. Agudath Israel of America currently aligns itself with two political parties in Israel, Agudath Yisrael (Hasidic) and Degel HaTorah (non-Hasidic). Despite its official non-Zionist position, American Agudath Israel has staunchly defended Israel, taking public positions on the hawkish side of the spectrum.[20] In its most recent position paper on the Middle East, Agudath Israel explicitly announced that it "joins with all other segments of the American Jewish community in urging that the United States continue to promote the security and well-being of Israel," a formulation anom-

---

[18]Lawrence Grossman, "Decline and Fall: Thoughts on Religious Zionism in America," in Waxman, ed., *Religious Zionism Post Disengagement,* pp. 36–38.

[19]For a critical assessment of the current state of Religious Zionism in the U.S., see ibid, pp. 31–54.

[20]A report issued by the organization said "that despite fundamental differences with the government of Israel, Agudath Israel's president met with President Kennedy at the White House in support of Israel's security needs, as well as other top government leaders over the years." *The Struggle and the Splendor: A Pictorial Overview of Agudath Israel of America* (New York, 1982), p. 117. I am grateful to Rabbi Avi Shafran for bringing this document to my attention.

alous for an organization that usually distances itself from other sectors of the American Jewish community.[21]

Conservative Judaism established a presence in Israel when it broke ground in 1958 for a center in Jerusalem opposite the campus of the Hebrew University on Givat Ram.[22] Neve Schechter, as it was named, initially served as a base for American Jews visiting Israel. By the mid-1970s, under the leadership of Gerson D. Cohen, then chancellor of the Jewish Theological Seminary, a far more ambitious set of goals was laid out, requiring all JTS rabbinical students to spend a year of study in Israel and envisioning Neve Schechter as a means to influence Israeli society and religion.[23] A year of study in Israel has remained a requirement for rabbinical and cantorial students at JTS and the Ziegler Rabbinical School in Los Angeles; a shorter Israel study period is required of education students. The Israeli presence of Conservative Judaism was further boosted by the establishment in 1979 of the Masorti (the Hebrew term for Conservative) movement, which offers support to roughly 44 synagogues in Israel, many with a heavy English-speaking population.[24] In 1984, Chancellor Ismar Schorsch transferred Neve Schechter into Israeli hands, and it became an educational training center for Masorti rabbis and teachers who would offer an alternative to Israeli Orthodoxy. Neve Schechter and these synagogues have served as a connecting point between American Conservative Jews and Israel, particularly when synagogue groups from the U.S. come to visit.

In the late 1980s, when the Conservative movement issued its first and only statement of principles, Israel figured prominently in the document as a source of religious inspiration:

---

[21]"National Public Policy Position Paper: 2008 National Leadership Mission to Washington, July 16, 2008," p. 21. The paper also calls Jerusalem "the eternal capital of Israel," and on p. 22 urges the U.S. government to refrain from pressuring Israel to "relinquish any of its sovereignty over the Holy City." I have not been able to determine when this formulation about joining "with all other segments" of the Jewish community was first introduced, but it was certainly before 1990.

[22]Earlier, in the 1920s, the Jewish Theological Seminary built the Yeshurun Synagogue on King George Street in Jerusalem, donating it as a gift to the city. This largess has long been forgotten.

[23]The background to this decision is discussed in detail in Eli Lederhendler, "The On-Going Dialogue: The Seminary and the Challenge of Israel," in Wertheimer, ed., *Tradition Renewed,* vol. II, pp. 233–43.

[24]On the Masorti movement, see http://www.masorti.org/about.html

> We rejoice in the existence of *Medinat Yisrael* (the State of Israel) in *Eretz Yisrael* (the Land of Israel), with its capital Jerusalem. We view this phenomenon not just in political or military terms; rather, we consider it to be a miracle reflecting Divine Providence in human affairs. We glory in Israel; we celebrate the rebirth of Zion . . . . The *brit* (covenant) between God and the Jewish people created an unbreakable bond between us and the Land of Israel. Throughout the ages we have revered, honored, cherished, prayed for, dreamed of, and sought to settle in Jerusalem and the Land of Israel.[25]

The Reform movement also has affirmed Israel in post-1948 declarations of principle. In 1976, its Centenary Platform declared Reform Jews to be "bound to . . . the newly reborn State of Israel by innumerable religious and ethnic ties . . . . We have both a stake and a responsibility in building the State of Israel, assuring its security and defining its Jewish character." At the same time, it affirmed the legitimacy of the Diaspora and the historic universalism of Reform Judaism: "The State of Israel and the Diaspora, in fruitful dialogue, can show how a people transcends nationalism even as it affirms it, thereby setting an example for humanity, which remains largely concerned with dangerously parochial goals." With this declaration, Reform highlighted its continuing belief that Zionism must fulfill a universal, rather than just a narrow national, mission.[26]

In 1997, the Central Conference of American Rabbis (CCAR), the Reform rabbinical association, addressed the subject of Israel, reaffirming both its Jewish and universal roles:

> The restoration of *Am Yisrael* [the Jewish People] to its ancestral homeland after nearly two thousand years of statelessness and powerlessness represents an historic triumph of the Jewish people, providing a physical refuge, the possibility of religious and cultural renewal on its own soil, and the realization of God's promise to Abraham: "to your offspring I assign this land." From that distant

---

[25]*Emet Ve-Emunah: Statement of Principles of Conservative Judaism* (New York, 1988), pp. 37, 38. For a critique of the gap between the Conservative movement's aspirations and its actual engagement with Israel, see Daniel Gordis, "Conservative Judaism, Zionism and Israel: Commitments and Ambivalences," in Danny Ben-Moshe and Zohar Segev, eds., *Israel, the Diaspora, and Jewish Identity* (Portland, Oreg., 2007), p. 71.

[26]"Reform Judaism: A Centenary Perspective," www.ccarnet.org/Articles/index.cfm?id=41&pge__prg__id=4687&pge__id=1656

moment until today, the intense love between *Am Yisrael* and *Eretz Yisrael* has not subsided.

We believe that the eternal covenant established at Sinai ordained a unique religious purpose for *Am Yisrael*. *Medinat Yisrael,* the Jewish State, is therefore unlike all other states. Its obligation is to strive towards the attainment of the Jewish people's highest moral ideals to be a *mamlechet kohanim* [kingdom of priests], a *goy kadosh* [holy nation], and *l'or goyim* [light unto the nations].

The statement also itemized obligations American Jews have toward Israel, including promoting its security, offering financial support, and recognizing Hebrew as indispensable to Jewish study. It even went so far as to address the charged question of aliyah:

While affirming the authenticity and necessity of a creative and vibrant Diaspora Jewry, we encourage aliyah to Israel in pursuance of the precept of *yishuv Eretz Yisrael* [settling the Land of Israel]. While Jews can live Torah-centered lives in the Diaspora, only in *Medinat Yisrael* do they bear the primary responsibility for the governance of society, and thus may realize the full potential of their individual and communal religious strivings.

Confident that Reform Judaism's synthesis of tradition and modernity and its historic commitment to *tikkun olam* [repairing the world] can make a unique and positive contribution to the Jewish state, we resolve to intensify our efforts to inform and educate Israelis about the values of Reform Judaism. We call upon Reform Jews everywhere to dedicate their energies and resources to the strengthening of an indigenous Progressive Judaism in *Medinat Yisrael.* [27]

Toward that end, the Reform movement has built an infrastructure in Israel. The World Union for Progressive Judaism (WUPJ) is based in Jerusalem. In 1978, the movement established the Association of Reform Zionists of America (ARZA) as an affiliate of what is now called the Union for Reform Judaism (URJ), its American congregational body. ARZA represents Reform in Israel and has founded the Israel Action Center, which lobbies and litigates for religious pluralism there. The Reform movement also built a campus in Jerusalem for a school that trains Israeli rabbis and cantors, and where American rabbinical and cantorial students spend their mandatory first year of study in Israel. While a Reform

---

[27] "Reform Judaism and Zionism: A Centenary Platform," http://ccarnet.org/Articles/index.cfm?id=42&pge__id=1606

kibbutz, Yahel, was established in the northern Negev in 1977, only recently has the movement taken concrete steps to encourage aliyah.[28]

Given their unofficial status in Israel, the non-Orthodox movements have had to contend with a common dilemma—how to support Israel, even as they sharply resent the way the government and the religious establishment treat them. During the first three decades of Israeli statehood Reform and Conservative leaders largely ignored the question of religious pluralism. But the issue came to a head in the 1980s, when efforts were made to solidify Orthodox control over "Who is a Jew." The debates in the U.S. that this struggle engendered will be discussed below.

How have the official pro-Israel positions espoused by the American Jewish religious movements filtered down to their members? Liturgy has been one important avenue. David Ellenson has noted that liturgical works "are ideal sources for examining how the State of Israel is envisioned by many modern American Jews. As religious documents, they incorporate the religious myths and symbolic language that provide the framework for how most American Jews view and understand Israel."[29] Given the low percentage of American Jews who attend synagogue services, skeptics may wonder how influential such compositions are, but for those who do attend, liturgy frames how Israel is to be understood as a religious phenomenon. Moreover, prayers specifically for Israel are often offered at dramatic and very public moments of the religious service, underscoring even more that country's significance.

The prime example is the "Tefila Li'shlom Ha-Medina" (Prayer for the Welfare of the State), recited just after the Torah reading

---

[28]Ben Harris, "Reform Promoting Aliyah," *New Jersey Jewish Standard,* August 3, 2007, http://www.jstandard.com/articles/3009/1/Reform-promoting-aliyah. On the impact of the year of study in Israel for Reform seminarians, see Lisa Grant and Michael Marmur, "The Place of Israel and the Diaspora," in Ben-Moshe and Segev, *Israel, the Diaspora, and Jewish Identity,* p. 102. The Reconstructionist movement, following the lead of its founder, Mordecai Kaplan, has maintained a Zionist platform, stressing the integral connection of all Jews and the role of Zionism in strengthening Jewish life throughout the world. Its most recent platform, "Zionism and Communal Covenant: A Reconstructionist Approach to Essential Jewish Principles," issued in 2004, can be accessed at http://www.jrf.org/re-sources/files/Zionism%20and%20Communal%20Covenant.pdf. Reconstructionism, however, has not established an infrastructure of institutions in Israel.

[29]Ellenson, "Envisioning Israel in the Liturgies," p. 121.

and before the return of the Torah scroll(s) to the ark on the Sabbath and festival days. In many congregations, it is customary to stand during its recitation. Composed toward the end of 1948 under the auspices of the Israeli Chief Rabbinate,[30] it appeals to God to protect the state and guide its leaders; bring peace to the land; and gather in Diaspora Jews. Most controversially, it begins and ends with messianic overtones, referring to the establishment of the state as the "first flowering of our redemption," and concluding with an explicit plea for the arrival of the Messiah "to redeem those who long for Your salvation." The prayer was adopted in its totality by Modern Orthodox congregations, but those of the Agudath Israel outlook, not to speak of those even more explicitly anti-Zionist, have rejected the prayer due to its messianic overtones.[31] Conservative, Reform, and Reconstructionist prayer books offer abridged versions, and in recent years the prayer's messianic and militaristic references have occasioned fresh debate among non-Orthodox Jews.[32]

Israel figures in the liturgies of the various movements in other ways as well. In every service, the traditional prayer book asserts the sanctity of the land of Israel and the historical aspiration for a Jewish return to Zion, and Modern Orthodox congregations unselfconsciously apply the theme to contemporary Israel.[33] Reform, Reconstructionist, and Conservative prayer books have reworked such references in keeping with the theological outlook each movement takes toward the current reality of Israel. Summing up his survey of these revisions, David Ellenson concludes:

---

[30]On the background to the composition of the prayer, see Ephraim Tabory, "The Piety of Politics: Jewish Prayers for the State of Israel," in Ruth Langer and Steven Fine, eds., *Liturgy in the Life of the Synagogue: Studies in the History of Jewish Prayer* (Winona Lake, Ind., 2005), pp. 232–38.

[31]The Art Scroll edition, the most widely sold Orthodox prayer book, omits the prayer. This prompted the Rabbinical Council of America, the Modern Orthodox rabbinical group, to commission its own edition of the Art Scroll prayer book, which includes it.

[32]Ellenson, "Envisioning Israel in the Liturgies," pp. 132–46; Eric Caplan, *From Ideology to Liturgy: Reconstructionist Worship and American Liberal Judaism* (Cincinnati, 2002), pp. 234–35; Ben Harris, "U.S. Jews Challenge Israel Prayer," Jewish Telegraphic Agency, April, 3, 2008, http://www.jta.org/cgi-bin/iowa/news/print/20080403030220081sraelPrayer.html

[33]On the adoption of Israeli synagogue practices by American Orthodox congregations see Chaim I. Waxman, "Israel in Orthodox Identity: The American Experience," in Ben-Moshe and Segev, eds., *Israel, the Diaspora, and Jewish Identity,* pp. 58–59. Waxman attributes these borrowings to young Orthodox Jews' year or more of study in Israeli yeshivas.

> The exclusively nationalistic or secular elements of the Zionist dream and contemporary incarnation of those political elements in the state are underplayed, if not entirely rejected. Israel, though a refuge for Jews in a time of persecution, is seen instead as an ultimate expression of the religious and moral hopes of the Jewish people. Universalism informs and animates this vision of the Jewish state, a vision that is highly consonant with the American and Diasporan context that inspired it.[34]

Since American Jewish religious movements express through liturgy both their religious conceptions of Israel and their self-understanding as American Jews, congregants attending synagogues of all stripes are exposed to repeated reminders of Israel's religious significance for them.

In addition, many synagogues hold special services in honor of Israel. These include celebrations of *Yom Ha'Atzma'ut* (Israel Independence Day) and *Yom Yerushalayim* (Jerusalem Day, marking the city's unification in 1967). "Hatikvah," the national anthem of Israel, and popular Israeli tunes are sung on such occasions, and some celebrations also feature Israeli-style foods. Many synagogues recite special prayers for Israel and host guest speakers on Israeli subjects. On the more somber side, some American congregations mark the eve of Israel Independence Day (what is called in Israel *Yom Hazikaron*) with a special service to mourn those who lost their lives in Israeli wars. Tisha B'Av, the fast day commemorating the destruction of the two temples and loss of Jewish sovereignty in ancient times, is marked in traditional synagogues with prayers for the restoration of that sovereignty, and non-Orthodox congregations as well sometimes incorporate Israel into the day's services.[35]

Synagogues of all stripes have organized group trips to Israel, often led by the rabbi or some other congregational leader. In a 2006 survey, for example, 80 percent of Reform educators reported that their congregations had organized such a trip in recent years.[36] The publicity surrounding these visits, and especially the subse-

---

[34]Ellenson, "Envisioning Israel in the Liturgies," p. 148.

[35]I have attended services on Tisha B'Av that conclude with the singing of "Hatikvah."

[36]Lisa Grant and Michael Marmur, "The Place of Israel in the Identity of Reform Jews: Israel/Diaspora Joint Commentators," in Ben Moshe and Segev, *Israel, the Diaspora, and Jewish Identity*, p. 131

quent reports of the participants, serve to cement the connection between Israel and the congregation even for members who stayed home.

Rabbis have devoted countless sermons and articles in synagogue bulletins to Israel. Sometimes these are occasioned by newsworthy events occurring in the Middle East, the anniversary of Israel's founding, or the presence of an eminent Israeli guest. The role of the synagogue as the "marshaling ground" to rally support for Israel was graphically illustrated when the 1973 war broke out on Yom Kippur, a time when most Jews were in the synagogue.

Although there is no record of the topics of all American rabbinic sermons, historian Marc Lee Raphael has scrutinized a sampling of sermonic material and synagogue bulletins in the first decades of the Jewish state in order to gauge the popularity of Israel as a theme. This is what he found:

> Of course, not every synagogue in the two decades prior to 1967 was sympathetic to Zionism, but overwhelmingly this was the case. Even the most superficial inspection of synagogue bulletins in these years reveals that rabbis regularly delivered sermons on the subject of Israel . . . . Whether, as Nathan Glazer has argued, this had "remarkably slight effect on the inner life of American Jewry," is hard to prove or disprove, but the evidence for its omnipresence is great.
>
> In Conservative and Reform synagogues all over the country, and in numerous Orthodox congregations as well, rabbis spoke about the War of Independence, the massive migration of Jews from Arab lands after this war, the Suez Crisis, and, regularly, the social, economic, political, and religious situation in Israel. In Baltimore, Chicago, Cleveland, Los Angeles, Miami, New York, Philadelphia, St. Louis, and Washington, D.C., printed collections of High Holiday sermons and sermon titles listed in synagogue bulletins indicate that it was commonplace for one of the four or five Holy Day sermons rabbis delivered (some preached during the Memorial Service on Yom Kippur, some did not) to dwell on the topic of Israel. And nearly every synagogue in the United States supported an appeal for Israel Bonds in the middle of a High Holiday worship service.[37]

It is of significance that appeals for Israel were delivered precisely on the days when the greatest number of Jews attended synagogue services. It should also be noted that Raphael refers to the

---

[37]Raphael, *Judaism in America*, pp. 129–30.

pre-1967 period; Israel has loomed even larger in synagogue discourse since then, sometimes to rally Jews on behalf of a beleaguered Israel, sometimes to bemoan the country's failings.[38]

In addition, Israel impinges on synagogue life in subtle ways that American Jews have come to take for granted. Most dramatically, in virtually every non-Orthodox synagogue prayers are pronounced in Israeli Hebrew—or at least in Sephardi Hebrew. Few American Jews have mastered the precise Israeli inflection, but Ashkenzi pronunciation has virtually disappeared, despite the fact that the preponderant majority of American Jews descend from Ashkenazi families.[39] Sephardi Hebrew is so ubiquitous that few can even remember when congregations altered their practices. As early as 1936, Hebrew Union College and the Central Conference of American Rabbis (Reform), the Jewish Theological Seminary (Conservative), and the National Council for Jewish Education signed a declaration in favor of transliterating Hebrew according to Sephardi pronunciation. Around the time of Israel's founding, the United Synagogue and the Rabbinical Assembly (both Conservative) endorsed such an approach, particularly for schools.[40]

It would take decades for the changeover to occur: as late as 1961–62, only 35 percent of Reform congregations reported using Sephardi Hebrew.[41] Rabbis and cantors may well have been the driving forces, and they, in turn, were shaped by the schools that trained them. Israelis serving as counselors at summer camps also accelerated the change. A history of the Reform movement's Olin-Sang-Ruby Union Institute traces the shift in pronunciation of Hebrew to a particular time and person, describing the influence of one Israeli "music and dance specialist" on the shift to Sephardi Hebrew. At the camp before 1961, the Hebrew word for Israel was transliterated as "Yisroel" and the day of rest was called "Shabbos," but afterward the campers were speaking of "Yisrael" and

---

[38]Raphael contends that Israel-centered activities in synagogues diminished in the late 1990s and were replaced by local Jewish concerns (p. 131), but he wrote this before the second intifada and the 2006 war in Lebanon, which may once again have cast Israel as a victim in need of help.

[39]See Linda Motzkin, *Aleph Isn't Tough: An Introduction to Hebrew for Adults* (New York, 2003).

[40]Emily Katz discusses these declarations of intent in "That Land Is Our Land," pp. 278–79.

[41]Ibid, p. 279.

"Shabbat." They undoubtedly brought the novel pronunciation back to their home synagogues.[42] Orthodox synagogues, for the most part, continue to adhere to the Ashkenazi pronunciation even today, mainly because so many of their members attended U.S. and Israeli yeshivas where the pronunciation of prayer and other religious texts continued to be Ashkenzi. However, it is not uncommon to hear Sephardi Hebrew in such synagogues as well.

Music has served as still another tool employed by synagogues to heighten consciousness about Israel. It has become common for Sabbath and festival prayers to be sung to the melodies of Israeli songs. Writing of his upbringing in an Orthodox synagogue during the 1950s, Lawrence Grossman recalls that "the *hazzan,* on festivals, would chant the prayer, '*ve-havienau le-tzion berinah*' ('bring us to Zion in joy') and the subsequent request for the restoration of the sacrificial system to the tune of *Hatikvah,* and the congregation would spontaneously rise."[43] Other examples of this same tendency in synagogues of all stripes are the singing of a passage from the *Kedushah,* the focal point of the cantor's recital of the service, to the tune of the (formerly) popular Israeli song, "Erev shel Shoshanim," and setting the words of the liturgy appealing to God to return to Jerusalem ("*veliyerushalyim irkha berachamim tashuv*") to the iconic Naomi Shemer song of 1967, "Yerushalayim Shel Zahav."

Cantors and prayer leaders routinely adapt to the words of the prayers Israeli pop tunes, melodies composed for Israeli song festivals, and Yemenite or other Middle Eastern Jewish tunes that arrive via Israel. Even the somber High Holy Day prayer *Unetaneh Tokef* is sung in some congregations to a modern Israeli melody. Musicologist Boaz Tarsi notes the significance of such deviations from the usual liturgical music: "The use of Israeli songs in designated sections of the liturgy [is] plainly not within the parameters of *nusah* [the accepted, age-old prayer melody]. But more than merely a departure from tradition, the deliberate superimposition of tunes from the new Jewish state transforms the practice into a separate genre . . . . The participants can be presumed to notice that the cantor deliberately departs from the tradition in order to

---

[42]Judah M. Cohen, "Singing Out for Judaism: A History of Song Leaders and Song Leading at Olin-Sang-Ruby Union Institute," in Michael M. Lorge and Gary P. Zola, eds., *A Place of Our Own: The Rise of Reform Jewish Camping* (Tuscaloosa, Ala., 2006), p. 190.

[43]Grossman, "Decline and Fall," p. 34.

include the Israeli tune."[44] One wonders if this is necessarily true. While these melodies may spark a conscious association with Israel for some congregants, for others they may represent the reverse: it has become so completely natural to incorporate such music that Israeli songs in the synagogue have become, unselfconsciously, part of the cultural heritage of American Jews.

Even more visible referents to Israel are present in synagogues. Many display the Israeli and American flags in the sanctuary or social hall. For a period of time, it was popular to face parts of the buildings, particularly sanctuaries, in Jerusalem stone.[45] Synagogue displays often include photographs of members taken during group trips to Israel. Not to be overlooked are Israeli-imported *kippot* (skull caps) and *talitot* (prayer shawls) donned by worshipers. And then there are the gift shops, which, in the words of one historian, have "introduced countless American Jews to Israeli culture and life."

> By making Bezalel [the principal Israeli art school] as accessible as Bloomingdales, the American synagogue gift shop provided an opportunity for American Jews to encounter the Holy Land without leaving home. The very concept of "home" is in fact key to understanding the selling of Israel in the American synagogue gift shop. Almost without exception, synagogue gift shops counted Israeli patina menorahs and mezuzahs, olivewood ashtrays and letter openers, coins fashioned into key chains and jewelry, as part of their inventory in the 1950s/60s. These objects and the context in which they were sold reveal a multiplicity of messages about the postwar American Jewish *home* and the then newly established Jewish *homeland* in the Middle East. They illuminate the explanatory potential of material culture, the power and agency of display, and the importance of the synagogue gift shop as a vehicle for forging a place for Israel in the American Jewish home.[46]

At a time when few American Jews traveled abroad, gift shops enabled average Jews to own a piece of Israel. And even after international air travel became more common and affordable, gift

---

[44]Boaz Tarsi, "Voices in the Sanctuary: Musical Practices of the American Synagogue," *Conservative Judaism* 55, Fall 2002, p. 67.

[45]The front of the sanctuary in the synagogue I attend is faced in Jerusalem stone.

[46]Joellyn Wallen Zollman, "Shopping for a Future: A History of the American Synagogue Gift Shop" (Ph.D. diss., Brandeis University, 2002), pp. 183–86, 201.

shops have continued to stock Israeli merchandise, serving as tangible links to the Jewish state.[47]

Clearly, synagogues—the religious institutions of American Judaism—help mediate Israel to American Jews, reminding them of their connections to that land. Less clear is whether the average congregant sees the State of Israel as a *religious* phenomenon, or, alternatively, as an aspect of Jewish *peoplehood.* This question has been studied only for the Reconstructionist movement. Summarizing their research, Steven Sharot and Nurit Zaidman write:

> Although the Reconstructionist ideology provided a clear rationale for regarding Israel as a symbolic focus of Judaism, most respondents appeared to think about Israel in ways that were divorced from what they regarded as their religious concerns. Reconstructionist prayer books, like Conservative and Reform prayer books, present Israel in religious terms; but the prayer book image of Israel appears to have little influence on how American Jews perceived the "real" Israel in relation to their religion.

Sharot and Zeidman contend that, for most Reconstructionist Jews, Israel "symbolizes the survival of the Jewish people."[48]

Jewish Education

During the first decades of Israeli statehood, synagogue schools were the primary educational vehicles of American Jews, but day schools have gradually emerged as important factors as well. Both types of schools (as well as some Jewish schools not under religious auspices) set themselves the goal of socializing young Jews as members of the Jewish people and forging a strong bond with Israel. A manifesto published in 1933 captured the aspirations of some educators who were reconceiving Jewish education in the U.S. as a Zionist enterprise with a sharp focus on the Jewish settlement of the land of Israel:

---

[47]Survey research conducted during the 1950s in one growing American suburb found that 43 percent of Jews claimed to have Israeli souvenirs in their homes, although most had never traveled to Israel. Marshall Sklare and Joseph Greenblum, *Jewish Identity on the Suburban Frontier: A Study of Group Survival in the Open Society* (2d. ed.; Chicago, 1979), p. 229.

[48]Stephen Sharot and Nurit Zaidman, "Israel as Symbol and as Reality: The Perception of Israel among Reconstructionist Jews in the United States," in Gal, ed., *Envisioning Israel,* p. 172.

> Palestine [should] become the dynamic, integrating force of our primary curriculum. It is Palestine, or Palestinianism, that gives meaning to our ceremonial observances, to our worship and prayers, to our language and literature, as well as to much of our present environment. Why then not make the introduction of Palestine the first step in the process of integrating the child into Jewish life?[49]

Translating this educational ideal into a classroom reality has not been easy. Not only must Israel vie with many other topics in the jam-packed hours devoted to Jewish study, but it also is quite distant, both geographically and conceptually, from most Jewish children, and there is no consensus among educators as to what Israel education should entail.

There are a few studies that track how Israel has been taught in Jewish schools. A perusal of curricula collected by bureaus of Jewish education in Buffalo, Cincinnati, New Haven, New York, Greater Miami, and St. Louis suggests that modern Israel was included in most religious and community schools during the 1940s and 1950s. In a survey of several Jewish communities conducted during the 1950s, however, only 48 out of 1,000 Jewish educators reported teaching about Israel as a discrete subject, although the authors note that Israel and Zionism were usually touched upon in lessons about Jewish history and current events.[50] Immediately after the Six-Day War, slightly under half of schools surveyed claimed to teach about Israel as a separate topic, with Reform and community-sponsored schools most likely to do so. The purpose of this instruction, according to the educators, was to create "a positive attitude toward Israel" in the children, and thereby influence the parents as well. [51]

The two decades after the Six-Day War marked a golden age for the publication of text books and other instructional materials about Israel by the religious denominations, Israel-based organizations, and commercial publishers. Furthermore, "in this period,

[49]William Chomsky, quoted in Walter Ackerman, "Israel in American Jewish Education," in Gal, ed., *Envisioning Israel,* pp. 178–79.

[50]Jonathan Krasner, "Israel in American Jewish Text Books, 1948–Present" (Paper delivered at the 2003 conference of the Midwest Jewish Studies Association), p. 3. I am grateful to Dr. Krasner for sharing this paper with me; Ackerman, *Israel in American Jewish Education,* p. 179.

[51]Alvin I. Schiff, "Israel in American Jewish Schools in the 1960s," *Jewish Education* 52, Winter 1984–85, p. 6.

Israelis (several hundred *shlihim* [emissaries sent by Israel or Israeli institutions] as well as many others living abroad) were becoming a quantitatively significant staff presence in American Jewish schools."[52] By the 1970s, a new survey concluded that 63 percent of schools taught about Israel as a separate subject, but also noted continuing confusion about the goals of such courses and about which aspects of Israel should be stressed.[53] Research conducted in the 1980s claimed that a staggering 98 percent of responding schools said they taught about Israel, with schools under Reform auspices ranking higher than the others. But the schools tended to focus on Israel to foster Jewish pride, and so presented an idealized Israel, with little emphasis on teaching about the reality of life in Israel, the religious implications of the establishment of the state, or the value of aliyah.[54]

Teaching about Israel seems to have lost much of its importance over the last two decades. Historian Marc Lee Raphael provides an example:

> [I]n one Seattle Reform congregation, the curriculum of the 1960s and 1970s had an Israel component in the fourth through sixth grades, an Israel component in the seventh through eighth grades, and an Israel component in the pre-confirmation and confirmation year. The 2000–01 curriculum did not have an Israel unit in any of those years, substituting in its place American Jewish community, ethics, holidays, prayer and (especially) prayer book, and the principles of Reform Judaism. Israel seemingly offered American Jews a strong sense of pride and identity in the 1950s and 1960s, but the ingredients of Judaic identity today come from sources other than the holy land.[55]

Similarly, a recent study of Israel education under Reform auspices concluded that "the goals of teaching about Israel continue to be expressed in broad and diffuse terms. Most [educators] . . . were unable to articulate a clear and precise vision for teaching Is-

---

[52]Barry Chazan, "Through a Glass Darkly: Israel in the Mirror of American Jewish Education," in Gal and Gottschalk, eds. *Beyond Survival and Philanthropy*, p. 127.

[53]Barry Chazan, "Israel in American Jewish Schools in the Mid-1970s," *Jewish Education* 52, Winter 1984–85, pp. 10–11. These results should be treated with caution since the response rate to the survey was very low.

[54]George Pollak, "Israel in American Jewish Schools in the 1980s," *Jewish Education* 52, Winter 1984–85, pp. 13–14.

[55]Raphael, *Judaism in America*, p. 131.

rael." Teaching about Israel was considered a good thing, but "what to teach, how to teach, and, most importantly, why to teach Israel to American Jews" were not thought through.[56]

Barry Chazan suggests a reason for the change: "Rabbis, teachers, principals, and Jewish communal leaders have openly shared their increasing ambivalence vis-à-vis teaching about Israel, and they sadly admit that their confusion has sometimes made it difficult for them to be effective gatekeepers of this subject," he writes.[57] One experienced teacher at a communal high school lamented that whereas in the 1980s students still identified with Israeli leaders as heroes, this was much more difficult 20 years later.[58]

Undoubtedly, media coverage of Israeli actions is one factor that helps explain the shift. Another element that should not be overlooked is the transformation that has occurred in the outlook of American Jews—a heightened preoccupation with personal meaning and interest in the building of local communities, at the expense of global collective Jewish identity, an attitudinal transformation we shall discuss below. Here is the grim assessment of Barry Chazan, who has tracked the teaching of Israel in American Jewish educational institutions over several decades:

> The state of Israel in American Jewish education is moribund. It is time to say loud and clear: Israel plays an insignificant role in the world of contemporary Jewish education, and contemporary Jewish education plays an insignificant role in shaping the world view of young Jews vis-à-vis Israel.[59]

Educators seem unwilling to discuss Israel in ways that challenge their students. Studies of curricula have repeatedly shown the extent to which Israel is viewed through the prism of American Jewish values. Material about Israel is "replete with themes central to the creed of American liberalism: humanitarian and social justice, modernism, progress, support for the underdog . . . . "[60] This example from a text written during the 1970s harks back to the arguments that Louis D. Brandeis, soon to be named to the U.S.

---

[56]Lisa D. Grant, "Israel Education in Reform Congregational Schools," *CCAR Journal* 54, Summer 2007, pp. 4–5.

[57]Chazan, "Through a Glass Darkly," p. 128.

[58]Personal conversation with the author in December 2007.

[59]Barry Chazan, "J'accuse," *Jewish Education News* 6, 1995, pp. 15–17.

[60]The analysis is that of Ackerman, "Israel in American Jewish Education," p. 182.

Supreme Court, made a century ago, identifying Zionism with Americanism:

> Israel's story is full of adventure . . . there are many similarities between America and Israel's history . . . . Both required pioneering under great hardship, a sharp break with the past, an open mind toward the future. Israel's founders in many ways repeated the struggles of America's pilgrims, colonial settlers, western pioneers . . . . [Israel] is a model, a pilot for undeveloped lands trying to become modern and independent.

A second example from another text book strives to generate sympathy for Israel using a different America-centered pitch:

> [It is] a country which has been through so many wars and terrorist attacks . . . has built so dramatically and achieved so much . . . has absorbed so many poor and downtrodden people and given so many shamed outcasts a sense of dignity.[61]

Such passages do not introduce a living, vibrant Israel with a distinctive culture and society, but a facsimile of America.

It has certainly not helped matters that Jewish supplementary schools and even, to some extent, day schools, have failed to teach modern Hebrew effectively, and thus a bridge to Israel that might have been constructed by language and literature cannot be crossed.[62] A survey conducted by Steven M. Cohen in 1986 asked Jewish adults to rate their competence in Hebrew. Claiming at least minimal competence were 41 percent of Orthodox Jews, 9 percent of Conservative Jews, and 5 percent of Reform Jews. Given that Orthodox Jews constituted less than 10 percent of the American Jewish population, it appeared that no more than 7 percent of American Jewish adults claimed any competence in Hebrew,[63] a finding that adds credence to Leonard Fein's observation that "Hebrew school in this country is mainly remembered as the place where Hebrew wasn't learned."[64]

---

[61]Both are quoted ibid, pp. 182–83.

[62]Krasner, "Israel in American Jewish Text Books," p. 4, n. 17. For a severe indictment of failures in Conservative supplementary schools, see Walter Ackerman, "Toward a History of the Conservative Congregational School," *Jewish Education* 48, Spring 1980, p. 25.

[63]Gilead Morahg, "Language Is Not Enough," in Alan Mintz, ed., *Hebrew in America: Perspectives and Prospects* (Detroit, 1993), p. 192.

[64]Leonard Fein, *Where Are We? The Inner Lives of America's Jews* (New York, 1988), p. 12.

The presence of large numbers of Israeli teachers in American Jewish schools adds another dimension to the challenge. The precise percentage of teachers of Israeli origin is a matter of scholarly disagreement. Writing in the mid-1990s, Walter Ackerman concluded, "Today it is doubtful that Jewish education in the United States could function without Israelis," but a subsequent study found that Israelis constituted only 9 percent of teachers in day and supplementary schools.[65] Their presence, in whatever quantity, serves to introduce young Jews to real-life Israelis who can speak with first-hand knowledge about contemporary Israel, thereby serving as authentic mediators between the American students and the Jewish state. But these teachers have emigrated from Israel, rendering them ambivalent at best about a country they themselves decided to leave behind, and thus, ironically, those educators who are best informed about Israel may not qualify as its ideal representatives.

Not surprisingly, there has been much discussion in Jewish educational circles about ways to improve Israel education. This is how David Breakstone, an Israeli, framed the issues more than two decades ago:

> The purpose [of Israel education] is not (or not only) to foster love for the country, to assure future pledges to the U.J.A., to create ties to the Jewish people, to provide a spiritual homeland, or to inspire positive attitudes. Rather, it is meant to produce "good" Jews, "authentic" Jews . . . in the sense of becoming conversant in the language of Judaism . . . not to Hebrew or any other spoken means of communication, but to a Jewish *gestalt*.

It is unlikely that this situation will change until a strong rationale and a coherent curricular focus for Israel education are developed that take into account the constraints of American Jewish educational institutions.[66]

Still, several factors suggest the need to temper the prevalent negative assessment of Israel education. As late as 1995, when

---

[65]Ayala Ronen Samuels, "Israeli Teachers in American Jewish Day Schools: The Teachers' Perspective" (Ph.D. diss., Jewish Theological Seminary, 1992), p. 4; Ackerman, "Israel in American Jewish Education," p. 188; Jewish Educational Service of North America (JESNA), *Educators in Jewish Schools Study* (New York, 2008), p. 6.

[66]David L. Breakstone, "The Dynamics of Israel in American Jewish Life: An Analysis of Educational Means as Cultural 'Texts'" (Ph.D. diss., Hebrew University, 1986), p. 233. The Melton Center for Jewish Education at the Hebrew University and the Jewish Agency

Conservative youths who had recently become bar/bat mitzvah were asked to identify "two people, dead or alive, that you consider to be Jewish heroes," the top vote-getters, excluding family members and Biblical figures, were Israeli leaders Yitzhak Rabin and Golda Meir.[67] While these results hardly attest to a deep knowledge of, or connection with, Israel, they do suggest the significance of Israeli heroes in the imagination of these young Jews. Whether similar responses would be given today, we do not know.

There remain many settings in which American Jews of all ages encounter modern Israeli society through instruction in Israeli Hebrew and texts about Israeli life.[68] American Jews can study modern Hebrew in any of the following settings: early-childhood programs in some communities run on the principle of complete immersion in Hebrew, to the point where it is the only language of conversation even in the playground;[69] Hebrew classes offered across a spectrum of Jewish day schools from Modern Orthodox through Reform; a few supplementary schools—most notably Kesher in Newton and Cambridge, Massachusetts—that provide Hebrew-speaking settings and have demonstrated records of success;[70] Hebrew language courses offered at almost 100 colleges and universities across the country;[71] and, finally, Ulpan courses sponsored by communities and organizations that place adults in

cosponsored a conference on Israel education in the summer of 2007, and the proceedings are scheduled to appear online. My thanks to Howard Deitscher for sharing the papers with me.

[67]Barry A. Kosmin, "My Hero: Insights into Jewish Education," in Jack Wertheimer, ed., *Jewish Identity and Religious Commitment* (New York, 1997), p. 12.

[68]In this paragraph I have relied greatly on a survey of Hebrew language programs conducted by Rachael T. Ellison, "Connecting the Dots: Mapping the Field of Hebrew Language Acquisition for Innovation and Advocacy" (Unpublished paper prepared for the Avi Chai Foundation, 2007).

[69]On the Maalah Program designed by the Davidson Graduate School of Jewish Education at the Jewish Theological Seminary, see Julie Gruenbaum Fax, "All Hebrew, All the Time: A growing number of L.A. schools now use a language-immersion program to get students beyond 'shalom,'" *Los Angeles Jewish Journal,* March 17, 2005, http://www.jewishjournal.com/articles/item/all_hebrew_all_the_time_20050318. Other programs, such as Nitzanim, Notzatzim, and Hebrew in America, sponsor programs in locales as diverse as San Diego, Detroit, and Bergen County, New Jersey.

[70]On Kesher, see www.kesherweb.org. Similar efforts in other communities are described at www.caje-co.org/high/hebrewimmersion.htm and www.keflisandiego.org

[71]As of 2003, Hebrew was offered in 93 college programs. The National Association for Professors of Hebrew (NAPH) has a membership of over 200. http://polyglot.lss.wisc.edu/naph/index.html

Hebrew-speaking environments.[72] Many of these varied programs make use of newspaper articles drawn from the Israeli press and videotapes of Israeli television, which serve as sources of information about modern Israel. To be sure, all of these together impact on no more than a fraction of American Jews and, for the most part, cannot claim that their graduates speak and read with fluency. They do, however, impart an understanding of aspects of Israeli culture, from the latest slang and hit songs, to insight into current political or social trends.

Another important point is the distinct difference between many of the day schools, on the one hand, and supplementary schools, on the other. Even the casual visitor to a day school—whether Modern Orthodox, Conservative, Reform, or communal—will notice walls festooned with reminders of Israel, time set aside for learning Israeli songs and dances, and attention paid to Israeli Hebrew and culture.[73] These schools also tend to hire a significant percentage of teachers who speak Israeli Hebrew (with the pluses and minuses this entails, as noted above). Day schools celebrate key commemorations of Israel's history, often inviting well-known guest speakers and alumni who have made aliyah to give presentations at such programs, and they serve as the backbone of Salute to Israel parades.

In the Orthodox sector, moreover, and to a lesser degree in other full-day Jewish high schools, students are strongly encouraged to spend a year in Israel after graduation before starting college (for the ultra-Orthodox, the subsequent college option is far more restricted). Some stay for another semester or even an extra full year.[74] To be sure, the primary purpose of such programs is not usually to strengthen the bond with Israel, but rather to bolster

---

[72]There seems to be no clearing-house for adult ulpanim, which are sponsored by Jewish community centers, federations, major organizations, colleges of Jewish studies, and synagogues.

[73]Two major curriculum projects for day schools, NETA for lower schools and Tal Am for secondary schools, both emphasize building strong connections with modern Israel. They have been adopted by several hundred day schools. See http://www.netahebrew.org/index.htm and http://www.talam.org/about.html

[74]Samuel C. Heilman, in *Sliding to the Right: The Contest for the Future of American Jewish Orthodoxy* (Berkeley, Calif., 2006), pp. 112–22, traces the history of the Orthodox "year in Israel" and describes the common phenomenon called "flipping out," when these young men and women "slide to the right" in religious observance and outlook, and bring their newfound piety back to the U.S. By the mid-1990s a researcher found that up to 90

Jewish identity through immersion in intensive Jewish religious or cultural experiences. Nevertheless, whatever the initial motivation, these high schools succeed in having their students spend significant time in Israel. Indicative of the status this confers on these schools in the community is that many of them "use the number of their graduates who go to Israel as part of their publicity campaigns for prospective students," and place advertisements in the local Jewish press that list, alongside the names of the colleges to which their graduates were accepted, the names of Israeli programs in which those graduates have enrolled.[75]

A period of serious study in Israel has thus become the norm for graduates of Orthodox day schools, and a serious option for products of non-Orthodox schools. The Jewish Agency, in fact, has set up an entire apparatus, called MASA, to help steer prospective high school graduates through the range of program options.[76] One cannot overstate the impact of intensive study in Israel upon at least two generations of Orthodox youth and an important sector of their non-Orthodox counterparts, both in the formation of their Jewish identities and their relationships to Israel.[77]

Informal Jewish educational experiences often complement what young American Jews are learning in school. One widespread albeit limited exposure to Israel comes through participation in Salute to Israel parades and other Israel-themed fairs and festivals held in Jewish communities around the country. As they construct

percent of graduates from Modern Orthodox day schools went on to yeshiva programs in Israel. This is undoubtedly an exaggeration, but peer and family pressures to go are certainly high. One educator said that "there are graduates who report their parents are forcing them to go to Israel for the year against their will . . . . There can be no doubt that the post-high-school yeshiva experience has become a mass movement within the Orthodox community." Waxman, "If I Forget Thee . . . ," pp. 417–18.

[75]Waxman, "If I Forget Thee . . . ," p. 418. See, for example, such ads in the *New York Jewish Week*, June 6, 2008, pp. 23 (Solomon Schechter School of Westchester), 25 (SAR Academy), 40 (The Frisch School), and June 20, 2008, pp. 8 (Ramaz), 13 (Yeshiva of Flatbush), and 18 (Westchester Hebrew High School).

[76]On the programs offered through MASA, see http://www.masaisrael.org/MASA/English/About+MASA/What+is+MASA.htm

[77]A study of the leadership cadre of American Jewish religious and organizational life would probably demonstrate that a high percentage of current leaders had studied in Israel. This hypothesis has been substantiated for participants in emergent minyanim. See Steven M. Cohen, J. Shawn Landres, Elie Kaunfer, and Michelle Shain, *Emergent Jewish Communities and Their Participants: Preliminary Findings from the 2007 National Spiritual Communities Study* (New York, 2007), pp. 23–24.

floats and exhibits, learn Israeli songs and dances, don special garb—even if only colorfully decorated T-shirts—tens of thousands of young people join with their teachers and, often, their parents, to celebrate Israel's independence each year. The longest-running of these events, initiated in 1964, is a mammoth parade up Fifth Avenue in Manhattan that usually draws over 100,000 participants and up to a million onlookers. If nothing else, these celebrations, and the smaller ones in other communities, have placed Israel on the mental calendar of huge numbers of American Jews of all ages. The founder of New York's parade went one step further, declaring that through this event, "The State of Israel gave Jews the freedom to appear in public as Jews." [78]

Informal educational experiences of longer duration have contributed richly to young people's evolving relationship to Israel. For those who are exposed to summer camps with rich Jewish programming, to Zionist youth movements, and to teen trips to Israel—admittedly a minority—Israel comes alive differently and often more immediately than in schools.[79]

Beginning around the time of Israel's establishment, a small number of summer camps were established with strong Zionist missions. A few, such as the Massad and Ramah networks, tried to conduct camp programs entirely in Hebrew, with bunks and buildings taking on Israeli place names, artwork depicting Israeli settings, and songs and dances drawn from the developing Israeli repertoire.[80] The Hebrew-speaking camps were augmented by oth-

---

[78]On the New York parade, see http://www.salutetoisrael.com/index.php?option=com__content&view=article&id=45&Itemid=55; and Marissa Gross, "The Salute to Israel Parade," Jerusalem Center for Public Affairs, June 15, 2008, http://www.jcpa.org/JCPA/Templates/ShowPage.asp?DRIT=4&DBID=1&LNGID=1&TMID=11&FID=253&PID=0&IID=2211&TTL=The__Salute__to__Israel__Parade

[79]The history of Jewish youth movements and summer camps has not been adequately studied. Some publications on the topic are J.J. Goldberg and Elliot King, *Builders and Dreamers: Habonim Labor Zionist Youth in North America* (New York, 1993); Shlomo Schulsinger-She'ar Yashuv, ed., *Kovetz Massad* [Hebrew] (Jerusalem, 1989); Zola and Lorge, eds., *A Place of Our Own;* Katz, "This Land Is Our Land," chap. 5; Michael Brown, "It's Off to Camp We Go: Ramah, LTF, and the Seminary in the Finkelstein Era," in Wertheimer ed., *Tradition Renewed,* vol. I, pp. 821–54; Seymour Fox with William Novak, *Vision at the Heart: Lessons from Camp Ramah on the Power of Ideas in Shaping Educational Institutions* (New York, 1997); Amy L. Sales and Leonard Saxe, *"How Goodly Are Thy Tents": Summer Camps as Jewish Socializing Experiences* (Hanover, N.H., 2004).

[80]Walter Ackerman, "A World Apart: Hebrew Teachers Colleges and Hebrew-Speaking Camps," in Mintz, ed., *Hebrew in America,* pp. 105–28.

ers, such as the Moshava camps of the Bnei Akiva religious Zionist youth movement; the Tel Yehudah camps run by Hadassah; and Habonim, sponsored by the youth movement of that name, all of them incubators of strong Zionist commitment. Also, camps under Modern Orthodox, Conservative, and Reform auspices featured significant Zionist content even though this was not their primary focus.

Reflecting on the Israel dimension of Zionist camps, one observer noted the extent to which "camp settings actually come closest to suggesting our idealization of Israeli life."[81] Housed in a rustic setting and evoking an ambience of communal living where campers might, at any moment, break out in Israeli song and dance, these camps have served as surrogates for an imagined Israel, devoid of warfare, urban blight or poverty. As one former camper explained: "Camp Moshava was my Israel. I had Israeli counselors and a world that felt more Israel to me than the real Israel. After one summer [in Israel] I never went again during the years I attended Moshava."[82]

Ethnographer Riv-Ellen Prell has argued that a disproportionate percentage of baby boomers who assumed leadership roles in American Jewish life came out of the Jewish camping experience of the 1950s and 1960s, much of it Zionist and Israel-oriented.[83] The same might be said of American Jews who made aliyah in the decade following the Six-Day War. However the ideologically driven Jewish camping movement has fallen on hard times. Hebrew-language-centered camping has virtually disappeared over the past two decades, as have a number of camps sponsored by Zionist youth movements. Insofar as Jewish camps today have an ideological slant, it is toward one or another of the religious movements. Israel is not their central concern, and only a portion of their programming is focused on it. While camps offering Jewish content still teach Israeli songs and dances, have Israel days, name their bunks after Israeli places, employ some Israeli Hebrew in

---

[81]William Cutter, "Response: Myths and Realities in Teaching Israel," in Gal and Gottschalk, eds., *Beyond Survival and Philanthropy*, p. 166.

[82]Quoted in Riv-Ellen Prell, "Summer Camp, Postwar American Jewish Youth and the Redemption of Judaism," in Bruce Zuckerman and Jeremy Schoenberg, eds., *The Jewish Role in American Life: An Annual Review* 5 (Ashland, Ohio, 2007), p. 96.

[83]Ibid, pp. 77–106.

camp activities, import Israelis to serve as counselors,[84] and in other ways expose campers to some aspects of Israeli culture, Zionism is not really on the agenda.

With the waning of Zionist-oriented summer camping, teen trips to Israel grew in popularity. Synagogues, schools, federations of Jewish philanthropy, and the religious movements have sponsored such trips, often billing them as a reward for participation in other programs. Thus the capstone of a high school program—full-day or supplementary—would be a heavily subsidized class trip to Israel for juniors or seniors, or participants in youth activities sponsored by a federation would receive a free trip. By the 1990s, the teen trip was no longer viewed primarily as an opportunity to express solidarity with the people of Israel, but rather as an educational experience needed for the socialization of young American Jews. An article on "Israel Experience" programs put it well: "This new conception of the Israel trip places it squarely within the context of the great twentieth-century search for methods and structures for teaching Jewish values and developing Jewish identity. According to this conception, the trip is a new Jewish educational framework for affecting the Jewish personality and identity of the young person who visits Israel."[85]

While there are no precise figures for how many Jewish teens have participated in Israel summer programs, the numbers certainly rose during the 1980s and 1990s. According to Barry Chazan, approximately 36,500 Jewish teens between the ages of 13 and 19 went to Israel on organized educational trips from 1992 through 1996. This number, Chazan writes, represented approximately 14 percent of all North American Jews in that age group, or roughly "2 percent of the eligible Jewish youth population in any one year."[86] Virtually all participants were affiliated with Jewish institutions—mainly the youth movements of the religious denominations, Jewish community centers, Young Judea, or B'nai B'rith Youth. In 1996, 100 sponsoring organizations offered nearly 250

---

[84]See Elan Ezrachi, "Encounters Between American Jews and Israelis: Israelis in American Jewish Summer Camps" (Ph.D. diss., Jewish Theological Seminary, 1995). Ezrachi found (p. 90) that in 1978 there were some 283 Israelis at 68 North American summer camps.

[85]Leora W. Isaacs and Devorah A. Silverman, "It's Israel, Chochem!: Factors Affecting Participation of Youth in Israel Experience Programs," *Journal of Jewish Communal Service* 74, Summer 1998, p. 204.

[86]Barry Chazan, *What We Know About the Israel Experience* (New York, undated), p. 5.

distinct programs for teens.[87] Safety concerns related to the outbreak of the second intifada in late 2000 brought a drop in the number of American participants, but enrollment in teen programs would have shrunk in any case, given the fact that students who waited just a few years could be eligible for free trips funded by Birthright Israel.[88]

Begun in late 1999, Birthright Israel—or Taglit, its Hebrew name—has sent some 200,000 Jews aged 18–26 from around the globe, but primarily from North America, on free trips to Israel. Funded primarily by philanthropists but also to some extent by federations of Jewish philanthropy and the Israeli government, Birthright represents the most dramatic effort to expose young Jews to Israel, albeit on a ten-day, whirlwind experience. Over two dozen organizations serve as subcontractors for the program, each with a slightly different emphasis. Some, for example, specialize in backpacking and hiking on nature trails, others stress visits to Jewish religious centers, and still others explore the Sephardi heritage. All trip operators are expected to include on their itineraries the main Israeli tourist venues—archaeological excavations; battlefields sites; key cities; political, social-welfare, and high-tech institutions of modern Israel; and holy places.[89]

Needless to say, this represents a huge financial undertaking. A recent study of the program presented its three overarching goals:

- To reach a sector of young American Jewry (popularly known as the "unaffiliated") that had been regarded as de-

---

[87]Ibid, p. 6. For a listing of over 20 summer programs for Cincinnati teens, see http://www.jewishcincinnati.org/page.aspx?id=56940. The New Orleans community's method of funding its Israel trips is presented at http://www.jewishnola.com/page.aspx?ID=105023. A good description of how the high school teen trip has become a focal point in one Jewish community, see Randal Schnoor with Billy Mencow, "Western Hebrew High: A Place for Social Belonging and Personal Meaning," in Jack Wertheimer, ed., *Learning and Community: Jewish Supplementary Schools in the Twenty-First Century* (Hanover, N.H., 2009).

[88]The head of one high school reported: "The intifada could not sink our trip; Birthright Israel did." Marilyn Henry, "Birthright Israel's Collateral Damage," *Jerusalem Post,* December 23, 2007, p. 14.

[89]A book-length overview of the program is Leonard Saxe and Barry Chazan, *Ten Days of Birthright Israel: A Journey in Young Adult Identity* (Hanover, N.H., 2008). A listing of parameters given to the tour operators appears on pp. 104–05.

tached or alienated from Jewish life and provide it with an Israel experience;

- To launch young, unaffiliated Jews on a "Jewish journey" that would lead them to a lifelong involvement with Jewish life;
- To create links among these young Jews, the State of Israel, and the Jewish community in the years to come.[90]

This list makes plain that Birthright is about far more than Israel, which represents but one dimension of a strategy to strengthen the Jewish identity and engagement of young Jews. The leadership of the American Jewish community, deeply concerned about securing the commitment of these Jews to engage in organized Jewish life, has come to see Israel as a means to jump-start the process. Indeed, studies of participants both in teen Israel programs and in Birthright Israel indicate a positive short-term effect. As Israeli sociologist David Mittelberg has put it, "interventions such as a focused, 'quality' Israel experience are shown to have a statistically significant and considerable positive impact on the various components of participants' Jewish identity."[91] Writing a few years later, the same scholar offered the following prescription: "The visit to Israel, and especially the well-crafted Israel experience, provides a window of opportunity. If structurally integrated into the first third of every Jewish American life, rather than into the last third of the lives of a third of America's Jews, it could help bring American Jewry safely into the next century with its ethnic identity intact."[92]

Close observers of Israel programs have puzzled over why they have such an impact. Some note that the participants spend their time in a "bubble," making scant contact with Israelis other than their bus driver, tour guides, and security guards. Anthropologist Harvey Goldberg went along on a high school tour sponsored by

---

[90]Ibid, p. 104.

[91]David Mittelberg, "The Impact of Jewish Education and an 'Israel Experience' on the Jewish Identity of American Jewish Youth," in Peter Medding, ed., *A New Jewry? America Since the Second World War*, Studies in Contemporary Jewry 8 (New York, 1992), p. 217.

[92]David Mittelberg, *The Israel Connection and American Jews* (Westport, Conn., 1999), p. 130. Saxe and Chazan, *Ten Days of Birthright Israel*, pp. 137–54, reach the same conclusion based on pre- and post-trip evaluations by the participants.

the Reform movement's National Federation of Temple Youth (NFTY). Noting that the group was "basically being insulated from its surroundings," Goldberg came to the conclusion that this was a deliberate strategy of the organizers to maintain their own authority and "merge modern Israel into the ideology and educational program of NFTY." Studying a similar program sponsored by a Zionist youth movement, sociologist Samuel Heilman was struck by the strong preoccupation of the teens with their peer group rather than with the larger Israeli environment. It seemed to him that "the primary product of the summer" was "not a set of connections to Israel but to one another . . . . In essence, as the group becomes one of the only constants in an ever-changing fluid environment, it grows in importance, filling the life-world of the participants." Both Israel and Judaism became secondary, serving as backdrops "for an American teen adventure."[93]

Sociologist Shaul Kelner observed similar patterns during a Birthright trip he studied. Much of the impact, he concluded, derived from its social dimension and group-building. Afterward, participants remembered the partying and dancing as vividly, if not even more vividly, than climbing Masada. Thus the social experience of those Kelner calls "pilgrim-tourists" invests the trip with meaning no less than the parts of Israel to which they are exposed. According to Kelner,

> for participants in programs like Birthright, Israel becomes an integrative symbol representing the individual's own fleeting experiences of collective effervescence and embodies sensations during a group tour of Israel. The symbol's other, more normative, associations [such as to ancient Jewish history and the heroism of the Israeli military] are not lost. Indeed, the symbol's ability to sustain new content attests to it robustness. The canonical meanings may even be reinvigorated by the infusion of the potent personal meanings.[94]

Such "pilgrim-tourism" can also take another form—visits to Israel by adults and family units. Although we lack precise statistics, trips taken by nuclear and extended families to mark bar and bat mitzvah milestones in Israel are extremely popular. Especially for the well-to-do, this experience has become a standard family-

---

[93]Kelner, "The Impact of Israel Experience Programs on Israel's Symbolic Meaning," p. 127.

[94]Ibid, p. 148.

bonding event, and a small industry has emerged that caters to families wishing to combine celebration with touring.[95] Family trips to Israel are also taken on other occasions, as is evident to any traveler to Israel during school vacation times, especially over the summer, when flights are filled with young families. And then there are the various missions organized by synagogues, Jewish organizations, and special-interest groups that range from gay and lesbian Jews[96] to adults volunteering at archaeological digs,[97] army bases, and social-service programs. All of these constitute engagement in informal education, although they serve social and recreational purposes too.

A surprisingly low number of American Jews avail themselves of this broad array of travel options. At no time since Israel's establishment has a majority of American Jews ever been to the Jewish state. The peak of visits to Israel was probably reached during the mid-1980s, when some 40 percent of American Jewish adults claimed to have traveled to the country at least once, and one in six said they had visited at least twice. There was a fall-off in travel beginning with the outbreak of the first intifada in late 1987, further exacerbated by the Gulf War of 1991.[98] By the time of the 2000–01 NJPS, the percentage of adults who claimed they had gone at least once had dropped to 35 percent, with more going from the Northeast and South than from the Midwest and West. Adults between the ages of 45 and 54 were the most likely to have been to Israel, perhaps reflecting the surge in travel in the decades after the Six-Day War. The survey also found a clear correlation with levels of Jewish affiliation: 58 percent of the highly affiliated had been to Israel as compared to just 25 percent of the unaffiliated. Synagogue members, participants in other Jewish organiza-

[95]A sample of opportunities for such trips can be found at http://www.goisrael.com/Tourism__Eng/Tourist+Information/Jewish+Themes/Bar-Bat+Mitzvah+in+Israel.htm

[96]Michael Lando, "Gays, Lesbians Take Pride in their Own Israeli Birthright," *Jerusalem Post*, May 18, 2008, http://www.jpost.com/servlet/Satellite?cid=1210668668557&pagename=JPost%2FJPArticle%2FShowFull

[97]For an example of a dig open to any and all adult volunteers, see "Archaeology Dig 2007: Tell Es-Safi/Gath," http://archaeology.about.com/b/2007/01/22/archaeology-dig-2007-tell-es-safigath.htm

[98]Steven M. Cohen, "Relationships of American Jews with Israel: What We Know and What We Need to Know," *Contemporary Jewry* 23, 2002, p. 135; Noam Monty Penkower, *At the Crossroads: American Jewry and the State of Israel* (Haifa, 1990), p. 7. The drop that occurred during the second intifada, 2001–04, was even sharper.

tions, donors to Jewish charities, and in-married Jews were far more likely than others to have traveled to Israel.[99]

Viewed comparatively, the 35 percent of today's adult American Jews who have been to Israel is dwarfed by the 66 percent of Canadians Jews and 73 percent of both Australian and French Jews who have.[100] It is hard to avoid the conclusion that although the free trips offered by Birthright Israel may well meet a particular need of American Jews, the fact that they are even necessary stands as damning evidence of a major weakness in the American Jewish connection to Israel: in most other wealthy, Western Jewish communities the majority of Jews have seen fit to spend their own money to visit the Jewish state.

Surveying the large infrastructure of formal and informal educational programs devised by American Jews to expose young people to Israel, an overall trend becomes apparent. During the first few decades of Israeli statehood, American Jews behaved as patrons to an Israel in need of material and political support; accordingly, the predominant emphasis of travel to Israel in the early years was philanthropic.[101] With the passage of time, the roles have reversed. It is now Israel that serves as a resource to help "needy" American Jew shore up the Jewish identity of their youth.

Birthright Israel, we recall, is not mainly about Israel per se, but about deepening the Jewish commitment of unaffiliated American Jews, and the available evidence suggests that, at least in the short term, it works—participants return claiming to be more engaged in Jewish life. While we are still unsure to what extent this is due to the enjoyable social experiences, the first-time encounter with a large and thriving Jewish society, or sparks of Jewish identity ignited by the people they meet and sites they visit, the desire of educators, communal professionals, and philanthropists to

---

[99]The figures are taken from NJPS 2000–01, "Connection with Israel," www.ujc.org/page.aspx?iod=46232. When only the estimated 4.3 million American Jews who identify as "strongly connected"to Judaism are considered, the percentage of travelers to Israel rises to 42 percent. The breakdown by subgroups is in David Mittelberg, "Jewish Continuity and Israel Visits," in Ben-Moshe and Segev, eds., *Israel, the Diaspora, and Jewish Identity*, p. 33.

[100]For comparative data, see David H. Goldberg, "Israel as a Source of Identification for Canadian Jewry," Erik H. Cohen, "The Role of Israel in French-Jewish Identity," and Suzanne D. Rutland, "Identity with Israel from Afar: The Australian Story," in Ben-Moshe and Segev, eds., *Israel, the Diaspora, and Jewish Identity*, pp. 217, 247, 255.

[101]Older American Jews can recall being asked to bring instant coffee, toilet paper, jeans, and pens to Israeli relatives and friends as late as the 1970s.

expose young American Jews to Israel—at considerable expense—highlights just how much the leaders of American Jewry are convinced they need Israel to ensure Jewish continuity in America. Deep, ongoing engagement with Israel is at best a secondary objective.

Jewish Culture

American Jewish culture has absorbed Israeli influences with growing intensity over the past 60 years. Indeed, it is often difficult to set a clear demarcation line between American Jewish and Israeli cultural expression. This is true of much Jewish dance, Jewish music—especially the large part of it that is in Hebrew—and Jewish food, as evident in the proliferation of Israeli-style kosher grill restaurants. In the realm of literature, American Jews are avid consumers of books about Israel and by Israelis. Although no quantitative information is available, it is almost certain that most American Jewish leaders regularly read online Israeli newspapers (in English) to keep up with developments in Israeli life. Rabbis and academics specializing in fields of Judaica routinely spend summers and sabbaticals in Israel. In sum, the most Jewishly engaged elites feel a need to immerse themselves in Israeli culture.

The importation of Israeli cultural influences began slowly during the first decades of statehood. In the 1950s and 1960s, several popular Israeli singers and dancers arrived on America's shores to perform. Songs were also imported by Israelis who came to work in Jewish summer camps and with youth movements. So much popular Israeli music found its way into the U.S. that several of the camps compiled songsters *(shironim)* consisting almost entirely of Israeli songs.[102] Over time, some of these songs came to be seen by Americans—Jews and non-Jews—as emblematic of Jewish music, even though they was previously unknown to American Jews or their European forebears. Thus when some representation of Jewish music is needed at baseball stadiums whose sound systems broadcast various types of ethnic music, the snappy "Jewish" tune

[102]A *shiron* released by the Reform movement camps in 1964 contained nearly triple the number of transliterated Hebrew songs as the previous edition. Cohen, "Singing Out for Judaism," pp. 190–91.

is *Havah Nagilah,* based on a Hasidic tune sung in Jerusalem and subsequently imported to the U.S.[103]

In the aftermath of the Six-Day War, Israeli popular songs such as Naomi Shemer's "Yerushalayim Shel Zahav" and Ron Eliran's "Sharm el-Sheikh" were the rage in American Jewish institutions. After a decline in interest that set in during the 1980s, a revival seems to have occurred in recent years, spurred by young Jews eager to bridge the cultural worlds. Observing a performance at the Museum of Jewish Heritage in New York given by Israeli singer-songwriter Din Din Aviv in 2008, a reporter noticed that the house was "packed with Israeli fans of Aviv who live in New York and American Jews clutching her CD. After the show, they jabber in a mix of Israeli-accented English and American-accented Hebrew while standing in line to pose for pictures with Aviv." The organizer of the event explained he was seeking to "bring Israelis and American Jews in New York closer together—and closer to Israel," and he was convinced that "there is a hunger to connect to Israel and the challenge is to satisfy that and give people a meaningful way to connect."[104]

A number of choral groups have also disseminated Israeli music in America. While most of these are local in their scope of operations, some travel around the country and even abroad. The best known is the Zamir Chorale, which was founded in 1960 by former Massad campers and continues to perform today. Its repertoire includes choral music drawn from various settings and eras in Jewish history, and it performs many Israeli compositions. For the baby-boomer generation that both provided its original singers and populates much of its audience today, Zamir supplied a trans-denominational and trans-political gateway to Israel by catering to the entire range of the Jewish religious and ideological spectrum. Describing a concert Zamir was planning to mark Israel's 60th anniversary, Mati Lazar, the conductor, observed: "These songs connect us to how we felt in the beginning about Israel. Music can stimulate memory. When you hear certain songs or prayers you can feel where you were when you first heard it, you can feel again the emotion you felt at the time .... It's easy to get stuck in intellec-

---

[103]"Who Wrote *Havah Nagilah?*" http://www.radiohazak.com/Havahist.html

[104]Uriel Heilman, "Israeli Music Strikes Chord in U.S.," Jewish Telegraphic Agency, May 6, 2008.

tual conversations about Israel, but music can bring you to another truth. You may not get every answer but you'll remember what you once knew." [105] This is a strong testament to the power of such concerts to evoke bonds with Israel.

Israeli dancing has played a parallel role. The decade of the 1950s saw a burst of interest in international folk dancing, and American Jews eagerly embraced Israeli dancing as their own distinctive style. Writing about "Hora Hootenannies and Yemenite Hoedowns," historian Emily Katz has traced how thousands of American Jewish young people participated in Israeli dance festivals held at Carnegie Hall in Manhattan, or, less formally, practiced Israeli dance steps in summer camps and youth programs at synagogues and Jewish community centers in many communities, in the process learning the Israeli songs to which the choreography was set. Here is one description from the early 1960s:

> Visit any group of young Jewish girls and boys, from Bangor, Maine, to Corpus Christi, Texas, from Vancouver, Canada, to San Diego, California—the length and breadth of the country, and see how those children dance a hora and sing Israeli songs . . . . We, the middle-aged folk of today, had nothing like it in our youth. As Jews, we lost our identity in . . . the jitterbug. A special Jewish dance for the young? Unthinkable when we were young, except at Jewish weddings.[106]

For American Jews, Israeli dancing at a time when folk dancing was all the rage provided a perfect medium for expressing "ethnic pride and a whiff of national difference without challenging the limits of American cultural pluralism."[107]

During the same period, a number of Jewish organizations—most notably the American-Israel Cultural Foundation—imported Israeli high culture to the U.S., ranging from visiting performances by the Israel Philharmonic Orchestra to traveling

---

[105]Jonathan Mark, "Zamir: They're Playing Our Song—Legendary Chorale Celebrates Israel with Musical Anthology," *New York Jewish Week,* March 28, 2008, pp. 16–17.

[106]*Women's League Outlook* of the Conservative movement, Fall 1962, cited in Katz, "That Land Is Our Land," p. 140. Katz devotes the second chapter of her dissertation to Israeli folk dance in America. A novelistic treatment of Jewish identity that begins and ends with Israeli folk dancing is Allegra Goodman, *Paradise Park* (New York, 2001).

[107]Katz, "That Land Is Our Land," p. 144. A parallel development worthy of exploration is the adoption of Israeli art, Yemenite jewelry, crocheted *kippot,* multicolored *talitot,* and other imported examples of Israeli material culture as a distinctive Jewish couture—indeed the only "Jewish" alternative to Hasidic garb.

exhibits of Israeli art. American fascination with Israeli archaeology was largely triggered by the arrival, in the fall of 1967, of an exhibit about Masada at New York's Jewish Museum that had been planned before the Six-Day War.[108] Those who backed these endeavors were trying both to aid Israel's fledgling economy and highlight its cultural sophistication. Their efforts succeeded as the arrival of high Israeli art and ancient artifacts was met with great enthusiasm both from critics and from Jewish audiences. Not accidentally, these displays also highlighted the cultural affinities between the emerging Jewish state and America, and affirmed the triumph of the Jewish people over the forces that had just recently nearly annihilated it.[109]

Israel also began to figure in American books during the first years of statehood. Between 1948 and 1967, well over 150 books on Israeli life rolled off the presses of American publishing houses. Some were written by non-Jewish admirers, such as Robert St. John (*Shalom Means Peace,* 1949); James McDonald, America's first ambassador to Israel (*My Mission in Israel,* 1951); and James A. Michener (*The Source,* 1965). Others were by Jewish writers, such as Ruth Gruber (*Israel Without Tears,* 1948) and Zelda Popkin (*Quiet Street,* 1951.) The popular breakthrough novel was, of course, Leon Uris's *Exodus* (1958), a panoramic description of Israel's struggle for independence, which sold over four million copies and was made, in 1960, into a motion picture that enjoyed great success (perhaps partially because the hero, played by Paul Newman, looked like a quintessential WASP, and fell in love with a non-Jewish woman).[110]

Since 1967 there has been a cascade of books, films, and television programs about Israel, the sheer volume of which is vastly disproportionate to the country's small size. The emergence of Israeli and Palestinian studies as academic fields has swelled the scholarly literature.[111] On the popular level, the emphasis gradually

---

[108]On the Masada exhibit, see Julie Miller and Richard I. Cohen, "A Collision of Cultures: The Jewish Museum and the Jewish Theological Seminary, 1904–71," in Wertheimer, ed., *Tradition Renewed,* vol. II, pp. 348–49.

[109]Katz, "That Land Is Our Land," p. 193.

[110]These books are discussed in Katz, "This Land Is Our Land," chap. 1. Michelle Mart examines images of Israel in American popular culture during the 1950s in *Eye on Israel: How America Came to View Israel as an Ally* (Albany, N.Y., 2007).

[111]For a listing of many dozens of academic books about Israel published over the past decade and a half, see http://aaupnet.org/news/bfu/israel/list.html

shifted away from *Exodus*-style heroism toward critical analyses of Israeli policies regarding the Palestinians and sober assessments of the country's internal challenges, as well as some satirical treatments. Compare, for example, the high-minded *Raid on Entebbe,* a made-for-TV movie about the rescue of hijacked Israelis in the Ugandan capital, aired in January 1977; *Munich,* the 2005 film describing, with considerable moral ambiguity, Israel's retaliation for the massacre of its athletes at the 1972 Olympics; and *You Don't Mess with the Zohan*, a 2008 movie that treated the (mis)adventures of an Israeli secret agent with utter irreverence.

Writers of serious American fiction have been slow to incorporate Israel into their work. Insofar as American novelists of Jewish origin touched upon Jewish themes at all in the post-World-War-II period, they generally addressed the immigrant experience and generational conflicts within families. Gradually, though, Israeli life began to impinge on the consciousness of American Jewish writers. Among the most notable explorations was Phillip Roth's *The Counterlife* (1987), partially set in Israel, in which the hero recreates himself as a right-wing "settler" in territory conquered during the Six-Day War. Surveying the literary scene at the end of the twentieth century, Sylvia Barack Fishman noted the extent to which works of fiction had begun to

> use Israel as a spiritual site for the exploration of the most basic existential issues. As American Jews journey psychologically and physically to and from Israel, they wrestle with their own personal counterforces. Israel is the place where the American Jewish writers confront the counterlife; it has become the sacral center, if not the geographical center, of the American Jewish psyche.[112]

Movies made in Israel have increasingly drawn the attention of American Jewish filmgoers. The annual Israel Film Festival, founded in 1981, plays in Los Angeles, Miami, and New York—the three largest American Jewish communities—and now showcases more than 60 Israeli films, old and new.[113] A perusal of the titles screened at the San Francisco Jewish Film Festival in July 2008 indicates that the theme with the most entries was "Israeli Di-

---

[112]Sylvia Barack Fishman, "Homelands of the Heart: Israel and Jewish Identity in American Jewish Fiction," in Gal, ed., *Envisioning Israel,* p. 292.

[113]"23rd Israel Film Festival: The Largest Showcase of Israeli Films in the U.S.," www.israelfilmfestival.com/the-festival/about us/

versity."[114] On the East Coast, the 2007 Boston Jewish Film Festival featured a panel discussion with three Israeli filmmakers who were assigned to address the following phenomenon: "Israeli films have roared into the limelight this year, winning critics' kudos and top prizes at major film festivals across the globe. Why has 2007 been so spectacular? What's the Israeli film industry's contribution to this success? Why are Israelis flocking to see homegrown films in unprecedented numbers? And what's the 'it' factor that makes Israeli cinema so stubbornly and astonishingly unique?"[115]

The fact that Meir Fenigstein, a Tel Aviv native who studied at the Boston College of Music, created the Israel Film Festival and remains its driving force exemplifies the role of Israelis as cultural mediators for American Jews. Some Israelis who have settled in the U.S. (or who regularly travel there on business) have come to play a key role in the transfer of Israeli culture to America. Though estimates vary, most authorities put the number of Israelis living in the U.S. at 100,000–150,000, most of them concentrated in the New York area, Los Angeles, Silicon Valley, and, more recently, Atlanta and San Diego.[116] There are several Hebrew-language newspapers—two in Los Angeles alone—and the Israeli expatriates import newspapers, musical performers, films, and other Israeli cultural products. And while Israelis have tended to avoid engagement with the organized American Jewish community, preferring to socialize within their own subgroup,[117] there is a definite cultural spillover effect on some American Jews.[118]

---

[114]http://sfjff.org/festival__2008/topics/?PHPSESSID=1727a4c461a0d28f08a87787ea5bf1c9

[115]"Spotlight on the Israeli Cinema," Boston Jewish Film Festival, November 4, 2007, http://www.bjff.org/festival__indiv__prog.php?prog__id=208

[116]"Israelis in the United States: Reconciling Estimates with the NJPS," http://www.ujc.org/page.html?ArticleID=46358. Sociologist Steven J. Gold—who believes there has been a significant uptick in the number of Israelis settling in the U.S. since 2000—has produced an illuminating survey of the occupational distribution of Israelis in various cities, "Educated and Entrepreneurial," http://www.israelisinamerica.org/articles/?p=6#-more-6, posted August 26, 2005. For press reports on the cultural and religious lives of Israelis in some American cities, see www.israelisinamerica.com

[117]The reasons for this segregation are explored in Steven J. Gold, *The Israeli Diaspora* (Seattle, 2002), esp. pp. 154–80; Moshe Shokeid, *Children of Circumstance: Israeli Emigrants in New York* (Ithaca, N.Y., 1988); and Fran Nachman Putney, "Can Sabras and Americans Find More Common Ground?" *Atlanta Jewish Times*, March 11, 2005.

[118]Lev Hakak, "Contemporary Hebrew Writing in America," http://www.israelisinamerica.org/articles/p=4#more-4, posted August 22, 2005.

Of the varied aspects of Israeli culture, highbrow literature has had the least impact on American Jews. True enough, English translations of the works of major Israeli poets and novelists began appearing as early as the 1960s, but sales have been disappointing. Commenting on this, literary scholar Alan Mintz writes:

> When it comes to the generality of committed Jewish laypeople who are affiliated with Jewish institutions and are involved with the life of the community, it is difficult to find much recognition of the names of Israeli writers, not to mention experience reading their works. In the elite of the community—the rabbis, the educators, the lay and professional leaders of organizations and federations—the name recognition may be there, but familiarity may extend only to the political views of the writers, say those of [Amos] Oz or [David] Grossman, and not to their main literary works. Even university teachers of Jewish Studies tend to regard Hebrew literature not as a source of current cultural creativity that makes claims upon them as intellectuals but as one area of academic specialization among many others. In the end, however, the muted reception of Israeli writing in America is less a reflection of the absolute number of its "users" than a sign of a failure of these writings to become part of the intellectual discourse of the American Jewish community and its cultural repertoire.[119]

Mintz contrasts the scant appreciation for serious Israeli literature with the popularity of sagas that glorify Israel, which serve the need of American Jews to shore up their own identities. "The glow of the heroic-romantic version of Israel abets this process; the moral realism of the Israeli literature . . . apparently does not."[120]

Summarizing Israel's impact on American Jewish religious, educational, and cultural life, it is hard to dispute the view that American Jews have only a shallow grasp of the real Israel.[121] They relate to Israel selectively, with an eye to their own preoccupations as Jews. This situation is really not surprising, nor is it likely to change. After all, how many Italian- or German-Americans can

---

[119]Alan L. Mintz, *Translating Israel: Contemporary Hebrew Literature and its Reception in America* (Syracuse, 2001), p. 3.

[120]Ibid, p. 41.

[121]The point has recently been made in a documentary by Paula Weiman-Kelman entitled "Eyes Wide Open," which follows American tour groups and some individuals as they encounter Israel.

read Italian or German, let alone follow the press and the literature produced in Italy or Germany? How many Korean or Japanese Americans keep up with high culture in their native lands? And we must recall, as well, that Israel is not a point of origin for most American Jews, and few have family members or close friends living there.

Sixty years after Israel's establishment, the goal of forging a strong global Jewish culture with Israel at its center is not only yet to be attained—it has not even been articulated by American Jewish leaders and educators. What has evolved instead is a more subtle and perhaps shallow connection, in which aspects of Israeli culture impinge on American Jews when they visit their local religious, educational, and cultural centers. Reminders of Israel abound in the public gathering places of American Jews and in many of their private homes. But American Jews cannot seriously engage with their Israeli counterparts so long as the two literally and figuratively speak different languages.[122]

ISRAEL AND THE AMERICAN JEWISH ORGANIZATIONAL WORLD

If American Jews in their private lives and their synagogues, schools, and Jewish community centers engage with Israel in a wide yet shallow fashion, the same cannot be said of their organizations. It is, in fact, impossible to understand the history of national Jewish organizations and many local ones without taking into account their intense involvement in Israel-related issues.

One of the remarkable transformations to occur in the first years of Israel's statehood was the eclipse of American Zionist organizations as the central agencies working with Israel and their replacement by the major national organizations. With the exception of some women's Zionist groups, the larger mechanisms of Zionist work in the U.S. were pushed aside by the mainstream agencies,

---

[122]To conduct such pan-Jewish discourse, of course, there would have to be Israeli partners, and the available evidence suggests that while Israelis maintain a strong interest in America, they have far less understanding of or patience for American Jewish concerns. A recent call for Israelis to rethink their attitude is Yehezkel Dror, "Revolutionizing Diaspora Ties," *Jerusalem Post*, April 28, 2008, http://www.jpost.com/servlet/Satellite?cid=1208870512370&pagename=JPost%2FJPArticle%2FPrinter

which took over as partners with Israel.[123] It is today hard to think of a large national American Jewish organization that does not include Israel in its portfolio, a point highlighted by the membership of no less than 55 "major Jewish organizations" in the Conference of Presidents of Major American Jewish Organizations, the umbrella body for agencies heavily invested in issues having to do with Israel.[124]

The rise of non-Zionist organizations as the dominant partners with Israel was promoted by David Ben-Gurion, Israel's first prime minister, who saw no difference between Zionists and non-Zionists after Israel's creation, since, he pointed out, neither fostered aliyah from the U.S. If, then, all that American Zionists were doing was helping Israel financially and politically, the same task could be taken up even more effectively by all American Jews. Hence Ben-Gurion did business with the leaders of non-Zionist organizations, and these proceeded to invade the turf of the Zionist Organization of America, taking over its roles as lobbyist and fund-raiser for Israel. Before long, the federations of Jewish philanthropy became the major arm of American Jewry in raising money for Israel, and a newly created American Zionist Committee for Public Affairs, founded in 1953 and later renamed the American Israel Public Affairs Committee (AIPAC), assumed responsibility for lobbying.[125]

Gradually, other organizations included Israel on their agendas. We have already noted the role of Jacob Blaustein of the American Jewish Committee as a go-between for the non-Zionist organizations and Israel, and in 1962 the formerly non-Zionist AJC opened an office in Israel; the Anti-Defamation League followed suit 15 years later.[126] After the 1967 war, Daniel Elazar wrote, "insuring the survival of Israel has become the heart of the defense

---

[123]Daniel J. Elazar, *Community and Polity: The Organizational Dynamics of American Jewry* (Philadelphia, 1976), p. 200. For a long time Hadassah was an exception to the decline of American Zionist organizations, perhaps because it was also deeply involved in American domestic-policy issues. But it too has been losing significant numbers over the past decade as veteran members die off. Judy Siegel, "Hadassah Confronts Financial Problems, Dwindling Membership," *Jerusalem Post,* June 16, 2008, http://www.jpost.com/servlet/Satellite?pagename=JPost/JPArticle/ShowFull&cid=1215330996081

[124]On the Conference of Presidents and its constituent groups, see http://www.conferenceofpresidents.org/index.asp

[125]These developments are chronicled in Urofsky, *We Are One,* pp. 278–97.

[126]Marianne Sanua, *Let Us Prove Strong: The American Jewish Committee, 1945–2006*

functions of the American Jewish community. Even the community-relations agencies are now spending a high proportion of their time and resources trying to increase support for Israel in the United States."[127] With the already noted involvement of religious, educational, and cultural agencies in the Israel arena, the prominent role played by federations in Israeli social welfare, and the advocacy carried out by American Jewish community-relations organizations, few national bodies were left out of the mix. Subsequently, many dozens of additional groups were founded by American Jews to serve as liaisons with Israel. The 2007 edition of the *American Jewish Year Book* lists over 100 organizations in the U.S. claiming an involvement with Israel, a figure that does not include all the "friends of" organizations established to raise funds for individual Israeli institutions.

What have these organizations done for Israel? Predominantly, they have raised money. Not surprisingly, the largest sums were donated in times of crisis. Describing the American Jewish response to the Six-Day War, for example, Arthur Hertzberg wrote: "It is ingrained in the American Jewish soul that the correct response to a danger is to give money. This was certainly the immediate reaction to the Middle East crisis [of 1967] . . . . There are innumerable stories from every Jewish community throughout the United States not only of giving on a fantastic scale by people of large means, but also of the literal sacrifice of their life savings by people of modest means."[128] After crises passed, some of the American organizations managed to identify new ones, and thus sustain "emergency" fund-raising year after year.

During the first 50 years of statehood, the federations, in conjunction with the United Jewish Appeal (UJA), became the primary fund-raising arm for Israel, channeling money through the United Israel Appeal (UIA) and the American Jewish Joint Distribution Committee (JDC). Israel used these funds for housing, vocational training, social welfare, rural settlement, youth care,

(Hanover, N.H., 2007), pp. 58–66; *ADL and Israel: 50 Years of Advocacy* (New York, 1998), p. 5.

[127]Daniel J. Elazar, "Decision-Making in the American Jewish Community," cited in Chaim I. Waxman, "The Centrality of Israel in American Jewish Life: A Sociological Analysis," *Judaism* 25, Spring 1976, p. 178.

[128]Arthur Hertzberg, "Israel and American Jewry, *Commentary* 44, August 1967, p. 69.

preschool and higher education, and, most important, absorption of new immigrants.[129] Over the first three decades of Israel's existence UJA transferred over $3.7 billion dollars to Israel via the UIA and the JDC, and during the next three decades sent double that sum.

However, the percentage of total funds raised by the federations that were allocated for Israel plummeted. In the prime year of crisis, 1948, nearly three-quarters of federation receipts went to Israel; in the next year of crisis, 1967, the figure topped 78 percent. By the decade of the 1990s, though, the percentage set aside for Israel dropped into the 40-percent range, and early in the twenty-first century it declined to under 25 percent.[130] The decline stems primarily from the flat campaigns of federations, which have led to cutbacks for all agencies. Since local needs, the first priority of federations, were becoming more pressing, and Israel's economy was improving substantially, it became difficult to justify continuing to send huge sums to Israel.

Another avenue through which American Jews contributed to the development of Israel's infrastructure was their purchase of Israel Bonds. Especially during the early years of statehood, these bonds were critically needed to sustain Israel's vast absorption and military costs. Describing the allure of bonds to Jews in Miami—consistently one of the top markets for them during the 1950s—historian Deborah Dash Moore writes:

> Unlike the Central Jewish Appeal [of the local federation], Israel Bonds gave Miami Jews a direct, continuous, and powerful tie with the Jewish state and a concrete means of building the Jewish homeland. Increasingly Miami Jews responded to the message of the constant campaigns. Israel became their homeland, too, through their wholehearted investment in its economic future. Lacking strong ties to their new homes, Miami Jews preferred to purchase bonds that gave them a stake in a surrogate home. Although government speakers often presented Israel as besieged, an island of democracy in a hostile sea, this imagery always accompanied an emphasis on defense, on action, on an aggressive preparedness. Jews in Miami could

---

[129]Edward Bernard Gluck, *The Triangular Connection: America, Israel and American Jews* (London, 1982), p. 109.

[130]These figures are graphically available in the entry "American Jewish Contributions to Israel (1948–2004)" at www.jewishvirtuallibrary.orgjsource/US-Israel/ujatab.html

> appreciate this stance in other Jews, especially when those others were ready to face the dangers. Israel provided an arena to implement frontier visions they could not imagine pursuing in Miami. Israel offered them a future, a chance to help create a new Jewish society, and the power and glamour of statehood. Since they could not seize these perquisites in Miami or even in Miami Beach, they encountered little resistance to adopting Israel as the source of their redemption. Israel guaranteed the Jewish future, and bonds guaranteed Israel. The link was simple, the identification was direct. Bonds were a powerful vehicle to implement dreams.[131]

By 1993, over $13 billion dollars had been invested in Israel Bonds, including over $1 billion in that year alone; for the rest of the decade annual sales hovered between $900 million and a bit over $1 billion. With the passage of time, though, many of these bonds were held by large banks and investment houses, and so stopped serving their earlier psychological function.[132]

In addition to general fund-raising for Israel, federations have also sought to play a more hands-on role through partnership programs. In the 1970s, Project Renewal was launched as a cooperative venture between the Israeli government and the federations to improve conditions in disadvantaged Israeli neighborhoods. Local community officials in Israel were given a direct say in how funds would be spent, and individual U.S. federations took on responsibility for a particular "twin" city, even exchanging visits with its inhabitants. Thus Project Renewal enabled American activists to come into direct contact with Israeli beneficiaries, providing the Americans a far more realistic understanding of Israeli conditions and of the flesh-and-blood individuals whom they supported.[133] By the late 1990s, another version of twinning was developed by federations jointly with the Jewish Agency for Israel, called Partnership 2000. Individual federations worked with a twin city, or area, in Israel, improving economic life, providing educational opportunities for young Israelis, delivering services to patients afflicted

---

[131]Deborah Dash Moore, "Bonding Images: Miami Jews and the Campaign for Israel Bonds," in Gal, ed., *Envisioning Israel*, pp. 265–66.

[132]Joel Bainerman, "End American Aid to Israel? Yes, It Does Harm," *Middle East Quarterly* 2, September 1995, pp. 3–12; Brian Mono, "Investing in Israel Grows More Complex," *Philadelphia Jewish Exponent*, March 4, 2002, p. 16.

[133]For an evaluation of the program, see Arnold Gurin and David Rosen, *Project Renewal and North American Jewish Communities: Ongoing Effects* (Waltham, Mass., 1991), esp. pp. 1, 26–29.

with Alzheimer's disease, and training Ethiopian immigrants, to cite a few examples.[134]

For several decades, funds sent by the federations dwarfed all other American Jewish aid to Israel. That began to change in the 1980s, and by the time Israel reached its 50th birthday American Jews were transferring twice as many dollars to Israel through the various "friends of" agencies as they were via UJA contributions.[135] Every major Israeli university, hospital, museum, and cultural center, as well as quite a few yeshivas and non-Orthodox religious institutions, established fund-raising vehicles in the U.S., and Israeli political parties have done so as well. Each of these makes possible targeted giving by American Jews eager to support a favorite cause.[136] Among the largest of the organizations is the New Israel Fund (NIF), founded in 1980 to support agencies it deemed "progressive causes in Israel." To date, the NIF has disbursed over $200 million to the Association for Civil Rights in Israel, various agencies that promote Arab-Israeli coexistence, Panim—Jewish Renewal, rape crisis centers, and the like.[137]

This tendency mirrors the shift occurring in American Jewish domestic philanthropy away from the federation umbrella structure to what some have called "boutique giving." While this change in form does not necessarily imply a decline in the overall amount of money allocated, it has generated anguished questions about the future of American Jewish philanthropy, and, in terms of Israel, has raised the prospect of a disengagement from Israel—if not from specific Israeli causes—by a great many American Jews.[138]

---

[134]Thus Washington, D.C., works with the city of Beit Shemesh and communities in Judaea; Chicago with three cities in the Negev; Boston with Haifa; New York with Jerusalem; and Los Angeles with Tel Aviv.

[135]Stephen G. Greene, "Making Friends in America," *Chronicle of Philanthropy,* June 13, 1996, p. 29. For a report on the accumulated gifts donated to specific "American friends" groups, see Sara Berman, "UJA Eclipsed by Targeted Gifts to Israel," *Forward,* March 6, 1998, p. 1.

[136]Jack Wertheimer, "Current Trends in American Jewish Philanthropy," *American Jewish Year Book* 97 (New York, 1997), pp. 33–40.

[137]http://www.nif.org/about

[138]See, for example, Karen Arenson, "Donations to a Jewish Philanthropy Ebb," *New York Times,* December 27, 1995, http://query.nytimes.com/gst/fullpage.html?res=9D02E7D61539F934A15751C1A963958260&scp=1&sq=Karen%20Arenson,%20Jewish%20philanthropy&st=cse; Charles Hoffman, "The 'Me' Generation and Israel," *Jerusalem Post International Edition,* June 17, 1989, p. 12; Marilyn Henry, "To Give and Receive," *Jerusalem Post,* April 23, 1999, p. 19.

One factor that helps explain the change is a general detachment of American Jews from organizations, a process parallel to the erosion of civic engagement in American society as a whole. Looking specifically at the moderately engaged Jewish population, Steven M. Cohen and Arnold M. Eisen, authors of *The Jew Within,* traced how "the forces of personalism and privatization" impelled many Jews to withdraw from the Jewish public sphere into a far more private domain. Regarding Jewish organizations as "remote and irrelevant," the Jews they studied were disenchanted not with Israel, but with organized American Jewish life.[139]

Another reason for the drop in UJA giving may be the shortening of distance between American Jews and Israel brought by quicker transportation and improved communications technology. One observer has noted the extent to which American Jews had, in the past, relied upon the UJA to serve as a mediating institution that informed them about ways to help Israel, but that function was now obsolete. "The high costs of gathering information about needs for and uses of donations encouraged the formation of a central organization. This suggests another explanation for the decline in funds donated overseas. The costs of information have declined, reducing the need for a central system to collect and distribute funds."[140]

We should also not minimize the dampening effect upon giving that Israeli leaders have when they publicly downplay the importance of American Jewish philanthropy. An Israeli ambassador to Washington recently crisscrossed the U.S. extolling Israel as the "land of milk and start-ups," and prime ministers of Israel have berated Jewish fund-raising campaigns for depicting hungry Israeli children. Most notably, Yossi Beilin, a one-time leading Israeli politician, has urged the UJA to get out of the social-welfare business entirely. The expression of such views makes it harder to convince American Jews to channel their money to Israel.[141]

---

[139]Steven M. Cohen and Arnold M. Eisen, *The Jew Within: Self, Family and Community in America* (Bloomington, Ind., 2000), pp. 137, 152. The broader tendency toward privatization and the depletion of "social capital" in American society was noted by Robert Putnam during the 1990s and explored in his book, *Bowling Alone: The Collapse and Revival of American Community* (New York, 2000).

[140]Helen Roberts, "American Jewish Donations to Israel," *Contemporary Jewry* 20, 1999, p. 201.

[141]Marilyn Henry, "Metro Views: The Crisis of American Jewish Philanthropy," *Jerusalem Post,* May 3, 2008, www.jpost.com/servlet/Sattelite?cid=1209626999320

Despite the changing patterns of giving, American Jews still contribute large sums to Israel. But even so, in the words of one observer, "because such giving is spread over a wide range of causes, its overall impact within Israel is by definition diffuse and the resulting influence, slight."[142] This has become the case especially in recent years, as Israel's Gross National Product has risen to unprecedented levels and the average income of Israelis compares favorably to that of workers in other Western countries, diminishing further the cumulative impact of American Jewish philanthropy. On the other hand, the recent scandal involving envelopes stuffed with cash given to Prime Minister Ehud Olmert suggests that the infusion of American Jewish dollars for particular ideological causes and on behalf of otherwise marginal groups has had greater impact than we know.

Beyond their financial contributions, American Jews have developed organizational mechanisms to advocate and lobby in support of Israel. Here, the community-relations field has been central. The large national organizations, which embraced the cause of Israel virtually since the founding of the state, seek to explain to the American government why it ought to side with Israel, stressing that country's democratic character and the parallels in its history to the American experience. Their efforts are complemented by local Jewish community relations councils, which also defend Israel, an activity generally encouraged by the national umbrella agency for these councils, the Jewish Council for Public Affairs (JCPA), formerly the National Jewish Community Relations Advisory Council (NJCRAC).[143] Several organizations concentrate on setting the record of Israel straight in the media, including CAMERA (Committee for Accuracy in Middle East Reporting in America), founded in 1982, and the Israel Project.[144]

Since the outbreak of the second intifada, dozens of additional groups have emerged to train Jews to interpret Israeli policies—especially regarding the conflict with the Palestinians—on campuses and in other civic settings. Many of these are run by

---

[142]Lederhendler, "The Diaspora Factor in Israeli Life," p. 127.

[143]On JCPA's Israel Advocacy Initiative, see http://www.jewishpublicaffairs.org/organizations.php3?action=printContentItem&orgid=54&typeID=1347&itemID=21305&User_Session=05d15482b4f2db774c4193a74d0fbd9d

[144]http://www.camera.org/index.asp?x_context=24; http://www.theisraelproject.org

federations, the Jewish campus organization Hillel, and the religious movements. A number of foundations have put resources into such endeavors. Thus the Charles and Lynn Schusterman Family Foundation, in cooperation with Hillel and a network of national Jewish organizations, created the Israel on Campus Coalition (ICC), and the Grinspoon Foundation has trained hundreds of college students as Grinspoon Israel advocacy fellows to act as campus organizers for Israel.[145]

Another model is the David Project for Jewish Leadership, which has developed over 100 high-school programs and 16 gap-year programs in Israel to prepare young American Jews to stand up for Israel when they enter college. In its own words,

> The David Project has a long-term strategy—to populate the campuses with educated, trained, and confident college students, to prepare high school students and Jewish teens to be proactive Israel activists, and to activate the Jewish community in response to the growing anti-Israel discourse. Our strategy is based on a unique analysis for understanding and communicating to others the nature of the Arab-Israeli conflict. Our approach enables participants to understand the complexities of the Arab-Israeli conflict by promoting critical thinking, historical accuracy, moral decision-making and activism.[146]

By arming young Jews with information about Israel's policies, such efforts give students the ability to stand their ground when Israel is bashed. But the programs also have certain drawbacks. For one thing, they make room for few if any doubts about Israeli policies, and so may seriously narrow their target population, alienating students who are generally pro-Israel but do not want to engage in apologetics.[147] And perhaps more important, they focus almost exclusively on geopolitics, thus losing the opportunity to expose American Jews to the lives of Israelis in all their complex-

---

[145]http://www.hgf.org/israel; http://www.hillel.org/israel/work/grinspoon.htm. Also see the video on Israel advocacy developed by the Jewish United Fund of Chicago, at http://www.juf.org/interactive/video.aspx?id=27886, and the Web page devoted to the issue by Women of Reform Judaism, http://www.womenofreformjudaism.org/programming/resolutions-statements/israel-advocy

[146]http://davidproject.org

[147]For a report on how Israel advocacy projects can impact negatively on some young people, see Jason Nielson, "Young Adults Avoid Israel Advocacy: People in their 20s and 30s Less Involved Than Others," *Boston Jewish Advocate,* June 19, 2003.

ity. This has been noticed by a competitor organization, the Orthodox outreach group Aish Hatorah, which proposes an alternative path to Israel advocacy, saying, "We need to show the world what Israel is beyond the conflict [with the Palestinians]; we need to show people how Israel innovates and creates."[148]

The most visible and controversial form of American Jewish advocacy for Israel is the lobbying that seeks to influence American government leaders. The most important lobbying group is AIPAC, which targets members of the U.S. Congress. With a membership said to exceed 100,000, AIPAC can enlist an army of volunteers anywhere in the U.S. to try to sway their representatives in Washington. In addition to AIPAC, at least 30 local pro-Israel political action committees (PACs) operate around the country, drawing mainly upon Jewish supporters. Among them are City PAC, based in Chicago, which, since 1984, has supported candidates for political office who are sympathetic to Israel, Florida Congressional Committee PAC, and Washington PAC, which bills itself as the second largest pro-Israel PAC, presumably after AIPAC.[149]

Lobbying for Israel has generated stiff criticism over the years. In response to the uptick in American economic and military aid to Israel following the 1973 Yom Kippur War, for example, some prominent Americans began to grumble about the undue influence of the Israel lobby. George Ball, the former undersecretary of state, expressed concern in the early 1980s that "America . . . seems disabled by domestic constraints from effectively promoting peace or restraining Israeli adventurism," and he was joined by Sen. Charles Mathias (R., Md.), who believed ethnic groups "sometimes press causes that derogate from the national interest."[150] As Israel-U.S. military and political ties grew, so did this type of criticism.

The most recent eruption occurred during the administration of President George W. Bush, which was extraordinarily sympathetic to Israel's security interests. In their book *The Israel Lobby and U.S. Foreign Policy,* John Mearsheimer and Stephen Walt charged

---

[148]"A New Paradigm for Israel Advocacy," http://www.aish.com/jewishissues/mediaob-jectivity/A__New__Paradigm__for__Israel__Advocacy.asp

[149]http://www.citypac.org/home/?page__id=18; http://fccpac.com; http://www.washingtonpac.com

[150]Both are quoted in Wolf Blitzer, "The AIPAC Formula: Why the American Israel Public Affairs Committee is Washington's Most Effective Lobby—and American Jewry's Newest Glamour Organization," *Moment* 6, November 1981, p. 25.

that the pro-Israel lobby—and most specifically AIPAC—was highly effective in pushing U.S. foreign policy in a pro-Israel direction even against American national interests—for example, in opposing the Palestinian cause, invading Iraq, and threatening Iran—while managing to spread the "myth" that what is good for Israel is also good for the U.S. According to Mearsheimer and Walt, the lobby holds considerable sway over the White House, the media, and especially Congress, deriving its clout from its army of activists who have the power to punish recalcitrant legislators at the ballot box.

Truth be told, their book is civil and polite toward the pro-Israel community when compared to the more rabid conspiracy theories about Jewish control of American institutions of government, which are, in turn, rooted in age-old anti-Semitic stereotypes. Even the most cursory Internet search will highlight the extent of the paranoia that surrounds discussion of lobbying efforts on behalf of Israel. Despite these attacks, American Jews who support Israel continue to invest their political capital on behalf of the Jewish state, a sure sign that they feel "at home" in America.

There are pro-Israel American Jews who express dissatisfaction with AIPAC for allegedly marching in lockstep with Israeli policies, and recently these dissenters have established a counterpart named J Street. With an initial operating budget of $1.5 million—as compared with AIPAC's $100-million endowment—J Street draws support from several small organizations with a dovish perspective, such as Americans for Peace Now; the Chicago-based Brit Tzedek v'Shalom (Jewish Alliance for Justice and Peace); and the Tikkun Community, centered around the magazine of that name. Its first public act was a set of endorsements of candidates for Congress in 2008.[151]

The J Street mission statement says:

> J Street was founded to promote meaningful American leadership to end the Arab-Israeli and Palestinian-Israeli conflicts peacefully and diplomatically. We support a new direction for American policy in the Middle East and a broad public and policy debate about the U.S.

[151]Neil A. Lewis, "U.S. Jews Create Lobby to Temper Israel Policy," *New York Times*, April 25, 2008, p. A20; Leila Krieger, "New Pro-Israel PAC Endorses First Congressional Candidates," *Jerusalem Post*, June 17, 2008, http://www.jpost.com/servlet/Satellite?cid=1212659749305&pagename=JPost%2FJPArticle%2FShowFull

> role in the region. We believe ending the Israeli-Palestinian conflict is in the best interests of Israel, the United States, the Palestinians, and the region as a whole.[152]

It is too early to speculate on J Street's eventual impact.

What motivates the large American Jewish organizational infrastructure that raises money for Israel and advocates on its behalf, even when no crisis confronts the Jewish state? Already during the 1950s, sociologists Marshall Sklare and Joseph Greenblum found extraordinary levels of support for both activities: 91 percent of Jewish respondents in the growing suburb they named Lakeville approved of raising money for Israel, and 63 percent favored influencing U.S. foreign policy in favor of Israel. A far smaller percentage belonged to Zionist organizations, leading the authors to conclude that "while willing to take a political stand in connection with their Jewish identity, the majority of our respondents do not favor Zionist organizations as the vehicle for exercising such influence. Zionist organizations are viewed as agencies whose sole concern is with Israel; the majority of our respondents reject the necessity of adherence to a specialized pro-Israel association." Instead, they wanted general-purpose Jewish organizations to assume the responsibility.[153]

Beyond the altruism and sense of solidarity that motivates American Jews to back Israel, we should not overlook the positive role such aid to Israel has played in building organized Jewish life in the U.S. Writing in the mid-1970s—a peak time for Israel activism—political scientist Daniel Elazar concluded:

> Jews who would deny the necessity for complete dedication to Israel's cause are, in effect, read out of Jewish communal life, while those who occupy the most important positions in Jewish communal life are usually people who can claim to be playing some significant role in the maintenance of Israel's security. Fund-raising for Israel, with its constantly accelerating demands, has become the most visible Jewish communal activity and has been the stimulus for the general increase in funds raised for across-the-board Jewish purposes in the

---

[152]http://www.jstreet.org/about/about-us

[153]Sklare and Greenblum, *Jewish Identity on the Suburban Frontier,* pp. 225, 226. Other factors shaping these attitudes were undoubtedly vicarious pride in Israel's successes and repressed guilt feelings over American Jewish failure to act on behalf of European Jews during the Holocaust.

> United States since the end of World War II. This has not only had certain direct effects, but also the substantial indirect effect of enhancing the Jewish federations, the organizations whose task it is to raise the funds.[154]

By dedicating resources to Israel, Jewish organizations achieved credibility with the large numbers of American Jews for whom this priority resonated.

Involvement with Israel has also given Jewish organizations a political role far transcending the small population of American Jews they claim to represent. As supporters of Israel, Jewish organizations have been thrust onto the international stage. Lay and professional leaders of the federation world, AJC, the Anti-Defamation League, and other pro-Israel organizations routinely host and visit the top echelon of American elected officials, and travel the globe to meet with heads of state, foreign ministers, and leaders of industry and finance, fulfilling their self-defined roles as advocates for Israel. It is hard to think of any other American ethnic group whose organizations command so much attention from the most powerful world leaders, attention they attract because of their involvement with Israel.[155]

Moreover, serious involvement with Israel has also given Jewish organizations a specifically Jewish purpose. Historian Eli Lederhendler has captured the point well:

> Links with Israel provide Diaspora philanthropy with an explicitly *Jewish* function that complements its health-and-welfare-related or social functions. In a very real sense, the ability to forge philanthropic ties with Israel is crucial to a Diaspora community's ability to carry on a more intensive organizational life. . . . Donating funds to Israel *is* an investment in Diaspora Jewish life, even as it represents tangible input into Israeli society . . . . When the Jewish Diaspora places financial resources at Israel's disposal, it must use its own *human* resources in particularly focused ways: it must exert leadership, articulate priorities, mobilize a following, and—not least—assert its role as a *Diaspora* vis a vis Israel.[156]

---

[154]Elazar, *Community and Polity,* pp. 80–81.

[155]The negative side to this high-powered political involvement, discussed above, is the routine grumbling, if not conspiratorial accusations, about the role played by the "Israel lobby."

[156]Lederhendler, "The Diaspora Factor in Israeli Life," p. 121.

Just as in an earlier era defense organizations asserted American Jewish primacy by virtue of their leadership role in combating anti-Semitism, during the years of Israel's statehood organizations that could demonstrate their effectiveness in channeling money to Israel or mobilizing strong lobbying on its behalf have gained credibility as leading actors in American Jewish life. For much of the past 60 years, intense involvement with Israel gave these agencies a positive Jewish mission, catapulting them into the limelight.[157]

WHAT AMERICAN JEWS THINK ABOUT ISRAEL

Surveying Jewish Attitudes

Despite all that American Jews do for and about Israel, the media and Jewish organizations show far more interest in tracing what American Jews think about Israel. For the general media, the ebb and flow of American Jewish attitudes make for interesting news stories, and if criticism of Israel is on the rise, reporters can focus on how American Jews are wracked by tensions and anguish. Jewish organizations, for their part, feel a need to take the pulse of their constituents, on the assumption that wavering feelings toward Israel may presage a broad decline in attachment among American Jews.

Within weeks after the establishment of Israel, AJC sponsored a survey of Jews and Christians in Baltimore to measure their attitudes toward the new state. The questions posed were themselves quite revealing of Jewish preoccupations at the time. For example, to test a respondent's knowledge of the situation, the survey asked where the fighting over the Jewish state was taking place, who were the participants, whether any Western country had been actively involved in governing Palestine, and what name was given to the new state. The pollsters found that Baltimore Jews passed with flying colors, three-quarters answering all questions correctly.

---

[157]During the course of interviewing several dozen Jewish leaders about American Jewish organizational life in 2006–07, I asked interviewees to identify the organizations they considered the most important in Jewish life. Almost invariably, organizations primarily involved with Israel were at the top of the lists.

They also found that native-born males with more education and higher incomes were most likely than others to answer all questions correctly.[158]

As some American Jews were fearful at the time that Jews might be charged with "dual loyalty" if they identified too closely with Israel, the survey probed this area too, finding that Jews with high levels of Jewish engagement expected domestic anti-Semitism to decline, whereas the least involved Jews were more worried about a rise. Still, the authors concluded, "being pro-Israel posed no threat, insofar as most of our respondents were concerned, to loyalty to the United States. The two countries stood for two different kinds of commitments and ties, neither of which clashed with the other and both of which were essential to our respondents' total image of themselves as American Jews." As for their views on the creation of Israel, 90 percent approved the establishment of the state and U.S. recognition of it. Finally, the survey found that while degree of commitment to Jewish life had no correlation with being pro- or anti-Israel, it did correlate with the intensity of a Jew's response to Israel.[159]

In a 1957 study of a community identified as Riverton, Marshall Sklare found that 94 percent of Jews expressed favorable feelings toward Israel.[160] A few years later Sklare and a colleague published another survey, of a community they called Lakeville, which first used a question that subsequently became a standard gauge for researchers to measure attachment to Israel: "If the Arab nations should succeed in carrying out their threat to destroy Israel, would you feel a very deep, some, or no personal sense of loss?" Ninety percent of respondents answered they would feel some loss, 65 percent describing it as "deep"; 10 percent said they would feel no sense of loss. The researchers probed for factors behind these responses. Some Jews considered such a tragedy tantamount to another Holocaust. Others saw it as a loss of pride in Israel's achievements ("They are fellow coreligionists who have struggled hard.

---

[158]Marshall Sklare and Benjamin Ringer, "A Study of Jewish Attitudes Toward the State of Israel," in Sklare, ed., *The Jews: Social Patterns of an American Group* (New York, 1960), p. 439.

[159]Ibid, pp. 448, 450, 440, 442.

[160]Cited in Eytan Gilboa, *Israel in the Mind of American Jews: Public Opinion Trends and Analysis* (London, 1986), p. 5.

They have done wonderful things. They're wonderful people; I'd hate to have anything happen to them."). And still others identified with Israeli Jews simply as fellow Jews ("Being a Jew, you can't help but feel for other Jews."). For those who expressed no sense of loss, humanitarian impulses apparently transcended any special feeling for fellow Jews ("I feel a deep sense of personal loss whenever a democratic nation is submerged.").[161]

Immediately after the Six-Day War, the authors of the Lakeville study returned to the scene and questioned Jews again. Most respondents reported feeling very concerned in the period leading up to the war in late May and early June 1967. Based on his interviews, Sklare described the mood as follows: "a psychological reaction probably occurred, namely, that if the Israelis are bearing the brunt of the struggle, the least that we comfortably situated American Jews can do is worry. Those who deprive us of this function will make us feel like bad Jews whereas we wish to consider ourselves to be good Jews."[162] The Jews of Lakeville also responded to the war by strongly supporting the Israeli position and increasing their philanthropic contributions during the crisis. Here, too, Sklare astutely took the measure of his interview subjects:

> Strange as it may seem, our respondents even today connect their own actions with the Israeli victory. If the winning of any war ever depends upon superior financial means, the Six-Day War was not such a war: by the time the first public (if not private) fund-raising meetings could be convened, victory was a foregone conclusion. But sober businessmen long experienced in problems of procurement, of manufacturing, and of transportation, acted as if the money they contributed one day could somehow miraculously be turned into the sinews of war the very next day. Because they wanted to believe in such a miracle, the emphasis was not upon pledges—the usual form of Jewish fund-raising—but on a different approach: the giving of cash.

Sklare goes on to note how completely the identification with Israel was acted out by Jewish givers: when the swift Israeli victory obviated the need for war aid, philanthropists quickly shifted their

[161]Sklare and Greenblum, *Jewish Identity on the Suburban Frontier,* pp. 215–19.

[162]Marshall Sklare, "Lakeville and Israel: The Six-Day War and Its Aftermath," in his posthumously published collection of essays edited by Jonathan Sarna, *Observing America's Jews* (Hanover, N.H., 1973), p. 110.

rationale and signaled that their largess would "keep Israel from losing the peace."[163]

For all of this immediate outpouring of worry and dollars, Sklare was forced to conclude that neither the crisis nor the war made a fundamental impact on the essential orientation of his interviewees in regard to Israel. Few changed their views on the types of support they were prepared to offer, whether through philanthropy, seeking to influence U.S. foreign policy, prioritizing Israel over local Jewish causes, encouraging their children to live in Israel, or immigrating there themselves.[164]

If the Six-Day War had only a limited impact on the behavior of American Jews, spurring them to higher levels of philanthropic and lobbying support but not forcing them to rethink their ways, it did have a greater impact on how American Jews thought about Israel. Writing in the wake of the Yom Kippur War, Norman Podhoretz explained the "Zionization" of American Jewry:

> When in 1967 and then again in 1973, the Jews of Israel were suddenly and violently hurled into mortal peril, the Jews of America responded not as people doing something in a philanthropic spirit for others; they responded as though their own lives, their own families and their own homes, were immediately and imminently at stake. The feeling was—and is—that if Israel were to be annihilated, the Jews of America would also disappear.[165]

American Jews, Podhoretz went on, feared they might cease to exist, either through physical annihilation for the second time in one century, or voluntarily, because "the burden of Jewish history is just too grievous to bequeath to one's descendants."[166] Whatever

---

[163]Ibid, p. 113.

[164]Ibid, pp. 123–24. A similar view is presented by Chaim I. Waxman, "The Limited Impact of the Six-Day War on America's Jews," in Eli Lederhendler, ed., *The Six-Day War and World Jewry* (Bethesda, Md., 2000), pp. 99–115. Lederhendler disagrees, speculating that the war "threw into relief the apparent gulf between Israelis (who could fend for themselves) and Jews (who could not). . . . While Jews celebrated their solidarity with Israel, they also became more conscious of what their own lives as non-Israeli Jews lacked in cultural and political terms—and hence, what was required to make such lives more worthwhile and more capable of being sustained. In this paradoxical cultural dialectic, the confrontation with a victorious Israel became the basis for an enlivened Diasporism." Eli Lederhendler, *New York Jews and the Decline of Urban Ethnicity, 1950–70* (Syracuse, 2001), pp. 190–91.

[165]Norman Podhoretz, "Now, Instant Zionism," *New York Times Sunday Magazine*, February 23, 1974, pp. 11ff.

[166]Podhoretz ascribes this phrase to Irving Kristol, ibid, p. 43.

their reasons, American Jews in the decade following the Six-Day War seemed more intensely focused on Israel, determined to provide the means it needed to ensure its survival.

They also incorporated Israel into their own self-conception as Jews. Writing in the mid-1980s about the "civil religion" of American Jews, Jonathan Woocher noted the "centrality of Israel" in that civil faith.[167] Striking evidence could be found in a survey of Reform Jews conducted in 1970, which found that 80 percent of respondents regarded support for Israel as essential to being a "good Jew."[168] Reform, a Jewish subgroup that was traditionally cool to Zionism and had, in the past, displayed relatively low levels of engagement with Israel, had shifted position dramatically.

Beginning in the 1980s, however, sociologists began to sense a weakening of this intensely pro-Israel posture in the American Jewish community as opinion research found evidence that declining percentages of American Jews felt a strong sense of engagement with Israel. Some of the change was attributable to the growing chorus of criticism expressed by some American Jewish elites about specific Israeli policies (the details will be discussed below), and American Jews may also have been influenced by declining sympathy for Israel among American non-Jews.[169]

In a series of surveys conducted over a 20-year period, sociologist Steven M. Cohen has tracked the ebb and flow of American Jewish attachment to Israel. Snapshots of his findings portray the nature of the changes:

> The result of the 1997 survey certainly point in the direction of diminished support for Israel [as compared to a survey conducted in 1988.]. When asked about their emotional attachment to Israel, just 9 percent answered "extremely attached" (as opposed to 13 percent in the 1988 study), and only another 18 percent said "very attached" (versus 24 percent in 1988). In other words, a total of just over a quarter (27 percent in 1997, versus 37 percent in 1988) defined themselves as at least very attached to Israel. When asked how close they feel to Israelis, 8 percent said "to a great extent" (against 19 percent

---

[167]Jonathan S. Woocher, *Sacred Survival: The Civil Religion of American Jews* (Bloomington, Ind., 1986).

[168]Leonard Fein, *Reform is a Verb: Notes on Reform and Reforming Jews* (New York, 1972), p. 69.

[169]See Cohen, "Relationships of American Jews with Israel," p. 134.

> in 1988), and 41 percent answered "to some extent" (versus 54 percent in 1988). About a third do see Israel as extremely important to their sense of being Jewish. These results place Israel well down on the list of symbols and concepts that seem to resonate with American Jews. . . . With respect to their ideas of the good Jew, just 20 percent thought it was essential for a good Jew to support Israel, and even fewer (18 percent) had similar views regarding visiting Israel during one's life. For most respondents, these behaviors were at least desirable, but about a third, in fact, found them irrelevant to their concept of a good Jew. Most respondents (52 percent) agreed that Israel is critical to sustaining American Jewish life. Three-quarters also rejected the view that Israel does not really need American Jewish charity any more (a view increasingly widespread among American Jewish donors).[170]

Almost a decade later, Cohen reported on another survey conducted in late 2004 and early 2005; in this case, his point of comparison was with opinion research he had conducted in 2002, during the peak of the second intifada. His overall finding: "Respondents were less likely than in comparable earlier surveys to say they care about Israel, talk about Israel with others or engage in a range of pro-Israel activities." Twenty-six percent claimed they were "very emotionally attached to Israel," compared with 31 percent who said so a couple of years earlier. Nearly two-thirds said they followed the news about Israel closely, down from 74 percent in 2002, while 39 percent said they talked about Israel frequently with Jewish friends, down from 53 percent in 2002. When respondents were asked how much "caring about Israel" mattered for their personal Jewish identity, 48 percent said it mattered "a lot," as compared to 58 percent in 2002. And on the question of whether "caring about Israel is a very important part of my being Jewish," 57 percent answered affirmatively, compared with 73 percent of respondents in a similar survey undertaken in 1989. As to their views of Israeli policies, more than two-thirds said they were at least sometimes "disturbed" by Israel's policies or actions, and nearly

---

[170]Ibid, pp. 140–41. Among Cohen's studies of American Jewish attitudes toward Israel, published by AJC, are *Ties and Tensions: The 1986 Survey of American Jewish Attitudes Toward Israel and Israelis* (New York, 1987); *Ties and Tensions: An Update: The 1989 Survey of American Jewish Attitudes Toward Israel and Israelis* (New York, 1989); and *After the Gulf War: American Jews' Attitudes Toward Israel: The 1991 National Survey of American Jews* (New York, 1992).

as many said they were "confused." Almost 40 percent said they were sometimes "alienated" by Israel, and 13 percent said they were "sometimes uncomfortable identifying as supporters of Israel," with an additional 14 percent "not sure." Finally, slightly more than a third said they were often or always "engaged" by Israel, while 47 percent said they were sometimes engaged and 18 percent said they were never engaged.[171]

The results of surveys conducted over a 60-year period indicate that American Jewish attitudes fluctuated, in part based upon how seriously Israel seemed to be in jeopardy and in part based on general American attitudes toward Israel. This was demonstrated most recently in a survey conducted after the 9/11 attacks: between January and October 2001, the percentage of American Jews who claimed to be "somewhat" or "very" attached to Israel rose from 72 to 82 percent; conversely, the self-described "not attached to Israel" Jews declined from 27 to 18 percent.[172] Clearly, the sense that Israel and the U.S. were facing similar threats and the feeling that non-Jewish Americans felt this kinship as well made American Jews more comfortable in attaching themselves to Israel. But the drop in the percentage of Jews expressing attachment to Israel from 2002 to 2004, noted above, shows that this did not last long.

Opinion research also makes it possible to study variations in attitudes toward Israel between American Jewish subgroups:

1. Gender: Beginning in the 1980s, researchers found that Jewish women tended to take more hawkish positions than men on Israeli policy, and were more likely to oppose political candidates deemed unfriendly to Israel. [173] Data from the National Jewish Population Survey (NJPS) of 2000–01 provided further evidence that women, on average, identified with Israel more than men. Respondents who said that Israel was "very important" to them broke down as follows: 55 percent of Orthodox men and 78 percent of Orthodox women; 50 percent of Conservative men and 54 percent of Conservative women; 42 percent of Reform men and 38 percent

---

[171]Steven M. Cohen, "Poll: Attachment of U.S. Jews Falls in Past 2 Years," *Forward*, March 4, 2005, pp. 1ff. Only people who claimed to be Jewish by religion were polled, the most Jewishly engaged American Jews.

[172]Steven M. Cohen, "Survey: Jewish Support Up For Israel, if Not Its Policies," *Forward*, Nov. 2, 2001, p. 1.

[173]Jay Y. Brodbar-Nemzer, "Sex Differences in Attitudes of American Jews toward Israel," *Contemporary Jewry* 8, 1987, pp. 50, 56–57.

of Reform women. When it came to visiting Israel, among in-married families with children, women outscored men in all three of the main religious movements: Orthodox—91 percent of women versus 81 percent of men; Conservative—61 percent of women versus 55 percent of men; and Reform—34 percent of women versus 32 percent of men.[174]

2. Denominational Affiliation: The difference between denominations was already evident in the weeks leading up to the Six-Day War, when, in a survey of opinion, Orthodox rabbis and synagogue leaders expressed the most concern about Israel's situation, outpacing Conservative rabbis and synagogue leaders, and even more so those affiliated with Reform.[175] Harris polls conducted in the early 1980s confirmed the same about rank-and-file members of these movements, as did a survey by Steven M. Cohen showing that more ritually observant Jews felt more attached to Israel than those less observant.[176] The 1990 NJPS asked respondents whether they had traveled to Israel: 58 percent of Orthodox Jews answered in the affirmative, as compared to 37 percent of Conservative Jews and only 22 percent of Reform Jews.[177]

That pattern has held consistently in a series of later surveys. Despite the strong similarities in the official positions of the three major movements about the importance of Israel, levels of attachment are highest among Orthodox Jews, lower among Conservative Jews, and lowest among Reform Jews. To cite one example, the 2000–01 NJPS found that 72 percent of Orthodox Jews claimed strong emotional attachment to Israel, as compared to 54 percent of Conservative Jews and 22 percent of Reform Jews.[178]

3. Marital Status: Jews married to other Jews have the highest

---

[174]Sylvia Barack Fishman and Daniel Parmer, *Matrilineal Ascent/Patrilineal Descent: The Gender Imbalance in American Jewish Life* (Waltham, Mass., 2008), pp. 61–62.

[175]Charles S. Liebman's survey cited in Gilboa, *Israel in the Mind of American Jews,* p. 11.

[176]Ibid, p. 12.

[177]David F. Schnall, "Orthodoxy and Support for Israel: Inferences from the 1990 National Jewish Population Survey," *Journal of Jewish Communal Service* 68, Summer 1992, p. 9.

[178]Chaim I. Waxman, "If I Forget Thee . . . ," p. 417. The figure for Reconstructionist Jews was 27 percent. For a denominational breakdown of the most recent study of New York's Jewish population, see Harriet Hartman and Moshe Hartman, "Denominational Differences in the Attachment to Israel of American Jews, *Review of Religious Research* 41, March 2000, pp. 394–417.

levels of attachment to Israel, followed by single Jews; Jews married to non-Jews lag far behind. A recent study of the interplay between marriage and Jewish connectedness finds that

> among those under 40, 86 percent of the in-married call themselves "pro-Israel," and so do 83 percent of the single. When presented with the statement, "Caring about Israel is a very important part of my being a Jew," fully 79 percent of the single respondents agree, as do 83 percent of the in-married. Of the in-married, 62 percent feel proud of Israel at least often (if not always), as do even more—67 percent—of the singles. By contrast, rates of attachment to Israel plummet among Jews who are intermarried.[179]

There has been some speculation that Jews who intermarry are already somewhat disconnected from Jewish life, and therefore their declining attachment to Israel is merely a symptom of their alienation. However, the high rate of identification with Israel that single Jews evince suggests that the act of intermarrying and the complications it brings constitute an important factor in dampening attachment to Israel.[180]

4. Age: Levels of attachment to Israel—and to the Jewish people—decline by age groups. One analysis based on the 2000–01 NJPS has found that

> those aged 35–44 are less likely than their elders, 55–64, to strongly agree that "Jews in the United States and Jews around the world share a common destiny" (35 percent vs. 44 percent). They are less likely to strongly agree that "when people are in distress, American Jews have a greater responsibility to rescue Jews than non-Jews" (25 percent vs. 32 percent); and they are less likely to strongly agree that "I have a special responsibility to take care of Jews in need around the world" (25 percent vs. 32 percent, again).

In response to a question asking whether they have "a strong sense of belonging to the Jewish people," the percentage answering "yes" slides down with each ten-year age cohort, so that 72 percent of Jews over age 65 agree, as compared to only 47 percent of adults under 35.[181] A recent report on attachment to Israel, based

---

[179]Steven M. Cohen and Ari Y. Kelman, *Uncoupled: How Our Young Singles Are Reshaping Jewish Engagement* (New York, 2008), pp. 16–17.

[180]Steven M. Cohen makes this argument in *A Tale of Two Jewries: The "Inconvenient Truth" for American Jews* (New York, 2006), pp. 11–12.

[181]Ibid, p. 5.

upon surveys conducted by AJC, concludes that "respondents 40 and above are more highly attached than those under 30, and those over 70 are markedly more highly attached."[182]

Why this should be so is a matter of debate among social scientists. Some contend that younger Jews have always expressed less attachment to Israel than their elders, and therefore their responses must be understood as an "age effect" due to their stage in life, and would presumably change when they got older. Others point to a drop in attachment to Israel among younger Jews specifically over the past few decades, suggesting that their views are attributable to a "cohort effect," their having a very different experience of Israel than older Jews, and so less likely to pass with time.[183]

5. Leadership Positions: Some surveys conducted in the 1980s and 1990s indicated that leaders of Jewish organizations exhibit far higher levels of engagement with Israel than rank-and-file Jews. The leaders travel to Israel more frequently, know more Israelis, display more knowledge about the country, may even have considered living there, and believe—much more than non-leaders—that were it not for Israel there would be much less "vitality in American Jewish life."[184] Some have used these findings to suggest that Jewish leaders are out of step with their communities and are unfit for leadership because they do not reflect the true wishes of their constituents. This view often emanates from critics on the left who want Jewish organizations to distance themselves from Israeli policies and espouse more dovish positions.[185]

---

[182]Theodore Sasson, Charles Kadushin, and Leonard Saxe, *American Jewish Attachment to Israel: An Assessment of the "Distancing" Hypothesis* (Waltham, Mass., 2008), p. 15.

[183]The age-effect analysis is presented ibid, pp. 16–19, and the cohort-effect analysis in Steven M. Cohen and Ari Y. Kelman, *Beyond Distancing: Young Adult American Jews and Their Alienation from Israel* (New York, 2007). The two studies rely upon different data sets.

[184]Steven M. Cohen, *Israel-Diaspora Relations: A Survey of American Jewish Leaders* (Tel Aviv, 1990), p. 8; and Gerald B. Bubis and Steven M. Cohen, "What Are the Professional Leaders of American Jewry Thinking about Israel?" *Jerusalem Letter* (Jerusalem Center for Public Affairs), March 15, 1989. I am not aware of any follow-up research on leadership attitudes since then.

[185]See, for example, Irving Litvag, "Democracy in the American Jewish Community: A Proposal for Change," *Tikkun* 11, November/December 1996, pp. 25–27, 77; and Michael Lerner, "The Israel Lobby: Bad for the U.S., Bad for Israel, Bad for the Jews," *Tikkun* 22, September/October, 2007, pp. 33–39, 74–83, esp. p. 37.

Debating Israeli Policies

One does not need opinion polls to know that American Jews do not share monolithic views about Israel. Indeed, while a strong consensus was successfully built in the early years of the state, since then communal discussions have more typically been marked by serious disagreement not only about Israeli policies but also over what, if any, limits should be placed on Jewish criticism of those policies.

In the decades before Israel's founding, the key dividing lines were over the desirability and feasibility of establishing a Jewish state. Debates between Zionists, non-Zionists, and anti-Zionists during the first four decades of the twentieth century created deep rifts in American Jewish life. In response to the Nazi menace and, eventually, the destruction of European Jewry, most opposition faded, but at the margins both the extreme religious right (such as the Neturei Karta) and the Reform left (embodied by the American Council for Judaism) opposed Israel—and still do.[186] Pro-Soviet communists also opposed Israel—except for the brief period that the Soviet Union supported Israel's creation—and their spiritual descendents have never completely disappeared.[187]

Once the state was established, a strong American Jewish consensus developed to support it. Aside from the left and right extremes, a wall-to-wall coalition of Jewish organizations promoted Israel as a bastion of democracy surrounded by totalitarian states that were directly linked to and armed by the Soviet bloc.[188] While this functional solidarity persisted well into the

---

[186]Neturei Karta today supports Iranian policy. Rabbi Dovid Weiss was quoted in Tehran expressing the hope that Israel would soon cease to exist—although with a minimum of bloodshed. See "Neturei Karta Rabbi to Iran Newspaper: Israel Will Cease to Exist," *Ynet*, August 16, 2006, http://www.ynetnews.com/articles/0,7340,L-3291956,00.html. The American Council for Judaism continues to function. See http://www.acjna.org/acjna/default.aspx

[187]Edward Alexander and Paul Bogdanor, eds., *The Jewish Divide Over Israel: Accusers and Defenders* (New Brunswick, N.J., 2006) includes several essays about radical leftist assaults on Israel. On p. xi it quotes Irving Howe, who wrote in 1970, "Jewish boys and girls, children of the generation that saw Auschwitz, hate democratic Israel and celebrate as 'revolutionary' the Egyptian dictatorship. Some of them pretend to be indifferent to the anti-Jewish insinuations of the Black Panthers; a few go so far as to collect money for Al Fatah, which pledges to take Tel Aviv."

[188]Arthur A. Goren, "The Golden Decade, 1945–55," in his collection of essays, *The Political and Public Culture of American Jews* (Bloomington, Ind., 1999), pp. 192–93.

1980s, cracks began to appear as early as 1973 both over Israeli policy in the territories conquered in 1967 and over whether mainstream American Jewish organizations should tolerate criticism of Israeli actions.

These issues came to the fore with the founding of Breira, an organization that disagreed with the Israeli position on the territories. According to its in-house, official history, Breira believed "that there can be an alternative to the endless cycle of war and violence between Israel and the Arabs, and that American Jews committed to a strong Jewish state could actually encourage Israel to do more than it was doing to initiate peace talks."[189] Although Breira's actual membership numbers were minuscule, some sympathizers held positions in major Jewish organizations, and so attracted attention to the group. Moreover, some Breira firebrands called for dismantling the existing Jewish communal structure, which they deemed unrepresentative, and suggested that American Jews should signal their displeasure by withholding financial contributions from those organizations and from Israel.

The response was swift, as opponents of Breira fiercely denounced it and publicly cast its members as traitors to the Jewish people and collaborators with the enemies of Israel; some Breira people lost their jobs as a result. Similar responses greeted a successor organization, New Jewish Agenda. The dissenters from the communal consensus, in turn, vilified their critics as witch-hunters, McCarthyites, and slanderers. It is doubtful that any other internal controversy has provoked such intemperate rhetoric and mudslinging in the American Jewish press and organizational world since World War II.[190]

Matters did not improve substantially afterwards. Beginning with the election of the first Likud government in Israel's history in 1977, American Jews were jolted out of their easy support for Israel by a series of uncomfortable developments. It was bad enough that a community consisting predominantly of political liberals found itself forced to swallow the elevation to prime min-

---

[189]Cited in Jack Wertheimer, "Breaking the Taboo: Critics of Israel and the American Jewish Establishment," in Gal, ed., *Envisioning Israel*, pp. 398–99.

[190]Michael E. Staub presents a sympathetic portrait of Breira in *Torn at the Roots: The Crisis of Jewish Liberalism in Postwar America* (New York, 2002), pp. 280–308.

ister of Menachem Begin, once an underground Revisionist leader and still an unapologetic hawk.[191] Then came the Israeli invasion of Lebanon in the summer of 1982, followed by the jailing, in 1985, of Jonathan Pollard, an American Jew who admitted to stealing military secrets for Israel.[192] By the end of 1987 the first intifada erupted, filling American TV screens with harsh scenes of violence on the West Bank. American Jews found it hard to stomach the seeming role-reversal of Palestinians with slingshots playing David to the Israeli Goliath.[193]

Fierce disagreements broke out within the American Jewish community over Israeli policies. The general press eagerly reported them and, not incidentally, fueled the debate. Headlines of articles told much of the story: "U.S. Jews Beginning to Go Public in Criticism of Israel,"[194] "What Does Loyalty Demand? As the Violence Mounts, American Jews Are Divided over Whether to Criticize Israel,"[195] "A Family Quarrel: Once American Jews Loved Israel Blindly. Now They're Learning to Ask Hard Questions,"[196] "The Agony over Israel,"[197] and "A Family Feud? American Jews Troubled by Shifts in Israel."[198] In the Jewish media, hundreds of articles and op-ed pieces addressed Israeli policies and debated the question, "Should American Jewish Organizations Publicly Criticize Israel on Peace Issues?"[199]

---

[191]William L. Chaze, "For Many U.S. Jews: Israel Yes, Begin No," *U.S. News and World Report,* February 28, 1983, pp. 20–21. For an analysis of how Likud's politics challenged the premises of American Jewish liberalism, see Jerold S. Auerbach, "Are We One? Menachem Begin and the Long Shadow of 1977," in Gal, ed., *Envisioning Israel,* pp. 337–51.

[192]See Shlomo Avineri, "Letter to an American Jewish Friend," *Jerusalem Post,* March 10, 1987, in which the prominent Israeli political scientist and former government official accused American Jews of timidity for not supporting Pollard.

[193]George E. Gruen, "The Impact of the Intifada on American Jews and the Reaction of the American Public and of Israeli Jews," in Robert O. Freedman, ed., *The Intifada: Its Impact on Israel, the Arab World, and the Superpowers* (Miami, 1991), pp. 220–66. The influence of all these developments on American Jewry is traced in Steven T. Rosenthal, *Irreconcilable Differences? The Waning of the American Jewish Love Affair with Israel* (Hanover, N.H., 2001).

[194]*Washington Post,* May 3, 1976, p. A2.

[195]*Newsweek,* February 22, 1988, pp. 77–78.

[196]Ibid, April 3, 1989, pp. 58–60.

[197]*Time,* May 7, 1990, pp. 28ff.

[198]*International Herald Tribune,* April 29, 1998, p. 6.

[199]The title of a typical debate, between Theodore R. Mann and Burton S. Levinson, in *Moment* 13, March 1988, pp. 18ff.

Since the signing of the Oslo Accords in 1993, the mood of American Jews—as of Israelis—has shifted sharply from euphoria at the prospect of Israeli-Palestinian peace, to disappointment at the continuation of the violence, to horror at the assassination of Prime Minister Yitzhak Rabin in 1995 by an Orthodox right-winger, to renewed hope in connection with the Barak-Arafat-Clinton summit at Camp David in 2000, to anger about the Palestinian refusal to accept the settlement offered and the second (or Al Aqsa) intifada that followed, to empathy and solidarity after the events of 9/11, and to worry over continuing anti-Israel rhetoric on American campuses. It is too soon to gauge the full impact of these rapid shifts on American Jewish sentiment.[200]

The Arab/Palestinian-Israeli conflict has not been the only issue to divide American Jews. During the 1970s and 1980s considerable rancor was generated over Israel's insistence on controlling the movement to rescue Soviet Jewry. Two major American organizations vied over policy: the National Conference on Soviet Jewry, created by the mainstream Jewish organizations, allied itself with Israeli policymakers and worked to channel emigrants to the Jewish state, while the grassroots Union of Councils for Soviet Jewry took the position that Jews from the Soviet Union, like other refugees, should be free to settle where they wished. Partisans of each group denounced the other as Israeli officials sought to stage-manage events behind the scenes.[201]

Most controversially, Israel has figured in the internal religious skirmishes of American Jewry. Between the mid-1980s and the mid-1990s (and continuing, in a milder form, since), American Jews stood at loggerheads over efforts by Israeli religious parties, which are Orthodox, to control Israeli domestic policy on matters of personal status. This "Who Is a Jew?" controversy included such questions as who may be registered as a Jew, who may au-

---

[200]For two preliminary analyses, see Aaron Ahuvia, "Six Degrees of Separation: 'Pro-Israel Realists' Versus 'Worried Jews,'" http://www.shalomctr.org/node/1439, and Ofira Seliktar, "The Changing Identity of American Jews, Israel and the Peace Process," in Ben-Moshe and Segev, *Israel, the Diaspora, and Jewish Identity*, pp. 124–137. The same author has also written a book-length study, *Divided We Stand: American Jews, Israel and the Peace Process* (Westport, Conn., 2002).

[201]The latest treatment of the subject is Henry L. Feingold, *"Silent No More": Saving the Jews of Russia, the American Jewish Effort, 1967–89* (Syracuse, 2007), chap. 5. For a study written from the perspective of the Union of Councils, see Stuart Altshuler, *From Exodus to Freedom: A History of the Soviet Jewry Movement* (Lanham, Md., 2005).

thorize religious conversions, which rabbis are qualified to officiate at marriages and convert non-Jews, and a host of related matters. The Israeli religious parties used their political clout as partners in governing coalitions to induce changes in policy that further strengthened the Orthodox monopoly on Israeli Judaism already embodied in the country's Chief Rabbinate.

These efforts have had powerful repercussions in the U.S., where adherents of the non-Orthodox movements far outnumber the Orthodox. Opinion surveys conducted during the most contentious "Who is a Jew?" controversies demonstrated that many American Jews believed that Israel was disenfranchising them.[202] Orthodox Jews, however, rallied to the defense of the Israeli Chief Rabbinate and supported the political hardball played by the religious parties.[203] Reform, Conservative, and Reconstructionist leaders—Reform being the most vocal—used their pulpits to rail against the absence of religious pluralism in Israel and to denounce the Chief Rabbinate and the religious parties. Some threatened to tell their congregants to withhold philanthropy from Israel, and there were synagogues that decided not to host Israeli politicians who cooperated with the Orthodox.[204]

The battles over religious pluralism highlighted and magnified a larger rift emerging in American Jewish life between Orthodox and non-Orthodox Jews. Survey research has demonstrated a significant gap between the two in regard to the disposition of the territories Israel captured in 1967, the Orthodox being far less willing to agree to territorial compromise on land they deem holy to Jews.[205] During the pullout from Gaza in 2005, Orthodox organizations

---

[202]Steven M. Cohen noted, "The theme running through responses is one of fear of potential rejection by Israel." Cohen, "Relationships of American Jews with Israel," p. 147.

[203]At least one prominent Orthodox rabbi in the U.S., the Lubavitcher Rebbe, actively fueled the flames and urged the religious parties on.

[204]Jack Wertheimer, *A People Divided: Judaism in Contemporary America* (New York, 1993), pp. xi–xii. Most recently, Israeli rabbinic courts have overturned conversions performed by some American Orthodox rabbis, a move that could drive a wedge between various factions within the Orthodox community of the U.S. See Gershom Gorenberg, "How Do You Prove You Are a Jew?" *New York Times Sunday Magazine,* March 2, 2008, pp. 46–51.

[205]David Berkman, "Gap Grows Between Orthodox and Others," *Los Angeles Jewish Journal,* February 7, 2008, http://www.jewishjournal.com/world/article/gap__grows__between__orthodox__and__others__20080208; Gary Rosenblatt, "Why the American Jewish Divide is Growing," *New York Jewish Week,* February 27, 2008, http://www.thejewishweek.com/viewArticle/c52__a4612/Editorial____Opinion/Gary__Rosenblatt.html

were sorely torn between their tradition of support for the Israeli government, on the one hand, and sympathy for the Israelis dispossessed of their homes, on the other. Using a baseball metaphor, one leader of the Union of Orthodox Jewish Congregations of America successfully urged his organization not to condemn the pullout, saying, "American Jewish Zionists have box seats, and we have the right and obligation to support our team. But we are not playing. Only members of the team, even those who are benched, have the right to take part in team meetings. We fans talk strategy, but the only ones with the right to decide matters are the team members."[206] Subsequently, however, Orthodox organizations mounted a campaign against turning over any part of Jerusalem to the Palestinians, and the Orthodox Union passed a resolution declaring that "in exceptional circumstances [it may] take public positions contrary to those of the Government of Israel."[207]

Writing of this shift, Lawrence Grossman notes that American Orthodox Zionism, which had previously kept silent even when it disagreed with particular Israeli policies, now "was no different from such dovish organizations as Americans for Peace Now and the Israel Policy Forum, except that its attacks on Israeli policies would presumably come from the right rather than from the left."[208] This observation brings into sharp relief a dramatic transformation of American Jewish attitudes toward Israel. Whereas American Jews once argued over whether to support or oppose the Zionist enterprise, and then over whether dissent from Israeli policies was even permissible, they are now arrayed in rival camps, arguing about how Israel should behave.

This was an inevitable development, given America's strong traditions of free speech and the outspoken nature of America's Jews. It was not only unrealistic to imagine that Jewish organizations could long stifle dissent, but also unhealthy. Debate over Israeli policies is a form of engagement and participation, if only from afar. Public silence or conformity in regard to Israel may signal indifference and apathy. [209]

---

[206]David Luchins, quoted in Yossi Shain, *Kinship and Diasporas in International Affairs* (Ann Arbor, 2007), p. 112.

[207]Quoted in Waxman, "If I Forget Thee . . . ," p. 427.

[208]Grossman, "Decline and Fall," p. 48.

[209]"In surveys of American Jews conducted . . . in the 1980s, those most critical of Israeli policies were also most attached to Israel." Cohen and Liebman, "Israel and American

It is highly significant that, for better or worse, the longest and most vituperative debates in American Jewish life over the last three decades have been about Israel. Other divisive issues, such as the role of women in Jewish life or the religious status of homosexuals, were resolved relatively swiftly within the individual denominations. However disagreements over Israeli policies in the territories and the proper relationship between synagogue and state in the Jewish state go on and on, and become increasingly bitter. They seem to have become a permanent feature of American Jewish culture, both causing and demonstrating deep fissures in the American Jewish community.

WHAT ISRAEL MAY MEAN IN THE AMERICAN JEWISH PSYCHE

Israel has played an enormous role in the American Jewish imagination and in virtually every nook and cranny of organized American Jewish life over the past 60 years. American Jews have celebrated Israel's triumphs and agonized over its intractable dilemmas. A minority of American Jews has taken the trouble to see Israel firsthand; many more have demonstrated identification with Israel, following its struggles and achievements, at times with swelling pride, at times with great concern. American Jews have rallied in the streets, collected billions of dollars of aid, and invested their political capital to influence their government to support Israel. And while mobilization has been the most dramatic expression of American Jews' connection with the Jewish state, Israel, in turn, has become a ubiquitous presence in their institutions and a powerful influence on their culture.[210]

Still, critics fault American Jews for their limited understanding of how Israeli society works and their scant grasp of Israeli Hebrew. How deep are the connections, they ask, when only a small minority has friends and relatives in Israel, or in other ways expe-

Jewry in the Twenty-First Century," p. 4. For a sweeping overview of debates among intellectuals in a number of countries over the changing meaning of Israel, see Yosef Gorny, *The Jewish State in Jewish Public Thought: The Quest for Collective Identity* (New York, 1994).

[210]For a different view, see Cohen and Liebman, "Israel and American Jewry in the Twenty-First Century," p. 5.

riences person-to-person contact with Israelis? Most disappointing to Israelis, only an infinitesimal fraction of American Jews has settled in Israel to join in the construction of the greatest Jewish project of recent centuries.[211]

This psychic and physical distance between most American Jews and Israel has led some to worry that the two Jewish communities will inexorably drift apart. According to one estimate, merely 5 percent of American Jews "can be classified as deeply personally attached to Israel," as measured by maintaining an active business or social connection with Jews living in Israel and receptivity to having their own children settle there.[212] Sixty years after Israel's founding, large percentages of American Jews maintain, at best, an episodic relationship with the Jewish state, paying closer attention only in times of crisis or when personally touched by Israel, as when a relative returns from a positive experience there, such as a Birthright trip.

The changeable quality of American Jewish interaction with Israel makes it difficult to determine easily what Israel means to large swathes of American Jewry. Can one speak of American Jews as Zionists if few orient their lives in America around Israel or seriously contemplate settling there? If not, is the term "pro-Israelism"[213] more suitable, because it speaks simply of the support American Jews have offered to insure the viability of a Jewish state they may never visit? Is Israel best understood primarily as a symbol of Jewish vulnerability, and therefore a cause to rally Jews when it appears to be endangered? Or should it be seen, in the formulation of the late Charles Liebman, as the *heim* of American Jews,

> the parents' home, or in the case of Israel the surrogate parents' and surrogate grandparents' home. One visits it on occasion, one sends money (without ever having the bad taste to inquire how that money is spent), and one wants very much to feel that life goes on there as

---

[211]Approximately 120,000 American Jews have settled in Israel. In recent years, some 2,000 have immigrated annually, the large majority of them Orthodox. "North American Immigration to Israel Continues to Climb," *Israel Insider*, July 4, 2007, http://web.israelinsider.com/Articles/Briefs/11628.htm

[212]Cohen and Liebman, "Israel and American Jewry in the Twenty-First Century," p. 20.

[213]On the difference between pro-Israelism and Zionism, see Sharot and Zaidman, "Israel as Symbol and as Reality," p. 151.

> it always has (which is why the type of Jew to whom Israel is *heim* expects and wants all Israelis to be religious, regardless of how uninterested he himself may be in religion).[214]

Or, as the Israeli political scientist Yossi Shain has recently argued, are American Jews in this transnational age no different from other diasporas in the ways they relate to their homelands, offering political and financial support as best they can out of a sense of kinship?[215]

Israel has emerged as a militarily and economically strong state, no longer as dependent as it had been earlier upon the largess and political aid of American Jews. As American Jews are less captivated by the mobilization model of rising to the defense of an embattled Jewish state, Israel-related causes that resonated in the past may have decreasing relevance for American Jews. In the decades to come American Jews will need to confront a different set of challenges.

First, they must come to terms with the full implications of Jewish sovereignty. How do Jews who have grown used to minority status and only limited self-government relate to a Jewish state that governs itself, manages its own social problems, and pursues its own policies? This question has already surfaced in regard to the difficult decisions Israel has taken in its decades-long struggle with antagonistic Arab neighbors, and, as time goes on, American Jews will have to confront further ramifications of Israeli sovereignty, some of which will not necessarily be to their liking, and certainly will be far from their own experience as a small minority whose relation to power has been very different.

Second, American Jewish thinkers will have to determine whether their own internal deliberations about Jewish identity, the nature of modern Judaism, and the meaning of being Jewish can be enriched by intensive contact with Israelis struggling with the same issues, or whether the two communities must go their separate ways. So far only small numbers of American Jews and Israelis have addressed these deeper issues *together*.

---

[214]Charles S. Liebman, *The Ambivalent American Jew* (Philadelphia, 1973), p. 106.

[215]"I consider the case of the Jewish diaspora and its links to Israel to be an archetypical rather than idiosyncratic one. This case provides a fully developed paradigm of relations between diaspora and homeland." Shain, *Kinship and Diasporas,* p. 161, n. 1.

Third, American Jews will have to think through how their own culture will intersect with Israel's. Until now, Israel's cultural influence has come almost via osmosis, in a largely unreflective fashion. Will American Jewish cultural leaders give priority to teaching the Hebrew language as a Jewish lingua franca, or at least as the indispensible key to Jewish literacy? Will they create a far more purposeful, self-conscious cultural interaction? Will Jewish intellectuals in the U.S. open a dialogue with their Israeli counterparts not only about geopolitics, but also about deeper questions of Jewish culture and values?

Fourth, American Jews will have to puzzle out the goals and direction of Israel education in their schools. What do they want their children to learn about Israel, and toward what ends? And now that trips to Israel have come to be seen as an essential vehicle to strengthen American Jewish identity, will the organizers of such programs give more thought to what they want "pilgrim tourists" to take away from these trips about Israel, Judaism, and Jewish identification?

Fifth, how will American Jews address the considerable psychological divide between themselves and Israeli Jews? Each Jewish community has developed distinctive ways to relate to such concepts as family, land, responsibility to fellow Jews, philanthropy, and pluralism.[216] Can these differences in outlook be bridged? Will the two communities even want to learn from and with each other?

Sixth, and most globally, as the nature of Jewish identity is redefined by succeeding generations of American Jews, how will they fit Israel into their emerging conceptions? Will the new social networking and Web-based technologies encourage stronger connections and more common ventures with Israelis, or will they drive these communities further apart?

With varying degrees of intensity, Israel has been a prime concern for those American Jews who have identified with some aspect of organized Jewish life over the past 60 years, and that is likely to remain so for the foreseeable future. Until now, American Jews have peered at Israel through a metaphorical kaleidoscope.

---

[216]This is the subject of Steven M. Cohen and Charles S. Liebman's book, *Two Worlds of Judaism: The Israeli and American Experiences* (New Haven, 1990).

Looking into the view-finder from the literal and psychological distance of America's shores, they have selectively seen shards of Israeli life. The colorful pieces of Israel they have noticed are far from the total reality; at best, they reflect only a partial set of images. Over time, moreover, their focus has changed: American Jews once were most proud of Israel's pioneering spirit and its creation of a haven of refuge for downtrodden coreligionists; later they most admired Israel's military might and its kibbutzim; and more recently they have focused on its technological prowess and scientific research. At different times, Israel symbolized very different aspects of Jewish civilization—liberation from exile, David fighting Goliath, Jewish cultural renaissance, concern for fellow Jews, and religious renewal. And alas, at other times it has come to represent, for some, religious intolerance, Goliath fighting the Palestinian David, chauvinism, and arrogance.

Looking through the other side of our figurative kaleidoscope, we see the last six decades of the American Jewish experience in sharper relief. Israel has figured prominently both in the pride of American Jews and their insecurities, their desire, on the one hand, to fit into America, but also, on the other, to express themselves as a distinctive group with its own culture and religion, songs and dances, institutions and leaders, making its mark on the international stage. American Jews have borrowed freely from Israeli forms in order to reconstruct their own culture. Israel has provided American Jews the opportunity to gather en masse in public places to demonstrate solidarity, and also to argue vociferously with each other about the meaning of being Jewish and the central values of Judaism.

Whatever the future may hold, the dynamically evolving and multilayered relationship with Israel has been the most sustained, exhilarating, maddening, controversial, and emotion-laden drama of American Jewish life over the past 60 years. It may also have been the most significant.

Review of the Year

UNITED STATES

United States

National Affairs

THE POLITICAL ARENA

The New Congress

The new Democratic-controlled Congress, sworn in January 4, 2007, was led by Rep. Nancy Pelosi (D., Calif.), the first woman speaker of the House of Representatives, and Sen. Harry Reid, the first Mormon majority leader of the Senate.

There were a record 13 Jewish senators and 30 Jewish representatives. Of the Senate's 49 Democrats, nine were Jewish, one of them newcomer Ben Cardin from Maryland. There were two Independents in the Senate, both of them Jewish: Joseph Lieberman, who failed to gain the Democratic nomination in Connecticut but won in a landslide on an Independent line, and Bernie Sanders, who handily won his Senate race in Vermont after many years of service in the House. There continued to be two Jewish Republicans, Norman Coleman of Minnesota and Arlen Specter of Pennsylvania. In the House, there were six Jewish freshmen: Steve Cohen (D., Tenn.); Gabrielle Giffords (D., Ariz.); Paul Hodes (D., N.H.); Steve Kagen (D., Wis.); Ron Klein (D., Fla.); and John Yarmuth (D., Ky.). The remaining 24 Jewish House members were all Democrats, except for Eric Cantor of Virginia. Also inaugurated were the first Muslim and first Buddhist members in the history of Congress.

House Democrats ran in 2006 on a pledge to enact a broad array of legislation during the "First 100 Hours." Votes were held during the early days of the session on many issues, including ethics reform, stem-cell research, homeland security, student-loan rates, minimum wage, and prescription drug prices, but little of it would become law (see below).

On September 17, President Bush nominated New York jurist Michael Mukasey to be attorney general. Upon confirmation, he became the second Jew to hold that post, following Edward Levi, who served under President Gerald Ford. The son of Russian immigrants, Mukasey graduated from the Ramaz School, an Orthodox Jewish day school in Manhattan, which his children would later attend and where his wife, Susan, would teach and serve as headmistress.

Senate Democrats threatened to delay the Mukasey confirmation hearings until they received access to documents regarding the surveillance and detention policies allegedly approved by Mukasey's predecessors Alberto Gonzales and John Ashcroft. When the hearings did begin the Democrats on the Judiciary Committee sought to determine where the nominee stood on controversial positions taken by the administration on civil liberties, presidential power, and the rule of law while fighting the "war on terror." Mukasey was grilled, for example, on whether he considered it torture to subject terror suspects to "waterboarding," an interrogation technique that simulates drowning and suffocation. While he avoided explicitly answering a number of politically sensitive questions, his performance was acceptable to Sens. Dianne Feinstein (D. Calif.) and Charles Schumer (D., N.Y.), two prominent majority members of the Judiciary Committee, and their support, added to that of the Republican members, ensured a positive committee recommendation. Mukasey was confirmed by the full Senate on November 8 by 53-40, the narrowest margin for the confirmation of an attorney general in more than 50 years.

A far lower-profile confirmation of another Orthodox Jewish nominee occurred three months earlier, on August 3, when the Senate unanimously approved Dr. Tevi Troy as deputy secretary of health and human services. Troy had served as White House liaison to the Jewish community during part of President Bush's first term.

In contrast to 2006 (see AJYB 2007, pp. 67–68), there were few battles over judicial nominations in 2007. Among the few exceptions was that of Leslie Southwick, nominated for the Fourth Circuit Court of Appeals. Pointing to some decisions by Southwick they considered insensitive to lesbians and African Americans, the National Council of Jewish Women (NCJW), People for the American Way, the Human Rights Campaign, and the Congressional Black Caucus announced their opposition. However Sen. Dianne Feinstein (D., Calif.) gave Senate Judiciary Committee Republicans the tenth vote they needed to report the nomination favorably out of committee, and Southwick was confirmed by the full Senate 59-38.

Presidential Politics

A national election loomed in 2008. For the first time in 80 years, there was no incumbent president or vice president running for either presidential nomination. The war in Iraq was increasingly unpopular among Americans—and even more so among American Jews. President George W. Bush's troop "surge" in Iraq was intended to secure some semblance of victory. Democrats, who controlled both houses of Congress, advocated a range of proposals, both foreign and domestic, to make pre-election political points, although many of these were assured presidential vetoes that could not be overridden. Both parties demonstrated strong support for Israel. Polls showed that although Jews made up a small percentage of the total electorate, they could play a pivotal role in the 2008 contest because of their disproportionate concentration in such key swing states such as Florida, Ohio, and Pennsylvania.

The candidates for president were off and running earlier than any time in memory, hoping to get their parties to coalesce quickly around them. States competed with each other to advance their primary and caucus dates even against party rules: Florida and Michigan jumped the line to enhance their status and influence as early campaign stops. The rough and tumble of presidential politics in 2007 demonstrated that little could be considered inevitable. As the incumbent Republican president languished in national polls, his party searched for a candidate who might maintain the formidable coalition of business and religious conservatives that had brought the party success in five of the past seven presidential contests. Democrats, meanwhile, found that despite large-scale popular antagonism toward the incumbent, it would be no cakewalk for them to get to 1600 Pennsylvania Avenue.

Although Senator Hillary Clinton of New York led the Democratic field throughout the year, her campaign was far from the juggernaut many had predicted from the former first lady. Clinton had a strong base of support in her home state, including a Jewish community that had overwhelmingly backed her in two Senate races. One poll found that she was also the favorite of Jews nationwide, and on May 31 the JTA reported that Clinton led the presidential pack in funds raised from Jews. Democratic consultant Steve Rabinowitz said the "overwhelming amount of establishment money is with Hillary," due to her ties to the Jewish community and those of her husband.

Clinton's "Jewish team" included Ann Lewis, a former staffer in Bill Clinton's administration and sister of Rep. Barney Frank of Massachusetts; Steve Grossman, the former head of the national Democratic Party and past chair of AIPAC; and Lionel "Lonnie" Kaplan, also a former AIPAC chair. She was also backed by a large group of Jewish elected officials, including her fellow senator from New York, Charles Schumer; Reps. Jerrold Nadler and Nita Lowey of New York and Debbie Wasserman Schultz of Florida; and Gov. Ed Rendell of Pennsylvania. Clinton drew praise from the Jewish community for sponsoring a resolution that called for the release of kidnapped Israeli soldiers. But her vote for allowing U.S. troops to be sent to Iraq in 2003 created problems for her with a Democratic base that had long grown weary of the war.

Clinton received a strong challenge from her Senate colleague from Illinois, Barack Obama. Many had though that Clinton's fund-raising machine would prove insurmountable, but at each federal election filing observers remarked at the fund-raising prowess of the Obama camp, which consistently matched or outpaced Clinton. His fund-raising chair was Penny Pritzker, a Chicago businesswoman, hotel heiress, and major donor to Jewish causes. Other prominent Jews backing Obama were fund-raiser Alan Solomont and several members of Congress: Steve Rothman of New Jersey, Adam Schiff of California, Janet Shackowsky of Illinois, and Robert Wexler of Florida.

Obama had a more difficult time with grassroots Jews, his Jewish poll numbers lagging behind those for the population at large. It was unclear to what extent this was due to an extensive e-mail campaign suggesting that Obama was a Muslim educated in radical Islamic schools, who was sworn into office on a Koran, and refused to recite the Pledge of Allegiance. Each charge was proven false, but the smears continued unabated, despite attempts from CNN, the Associated Press, and the Obama campaign itself to dispute them.

John Edwards, the former senator from North Carolina who had been the party's 2004 vice-presidential nominee, had an uphill battle all year, consistently running third in most polls. Edwards was supported by Marc Stanley, who was vice chair of the National Jewish Democratic Council (NJDC). Despite what was considered a pro-Israel track record during his Senate tenure and the 2004 campaign, Edwards faced criticism from pro-Israel quarters after naming as his campaign manager former Michigan congressman David Bonior, a strong critic of Israel. Sen. Joseph Biden of Delaware was supported for the nomination by Michael Adler, the NJDC chair. Governor Bill Richardson of New Mexico, despite close ties to the pro-Israel community, fumbled when he suggested that, if elected, he might tap former secretary of state James Baker—perceived as hostile to Israel—as a Mideast peace envoy. Sen. Christopher Dodd of Connecticut, another stalwart friend of the Jewish community, failed to break from the large pack of presidential hopefuls.

On the Republican side, former New York mayor Rudy Giuliani led the early stages of the race in both name recognition and Jewish backing—he enjoyed a 75-percent approval rating among Jewish Republicans. Giuliani's celebrity status had been cemented in the early hours of September 11, 2001, as the nation watched him take charge after the attacks. Giuliani, however, was plagued by some of his associations. On November 7, he was endorsed by televangelist Rev. Pat Robertson. While that would presumably shore up support among Christian conservatives wary of Giuliani's liberal stance on gay rights and abortion, it raised eyebrows among moderates. The very next day, New York's former police commissioner, Bernard Kerik, was indicted for a range of alleged business and personal misdeeds. In 2004 Giuliani had enthusiastically backed Kerik for the position of U.S. secretary of homeland security (revelations that Kerik had hired an illegal nanny torpedoed his chances). The indictment had a caustic affect on Giuliani's law-and-order reputation. As his poll numbers slipped, Giuliani pinned his candidacy on a strong showing in Florida's January primary.

Sen. John McCain's bid for the nomination received strong support from some Jewish stalwarts. Fred Zeidman, chair of the U.S. Holocaust Memorial Council, had helped lead Jewish outreach for the Bush campaigns in 2000 and 2004, and would now take on the same task for McCain. In December, McCain was endorsed by Sen. Joseph Lieberman of Connecticut. The nod from the 2000 Democratic nominee for vice president bolstered the Arizona senator's reputation for working across the political aisle, although it increased the alienation of Lieberman from the Democrats, with whom he still caucused in the Senate despite his self-identification as an Independent.

McCain touched off a controversy when he asserted that the Constitution established America "as a Christian nation" and that he would back a Christian presidential candidate over one who was Muslim. Later, he clarified that he would back a Muslim candidate if he judged that person "best able" to run the nation. Several Jewish organizations called upon McCain to withdraw his assertion about the Christian nature of the Constitution, and AJC held a private meeting with him to clarify his views. McCain defended himself from charges of anti-Semitism by saying he had intended to stress the "Judeo-Christian values" that were imbued in the Constitution. According to an AJC survey, McCain was viewed favorably by half of Jewish Republicans—second to Giuliani, but far outpacing the rest of the Republican field.

Two evangelical Christian candidates also stirred debate in the Jewish community. Sen. Sam Brownback of Kansas suggested disbanding the Palestinian Authority and joining the Palestinians with Jordan in a confederation. Brownback exited the race in October. Former Arkansas governor Mike Huckabee held on throughout the year, but was dogged by accusations that his campaign was suffused with Christian religious themes. AJC criticized his views as "a prescription for theocracy," while the ADL questioned whether Huckabee indeed wanted to be the president of all Americans and rebuked him for using Holocaust imagery when discussing abortion.

The NJDC attacked another Republican hopeful, former Massachusetts governor Mitt Romney, for selecting the Henry Ford Museum in his hometown of Detroit, Michigan, to announce his candidacy, citing Ford's strident anti-Semitism. Romney was nonplused and made a strong play for Jewish support, extolling his hawkish stance on Iran and strong support for Israel. The head of the Republican Jewish Coalition (RJC), St. Louis businessman Sam Fox, supported Romney (Fox would head to Belgium in April to become the U.S. ambassador). Romney did well in early polls, led the Republican pack in fund-raising, and won the August 12 Republican "straw poll" in Iowa. However he had trouble throughout the campaign in reconciling ostensibly pro-choice and gay-rights positions he had taken earlier in his political career with the more conservative views he was expressing in the presidential race.

The 2008 presidential field was also remarkable for its little-known contenders. Two of them worried pro-Israel voters. In the Republican race, Rep. Ron Paul of Texas showed great fund-raising ability, in part because his opposition to the Iraq war appealed to many Americans who connected to politics not through rallies and speeches, but via the Internet. On the Democratic side, Rep. Dennis Kucinich of Ohio made his second run for the highest office in the land. Both these candidates shared a disdain for the current U.S.-Israel relationship. Paul said he would end aid to Israel and other American allies, and strongly opposed military intervention to prevent Iran from gaining nuclear weaponry. He had voted against the House resolution condemning attacks on Israel during the Lebanon war. Kucinich, who opposed Israeli use of force in the Palestinian areas, had been the keynote speaker at a 2006 conference for the

Friends of Sabeel North America, a group known for its scathing criticism of Israel, and in March 2007 Kucinich hired for his campaign a former organizer for the U.S. Campaign to End the Israeli Occupation.

THE INTERNATIONAL ARENA

Israel and the Palestinians

The Gaza Strip during 2007 was both a launching pad for attacks against Israelis and the site of an internecine Palestinian war. Israeli citizens in Sderot and neighboring areas came under attack throughout the year, causing several fatalities and hundreds of injuries. Rockets from Gaza also damaged property, including synagogues, hospitals, schools, homes, public buildings, an electric-power grid, and local factories.

More than 100 Palestinians were killed and another 500 injured by fellow Palestinians during military clashes between Hamas and Fatah during the week of June 7–15 that saw Hamas seize control of the Gaza Strip. The fighting settled a score begun in January 2006, when Hamas won legislative elections. This marked a serious setback for U.S. and Israeli policy, which had sought to isolate and undermine Hamas while bolstering Fatah's leader, President Mahmoud Abbas.

Israeli prime minister Ehud Olmert told members of the Conference of Presidents of Major American Jewish Organizations in New York that Israel would extend economic and military support to Abbas's government so long as it avoided "any compromise and agreements with Hamas." The new situation in Gaza relegated to the back burner Olmert's plans for inserting an international force into Gaza. Shortly afterward, northern Israeli towns experienced their first attacks from Lebanon since the end of the 2006 war. Olmert said the violence was the work of the Al Qaeda Palestinian Arab faction in Lebanon.

U.S. secretary of state Condoleezza Rice engaged in a stepped-up round of shuttle diplomacy in the Middle East early in the year. A three-way summit with Olmert and Abbas on February 19 focused on the "political horizon" of renewed peace talks—after six years of stalled negotiations—and prescribed that the Fatah-Hamas unity government must meet international demands on recognition of Israel and rejection of violence. Rice reported that the "three of us affirmed our commitment to a two-state solution [and] agreed that a Palestinian state cannot be born of violence and terror."

As his administration approached its final year, President Bush called for a Middle East peace summit, the first ever in which all parties would take for granted the inevitability of a Palestinian state. The summit opened on November 27 in Annapolis, Maryland, hosted by Secretary Rice. Among the participants were Olmert, Abbas, and representatives of more than 40 other countries, including Egypt and Jordan, which had relations with Israel, and Saudi Arabia and Syria, which did not. According to President Bush, the conference would "signal international support for the Israelis' and Palestinians' intention to commence negotiations on the establishment of a Palestinian state and the realization of peace between these two peoples."

Iranian president Ahmadinejad joined Hamas in condemning the summit. Most American Jewish organizations voiced qualified support for the talks. The Conference of Presidents called it "a significant step towards launching meaningful, bilateral negotiations" and an "opportunity to bring change" that might "herald a new era in which Israel will not just be recognized but fully accepted as a Jewish state and neighbor." The Jewish Council for Public Affairs (JCPA) expressed hope that the gathering might mark "the beginning of a renewed process that leads to two states living side by side in security and peace." Both groups pointed out the need for Palestinians to reform their political and economic institutions.

Some of the more hawkish American Jewish organizations—the National Council of Young Israel, the Rabbinical Council of America, the Union of Orthodox Jewish Congregations of America, and the Zionist Organization of America—responded to the summit by setting up a new entity, the Coordinating Council on Jerusalem, to oppose Israeli territorial concessions in any part of Jerusalem.

Foreign Aid and Other Legislation

In June, the House approved the annual foreign-aid appropriations bill by 241-178. It contained $2.44 billion for Israel, including $2.4 billion in military aid and $40 million in assistance for the resettlement of Soviet, Eastern European, and Ethiopian refugees. The Senate approved a similar package in September. When finally adopted by both houses in December, there was a slight decrease to $2.38 billion in military aid and $39.6 million in resettlement aid. An across-the-board .81 percent funding reduction was necessary to bring the bill into compliance with overall budget numbers, based on a compromise reached by House and Senate lawmakers.

This Israeli aid package marked the final step in a ten-year plan that phased out economic aid in favor of military aid. While Prime Minister Olmert was in the U.S. in June, President Bush announced a plan for the next decade, in which the U.S. would give Israel an average of $3 billion a year for a total of $30 billion, an increase of 25 percent. The increase was explained as a means of balancing a U.S. arms package for Saudi Arabia and the Gulf states, estimated to top $20 billion over the next decade, designed to upgrade missile defenses, air force, and naval capabilities. Olmert said that the Israeli government "understands the United States' need to assist the moderate Arab states, which are standing in one front with the United States and us in the struggle against Iran."

Aid to Palestinians—$150 million in direct assistance to the Palestinian Authority—was conditioned on the fulfillment of "benchmarks" that included combating terror, denying assistance to organizations connected to or engaged in terrorism, implementing economic and government reforms, and permitting financial oversight. According to AIPAC, the aid package prohibited the PA from using the funds toward government salaries in Hamas-controlled Gaza, and continued the policy of no contact or negotiations with Hamas until it agreed to recognize Israel and meet international standards of conduct. Congress also tied $100 million of U.S. aid to Egypt to that country's efforts to curtail the smuggling of arms from Sinai into Gaza. The U.S. secretary of state would have to certify adequate compliance before the money could be paid.

A bill titled the United States-Israel Energy Cooperation Act was introduced by Sens. Jeff Bingaman (D., N.M.), Mary Landrieu (D., La.), and Gordon Smith (R., Oreg.) on March 12. A priority of the American Jewish Congress, the bill would have authorized funding through a grant program for joint ventures in alternative and renewable energy research between U.S. and Israeli businesses, nonprofits, universities, and government entities. A new International Energy Advisory Board would advise the government in the grant-making process. The bill had passed the House in the prior Congress, and was now referred to the Senate Committee on Energy and Natural Resources. No further action was taken in 2007.

Congress adopted numerous resolutions demonstrating support for Israel. On April 26, the House passed one introduced by Rep. Ileana Ros-Lehtinen (R., Fla.) "expressing deep concern over the use of civilians as 'human shields' in violation of international humanitarian law and the law of war during armed conflict, including Hezballah's tactic of embedding its forces among civilians to use them as human shields during the recent conflict between Hezballah and the State of Israel." On June 5, both houses passed resolutions commemorating the 40th anniversary of the "unprovoked" Six-Day War. It commended Israel for its administration of an undivided Jerusalem over four decades and reiterated Congressional commitment to relocating the U.S. embassy from Tel Aviv to Jerusalem and to a two-state solution to the conflict.

A resolution was introduced in June by Sens. Dianne Feinstein (D., Calif.) and Richard Lugar (R., Ind.) urging the president to intensify U.S. diplomatic efforts in pursuit of a "true and lasting solution to the Israeli-Palestinian conflict, based on the establishment of two states, the State of Israel and Palestine, living side by side in peace and security, with recognized borders." The resolution also denounced terrorism and reaffirmed Israel's right to defend herself. In addition to Feinstein and Lugar, the resolution was also cosponsored by, among others, Sens. Carl Levin (D., Mich.), Herb Kohl (D., Wis.), Russ Feingold (D., Wis.), and Ron Wyden (D., Oreg.). It was backed by Churches for Middle East Peace and by dovish Jewish groups such as Americans for Peace Now and B'rit Tzedek v'Shalom. Other national Jewish groups took no position on the measure.

The plight of the three captured Israeli soldiers evoked congressional resolutions and rallies, but did not return Ehud Goldwasser, Eldad Regev, and Gilad Shalit to their families as they entered their second year of captivity at the hands of Hamas and Hezballah. On March 1, Sens. Hillary Clinton (D., N.Y.) and George Voinovich (R., Ohio) introduced a resolution calling for their immediate and unconditional release. Also signing on were their colleagues Sherrod Brown (D., Ohio), Sam Brownback (R., Kans.), Norman Coleman (R., Minn.), Dianne Feinstein (D., Calif.), Frank Lautenberg (D., N.J.), Joseph Lieberman (I., Conn.), Barbara Mikulski (D., Md.), Bill Nelson (D., Fla.), and Charles Schumer (D., N.Y.). In the House, a similar measure was introduced by Rep. Gary Ackerman (D., N.Y.) and 68 cosponsors.

On July 16, a national rally in New York City and smaller rallies around the country were held to mark the anniversary of their capture. The national gathering was sponsored by the American Zionist Movement, the Conference of Presidents, JCPA, the New York Jewish Community Relations Council, United Jewish Communities (UJC), and UJA-Federation of New York. The same day, Rep. Ron Klein (D., Fla.) spoke on the House floor to call attention to their plight and reiterate the U.S. demand for their return. Klein also introduced into the record similar statements by other members of Congress.

A House resolution calling the Ottoman Turkish killings of more than a million Armenians during World War I "genocide" caused great difficulties for Jewish organizations. Turkey, a key ally of Israel, had long opposed labeling the events of that period genocide, and Jewish groups had studiously avoided the topic even though the massacres of the Armenians marked a precedent that Hitler followed in his treatment of the Jews. The "genocide" resolution was sponsored by Adam Schiff (D., Calif.) and cosponsored by three-fourths of the Jews in Congress.

When the large Armenian community in the Boston area dropped its participation in A World of Difference, the Anti-Defamation League's signature multicultural education program, to show its displeasure with the Jewish group's silence on the measure, the regional ADL endorsed the House resolution. National ADL and other Jewish groups did not do so, although ADL national director Abraham Foxman went so far as to declare what happened to the Armenians "tantamount to genocide." The House Foreign Affairs Committee approved the resolution on October 11, prompting the prime minister of Turkey to recall its ambassador "for consultations" and to threaten withdrawing permission for supplies to be shipped through Turkey to American-led forces in Iraq.

On October 30 the House passed a resolution introduced by Rep. Henry Waxman (D., Calif.) recognizing the 40th anniversary of the Soviet Jewry movement and the 20th anniversary of the landmark 1987 rally for Soviet Jewry in Washington. The Senate version was introduced by Sen. Joseph Lieberman (I., Conn.). Approval came on November 16.

AIPAC

AIPAC, the premier pro-Israel lobby, did not appear weakened by the pending espionage trials of two former veteran staffers, Steven Rosen and Keith Weissman (see AJYB 2007, p. 78), who during the year, filed motions to force the government to present evidence in open court, daring prosecutors to reveal clandestine sources, methods, and other confidential information. More than 6,000 pro-Israel activists attended AIPAC's annual policy conference in March, including 1,200 students. Speakers included Vice President Dick Cheney, Senate Majority Leader Harry Reid, House Speaker Nancy Pelosi, Republican Congressional leaders Mitch McConnell and John Boehner, Christian Zionist Pastor John Hagee (see below), Israeli foreign minister Tzipi Livni, and Likud leader Benjamin Netanyahu. Prime Minister Olmert addressed the gathering via satellite.

But AIPAC's preeminent position and a string of legislative victories—from foreign aid to Iran sanctions—generated a backlash both inside and outside the Jewish community. Following the policy conference came public critiques from *New York Times* columnist Nicholas Kristof (Mar. 18), who decried the lack of "serious public debate" by either party about U.S. policy in the Middle East, and billionaire investor and philanthropist George Soros, who, in the *New York Review of Books* (Apr. 12), charged that AIPAC had been "remarkably successful" in squelching criticism of U.S. policy by raising the specter of anti-Semitism.

In September, two professors, Stephen Walt of Harvard and John Mearsheimer of the University of Chicago, published *The Israel Lobby and U.S. Foreign Policy,* which repeated in greater detail and sophistication accusations made in their controversial 2006 essay (see AJYB 2007, pp. 76–77). Israel, they said, was a "strategic liability" for the U.S., supported only because of the aggressive pro-Israel lobby, which, they wrote, bore responsibility for leading America into war in Iraq and was seeking to provoke another war with Iran. Although the book targeted a broad constellation of pro-Israel groups, including Christian Zionist organizations, the brunt of its disapproval fell on AIPAC.

The reaction from mainstream Jewish leaders to the barrage was swift and furious. In the *Jerusalem Post,* AJC executive director David Harris charged that Kristof had a "blind spot" and had "sanctimoniously lectured" Israel. As reported in the *Forward, New Republic* editor Martin Peretz called Soros, a Hungarian-born Holocaust survivor, a "cog in the Hitlerite wheel." In the pages of the *Washington Post,* Johns Hopkins professor Eliot Cohen pronounced Walt and Mearsheimer's work anti-Semitic. In the September 3 issue of the *New Yorker,* however, David Remnick argued that their book was not anti-Semitic, although it did provide a one-sided narrative that "recounts every lurid report of Israeli cruelty as indisputable fact but leaves out the rise of Fatah and Palestinian terrorism before 1967; the Munich Olympics; Black September; myriad cases of suicide bombings; and other spectaculars."

Combating Boycotts

Campaigns to single out Israel and companies operating there for boycott, sanction, and divestment continued to capture the imagination of Israel's detractors, but achieved little.

The main anti-Israel push came from Great Britain. On April 13, the leadership of that country's 35,000-member National Union of Journalists voted 66-54 to boycott Israeli products. Later, the University and College Union (UCU)—formed by a merger of the two British lecturers' unions, NATFHE and AUT—declared an academic boycott of Israel. And the London *Guardian* published a call by a fringe group of 130 British doctors to expel the Israel Medical Association (IMA) from the World Medical Association (WMA).

Hadassah, the women's Zionist organization that specialized in providing health services, stated in a press release that it had "confidence that the World Medical Association, proudly led by Chairperson of Council, Israeli physician Yoram Blachar, will stand strong against these baseless accusations and proceed with its valuable work of medical collaboration and cooperation."

The threatened academic boycott drew the most sustained American denunciations. Robert J. Birgeneau, chancellor of the University of California at Berkeley, said that the UCU's "threat to cut off all funding, visits, and joint publishing with Israeli institutions violates the fundamental principles of academic freedom." Columbia University president Lee Bollinger declared that his institution would "embrace Israeli scholars and universities that the UCU is now all too eager to isolate." On May 31, Sen. Christopher Dodd (D., Conn.) sent a letter to the UCU's joint general secretary complaining that the boycott "compromises the principles of objectivity, fairness, and dialogue that are at the foundation of all academia."

The American Jewish Congress released a statement on June 26 signed by two dozen former Rhodes scholars protesting the proposed boycott, which the scholars called "unjustified and an egregious violation of the basic rules of the academic community." On July 11, the House of Representatives adopted a resolution sponsored by Rep. Patrick Murphy (D., Pa.) condemning the academic boycott. Speaking in favor of the measure were Reps. Sheila Jackson-Lee (D., Tex.), Ileana Ros-Lehtinen (R., Fla.), Henry Waxman (D., Calif.), Elliot Engel (D., N.Y.), and Debbie Wasserman Schultz (D., Fla.). The sole opposing voice was that of Rep. Ron Paul (R., Tex.), who had declared his candidacy for president. The isolationist Paul questioned whether the "U.S. government should be sticking its nose into a dispute between British and Israeli academics."

The *New York Times* of August 8 carried an ad placed by AJC listing 300 college and university presidents endorsing Bollinger's denunciation of the academic boycott. Among the signatories were the presidents of Berkeley, Georgetown, Johns Hopkins, New York University, and Princeton. The ad encouraged British academics opposed to the boycott, several of whom urged their colleagues not to go along with it. Referring to the AJC ad, Prof. Mark Pepys, head of University of London's Department of Medicine, said: "The robust position of 300 U.S. institutions in defense of the universally recognized principle of academic freedom cannot be ignored. American academia, with its depth, breadth and scale, has enormous impact in the UK at all levels of academic life."

The Jewish Labor Committee was successful in its efforts to keep American unions from following the lead of their British counterparts. The JLC organized a statement by the leaders of more than two dozen American unions in opposition to boycotts of Israel. The labor leaders agreed that "[r]ather than divestment from Israel, we believe that investment of time, energy and material aid is the best means to alleviate the ongoing suffering of Palestinians and Israelis." Signatories included AFL-CIO president John J. Sweeney, as well as the heads of unions representing teamsters, miners, electrical and communications workers, government employees, and others.

One notable academic supporter of anti-Israel boycotts, political scientist Norman Finkelstein, was denied tenure at DePaul University. Finkelstein was notorious for attacks on Israel and assertions that Jews exploited the Holocaust for political and financial gain. The case against Finkelstein had been championed by Professor Alan Dershowitz of Harvard Law School.

Iraq

President Bush, on January 10, announced plans for an escalation, or "surge," of more than 20,000 troops to be sent to Iraq to quell the violence that had, to date, resulted in more than 3,000 American military causalities and many more wounded. Polls continued to show American Jews opposed to the war in large numbers, with more than three-quarters agreeing that it was a mistake. As the war entered its fifth year, Jewish organizations wrestled with the dilemma of whether to speak out publicly against it.

ADL national director Foxman, in an interview with the JTA, suggested that muted Jewish criticism of the war reflected gratitude to President Bush for his support of Israel, especially at a time when action might have to be taken against Iran. But Rabbi David Saperstein, director of the Reform movement's Religious Action Center (RAC), disagreed. In a February 22 op-ed in the *Forward,* he urged "the Jewish community to weigh in and determine what insights Jewish values and interests can offer, not only because our prophetic tradition mandates that we speak out on the great moral issues of the day . . . but also because Israel's interests and security are so clearly at stake." On March 12, the Union for Reform Judaism's executive committee adopted a resolution opposing the troop escalation and calling on the president to set a timetable for troop withdrawal. The Reconstructionist Rabbinical Association also issued a call for a "rapid and responsible" troop withdrawal.

Although no national Jewish group had taken a position in favor of the war, some critics—in the spirit of Mearsheimer and Walt—were willing to draw the conclusion. Rep. James Moran (D., Va.) blasted the pro-Israel lobby for allegedly promoting the war. In the September/October issue of *Tikkun* magazine, Moran repeated a charge he had made in 2003 (see AJYB 2004, p. 81), alleging that AIPAC and its "wealthy" and "powerful" members "pushed this war from the beginning." The National Jewish Democratic Council issued a statement deriding Moran for making a "phony" connection between AIPAC and the war.

In Congress, Democrats were not only unable to follow through on their 2006 election-year promise to end the war, but they also failed to block the surge. The most they could accomplish was pass a resolution in the House condemning the plan. Sen. Carl Levin (D., Mich.), joined by Sen. John Warner (R., Va.), led unsuccessful efforts in the upper house to express disapproval for increasing the number of American fighters. The president and Congress sparred over funding for the war itself, with the White House successfully defeating language that would have called for specific timetables for troop withdrawal.

Iran

The Jewish community and Israel took very seriously the continuing threats of Iranian president Mahmoud Ahmadinejad to "eliminate" the Jewish state. On December 13, 2006, for example, Reuters reported the bombastic leader as professing his desire for "the Zionist regime" to be "wiped out." Compounding this rhetoric was the Iranian nuclear program, which appeared to progress unabated despite UN resolutions and sanctions against it in 2006. Iran proclaimed its intent was energy production for peaceful purposes, but skeptics abounded and rhetoric soared, especially as American military officials charged Iran with supplying weapons to rebels in Iraq. The UN Security Council expanded its sanctions regime in March 2007 to cast a wider net over financial institutions and transportation of materials that could potentially be used for the production of nuclear missiles. On April 9, Iran reported that it had 3,000 centrifuges that could enrich uranium, a necessary precursor for nuclear-weapon production.

On June 20, the House passed a resolution calling for the UN to charge Ahmadinejad with violation of the UN Charter and the 1948 UN Convention on Genocide, for his threats against Israel. On August 30, the International Atomic Energy Agency (IAEA) reported that the Iranian nuclear program remained intact, but that the agency could not verify some critical data, including those related to advanced centrifuge research. At the end of the year Ahmadinejad intimated that he might seek enriched uranium from another country, such as Switzerland.

The tightrope that Jewish agencies walked in response to the Iranian nuclear program was even trickier than the one involving Iraq: deep concern about the existential threat to the Jewish state had to be weighed against the need to demonstrate that the movement to stop Iran was not solely a Jewish campaign. As policy makers debated the merits of a preemptive effort to destroy Iran's nuclear capacity should negotiations and sanctions fail, fears mounted that the Jewish community would open itself to charges that it was beating the drums for war with Iran. Therefore Jewish leaders framed economic alternatives as an option short of military intervention.

At the JCPA Plenum in February, a last-minute motion to recommend divestment from Iran was referred to a committee for further review, and on March 27 the JCPA board, noting that "the threat of Iran obtaining nuclear weapons is a matter of the gravest concern and utmost urgency," called on political, civic, and religious leaders to "utilize all diplomatic and economic measures necessary to deter Iran from continuing its quest for nuclear weapons, while respecting the humanitarian needs of the Iranian people." The term "economic measures" was defined to include sanctions, targeted divestment, and restrictions on bank transfers. UJC passed a resolution on June 4 instructing its investment committee to divest its endowment and pension funds of holdings directly invested in companies that conducted business, not of a humanitarian nature, with either Sudan or Iran, relying on data provided by the U.S. Department of Energy, the Congressional Research Service, and other government or research agencies. It also directed federation leaders to advance such divestment at the state and local levels.

Steam also gathered elsewhere in support of using American financial markets against Iran and other regimes accused of terror. The Center for Security Policy, led by Frank Gaffney, launched a divestment campaign aimed at getting states, colleges, pension funds, and other investors to divest from Iran. Several of the largest states embraced "terror-free" investing. On June 8, Florida governor Charles Crist signed a measure directing the state's retirement program to contact companies with business ties to Iran or Sudan to seek their withdrawal from those countries, and to divest 90 days after communication if the ties continued. In June, Illinois governor Rod Blagojevich allowed divestment legislation to come into effect without his signature. On September 25, Texas governor Rick Perry directed the state pension fund to divest from Iran. California governor Arnold Schwarzenegger signed a bill on October 26 ordering the state's two largest pension funds to divest from companies with business ties to Iran's petroleum, natural gas, nuclear, or defense sectors. And on December 17, the New Jersey State Senate adopted a measure passed in June by the Assembly to prohibit state pension investment in Iran.

The U.S. Congress began work on a legislative initiative to allay concerns that such measures might run afoul of a constitutional prohibition against states engaging in foreign affairs. In May, Sen. Barack Obama (D. Ill.) and Reps. Barney Frank (D., Mass.) and Tom Lantos (D., Calif.) introduced the Iran Sanctions Enabling Act to shield fund managers and state pension programs from shareholder lawsuits if they divested stakes in energy companies that had at least $20 million invested in Iran's energy sector. The measure passed the House on June 30, but the Senate did not take action on it. Sens. Lautenberg (D., N.J.) and Clinton (D., N.Y.) introduced a bill to deter subsidiaries of U.S. companies from doing business in Iran. Known as the Stop Business with Terrorists Act of 2007, this measure would strengthen the sanction provisions that prevented American companies from doing business in countries that sponsored terror.

Public and private protests greeted President Ahmadinejad when he visited New York City for the opening of the UN General Assembly session in September. The Conference of Presidents and the New York JCRC, in cooperation with the JCPA, UJC, and UJA-Federation of New York, sponsored a rally on September 24 to protest Iranian nuclear ambitions and anti-Israel rhetoric. There were additional protests when Ahmadinejad spoke at Columbia University to an audience of 600 faculty, students, and administrators at the university's School of International and Public Affairs.

On October 25, the U.S. government announced a unilateral effort against Iran, making it unlawful for anyone subject to U.S. legal jurisdiction knowingly to provide material support or resources to the Quds division of the Iranian Revolutionary Guard Corps. And at the end of the year, the administration released a National Intelligence Estimate dated December 3 stating that Iran had actually halted its nuclear-weapons program in 2003 in response to the U.S.-led invasion in Iraq. But while the finding, developed by the nation's 16 intelligence agencies, expressed "high confidence" about the 2003 suspension, it could only say with "moderate confidence" that the program had not resumed afterwards.

Jewish Refugees from Arab Lands

An international campaign led by B'nai B'rith International, Justice for Jews from Arab Countries (JJAC), and Jews Indigenous to the Middle East and North Africa (JIMENA), brought new focus to the expulsion and mass departure of more than 800,000 Jews who lived in Arab countries prior to the 1948 Arab-Israeli War—a number larger than the 711,000 Palestinians who left their homes and property at the time of the creation of Israel

In February, resolutions were introduced in both houses of Congress acknowledging the human rights of all Middle East refugees. They were sponsored in the House by Rep. Jerrold Nadler (D., N.Y.) and in the Senate by Sen. Frank Lautenberg (D., N.J.). The House resolution, adopted April 1, called on the president to ensure that, at international forums attended by the U.S., all references to the Palestinian refugee situation were matched by "a similarly explicit reference to Jewish and other refugee populations." There were also two House hearings on this issue. The first, on May 8 in the Foreign Affairs Committee's Subcommittee on the Middle East and South Asia, was chaired by Rep. Ackerman (D., N.Y.), and the second was conducted by the Congressional Human Rights Caucus (CHRC), chaired by Rep. Lantos (D., Calif.).

In November, the JJAC held a conference in New York at which it distributed copies of a memo composed in 1947 by the Arab League calling for measures against Jews living in Arab lands. According to a report on the subject published in the *New York Times* (Nov. 2), the World Jewish Congress had informed the UN Economic and Social Council in 1948 of the document, with a warning that "all Jews residing in the Near and Middle East face extreme and imminent danger." The *Times* further reported that in March 1948, Charles Malik, the Lebanese ambassador then serving as president of the council, used parliamentary tactics to quash consideration of the Arab League memo and that, despite some news coverage at the time, the issue had been almost forgotten. At the conference, Irwin Cotler, the former Canadian minister of justice, accused the UN of "expunging this experience from the Mideast narrative."

Darfur

February marked the fourth year of the conflict in the Darfur region of Sudan, as proposed ceasefires and tentative truces gave way to continued mayhem and violence directed at the civilian population and humanitarian aid workers. At year's end the total death toll was estimated at more than 400,000, with an additional two and a half million displaced since 2003.

In February, Academy Award-winning film director Steven Spielberg, along with actress Mia Farrow, urged China, the largest investor in the Sudanese oil industry, to exert political leverage on its government to help end the crisis in Darfur. Spielberg announced that he would not serve as artistic advisor to the 2008 Olympic Games in Beijing, due to Chinese inaction on the matter.

Save Darfur, a coalition of 180 faith-based organizations, tried to draw attention to the crisis and the need for a strong and coordinated response. Among its members were three dozen Jewish agencies representing a broad spectrum of religious views. On April 29, the coalition sponsored its third "Global Day for Darfur." The rally, held in Washington's Lafayette Park, was one of more than 400 such events in 287 cities and 47 states. Speakers included Elie Wiesel; Rev. Richard Cizik (National Association of Evangelicals); Larry Cox (Amnesty International); Mia Farrow (UNICEF goodwill ambassador); Rabbi Steve Gutow (JCPA); Gov. Jon Corzine (D., N.J.); Theodore Cardinal McCarrick (Washington, D.C.); Dr. Richard Land (Southern Baptist Convention); Rabbi David Saperstein (RAC of Reform Judaism); Ruth Messinger (American Jewish World Service); and Paul Rusesabagina, recipient of the Presidential Medal of Freedom, who risked his life to save more than 1,000 people during the genocide in Rwanda.

As noted above in connection with Iran, several Jewish agencies passed targeted divestment resolutions against Sudan. JCPA policy called for the removal of investments in companies that directly or indirectly helping the Sudanese government perpetuate genocide. A campaign focused on Fidelity Investments gained some traction, as the mutual-fund company dramatically reduced its holdings in PetroChina, a company linked to the government in Sudan. However Fidelity denied that it was reacting to the public campaign.

Despite speculation that he would wield his veto pen, President Bush, on the last day of the year, signed the Sudan Accountability and Divestment Act. It authorized state and local governments to divest assets in companies that conducted business operations in Sudan, and put an end to U.S. government contracts with such companies. Some 26 states had already initiated divestment initiatives.

THE DOMESTIC-POLICY ARENA

Homeland Security

The Democratic majorities in both houses of Congress moved swiftly to shore up their bona fides on homeland security, traditionally a province of Republicans. On January 9, during the "First 100 Hours," the House passed a measure to implement the report of the 9/11 Commission, and the Senate subsequently passed a similar measure. The differences were resolved in conference, and the Improving America's Security Act was agreed to by the House on July 26 and the Senate the next day.

Included in the bill were provisions to give homeland-security grants on the basis of degree of risk, screen all cargo entering the country, improve cooperation among intelligence agencies, revise visa programs, and experiment with "enhanced drivers licenses." The bill also set up an Office of International Cooperation within the Department of Homeland Security that would help pair domestic and overseas entities for homeland-security research activities. This provision was touted by AIPAC because it identified Israel as one of five countries that might be potential partners for the program.

The Military Commissions Act of 2006 had removed from federal judicial purview the authority to hear habeas corpus petitions for individuals identified as "enemy combatants," and as the issue wended its way to the U.S. Supreme Court (see below), Congress debated whether to restore that authority. Legislation to that effect, the Habeas Corpus Restoration Act, was sponsored by Sens. Patrick Leahy (D., Ver.) and Arlen Specter (R., Pa.) in the Senate, and Reps. Jerrold Nadler (D., N.Y.) and Jane Harman (D., Calif.) in the House. A broad array of Jewish groups signaled support for the measure. American Jewish Congress president Richard Gordon said passage would mark "a welcome return to the very first principles upon which our government was founded," and rejected arguments that the bill would undermine the war on terror by noting that, under its provisions, detainees would not be automatically released, but rather would have access to judicial review.

Citing concerns about the capacity of U.S. law enforcement to intercept electronic communications, the president signed into law the Protect America Act of 2007 on August 5. It removed the warrant requirement for surveillance of intelligence targets, including U.S. citizens, if law enforcement "reasonably believe" one of the parties being monitored is outside the U.S. Investigators would have power, under the law, to eavesdrop on telephone and Internet communications between people in the U.S. and people abroad without a court order. The bill replaced the warrant requirement of the Foreign Intelligence Security Act (FISA) with a system of internal controls. Mired in controversy over whether to grant retroactive immunity to telecommunications companies that cooperated with law enforcement, the law was slated to expire in February 2008. The RAC of Reform Judaism complained that the act broke down checks and balances that had been built into the FISA system, and permitted wiretapping with minimal or no judicial oversight. A RAC action alert cited biblical and Talmudic authority that "surveillance of private space was deemed to be a violation of privacy rights."

The term "waterboarding" entered the national lexicon as news emerged that the Central Intelligence Agency had used such extreme interrogation techniques as pouring water over an immobilized suspect's head to simulate drowning. Civil-liberties and human-rights agencies expressed outrage at a Department of Justice memorandum permitting this technique and others, such as placing detainees in hypothermic chambers, head slapping, and sleep deprivation. Waterboarding was debated during the Senate hearings to confirm Michael Mukasey as U.S. attorney general (see above).

On December 10, AJC announced its backing for legislation to ban the use of torture by American military, intelligence, and law-enforcement personnel. The bill was being pushed by a coalition of 140 groups—including the Union for Reform Judaism and Rabbis for Human Rights-North America—under the banner of the National Religious Campaign Against Torture. The JCPA also called on its members to support the ban. The American Jewish Congress, in a statement welcoming the appointment of Mukasey as attorney general, called for Congress to declare waterboarding illegal. Most of the mainstream Jewish organizations, however, remained silent. Rabbi Brian Walt, executive director of Rabbis for Human Rights-North America, explained to the *Forward* that "the reluctance of a large segment of the organized Jewish community to speak out against harsh interrogation techniques stems partly from the belief that torture may help to prevent terrorist attacks, as well as from concern that heightened scrutiny of American security forces' methods could draw increased attention to Israel's own interrogation practices." Walt called this stance ironic, since the Israeli Supreme Court had banned torture in 1999, and "Israel has a better record than the U.S. on this."

On December 6, Sen. Dianne Feinstein (D., Calif.), with the support of her colleagues Chuck Hagel (R., Neb.), Sheldon Whitehouse (D., R.I.), and Russ Feingold (D., Wis.), added provisions to the Intelligence Authorization Conference Report that would require all U.S. agencies, including the CIA, to follow the interrogation guidelines laid out in the *Army Field Manual*. The House passed a similar bill on December 13.

Immigration

Despite significant lobbying and media attention, immigration reform did not occur in 2007. Jewish organizations, spearheaded by HIAS, favored so-called Comprehensive Immigration Reform (CIR), which combined disparate proposals such as an earned path to citizenship for those in the U.S. illegally; guest-worker programs; reduction of family reunification backlogs; and increased border security and enforcement of immigration laws. In the end, Congress adopted a proposal heavily weighted to enforcement.

The Comprehensive Immigration Reform Act of 2007—also known as the Secure Borders, Economic Opportunity and Immigration Reform Act—was introduced in May in the Senate, where it was described as a compromise evidencing compassion for those already in the U.S. while simultaneously doing more to prevent further illegal immigration. The bill would have provided a circuitous route to citizenship for approximately 12 million noncitizens, and also included the DREAM Act, a special provision to facilitate legal status and higher education for undocumented immigrant children. The legislation sought to augment border security by funding 300 miles of vehicle barriers, more than 100 camera and radar towers, and a surge of 20,000 border police. It would also have restructured visa criteria for skilled workers. Heated debate swirled around the bill, particularly the citizenship provision, which was derided as an "amnesty" plan.

A Senate filibuster ensued, and on June 8 HIAS president Gideon Aronoff expressed disappointment that "the Senate was unable to overcome politics to produce the kind of solution that this nation deserves."

He said HIAS was dismayed at the Senate deadlock, and "extremely concerned" about provisions that had worked their way into the bill that would have undermined family reunification. Aronoff called current immigration policy "inconsistent and haphazard," including a "chaotic and wasteful border and interior enforcement scheme that places the United States' security in jeopardy."

In August, HIAS decried an enforcement-only immigration reform proposal issued by the White House. Hopes for the progressive elements of CIR were dashed one last time on October 24, when Senate backers of the DREAM Act legislation failed to get sufficient votes to end a filibuster and permit debate to continue.

Hate Crimes

Proponents of a federal hate-crimes law came closer than ever to seeing enactment of a bill that would expand the definition of such crimes to include acts committed because of animus against the victim's real or perceived gender, gender-identity, sexual orientation, or disability, and would give the Department of Justice greater authority to investigate and prosecute hate crimes. There was a concerted effort this time to mobilize the support of religious individuals and organizations, including the formation of Clergy Against Hate, which set up a Website with resources to advocate for the measure.

On May 3, the House approved the Local Law Enforcement Hate Crimes Prevention Act by 237-180. Jewish organizations, led by the ADL, hailed the vote. In September, the Senate, by voice vote, added the measure to the Defense Authorization Act, a step taken after a 60-39 vote to invoke cloture ended a filibuster. But in December, the conference committee charged with reconciling the House and Senate versions of the Defense Authorization Act removed the hate-crimes provisions to avert a threatened presidential veto.

Head Start

The Jewish community found itself locked in a painful conflict over reauthorization of Head Start, an early-childhood education program for children from low-income households. An amendment was proposed to exempt religiously affiliated groups that administered Head Start from certain civil rights laws, allowing such operators to hire and fire government-funded employees on the basis of religion. Jewish and other groups favoring Head Start but opposed to the amendment played a game of brinksmanship, threatening to oppose final passage of the bill unless the exemption language was removed. In the end, the amendment failed both in committee and in a motion to recommit on the House floor.

Voting Rights

Several mainstream Jewish organizations lined up with civil rights groups in support of granting voting representation in Congress to residents of the District of Columbia. Although the District already had a delegate with the right to vote in House committee, that delegate had no vote on the House floor, and since the vast majority of D.C. residents were members of racial and ethnic minorities, the civil rights issue was clear. Opponents of the initiative pointed to language in the Constitution reserving full House representation for admitted states.

A compromise bill was offered by Delegate Eleanor Holmes Norton (D., D.C.) and Rep. Tom Davis (R., Va.) that would have expanded the number of representatives by two. The District—which was heavily Democratic—would receive a single permanent seat. The second new seat would be awarded to the predominantly Republican state of Utah until the 2010 census, after which it would be distributed through the general reapportionment process. (Utah was widely considered likely to gain a seat after the census.) The House passed the bill, but Senate proponents were unable to muster the 60 votes necessary to stop debate and move to a vote.

Stem-Cell Research

As part of its "First 100 Hours" agenda, Congress endeavored to address stem-cell research. Medical researchers held out the hope that embryonic stems cells might hold the key to treating and curing a range of maladies, such as Parkinson's disease, spinal-cord injuries, and certain forms of cancer. The Stem-Cell Research Enhancement Act of 2007 was designed to promote such research by increasing the number of embryonic stem-cell lines that could be used in federally funded research. The bill would ostensibly overturn an executive order issued by the president in August 2001 that limited federal funding to cell lines created before that date. Jewish agencies, including the denominational bodies, supported the research—within ethical parameters—and opposed efforts to restrict or penalize scientists, clinicians, or patients for participating in stem-cell therapeutic technology.

An attempt to pass similar legislation in 2006 had drawn the first veto of President Bush's administration. The 2007 attempt once again passed both houses, but fell short of the two-thirds margin necessary to override a veto, and so was given up. There was greater success at the state level, though. In New York, Hadassah leaders hailed the State Legislature for providing $100 million to fund stem-cell research and regenerative medicine, with an expectation of a billion dollars over the next ten years.

Holocaust-Related Matters

The second annual observation of International Holocaust Remembrance Day took place at the UN on January 29. Among the speakers were Secretary General Ban Ki-moon (by video), Israeli ambassador to the UN Dan Gillerman, a Jewish survivor, and representatives of other groups persecuted by the Nazis. The UN's New York headquarters also hosted exhibits highlighting different aspects of the Holocaust and their contemporary relevance.

Members of Congress and Jewish community organizations sought greater access to the trove of millions of pages of Holocaust-era documents housed in archives in Bad Arolsen, Germany, that recorded what happened to more than 17 million victims of the Nazis. These were under the control of the International Tracing Service (ITS), which was governed by a multinational board. While a recent agreement made the documents available to family members and researchers, many of the ITS member nations had not yet ratified the agreement. Reps. Alcee Hastings (D., Fla.), Robert Wexler (D., Fla.), and Mark Kirk (R., Ill.) organized letters to the German ambassador and representatives of the European nations whose approval was needed.

Adding a sense of urgency was the fact that the International Commission on Holocaust Era Insurance Claims (ICHEIC), set up ten years earlier to compensate survivors for unpaid insurance policies, was winding down its work. It was hoped that information from the Bad Arolsen archives might bolster claims against insurers.

In March, Rep. Ileana Ros-Lehtinen (R., Fla.) introduced a controversial measure, the Holocaust Insurance Claims Accountability Act. This bill would require insurance companies doing business in the U.S.

to disclose information about Holocaust-era insurance policies, and established a federal cause of action for claims arising from these policies. Ros-Lehtinen and the survivors groups supporting her felt that ICHEIC had allowed insurers to drag their feet on producing information, and had allowed inadequate listings and settlements. Mainstream Jewish organizations, however, did not support the bill. According to the *Forward,* their leaders felt the measure would threaten existing international compensation agreements, which were premised on voluntary monetary payouts in exchange for immunity from further lawsuits. The agreements had yielded payments of more than $300 million to almost 50,000 survivors. One-third of the payments were settlements on policies, and the remainder consisted of $1,000 "humanitarian awards" in cases where existence of the insurance policies could not be definitively proved. The proposed legislation, then, put some survivors groups on a collision course with one another, Jewish organizations, the courts, and the U.S. government.

Health Care

Jewish agencies, conscious of the graying of the general population and the Jewish community in particular, played an active role in the continuing debate over Medicare, Medicaid, and prescription-drug benefits. Legislation was introduced to require the government to negotiate directly with pharmaceutical companies for lower drug prices for people in the Medicare program. The House passed the Medicare Prescription Drug Price Negotiation Act of 2007 on January 12 by 255-170, but it was not taken up by the Senate. UJC expressed displeasure that the president's budget recommended reducing spending on Medicare and Medicaid by nearly $100 billion, cutting $95.9 billion from entitlement spending over the next five years, $309 billion over ten years.

A health-care program for children took center stage as well: many felt that the battle over the State Children's Health Insurance Program (SCHIP) had significant implications both for those who might gain or lose health coverage and for members of Congress seeking to maintain their seats. Congress debated reauthorization of the 1997 federal program that funded state programs for families with children. The bill drew fire over funding levels, eligibility for the children of illegal immigrants, state flexibility on eligibility levels and citizenship documentation, incentives for state outreach and enrollment, and expanding SCHIP to include comprehensive coverage for children.

In addition to maintaining coverage for more than six million children currently covered, the bill would have expanded coverage to an additional three million in households with incomes up to three times the federal poverty level. It would also provide mental health parity and the option of dental coverage, but not extend eligibility to children of illegal immigrants. House Democrats agreed to limit the increase in SCHIP spending to $35 billion, matching the Senate proposal, paid for completely by a 61-cent increase in the tobacco tax.

President Bush vetoed SCHIP twice. The first veto, on October 3, derailed a measure that had passed the Senate by a 67-29 veto-proof majority. In the House, though, it came up 25 votes short of the 290 needed to override a veto. Jewish agencies made a strong effort to garner support. NCJW president Phyllis Snyder, in a JTA op-ed, recalled that the Jewish greeting for a happy and healthy new year had "added meaning this year," as Congress had the "opportunity to ensure a healthy new year for millions of America's children." Efforts to address opposition concerns on income eligibility, undocumented immigrants, and the phase-out timetable for childless adults receiving SCHIP benefits failed to sway enough votes to reach the two-thirds mark, and on October 18, the House fell just 16 votes short of the number needed to override. The second veto came on December 12, after which Congress adopted a long-term reauthorization of the program without the additional coverage. That bill was signed December 21.

Poverty

As part of the "First 100 Hours" agenda, the new Congress moved to increase the minimum wage from $5.15 to $7.25. The bill was introduced January 5 and signed by the president on May 25, as part of legislation providing funds for troops, veterans, and Hurricane Katrina recovery, along with tax breaks for small businesses.

For the first time, the farm bill became a major focus for Jewish agencies, spearheaded by the JCPA. This was so because the food-stamp federal entitlement was technically an agricultural program, and funded in the farm bill. Rabbi Steve Gutow, the JCPA executive director, issued a "Food Stamp Challenge," pledging to eat over the course of one week only as much food as could be purchased with $21, the average amount ($1/meal) provided to food-stamp recipients. His challenge was designed to call attention to the inadequacy of the food-stamp benefit and to galvanize support for a strong reauthorization of the nutrition title of the farm bill.

The Feeding America's Family Act, sponsored by Reps. James McGovern (D., Mass.) and Joanne Emerson (R., Mo.), was embraced by anti-hunger advocates. It would have added $20 billion to nutritional programs by increasing the minimum benefit, restoring food stamps to all legal immigrants, and streamlining outreach efforts. In the Senate, advocates pushed for the Food Stamp Fairness and Benefit Restoration Act of 2007, introduced by Sens. Harkin (D., Iowa) and Lugar (R., Ind.) to improve the benefit formula and reverse the trend of decreasing U.S. government donations to community food banks and food pantries.

Rep. Steve King (R., Iowa) offered two amendments, one barring for life anyone who had ever been without status in the U.S.—including refugees and asylum-seekers—from the food-stamp program; and the other mandating that extremely poor legal immigrants count their sponsor's income when determining eligibility for food stamps, even after the expiration of a five-year window. Several Jewish agencies vigorously opposed these amendments, and they were not included in the final version of the bill.

As Thanksgiving neared, the Senate remained deadlocked. An agreement in December finally enabled the Senate to pass a five-year, $286-billion reauthorization of the farm bill by a vote of 79-14. And at year's end, conferees were lining up to iron out an agreement on a $5.1-billion disaster fund to assist farmers during droughts, floods, and fires, a provision that was not in the House proposal.

Energy and the Environment

Congress debated a broad range of measures to address the sometimes complementary and sometimes conflicting priorities of energy independence and environmental protection. But fault lines formed on whether domestic policy should be weighted toward conservation, development of alternative fuels, or drilling for oil at home, including the Arctic National Wildlife Refuge in Alaska. Compounding the issue was a growing consensus that the earth was warming, in part because of human factors, such as greenhouses gases, and that climate change posed a dire threat to the planet and life on it.

The Energy Independence and Security Act raised the required average fuel economy of cars and light trucks to 35 miles per gallon by the year 2020, the first increase in more than 20 years. Stricken from the measure was a requirement that 15 percent of American energy come from renewable sources by 2020. Congress also inched closer to adopting a policy on global warming. The House passed a resolution calling for mandatory limits on greenhouse gases. Sen. Lieberman (I., Conn.) teamed up with Sen. Warner (R., Va.) to sponsor the Climate Security Act, an effort to lower greenhouse gas emissions by as much as 19 percent below 2005 levels by the year 2020, and as much as 63 percent by mid-century. Action was expected in 2008.

There was a solid Jewish consensus that dependence on energy produced in often hostile countries had rendered Americans less secure. Seventeen Jewish agencies wrote members of Congress on October 24 to advocate for energy policies that "reduce our dependence on foreign sources, sustain our fragile environment, and build a robust national economy." Public investment in alternative fuels, in continued, would help avoid "pouring billions of dollars into the coffers of some of the world's most despotic and anti-American regimes." The Coalition on the Environment and Jewish Life organized a grassroots campaign to send postcards to members of Congress through its campaign, "A Light Among the Nations: How Many Jews Does it Take to Change a Light Bulb?" And AJC offered financial incentives to its employees to purchase fuel-efficient, environmentally friendly vehicles.

Life Insurance

The House of Representatives approved the Life Insurance Fairness for Travelers Act, prohibiting insurers from using locations of past or prospective travel as a basis for decisions on granting life insurance. The insurers had used the State Department's "watch list" as a proxy for risk, and charged higher premiums or denied policies to those intending to travel to countries deemed dangerous, such as Israel. Introducing the bill, Rep. Debbie Wasserman Schultz (D., Fla.) cited her own difficulties in obtaining insurance coverage because of her travels. Similar measures on the state level had already passed in California, Colorado, Connecticut, Florida, Georgia, Illinois, Maryland, Massachusetts, New York, and Washington.

Civil Rights and Civil Liberties

HABEAS CORPUS

In August, a broad range of Jewish groups—including AJC, ADL, JCPA, and the URJ—submitted amicus briefs to the Supreme Court in support of detainees held at Guantánamo Bay, Cuba, who were seeking review of the legality of their detentions in federal court, as well as challenging the constitutionality of the Military Commissions Act of 2006. Oral arguments in the combined case of *Boumediene v. Bush* and *al Odah v. U.S.* were held on December 5.

Many other civil-liberties groups also backed the rights of the detainees, including Human Rights First, Human Rights Watch, the Constitution Project, and the Rutherford Institute, as did the American-Arab Anti-Discrimination Committee, the Muslim Public Affairs Council, and the National Council of the Churches of Christ in the U.S.A.

Gay and Lesbian Rights

The fall 2006 elections had increased the number of political liberals in Congress, raising hopes for passage of the Employment Non-Discrimination Act (ENDA), popularly known as the gay rights bill. Introduced in the House by Reps. Barney Frank (D., Mass.), Christopher Shays (R., Conn.), Tammy Baldwin (D., Wis.), and Deborah Pryce (R., Ohio), it would have prohibited discrimination on the basis of sexual orientation or gender identity. The latter provision, affording civil-rights protection to transgendered individuals, triggered controversy: with a national election coming up in 2008, there was fear of a backlash against the bill's supporters. Another bone of contention was language inserted in the bill to ease fears of religious groups that they might be forced by it to violate the teachings of their faiths.

In the hope of securing passage, Rep. Frank and others proposed limiting the measure to the less controversial subject of discrimination on the basis of sexual orientation, leaving the situation of transgendered people for later legislation. The NCJW joined in a letter sent on October 1 to the chair of the House Education and Labor Committee opposing Frank's strategy. Frank went ahead and introduced the narrower ENDA, with the gender-identity provision stripped away. He also chose to revert to the religious exemption language from prior years. The bill was passed by the House on November 7 by 235 to 184, the first time such a measure had ever passed in either house. No action was taken in the Senate.

Reproductive Rights

On June 7, the National Council of Jewish Women unveiled its "Plan A" campaign to press for reproductive rights and unfettered access to contraceptives through education and advocacy initiatives at the community, state, and national levels. NCJW sections in many parts of the country reported considerable activity, including ensuring that local pharmacies stocked emergency contraception, asking school boards to require comprehensive sex-education programs, and advocating for affordable contraception on college campuses.

In a 5-4 decision, the U.S. Supreme Court, in *Gonzales v. Carhart,* upheld the Partial-Birth Abortion Ban Act. Justice Anthony Kennedy's decision said that the ban on the rarely used intact dilation and extraction procedure to end late-term pregnancies did not place an undue burden on the due process rights of women, even in the absence of an exception for the health of the mother.

Several Jewish organizations expressed fear that this ruling could ultimately lead to an end to all abortion rights. The National Council of Jewish Women, in a statement, declared that the Supreme Court had "dealt a devastating blow to *Roe v. Wade* and the right of women to safe and legal abortions." Hadassah president June Walker said: "We are concerned that interference of this kind may place the health of a pregnant woman in jeopardy, something that is considered unacceptable by the Jewish religion, which places the health of the mother above all other considerations." But Rabbi Avi Shafran, director of public affairs for Agudath Israel of America, disagreed sharply, stating that from the perspective of Jewish law, the ban on partial-birth abortion prohibited "little if anything short of murder."

Genetic Information

The Genetic Information Nondiscrimination Act of 2007 was introduced in the House by Reps. Louise Slaughter (D., N.Y.), Judy Biggert (R., Ill.), Anna Eshoo (D., Calif.), and Greg Walden (R., Oreg.). A companion bill was introduced in the Senate by Olympia Snowe (R., Me.), Edward Kennedy (D., Mass.), Mike Enzi (R., Wyo.), and Christopher Dodd (D., Conn.). The legislation would prohibit employers from using genetic information to discriminate in employment decisions, and both employers and insurance companies from using such information to determine eligibility for insurance or to set insurance rates. It had been a key legislative priority of Hadassah and other Jewish organizations for many years. The House passed it by 420-9 on April 25, but Sen. Tom Coburn (R., Okla.)—a physician—put a "hold" on the bill in the Senate, ending its chances for passage in 2007.

Desegregation

The Supreme Court, hearing a pair of school desegregation cases together, ruled 5-4 that two voluntary integration programs were unconstitutional. In *Parents v. Seattle* and *Meredith v. Jefferson County,* Chief Justice Roberts's decision found that the school systems could not justify using race to remedy past discrimination because, in the Seattle case, the schools had never been legally segregated, and, in Jefferson County, Kentucky, they were no longer segregated. The court further held that while race could be used to achieve diversity, these particular programs failed to use other means to reach this goal.

Jewish organizations generally supported the school systems, the ADL filing its own brief and AJC joining with a number of other agencies.

A Racial Incident

A civil rights rally in Jena, Louisiana, on September 20 drew thousands of activists to protest what they asserted was a racially biased justice system in the small town. After several African American students sat under a tree where white students generally ate lunch, a noose was hung from the tree. Several racially charged incidents followed, and charges of attempted murder were made against six black students. The charges were later reduced. The ADL expressed "deep concern," and offered to help heal tensions.

Church-State Issues

Faith-Based Initiatives

The Union of Orthodox Jewish Congregations of America (UOJCA) welcomed Justice Samuel Alito's decision in *Hein v. Freedom From Religion Foundation (FFRF),* which found that that ordinary citizens having no particular standing, such as a demonstration of injury, had no right to challenge government activities they felt violated the First Amendment's prohibition on the establishment of religion. The FFRF had objected to conferences held by the White House Office of Faith-Based and Community Initiatives.

Other Jewish organizations, such as AJC, ADL, and the American Jewish Congress, filed amicus briefs in favor of the FFRF, along with the

ACLU, Americans United for Separation of Church and State, the Baptist Joint Committee, People for the American Way Foundation, and American Atheists. After the decision was handed down, the American Jewish Congress called for Congress to pass legislation allowing such suits. "The balance of powers is out of sync, and it needs to be set straight," it said in a statement.

Religious Workers

Another year passed without adoption of legislation to protect the rights of religious workers. In the house, the Workplace Religious Freedom Act (WRFA) was introduced by Reps. Carolyn McCarthy (D., N.Y.) and Mark Souder (R., Ind.). It would require employers to make reasonable accommodation for an employee's religious practice, such as observing the Jewish Sabbath.

An article by Judith Moldover that appeared in the *New York Law Journal* in October discussed concerns by some supporters of the WRFA that adoption of ENDA, protecting the rights of gays and lesbians in the workplace (see above), could present a conflict for those seeking religious accommodation. According to Moldover, conflict between sexual-orientation discrimination and religious accommodation might occur in three situations: "refusal to service homosexual clients, refusal to participate in diversity programs and training, and supervisory conduct."

The Military

Responding to a request by the Military Religious Freedom Foundation—a watchdog group formed by retired Air Force lawyer Michael Weinstein—the Defense Department's inspector general issued a report in August charging that four generals and three other military officers had violated ethics rules when they participated in a video touting an evangelical Christian group. The ten-minute fund-raising video for Christian Embassy, filmed in 2005, included uniformed officers appearing in the halls of the Pentagon. The inspector general recommended that Army and Air Force leaders take "corrective action" against the men. In addition, a retired Army colonel was rebuked for providing Christian Embassy staff unescorted access to the Pentagon in order to make the video.

INTERFAITH RELATIONS

The Israeli-Palestinian conflict continued to be the major focus of the interfaith encounter.

This was evident on November 1, when a broad array of religious leaders, under the banner of the National Interreligious Leadership Initiative for Peace in the Middle East, sent a letter to Secretary of State Rice calling for greater U.S. involvement in solving the Middle East conflict, including mediation of a two-state settlement between Israelis and Palestinians and peace between Israel and its northern neighbors, Syria and Lebanon. The group acknowledged that the Saudi-sponsored Arab Peace Initiative "represents an historic positive development in the history of this conflict." Signatories included two Catholic cardinals—Theodore McCarrick of Washington and William Keeler of Baltimore; the leaders of the mainline Congregational, Episcopal, Lutheran, Methodist, and Presbyterian denominations; the patriarchs of the Greek Orthodox and Armenian churches; the heads of the Reconstructionist, Reform, and Conservative Jewish movements; and top officials of the Islamic Society of North America, the Islamic Circle of North America, and the American Society for Muslim Advancement.

Mainline Protestants and Jews

American mainline churches continued to reevaluate their positions on the Israeli-Palestinian conflict, adopting somewhat more nuanced policies than they had in the past.

In June, the United Church of Christ (UCC) advanced a resolution calling for a "balanced" approach. The UCC General Synod, held in Hartford, acknowledged that two resolutions adopted in 2005 were focused only on the actions of Israel, and "may have overlooked many aspects of an extremely complicated situation." Those resolutions had condemned Israel's security barrier and endorsed the use of economic leverage, including divestment, as means to advance Israeli-Palestinian peace. The new resolution stated: "We cannot raise our voices only to point out the transgressions of one side," adding that the UCC "has yet to fully address other forces contributing to the ongoing violence, oppression and suffering in the region." And it called for the creation of a task force to "engage in ongoing and balanced study of the causes, history, and context of the conflict" that would report its findings in 2009. Jewish organizations welcomed the resolution.

The Evangelical Lutheran Church in America (ELCA), the largest

Lutheran group in the U.S., became the first mainline Protestant body to rule out divestment as a matter of policy. The ELCA Churchwide Assembly, meeting in August in Chicago, resolved to explore the church's "entire investment activity," but the delegates added an amendment stating that such exploration "would exclude the option of divestiture." Nevertheless, the church left the door open for a possible boycott of goods made in Israeli settlements. The ELCA resolution called for increased awareness, advocacy, and "economic stewardship" to advance peace between Israelis and Palestinians, and, as amended, added that economic initiatives "could include purchasing of products from Palestinian providers and exploration of the feasibility of refusing to buy products produced in Israeli settlements."

Among the low points for the year was a conference held in Boston in October by the American arm of the stridently anti-Zionist Sabeel Ecumenical Liberation Theology Center. Titled "The Apartheid Paradigm in Palestine-Israel: Issues of Justice and Equality," its keynote speaker was Anglican archbishop and Nobel laureate Desmond Tutu of South Africa. Also on the rostrum was an American Episcopal bishop. Tutu compared the Jewish state to apartheid-era South Africa, and lifted passages from the Hebrew Bible to argue that the God worshiped by Jews would side with the Palestinians. "If you reject your calling," Tutu admonished Israel, "you may survive for a long time, but you will find it is all corrosive inside, and one day you will implode." The archbishop made no mention of Arab hostility toward Jews.

An American Christian group emerged as an independent voice in church policy toward the Israeli-Palestinian conflict. Christians for Fair Witness on the Middle East praised the UCC call for balance (see above) while rebuking views such as that taken by Churches for Middle East Peace (CMEP), which accused Israel of provocation for archaeological work near the Temple Mount. Fair Witness called the CMEP reaction "biased and inflammatory." Rev. Dr. Peter Pettit, a Fair Witness leader as well as director of the Institute for Jewish-Christian Understanding at Muhlenberg College, asked, "[s]houldn't our role as Christian peacemakers be to restore calm to the situation by explaining the facts and encouraging a peaceful return to a project intended only to provide safety to visitors to a site holy to all three religions?"

In February, 13 American Christian leaders travelled to Tehran to meet with Iranian religious figures and the president. The trip was organized by the American Friends Service Committee (Quakers) and the Mennonite Central Committee, with the stated intent of fostering dialogue.

Representation came from the United Methodist Church, the Episcopal Church USA, and the Evangelical Lutheran Church in America. A statement released upon their return quoted Ahmadinejad as saying that "the Israeli-Palestinian conflict can only be solved through political, not military means," a sentiment that the Iranian president never expressed in public. The ADL charged that the trip represented a breach in Christian-Jewish relations.

Evangelicals and Jews

In contrast to mainline coolness toward Israel, the only problem some Jews had with evangelicals was that they seemed somewhat too enthusiastic about the Jewish state. A prime example was Rev. John Hagee. The leader of a mega-church in San Antonio, Texas, Hagee had taken his "Night to Honor Israel" program to more than two dozen communities and raised more than $10 million for social services in Israel, along the way earning acceptance by some Jewish communal leaders. The programs, which originated in Hagee's backyard, had become routine events not just in the Bible Belt, but in places not known for their evangelical demographic, including Fresno, California; Concord, New Hampshire; Albany, New York; Philadelphia, Pennsylvania; and Madison, Wisconsin. And he now had a national organization, Christians United for Israel, launched in early 2006.

Acceptance of Hagee came, in part, because he had deftly dodged the third rails of the Jewish-evangelical encounter by actively opposing proselytization of Jews and muting his concerns over Israeli disengagement from Gaza in 2005. On March 11, AIPAC granted him a prime-time speaking slot at its annual policy conference in Washington, providing Hagee his largest predominantly Jewish audience to date. In his speech, Hagee described 50 million American Christian Zionists as a "sleeping giant" that had been awakened by the threats posed by Iran and other enemies of Israel. Hagee declared to the cheering crowd, "Israel, you are not alone," and led the gathering in a chorus of "Israel Lives!"

Hagee was not without prominent and vociferous Jewish critics. One was Rabbi Eric Yoffie, president of the URJ and the most prominent leader of the Reform movement. In an address to the Central Conference of American Rabbis, Yoffie called on Jewish organizations, particularly federations, to reconsider their embrace of Hagee, whom he called "extremist." Yoffie felt that the views of Hagee and many other Christian Zionists, which encouraged Israel not to compromise on territory, "may advance their theology but they do so at the expense of Israel's security and well-being." He also rebuked Hagee for his disparaging comments about Catholics and Muslims. Rabbi James Rudin, senior AJC adviser on interreligious affairs, criticized AIPAC for unduly focusing on Hagee's tactical support and ignoring his "apocalyptic claims" about an imminent second coming. At its biennial conference, the Reform movement welcomed Pastor Rick Warren, a prominent evangelical minister who generally stayed out of the political crosshairs.

Catholics and Jews

Jewish relations with the Catholic Church remained generally positive throughout the year, with one exception. On July 7, Pope Benedict XVI issued a *motu proprio,* a letter signed personally by the pope, solely on his authority, titled *Summorum Pontificum,* which allowed greater freedom to use the Tridentine liturgy, more commonly known as the Latin Mass. Previously, a congregation required permission from the local bishop to use the ancient service, dating to 1570. Its Good Friday liturgy had long been offensive to Jews. Although the reference to "faithless" or "perfidious" Jews was removed in 1959, still included in the "intercessions" was a "Prayer for the Conversion of the Jews" asking God to take "the veil from their hearts" so that they might recognize the divinity of Jesus, and that God's mercy be given "even to the Jews."

Most observers did not believe that the pope was even thinking about Jews when he authorized use of this mass; rather, he was trying to reach out to Traditionalist Catholics, who had long rejected modifications made to the mass and the substitution of vernacular languages for Latin. The dissident movement had gained some notoriety in recent years with the swirl of publicity around filmmaker Mel Gibson and his father, both of whom were considered followers.

The day before the pope officially released his letter, ADL national director Abraham Foxman issued a statement calling it "a theological setback in the religious life of Catholics and a body blow to Catholic-Jewish relations." Foxman later backtracked somewhat, saying, "the Vatican is not an enemy of the Jewish people, nor is Pope Benedict XVI," but he warned that wider use of the Latin Mass could jeopardize the progress made since Vatican II and encourage "retrograde forces" within the Church.

AJC took a contrary stance, expressing concern but calling the *motu proprio* "nothing new." AJC welcomed a confirmation by Pope Benedict

XVI that the changes in policy regarding the mass would in no way affect the positive changes of Vatican II.

The papal decision about the mass, in fact, would have virtually no practical impact. Almost all Catholics around the world would continue to participate in masses in their local languages, using the liturgy set forth in 1970 in which the so-called conversion prayer had been revised and a positive statement recognizing an "eternal" Jewish covenant with God was included.

Muslims and Jews

Jewish organizations maintained a policy of avoiding contact with most Muslim organizations, especially the Council on American-Islamic Relations (CAIR), which was suspected of backing terrorism.

Rabbi Eric Yoffie, president of the Union for Reform Judaism, generated considerably controversy by accepting an invitation to address the Islamic Society of North American (ISNA)—considered to be relatively moderate—on August 31. Yoffie told the audience that Americans were generally ignorant of Islam, largely because both the media and Christian fundamentalists focused on the most extreme expressions of the religion. As a result, he said, there was pervasive discrimination against Muslim Americans, often justified in the name of homeland security.

On December 16, ISNA president Ingrid Mattson returned the visit and addressed the biennial URJ conference. She spoke of a diverse and transformed Muslim American community that was ready for meaningful dialogue with Jews.

ETHAN FELSON

Jewish Communal Affairs

American Jews and the Middle East

Israel, Iran, Iraq

In December 2006, AJC issued a pamphlet, *'Progressive' Jewish Thought and the New Anti-Semitism,* by Prof. Alvin Rosenfeld of Indiana University, which pointed to specific examples of left-of-center Jewish critics of Israel who went so far as to question the right of the Jewish state to exist, a position that Rosenfeld considered anti-Semitic. Few knew of the publication until an article about it appeared in the *New York Times* on January 31, 2007, and then it became a focus of public dispute.

A number of discrete issues were debated back and forth, such as inaccuracies in the *Times* characterization of AJC and of Rosenfeld's thesis, whether Rosenfeld had erred in lumping together friendly critics of Israel with virulent foes, and whether, as some critics alleged, his real agenda was to push an alleged Jewish neoconservative alliance with the Bush administration and Christian conservatives in support of the Iraq war. The most serious charge was that *'Progressive' Jewish Thought* was meant to censor all liberal criticism of Israel by tarnishing it with the label of anti-Semitism. Rosenfeld countered that he could not see how pointing out the anti-Semitic implications of those who wanted Israel dismantled amounted to censorship, and suggested that those making the charge were themselves engaging in censorship by seeking to silence Israel's defenders.

As 2007 began American Jewish groups were focused on a potentially nuclear Iran whose president made no secret of his intention to destroy Israel. In January, the Conference of Presidents of Major American Jewish Organizations prepared for a visit to the Persian Gulf states, where discussions would be held on the dangers the Sunni regimes faced from Shi'ite Iran. The strategy of generalizing the case against Iran reflected fear that American opinion might blame the pro-Israel community for any potential conflict with Tehran, especially at a time when the administration, which was arguing for a hard line, was deeply unpopular. Martin Raffel, associate director of the Jewish Council for Public Affairs (JCPA) told the *New York Jewish Week* (Feb. 9), "It would be a big mistake for us to frame this as an Israeli or Jewish issue."

If any proof of the need for caution was needed it came from what was already being said about the Iraq war's connection to Jews and Israel. A new biography of former secretary of state Colin Powell quoted him as citing the influence of the "JINSA [Jewish Institute for National Security Affairs] crowd" upon the decision to go to war. After a large January 27 rally in Washington against the war, United for Peace and Justice, the sponsoring group, announced it would join with the U.S. Campaign to End the Israeli Occupation in a two-day mobilization in June, under the title, "The World Says No to Israeli Occupation."

Most alarming to pro-Israel groups was the report issued by the bipartisan Iraq Study Group, whose members were respected figures in American life. One of the report's conclusions was that "the United States will not be able to achieve its goals in the Middle East unless the United States deals directly with the Arab-Israeli conflict." This assertion not only raised the specter of American pressure on Israel, but also set Israel up as the potential scapegoat for failure in Iraq. Staff members of the study group expressed surprise that reference to Israel found its way into the report, and it remained unclear who inserted it.

A Gallup report released in late February found that American Jews were considerably more opposed to the Iraq war than non-Jews. Drawing together data from 13 polls conducted since 2005, Gallup said that 77 percent of Jews considered the war a mistake, as compared to 52 percent of all Americans. But almost all the mainstream Jewish organizations—fully aware that opposing the war meant challenging the pro-Israel administration—remained noncommittal. The only major Jewish bodies that publicly reflected the majority Jewish view were the Union for Reform Judaism (see below, p. 136) and the National Council of Jewish Women, which adopted an antiwar stance in December. JCPA, the umbrella body for the national agencies and local community relations councils, took no stand on the issue at its plenum in February, although the war was discussed at a sparsely attended evening session.

Iraq was brought up somewhat perfunctorily at the AIPAC Policy Conference in March, the pro-Israel lobby's annual event that drew thousands of activists and hundreds of political figures. Vice President Dick Cheney denounced antiwar resolutions proposed in Congress on the grounds that they undermined the war effort, and Israeli prime minister Olmert, on the phone from Jerusalem, said, "When America succeeds in Iraq, Israel is safer. The friends of Israel know it." Clapping in the audience was noticeably restrained.

The policy conference paid considerably more attention to Iran—the recent fear of Jews being blamed for a new war at least temporarily forgotten—and the *New York Jewish Week* (Mar. 16) aptly headlined its story "Apocalypse Now." AIPAC executive director Howard Kohr warned that "the Mullahs in Iran are watching Washington very closely . . . any sign of weakness, any sense that we are willing to take options off the table will be taken as a signal that they can proceed with their plans." Rev. John Hagee, the pro-Israel evangelical preacher, was greeted by loud cheers when he compared President Ahmadinejad to Hitler. Politicians of both parties, eager to curry favor with the pro-Israel electorate, competed with each other in their denunciations of the Tehran regime, and a section of a bill pending in the House of Representatives that required congressional authorization for any attack on Iran was removed, reportedly because of AIPAC influence.

But critics of the lobby were hardly intimidated. An article in the *Economist* (Mar. 17) reported: "The Iraq debacle has produced a fierce backlash against the pro-war hawks, of which AIPAC was certainly one. It has also encouraged serious people to ask awkward questions about America's alliance with Israel. And a growing number of people want to push against AIPAC." Nicholas Kristof, writing in the *New York Times* in the wake of the policy conference (Mar. 18), wondered why "there is no serious debate among either Democrats or Republicans about our policy toward Israelis and Palestinians."

Considerable interest focused on billionaire investor and philanthropist George Soros, who, in 2006, had made preliminary moves to set up a dovish alternative to AIPAC (see AJYB 2007, p. 115). An article he published in the April 12 issue of the *New York Review of Books*, "On Israel, America, and AIPAC," suggested that he might renew the attempt. Soros charged that AIPAC endangered Israel by encouraging hard-line policies and opposing moves toward peace. But one of his aides told the *New York Jewish Week* (Mar. 23) that Soros felt he lacked "the necessary standing in the community" to lead an anti-AIPAC.

With Soros apparently out of the picture, reports surfaced of a possible merger between three dovish groups, Americans for Peace Now, Israel Policy Forum, and Brit Tzedek v'Shalom, to form a unified pro-peace lobby. Those involved said that this was not an attempt to fight AIPAC, but rather to present an alternate voice. The immediate goal was to raise $10 million from current donors to the three groups and from outside sources, including Hollywood figures and young liberal Jews. Insiders began humorously referring to the hypothetical lobby as the J Street Project, as the letter J was not a street name in Washington.

A two-day conference at Queens College, April 22–23, explored the question, "Is It 1938 Again?" The choice of speakers was well-balanced, including such figures as retired *Commentary* editor Norman Podhoretz and Conference of Presidents executive vice president Malcolm Hoenlein, who argued that the threat posed by Iran and by politicized Islam was comparable to the Nazi menace, and others, such as Princeton University political scientist Michael Walzer and journalist Leonard Fein, who felt that the threat was overblown. The event drew a standing-room-only crowd, evidence that the situation was of grave concern to the heavily Jewish community near the campus.

With all the attention being given to Iran, it came as something of a surprise when, in May, Secretary of State Condoleezza Rice departed from the administration's previous passivity on the Israeli-Palestinian front and announced a new push to arrive at a peace settlement. While it remained unclear whether and how hard the U.S. planned to prod Israel into concessions, pro-Israel groups took notice.

The Rice initiative coincided with preparations for the 40th anniversary of the Six-Day War of 1967, the conflict in which Israel gained control over the territories in dispute. With strong AIPAC backing, both houses of Congress passed a nonbinding resolution on June 5 hailing Israel's 1967 victory and praising Israel's administration of an "undivided city of Jerusalem for the past 40 years, during which Israel has respected the rights of all religious groups." It also reiterated calls for the administration to move the U.S. embassy to Jerusalem, a step that presidents had consistently favored rhetorically but avoided carrying out.

The resolution came in for criticism from dovish Jewish groups for failing even to mention the possibility of territorial compromise—specifically, the likelihood that East Jerusalem would become the capital of a Palestinian state. Five days later, June 10, the previously planned demonstration against Israeli occupation of the West Bank, sponsored by United for Peace and Justice and the U.S. Campaign to End Israeli Occupation, took place in Washington. Organizers asked participants to refrain from anti-Jewish language so that critics would not be able to impute anti-Semitism to the anti-occupation cause.

The very next day Hamas began its takeover of Gaza, and completed it three days later. PA president Abbas created a separate Fatah-led government on the West Bank. Both Prime Minister Olmert, visiting President Bush in Washington, and AIPAC publicly supported U.S. aid to Abbas's Palestinian Authority. But the pro-Israel community worried about possible U.S. pressure on Israel to grant Abbas concessions in order to strengthen his position in the intra-Palestinian struggle. And while Jewish leaders understood that Abbas was preferable to his rejectionist opponents, some felt that he had proven too weak to make a difference, and that Israel would have no choice but to negotiate with Hamas.

During the summer, Jewish attention to Middle East policy questions was temporarily diverted to the discussion of a potentially damaging book, *The Israel Lobby and U.S. Foreign Policy,* by John J. Mearsheimer and Stephen M. Walt. Its publication in August came as no surprise, as the authors had laid out their arguments in an article that appeared in 2006 (see AJYB 2007, pp. 117–18). The book, like the article, claimed that an "Israel lobby" made up of Jews and others stifled dissent in order to secure a stranglehold on American policy in the Middle East, which it used for what it saw as the benefit of Israel, against the interests of the U.S. and, ultimately, of Israel itself. Mearsheimer and Walt included chapters on the alleged role of the lobby in getting the U.S. to attack Iraq and on what they saw as its current push to have American force used against Iran.

The book presented the Jewish community with several daunting challenges. Although carefully avoiding even the appearance of anti-Semitism, it seemed to resurrect the old canards that Jews were guilty of dual loyalty and that they controlled events from behind the scenes. It also reiterated in stark and explicit terms the thesis that the pro-Israel community bore guilt for the unpopular Iraq war, and that it was trying to do the same in Iran, the latter charge virtually forcing Israel's advocates to pull their punches in addressing the threat from that country.

The first published critique of Mearsheimer and Walt was actually in the bookstores before their book was. *The Deadliest Lies: The Israel Lobby and the Myth of Jewish Control* was written by ADL national director Abraham Foxman in response to the 2006 article that preceded it (and to Jimmy Carter's 2006 book *Palestine: Peace Not Apartheid*), on the assumption that the book would mirror the article. Foxman concentrated on *The Israel Lobby*'s use of classic anti-Semitic motifs, denied that he or his organization had engaged in suppressing free expression, affirmed the right of interest groups to lobby in a democracy, and demonstrated that the government figures who initiated the Iraq war were not Jewish.

Subsequent reviews of *The Israel Lobby* were almost uniformly negative, reiterating Foxman's points and adding others. The two most telling criticisms of Mearsheimer and Walt were, first, that they did not interview anyone associated with AIPAC or other pro-Israel groups and thus were unable to describe exactly how the lobby managed to impose its will on the government, and second, that they left out of their account the strong cultural and political affinity that so many Americans felt for Israel, which was far more central in explaining American concern for its well-being than the operations of a lobby.

But *The Israel Lobby* quickly made the best-seller lists, and Mearsheimer and Walt drew large audiences as they traveled the country promoting it. What impact the book had on public opinion was unclear. In October, the ADL released the results of a poll showing that 31 percent of Americans agreed with the statement that "Jews are more loyal to Israel than America." While Foxman considered that figure "very troubling," it was down somewhat from the last time the question was asked, in 2005.

The other object of Foxman's ire, Jimmy Carter, also resurfaced in October. Having drawn cheers from Brandeis University students when he spoke before them earlier in the year (see below), Carter hoped to repair relations with the organized Jewish community, and invited leaders of Jewish organizations to meet with him about the Middle East situation. Only the Reform movement's Religious Action Center (RAC) and four small left-of-center organizations sent representatives. Foxman, explaining why he stayed away, told the *Forward* (Nov. 2), "I didn't want to be used." And at a closed-door meeting that he requested with Jewish members of Congress, Carter received a hostile reception and was urged to apologize for his book.

News that the U.S. planned to host a Middle East summit in Annapolis in late November raised—not for the first time—considerable perplexity in the Jewish community over whether the Bush administration was just going through the diplomatic motions or whether this was a serious initiative to move toward peace, and if the latter, how much Israel would be asked to concede. Prime Minister Olmert's domestic political problems weakened his diplomatic leverage, and this added to the mood of skepticism. David Harris, the AJC executive director, told the *New York Jewish Week* (Oct. 26), "We're watching the way things unfold, and we don't want to see expectations race ahead of realities."

As the summit date neared, the administration strongly signaled that it was serious about Annapolis. Addressing the General Assembly of the United Jewish Communities (UJC) on November 13, Secretary of State Rice said "failure is not an option" since "what is at stake is nothing less than the future of the Middle East." Sensitive to this mood of urgency,

AIPAC, in a gesture of conciliation, gave tacit approval to a congressional letter favoring an increase in aid for the PA, prompting Sheldon Adelson, a major giver, to chastise the pro-Israel lobby. Informed that Israel had no objection to the aid, Adelson told the JTA, "If someone is going to jump off a bridge, it is incumbent upon their friends to dissuade them." The hard-line Zionist Organization of America, hoping to counter the Jewish community's growing acceptance of a renewed peace process, asked the Conference of Presidents to insist on Fatah revising certain anti-Israel clauses of its constitution as a condition for negotiations, but the move fell through when Israel indicated that it did not take that constitution seriously.

The issue that aroused the greatest fears among American Jews wary of Annapolis was the fate of Jerusalem. Taking the lead in this battle was a new Coordinating Council for Jerusalem, made up primarily of Orthodox groups and led by the Union of Orthodox Jewish Congregations (OU), which had a long record of opposition to dividing the holy city. More surprising was the involvement of Agudath Israel, the non-Zionist, *haredi* Orthodox organization that had previously confined its public statements to religious and educational matters, but now said it was "deeply pained and concerned about the prospect of Israel relinquishing parts of Jerusalem to Palestinian sovereignty." Upon his arrival in the U.S. for the summit, Prime Minister Olmert infuriated the Orthodox by denying them a voice in the decision, saying: "the government of Israel has a sovereign right to negotiate anything on behalf of Israel."

When the negotiators met at the U.S. Naval Academy in Annapolis on November 27, two small, rival groups of Jewish demonstrators rallied outside, one calling for a united Jewish Jerusalem and the other for advancing the peace process. The agreement that resulted—a promise of direct American involvement in monitoring compliance with the "road map" in the hope of concluding an Israeli-Palestinian peace deal by January 2009—elicited little enthusiasm from American Jews, as it sounded very much like earlier deals that went nowhere.

American Jewish misgivings were illustrated by the actions of the Conference of Presidents. As reported in the *Forward* (Nov. 30), the conference issued a statement saying that the Annapolis summit "can be a significant step toward launching meaningful, bilateral negotiations." Yet it also hosted the Orthodox mayor of Jerusalem, who adamantly opposed ceding control of any part of the city. Israel Policy Forum president Seymour Reich complained, "I am troubled by the invitation, because there is a perception that he came to undermine Annapolis, and the conference should not have given him a platform."

AJC's annual *Survey of American Jewish Opinion,* released in early December, confirmed both a continuing pessimism about prospects for peace and a growing Orthodox–non-Orthodox divide over specific issues. Only 37 percent of the sample thought that a time might come when Israel and its Arab neighbors would live in peace, and 82 percent believed that the Arab goal was "not the return of occupied territories but rather the destruction of Israel." Forty-six percent overall favored the creation of a Palestinian state as compared to just 20 percent of the Orthodox, and while 58 percent of American Jews opposed compromise on the status of Jerusalem in the context of an overall Israeli-Palestinian agreement, the figure jumped to 77 percent among Orthodox respondents.

Iran came to the top of the Jewish agenda again at the end of the year. Weeks after a Zogby poll showed more than two-thirds of American Jews (as compared to a bit more than half of all Americans) in favor of attacking Iran before it went nuclear, a National Intelligence Estimate (NIE) stated with "high confidence" that Iran had jettisoned its nuclear-weapons program in 2003. Unlike Israeli officials who outright rejected the NIE conclusion, both the Conference of Presidents and AIPAC sought to convince the U.S. government that a tough line against Iran was still warranted even under the new findings. They noted the NIE's assessment that uranium enrichment was continuing, and that could be used for the production of bombs.

The Campus

The importance of securing the pro-Israel allegiance of college-age Jews was underlined in a new survey, *Beyond Distancing: Young Adult American Jews and their Alienation from Israel,* published in early September. Researchers Steven M. Cohen and Ari Kelman traced a consistent pattern: the younger the age group, the lower the degree of attachment to Israel. And they ominously predicted, "Insofar as younger Jews are less attached to Israel, the inevitable replacement of the older population with younger birth cohorts leads to a growing distancing in the population overall."

Could anything be done to counter the trend? For some time the organized pro-Israel community had faced a dilemma on college campuses, whether to encourage and fund only programs that echoed the positions of the Israeli government, possibly alienating those with different views, or to back other initiatives as well, even at the risk of enabling criticism of Israeli policies. The problem arose again in 2007.

As the year began, a group of eight philanthropic couples who gave charitable grants through UJA-Federation of New York to causes of their choice declined to renew a $30,000 grant it gave in 2006 to the Jewish Student Press Service for publication of *New Voices,* a Jewish campus magazine. The decision was made when the givers discovered that *New Voices* included pieces critical of mainstream Israel advocacy, for example, questioning the Birthright Israel program.

Also in January, the Israel on Campus Coalition (ICC), a group of 31 Jewish organizations dedicated to building pro-Israel sentiment at colleges, debated whether to exclude the Union of Progressive Zionists, active on about 60 campuses, which sometimes sponsored visits by former Israeli soldiers who belonged to Breaking the Silence, which opposed Israeli actions in the territories. The Zionist Organization of America urged ousting the union unless it severed ties with Breaking the Silence, but the proposal was defeated unanimously by the ICC's nine-member executive committee on January 19.

Other serious problems arose on campus for Israel advocates. On January 23, former president Jimmy Carter appeared at Brandeis University to promote his recent book *Palestine: Peace Not Apartheid,* which condemned Israeli policy toward the Palestinians, comparing it to the old South African separation of the races, and alleged that pro-Israel elements enjoyed disproportionate leverage in formulating U.S. Middle East policy (see AJYB 2007, p. 117). As the visit came soon after the Central Conference of American Rabbis canceled a planned visit to the Carter Center in Atlanta (see below), and 14 Jewish members of the center board resigned to protest the book, many wondered why Brandeis, a Jewish-sponsored university, was giving the former president a forum.

It turned out that the school administration had invited Carter to debate Harvard Law School professor Alan Dershowitz, but Carter insisted on appearing alone, and a faculty-student committee invited him to do so. University president Jehuda Reinharz, who was on a fund-raising trip, did not come, a fact that seemed to distance the institution even more from the invitation. After a brief presentation, Carter answered prescreened question for about 45 minutes. He won over the large audience with charm and humor, even conceding that a passage in his book that seemed to justify terrorism was sloppily phrased and would be corrected.

He received two standing ovations. Dershowitz made an appearance after Carter left and sought to punch holes in arguments that Carter made in his book.

Reactions to the Carter appearance varied widely. The position taken by the university and shared by much of the faculty and many students was that the event was a successful example of academic openness to all viewpoints. Others, however, noting the prescreening of questions, the refusal to have a face-to-face debate, and the banning of protests or even posters, charged that openness was precisely what was lacking. Meanwhile, some major givers to Brandeis, already unhappy about earlier actions by the university (see AJYB 2007, pp. 118–19), were reportedly so upset at Carter's appearance that they contemplated withholding their gifts. And according to an article that appeared in the student newspaper, the Brandeis administration was seeking to prevent the appearance on campus of other controversial speakers on the Middle East.

In June, Lee Bollinger, president of Columbia University, condemned a threatened boycott of Israel by British academics, challenging its advocates with the words, "add Columbia to the boycott list." Jewish groups, which had had their differences with Bollinger over alleged anti-Israel bias by Columbia professors and the 2006 appearance of Iranian president Ahmadinejad on campus, applauded him. AJC issued a statement praising his "deep understanding that this is a watershed moment for academic freedom which requires firm action." Bollinger told the *New York Jewish Week* (June 15) that he was surprised that no other American university presidents had denounced the planned boycott.

Pro-Israel advocates received another piece of good news that month, De Paul University's denial of tenure to Norman Finkelstein, who, orally and in print, had denounced Israel for crimes against the Palestinians and accused Jewish organizations of exploiting the Holocaust for financial and political purposes. Many—and no one more vociferously than Alan Dershowitz—had charged Finkelstein with shoddy scholarship, but Finkelstein claimed he was the victim of pro-Israel forces. The university said that the decision to deny tenure was made on academic, not political, grounds.

Another tenure dispute was resolved at Barnard College in the fall. Abu El-Haj, an assistant professor of anthropology, was the author of *Facts on the Ground: Archaeological Practice and Territorial Self-Fashioning in Israeli Society,* which argued that Israelis, who had no historical connection to the land of Israel, misused archaeology to invent a Jewish past in the area and suppress Palestinian roots there. Two online petitions, one pro-tenure and the other anti-tenure, each gathered well over 2,000 signatures. Tenure was granted on November 2.

Jewish Continuity

Research

Questions raised about the accuracy of the 2000–01 National Jewish Population Survey (NJPS) and the likelihood that no decennial survey would be attempted in 2010 left the field open for a variety of research methodologies. Several studies appeared during the year that had significant implications for American Jewish demography.

Issued in early February, *Reconsidering the Size and Characteristics of the American Jewish Population,* conducted by the Steinhardt Social Research Institute at Brandeis University, suggested an upward revision of the low number of American Jews, 5.2 million, found by the NJPS. On the basis of the combined responses of Jews to over 30 national surveys, the researchers came up with a Jewish population of over six million, and, if all people of Jewish parentage were included, 7.5 million. The NJPS, in their view, had undercounted young adults and those less Jewishly affiliated.

Published around the same time, *A Tale of Two Jewries,* prepared by Prof. Steven M. Cohen for the Jewish Life Network/Steinhardt Foundation, analyzed the differences between in-married and intermarried Jews. Cohen found the in-married far more involved in Jewish life, leading him to suggest that "intermarriage does indeed constitute the greatest single threat to Jewish continuity today." Predictably, this aroused the ire of advocates of outreach to the intermarried. Ed Case, who ran InterfaithFamily.com, told the *New York Jewish Week* (Feb. 9) that such denigration of mixed-religion families only served to push them further away from Jewish life.

Another research report, put out in December by Brandeis University's Cohen Center for Modern Jewish Studies, took direct issue with Steven M. Cohen. *It's Not Just Who Stands under the Chuppah: Jewish Identity and Intermarriage* found that the in-married/intermarried gap shrank considerably when the degree of Jewish involvement of the Jewish partner was factored in. This suggested that the fact of intermarriage was less significant than Jewish education for both spouses. More support for this thesis came from research done in Boston by the city's Combined Jewish Philanthropies, which found that 60 percent of intermarried families were raising their children as Jews, and that their Jewish profile differed little from that of in-married families.

Cohen, together with Ari Kelman, published a survey in May, *The Continuity of Discontinuity,* sponsored by the Andrea and Charles Bronfman Foundation, that took an optimistic view of young-adult, unmarried Jews. While that age cohort was, to a great extent, alienated from organized Jewish life, Cohen and Kelman found that many had created their own semi-formal Jewish groups dedicated to Jewish culture, literature, social action, and music. There was even a published, regularly updated guide to such activities, *Slingshot*. The authors also noted that federations and other establishment Jewish bodies were beginning to accommodate the needs of this age group.

Seeking Solutions

As the social scientists argued, American Jews interested in enhancing Jewish identity supported many different strategies.

One was the experience of spending time in Israel. In February, the Adelson Family Charitable Foundation—casino mogul Sheldon Adelson was the third richest American, according to *Forbes*—pledged an annual $25-million gift to Birthright Israel, which Birthright estimated could double the number of young American Jews it brought to Israel each year. The foundation stated that it would continue to provide this amount so long as other funders maintained their contribution levels.

Jewish education was widely considered another potent means of strengthening Jewishness. Two important studies of Jewish education appeared in the spring. Brandeis's Cohen Center released *The Impact of Day School: A Comparative Analysis of Jewish College Students,* commissioned by the Partnership for Excellence in Jewish Education. Surveying over 3,000 day-school graduates, it found that such schools were successful not only in buttressing Jewish identification, but also in preparing students for university life. And *Recent Trends in Supplementary Jewish Education,* prepared by Prof. Jack Wertheimer for the Avi Chai Foundation, pointed to innovative programs being introduced in these educational settings.

A new element entered the educational picture in 2007, the prospect of Jewish charter schools, which some viewed as a threat to the day schools. The first such charter school, Ben Gamla, in Hollywood, Florida, began operation in late August. Publicly funded, it was open to children of any or no religion. The school did not teach Judaism, but offered instruction in Hebrew language and secular Jewish culture, along with the standard public-school curriculum. Peter Deutsch, its founder, hoped to set up 100 more such schools around the country. But while he and his backers saw this as a way of bringing Jewish instruction to thousands of children whose parents would never consider day school—either because of cost or ideology—others worried not only about possible violations of Church-State separation, but also that the charter schools would draw students who might otherwise attend day schools.

Many considered Jewish summer camps potent agents of Jewish identification since campers were immersed in a Jewish environment 24 hours a day. In May, a donor who wished to remain anonymous gave $15 million to the Foundation for Jewish Camping. From this money, families that were sending children to a Jewish camp for the first time could receive up to $1, 250. The donor also included an incentive provision: local federations would have to match whatever funds were disbursed. Soon afterward the San Francisco-based Jim Joseph Foundation granted $11.2 million for families sending children to Jewish camps in the western part of the country, $1,800 for each first-time camper and $1,000 for each second-year returnee. Another $11 million was channeled to Jewish camping through matching programs initiated by the Harold Grinspoon Foundation.

A number of innovative suggestions for revitalizing the Jewish community came from businessman and philanthropist Scott Shay, in his book *Getting Our Groove Back: How to Energize American Jewry*. Among them were a ceremony renewing bar/bat mitzvah every 18 years following the original celebration; lowered day-school tuitions; earlier marriage, more children, and communal funding for childbearing by single women; conversion of children of Jewish fathers and non-Jewish mothers; and reconstituting Conservative Judaism as a "broad tent" rather than a denomination.

Others looked for even bolder, more innovative solutions to the challenge of maintaining Jewish continuity. In late August, the Samuel Bronfman Foundation hosted some 40 leading Jewish thinkers and communal professionals from the U.S. and abroad for three days of study and conversation in Park City, Utah. The theme was "Why Be Jewish?" At the conclusion of the program, the foundation said it would continue the effort through an ongoing Bronfman Vision Forum. And in October, the Andrea and Charles Bronfman Foundation announced a search for "The Next Big Jewish Idea." The winner would receive a two-year faculty appointment at Brandeis University with a six-figure salary, enabling him or her to work on a book setting forth the "Idea."

Religion

Perhaps the most widely reported story about American Judaism in 2007 was the work of three prominent Jewish media figures—Michael Lynton, chairman and CEO of Sony Pictures; Gary Ginsberg of Rupert Murdoch's News Corporation; and Jay Sanderson, CEO of the Jewish Television Network—who compiled a list of the "Top 50" American rabbis and got *Newsweek*'s Website to post it on April 2. Admittedly unscientific, the rankings heavily favored males, residents of the West Coast, and people with national reputations, reflecting the biases of the Hollywood executives who initiated the project. Both those rabbis who made the list and those who did not downplayed its significance.

If some rabbis were getting positive publicity, many synagogues were not. "Going, Going, Gone" was the title of a Stewart Ain article in the *New York Jewish Week* (Sept. 14) about non-Orthodox congregations across the country that were hemorrhaging members and having difficulty paying fixed costs such as salaries, upkeep, mortgage, and insurance. Dues were already at record levels and further increases would only drive away more members. In some communities mergers between synagogues had become financially necessary. Ain quoted a new survey conducted by STAR (Synagogues: Transformation and Renewal) noting that 12 percent of rabbis believed that the affordability of Jewish life was the most serious problem facing American Jewry, up from 5 percent in 2006.

The search for a "magic bullet" to revitalize the synagogue could take unusual forms. In his "On Religion" column in the *New York Times* (Nov. 3), Samuel G. Freedman reported on Synagogue 3000, an organization dedicated to invigorating synagogue life, and its attempt to replicate the success of the Christian mega-churches. Of particular interest to the group's leaders was Saddleback Church in California, where Rev. Rick Warren preached before thousands of rapt listeners each Sunday. Ron Wolfson of Synagogue 3000 told Freedman that, as strange as it sounded, "Jews need to be more quote unquote evangelical."

Another potential challenge to American Judaism was the sudden proliferation of well-publicized books denigrating religion as destructive and advocating atheism, such as Richard Dawkins's *The God Delusion,* Sam Harris's *Letter to a Christian Nation,* and Christopher Hitchens's

God Is Not Great. One might have thought, under the circumstances, that Humanistic Judaism, the small movement that practiced a form of the religion that did not acknowledge a supreme being, would gain a new lease on life. In fact the Humanists, badly shaken by the sudden death of their longtime leader, Rabbi Sherwin Wine, in July (see below, p. 722), seemed uncertain of their future. Sociologist Steven M. Cohen explained the apparent paradox in the *Forward* (Oct. 19) by noting that American Jews did not need to become Humanists, since God was not central to American Judaism anyway. He said, "Most Jews . . . affirm a nominal belief in God, but God doesn't play a major role in their thinking about what it means to be a Jew or even a good person."

A study issued toward the end of the year, *Emergent Jewish Communities and Their Participants,* lent scholarly credence to the view that American Judaism was likely to become increasingly postdenominational. Sponsored by Synagogue 3000, the Synagogue Studies Institute, and Mechon Hadar, it found at least 80 "independent" congregations across the country with e-mail lists of close to 20,000 people, almost all of them in their twenties and thirties. A similar preference for blurring denominational boundaries could be discerned on the rabbinic level: the Charles and Lynn Schusterman Foundation announced it would fund a five-year joint rabbinic-training program for Reform and Conservative seminarians, and the nondenominational rabbinical school at Hebrew College in Boston was poised to graduate its first class in 2008.

But it no sense were the Jewish denominations on the verge of collapse. Not only were those 20,000 names on e-mail lists a drop in the bucket compared to the numbers formally associated with established congregations, but the institutions representing the denominations involved themselves in a much broader range of activities, and far more deeply, than the small, independent groups.

Reform Judaism

In 2005, the Union for Reform Judaism (URJ), which represented some 900 synagogues, became the first major Jewish body to criticize the American administration's policies in Iraq and to call for a "clear exit strategy" (see AJYB 2006, p. 102). By early 2007 some elements within the URJ, citing poll evidence of widespread opposition to the war among American Jews, wanted the organization to denounce administration policy even more explicitly, along the lines laid out by the much smaller 140-

member Association of Rabbis for Jewish Renewal, which, in January, denounced the planned "surge" in Iraq and called for a "firm timetable for ending the military presence of U.S. forces in Iraq."

The Reform movement's Commission on Social Action recommended such a statement in February, and the URJ set up a special Website providing congregations and their members material for debating the issue and giving feedback. A vote on the statement was scheduled for the March 12 meeting of the URJ executive committee. Despite sharp public opposition from the Republican Jewish Coalition (RJC) and some pro-administration executive committee members, the resolution passed overwhelmingly. Movement leaders expressed gratification that Reform had maintained its position at the forefront of what they considered a "moral" cause.

Reform also continued to play its traditional role in support of progressive domestic causes. It advocated federal funding for stem-cell research and, quoting Maimonides, spearheaded a lobbying effort to raise the minimum wage from $5.15 to $7.25 an hour.

The movement was very active on Israel-related matters. In January, the Central Conference of American Rabbis (CCAR), which represented 1,500 Reform rabbis, canceled a tour of the Carter Center that had been scheduled for March as part of the group's annual conference, held this year in Atlanta. The decision was intended as a rebuke to Carter for his book *Palestine: Peace Not Apartheid,* which, according to CCAR's president, had an anti-Israel and anti-Jewish effect.

Twice during April the Reform movement protested actions by Israeli Orthodox rabbis. The first instance was a statement by former Sephardi chief rabbi Mordechai Eliyahu attributing the rise of Nazism in Europe to the "sin" of Reform Judaism, and the second was the refusal of local rabbis in the town of Hod Hasharon to allow a Reform rabbi to offer a public prayer at Yom Hazikaron (Memorial Day) ceremonies honoring Israel's fallen soldiers. Reform was also highly critical of a vote in the Israeli Knesset in July restricting the sale of Jewish National Fund lands to Jews, which was designed to override a court decision barring such discrimination (see below, p. 295). Rabbi Eric Yoffie, the URJ president, called the legislation undemocratic and pointed out that Jews would be justly outraged should any country seek to ban Jews from buying land.

In 2007, American Reform for the first time emphasized aliyah, immigration to Israel, as a priority. This was not simply expressed in abstract terms. The Association of Reform Zionists of America announced—in cooperation with the municipality of Modi'in—a package of financial incentives for Reform families that would move in to the town, located between Jerusalem and Tel Aviv, which already had a functioning Reform community.

Yoffie set off a storm of controversy in September by accepting an invitation to address the annual conference of the Islamic Society of North America. In his talk Yoffie denounced anti-Muslim prejudice in the U.S., including racial profiling, and attributed the situation to Americans' "profound ignorance" of Islam. Yoffie also called for greater Muslim-Jewish dialogue and joint backing for a two-state solution for Israel and the Palestinians. While the URJ justified Yoffie's appearance at the conference with the claim that the Islamic Society had renounced violence, others, including David Harris, executive director of AJC, noted that the organization had been named as an unindicted co-conspirator in a major terrorism trial. Undeterred, Yoffie announced a new initiative to encourage dialogue on the local level between Reform synagogues and mosques.

History was made as the year began when Barbara Benioff Friedman assumed the post of board chair of Hebrew Union College (HUC), Reform's rabbinical and cantorial seminary, thus becoming the first female chair of any major American Jewish seminary. In a move that was not as well received, HUC closed down its New York Kollel, which had provided extremely popular adult education classes for 12 years. The decision was made for financial reasons.

On religious issues, the Reform movement continued to innovate in a number of areas. The appointment of Debbie Friedman, the popular singer and songwriter, to teach at the HUC School of Sacred Music in the fall was widely seen as the final victory of the folk-song style—some derisively called it "campfire music"—over traditional cantorial chanting in Reform congregations. In August, the URJ issued a new edition of its resource manual for gay, lesbian, bisexual, and transgender Jews that contained not only liturgy for same-sex unions and divorces and a "coming-out" prayer, but also two new blessings to be recited when transitioning between genders. Also in August, Rabbi Richard Address, director of the URJ Department of Jewish Family Concerns, suggested in the pages of the *Forward* (Aug. 17) that intimate relations with a third party entered into while a spouse suffered from Alzheimer's should not be considered adultery.

At the same time, elements of the Reform movement—particularly many young people—sought at least a partial return to tradition. "Reform Youth Flexing Their Ritual Muscle" was the headline in the *New*

York Jewish Week (Aug. 10) for a story about Kutz Camp, the Reform summer camp in upstate New York. Reporter Debra Nussbaum Cohen recounted what happened at evening services on the Fourth of July, when a noticeable number of campers—around a quarter of the total—walked out on the jazz-inflected prayers and organized their own more traditional evening service. Upon further investigation Nussbaum Cohen learned that "a small but growing number of campers and young faculty" wore "yarmulkes or tzitzit, even tefillin along with prayer shawls." One camper had perfected "shuckling," rocking back and forth during prayer. There were even "rumblings" about switching the "kosher-style" camp cuisine to kosher.

The pull of tradition was hardly confined to the camper generation. No less a Reform personage than Rabbi Yoffie, in the same December biennial address that urged outreach to Muslims, called for revitalization of Reform Shabbat observance, specifically urging the restoration of the Saturday morning service to prominence and making Shabbat a full, 24-hour experience. "In the absence of Shabbat," Yoffie declared, "Judaism withers." Another, less traditional feature of the biennial was a prayer service modeled on Rick Warren's Saddleback mega-church in California, complete with five-piece band (see above, p. 134).

Conflict between avant-garde and traditional forces in Reform had been festering for some time over the question of whether rabbis should perform marriages between Jews and non-Jews, and it burst into the open in June with the resignation of Rabbi Jeffrey Salkin from The Temple in Atlanta, one of the largest Reform congregations in the nation. Salkin said that one important reason for his decision was "a synagogue culture that had become accustomed to rabbinic officiation at interfaith weddings," something that he refused to do.

Many other rabbis agreed that this had become a serious problem for the movement, and the CCAR had in fact set up a task force to study it two months before Salkin resigned. The official CCAR position was against officiation, but rabbis were given autonomy to decide the matter for themselves, and it was believed that some 40 percent of Reform rabbis performed intermarriages. Even though the institutions of Reform Judaism instructed synagogue search committees not to question rabbinic candidates about their attitudes on this question, many did anyway, and automatically eliminated the applications of non-officiators from consideration. At the same time, rabbis who did perform intermarriages complained that their more traditional colleagues looked down upon them, and organizations that stood for greater outreach to interfaith families urged the CCAR to alter its official policy of discouraging officiation.

A new Reform prayer book, the first in 32 years, was released in the fall, and it reflected all the complexities of a movement that, the *New York Times* reported (Sept. 3), "is growing in different directions simultaneously." The prayer book, *Mishkan Tefilah,* featured gender-neutral language, took into account the presence at services of interfaith families, and provided four versions of the prayers ranging from traditional (even affirming the doctrine of the resurrection of the dead) to atheist.

A second Reform publication came out soon afterward, *The Torah: A Women's Commentary*. Sponsored by Women of Reform Judaism, it was the subject of a scholarly panel discussion at the annual joint meeting of the Society of Biblical Literature and the American Academy of Religion in November.

Conservative Judaism

2006 had been a year of significant change for the Conservative movement in two respects. First, it's Committee on Jewish Law and Standards (CJLS) approved each of two competing resolutions on the religious status of homosexuals, one affirming the old restrictions and the other liberalizing them and opening the door for ordination of openly gay and lesbian rabbis as well as rabbinic officiation at same-sex unions. Second, Arnold Eisen, a Stanford University academic who was not a rabbi, was chosen chancellor of the Jewish Theological Seminary (JTS), the major Conservative rabbinical school (see AJYB 2007, pp. 128–30).

The year 2007 was far quieter for the movement as its institutions and members gradually absorbed and began to address the implications of these momentous decisions. As the year began JTS sent out a confidential, eight-part survey to Conservative rabbis, cantors, educators, and lay leaders to gauge the impact of the change in the religious status of homosexuals, and, more broadly, to discover what they thought of the movement's direction and prospects. The survey was completed and returned by 5,583 people.

Sociologist Steven M. Cohen, who directed the project, reported the results in early February. Solid majorities in each category of respondents said they favored JTS adoption of the liberal CJLS opinion; among the rabbis 68 percent backed such a step and 28 percent opposed it. Canadian Conservatives were noticeably less enthusiastic about the change than those living in the U.S., 82 percent of the rabbis north of the border opposing it (see below, p. 326).

Yet even many who approved the movement's new stance were uneasy about its possible consequences. About half of all respondents doubted whether it conformed to Jewish law, and a majority of the lay and professional leaders considered the CJLS issuance of more than one opinion about the status of gays a source of confusion. Other potential danger signals were that about a third of respondents did not like the long-term "move to greater liberalization," 42 percent of the clergy felt that the changes on the subject of homosexuals "blur the boundary between Conservative and Reform Judaism," and 83 percent of the rabbis and rabbinical students thought they "widen the gap between Conservatism and Orthodoxy." Yet the perception of a sharp turn to the left was complicated by strong majorities opposing two practices associated with Reform, rabbinic officiation at mixed-religion marriages and adoption of patrilineal descent, the recognition of children of Jewish fathers and non-Jewish mothers as Jews (*New York Jewish Week,* Feb. 2).

Two Conservative seminaries, buttressed by the findings of the survey, quickly opened their doors to gay and lesbian students. First out of the gate was the Ziegler School of Rabbinic Studies, part of the University of Judaism in Los Angeles. In early March the school accepted its first two openly gay students, a man and a woman. By the end of the month the JTS rabbinical school—whose new dean, appointed in January, had coauthored the CJLS opinion permitting the ordination of homosexuals and officiation at gay unions—announced that it too would admit students "without regard to sexual orientation," even extending the application period to enable more to seek admission. But the Schechter Rabbinical Seminary, the movement's school in Israel, did not go along. Its dean, Rabbi Einat Ramon, told the *Forward* (Mar. 30) that the traditional heterosexual family was fundamental to Judaism and that "in Israel the movement has to be consistently Halakhic, otherwise it will unite with the Reform movement."

Realizing that implementation of the new approach would not be simple, Conservative institutions set up mechanisms to ease the transition. Chancellor Eisen said that JTS would convene forums on integrating gays and lesbians into seminary life, and that faculty had been requested to speak about the matter to their classes. The Rabbinical Assembly (RA), the movement's rabbinic body, created a committee to examine what exactly same-sex commitment ceremonies entailed and to what extent Jewish divorce law applied to such unions.

Conservative leaders were virtually unanimous in their positive assessment of how the movement had addressed the issue. All constituencies had been consulted, decisions had been reached through appropriate procedures, and—confounding the pessimists—no schism had ensued. "I'm hoping that the whole process that surrounded the decision will revitalize the sense that Conservative Judaism is a living organism," said Eisen. But Rabbi Joel Roth, a leading traditionalist scholar who had resigned from the CJLS in protest, pointed out that the movement still retained the traditional position on homosexuality as a valid Conservative option along with the new permissive view, and warned that Conservative Judaism would suffer severely if those adhering to the old heterosexual standards "no longer feel they have a place in the movement."

Great, perhaps unrealistic, expectations accompanied Arnold Eisen's assumption of the JTS chancellorship. For some time the Conservative movement had suffered from declines in numbers, fund-raising, and morale as its pragmatic and nonideological form of Judaism that had thrived in mid-twentieth-century America lost much of its appeal to younger Jews in more religiously polarized times. How would the new chancellor reverse the downward spiral?

In his inaugural address delivered September 5, Eisen noted that in the course of numerous visits to Conservative communities around the country he saw great enthusiasm and energy, causing him to reject any notion that the movement was in decline. But equally evident was confusion over what Conservative Judaism stood for. Eisen believed that the answer was the concept of mitzvah, Divine commandment. He did not plan to tell Jews which commandments they were required to perform, but would rather have rabbis "facilitate and guide a grassroots conversation about mitzvah" so that Jews could thrash out among themselves "what obligates them; what they feel responsible for; what engages them . . . ." JTS, he announced, would begin with a pilot program in ten synagogues.

Eisen's diagnosis of Conservative Judaism's ills and his proposed cure were by no means uncontested, as others suggested different approaches. Rabbi Elliot Cosgrove, in a widely noted article in the spring issue of *Conservative Judaism* magazine, argued that the primary conflict that had to be bridged was theological, between Conservative Jews who viewed Scripture as God's word and those for whom it was a human product, and unless a way were found to reconcile the two the movement could split. Prof. Jack Wertheimer, who had recently stepped down as JTS provost, wrote in the September issue of *Commentary* that emphasis on traditional Jewish practice and learning remained the key to Conservative survival.

The movement's problems were set aside for a least one day, December 9, when the Center for Jewish History hosted a daylong conference on the legacy of Rabbi Abraham Joshua Heschel, who taught at JTS from 1945 until his death in 1972. Most of the speakers concentrated on Heschel's social activism, although Eisen's presentation stressed the Judaic roots of his passion for justice and delved into his sometimes rocky career at JTS.

Orthodox Judaism

One rather obscure news item late in the year epitomized Orthodoxy's great American success story. In November, when U.S. Supreme Court justices announced the appointment of their new clerks, both of Justice Antonin Scalia's choices were not only kippah-wearing Orthodox Jews, but they had Hebrew first names, Moshe Spinowitz and Yaakov Roth. Roth told the *Forward* (November 23), "I think it's sort of a coincidence. Things just sort of worked out that way this year, but it is 20 percent of a minyan." Given the history of anti-Jewish discrimination at the higher levels of the legal profession until at least the 1960s, and the tiny proportion of Orthodox Jewish lawyers, the fact that these appointments went almost unnoticed indicated how seamlessly Orthodox Jewry had integrated into elite American circles.

However, another aspect of Orthodoxy's success triggered great interest from the media in 2007, along with some trepidation. The *New York Times,* during the course of the year, ran four long feature stories about burgeoning Orthodox communities in the New York area, in each case noting problems their growth had caused. In its February 18 issue it recounted how the Orthodox, "the fastest-growing group in town," had taken political control of Teaneck, New Jersey, leaving "bad feelings." On May 17 the *Times* informed its readers of a new Orthodox presence in Waterbury, Connecticut, complete with synagogue, yeshiva, and kosher butcher, but also with complaints to the zoning commission about the yeshiva dormitories and "a sudden rash of vandalism and robberies" of Jewish homes. Tensions between blacks and the exploding Orthodox Jewish community of Lakewood, New Jersey, attracted the *Times*'s attention on December 10. And the Satmar Hasidic community of Kiryas Joel, in Orange County, New York—according to census figures, the fastest growing municipality in the state—was the subject of a December 16 article about alleged harassment of a woman living there whose dress was not modest enough to suit local Hasidic authorities.

The battle over the future of Modern Orthodoxy continued. Rabbi Marc Angel, who retired after serving as rabbi for 38 years at Congregation Shearith Israel (the Spanish and Portuguese Synagogue) in New York City, shocked many when he charged that Modern Orthodoxy had jettisoned its "modern" character. In an interview with the *New York Jewish Week* (June 22), Angel accused it of "slipping over the line to a cultic superstitious kind of religion." During his years in the rabbinate, Angel noted, Orthodoxy had become more "insular," shunning "innovative thought" and relying increasingly on "so-called authorities." He announced the creation of a new body, the Institute for Jewish Ideas and Ideals, "to foster an appreciation of legitimate diversity within Orthodoxy." Subsequent critical letters to the editor took two forms, one denying the shift that Angel perceived and the other justifying it as a return to a more authentic Orthodoxy.

The controversy over American Orthodox conversions, begun in 2006 when the Israeli Chief Rabbinate announced it would no longer accept those performed by rabbis not on an "approved" list (see AJYB 2007, p. 126), escalated. The Rabbinical Council of America (RCA), the Modern Orthodox rabbinic organization, at its annual convention in the spring, discussed proposed new conversion guidelines that would, it was hoped, gain approval from the Chief Rabbinate and thus avoid the situation of American converts having their Jewish identity challenged in Israel: the convert would commit to belonging to an Orthodox synagogue within walking distance, observing Shabbat and kashrut, and sending children to an approved Orthodox day school for 12 years. Rabbi Angel and others denounced the plan for subordinating the American rabbinate to the Israelis and depriving individual rabbis of their traditional autonomy in performing conversions.

The RCA called a press conference for April 30 to announce an agreement with the Chief Rabbinate that would entail the establishment of some 20 regional conversion courts across America that would act according to the new guidelines, but it was canceled when the Israelis were quoted as insisting that in order for their conversions to be accepted, American rabbis would have to pass a test given in Israel. Yet another complication arose in September, when Israel's Interior Ministry announced even more stringent criteria for acceptance of foreign conversions (see below, pp. 291–92). Rabbi Shlomo Amar, the Sephardi chief rabbi of Israel, arrived in the U.S. in October for talks with the RCA about the conversion issue. The substance of the discussions was not disclosed, but the RCA said it was going ahead with its plan for regional courts.

The National Council of Young Israel, a network of about 150 Modern Orthodox synagogues across the country, took steps that gave credence to Angel's complaint about a turn to the right. In an August 1 memorandum sent to all member congregations, the council prohibited its branches from holding or sponsoring women's prayer groups and megillah readings, barred women or converts from serving as synagogue presidents, and stated that any movement synagogue looking to hire a rabbi would first have to get authorization from the National Council, which would examine his scholarly and ideological credentials—a requirement clearly intended to block the hiring of anyone with unconventional views.

Ironically, the most explosive challenge to Modern Orthodoxy in 2007 came not from those who considered it insufficiently Orthodox, but from someone within its own ranks who thought it insufficiently modern. On July 22, the *New York Times Sunday Magazine* carried an article titled "Orthodox Paradox" by Noah Feldman, an Orthodox man who had graduated from the elite Maimonides day school in Boston, went on to Harvard and Oxford, and was now a professor at Harvard Law School. Feldman claimed that Maimonides had left pictures of him and his Korean girlfriend out of a published class reunion photo taken in 1998, and subsequently refused to publish news about their marriage and later family events he sent to the school's alumni bulletin.

For Feldman these snubs symbolized the underlying flaw of Modern Orthodoxy: its inability to accept intermarriage in today's open society gave the lie to its fundamental claim, that one could be both a faithful Orthodox Jew and a modern American. For good measure, Feldman cited other examples of unethical and even violent teachings of Orthodoxy that its modern exponents had not eliminated. Even though it later emerged that there had been no deliberate cropping of the reunion photo—Feldman and his then-girlfriend did not appear because they were standing on the far edge of the group, outside camera range—his charges provoked considerable debate within the Orthodox community over whether Modern Orthodoxy was indeed a contradiction in terms (if so, perhaps more insular Orthodoxy was the answer) and over the specific issue of whether intermarriage, which today no longer necessarily implied abandonment of the tradition, should be treated more leniently by Orthodox Judaism.

Far angrier than Feldman was writer Shalom Auslander, whose best-selling memoir *Foreskin's Lament* denounced Orthodox Judaism in no uncertain terms. Raised in a strict Orthodox manner, Auslander, now no longer observant, still could not shake the cruel God he was educated to believe in. His book, both religiously blasphemous and bitingly funny, was reportedly read surreptitiously by many Orthodox Jews.

One common criticism of Orthodoxy, its treatment of women, drew considerable attention during the year. In February, the tenth annual conference of the Jewish Orthodox Feminist Alliance (JOFA) stressed the *agunah* problem, the plight of women whose estranged husbands refused to grant a Jewish divorce, thus preventing them from remarrying. A rabbinic conference on the matter scheduled for November 2006 in Israel had been canceled by the Chief Rabbinate at the last moment (see AJYB 2007, pp. 263–64), and some of the JOFA speakers advocated more militant tactics, but no consensus emerged on strategy. JOFA did run a multipage ad on the subject, "A Call to Action for Rabbis and the Orthodox Community," in Jewish newspapers in early March, signed by hundreds of people, asking, "Does Anybody Hear? Does Anybody Care?" and demanding "an end to this injustice—a disgrace for every Jew who adheres to Halakhah."

Action was taken in November against a rabbi who was said to aid men in remarrying without giving their first wives Jewish divorces. Led by a number of well-known Orthodox scholars, RCA rabbis picketed the rabbi's Brooklyn yeshiva to publicize his actions. The rabbi eventually appeared and told reporters that the charges against him were untrue.

Another theme voiced at the JOFA conference was the anti-feminist effects of the year that most Orthodox young women spent studying in Israel after high school. Emily Shapiro Katz, who taught American students in Israel for six years, decried the tendency of the Israeli schools to stress standards of modesty in dress over academic achievement, place rabbinic faculty on a higher pedestal than female teachers, and treat the very word "feminist" as a threat to Orthodoxy.

Complaints raised in 2006 about conditions at the large Agriprocessors kosher slaughterhouse in Postville, Iowa (see AJYB 2007, p. 125), multiplied in 2007. In late March, 23 workers at the plant filed a class-action suit against the company claiming that workers were not compensated for time spent preparing for work and cleaning up. In early May hundreds of workers walked out for several hours after management notified all workers—many of whom were believed to be in the U.S. illegally—that they had to supply social security numbers. People for the Ethical Treatment of Animals (PETA) released yet another video in July, recorded in May, this one showing substandard conditions at a Nebraska kosher slaughterhouse owned by the same man who owned Agriprocessors. A new charge surfaced in August, the U.S. Department of Agriculture citing Agriprocessors on multiple charges of food-safety violations committed during 2006.

A major event in the intellectual life of American Orthodoxy was the publication of *How to Read the Bible: A Guide to Scripture, Then and Now,* by James L. Kugel, for many years professor at Harvard University and now teaching in Israel, who identified himself as an Orthodox Jew. Opening up to an Orthodox audience the explosive question of whether reconciliation was possible between the traditional Jewish understanding of the Bible as God's word and modern critical approaches, the book surveyed each book of the Bible, comparing old and new ways of understanding.

The future paths of the two largest American Hasidic communities were largely dependent on lawsuits. 770 Eastern Parkway in Crown Heights, Brooklyn, the headquarters of Chabad (Lubavitch), had been contested ground since the death of the movement's last rebbe, Rabbi Menachem Mendel Schneerson, in 1994. The basement synagogue where the rebbe had prayed was controlled by the local Chabad community, which believed that Schneerson had not actually died and would soon emerge as the messiah. Suing to wrest it away was the official global Chabad organization, which held possession of the building above. It ran a sophisticated network of Chabad branches around the world and publicly rejected the view that the rebbe was the messiah. In March a state judge ruled that the case should go to trial.

The long-running feud between two sons of the late Satmar rebbe, Rabbi Moshe Teitelbaum, over the succession (see AJYB 2007, p. 126) was apparently settled by the New York State Court of Appeals in November. Under terms of the decision, the younger son, Rabbi Zalman Teitelbaum, was expected to retain control of the main Satmar community in the Williamsburg section of Brooklyn, while his older brother, Rabbi Aaron Teitelbaum, would run the satellite Kiryas Joel community upstate.

The Organizational World

Presidents Conference

In April, the Conference of Presidents of Major American Jewish Organizations, the umbrella body for 52 national Jewish organizations, chose June Walker as its new chair. Walker, national president of Hadassah, the women's Zionist organization, would be the second woman to chair the conference. She was believed to be among those who had complained in the past about the conference leadership's lack of consultation with member organizations.

UJC

United Jewish Communities (UJC) was formed in 1999 in an effort to streamline American Jewish philanthropy and make it more effective through a merger of the Council of Jewish Federations, United Jewish Appeal, and United Israel Appeal. Almost from the outset UJC was the object of criticism from many quarters, and contributions and donor bases of federations continued to decline. A UJC memo dated March 16, 2007, reflecting ideas put forward at a meeting of lay and professional leaders, recommended major restructuring. The four "pillars" of UJC's work—Campaign/Financial Resource Development, Israel/Overseas, Human Services and Social Policy, and Jewish Renaissance and Renewal—would be dissolved, and an office in Israel would play a major role in attracting philanthropy from outside the U.S.

At UJC's annual General Assembly in November, held this year in Nashville, the focus was on attracting younger givers who often felt that federations did not reflect their concerns or interests, and on the growing number of major donors who preferred to set up their own "boutique" charities geared to their personal interests rather than donating to federations. Many of the federations had devised mechanisms whereby contributors could direct money to their particular favorite causes via federation channels.

The 3,500 General Assembly attendees barely had time to return home when reports circulated that the Jewish Federation of Metropolitan Detroit, the fourth largest federation, was withholding its UJC dues on the grounds that its dues allocation did not reflect its community's loss of Jewish population, and that the South Palm Beach Federation was also requesting a cut in its designated dues.

AIPAC

The federal case initiated in 2004 against former AIPAC staffers Steven Rosen and Keith Weissman, charging them with passing classified information to unauthorized persons, continued on into 2007. In March, officials of three Jewish organizations, following the policy of distancing such organizations from the two accused men, turned down requests to testify for them. Defense attorneys had hoped that testimony about the attendance of these officials at a meeting with an administration figure would show that exchange of government information was routine in Washington, and thus that Rosen and Weissman did nothing illegal.

The April 2 *Wall Street Journal* carried a biting critique of the government's actions by Dorothy Rabinowitz. This prosecution, she wrote, "had brought new life to the obsessed," feeding charges of a pro-Israel conspiracy to control U.S. policy. Rabinowitz detailed how weak was the case against Rosen and Weissman, and warned that a conviction would raise the possibility "for countless others to face trials in the future, for newly invented crimes unearthed by willing prosecutors."

Better news for the defense came later that month, when Judge T.S. Ellis III, who would preside over the trial, ruled that any evidence produced by the government would have to be open to the public.

WJC

Stung in 2006 by proof of significant financial irregularities (see AJYB 2007, p. 123), the World Jewish Congress went through more tribulations in 2007. In March, President Edgar Bronfman dismissed his longtime trusted associate, Israel Singer, for allegedly taking money that did not belong to him. This firing raised the question of whether Singer should continue as president of the Conference on Jewish Material Claims against Germany, especially as a new scandal surfaced in early May about questionable payments to a Singer confidant in connection with the March of the Living program, funded mainly by the Claims Conference. Singer announced in June that he would not be a candidate for reelection as conference president when his term expired in July.

Edgar Bronfman resigned as WJC president in May, and on June 10 WJC delegates elected Ronald Lauder—the cosmetics heir who had been an ambassador, president of the Jewish National Fund, and chairman of the Presidents Conference—as the new president. He received 59 votes, easily defeating Mendel Kaplan of South Africa, who got 17. Matthew Bronfman, Edgar's son, ran unopposed for the position of chairman. In August—as new WJC lawsuits were announced to reclaim money from Singer—Lauder announced the appointment of Michael Schneider as general secretary, the top WJC professional position. Schneider had previously served as executive vice president of the American Jewish Joint Distribution Committee.

ORT

Tensions among the various national components of ORT (Organization for Rehabilitation and Training), which ran a network of technical and vocational schools in Israel and elsewhere, affected ORT America. ORT Israel separated itself from World ORT in 2006. While the Israelis said this was because they were getting insufficient funding and could get more by striking out on their own, ORT America, fearful that its donors would now be approached by ORT Israel, informed its supporters that donations to ORT Israel were not tax deductible, and charged that the Israeli body lacked financial transparency. In January, World ORT announced it would fund Israeli schools directly, without going through ORT Israel. ORT America denied ORT Israel the use of the "ORT" trademark to fund-raise in the U.S., causing ORT Israel to sue in an American court, arguing that ORT had become a generic name that could not be restricted. In Israel, meanwhile, ORT Israel sought to bar World ORT from using the name, and a Haifa court ruled in April that the dispute should be mediated.

Culture

The disproportionate number of Jews who excel in intellectually demanding fields—a subject that had attracted numerous attempts at explanation—received renewed attention in the April issue of *Commentary,* which featured "Jewish Genius" by Charles Murray. Already controversial as the author of *The Bell Curve,* which argued that intelligence had some basis in genetics, Murray noted that Jewish IQ scores were higher than others, and suggested that factors in Jewish history, such as the centrality of Torah study for men and the development of the Talmud, "intertwined" Judaism with "intellectual complexity," so that males of inferior intelligence were marginalized and eventually left the fold. Murray's thesis was harshly criticized by some other social scientists for racial stereotyping.

A significant new reference work appeared as the year began, a new edition of *Encyclopedia Judaica,* meant to replace the first edition published in 1972. Many of the old entries were updated, and new ones, reflecting changes in the Jewish world and advances in scholarship, were included. This was true not only for specific facts, people, and institutions, but entire themes were vastly expanded, such as the role of Jewish women. In addition, while the 1972 version was oriented toward Israel, the second edition gave far more space to Diaspora matters.

Two important Jewish cultural institutions announced major changes in 2007. What had been called the National Foundation for Jewish Culture dropped the word "National" from its name and approved a new strategic plan aimed at making the foundation "THE destination for those interested in culture as a vehicle for exploring Jewish experience." Elise Bernhardt, the president and CEO, also hoped to triple the foundation's $3 million endowment over five years. And the National Yiddish Book Center, located in Amherst, Massachusetts, broke ground for a new facility that would include an educational center, student center with kosher kitchen, performance hall, and book repository with space for up to 500,000 volumes.

A most unusual daylong conference took place in New York on April 29, sponsored by Nextbook, entitled "What's He Doing Here? Jesus in Jewish Culture." Exploring—and disagreeing about—the place of Jesus in Jewish tradition were well-known academics, rabbis, and writers. In the *Forward* (May 4), Nextbook editor Jonathan Rosen explained, "A one-day conference devoted to a marginal figure in Judaism who nevertheless is a central figure to much of the world had a kind of logic to it."

LAWRENCE GROSSMAN

Jewish Population in the United States, 2008*

Methodology

The Jews of the U.S. are what demographers call a "rare population," one that is very difficult to count. [1]

Given that constraint, we have endeavored since 2006 to provide readers with the most accurate estimates of local Jewish population data available. This effort is ongoing, as every year new local studies are added and numbers are updated. A by-product of our effort is that the aggregation of all of these local estimates—based on scientific surveys, informant estimates, and Internet estimates—yields an estimate of the total U.S. Jewish population, one that is likely to be at the high end, for reasons described in our 2006 article.[2]

To develop this year's estimates, we have changed our methodology somewhat. The current estimates are derived from three sources:

1. *Scientific Estimates.* These are based upon the results of some type of scientific study of a community, which, in almost all cases, involves the use of random digit dialing (RDD) telephone surveys. RDD is the currently accepted best methodology for developing population estimates.[3]

When results are from a non-RDD study, three asterisks appear next

---

**Note:* The authors, Ira Sheskin of the University of Miami and Arnold Dashefsky of the University of Connecticut, are both affiliated with the Mandell L Berman Institute-North American Jewish Data Bank (http//www.jewishdatabank.org), the former as a board member and the latter as director. This article is a productive partnership between them and the Data Bank. The authors thank Dr. Jim Schwartz, Jeffrey Scheckner, and Dr. Barry Kosmin, who authored this AJYB article in previous years; many population estimates in this article were based on their efforts. We also thank Dinur Blum, graduate assistant, and Lorri Lafontaine, program assistant, both at the Data Bank at the University of Connecticut, for their assistance. Thanks are also extended to Ron Miller and Bruce Phillips for helpful comments on an earlier draft.

[1]The reasons are noted in Ira M. Sheskin and Arnold Dashefsky, "Jewish Population in the United States, 2007," AJYB 2007, p. 133.

[2]Ira M. Sheskin and Arnold Dashefsky, "Jewish Population in the United States, 2006," AJYB 2006, pp. 134–139, which also discusses the discrepancy between the population estimate we offer and that of our colleague, Sergio DellaPergola, in his article on world Jewish population.

[3]For a brief description of RDD in local Jewish community studies see Ira M. Sheskin, *How Jewish Communities Differ: Variations in the Findings of Local Jewish Demographic Studies* (New York, 2001), p. 6, a publication of the North American Jewish Data Bank.

to the date of the study. In most cases, these non-RDD studies involve the use of distinctive Jewish names (DJNs) to estimate the Jewish population of counties surrounding a county in which a scientific study was completed.[4]

2. *Informant Estimates.* E-mail was used as the principal method to contact local Jewish communities served by Jewish federations. For those communities that did not reply, estimates have been retained from previous years. For some communities in which no scientific study has been completed, a local informant was contacted. These informants generally have access to information on the number of households on the local Jewish federation's mailing list and/or the number that belong to various synagogues and local Jewish organizations.

Because of the number of estimates in Table 3, it is impossible to contact all informants in one year. Thus, beginning this year, we have undertaken what we believe will be a multiyear effort to update the estimates for communities that have no scientific study. We began with four states in each of the four regions of the U.S.: Vermont in the Northeast, Mississippi in the South, North Dakota in the Midwest, and Wyoming in the West. These new estimates are documented with "2008" appearing in the column headed "Data of Informant Confirmation."

Relying on an Internet search of relevant Websites, we began by identifying Jewish organizations and religious congregations in each of these four states. We then initiated phone interviews or e-mail contacts with designated leaders of these groups and asked a series of questions, including the number of Jewish households, the proportion of persons in these households who are Jewish, and the proportion of households spending less than eight months of the year in the area. This information provided the raw data that allowed us to estimate a community's size. Readers should note that these figures are simply estimates of an elusive population.

---

[4]For example, DJN estimates were made for seven counties surrounding San Antonio (Bexar County), Texas. The ratio between counts of DJN households in Bexar County and the RDD estimate of Jewish households in Bexar County was applied to the DJN household count in the seven counties surrounding Bexar to estimate Jewish households in these seven counties. The household size and the percentage of persons in Jewish households who are Jewish from Bexar County were then applied to the estimate of the number of households in the surrounding counties to derive an estimate of Jews in the seven counties surrounding Bexar. While this procedure can be criticized, we believe it provides reasonable estimates that are almost certainly better than informant estimates.

3. *Internet Estimates.* In a number of cases, we have been able to locate estimates of the number of Jews in an area on the Internet, provided by newspapers, synagogue Websites, and other such sources. For example, the Goldring/Woldenberg Institute of Southern Jewish Life (http://www.isjl.org/history/archive/index.html) has published vignettes on every known Jewish community, existing and defunct, in five Southern states (Alabama, Arkansas, Louisiana, Mississippi, and Tennessee). This helped us update the estimates for a number of communities in these states, as well as delete and add some communities.

Scientific studies enabled us to count more than 80 percent of the total number of Jews estimated by this article; only 20 percent were determined by the less reliable informant or Internet procedures—although an analysis we presented in AJYB 2007, pp. 136–38, strongly suggests that informant estimates are more reliable than previously assumed. Also note that less than 0.1 percent of the total estimated number of Jews derives from communities for which the informant estimate is more than ten years old.

All estimates are for Jews living in households and institutions, and do not include non-Jews living in households with Jews. The estimates of Jewish population include both Jews who are affiliated with the Jewish community and Jews who are not.

Population estimation is not an exact science, and therefore readers should not assume that because the number of Jews in a community listed in this year's article differs from the number reported last year, the change all occurred during the past year. Rather, it most likely occurred over a longer period of time, but has only recently been substantiated.

Readers are invited to offer suggestions for improving the accuracy of the estimates and the portrayal of the data. Please send all correspondence to Ira M. Sheskin at isheskin@miami.edu.

Features in the Local Population Estimates

Table 3 provides estimates for almost 1,000 Jewish communities and parts of communities. In some cases, the geographic areas in Table 3 are Jewish federation service areas. In other cases, where data are available, we have disaggregated Jewish federation service areas into smaller geographic units. Thus, separate estimates are provided for such places as Boulder, Colorado, and Boynton Beach, Florida.

For each community, Table 3 indicates whether the estimate is based on a scientific study or on an informant or Internet estimate. Estimates for communities in boldface type are based on a scientific study. Almost all of them used random digit dialing (RDD) techniques. The boldface date is the year the field work for a scientific study was conducted. If an asterisk appears next to the date, as mentioned above, the estimate was based upon a scientific study that did not employ RDD.

Estimates for communities that are not boldface are based on the informant methodology or the Internet methodology. Because detailed records supplying the date of the last informant contact are not available in many cases, only a range of years (pre-1997 or 1997–2001) is presented for many communities. In those communities for which the date in the "Date of Informant Confirmation or Latest Study" column of Table 3 is more recent than the date of the latest study shown in boldface type, the study estimate has been either confirmed or updated by a local informant at a date later than the scientific study.

Finally, the number of Jews who live in part-year households (between three and seven months of the year) is presented for communities about which such information is available. Jews in part-year households are an essential part of some Florida Jewish communities, joining local synagogues and making donations to local Jewish charities. Our methodology allows the reader to gain a better perspective on the size of certain Jewish communities without double-counting the persons in these households in the totals produced in Tables 1–2. Note that Jews in part-year households are reported with respect to the community that constitutes their "second home." Finally, note that the "part-year population" in the final column of Table 3 is not included in the Jewish population column, but is in addition to the number of Jews in that column.

Local Population Changes

Because population changes based upon scientific studies have a greater degree of validity than those based upon local informants or Internet methods, this section divides the discussion of local population changes into updates based on new scientific studies and those based on new informant estimates. In all, more than 125 changes were made this year in Table 3.

NEW SCIENTIFIC STUDIES

In the past year, five new local Jewish community studies or "small update studies" were completed: Cincinnati, Ohio; Denver/Boulder, Colorado; Lehigh Valley, Pennsylvania; and MetroWest and Middlesex County, both in New Jersey.

Based on the new Cincinnati study, the estimate in Table 3 increased by 4,500, from 22,500 to 27,000. This should not necessarily be interpreted as reflecting population growth, but as the replacement of an inaccurate informant estimate with a more accurate scientific estimate. This study also replaced the informant estimate of 500 for Covington-Newport, Kentucky, with a scientific estimate of 300.

While preliminary estimates from the Denver/Boulder study were presented last year, the final results showed 83,900 Jews rather than the 81,500 reported then. The adjustment accounts for inclusion of an estimate of cell-phone-only households.

Based on a new study in the Lehigh Valley, the estimate decreased by 450, from 8,500 to 8,050. This should not necessarily be viewed as an actual decrease; rather, an inaccurate informant estimate has been replaced by a more accurate scientific estimate. This study also produced a first-ever estimate for two counties to the north of the Lehigh Valley and one in New Jersey. The estimate for Carbon County (Pennsylvania) is 600; for Monroe County (Pennsylvania) 2,300; and for Warren County (New Jersey) 900.

A small update study in MetroWest, using Distinctive Jewish Names (DJNs), suggested that the Jewish population of MetroWest (Essex, Morris, Sussex, and northern Union counties) had decreased by about 5,000 since the last study in 1998. This study also entailed a reevaluation of the results of the 1998 study (see the vignette on Essex-Morris below), which would render the actual decrease in Jewish population in this area nowhere near as significant as suggested by the reported decrease in Table 3 for Essex County (from 76,200 to 48,000) and for Morris County (from 33,500 to 29,700). This study also produced a new estimate for Sussex County of 4,300, up from 4,100 in 1998, as well as a first-ever estimate for northern Union County of 8,200.

Based on a new study, the estimate for Middlesex County increased by 7,000, from 45,000 to 52,000. Once again, this should not be interpreted as reflecting population growth. Rather, an inaccurate informant estimate has been replaced by a more accurate scientific estimate. This study also produced a first-ever estimate for the city of Somerset (3,500) in Somerset County.

NEW INFORMANT/INTERNET ESTIMATES

Based on new informant or Internet estimates, significant increases are reported for Howard County, Maryland (increase of 6,500); Long Beach, California (5,750); Anchorage, Alaska (2,700); Maui, Hawai'i (1,290); and Nantucket, Massachusetts (500). A significant decrease (325) was reported for Rutland, Vermont. The new estimates for Alaska and Hawai'i are based upon the work of Prof. Bernard Katz, posted on the Website of the Nahum Goldmann Museum of the Diaspora.

Estimates are provided for the first time for Nantucket (500 full-year and 200 part-year Jewish residents); Jackson Hole, Wyoming (300); Sedona, Arizona (300); Bristol-Johnson City-Kingsport, Tennessee (200); Lafayette, Louisiana (200); Middlebury, Vermont (200); Bentonville, Arkansas (100); and North Conway, New Hampshire (100 full-year and 70 part-year Jewish residents). Note that Bentonville is the home of Wal-Mart. Although these communities have certainly existed for a while, our new procedures have "found" them, enabling their addition to Table 3.

National, State, and Regional Totals

Based upon a summation of local Jewish community studies (Table 3), the estimated size of the American Jewish community in 2008 is 6,489,110 (Table 1), compared to an estimate of 6,443,805 in 2007. The new figure is about 1.3 million more than the Jewish population estimate reported in United Jewish Community's 2000–01 National Jewish Population Survey (NJPS 2000–01). In AJYB 2006, pp. 135–38, we offer explanations for the difference.[5]

The increase of about 45,000 Jews from last year to this year should not necessarily be interpreted to imply that the number of Jews in the U.S. is increasing. Rather, we have new estimates for some communities that are higher than the previous informant estimates, which were too low. In other cases, our research has found communities that existed last year as well, but were not included in last year's Table 3.

---

[5]See also Ira M. Sheskin, "Four Questions about American Jewish Demography," *Jewish Political Studies Review* 20, Spring 2008, pp. 23–42.

Also, for reasons discussed in AJYB 2006, pp. 136–37, it is unlikely that the number of American Jews is actually approaching 6.5 million. Rather, the number is probably between 6.0 and 6.4 million. Briefly, some part-year households (those that spend part of the year in one community and part in another), some college students (who live in two communities), and some households that moved from one community to another in the interim between implementation of local Jewish community studies are, to some extent, being double-counted in Table 3.

Tables 1 and 2 show the total Jewish population of each state, Census Region, and Census Division. Overall, about 2.2 percent of Americans are Jewish, but the percentage is 4 percent or higher in New York (8.4 percent); New Jersey (5.5 percent); Washington, D.C. (4.8 percent); Maryland (4.3 percent); and Massachusetts (4.3 percent). Eight states have a Jewish population of 200,000 or more: New York (1,618,000); California (1,200,000); Florida (655,000); New Jersey (479,000); Pennsylvania (287,000); Illinois (279,000); Massachusetts (278,000); and Maryland (241,000). The four states with the largest Jewish populations account for more than 60 percent of the approximately 6.5 million American Jews reported in Table 3. Note that in addition to the state totals shown in Table 1, Florida has 84,000 Jews who reside there from three to seven months of the year.

Table 2 shows that, on a regional basis, the Jewish population is distributed very differently from the American population as a whole. While only 18 percent of Americans live in the Northeast, 44 percent of Jews live there. While 22 percent of Americans live in the Midwest, 11 percent of Jews do. While 37 percent of Americans live in the South, 22 percent of Jews do. Approximately equal percentages of all Americans (23 percent) and Jews (24 percent) live in the West.[6]

Vignettes of Recently Completed Local Studies

Three local Jewish demographic studies were completed for Jewish federations since the last article on Jewish population in the U.S. appeared in AJYB 2007: Denver, Colorado; Lehigh Valley, Pennsylvania; and

---

[6]For an analysis of changes in Jewish geographical distribution over time see Ira M. Sheskin, *Geographic Differences Among American Jews*, United Jewish Communities Series on the National Jewish Population Survey 2000-01, Report Number 8 (2005), available at http://www.ujc.org/local__includes/downloads/6760.pdf

Southern Maine. In addition, a small update study was completed for United Jewish Communities of MetroWest New Jersey (Essex, Morris, and Sussex counties). Local studies produce a wealth of information about a Jewish community, including the geographic distribution of the Jewish population, migration patterns, basic demographics (such as age, marital status, and income), religiosity, intermarriage, memberships in synagogues and Jewish organizations, levels of Jewish education, familiarity with and perception of Jewish agencies, social service needs, Israel, anti-Semitism, use of the Jewish and general media, philanthropic giving, voting patterns, and many other topics. This section presents a few of the major findings of each of these three recent studies. Note that although updated population estimates for Cincinnati and Middlesex County, New Jersey, appear in Table 3 based upon new local demographic studies, vignettes for them will appear in AJYB 2009.

In addition, it is the intention of the authors to present the summarized results of all local Jewish community studies completed since 2000 for which reports have been published. This year, the electronic version will include vignettes on Bergen County, New Jersey (2001); Columbus, Ohio (2001); Sarasota, Florida (2001); Seattle, Washington (2000); Tidewater, Virginia (2001); and Westport, Connecticut (2000). This will be available by June 2009 at www.ajc.org and at www.jewishdatabank.org.

In reading these vignettes, it is important to bear in mind the difference between the number of Jews in a community and the number of persons in Jewish households, which also includes non-Jewish spouses and children not being raised Jewish. Also, in these vignettes, when a community is compared to other Jewish communities, the comparison is to communities that have completed scientific studies since 1993. Full reports of the results of these studies are available from the North American Jewish Data Bank at www.jewishdatabank.org. Finally, while random digit dialing (RDD) produces the most truly random sample, most studies, for economic and other reasons, combine RDD sampling with the use of distinctive Jewish name (DJN) sampling or with sampling from mailing lists (known as List sampling). In all surveys employing either DJN or List sampling, weighting factors are used when combining these samples with the RDD sample to remove much of the bias introduced by their use.

METRO DENVER/BOULDER, COL. (2007)

This study covered the seven-county Metro Denver/Boulder area (called simply "Denver" in this vignette), which includes Adams, Arapahoe, Boulder, Broomfield, Denver, Douglas, and Jefferson counties, Colorado. Jack Ukeles and Ron Miller were the principal investigators for this study, which was based upon 227 RDD; 1,102 List; and 70 DJN telephone interviews. This was the first scientific survey of the Jewish population of this area since 1997.

About 117,200 persons live in 47,500 Jewish households in Denver, in which 83,900 persons (72 percent) are Jewish. Denver is the fourth largest Jewish community in the West, after Los Angeles, the San Francisco Bay area, and San Diego. It is the 16th largest Jewish community in the U.S., with Jews comprising about 3.2 percent of the total population.

The number of Jews in Denver has increased from 38,600 in 1981 to 63,300 in 1997 and 83,900 in 2007. Fifteen percent of Denver Jewish households have moved to the community within the past five years, and the newcomers are disproportionately younger adults. During this period, the percentage of persons in Jewish households who are not Jewish has increased from 9 percent to 19 percent to 28 percent.

A significant geographic shift has occurred in the location of the Jewish population. The percentage of Jewish households living in Denver County decreased from 41 percent in 1997 to 34 percent in 2007. The percentage of Jewish households in South Metro increased from 13 percent in 1997 to 21 percent in 2007. All geographic areas showed increases in the number of Jewish households: Denver County by 23 percent; South Metro by 133 percent; Boulder by 25 percent; North and West Metro by 26 percent; and Aurora by 46 percent.

Denver is one of the most geographically dispersed Jewish communities. The 10 percent of Jewish households living in one of the top three zip-code areas for Jewish households is the second lowest of about 45 comparison Jewish communities. Such a situation generally makes it more difficult for local institutions to provide services to their target populations.

Denver is a relatively young Jewish community. While the 22 percent of persons in Jewish households who are age 0–17 is about average among about 50 comparison Jewish communities, the 12 percent of persons in Jewish households who are age 65 and over is the sixth lowest, and the 5 percent who are age 75 and over is the fourth lowest, of about 45 comparison Jewish communities. However, the 26 percent of persons in Jewish households age 50–64 is the third highest among about 40 comparison Jewish communities. Thus as this groups ages over the next 15 years—if they remain in the area—the community can expect a significant increase in persons age 65 and over.

Diversity within the Jewish community is reflected by the fact that 3 percent of households contain a gay, lesbian, bisexual, or transgender household member, and just under 2 percent contain a same-sex couple. Nine percent of the Jewish households are multiracial and another 4 percent identify as Hispanic.

Twenty-six percent of Jewish households report they are either just managing financially or cannot "make ends meet." The median household income of $75,000 (in 2007 dollars) is below average among about 50 comparison Jewish communities.

Two percent of Jewish households report they are Orthodox; 16 percent Conservative; 6 percent Traditional; 5 percent Reconstructionist; 39 percent Reform; 3 percent Jewish Renewal; and 28 percent Just Jewish. The percentage of Conservative households is the second lowest, and the percentage of Orthodox households, Reform households, and Just Jewish households are all about average, among about 50 comparison Jewish communities. These percentages did not change significantly since 1997.

Issues exist in terms of Jewish continuity. While the 19 percent of households that always or usually light Shabbat candles and the 13 percent of households that keep a kosher home are both about average among some 50 comparison Jewish communities, the 66 percent of households that always or usually light Hanukkah candles is the fifth lowest, and the 57 percent of households that always or usually participate in a Passover Seder the third lowest.

The 53 percent couples-intermarriage rate is the fourth highest of about 50 comparison Jewish communities, and has increased dramatically from 39 percent in 1997. The 18 percent of children being raised Jewish in intermarried households is the lowest of about 50 comparison Jewish communities.

The 32 percent of households that contain current synagogue members is the eighth lowest of about 50 comparison Jewish communities, and has decreased from 37 percent in 1997. Only 13 percent of intermarried households contain current synagogue members, which is below average among about 50 comparison Jewish communities. The 16 percent of respondents who are members of a Jewish organization, such as B'nai

B'rith or Hadassah, is the third lowest of about 40 comparison Jewish communities.

The 24 percent of respondents who experienced anti-Semitism in the local community in the past year is the third highest of about 35 comparison Jewish communities.

The 23 percent who made a donation to the Jewish federation in the past year is the fourth lowest of about 50 comparison Jewish communities, and the 44 percent who report a donation to any Jewish charity in the past year is the lowest of about 45 comparison Jewish communities.

METROWEST (ESSEX, MORRIS, SUSSEX, AND NORTHERN UNION COUNTIES), N.J. (2008)

This small 2008 update study involved no new telephone interviewing but did include counts of DJN households by zip code in Essex, Morris, Sussex, and northern Union counties. Ira Sheskin of the University of Miami was the principal investigator, assisted by Ron Miller, associate director of the North American Jewish Data Bank, and Jonathon Ament, then of the United Jewish Communities Research Department.

During the course of this update it became evident that the larger 1998 MetroWest study had not been clear about the difference between persons in Jewish households and Jewish persons, and thus was interpreted by users as recording 117,000 *Jews* living in about 47,000 households, instead of 117,000 *persons* living in those households. In fact, the 1998 report did not provide information on the percentage of persons in Jewish households who were Jewish. Also, the data from this study are neither in the North American Jewish Data Bank nor are they available from the researcher.

The median value for the *percentage of persons in Jewish households who are Jewish* is 82 percent, not only for all 50 comparison Jewish communities that have completed Jewish community studies since 1993, but also for the 20 Northeastern communities that have completed studies since 1993. Thus, if we assume that 82 percent of persons in MetroWest Jewish households in 1998 were Jewish, then 96,000 Jews lived there at that time. While this procedure certainly leaves something to be desired, the 96,000 estimate is clearly closer to the truth than the 117,000 stated in the original report.

The population estimate for 2008 shown in Table 3 is derived by calculating a ratio between the RDD estimate of the number of Jewish households from the 1998 study and the number of households with a DJN in the 1998 telephone directory, and applying this ratio to the DJN count from the 2008 telephone directory. Based upon these counts, the number of Jewish households decreased by 5 percent (2,500 households) from 1998 through 2008. Assuming that both the 82 percent of persons in Jewish households who are Jewish and the average household size have not changed in the past decade, the number of Jews living in MetroWest in 2008 is 91,000. A decrease of 5,000 from 96,000 in 1998 may well be within the margin of error of the DJN update methodology.

This study shows that although the geographic distribution of Jewish households at the county level did not change significantly from 1998 to 2008, the number of DJN households in East Essex (including Newark) shows a 34-percent decrease. While current popular belief suggested an increase in Jewish population in Morris County, the study actually showed a small (6 percent) decrease in the number of DJN households. Livingston, Montclair, and Pompton showed significant increases in DJN households, and Bloomfield, Morristown, Parsippany, and West Orange showed important decreases.

The purpose of this study was to examine the changes in the Jewish population of the service areas of the Lautenberg Family JCC-Aidekman Campus in Morris County and the Cooperman JCC in Essex County. From 1998 to 2008, the number of DJN households in the Lautenberg service area decreased by 9 percent and the number in the Cooperman service area decreased by 6 percent. These were important findings to consider as the community embarked upon an assessment of its MetroWest campuses.

Lehigh Valley, Pa. (2007)

This study covered Lehigh and Northampton counties. Allentown is the major city in Lehigh County; Bethlehem and Easton are the major cities in Northampton County. Ira Sheskin of the University of Miami was the principal investigator. The study was based upon 537 telephone interviews, of which 217 were completed using RDD sampling and 320 using DJN sampling. This was the first scientific survey of the Lehigh Valley's Jewish population.

Of the approximately 9,800 persons living in 4,000 Jewish households in the Lehigh Valley, about 8,000 (82 percent) are Jewish. An additional 50 Jewish persons, without their own telephone numbers, live in institutions. This total of 8,050 Jews comprises about 1.3 percent of the total population of Lehigh and Northampton counties. An additional 3,800 Jews are estimated to live in the surrounding counties of Carbon and Monroe (Pa.), and Warren (N.J.).

The study shows that the Jewish population of the Lehigh Valley is relatively stable. Based upon counts of DJN households, the number of Jewish households decreased by 7 percent (300) from 2000 through 2007. Survey results suggest that migration into the Lehigh Valley is about equal to migration out of it. The number of donors to the Jewish federation annual campaign remained about the same, 1,533, as compared to 1,574 in 2001. Only about one-third of adult children remain in the Lehigh Valley after leaving their parents' homes.

The geographic distribution of Jewish households in the Lehigh Valley has not changed significantly in recent years. In 2007, 71 percent of households lived in Lehigh County; 16 percent in the Bethlehem area; and 13 percent in the Easton area. One zip code (18104) contained 34 percent of Jewish households, making this one of the more geographically concentrated Jewish communities in the country. The high concentration facilitates the provision of services.

The Lehigh Valley is an older Jewish community. The 23 percent of persons age 65 and over in Jewish households is above average, and the median age of 51.6 years is the eighth highest among about 45 comparison Jewish communities. A significant increase in the number of persons age 65 and over in Jewish households is to be expected in the Lehigh Valley, as it currently has the highest percentage of persons in Jewish households age 50–64 (30 percent) among about 40 comparison Jewish communities.

The study finds that the Lehigh Valley is an average Jewish community in many ways. This is certainly so on measures of Jewish religiosity. Among about 35–50 comparison Jewish communities (the number depending upon the specific practice in question), the Lehigh Valley has an average percentage of households who always or usually light Hanukkah candles (73 percent); always or usually participate in a Passover Seder (70 percent); have a mezuzah on their front door (68 percent); always or usually light Shabbat candles (22 percent); keep a kosher home (11 percent); keep kosher both in and out of the home (5 percent); and refrain from using electricity on Shabbat (2 percent). The 29 percent of respondents who never attend services is also average among about 45 comparison Jewish communities, as is the 23 percent of respondents who attend services once per month or more.

The 36 percent of married couples who are intermarried (the *couples intermarriage rate*) in the Lehigh Valley is about average among about 50 comparison Jewish communities. However, unlike many of the others, the trend in the Lehigh Valley is for high intermarriage rates among all age groups. Forty-one percent of married couples in households age 35–49 are intermarried, as are 37 percent in households age 50–64, 25 percent in households age 65–74, and 21 percent in households age 75 and over.

It is in Jewish community participation where the Lehigh Valley shows particular strength. Current synagogue membership, 51 percent, is above average among about 50 comparison Jewish communities, and the 81-percent figure for lifetime synagogue membership—the percentage of households belonging to a synagogue at some time during their adult lives—is about average among about 30 comparison Jewish communities. Jewish community center (JCC) membership, 18 percent, is about average among about 45 comparison communities, but the 43 percent of Jewish households that participated in a JCC program during the past year is well above average among about 45 comparison communities. The JCC's 39-percent market share of the fitness facility and health club market among Jewish households is about average among about 25 comparison communities. The 62 percent of households that are *associated* with the Jewish community (anyone in the household is a member of a synagogue, the JCC, or a Jewish organization) is above average among about 40 comparison Jewish communities.

As in many other communities, synagogue membership shows a strong correlation with median household income. Membership increases from 41 percent of households earning under $50,000 a year to 47 percent of those earning $50,000–$100,000, 56 percent of those earning $100,000–$200,000, and 73 percent of those earning $200,000 and over.

The 39 percent of elderly single households in the Lehigh Valley that have experienced a physical, mental, or other health condition lasting six months or more that limits or prevents employment, educational opportunities or daily activities is the highest among about 35 comparison Jewish communities. Clearly, there is a need for the community to prioritize services to this group through programs by Jewish family service and other agencies. Furthermore, Lehigh Valley has the highest percentage, among about 50 comparison communities, of persons in Jewish households who are age 50–64, a situation that will lead to a significant increase in the percentage of elderly over the next 15 years.

The local Jewish newspaper, *Hakol,* is always or usually read by 47 percent of respondents, the fifth highest readership percentage of about 25 comparison Jewish newspapers. The 52 percent of households that reported donating to the Jewish federation in the past year is the seventh highest of about 50 comparison Jewish communities. The $581 average donation per household to the Jewish federation is well above average among about 45 comparison Jewish communities. Of the donating households, 22 percent donated $1,000 and over, the third highest of about 40 comparison Jewish communities.

While Lehigh and Northampton counties are very similar demographically (except for the former's median Jewish household income of $90,000 and the latter's $73,000), they are quite different in terms of Jewish behavior and connections, almost certainly reflecting the presence of the JCC and the organized Jewish community in Allentown (Lehigh County). For example, 25 percent of households in Lehigh County always or usually light Shabbat candles, compared to 15 percent in Northampton County. Similar differences are seen for having a mezuzah on the front door, always or usually participating in a Passover Seder, and always or usually lighting Hanukkah candles. The percentage of married couples in Jewish households who are intermarried is lower in Lehigh County (31 percent) than in Northampton County (45 percent).

SOUTHERN MAINE (2007)

This study covered Cumberland and York counties, Maine. Portland is the principal city in Cumberland County. Ira Sheskin of the University of Miami was the principal investigator for this study, which was based upon 421 telephone interviews, of which 150 were completed using RDD sampling and 271 using DJN sampling. This was the first scientific survey of the Jewish population of this area.

About 11,825 persons live in 4,300 Jewish households in Southern Maine, in which 8,350 persons (71 percent) are Jewish. Jews comprise about 1.7 percent of the total population of the two counties. An additional 1,750 Jews are estimated to live in the surrounding counties of Androscoggin, Oxford, and Sagadahoc.

From 1995 to 2005 the number of Jewish households in Southern Maine remained about the same, with perhaps a small geographic shift out of the Core Area (Portland) to other areas of Cumberland and York counties.

The study's findings on migration suggest that this population stability will probably continue. The 10 percent of Jewish households in Southern Maine that moved in over the past five years suggests that an average of 86 current households currently in Southern Maine moved into the community annually over the past five years (the in-migration rate). The 6 percent of Jewish households indicating they will definitely (2.5 percent) or probably (3.7 percent) move out of Southern Maine within the next three years suggests that an average of between 36 and 89 Jewish households will move out annually over the next three years (the out-migration rate). Assuming these rates continue for the next few years, the number of Jewish households in Southern Maine will probably not change significantly.

Jewish identity and continuity confront significant problems in Southern Maine. The 48 percent of Jewish respondents who consider themselves Just Jewish is the highest of about 50 comparison Jewish communities. Among the comparison Jewish communities, Southern Maine has the lowest percentage of households that keep a kosher home (3 percent); the second lowest percentages of households that have a mezuzah on their front door (50 percent), always or usually light Shabbat candles (13 percent), and keep kosher in and out of the home (3 percent); and the third lowest percentage of households that always or usually participate in a Passover Seder (60 percent). Its 70 percent of households that light Hanukkah candles and 1 percent that refrain from using electricity on Shabbat are both about average among the comparison communities. The 48 percent of households that always, usually, or sometimes have a Christmas tree in their home is the highest of about 40 comparison Jewish communities. Among about 50 comparison Jewish communities, Southern Maine has the highest percentage of married couples in Jewish households that are intermarried, 61 percent.

The 33 percent of households claiming membership in a synagogue is well below average among the comparison Jewish communities, the 65 percent belonging to a synagogue sometime in their lives is the lowest, and the 39 percent of households with children that belong to a synagogue is the fifth lowest. In addition, Southern Maine has the second lowest percentage of Jewish respondents who attend synagogue services once per month or more, 15 percent, and the highest percentage who never attend (or attend only for special occasions), 45 percent.

The 36 percent of Jewish respondents who feel very much or somewhat a part of the Southern Maine Jewish community is the second lowest of about 25 comparison Jewish communities. The 33 percent of Jewish respondents who are extremely or very emotionally attached to Israel is the second lowest of about 30 comparison Jewish communities. And the 34 percent of Jewish respondents age 40 and over who would very much prefer Jewish-sponsored adult-care facilities is the lowest of about 20 comparison Jewish communities. Thus not only are levels of Jewish religious practice and Jewish organizational membership low in Southern Maine, but so are feelings of identification with, and ethnic attachment to, the Jewish people.

Philanthropic patterns bear this out as well. The 25 percent of Jewish households that donated to the federation (called the Jewish Community Alliance) in the past year is the fifth lowest of about 50 comparison Jewish communities, and the 50 percent that donated to any Jewish charity (including the JCA) in the past year is the fourth lowest of about 45 comparison Jewish communities. Conversely, the 89 percent of households that donated to non-Jewish charities in the past year is the second highest of about 45 comparison Jewish communities, and the 41 percent that donated to non-Jewish charities but not to Jewish charities is the highest of about 45 comparison Jewish communities.

Finding programs that provide compelling reasons for those Jews in Southern Maine who are emotionally unengaged in Jewish life to become involved represents a significant challenge. Currently, the JCA (which includes a preschool and day camp) and the Jewish family service agency (operating from a small, one-room office) are in one location, and the Jewish nursing home and the Levey Day School, with an enrollment of less than 40, are elsewhere. The study pointed to the need for a Jewish community campus that would house all of these in once place, so as to build Jewish community and strengthen Jewish connections in Southern Maine.

Comparisons among Local Jewish Communities

Since 1993, more than 50 American Jewish communities have completed one or more *scientific* Jewish community studies. Each year this article presents and discusses several tables comparing these studies. This year, tables are presented on synagogue membership (Table 4), membership in the local Jewish community center (Table 5), observance of kashrut (Table 6), and the need for in-home health care for the elderly in the past year (Table 7).

Excluded from the tables are the results of older community studies that are too dated for current comparisons or for which more recent results are available. (For example, while studies were completed in Miami in 1994 and 2004, the tables show results only for 2004.) Comparison tables are available elsewhere containing the results of Jewish community studies completed between 1982 and 1999.[7]

The comparisons among Jewish communities should be treated with caution for three major reasons: the studies were not done at the same time, but over a 15-year period; they used different sampling methods; and they used different questionnaires.[8]

Despite these issues, examination of community comparisons is important because it helps put the results of each individual Jewish community study in context. The communities shown in Tables 4–6 have a combined Jewish population that comprises about 75 percent of the total U.S. Jewish population estimated in Table 1. Generally, for two percentages in these tables to be considered substantially different, the gap needs to be at least five percentage points.

Synagogue Membership

Table 4 shows the percentage of households that report belonging to synagogues for 50 Jewish communities. In most instances, these are overestimates of the actual percentages of synagogue-member households. This is attributable to several factors. First, not all potential respondents cooperate with a telephone survey. It is likely that synagogue-member households respond at a disproportionately high rate, in part because they are more interested in the subject matter and in part because survey publicity is more likely to reach synagogue members. Second, former synagogue members may still attend services on the High Holidays and for other functions, and so may report membership when in fact they are not actually members. Third, even with an anonymous survey, there may be reluctance on the part of some respondents to admit to not being syna-

---

[7]Sheskin, *How Jewish Communities Differ*, presents 124 comparison tables containing older data.

[8]For a more complete discussion of the difficulties of comparing local Jewish community study results, see AJYB 2007, p. 153; and Ira M. Sheskin, "Comparisons between Local Jewish Community Studies and the 2000–01 National Jewish Population Survey," *Contemporary Jewry* 25 (2005), pp. 158–192.

gogue members, and they claim falsely to be members. Fourth, despite assurances to the contrary, some respondents may feel that questions concerning synagogue membership answered in the negative will lead to an appeal for membership, leading some non-member respondents to claim that they are synagogue members.[9]

The percentage of households reporting synagogue membership varies from a low of 14 percent in Las Vegas to a high of 58 percent in Tidewater, Virginia. The median value is 45 percent. Of the ten communities with the lowest synagogue membership, seven are in the West: Denver (32 percent); Tucson (32 percent); San Diego (29 percent); Phoenix (29 percent); San Francisco (22 percent); Seattle (21 percent); and Las Vegas (14 percent). The other three are Florida retirement communities—South Palm Beach (33 percent); West Palm Beach (30 percent); and Broward County (27 percent). In each of these ten communities, the percentage of locally born Jews is low and the percentage of new residents is high. In these situations, many households break ties with synagogues in the community they have left and then fail to join a synagogue in their new community. Social scientists have noted that households that move to the West are often those that are least traditional, and national studies of American religious behavior have noted that the West contains the greatest percentage of "unchurched" households.[10]

Tidewater (Norfolk/Virginia Beach), whose 58-percent synagogue-membership rate is the highest of the 50 communities in the table, is an interesting case study. Given that intermarriage in this community is very high and levels of home religious practice are about average, the high membership rate may be surprising—as is the 37 percent of intermarried couples that belong to synagogues, the highest of 40 comparison communities. However, in small Southern communities church membership is quite high, and assimilation may actually be expressed by joining the "Jewish church." Note that the other small Southern communities in the table (with the exception of Orlando, which has many new residents) have synagogue membership rates at the median or higher: Richmond (45 percent); Charlotte (49 percent); Jacksonville (49 percent); and San Antonio (52 percent).

---

[9]For an analysis of the disparity between reported and actual synagogue membership, see Ira M. Sheskin, *The Jewish Community Study of the Lehigh Valley* (Allentown, Pa., 2008), pp. 7-20–7-24.

[10]See, for example, Barry A. Kosmin and Seymour P. Lachman, *One Nation Under God: Religion in Contemporary American Society* (New York, 1993).

Larger communities tend to have low synagogue-membership rates. All seven of the largest communities in the table (excluding the Florida retirement communities) have rates that are below median: New York (43 percent); Chicago (42 percent); Washington (37 percent); Philadelphia (37 percent); Los Angeles (34 percent); Atlanta (33 percent); and San Francisco (22 percent). This finding is consistent with the view of sociologists that residents of large cities tend to be less involved in their communities than those in small cities.

Jewish federations, responsible for central planning for each community, should take note of their position in Table 4. While a goal of every Jewish federation and Jewish community may be to increase synagogue membership, the relative priority given to such efforts ought to be informed by this data. Communities toward the top of the table should recognize that their chances of increasing membership significantly are probably not great. Communities toward the bottom of the table, on the other hand, may have a greater potential for increasing membership. Also, a federation can use this information to compare its community with other similar communities. For example, a Western community should understand that all communities in that region have synagogue-membership rates below 34 percent, and that moving its rate above that level may be an unrealistic short-term goal.

Jewish Community Center Membership

Table 5 shows the percentage of households that report Jewish community center (JCC) membership for 47 communities. As was the case in regard to synagogue membership, these figures likely overestimate the actual percentages, and for similar reasons. First, JCC member households are more likely to respond to a telephone survey, in part because they are more interested in the subject matter and in part because survey publicity is more likely to reach them. Second, former JCC members who may still attend various JCC events may report membership when in fact they are not currently members. Third, even with an anonymous survey, there may be respondents who are reluctant to admit that they are not JCC members, and therefore falsely claim to be members. Fourth, despite assurances to the contrary, some respondents may feel that questions concerning JCC membership will lead to an appeal for them to join, and so they claim that they are members. Fifth, some respondents confuse a JCC with a synagogue, particularly in communities where some synagogues have the words "Jewish Center" or "Jewish Community Center" in their names, and so claim to be JCC members when they are not.[11]

The percentage of households reporting JCC membership varies from 1 percent in Broward County (Soref) to 36 percent in St. Paul. The median value is 14 percent. Three JCCs are not full-service facilities, a fact that almost certainly explains the low percentages of membership: Miami (Miami Beach), 5 percent; Monmouth County (Western), 5 percent; and Las Vegas, 3 percent. Miami operates from a converted mansion and Monmouth and Las Vegas are housed in office buildings.

Similar to the results for synagogue membership, JCCs in Florida do not attract large percentages of the community. Only the Alper JCC, located in a young area of Miami where lengths of residence are relatively long, has membership around the median value (13 percent). The other Florida JCCs, all with relatively low membership rates, are Miami (Russell), 10 percent; St. Petersburg, 10 percent; West Palm Beach (Kaplan), 7 percent; Broward (Posnack), 6 percent; West Palm Beach (Boynton), 5 percent; Miami (Miami Beach), 5 percent; South Palm Beach, 4 percent; and Broward (Soref), 1 percent. Aside from the factors mentioned earlier about the low synagogue-membership percentages, other reasons for low JCC membership rates in Florida are the large number of elderly people who do not need preschool, day camp, and after-school care; the fact that much of the Florida population comes from the New York metropolitan area, where JCCs are not well known; and the mostly Jewish condominium developments that are home to much of the South Florida Jewish population, where the clubhouses provide JCC-type activities.

Charlotte, where 36 percent say they belong to the JCC, is an interesting case study. While many JCCs are on a "campus" that often also includes the Jewish federation, a Jewish day school, and a Jewish family service, the Charlotte campus (Shalom Park) also includes Reform and Conservative synagogues and a Chabad house. The classrooms for the synagogues are in the JCC. Undoubtedly, those joining a synagogue will visit the JCC and possibly decide to join, so as to take advantage of JCC activities while their children are involved in Jewish education.

---

[11]For an analysis of discrepancies between reported and actual JCC membership, see Sheskin, *Jewish Community Study of the Lehigh Valley,* pp. 7-41–7-44.

Monmouth County, New Jersey (Deal), where 27 percent of households claim JCC membership, is another unusual case study. The membership rate here is augmented by a large Sephardic (predominantly Syrian) population that comes from Brooklyn to spend the summer in the Deal area. The JCC day camp is largely comprised of children of these seasonal families.

JCCs should take note of their position in Table 5. While a goal of every JCC is to increase membership, the priority given to such efforts should be informed by this table. Communities toward the top of the table should recognize that their chances of increasing membership significantly are not great, while those toward the bottom may have significant potential for increasing membership. Also instructive is comparison of a given community with other similar communities. For example, a Florida retirement community should appreciate the fact that all such communities have low membership rates. Some understanding of these rates is also helpful for a JCC's self-perception. In one recently studied community, for example, the JCC wanted to determine why membership had recently declined by several hundred. Not only did the demographic study provide explanations for the decrease, but the community learned from Table 5 that their membership rate was still above the median.

Keeping Kosher

Table 6 shows that, among 49 communities, the percentage of households that say they keep a kosher home varies from 3 percent in Portland, Maine, to 29 percent in Bergen County, New Jersey. The median value is 13 percent. Table 6 also shows that the percentage saying they keep kosher both in and out of the home, for 32 Jewish communities, varies from 1 percent in Westport, Connecticut, to 18 percent in Bergen County. The median value is 5 percent. Of course, definitional issues arise as to the meaning of "kosher." In almost all the communities, if respondents asked what definition to use, they were told to define "kosher" for themselves.

Clearly, both these measures correlate with the percentage of a community that is Orthodox (see Table 6 in AJYB 2007, pp. 201–202). Bergen (29 percent Orthodox), New York (28 percent), Monmouth (26 percent), Harrisburg, Pennsylvania (23 percent), Detroit (22 percent), Miami (22 percent), and Baltimore (22 percent) all have significant Orthodox populations.

The percentages for keeping kosher at home of all the Western communities are at or below the median: Palm Springs (13 percent), Tucson (11 percent), Los Angeles (11 percent), Phoenix (9 percent), San Diego (8 percent), Las Vegas (5 percent), and Seattle (5 percent). This is consistent with the findings noted above for synagogue and JCC membership, and with findings from the NJPS 2000–01. [12]

Three of the Florida retirement communities have values above the median for keeping kosher at home (Miami, 22 percent, Broward, 16 percent, and South Palm Beach, 14 percent), while three have values below the median (St. Petersburg, 10 percent, West Palm Beach, 9 percent, and Sarasota, 6 percent). Note that most Jews moving to Florida for retirement purposes who desire to maintain a kosher lifestyle select the east coast of the state, where there is a kosher infrastructure, rather than the west coast.

An interesting contrast can be seen between South Palm Beach (14 percent), which includes the two southernmost communities of Boca Raton and Delray Beach in Palm Beach County, and West Palm Beach (9 percent), which includes the remainder of the county. South Palm Beach contains a concentration of young Orthodox Jews. They support kosher establishments that are not found in West Palm Beach, such as food marts, restaurants, and catering services.

The typical pattern a generation ago was that much higher percentages of Jews kept kosher only in the home than both in and out of the home. This is still somewhat evident in Monmouth (15 percent in the home only and 11 percent both in and out), Harrisburg (15 percent and 8 percent), Rochester (13 percent and 8 percent), Hartford (11 percent and 6 percent), Broward (11 percent and 5 percent), and South Palm Beach (9 percent and 5 percent). But this pattern has clearly changed in most communities, where the home-only percentage is about equal to the in-and-out percentage. Interestingly, in two communities the trend is reversed: Bergen (11 percent in the home only and 18 percent in and out of the home), and Detroit (8 percent and 14 percent).

Purveyors of kosher products will find this data useful. In Miami, for example, the 22 percent of Jewish households that keep kosher in the home amounts to 12,000 households. Given their average household size,

---

[12]See Sheskin, *Geographic Differences Among American Jews,* for an analysis of levels of religiosity by geographical region.

that means 31,000 persons live in kosher households. Similarly, the 12 percent of Miami Jewish households that keep kosher both in and out of the home comprises about 19,000 persons.

Need for In-Home Health Care

Jewish demographic studies collect data on the social service needs of a community in three ways. First, the need for social services is determined in part by the size of various demographic groups—a community with a higher percentage and number of elderly, for example, is likely to need more in-home health care than one with a lower percentage and number. Second, respondents are sometimes asked, in a variety of ways, how important various types of services are to their households. Third, respondents are asked if they needed a given service in the past year and, if so, whether that need was met.

Table 7 shows the responses to a question asked in 32 Jewish communities about the need for in-home health care over the past year in households with elderly persons. The percentage of households with elderly persons that needed such care varied from 6.0 percent in Charlotte to 18.5 percent in Miami. The median value is 14.0 percent.

The extent to which organizations like Jewish family service should prioritize the provision of home health care may be viewed in the context of this table. Communities toward the top, with the highest percentages needing home health care, like Miami (18.5 percent), Jacksonville (18.0 percent), and Minneapolis (17.2 percent), might give this service a higher priority than those communities toward the bottom, like Harrisburg (8.1 percent), San Francisco (8.0 percent), and Charlotte (6.0 percent).

The percentage needing home health care is somewhat related to the percentage of the elderly, age 75 and over. In the four Florida retirement communities with a need for home health care above the median—Miami (18.5 percent), Broward (15.1 percent), South Palm Beach (15.0 percent), and West Palm Beach (14.7 percent)—an average of 61 percent of the elderly are age 75 and over. For the two Florida retirement communities whose need for home health care is below the median—St. Petersburg (10.5 percent) and Sarasota (10.1 percent)—an average of 52 percent of the elderly are 75 and over.

In 31 of the 32 communities (the exception was St. Louis), when respondents reported that their households needed in-home health care, they were asked whether the care had been received. If the households received the care, the respondents were asked whether the care had been received from a Jewish source. The general pattern among the comparison Jewish communities is that most households needing the care received it, and most households receiving it used non-Jewish sources.

In this particular table, comparisons between communities are particularly important for some of the smaller communities whose demographic studies use small-size samples. For example, in Charlotte, only 103 households contained elderly persons, and thus the sample size for the rightmost three columns in Table 7 is rather small. However, since the pattern in Charlotte (most households needing in-home health care received it, and most receiving it got it from non-Jewish sources) is similar to that in every other community. Therefore the Charlotte community can be confident that the results reflect reality, despite the small sample size.

State Maps of Jewish Communities

Starting with this issue of the AJYB, we introduce a new feature: state-level maps showing the approximate sizes of each Jewish community. Table 3 should be used in conjunction with the maps, as the table provides more exact estimates for each community and sometimes a more detailed description of the geographic areas included within each community. This year, maps are provided for New York and California, the two states with the largest Jewish populations.

The map of New York shows that the largest Jewish populations are in the New York metropolitan area (the five boroughs of New York City, Nassau, Suffolk, and Westchester), and in Rockland County. The four largest communities in upstate New York are Rochester, Buffalo, Albany, and Syracuse. Note that three of the estimates are based on scientific studies: Buffalo (1995); Rochester (1999); and the New York City metropolitan area (2001). All others are informant estimates.

The map of California shows that the largest Jewish populations are along the coast of southern California from Santa Barbara to San Diego, and in the San Francisco-East Bay (Oakland) area. No other significant (5,000 or over) Jewish communities exist outside these two areas. Six of the estimates are based on scientific studies: East Bay (1986); San Jose (1986); Los Angeles (1997); Palm Springs (1998); San Diego (2003); and San Francisco (2004). All others are informant estimates.

Errata

Table 3 in AJYB 2007, p. 177, omitted the community of North Shore in Massachusetts. We thank Dr. Jonathon Ament, formerly of United Jewish Communities, for bringing this to our attention.

Table 7 in AJYB 2007, p. 204, reported a 50-percent couples-intermarriage rate for Essex-Morris (MetroWest) New Jersey. However, this value was based upon an unclear statement in the report for that community. As the original data are not available, the correct value is unknown.

IRA M. SHESKIN
ARNOLD DASHEFSKY

TABLE 1: JEWISH POPULATION IN THE UNITED STATES, 2008

State	Estimated Jewish Population	Total Population*	Estimated Jewish Percent of Total
Alabama	8,900	4,627,851	0.2%
Alaska	6,200	683,478	0.9%
Arizona	106,400	6,338,755	1.7%
Arkansas	1,725	2,834,797	0.1%
California	1,199,940	36,553,215	3.3%
Colorado	90,120	4,861,515	1.9%
Connecticut	112,830	3,502,309	3.2%
Delaware	15,100	864,764	1.7%
Washington, D.C.	28,000	588,292	4.8%
Florida	655,235	18,251,243	3.6%
Georgia	127,745	9,544,750	1.3%
Hawaii	8,200	1,283,388	0.6%
Idaho	1,100	1,499,402	0.1%
Illinois	278,520	12,852,548	2.2%
Indiana	17,420	6,345,289	0.3%
Iowa	6,140	2,988,046	0.2%
Kansas	18,225	2,775,997	0.7%
Kentucky	10,850	4,241,474	0.3%
Louisiana	9,875	4,293,204	0.2%
Maine	13,915	1,317,207	1.1%
Maryland	241,050	5,618,344	4.3%
Massachusetts	277,805	6,449,755	4.3%
Michigan	87,270	10,071,822	0.9%
Minnesota	46,685	5,197,621	0.9%
Mississippi	1,550	2,918,785	0.1%
Missouri	59,165	5,878,415	1.0%
Montana	850	957,861	0.1%
Nebraska	6,850	1,774,571	0.4%
Nevada	69,600	2,565,382	2.7%
New Hampshire	10,170	1,315,828	0.8%
New Jersey	479,200	8,685,920	5.5%
New Mexico	11,250	1,969,915	0.6%
New York	1,617,720	19,297,729	8.4%
North Carolina	27,745	9,061,032	0.3%
North Dakota	400	639,715	0.1%
Ohio	149,155	11,466,917	1.3%
Oklahoma	5,050	3,617,316	0.1%
Oregon	31,850	3,747,455	0.8%

TABLE 1: JEWISH POPULATION IN THE UNITED STATES, 2008 (CONTINUED)

State	Estimated Jewish Population	Total Population	Estimated Jewish Percent of Total
Pennsylvania	286,70	12,432,792	2.3%
Rhode Island	18,750	1,057,832	1.8%
South Carolina	11,335	4,407,709	0.3%
South Dakota	295	796,214	0.0%
Tennessee	19,350	6,156,719	0.3%
Texas	130,170	23,904,380	0.5%
Utah	4,400	2,645,330	0.2%
Vermont	5,385	621,254	0.9%
Virginia	98,040	7,712,091	1.3%
Washington	43,135	6,468,424	0.7%
West Virginia	2,335	1,812,035	0.1%
Wisconsin	28,330	5,601,640	0.5%
Wyoming	1,000	522,830	0.2%
TOTAL	6,489,110	301,621,157	2.2%

*July 1, 2006 http://factfinder.census.gov

TABLE 2: DISTRIBUTION OF U.S. JEWISH POPULATION BY REGIONS, 2008

	Total Population	Percent Distribution	Jewish Population	Percent Distribution
Northeast	54,680,626	18.1%	2,822,475	43.5%
Middle Atlantic	40,416,441	13.4%	2,383,620	36.7%
New England	14,264,185	4.7%	438,855	6.8%
Midwest	66,388,795	22.0%	698,455	10.8%
East North Central	46,338,216	15.4%	560,695	8.6%
West North Central	20,050,579	6.6%	137,760	2.1%
South	110,454,786	36.6%	1,394,055	21.5%
East South Central	17,944,829	5.9%	40,650	0.6%
South Atlantic	57,860,260	19.2%	1,206,585	18.6%
West South Central	36,649,697	11.5%	146,820	2.3%
West	70,096,950	23.2%	1,574,125	24.3%
Mountain	21,360,990	7.1%	284,720	4.4%
Pacific	48,735,960	16.2%	1,289,405	19.9%
TOTAL	301,621,157	100.0%	6,489,110	100.0%

TABLE 3: COMMUNITIES WITH JEWISH POPULATION OF 100 OR MORE, 2008

State	Date of Informant Confirmation or Latest Study	Geographic Area*	Jewish Population	Regional Totals	Part-Year Jewish Population**
ALABAMA					
	1997-2001	Birmingham (Jefferson County)	5,300		
	2008	Dothan	150		
	2008	Florence-Sheffield	100		
	1997-2001	Huntsville	750		
	1997-2001	Mobile (Baldwin and Mobile Counties)	1,100		
	2008	Montgomery	1,100		
	2008	Tuscaloosa	200		
	2008	Other Places	200		
		Total Alabama	8,900		
ALASKA					
	2008	Anchorage (Anchorage Borough)	5,000		
	2008	Fairbanks (Fairbanks and North Star Borough)	600		
	2008	Juneau	300		
	1997-2001	Kenai Peninsula	200		
	1997-2001	Other Places	100		
		Total Alaska	6,200		
ARIZONA					
	2002	**Cochise County (2002)** ***	450		
	1997-2001	Flagstaff (Coconino County)	500		
	1997-2001	Lake Havasu City	200		
	2002	**Northwest Valley (Glendale-Peoria-Sun City) (2002)**	10,900		
	2002	**Phoenix (2002)**	23,600		
	2002	**Northeast Valley (Scottsdale) (2002)**	34,500		
	2002	**Tri Cities Valley (Ahwatukee-Chandler-Gilbert-Mesa-Tempe) (2002)**	13,900		
	2002	**Phoenix Total (2002)**		82,900	
	2008	Prescott	300		
	2008	Sedona	300		50

*Estimates for communities with boldface type are from a scientific study in the year shown. **Part-year population shown only for where such information is available. ***Indicates a study that did not include random digit dialing to estimate the Jewish population size.

State	Date of Informant Confirmation or Latest Study	Geographic Area*	Jewish Population	Regional Totals	Part-Year Jewish Population**
	2005	**West-Northwest (2002)**	3,450		
	2005	**Northeast (2002)**	7,850		
	2005	**Central (2002)**	7,150		
	2005	**Southeast (2002)**	2,500		
	2005	**Green Valley (2002)**	450		
	2005	**Tucson (Pima County) Total (2002)**		21,400	1,000
	1997-2001	Yuma	150		
	2002	**Santa Cruz County (2002)*** **	100		
	1997-2001	Other Places	100		
		Total Arizona	106,400		1,050
ARKANSAS					
	2008	Bentonville	100		
	2008	Fayetteville	175		
	2001	Hot Springs	150		
	2001	Little Rock	1,100		
	2008	Other Places	200		
		Total	1,725		
CALIFORNIA					
	1997-2001	Antelope Valley-Lancaster-Palmdale	3,000		
	1997-2001	Bakersfield (Kern County)	1,600		
	1997-2001	Chico-Oroville-Paradise (Butte County)	750		
	1997-2001	Eureka (Humboldt County)	1,000		
	1997-2001	Fairfield	800		
	1997-2001	Fresno (Fresno County)	2,300		
	2008	Long Beach (in Los Angeles County: Cerritos-Hawaiian Gardens-Lakewood-Rossmoor-Signal Hill and, in Orange County: Cypress-Huntington Harbor-Los Alamitos-Seal Beach	23,750		

1997	**Malibu-Palisades (1997)**	27,190	
1997	**Santa Monica-Venice (1997)**	23,140	
1997	**Airport Marina (1997)**	22,140	
1997	**Fairfax (1997)**	54,850	
1997	**Beverly Hills (1997)**	20,500	
1997	**Cheviot-Beverlywood (1997)**	29,310	
1997	**Westwood (1997)**	20,670	
1997	**Central City (1997)**	4,710	
1997	**Hollywood (1997)**	10,390	
1997	**Culver City (1997)**	9,110	
1997	**Central Valley (1997)**	27,740	
1997	**Burbank-Glendale (1997)**	19,840	
1997	**Encino-Tarzana (1997)**	50,290	
1997	**Southeast Valley (1997)**	28,150	
1997	**Simi-Conejo (1997)**	38,470	
1997	**High Desert (1997)**	10,920	
1997	**North Valley (1997)**	36,760	
1997	**West Valley (1997)**	40,160	
1997	**Beach Cities (1997)**	17,270	
1997	**Central (1997)**	11,600	
1997	**Palos Verdes Peninsula (1997)**	6,780	
1997	**San Pedro (1997)**	5,310	
1997	**Eastern Belt (1997)**	3,900	
1997	**Los Angeles-Pasadena-Santa Monica (1997)**		519,200
1997-2001	Mendocino County (Redwood Valley-Ukiah)	600	
1997-2001	Merced County	190	
1997-2001	Modesto (Stanislaus County)	500	
1997-2001	Monterey Peninsula	2,300	
1997-2001	Murrieta Hot Springs	550	
1997-2001	Napa County	1,000	
1997-2001	Orange County (most of Orange County-excluding parts included in Long Beach)	60,000	

State	Date of Informant Confirmation or Latest Study	Geographic Area*	Jewish Population	Regional Totals	Part-Year Jewish Population**
	1998-2002	**Palm Springs (1998)**	4,400		
	1998-2002	**Cathedral City-Rancho Mirage (1998)**	3,100		
	1998-2002	**Palm Desert-Sun City (1998)**	2,500		
	1998-2002	**East Valley (Bermuda-Dunes-Indian Wells-Indio-La Quinta) (1998)**	1,300		
	1998-2002	**North Valley (Desert Hot Springs-North Palm Springs-Thousand Palms) (1998)**	700		
	1998-2002	**Palm Springs Total (1998)**		12,000	5,000
	1997-2001	Redding (Shasta County)	150		
	1997-2001	Riverside-Corona-Moreno Valley	2,000		
	1997-2001	Sacramento (El Dorado, Placer, Sacremento, and Yolo Counties)	21,300		
	1997-2001	Salinas	1,000		
	1997-2001	San Bernardino-Fontana area	3,000		
	2003	**North County Coastal (2003)**	24,000		
	2003	**North County Inland (2003)**	18,100		
	2003	**Greater East San Diego (2003)**	18,900		
	2003	**La Jolla-Mid-Coastal (2003)**	14,400		
	2003	**Central San Diego (2003)**	12,200		
	2003	**South County (2003)**	1,400		
	2003	**San Diego (San Diego County) Total (2003)**		89,000	
	2006	**Alameda County (Oakland) (1986)**	60,000		
	2006	**Contra Costa County (1986)**	40,000		
	2006	**East Bay Total (1986)**		100,000	
	2007	**Marin County (2004)**	26,100		
	2007	**North Peninsula (2004)**	40,300		
	2007	**San Francisco County (2004)**	65,800		

State	Date	Area	Population	Subtotal	Other
	2007	**Sonoma County (Petaluma-Santa Rosa) (2004)**	23,100		
	2007	**South Peninsula (Palo Alto) (2004)**	72,500		
	2007	**San Francisco Total (2004)**		227,800	
	2006	**San Jose (Silicon Valley) (1986)**	63,000		
		San Francisco Bay Area		390,800	
	1997-2001	San Gabriel and Pomona Valleys-Ontario (Alta Loma-Chino-Calremon-Cucamonga-La Verne-Montclair-Ontario-Pomona-San Dimas-Upland	30,000		
	1997-2001	San Luis Obispo-Paso Robles (San Luis Obispo County)	2,000		
	1997-2001	Santa Barbara (Santa Barbara County)	7,000		
	1997-2001	Santa Cruz-Aptos (Santa Cruz County)	6,000		
	1997-2001	Santa Maria	500		
	1997-2001	South Lake Tahoe (El Dorado County)	150		
	1997-2001	Stockton	850		
	1997-2001	Sun City	200		
	1997-2001	Tulare and Kings Counties (Visalia)	350		
	1997-2001	Vallejo area	900		
	1997-2001	Ventura County	15,000		
	1997-2001	Other Places	200		
		Total California	1,199,940		5,000
COLORADO					
	1997-2001	Aspen	750		
	1997-2001	Colorado Springs	1,500		
	2007	**Denver (2007)**	28,700		
	2007	**South Metro (2007)**	19,800		
	2007	**Boulder (2007)**	12,900		
	2007	**North and West Metro (2007)**	11,400		
	2007	**Aurora (2007)**	6,600		
	2007	**North and East Metro (2007)**	4,500		
	2007	**Greater Denver (Adams, Arapahoe, Boulder, Broomfield, Denver, and Jeffesrson Counties) Total (2007)**		83,900	

State	Date of Informant Confirmation or Latest Study	Geographic Area*	Jewish Population	Regional Totals	Part-Year Jewish Population**
	1997-2001	Fort Collins-Greeley-Loveland	2,000		
	1997-2001	Grand Junction (Mesa County)	320		
	1997-2001	Pueblo-Lamar-Trinidad	425		
	1997-2001	Steamboat Springs	250		
	pre-1997	Telluride	125		
	1997-2001	Vail-Breckenridge-Eagle (Eagle and Summit Counties)	650		
	1997-2001	Other Places	200		
		Total Colorado	90,120		
CONNECTICUT					
	1997-2001	Bridgeport-Shelton (Easton-Fairfield-Monroe-Shelton-Stratford-Trumbull)	13,000		
	1999-2001	Danbury-Newtown (Bethel-Brookfield-Danbury-New Fairfield-Redding-Ridgefield-Sherman)	3,200		
	2008	Greenwich	7,000		
	1997-2001	Stamford-Darien-New Canaan	9,200		
	2001	**Westport (2001)**	5,000		
	2001	**Weston (2001)**	1,850		
	2001	**Wilton (2001)**	1,550		
	2001	**Norwalk (2001)**	3,050		
	2001	**Westport-Weston-Wilton-Norwalk Total (2001)**		11,450	
		Fairfield County Total		43,850	
	2000	**Bloomfield-Hartford-West Hartford (2000)**	15,800		
	2000	**East Hartford-Glastonbury-Manchester-South Windsor (and adjacent Tolland County) (2000)**	4,800		
	2000	**Farmington Valley (and adjacent Litchfield County) (2000)**	6,400		
	2000	**Bristol-New Britain-Middletown (adjacent Middlesex County)–Meriden-Wallingford (adjacent New Haven County)-Plymouth-Terryville (adjacent Litchfield County) (2000)**	5,000		
	2000	**Windsor-Suffield (2000)**	800		

2000	**Hartford County Total (including northern Middlesex County, western Tolland County, eastern Litchfield County, northern New Haven County) (2000)**		32,800
1997-2001	Torrington	580	
	Other Places in Litchfield County	50	
	Litchfield County Total (excluding towns in adjacent Hartford County)		630
1997-2001	Lower Middlesex County (Branford-Clinton-Durham-Guilford-Killingworth-Madison-Old Saybrook-Old Lyme-Westbrook)	1,600	
	Middlesex County Total (excluding towns in adjacent Hartford County)		1,600
1987	**New Haven (Ansonia-Bethany-Branford-Derby-East Haven-Guilford-Hamden-Madison-Meriden-Milford-North Haven-Orange-Quinnipiac-Seymour-Wallingford-West Haven-Woodbridge) (1987)**	24,300	
1997-2001	Waterbury-Cheshire (Bethlehem-Litchfield-Middlebury-Morris-Naugatuck-Oakville-Oxford-Plymouth-Prospect-Roxbury-Southbury-Southbury-Southington-Thomaston-Torrington-Washington-Waterbury-Watertown-Wolcott-Woodbury-and other parts of Litchfield County and northern New Haven County	4,500	
	New Haven County Total (excluding towns in adjacent Hartford County)		28,800
pre-1997	Colchester-Lebanon; Hebron (adjacent Tolland County)	300	
1997-2001	New London-Norwich (central and southern New London County and parts of Middlesex and Windham Counties)	3,850	
	New London County Total (including adjacent Tolland County)		4,150
2006	Storrs-Columbia	400	
2006	Other Places in Tolland County	100	
	Tolland County Total (excluding towns in adjacent Hartford and New London Counties)		500

State	Date of Informant Confirmation or Latest Study	Geographic Area*	Jewish Population	Regional Totals	Part-Year Jewish Population**
	pre-1997	Danielson	100		
	2006	Willimantic	300		
	2006	Other Places in Windham County	100		
		Windham County Total		500	
		Total Connecticut	112,830		
DELAWARE					
	2005	**Kent and Sussex Counties (Dover) (2005)***	3,200		
	2005	**Newark area (2005)**	4,300		
	2005	**Wilmington area (2005)**	7,600		
		Total Delaware	15,100		
DISTRICT OF COLUMBIA					
	2003	**District of Columbia (2003)**	28,000		
	2003	**Lower Montgomery County (2003)**	88,600		
	2003	**Upper Montgomery County (2003)**	24,400		
	2003	**Prince Georges County (2003)**	7,200		
	2003	**Arlington-Alexandria-Falls Church (2003)**	27,900		
	2003	**South Fairfax-Prince William County (2003)**	25,000		
	2003	**West Fairfax-Loudoun County (2003)**	14,500		
	2003	**Greater Washington Total (2003)**		215,600	
FLORIDA					
	1997-2001	Brevard County	5,000		
	pre-1997	Crystal River	100		
	1997-2001	Fort Myers-Arcadia-Port Charlotte-Punta Gorda (Charlotte, De Soto, and Lee Counties)	8,000		
	1997-2001	Fort Pierce	1,060		
	2008	Gainesville	2,500		

2002	**Jacksonville Core Area (2002)**	8,800		
2002	**The Beaches (Atlantic Beach, Neptune Beach, Jacksonville Beach, Ponte Verde Beach) (2002)**	1,900		
2002	**Other areas of Duval, Nassau, Clay, and St. Johns Counties (including St. Augustine) (2002)**	2,200		
2002	**Jacksonville Total (2002)**		12,900	200
1997-2001	Key West	650		
pre-1997	Lakeland	1,000		
1997-2001	Naples (Collier County)	4,200		
1997-2001	Ocala (Marion County)	500		
1997-2001	**North Orlando (Seminole County and southern Volusia Counties) (1993)**	7,800		
1997-2001	**Central Orlando (Maitland-Orlando-Winter Park) (1993)**	7,700		
1997-2001	**South Orlando (Orlando and northern Osecola Counties) (1993)**	5,200		
1997-2001	**Orlando Total (1993)**		20,700	400
1997-2001	Pasco County (New Port Richey)	1,000		
1997-2001	Pensacola (Escambia and Santa Rosa Counties)	975		
1997-2001	**North Pinellas (Clearwater) (1994)**	9,850		
1997-2001	**Central Pinellas (Largo) (1994)**	4,050		
1997-2001	**South Pinellas (St. Petersburg) (1994)**	10,300		
1997-2001	**St. Petersburg (Pinellas County) Total (1994)**		24,200	1,500
2001	**Sarasota (2001)**	8,600		1,500
2001	**Longboat Key (2001)**	1,000		1,500
2001	**Bradenton (Manatee County) (2001)**	1,750		200
2001	**Venice (2001)**	850		100
2001	**Sarasota Total (2001)**		12,200	3,300
2005	**East Boca (2005)**	8,900		
2005	**Central Boca (2005)**	33,800		
2005	**West Boca (2005)**	17,000		
2005	**Boca Raton Subtotal (2005)**		59,700	13,000

State	Date of Informant Confirmation or Latest Study	Geographic Area*	Jewish Population	Regional Totals	Part-Year Jewish Population**
	2005	**Delray Beach (2005)**	47,800		10,800
	2005	**South Palm Beach Subtotal (2005)**		107,500	23,800
	2005	**Boynton Beach (2005)**	45,600		10,700
	2004	**Lake Worth (2005)**	21,600		3,300
	2005	**Town of Palm Beach (2005)**	2,000		2,000
	2005	**West Palm Beach (2005)**	8,300		2,000
	2005	**Wellington-Royal Palm Beach (2005)**	9,900		1,400
	2005	**North Palm Beach-Palm Beach Gardens-Jupiter (2005)**	13,950		3,500
	2005	**West Palm Beach Subtotal (2005)**		101,350	22,900
	2005	**Palm Beach County Total (2005)**		208,850	46,700
	2004	**North Dade Core East (Aventura-Golden Beach-part of North Miami Beach) (2004)**	34,000		
	2004	**North Dade Core West (Ojus and parts of North Miami Beach) (2004)**	13,100		
	2004	**Other North Dade (north of Flagler Street) (2004)**	3,800		
	2004	**North Dade Subtotal (2004)**		50,900	4,500
	2004	**West Kendall (2004)**	13,750		
	2004	**East Kendall (parts of Coral Gables-Pinecrest-South Miami) (2004)**	15,650		
	2004	**Northeast South Dade (Key Biscayne-parts of City of Miami) (2004)**	8,300		
	2004	**South Dade (2004)**		37,700	800
	2004	**North Beach (Bal Harbour-Bay Harbor Islands-Indian Creek Village-Surfside) (2004)**	3,700		
	2004	**Middle Beach (parts of City of Miami Beach) (2004)**	10,300		
	2004	**South Beach (parts of City of Miami Beach (2004)**	3,700		
	2004	**The Beaches (2004)**		17,700	1,700
	2004	**Miami-Dade County Total (2004)**		106,300	7,000

	1999	**Hollywood-Hallandale (1999)**	32,900		3,400
	1999	**Pembroke Pines-Cooper City-Davie-Weston (1999)**	44,200		1,900
	1999	**Plantation-North Lauderdale-Tamarac-Lauderdale Lakes-Sunrise (1999)**	65,600		5,700
	1999	**Coral Springs-Parkland (1999)**	28,000		0
	1999	**Margate-Coconut Creek-Wynmoor-Palm Aire-Century Village (1999)**	30,300		7,400
	1999	**Fort Lauderdale (1999)**	11,300		2,400
	1999	**Broward County Total (1999)**		212,300	20,800
		Southeast Florida (Miami-Dade, Broward, Palm Beach Counties)		527,450	74,500
	2005	**Stuart (Martin County) (2005)**	2,900		
	2005	**Southern St. Lucie County (Port St. Lucie) (2005)**	2,900		
	2005	**Stuart-Port St. Lucie Total (2005)**		5,800	900
	1997-2001	Tallahassee	2,200		
	1997-2001	Tampa (Hillsbourough County)	20,000		
	1997-2001	Vero Beach (Indian River County)	400		
	2007	Volusia and Flagler Counties (Daytona Beach)	4,000		
	pre-1997	Winter Haven	300		
	1997-2001	Other Places	100		
		Total Florida	655,235		84,100
GEORGIA					
	1997-2001	Albany Area	200		
	1997-2001	Athens	600		
	2005	**Intown (2005)**	28,900		
	2005	**North Metro Atlanta (2005)**	28,300		
	2005	**East Cobb Expanded (2005)**	18,400		
	2005	**Sandy Springs-Dunwoody (2005)**	15,700		
	2005	**Gwinnett-East Perimeter (2005)**	14,000		
	2005	**North and West Perimeter (2005)**	9,000		
	2005	**South (2005)**	5,500		
	2005	**Atlanta Total (2005)**		119,800	

State	Date of Informant Confirmation or Latest Study	Geographic Area*	Jewish Population	Regional Totals	Part-Year Jewish Population**
	1997-2001	Augusta (Burke, Columbia, and Richmond Counties)	1,300		
	1997-2001	Brunswick	120		
	1997-2001	Columbus	750		
	1997-2001	Dalton	125		
	1997-2001	Macon	1,000		
	2008	Savannah (Chatham County)	3,500		
	1997-2001	Valdosta	100		
	1997-2001	Other Places	250		
		Total Georgia	127,745		
HAWAII					
	1997-2001	Hawai'i (Hilo)	280		
	1997-2001	Oahu (Honolulu)	6,400		
	1997-2001	Kau'ai	100		
	2008	Maui	1,500		1,000
		Total Hawai'i	8,280		1,000
IDAHO					
	1997-2001	Boise (Ada and Boise Counties)	800		
	1997-2001	Ketchum	100		
	1997-2001	Moscow-Lewiston	100		
	1997-2001	Other Places	100		
		Total Idaho	1,100		
ILLINOIS					
	1997-2001	Aurora area	750		
	1997-2001	Bloomington-Normal	500		
	2007	Champaign-Urbana (Champaign County)	1,400		
	2000	**Chicago (Cook and DuPage Counties and parts of Lake County) (2000)**	270,500		

State	Date	Place	Population	
	1997-2001	DeKalb	180	
	1997-2001	Elgin (northern Kane County and southern McHenry County)	500	
	1997-2001	Joliet (Will County)	210	
	1997-2001	Kankakee	100	
	1997-2001	Peoria	800	
	1997-2001	Quad Cities-Illinois portion (Moline-Rock Island)	400	
	1997-2001	Quad Cities-Iowa portion (Davenport) (Scott County)	500	
	1997-2001	Quad Cities Total		900
	1997-2001	Quincy	100	
	1997-2001	Rockford-Freeport (Boone, Winnebago, and Stephenson Counties)	1,100	
	1997-2001	Southern Illinois (Carbondale-East St. Louis) (all of Illinois south of Carlinville)	500	
	2008	Springfield-Decatur (Morgan, Sangamon, and Macon Counties)	930	
	1997-2001	Waukegan	300	
	1997-2001	Other Places	250	
		Total Illinois	278,520	
INDIANA				
	1997-2001	Bloomington	1,000	
	1997-2001	Evansville	400	
	1997-2001	Fort Wayne	900	
	1997-2001	Gary-Northwest Indiana (Lake and Porter Counties)	2,000	
	2006	Indianapolis	10,000	
	1997-2001	Lafayette	550	
	1997-2001	Michigan City (La Porte County)	300	
	1997-2001	Muncie	120	
	1997-2001	South Bend-Elkhart (St.Joseph and Elkhart Counties)	1,850	
	1997-2001	Terre Haute (Vigo County)	100	
	1997-2001	Other Places	200	
		Total Indiana	17,420	

State	Date of Informant Confirmation or Latest Study	Geographic Area*	Jewish Population	Regional Totals	Part-Year Jewish Population**
IOWA					
	1997-2001	Cedar Rapids	420		
	1997-2001	Council Bluffs	150		
	1997-2001	Des Moines-Ames	2,800		
	1997-2001	Iowa City (Johnson County)	1,300		
	1997-2001	Postville	150		
	1997-2001	Quad Cities-Illinois portion (Moline-Rock Island)	400		
	1997-2001	Quad Cities-Iowa portion (Davenport) (Scott County)	500		
	1997-2001	Quad Cities Total		900	
	1997-2001	Sioux City (Plymouth and Woodbury Counties)	400		
	1997-2001	Waterloo (Black Hawk County)	170		
	1997-2001	Other Places	250		
		Total Iowa	6,140		
KANSAS					
	2006	**Kansas City area-Kansas portion (1985) (Johnson and Wyandotte Counties)**	16,000		
	2006	**Kansas City area-Missouri portion (1985)**	4,000		
		Kansas City Total		20,000	
	1997-2001	Lawrence	200		
	pre-1997	Manhattan	425		
	1997-2001	Topeka (Shawnee County)	400		
	1997-2001	Wichita (Sedgwick County and Salina-Dodge City-Great Bend-Liberal-Russell-Hays)	1,100		
	1997-2001	Other Places	100		
		Total Kansas	18,225		
KENTUCKY					
	2008	**Covington-Newport area (2008)**	300		
	1997-2001	Lexington (Bourbon, Clark, Fayette, Jessamine, Madison, Pulaski, Scott, and Woodford Counties)	2,000		
	2006	**Louisville (Jefferson County) (2006)*****	8,300		

State	Year	Place	Population	Subtotal
	1997-2001	Paducah	150	
	1997-2001	Other Places	100	
		Total Kentucky	10,850	
LOUISIANA				
	1997-2001	Alexandria (Allen, Grant, Rapides, and Vernon Parishes)	175	
	1997-2001	Baton Rouge (Ascension, East Baton Rouge, Iberville, Livingston, Pointe Coupee, St. Landry, and West Baton Rouge Parishes)	1,600	
	2008	Lafayette	200	
	2008	Lake Charles area	200	
	2007	New Orleans (Orleans and Jefferson Parishes)	7,000	
	2007	Shreveport-Bossier area	450	
	2007	Monroe-Ruston area	150	
	2007	North Louisiana (Caddo and Bossier Parishes) Total		600
	2008	Other places	150	
		Total Louisiana	9,875	
MAINE				
	pre-1997	Augusta	140	
	1997-2001	Bangor	3,000	
	2007	**Androscoggin County (Lewiston-Auburn) (2007)*** **	600	
	2007	**Oxford County (2007)*** **	750	
	pre-1997	Rockland area	300	
	2007	**Sagadahoc County (2007)*** **	400	
	2007	**Portland Area (2007)**	4,425	
	2007	**Other Cumberland County (2007)**	2,350	
	2007	**York County (2007)**	1,575	
	2007	**Southern Maine Total (2007)**		8,350
	pre-1997	Waterville	225	
	1997-2001	Other places	150	
		Total Maine	13,915	

State	Date of Informant Confirmation or Latest Study	Geographic Area*	Jewish Population	Regional Totals	Part-Year Jewish Population**
MARYLAND					
	1997-2001	Annapolis area	3,000		
	1999	**Owings Mills-Reisterstown (1999)**	22,300		
	1999	**Pikesville-Mt. Washington (1999)**	34,100		
	1999	**Park Heights (1999)**	8,680		
	1999	**Randallstown-Liberty Road (1999)**	3,840		
	1999	**Central Baltimore (1999)**	9,230		
	1999	**Towson-Lutherville-Timonium Corridor (1999)**	6,580		
	1999	**Carroll County (1999)**	2,650		
	1999	**Other Places (1999)**	4,020		
	1999	**Baltimore Total (1999)**		91,400	
	1997-2001	Cumberland	275		
	1997-2001	Easton (Talbot County)	100		
	1997-2001	Frederick (Frederick County)	1,200		
	1997-2001	Hagerstown (Washington County)	325		
	1997-2001	Harford County	1,200		
	2008	**Howard County (Columbia) (1999)**	22,500		
	2003	**Lower Montgomery County (2003)**	88,600		
	2003	**Upper Montgomery County (2003)**	24,400		
	2003	**Prince Georges County (2003)**	7,200		
	2003	**Greater Washington Total in Maryland (2003)**		120,200	
	1997-2001	Ocean City	200		
	1997-2001	Salisbury	400		
	1997-2001	Other places	250		
		Total Maryland	241,050		
MASSACHUSETTS					
	1997-2001	Amherst area	1,300		
	1997-2001	Andover-Lawrence (Boxford-Dracut-Methuen-North Andover-Tewksbury)	2,850		

	2002	**Attleboro area (2002)*** **	800		
	2005	**Brighton-Brookline-Newton and Contiguous Areas (2005)**	61,500		
	2005	**Central Boston-Cambridge and Contiguous Areas (2005)**	43,400		
	2005	**Greater Framingham (2005)**	18,700		
	2005	**Northwestern Suburbs (2005)**	24,600		
	2005	**Greater Sharon (2005)**	21,000		
	2005	**Other Towns (2005)**	41,300		
	2005	**Boston Region Total (2005)**		210,500	
	1997-2001	Cape Cod-Barnstable County	3,250		
	1997-2001	Fall River area	1,100		
	1997-2001	Greenfield (Franklin County)	1,100		
	1997-2001	Haverhill	800		
	1997-2001	Holyoke	600		
	1997-2001	Lowell area	2,000		
	2008	Martha's Vineyard (Dukes County)	375		200
	2008	New Bedford (Dartmouth-Fairhaven-Mattapoisett)	3,000		
	1997-2001	Newburyport	280		
	1997-2001	North Adams (northern Berkshire County)	400		
	1995	**North Shore (1995)**	18,600		
	1997-2001	North Worcester County (Fitchburg-Gardener-Leominster)	1,500		
	2008	Nantucket	1,200		100
	1997-2001	Northampton	500		
	1997-2001	Pittsfield (Central and Southern Berkshire County)	4,000		
	1997-2001	Plymouth area	1,000		
	1997-2001	South Worcester County (Southbridge-Webster)	500		
	1997-2001	Springfield (Agawam-East Longmeadow-Hampden-Longmeadow-West Springfiled Wilbraham)	10,000		
	1997-2001	Taunton area	1,000		
	1997-2001	**Worcester (central Worcester County) (1986)**	11,000		
	1997-2001	Other places	150		
		Total Massachusetts	277,805		300
MICHIGAN					
	1997-2001	Ann Arbor (Washtenaw County)	7,000		
	2007	Bay City	150		

State	Date of Informant Confirmation or Latest Study	Geographic Area*	Jewish Population	Regional Totals	Part-Year Jewish Population**
	2007	Benton Harbor-St. Joseph	150		
	2007	**West Bloomfield (2005)**	19,000		
	2007	**Bloomfield Hills-Birmingham (2005)**	6,500		
	2007	**Farmington (2005)**	12,500		
	2007	**Oak Park-Huntington Woods (2005)**	12,500		
	2007	**Southfield (2005)**	7,000		
	2007	**East Oakland County (2005)**	2,000		
	2007	**North Oakland County (2005)**	3,800		
	2007	**West Oakland County (2005)**	2,500		
	2007	**Wayne County (2005)**	5,600		
	2007	**Macomb County (2005)**	600		
	2007	**Total Detroit (2005)**		72,000	
	2007	Flint (Genesee County)	1,300		
	2007	Grand Rapids (Kent County)	2,000		
	2007	Jackson	200		
	1997-2001	Kalamazoo (Kalamazoo County)	1,500		
	2007	Lansing area	2,100		
	2007	Midland	120		
	2007	Mt. Pleasant (Isabella, Mecosta, Gladwin, and Gratiot Counties)	75		
	2007	Muskegon (Muskegon County)	210		
	2007	Saginaw (Saginaw County)	115		
	2007	Traverse City	150		
	2007	Other places	200		
		Total Michigan	87,270		

State	Date	Place	Population	Subtotal
MINNESOTA				
	1997-2001	Duluth (Carlton and St. Louis Counties)	485	
	1997-2001	Rochester	550	
	2004	**City of Minneapolis (2004)**	5,200	
	2004	**Inner Ring (2004)**	16,100	
	2004	**Outer Ring (2004)**	8,000	
	2004	**Minneapolis Subtotal (2004)**		29,300
	2004	**City of St. Paul (2004)**	4,300	
	2004	**Southern Suburbs (2004)**	5,900	
	2004	**Northern Suburbs (2004)**	700	
	2004	**St. Paul Subtotal (2004)**		10,900
	2004	**Twin Cities Sorrounding Counties (Anoka, Carver, Goodhue, Rice, Scott, Shelburne, Washington, and Wright Counties) (2004)*** **	5,300	
	2004	**Twin Cities Total (2004)**		40,200
	1997-2001	Other places	150	
		Total Minnesota	46,685	
MISSISSIPPI				
	1997-2001	Biloxi-Gulfport	250	
	2008	Greenville	120	
	2008	Hattiesburg (Forrest and Lamar Counties)	130	
	2008	Jackson (Hinds and Rankin Counties)	650	
	2008	Other places	400	
		Total Mississippi	1,550	
MISSOURI				
	1997-2001	Columbia	400	
	1997-2001	Joplin	100	
	2006	**Kansas City area-Kansas portion (1985)**	16,000	
	2006	**Kansas City area-Missouri portion (1985)**	4,000	
	2006	Kansas City Total (1985)		20,000
	1997-2001	St. Joseph (Buchanan County)	265	

State	Date of Informant Confirmation or Latest Study	Geographic Area*	Jewish Population	Regional Totals	Part-Year Jewish Population**
	2006	**St. Louis City (1995)**	2,400		
	2006	**Chesterfield-Ballwin (1995)**	9,900		
	2006	**North of Olive (1995)**	12,000		
	2006	**Ladue-Creve Coeur (1995)**	10,000		
	2006	**Clayton-University Cities (1995)**	7,300		
	2006	**Other Parts of St. Louis and St. Charles Counties (1995)**	12,400		
	2006	**St. Louis Total (1995)**		54,000	
	1997-2001	Springfield	300		
	1997-2001	Other Places	100		
		Total Missouri	59,165		
MONTANA					
	1997-2001	Billings (Yellowstone County)	300		
	1997-2001	Butte-Helena	100		
	1997-2001	Kalispell (Flathead County)	150		
	1997-2001	Missoula	200		
	1997-2001	Other places	100		
		Total Montana	850		
NEBRASKA					
	1997-2001	Lincoln-Grand Island-Hastings	700		
	1997-2001	Omaha	6,100		
	1997-2001	Other places	50		
		Total Nebraska	6,850		
NEVADA					
	2005	**Northwest (2005)**	22,000		
	2005	**Southwest (2005)**	16,000		
	2005	**Central (2005)**	6,300		

State	Date	Area	Population	Total	Part-year
	2005	**Southeast (2005)**	16,400		
	2005	**Northeast (2005)**	6,800		
	2005	**Las Vegas Total (2005)**		67,500	
	1997-2001	Reno-Carson City (Carson City and Washoe Counties)	2,100		
		Total Nevada	69,600		
NEW HAMPSHIRE					
	1997-2001	Concord	500		
	1997-2001	Franklin-Laconia-Meredith-Plymouth	270		
	pre-1997	Hanover-Lebanon	600		
	pre-1997	Keene	300		
	1997-2001	Littleton area	200		
	1997-2001	**Manchester area (1983)***	4,000		
	1997-2001	Nashua area	2,000		
	2008	North Conway-Mount Washington Valley	100		70
	1997-2001	Portsmouth-Exeter	1,250		
	1997-2001	Salem	150		
	2007	**Strafford (Dover-Rochester) (2007)*****	700		
	1997-2001	Other places	100		
		Total New Hampshire	10,170		70
NEW JERSEY					
	2004	**Atlantic County (2004)**	11,700		7,300
	2004	**Cape May County-Wildwood (2004)**	500		900
	2004	**Atlantic and Cape May Counties Total (2004)**		12,200	8,200
	2001	**Pascack-Northern Valley (2001)**	11,900		
	2001	**North Palisades (2001)**	16,100		
	2001	**Central Bergen (2001)**	17,200		
	2001	**West Bergen (2001)**	14,300		
	2001	**South Bergen (2001)**	1,000		
	1997-2001	Other Bergen	23,200		
	2001	**Bergen County (Total) (2001)**		83,700	
	1997-2001	Bridgeton	110		

State	Date of Informant Confirmation or Latest Study	Geographic Area*	Jewish Population	Regional Totals	Part-Year Jewish Population**
	2006	**Cherry Hill (1991)**	22,100		
	2006	**Haddonfield/Haddon Heights, Voorhees, and Pennsauken in**			
	2006	**Camden County and Marlton, Mt. Laurel, and Moorestown**			
	2006	**in Burlington County (1991)**	12,900		
	2006	**Other Burlington and Gloucester Counties (1991)**	14,200		
	2006	**Cherry Hill-Southern N.J. (Camden, Burlington, and Gloucester Counties) Total (1991)**		49,200	
	2008	**South Essex (1998)**	12,000		
	2008	**Livingston (1998)**	10,200		
	2008	**North Essex (1998)**	13,700		
	2008	**West Orange-Orange (1998)**	9,100		
	2008	**East Essex (1998)**	3,800		
	2008	**Essex County (Newark) Total (1998)**		48,800	
	2001	**North Hudson County (2001)**	2,000		
	1997-2001	Bayonne	1,600		
	2006	Hoboken	1,800		
	1997-2001	Jersey City	6,000		
	2001	Hudson County Total		11,400	
	1997-2001	Hunterdon County (Flemington)	2,000		
	2008	**North Middlesex (Edison, Piscataway, Woodbridge) (2008)**	3,600		
	2008	**Highland Park-South Edison (2008)**	5,700		
	2008	**Central Middlesex (New Brunswick, East Brunswick) (2008)**	24,800		
	2008	**South Middlesex (Monroe Township) (2008)**	17,900		
	2008	**Middlesex County Total (2008)**		52,000	
	2006	**Western Monmouth (Marlboro-Freehold-Manalapan-Howell) (1997)**	37,800		
	2006	**Eastern Monmouth (Deal-Asbury Park-Long Branch) (1997)**	17,300		

	2006	**Northern Monmouth (Highlands-Middletown-Hazlet-Union Branch) (1997)**	8,900		
	2006	**Monmouth County Total (1997)**		64,000	6,000
	2008	**West Morris (1998)**	13,300		
	2008	**North Morris (1998)**	13,000		
	2008	**South Morris (1998)**	3,400		
	2008	**Morris County Total (1998)**		29,700	
	2007	Lakewood	40,000		
	2007	Other Ocean County	8,000		
	2007	Ocean County Total		48,000	
	1997-2001	Passaic County	17,000		
	1997-2001	Princeton area	3,000		
	2008	**Somerset (City of) (2008)*** **	3,500		
	1997-2001	Other Somerset County	10,500		
		Somerset County Total		14,000	
	2008	**Sussex County (1988)**	4,300		
	1997-2001	Trenton (most of Mercer County)	6,000		
	2008	**Northern Union County (Springfield-Berkeley Heights-New Providence-Summit (1988)**	8,200		
	2008	Other Union County (Elizabeth) and adjacent areas of Somerset County	22,600		
	2008	Union County Total		30,800	
	1997-2001	Vineland (incuding most of Cumberland County and parts of Salem County)	1,890		
	2007	**Warren County (2007)*** **	900		
	1997-2001	Other Places	200		
	2008	**MetroWest Total (Essex-Morris-Sussex-Northern Union Counties) (1988)**		91,000	
		Total New Jersey	479,200		14,200
NEW MEXICO					
	1997-2001	Albuquerque (Bernalillo)	7,500		
	1997-2001	Las Cruces	600		
	pre-1997	Los Alamos	250		
	1997-2001	Santa Fe-Las Vegas	2,500		
	pre-1997	Taos	300		
	1997-2001	Other Places	100		
		Total New Mexico	11,250		

State	Date of Informant Confirmation or Latest Study	Geographic Area*	Jewish Population	Regional Totals	Part-Year Jewish Population**
NEW YORK					
	1997-2001	Albany (Albany County)	12,000		
	1997-2001	Amsterdam	100		
	1997-2001	Auburn (Cayuga County)	115		
	1997-2001	Binghamton (Broome County)	2,400		
	2006	**Buffalo (Erie County) (1995)**	18,500		
	1997-2001	Canandaigua-Geneva-Newark-Seneca Falls	300		
	1997-2001	Catskill	200		
	1997-2001	Cortland (Cortland County)	150		
	1997-2001	Ellenville	1,600		
	1997-2001	Elmira-Corning (Chemung, Schuyler, and Tioga Counties)	950		
	1997-2001	Fleischmanns	100		
	1997-2001	Glens Falls-Lake George (Warren, Washington, southern Essex, and northern Saratoga Counties)	800		
	1997-2001	Gloversville (Fulton County)	300		
	1997-2001	Herkimer (Herkimer County)	130		
	1997-2001	Hudson (Columbia County)	500		
	1997-2001	Ithaca (Tompkins County)	2,000		
	1997-2001	Jamestown	100		
	1997-2001	Kingston-New Paltz-Woodstock (eastern Ulster County)	4,300		
	2002	**Kingsbridge-Riverdale (2002)**	21,500		
	2002	**Northeast Bronx (2002)**	13,900		
	2002	**Other Bronx (2002)**	9,600		
	2002	**Bronx Subtotal (2002)**		45,000	
	2002	**Bensonhurst-Gravesend (2002)**	40,000		

2002	**Borough Park (2002)**	76,600	
2002	**Coney Island- Brighton-Sheepshead Bay (2002)**	49,700	
2002	**Flatbush-Midwood-Kensington (2002)**	101,100	
2002	**Kingsbay-Madison (2002)**	33,700	
2002	**Williamsburg (2002)**	52,700	
2002	**Crown Heights-Prospect-Lefferts Gardens (2002)**	15,700	
2002	**Brooklyn Heights-Park Slope (2002)**	23,000	
2002	**Canarsie-Flatlands (2002)**	33,100	
2002	**Other Brooklyn (2002)**	30,400	
2002	**Brooklyn Subtotal (2002)**		456,000
2002	**Gramercy Park-Murray Hill (2002)**	32,500	
2002	**Lower Manhattan (2002)**	41,100	
2002	**Upper East Side (2002)**	64,700	
2002	**Upper West Side (2002)**	59,400	
2002	**Chelsea-Clinton (2002)**	24,600	
2002	**Washington Heights (2002)**	8,800	
2002	**Other Manhattan (2002)**	11,900	
2002	**Manhattan Subtotal (2002)**		243,000
2002	**Fresh Meadows-Kew Garden Hills-Hillside (2002)**	28,200	
2002	**Northeast Queens (2002)**	24,100	
2002	**Rego Park-Forrest Hills (2002)**	39,100	
2002	**The Rockaways (2002)**	10,700	
2002	**Other Queens (2002)**	83,900	
2002	**Queens Subtotal (2002)**		186,000
2002	**Mid-Staten Island (2002)**	29,500	
2002	**Other Staten Island (2002)**	12,500	
2002	**Staten Island Subtotal (2002)**		42,000
2002	**East Meadow-Bellmore (2002)**	30,100	
2002	**Five Towns-Atlantic Beach (2002)**	41,400	
2002	**Great Neck (2002)**	47,900	
2002	**Northeast Nassau (2002)**	37,500	
2002	**South Shore (2002)**	25,200	
2002	**Other Nassau (2002)**	38,900	

State	Date of Informant Confirmation or Latest Study	Geographic Area*	Jewish Population	Regional Totals	Part-Year Jewish Population**
	2002	**Nassau County Subtotal (2002)**		221,000	
	2002	**Western Suffolk (2002)**	36,500		
	2002	**Central Suffolk (2002)**	34,200		
	2002	**Eastern Suffolk (2002)**	13,400		
	2002	**Other Suffolk (2002)**	5,900		
	2002	**Suffolk County Subtotal (2002)**		90,000	
	2002	**Southeastern Westchester (2002)**	21,900		
	2002	**Central-Southeastern Westchester (2002)**	56,800		
	2002	**Northern Westchester (2002)**	45,000		
	2002	**Other Westchester (2002)**	5,300		
	2002	**Westchester County Subtotal (2002)**		129,000	
	2002	**New York City Total (2002)**		972,000	
	2002	**New York (New York and Nassau, Suffolk, and Westchester Counties) Total (2002)**		1,412,000	
	1997-2001	Niagara Falls	150		
	1997-2001	Olean	100		
	1997-2001	Oneonta (Delaware and Otsego Counties)	300		
	1997-2001	Orange County (Middletown-Monroe-Newburgh-Port Jervis)	19,000		
	1997-2001	Plattsburgh	250		
	1997-2001	Potsdam	200		
	2007	Poughkeepsie (Dutchess County)	4,200		
	1997-2001	Putnam County	1,000		
	2008	**Brighton (1999)**	10,700		
	2008	**Pittsford (1999)**	3,100		
	2008	**Other areas of Monroe County and Victor in Ontario County (1999)**	7,250		
	2008	**Rochester Total (1999)**		21,050	

State	Date	Area	Population
	1997-2001	Rockland County	90,000
	1997-2001	Rome	100
	1997-2001	Saratoga Springs	600
	1997-2001	Schenectady	5,200
	pre-1997	Sullivan County (Liberty-Monticello)	7,425
	1997-2001	Syracuse (Onondaga County, western Madison County, and most of Oswego County)	9,000
	1997-2001	Troy area	800
	2007	Utica (southeastern Oneida County)	1,100
	1997-2001	Watertown	100
	1997-2001	Other places	600
		Total New York	1,617,720
NORTH CAROLINA			
	1997-2001	Asheville (Buncombe, Haywood, and Madison Counties)	1,300
	1997-2001	**Charlotte (Mecklenburg County) (1997)**	8,500
	2007	Durham-Chapel Hill (Durham and Orange Counties)	6,000
	1997-2001	Fayetteville (Cumberland County)	300
	1997-2001	Gastonia	210
	1997-2001	Greensboro-High Point (Guilford County)	2,500
	1997-2001	Greenville	240
	1997-2001	Hendersonville (Henderson County)	250
	1997-2001	Hickory	260
	1997-2001	Raleigh (Wake County)	6,000
	1997-2001	Southeastern North Carolina (Elizabethtown-Jacksonville-Whiteville-Wilmington)	1,200
	1997-2001	Winston-Salem	485
	1997-2001	Other places	500
		Total North Carolina	27,745
NORTH DAKOTA			
	2008	Fargo	150
	2008	Grand Forks	150
	1997-2001	Other places	100
		Total North Dakota	400

State	Date of Informant Confirmation or Latest Study	Geographic Area*	Jewish Population	Regional Totals	Part-Year Jewish Population**
OHIO	2006	**Akron-Kent (1999) (Portage and Summit Counties)*** **	3,500		
	pre-1997	Athens	100		
	2006	**Canton-New Philadelphia (Stark and Tuscarawas Counties) (1955)*** **	1,000		
	2008	**Downtown Cincinnati (2008)**	700		
	2008	**Hyde Park-Mount Lookout-Oakley (2008)**	3,100		
	2008	**Amberley Village-Golf Manor-Roselawn (2008)**	5,100		
	2008	**Blue Ash-Kenwood-Montgomery (2008)**	9,000		
	2008	**Loveland-Mason-Middletown (2008)**	5,500		
	2008	**Wyoming-Finneytown-Reading (2008)**	2,000		
	2008	**Other areas of Cincinnati (2008)**	1,300		
	2008	**Covington-Newport, Kentucky (2008)**	300		
	2008	**Cincinnati Total (2008)**		27,000	
	2006	**Inner Core (1996)**	24,200		
	2006	**Outer Core (1996)**	17,100		
	2006	**Northern Heights (1996)**	17,000		
	2006	**Northeast (1996)**	5,600		
	2006	**Southeast (1996)**	4,600		
	2006	**Cleveland Cuyahoga (1996)**	13,000		
	2006	**Cleveland (Cuyahoga and parts of Lake, Geauga, Portage, and Summit Counties) Total (1996)**		81,500	
	2001	**Perimeter North (2001)**	5,450		
	2001	**Bexley area (2001)**	6,800		
	2001	**East-Southeast (2001)**	3,550		
	2001	**North-Other areas (2001)**	6,200		
	2001	**Columbus Total (2001)**		22,000	
	1997-2001	Dayton (Greene and Montgomery Counties)	5,000		
	1997-2001	Elyria-Oberlin	155		
	1997-2001	Hamilton-Middletown-Oxford	900		

State	Date	Location	Population
	1997-2001	Lima (Allen County)	180
	pre-1997	Lorain	600
	1997-2001	Mansfield	150
	1997-2001	Marion	125
	1997-2001	Sandusky-Freemont-Norwalk (Huron and Sandusky Counties)	105
	1997-2001	Springfield	200
	1997-2001	Steubenville (Jefferson County)	115
	2006	**Toledo-Bowling Green (Fulton, Lucas, and Wood Counties) (1994)*** **	3,900
	1997-2001	Wooster	175
	1997-2001	**Youngstown-Warren (Mahoning and Trumbull Counties) (2002)*** **	2,300
	1997-2001	Zanesville (Muskingum County)	100
	1997-2001	Other Places	350
		Total Ohio	149,155
OKLAHOMA			
	1997-2001	Oklahoma City-Norman (Oklahoma and Cleveland Counties)	2,300
	1997-2001	Tulsa	2,650
	1997-2001	Other places	100
		Total Oklahoma	5,050
OREGON			
	1997-2001	Bend	500
	1997-2001	Corvallis	500
	1997-2001	Eugene	3,250
	1997-2001	Medford-Ashland-Grants Pass (Jackson and Josephine Counties)	1,000
	2007	Portland	25,500
	1997-2001	Salem (Marion and Polk Counties)	1,000
	1997-2001	Other places	100
		Total Oregon	31,850
PENNSYLVANIA			
	2007	Altoona (Blair County)	550
	1997-2001	Butler (Butler County)	250
	2007	**Carbon County (2007)*** **	600
	1997-2001	Chambersburg	150

State	Date of Informant Confirmation or Latest Study	Geographic Area*	Jewish Population	Regional Totals	Part-Year Jewish Population**
	1997-2001	Erie (Erie County)	850		
	1997-2001	**East Shore (1994)**	5,300		
	1997-2001	**West Shore (1994)**	1,800		
	1997-2001	**Harrisburg Total (1994)**		7,100	
	1997-2001	Beaver Falls (northern Beaver County)	180		
	1997-2001	Hazelton-Tamaqua	300		
	1997-2001	Johnstown (Cambria and Somerset Counties)	275		
	1997-2001	Lancaster area	3,000		
	1997-2001	Lebanon (Lebanon County)	350		
	2007	**Allentown (2007)**	5,950		
	2007	**Bethlehem (2007)**	1,050		
	2007	**Easton (2007)**	1,050		
	2007	**Lehigh Valley Total**		8,050	
	2008	**Monroe County (2007)*****	2,300		
	1997-2001	New Castle	200		
	1997-2001	Oil City	100		
	2006	**Bucks County (1997)**	34,800		
	2006	**Chester County (Oxford-Kennett Square-Phoenixville-West Chester) (1997)**	10,100		
	2006	**Delaware County (Chester-Coatesville) (1997)**	15,700		
	2006	**Montgomery County (Norristown) (1997)**	58,900		
	2006	**Philadelphia (1997)**	86,600		
	2006	**Philadelphia Total (1997)**		206,100	
	2008	Pike County	300		
	2002	**Squirrel Hill (2002)**	13,900		
	2002	**Squirrel Hill Adjacent Neighborhoods (2002)**	5,700		
	2002	**South Hills (2002)**	6,400		
	2002	**East Suburbs (2002)**	5,500		

State	Date	Area	Population	Total
	2002	**Fox Chapel-North Hills (2002)**	5,000	
	2002	**Western Suburbs (2002)**	1,600	
	2002	**East End (2002)**	1,700	
	2002	**Mon Valley (2002)**	800	
	2002	**Other Areas of Greater Pittsburgh (2002)**	1,600	
	2002	**Pittsburgh (Allegheny and parts of Washington, Westmoreland, and Beaver Counties) Total (2002)**		42,200
	1997-2001	Pottstown	650	
	1997-2001	Pottsville	120	
	1997-2001	Reading (Berks County)	2,200	
	2008	Scranton (Lackawanna County)	3,100	
	1997-2001	Sharon-Farrell	300	
	1997-2001	State College	700	
	1997-2001	Sunbury-Lewisburg-Milton-Selinsgrove-Shamokin	200	
	1997-2001	Uniontown area	150	
	2008	Wayne County (Honesdale)	500	
	1997-2001	Wilkes-Barre (Luzerne County, except Hazelton-Tamaqua)	3,000	
	1997-2001	Williamsport-Lock Haven (Clinton and Lycoming Counties)	225	
	1999-2001	**York (1999)**	1,800	
	1997-2001	Other places	900	
		Total Pennsylvania	286,700	
RHODE ISLAND				
	2007	**Providence-Pawtucket (2002)**	7,500	
	2007	**West Bay (2002)**	6,350	
	2007	**East Bay (2002)**	1,100	
	2007	**South County (Washington County) (2002)**	1,800	
	2007	**Northern Rhode Island (2002)**	1,000	
	2007	**Newport County (2002)**	1,000	
		Total Rhode Island	18,750	
SOUTH CAROLINA				
	1997-2001	Charleston	5,500	
	1997-2001	Columbia (Lexington and Richland Counties)	2,750	
	1997-2001	Florence area	220	

State	Date of Informant Confirmation or Latest Study	Geographic Area*	Jewish Population	Regional Totals	Part-Year Jewish Population**
	1997-2001	Greenville	1,200		
	1997-2001	Myrtle Beach-Georgetown (Georgetown and Horry Counties)	475		
	1997-2001	Rock Hill-York	100		
	1997-2001	Spartanburg (Spartanburg County)	500		
	1997-2001	Sumter-Kingstree (Clarendon, Lee, Sumter, and Williamsburg Counties)	140		
	1997-2001	Other places	450		
		Total South Carolina	11,335		
SOUTH DAKOTA					
	1997-2001	Sioux Falls	195		
	1997-2001	Other places	100		
		Total South Dakota	295		
TENNESSEE					
	2008	Bristol-Johnson City-Kingsport	200		
	2008	Chattanooga	1,400		
	2008	Knoxville	1,800		
	2006	**Memphis (2006)*** **	7,800		
	2008	**Nashville (2002)*** **	7,800		
	1997-2001	Oak Ridge	250		
	2008	Other places	100		
		Total Tennessee	19,350		
TEXAS					
	1997-2001	Amarillo (Carson, Childress, Deaf Smith, Gray, Hall, Hutchinson, Moore, Potter, and Randall Counties)	200		
	1997-2001	Austin (Travis County)	13,500		
	pre-1997	Baytown	300		
	1997-2001	Beaumont	500		
	1997-2001	Brownsville-Harlingen-South Padre Island (Cameron County)	450		

pre-1997	College Station-Bryan	400	
1997-2001	Corpus Christi (Nueces County)	1,400	
2006	**Near North Dallas (1988)**	12,300	
2006	**Far North Dallas-Richardson (1988)**	9,900	
2006	**East and Northeast Dallas-West Garland (1988)**	5,700	
2006	**Plano-Carrollton (1988)**	6,900	
2006	**Other areas of Dallas (1988)**	10,200	
2006	**Dallas Total (1988)**		45,000
1997-2001	El Paso	5,000	
1997-2001	Fort Worth (Tarrant County)	5,000	
1997-2001	Galveston	400	
2008	**Braeswood (1986)**	16,000	
2008	**Bellaire-Southwest (1986)**	5,100	
2008	**West Memorial (1986)**	5,000	
2008	**Memorial Villages (1986)**	2,500	
2008	**Rice-West University (1986)**	3,300	
2008	**University Park-South Main (1986)**	450	
2008	**Near Northwest (1986)**	2,700	
2008	**Northwest-Cypress Creek (1986)**	3,000	
2008	**Addicks-West Houston (1986)**	2,100	
2008	**Clear Lake (1986)**	1,350	
2008	**Other areas of Harris County (1986)**	3,500	
2008	**Houston (Harris, Montgomery, and Fort Bend Counties, and parts of Brazoria and Galveston Counties) Total (1986)**		45,000
1997-2001	Laredo	130	
1997-2001	Longview	100	
1997-2001	Lubbock (Lubbock County)	230	
1997-2001	McAllen (Hidalgo and Starr Counties)	500	
1997-2001	Midland-Odessa	200	
1997-2001	Port Arthur	100	
2007	**Inside Loop 410 (2007)**	2,000	
2007	**Between the Loops (2007)**	5,600	
2007	**Outside Loop 1604 (2007)**	1,600	
2007	**San Antonio Surrounding Counties (Atascosa, Bandera, Comal, Guadalupe, Kendall, Medina, and Wilson Counties) (2007)*** **	1,000	
2007	**San Antonio Total (2007)**		10,200

State	Date of Informant Confirmation or Latest Study	Geographic Area*	Jewish Population	Regional Totals	Part-Year Jewish Population**
	1997-2001	Tyler	400		
	1997-2001	Waco (Bell, Coryell, Falls, Hamilton, Hill, and McLennan Counties)	300		
	1997-2001	Wichita Falls	260		
	1997-2001	Other places	600		
		Total Texas	130,170		
UTAH					
	1997-2001	Ogden	150		
	1997-2001	Salt Lake City (Salt Lake County)	4,200		
	1997-2001	Other places	50		
		Total Utah	4,400		
VERMONT					
	1997-2001	Bennington area	500		
	2008	Brattleboro	350		
	1997-2001	Burlington	2,500		
	1997-2001	Manchester area	325		
	2008	Middlebury	200		
	2008	Montpelier-Barre	550		
	2008	Rutland	300		
	1997-2001	St. Johnsbury-Newport (Caledonia and Orleans County)	140		
	1997-2001	Stowe	150		
	pre-1997	Woodstock	270		
	1997-2001	Other places	100		
		Total Vermont	5,385		
VIRGINIA					
	1997-2001	Blacksburg-Radford	175		
	1997-2001	Charlottesville	1,500		

State	Date	Location	Population	Total
	1997-2001	Danville area	100	
	1997-2001	Fredericksburg (parts of Spotsylvania, Stafford, King George, and Orange Counties)	500	
	1997-2001	Lynchburg area	275	
	1997-2001	Martinsville	100	
	1997-2001	Newport News-Hampton-Williamsburg-James City-York County, and Poquoson City	2,400	
	2008	**Norfolk (2001)**	3,550	
	2008	**Virginia Beach (2001)**	6,000	
	2008	**Chesepeake-Portsmouth-Suffolk (2001)**	1,400	
	2008	**Norfolk-Virginia Beach Total (2001)**		10,950
	2003	**Arlington-Alexandria-Falls Church (2003)**	28,000	
	2003	**South Fairfax-Prince William County (2003)**	25,000	
	2003	**West Fairfax-Loudoun County (2003)**	14,500	
	2003	**Greater Washington Total in Northern Virginia (2003)**		67,500
	1997-2001	Petersburg-Colonial Heights	350	
	2006	**Central (1994)**	2,200	
	2006	**West End (1994)**	2,400	
	2006	**Far West End (1994)**	4,800	
	2006	**Northeast (1994)**	1,200	
	2006	**Southside (1994)**	1,900	
	2006	**Richmond (Henrico and Chesterfield Counties) Total (1994)**		12,500
	1997-2001	Roanoke	900	
	1997-2001	Staunton-Lexington (Augusta, Bath, Highland, Page, Rockingham, and Shenandoah Counties)	370	
	1997-2001	Winchester (Clarke, Frederick, Warren, and Winchester Counties)	270	
	1997-2001	Other places	150	
		Total Virginia	98,040	
WASHINGTON				
	1997-2001	Bellingham	525	
	1997-2001	Kennewick-Pasco-Richland	300	

State	Date of Informant Confirmation or Latest Study	Geographic Area*	Jewish Population	Regional Totals	Part-Year Jewish Population**
	1997-2001	Olympia (Thurston County)	560		
	pre-1997	Port Angeles	100		
	2000	**Eastside (2000)**	11,200		
	2000	**Seattle-Ship Canal South (2000)**	10,400		
	2000	**North End-North Suburbs (2000)**	12,600		
	2000	**Other Areas of Seattle (2000)**	3,000		
	2000	**Seattle (Kings County and parts of Snohomish and Kitsap Counties) Total (2000)**		37,200	
	1997-2001	Spokane	1,500		
	1997-2001	Tacoma (Pierce County)	2,000		
	1997-2001	Vancouver-Longview-Kelso	600		
	1997-2001	Yakima-Ellensburg (Kititas and Yakima Counties)	150		
	1997-2001	Other places	200		
		Total Washington	43,135		
WEST VIRGINIA					
	pre-1997	Bluefield-Princeton	200		
	2007	Charleston (Kanawha County)	975		
	1997-2001	Clarksburg	110		
	1997-2001	Huntington	250		
	1997-2001	Morgantown	200		
	pre-1997	Parkersburg	110		
	1997-2001	Wheeling	290		
	1997-2001	Other places	200		
		Total West Virginia	2,335		
WISCONSIN					
	1997-2001	Appleton area	100		
	1997-2001	Beloit-Janesville	120		

State	Date	Place	Population	Total
	1997-2001	Green Bay	500	
	1997-2001	Kenosha (Kenosha County)	300	
	1997-2001	La Crosse	100	
	2008	Madison (Dane County)	5,000	
	2006	**City of Milwaukee (1996)**	3,100	
	2006	**North Shore (1996)**	11,000	
	2006	**Mequon (1996)**	2,300	
	2006	**Metropolitan Ring (1996)**	4,700	
	2006	**Milwaukee (Milwaukee, eastern Waukesha, and southern Ozaukee Counties) Total (1996)**		21,100
	1997-2001	Oshkosh-Fond du Lac	170	
	1997-2001	Racine (Racine County)	200	
	1997-2001	Sheboygan	140	
	1997-2001	Wausau-Antigo-Marshfield-Stevens Point	300	
	1997-2001	Other places	300	
		Total Wisconsin	28,330	
WYOMING				
	1997-2001	Casper	150	
	2008	Cheyenne	300	
	2008	Jackson Hole	300	
	2008	Laramie	200	
	1997-2001	Other places	50	
		Total Wyoming	1,000	

TABLE 4: SYNAGOGUE MEMBERSHIP

Base: Jewish Households

Community	Year	%	Community	Year	%
Tidewater	2001	58%	Richmond	1994	45%
St. Paul	2004	56%	Atlantic County	2004	44%
Essex-Morris	1998	56%	New York	2002	43%
St. Louis	1995	56%	Rhode Island	2002	43%
Minneapolis	2004	54%	Chicago	2000	42%
Rochester	1999	54%	St. Petersburg	1994	40%
Pittsburgh	2002	53%	Miami	2004	39%
Hartford	2000	53%	Howard County	1999	38%
San Antonio	2007	52%	Washington	2003	37%
Baltimore	1999	52%	Philadelphia	1997	37%
Cleveland	1996	52%	Martin-St. Lucie	1999	36%
Lehigh Valley	2007	51%	Los Angeles	1997	34%
Detroit	2005	50%	Orlando	1993	34%
Bergen	2001	50%	Portland (ME)	2007	33%
Columbus	2001	50%	Atlanta	2006	33%
Jacksonville	2002	49%	South Palm Beach	2005	33%
Palm Springs	1998	49%	Denver	2007	32%
Charlotte	1997	49%	Tucson	2002	32%
Harrisburg	1994	49%	West Palm Beach	2005	30%
Monmouth	1997	48%	San Diego	2003	29%
Milwaukee	1996	48%	Phoenix	2002	29%
Westport	2000	46%	Broward	1997	27%
Wilmington	1995	46%	San Francisco	2004	22%
Sarasota	2001	45%	Seattle	2000	21%
York	1999	45%	Las Vegas	2005	14%

TABLE 5: MEMBERSHIP IN THE LOCAL JEWISH COMMUNITY CENTER

Base: Jewish Households

Community	Year	%	Community	Year	%
St. Paul	2004	36%	Atlanta	2006	10%
Charlotte	1997	36%	Miami (Russell)*	2004	10%
Harrisburg	1994	31%	Washington (DCJCC)*	2003	10%
San Antonio	2007	29%	Rhode Island	2002	10%
Rochester	1999	28%	Bergen (YJCC)*	2001	10%
York	1999	27%	St. Petersburg	1994	10%
Monmouth (Deal)*	1997	27%	Philadelphia	1997	8%
Jacksonville	2002	26%	W Palm Beach (Kaplan)*	2005	7%
Cleveland	1996	24%			
Milwaukee	1996	24%	Broward (Posnack)*	1997	6%
St. Louis	1995	24%	W Palm Beach (Boynton)*	2005	5%
Richmond	1994	24%			
Pittsburgh	2002	23%	Miami (Miami Beach)*†	2004	5%
Wilmington	1995	23%			
Hartford	2000	22%	Washington (NOVA)*	2003	5%
Bergen (Palisades)*	2001	21%	Seattle	2000	5%
Tidewater	2001	19%	Monmouth (Western)*†	1997	5%
Lehigh Valley	2007	18%			
Minneapolis	2004	17%	South Palm Beach	2005	4%
Tucson	2002	17%	Las Vegas†	2005	3%
Orlando	1993	17%	Westport[1]	2000	1%
Detroit	2005	15%	Broward (Soref)*	1997	1%
Atlantic County	2004	14%			
New York	2002	14%	Total in Communities with 2+ JCCs		
Miami (Alper)*	2004	13%	Bergen	2001	18%
San Francisco	2004	13%	Monmouth	1997	13%
Sarasota	2001	12%	Miami	2004	11%
Washington (Gr. Wash)*	2003	11%	Washington	2003	9%
			West Palm Beach	2005	7%
Los Angeles	1997	11%	Broward	1997	4%

*In communities with more than one JCC and where data are available for each JCC, results reflect only the membership of households who live in the service area of each JCC.
†JCC is not a full service facility.
[1]Membership is in JCCs in neighboring communities, since there is no local JCC.

TABLE 6: KEEP KOSHER

Base: Respondents

Community	Year	Total In Home	In Home Only	In and Out of Home
Bergen	2001	29%	11%	18
New York†	2002	28%	NA	NA
Monmouth	1997	26%	15%	11
Harrisburg	1994	23%	15%	8
Detroit	2005	22%	8%	14
Miami	2004	22%	10%	12
Baltimore†	1999	22%	NA	NA
Essex-Morris†	1998	22%	NA	NA
Rochester	1999	20%	13%	8
Pittsburgh†	2002	19%	NA	NA
Cleveland†	1996	18%	NA	NA
Philadelphia	1997	17%	9%	8
Hartford	2000	17%	11%	6
Buffalo†	1995	17%	NA	NA
Rhode Island	2002	16%	8%	8
Broward	1997	16%	11%	5
St. Paul	2004	14%	6%	9
South Palm Beach	2005	14%	9%	5
Howard County†	1999	14%	NA	NA
Minneapolis	2004	13%	7%	6
York	1999	13%	8%	6
Milwaukee	1996	13%	8%	5
Denver†	2007	13%	NA	NA
Atlanta†	2006	13%	NA	NA
Columbus*	2001	13%	NA	NA
Palm Springs†	1998	13%	NA	NA
Washington	2003	12%	5%	7
Wilmington	1995	12%	7%	5
Tucson	2002	11%	5%	6
Lehigh Valley	2007	11%	5%	5
Los Angeles†	1997	11%	NA	NA
San Antonio	2007	10%	4%	5
Jacksonville	2002	10%	5%	5
Tidewater	2001	10%	5%	5
Atlantic County	2004	10%	6%	4
St. Petersburg	1994	10%	6%	4
Richmond	1994	10%	6%	3
Boston[1]	2005	10%	NA	NA
West Palm Beach	2005	9%	6%	3
Orlando	1993	9%	6%	3
Phoenix†	2002	9%	NA	NA

TABLE 6 Continued

Base: Respondents				
Community	Year	Total In Home	In Home Only	In and Out of Home
St. Louis*	1995	9%	NA	NA
Charlotte	1997	8%	5%	3
San Diego†	2003	8%	NA	NA
Sarasota	2001	6%	4%	3
Westport	2000	6%	4%	1
Las Vegas	2005	5%	3%	3
Seattle†	2000	5%	NA	NA
Portland (ME)	2007	3%	1%	3

*Question was only asked about keeping two sets of dishes in the home.
†Question was only asked about keeping kosher in the home.
[1]Question was only asked about following Jewish dietary laws in the home.

TABLE 7: HOME HEALTH CARE FOR THE ELDERLY IN THE PAST YEAR

Base: Jewish Households with Elderly Persons

Community	Year	Total Who Needed In-Home Health Care	Received Jewish In-Home Health Care	Received Other In-Home Health Care	No In-Home Health Care Received
Miami	2004	18.5%	2.0%	14.5	2.0
Jacksonville	2002	18.0%	0.0%	16.7	1.3
Minneapolis	2004	17.2%	2.8%	13.0	1.4
Monmouth	1997	16.7%	0.0%	14.3	2.4
San Antonio	2007	16.5%	0.6%	15.6	0.3
Rochester	1999	16.2%	0.9%	14.2	1.1
Wilmington	1995	16.2%	0.0%	16.2	0.0
St. Paul	2004	16.1%	2.0%	14.1	0.0
Lehigh Valley	2007	16.0%	1.1%	14.9	0.0
Rhode Island	2002	15.3%	2.3%	12.6	0.4
Broward	1997	15.1%	0.3%	13.4	1.4
South Palm Beach	2005	15.0%	0.7%	13.6	0.7
York	1999	15.0%	0.0%	14.4	0.6
West Palm Beach	2005	14.7%	1.0%	13.1	0.6
Hartford	2000	14.2%	2.3%	11.4	0.5
Detroit	2005	14.0%	2.3%	11.1	0.6
Milwaukee	1996	13.6%	1.2%	11.2	1.2
Tucson	2002	13.1%	0.7%	9.9	2.5
Portland (ME)	2007	12.8%	0.0%	9.9	2.9
Bergen	2001	12.0%	0.0%	11.4	0.6
Atlantic County	2004	11.7%	0.3%	10.8	0.6
Las Vegas	2005	10.9%	0.2%	9.4	1.3
Richmond	1994	10.9%	1.6%	8.5	0.8
St. Petersburg	1994	10.5%	0.4%	10.1	0.0
Sarasota	2001	10.1%	0.0%	10.1	0.0
Westport	2000	9.3%	0.0%	9.3	0.0
St. Louis	1995	9.0%	9.0%	NA	NA
Washington	2003	8.5%	1.5%	7.0	0.0
Tidewater	2001	8.5%	4.2%	3.6	0.7
Harrisburg	1994	8.1%	1.1%	6.7	0.3
San Francisco	2004	8.0%	2.0%	5.0	1.0
Charlotte	1997	6.0%	0.0%	6.0	0.0

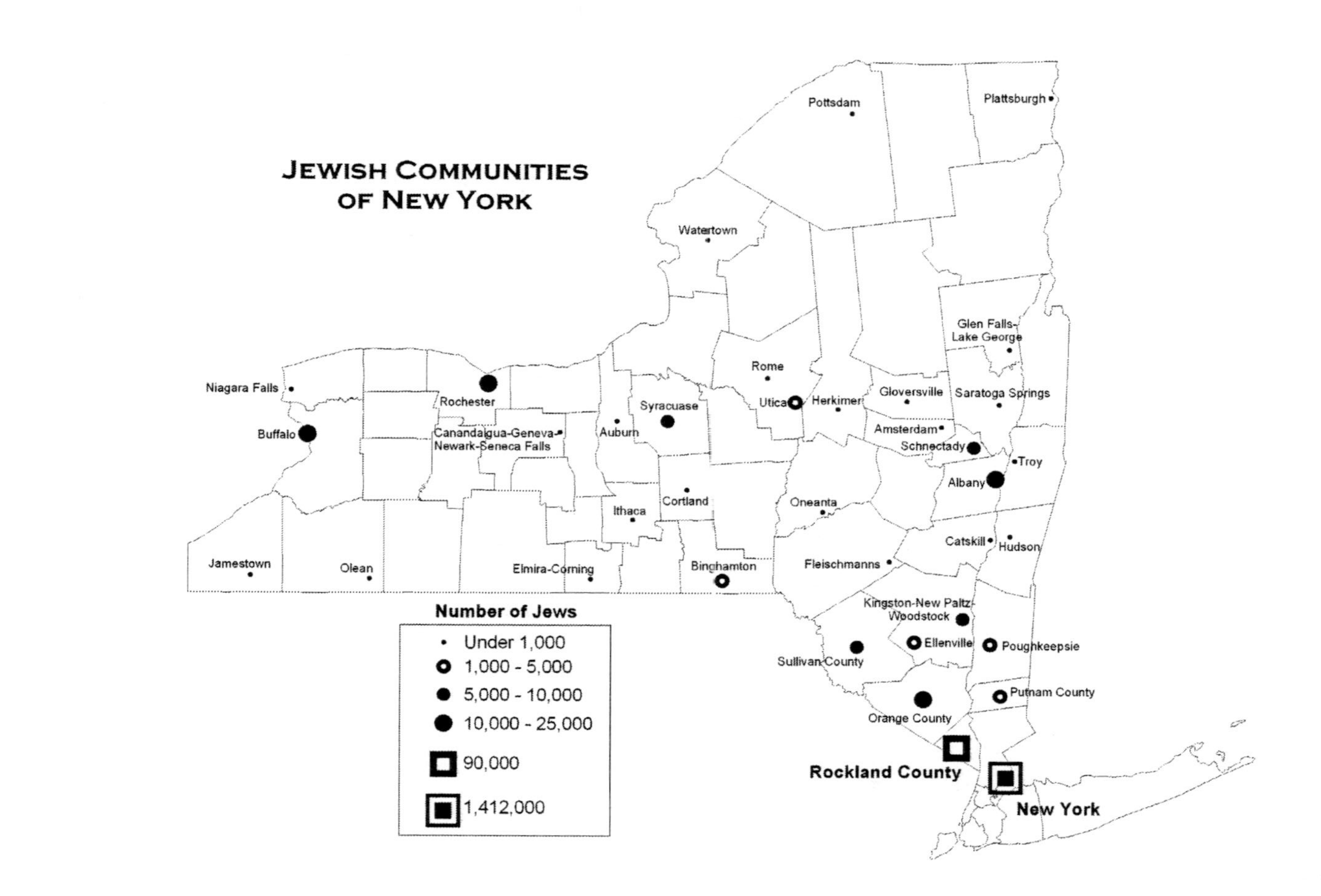
JEWISH COMMUNITIES OF NEW YORK
Pottsdam
Plattsburgh
Watertown
Glen Falls-Lake George
Rome
Niagara Falls
Rochester
Syracuase
Utica
Herkimer
Gloversville
Saratoga Springs
Buffalo
Canandaigua-Geneva-Newark-Seneca Falls
Auburn
Amsterdam
Schnectady
Troy
Albany
Cortland
Oneanta
Ithaca
Catskill
Hudson
Jamestown
Olean
Elmira-Corning
Binghamton
Fleischmanns
Kingston-New Paltz-Woodstock
Ellenville
Poughkeepsie
Sullivan County
Putnam County
Orange County
Rockland County
New York
Number of Jews
Under 1,000
1,000 - 5,000
5,000 - 10,000
10,000 - 25,000
90,000
1,412,000

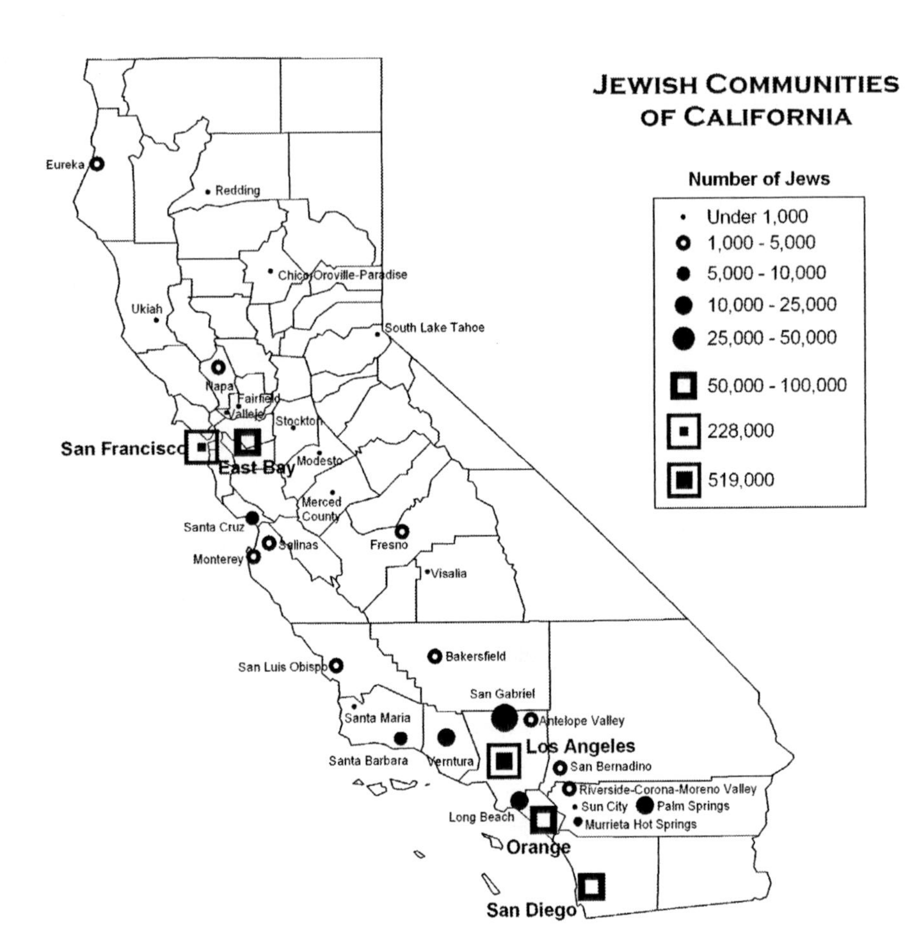

JEWISH COMMUNITIES OF CALIFORNIA
Number of Jews
Under 1,000
1,000 - 5,000
5,000 - 10,000
10,000 - 25,000
25,000 - 50,000
50,000 - 100,000
228,000
519,000
Eureka
Redding
Chico
Oroville-Paradise
Ukiah
South Lake Tahoe
Napa
Fairfield
Vallejo
Stockton
San Francisco
East Bay
Modesto
Merced County
Santa Cruz
Salinas
Fresno
Monterey
Visalia
Bakersfield
San Luis Obispo
San Gabriel
Santa Maria
Antelope Valley
Los Angeles
Santa Barbara
Verntura
San Bernadino
Riverside-Corona-Moreno Valley
Sun City
Palm Springs
Long Beach
Murrieta Hot Springs
Orange
San Diego

Review of the Year

OTHER COUNTRIES

Israel

TWO WATERSHED EVENTS that occurred the year before—the Hamas victory in the Palestinian Authority elections and the disappointing and inconclusive war in Lebanon—deeply influenced Israeli life during 2007. Hamas took over Gaza through a bloody coup in June, the intermittent barrage of rockets from Gaza into southern Israel intensified, and few were optimistic about a new U.S.-sponsored round of Israeli-Palestinian peace talks that began in December. Meanwhile, Israel's already strife-torn internal politics were further embittered by investigations into the decision to fight in Lebanon and how the war was conducted—and these did not even touch upon the financial and sexual scandals, both proven and rumored, that implicated a number of the country's top leaders. Despite several reports that turned out to be false, no progress was made on obtaining the release, or even reliable information about, the three Israeli solders kidnapped in 2006, Gilad Shalit, taken near Gaza, and Eldad Regev and Ehud Goldwasser, abducted near the northern border.

The bright spots for Israel during 2007 also grew out of policies conceived earlier. With the exception of residents of the towns near Gaza subject to bombardment, ordinary Israelis had never been more physically secure, as precautionary measures and the security barrier in the West Bank drastically reduced the number of suicide bombings and other attacks. Also, Israel's economy continued the impressive performance powered by its industrial sector, especially high-tech.

Looming over Israel's future was the ongoing threat of a potential Iranian nuclear capacity in the hands of a regime that made no secret of its intention to wipe Israel off the map. Israel's bombing and dismantling, in September, of what was apparently a nuclear facility in Syria underlined the danger posed by Iran, whose installations was far less susceptible to Israeli attack.

SECURITY AND DIPLOMACY

A Year of Tensions and Disappointments

JANUARY: PEACE FEELERS

Israel began easing restrictions on Palestinian movement in the West Bank on January 1, in fulfillment of a promise Prime Minister Ehud Olmert made to PA president Mahmoud Abbas at a meeting on December 24, 2006. By mid-January Olmert said that 44 of the 160 West Bank roadblocks had been removed and that this was only the first stage. He also pledged that the waiting time for Palestinian trucks to pass through checkpoints would be streamlined from an average of 40 minutes to 15.

Egyptian president Hosni Mubarak, meeting with Olmert in the Sinai town of Sharm al-Sheikh on January 5, reiterated Egypt's longstanding position that the Middle East should be free of all unconventional weapons—including those of a biological and chemical nature as well as nuclear bombs—but suggested nonetheless that Egypt might have to seek a nuclear capacity. "We don't want nuclear weapons, but since they appear highly present in the region, we must defend ourselves," he said, clearly referring to Iran. Olmert, for his part, voiced the traditional Israeli view that the Jewish state would not be the first to introduce nuclear weapons to the area, but added that Iran's intention to obtain such arms and use them was "cause for concern" to Israel, Egypt, other regional states, and Europe.

Olmert paid a visit to China on January 9–11 to mark the 15th anniversary of relations between the two countries. He met with President Hu Jintao and other top officials in Beijing and attended a gala concert featuring Israeli singer David D'Or, famed for his falsetto voice, and Chinese singers Yao Hong and Wang Haitao. This was the third visit by an Israeli prime minister since relations were established in 1992.

Al Qaeda had sent "dozens, if not hundreds" of terror operatives to the countries surrounding Israel, Maj.-Gen. Amos Yadlin, chief of Military Intelligence, told the Knesset Foreign Affairs and Defense Committee on January 9. In addition to Syria, Lebanon, Jordan, and Egypt, Yadlin said that a handful of agents had been sent to the Gaza Strip as part of an Al Qaeda directive to deploy in the area.

Hamas responded with threats of assassination to Abbas's declaration in early January banning six Hamas-linked security organizations. Referring to the PA president as "the president of the Oslo Authority," Hamas announced on January 8 that it held him "responsible for every drop of blood that will be shed by our kinsmen because of his decision . . . ." Abbas indeed narrowly escaped an attempt on his life, according to a January 28 report on the Website of *Yediot Aharonot*. The attempt had occurred near Ramallah the previous week as Abbas was on his way to meet Hamas prime minister Ismail Haniyeh for discussions about forming a unity government: roadside explosives were detonated by Abbas's presidential guard and the convoy of vehicles was diverted back to Ramallah. The negotiations for a unity government stalled and the confrontation between Hamas and Fatah forces in Gaza continued. Some 20 people were reported killed and 66 wounded in clashes on January 26–27.

U.S. secretary of state Condoleezza Rice toured the region for five days in mid-January, in the course of which she met with Prime Minister Olmert, Foreign Minister Tzipi Livni, and Defense Minister Amir Peretz, as well as PA president Abbas. En route to Israel she told reporters on the plane, "I'm not coming with a plan. I don't think a plan can be made in America."

Three Israelis—Michael Ben Sa'adon, 27, Emil Elmaliyah, 32, and Israel Samoliya, 26—were killed and dozens more wounded in a January 29 suicide bombing outside a bakery in the Izidor neighborhood of Eilat, the first terror bombing in the history of the Red Sea resort city. A higher toll was apparently averted when Lt. Col. Yossi Woltinsky became suspicious of a hitchhiker he had picked up on the assumption that the man worked in one of Eilat's hotels, and dropped him off on the outskirts of town rather than in the center.

February: Toward PA Unity

In early February, Defense Minister Peretz announced the choice of Iron Dome, built by the government-owned firm Rafael Arms Development Authority Ltd., as Israel's defense against short-range rockets. The decision followed several months of deliberations occasioned by the intermittent rain of Palestinian Qassam rockets and mortar fire on Israeli towns and villages in the area near the Gaza Strip. Development was expected to take about three years: Rafael would develop projectiles to intercept incoming rockets and the control system to fire them, while the Elta subsidiary of the government-owned Israel Aerospace Industries (formerly called Israel Aircraft Industries) would refine the radar system. Peretz, criticizing his predecessors for failing to move more quickly, announced that the system would be installed first in the border town of Sderot. The cabinet had allocated NIS 811 million (about $200 million) for the first stage of development the previous December.

The foreign ministers of the Quartet (U.S., UN, EU, and Russia) met in New York on February 2. Rice, German foreign minister Frank-Walter Steinmeier, Russian foreign minister Sergei Lavrov, and UN secretary general Ban Ki-moon agreed on the primacy of the "road map" in the peace process, reviewed and reaffirmed the conditions under which aid would be given to the PA, and differed over the prospects for talks with Syria.

Violence between Fatah and Hamas accelerated the very day of that meeting as Hamas gunmen blew up the Fatah-affiliated Voice of Labor radio station in the Gaza Strip, pulling down the Palestinian flag after conquering the building and raising the Hamas green banner. And on the other side, between five and eight Iranian student collaborators with Hamas were reportedly arrested in a raid by Fatah-controlled national security police on the Islamic University in Gaza, and hundreds of weapons, as well as a lathe used to manufacture Qassam rockets, were said to have been seized. Fighting spilled over to the Gaza beachfront over the next few days, terrifying local residents. One man, who lived in a building that Hamas threatened to blow up unless Fatah men fortified inside surrendered, asked the Associated Press: "Who will protect us? What is our fault? We are neither Fatah nor Hamas." AP reported that more than 70 people had been killed on both sides since fighting erupted in December 2006.

An IDF patrol on the northern border found four bombs, disguised as boulders for "safe-keeping" and placed on the Israeli side of the border with the clear intention of hitting Israeli frontier patrols, on February 6. The Defense Ministry protested to UN forces policing the cease-fire there about this "severe incident."

PA president Abbas and Damascus-based Hamas leader Khaled Mashal met with King Abdullah of Saudi Arabia in Mecca on February 7 in a last-ditch effort to reach an agreement on a Palestinian unity government and a truce that would quell spiraling internecine violence in Gaza. Over the previous weekend at least 27 people were killed in fighting between Fatah and Hamas in the Strip. The Saudi-brokered agreement that emerged—which did not provide for recognition of Israel—gave Hamas an 11-8 edge in cabinet positions and allocated four ministries to other Palestinian parties; directed that disputes between the two sides would be solved by peaceful means rather than violence; sought to speed internal reforms within the Palestine Liberation Organization; and made Hamas, for the first time, a member of the PLO. (The unity government would be sworn in March 17.)

Olmert, Abbas, and Rice met in Jerusalem on February 19, and afterward issued a statement declaring that the Israeli and PA leaders "reiterated their acceptance of previous agreements and obligations," including the "road map." Rice added that those leaders welcomed U.S. participation "to overcome obstacles, rally regional and international support, and move forward toward peace." While the American had no comment on the Mecca agreement, Livni told reporters that the provisions "do not meet the requirements of the international community." Robert Satloff, executive director of the Washington Institute for Near East Policy think tank, commenting on the Saudi-sponsored plan, said: "nothing in the accord can be viewed as addressing the first two of the Quartet's conditions [recognition of Israel and renunciation of violence] and only through a tortuous interpretation of the final clause can even a loose connection be made to the third condition [accepting previous Israeli-Palestinian agreements]." It only asked Hamas to "respect" unspecified Palestinian and Arab commitments and UN resolutions.

Three days later Hamas's Izz al-Din al-Qassam Brigades called for an end to the cease-fire with Israel that had been declared the previous November (see AJYB 2007, p. 236). What provoked this first open disavowal by a Hamas body of the three-month lull in hostilities was the killing by Israeli forces of Mahmoud Qassem, a West Bank Islamic Jihad commander linked to a failed suicide-bomb attack in Tel Aviv.

Jerusalem quickly became a flashpoint for violence after Israeli authorities approved construction of a new ramp providing access from the Mughrabi Gate to the Temple Mount, to replace the earthen ramp that collapsed in 2005. This gate was the nearest on the Mount to Al-Aqsa, the third holiest site in Islam. Under Israeli law a "salvage dig" was required to precede any construction in the Old City of Jerusalem, and the onset of the digging in early February triggered several days of riots by Palestinian and Israeli Arabs. Violence peaked after Israeli police stormed the Mount in a move that Israel explained as intended to prevent rioters from stoning Jews worshiping at the Western Wall below. Dismissing Israeli claims that repairs to the area were necessary to guarantee access to the Muslim holy site, Arab League secretary general Amr Moussa charged on February 11 that the digging signified Israel's intention to tighten its control over Jerusalem. Moussa, a former Egyptian foreign minister, called on the international community to stop the work. At the same time the Islamic Action Front, the largest opposition group in Jordan, called for jihad, holy war, to "liberate" Al-Aqsa and "save it from destruction and sabotage by Jewish usurpers. The mayor of Jerusalem announced a moratorium on the project. On February 15, during a visit to Turkey, Prime Minister Olmert spoke to his Turkish counterpart, Recep Tayyip Erdoğan, about having Turkey, a Muslim country that had relations with Israel, send in a team to inspect the site and report on the project. Olmert said that Israel "has nothing to hide." During the visit, however, Muslim protesters denounced Olmert as a "murderer."

Erez Levanon, 42, of Bat Ayin in the Gush Etzion bloc near Bethlehem, was killed by terrorists on February 25. His body was found in an alleyway in Beit Omar, a Palestinian village north of Hebron. Islamic Jihad claimed credit for the killing, saying that two members of its al-Quds Brigades lured Levanon into an agricultural area and stabbed him to death. The next day the Shin Bet arrested two Palestinian teenagers who said they had attacked and killed Levanon while he was praying. The Shin Bet believed that the youths were acting on their own and not as part of any Palestinian group. That same day 25 Palestinians were arrested in a large-scale IDF operation in the city of Nablus, on the northern West Bank. Troops closed the entrance to the city and placed about 50,000 civilians under curfew during the operation.

March: The Saudi Plan Revived

National Infrastructure Minister Binyamin Ben-Eliezer postponed an early March trip to Cairo after a furor in the Egyptian press over claims, in an Israel documentary film, that troops under his command had killed as many as 250 Egyptian prisoners during the 1967 Six-Day War. A spokesman for Ben-Eliezer said the claims were entirely false. Ran Edelist, the film's producer, said the film actually portrayed members of a Palestinian commando battalion killed in the heat of battle, and was distorted by the Egyptian press.

Eighteen wanted Al-Aqsa Martyrs Brigades and Fatah fugitives were taken into custody in a March 7 IDF raid into Ramallah. The terrorists, who had taken shelter in a Palestinian intelligence service compound, were accused of perpetrating dozens of attacks on Israeli soldiers and civilians.

Olmert and Abbas had a meeting scheduled for March 11 in Jerusalem. Ignoring advice from two Likud Knesset members—former foreign minister Silvan Shalom and Yuval Steinitz, former head of the Knesset Foreign Affairs and Defense Committee—to call the meeting off because it was pointless, Olmert did attend the session with Abbas, who raised the 2002 Saudi initiative, adopted by the Arab League, which offered full diplomatic relations with Israel in exchange for full Israeli withdrawal from the territories captured in 1967, the creation of a Palestinian state with East Jerusalem as its capital, and a "just solution" to the Palestinian refugee problem. Earlier, the Israeli prime minister had called that initiative "an issue that we would be willing to take seriously."

The Israeli Supreme Court on March 13 rejected petitions by six human rights groups to open border crossings into Gaza so as to facilitate the flow of humanitarian aid into the Strip. In expressing the court's view, its president, Dorit Beinish, said that changes in the security situation had made border closure permissible. Beinish said she was convinced the army was doing its best to ensure that all the crossings closed after the 2006 kidnapping of soldier Gilad Shalit would to be opened whenever feasible.

On March 20, three days after the official formation of the Palestinian unity government, the Israeli Foreign Ministry called off a scheduled meeting with Norwegian deputy foreign minister Raymond Johansen. The day before Johansen was in Gaza to meet PA prime minister Ismail Haniyeh, thus becoming the first Western dignitary to meet formally with Hamas officials since the formation of the PA unity government.

Olmert's office refused, on March 25, to comment on reports that the prime minister had met some months earlier with a senior Saudi official. Citing Arab sources, *Ha'aretz* identified the official as Prince Bandar bin Sultan, the Saudi national security adviser, and said that the two had met in Jordan. Another indication of Saudi involvement came from UN secretary general Ban Ki-moon, who, arriving for a visit to Israel and the PA, said that he saw a determination in the Arab world to restart the Saudi/Arab League peace initiative. In a March 30 interview with the *Jerusalem Post,* Olmert called Saudi king Abdullah "a remarkable leader" and noted that the initiative he launched while serving as foreign minister in 2002 "was very interesting."

Meanwhile, the *Yediot Aharonot* Website reported on March 28 that Saudi, Israeli, and American diplomats had been holding secret talks in Washington in an attempt to work out a financial compensation plan for Palestinian refugees that would preempt their demand for a "right of return" to homes and property lost in Israel's 1948 War of Independence. According to the report, Palestinians would only be allowed to return to a Palestinian state, not to Israel.

An Arab League summit held March 29 in Riyadh unanimously passed a resolution calling for reaffirmation of the 2002 Saudi initiative by all Arab states, and Javier Solana, the European Union foreign policy chief who was a guest at the summit, called it a basis for further negotiations. In an interview with London's *Daily Telegraph* a day before the summit, Prince Saud al-Faisal, the Saudi foreign minister, said that the Arab world had now done "what we have the power to do," and that now "it is up to the other side, because if you want peace, it is not enough for one side only to want it. Both sides must want it equally." The prince cast the entire blame for not achieving peace on Israel. "It has never been proven that reaching out to Israel achieves anything," he told the British newspaper. "Other Arab countries have recognized Israel and what has that achieved? The largest Arab country, Egypt, recognized Israel and what was the result? Not one iota of change happened in the attitude of Israel towards peace."

Other diplomatic activity proceeded as well. Secretary of State Rice, in Jerusalem on March 27 as part of another Middle East tour, said that Olmert and Abbas had agreed to meet every two weeks to discuss PA-Israeli issues and to map out a "political horizon," even though the two leaders were "not yet at final-status negotiations." German chancellor Angela Merkel was in the region in late March and early April. In addition to talks with top Israeli leaders, Merkel met with the families of the missing Israel soldiers. And in Ramallah, Palestinian officials, according to the *Jerusalem Post,* said her talks with Abbas focused on efforts to release Gilad Shalit, held in Gaza since the preceding June. A Palestinian official complained that Merkel "appeared to be obsessed" with the Shalit case "but refused to even acknowledge the fact that we have more than 10,000 prisoners in Israel."

Israeli forces attacked targets in the Gaza Strip on March 29, ending the policy of restraint exercised there since the November 2006 cease-fire. The reported target was a Qassam rocket-launching cell that was about to fire into Israel.

April: A Message to Syria?

Speaker of the House Nancy Pelosi, after a trip to Israel, met with Syrian president Assad in Damascus on April 5. She later told reporters that she and the other members of a congressional delegation "were very pleased" with Assad's assurance that he was ready to resume negotiations with Israel. She added that the group had also raised the subject of the three kidnapped Israeli soldiers. Syrian information minister Muhsen Bilal told the reporters accompanying Pelosi that Israel needed to prove that it was serious about peace and "declare this in a clear manner."

The next day the Prime Minister's Office in Jerusalem strongly denied a report that Pelosi had carried a secret message from Olmert to Assad. The prime minister, in fact, was caught in the thicket of American politics, as the Bush administration was strongly critical of the visit of Pelosi, a Democrat, at a time that the Republican president was imposing a diplomatic freeze on Syria. The Prime Minister's Office was quoted by *Ha'aretz* as saying, "Pelosi took part of the things that were said at the meeting [with Olmert] and used what suited her," and that "we have not intervened in the internal debate in the United States, and we did not harm anyone."

Whether or not Pelosi had been carrying a message from Olmert, Israeli-Syrian relations showed no signs of easing. Division-strength maneuvers simulating a possible conflict with Syria, perhaps involving a surprise attack by Damascus, were staged in the Judean Desert in April, according to a report in the *Jerusalem Post.* The war games involved hundreds of tanks and thousands of soldiers, with air support from helicopters and UAVs (unmanned aerial vehicles).

On April 18–19, U.S. defense secretary Robert Gates met with Prime Minister Olmert, Foreign Minister Livni, and Defense Minister Peretz. This was the first visit by a senior Pentagon official to Israel in eight years.

Hamas launched a major barrage of Qassam rockets and mortars against Israel on April 24; military sources said that ten Qassams and 12 mortar shells fell on Israeli territory, causing no damage or injuries. Israel believed that this attack was intended as "cover" for an attempt to kidnap another Israeli soldier, similar to the June 2006 snatching of Gilad Shalit.

May: Sderot under Fire

Early May brought more diplomatic activity on the Syrian front. Secretary of State Rice met with Syrian foreign minister Walid al-Muallem for 30 minutes on May 3, during an international conference at Sharm al-Sheikh designed to muster support for U.S. policy in Iraq. The meeting, according to Rice, was "professional . . . I didn't lecture him and he didn't lecture me." The Syrian asked the U.S. to return its ambassador, withdrawn two years earlier, to Damascus. "We hope the Americans are serious because we in Damascus are serious about improving relations with America," Muallem said. The U.S. position was that normalized relations would come only after Syria stopped allowing jihadists to cross its border into Lebanon, cut its ties with Iran and Hezballah, and closed the headquarters that terror organizations like Hamas and Islamic Jihad maintained in Damascus.

Rice, on May 8, said she was postponing a scheduled May 15 visit to Israel, part of a still-planned Middle East swing. State Department spokesman Sean McCormack said the postponement was necessary because "the political situation in Israel has become a bit more complex in the near term," a clear reference to the interim report of the Winograd Commission investigating the 2006 war in Lebanon and a possible political crisis in the Olmert government (see below, pp. 274–75).

A World Bank report issued on May 9 suggested that Israeli security measures were preventing a Palestinian economic recovery. "The system has created such a high level of uncertainty and inefficiency that normal conduct of business in the West Bank has been stymied," said David Craig, World Bank director for Israel and the PA. "Restoring sustainable Palestinian economic growth is dependent on its dismantling." Rejecting Craig's claim, Israeli Foreign Ministry spokesman Mark Regev said Israel "has no interest whatsoever in seeing a failed Palestinian economy." He suggested that the PA's economic problems were largely due to terrorism, violence, instability, "and the overall anarchy that exists." Meanwhile factional violence between Hamas and Fatah in Gaza escalated, and on May 14 PA interior minister Hani Kawasmeh, who was responsible for trying to calm the situation, resigned in frustration.

During a visit to Sderot by Olmert and Peretz on May 18, the *Tzeva Adom* (Color Red) alarm for incoming rockets was sounded and the two leaders took cover. Less than an hour after their departure a rocket hit a synagogue in the town. There were no injuries because all of the approximately 300 people attending a Torah scroll dedication there had already left. "If people had not gone home, many would have been killed," one resident told *Yediot Aharonot,* "God rescued us."

Seeking to stop such attacks on Israeli towns near the Gaza Strip, the security cabinet on May 20 voted to "intensify operational measures," meaning the resumption of targeted killings. National Infrastructure Minister Ben-Eliezer said that targets might include Hamas politicians as well as military commanders. "I don't distinguish between those who carry out the attacks and those who give the orders. I say we have to put them all in the cross-hairs," he told Israel Radio. And a few hours later, a rocket attack on the Gaza home of Khalil al-Haya, a Hamas member of the Palestinian National Assembly, killed eight people, seven of them members of al-Haya's family. Hamas responded by saying that now it would target Israeli politicians.

Defense Minister Peretz declared a "special home-front situation" for the Sderot area, a change of status that could help residents obtain government compensation for property and income lost because of attacks from Gaza. But Qassam fire continued on Sderot, taking a toll of about 20 hits a day. On May 21, Shirel Friedman, 32, was killed when a Palestinian rocket hit a car near a bakery in the commercial area of Sderot, and on May 27, Oshri Oz, a 36-year-old computer technician from Hod Hasharon in the center of the country who was visiting Sderot as part of his job, was killed by a Qassam that hit near his car.

In the Jerusalem area, two Palestinians were killed by security men after they opened fire on a routine patrol in the village of Sheikh Said, near the Jewish neighborhood of Armon Hanatziv on the southeastern edge of the city, on May 27.

Khaled Shawish, a senior commander of the Fatah-linked Al-Aqsa Martyrs Brigade, was arrested by Israeli security forces in Ramallah on May 28. Shawish, who was reportedly responsible for killing Binyamin Ze'ev Kahane, son of the late Meir Kahane, and his wife, Talia, in 2000, was arrested in the parking lot of the Muqata government complex, not far from Yasir Arafat's grave.

Fatah, on May 29, accepted an Egyptian proposal for a Cairo meeting with Hamas in an effort to put a halt to the internal bloodshed between the two groups. At about the same time, the office of PA president Abbas said that he would meet the following week with Prime Minister Olmert. The two men had last met in April.

The next day the Israeli cabinet turned down feelers from Hamas about a possible cease-fire deal. A statement from the Prime Minister's Office said that Israel "is not conducting any negotiations with a terrorist organization," and that "attacks and military pressure on terror groups, mainly Hamas and Islamic Jihad," would continue. Some in the Israeli government felt that even this was not enough. Strategic Affairs Minister Avigdor Lieberman proposed dealing with the Qassam problem by declaring Gaza "a hostile entity." He explained: "Gaza will be isolated from Israel and the West Bank. There will be no safe passage between the two Palestinian entities—not for goods, not for people, not for Abbas. Israel will complete the disengagement from Gaza by gradually cutting all ties—including the supply of water and electricity, trade, taxes, and so forth." He urged that Israel regard Gaza—at that point still ruled by Abbas's PA—and the West Bank as separate entities. Food and other essential supplies, he said, could be brought into Gaza via Egypt.

June: Hamas Seizes Gaza

On June 1, as Qassams and rockets continued to fall on Sderot, about 100 IDF reservists from that town published an open letter to Olmert saying they would find it difficult to report for military duty so long as the government "abandons Sderot's residents." "We have stopped believing that someone is doing everything he can in order to protect us," the reservists wrote, "we cannot accept that our children and the rest of the residents of the region will continue to be the cannon fodder of the State of Israel." The letter did not go so far as to say that its authors would disobey the law and refuse to serve.

A 45-page Amnesty International report, released on June 5 to mark the 40th anniversary of the start of the Six-Day War, strongly criticized Israel for the deteriorating humanitarian situation in the West Bank and Gaza, and said Israel "should lift the regime of blockades and restrictions . . . halt the construction of the fence/wall inside the West Bank, and remove sections already built there." It also called on Israel to stop building new settlements "as a first step towards removing Israeli settlements and outposts." At the same time, it urged Palestinians to stop attacks on Israeli civilians and for the PA to act to prevent such attacks. The report was denounced by Vice Prime Minister Shimon Peres, who said Israel had not built the security fence "as some sort of caprice. It was the right way to defend life within Israel—something that every country is obligated, not only entitled, to do." The Israeli Justice Ministry issued a statement denouncing the report's "lack of emphasis on the centrality of Palestinian terror."

That same day, Chief of Staff Gabi Ashkenazi, visiting the Shizafon Armored Corps base in southern Israel, said the army was preparing for an escalation against both the Palestinians and on the northern front. After witnessing the continuing large-scale maneuvers simulating the conquest of a Syrian village, Lt.-Gen. Ashkenazi declared, "The Israel

Defense Force's goal is to improve our readiness, while at the same time continuing the war on terror. The display seen here today is quite impressive: Only one element is lacking, an enemy."

However Defense Minister Peretz said he "hoped the Syrians won't misinterpret" the army's constant training. "We have no intelligence indicating that Syria is interested in starting a war," he noted, adding, "I hope that the escalation in words does not bring about an escalation in actions." Yet a third view came from Maj.-Gen. Amos Yadlin, director of Military Intelligence, who spoke of Syrian preparations that could be ominous, including "cleaning army posts, conducting large maneuvers, and strengthening defenses. They are reaching a greater state of readiness for war than in the past, but that doesn't mean they will be ready for war tomorrow."

On June 11 Israel successfully launched its latest intelligence satellite, Ofeq-7, on an Israeli-made Shavit rocket from the Palmahim launch site south of Tel Aviv. Security sources said that the launch was not timed to correspond with threats from Iran or Syria, but had been planned for some time. They said that Ofeq-7—which replaced Ofeq-5, launched five years earlier—represented a "significant upgrade" in Israel's capacity to gather intelligence. The main contractor was Israel Aerospace Industries, and Israel Military Industries produced the rocket engine for the launch vehicle.

Clashes between Hamas and Fatah in Gaza, which had continued intermittently at the cost of some 150 lives since the beginning of the year, accelerated, and Hamas carried out a carefully planned takeover of the Gaza Strip. On June 11 Hamas declared it had taken over the town of Beit Hanoun at the northern edge of the Strip, the area from which most of the Qassam rocket fire on Sderot had been initiated. It then surrounded and conquered Fatah headquarters in Gaza City, unsuccessfully guarded by 500 armed men, the next day. On June 13 Hamas took control of all of the area north of Gaza City, and proceeded to blow up the southern Gaza headquarters of the Preventive Security Force in Khan Younis, killing 13. After taking Khan Younis and Rafiah, the two main towns in the southern Strip, Hamas solidified its control by overrunning the two remaining Fatah posts in Gaza City on June 14, as well as both main arterial roads traversing the Strip.

An official casualty count was never released, but it was clear that well over 100 were killed on both sides. There were also reports of numerous atrocities—Fatah activists and their entire families taken from their homes and executed in the street; President Abbas's cook being bound and gagged and thrown to his death from atop a 15-story building; and the murder of unarmed civilians and hospital patients. The carnage took place on both sides, and Sarah Leah Whitson, Human Rights Watch's Middle East director, said, "These attacks by both Hamas and Fatah constitute brutal assaults on the most fundamental humanitarian principles. The murder of civilians not engaged in hostilities and the willful killing of captives are war crimes, pure and simple."

Abbas, who remained in the Fatah-controlled West Bank, dissolved the unity government headed by Haniyeh, and said that he, as president, would rule the West Bank by decree. Hamas denounced the move as "worthless" and insisted that Haniyeh "remains head of government."

Abbas moved quickly. On June 15 he appointed Salam Fayyad, the former finance minister who was regarded in the West as a symbol of Palestinian reform, as prime minister. At about the same time, Fatah armed units cracked down hard on Hamas in the West Bank. "There was a decision by the leaders of the security forces to go after Hamas and to arrest them, before they think of bringing the war here," said Issam Abu Bakr, a Fatah leader in Nablus. "This is true for all of the West Bank. Perhaps it was a belated decision, but now we can stand against Hamas and defend ourselves."

There were widespread arrests of Hamas activists in Jenin, Nablus, Jericho, Ramallah, and Bethlehem, where security forces wore ski masks to avoid being identified. Fatah-allied students took over Al-Quds University in Ramallah. Earlier, on June 12, Fatah armed units had stormed the building housing the Palestinian Legislative Assembly in Ramallah and torched the first floor. But Hamas leader Mahmoud al-Zahar said in Gaza on June 20 that continued Fatah efforts to drive his organization out of the West Bank would result, ultimately, in Fatah's overthrow there.

The Hamas takeover of Gaza drew dire predictions from some former military men in Israel who were identified with the political right. Ya'akov Amidror, who had served as deputy chief of Military Intelligence, said that Hamas was poised to "turn Gaza into Hamastan like Hezballah in Lebanon, with Iranian and Al Qaeda elements. We will have a full-fledged terrorist state on our borders." The ex-general claimed that Fatah's collapse in Gaza was the disastrous fulfillment of the 2005 disengagement from Gaza and the northern West Bank. "Israel's irresponsible departure," he said, "enabled Hamas to get stronger with tremendous quantities of explosives, weapons, training, money and more." The only solution, he felt, was for Israel "to enter Gaza and remain there for years."

Former chief of staff Moshe (Bogie) Ya'alon, who, after a year at the Washington Institute for Near East Policy in the U.S. capital, returned to join the right-leaning Shalem Center think tank in Jerusalem, agreed, saying that current events in Gaza were "just the first step . . . . Our entry into Gaza is inevitable; no one else will do it for us. There are many questions and dilemmas, of course, but the writing is already on the wall. We must enter before the threat reaches Ashdod and elsewhere." Ya'alon had opposed the 2005 disengagement when he was head of the army.

On the other hand, Labor MK Matan Vilna'i, a former deputy chief of staff, expressed confidence that the Egyptians, who were Israel's allies against Gaza terror, had the ability to stop the smuggling of weapons into the Strip. Israel, in his view, had to "resume targeted killings, air strikes, and special forces in Gaza," but not an invasion of the Strip, and also engage in "diplomatic moves vis-à-vis the Palestinian Authority."

In the aftermath of the Hamas takeover, Ayman al-Zawahri, the Al Qaeda second-in-command, called on Hamas to implement sharia, Islamic law, in the Gaza Strip. "Taking over power is not a goal but a means to implement Allah's word on earth," he said in a message over the Internet, in which he also called on all Muslims to support Hamas.

Prime Minister Olmert said on June 17 that Israel would not allow Gaza to sink into a humanitarian crisis. Israel, he declared, would find ways of supplying food and medications to the Strip through international aid groups. The prime minister was responding, in part, to calls by Meretz MK Zahava Gal-On, who said that Israelis could not "stand aloof. The international law and the laws of morality do not allow us to be indifferent and say, 'let the Arabs kill themselves.'"

The right, predictably, had a very different view of Israel's responsibilities. "An Islamic country has been established in Gaza, which is in our backyard. The country controlling Gaza today is Iran, and from this point we must derive our decisions regarding the humanitarian aid to the Strip," said MK Effi Eitam of the National Religious Party-National Union. According to Eitam, Egypt should now be responsible for aid to Gaza.

National Infrastructure Minister Ben-Eliezer, a leader of the Labor Party, recommended at least a temporary halt to all aid to Gaza while stepping up the separation between the West Bank and Gaza. His Labor colleague, Deputy Defense Minister Ephraim Sneh, told Army Radio that aid to Gaza could not be completely halted, but that even if aid kept getting in "there will be a crisis in Gaza because it's being controlled by gangs who show no responsibility to the public . . . Israel is not [Hamas head]

Ismail Haniyeh's welfare office." The suspension of supplies to Gaza began in mid-June, as the Israeli company Dor Alon, the only fuel supplier to the Strip, restricted its provision of fuel to Gaza's power plant.

Olmert, who was due to meet Bush in Washington, favored total separation of Gaza—the de facto Hamastan—and the Fatah-controlled West Bank, and advocated deployment of an international force to intercept and put an end to arms shipments to Gaza through smugglers' tunnels at the southern end of the Strip. Foreign Ministry spokesman Mark Regev called the new reality "a serious strategic challenge and a threat," and said, "We'll want to engage with the international community on how to prevent the upgrade." But Saeb Erekat, a top advisor to Abbas, pleaded for Israeli moderation and forbearance. "Residents must not be punished for the bloody coup staged by Hamas," he declared.

Meeting with Olmert in Washington on June 19, Bush was highly critical of the Hamas takeover. "They made the choice of violence," he said, adding that he hoped that Abbas, whom he called "the president of all the Palestinians," and Prime Minister Fayyad, "who's a good fellow, will be strengthened to the point where they can lead the Palestinians in a different direction." For his part, Olmert said he was willing to carry out conciliatory moves to help Abbas.

Egypt hastily convened a four-way summit involving its president, Hosni Mubarak, King Abdullah II of Jordan, Olmert, and Abbas for late June in Sharm al-Sheikh. In announcing the summit Mubarak called the Hamas move "a coup against legitimacy." The Sharm meeting opened on June 26. As expected, the four leaders reiterated a commitment to the search for Middle East peace. Olmert stole the headlines by announcing that Israel would release 250 Palestinian prisoners as a goodwill gesture to Abbas. (They were released on July 21.)

According to *Ha'aretz,* Olmert had not at first planned to release prisoners. Rather, his original package of gestures to bolster Abbas had included the transfer to the PA of funds Israel collected as Palestinian taxes on behalf of the PA (Israel had withheld about $600 million in such taxes since the election of the Hamas government in early 2006) and the removal of West Bank roadblocks and other "alleviations" of pressure on Palestinian daily life in the West Bank. Apparently after consultations with Defense Minister Ehud Barak (who had replaced Peretz in that position and as Labor leader), Foreign Minister Livni, and Transport Minister Shaul Mofaz—a former defense minister and chief of staff—Olmert decided to release 250 Fatah prisoners from the West Bank with no "blood on their hands" since it would strengthen Abbas and increase the pressure on Hamas, whose own prisoners in Israel would not be released.

Ha'aretz pointed out that the number of prisoners to be released was small compared to previous Israeli gestures Ariel Sharon made to help Abbas. And since the Olmert offer included neither Fatah veterans jailed since before the Oslo agreements nor West Bank Fatah Tanzim leader Marwan Barghouti, serving five life terms for ordering terrorist murders during the second intifada, the paper deemed it unlikely that this prisoner release would enhance Abbas's credentials with the Palestinians. Criticism also came from the right, which held that concessions to the Palestinians only emboldened the radicals: Likud leader Benjamin Netanyahu, speaking to the Jewish Agency Assembly in Jerusalem, said that the moves sent "a wrong, harmful message that will not strengthen the Palestinian Authority. It will only weaken it."

Meanwhile, the first-ever official Arab League delegation visited Israel on June 25. It consisted only of the foreign ministers of Egypt and Jordan, both of which had diplomatic relations with Israel. They came to promote, once again, the 2002 Arab League initiative first proposed by Saudi Arabia,

On the eve of the June 26 Sharm al-Sheikh summit, which was also exactly a year since Gilad Shalit's abduction, Hamas released a recording of the soldier's voice on a Hamas Website. Speaking in Hebrew, he said, in part, "Mom and Dad, brother and sister, my comrades in the IDF—I send you from jail my regards and my longing for all of you. I've gone through a whole year in jail, and my health is still deteriorating and I'm in need of prolonged hospitalization. I regret the lack of interest shown by the Israeli government and the IDF in my case and their lack of response to the demands of the Islamic Brigades." Shalit, now 20, called on the Israeli government to exchange prisoners with the Palestinians, "especially as I was part of a military operation under military orders." He continued, "Just as I have parents, a mom and dad, the thousands of Palestinian prisoners also have mothers and fathers whose children must be returned to them."

Israeli officials told the *Jerusalem Post* that release of the tape may have been a goodwill gesture indicating Hamas's desire to reach a deal and prisoner swap for Shalit, and a Hamas spokesman in Gaza told Channel 2 TV that this was indeed the case. The kidnapped soldier's father agreed that the tape might be a positive sign. Noam Shalit said, "We hope that in light of the new situation in Gaza, Hamas has an interest in proving to the Palestinian people they have achievements." Except for a letter from their son received in September 2006, the Shalits had not heard from Gilad since his capture.

Hours after Tony Blair stepped down as Britain's prime minister on June 27, the Quartet—the U.S., UN, EU, and Russia—announced his appointment as its special Middle East envoy. His mission, according to an official statement, was to mobilize international financial and humanitarian support for the Palestinians. Clearly referring to the violent Hamas takeover of the Gaza Strip a fortnight earlier, a Quartet statement said that "the urgency of recent events has reinforced the need for the international community . . . to help Palestinians as they build the institutions and economy of a viable state in Gaza and the West Bank, able to take its place as a peaceful and prosperous partner to Israel and its other neighbors." Blair replaced the previous envoy, former World Bank president James Wolfensohn, who resigned in frustration after less than a year. Blair, based in Jerusalem, was to work with a small team of experts.

That same day at least 12 Palestinians were killed and 40 wounded when Israeli troops went into southern Gaza. Armor and aircraft supported the strike against suspected terrorists in the kind of incident that had become almost routine along the Gaza border.

July: A Conference Is Called

In fulfillment of its promise to bolster Abbas, Israel transferred $118 million in taxes it had collected for the Palestinian Authority to the PA on July 1. The money would be used to pay government workers. Also, after a hiatus of about 18 months, Israeli and Palestinian officials resumed security talks. According to an AP report, these "included discussions on the movement of Palestinian forces and guarantees of safety for security installations during Israel Defense Force operations." Regular contacts between Israeli and Palestinian security officers, which first began about the time of the PA's establishment, were interrupted by the outbreak of the second intifada in 2000, and occurred again on an intermittent basis until discontinued with the election of a Hamas government in 2006.

Alan Johnston, a BBC reporter and the only Western correspondent working full-time in Gaza, was freed by his Army of Islam captors on July 4 after 16 weeks of captivity. Johnston had been kidnapped by an Al Qaeda affiliate with links to one of Gaza's most powerful clans. Hamas had applied pressure on his captors to release him.

Eight Hamas gunmen were killed in an Israeli antiterror incursion that escalated into a fierce battle in the Gaza Strip on July 5. The fighting included air support by Israeli forces, tanks, and bulldozers. Hamas later said that its men had discovered an Israeli undercover unit operating in the area, about half a mile inside Palestinian territory. Among the Hamas dead was Muhammad Siam, the organization's chief field commander in the central Gaza area. In another Israeli raid, conducted on July 13 by a Givati Brigade unit near the al-Bourej refugee camp in central Gaza, Sgt. Arbel Reich, 21, was killed. This was the IDF's first combat death in 2007.

On July 10, the authoritative French newspaper *Le Monde* published an open letter to Quartet envoy Tony Blair from the foreign ministers of all ten of the EU's Mediterranean states—Bulgaria, Cyprus, Spain, France, Greece, Italy, Portugal, Malta, Romania, and Slovenia. In it they told Blair that the Quartet-backed "road map" had failed and that there was a need to "redefine our objectives" to include getting Israel to make "concrete and immediate measures in favor of Mahmoud Abbas." The specifics were familiar: transfer of more of the tax monies collected by Israel for the PA, release of prisoners ("thousands . . . without blood on their hands"), a settlement freeze, and the evacuation of unauthorized outposts. In a clear reference to imprisoned Fatah leader Marwan Barghouti, the letter requested "release as well of the main Palestinian leaders to ensure succession within Fatah."

A promising agreement was reached four days later: Israel agreed to grant safe passage to 178 wanted members of Fatah's Al-Aqsa Martyrs Brigades who were fugitives from justice on condition that they turn in their arms and sign a pledge renouncing terrorist activities. By early August only about 60 percent of the men had relinquished their weapons and Israel announced that the deal was dead. Israel then arrested two of the militants previously granted amnesty, and on August 22 a Brigades spokesman said it was calling off the truce it had maintained with Israel since the understanding had been reached and called on its members to rearm.

In July, the families of Eldad Regev and Ehud Goldwasser, kidnapped by Hezballah in 2006, dismissed reports from German sources quoted in the Lebanese daily *An-Nahar* that one of the two men had died, either in captivity or during the kidnap operation. Though *An-Nahar* was associated with opposition to Hezballah inside Lebanon, Miki Goldwasser called the dispatch "a cynical attempt to play with the emotions of the reservists' families." She told Army Radio: "They can't play with my feelings, and I know that they wouldn't just release information to [a] newspaper." Shlomo Goldwasser, Ehud's father, was similarly skeptical, commenting, "When information existed as though both soldiers were alive and well, we did not take them seriously. Since the abduction we receive this or that message that Red Cross representatives will be allowed to visit or will be given details that could indicate with certainty at their condition." The *An-Nahar* report was also discredited by Sheikh Hassan Nasrallah, the Hezballah leader, who said he would never leak information without extracting a price from Israel for it. According to a *Ha'aretz* report, the UN was conducting talks between Israel and Hezballah about the soldiers, apparently through a German intelligence operative.

A week earlier, Nasrallah had said that Hezballah now had arms that could strike "anywhere in Israel," in what appeared to be an attempt to extort concessions from Israel. And on July 24, an Israeli military official was quoted by the *Jerusalem Post* as saying that Hezballah had restored its military capability, alleging that arms were being smuggled to it by Syria with the knowledge and compliance of the Lebanese army.

President George W. Bush delivered a major address devoted entirely to the Israeli-Palestinian conflict on July 17. Recalling that he had been "the first American president to call for the creation of a Palestinian state" five years earlier, Bush listed the "many changes" that had occurred since then, some of them "hopeful": Israel's withdrawal from Gaza and parts of the West Bank, Palestinian elections, and the floating of the Saudi-Arab League peace plan. But then, he continued, "confronted with the prospect of peace, extremists have responded with acts of aggression and terror. In Gaza, Hamas radicals betrayed the Palestinian people with a lawless and violent takeover. By its actions, Hamas has demonstrated beyond all doubt that it is [more] devoted to extremism and murder than to serving the Palestinian people."

The Palestinians faced a stark choice, the president declared, between, on the one hand, the "chaos and suffering" offered by Hamas, a "surrender of their future" to Syria and Iran, and, on the other, "the vision of President Abbas . . . a peaceful state called Palestine as a homeland for the Palestinian people," including "the institutions of a modern democracy . . . competent ministries that deliver services without corruption . . . and the rule of law."

To help the Palestinians make the right choice he announced that the U.S., in consultation with the rest of the Quartet, was taking a series of steps: increases in financial assistance for humanitarian relief, reform of Palestinian security services, and loans to businessmen; intensification of diplomatic efforts in pursuit of a "political horizon" for a Palestinian state; and help in building the institutions of such a state. But he cautioned both sides that concessions would be necessary. "The Palestinian government must arrest terrorists, dismantle their infrastructure, and confiscate illegal weapons . . . . They must work to stop attacks on Israel, and to free the Israeli soldier held hostage by extremists. And they must enforce the law without corruption, so they can earn the trust of their people, and of the world." As for Israel, "Prime Minister Olmert must continue to release Palestinian tax revenues" and also make clear "that Israel's future lies in developing areas like the Negev and Galilee—not in continuing occupation of the West Bank . . . . unauthorized outposts should be removed and settlement expansion ended."

Bush announced the convening, in the fall, of a regional international conference aimed at restarting the stalled peace process. This, he said, would "provide diplomatic support for the parties in their bilateral discussions and negotiations, so that we can move forward on a successful path to a Palestinian state." The key participants, he said, would be "the Israelis, the Palestinians, and their neighbors in the region. Secretary Rice will chair the meeting."

Foreign Ministry spokesman Mark Regev confirmed on July 18 that Israel had for some time been maintaining contacts with Syria via third parties, including Turkey, the U.S., and European countries. He told *Yediot Aharonot* that given this ongoing situation, the problem hampering relations between the two countries was not any lack of communication but rather Syrian intentions. Regev doubted whether Syria's talk of peace with Israel was anything more than an attempt to "play the Israeli card cynically in attempts to solve their diplomatic problems with the countries of Europe and North America, without any real intentions to change their relationship with Israel."

On July 19 the *Jerusalem Post* reported that Hamas had succeeded in smuggling much more sophisticated arms into Gaza—antiaircraft and antitank missiles and old-model Katyushas—since the 2005 Israeli disengagement, and had accumulated a virtual army there of about 13,000 men organized into four brigades. It quoted a senior IDF officer as saying that Israel was on a "collision course" with Hamas, and urged quick action before the Islamic terror organization built up its military capabilities even more.

Police completed the forced evacuation of hundreds of right-wing activists from the former Samarian settlement of Homesh on July 23. Some were arrested while others escaped to nearby hills or fled to a Palestinian village. The demonstrators, some of whom were prevented by police from reaching the site of the northern West Bank settlement evacuated in the 2005 disengagement, attempted to build a synagogue with bricks they had brought with them and to put up a wooden tower to mark the two-year anniversary of the pullout. Organizers of the march complained of brutality by security forces.

Secretary of State Rice began yet another Middle East tour on July 31, accompanied by Defense Secretary Robert Gates. Upon their arrival Rice signed a joint statement with Egypt, Jordan, and six Persian Gulf states endorsing the 2002 Arab peace initiative. Speaking at a joint news conference with Rice at the Egyptian Red Sea resort of Sharm al-Sheikh, where the conference took place, Egyptian foreign minister Ahmed Aboul Gheit said he would like to see the agenda for the upcoming international Middle East peace conference attach high priority to the establishment of a Palestinian state in the near future.

August: Talks and Qassams

From there it was on to Jerusalem on August 1, where Rice told Israeli leaders about Bush's plans for the conference and passed on encouraging news about the possibility that Saudi Arabia might attend. The next day she briefed Abbas in Ramallah and met with the new government of Prime Minister Salam Fayyad, installed after the Hamas takeover of the Gaza Strip, and signed an agreement granting the PA $80 million in U.S. aid to beef up its security forces.

Israel's security cabinet met on August 8 for the sixth time in six weeks to discuss tensions with Syria. Olmert explained the meeting in reassuring terms, say that "there is concern that someone might mistakenly think that there will be an offensive and a war in which no one is interested . . . therefore, we must prepare for any scenario." Though unknown to the public at the time, the meeting also touched on secret plans for an air-and-ground strike against a suspected nuclear facility under construction near the Euphrates River in eastern Syria (see below, pp. 266–67).

Ahmad Khatib, 20, from Kafr Manda in the Galilee, was shot dead by an Israeli security guard in Jerusalem's Old City on August 13. Surveillance videos clearly showed Khatib following two Israeli security men along the Old City's narrow lanes and grabbing the pistol of one of them. Khatib was killed in the ensuing gunfight as he fired back at the pursuing guards. A careful examination of the videos did not substantiate charges by Khatib's family that one of the guards had "verified his death" by shooting him in the head as he lay wounded and helpless on the pavement. Galilee Freedom Brigades, an unknown group, claimed credit for Khatib's attempted attack, saying it was in revenge for a 2004 killing.

Qassam fire on southern Israel continued on an almost daily basis: at the end of the month the IDF reported that 92 Qassams and 118 mortar shells were fired from Gaza into Israel during August. There were also frequent skirmishes along the Gaza border between armed terrorists and Israeli forces, and Israel kept up the pressure with strikes against key terror leaders, particularly those affiliated with Islamic Jihad. A major tragedy was averted on August 6, when a Qassam rocket that fell in the yard of a kindergarten in the border town of Sderot exploded, causing damage but no injuries. Israel continued to conduct almost daily raids into the Gaza Strip to thwart terror operations in the making and to prevent the flow of arms into the Strip from the Philadelphi corridor at its southern end. On August 14, for example, two Hamas militants were killed when Israeli units moved in to search for the tunnels used by smugglers to move arms and drugs into the Strip from Egyptian Sinai.

Two young Palestinians, aged 9 and 12, were killed on August 22 when an Israeli tank fired on them as they were attempting to retrieve Qassam rocket launchers just after the rockets had been fired on Israel from northern Gaza. Explaining that the tank crew had not identified the shadowy figures near the launchers as children, the army issued a statement saying, "Children have no business being near rocket launchers" and decrying what it called the "cynical use of children" by terror groups. A similar tragedy occurred on August 30, when three young Bedouin cousins were killed in an Israeli attack on rocket launchers in the Beit Hanun area. It was not clear whether the victims were near the launchers at the time because they had been hired by terrorists to retrieve them, or whether they approached out of childish curiosity. A relative told *Ha'aretz,* "We are victims of the occupation and of the misbehavior of some of our fighters, who randomly choose our area to target Israel."

In mid-August seven soldiers were suspended from duty for refusing to facilitate the forced evacuation of Israeli squatters from the disputed wholesale market area in the old city of Hebron. The soldiers, from an ultra-Orthodox unit of the Nahal Brigade, would not do guard duty on the roads surrounding the area where the ouster took place, saying that would be aiding and abetting the evacuation.

Parents of other soldiers who refused to take part in the evacuation itself gathered at their sons' bases to show support. Some held up signs saying, "Son, do not expel." One father said his son "enlisted in the army to fight the enemy—Jews are not the enemy." MK Arye Eldad of the right-wing National Union said the soldiers had been called on to be "the executors of an immoral decision tainted with political motives, whose purpose is to exile Jews from their Jewish property." According to attorney Ya'akov Ne'eman, the former finance minister who now represented the settler families, Jews had owned the property in the market before being forced out during the Arab riots of 1929.

Olmert and Abbas held two meetings in August. The first took place in the West Bank city of Jericho on August 6, the first time that an Israeli prime minister had been in PA territory since a May 2000 get-together between then-prime minister Ehud Barak and the late PA leader Yasir Arafat. Both sides projected a sense of progress in a visit that, according to an Olmert spokesman, was intended at least in part "to show good will and foster good relations." After the three-hour meeting Olmert said the talks had focused on "fundamental issues which are the basis of the establishment of a Palestinian state." Israel, his office quoted him as saying, intended "to bring about two states for two peoples living side-by-side in security, as soon as possible." Abbas aide and associate Saeb Erekat told reporters that Abbas "did not come to the meeting with a magic wand, and neither did Mr. Olmert." Though not made public at the time, Palestinian authorities acting on an Israeli tip arrested several members of Abbas's own Fatah movement who had planned an attempt on the life of the Israeli prime minister during the summit. The men's arrest and subsequent release were only announced in October (see below, p. 254).

A second set of talks, on August 28, produced no concrete results. PA negotiator Erekat termed the session "good," but said the two sides had not "discussed any details related to the fundamental issues" or "reached the stage of exchanging documents." He declared that the Palestinians wanted "peace, but not at any price," and indicated that the Palestinians would settle for nothing less than an Israeli withdrawal from all territories conquered in the 1967 Six-Day War.

A few days earlier, Abbas, during a meeting with Israeli Arab MK Muhammad Barakeh, said he did not favor the idea of a territorial exchange in which Arab-populated areas of Israel, along with their residents, would be swapped for West Bank lands containing Israeli settlements. Barakeh agreed with him, saying that Israel's Arab citizens were "not real estate to be negotiated over in order to validate the evils of the occupation." A proposal for such a territorial exchange was being floated by Strategic Planning Minister Avigdor Lieberman, leader of the hard-line party Yisrael Beitenu.

Representatives of three EU intelligence agencies met secretly with officials of Hamas, who were eager to get the Europeans to help end the Gaza boycott and pressure Israel to reopen the border crossing at Rafiah, at the southern end of the Gaza Strip, the *Jerusalem Post* reported on August 29, although neither Israeli nor EU officials would confirm the story.

September: Gaza Terror Escalates

On September 3 a Qassam landed in the courtyard of a day-care center in Sderot, and Islamic Jihad called it "a present for the start of the school year." The next day the *Jerusalem Post* carried a story indicating that the army would soon receive orders to resume targeted killings of terrorists involved in planning and carrying out rocket and mortar attacks on southern Israel. Prime Minister Olmert said that the Palestinians, who had paid dearly in the past for Qassam attacks, "will also pay a heavy price in the future." Israel, he went on, "will not compromise . . . and we will hit at those who operate these systems and the chain of command." But a major Israeli thrust into Gaza to stop the Qassam fire would inevitably involve heavy casualties on both sides, and Foreign Minister Livni advocated other alternatives. At a September 4 press conference with visiting EU foreign policy chief Javier Solana she said: "We must use additional means apart from military ones, to make clear to Gaza residents that their way of life is dependent on Israel."

Two cars carrying six terrorists with suicide belts, explosives, automatic rifles, grenades and RPGs (rocket-propelled grenades) were intercepted by Israeli forces and killed near the Gaza border on September 6. The terrorists, belonging to the Al-Aqsa Martyrs Brigades and Islamic Jihad, were driving at high speed towards the border fence. In the encounter, Israeli Air Force planes were called in to provide support for the ground forces.

One of two Qassam rockets fired at the Zikkim army basic-training facility just north of the Gaza Strip landed near unfortified barracks inside the base, wounding about 60 trainee soldiers on September 10. Four of the injuries were serious. The attack, against recruits being prepared for noncombat army jobs, raised a panic among parents, many of whom rushed to the base to check on the welfare of their sons and demanded that they be moved to a safer base—or that Zikkim itself be made more secure—for the remainder of their training period.

On September 18, Sgt. Benzion Haim Henman, 22, was killed in a clash at the Ein Beit Ilma refugee camp near Nablus, in the northern West Bank. Henman's unit was on an antiterrorist operation.

The Israeli security cabinet declared the Gaza Strip a "hostile entity" on September 19, and said this would create the legal basis for cutting electricity and fuel supplies to the Hamas-run territory. Hamas spokesman Fawzi Barhoum called the decision "a declaration of full-fledged war on the Gaza Strip" and claimed that "the steps are in preparation for a military operation that is looming with the Zionist occupation forces."

Secretary of State Rice was in Israel that day. After meeting with Foreign Minister Livni, she said the U.S. "will not abandon the innocent Palestinians in Gaza," but reiterated U.S. concerns over the Hamas takeover there. Livni, for her part, added that Palestinians must absorb the lesson "that supporting Hamas won't help them." Rice also met with Olmert and with Defense Minister Barak, who told her that Israel was not seeking to create a humanitarian crisis in Gaza. Earlier, the secretary of state said she was trying to get the Israelis and the Palestinians to agree on terms for the planned Middle East peace conference. "We can't simply continue to say we want a two-state solution, we have got to start to move towards one," she told reporters. "The international meeting is also going to be doing exactly that." Although it would not be made public until December, David Landau, the editor of *Ha'aretz,* urged Rice to impose a peace settlement on Israel, saying that Israel wanted to be "raped" by the Americans.

At least 12 Qassam rockets and 20 mortar shells were fired on Sderot on September 26. There were no injuries. Several hours later, five Palestinians riding in a jeep were killed when their vehicle was hit by an IDF rocket in the Zeitoun neighborhood of Gaza City. It was carrying firing-ready rockets, according to an army statement. That same day Israeli security forces found several rocket casings and launchers near Beit Jalla, a Palestinian suburb of Bethlehem and Jerusalem inside PA territory.

On September 27, after yet another rocket and mortar barrage, Israel launched new strikes into Gaza, killing 11 Palestinian militants. Abbas, in New York for the opening of the UN General Assembly, called on the world body to "stop the massacre of Palestinians being carried out by the army of occupation in the Gaza Strip." Hamas, for its part, vowed that Israel would "pay heavily."

Foreign Minister Livni and her Syrian opposite number, Walid Muallem, met secretly in New York where they were both attending the

UN General Assembly, according to a report in *a-Sinara,* an Israeli Arab newspaper published in Nazareth. The paper said the meeting, which had the prior approval of Prime Minister Olmert, was also attended by Dan Gillerman, Israel's ambassador to the UN, and the Syrian ambassador to Washington. *Yediot Aharonot* quoted an Arab source as saying that Muallem, at the meeting, complained that Israel on one hand violated Syrian airspace and on the other called for peace, and asked for clarification of its real position. Muallem and aides of Livni denied that the meeting took place.

October: Preparing for the Conference

Israel released 57 Palestinian prisoners, mostly Fatah members, on October 1, as a gesture to strengthen PA president Abbas. This was in addition to the 250 released earlier in fulfillment of the promise Olmert made at the Sharm al-Sheikh summit in June.

A plan to restore "dignity" to the Palestinians while annexing the West Bank to Israel was proposed by MK Benny Elon, head of the far-right National Religious Party-National Union, on October 7. "The establishment of the State of Israel did not deprive the Palestinians of their state—there never was such a state," he said. "But Israel took from them their houses and their dignity. We can return to the Palestinians their dignity, to give them homes and hope for a new life, by changing their refugee status," declared Elon. He proceeded to announce what he called the "Israeli initiative," which he described as "a new way of thinking that allows for real peace." Simply put, Israel would annex the West Bank but allow Palestinians to stay there if they took Jordanian citizenship. He said hundreds of thousands of refugee-camp residents could be given money to build new homes, allowing the camps themselves to be razed.

Eight mortar shells, three Qassam rockets, and one Grad-type Katyusha landed in Israel that day. The Katyusha, of a type used by Hezballah in Lebanon, landed less than a quarter-mile from the town of Netivot, about seven miles from the Gaza border. This was the first time Palestinian rockets had reached as far as Netivot.

Opening the Knesset's winter session on October 8, Prime Minister Olmert said that Israel should move ahead with the peace process while simultaneously battling terror. "We must give negotiations a chance," he said. "Israel has excellent excuses to justify stagnation in the talks. I don't intend to look for excuses. I am determined to give a chance to a meaningful diplomatic process . . . . Any other option means a demographic battle, drowned in blood and tears, which does not serve the State of Israel in any way."

The next day, October 9, witnessed the start of talks on the declaration of principles for the November Middle East summit, scheduled for Annapolis, Maryland. Olmert said that "the peace process requires determination to make brave, unavoidable decisions, which involve relinquishing the full realization of the dreams that fed our national ethos for many years . . . . The Palestinians will also have to confront the need to relinquish the fulfillment of some of their dreams in order to create with us a reality that might not be ideal and might not be perfect, but one that will give us all stability, security, happiness and peace." But three days later PA president Abbas was quoted by the AP as telling Palestinian TV: "We have 6,205 square kilometers in the West Bank and the Gaza Strip. We want it as is." On October 12, PA negotiator Saeb Erekat said that the summit would have to be postponed if Israel and the Palestinians could not come to an agreement in advance. He "really doubted" that the Americans would issue invitations if "decisions are not made" by Olmert and Abbas.

That day London's *Guardian* newspaper quoted Vice Prime Minister Haim Ramon as saying that, in a peace settlement, Jewish areas of the Holy City would remain Israeli and some Arab areas might be transferred to the PA. He asked, "Wouldn't it be the right deal today for the Western world and the international community to recognize annexation of [Jewish] neighborhoods and for us to quit Arab neighborhoods?" At the same time Ramon admitted that decisions on what to do with the Old City's holy sites might have to be deferred. "We need to say that there will be a special regime in the 'Holy Basin,' which we will talk about in the future," Ramon noted.

The cabinet, on October 11, authorized development of technology to protect Israeli civilian aircraft from rocket attack, to begin in 2008. According to the *Jerusalem Post,* this decision was in response to advances in antiaircraft missile technology and its increased availability to terrorists, and reports that international terror groups planned to target Israeli planes. The cabinet also approved Transport Minister Shaul Mofaz's plan to protect civilian planes, until the new system was developed, with technology previously only used for the military.

During an October visit to Washington, Defense Minister Barak—who had earlier said no pullout from the West Bank was possible unless Israel had an adequate missile-defense system in place—discussed strategic issues with U.S. officials, including protection against various kinds of rockets. Those defenses would ultimately constitute three tiers: the short-range Iron Dome (to deal with Qassams), the middle-range David's Sling (designed to intercept and shoot down rockets fired from 25–50 miles away, such as Katyushas and Iranian-made rockets in Hezballah's possession), and the already deployed Arrow, still the world's only operational antimissile missile system developed with Israeli technology and U.S. funding. Labor Knesset member Ephraim Sneh, a former deputy defense minister, was optimistic about the triple system. "When deployment of the three systems is in place," he said, "I believe that the citizens of Israel will have perfect protection."

Sgt. Ben Kubani, 20, was killed by Palestinian fire during a gun battle near Khan Younis in the southern Gaza Strip on October 17. Kubani's unit was engaged in operations against the terror infrastructure that took place daily along and inside the Strip.

The Quartet Middle East envoy, Tony Blair, proposed a number of economic steps to improve the condition of the Palestinians, according to an October 17 report in *Ha'aretz*. These moves, already brought up in talks with Israel, the PA, and the U.S., included the establishment of a new Palestinian city near Ramallah to house tens of thousands now living in refugee camps.

Rumors swirled, in October, about the fate of the kidnapped Israeli soldiers. On October 14 the London-based Arab newspaper *a-Shara al-Awsat* said that Ehud Goldwasser and Eldad Regev, the two abducted by Hezballah in 2006, were no longer alive and that their bodies had been sent to Iran. Three days later the Saudi newspaper *al-Watan* reported that they were alive, and that Israel and Hezballah had agreed on an exchange of nine Lebanese prisoners for the kidnapped soldiers. And speaking on Hezballah's al-Manar TV station, Sheikh Hassan Nasrallah, the Shi'ite organization's leader, referred to "strenuous negotiations, continuing sessions that will be resumed within days."

On October 17, Israel exchanged one mentally ill Hezballah prisoner and the remains of two Hezballah fighters for the body of Gabriel Dawit, an Israeli citizen who had disappeared in 2005. Dawit apparently drowned in the Mediterranean and his body washed up in Lebanon. On October 22, authoritative *Yediot Aharonot* journalist Shimon Shiffer reported that as part of the exchange Hezballah also gave Israel a letter written by missing airman Ron Arad to his wife, Tami, in 1986, along with a photograph of Arad and parts of a Hezballah internal report detailing unsuccessful efforts it made to discover what became of him. But the information did not satisfy Israel. Ofer Dekel, the former Shin Bet official designated to handle prisoner-exchange negotiations, said that Israel would not free Samir Kuntar, the Lebanese captured in the 1979 terrorist attack in which three members of the Haran family were killed, without getting "concrete evidence" about the whereabouts or fate of Arad. At the same time, Dekel reported that, contrary to rumors, there had been no progress in efforts to obtain the freedom of Regev and Goldwasser.

On October 26, Shin Bet security service head Yuval Diskin disclosed that three Fatah militants who had plotted to assassinate Prime Minister Olmert during his August 6 visit to Jericho for a meeting with PA president Abbas (see above, p. 248) had been arrested by the PA and freed two months later. Commenting on the release, the Prime Minister's Office said in a statement that Israel viewed it with "severity." Diskin said that Israel had received exact information on the assassination plot prior to Olmert's trip to Jericho. "The information was handed over immediately to the Palestinian security services, which arrested the cell members. However, they've recently been released for some reason, and we have made our objection known to the Palestinians." Likud MK Yuval Steinitz, former chairman of the Knesset Foreign Affairs and Defense Committee and a close ally of party leader Benjamin Netanyahu, said that the planned attack and the release showed it was not the time to negotiate peace agreements with the Palestinians.

Olmert met with Prime Minister Gordon Brown during a visit to London on October 23. At a press conference afterward, Brown said that Britain was "ready, and will push for, further sanctions against Iran . . . . We want to make it clear that we do not support the nuclear ambitions of that country." But Olmert suggested that sanctions might not be enough. "Economic sanctions are effective," he said. "They have an important effect already, but they are not sufficient. So there should be more. Up to where? Up until Iran will stop its nuclear program." From there Olmert flew to Paris where he talked about the Iranian threat and the Palestinian negotiations with French president Nicolas Sarkozy. The two reportedly had "identical" views on several key issues. After the meeting, the French leader said, "They say that I support Israel because my grandfather was Jewish, but this isn't a personal matter." He called Israeli security "a clear red line" and said it was "an inviolable condition, which we will never concede."

Two Israelis were wounded, one of them seriously, in a drive-by shooting at a hitchhiking post outside the settlement-city of Ariel, the de facto Israeli capital of the northern West Bank, on October 24. That same day Defense Minister Barak, responding to increased mortar and Qassam rocket attacks on Israeli towns and villages around the Gaza Strip, said he planned to approve a number of sanctions against the Strip and asked his deputy defense minister, Matan Vilna'i, to recommend limitations on the delivery of various types of fuel, services, and merchandise.

Among the specific recommendations was the cutting off of electricity for a specified time following Qassam attacks, a policy option that was made legal on September 19, when Israel declared Gaza a "hostile entity." Since that change in status Israel had blocked the shipment of certain merchandise into the Strip, including cigarettes and electrical appliances. When Gaza-based terror groups tried to hide potassium for use in explosives in sacks of sugar, Israeli authorities also began checking sugar shipments into Gaza. "We do not want to cause a humanitarian crisis," said an unnamed defense official. "But we do want to send a clear message that the rocket fire will not be tolerated."

Also on October 24, Amnesty International criticized both Hamas and Fatah for serious human rights abuses during internecine fighting between the two rival groups. "The leaders of both the PA and Hamas," the Amnesty report said, "must take immediate steps to break the cycle of impunity that continues to fuel abuses, including arbitrary detentions, abductions, torture and ill-treatment by their forces." These violations, it said, exacerbated "the human rights and humanitarian crisis caused by the Israeli military campaigns and blockades." It said that both Hamas and Fatah showed "flagrant disregard for the safety of the civilian population" by starting "indiscriminate attacks and reckless gun battles" in civilian neighborhoods.

Sgt. Maj. Ehud Efrati, 34, a reservist in a paratrooper reconnaissance unit, was killed when his unit came under heavy fire from Palestinian gunmen near the Sufa Crossing in southern Gaza on October 29. A Palestinian combatant was killed and two other Israeli soldiers were wounded lightly in the engagement. Four Palestinians were killed in a barrage of ten mortar shells during an Israeli Air Force missile strike in the southern Gaza Strip the next day. In the raid, a Palestinian residence was also hit, injuring six civilians.

As Israeli and Palestinian negotiating teams continued to seek a formula that would allow a statement of principles at the U.S.-sponsored Annapolis conference set for November, Strategic Planning Minister Avigdor Lieberman, head of the rightist Yisrael Beitenu, said on October 28 that his party would bolt the government and cause its collapse if Israel were to discuss "core issues" like Jerusalem, refugees, and borders before the PA proved it could carry out its commitment to fight terror. He also rejected the idea of providing a safe passage between Palestinian territory in the West Bank and Gaza.

NOVEMBER: NEGOTIATIONS IN ANNAPOLIS

Seven Palestinians were killed and about 100 wounded on November 12, when Hamas security forces fired into a throng of about 250,000 Fatah supporters marking the third anniversary of the death of Yasir Arafat. Hamas said there had been shooting from both sides, though the *New York Times* and other foreign media quoted Gaza hospital sources as saying all the victims were aligned with Fatah. The office of President Abbas blamed Hamas for the carnage, issuing a statement that declared: "This heinous crime is decisive evidence that the coup leadership of Hamas is out of step with the national values and customs and is using blind force and the most bloody and brutal techniques against our people in Gaza." Another leading Fatah figure, former Gaza strongman Muhammad Dahlan, said, "The shooting and killing, these sad and shameful scenes carried out by the Hamas gangs against innocent people and civilians today, are a sign of the failure and breakdown of Hamas's path."

Ido Zoldan, a resident of the settlement of Shavei Shomron, was driving toward the neighboring settlement of Karnei Shomron in the northern West Bank on November 19, when gunmen in a passing vehicle opened fire, critically wounding him. About ten days later Israeli forces arrested three men, two of them members of Palestinian National Security, the PA police force, who were the alleged perpetrators. Zoldan, 29, was married and the father of two small children.

That day the cabinet approved the release of another 441 Palestinian prisoners held on security charges. None had "blood on their hands," and 16, all Fatah members, were from the Gaza Strip. In another goodwill gesture two days later designed to strengthen Abbas, Olmert approved the delivery of 25 armored vehicles for use by Palestinian police in the West Bank. Responding to criticism by right-wing ministers, an official in the Prime Minister's Office said, "We are asking the Palestinians to fight terror. How are they supposed to do that, with stolen Israeli cars?"

After weeks of diplomatic maneuvering over who would attend, and tortured attempts to reach agreement on a declaration of principles, the U.S. announced on November 21 that the long-mooted Middle East summit would take place on November 27 at the U.S. Naval Academy in Annapolis. The U.S., as host, invited 49 nations, groups of nations (including the Arab League), financial institutions, and individuals. Both Saudi Arabia and Syria were invited.

Prior to leaving for the conference, Olmert expressed a sense of urgency and apprehension about the consequences of failing to move towards some kind of deal for separate Israeli and Palestinian states. "If the day comes when the two-state solution collapses, and we face a South African-style struggle for equal voting rights, then, as soon as that happens, the State of Israel is finished," he told *Ha'aretz* in an interview. What he clearly meant was that both the U.S. and world Jewry would withdraw their support of Israel if it were perceived as an apartheid country.

On both sides, pressure from hard-liners at home, including protests on the streets of Jerusalem and Gaza, made a breakthrough improbable. Hamas warned that concessions to Israel would make Abbas "a traitor," while the leader of the Israeli opposition, Likud head Benjamin Netanyahu, said Palestinians were "not lifting a finger to halt terror," and the leaders of two parties in Olmert's coalition, Shas and Yisrael Beitenu, threatened that giving in too much on such core issues as Jerusalem and the "right of return" of Palestinian refugees would lead those parties to bolt the coalition. Outsiders were just as vocal: from Tehran came the comment of Ayatollah Ali Khamenei that "this conference has already failed. The U.S. and its accomplices hope to preserve their reputation by this conference and compensate for past failures of the fake Zionist regime."

On the evening before the talks were to begin, Bush held separate meetings with Olmert and Abbas at the White House in an effort to reach a joint declaration of principles. At a pre-meeting dinner for delegates hosted by Secretary of State Rice, the president predicted tough bargaining ahead and the need for concessions by both sides. "We've come together this week because we share a common goal: two democratic states, Israel and Palestine, living side-by-side in peace and security," he said. "Achieving this goal requires difficult compromises, and the Israelis and Palestinians have elected leaders committed to making them."

The conference produced a vaguely worded joint declaration in which Israel and the Palestinians agreed to restart talks—suspended seven years earlier—on December 12, but did not set a firm deadline for their conclusion. President Bush, announcing this agreement on November 27, tried to make that sound good. "Our purpose here in Annapolis is not to conclude an agreement. Rather, it is to launch negotiations between the Israelis and Palestinians," he said. "For the rest of us, our job is to encourage the parties in this effort and to give them the support they need to succeed." The time was right, Bush contended, because the PA and Israel had leaders who were determined to achieve peace, and because "we must not cede victory to the extremists."

Israel was prepared to make painful compromises and would address all the issues "we have avoided" in direct and continuous negotiations, Olmert said. His speech included an open acknowledgment that the Palestinians had suffered for many years, with many living in poverty and neglect for decades in camps. "We are not oblivious to the tragedies that you have experienced," the Israeli leader said.

Although many dismissed the conference as a glorified photo-op that would produce no real results, there appeared to be several accomplishments. For one thing, Israel insisted on, and the Palestinians agreed to, commitments by both sides to "immediately implement their respective obligations under the performance-based 'road map,'" with monitoring and evaluation of these efforts designated as a task of the U.S. The major Palestinian obligation was to dismantle the terror apparatus, while Israel had to freeze all settlement activity and take down outposts put up since March 2001.

A second accomplishment was the attendance of Arab League nations—particularly Syria, which sent a deputy foreign minister, and Saudi Arabia. Though there was no substantive contact between Israel and these nations at the sessions, their very presence represented a diplomatic accomplishment for the U.S., if not for Israel. As it turned out, Israeli efforts to use the conference as an opening to new contacts with Arab states were largely unsuccessful. Foreign Minister Livni, who attempted to set up meetings with representatives of 15 Arab countries that did not have ties with Israel at or after Annapolis, only met with Foreign Minister Salaheddin al-Bashir of Jordan, which already had full diplomatic ties with Israel. And according to a report in the *Jerusalem Post,* a plan for Livni to stop off in a North African country—either Morocco or Tunisia—on her way home from the U.S. failed to materialize. Nor did Olmert meet publicly with any Arab representative at or after Annapolis—though he did exchange brief comments and handshakes with the delegates from Qatar, Morocco, Bahrain, and the Muslim but non-Arab Pakistan after his Annapolis speech.

According to *Washington Post* reporter Glenn Kessler's account of the closed-door session that followed the public declarations, Livni challenged the 16 Arab League representatives in the room. "Why doesn't anyone want to shake my hand," Kessler quoted Dutch representative Franz Timmerman as saying that Livni asked. "Why doesn't anyone want to be seen speaking to me?" Kessler wrote: "She was saying, 'Stop treating me as a pariah,'" Timmerman told him, "They shun her like she is Count Dracula's younger sister." The Israeli Foreign Ministry had a somewhat different version of Livni's statement, quoting her as saying that she would not ask for handshakes.

At the same gathering, Rice, who also received cool treatment from Arab delegates, spoke movingly about parallels between her childhood in Birmingham, Alabama, and the situation of Palestinians and Israelis. "Like the Israelis, I know what it is like to go to sleep at night not knowing if you will be bombed, of being afraid to be in your own neighborhood, of being afraid to go to your church," Kessler reported her saying in his *Washington Post* account. "I know what it is like to hear you cannot go on a road or through a checkpoint because you are Palestinian. I understand the feeling of humiliation and powerlessness."

In the aftermath of the conference, the U.S., on November 30, suddenly withdrew a UN Security Council resolution endorsing the Annapolis declaration. This was done in deference to Israel, which feared that even though the resolution was unobjectionable, its passage might lead to unwanted Security Council involvement in the restarted peace process. Of particular concern, some reports suggested, was the possibility that the Council might impose an end-of-2008 deadline for the conclusion of an agreement instead of the declaration's vague hope for such an ending.

That same day a three-judge Israeli Supreme Court panel ruled on a legal challenge mounted by a coalition of human-rights organizations against Israel's decision to reduce fuel and electricity supplies to the Gaza Strip. The fuel cuts had begun in October and the electricity reduction was due to start in December. Opponents of the policy argued that it constituted collective punishment against all residents of Gaza for the Hamas seizure of control there in June.

The judges decided that reduction of fuel supplies could continue since "we were not convinced that the decision by [the state] to limit the amount of fuel transferred to the Gaza Strip harms, at this point, vital humanitarian needs in the Strip." Nevertheless, they said, the proposed electricity cut should be suspended. "We welcome the delay in electricity cuts and expect that at the end of the day the court will prevent the military from cutting electricity to Gaza, but we are concerned about the court's failure to intervene in the fuel cuts," said Sari Bashi of Gisha, one of the rights groups spearheading the legal challenge. The government claimed that the electricity cuts would be minor and not affect installations such as hospitals, water pumps, and sewage plants.

DECEMBER: NO IMPROVEMENT

Israel released 429 more Palestinian prisoners on December 2 as another confidence-building measure intended to strengthen Abbas. The release had originally been planned to take place before the Annapolis conference. Marwan Barghouti, the Fatah leader serving five life terms for terrorist murders he ordered during the second intifada, called the release "a joke," asserting that most of the prisoners would have been released anyway in the next few months.

As prescribed in the Annapolis declaration, formal talks between Israel and the PA resumed on December 12. Teams headed by Tzipi Livni and Ahmed Querei (Abu Ala) met in an atmosphere that was described as tense. In the course of the 90-minute session, PA negotiator Saeb Erekat blasted Israel for authorizing construction of 300 new apartments in the disputed Har Homa neighborhood of Jerusalem, a move he said violated the pledge Israel made in Annapolis to halt all settlement activity. The Israeli delegation, for its part, focused on the continuing rocket attacks on its southern towns from the Gaza Strip.

The very next day, enraged by the continuing damage to his town, Sderot mayor Eli Moyal resigned, saying, "I cannot take the responsibility to manage a city that is under attack for seven years. If 20 children are killed tomorrow from a rocket, I will be asked, 'Why did you open the kindergarten?' I have been deliberating matters pertaining to human life for years now, and I cannot continue." A few hours later he retracted his resignation.

Even before returning home from Annapolis in November, Prime Minister Olmert came under heavy criticism from parties within his own coalition, especially the right-wing Israel Beitenu and the ultra-Orthodox Shas, both of which could be expected to leave the government if Israel made substantial concessions. Seeking to blunt their threats to scuttle the government, Olmert stressed that there was no firm timetable for the completion of talks.

There was also skepticism on the Palestinian side. PA president Abbas, despite his apparent commitment to negotiate a settlement, refused to recognize Israel as a Jewish state, a demand that was key to Israel's negotiating position in opposition to the "return" of Palestinian refugees to Israeli territory. Beyond that, many Palestinians, most prominently Hamas, challenged Abbas's authority to make a deal even if he wanted to, on the grounds that he did not represent the Palestinian people.

The construction in Har Homa was a particular sore point for the

Palestinians, and Israel seemed confused about how to handle it. According to some press reports, Olmert and Livni had not even been aware of the decision to build, which seemed, on its face, to contradict Israel's commitment at Annapolis to halt settlement activity. Reuters quoted a senior Israeli official as saying that the Jewish state "does not need American approval to do something that we think, as a sovereign state, we should do." He added that if someone had bought an empty lot in a settlement ten years earlier, and now decided to build on it, "the government of Israel cannot do anything about it." According to a report in the right-wing *Makor Rishon* newspaper, on December 23 Housing Minister Ze'ev Boim, on Olmert's direct instructions, canceled a tender for bids to build 120 of the Har Homa residences. But at the same time, Minister for Jerusalem Affairs Rafi Eitan said construction would go on. "Har Homa is an integral, organic part of Jerusalem," he told a radio interviewer. "No promise was ever given to anyone that we wouldn't continue to build in Har Homa."

Despite the doubts on both sides, Secretary of State Rice expressed optimism about the chances for an agreement. Asked to comment about the apparent lack of progress, Rice said on December 20 that she had "never myself been a part of a negotiation nor have I ever studied, as a professor, a negotiation that didn't start out a little slowly." She claimed that "the parties have said they believe they can reach an agreement by 2008"—a view expressed only as a "hope" but not a firm pledge in the Annapolis statement itself. "I certainly believe that within a year the parties can come to terms about what will constitute a Palestinian state," she elaborated, adding that implementation of an agreement would, of necessity, take "a while longer." Rice added that both sides had to fulfill their obligations under the "road map."

Three days before, on December 17, international donors pledged $7.4 billion, $1.8 billion more than anticipated, to the PA at a conference in Paris. Secretary of State Rice had told attendees from 90 states that the PA was in "serious budgetary crisis" and that the meeting represented a last chance to avoid a PA bankruptcy. The U.S. pledged $555 million for 2008. The host of the meeting, President Sarkozy of France, called it a turning point in the long-stalled peace negotiations, and Tony Blair, the Quartet's special envoy, said it was a "state-building conference."

Israel meanwhile escalated its antiterror operations, killing at least 11 Islamic Jihad operatives on December 16 and 17. Among the dead were Tariq Abu Ra'ali, head of Islamic Jihad in Jenin in the West Bank, Majad Harazin, a senior operative in charge of squads firing Qassams in the

Gaza Strip, and four members of Jihad's Al-Quds Brigades. "We will continue to seek out the heads of terror organizations and strike at them," Prime Minister Olmert said on December 18.

A few days earlier, on December 14, a top adviser to PA prime minister Fayyad was kidnapped while on a visit to the Gaza Strip for the funeral of his mother-in-law. Omar al-Ghoul was taken away by men in civilian clothes shortly after his arrival from Ramallah. Information Minister Riad al-Malki blamed "criminals working for Hamas" for the abduction and called for Ghoul's immediate release. He said that the incident showed Fatah leaders that "Gaza is closed to them." A Hamas spokesman said that Ghoul, a harsh critic of the Hamas takeover of Gaza, was being interrogated for "illegal activities." By year's end he had still not been released.

An explosion near a funeral procession in Gaza killed three people and injured at least 30 others on the day Ghoul was abducted. PA police said it may have been caused by a grenade dropped by a gunman taking part in the funeral march.

Israel's tough actions in Gaza finally appeared to produce results in late December, as reports indicated that Hamas was seeking ways to reach a *hudna,* an informal cease-fire. According to these reports, Hamas would stop its own attacks against Israel in exchange for a suspension of the targeted killings policy and a loosening of the Israeli blockade of the Strip. Israeli defense officials, however, said that Hamas had to do more, such as stopping other militant groups, particularly Islamic Jihad, from firing rockets and mortars at Israel. On December 20, National Infrastructure Minister Ben-Eliezer added other conditions: an end to the smuggling of arms into the Gaza Strip and the opening of talks for the release of kidnapped soldier Gilad Shalit.

At the same time, *Ha'aretz* reported that many on the Israeli side, including the prime minister, were deeply suspicions of the Hamas offer and did not feel that under prevailing conditions there was room for negotiations. But that could change, the paper reported, if Haniyeh, the former PA prime minister, managed to rein in the militants. Nevertheless, two members of Olmert's cabinet, Transport Minister Mofaz and Minister without Portfolio Ami Ayalon, said on December 19 that they would not rule out talks with Hamas. Mofaz, a former Likud defense minister, said he would consider such talks only via an intermediary and only if Israel continued its strikes against terrorists. But Ayalon, a former head of the Shin Bet security service and member of the dovish wing of Labor, said he would "talk to anyone" for the purpose of ending Qassam rocket fire.

Negotiating, he added, "is not a dirty word, as long as it does not allow them only to get stronger."

On the eve of the second round of talks between teams headed by Livni and Abu Ala, an unidentified Israeli official warned of impending outside pressures. "Israel has created a series of far-reaching expectations in the international arena," the official told *Ha'aretz* on December 23, referring to Israel's pledge to curtail settlements, "but this is not going to happen." Since there was little support for concessions in the coalition and the Olmert government was inherently weak, the official added, "There is no political capability either to evacuate settlements or freeze construction in the settlements."

In mid-December, Internal Security Minister Avi Dichter called off a trip to Britain scheduled for early 2008 to avoid possible arrest by British authorities. Concerns about the minister's possible arrest were linked to his role as head of the Shin Bet in 2002, when an attack on the Gaza home of Hamas military commander Salah Shehadeh resulted in also killing 13 innocent civilians (see AJYB 2003, p. 218). British law allowed individuals to seek warrants for the arrest of those suspected of serious human rights abuses abroad.

Identifying Israel as a Jewish state discriminated against non-Jews, said Latin Patriarch Michel Sabbah in his annual pre-Christmas news conference in Jerusalem. Sabbah, a Palestinian, said Israel should become a state for all its residents, Jews, Muslims, and Christians. "This land cannot be exclusive for anyone," he stated. In response, a Foreign Ministry spokesman said, "We reject his claim that other religions are not enjoying equal rights in Israel."

Defense Minister Barak paid a brief visit to Egypt on December 27, meeting with President Mubarak and Egyptian security chief Omar Suleiman in Sharm al-Sheikh. Afterward Barak said that the two countries would continue their joint struggle against terror. Mubarak, for his part, rapped Foreign Minister Livni for criticizing, before the Knesset Foreign Affairs and Defense Committee, what she called Egypt's "dismal failure" to stop arms smuggling into Gaza. "It's very easy to sit in an office in Jerusalem and hand out grades on our performance in the field," Mubarak said. "But it makes for a tense atmosphere, and our relationship with Israel is very important to me."

The pressure on Palestinian terror groups in the Gaza Strip continued on December 27, with IDF and Shin Bet forces killing eight Hamas and Islamic Jihad gunmen. Among the dead was Muhammad Abd-allah Abu Murshad, the Jihad's head of rocketry in Gaza.

Hikers Ahiam Amihai and David Rubin, soldiers on leave from their units and out of uniform, were shot to death by Palestinians in the Hebron Hills on December 28. Both were residents of Kiryat Arba, as was a young woman who was with them and survived the attack. Islamic Jihad and the armed wing of Fatah each claimed responsibility, and PA foreign minister Riyad al-Malkhi vowed that the perpetrators would be dealt with harshly. The Shin Bet security service later said that the PA had detained two suspects, both of whom were connected to the Palestinian security forces. PA Interior Minister Abdel-Razak al-Yahya reacted to the incident by saying that his government was dismantling armed groups. "There is no Al-Aqsa Martyrs Brigades any more," he told Palestinian radio.

The signers of a leaflet distributed in Gaza might have disputed Yahya's claim. Under the name of the Al-Aqsa Martyrs Brigades, it called for killing PA prime minister Fayyad for alleged collaboration with Israel and the U.S. In a December 31 report by its Arab affairs writer, Khaled Abu Toameh, the *Jerusalem Report* noted that Fayyad was under heavy criticism from activists inside the Fatah movement for denying them funds and seeking to diminish their power. Others, according to Abu Toameh, accused Fayyad of attempting to consolidate his own position in the hope of undermining President Abbas.

At year's end, about 2,000 Palestinians who had visited Mecca for the Muslim hajj pilgrimage found themselves stranded on the Egyptian side of the Rafiah checkpoint. At the request of Israel, which suspected that some of the pilgrims were carrying large sums of cash back to the Gaza Strip and that others might be terrorists, Egypt insisted that the multitude go home through the Israeli-controlled Kerem Shalom checkpoint. (On January 2, 2008, Egypt would cave in to Hamas pressure and open the Rafiah crossing-point for the pilgrims.)

Smuggling into the Gaza Strip continued. On December 29 the army announced that 6.5 tons of potassium nitrate, an ingredient used in the manufacture of home-made explosives like those in suicide bombs and Qassam rockets, was discovered in bags marked "sugar" that were destined for the Gaza Strip. Markings on the bags also indicated, falsely, that they were part of an EU humanitarian aid shipment.

A "Peace Index" survey using a sample of almost 600 Israelis, conducted by two Tel Aviv University professors, was published in late December. It showed that an overwhelming 81 percent of Jewish respondents favored targeted killings of Qassam firing teams and their dispatchers, and that 76 percent did not believe that Egypt was seriously trying to stop arms smuggling into Gaza. Only a bare majority, 51 percent, thought Israel should live up to the understandings reached with the Palestinians at Annapolis, 53 percent supported a settlement freeze, and 57 percent thought that Israelis had no business in areas under Palestinian rule. Seventy-five percent of the national sample said that "on the personal level" 2007 had been "good" or "very good" for them.

A Security Summary

Thirteen Israelis—seven civilians and six military personnel—were killed in terror attacks in 2007, the lowest number since the start of the second intifada in 2000. There was only one "successful" suicide bombing during the year, the one in Eilat in January (see above, p. 227), compared to six in 2006 and the high of 60 in 2002. According to a Shin Bet security service report, the drop was entirely attributable to Israeli actions: construction of the separation fence, securing timely intelligence about possible attacks, and the army's near-complete freedom of action to intercept terrorists on the West Bank before they were able to launch attacks.

Palestinians fired 1,263 rockets and 1,511 mortar shells into Israel from the Gaza Strip in 2007, compared to 1,722 rockets and 55 mortars in 2006. Israeli forces killed 373 Palestinians in 2007, a 43-percent decline from the preceding year, according to a year-end report by B'Tselem, the Israeli human-rights organization. The percentage of noncombatant civilians among the killed also decreased, from 54 percent in 2006 to 35 percent in 2007. Of the Palestinians killed, 53 were minors. At the same time, B'Tselem said, 344 Palestinians were killed in internal conflict, mostly in clashes between Fatah and Hamas.

According to a report presented to the cabinet in early 2008 by Yuval Diskin, head of the Shin Bet internal security services, Israel killed 810 Palestinians in the territories during 2006–07, about 200 of whom were not clearly linked to terrorist organizations. Diskin estimated the total number of terrorist fighters at around 20,000. He also noted that about 3,000 residents of Sderot, the border city hardest hit by Hamas and Islamic Jihad mortar and Qassam rocket fire from Gaza, had left town. Diskin's report stated that the political leadership was generally pleased with the impact of the Israeli attacks into Gaza, but since military efforts to stop the rockets had not been effective, an investment of NIS 320 million (about $80 million) would be necessary to build shelters and safe rooms in Sderot and other border towns.

Strike into Syria

Israeli F-15 aircraft struck deep into Syria to destroy what apparently was a nuclear facility under construction near the Euphrates River in the eastern part of the country on September 6. The daring raid first came to light when a Syrian spokesman said that its air defenses ran off Israeli warplanes that violated its airspace. After the intruders were confronted by Syrian defense units, the Syrian said, the planes "dropped some ammunition in deserted areas and fled." Syria warned that it would retaliate at the time and place of its own choosing against "this flagrant, aggressive act."

The incident remained a mystery for more than a week, as Israel maintained an official silence and even the most talkative defense officials kept mum on the subject. Eventually it emerged that the target had been a nuclear facility, and it had been destroyed. There were also reports that Israeli commando units on the ground not only guided the bombers but also succeeded in taking away some nuclear materials, in order to convince the Americans that what Israel had hit was actually a nuclear plant.

Israel never officially confirmed that the raid took place. Opposition leader Benjamin Netanyahu was the only top Israeli who talked about it. In an interview with Channel 1 news anchor Haim Yavin on September 14, Netanyahu boasted that, as opposition leader, he had supported the plan for the raid. "When the prime minister takes action in important and necessary matters, and generally when the government is doing things for the security of Israel, I give it my endorsement," Netanyahu told Yavin. "I was party to this matter, I must say, from the first minute, and I gave it my backing, but it is still too early to discuss this subject." Netanyahu's remarks drew criticism from both sides of the Israeli political divide, as the Likud leader was charged with irresponsibility for lifting, albeit briefly and vaguely, the veil of silence that had been imposed on information about the raid.

London's *Sunday Times* reported on September 16 that Israel planes, guided with laser beams by commandos from the Shaldag reconnaissance unit, who had been infiltrated in the day before, literally "blew apart" a nuclear cache, uranium-enrichment facilities, or other nonconventional weapons equipment that North Korea had provided Syria. Citing what it said were Israeli sources, the story identified the attacking unit as the 69th Squadron, consisting of American-made Israeli F15-I aircraft, and the target as 50 miles from the Syrian-Iraqi border.

The British newspaper claimed that planning for the audacious raid—

in which Syria's Russian-made antiaircraft defense system was paralyzed or blinded—had been going on for almost six months, ever since Mossad overseas intelligence chief Meir Dagan presented Olmert with evidence that Syria was seeking to buy a nuclear device from North Korea, apparently for mounting on Scud-C missiles also produced in North Korea. "This was supposed to be a devastating Syrian surprise for Israel," the *Times* quoted its Israeli source as saying. "We've known for a long time that Syria has deadly chemical warheads on its Scuds, but Israel can't live with a nuclear warhead."

Using the Ofek-7 intelligence satellite and other means, Israel was monitoring what purported to be an agricultural research center at Deir al-Zor on the Euphrates. The paper said that Ofeq-7, launched in June (see above, p. 237), was diverted from Iran to Syria and sent out high-quality images of northeastern Syria every 90 minutes.

Preparations for the attack may have been behind the mixed signals sent to the Syrians during the summer regarding possible war, including the reinforcement of Israeli forces in the Golan Heights. The Syrians, in response to the Israeli moves, also escalated preparations for a possible confrontation. Later, Defense Minister Barak tried to lower the pressure, pulling some Israeli forces out of the Golan and eliciting a reciprocal Syrian response. The *Sunday Times* said that there was an alternate theory in Washington to the effect that the air strikes were actually "a diversion for a daring Israeli commando raid, in which nuclear materials were intercepted en route to Iran and hauled to Israel."

Imad Moustapha, the Syrian ambassador to the U.S., called all these reports "absolutely totally fundamentally ridiculous and untrue," in an interview with *Newsweek*. But additional proof of Syrian intentions appeared in a September 18 report in *Jane's Defense Weekly* that dozens of Iranian engineers and about 15 Syrian officers were accidentally killed while trying to attach a warhead filled with deadly Sarin nerve gas to a Scud missile. Syrian media had reported that the incident, which took place in June, involved a blast at an arms depot near Aleppo in northern Syria. According to *Jane's*, the Syrians and Iranians were working on modifying Scuds to carry nonconventional armaments.

In mid-October, the UN actually changed a statement made by Syrian ambassador Bashar al-Jaafari to a UN committee in which, by an apparent slip of the tongue, he confirmed the charges against his country. Initial reports of his speech, relayed by *Ha'aretz* and confirmed by the Foreign Ministry, had Jaafari saying: "Israel was the fourth largest exporter of weapons of mass destruction and a violator of other nations' airspace, and it had taken action against nuclear facilities, including the 6 July attack in Syria [an apparently mistaken date, in reference to the September 6 attack]." But the crucial paragraph in the revised UN document read: "Moreover, the entity that was the fourth largest exporter of lethal weapons in the world, that which violated the airspace of sovereign states and carried out military aggression against them, as had happened on 6 September against Syria, such an entity, with all those characteristics and more, had no right to go on lying without shame."

Photographs taken by a commercial satellite and released on October 24 seemed to indicate that the Syrians had razed the structures hit in the Israeli attack, according to an Associated Press report. The wire service said that the cleanup might indicate a Syrian effort to conceal evidence of the purpose of the structures that might be gathered by a proposed international inquiry. Syria, said David Albright, president of the Institute for Science and International Security, which examined the satellite images, "took down this facility so quickly it looks like they are trying to hide something." Albright said Syria might have acted in haste because the Israeli attack blew a hole in the roof, exposing the interior to spy planes and satellites. And the fact that the roof was built early in the construction process indicated that it was likely a reactor. "From what we understand," he explained, "North Korea builds reactors in an old-fashioned way; the roof goes on early."

But Prof. Uzi Even of Tel Aviv University said in late November that an analysis of satellite photos published in the media brought him to the conclusion that the structure destroyed in the attack was not a nuclear reactor. Even told reporter Yossi Melman of *Ha'aretz:* "In my estimation this was something very nasty and vicious, and even more dangerous than a reactor. I have no information, only an assessment, but I suspect that it was a plant for processing plutonium, namely a factory for assembling the bomb."

In mid-December Assad said that Syria had turned down an offer of nuclear missiles, apparently contained in a letter from smugglers who said they were representing Abdul Kadir Khan, father of the Pakistani nuclear-weapons program. In an interview with an Austrian newspaper, the Syrian president said his country "does not know if the letter was genuine, or an Israeli trap." Assad added that "we are not interested in nuclear weapons or a nuclear facility and I never met Khan."A different signal, though, came from Muhammad Habash, a member of the Syrian parliament, who said that though Syria had no interest in escalating tensions with Israel, the Israeli nuclear reactor in Dimona was well within

round-trip for the purpose of blowing up an Iranian site, using a combination of precision laser bombs and low-yield nuclear bunker-buster munitions. According to the report, the nuclear bombs in the attack would each have a force equal to about one-fifteenth of the atom bomb dropped on Hiroshima in 1945. "It will be one mission, one strike, and the Iranian nuclear project will be demolished," the *Times* quoted one of the sources as saying. Three possible targets for a purported Israeli strike were named: Natanz, which housed centrifuges used to enrich uranium, a conversion facility for uranium near Isfahan, and a heavy-water reactor at Arak.

A source in the U.S. Defense Department speculated that the leak may have been intentional. "In the cold war," the American reportedly said, "we made it clear to the Russians that it was a virtual certainty that nukes would fly and fly early. Israel may be adopting the same tactics: 'You produce a weapon; you die.'"

At least in part due to the Iranian nuclear threat, the U.S. announced that deliveries to Israel of the Joint Strike Fighter, a new, advanced aircraft, would begin in 2012, earlier than originally planned. Speaking to the *Jerusalem Post,* one Israeli defense official praised the plane's stealth capabilities. "It can fly to downtown Tehran without anyone knowing," he was quoted as saying.

Israel reacted with skepticism to the U.S. National Intelligence Estimate issued in early December that said that Iran had ceased its nuclear armaments program in 2003. Prime Minister Olmert said that Israel's attitude towards the Iranian nuclear threat would not change and that the world had to keep up the pressure on Iran, including sanctions aimed at blocking further nuclear development. Speaking to the cabinet a few days after the American report was released, Olmert said: "According to the assessment, Iran had a nuclear weapons program until at least 2003, and there is no positive report giving any explanation of where this program has disappeared to." Israel dispatched a delegation of high intelligence officials to gather more information about the American report, much of which was classified as secret, and to present confidential Israeli intelligence in an effort to persuade the Americans that Iran was still actively working on the development of nuclear arms.

Internal Security Minister Avi Dichter publicly expressed doubts about the U.S. report, saying it was based on a "misconception." Speaking to a weekend cultural gathering in Bat Yam, south of Tel Aviv, the former head of the Shin Bet internal security service said that the mistaken U.S. report could have disastrous repercussions, possibly triggering a "re-

'e vice president of the American Jewish Joint

ious national components of ORT (Organiza-
l Training), which ran a network of technical
Israel and elsewhere, affected ORT America.
' from World ORT in 2006. While the Israelis
vere getting insufficient funding and could get
:ir own, ORT America, fearful that its donors
by ORT Israel, informed its supporters that
'ere not tax deductible, and charged that the
al transparency. In January, World ORT an-
aeli schools directly, without going through
. denied ORT Israel the use of the "ORT"
the U.S., causing ORT Israel to sue in an
t ORT had become a generic name that could
meanwhile, ORT Israel sought to bar World
ınd a Haifa court ruled in April that the dis-

ıber of Jews who excel in intellectually de-
ıat had attracted numerous attempts at ex-
attention in the April issue of *Commentary,*
us" by Charles Murray. Already controver-
l Curve, which argued that intelligence had
ıy noted that Jewish IQ scores were higher
ıt factors in Jewish history, such as the cen-
ı and the development of the Talmud, "in-
ıtellectual complexity," so that males of
ginalized and eventually left the fold. Mur-
ed by some other social scientists for racial

vork appeared as the year began, a new edi-
neant to replace the first edition published
es were updated, and new ones, reflecting

gional Yom Kippur"—referring to the surprise attack on Israel by Syria and Egypt in 1973. Dichter said that the Iranian threat was "ongoing and palpable," threatening not only Israel but the whole region, including Europe and North Africa, which were also in range of Iranian missiles. There were various reports that the U.S. estimate had been tainted by a concerted Iranian effort at disinformation. London's *Sunday Telegraph* quoted a senior British intelligence official's assessment that the Americans had been tricked, and the French-based National Council for Resistance in Iran said that Tehran was using double agents to mislead the Americans.

U.S. Aid

Israel and the U.S. signed a ten-year defense-aid agreement worth $30 billion in late September. The memorandum of understanding (MOU), signed in Jerusalem, substantially increased the amount of U.S. defense assistance to the Jewish state.

The agreement represented a new approach to U.S. aid to Israel. Prior to 1998, military aid to Israel amounted to $1.8 billion a year, and Israel received an additional $1.2 billion in civilian aid, which was mostly used to service the debt incurred for arms purchases in the 1970s, when American defense aid came in the form of loans rather than grants. Under an agreement reached in 1998 under then-prime minister Benjamin Netanyahu—and because Israel was paying off the massive debts to the U.S.—Washington agreed to Israel's request to gradually reduce the amount of civilian aid by $120 million a year while raising military assistance by an annual $60 million. As a result, in 2008 Israel was to receive $2.4 billion in defense aid, and, for the first time, no civilian aid at all. The new deal, to go into effect in 2009, required Israel to use 73.7 percent of the aid package for purchases from U.S. suppliers, and the remaining 26.3 percent for purchases from Israeli contractors.

The $30-billion U.S. aid package turned out to be larger than that envisioned by an Israeli committee, which recommended an increase over ten years of NIS 100 billion (about $25 billion at current exchange rates) in defense budget spending levels.

In late July, possibly as a precursor to its own arms deal, Israel unexpectedly dropped its objections to an American plan to sell $20 billion worth of advanced arms, including satellite-guided bombs, naval vessels, and fighter aircraft, to Saudi Arabia. Earlier, a number of members of Congress, including Democrats Tom Lantos of California and Anthony

Weiner and Jerrold Nadler of New York, said they would try to block the Saudi arms package, which included Joint Direct Attack Munitions (JDAM), a relatively low-cost kit that transformed ordinary free-falling bombs into precision-guided munitions.

Unfinished Business

Former MK Azmi Bishara, leader of the Arab Balad party, fled the country in early April while under investigation for treason and espionage allegedly committed during the war in Lebanon in the summer of 2006. On May 2—the same day that a Petah Tikva Magistrate's Court lifted a gag order that had cast a veil of secrecy over the case—Bishara appeared at the Israeli embassy in Cairo to turn in his resignation from the Knesset. A Shin Bet official told reporters that the charismatic Bishara had been in contact with Hezballah operatives during the war, providing "information, suggestions and recommendations" about the advisability of sending rockets deep into Israel.

Reportedly, Bishara had been questioned twice by Israeli police before his departure from the country. Speaking by telephone from abroad to supporters in Nazareth, Bishara said he might stay away since he was unlikely to get a fair trial, and conviction would mean a long jail sentence and an end to his political career. "My guilt is that I love my homeland," he continued, "our intellect and our words are our weapons. Never in my life did I draw a gun or kill anyone." Said Nafa, who took Bishara's seat in the Knesset, accused the Shin Bet of a frame-up.

Intelligence agencies were quoted as saying that Bishara had brought large sums of money from foreign sources into Israel, but that they were not sure whether he had done so for himself or as a courier. According to *Ha'aretz,* the Shin Bet—which did not expect Bishara to return anytime soon—also had other serious, undisclosed suspicions about Bishara.

An Israeli Arab, Ashraf Keisi, was given five life sentences plus 20 years in prison for driving a suicide bomber to the Stage nightclub in Tel Aviv in February 2005 for an attack in which five Israelis were killed (see AJYB 2006, p. 237). He was convicted of five counts of murder, one count of attempted murder, and other offenses. In handing down the sentence on October 18, Saviona Rotlevi, presiding judge of the Tel Aviv District Court, dismissed Keisi's claim "that he had regrets during the drive but could not act on them because of the suicide bomber's threats." Keisi helped the bomber choose a location that would allow for the highest number of victims, and received $5,000 in advance for his part in the bombing. He was promised, but never paid, another $14,000.

Three Israelis convicted of transporting a suicide bomber to Netanya for a July 2005 attack in which five Israelis died and 30 were injured (see AJYB 2006, p. 249) were each sentenced to 13 years in jail on April 12. The men—Kfir Levy of Ramat Gan and Israeli Arabs Sif Azam and Abed Abu Moch—were convicted of manslaughter and causing severe injury. Each drove the terrorist part of the way from the West Bank to Netanya's Hasharon mall, where he blew himself up. Yaron Horowitz, whose 16-year-old daughter was killed in the blast, said the accused deserved life sentences because they were "partners to the murder—especially Levy, who succeeded in getting the perpetrator into Israel because he is Jewish."

POLITICAL DEVELOPMENTS

Apportioning Blame

In the summer of 2006 Israel fought a 34-day war against Hezballah in southern Lebanon in which 119 soldiers and 43 civilians were killed and many more wounded. The aims of the war—return of two kidnapped soldiers and removal of the Hezballah threat to northern Israel—were not attained, although the government viewed the stationing of a UN force on the Lebanese border after hostilities ended as an accomplishment, and Hezballah undoubtedly was weakened, at least temporarily, as a fighting force (see AJYB 2007, pp. 238–247).

The Israeli public demanded an accounting, and in September 2006 an investigative panel was set up under the chairmanship of Eliyahu Winograd, a retired judge, to look into the performance of the government. The Winograd Commission issued an interim report on April 30, 2007, that dealt only with the period from Israel's withdrawal from its "security zone" in southern Lebanon in 2000 through the start of the war in the second week of July 2006.

It accused Prime Minister Olmert of "severe failure" in leading the country into war, stressing that Olmert, who "bears supreme and comprehensive responsibility" for both the government and the army, acted hastily, without an overall plan for the conflict into which he led the country. But blame was shared by his colleagues as well, as the entire government had voted to go to war without understanding the implications of its actions. It "did not consider the whole range of options," the report claimed, "including political moves combined with military strikes, which would have kept the conflict below the 'escalation level.'" To be sure, the commission noted that the lack of readiness for war was to some extent due to neglect and lack of advance planning by previous governments (principally, though not explicitly stated, those headed by Ariel Sharon).

The report also sharply criticized Defense Minister Amir Peretz and the IDF chief of staff during the war, Dan Halutz, who had resigned on January 17. It said that Peretz, whose primary previous experience before taking the reins of the Labor Party was as a union leader, "did not have the knowledge or experience in military, political or governmental matters" nor did he grasp the "basic principles of using military force to achieve political goals." Nevertheless, Peretz made vital decisions as defense minister without properly consulting "experienced political and professional experts." Halutz, the commission said, had not prepared the army properly, particularly for the predictable occurrence of a Hezballah kidnapping of Israeli soldiers. It also accused him of acting impulsively and failing to present alternative courses of action to the political leadership. As chief of staff, the report went on, Halutz bore special blame as he should have taken into consideration the inexperience of both Olmert, who had been prime minister for only a few months, and Peretz, a complete tyro in matters of national defense.

This interim report did not make personal recommendations about the individuals involved, but the commission held out the possibility that it would do so in its final report, which was expected in the summer (it was ultimately delayed until early 2008). Nevertheless, demands for the heads of the two main targets of criticism still in office mounted quickly. Foreign Minister Livni, after an hour-long meeting with Olmert on May 2, said she had told the prime minister to resign. "It's not a personal matter," she said. "The issue is more important than both of us." Livni said she did not support the nomination of a prime minister from another party, and thought that Kadima, where she nominally held the number-two post, would be able to form a new government. She told reporters she had contemplated resigning, but that "resignation is a form of protest, not necessarily an act of leadership."

Calls for Olmert to step down also came from MKs in Labor, his principal coalition partner, but only one, Minister without Portfolio Eitan Cabel, resigned from the government. Inside his own party, Kadima,

Knesset coalition chairman Avigdor Yitzhaki, a former director general of Ariel Sharon's Prime Minister's Office, circulated a petition among party MKs seeking to force Olmert out, but the prime minister got the public backing of Kadima ministers Meir Sheetrit (Housing) and Avi Dichter (Public Security). And at a meeting where Yitzhaki tendered his resignation as coalition chairman but not as MK, a majority of Kadima Knesset members said they stood behind the prime minister.

On May 3 a crowd estimated by police at 100,000 (the organizers claimed 200,000) gathered at Tel Aviv's Rabin Square to demand the ouster of Olmert and Peretz. "Ehud Olmert, you said you work for us. Olmert, you are fired!" said the event's keynote speaker, author Meir Shalev, referring to an earlier Olmert speech in which the prime minister said that taking responsibility and making tough, often unpopular decisions was "my job." Retired general Uzi Dayan, head of the small and so far unsuccessful Tafnit (Turning Point) political party and the organizer of the rally, called on Olmert not to delay until the final report was issued, but to "do the right thing and go home."

Public sentiment was heavily anti-Olmert. A poll conducted by *Ha'aretz* 24 hours after the release of the interim Winograd report showed that 68 percent of respondents wanted him to resign and only 23 percent thought he ought to stay on. The figures for Peretz were even worse—85 percent wanted him out as defense minister. Meanwhile, former chief of staff Amnon Lipkin-Shahak was named to head a committee dealing with implementation of the Winograd recommendations.

In late May, making his first appearance before the Knesset since the publication of the interim report, Olmert defended his decision not to resign. He claimed that the war, painful as it had been, had restored quiet to the northern border, which he had visited two weeks earlier. Olmert said that the government's main goals in going to war were the implementation of Security Council Resolution 1559, deployment of the Lebanese Army on the border, a cease-fire, and the return of captured soldiers Eldad Regev and Ehud Goldwasser—although he knew at the time that the chances of bringing them back through a military operation were "slim." While admitting that the numerous failures in the war were his responsibility, Olmert pointed out that the report had cited instances of "effort and decision-making ability" on the part of the government. Finally, he said that during the war opposition leader Benjamin Netanyahu had "offered his full and unconditional support. He too would do the same thing, he told me."

The prime minister was notably absent from a ceremony at Jerusalem's

Mt. Herzl on July 2 marking the first anniversary of the war on the Hebrew calendar. His office said that the decision not to attend was due to security considerations.

In an October 29 TV address, Prime Minister Olmert added a new factor to the political picture by announcing that he had prostate cancer and was likely, but not certain, to need surgery. He said the disease and the possible operation would not interfere significantly with his ability to carry out his duties. The cancer was discovered during a routine checkup, and his doctors said it was "of no danger to him."

At the very end of the year, on December 31, the Knesset Foreign Affairs and Defense Committee issued its own 150-page report on the Lebanon war. All 17 committee members signed their names to it and about a third of them also made additional comments in a minority opinion. The committee had begun its investigation in September 2006, soon after the fighting ended, and most of the work was done by its classified subcommittees. The report rapped the policy of restraint followed by several Israeli governments in southern Lebanon following the May 2000 withdrawal from the security zone for creating "a state of paralysis and slack" in the army, and criticized the Olmert government for delaying the ground offensive, which it said should have been launched earlier and on a much broader scale than the limited—and costly—thrust north in the last days of the war. It found that by not mounting that ground offensive earlier, the Israeli military had "failed to achieve the war's central objective, combating Katyusha fire." The Knesset panel was extremely critical of the senior army command, saying that its mistaken tactics and "blindness" played into Hezballah's hands, and that the lack of a prepared plan of attack was "a grievous blunder."

Leaving personal recommendations to the final Winograd Report—due to be released in about a month—the Knesset report offered a number of recommendations on how to improve military performance in future confrontations. In the 2006 war logistical information was often not relayed in real time. "Improved communication would have thwarted many errors," said the report. From now on, "units should carry their own logistical information with them rather than referring back to central command." Halutz's overreliance on air power to knock out Hezballah's infrastructure also came under fire, and the committee pointed to the necessity of utilizing infantry to secure territory, since without that ground presence air power could have only a limited effect. "Locating Katyusha rockets from the air," it noted, "was a nearly impossible mission, and neutralizing them could not be accomplished solely from the air."

Also on the last day of the year, a subcommittee of the full Foreign Affairs and Defense Committee issued a separate report slamming the Foreign Ministry's public-relations efforts during the war, focusing especially on the lack of a coordinated plan anticipating that conflict would break out in the north. The subcommittee was headed by Kadima MK Amira Dotan, a former IDF officer and the first woman to attain the rank of brigadier general.

Tel Aviv University's "Peace Index" survey, conducted in late 2007, showed that Olmert's public standing remained quite low. Sixty-one percent of the respondents said that if the final Winograd Report included sharp criticism of Olmert the prime minister should resign, and only 20 percent thought he should stay on under such circumstances.

A President under Fire

At a January 23 press conference and in a letter to the accused, Attorney General Menahem Mazuz announced that, having examined the file with evidence that the police had given him the previous October, he would consider charging President Moshe Katzav on several counts. The final decision on whether to bring charges, Mazuz said, would come after a "hearing" with Katzav and his attorneys, a kind of mini-presentation of the respective cases that is sometimes conducted in Israel when public figures are suspected of criminal offenses.

Katzav was accused of sexual offenses against four women. Three of them worked at Beit Hanassi, the official presidential residence and offices, during his term, and the fourth was an employee at the Ministry of Tourism when Katzav's served as minister there (see AJYB 2007, pp. 222–24). Mazuz indicated that he contemplated charges of forcible rape in the Tourism Ministry case: the woman there was identified in public by the letter Aleph, as was one of the Beit Hanassi employees. In the case of the latter Aleph, Mazuz would not accept the police recommendation of a rape charge, but would charge Katzav with indecent acts, sexual harassment, and exploiting his status as an employer to gain sexual favors.

In the two other cases Mazuz indicated that he would only press charges of sexual harassment and indecent acts. He would not try to bring charges made by yet a fifth complainant, and the statute of limitations had passed in five other possible cases. Also, there would be no charges based on accusations of irregularities and cronyism in Katzav's granting of president pardons to those convicted of crimes, or of illegal wiretapping at Beit Hanassi. Police had recommended criminal indictments on both these charges. It had taken Mazuz several months to make a decision, the Justice Ministry said, because both sides had kept on providing him with new material. The hearing with the president and his lawyers was not expected to take place for several months.

Mazuz's announcement fueled demands from politicians and the public that Katzav step down and leave Beit Hanassi rather than waiting for Mazuz's final decision on whether to prosecute. Some called for Katzav to suspend himself voluntarily pending the legal findings, but others argued that he should be removed from office by the Knesset.

Katzav did not respond immediately and scheduled a press conference for the following day. But one member of his defense team, top criminal lawyer Tzion Amir, said that Katzav had been mistreated. The president, he said, "had a clear understanding . . . that the evidence in the investigation file would lead to a different decision. [Mazuz's] decision came down on his head like cold water, but it's important to emphasize that there are holes in this case."

In an extraordinary public display, Katzav lashed back at his accusers the next day, January 24, in an event labeled a press conference but where the press was not allowed to ask questions. Calling the accusations against him "lies," "libels" and a "frame-up," Katzav said he was the victim of a "lynch" accompanied by unprecedented media brain-washing. In addition, he accused the police of doing everything they could against him. Behind this vendetta, he suggested, was a clique that had been after him since he defeated Shimon Peres for the presidency in July 2000. "I saw myself as a symbol of all those who don't belong to the same clique, elite, rich, close to others. And only they have the right to represent Israel," he said. Katzav dismissed his accusers as "people fired by me or who didn't get what they wanted from me."

Katzav's performance drew angry reactions from the political establishment. Prime Minister Olmert, speaking at the annual Herzliya Conference on Security, called it "a sad day for the State of Israel" and said he had no doubt that Katzav would have to leave Beit Hanassi because he could no longer function in office. Yossi Beilin, head of the left-wing party Meretz, said Katzav's "horror show proved that he shouldn't serve another day, and should resign immediately." United Arab List MK Taleb a-Sana said Katzav "fired wildly, in every direction," and had missed "his final chance to save his last shred of dignity." Internal Security Minister Avi Dichter, who was responsible for the police, said that the president should apologize to the police and the public "for the things he said in his emotional frenzy."

But Katzav claimed that the public was behind him. Presidential spokesperson Hagit Cohen was quoted by the settler-linked Arutz 7 radio and Internet news organization as saying that she had never seen "such a deluge of expressions of support." The president's attack on the media, she said, had struck a particularly responsive chord. Despite the Katzav camp's claims, however, a poll conducted by the Dahaf organization for *Yediot Aharonot* and its Ynet Website indicated that 71 percent of Israelis favored Katsav's resignation. The poll, using a sample of 516 people, was carried out after Katzav's "press conference."

Political wheels moved quickly. Already on January 25 Katzav requested a temporary suspension from office, and the Knesset House Committee approved it 13-10. This meant that although Katzav remained on technically as president, Knesset Speaker Dalia Itzik moved up to become acting president. Katzav indicated that he would only relinquish the formal title if and when an indictment was filed against him.

Five days later the Knesset formally approved the framework for impeachment proceedings. Efforts to impeach Katzav, however, failed on March 7, after only seven members of the committee—far short of the necessary 19 in the 25-member body—voted in favor. Six of them were women—Sheli Yahimovitch, Nadia Hilu, and Collette Avital of Labor; Limor Livnat of Likud; and Zahava Gal-On of Meretz. The Likud's Gideon Sa'ar was the lone male MK voting to impeach.

After several sessions in the "hearing" process and extensive discussions with Katzav's legal team, a deal for a plea bargain was reached. Under its terms, the most serious charge against Katzav, forcible rape, would be dropped, and he would be indicted on lesser charges of indecent acts, sexual harassment, and obstruction of justice. The president would resign from his post (the deal was announced only two weeks before Katzav's six-year term of office was to expire anyway), he would serve no jail time, but would pay compensation to two of the complainants.

Mazuz justified the plea bargain on the grounds that some of the charges he had originally recommended might be difficult to prove in court, and that during the hearing process Katzav's lawyers had presented new evidence causing him to modify his original position. The lead defense attorney substantiated this view, writing in *Yediot Aharonot* that material from the investigation file made it apparent to him that the case against Katzav would "go up in smoke." Katzav resigned on June 30.

Many reacted to the deal with outrage. At a news conference televised a few hours after it was announced, Aleph from Beit Hanassi called Katzav a "serial sex offender" and a "pervert," and said the decision to let him off without jail time "gives legitimacy to sex offenders." (The complainant's face was electronically blurred during the broadcast so she could not be identified.) About a week later, Aleph's attorneys, protesting the fact that her complaint had been excluded in the plea-bargain deal, produced phone records showing that Katzav called her 689 times, sometimes after midnight, from his office or mobile phone. Most political commentators called the plea bargain scandalous, Sima Kadmon of *Ma'ariv* writing that Mazuz should step down as attorney general.

A few days later, on June 30, 20,000 protesters demonstrated against the plea deal in Tel Aviv's Rabin Square, and several public opinion surveys showed about 70 percent of the public opposed to letting Katzav off so easily. There were also expressions of outrage at claims made by Katzav and his lawyers that the agreement proved that there was nothing to the original accusations, and that the president had signed the agreement admitting to at least some sexual offenses to spare the Israeli people, and especially his own family, the ordeal of a long public trial.

The Supreme Court began hearing legal arguments on petitions to overturn the deal in mid-July. The court had the power to overturn it entirely or to require that it be redrafted. No decision on the petitions had been reached as the year ended.

A New President

Shimon Peres, 83, was elected Israel's ninth president by the Knesset on June 13, on the second ballot, by 86 to 23, with eight abstentions and two defective ballots. After the first ballot, which Peres led with 58 votes, three short of the required 61-vote majority, candidates Reuven (Ruby) Rivlin of Likud, who had 37 votes, and Labor's Collette Avital, with 21, stepped down. Knesset Speaker Dalia Itzik, who was to remain acting president until Peres took office a month later, noted that on assuming the presidency Peres would be leaving the Knesset for the first time since 1958. Peres thanked Prime Minister Olmert and Kadima, the party to which he belonged, and said that "the president does not deal with politics and partisanship: He represents unity in a strong voice and expels despair from our midst." He praised the Knesset for showing "nobility and camaraderie."

After making the obligatory visit to the Western Wall in Jerusalem's Old City, Peres traveled to the Har Nof neighborhood on the other side of town for an audience with Rabbi Ovadia Yosef, the Shas spiritual leader, who had instructed members of his party to support Peres for president. "I am an admirer of the rabbi," Peres said. "He is a genius and the nation of Israel must be thankful to him."

Peres, born Szymon Perski in Poland in 1923, immigrated to Palestine with his family as a boy. He had been prime minister on three separate occasions, served in 12 different cabinets, and held the posts of foreign minister, defense minister, minister for the Negev and Galilee, and, in the Olmert administration, vice prime minister. In 1994 he won the Nobel Peace Prize together with the late Yitzhak Rabin and Yasir Arafat for their work in crafting the Oslo Accords.

Labor Picks a Leader

Former prime minister Ehud Barak was elected chairman of the Labor Party, defeating former Shin Bet security services and Israel Navy commander Ami Ayalon in a run-off after neither candidate received the required 40 percent of ballots in the first round. The other candidates were the incumbent, Defense Minister Amir Peretz, whose chances to continue were seriously impaired by criticism of his performance during the war in Lebanon; former minister Ofir Pines-Paz, who resigned from the Olmert cabinet in October 2006 to protest bringing the right-wing Yisrael Beitenu into the government; and Dani Yatom, a former IDF general who headed the army's Central Command and went on to became director of the Mossad and then security adviser when Barak was prime minister in 1999–2001.

Even though Barak led in the first round, garnering 36 percent to Ayalon's 31, most pundits made Ayalon the favorite for the second round after the outspoken dove got the endorsement of Peretz, who had come in third with 22 percent. But in the run-off, Barak, who conducted a relatively quiet campaign that concentrated on party activists and avoided the news media, won by 51.2 to 47.8 percent. Within a week Olmert named Barak defense minister to replace Peretz, and on June 17 the change was approved by the Knesset. Ayalon, who had said during the campaign that he would not serve in a cabinet headed by Olmert, was appointed minister without portfolio on September 12, and would be part of the security cabinet.

It was uncertain how long a Barak-led Labor would remain in the government. During a news conference at Kibbutz Sdot Yam during the campaign for party leadership, Barak said he would move for new elections if he got the top Labor spot. Alternatively, he suggested that the prime minister, on his own, would "find the appropriate way to reach personal conclusions," that is, resign. But at year's end Barak had still given no indication that he would leave the government or bring it down. Labor activists as well as their opponents anxiously awaited the issuance of the final Winograd Report in late January 2008 to see what move Barak would make, if any.

A New Face at Justice

Daniel Friedmann, a Tel Aviv University law professor, was appointed minister of justice in February, when Tizpi Livni vacated the post to become foreign minister. He was a longtime and very vocal opponent of the growing power of the Supreme Court under the activist leadership of former court president Aharon Barak and Barak's successor, Dorit Beinisch. It was widely assumed that Prime Minister Olmert chose him precisely for that reason. There were also suggestions of personal animosity between Friedmann and Beinisch due to the judge's successful opposition to the appointment of Prof. Nili Cohen, Friedmann's Tel Aviv University colleague, to the Supreme Court. Friedmann, an Israel Prize winner, was an internationally recognized expert on the law of torts.

Allegations and Convictions

In January, Attorney General Mazuz ordered a criminal probe into Prime Minister Olmert over alleged abuse of influence in the privatization of Bank Leumi, Israel's second largest bank. The case focused on suspicions that Olmert, while acting finance minister in 2005, tried to steer the sale of the bank toward his friend, Australian real estate baron Frank Lowy, who, in the end, did not purchase it. But in late November police investigators recommended that the case be closed since there was insufficient evidence to bring criminal charges. The file was transferred to the State Attorney's Office for a final decision on the police recommendation.

Investigations against Olmert in other cases were still pending at year's end. They included charges of illegal political appointments while he served as minister of trade, industry and labor early in Ariel Sharon's second term as prime minister, and suggestions that he paid an illegally low price for a home in Jerusalem's German Colony neighborhood. On November 11, police sent 100 detectives to 20 locations to gather evidence in the various cases. These places included the Ministry of Trade, Industry and Labor; the Israel Lands Administration; the Small Business Administration; the offices of Uri Messer, Olmert's attorney; the Municipality of Jerusalem, where Olmert served as mayor for a decade; and Alumot, the company involved in the sale of the house on Cremieux Street to Olmert.

Haim Ramon, who resigned as justice minister in August 2006, was convicted of indecent sexual conduct on January 31, 2007. His resignation had come in response to a police investigation of allegations that he kissed a female soldier during a farewell party for the young woman at the government complex in Tel Aviv. Ramon was subsequently indicted. In a unanimous opinion, a three-judge Tel Aviv Magistrate's Court panel found that Ramon had sexually harassed the soldier by "placing his lips on her lips and inserting his tongue in her mouth." The judges said that the kiss was not indicative of affection, as Ramon claimed, but rather had "all the elements of a sex offense." The crime carried a maximum penalty of three years in jail, but, after the prosecution urged leniency, Ramon was sentenced to 120 hours of public service and fined 15,000 shekels.

Ramon subsequently returned to the cabinet as vice prime minister, even though women's groups and others charged that he was disqualified from a ministerial position since his crime involved moral turpitude. The Supreme Court found in Ramon's favor in this instance. In her ruling, Justice Ayala Procaccia said that Ramon's offense was apparently "a one-time slip that does not attest to an innate moral defect that might constitute grounds to disqualify him from holding public office." Dissenting, Justice Edna Arbel said that the fact that Ramon's sexual offense was not severe should not obscure the reality that he was "in fact convicted of criminal offenses."

Finance Minister Avraham Hirschson, a close confidant of Prime Minister Olmert, resigned on July 1 in the wake of a police investigation of embezzlement and other charges against him. He had suspended himself from office in late April, issuing a statement to the effect that the public had made up its mind about his guilt without hearing his side of the story, and saying that he preferred to be with his family during "a difficult time—one of the most difficult I have ever known."

The investigation centered on events in 2003, when Hirschson headed the National Workers Union, a Likud-affiliated body. An initial probe explored suspicions that a lower-ranking union official, Ovadia Cohen, had embezzled NIS 5 million from a union-linked educational fund, but suspicions later shifted to Hirschson as the recipient of the purloined money. One former staffer claimed to have seen Hirschson accept cash-filled envelopes from Cohen. In addition, Hirschson was suspected of having the union finance medical treatment for him and of diverting money from the March of the Living, the international organizer of Holocaust memorial trips to Polish concentration camps, which Hirschson founded and led.

Interior Minister Ronnie Bar-On, another longtime friend and associate of Olmert, and, like the prime minister, a former chairman of the Likud-linked Betar Jerusalem soccer club, was named to replace Hirschson at the Treasury. Bar-On's spot at Interior went to Meir Sheetrit, who was replaced at the Housing and Construction Ministry by Ze'ev Boim. All three ministers, like Hirschson, were members of Kadima.

Moshe Karadi, the national police chief, resigned in February in the wake of revelations reported by an investigative committee about a case of corruption among police in the Southern District during 1999, when Karadi was the commander there. No wrongdoing was imputed to Karadi himself. Public Security Minister Avi Dichter immediately appointed Ya'akov Ganot, head of the Prisons Service, to replace him, but the choice came under fire since Ganot, back in the 1990s, had admitted at a police disciplinary hearing that he had violated the force's rules about accepting favors, and was suspended for three years. Granot withdrew, and Dichter named veteran policeman David (Dudi) Cohen to head the national police.

Jacky Matza, commissioner of the Tax Authority, resigned in January after a police investigation into possible influence-peddling, bribery, and tax-fixing became public. Matza had been appointed to the post while Olmert was finance minister, and the investigation also involved Shula Zaken, a longtime Olmert aide, office manager, and current bureau chief in the Prime Minister's Office; her brother, alleged "fixer" Yoram Karashi; former Tax Authority head Eitan Rub; and other senior tax officials. Police later recommended that Matza be indicted. Zaken was first placed under house arrest, was then suspended, and returned to her job late in the year.

In an annual poll conducted by the Ma'agar Mohot organization in advance of the Sderot Conference for Social and Economic Policy in November, Olmert and Hirschson topped the list of politicians the public considered most corrupt, each scoring 56 percent. In polling for the most honest minister in the same survey, Foreign Minister Livni rated highest at 46 percent, followed by Education Minister Yuli Tamir, 40 percent, and Transport Minister Shaul Mofaz, 34 percent. An alarming 69 percent of respondents said they believed that Israeli politics and government were corrupt; 29 percent considered the police corrupt; and 12 percent said the same of the IDF. Uzi Dayan, the conference organizer, said the survey proved that the public saw corruption as "public enemy No. 1."

DOMESTIC DEVELOPMENTS

Demography

Israel's population stood at 7,242,000 at the end of 2007, the Central Bureau of Statistics reported. Of that total, 5,477,000 (75.6 percent) were Jews, 1,449,000 were Arabs, and the remaining 4.4 percent were of other ethnicities. The population grew by 1.7 percent in 2007, with 124,000 new Israelis, as compared to 1.8 percent in 2006. Approximately 18,000 new immigrants arrived in Israel during the year, down from about 19,000 in 2006 and about 21,000 in 2005. Some 149,000 babies were born in 2007.

Israel had 41 percent of the world Jewish population of 13.2 million as of January 2007, according to a report published by the Jerusalem-based Jewish People Policy Planning Institute. The JPPPI estimated that the Jewish population of Israel grew by 80,000 during 2006 while the Diaspora suffered a net loss of about 20,000.

The National Council for the Child issued its yearbook in December 2007. It featured considerable data about Israeli families, not all of it reassuring. Of all children in Israel, 69.1 percent were Jewish, a decline from 75 percent in 1997. Single-parent families contained 8.5 percent of Israeli children as compared to 6.8 percent a decade earlier. At the start of the year, 166,000 families had four or more children. That amounted to 17 percent of all families, up from the 2000 figure of 150,000 families, which was then 16.3 percent of the total. The percentage of these large families living under the poverty line increased from 54.7 percent in 2004 to 60 percent in 2007. Of all Israeli children, a third lived below the poverty line; for Bedouin the figure was 70 percent. Among Israeli Jews, religious families had, on average, far more children than secular families. Thus the country's youngest city was Betar Illit, a *haredi* center southwest of Jerusalem, where children constituted 62.6 percent of the population, whereas only about 20 percent of the people in Tel Aviv, the secular metropolis, were children.

The yearbook also published data about the use of new technology. It found that 93 percent of Israeli children had computers at home and 80 percent had their own cell phones. Israeli adults were not far behind. A TNS/Teleseker survey found that four million Israelis aged 13 and up used the Internet and that 73 percent of households had an Internet connection. The annual rise in Israeli Internet use for 2007 was about 2 percent, slightly ahead of population growth.

The Economy

Continued Growth

The Israeli economy, as measured by Gross Domestic Product (GDP), grew by 5.3 percent in 2007, according to the Central Bureau of Statistics, continuing four and a half years of rapid expansion after the lean recession years of the early-twenty-first century. In 2006 the growth rate had been 5.2 percent, and the average rate since the implementation of far-reaching economic reforms in the mid-1980s was 4.5 percent. Another key indicator, business sector GDP, was up 6.3 percent. Per-capita growth—the expansion of GDP minus the increase in population—rose by 3.5 percent for the year to reach $28,800, almost on par with the "second economic tier" of EU countries, such as Italy ($31,000) and Greece ($30,800). Israel's foreign currency reserves stood at $28.42 billion in December 2007, down fractionally from $29 billion in December 2006.

This growth—more rapid than that of any other Western economy—was spurred both externally and domestically. Exports of goods and services rose by 8.6 percent to $45.9 billion. Imports were up even more, by 12.6 percent to $56.1 billion, resulting in a 30-percent widening of the annual trade deficit to $10.2 billion. Per-capita consumption rose by 3.6 percent, powered especially by a 22.6-percent jump in per-capita consumption of durable goods, such as automobiles and electrical appliances. At the same time, Agriculture Minister Shalom Simhon announced that exports of produce rose by 27 percent in the course of the year to $1.5 billion. He attributed this to improved productivity and exploitation of niche markets for Israeli products.

Perhaps the most striking statement about the economy came in the government budget, which originally planned for a NIS 8.1 billion (about $2 billion) deficit, 2.9 percent of GDP, due to the lingering effects of the 2006 war in Lebanon. But much higher than expected revenues from taxes, triggered by the rapid pace of economic activity as well as by one-time payments from the privatization of government companies and taxes from the sale of Israeli companies, resulted in a negligible deficit of NIS 100 million (about $25 million).

The strength of the economy was reflected by the local stock market, the Tel Aviv Stock Exchange (TASE). The Tel Aviv 25 Index rose by 31.39 percent in 2007, ending the year at 1,217.07. The Tel Aviv 100 finished its fifth consecutive year of positive results with a gain of 25.27 percent. For 2007, the shekel strengthened against the U.S. dollar by 9 percent, closing the year at NIS 3.845 to the dollar.

Trading volume on the TASE rose sharply in 2007. Equities trading averaged about $500 million a day, up 55 percent over 2006, while bond trading, at $800 million daily, more than doubled the average of the preceding year. It also proved much easier to raise capital, $5 billion being raised in offerings of equities, up 85 percent over 2006, and $21 billion in bonds, a 90-percent rise. In 2007, 150 equity-traded funds (linked to various share, bond, and commodity indexes in Israel and abroad) were added, bringing the number of ETFs to 240. Public holdings in ETFs reached $6 billion, the TASE reported. According to Esther Levanon, the TASE head, extensive changes were instituted to make the exchange more attractive to foreign investors and to induce Israeli firms to dual-list on the TASE and a foreign bourse, rather than continue the current practice of many of them that offered their shares and raised capital only on foreign exchanges.

Though the Israeli economy's fundamentals—including balance of payments, a lowered foreign and domestic debt, growth figures, and falling unemployment—were positive, there were fears that a downturn in the global economy, particularly in the U.S., might affect continued expansion in 2008, since markets for many Israeli products, particularly in the high-tech sector, were located outside the country.

The Consumer Price Index rose by 3.4 percent in 2007, capped by a 0.6-percent increase in December, as calculated by the Central Bureau of Statistics. This annual inflation rate topped the government's target of 1–3 percent, included in the budget for 2007, and the monthly rise was the highest December CPI since 2006. For the year, basic inflation (the CPI minus fruits and vegetables) was up 3.3 percent, and the CPI excluding housing was up 3.9 percent. Despite the shekel's gain in value against the U.S. dollar, housing prices—customarily dollar-denominated—rose by only 3.6 percent in shekel terms.

Investment in technology reached its highest levels in seven years, according to the year-end report of the IVC Research Center. It said that in 2007, 462 Israeli technology companies raised $1.76 billion from local and foreign investors, 8.5 percent more than the amount raised in 2006 and 31.5 percent higher than the 2005 figure. Sources inside the industry, however, were not sure that the upward trend would continue into 2008.

Foreign investment in Israel fell by $11 billion from 2006's record figure of $22.5 billion, according to the Bank of Israel. The drop was due to fewer mergers and acquisitions by overseas companies and the sale by foreigners of a net $623 million in Israeli corporate and government bonds, after purchasing a net $2.2 billion in 2006. Financial sources noted, though, that 2006 had been a special year, with figures bolstered by once-in-a-lifetime deals like the $4-billion purchase of 80 percent of the Iscar precision-tool-making firm by Warren Buffett.

At year's end economists and political leaders were carefully watching two key indicators: the potential effect of an anticipated slowdown in the U.S., which accounted for about 40 percent of Israel's exports, and the shockwaves of the sub-prime mortgage crisis on the world economy.

Business Developments

Israel led the world in proportional R&D investment, according to figures released in early August by the Central Bureau of Statistics. The Israeli R&D expenditure for 2007 was NIS 28.3 billion (just over $6.7 billion), amounting to 4.5 percent of GDP. That topped Sweden's 3.7 percent, Finland's 3.5 percent, Japan's 3.3 percent, the U.S.'s 2.1 percent, and Canada's 1.7 percent. The Israeli business sector contributed 77 percent of the R&D expenditure. Israeli R&D received a further boost on December 19, when the U.S.-Israel Joint Energy Bill was signed into law by President Bush. The legislation, passed a week earlier by Congress, provided funding for R&D into sources of renewable alternative energy, including solar, biomass, wind, geothermal, wave, and tidal energy.

Israeli exports of polished diamonds were up 7 percent over 2006 to $7.08 billion. The U.S. was the largest market for Israeli stones, at $3.73 billion, followed by Hong Kong's $1.31 billion, Belgium's $562 billion, Switzerland's $428 billion, and India's $109 billion. There was also a substantial trade in unpolished stones between India and Israel, two of the world's largest processors, cutters, and polishers of diamonds. Despite the impressive figures, the diamond industry—which represented little added value due to the high cost of raw materials—had, as usual, minimal impact on the national economy.

Sales at IKEA Israel rose by 9.7 percent in 2007 to NIS 469 million, the retailer reported. It said that 2.6 million Israelis had visited the store, located at the Poleg interchange near Netanya, in the course of the year. Plans for a second store, in Rishon Lezion south of Tel Aviv, were held up by zoning and licensing disputes.

Israeli defense exports to the U.S. more than quadrupled in the seven years from 1999 to 2006, from $250–$270 million to $1.2 billion, according to Defense Ministry figures released in June. In addition, the $3.4 billion in defense exports in 2006 put Israel in fourth place among arms-exporting countries, after the U.S., Russia, and France, and ahead of Britain. Maj.-Gen (res.) Yossi Ben-Hanan, head of Sibat, the Defense Ministry's branch that dealt with military cooperation and exports, said that restrictions on arms sales imposed at the request of the U.S. had "cost" Israel only $300 million in military exports.

Israel and India expanded their already considerable cooperation in missile development with a longer-range version of the Barak naval-defense system for the Indian Air Force, according to an early July report in the authoritative *Defense News.* The four-year, $300-million deal was part of an agreement signed in June with Israel Aerospace Industries, following a $480 million contract signed by IAI and the Indian Defense Research Development Organization in 2006. According to a report on the Walla! Hebrew Website, the agreement was part of a larger deal being negotiated by IAI and Indian defense authorities that could amount to as much as $1.5 billion in joint production. In a separate report, *Defense News* said that India was interested in joint production with Israel of unmanned helicopters. And according to *Yediot Aharonot,* IAI was also seeking contracts worth hundreds of millions of dollars for the upgrade of 51 Indian Air Force Mirage-2000 aircraft.

Four Israeli companies—Israel Aerospace Industries (IAI), Elbit Systems, Rafael Arms Development Authority Ltd., and Israel Military Industries—were among the 100 largest defense firms, according to the 2007 rankings compiled by *Defense News.* IAI was in 33d place with sales of $1.7 billion; Elbit was 39th with $1.4 billion; Rafael was number 49 with $1.05 billion; and IMI was 84th with $482 million. Elbit also ranked 17th in 2006 performance in a ranking of leading public companies published by *Aviation Week.*

Arkady Gaydamak, the Israeli-Russian billionaire businessman, was extremely active during 2007. Already the owner of the Betar Jerusalem soccer club, he purchased Gilon Investments Ltd. and Ameris Holdings Ltd.—which controlled the Israel Petrochemical Enterprises Ltd. chain of gas stations—and the real estate company Ocif Investment. Gaydamak was also in the headlines for funding brief vacations away from the Gaza border for residents of embattled Sderot, running a large camp in southern Israel for residents of the North during the 2006 war in Lebanon, and donating to other popular and populist causes. Reportedly an ally of Likud leader Benjamin Netanyahu, Gaydamak founded a political movement and said he would run for mayor of Jerusalem. He failed, however, in his plan to purchase the non-kosher Tiv Taam supermarket chain and turn it kosher.

Solel, which manufactured solar-powered thermal systems for the generation of electricity, made a breakthrough deal, through an American subsidiary, for construction of a $2-billion solar generating plant in California's Mojave Desert, with Pacific Gas and Electric. To be called the Mojave Solar Park, the plant was expected to supply 553 megawatts of electricity.

Employment

The average salary of employed Israelis was NIS 7,957 in 2007, the Central Bureau of Statistics reported. A record 2.81 million people were employed: 2.72 million Israelis, 72,000 foreign workers, and 21,000 Palestinians. The average salary of foreign workers was NIS 4,700. High-tech workers in Israel made NIS 16,000–20,000. The rate of participation in the labor force—a key issue in Israel, where many ultra-Orthodox men and Israeli Arab women did not seek out jobs—rose by a significant 2 percent to 56.7 percent. Unemployment was 6.6 percent at year's end, down from 7.9 percent in January 2007 and 8.3 percent in January 2006.

Trade, Industry and Labor Minister Eli Yishai signed an order on December 31 obligating all employers to allot part of their workers' salaries to pension funds, making about a million Israelis eligible for pensions they never had before. The order came in the wake of an agreement reached in June by the Histadrut trade union federation and employers under which 2.5 percent of an employee's salary would go toward a pension. Central Bureau of Statistics figures indicated that before this change 47 percent of Israel's workers had no pension plans other than the National Insurance benefits given to senior citizens. Only 28 percent of

Arabs and 38 percent of immigrants had pension plans, according to a report in *Ha'aretz.*

The Israeli educational sector experienced a series of strikes in 2007. In April, university students struck to protest increases in tuition and the failure to implement cuts in fees that had been recommended by a government commission in 2001. Students blocked roads and some were arrested. After three weeks, university presidents warned that students who did not return to class by May 8 would not receive credit for the semester. But the day before the deadline, strike leaders sealed off the universities with chains so no one could enter. It was not until May 14—41 days into the strike—that a settlement was reached with the government.

Middle- and secondary-school teachers went on a "rolling" strike in the spring, demanding an 8.5 percent pay increase and a reduction in class size. The teachers unions, unwilling to paralyze Israel's entire school system, struck in different regions on different days, exempting completely the schools near the Gaza border. In the fall, however, after one union, the National Teachers Union, reached a deal, the Secondary School Teachers Organization (SSTO) nationalized their strike, shutting down 1,200 high schools and over 40 percent of junior high schools. On December 13, 15 minutes before a restraining order by an Israeli Labor Court would have forced the teachers back to work, the SSTO reached a settlement with the government that called for raises, and included a personal promise from the prime minister to reduce class size. This strike, lasting more than 60 days, was the longest in the history of the Israeli educational system.

Senior faculty at the universities called a strike at the opening of the fall semester. It was not settled until mid-December, after Hanukkah. To make up for the missed class time the academic year was extended until July 10, 2008.

Religion, State, and Society

Conversion

In September, the Interior Ministry, controlled by the Orthodox Shas party, drafted new criteria that would make it more difficult for converts to Judaism elsewhere in the world to immigrate to Israel. The purpose was to prevent non-Jews with ulterior motives from entering the country as Jews. Among other requirements, a convert would have to attend classes for at least nine months prior to conversion in the Diaspora country, and be active in his or her home community's religious life. Rabbi Seth Farber, head of the Jerusalem-based Itim Jewish Life Information Center, said that the new regulations were counterproductive. "There are some total idiots in the Interior Ministry who exhibit utter ignorance on the issue of conversions abroad," Farber said, urging that rabbis overseas should be trusted. "If they are permitted to hold conversions, they should be considered responsible enough not to convert would-be foreign workers and terrorists who are only after Israeli nationality."

In December, Itim, which, among other activities, helped conversion candidates deal with the bureaucracy, asked the High Court of Justice to order the Interior Ministry to show cause why Italian-born Rachel del Conte, a 2006 convert, not be given the status of a new immigrant. The woman had studied in Israel and went overseas for the conversion, and the courts had ruled in 2005 that such conversions from recognized foreign Jewish communities must be recognized. Farber accused the ministry of "thumbing its nose" at court decisions.

From the standpoint of the government, expedited conversion procedures were a priority: there were about 300,000 non-Jews, mostly from the former Soviet Union, who immigrated to Israel as family members of Jews under the Law of Return. Some had already converted via a special army program, but most had not.

An interministerial committee headed by Erez Halfon, director general of the Absorption Ministry, had been charged with developing a plan to make the conversion process more efficient. His report—which, among other things, called for the appointment of more religious court judges to deal with conversions—was completed in late summer. It provoked predictable reactions. Absorption Minister Ya'akov Edri called converting the non-Jews—who otherwise could not marry in Israel—a "national and strategic mission of vital importance to the future of the State of Israel." But *Yated Ne'eman,* the ultra-Orthodox daily with strong links to Rabbi Shlomo Yosef Elyashiv, the nonagenarian Lithuanian rabbinical powerhouse, blasted the proposal as authorizing "fake" conversions, and Rabbi Gilad Kariv of the Reform movement's Israel Religious Action Center said the recommendations were not only insufficient and "useless," but, by strengthening the position of the Chief Rabbinate, they "might deepen the ongoing conversion crisis."

Opposition from the Sephardi Orthodox party Shas, which belonged to the government coalition, ensured that no steps would be taken to implement the Halfon report. Nevertheless, it was widely believed that the Prime Minister's Office hoped that the objections could ultimately be overcome with the help of the Sephardi chief rabbi, Shlomo Amar, who was considered a moderate.

In October, with no action being taken to provide more judges for the religious courts, 45 Modern Orthodox rabbis, most of them from the Religious Kibbutz Movement, agreed to serve on new independent conversion courts, outside the jurisdiction of the Chief Rabbinate. Few revealed their names. One who did was Rabbi Benny Lau of Jerusalem's Ramban Synagogue, who said that some American-born members of his own congregation who had rabbinic ordination and considerable experience with performing conversions could serve on these independent courts. "I think there will be no alternative," Lau told *Ha'aretz.* "The rabbinate is undergoing a process of dissolution . . . and conversion is the core of the matter. One of our roles as rabbis is to serve the public, and I see this issue as fulfilling that function."

That same month, during a U.S. visit, Rabbi Amar discussed conversions with Orthodox leaders. It was reported that as a result of these talks the Rabbinical Council of America, the main American Orthodox rabbinical body, planned to open 20 conversion courts across the country as part of an effort to standardize conversion procedures and thereby ensure that U.S. conversion would be recognized in Israel (see above, p. 143).

In late December, *Haaretz* reported that the prime minister had charged Oded Yehezkel, the cabinet secretary, with handling the politically thorny issue of conversions, and that Yehezkel had informed 14 senior officials that Olmert, who considered the matter a priority, wanted to "improve, streamline, and expand Israel's conversion system" so as to make as many as possible of the non-Jewish immigrants Jews.

Civil Marriage

Rabbi Amar and Justice Minister Daniel Friedmann announced in early July that they had reached agreement on legislation allowing civil marriage for non-Jewish Israeli couples who were not listed by the Interior Ministry as belonging to any other religion. According to *Ha'aretz,* the law would affect 264,000 Israelis, most of them immigrants from the former Soviet Union who, previously unable to marry in Israel, had to travel abroad to do so.

Friedmann, noting the small number of individuals covered by the bill, called the agreement imperfect, but nevertheless said it was "a meaningful step towards expanding marriage rights in Israel." But Rabbi Yoram Mazor of the Reform movement complained that this was "not a civil-marriage bill" and represented a "fictitious solution" for only about one-third of the immigrants from the former Soviet Union. Under it, he pointed out, couples in which one partner was Jewish and the other was not would still have to go abroad to marry.

Shmitta

The onset of the new Jewish year in September brought with it problems relating to *shmitta,* the seventh, sabbatical, year of the biblical agricultural cycle during which, according to Jewish law, no produce on Jewish-owned fields in Israel could be grown or sold, and the land had to lie fallow. With the proliferation of Jewish settlements in Palestine in the late-nineteenth century, some rabbinic authorities took into account the realities of modern agriculture and devised the *heter mekhira* (permit of sale) through which the land was fictitiously sold to non-Jews so as to avoid the *shmitta* strictures.

Every seven years the Chief Rabbinate utilized the *heter mekhira,* while the more rigorously Orthodox, who did not accept its validity, generally purchased produce that was imported or grown by non-Jews. However for the *shmitta* year that began in 2007, the Chief Rabbinate, under increasing influence of the ultra-Orthodox, for the first time dropped its blanket authorization of the *heter mekhira* and gave local rabbinical authorities the option of accepting or rejecting it.

A group of Orthodox Zionist rabbis brought suit against the Chief Rabbinate, and in late October the Supreme Court disallowed the new policy, saying that reducing the amount of land covered by *heter mekhira* would lead many more observant Jews to buy Arab and foreign produce, and thus cause substantial losses to Israeli agriculture. The ruling drew praise from secular Israelis (who did not observe *shmitta* in any event), with Agriculture Minister Shalom Simhon calling it a "victory for sanity," and from the National Religious Party, whose leader, MK Zevulun Orlev, said it had prevented "surrender to the methods of the ultra-Orthodox."

The latter, of course, rejected both the court decision and *heter mekhira.* Rabbi Yosef Sholom Elyashiv, leader of the Lithuanian ultra-Orthodox in Israel, said there was no getting around *shmitta.* Comparing it to eating chicken and milk together, he ruled that even the pots used to cook food raised under the *heter mekhira* would be unkosher.

INDISCREET WORDS

Rabbi Ovadia Yosef, the former Sephardi chief rabbi whose acid tongue had often sparked controversy, was at it again in late August, suggesting that soldiers had been killed in the Lebanon war because they were not religious. "Is it a wonder that soldiers who don't observe the Torah, don't pray every day and don't put on tefillin every day are killed in war? It is no wonder," Yosef was quoted as saying in his weekly Saturday night sermon, delivered at his synagogue in Jerusalem. "Soldiers who are believers and who pray, God helps in wars. They are not killed."

Eli Ben-Shem, chairman of Yad Lebanim, which worked with the families of fallen soldiers, called Yosef's remarks "shameful" and said that his organization had received angry phone calls from bereaved parents, particularly those from religious families, who, he said, "were hurt very badly," adding that secular people "don't pay much attention anyway" to Rabbi Yosef.

The rabbi was the patron of the Shas party, and its leader, Eli Yishai, was hard-pressed to defend him. Yishai said that Yosef's remarks were taken out of context. "The rabbi referred to a Gemara [part of the Talmud], a quote from a time when righteous and God-fearing people used to join the army," he told Galei Zahal, the Army Radio. "The rabbi didn't invent it. He just said that from the Gemara's point of view, the people of Israel are all responsible for one another. If I sin, it can have an effect on soldiers."

Other Domestic Developments

LAND SALES

In a clear attempt to bypass a 2004 court ruling directing the Israel Lands Administration to accept bids for purchases of Jewish National Fund land from Arabs as well as Jews, the Knesset, in July, gave preliminary approval to a bill restricting JNF sales to Jews only. The vote was 64 to 16. JNF holdings amounted to about 13 percent of all state land. Arab MKs, the leftist Meretz party, and the *Ha'aretz* editorial page denounced the bill as racist, but its proponents countered that the original purpose of JNF was to buy land for Jewish settlement, and that this was the understanding under which contributors donated money to the organization.

A compromise was reached in September whereby JNF would sell land to both Jews and Arabs, but that the Israel Lands Administration would reimburse it for land sold to non-Jews, ensuring that the overall amount of land owned by Jews remained the same. A public-opinion poll taken in early October showed that 81 percent of Israelis wanted JNF to sell only to Jews.

In a related story, the Jerusalem District Court approved the first-ever appointment of an Arab, Ra'adi Sfori, as a member of the JNF board of directors. The judges ruled that "as this is one director among a large number, there is no chance that he will have the opportunity to cancel the organization's goals."

Darfur Refugess

There was no reliable estimate of the number of refugees from the war-torn Darfur region of southern Sudan who were living in Israel. Estimates ranged from the hundreds cited by official sources to as many as several thousand. At least 190 Darfur refugees who got to Israel via Egyptian Sinai were held in prison.

Israeli policy, which provoked widespread criticism both domestically and abroad, had gone through several stages, at one point insisting on sending the refugees back to Egypt but not to Sudan, and at another denying them the possibility of applying for asylum on the technical ground that Sudan was an enemy country. In late 2007, the Hotline for Migrant Workers in Tel Aviv petitioned the Supreme Court to prevent Israel from invoking an anti-infiltration law allowing those caught crossing the border to be held without resort to the courts, arguing, instead, that the Darfuris be released from prison unless they were criminals or security threats. Several refugee-rights groups urged that the refugees be allowed to apply for asylum.

Interior Minister Meir Sheetrit said in September that Israel would grant citizenship to some of them. He noted that "Israel, with its history, must offer assistance," and "can't stand by." At year's end, though, no move to grant residency rights or citizenship had been approved.

Amir Circumcision

The infant son of Yigal Amir, convicted assassin of Yitzhak Rabin, was circumcised in a religious ceremony on November 4, the 12th anniversary of the day his father shot the then-prime minister to death in Tel Aviv. Protesters gathered outside the Ayalon prison, where Amir was serving a life sentence, raising signs and shouting as Amir's wife, Larissa Trimbobler, arrived with the baby.

Court rulings in 2006 had allowed conjugal visits by Trimbobler, after Amir had tried to have some of his sperm smuggled out of jail (see AJYB 2007, p. 268). Despite considerable public disapproval, Amir was allowed to attend the brit after the Supreme Court upheld a Tel Aviv District Court decision allowing Amir to be present. The previous evening, more than 100,000 people attended the annual public Rabin memorial assembly at the site of the assassination, the former Malhei Yisrael Square, which was renamed Rabin Square shortly after the killing.

The Evangelical Factor

For some time Israelis had debated the wisdom of relying on the political and financial help of evangelical Christians. While this aid came in handy at a time of heightened anti-Israel sentiment around the world, there was suspicion of ulterior motives. The issue emerged again late in 2007. According to a December 21 report in *Ha'aretz,* the Jewish Agency and Rabbi Yechiel Eckstein, whose International Fellowship of Christians and Jews had raised tens of millions of dollars to finance Jewish immigration to Israel, had agreed to place a Christian on the Agency's board of directors. This aroused considerable controversy since it looked like an evangelical effort to use financial clout in order to build influence within a Jewish organization that handled aliyah.

Around the same time, the Fellowship and the Agency gave critics more reason to worry when 40 Iranian Jews, new immigrants to Israel, stepped off a plane at Ben-Gurion Airport to be greeted by fanfare and TV cameras (their faces were blurred in broadcast pictures to obscure their identities and avoid reprisals against relatives back in Iran). The Fellowship, it turned out, bankrolled the $10,000 grant given to each of the newcomers. *Ha'aretz* journalist Yossi Melman criticized the media circus. Rabbi Eckstein, however, played the event for all it was worth, comparing the situation of Iran's 20,000–25,000 remaining Jews to that of European Jews before the Holocaust. "It's like sitting on the side of a volcano," the Jewish Telegraphic Agency quoted him as saying. "Lava is gathering but you can still live there. The haunting question is if the volcano were to erupt."

Law of Return

For years suggestions had been made to amend the Law of Return, which granted immediate citizenship to any Jew in the world arriving in Israel and to certain categories of relatives as well. As noted above, the law had enabled hundreds of thousands of people to live in Israel who were not Jewish according to Jewish law, mostly from the former Soviet Union, and often their background and intentions were unclear and their interest in assimilating into Israeli life questionable.

Interior Minister Meir Sheetrit, a former treasurer of the Jewish Agency, told the Agency Board of Governors meeting in Jerusalem in October that while he favored granting Israeli citizenship to Jews coming to Israel, it need not be done "five minutes after they arrive." He proposed waiting a few years to make sure the immigrant was not a fugitive from the law in another country, and that he or she had started learning Hebrew and the basics of Israeli identity. "There is a need to change the Law of Return," Sheetrit said, "so that Israel can conduct itself as a country, and not a committee for the Jewish people."

Blood Libel Returns

In early February, Italian-born historian Ariel Toaff, a professor at Bar-Ilan University, published a book in Italian, *Pasque di sangue* (Bloody Passovers) that raised the possibility that some Jews in the Middle Ages—specifically Ashkenazim living in Italy—might indeed have used Christian blood. As the book was published in Italy, and Toaff's father was a highly esteemed former chief rabbi of Rome, the first cries of outrage were voiced there (see below, p. 444), but they quickly spread to Israel. Various theories were put forward as to why a Jewish scholar would support an anti-Semitic libel, and there were calls for Toaff's dismissal from Bar-Ilan, in turn triggering debate over whether academic freedom applied to a case like this. Prof. Yisrael Yuval of the Hebrew University, who had dealt with much of the same material in his own work but rejected Toaff's conclusions, suggested that the greatest danger lay "in the Islamic world, where a story like this could ignite passions and be utilized for other purposes."

After its president had a closed-door meeting with Toaff, Bar-Ilan issued a statement expressing "great anger" and "extreme displeasure" at the book. At first Toaff defended his findings and argued that they were being misinterpreted, as he never actually claimed to have proof that any Jew committed ritual murder, only that "there was always the possibility that some crazy person would do something." "I am being presented as the new Yigal Amir," he told a *Ha'aretz* reporter, "but one shouldn't be afraid to tell the truth." On February 14, Toaff instructed his Italian publisher to halt distribution of the book so that he could rewrite certain passages and thus make its thesis clearer. And to emphasize his hatred of anti-Semitism, Toaff said he would donate the royalty money for books already sold to the Anti-Defamation League. This did not stop the Knesset, a week later, from a public discussion of the matter, with some MKs going so far as to advocate legal action against the author for allegedly libeling the Jewish people. A revised edition of the book, which specified that Jews were not guilty of ritual murder, came out in February 2008.

Selling Israel

The drive, over the last several years, to change Israel's international image from that of a beleaguered garrison state into one that promised the "good life" encountered problems in 2007. Apparently convinced that sex sells, the Israeli consulate in New York, at the behest of the government, placed a feature article about "Women in the IDF" in the men's magazine *Maxim* that included risqué photographs, and, on an invitation to a consulate event, ran a picture showing Gal Gadot, a former Miss Israel, in a skimpy bikini, provocatively reclining against a background of the New York City skyline.

Female Knesset members voiced strong objections. "This pornographic campaign, sponsored by the Foreign and Tourism ministries, is an outrage," said Labor MK Collette Avital, who had previously served as consul general in New York. "I wonder if the best way to encourage tourism is by advertising sex."

Tel Aviv Centennial

Preparations were under way for the celebration of Tel Aviv's centennial in 2009, which was expected to cost $20 million. Among the events planned was the erection of a statue of Meir Dizengoff, the first mayor, on Rothschild Boulevard, completion of the renovated Habimah national theater building and other historic sites, and an appearance by Milan's La Scala opera company at the Ganei Yehoshua (Yarkon) park on the northern edge of town.

SPORTS

The much-anticipated Israel Baseball League played its first season in 2007, starting with six teams based in Tel Aviv, Netanya, Bet Shemesh, Petah Tikva, Modi'in, and Ra'anana. Some of the managers were Jewish former major leaguers. The season, which began on June 24, was 45 games and eight weeks long. Games went seven innings instead of nine, and ties were decided by a "home run derby" instead of extra innings. The opening game was aired by PBS in six American cities.

Despite considerable publicity, relatively few Israelis showed enthusiasm for the game, probably because baseball was too slow-moving and its rules rather arcane for fans used to soccer and basketball. Other problems emerged as well. After the inaugural season ended, the commissioner—Dan Kurtzer, a former U.S. ambassador to Israel and Egypt—and nine members of the advisory board resigned, complaining that the league would not divulge financial information. The future of the league remained in doubt. Nonetheless, eight of the players were signed by American professional teams.

Israel's national soccer team racked up some diplomatic points and English goodwill on November 17 by defeating Russia 2-1 in a European Championship qualifying match at Ramat Gan Stadium. The win kept alive England's chances of reaching the European final 16, to be played in Austria and Switzerland in the summer of 2008. The British, however, lost to Croatia the following week and failed to qualify.

The Maccabi Tel Aviv soccer club, which, since its founding, had won the National League (now Premier League) championship 18 times and the State Cup 22 times, was sold to a group headed by Canadian metals dealer Alex Shnaider for a reported NIS 60 million ($15 million). The *Globes* business daily reported in January that Midland Resources Holding Co., through which Shnaider and his partner, Edouard Shyfrin, bought the club, was a partner in a Russian firm that sold air-defense systems to Syria.

Dudi Sela, 22, at the time ranked 105th in the world, scored a stunning upset of sixth-ranked Fernando Gonzales to propel Israel past Chile and into the top-ranked Davis Cup World Group. The triumph in the deciding match at the Ramat Hasharon Tennis Center on September 23 placed Israel among the top 16 nations in the international tennis competition. Sela, from Kiryat Shmona near the northern border, ended the year ranked 64th, after winning $150,000 in prize money in 2007. Israel's top woman player, 20-year-old Shahar Peer, ended the year ranking 17th, down slightly from her career high of 15th earlier in 2007. A quarterfinalist at the Australian Open and the U.S. Open, Peer collected over $800,000 in prize money during 2007. Men's doubles team Andy Ram and Yoni Erlich, ranked 18th in the world, had prizes of $288,000 for the year.

Also in tennis, Israel defeated Austria 4-1 in July to reach the World Group of the top eight national teams in the Federation Cup, the women's equivalent of the Davis Cup. Other teams in the top-ranked group were China, France, Germany, Italy, Spain, the U.S., and Russia, which Israel was due to meet in the 2008 tournament quarterfinals.

The first World Jewish Ice Hockey Championships took place on artificial ice at the rink in the town of Metulla, near the Lebanese border, July 15–20. The U.S. won the gold medal and teams from France, Canada, and Israel also competed.

Betar Jerusalem, owned by Arkady Gaydamak, won the Israeli soccer Premier League Championship. Israel soccer's State Cup was won by Hapoel Tel Aviv, which defeated Hapoel Ashkelon 5-4 on May 16. The winner of Israeli basketball's Premier League Championship was Maccabi Tel Aviv.

Personalia

Honors and Awards

The 2007 Israel Prizes went to Tel Aviv University emeritus prof. Elisha Efrat (Geography); Hebrew University emeritus prof. Amnon Cohen (Israel Studies); Hebrew University emeritus prof. Shalom Schwartz (Psychology); Hebrew University prof. and Bank of Israel consultant Nisan Leviatan (Economics); Hebrew University emeritus prof. Zvi Selinger (Biology); Tel Aviv University emeritus prof. Zvi Hashin (Engineering); Ya'akov Yaar and Ada Karmi-Melamede (Architecture); Shenkar Institute Design Faculty chair Yarom Vardimon (Design); *Yediot Aharonot* columnist Nahum Barnea (Journalism); industrialist-philanthropist Dov Lautman, the Gevatron Choir, feminist activist and educator Prof. Alice Shalvi, and the Joint Distribution Committee Israel (Lifetime Achievement); and Bar-Ilan University's Responsa Project (Torah Literature).

Winners of the 2007 Wolf Prizes were Profs. Ronald Philips of the University of Minnesota and Michael Georges of the University of Liege, Belgium (Agriculture); Profs. Ada Yonath of the Weizmann Institute of Science and George Feher of the University of California, San Diego

(Chemistry); Profs. Stephen Smale of the University of California Berkeley and Hillel (Harry) Furstenberg of the Hebrew University of Jerusalem (Mathematics); Anthony Pawson of Mt. Sinai Hospital, Toronto, Alexander Levitzki of the Hebrew University of Jerusalem, and Anthony Hunter of the Salk Institute, La Jolla, California (Medicine); Albert Fert of Unité Mixte de Physicque CNRS-Thales, Orsay, France, and Peter Gruenberg, IFF, Juelich, Germany (Physics); and Michelangelo Pistoletto, Biella, Italy (Arts).

The EMET prizes were awarded to Profs. Micha Sharir and Vitali Milman, Tel Aviv University, and Shmuel Agmon, Hebrew University (Exact Sciences); former Supreme Court president Aharon Barak and Bar-Ilan and Tel Aviv University prof. Shlomo Giora Shoham (Social Sciences); Tel Aviv University prof. Eliora Ron and Weizmann Institute prof. Yosef Yarden (Life Sciences); Haifa University prof. Myrian Yardeni and retired philosophy prof. Avishai Margalit (Humanities); and authors David Grossman and Sami Michael (Culture and Arts).

The Sokolow Prizes for Journalism went to *Ha'aretz* film critic Uri Klein; Channel 10 Arab-affairs reporter Shlomi Eldar; *Ha'aretz* health reporter Ran Reznik; and TV-and-radio personality Yaron London for his life's work.

The winner of the $100,000 Charles Bronfman Prize was Dr. Amitai Ziv, founder and director of the Israel Center for Medical Simulation. The "Andy" Prize, given by Mr. Bronfman in the name of his late wife Andrea Morrison Bronfman, was awarded to Israeli jeweler-artist Itai Noy in January, on the first anniversary of Andrea Bronfman's death.

The $1 million Dan David Prizes, awarded by the Tel Aviv University-headquartered Dan David Foundation, went to French historian Jacques Le Goff ("past"); conductor Zubin Mehta and composer Pascal Dusapin ("present"); and scientists James Hansen, Sarah Kurtz, and Jerry Olsen ("future").

The third annual Institute of International Education Victor J. Goldberg IIE Prize for Peace in the Middle East was given to Amin Khalaf and Lee Gordon, veteran Israeli educators and cofounders of Hand in Hand, which, since its founding in 1997, had established three bilingual, multicultural Jewish-Arab schools.

The Ministry of Environmental Protection's first Green Campus Award went to the Sami Shamoon College of Engineering. The college, with 2,500 students on campuses in Beersheba and Ashdod, was the first engineering school in Israel to offer students courses in protecting the environment.

Prof. Saul Friedländer, the Czech-born Israeli Holocaust historian, received the top prize at the 2007 Frankfurt Book Fair. Friedlander, who managed to avoid arrest by the Nazis in France, where his parents had fled from Czechoslovakia only to be deported later to Auschwitz, now taught at the University of California.

The award for best actor at the Berlin Film Festival was given to an Israeli, Sasson Gabay, for his portrayal of the director of an Egyptian police band that mistakenly ends up in a small Negev town on a visit to Israel, in *The Band's Visit*. Eran Kolirin, director of the film, was named European discovery of 2007. *The Band's Visit* also won awards at the Tokyo Film Festival, the Cannes Film Festival, and festivals in Kiev, Sarajevo, Flanders, and Zurich. It also swept the Israeli Film Academy's "Oscars," taking seven prizes.

Oded Balilty, an Israeli photographer for the Associated Press, was awarded a Pulitzer Prize in the category of breaking-news photography for his picture of a lone Jewish woman facing security forces during the evacuation of Amona, a West Bank outpost near Ramallah, in February 2006.

Deaths

Israeli linguist and former Tel Aviv University professor Tanya Reinhart, 63, harsh critic of Israeli policies who had been teaching at NYU, at Montauk, New Jersey, on March 17; Shimon Tzabar, 81, former Israeli journalist who claimed to have been a member, at various times, of the Hagana and of the IZL and LEHI undergrounds, turned communist and immigrated to England after the 1967 war, in London, on March 19; Liviu Librescu, 76, Holocaust survivor, aerospace engineer, professor, killed April 16 protecting his students during the Virginia Tech massacre, buried April 20 in Ra'anana; Hebrew University sociologist Baruch Kimmerling, 67, "new historian" who applied postcolonial theory to the Zionist movement and Israel, in Jerusalem, on May 20; Ze'ev Schiff, 74, French-born *Ha'aretz* defense correspondent, dean of Israeli military reporters, and coauthor of best-selling books on Israeli wars, in Tel Aviv, on June 19; Yair Levy, 68, former official of the Israel Export and International Cooperation Agency, on July 28; Amos Manor, 89, Romanian-born head of the Shin Bet from 1953 to 1963, on August 5; Dr. Haider Abdel-Shafi, 88, Gaza physician who dabbled in politics, leader of the Palestinian delegation to the 1991 peace talks, polled the most votes in elections to the Palestinian National Assembly in 1996 and walked out three years later in a dispute with Yasir Arafat, in Gaza, on September 25; former Ashkenazi chief rabbi Avraham Shapira, 94, opponent of any territorial compromise, in Jerusalem, on September 28, his funeral attended by some 25,000 mourners; Mordecai (Motel) Kreiner, 79, former manager of Supersol and pioneer of the Israeli supermarket, in Savyon, on October 12; John Strugnell, 77, controversial Christian editor and translator of the Dead Sea scrolls and professor of Christian origins at Harvard Divinity School, in Cambridge, Massachusetts, on November 30; Moroccan-born Sa'adia Marciano, 58, leader of the Black Panther movement that emerged from Jerusalem's Musrara slum area in the early 1970s to espouse the cause of Israel's long-neglected poor and underprivileged, in Jerusalem, on December 21.

HANAN SHER

The Americas

Canada

National Affairs

CANADA ENJOYED A YEAR of political stability and relative prosperity. The minority Conservative government, which gained power in 2006, survived in the four-party House of Commons largely because the other parties were unwilling to force another election. The economy grew, unemployment was lower than it had been in decades, and the dollar ascended with surprising rapidity, exceeding par with its American counterpart for the first time in 30 years. Political highlights included elections in the two largest provinces, Ontario and Quebec, neither of them leading to a change of government.

In preparation for the Quebec election in March, Montreal's Jews were concerned because of their strong aversion to the secessionist Parti Québecois (PQ). While the governing Liberals had lost popularity since winning a majority in 2003, they were able to hang on to a narrow plurality in a National Assembly that was split among three parties, resulting in the first minority government for the province in over a century. The fact that the PQ was relegated to third place provided a measure of satisfaction to the Jewish community. Although Lawrence Bergman and Russell Copeman, both Liberals, were reelected, Premier Jean Charest left Bergman out of his new cabinet, the first time in decades that a Liberal premier with Jews in his caucus had failed to include at least one. In November, a delegation from the Canadian Jewish Congress (CJC) met with Charest and expressed the community's dissatisfaction at the lack of Jewish cabinet representation. The biggest story of the election was the emergence of Action Démocratique du Québec (ADQ) as the second largest party, and thus the official opposition. Jews had very little connection with the ADQ, and, as usual, gave almost all their votes to the Liberals.

Ontario's election in October (originally scheduled for the Jewish holiday of Shemini Atzeret but then changed after strenuous protests) focused on the issue of public funding for religious schools other than Catholic. Several successive provincial governments had refused to grant these schools the funding granted to Catholic education, and as a result day-school tuitions were substantially higher than in the five Canadian provinces that did provide support. There were about 40 Jewish day schools in Ontario—in Toronto, Ottawa, Hamilton, and London—enrolling some 13,000 students.

In this election campaign, Conservative leader John Tory made the extension of funding to other religions the central plank of his platform, calculating perhaps that the move would attract additional votes to his party, which traditionally had not done well among minorities. Unfortunately for Tory, his party, and the various religious schools, the move backfired and Dalton McGuinty's Liberal Party won a second majority government. Despite the efforts of Jews and other religious groups, polls showed that most Ontarians opposed the Conservative position. There was no evidence that any substantial part of the electorate, aside from members of religious groups that would have benefited directly, had warmed to the idea. University of Toronto political scientist Nelson Wiseman described the Conservative school-funding initiative as follows: "They pulled a grenade and it blew up in their face."

The tenor of the debate about the proposal during the campaign alarmed many Jews and made some of them regret that the matter had ever been raised. *Canadian Jewish News* (*CJN*) editor Mordechai Ben-Dat pointed to the "overwhelming hostility" of the electorate toward the proposal and "the shameful, incendiary incitement of this hostility by the premier and other leading Liberals." After the election, a B'nai Brith Canada (BBC) press release noted that the contest had been "fraught with bigotry and prejudice, much of it feeding misconceptions about the . . . issue of fair funding." Accepting the verdict of the voters, Tory formally abandoned his pledge to support funding the religious schools. The prospect of direct government funding, a long-sought goal of the Jewish community, now seemed dead for the foreseeable future.

Among those elected as Liberals were Monte Kwinter and David Caplan, both cabinet ministers in the previous government. However, McGuinty dropped Kwinter from the new cabinet while retaining Caplan. Others elected to the provincial legislature were Liberals David Zimmer and Conservative Peter Shurman. Shurman's victory probably reflected a rise in Jewish support for the Conservatives because of the school-funding issue.

In a federal by-election in the Montreal constituency of Outremont, Liberal leader Stephane Dion's hand-picked candidate, academic Jocelyn Coulon, raised concerns among Jews because of his views on the Middle East. B'nai Brith spokesman Moïse Moghrabi claimed that Coulon, an international-affairs expert frequently quoted in the media, was biased against the U.S. and Israel. However Liberal MP Irwin Cotler defended Coulon as a "critical friend" of Israel whose views were consistent with the basic principles of Canadian foreign policy. Coulon met with Jewish community representatives before the September election and sought to reassure them by backtracking on his earlier call for Israel to negotiate with Hamas. As it turned out, Coulon lost the election, at least in part because some Jews, though habitual Liberals, would not vote for him. Coulon's defeat was also a significant political blow to Dion.

Terrorism and Militant Islam

In February, Parliament considered extending two key parts of antiterrorism legislation that had been enacted for a five-year period after the 9/11 attacks. These enabled police to make preventive arrests and detentions, and provided for investigative hearings where testimony could be compelled. The government supported extension while the opposition Liberals opposed it due to civil liberties concerns. Liberal MP Irwin Cotler, however, a former justice minister and staunch advocate of human rights, defied his party and expressed support for the bill, but finally abstained. The bill failed because all three opposition parties voted against it. Jewish groups expressed their disappointment. CJC asserted that security had been "significantly eroded." BBC executive vice president Frank Dimant contended that the defeat was "political theatrics at the expense of vital security concerns." Brent Belzberg, cochair of the Canadian Council for Israel and Jewish Advocacy (CIJA), asserted that the Conservative approach was correct and urged the other parties to join in passing a new law quickly. He argued that "our communal safety is too precious to risk in the name of some perceived parliamentary insult or gamesmanship."

Sen. Jerry Grafstein introduced a private member's bill to make suicide bombing a criminal offense. It passed the first of the required three readings but got no further, despite the backing of numerous prominent public figures. Grafstein viewed his bill as an opportunity for Canada to take the lead among democratic states in giving the government the tools to pursue those who plan such attacks and assist in them. But a Conservative leader in the Senate indicated that his caucus would oppose the bill as unnecessary.

A billboard that glorified Hezballah leader Hassan Nasrallah was erected in Windsor in August. As Canada classified Hezballah as a terrorist organization, there were immediate complaints from both Jews and non-Jews. The billboard was removed after three days.

In October *Le Figaro* revealed that Canada had identified a Lebanese-Canadian as a suspect in the bombing of the synagogue on Rue Copernic in Paris in 1980 (see AJYB 1982, pp. 197–98). France was still investigating the unidentified man and it was unclear if and when there would be an extradition request. Bernie Farber, CEO of the CJC, expressed the hope that he would be extradited, but noted that two terrorists from the Popular Front for the Liberation of Palestine had long been the subject of deportation proceedings yet remained in Canada. One of them, Issam al-Yamani, faced a deportation hearing in March. Yamani, who arrived in Canada in 1985, admitted his former PFLP membership but contended that the organization was a constitutionally protected political association.

The Victoria Philharmonic Choir in British Columbia presented Handel's *Samson* oratorio in March from a new angle, transforming the biblical hero into a terrorist, a precursor of today's suicide bombers. The same theme was broadcast on the VPC Website. The production set the scene in Jerusalem in 1946, and had Samson blow himself up at British headquarters.

Israel and the Middle East

The government of Prime Minister Stephen Harper remained quite supportive of Israel. For example, Foreign Minister Peter MacKay, speaking at the Herzliya Conference in January, defended his decision not to meet with Hamas officials while in the region, depicting it as part of Canada's antiterrorism stance. He also emphasized that "the regime in Iran cannot be allowed to acquire nuclear weapons." MacKay did level some criticisms at Israel, particularly about its conduct at border crossings and the route of the security fence.

Harper's policies came under attack from a surprising source, former prime minister Joe Clark, the man who made the aborted promise to move the Canadian embassy to Jerusalem during the 1979 campaign. In a speech in Montreal in January, Clark accused Harper of jeopardizing Canada's "balanced and careful" Middle East policy through the pro-

Israel tilt during the Lebanon war in 2006, the suspension of aid to Hamas, and alleged closeness with the Bush administration.

MP Cotler took a broad view of the Middle East situation in a Jerusalem speech in July. Referring to a variety of regional threats, including Iran, he contended that the Jewish people was facing "a gathering storm without parallel or precedent since the 1930s," musing that in some respects 2007 resembled 1938. But he concluded that "it is not 1938. There is a Jewish state as an antidote to Jewish vulnerability."

In a rebuff to those who considered Jerusalem to be an integral part of Israel, in July the Federal Court of Appeal upheld a lower court's decision that the government properly declined to allow a citizen's birthplace to be designated as "Jerusalem, Israel" on his passport. The government's policy was to use only the city name in the case of Jerusalem because its status has not yet been determined by negotiations. The court emphasized that the 1947 UN partition resolution did not contemplate Israeli sovereignty over Jerusalem. The teenage petitioner, Eliyahu Veffer, had contended that the government's position violated his constitutional right to freedom of religion, an argument that the court rejected.

Canada's actions at the UN and its agencies were somewhat more sensitive to Israel's position than in the past. UN Watch, which monitors the UN human rights scene, issued its Human Rights Scorecard in March and ranked Canada first among the member states on the Human Rights Council for its record on human rights, in particular for its opposition to biased resolutions against Israel. In June, the Canadian representative to the council objected strongly to a statement by the president that a package of measures singling out Israel for special scrutiny had been approved by consensus. Then, after the council voted by 46 to 1 (Canada) to back the president's assertion of a consensus, Canada protested. Foreign Minister MacKay expressed Canada's great disappointment in the council's actions, saying that "Canada cannot accept the inclusion of a permanent agenda item on Palestine and the occupied Arab territories, as it singles out one situation for highly politicized, partial and subjective treatment of a complex issue." This stand evoked praise from the Canada-Israel Committee (CIC) and from Israel's foreign minister, Tzipi Livni. Jon Allen, the ambassador to Israel, stressed that his government recognized Israel's need for self-defense in a "tough neighborhood."

However, Louise Arbour, a Canadian who was serving as UN high commissioner for human rights, expressed "her appreciation to all those who contributed to launching the council on a consensual basis." And in September Arbour came under tough criticism from Hillel Neuer, director of UN Watch, for lack of balance and for attending a human rights conference in Iran while ignoring that country's genocidal threats against Israel. He noted that "she has never once issued a stand-alone statement against Palestinian terrorism" and that she repeatedly resorted "to a one-sided narrative that denies Israelis their essential right to self-defense." Neuer further criticized Arbour in November for failing to take any action against anti-Semitism.

At the annual CIJA Parliamentary Dinner in February, Prime Minister Harper, referring to the 2006 Lebanon War, told the group that "Israel had a friend when it mattered, and that, my friends, is the only thing that really counts." He added that a struggle between a democracy and a terrorist group "is not a matter for shades of gray, it is a matter of right and wrong." Harper also promised that "Israel will always have a steadfast friend in Canada's new government." His remarks were welcomed enthusiastically by the audience. Not to be outdone, Stephane Dion, the opposition leader, declared that "Israel's fight for existence is our fight. Her struggle for peace and security is our struggle."

Foreign Minister Livni visited Ottawa in March and thanked the government for its support of Israel and its role in the international struggle against terrorism. She met her counterpart, Peter MacKay, as well as Public Safety Minister Stockwell Day. At a meeting of the Canada-Israel Chamber of Commerce she spoke of the prospects for foreign investment in Israel, emphasizing her country's dynamic economic growth, and praised the benefits of the free-trade agreement with Canada. She was preceded by Minister of Public Security Avi Dichter, who addressed a CIJA luncheon in February. He praised Canada, describing it as a "true friend and ally." During his visit he met with the prime minister, Stockwell Day, and the commissioner of the Royal Canadian Mounted Police, and briefed the House of Commons Public Safety and National Security Committee about Iran and about Israel's counterterrorism experience.

Shortly after the Annapolis conference on the Middle East in November, Israeli prime minister Ehud Olmert asked his Canadian counterpart for help in the forthcoming peace negotiations. Stephen Harper told the House of Commons that "Canada stands ready to assist the process in any way that we can." Michael Ignatieff, the Liberal deputy leader, visited Israel around the same time, and expressed optimism about the prospects for peace while recognizing the threat posed by Iran. Later, the new foreign minister, Maxime Bernier, issued a statement saying that Canada continued to support "the security and well-being of Israel and its legitimate place within the Middle East and the international community."

The Canada-Israel trade agreement was acknowledged as a big success. Ephraim Shoham, leaving his post as Israeli trade commissioner after four years, pointed out that during his posting Israeli exports to Canada increased by 80 percent while trade in the opposite direction was up 50 percent. The most recent figure for total trade was $951 million. Israel and Quebec signed a cooperation agreement in December pertaining to health, education, trade, science, and technology that expanded a pact originally signed in 1997. Israeli consul general Yoram Elron described it as a "milestone agreement" that would reinforce the bilateral relationship. He spoke about a significant growth in Quebec imports from Israel, especially in the areas of medicine, aerospace, and petroleum technology, and pointed to joint ventures as examples of the benefits of the prior agreement.

A number of requests by Russian Israelis for asylum in Canada charged that immigrant children were mistreated in the Jewish state. According to a story in *Ha'aretz,* Canada's Immigration and Refugee Board (IRB), looking into the allegations, sent a query to the National Council for the Child in Israel as to whether children from the former Soviet Union faced abuse or official harassment. The council replied in the negative, and the Israeli embassy in Canada angrily accused the purported refugees of "deliberately misleading" the Canadian government. In another immigration matter, the IRB rejected an Israeli woman's claim for refugee status. She claimed that, as a victim of terrorist attacks, she feared for her life in Israel, but the IRB said that she did not qualify as a victim of persecution because she was not targeted because of her religion.

Following Foreign Minister MacKay's visit to the Middle East in January, the Canadian International Development Agency (CIDA) decided to increase its aid to the Palestinian Authority, earmarking $12–15 million for humanitarian assistance. In 2006 Canada had suspended aid to the PA after Hamas, classified as a terrorist organization, won control of the government in Gaza. The new aid would be routed through the Temporary International Mechanism, which bypassed Hamas, and was on top of some $20 million spent during the previous year in direct aid to Palestinians. A further $1.2 million was committed to aid in the construction of a border crossing between Israel and Gaza. Some announced aid projects were suspended.

Opposition leader Dion called for the restoration of aid in June, contending that the Hamas government of the PA had in fact dissolved. He claimed that the flow of funds would strengthen Palestinian president Mahmoud Abbas. Within a month the government indeed resumed some aid, directed mainly to the West Bank, in recognition of the more moderate policies of the PA after the ouster of Hamas from the government. Later, in December, at the Paris donors' conference, Canada promised a total of $300 million over five years. A spokesperson for the Department of Foreign Affairs assured the public that "Canada will insure that Canadian funds do not directly or indirectly benefit Hamas or other terrorist groups listed under Canadian law."

But Gerald Steinberg, a political scientist at Bar-Ilan University, attacked CIDA in a March column in the *Canadian Jewish News*. He contended that the agency indirectly promoted the Palestinian position against Israel. It had, for example, provided support for the publication of a book hostile to Israel, and had, according to a report by the Canadian Coalition for Democracies (CCD), allowed funds to go to groups that followed "radical anti-Israel policies." The column provoked harsh criticism from both Canadian and Israeli academics.

When Palestinian minister Mustafa Barghouti visited Canada in March, MacKay declined to meet with him. However some MPs from the Liberal and New Democratic (NDP) parties and the Bloc Québecois did, and taunted MacKay on the floor of the House over his failure to do so. Barghouti suggested publicly that Canada was too influenced by Israel, an assertion that was strongly rejected by CIC officials. They declared that meeting with Barghouti was "entirely inappropriate" because he was a member of the Hamas government. Also in March, some 37 parliamentarians from all parties formed a Canada-Palestine Friendship Association, in part to insure "that Canada's foreign policy for the Middle East is in the best interests of the Palestinian people."

There was considerable anti-Israel activity in a number of sectors. Some of it was targeted at the Conservative government. Mohamed Elmasry, president of the Canadian Islamic Congress, charged in January that Foreign Minister MacKay was "not accessible to the Canadian Arab and Muslim community." The Canadian Arab Federation joined together with Elmasry's organization in a campaign to dissuade members of various groups from voting Conservative in the next election.

NGO Monitor, an Israeli publication, alleged in May that Alternatives, a Montreal-based organization that received half of its funding from the Canadian government, demonized Israel and promoted political activity against it.

In December an Ontario conference of the Canadian Union of Postal Workers (CUPW) adopted a resolution supporting a boycott and sanctions against Israel and endorsing an educational campaign to inform the public about Israel's "apartheid nature." In explaining the resolution, union leader Gerry Deveau said that "Israel is assembling the wall and it's causing social, economic, and medical hardship to the people in the area." In contrast, high school teachers in Toronto rejected, in January, a motion to support a boycott of Israel. Throughout the year a group called Boycott Israeli Apartheid Campaign tried to mount boycotts of Chapters and Indigo bookstores to protest the support that owners Heather Reisman and Gerald Schwartz gave to an organization that helped Israeli soldiers.

Employees of the UJA-Federation of Greater Toronto and CJC's Ontario Region decertified their union local from the Canadian Union of Public Employees in May, because of CUPE's antagonistic stance toward Israel over several years. A particularly nasty resolution employing apartheid terminology and calling for a boycott and sanctions, adopted in 2006, was the final straw (see AJYB 2007, pp. 287–88). The employees formed their own association.

Several elected officials and other political figures joined a June demonstration in Montreal that denounced Israel's allegedly illegal occupation and apartheid practices. Opposition members of Parliament and the Quebec National Assembly, along with various candidates, were prominent among the marchers. Several labor federations organized the protest, and they called upon the federal government to revoke the Jewish National Fund's tax-exempt status.

Also in June a group called the Palestinian Media Collective sought to paint the *Vancouver Sun* as pro-Israel and anti-Palestinian by publishing a parody edition of the paper. The *Sun* was part of the CanWest chain of newspapers, controlled by the Asper family of Winnipeg. CanWest launched a lawsuit in response. In October, an "alternative" bimonthly in Toronto, *This Magazine,* devoted an issue to Israel, entitling it "The New Apartheid." The editor declared the focus to be the "clear . . . injustices perpetrated by the Israeli state against Palestinians."

Several Canadian and U.S. legislators, concerned about the prospects for a second UN World Conference against Racism (the so-called Durban II), slated for 2009, proposed a parallel and competing international human rights meeting. A leading advocate was Sen. Jerry Grafstein, who said that the goal was to "insure that if there's a debate on human rights, it's fair and not distorted." The organizing committee for the upcoming UN conference was chaired by Libya and included Iran.

MP Jason Kenney, a member of the federal cabinet, speaking at a Montreal synagogue in March, pledged that the government would act vigorously to prevent Iran from acquiring nuclear weapons, saying that the prime minister was unwavering in his support for Israel and that he "understands its existential fight." MP Cotler, speaking at the same event, called for the indictment under international law of Iran's President Mahmoud Ahmadinejad for "incitement to genocide." In remarks to the press in August, Cotler argued for tough economic sanctions on Iran. Independently, BBC urged that the Iranian president be indicted and barred from Canada.

A dual Canadian and Egyptian citizen, Mohammed Essam Ghoneim al-Attar, was arrested in Cairo in January, put on trial in February, and convicted and sentenced in April to 15 years for spying for Israel. Al-Attar claimed that he confessed under torture. Israel's public security minister emphatically denied that the man was a spy for Israel and denounced the allegations as "nonsense."

VisionTV, a multifaith religious cable channel, ran two lectures in July by a Pakistani fundamentalist, Israr Ahmad, who was known for his anti-Semitic writings. Although he did not express such sentiments during those lectures, he did appear to endorse violence in pursuit of jihad. After CJC spokesperson Len Rudner questioned the appropriateness of his appearances, the channel's president issued a statement condemning any endorsement of violence and announced that no further programs by Ahmad would be offered.

Former grand chief of the Assembly of First Nations Ovide Mercredi visited Israel for the first time in April and May, along with several other native leaders, in a trip coordinated by the Jewish National Fund. He came away "reflecting on how we could use Israel's model for the benefit" of his own people.

The Campuses

There was strong negative reaction from university presidents to the call by the University and College Union in Britain for a boycott of Israeli universities. Among those who took the lead was McGill's Heather Munroe-Blum, who quickly issued a statement calling the move "a gross violation of the values which form the foundation . . . of civil society" and added that if they "choose to isolate Israeli universities" they should add McGill to their boycott list. She promised to "stand steadfast against those who seek to undermine academic freedom." Other presidents taking similar positions were those heading British Columbia; Concordia; York; Simon Fraser; Queen's; Ryerson; Toronto; Montreal; Dalhousie; Ottawa; Western Ontario; Quebec; Manitoba; Winnipeg; Calgary; and Alberta.

The presidents of Ryerson and Queen's universities were criticized by elements of their student bodies for opposing the proposed boycott. The Ryerson Students' Union (RSU) drafted a motion over the summer calling on the university president to retract his statement on the matter and engage in a process of consultation with the campus community. The Queen's Coalition for Racial and Ethnic Diversity called its principal's anti-boycott stand "a defamation of Queen's community members . . . who strongly oppose your stance."

The RSU, in fact, brought a motion to the general meeting of the Canadian Federation of Students in November in Toronto that called for a boycott, divestment, and sanctions campaign against Israel, but it was rejected by more than a two-thirds majority on a technical motion. Later that month RSU ran a program featuring four professors with diverse views about a boycott, although all were anti-Israel and pro-Palestinian. Yet a survey taken in August of 900 students at the University of Toronto and Ryerson showed that 90 percent of respondents opposed a boycott and 71 percent opposed funding anti-Israel campus groups from the mandatory fees paid by students.

Anti-Israel activists exerted considerable pressure on several campuses. "Israeli Apartheid Weeks" were held in February to highlight alleged violations of human rights and repression of Palestinians. In 2007, 40 years after the 1967 Six-Day War, the emphasis was on "Zionist ethnic cleansing, colonization and occupation of Palestine." The Arab Students' Collective and Solidarity for Palestinian Human Rights (SPHR) coordinated activities at York, McMaster, Concordia, Toronto, and elsewhere. Israeli Arab MK Jamal Zahalka spoke at several of these on "Debunking the Myth of Israeli Democracy." At Hamilton's McMaster University an American law professor, formerly legal adviser to the PLO, appeared in January to advocate divestment and accuse Israel of genocide. In February Norman Finkelstein, the controversial former DePaul University professor who was denied tenure, spoke on campus. At the University of Toronto, Finkelstein lectured in November, and there was also an anti-Israel rally there.

Jewish student groups, unable to convince university authorities to take steps against these activities, sought to counter their effects by hosting events of their own. For example, they invited Israeli ambassador Alan Baker to speak at the University of Toronto, where he declared that to label Israel as practicing apartheid was "a celebration of ignorance, hypocrisy, academic dishonesty, and crude propaganda." In March, at that university, Jewish groups joined with others to sponsor Freedom and Democracy Week, which included lectures on terrorism and extremism, with reference to the Canadian experience. At York, a new Campus Coalition of Zionists (CCZ) set up a table to distribute literature, mostly about Iran. On November 20, students manning the table were "physically and verbally intimidated" by anti-Israel agitators who forced them to leave and then destroyed their materials. The next day CCZ and other groups sponsored a lecture by Itamar Marcus, director of Palestinian Media Watch. After his talk anti-Israel students in the audience shouted invective at Marcus, and subsequently some students demanded that the York senate discipline CCZ for spreading hate speech on campus. Although several senators expressed support, there was no action by year's end. The Jewish student group Hillel avoided confrontational events, preferring dialogues and "positive educational programs." Thus Hillel joined with several other Toronto-area student groups to organize Holocaust and Genocide Awareness Week in November, highlighting not only the Jewish experience under the Nazis but also the suffering of Armenians, Rwandans, Darfuris, and Cambodians.

The Canadian Institute for Jewish Research, based in Montreal, established a training program for students interested in advocating for Israel. The Student Israel Advocacy Seminars began in the fall and ran for the rest of the academic year, combining academic lectures by professors with practical seminars on advocacy techniques. Although students who had worked with CIJR in the past often went on to professional pro-Israel work, director Frederick Krantz felt the need for more systematic preparation for larger numbers of students. He said that pro-Israel students were not generally well prepared with an ideological focus and often did not have an adequate historical background.

York professor David Noble won a labor arbitration case against his university in November, and was awarded $2,500. The arbitrator found that the administration had violated the collective agreement by issuing a press release in 2004 that condemned a flyer he was distributing on campus that made accusations about connections between pro-Israel donors and the university (see AJYB 2005, p. 296). Another case arising from the Noble incident was also resolved during the year. For his actions during two campus protests in defense of the Noble flyer, student Daniel Freeman-Maloy had been suspended for three years. Although the suspension was lifted after only three months, Freeman-Maloy sued. The suit was settled in May 2007 without disclosure of the terms, and Freeman-Maloy enrolled as a graduate student at York in the fall.

The University of Windsor law school ended a 34-year-old policy of canceling classes on the High Holy Days. While Noble has been campaigning against a similar practice at York, there was no indication that his efforts had any effect at Windsor. The dean said that the school would develop a new policy to accommodate all minority religious groups, not just Jews. This left York and the University of Toronto as the only law schools canceling classes on those days.

Shiraz Dossa, a political science professor at St. Francis Xavier University, encountered considerable hostility from colleagues in January after he returned from the Tehran Holocaust-denial conference held in late 2006. Over 100 professors signed a letter declaring "profound embarrassment" over his participation, and the university president termed Holocaust denial "abhorrent."

Anti-Semitism and Racism

There were several anti-Semitic incidents in various parts of the country during the year. One of the most upsetting was the firebombing of the YM-YWHA in Montreal on the night of the Passover seder in April, with a Molotov cocktail. There were no damages or injuries. Two men, Azim Ibragimov and Omar Bulphred, were arrested for that incident as well as for a similar 2006 attack on a Hasidic school in Outremont (see AJYB 2007, p. 291). Both men were Muslim immigrants who had become Canadian citizens. The police declared that anti-Semitism had been a motivating factor in both cases, making the crimes more serious than ordinary arson.

Vandals threw rocks through the windows of a Chabad center in Toronto in March. A similar incident occurred in October at a synagogue in the Montreal area, and the young man who was caught and charged was wearing Nazi gear and insignia. An arson attack destroyed a Satmar home in Val David, a resort community north of Montreal, in June. Anti-Semitic graffiti were painted on synagogues in Edmonton and Montreal in January. The same happened to a synagogue in the Vancouver area in April, and two teenagers were caught and charged. In the small Ontario town of Bowmanville, a rental home owned by Jews was damaged and defaced with anti-Semitic graffiti in September. There were also two incidents in the York region north of Toronto: in October, nine vehicles were painted with anti-Semitic graffiti, and in December, a home was similarly defaced and the car parked there burned. Jewish high-school students in Winnipeg were the targets of anti-Semitic slurs and a death threat during a visit to another high school in November.

Internet promulgation of hatred was a persistent problem. In January,

Sebastien Presseault of Montreal pleaded guilty to promoting racial hatred and was sentenced to six months in jail. He had been using a U.S.-based Web-hosting service, which responded to pressure from BBC and agreed to drop his site. The judge described the Website as "vile, despicable and nauseating" in its descriptions of blacks, Jews, and other minorities. Richard Warman, an Ottawa anti-hate activist who was not Jewish, was responsible for two successful prosecutions of offensive Internet sites during the year. In February he initiated a case with the Canadian Human Rights Tribunal regarding Bobby James Wilkinson of Ottawa, who ran a Website of the Canadian Nazi Party. Wilkinson was fined $4,000 and ordered to stop using the Internet to foment hatred. In another case initiated by Warman in November, Jessica Beaumont of Calgary was fined $1,500 by the Tribunal and ordered to pay Warman another $3,000. She had posted hate messages directed at various minorities.

The long-running case of the former aboriginal leader David Ahenakew reached a new stage in 2007. Ahenakew was convicted in 2005 for promoting hatred against Jews through his public statements, but the conviction was overturned and a new trial ordered in 2006 (see AJYB 2007, p. 292). The government's appeal of that decision began in June 2007. The question at issue was whether Ahenakew had intended to promote hatred with his anti-Semitic remarks. The Crown prosecutor contended that he did, and BBC used its intervenor status to argue that the most important consideration was the content of his words, which did convey hatred, whatever his intentions may have been.

White supremacist Paul Fromm, a longtime public school teacher, had his teaching license lifted by a disciplinary tribunal of the Ontario College of Teachers in November. The action was based on his activities over many years outside the classroom that were "inconsistent with the values of the profession," including the use of "racist language in relation to Jews."

A Toronto synagogue held a forum on anti-Semitism in the media in November, where *National Post* columnist Robert Fulford suggested that anti-Israel bias, especially in the liberal media, had spilled over into anti-Semitism.

The Quebec Press Council found that *National Post* columnist Barbara Kay had unfairly portrayed francophone Quebecers, particularly the separatists, as anti-Semitic and weak on the terrorism issue. In a column published during Israel's 2006 war in Lebanon entitled "The Rise of Quebecistan," Kay was commenting about a Montreal protest march against the war, attended by Quebec politicians, which featured many anti-Israel expressions (see AJYB 2007, pp. 284–85). The council ruled in March that her article lacked "balance, rigor, level-headedness, and . . . respect for certain social groups." Both Kay and her paper dismissed the decision, and she charged the council with a "Kafkaesque" attempt to intimidate critics of Quebec political life.

Business executive Tony Comper and his wife, Elizabeth, were honored at a Montreal dinner in April for their leadership in organizing non-Jewish business leaders to combat anti-Semitism (see AJYB 2007, p. 292). They received the Scopus Award from Canadian Friends of the Hebrew University of Jerusalem.

Cardinal Marc Ouellet, archbishop of Quebec, wrote an open letter in November that appeared in several newspapers acknowledging mistakes made by the Roman Catholic Church in Canada. Among them was "the narrow-minded attitudes of certain Catholics, before 1960, that favored anti-Semitism."

Holocaust-Related Matters

Justice for aging accused Nazi war criminals proceeded at a very slow pace. Michael Seifert, wanted for years by Italian authorities for torture and murder at a transit camp near Bolzano, lost his appeal in August, as the British Columbia Court of Appeal rejected his lawyer's arguments that his client was too sick and frail to go to prison and that Irwin Cotler, then serving as minister of justice, was biased when he acted on an earlier court ruling. Another step against Seifert was taken in November, when a Federal Court judge ruled that he had obtained his citizenship "by misrepresenting and concealing his activities during the war and his place of birth." This made it possible for Seifert's citizenship to be revoked, a necessary prelude to deportation to Italy. (His final appeal to the Supreme Court of Canada was rejected in early 2008.)

In May the cabinet ruled on the citizenship revocations of four men. It decided not to revoke those of Wasyl Odynsky and Vladimir Katriuk, both of whom had been found earlier to have lied about their wartime activities on their applications for immigration. BBC went to court to try to force the government to change its position. The cabinet did revoke the citizenship of Helmut Oberlander and Jacob Fast, who were found to have lied about their participation in Nazi units when they applied for admission to Canada. This was the second revocation for Oberlander, who had gotten the earlier one reversed by the Federal Court in 2004. Justice Minister Rob Nicholson, announcing the decision, stated that

"Canada will not become a safe haven for anyone who has been involved in war crimes, crimes against humanity, or genocide."

Nevertheless, the Simon Wiesenthal Center gave Canada a grade of "F" in its annual evaluation of international efforts against Nazi war criminals. The center's director, Efraim Zuroff, asserted that "Canada has not been able to deport eight Nazi collaborators who have been stripped of their citizenship. The entire process has broken down and it's an embarrassment." He was particularly critical of Canada's lenient appeals process and what he considered a lack of political will to bring cases to a conclusion. Since 1994, when the present system for such deportations was adopted, 21 cases had been initiated but not a single deportation carried out. In January, CJC, joined by representatives of the Armenian, Roma, and Rwandan communities, held a press conference where the speakers called on the government to act promptly in the matter of aging war criminals such as Oberlander, Katriuk, Fast, Odynsky, Jura Skomatchuk, and Josef Furman.

The effort to recover paintings looted by the Nazis from art dealer Max Stern, who later settled in Canada, continued in several countries (see AJYB 2007, p. 293). Stern's estate (three universities in Canada and Israel were the beneficiaries) was seeking to recover up to 200 artworks that Stern was forced to sell under duress in 1937. One painting was located in Spain. The owner, a foundation that had acquired it some years earlier, was persuaded to transfer title to the estate, but the painting was allowed to remain on permanent loan to the foundation. Another painting was owned by a Rhode Island woman, who moved it to Germany when the estate began to inquire about it. In June, a U.S. District Court judge ordered her not to move it again, pending the outcome of legal proceedings. In December, the judge ruled that the forced sale in 1937 amounted to theft and ordered the painting turned over to the Stern estate. According to an announcement in December, a third painting was recovered, which would be put on display at the Montreal Museum of Fine Arts.

Prime Minister Harper addressed a gathering on Parliament Hill on Holocaust Memorial Day in April and drew a connection between the destruction of European Jewry and the threat that Israel now faced. Harper said that political leaders "must stand up to those who advocate the destruction of Israel and its people today and they must be unequivocal in their condemnation of anti-Semitic despots, terrorists and fanatics."

The first Echenberg Family Conference on Human Rights was held at Montreal's McGill University in October. Focusing on the prevention of genocide, the program featured first-person testimony from survivors of the genocides in Armenia, Rwanda, the former Yugoslavia, Cambodia, and Darfur, joined by Jews and Roma who gave accounts of the Nazi annihilation programs. Attention was also given to scholarly analyses of how to identify incipient genocides and prevent them. Hermann Gruenwald's new book, *After Auschwitz: One Man's Story,* was launched during the conference.

In November, the Azrieli Foundation's Memoir Project held a public event in Toronto to launch the publication of its first series of six memoirs of Canadian survivors.

JEWISH COMMUNITY

Demography

A study of Jewish mobility patterns, based on 2001 census data, was released in March. Demographer Charles Shahar found confirmation of a trend that had been observed for several decades: Toronto was the leading destination for Jews moving within Canada, while Montreal continued to lose Jews. Between 1996 and 2001, Toronto's Jewish community attracted about 2,300 internal migrants, about the same number that left Montreal. Ottawa and Calgary gained about 300 Jews each, and Hamilton showed a rise of 170. Vancouver and Halifax lost 30–40 Jews each, while Winnipeg lost about 265. The data also showed that Toronto attracted the most Jews from outside Canada, about 10,400, while about 3,000 went to Montreal and 1,750 to Vancouver. Immigration into Winnipeg was estimated at about 750, meaning a net gain of perhaps 500 Jews into a community that had been declining for some time. The latest estimate for the total Jewish population in Canada was around 370,000.

Communal Affairs

The Canadian Jewish Congress held its triennial plenary in Ottawa in June. One of the highlights was the election, for the first time in CJC history, of co-presidents, Rabbi Reuven Bulka and Sylvain Abitbol. A major issue discussed at the plenary was a proposal to change the internal operations of CJC: instead of national elections, the senior officers would henceforth be appointed by a board representing the three largest federations (Toronto, Montreal, and Vancouver), Congress regions, and the

Canadian Council for Israel and Jewish Advocacy (CIJA). The idea raised the ire of Congress veterans, who valued its democratic traditions and saw elections as a key element in the body's legitimacy. Abitbol, a former president of the Montreal federation, strongly advocated the new by-law, believing it would streamline CJC's operation. Bulka, however, before his election as co-president, had expressed reservations. After the proposal to approve the change passed, Bulka assured the delegates that "Congress will continue to be the voice of the Jewish people in Canada."

In a series of articles in the *Canadian Jewish News* in March, Prof. Harold Waller of McGill University analyzed developments in Canadian Jewish organizational life in recent years, with special emphasis on the changing role of CJC and its relationship with the local federations. Since CJC lacked a dependable funding base, he argued, it had become increasingly dependent on the federations for its survival, and in the process lost some of its autonomy. Furthermore, when CIJA was established in 2004 it was given the major responsibility for community advocacy, meaning that CJC's budget allocations would now come through that body, further reducing its autonomy. The new corporate-type structure was defended by some Congress leaders, as the advocacy function within the organized community, with its multitude of organizations, was now more clearly defined and, perhaps, more effective.

Waller's articles stimulated considerable discussion, notably on the letters page of the *CJN*. Another article appearing in the paper in June, by Prof. Michael Brown of York University, dealt with the impact of the move away from traditional elections. He opined that "Congress was once the pride of Canadian Jewry, the kind of organization that American Jews have never been able to establish, a truly representative body." He continued that "assisted suicide is proposed for the parliament of the Jewish people of Canada, which would end its role as a representative communal spokesperson and give it a new role as the mouthpiece for those 'who know best.'" In his view the structural changes "will mark the final step in . . . the move from democracy to plutocracy." This provoked a strongly worded response, published in the *CJN*, from numerous CJC, federation, and CIJA officials. They dismissed Brown's critique as nonsense and argued that the new arrangements would enhance CJC's effectiveness. They concluded that "holding on to false vestiges of the past to forgo change is not in the best interests of *amcha.*"

Internal strife that B'nai Brith Canada faced was equally intense. A number of senior officials, including former presidents Morley Wolfe and Harvey Crestohl, charged that the organization had become too centralized and that the head office was not accountable to members. Specifically, they claimed that changes in the constitution had not been legally approved at the 2005 annual general meeting, despite a finding to the contrary by the B'nai Brith International appeals court. Crestohl claimed that up to a quarter of BBC's membership was unhappy with the situation. The dissidents began publishing a newsletter in May, in the hope of restoring BBC "to its once prominent position as a respected and admired organization."

Efforts were made in Toronto to avoid a repetition of what occurred surrounding the community commemoration of Yom Hashoah in 2006. That year the Orthodox rabbinate complained about the scheduled participation of the mixed-gender Renanim Youth Choir in the ceremonies because of the Orthodox prohibition on *kol ishah* (men hearing women sing). When the choir was then removed from the program, the cross-denominational Toronto Board of Rabbis dropped out of the event in protest. The solution, for 2007, was a mixed choir of students below the age of bar and bat mitzvah. With that compromise, both the board and the Orthodox Vaad Harabonim participated. The keynote speaker was Baroness Sibylle Niemoeller von Sell, herself a resister against the Nazis and later a convert to Judaism.

The government of Ontario gave UJA Federation of Greater Toronto $15 million toward the construction of three new community centers that were central to the federation's future plans.

Israel-Related Activities

In a major reorganization, the Canada-Israel Committee (CIC) eliminated nine staff positions in June. The move reflected budgetary stringencies as well as a shift in strategic priorities. CIC, now funded by CIJA, was deemphasizing its research function and stressing government and media relations and missions to Israel. CIJA CEO Hershell Ezrin, commenting on the action, claimed that pro-Israel advocacy remained his organization's highest priority.

In July, the Alliance of Concerned Jewish Canadians, which claimed 115 members, was rejected for a second time in an attempt to become a part of CJC. The group opposed Israel's policies in Gaza and the West Bank and supported calls by labor unions for a boycott of Israel. Announcing its negative decision, CJC explained that the alliance's goals were inconsistent with those of Congress. CJC president Ed Morgan, in fact, took a strong stand against the proposed boycott of Israeli academic institutions in a June letter to the British Association of University Teachers. He suggested, perhaps tongue in cheek, that British academics and universities should be boycotted because of their country's invasion and occupation of Iraq.

Zeev Bielski, head of the Jewish Agency and the World Zionist Organization, praised the Canadian federations for their quick response and financial support of the beleaguered citizens of Sderot, the target of continuous rocket attacks. The funds collected enabled children to spend part of the summer in camps far from hostilities.

Family members of the three kidnapped Israeli soldiers, Eldad Regev, Ehud Goldwasser, and Gilad Shalit, addressed members of the Toronto community in November at Shaarei Shomayim Congregation. Although Consul General Amir Gissin and the family representatives commended the Canadian government for its actions on behalf of the soldiers, MP Anita Neville, speaking in Winnipeg a day earlier, charged that the government's efforts were inadequate.

Justice for Jews from Arab Countries issued a report in November regarding events in the 1947–48 period that affected those Jews. Several Canadians were involved in preparing and then releasing the report. Their main finding was that several key Arab countries had proposed draft laws that would have declared their Jewish residents to be "members of the Jewish minority in the state of Palestine," frozen their bank accounts and used the funds to support "resistance to Zionist ambitions in Palestine," interned "active Zionists," and confiscated their assets. Stanley Urman, executive director of the organization, revealed that the exodus of nearly one million Jews from Arab countries "did not occur by happenstance. It was state-organized state collusion, led by the Arab League as a weapon in their struggle against the State of Israel." David Matas, chair of JJAC's legal advisory committee, asserted that the deportations and forcible displacements ought to be considered crimes against humanity. MP Irwin Cotler termed the actions "state-sponsored oppression."

Radio Shalom, a unique trilingual station in Montreal, went on the air in May featuring music, talk, and news from Israel. The station did not broadcast on Shabbat and Jewish holidays.

Religion

Toronto's Orthodox rabbinate suspended the performance of all conversions at the beginning of the year in order to reevaluate its standards, in light of developments in the U.S. and Israel (see AJYB 2007, p. 126). Rabbi Reuven Tradburks, head of the bet din (religious court), said that he and his colleagues were waiting for the Rabbinical Council of America to determine its position first. The main impact of potentially more stringent standards would be on families seeking to convert adopted children. In recent years there had been about 50 such conversions annually, about half of them below bar/bat mitzvah age and half above. Anonymous rabbinical critics cited in the *CJN* contended that changes under consideration represented a further move to the right by Toronto Orthodoxy, and even an attempt to "remake Orthodoxy in the *haredi* image." Rabbi Tradburks, however, said the aim was to maintain a consistent definition of Jewishness throughout the Jewish world.

A key aspect of the issue was what level of religious observance to require of parents of adopted children. In May the bet din endorsed an RCA decision allowing only conversions by approved religious courts in accord with broadly accepted Halakhic guidelines, including the demand that parents of adopted children agree to follow an Orthodox lifestyle. This policy had never before been applied in Toronto.

There were a number of issues involving kashrut during the year. In Toronto, the previous monopoly of the Kashruth Council of Canada (COR) was challenged by a new organization, Mehadrin Kosher Supervision, which signed up six restaurants as clients. While Rabbi Tradburks, speaking for the Vaad Harabonim, reaffirmed the view that having one overall authority was best for the community, Mehadrin claimed that competition could only be helpful for the consumer. By year's end at least two of the establishments supervised by Mehadrin had switched to the established COR.

In Winnipeg, Omnitzky Kosher Food ran into trouble with its rabbinic supervisors and had its kashrut certification removed. This encouraged the opening of a new kosher butcher shop, but it failed after three months and Omnitzky regained its certification.

In Montreal, the community *mikveh* (ritual bath) became a source of controversy when its operators banned use of the facility for any conversions. Since there were other *mikvaot* available for Orthodox conversions, the decision forced non-Orthodox rabbis to seek an alternative, and thus it became necessary to travel 120 miles to Ottawa to complete the conversion process. Although Rabbi Itche Gurary, who was in charge of the *mikveh,* claimed that the rule banning conversions was due to problems of hygiene caused by overuse, critics contended that the closure was deliberately aimed at blocking non-Orthodox conversions. Two Orthodox rabbis, Michael Whitman and Mordechai Zeitz, expressed support for restoration of the status quo ante.

Toronto's venerable Holy Blossom Temple, the city's leading Reform congregation, considered significant renovations during the year. One of the proposals was to reorient the sanctuary 180 degrees so that it would face east, toward Jerusalem, which is the arrangement in traditional synagogues. The suggestion evoked intense opposition from members aligned with Classical Reform, but a congregational vote in July approved the change. However an ad hoc Holy Blossom Temple Sanctuary Legacy Group continued to oppose the move and sent an open letter to the board in September urging a halt to the project.

Temple Shalom, a Reform congregation in Winnipeg, established its own *hevra kadisha* (group that prepared Jewish bodies for burial) because the city's only Jewish funeral chapel, Chesed Shel Emes, refused to perform the traditional preparation for bodies that were not going to be "buried in a Halakhically acceptable cemetery." Seven years earlier the temple had purchased land in a non-Jewish cemetery in order to accommodate members who were married to non-Jews and wished to be buried next to them.

The Jewish Theological Seminary's decision in March to admit gays and lesbians to its rabbinical school encountered significant opposition from Toronto's Conservative rabbinate. Rabbi Wayne Allen, president of the Ontario region of the Rabbinical Assembly, declared that "this is an abandonment of traditional Judaism, and as such I can have no part of it." Rabbi Steven Saltzman asked, in light of the decision, what the movement really stood for and how it differed from Reform. Several other rabbis spoke out as well. In a survey released by JTS, 82 percent of Canadian Conservative rabbis and cantors opposed ordination of gays and lesbians, compared to 69 percent in favor in the U.S.

At a panel discussion in Toronto in April, Rabbi Reuven Bulka, a leading Orthodox spokesman, declared that donating an organ or tissue from a deceased person was a matter of *pikuah nefesh* (saving human life) and therefore a religious obligation.

Education

Toronto's Board of Jewish Education changed its name in July to the Centre for Enhancement of Jewish Education, to be known informally as the Mercaz. The change was one of several to result from a 2006 study of Jewish education in the city. Other anticipated innovations included the establishment of a $100-million endowment fund and, on a trial basis, a loan program for tuition. Fiscal matters, such as tuition subsidies and new financing mechanisms, were central to the new body's mandate. In addition, the Mercaz would support adult and other types of informal education.

In Montreal several Orthodox day schools were in trouble with the Quebec government, which partially funded them, because they were not teaching the compulsory government curriculum. Education Minister Michelle Courchesne said that certain unnamed high schools for religious boys were not devoting sufficient time to subjects other than Judaism, and gave them three years to comply with regulations. Marc Gold, president of Federation CJA, supported the government position but noted that the matter was delicate because of "the religious sensibilities of a particular segment of the Orthodox Jewish community." It was estimated by the newspaper *La Presse* that some 700 students attended the Jewish schools in question. Some schools run by other religious groups were in a similar position.

Another issue involving the Montreal day schools and the Quebec government involved a new compulsory course on comparative religion called Ethics and Religious Culture, scheduled to begin in 2008, aimed at encouraging tolerance and mutual respect among people of different faiths. A number of *haredi* schools expressed concern that teaching about other religions would compromise the convictions of their own young children, and leaders of some Hasidic schools said that they simply could not teach the course. CJC took the position that the program should begin only in high school, to ease the fears of Orthodox parents of young children. The Solomon Schechter Academy introduced the course early and found that it worked well.

United Talmud Torahs, a Montreal day school, announced in November that it would close its suburban St. Laurent branch because of inadequate enrollment and financial problems and shift the students to the main Montreal location. However, parents mounted a vigorous and ultimately successful initiative to reverse the decision. An ad hoc parents group raised about $160,000 and launched a campaign to encourage more families to join the school. Its closure would have been a blow to the Jewish community in St. Laurent.

A new adult Jewish studies program for the Toronto area and nearby Hamilton, the Maimonides Schools for Jewish Learning, planned to offer Master's degrees as well as nondegree programs. The founder, Prof. Hindy Najman, said the new program "is intended to raise the bar of Jewish education throughout the city." The clientele was expected to include professionals and teachers holding Jewish community positions as well as people who simply wanted to learn more about Jewish civilization.

Community and Intergroup Relations

A national survey in August showed that 78 percent of Canadians had a favorable opinion of Jews. But the results of other surveys were troubling. In one, 53 percent of respondents agreed that minorities should fully adapt to Canadian life, while only 18 percent were prepared to accommodate their disparate needs. In Quebec the numbers were even more dramatic: 77 percent said that minorities should adapt while only 5 percent would agree to accommodate. This gap was consistent with other polls that showed Quebecers as much less willing than other Canadians to tolerate cultural differences.

The overriding intergroup-relations issue in Quebec was over "reasonable accommodation" of minority groups. It was triggered by a series of incidents involving members of minorities, often Muslim immigrants, and brought to a head by the comments of provincial opposition leader Mario Dumont, who asked whether the majority French Québecois group had gone so far in accommodating diverse practices that they stood at risk of losing their own culture.

Although Jews were not the main focus of the discussion, a number of incidents took place in recent years that involved Jews or Jewish institutions, and so Jews were drawn ineluctably into the debate. There were complaints that Hasidic men refused to take driving examinations with female evaluators or deal with female police officers; that Jewish teachers in public schools got paid time off for religious holidays; that a YWCA was badgered to frost its windows so that male Hasidic students from a nearby yeshiva could not view women in exercise garb (after about a year the frosting was removed); and that Jewish General Hospital refused to allow two ambulance drivers to bring their nonkosher lunches into the kosher cafeteria (the hospital was later fined $10,000 for this by the Quebec Human Rights Commission.)

Both the electronic and print media covered the issue extensively, often in provocative, even inflammatory, terms. Then the small town of Herouxville—a place unlikely to attract members of minority groups—issued a public manifesto setting out what it expected of minorities who wanted to settle there.

Amid all the fuss, the Quebec government, in February, set up a commission to evaluate the situation and make recommendations. In his announcement, Premier Charest referred to four examples indicating why a commission was needed, three involving Jews: the hospital cafeteria incident, guidelines given to female police officers not to deal with Hasidic men, and the frosted window at the Y. Charest declared that "these are not reasonable accommodations. These are arrangements contrary to the values of our nation." He added that immigrants must adapt to Quebec values. *CJN* columnist Gil Troy argued in March that the whole idea was flawed because it assumed that the majority collectively defines a culture to which minorities must adapt, signifying that minorities had no rights of their own. Troy called for a "glorious collaboration" to build a civil society.

The commission, consisting of academics Gérard Bouchard and Charles Taylor, went on the road for months, holding hearings in various parts of the province. Many of the hearings, which were televised, afforded an opportunity for the expression of very hostile and intolerant views toward minority groups and their practices. CJC regional president Victor Goldbloom said that "we are obviously uncomfortable with the way the hearings are unfolding," and Rabbi Reuben Poupko called the "very painful" hearings "a magnet for the most extreme and dangerous voices in Quebec. That people have the confidence to say what they do in public has shocked me." Poupko also lamented the absence of public denunciations of the expressed intolerance. B'nai Brith's national legal counsel, Steven Slimovitch, said the hearings had "turned into a soapbox for venting racism."

In a brief on immigration policy submitted to a legislative committee in October, CJC and Jewish Immigrant Aid Services said that prospective immigrants to Quebec should be asked to sign a "moral contract" to accept the province's "common values." CJC filed another brief the next month with the Bouchard-Taylor commission urging the government not to amend the Charter of Human Rights and Freedoms. This request was aimed at Premier Charest's suggestion that the charter be amended to give gender equality precedence over religious freedom; CJC rejected the concept of a hierarchy of rights. The brief also systematically refuted the many allegations against Jews made during the hearings, including the charge that all consumers pay more for food products because of kosher certification. It stressed the community's determination to maintain kashrut and holiday observances at its institutions with no diminution of respect for non-Jewish staff and patients.

In an appearance before the commission, Victor Goldbloom of the CJC defended the practice of government funding of Jewish day schools on the grounds that they taught the required curriculum and performed a public service. He also justified the wearing of religious symbols by individuals who worked in the public service. B'nai Brith's commission brief bucked the tide of public opinion by urging greater accommodation of religious practices in the public sphere, not less. *CJN* columnist Gerald Gall was pessimistic, expressing the fear that the commission's work "will result in diminished accommodation for minority religious beliefs and practices."

The commission was expected to report its conclusions early in 2008. In the meantime, some changes were enacted at Jewish institutions. In April the Jewish General Hospital announced it was setting up nonkosher sections in its cafeterias for people who brought their own food. It also settled the case of the complaining ambulance drivers by paying each of them $7,500. (The Human Rights Commission had originally assessed a $10,000 fine for religious discrimination and restricting access to public places.) In addition, the Jewish Rehabilitation Hospital decided to "review its dietary practices" in the wake of complaints by a doctor, other staff, patients, and visitors about Passover restrictions. Meanwhile, another case involving the Jewish General Hospital went to the Quebec Human Rights Tribunal. It accused the institution of discriminating against female employees by accommodating patient wishes to receive "intimate care" by a person of their own sex. In October, the tribunal ordered the hospital and the employees union to pay $15,000 to two female patient attendants who had not been given the opportunity to work as orderlies.

In December, the Supreme Court of Canada announced a landmark decision. It upheld a judgment for damages against a man who had withheld a get (Jewish divorce) from his wife for 15 years after they had obtained a civil divorce, thus preventing her from remarrying and having more children. The court, by a 7-2 margin, held that it was a matter of enforcing a civil contract, not a decision based on religion, because the husband had previously agreed in writing to deliver the get at the time of the civil divorce.

Montreal Hasidim who spent vacation time in the nearby Laurentian Mountains encountered problems in their relations with the local inhabitants. For example, a Satmar group bought a resort in the town of St. Adolphe d'Howard to accommodate members of the community who wanted to spend the summer in the mountains. But the director general of the town expressed concern, saying, "Honestly, we believe that there will be anxiety over this community, which will not integrate into the community of St. Adolphe, making a sort of ghetto of this complex." An apology followed a week later. In September, Belz Hasidim appealed to Quebec's top court against a judgment that houses that were being used as a synagogue and a school in Val Morin violated zoning laws. At a regional hearing of the Bouchard-Taylor Commission that same month, numerous citizens expressed a variety of complaints against the Hasidim in their midst, focusing on the way they separated themselves from their neighbors.

David Moyal of Toronto launched cases in the Ontario Human Rights Commission and the Ontario Rental Housing Tribunal alleging that his landlord had prevented him from erecting a sukkah on the holiday of Sukkot. He charged that he had suffered discrimination and that the enjoyment of his apartment had been diminished.

In Winnipeg, the family of Sam Golubchuk, an Orthodox Jew, was fighting in December to keep him on life support despite the decision of the physician and hospital to remove him because of minimal brain function and no hope of recovery. The family claimed that such a move would violate his religious principles. As the year ended, the issue was not yet resolved.

Culture

What used to be the Saidye Bronfman Centre for the Arts in Montreal was renamed the Segal Centre for the Performing Arts at The Saidye, as the result of a major gift from Leanor and Alvin Segal. After major renovations, the centerpiece remained the theater, but there were also venues for many different kinds of performances, including music, dance, and film, as well as educational activities. An Academy of Performing Arts for students was also part of the new complex.

Toronto's Harold Green Jewish Theatre Company, a nonprofit professional organization, announced it would begin presenting plays in 2008. Artistic directors David Eisner and Avery Saltzman said they wanted to "illuminate humanity through a Jewish perspective."

Antigone: Insurgency by Adam Seelig opened in Toronto in November. Seelig adapted the ancient Greek play to deal with the current terrorist threat. The play dealt with the question of how to maintain democratic principles in a time of war and how to balance national security and individual rights. Hannah Moscovitch's new play *East of Berlin,* which opened in Toronto in October, was about the son of a Nazi doctor who tries, after the war, to deal with his father's guilt.

The Toronto Jewish Film Festival in May presented a number of documentaries, many with Holocaust themes. *Once a Nazi,* by Frederic Bohbot and Evan Beloff, told the story of Adalbert Lallier, a concentration camp guard in the Waffen SS, who immigrated to Canada and lived an ordinary life as an economics professor. Some 50 years later his conscience compelled him to disclose what he knew about crimes he had witnessed, and his testimony led to the imprisonment of another former guard. Montreal's Jewish Film Festival announced its dissolution after founder Susan Alper resigned in May. The main reason was a lack of dependable funding. The Voices Forward festival, held in Toronto during May and June, featured ten films about Palestinians and Israelis.

The world premiere of a documentary about Phyllis Lambert, the architect and heritage activist, took place in March. The film, by Teri Wehn-Damish, traced Lambert's emotional and professional development. Israeli Dan Geva's *Description of a Memory,* an analysis of Israel past and present, took first prize at the Recontres Internationales du Documentaire de Montréal in November.

The controversial filmmaker Simcha Jacobovici made *The Lost Tomb of Jesus,* which appeared on television in Canada and the U.S. In it he claimed that ossuaries found in a Jerusalem vault were those of Jesus and his family. In a lecture at a Montreal synagogue in May, Israeli archaeologist Eliezer Oren said that scholars would have to take Jacobovici's findings seriously but that a number of issues remained open. Other commentators were sharply critical. Another Jacobovici film, *Charging the Rhino,* premiered on television in November. It chronicled his visit to his Romanian birthplace and traced the stories of his father and cousin during and after the war. Also included was a fascinating interview with an unrepentant Iron Guard leader.

Igal Hecht had two new films on television. The first, *In the Shadow of the Messiah,* showed a group of Canadian and Dutch messianic Jews traveling around Israel and trying to explain their views on Jesus to Israelis. His *Journey of Miracles* was about Canadian Holocaust survivors trying to explain their experiences to young people. Hecht's film *Streets of Jerusalem* premiered at a Toronto theater in May. He interviewed eight Jerusalemites—Jewish, Christian, and Muslim—about life in the city. Other films released during the year included Bryan Friedman's *The Bodybuilder and I* and Elliot Halpern's *Vimy Ridge: Heaven to Hell.*

The Canadian Museum for Human Rights, established by the Asper family in Winnipeg, became the first institution outside Ottawa to be designated a national museum. The federal government promised to provide annual funding once the museum would open in 2011. The Jewish Museum and Archives of British Columbia opened in Vancouver in March. Its collection focused on the development of the province's community since its founding over a century ago.

Quebecers connected to KlezKanada organized a klezmer cruise down the Dnieper River in Ukraine in May, which visited featured sites of Jewish significance. The National Film Board commissioned Gary Beitel and Barry Lazar to make a film of the trip and provided real-time shots of events on its website. A concert of Sephardi liturgical music, *La Magie du Sacre,* was featured at Montreal's Festival Sépharade in June. Israeli Yiddish singer Vira Lozinsky made her North American debut at August concerts in Montreal and Toronto, and subsequently performed at the KlezKanada Festival in the Laurentians.

A conference on the poetry of A.M. Klein was held at Montreal's Concordia University in October. Trent University professor Elizabeth Popham, who was in the process of editing a volume of Klein's letters, told the attendees that Klein suffered "terrible anxiety about not being accepted" outside the community of immigrant Jews in Canada. Klein's insecurity eventually led to a breakdown and his withdrawal from creative activity.

Publications

Derek Penslar's *Israel in History: The Jewish State in Comparative Perspective* analyzed how Israel's historical development affected its contemporary society. Harold Troper's *The Rescuer* was about Judy Feld Carr, who, over the course of decades, ran a covert operation to ransom more than 3,000 Jews out of Syria. It was an updated version of his earlier book with a new title.

The 9/11 terror attacks had a profound impact on David Solway, a committed leftist who had supported the Palestinian cause. Afterwards he began to reexamine his convictions, and eventually arrived at conclusions fundamentally at odds with his previous beliefs. In *The Big Lie: On Terror, Antisemitism and Identity,* Solway sounded the alarm on what he considered the Muslim threat to Western civilization. A. Alan Borovoy's *Categorically Incorrect* dealt with Canada's response, both foreign and domestic, to the 9/11 attacks. While cognizant of the need to combat terror, Borovoy argued that the laws passed infringed excessively on civil liberties. On the other hand, he criticized the government for an inadequate response overseas.

The Holocaust memoirs published during the year included *163256: A*

Memoir of Resistance by Michael Englishman; *A Long Labor: A Dutch Mother's Holocaust Memoir* by Rhodea Shandler; *Legacy and Redemption: A Life Renewed* by Joseph E. Tenenbaum; *They Called Me Mayer July: Painted Memories of a Jewish Childhood in Poland Before the Holocaust* by Mayer Kirshenblatt and Barbara Kirshenblatt-Gimblett; and *Missing Pieces: My Life as a Child Survivor of the Holocaust* by Olga Verrall. Yehudi Lindeman edited interviews of survivors for the McGill University Living Testimony Archive and published them in *Shards of Memory: Narratives of Holocaust Survival.*

There were several nonfiction works on Jewish themes. Among them were *The Jews of Windsor, 1790–1990: A Historical Chronicle* by Jonathan V. Plaut; *A Joyful Harvest: Celebrating the Jewish Contribution to Southern Alberta Life 1889–2005,* published by the Jewish Historical Society of Southern Alberta; Anna Porter's *Kasztner's Train,* about the escape to Switzerland of nearly 1,700 Hungarian Jews that became a controversial issue in Israel well after the war; *The Volunteer: A Canadian's Secret Life in the Mossad* by Michael Ross; *Arguing with the Storm: Stories by Yiddish Women Writers,* edited by Rhea Tregebov; Rabbi Reuven Bulka's *Turning Grief into Gratitude: Reflections and Recommendations on Mourning and Condolence;* Rabbi Gedalia Zweig's *Living Kaddish;* Thomas Hecht's autobiography written with Joe King, *Czech Mate: A Life in Progress; Rather Laugh than Cry* by Malka Zipora; and Ann Weinstein's *Me and My Tormentor: Saul Bellow—A Memoir of My Literary Love Affair*. Other significant nonfiction books were Andrew Cohen's *The Unfinished Canadian, The People We Are*; Rosalie Wise Sharp's memoir *Rifke: An Improbable Life;* Misha Aster's *The Reichs-Orchestra: The Berlin Philharmonic and National Socialism* (in German); Jonathan Garfinkel's *Ambivalence: Crossing the Israel/Palestine Divide*; Tilda Shalof's *The Making of a Nurse; What is a Canadian?* by Irvin Studin; *An Apple a Day: The Myths, Misconceptions and Outright Exaggerations About Diet, Nutrition and the Foods We Eat* by Joe Schwarcz; and *Brothers of Iron* by Joe Weider and Ben Weider with Mike Steere.

Fiction works included the first English translation of Yves Theriault's *Aaron*, translated by Paul Socken and W. Donald Wilson; *Notebooks: Selections from the A.M. Klein Papers,* edited by Zailig Pollack and Usher Caplan; *Anna's Journal* by Harry Pollack; *A Sharp Intake of Breath* by John Miller; Guy Gavriel Kay's *Ysabel;* Sidura Ludwig's *Holding My Breath: A Novel;* and Alvin Rakoff's *Baldwin Street: A Novel.*

There were several books of poetry published. Among them were *The Fiery Mountain* by Simcha Simchovitch; *Black River* by Kenneth Sherman; *Poetry Pure and Simple* by David Zaretsky; and Pierre Anctil's translation of the poetry of Sholem Shtern, *Nostalgie et Tristesse.*

Winners of Canadian Jewish Book Awards were Susan Glickman for *The Violin Lover;* Rosemary Sullivan for *Villa Air-Bel;* Eric Koch for *I Remember the Location Exactly;* Bernice Eisenstein for *I Was a Child of Holocaust Survivors;* Carol Matas for *Turned Away: The World War II Diary of Devora Bernstein;* Michael Wex for *Born to Kvetch;* Shirley Kumove for *Drunk from the Bitter Truth: The Poems of Anna Margolin;* Rafi Aaron for *Surviving the Censor: The Unspoken Words of Osip Mandelstam;* and Seymour Mayne for *September Rain.* Sherry Simon won the Gabrielle Roy Prize for *Translating Montreal: Episodes in the Life of a Divided City.* David Solway received the A.M. Klein Prize for Poetry for *Reaching for Clear: The Poetry of Rhys Savarin.* Faydra Shapiro won a National Jewish Book Award in the U.S. for *Building Jewish Roots: The Israel Experience.*

Personalia

Stanley Kershman was appointed to the Superior Court of Justice of Ontario; Audrey Lampert was appointed to the New Brunswick Human Rights Commission; Mark Cohon became commissioner of the Canadian Football League; Sarah Fulford became editor of *Toronto Life* magazine; Marcy Grossman was appointed consul general in Miami; Rabbi Chaim Mendelsohn became the first Jewish military chaplain since World War II; and Israel appointed Amir Gissin and Yoram Elron as consuls general, in Toronto and Montreal, respectively.

The following received the Order of Canada: Companion—Barney Danson; Officers—Chaviva Hosek, Arthur Hiller, Cyril Kay, Jacob Masliyah, Ben Weider, Edward Lyons, and Leon Katz; Members—Howard Engel, Avrum Morrow, Evelyn Shapiro, Muriel Gold, Lola Rasminsky, and Leon Rooke. Naim Kattan was awarded the Prix Hervé Duluen by the Académie Française while Barney Danson received the distinction of being named a chevalier of the French Legion of Honor. Victoria Kaspi received the Rutherford Medal for physics. The federal government named writer A.M. Klein and journalist Hirsch Wolofsky, both deceased, as national historic figures.

Henry Molot received the civil service's highest honor, the Public Service Award for Excellence. Three filmmakers won an Emmy award for their documentary *Sex Slaves:* Ric Esther Bienstock, Felix Golubev, and Simcha Jacobovici.

Barbara Farber was elected president of the United Israel Appeal Federations Canada, Marc Gold president of Federation CJA in Montreal, and David Koschitzky board chair of UJA Federation of Greater Toronto. Rabbi Yonasan Weiss became chief rabbi of Montreal. Victor Goldbloom and Gerry Cutler ware elected presidents of the Quebec and Pacific regions, respectively, of the Canadian Jewish Congress, while Daniel Amar and Len Rudner were appointed executive directors of the Quebec and Ontario Regions, respectively. Sara Horowitz was elected president of the Association for Jewish Studies and Dina Kutner was appointed general manager for Canada of El Al Israel Airlines.

Anat Ekhoiz and Carol Leszcz won Grinspoon-Steinhardt Awards for Excellence in Jewish Education. *Canadian Jewish News* writers Paul Lungen, Norman Ravvin, and Jenny Hazan won Rockower Awards for excellence in Jewish journalism.

A number of well-known members of the community passed away during the year. In January: internationally known Cantor David Bagley, aged 74; pioneering television weatherman Percy Saltzman, aged 91; mathematician, game theorist, and peace activist Anatol Rapoport, aged 95; psychologist and vocational counselor Ruth Borchiver, aged 78; and Sydney Shulemson, the most decorated Canadian Jewish veteran of World War II, aged 91. In February: Abraham Lieff, the first Jew on the Ontario Supreme Court and an expert in family law, aged 103; Quebec pop music promoter Ben Kaye, aged 68; and economist, development specialist, and civil libertarian Irving Brecher, aged 84. In March: family matriarch Helen Steinberg, aged 98; Rabbi Yitzchok Hendel, chief judge of Montreal's bet din and founding head of the city's Lubavitch yeshiva, aged 90; and retired judge Sam Filer of the Superior Court of Justice in Ontario and community leader, aged 71. In April: retired Jewish Family and Child Service director Gordon Wolfe, aged 70; award-winning filmmaker Harry Rasky, aged 78; decorated war veteran and career soldier Sam Cohen, aged 101; and businessman, former CJC president, and community leader Sol Kanee, aged 97. In May: acclaimed novelist and poet Monique Bosco, aged 79; community leader Albert Benchetrit, aged 75; and basketball coach Harvey Liverman, aged 58. In June: Edmund Yehuda Lipsitz, educator, author, and community civil servant, aged 81; and noted composer Oskar Morawetz, aged 90. In July: Carol Goldman, Jewish educator for children with special needs, aged 60; businessman and theater impresario Edwin "Honest Ed" Mirvish, aged 92; Leonard Mendelsohn, professor of Hasidic literature, aged 70; Sara Pachter, who led 100 tours to Israel, aged 93; and Bluma Appel, philanthropist, arts patron, and social activist, aged 86. In September: journalist and broadcaster Sidney Katz, aged 91; and advertising executive and political strategist Menachem Dunsky, aged 77. In October: lawyer and community leader Samuel Godinsky, aged 101; and retired educator and community executive Harold Malitzky, aged 80. In November: pioneering geriatrician Dr. Ruhla Brohovici, aged 102; and comedy writer Mel Tolkin, aged 94. In December: businessman and former mayor of Dartmouth, Nova Scotia, Joseph Zatzman, aged 95; Michael Lawrence (Larry) Bessner, war veteran, professor, and community leader, aged 86; and former MP Milton Klein, aged 97.

HAROLD M. WALLER

Venezuela

National Affairs

On December 3, 2006, Hugo Chávez Frías, Venezuela's president since 1999, won reelection to a six-year term, with 63 percent of the vote. The Venezuelan opposition, convinced that he won through fraud, sank into despair. But a year later, on December 2, 2007, the tables were turned when voters defeated by referendum constitutional changes proposed by Chávez that would have increased his power enormously.

The Chávez Phenomenon

Starting as an obscure army officer, Chávez launched his political career with an unsuccessful coup in 1992 and landed in jail. Given amnesty in 1994, he was elected president four years later at the head of his Movimiento Quinta República (MVR) party, which appealed to the poor with a socialist platform. When he took the oath of office for the first time in February 1999, he declared the country's constitution "moribund" and announced elections for a National Assembly that would write a new one. In those elections, Chávez's supporters won 122 seats and the opposition only six.

The new constitution that would become the basis of what Chávez called the "Bolivarian Revolution" was approved by popular vote that December. At the same time a new National Assembly was installed in which the president's supporters held 130 seats and his opponents 37. The Chavist majority proceeded to appoint new members of the Supreme Court and the National Electoral Council (in charge of the electoral process), as well as a new attorney general, comptroller general, and ombudsman—all of whom were unconditional followers of Chávez. Similarly, the president was given absolute control over all public agencies, the presidential term was extended from five years to six, and Chávez himself was immediately reelected to a second term.

From the day he took office Chávez never hid his aim of emulating communist Cuba. This was symbolized by his frequent trips to the island and the economic support he provided Castro's government. Oil-rich Venezuela sent 50,000 barrels of oil daily to Cuba, and in exchange, Castro sent Cuban teachers, doctors, and paramedics to Venezuela. In 2006 such Cuban personnel in Venezuela totaled more than 30,000. Chávez, like Castro, declared himself an anti-imperialist and challenged the American government, becoming, in 2000, the first Western head of state to visit Saddam Hussein after a decade of isolation, and subsequently accusing the U.S. of orchestrating the 9/11 attacks in order to justify the invasion of Iraq. Domestically, the government sought to introduce socialist, "anti-imperialist" ideology through the educational system, both public and private, but this drew so much opposition that the plan for the private schools had to be withdrawn.

On April 11, 2002, government supporters shot into a crowd that was demonstrating for Chávez's resignation, killing 19 people and injuring 200. An army-led coup then removed him from office and the U.S. quickly recognized the provisional government that replaced him. But the military chiefs could not agree among themselves, and Chávez was back in power 72 hours later.

In 2003, after a protracted strike, Chávez fired 20,000 directors, managers, and other employees of the state-owned company Petróleos de Venezuela (PDVSA) and made it an arm of the government, a *caja chica* (petty-cash box) where he got the money to support his social programs for the poor *(Misiones)* and lavish gifts outside the country for political purposes, such as deeply discounted oil to Cuba, other Latin American countries, and inner-city U.S. neighborhoods, and cheap gasoline for London buses.

A national referendum to remove him from office, held in 2004 at the initiative of the opposition, was defeated easily. Suspicions of large-scale fraud that marred the vote convinced Chávez's opponents that the president's control of the electoral machinery made fair voting impossible, and so the opposition boycotted the National Assembly elections in December 2005. Chávez's supporters won all 167 seats, and the new body increased the president's control over the appointment of judges and other high officials.

Learning the lesson from Fidel Castro's failure to export the Cuban revolution by force of arms, Chávez sought to spread his revolution through money, backing the Colombian narco-guerrilla group Revolutionary Armed Forces of Colombia (FARC), helping Evo Morales win the Bolivian election of December 2005, and trying—unsuccessfully—to do the same for leftist presidential candidates in Peru (Ollanta Humala) and Mexico (Andrés Manuel López Obrador) in 2006. Even in the face of these defeats, Chávez celebrated as private victories the election later that year of Rafael Correa in Ecuador and former guerrilla Daniel Ortega in Nicaragua. In 2007, there thus emerged a Chávez-Morales-Correa-Ortega axis that tried to supplement the socialist rallying cry with "indigenism," a political movement of revenge and neo-racism aimed against people with European ancestry.

Venezuelan diplomacy worked in two parallel lines. Beside the traditional, state-to-state relationships, the regime created organizations and support networks for the Bolivarian Revolution. It provided financial support for the creation of *Círculos Bolivarianos* (Bolivarian Circles) all over the world, which not only promoted the revolution in their own countries but also acted against any group opposing Chávez.

According to a Justice and Democracy Foundation report issued in November 2007, Chávez had designated a total of $38 billion as gifts to other countries. Just 5 percent of that sum could have paid the minimum wage of the one million unemployed Venezuelans. Some of the money went to buy helicopters, refineries, and health clinics in those other countries, and some was used to buy external debt bonds of Cuba, Argentina, Brazil, Nicaragua, Bolivia, and Ecuador. In addition, the report noted an investment of $10 million in the Latin American TV channel Telesur, a Chavist project that tried to copy CNN. Cristina Moure, director of research and analysis for the foundation, warned that "if you ask the government about these donations, it will reply that they are about Latin American solidarity. But it is just the buying of support for Chávez's goal of extending his revolution to other countries."

Chávez's dream of becoming an "anti-imperialist and multipolar" world leader was also promoted through the investment of millions of dollars in public relations. Foreign journalists were often used to promote the Bolivarian Revolution. American journalist Barbara Walters, for example, was brought to Caracas in March 2007 to interview Chávez and create a favorable impression of the regime. Other celebrities who were hosted and used for the same purpose were actors Danny Glover, Kevin Spacey and Sean Penn, and supermodel Naomi Campbell.

A New Presidential Term

Chávez's reelection at the end of 2006 emboldened his followers toward greater radicalism. Chavist bands—sometimes supported by military men or public officials—invaded and stole from farms that produced sugar cane, meat, milk, and chickens. On other occasions the army directly occupied properties, under orders given by Chávez on his Sunday program *"Aló Presidente!"* (Hello President!), broadcast on radio and TV for anywhere between four and nine hours.

The food shortages that the country suffered in late 2007 were partly the result of these invasions. Another factor in the shortages was government regulation that set the price of food well below the inflation rate. Staples disappeared from supermarkets, and sometimes it was only possible to find them at street vendors' stands, a kind of black market tolerated by the authorities.

Another form of assault on private property was invasion of, and stealing from, apartment buildings in Caracas and other cities. These tended to be either old buildings that were going to be demolished or renovated, or else new construction projects that were in the process of selling their apartments. Organized gangs protected by government officials and popular Chavist leaders were behind the invasions.

There was a marked increase in emigration, and by late 2007 an estimated 450,000–500,000 citizens were thought to have left the country since Chávez came to power. The bulk of the emigrants were between 24 and 45 years old, and their preferred destinations were the U.S. (mostly Florida), Canada, Spain, and Italy. Many were physicians—some 2,700 in 2007 alone—whom Chávez called traitors to the country and replaced with Cuban doctors and paramedics. The most recent wave of emigrants also included many other professionals and middle-class businessmen, and a good number of them left properties in Venezuela in the hope that they might some day return.

Apart from economic reasons, the most important factor driving emigration was the increasing lack of personal safety. Opinion polls showed that most Venezuelans, regardless of social class or region, considered this the greatest threat to their own personal lives. Venezuela had the highest rate of homicide in Latin America: in 2007 there were 12,000 murders, most of them by firearms. There were also 382 kidnappings, mainly of ranchers and businessmen; nine of those kidnapped were killed. In Caracas alone, 9,875 cars were stolen, mostly under firearm threats. Many crimes went unreported due to lack of trust in the police.

The crime problem was largely due to the amount of firearms in the hands of the population, rising alcohol and drug consumption, incompetence of judges and prosecutors, and extensive corruption. Many crimes—especially the murders and kidnappings—were widely attributed to policemen and military officers. A report by Transparency International published in September 2007 ranked Venezuela 162d in its corruption perception index out of 180 countries studied.

Venezuela was a paradise for drug trafficking and other international crime syndicates. The former Venezuelan minister Moisés Naim, editor-in-chief of *Foreign Policy* magazine, published an article in *El País,* a leading Spanish newspaper (Nov. 4), titled "Venezuela's Hidden Story," describing the situation. He pointed out the irony that Chávez, a consistent critic of globalization, had allowed Venezuela to be globalized "by criminal gangs." Naim concluded, "it is a globalization that depends on corruption, crime and death. And that may be more critical in shaping Venezuela's future than any of Chávez's political experiments."

On December 28, 2006, the reelected president announced his intention not to renew the broadcast license of the privately owned Radio Caracas Television (RCTV) because its owners, he claimed, had been implicated in the coup that tried to overthrow him in April 2002. On January 10, 2007, Chávez ramped up his rhetoric, announcing the "Socialism of the Twenty-First Century." From now on, he explained, there would be only one political party in Venezuela, his own, and he proposed to alter the 1999 constitution. On January 18, the National Assembly bestowed on the president special powers until July 31, 2008, to allow him to pass laws he considered necessary.

On February 4, Chávez ordered a military parade to celebrate the 15th anniversary of the failed coup he led in 1992, and on that day the four branches of the Venezuelan armed forces adopted as obligatory the salute of the Cuban revolution: *Patria, Socialismo o Muerte!* (Homeland, Socialism or Death!)

During 2007 Chávez significantly increased the already high number of military officers holding high positions in government and at the head of state-run companies.

Chávez presented to the National Assembly his proposal to reform 69 articles of the constitution on August 15. The more controversial points were:

1. Increasing the length of presidential terms from six years to seven and allowing indefinite reelection of the president;

2. Ending the independent powers of governors and mayors, and enabling the president to change territorial boundaries and appoint vice presidents for the different regions;

3. Changing the rules on the legal status of different types of property, in effect eliminating private property;

4. Creating communal councils similar to the committees of the Cuban revolution;

5. Eliminating the legal force of international human-rights treaties within Venezuelan borders;

6. Officially designating the military as "Bolivarian" and identifying it as socialist and anti-imperialist;

7. Implementing "popular and socialist" education "to demolish the old values of capitalism and individualism."

But the radicalism that emerged with Chávez's reelection brought a strong backlash. Already in February 2007 opinion polls began to show considerable resistance: indefinite reelection of presidents was opposed by 60 percent; Cuban-style socialism by 86 percent; curtailing private-property rights by 78 percent; the closure of RCTV by 75 percent; and confrontation with the U.S. by 78 percent.

The government nevertheless closed down RCTV on May 27, the regime's most serious infringement on free expression yet. Forced to close its open signal in Venezuela, it become an international cable channel. The move against RCTV drew widespread condemnation internationally, the U.S. Senate unanimously approving a resolution deploring the action. In Venezuela, street protests proliferated. The attack on freedom of expression served to mobilize a new element of opposition to the regime: graduate and undergraduate students who believed that the autonomy of their universities would be targeted next.

Chávez, however, did not appear fazed. He harshly criticized the Venezuelan Catholic Church for defending freedom of speech, and called José Miguel Insulza, secretary general of the Organization of American States (OAS), who opposed the RCTV closure, "stupid" [using a vulgar expression], "dull," and "viceroy of the Empire."

There were also other attempts to stifle dissent: physical attacks on journalists, destruction of television equipment, and the use of the penal code to persecute journalists and opponents of the regime. Thus Gen. Francisco Usón, a former Chávez collaborator, was sentenced to five years in prison because of opinions he expressed on a TV program.

The Gutenberg University of Sweden and the Andrés Bello Catholic University of Caracas, in a joint project that studied free expression in Venezuela, concluded that the government owned or controlled nine of the twelve national TV stations, in addition to several local stations. During 2007, the pro-government TV and radio stations did not give opposition leaders any opportunity to express their opinions about the proposed constitutional reforms. On the contrary, each day these media promoted the changes.

The economic aspect of "Socialism of the Twenty-First Century" entailed the nationalization of "strategic" companies. The energy sector was first: Exxon Mobil, Conoco Phillips, the French company TOTAL, British Petroleum, and the Norwegian firm Statoil. This was not, strictly speaking, expropriation, because the government paid the oil companies the value of the shares it took over, and allowed them to retain a minority stake. When nationalization was carried out in April, the government orchestrated a grand demonstration, mobilizing the army and Chávez followers in the Orinoco Petroleum Belt.

In May came the turn of the telecommunications company CANTV to be nationalized. Afterwards, there were persistent rumors that Venezuelan directors and managers would become officers of the Cuban Intelligence Service G-2, with the power to tap telephones and Internet communications. The government took over Electricity of Caracas in June, a company that had been privately owned since its establishment in 1895.

In July Chávez traveled to Belarus and Russia to buy arms. He declared in Minsk: "We have created a truly strategic alliance between Venezuela and Belarus. We should protect our homelands and oppose external threats." Greeting President Lukashenko (described by Washington as "the last dictator in Europe"), Chávez told him: "If we have done so much in less than a year, I can't imagine how much more we can do in the next 20 years in power." Chávez called on the Belarusian government to "oppose a fake democracy that is really an elitist and transnational oligarchy."

On August 4, five days before an official visit by Chávez to Buenos Aires, Argentinean customs authorities seized a suitcase containing $790,000 from a Venezuelan-American citizen, Guido Antonini Wilson. He was traveling in an airplane rented by ENARSA, the Argentinean State Energy Company, together with officials close to Julio de Vido, Argentina's minister of federal planning, and with employees of Venezuela's oil company, PDVSA. Antonini was not arrested, and a few days later traveled to his home in Florida. He went to the FBI and claimed that he was receiving threats from people linked to the Chávez government.

In Florida on December 12, the FBI arrested Carlos Kaufman and Franklyn Durán, Venezuelan businessmen suspected of acting as foreign agents. Both men had pressured and threatened Antonini Wilson not to say that the cash seized by Argentina's customs was sent by the Venezuelan government to help fund the electoral campaign of Argentinean presidential candidate Cristina Fernández de Kirchner. For several weeks the scandal occupied the front pages of newspapers and television news programs in Venezuela and Argentina. Chávez and senior officials said that the case of Antonini Wilson's "suitcase" was a conspiracy orchestrated by the "Empire" and President Bush.

Referendum

As the December 2 referendum on Chávez's constitutional changes neared, most opinion polls showed a majority against him. Nevertheless, it was assumed that many of his opponents, convinced that the result was fixed in advance, would stay away from the polls. Thus it came as a great surprise when, early in the morning of December 3, the Chavist president of the National Electoral Council announced to the country that the presidential proposals had been rejected, 51 percent to 49. More than three million people who had voted for Chávez's reelection in December 2006 voted against him one year later. Chávez acknowledged defeat at 2:50 a.m., and rumor had it that the military leadership had to convince him to do so. But two days later Chávez used obscenities in referring to the outcome. Calling the opposition's victory "Pyrrhic," he threatened to carry out his socialist vision even against the electorate's manifest will.

There were several reasons Chávez lost the referendum. Clearly, a majority of Venezuelans rejected Cuban-style socialism, threats to property rights, and the antidemocratic idea of a president for life. Furthermore, the newly energized student movement provided fresh leadership to anti-Chavist ranks. The shortages of basic food items also hurt the government's cause. Another factor was an incident at the 17th annual Iberian-American Summit, held in Chile, where Chávez was made to look ridiculous. After he interrupted Spanish president Rodríguez Zapatero's remarks by shouting insults against that country's former president, José María Aznar, King Juan Carlos of Spain exclaimed to Chávez, "*¿Por qué no te callas?*" (Why don't you shut up?). The scene was immediately broadcast on YouTube, and the international media had a field day mocking Chávez.

Also hurting Chávez was that some former friends turned against him. On November 5, Gen. Raúl Isaías Baduel, who had been a key ally and defense minister until July 2007, informed the media that the proposed constitutional changes amounted to a coup d'état. And on November 27, María Isabel Rodríguez, Chávez's recently divorced second wife, gave a press conference asking people to vote against the changes, since they would convert Venezuela into a second Cuba.

Furthermore, Chávez damaged his own cause. He used his Sunday TV and radio program on November 25 to criticize and insult Colombian president Álvaro Uribe, threatening to break off diplomatic and commercial relations. Uribe responded: "President Chávez, the truth is that if you are fomenting an expansionist project in the continent, that project does not have any place in Colombia. You cannot set the continent on fire talking about imperialism when you, helped by your budget, want to form an empire." It is likely that this tiff convinced a good number of the nearly three million Colombians with Venezuelan citizenship to vote against the constitutional changes.

The most important consequence of the December 2 referendum was that it demonstrated to the opposition the realistic possibility of defeating Chávez at the ballot box through unity and wise strategy. The result also convinced many upper- and middle-class Venezuelans—including Jews—who had considered emigrating to remain in the country.

Israel and the Middle East

Chávez showed special interest in relations with the Arab and Muslim world. In 2004 he traveled to Tripoli to receive the Muammar Gaddafi Human Rights Prize from the Libyan president. Chávez declared support for the nuclear program of his "brother," Iranian president Ahmadinejad, and visited Tehran a total of seven times; Ahmadinejad visited Venezuela three times. In 2007, Iran Air inaugurated regular flights to Venezuela, and Conviasa, the Venezuelan airline, began offering flights to Tehran and Damascus. By 2007 the value of Venezuela's trade with Iran exceeded $10 billion, making Iran Venezuela's second largest commercial partner.

The Chávez government was also linked to Middle Eastern terrorist groups. On March 5, 2004, Phil Gunson, president of the Foreign Press Association in Venezuela and a correspondent for the *Miami Herald,* published an article about the recent appointment of Hugo Cabezas and Tarek El Aissami as director and deputy director of ONIDEX, Venezuela's National and Foreigners Identification Office, the body that provided identification cards and passports for natives and for foreigners living in the country. According to Gunson, the two men were linked to extremist groups in Los Andes University (ULA), and El Aissami, whose father was Iraqi, was possibly connected with Islamic fundamentalist movements in the Middle East. On February 2, 2007, President Chávez appointed El Aissami vice minister of internal affairs and justice.

When university students protested in Caracas streets in defense of freedom of expression, they were brutally repressed by the police forces under the orders of El Aissami.

During Israel's war in Lebanon in 2006, Chávez repeatedly accused Israel of genocide and compared its actions to Hitler's Germany; visited Syria and Iran to express solidarity with Hezbollah and the Palestinians; and ordered the closing of Venezuela's embassy and consulate in Israel. The government also organized an anti-Israel demonstration in front of the Israeli embassy in Caracas. Chávez's speeches since the end of the war—especially during his visits to Muslim countries—and the government-controlled media's statements were consistently hostile to Israel. Among the government-supported anti-Israel activities that took place during 2007 was the exhibition "Palestine, an 11,000-Year History," financed by the state oil company PDVSA and two Chavist mayors. There were also organized activities to raise money for the release and repatriation of the terrorist Carlos Ilich Ramírez, the "Jackal," who was serving a life sentence in France.

Anti-Semitism

Venezuela was historically a country open to immigration, with low levels of anti-Semitism and xenophobia. This remained true of the great bulk of ordinary Venezuelans even during the Chávez years.

Argentinean sociologist Norberto Ceresole, a self-declared anti-Semite and Holocaust denier, is believed to have had a formative influence on Chávez's attitudes. Unlike all previous democratically elected presidents of Venezuela, Chávez refused any communication with Venezuelan Jewish organizations. During the early years of his presidency Chávez did not even mention Jews. Meanwhile, other important Chavist figures and the government-controlled media expressed clear anti-Israel and sometimes anti-Semitic views, leading the Confederation of Israelite Associations of Venezuela (CAIV), the representative body of Venezuelan Jewry, to send numerous letters of protest. CAIV's requests to meet with ministers and other public officials usually went unanswered.

In November 2004, DISIP, the regime's political police, got a court order allowing it to raid the site of the Hebraica School and the Hebraica Club in Caracas "to search for arms." There was never an explanation for the move, only accusations by some Chavists leaders that the Mossad (Israel's secret service) had planned the assassination of state prosecutor Danilo Anderson.

In his Christmas address on December 24, 2005, Chávez said, "the minorities descended from those who killed Christ are the same ones who today control the riches of the world." The Simon Wiesenthal Center in Buenos Aires responded by organizing an open letter signed by more than 300 Venezuelan intellectuals and scientists—mostly non-Jews—protesting the anti-Semitic remarks and also denouncing Chávez's invitation to Iranian president Ahmadinejad to visit Venezuela.

On March 24, 2007, CAIV celebrated its 40th anniversary at an event held at the Hebraica Club and School. Cristina Fernández de Kirchner, Argentina's first lady, was the guest of honor. Representatives of AJC, the World Jewish Congress, the Latin American Jewish Congress, and the Latin American Sephardic Federation also attended. President Chávez, several ministers, and other senior officials were invited, on the assumption that since Cristina Kirchner and her husband had a close relationship with Chávez, members of the government might attend as a show of courtesy, and their presence could improve the relationship between the regime and the Jewish community. But none of the official guests came, and Jewish leaders interpreted this as further evidence of the government's lack of sympathy for the Jews.

The CAIV event prompted a disturbing dialogue on the National Radio program *"La Noticia Final"* between interviewer Cristina González and Argentinean writer Carlos Asnárez, author of *Palestine, A Nation and a People.* González, who had drawn many earlier complaints from CAIV for negative remarks about Jews, referred to CAIV's anniversary as follows: "There was recently a Jewish meeting. Many Jews came to Venezuela to celebrate. . . . Everybody knew how many came into the country, but nobody knew how many stayed. No one checked how many left, and maybe a good number of people from the Mossad could have come." Asnárez replied: "This has to do with the impunity that these Zionists have, to operate worldwide with very strong economic power, an extremely strong media power. In Argentina the Jewish lobby is tremendously powerful and we can compare it with the American Jewish lobby. Unfortunately they play with guilt. Some political leaders who do not share Zionist ideas attend events organized by the Zionists because they feel obligated in order to appear in the photo so they will not be accused of anti-Semitism, the first accusation they like to use."

The U.S. Department of State, in its *International Religious Freedom Report* published in September 2007, stated about Venezuela: "The president, government officials, and government-affiliated media outlets promoted anti-Semitism through numerous anti-Semitic comments that created a spillover effect into mainstream society. There was a rise in anti-Semitic vandalism, caricatures, slogans at rallies, intimidation, and physical attacks against Jewish institutions." Foreign Minister Nicolas Maduro dismissed the report, saying it was part of America's psychological warfare against Venezuela.

Besides Cristina González, the journalists who most frequently expressed anti-Semitic opinions were Mario Silva and Vladimir Acosta, both of whom indulged in conspiracy theories directed at Israel, the "Zionist lobby," and individual Jews, such as Pynchas Brener, rabbi of the Ashkenazi community. Chávez often said that Silva's show, *"La Hojilla"* was his favorite program, and during the weeks leading up to the December 2 referendum he arranged to have himself interviewed on it three times. Israel and the Jewish community were also regularly attacked in the official government newspapers *VEA, Las Verdades de Miguel,* and *El Diario de Caracas*. The complaints that CAIV sent to government officials, the attorney general, and the directors of the national radio and TV stations about the media were ignored.

The most serious physical threat to the Jewish community during 2007 took place at midnight on December 1, a few hours before the vote on the referendum, when police once again raided the Hebraica Club and School in Caracas while a large wedding was taking place. This generated great anxiety in the community, which was relieved by the announcement of the electoral result.

JEWISH COMMUNITY

The great majority of the 14,500 Jews of Venezuela lived in the capital city of Caracas. Sephardi Jews began arriving from Morocco and elsewhere in the Middle East beginning in the 1930s, and especially after Morocco achieved independence in 1956. Ashkenazi Jews were generally the descendents of World War II refugees. The two communities differed only in their liturgies; they jointly supported a school, a cultural and sports center, a weekly newspaper, and a social-service agency. The local synagogues varied by their congregants' place of origin and degree of religious Orthodoxy. An estimated 8–10 percent of Jews required financial aid because they are old, disabled, or unemployed.

When Chávez was first elected president, Jews had the same preoccupations about their future as other Venezuelans, but when the government's hostility towards Israel and Jews become evident, many considered leaving the country. The Jewish community lost about 25 percent of its members since 1999, especially young couples seeking to educate their children in a safe environment and college graduates who continued their education in the U.S. or elsewhere and did not return to Venezuela upon completion of their studies.

In 1997 the Hebrew day school had 2,000 students; in 2007 enrollment was down to 1,400. Nevertheless, Jewish life remained dynamic, with extensive cultural, sports, and social activities. Zionism was traditionally strong in Venezuela, and that remained true even in the face of the Chavists' constant attacks against the State of Israel.

PAULINA GAMUS

Western Europe

Great Britain

National Affairs

PRIME MINISTER Tony Blair resigned on June 27 after ten years in office. The longest-serving prime minister in Labour Party history, he led the party to an unprecedented three consecutive general-election victories.

Over the months preceding his resignation it was clear that the government was in trouble. In January police questioned Blair about allegations that honors were being offered for money (see AJYB 2007, p. 334), and it was not until July that the Crown Prosecution Service ruled that there was "insufficient evidence" to bring charges. In March, 15 Royal Navy sailors serving on the *HMS Cornwall* were captured by Iran, held for 12 days, and finally released and pardoned by President Ahmadinejad in a televised ceremony. Afterward, Defense Secretary Dan Browne was strongly criticized for allowing the sailors to tell reporters their unimpressive story. By June Labour had slumped 30 percent in the polls.

To be sure, there were accomplishments as well. In May, devolved government was restored in Northern Ireland. The month before, the pound hit $2.0131, a 26-year high against the dollar. Indeed, Blair could take credit not only for a strong currency, but also for significant economic growth during his tenure, 2.8 percent. In addition, inflation was under control and employment at record levels.

The public held high hopes for Blair's successor, Gordon Brown, who had been his chancellor of the exchequer over the entire ten years. Soon after the transfer of power an ICM survey conducted for the *Guardian* showed a significant jump in Labour's standing with the public.

Brown sought to distance himself from the tired Blair administration. His cabinet included the first-ever female home secretary, Jacqui Smith, and he put together a government of "all the talents" so as to draw on members of other parties for advice. They included two Liberal Democrat peers who were Jewish, Baronness Rabbi Julia Neuberger and human-rights lawyer Lord Lester of Herne Hill. However Brown was immediately beset with crises. At the end of June, only the vigilance of emergency workers prevented terrorist nail-bombs from exploding at two sites in central London. And when a flaming vehicle was driven at full speed into a Glasgow airport terminal on June 30, the government raised the UK threat level to "critical."

In July, Labour won a by-election in Ealing Southall, West London, with the Tories coming in third. According to an ICM poll for the *Sunday Telegraph,* Labour was now backed by 40 percent of the public and the Tories by 33 percent, leading to speculation that Brown might capitalize on his popularity to call a general election and confirm his mandate to govern. The country waited with bated breath. By September Labour's lead had stretched to double figures, and the prime minister's rating as a "strong leader" had also jumped. But on October 6, in the wake of a successful Tory conference at which shadow chancellor George Osborne announced a popular plan to raise the threshold for inheritance tax to £1m, Brown announced that there would be no election.

It was a decision he might have come to regret, as misfortunes multiplied. Record summer rains completely flooded large areas of central and northern England. In foreign policy, a diplomatic row blew up between Britain and Russia when Moscow refused to extradite ex-KGB officer Andrei Lugovoi, suspected of murdering Alexander Litvinenko, himself an ex-KGB agent, in Britain. In September came the first hints of a threat to the economy that would only grow worse with the collapse of the U.S. subprime mortgage market. A British bank, Northern Rock, was forced to ask the Bank of England for an emergency loan. In October, for the first time since Brown took office, the Tories outscored Labour in the opinion polls, 40 percent to 34.

In November, Chancellor of the Exchequer Alistair Darling admitted in the House of Commons that confidential personal and financial details about 25 million people had been lost, and that same month Transport Secretary Ruth Kelly revealed that the personal information of three million drivers had been similarly lost. The year ended with a final blow: it emerged that property magnate David Abrahams (who was Jewish) had illegally used third parties to disguise donations of £6m to Labour MPs, and police launched an investigation. A poll taken at the time showed the Tories leading Labour 38 percent to 34.

Israel and the Middle East

THE GOVERNMENT

The new prime minister brought little change to Britain's Middle East policy. The new foreign secretary, David Miliband, pledged in June that British diplomats would be "unstinting" in pursuit of a two-state solution. There would be no contact with Palestinian rejectionists; the UK would support all those on both sides of the divide who were committed to peace; and there would be frank engagement with Israel over the building of Jewish settlements that were "contrary to international law." BBC world affairs correspondent Paul Reynolds commented that Miliband's Jewish origins would allow him "freedom to criticize Israel without being accused of anti-Semitism."

Britain also continued to regard the "road map" as the best hope for a peaceful solution, despite representations from her European partners in July that it had failed and should be replaced by an international force to patrol the Palestinian territories. In August the Commons All-Party Foreign Affairs Committee described the international community's embargo on contacts with Hamas as counterproductive and urged the government to defy it, suggesting that the UK open relations with "moderates" among the Palestinian rejectionists. Here again, the government held firm, reiterating that any engagement with Hamas depended on it renouncing violence, recognizing Israel, and adhering to previously accepted agreements between Israel and the Palestinians.

Brown's major Middle East policy statement came in September, with the publication of *Economic Aspects of Peace in the Middle East,* written by MP Ed Balls, the prime minister's close associate, and Jon Cunliffe, his adviser on international economic affairs. Originally intended for publication in 2006 but delayed by Hamas's election victory and the ensuing violence, it stressed that development of the Palestinian economy was essential to hopes for peace. The Israeli government, for its part, had to recognize that the long-term security of both Israel and Palestine depended on Palestinian economic development, and therefore Israel had to remove roadblocks on the West Bank and install border crossings with specific open hours for transport of goods and people to and from Gaza. Israel's closure regime, the report stated, "exerts a heavy toll," and regeneration could not occur in such an "insecure environment." The Palestine Authority was urged to prevent terrorist attacks.

Miliband visited the region in November, meeting with Israeli foreign minister Tzipi Livni and with the Palestinian president and prime minister, Mahmoud Abbas and Salam Fayyad. Afterward, the foreign secretary announced that the UK was ready to offer almost £250m to bolster the economy in the West Bank and Gaza if there was "tangible progress in security" and "a framework document on a two-state solution."

Secretary of State for International Development Douglas Alexander arrived in Israel for a fact-finding mission in December. He said that his department had given £15m in the current fiscal year to the Temporary International Mechanism established to deliver aid directly to the Palestinians, bypassing Hamas, plus a further £15m to the UN Relief and Works Agency (UNRWA), which cared for Palestinian refugees. Israel and the Palestinians had reached "a moment of possibility for peace," he said, welcoming Fayyad's three-year reform plan intended to maximize the efficiency of international aid and promote good governance.

In the second half of the year there were minor signs of friction between Israel and Great Britain. In August Israeli lawyers rejected renewed British demands to reopen the case against an Israeli soldier suspected of killing British peace activist James Miller (see AJYB 2007, p. 338). Israel's public security minister, Avi Dichter, canceled a trip to Britain in December, fearing arrest for alleged war crimes against Palestinians. The Israel Project, an organization dedicated to boosting Israel's image in the international media, issued a survey that month showing that 16 percent of the British public supported the Palestinians and 11 percent supported Israel. The overwhelming trend, the survey concluded, was lack of interest in the entire Middle East conflict.

Israel enjoyed a moment of unprecedented popularity with the British public in November, when its soccer team defeated Russia 2-1, thus giving the British team a second chance of qualifying for the 2008 European championship.

Tony Blair, Special Envoy

In July, following his retirement from British politics, Tony Blair was appointed the Quartet's special envoy to the Middle East. He saw his new role as helping rebuild the legal, governmental, and economic institutions in the region. While his brief did not include participating in peace negotiations, Blair said he would support moderate factions in Palestine, including the Palestinian president, and hoped to play a part in gaining statehood for the Palestinian people.

After a meeting between Blair, Fayyad, and Israeli defense minister Ehud Barak, a series of agreements on economic matters were announced in November. Aimed at providing jobs for Palestinians and improving conditions in the territories, they included construction of an agro-industrial park in Jericho, emergency sewerage work in Gaza, and housing and educational development in the territories. These, said a British official, were "quick impact" projects designed to give impetus to the forthcoming Annapolis summit.

Anti-Israel Acitivity

In January, a new group calling itself the Enough Coalition was launched by a group of actors, writers, politicians, and intellectuals eager to present the Palestinian viewpoint on the 40th anniversary of the Six-Day War. Although it claimed to support a just peace for both Israelis and Palestinians, the inaugural gathering included only representatives of pro-Palestinian organizations such as the Muslim Public Affairs Committee, War on Want, and Jews for Justice for the Palestinians. Their efforts culminated in a large-scale rally in London's Trafalgar Square in June, organized by the Palestine Solidarity Campaign and assisted by the Stop the War coalition and War on Want. Trade unions were also involved, despite attempts by Trade Union Friends of Israel (TUFI) to persuade British unions to withhold support. A delegation from the anti-Zionist Orthodox Jewish faction Neturei Karta was present.

Several British charities seemed bent on discrediting Israeli policy. In June Christian Aid urged its supporters to write the foreign secretary to urge the building of "bridges, not walls, in the Middle East." Israel's defensive barrier on the West Bank, it argued, symbolized the impasse in the area and also had "a hugely damaging impact" on the livelihood of Palestinians. In August, a booklet published by War on Want—a leading member of the Enough Coalition and the Stop the War organization—advised: "Investment in Israel should be presented in public as investment in a system of occupation, injustice and apartheid."

Some 400 people attended a pro-Palestinian rally in central London in October to mark Al-Quds Day, an annual event launched about 30 years earlier to assert Muslim claims to Jerusalem. It was organized by the Justice for Palestine Committee and among its supporters were Hezballah, Respect, and Neturei Karta.

Communities Minister Hazel Blears announced in November a £70m government initiative to confront and isolate Muslim extremists. It was, she said, imperative to equip people "with the skills and strength to withstand the messages of those preaching division and hatred." Of the total, her ministry would invest £25m in a scheme to help mainstream Muslim clerics and community leaders counter extremism; the remainder would be available to local authorities and other groups. Jon Benjamin, chief executive of the Board of Deputies of British Jews, said the move "rightly recognizes that the battle against extremism is more than about increased security." Nonetheless, that same month the Home Office allowed senior Hezballah official Ibrahim Mousawi to enter Britain, ignoring the protests of MPs and Jewish leaders who sought to get Whitehall to reverse the decision. Mousawi, editor of Al Manar, Hezballah's Beirut-based TV station, was in Britain for a Stop the War conference.

In December, the Muslim Council of Britain reversed its boycott of Holocaust Memorial Day and for the first time agreed to send representatives "for the sake of the common good." Since the launch of the commemoration in 2001 the council had refused to participate, calling for its replacement by a Genocide Memorial Day.

Plans for boycotting Israel, however, remained alive throughout the year. In anticipation, the Board of Deputies and the Jewish Leadership Council launched a Fair Play Campaign in January to provide a quick and effective communal response. The next month the group's representatives met with heads of Israeli universities to coordinate a response to any potential academic boycotts.

The annual meeting of the National Union of Journalists (NUJ), whose 40,000 members made it Britain's largest journalist union, took place in Birmingham in April. It passed a resolution to boycott Israel; called for an end to Israel's alleged aggression in Gaza and the occupied territories; and instructed its national executive to support such organizations as the Palestine Solidarity Campaign and Jews for Justice in Palestine. Some 300 members of NUJ who worked for the BBC signed a petition condemning these steps as inconsistent with their professional duty to report the news impartially.

In May, despite pleas from its own leadership and a concerted campaign by pro-Israel supporters and academics, members of the University and College Union (UCU) voted to circulate a boycott motion initiated by the universities of East London and Brighton for discussion by the membership. Another resolution agreed to was one proposed by the University of Birmingham, calling for a moratorium on research and cultural collaboration with Israel and for the European Science Foundation to withdraw funding from Israel until that nation abided by UN resolutions.

That same month Unison, the 1.3-million-member union of public-sector workers, held its annual conference in Brighton. It voted approval for a motion suggested by its Wolverhampton branch to support an "economic, cultural, academic and sporting boycott" of the Jewish state. Similarly, the annual conference of the Transport and General Workers' Union (TGWU), which had 800,000 members, voted to impose a boycott on Israeli goods, deploring the Israeli government's treatment of the Palestinian people and its failure to recognize their legitimate aspiration for a Palestinian state. The union emphasised that the boycott was not anti-Semitic.

The tide turned somewhat in midsummer, after a "Stop the Boycott" campaign was launched by Bicom (Britain-Israel Communications and Research Center) and the Jewish Leadership Council. Full-page advertisements appeared in the major newspapers signed by 250 eminent academics; notices appeared in the British press inserted by the Anti-Defamation League (ADL); and criticism of the boycott came from Nobel prize-winners, research bodies, British and American Jewish leaders, and Israeli politicians and academics. "The [UCU] resolution does absolutely no good for the peace process," declared Prime Minister Blair in the House of Commons in June. A poll that month of some 1,000 business, cultural, and political leaders commissioned by Bicom and conducted by Populus found 86 percent opposed to the boycott, although 67 percent did not think it was anti-Semitic.

As for the NUJ resolution, a rank-and-file rebellion spearheaded by BBC staff in July forced the union to abandon its boycott decision. Then in August, Unison secretary Dave Prentis wrote to the head of Histadrut, the Israeli labor federation, that his group's boycott resolution "did not commit Unison to boycott Israel or Israeli organizations," but had rather been one way to induce Israel to change its policies. The UCU called off its boycott plan in September after lawyers advised that it would be a form of discrimination "beyond the union's powers and unlawful."

In December 2006 the executive committee of the National Union of Students (NUS) had declared that Jewish students themselves had the right to define what constituted campus anti-Semitism, implying that manifestations of anti-Zionism might be included in that category (see AJYB 2007, p. 341). This was followed up by an NUS announcement in January 2007 of plans for a major symposium on the spillover from anti-Israel campus activity to anti-Semitism. The group's Leeds branch, however, did not endorse the policy until March, when it finally annulled its rule permitting the student union to ignore Jewish Society complaints "as long as Judaism as a faith was not offended," and passed a motion defining as "racist" any incident perceived as such by the affected minority group. The NUS annual Blackpool conference that month reiterated the policy and added an amendment calling for a ban on the use of classic anti-Semitic rhetoric and imagery to criticize Israel.

Leeds remained a focus of activity throughout the year. In May an extraordinary general meeting of UCU's Leeds branch castigated the university for canceling a March lecture by Dr. Matthias Küntzel of the Hebrew University on "Hitler's Legacy: Islamic Anti-Semitism." Security concerns had been cited as grounds for the decision, but pressure from Islamic undergraduates was also suspected to have played a role. The UCU branch voted to demand that Küntzel be reinvited as a demonstration of the university's commitment to free speech.

With the opening of the fall semester, Union of Jewish Students (UJS) campaign director Ya'ir Zivan warned that Jewish students should beware of intensifying activity on the part of the far-left Hizb ut-Tahrir, which could be operating at as many as 25 universities. Zivan also noted that although UCU had dropped its academic boycott plans, the campaign had strongly affected the atmosphere on campus and anti-Israel elements would surely attempt to ride on its momentum.

Already in August, literature calling Jews "a race of cruel bloodsuckers" for killing children in Gaza was distributed to student unions in Edinburgh and Bangor. In October the Palestinian Solidarity group at Leeds attacked Israel for its environmental record, linked with its treatment of the Palestinians. At Manchester University that same month Jewish students protested a twinning arrangement with the student body at Al-Najah University in Nablus, which had been approved by a vote of the student union in March. In November that student union erected a mock-up of Israel's security barrier as an "apartheid wall" during Solidarity with Palestine Week.

British Jews and Israel

The Jewish community campaigned throughout the year for the release of Israeli soldiers captured by Hezballah and Hamas. Prayers were recited weekly in the synagogues, and the Zionist Federation together with Christian Friends of Israel organized a mass lobby of the House of Commons in January. More than 100 MPs signed an early-day motion demanding the soldiers be freed, and a petition bearing 11,500 signatures calling on Britain to press for their release was presented to Foreign Secretary Margaret Beckett. This matter was high on the government's agenda, said the head of the Foreign Office's Arab/Israel and North African group, noting that British diplomats had been in contact with their opposite numbers in Lebanon and the Palestinian territories about the soldiers.

The release in July of Alan Johnston, a BBC journalist kidnapped in Gaza and held hostage for four months, gave new impetus to the campaign for the abducted Israelis. Israel's Knesset speaker, Dalia Itzik, appealed to Prince Charles and Tony Blair to use their influence in the Arab world. A campaign under the name "Free the Three" took out full-page advertisements in leading newspapers featuring the slogan, "One Alan Johnston is Free . . . Three Alan Johnstons aren't." Seven hundred people demonstrated outside Syria's London embassy and 250 in Manchester's town center. In November, Foreign Office minister Kim Howells assured the father of abducted soldier Ehud Goldwasser of the government's support.

But British Jewry was hardly united in regard to Israeli policies. In February more than 100 Jewish intellectuals and other prominent figures publicly dissociated themselves from mainstream Jewish support for Israel by launching Independent Jewish Voices (IJV) with full-page advertisements in the major British newspapers and the *Jewish Chronicle*. "Born of our frustration with the widespread misconception that the Jews of this country speak with one voice . . . which supports the Israeli government's policies," IJV stood for the rights of Palestinians and Israelis "to peaceful and secure lives." It condemned anti-Semitism, anti-Arab racism, and Islamophobia. "The battle against anti-Semitism," it proclaimed, "is undermined whenever opposition to Israeli government policies is automatically branded as anti-Semitic," and was "contradicted when those who claimed to speak on behalf of Jews in Britain and other countries consistently put support for the policies of an occupying power above the human rights of an occupied people."

Anti-Semitism

"We will not tolerate racially motivated crime of any kind," Race and Faith Minister Phil Woolas told the *Jewish Chronicle* in March. He also revealed that the 2006 All-Party Parliamentary Enquiry into Anti-Semitism (see AJYB 2007, p. 343) had been granted the status of an ongoing select committee, and in that capacity would continue to monitor anti-Semitism. The government, he promised, was taking a zero-tolerance approach.

In July, a working group composed of civil servants and Jewish leaders began discussing implementation of 35 government recommendations to tackle anti-Semitism that had been suggested in response to the Enquiry. By November it could report that the government had set up a task force on anti-Semitism chaired by MP Parmjit Dhanda, parliamentary undersecretary at the Department for Communities and Local Government; pledged that by 2009 all 43 British police forces would be using the same system to report anti-Semitic incidents; appropriated £2m to extend across the nation the Schools Linking Network that combated extremism by making connections between schools of different faiths and backgrounds; and agreed to help meet the spiraling costs of security at Jewish schools that were currently paid by parents. In addition, the Crown Prosecution Service (CPS) was conducting an internal review of how it dealt with cases of race hatred and incitement. In September the government gave the Parliamentary Group against Anti-Semitism £20,000 to fund efforts to persuade foreign parliaments to set up similar investigations into anti-Semitism.

The Community Security Trust (CST), which monitored anti-Semitic activity for the Jewish community, recorded 547 incidents in 2007, the second highest annual total since these counts began in 1984 but 8 percent below the 2006 total of 594. CST attributed the fall to the absence of "trigger events" such as the 2006 Israeli war in Lebanon rather than to any change in the rising long-term trend. The 2007 figure included 114 violent assaults (as compared to 112 in 2006); 62 incidents of damage and desecration of Jewish property (70 in 2006); and 328 incidents of abusive behaviour (365 in 2006).

The resolution of one particular case of anti-Semitism, a racially aggravated assault on an Orthodox young man in Manchester in 2006, evoked protest from the Jewish community. After the CST complained that the sentences handed down "send out an entirely wrong message to both the perpetrators and the Jewish community," the solicitor general referred the sentences to the Court of Appeal for review in August.

Although the far-right British National Party (BNP) fielded 750 candidates in the May local elections, it gained only two more seats than it had before, increasing its nationwide total to 51. This followed a large-scale "Hope Not Hate" anti-BNP campaign in London, Manchester, and Leeds conducted by the antifascist Searchlight organization in conjunction with local political parties, trade unions, communal groups, and the *Daily Mirror,* and supported by the Holocaust Educational Trust.

Tempers ran high in Oxford in November when the Oxford Union debating society invited Holocaust denier David Irving and BNP leader

Nick Griffin to lead "A Night of Discussion on The Limits of Free Speech." Although they could not prevent the event from taking place, students, interfaith groups, trade unions, and political organizations succeeded in considerably limiting its scope by conducting mass demonstrations both outside and inside the union.

The Board of Deputies launched "Racism: It's Not Kosher" in December. This was a campaign to put the Jewish community in the forefront of the fight against racism, and specifically to prevent BNP from winning a by-election for a seat on the Greater London Assembly for Harrow, North London. The BNP candidate lost badly, polling only 56 votes, and the campaign claimed credit for the result.

In September, the Racial and Religious Hatred Act became law. This was designed to close a loophole in the existing racial hatred law that had protected Jews but not Muslims or Christians.

It was announced in January that a European Institute for the Study of Contemporary Anti-Semitism would be established in Great Britain.

JEWISH COMMUNITY

Demography

In December, the Board of Deputies Community Policy Research Group (formerly called the Community Research Unit, see below, p. 364) issued *Britain's Jewish Community Statistics 2006,* prepared by David Graham and Daniel Vulkan. It calculated the number of births partly on the basis of circumcision records. The number of circumcisions in 2006 fell to 1,695 from a revised total of 1,709 in 2005, leading to an estimate of 3,314 births that year, down from a revised figure of 3,339 for 2005. The number of marriage performed under Jewish religious auspices also fell, from 1,000 in 2005 to 894 in 2006, and the number of gittin (religious divorces) granted in 2006 amounted to 248 as compared to 251 for 2005. Burials and cremations under Jewish religious auspices also declined, from 3,221 in 2005 to 3,107 in 2006. 2007 statistics on conversions to Judaism were available only for the Reform Synagogues of Great Britain, which accepted the conversions of 101 adults and 30 children, as compared to 113 adults and 51 children in 2006.

The report also introduced new data for *shalom zakhor* celebrations held by strictly Orthodox Ashkenazi Jews after the birth of a boy. Based on their number, it calculated a figure of 1,055 strictly Orthodox births, almost one-third of total UK Jewish births. They were concentrated in North London's predominantly *haredi* Stamford Hill area and in the city of Manchester.

Other demographic studies of British Jewry also demonstrated the growth of the ultra-Orthodox community. An in-depth analysis of the 2001 census by the Institute for Jewish Policy Research (JPR), published in May, noted a "young, rapidly growing cohort of [strictly Orthodox] Jews who are bucking the demographic trend in a remarkable way." The 116-page report, *Jews in Britain: A Snapshot from the 2001 Census,* by David Graham, Marlena Schmool, and Stanley Waterman, predicted that "the demographic make-up of British Jewry and probably also its religious structure will be very different in just a generation." Whereas, in British Jewry as a whole, intermarriage, cohabitation, and a growing incidence of adult singlehood were eroding the traditional Jewish family, "the very young population structure of strictly Orthodox groups points to a demographic future far more secure than the rest of the Jewish population."

Similarly, Dr. Yaakov Wise, honorary research fellow at Manchester University's Center for Jewish Studies, claimed, on the basis of the Manchester data, that three out of every four Jewish births in 2007 would be *haredi,* a pattern that would lead to that sector forming the majority of British Jewry within three decades. His calculations assumed the continuation of the current stark differences between demographic trends in that community and those among non-*haredim.* There was no consensus on the size of the current *haredi* population in the country. Wise believed there were 45,500, but David Graham, senior research officer of the Board, claimed there were only 25,000–35,000. Estimates of the total Jewish population ranged from 275,000 to 300,000.

Communal Affairs

A highly self-critical internal review of the Union of Jewish Students (UJS) was released in May entitled "Change in a Changing Environment." It found that the organization lacked "a clear and focused sense of mission, role, and purpose," and suffered from "serious logistical, administrative, and management deficiencies." The review recommended the appointment of a "turn-around professional" to fix these problems. UJS, "the only grass-roots, national representative Jewish student organization in the UK," had a membership of 8,000 on 80 campuses, the largest of them located in Leeds and Birmingham. Aimed primarily at defending and protecting Jewish student rights on campus, it was largely funded by UJIA, the Hillel Foundation, and CST.

A *Jewish Chronicle* investigation published in January found serious poverty in the Jewish community that was burdening already heavily challenged charities. Figures based on the 2001 census and surveys provided by the Shoresh Trust showed that up to 40 percent of the total caseload of Norwood, the Jewish family service, comprised people who could not support themselves, with the percentage rising to 78 percent in Hackney, North London, where many Orthodox Jews lived. Some 3,000 Jewish children in the UK lived below the poverty line (defined as 60 percent of the average wage), and 4 percent of children at state-aided Jewish schools qualified for free school meals.

The shortage of suitable housing for Hackney's expanding strictly Orthodox Jewish community caused considerable concern. The JPR report noted above found that Hackney Jews experienced higher levels of social deprivation than Jews elsewhere in the country, 34.5 percent of them living in public housing. In September the Agudas Israel Housing Association opened two £10m "affordable" housing developments and the local planning committee granted permission for two more, but even these were beyond the means of large *haredi* families with low incomes. In September, Greater London Authority officials met with representatives of communal organizations, including the London Jewish Forum, and agreed to look into possible sites such as Thames Gateway and Olympic boroughs for new *haredi* homes. "We should be able to address the needs of the Orthodox community," Mayor Ken Livingstone told the Forum's annual meeting in November. In December, Diane Abbott, MP for Hackney North and Stoke Newington, filed an early-day motion in Parliament calling for more government research into the "hidden deprivation" of Hackney's Jewish community.

Outside London, the *Jewish Chronicle* reported, more than one out of every eight Jews in Leeds and one out of every 15 in Manchester relied on charity to get by. To address the problem, Manchester's Jewish Project to Reorganize Communal Organizations set up an operation called Community First in January to promote the social and economic health of the Jews there. The Board of Deputies opened a branch office in Manchester, its first outside London, in July, aimed at improving and expanding relations with local government. In November, the £450,000 Aguda Center for children and families in North Manchester opened in Salford, offering a wide range of social services to 250–300 families per month.

Ironically, the prosperity of some sectors of British Jewry was also blamed for social ills. In February, Norwood's chief executive, Norma Brier, suggested that increased affluence was a possible cause of the growing numbers of family break-ups.

In January, Norwood confirmed that gay Jewish couples could adopt Jewish children. The Board of Deputies established a Jewish volunteer network in June to enable all Jewish charitable organizations to recruit volunteers through a single channel. In August, the Board replaced its Community Research Unit with a Community Policy Research Group, which was expected to function as an academic research body that would help shape British Jewry's long-term planning strategy. "We are trying to use methods similar to those of modern policy-makers," said Alex Goldberg, the Board's community-issues director.

Religion

In March, with its lease on Adler House due to expire, the United Synagogue (US) bought new headquarters in Finchley Road, Northwest London, for £3.6m. Rabbi Saul Zneimer, the first rabbi to serve as chief executive officer of the US, resigned in August after six years. In the Sephardi community, the Board of Elders of the Spanish and Portuguese Jews' Congregation announced in April that Dayan (religious judge) Saadia Amor would replace Dayan Pinchas Toledano as head of the Sephardi Bet Din (religious court).

In July, the Hertsmere Borough Council's planning committee gave permission for the construction of an *eruv* (symbolic boundary enabling carrying on the Sabbath) in Borehamwood. This would be Great Britain's third *eruv* and the first outside a London borough. Plans were afoot in August for yet a fourth, in north Manchester.

The Chief Rabbi's Office produced a report in September calling for more young Jews to participate in interfaith activities, a sphere that currently attracted mainly rabbis. Plans included a course at the London School of Jewish Studies on Jewish attitudes toward interreligious dialogue, and programs on interfaith issues in regional communities.

There were a number of developments during the year regarding synagogue buildings. London's New West End Synagogue, built in 1879, was designated a Grade 1 listed building in August; the only other synagogue so listed was the seventeenth-century Bevis Marks in the City of London. In August it was announced that Fieldgate Street Great Synagogue, opened in 1899 in London's East End, was to close. In Liverpool, Greenbank Drive Hebrew Congregation closed in December after a levy on its 400 members failed to meet the costs of staying open for another year. The closure was part of a plan to consolidate the community's buildings in line with falling Jewish population figures.

In December, Chabad closed its Gaon Club for young Jewish businesspeople in London's West End after admitting a £1.5m deficit. Complaints had been made of "lavish expenditure" on the club, run by Rabbis Yosef and Mendy Vogel. A rift opened between their father, the prominent Chabad figure Rabbi Faivish Vogel, and his fellow trustees after a bet din hearing found the brothers guilty of diverting money that had been designated for other activities.

Rabbi Shoshana Boyd Gelfand was appointed executive director of the Reform movement in April, placing upon her shoulders the responsibility for carrying out the 2020 Vision project to reinvigorate Reform Jewry. Rabbi Tony Bayfield was appointed the movement's first full-time head. The first same-sex wedding in Britain conducted by a rabbi was held in a Reform synagogue in October.

In August, Rabbi Aaron Goldstein, Liberal Judaism's outreach director, quoted unofficial statistics showing that requests for rabbinic officiation at mixed-faith unions had risen from 30–40 in 2006 to around 60 in 2007. In 2003 Liberal Judaism had begun to allow its rabbis to perform such ceremonies even in synagogues so long as the couple made "a commitment to be part of the community and raise Jewish children."

Education

According to *The Future of Jewish Schools—A Consultation Document,* published by the Jewish Leadership Council in October, the supply of places at mainstream Jewish schools could exceed demand within five years. For one thing, enrollment figures for 2005/6 showed over half the children from mainstream London families attending non-Jewish primary schools. Furthermore, given the demographic trends, the document estimated a fall of up to 20 percent in the primary-school-age population over the next decade, and if the take-up rate for places at Jewish primaries remained at its current 45 percent, nearly one out of three classroom seats would be vacant in London mainstream Jewish primaries by 2016. Jewish primary schools in Northeast London (mainly in Redbridge) already had about 20 percent spare capacity, and in Manchester only 880 out of 1,065 places were filled in 2005/6. The Jewish primary school in Brighton, Sussex, closed in 2007.

In the secondary sector, London mainstream schools (particularly those in Northwest London) were close to capacity in 2005/6 with 4,438 students, an estimated 42 percent of the Jewish pupil population. But the projected number of additional places to be created through the expansion of existing establishments and the planned creation of new ones would, the report said, increase capacity to some 7,000 by 2016. Given the fall in numbers at the primary level, these secondary schools would be nearly 50 percent over capacity by 2016 unless demand for places increased.

Meanwhile, plans for Britain's first Jewish cross-community secondary school (JCoss) proceeded apace (see AJYB 2007, p. 349). In April it secured a government grant of approximately £40m, and in August planning permission was received from Barnet Council for its 14,000-square-meter site. The project's president, property magnate Gerald Ronson, announced in December a £10m fund-raising campaign for JCoss. He claimed that the new school would open up the choice of a Jewish education to a whole new group of parents and reengage many "who otherwise will be lost to our community."

The strictly Orthodox community had the opposite problem, the Leadership Council's document found. It could not expand or build schools fast enough to meet the needs of its children, who now formed half the Jewish school population. This sector had significant funding problems, as many of the schools were private to avoid having to teach the national curriculum, and therefore did not receive government money.

Conflict between mainstream and *haredi* sectors went public in August, when leaders of the former announced their support for *Faith in the System,* a government publication aimed at promoting social cohesion and tolerance in faith-based schools. The Union of Orthodox Hebrew Congregations disassociated itself from the document. Though it approved the broad aims, some of the practical recommendations, such as a program of visits between schools of different religions, were deemed inappropriate for strictly Orthodox schools. Moreover, said the Union, "neither the United Synagogue [which supported the document] nor the Board [of Deputies] has any status to speak on behalf of the entire Jewish community." The Board agreed it did not speak for the *haredi* sector, which had withdrawn from that body two years earlier, when the Reform representatives joined. But, said the Board chief executive, Jon Benjamin, "we have to show where faith schools can work in a context that is not insular and that our children understand the wider world in which they live."

In May, the United Jewish Israel Appeal announced it would fund a three-year fellowship in Israel studies at the Oxford Center for Jewish Studies. And in June, Bolton University and Ma'alot Greater Manchester—a Jewish studies program—announced it would offer a new B.A. combined degree in business and Jewish studies.

Foreign Aid

World Jewish Relief (WJR) remained British Jewry's leading international charity. Chairman Nigel Layton reported in July that the funds raised for its Gifts in Kind program, which sent items of all types to impoverished Jews in Ukraine, Belarus, Moldova, Serbia, and Hungary, had risen from £1m to £5m annually. He also noted that WJR bought goods valued at £2.5m per year from In Kind Direct, a project started by Prince Charles to buy surplus goods that would otherwise be thrown away and to distribute them to those in need. The Prince was guest speaker at WJR's annual dinner in December.

Visits between UK congregations, groups or individuals and twinned East European communities continued. In March the rabbi and members of Elstree Liberal Synagogue paid their first visit to their twin community, Lutsk, Ukraine, where they had funded the establishment of classes in Jewish studies, Hebrew, and religion. In June, Hendon Reform Synagogue hosted groups of children from its twin congregation, Bobruisk, Belarus. It was reported in April that the number of participants in WJR's bar mitzvah twinning scheme had risen from 39 in 2005 to 50 in 2006.

In October, Rabbi Abraham Ginsburg, director of the Stamford Hill-based Committee for the Preservation of Jewish Cemeteries in Europe, led an international campaign to halt the destruction of the ancient Snipiskes Jewish cemetery in Vilnius, Lithuania, the site of major redevelopment.

Publications

The 2007 Jewish Quarterly/Wingate prize was won by Howard Jacobson for his novel, *Kalooki Nights*. A new prize for journalism was created honoring the late Chaim Bermant, noted author and long-time *Jewish Chronicle* columnist.

Works of fiction published in 2007 included *Everything Passes,* a poetic novel by Gabriel Josipovici; *Beethoven Was One-Sixteenth Black* by Nadine Gordimer; *Fame and Fortune,* a sequel to Frederic Raphael's *Glit-*

tering Prizes; The Song Before It Is Sung by Justin Cartwright; *Unused Language,* a first short-story collection by Jennifer Wingate; *Mrs. Zhivago of Queen's Park* by Olivia Lichtenstein; *The Brodsky Touch* by Lana Citron; *The Last Testament* by Sam Bourne (the alias of journalist Jonathan Freedland); *When We Were Romans* by Matthew Kneale; Jonathan Wilson's historical crime romance *A Palestine Affair;* and *Love Falls* by Esther Freud.

Historical studies were *Rome and Jerusalem: The Clash of Ancient Civilizations* by Martin Goodman; *Historians* by Daniel Snowman; *Barbarism and Civilization: A History of Europe in Our Time* by Bernard Wasserstein; *Churchill and the Jews* by Martin Gilbert; *Betrayal: France, the Arabs and the Jews* by David Pryce-Jones; *Judaism Without Jews* by Elaine Glaser; *Last Days in Babylon* by Marina Benjamin; Nick Lambert's *Jews and Europe in the 21st Century: Thinking Jewish;* and *On Brick Lane,* an oral history of London's East End by Rachel Lichtenstein. Two books on the refugee phenomenon were *Remembering Refugees: Then and Now* by Tony Kushner and *From Outside In: Refugees and British Society* by Nushin Arbabzadah.

Works of poetry included *Femenismo,* Joanne Limburg's poems about being a Jewish woman in Britain; *Out of the Blue* by Nadine Brummer; *New Departures,* a book-length poem by Michael Horovitz; *Musica Transalpina* by Michelene Wandor; *Moon Wheels* by Ruth Fainlight; *Wide Skies, Salt and Best Bitter* by Peter Philips; and *Galatea* by Melanie Challenger. In the field of literature, Risa Domb, who died in 2007 (see below, p. 369), published *Identity and Modern Israeli Literature.* The second volume of *New Women's Writing from Israel,* which she edited, also appeared.

Works by rabbis included *Rabbis in Danger,* Jonathan Romain's account of rabbinical occupational hazards; a new translation of and commentary on *The Authorised Daily Prayer Book* by Chief Rabbi Sir Jonathan Sacks, who also published *The Home We Build Together,* which cast a critical eye at multiculturalism and assimilation; and *Liberal Judaism: A Judaism for the Twenty-First Century* by Rabbi Pete Tobias. Closely related were *British Chief Rabbis 1664–2006* by Derek Taylor, and *Law, Medicine and Ethics,* published by the Cancerkin breast cancer charity in honor of the late chief rabbi, Lord Immanuel Jakobovits. Other publications on religious themes included *Orthodox Judaism in Britain since 1913: An Ideology Forsaken* by Miri Freud-Kandel; *Undercurrents of Jewish Prayer* by Jeremy Schonfield; *What Do Jews Believe?* by Edward Kessler; and *Jewish Thought: An Introduction* by Oliver Leaman.

Holocaust literature included *Roman's Journey* by Roman Halter; *The Crime of My Very Existence: Nazism and the Myth of Jewish Criminality* by Michael Berkowitz; *The Mascot* by Mark Kurzem; *The Single Light* by Ernest Levy; and *A Garden of Eden in Hell* by Melissa Müller and Reinhard Piechocki, about the life of pianist and Holocaust survivor Alice Herz-Sommer.

Biographies and autobiographies included *Some Sort of a Life* by actress Miriam Karlin; *Before I Forget: A Family Memoir* by Brian Tesler; *Take Off Your Party Dress,* in which Dina Rabinovitch recorded her fight against cancer (see below, p. 370); *Making Trouble: Life and Politics* by Lynne Segal; and *West End Chronicles* by Ed Glinert. Poet Dannie Abse mourned the death of his wife in poetry in *Running Late,* and in prose in *The Presence.*

Books about Israel were *The Jewish Divide Over Israel: Accusers and Defenders*, edited by Edward Alexander and Paul Bogdanor; *The Politics of Acopalypse: The History and Influence of Christian Zionism* by Dan Cohn-Sherbok; and *What Zionists Really Think* by Colin Schindler.

Borat Sagdiyev (comedian Sacha Baron-Cohen) published *Touristic Guidings to Glorious Nation of Kazakhstan.*

Personalia

Honors conferred on British Jews in 2007 included knighthoods to treasury adviser James Sassoon for services to the financial industry and public service; solicitor Geoffrey Bindman for services to human rights; Norman Rosenthal for his 30 years as exhibitions secretary at the Royal Academy of Arts; and Leigh Lewis for his work as permanent secretary in the Department for Work and Pensions.

Notable British Jews who died in 2007 included Harry Crivan, Zionist personality and metallurgist, in Glasgow, in January, aged 99; Clive Bourne, philanthropist, in Nevis, West Indies, in January, aged 64; Nathan Vogel, founder of the Chabad senior boys' school, in London, in January, aged 82; Paul Oppenheimer, pioneer of Holocaust education, in Birmingham, in January, aged 78; Sam Cohen, communal worker, local Labour government politician, and Zionist, in London, in January, aged 103; Alexander Brown, Blackpool religious official and ritual slaughterer, in Manchester, in January, aged 95; Risa Domb, founder-director, Cambridge University Center for Modern Hebrew Studies, in Cambridge, in January, aged 69; George Garai, Zionist journalist, in London, in February, aged 80; Philip Kleinman, journalist, in London, in February, aged 74; Jack Goldwhite, founder of the Wingate football club, in London, in February, aged, 89; Jakov Lind, Holocaust diarist, in London, in February, aged 80; Teddy Isaacs, Sheffield communal personality, in London, in February, aged 96; Leslie Gatoff, Jewish educator, in London, in February, aged 86; Helena Wolman, social worker, in Manchester, in April, aged 82; Josef Dunner, senior leader of Britain's strictly Orthodox community, in London, in April, aged 94; Susi Bradfield, prominent WIZO figure and philanthropist, in London, in May, aged 77; Michael Hamburger, poet and translator, in Suffolk, in June, aged 83; Maurice Wohl, philanthropist, in London, in June, aged 84; Natalia Karp, pianist, in London, in July, aged 96; Sourie Somers, Whitechapel Road Pavilion Yiddish Theater Company star, in London, in July, aged 99; Abraham Wulwik, for 31 years headmaster of Northwest London Jewish Day School, in London, in July, aged 90; Monty Richardson, active in all aspects of Jewish communal life, in London, in July, aged 89; Frank Cass, publisher of Jewish books, in London, in August, aged 77; Kalman Fausner, for 54 years Hove synagogue cantor, in Hove, in September, aged 98; John Bull, Westminster city councilor for 31 years and prominent Jewish personality, in London, in September, aged 79; Judy Goldkorn, Federation of Women Zionists stalwart, in London, in September, aged 91; Alan Coren, humorist and first Jewish editor of *Punch* magazine, in London, in October, aged 69; Dina Rabinovitch, journalist, in London, in October, aged 44; Michael Harris, US council member for 22 years, on the Board of Deputies for 48, in London, in October, aged 78; Peter Lipton, philosopher of science and Cambridge Jewish personality, in Cambridge, in November, aged 53; Leonard Tann, long-serving Birmingham rabbi and educator, in Birmingham, in November, aged 62; Norman Pearlman, amateur entertainer and a founder of the Jewish Theater Group, in Manchester, in November, aged 80; Hayim Pinner, Labor Zionist, Board of Deputies secretary general, 1977–91, in London, in November, aged 82; Ruth Winston-Fox, social worker and communal personality, in London, in November, aged 95.

MIRIAM KOCHAN

France

National Affairs

On May 6, French voters elected Nicolas Sarkozy, the center-right candidate, president of France for a five-year term. He defeated the Socialist candidate Ségolène Royal by 53.06 percent to 46.94 percent in the second-round run-off. Turnout was high, 83.97 percent of registered voters, which was not surprising given the intense public interest the campaign aroused.

The run-off was necessary because no candidate won an absolute majority in the first round of voting on April 21. Sarkozy was first in that contest with 31.18 percent, followed by Royal at 25.87 percent and centrist François Bayrou at 18.57 percent. Finishing fourth with 10.44 percent was ultra-rightist Jean-Marie Le Pen, whose National Front party suffered a major setback. In the previous presidential election in 2002 Le Pen came in second, albeit because the far stronger left-wing vote was divided among a multitude of first-round candidates. Le Pen that year received 16.86 percent in the first round and 17.79 in the run-off, when he was beaten by Jacques Chirac.

In 2007, eight candidates other than the top four shared the remainder of the first-round vote, with ultra-leftist Olivier Besancenot the only one to garner more than a million votes (4.08 percent). The others included hard-rightist Philippe de Villiers, Communist Marie-George Buffet, and Dominique Voynet of the Greens. As Buffet attracted less than 2 percent, the election confirmed the near-demise of the Communist Party, which, less than half a century earlier, when there was still a blue-collar, ethnic, French working class, regularly got more than a quarter of the vote. The French Greens, who hoped for electoral successes similar to those of their ideological soul mates in neighboring Germany, also saw their hopes dashed.

A non-practicing Roman Catholic who was largely raised by a Jewish-born grandfather after his parents divorced, the 52-year-old Sarkozy enjoyed the support of the vast majority of France's 600,000-strong Jewish community because of a long record of support for Israel and Jewish causes. Although Jews represented only 1 percent of the French population, they were credited by friends and foes alike with an influence beyond their numbers due to their relatively strong presence in the media and other key sectors.

Sarkozy had been preparing his candidacy for years, but officially began it on January 14 with a mass rally in Paris of his Union for a Popular Movement (UMP). Organizers said that 78,000 party members attended. Sarkozy spoke immediately after the results were announced of an internal party vote in UMP branches across France in which, according to UMP officials, just over 69 percent of the almost 340,000 members took part and 98.1 percent of them designated Sarkozy as their preferred candidate.

"Sarko" told those present that with his designation as candidate he had ceased to represent the party only, and aspired to be "the person who unites all the French people." "My France is that of all the French," he said in a lyrical speech that referred to a long string of national heroes stretching from the Middle Ages until the present, who, he said, had inspired his career. Along with such obvious names as Charles de Gaulle and philosophers Pascal and Voltaire he threw in lesser-known figures, including Georges Mandel, the French Jewish politician murdered by Nazi collaborators during World War II and about whom Sarkozy wrote a biography in 1994.

"All of them," he said, referring to these listed role models, "have taught the little Frenchman of mixed blood who I am, the love of France and the pride in being a Frenchman." Three of Sarkozy's grandparents were foreign-born: his father, who arrived in France as a political refugee after the war, was a Catholic minor Hungarian aristocrat, and his maternal grandfather was born in the Jewish community of Salonica, now in Greece but then in the Ottoman Empire. Sarkozy also mentioned events and places he had visited that, he said, forged his personality, including the hall at Jerusalem's Yad Vashem Holocaust memorial that was specially dedicated to the one million children killed.

Among those present at the rally, but who discreetly and nonetheless demonstratively left after less than an hour, was Dominique de Villepin, the serving prime minister, who was Sarkozy's main rival for the position of center-right presidential candidate. Despite smiles, the two men had been at daggers drawn for months. And shortly after Sarkozy was elected, an instructing magistrate placed de Villepin under judicial investigation—one small step short of being criminally charged—for participation in a complicated pre-election plot to disseminate false rumors alleging that Sarkozy had secret bank accounts abroad containing large sums of shady origin. President Jacques Chirac, who had at one point harbored ambitions of running for a third term, was conspicuously absent from the rally.

Ségolène Royal, the first woman to represent a major party in a French presidential election, had eliminated her Socialist rivals from contention in late 2006. She outlined her campaign platform, contained in a 100-point "Presidential Pact," at a major rally in the Paris suburbs on February 11. In an effort to break with the past practice of having a small group draw up the platform, Royal had promised that the public would help formulate hers, and some 6,000 town-hall-style meetings were held across the country in the months preceding the rally. Royal said she also had received 135,000 suggestions by Internet. "I have tried to listen to all of you. I wanted the citizens of this country to speak so that I could carry their voice, because you are fed up with programs written in the shadows and ignored as soon as they are written. Promises must be kept and must be credible," she said.

The program she presented was only moderately left wing, far closer to the center of politics than previous Socialist platforms. On the international scene, she called for strengthening the European Union by tightening the links between its members. She also proposed that the EU take the initiative for an "International Conference for Peace and Security in the Middle East."

Royal's campaign, at first buoyed by the novelty of a woman's candidacy backed by her own Mona Lisa-type good looks, started to wear thin once the campaign was underway. It did not help that she was sniped at by many within her own party, particularly former prime minister Laurent Fabius and former finance minister Dominique Strauss-Kahn, both of whom she had beaten out for the Socialist nomination.

The big surprise of the campaign was centrist candidate François Bayrou, whose political identity as someone who was neither part of the left or the right appealed to many French people who were fed up with that endless split that had characterized French politics since the French Revolution of 1789. Bayrou rose steadily in the polls and by early March tied Royal at 23 percent. At that point Sarkozy was at 28 percent and his camp worried about the prospect of a Sarkozy-Bayrou run-off, in which case many Royal sympathizers, whose main aim was to stop Sarkozy, would back Bayrou. In the Sarkozy-Royal tussle that did materialize, first-round Bayrou voters split between Sarkozy and Royal in the run-off.

Although both Sarkozy and Royal had visited Israel in 2006 and Sarkozy had assiduously courted French Jewry for years, the Arab-Israeli conflict and Jewish issues in general were absent from the election campaign. It was considered a foregone conclusion that the bulk of Jewish voters would back Sarkozy, but since it was illegal to ask about religion in opinion polls there was no way to verify the breakdown of the Jewish vote. One indication, however, came from the 45,000 French citizens residing in Israel, nearly all of whom were Jewish. Over 82 percent voted for Sarkozy when they cast their ballots in French consulates in Jerusalem, Haifa, and Tel Aviv.

Sarkozy's popularity with Jews was demonstrated on January 23 at the annual gala dinner of CRIF (Conseil Représentatif des Institutions Juives de France), the umbrella body of French Jewish groups. The CRIF dinner, instituted in 1985, was attended by the "who's who" of the French political world as well as by French Jewish leaders, and was traditionally addressed by the serving French prime minister and by CRIF's president. The guest speaker at the 2007 event was Prime Minister de Villepin, but all eyes were turned to Interior Minister Sarkozy, whose arrival caused a rugby-type scrum around him by the media and well-wishers. He stayed through the pre-dinner cocktails, surrounded by Jewish personalities seeking to have their photos taken with him. But he left before the dinner, possibly in order not to seem to be taking second place to the prime minister when the latter spoke. Royal, who, a week before, had told CRIF officials that she would not attend, showed up for the cocktails, as did Bayrou. During his welcoming speech, outgoing CRIF president Roger Cukierman pledged that the body would be neutral in the forthcoming presidential poll.

Sarkozy's election chances received an unexpected boost on March 28 when a major riot broke out at the Gare du Nord train station in Paris over the arrest of an illegal immigrant from Congo-Brazzaville who had leapt over a turnstile without paying his fare. The man, who had a long police record for minor criminal offences, tried to resist arrest because he was under a court order that he be expelled from France if apprehended. The train station with its many underground shops was a meeting place for African immigrants and young French blacks, who congregated there by the hundreds each day. When they saw police chasing the suspect, pouncing on him and holding him on the ground, they erupted in anger. Shops were looted and station equipment destroyed, and the air was thick with tear gas as the rioters, soon joined by ethnic French anarchists tipped off by radio news bulletins, fought it out with police inside the labyrinth-like station's maze of corridors. The proceedings were filmed by fast-arriving television-camera crews. A large segment of the French public, still feeling the shock of the October 2005 riots that raged for nearly three weeks across immigrant ghetto suburbs, expressed renewed anger at street violence by Third World immigrants, a favorite Sarkozy campaign theme.

Sarkozy had resigned as Interior Minister earlier that month to devote himself to full-time campaigning, and so he had no direct responsibility for dealing with the riot. Left-wingers nevertheless blamed it on Sarkozy, saying that his constant harping on law-and-order combined with calls for tougher immigration regulations had helped create a climate in which immigrants felt hounded by authorities. Fears of more violence to come proved unfounded, and it was a good-natured crowd of tens of thousands of Sarkozy supporters who gathered in the Place de la Concorde in central Paris when the final results were announced on May 6. There were only a few scattered protests, including the burning of cars in Paris suburbs, over the next 48 hours, mostly by small groups of ethnic French anarchists.

One subject that came immediately to the fore on election day itself was the new president's stormy relationship with his wife Cécilia, a matter that soon affected Sarkozy's political fortunes and saw him drop sharply in opinion polls. The couple, who married in 1996 after long and messy divorces from their former spouses, separated in 2005 when Cécilia went off to live in New York with French Jewish advertising executive Richard Attias. The French press reported at the time that Sarkozy was himself romantically involved with a woman journalist. But Cécilia, who had long played a key role in her husband's political career, came back to her husband in 2006, apparently on Sarkozy's insistent bidding. He proceeded to publicly flaunt their renewed relationship. Later newspaper reports said Cécilia returned because she did not wish to be blamed in case Sarkozy lost the election.

On election day Cécilia failed to accompany Sarkozy to vote (the two grown daughters from her first marriage did), and it turned out that she failed to vote altogether. Cécilia showed up late that evening. It was subsequently learned that the couple had already effectively separated again, and only reunited for his inauguration ceremony. It was carried on live television, and Sarkozy made several affectionate gestures towards his wife as the press photographers clicked away, but Cécilia looked embarrassed and distant. The proceedings were front-page news, and celebrity and gossip magazines had a field day, vastly increasing their circulations for months.

In August, the couple and their 11-year-old son Louis went on vacation with friends to Wolfeboro, New Hampshire. During their stay they were invited for a family lunch at the Bush residence in nearby Kennebunkport. Cécilia canceled her participation at the last minute, citing ill health. French journalists tailing the Sarkozys separately said they saw her shopping in Wolfeboro the same day. Before the visit, however, Cécilia had apparently played a role in the dramatic diplomatic mission to free five Bulgarian nurses and a Palestinian doctor who had been in Libyan jails for years on trumped-up charged of inoculating children with the HIV virus (see below, p. 382). Cécilia then dropped from public sight, and on October 18 it was announced that the couple had divorced. Cecilia apparently went straight back to Attias, telling reporters that attempts to repair her marriage with Sarkozy had failed. (Cécilia and Attias would wed in New York in March 2008.)

Within weeks Sarkozy was involved in a whirlwind romance with a Paris-based Italian singer-fashion model, Carla-Bruni Tedeschi (who like Sarkozy, had one Jewish grandfather), again amid a flurry of media attention clearly encouraged by the president. This proved a miscalculation as his popularity rates began to plummet. Many French people complained that the president had lost all dignity and was turning his office into the setting for a "Dallas"-like TV series. By the end of the year Sarkozy's approval rating had fallen from around 70 percent to half that figure, spelling major political trouble ahead.

Oddly enough, marital woes might also have affected Royal had she been elected. Her longtime companion and father of their four children was Socialist Party secretary general François Hollande, and during the campaign the press speculated about Hollande's potential role as male companion of the first woman president. But the couple almost never appeared together in public, and the one time they did, for a major election rally when they were both on stage, Hollande pressed a clumsy kiss on the candidate's cheek and Royal turned her head away, sparking much speculation. Shortly after her defeat, Royal issued a press communiqué saying that the couple had in fact separated some months before, apparently because Hollande was having an affair with another woman. "I wish him all the best in his new life," she said.

Aside from family issues, Sarkozy's presidency started out on a good footing as he received credit for clever high-level appointments, including some top figures lured from the opposition Socialists. Chief among these was humanitarian crusader Bernard Kouchner, a longtime health minister under President François Mitterrand, whom Sarkozy named foreign minister. Kouchner, whose father was Jewish, had long harbored his own presidential ambitions bolstered by strong personal popularity among the French public for his decades of media-attracting action as head of Médecins Sans Frontiers (Doctors Without Borders), an international disaster-relief group. Precisely because he was far more popular than any other left-wing politician, Kouchner was always a figure of suspicion in his own party, and his Socialist rivals blocked him from running for president. This made it all the easier for him to accept Sarkozy's offer of the prestigious foreign-affairs portfolio.

Another leading Socialist who allowed himself to be lured by Sarkozy was Dominique Strauss-Kahn, the Jewish former finance minister who had been one of the three finalists for his party's presidential nomination. Sarkozy told Strauss-Kahn that France would support him if he stood for the office of managing director of the Washington-based International Monetary Fund (IMF). Strauss-Kahn accepted the offer and the IMF indeed appointed him its head on September 28. Also lured from Socialist ranks were Jacques Lang, former culture minister, and Jacques Attali, long a close Mitterrand adviser. Both men (who were Jewish) accepted positions as members of top state advisory committees. Like Kouchner and Strauss-Kahn, they were assured of government-supplied offices and honors and were removed from the ranks of the active opposition.

An appointment of particular interest to Jews was that of Jean-David Levitte, France's ambassador to the U.S., as personal foreign-policy adviser to the president. Although his mother was not Jewish, Levitte's father was a major figure in the Jewish community during the late 1940s and 1950s, whose own parents were both murdered in the Holocaust. The younger Levitte belonged to the French Jewish Scout movement before entering university. During his years in the French diplomatic service he was not considered particularly friendly to Jewish concerns, especially when he was diplomatic adviser to President Chirac and later ambassador to the UN. But he seemed to warm to Jewish issues when serving as ambassador in Washington.

Sarkozy also scored coups by appointing Rachida Dati, 41, a little-known female magistrate born into a poor family of North African Muslim immigrants, as justice minister, and Senegalese-born Rama Yade, 30, as deputy foreign minister in charge of human rights. The moves were clearly overtures to the immigrant Arab and black African communities that distrusted Sarkozy because of his stance on immigration. Yade was married to a Jew, Joseph Zimet, son of a famous French Yiddish-language singer.

Sarkozy, who long had the reputation of being the most pro-American politician on the French scene but avoided foreign policy issues during the campaign, made a high-profile visit to the U.S. on November 6–7 that included an address before Congress that was interrupted about 20 times by applause. Presidential spokesman David Martinon told journalists as the visit began that its aim was to renew good relations that had soured after President Chirac actively campaigned to prevent the U.S. from launching the second Gulf War in 2003. While in the U.S. Sarkozy received the American Jewish Committee's "Light Unto the Nations" Award.

Elections for the National Assembly were held in June. Sarkozy supporters won 341 seats, a comfortable majority in the 577-seat lower house of France's parliament, but fewer than the 397 seats they won in the last such election in 2002.

Israel and the Middle East

Israel

"I have the reputation of being a friend of Israel. It's true. I will never compromise with Israel's security." French Jews were used to hearing such statements from the country's politicians before an election, but this time it was made by President Sarkozy after his election, and addressed to France's ambassadors abroad, summoned to a conference in Paris on August 27. In the same speech Sarkozy said that the prospect of a nuclear-armed Iran was the worst crisis facing the world and that Iran's possession of nuclear weapons was unacceptable to France. The major powers, he went on, should ratchet up sanctions against Tehran while at the same time showing openness to talks should Iran suspend its nuclear activities. The choice was clear, he declared, "the Iranian bomb or the bombing of Iran."

French Jewish leaders expressed hope that policy towards Israel would change notably for the better under the new government. Roger Cukierman, outgoing president of CRIF, told reporters soon after the election: "I hope to now see an improvement of relations between France and the Middle East, and especially, a true re-equilibrium of French policy towards the region. Until now Israel's friends were often former ministers and future ministers, but rarely serving ministers." Joël Mergui, president of the Paris Consistory, the board that administered synagogues and Jewish affairs in the capital, recalled that he had accompanied Sarkozy when the politician made his first visit to Israel, which was when it came under missile fire from Iraq during the first Gulf War in 1991: "Nicolas Sarkozy then came to demonstrate his solidarity with Israel. That act today still symbolizes his closeness to the State of Israel."

French Jews were especially heartened that Sarkozy chose Kouchner as foreign minister. Although coming from Socialist ranks, Kouchner was one of the rare French politicians to strongly back U.S. intervention in Iraq in 2003, and was a longtime proponent of a hard line against Iran and its nuclear ambitions, proposing sanctions and economic boycotts. During Israel's 2006 war in Lebanon, Kouchner said in an interview that France should "actively defend the citizens of Israel who have been attacked" and that UN forces should be given a mandate to disarm Hezbollah, although he did add that the movement could probably not be destroyed by force. Kouchner's positions led the Franco-Palestinian Solidarity Association to state that his nomination "was bad news for the Arabs." Kouchner, who received an honorary doctorate from the Hebrew University in Jerusalem in 2005, was Jewish on his father's side but did not have community ties. Two of his grandparents were killed in Auschwitz.

The improvement in ties between France and Israel following Sarkozy's election was highlighted during a three-day official visit to France, October 21–23, by Israeli prime minister Ehud Olmert, who held meetings with Sarkozy and other French leaders. His stay in France followed a preparatory visit by Foreign Minister Tzipi Livni in July. Olmert told journalists after meeting Sarkozy that France and Israel had identical views on the Iranian threat. "I couldn't have heard on the Iranian issue things that could more fall in line with my expectations," said Olmert. He noted that they did not discuss possible military action against Iran's nuclear program but focused rather on tougher sanctions. Just a month before, Kouchner had created a stir when he said in a radio interview that the world might have to get ready for war over Iran's nuclear ambitions. Dr. Richard Prasquier, the new head of CRIF, said that Sarkozy told Olmert "he did not understand how the Palestinians could still think of 'returning' to Israel, a country whose reason for being was to be a Jewish state. He said that with great conviction and understanding of Israeli realities. I can only hope that his position will remain the same."

Olmert also held emotional meetings with the French Jewish community, which he hailed as the "the warmest and closest to Israel in the world." It was later announced that Israeli president Shimon Peres would visit France in March 2008 and that Sarkozy would go to Israel several months later.

During the year, Foreign Minister Kouchner visited Israel twice, pledging friendship and support but also making clear that French backing was not unconditional. In his typically direct style, he told journalists on arrival: "I will tell the Israelis that settlement activity [across the Green Line] is not only illegal, it is also politically the main obstacle to peace. Increased settlement activity reinforces the [Palestinian] feeling of injustice and therefore increases lack of security."

On October 19, Paris mayor Bertrand Delanoë officially marked the erection, in the Yitzhak Rabin public garden in southern Paris, of a large scaffolding containing portraits of Gilad Shalit, Eldad Regev, and Ehud Goldwasser, the three Israeli soldiers held captive in the Gaza Strip and Lebanon since the summer of 2006. The ceremony was initiated by Siona, a Jewish group that campaigned to make the plight of the three known to the general public. In the weeks that followed the portraits were defaced several times by anti-Israel activists.

The Middle East and Radical Islam

Soon after his election Sarkozy sent Foreign Minister Kouchner on the first of a series of visits to Lebanon to try to reconcile the factions there and bolster the pro-Western administration of Prime Minister Fouad Siniora. Kouchner met with little success. On his first visit, May 24, he made clear that France wanted to keep Syria at arms length. He said he had come "to meet the personalities and political groups who are in favor of Lebanese unity, autonomy and territorial integrity. That means very clearly that we don't have to speak to Syria's leaders." He recalled that France strongly supported an international probe and international tribunal for the killers of former prime minister Rafiq Hariri, and claimed that the Lebanese national army was fully justified in trying to disarm Islamist militants who had taken over the Palestinian refugee camp at Nahr el-Bahred in northern Lebanon.

Kouchner organized talks at Le Celle St. Cloud, outside Paris, for July 14–15, inviting 28 representatives from 14 Lebanese factions including Hezballah, plus five representatives of "civil society." The sessions were inconclusive. Several French Jewish groups protested Hezballah's participation. Kouchner wrote a letter to them on July 25 saying that "there were several arguments that made it politically necessary to invite this group." One of these arguments was presumably the opportunity to learn the fate of the two Israeli soldiers kidnapped by the group in 2006, but no new information was forthcoming. There were at least eight visits to the region by Kouchner or his aides, plus telephone calls by Sarkozy to Syrian president Bashar Assad, before Sarkozy called it quits and said he was freezing diplomatic ties with Damascus.

Paris was also the scene, on December 16–17, of a conference of international donors for the Palestinians, at which a record seven billion dollars in aid was pledged by 68 countries and organizations. Top donors included the EU ($650 million in 2008); the U.S. ($555 million in 2008); Great Britain ($490 million over three years); Germany ($290 million over three years); and Japan ($150 million). U.S. secretary of state Condoleezza Rice said at the meeting that "this conference is literally the [Palestinian] government's last hope to avoid bankruptcy." Attended by Israeli foreign minister Livni, this meeting followed the U.S.-organized Middle East conference at Annapolis, Maryland, in November, which launched negotiations aimed at creating a Palestinian state within a year.

President Sarkozy paid a visit to Algeria on December 3–5 despite a major, last-minute roadblock. Algeria's minister of veterans' affairs, Mohammed Cherif Abbes, himself a veteran of Algeria's war of independence against France, said in a newspaper interview several days before the French leader's arrival that "Sarkozy is not welcome in Algeria. We know his origins and we know who brought him to power . . . the Jewish lobby, which dominates those who decide things in France and who hold a monopoly over its industries."

The statement came amid a campaign by Algerian authorities to dissuade Sarkozy from including the Algeria-born French Jewish singer Enrico Macias (born Gaston Grenassia) in his official party. Prime Minister Abdelaziz Belkhadem said he would refuse to shake Macias's hand if he came. Macias, who was enormously popular since emerging on the French scene shortly after fleeing independent Algeria together with more than 100,000 other Jews, was a longtime and highly committed backer of Israel. His popularity extended to the Algerian public as well, and Macias had often expressed the wish to revisit his homeland.

As the affair escalated with more anti-Semitic vitriol against both Sarkozy and Macias, there were calls in France for the president to cancel his own visit. Algerian president Abdelaziz Bouteflika finally telephoned Sarkozy to say that Abbes had spoken in his own name only and that his views did not reflect those of the Algerian government. But Sarkozy finally asked Macias to withdraw from the visit, telling him to "have patience."

The visit began in an extremely tense atmosphere when Sarkozy made clear, on Algerian soil, that he would not issue the public apology Algerian leaders expected for French colonial rule of the country that lasted from 1830 through 1962. However Sarkozy was accompanied by 150 French business leaders who arrived with promises of huge investments, and returned with $7 billion in contracts, including for civilian nuclear power stations. While he was in the country Sarkozy took a swipe at Algerian anti-Semitism in a speech, but also explained to journalists that it was necessary to maintain good ties with Algeria if only to combat a continuing, mostly low-key, but often bloody Islamic fundamentalist insurrection that Algerian authorities were trying to crush.

Yet another controversy erupted when Libyan leader Muammar Qaddafi arrived in France on December 10 for a five-day visit. This had been one of the conditions Qaddafi set in July when he released into French hands a group of Bulgarian nurses and a Palestinian doctor who had been held for years in Libyan jails on trumped-up charges that they had inoculated Libyan children with the HIV virus. The visit was roundly criticized by the French press not only because the motorcades snarled Paris traffic for days, but also because the Libyan leader made outlandish comments denying that his was a dictatorial state. Several Jewish groups issued statements recalling the role of Qaddafi's Libya in international terrorism, but they remained relatively low key and avoided blaming Sarkozy personally for the visit. The president's office said it was better to bring Libya back in "out of the cold" than to reject it and possibly induce it to resume with its old ways. The meetings also yielded close to $10 billion in contracts for France.

On January 3, French authorities expelled an extremist Muslim imam back to his native Morocco after several unheeded warnings about his lecturing in a prayer hall near Paris against Jews, woman, and non-Muslims. Ahmed al-Fatmi, 62, had resided in France for ten years and preached in Grigny, an area where clashes between police and local Arab youths were common. This expulsion followed another two weeks earlier (in late 2006) to Tunisia of Bilal Chouhir, a preacher in the central France city of Lyons. Chouhir was reported to have made death threats against French government ministers and journalists, and to have "publicly incited for holy war against Western society by all possible means."

During the course of the year police announced the arrests of 89 Islamic fundamentalists. Eleven of them were picked up on February 14 in southwest France and in the greater Paris area as part of a crackdown on an Islamist network that sent young French Arabs to fight against the U.S.-led coalition in Iraq. These arrests followed the return to France the previous day of two French Arabs arrested in Syria and sent back to France by that country, who then gave information about the others. Among those arrested was a Zairean Muslim, the first time a sub-Saharan African was arrested in France in connection with the Iraq conflict.

A French court, on October 10, rejected a request for parole submitted by Lebanese national Georges Ibrahim Abdallah, who had been jailed for life since 1984 on charges of murdering a U.S. defense attaché, Colonel Charles Ray, and Israeli diplomat Yaacov Bar Simantov in 1982. A note from DST, the French counterespionage agency, was read before the court saying Abdallah was still a threat to France and that his release would be celebrated as a victory by extremist groups. Now aged 57, Abdallah was acting on behalf of a faction within the Popular Front for the Liberation of Palestine when arrested. The court said one reason for its decision to deny parole was that Abdallah had never expressed regret for his acts.

The Palestine Liberation Organization (PLO) office in France and the Franco-Palestinian Solidarity Association appealed before a French court on October 29 for the nullification of a contract under which the French firms Alstom and Véolia would build a light railway in Jerusalem. Since the route would include areas of the city taken over during the June 1967 war and reach the new Jewish neighborhoods of Pisgat Ze'ev and French Hill, the Arab groups declared this a violation of the Geneva Convention banning the settlement of populations in occupied areas. Lawyers for the firms countered that French courts had no jurisdiction over the case since the contract was being executed abroad. A decision was expected in 2008.

Racism and Anti-Semitism

In one of his last major speeches before leaving office, outgoing president Chirac delivered a televised exhortation to the French on March 11: "Never compromise with extremism, racism, anti-Semitism or the rejection of 'the other.' In our history, extremism nearly led us into the precipice. It is a poison which divides, which perverts, and which destroys. The soul of France says no to extremism." Chirac said that "in the face of religious extremism, France must defend tolerance, dialogue and respect between men and cultures. Failure to do this will endanger peace and the security of mankind." He concluded with a personal testament: "All my life, I have fought for justice, for progress, for peace, and for the grandeur of France." French Jews, who generally felt that Chirac had been consistently aloof, even cold, toward the State of Israel, gave him credit for being highly attuned to domestic Jewish sensitivities.

The annual report on racist violence published by the state-run National Consultative Commission on Human Rights counted 386 anti-Semitic acts in France in 2007, a drop of 32.5 percent from the 571 such acts reported in 2006. Jews were not the main victims of racism, the report showed, as 68 percent of those subjected to racist violence in France and 60 percent of those receiving racist threats were of North African Arab origin. To be sure, that community, constituting between five and six million people, was ten times larger than French Jewry.

Another audit of anti-Semitic acts during 2007 was prepared by the Service de Protection de la Communauté Juive (Jewish Community Protection Service, or SPCJ), the Jewish organizations' own security service that worked in close coordination with the police. It counted 256 incidents, down 31 percent from the 371 in 2006 (the 2005 figure was exactly 300). Included in the 2007 figure were 143 acts of violence against people and property, as compared to 213 in 2006, a 33-percent decline. The number of physical attacks on people was 71; there were 112 in 2006. The figure for threats, either direct or by mail or telephone, dropped 28.5 percent, from 158 in 2006 to 113.

The SPCJ report cautioned that the picture it gave might understate the problem, since the data only included cases where the anti-Semitic motive was proved beyond the shadow of a doubt. Excluded were "opportunistic" crimes, for example young French Arabs beating up a young Jew they happen upon by chance in the subway, where the anti-Semitic factor may be an aggravating factor in general delinquency. Since 2004, the report noted, the monthly trend of anti-Semitic acts no longer followed the levels of tension in the Middle East, as had been the case from 2000 through 2004. In fact for 2007 "references to the conflict between Israel and Palestine are almost completely absent . . . from statements and gestures that accompany or motivate anti-Semitic acts. " Despite the lower numbers, warned the report, "We still have a feeling of uncertainty with regard to the phenomenon; it is unstable, unpredictable and likely to change in unexpected ways; it requires extreme vigilance, both by the government and by the CRIF and the SPCJ."

A specially prepared brochure was published highlighting examples of anti-Semitic incidents in 2007. Among them were the following:

April 7: An Algerian man drove his car directly at two yarmulke-wearing youths in the city of Lyons, hitting one of them. The victim was thrown over the hood of the car and suffered injuries to the face and to one knee. The perpetrator was arrested.

April 22: The mezuzah was violently torn off the main entrance hall of the Jewish community center at Neuilly-sur-Seine, an affluent Paris suburb.

May 6: Two petrol bombs were thrown into a yeshiva in the town of Saint Louis in eastern France. There were no injuries and no damage.

June 23: A 13-year-old Jewish boy was attacked in the rough east Paris suburb of Villemomble by a group of men who punched him and threw him against a parked car, shouting such taunts as "We're going to get this Jew." The youth suffered a concussion but his family refused to press charges for fear of reprisals.

August 24: Arson caused serious damage to a Jewish prayer hall, once again in Saint Louis. No injuries were reported.

September 21: A group of 25 people wearing yarmulkes were the target of stones thrown by a group of nine individuals, who resisted arrest when police arrived. The incident took place in a rough Paris suburb.

November 14: A bottle containing firecrackers was thrown into the home of a Jewish family in Gagny, also a tough suburb of the French capital. The assailants could not be identified, but Gagny had a large Muslim minority and particularly active street gangs. The same family had been the object of earlier death threats and anti-Semitic insults.

The French press during the year reported many other stories relating to anti-Semitism. The first was on January 18, when a Paris court fined Bruno Gollnisch, the number-two figure in Jean-Marie Le Pen's National Front, 55,000 euros for challenging the truth of crimes against humanity, an offense under French law. During a news conference in 2004, Gollnisch said he did not doubt that millions had died in concentration camps or that gas chambers had existed, but added, "On the subject, however, of how people died there, I believe a debate should be held. I am not a specialist on such issues and I believe that historians should discuss this issue freely." The presiding judge said Gollnisch's remarks strongly insinuated that millions had not been killed in gas chambers

A juvenile court on March 19 sentenced two youths of North African Arab origin and another of Asian origin to suspended nine-month terms for throwing improvised explosive devices into the recreation yard of a Jewish school in Paris in 2005. The prosecutor told the youths that they were getting off lightly only because they had no prior criminal records.

Two anti-Semitic incidents occurred in March. A kippah-wearing 13-year-old Jewish boy was attacked and beaten up by fourth youths of black African origin on his way home from school in a tough north Paris neighborhood on March 20. And on the last day of the month about 50 tombstones were overturned in the Jewish section of a municipal cemetery at Lille in northern France. There was no indication of who was responsible. Outgoing president Chirac sent a message of sympathy to the local Jewish community condemning the outrage.

Orthodox rabbi Élie Dahan was attacked on April 19 by a man of black African or West Indian origin in the Gare du Nord train station in Paris and suffered facial injuries. The rabbi, easily identifiable by his clothing and beard, was walking in the station when his assailant shouted at him: "Don't look at me, dirty Jew. I'm going to hit you, dirty Jew !" The attacker fled immediately and was not apprehended.

A Paris court on May 21 dismissed a libel suit brought by former university professor Robert Faurisson, a Holocaust denier, against former French justice minister Robert Badinter. The ex-minister, a Jew whose father was killed at Auschwitz, had described Faurisson during a television appearance in November 2006 as "already sentenced before courts as a falsifier of history." The court, agreeing with Badinter's defense that Faurisson falsified history by saying there were no gas chambers, threw out the case and ordered Faurisson to pay 5,000 euros for court expenses.

Two days later a Paris appeals court dismissed as unfounded a libel suit brought by leftist Israeli filmmaker Eyal Dayan against French Jewish philosopher Alain Finkielkraut, who had accused Dayan of being "an anti-Semitic Jew." Finkielkraut leveled the charge in 2003 on a radio program while commenting on a full-length documentary film made by Sivan, who lived in Paris, about the Israel-Palestinian conflict. The court found that Finkielkraut's words did not constitute libel.

In June, in the eastern France city of Reims, a handicapped Jewish woman who was swimming in a local public pool asked some youths to let her pass. One of them, seeing the Star of David around her neck, responded with anti-Semitic insults and struck her in the back. The 15-year-old boy—who, as it turned out, already had a police record—was charged with assault and public expression of anti-Semitism.

An appeals court in Dijon in central France confirmed a sentence on June 28 against a teenage girl of North African Arab origin who proffered anti-Semitic insults against Franco-Israeli singer Shirel during a concert in the region in 2004. The accused was sentenced to 140 hours of community service, as well as payment of a symbolic one euro in damages and 1,500 euros in legal fees. The accused had denied responsibility when the case was tried in a lower court, but the appeals court confirmed the sentenced after seeing television news footage of the incident.

That same day a court in Chartres, south of Paris, sentenced black nationalist Stelio Capo Chichi, also known as Kemi Seba, to a six-month suspended prison term and a fine of 1,500 euros for making violently anti-Semitic public statements in February 2007, when addressing customers emerging from a local supermarket. Another member of the same group, Cyrille Kamdem, got a three-month suspended sentence and a 750-euro fine on the same charge, and also had to pay 1,000 euros in damages to an antiracist group.

On August 28, a Paris court sentenced Nizar Ouedrani to nine months in prison for seriously injuring Yosef Zekri with a lead pipe in July as the latter was on his way to his Paris synagogue. The accused, who was of North African Arab origin, said he did not act out of anti-Semitic motives, but rather lost his temper during a traffic argument. Witnesses, however, testified that Ouedrani shouted, "I'm going to finish you off dirty Jew," as he attacked Zekri, who suffered a broken arm, needed stitches for a head wound, and had to wear a neck brace for several weeks.

Three French neo-Nazis were sentenced on September 12 to prison terms ranging up to 30 months for daubing Nazi graffiti on 117 graves in the centuries-old Jewish cemetery at Herrlisheim in Alsace on April 30, 2004, Hitler's birthday. The principal accused, Emmanuel Rist, was also facing the prospect of a separate trial for the murder, in 2001, of a Moroccan shopkeeper, a crime to which he admitted but that he insisted had no racial motive. The two other accused, Laurent Boulanger and Laurent Petterschmidt, respectively received terms of 18 months and one year plus six months suspended for the cemetery affair.

A Paris court on October 16 sentenced Franco-Ivorian Youssouf Fofana, the main suspect in the Ilan Halimi murder case of 2006, to a year's imprisonment on the charge of insulting magistrates. Fofana had been in prison since his extradition from the Ivory Coast, where he had fled after the tortured body of the Jewish telephone salesman was found abandoned near Paris on February 13, 2006. The death of Halimi, who had been kidnapped for ransom because he was a Jew, was one of the greatest shocks suffered by French Jewry since the end of World War II (see AJYB 2007, pp. 360–62). At a yet-to-be-determined date in 2008, 20 people were to stand trial for their roles in Halimi's murder.

Fofana's October 16 trial appearance followed a letter he wrote to instructing magistrate Corinne Goetzmann, saying "I s . . . on you." Fofana initially refused to answer questions, and then donned a religious Muslim's skullcap and declared: "I am a symbolic war trophy . . . . I am the ally of the Muslims and the Africans against the bearded kippah-wearers. In the name of Allah, I shall be freed by commandos backed by oil money." Halimi's body, which had been buried near Paris, was reburied on February 9 at the Givat Shaul cemetery in Jerusalem in an emotional ceremony addressed by French chief rabbi Joseph Sitruk and French ambassador to Israel Jean-Michel Casa.

A court in the Alsatian town of Saverne sentenced already convicted Holocaust denier Vincent Reynouard to a year in prison and a fine of 10,000 euros for writing, having published, and having distributed to various public institutions, such as museums and city halls, a 16-page brochure entitled *The Holocaust — What Is Hidden from You.* Raynouard had previously been sentenced to a suspended prison term and fine in 1996 on similar charges. He was then fired from his job as a public school teacher and moved to Belgium. Reynouard was arrested during a visit to France. He immediately appealed the sentence, and, allowed to remain free until the appeals trial, went back to Belgium. Should he lose the appeal Reynouard would have to be extradited to serve his sentence.

A Paris appeals court confirmed, on November 15, a lower court ruling sentencing "comedian" Dieudonné M'bala M'bala to a 5,000-euro fine for incitement to racial hatred against Jews. Dieudonné, the son of a black father from Cameroon and a French white mother, had for some years indulged in anti-Semitic "humor." After Jews demonstrated against him during one of his performances, he told a newspaper interviewer that the demonstrators were "reconverted former slave traders" who now "specialized in banking, entertainment and terrorism, and who support Arik Sharon," and reiterated that "those who attack me made their fortunes in the slave trade." After being sued by several Jewish and antiracist groups for these remarks, he attempted to enlist support among black nationalist groups in France. Dieudonné told the appeals court that his initial statements were aimed solely at "Israeli diamond dealers" who, he said, backed the former apartheid regime in South Africa. The court rejected his defense, ruling that the incriminating interview was clearly aimed at all Jews.

On November 22, a Paris appeals court heard a request for reopening legal proceedings in the case of Sébastien Selam, a Jewish disc jockey who was 23 years old when he was murdered in 2003 by Abdel Amastaibou, a Moroccan-born neighbor. Amastaibou, then 20, knifed Selam to death in the basement garage of their apartment building, disfigured his body, and was arrested when he appeared on the street covered in blood and shouting, "I am going to heaven because I killed a Jew." He had been declared insane at the time and was committed to a mental hospital. Now, however, he was allowed to leave for occasional family visits, and Selam's family wanted a new psychological examination and a trial if he were found sane. Lawyer Axel Metzker recalled that, when the murder took place, Amastaibou had already been accused in court of making death threats and anti-Semitic insults against a neighborhood rabbi. (The court, on January 21, 2008, would accept the family's request and order a new examination.)

Jews were sometimes the aggressors. On January 7, Jewish youths beat up and injured two black sanitation workers in the Rue de Roisiers, the heart of the Jewish neighborhood of the Marais district in central Paris. The victims were driving a garbage truck and picking up refuse when the youths hurled insults at them, provoking the driver to come down from the vehicle. He was then assaulted and beaten with wooden stools from a nearby open-air restaurant and with heavy motorcycle helmets, as was his partner who came to his rescue. Police arrested four of the assailants. There had been several previous incidents in the area involving Jewish toughs who harassed passersby they felt "should not be in the neighborhood." Police sources said the same youths were often found in the sometimes violent demonstrations organized by the French branch of the Jewish Defense League.

The latest attack was condemned by CRIF and by the mayor of Paris, while black nationalist groups threatened retaliation. Members of "Tribu Ka," a black extremist group that had been banned by the authorities, demonstrated outside the neighborhood police station to protest what they said was police inaction against the Jewish gang. The blacks also threatened to track down the perpetrators themselves, as they tried to do in May 2006 when several dozen of them threw their weight around the Rue des Rosiers for 30 minutes before the arrival of police (see AJYB 2007, p. 368).

Holocaust-Related Matters

President Chirac officiated at the January 18 national day of tribute for French nationals declared "Righteous among the Nations" by Jerusalem's Yad Vashem for saving Jews during World War II. The main ceremony took place at the Panthéon, in the heart of the Latin Quarter in Paris, where French national heroes were buried. Chirac's speech, widely considered among the best he had ever made, repeated some of the themes from the ground-breaking address he made in July 1995, shortly after taking office, when he officially acknowledged Vichy French responsibility in the Holocaust. "The Talmud says that to save a life is to save the universe . . . and the memory of the righteous shall be cherished for generations," he said.

The Panthéon was transformed for a week, made into an exhibit hall in honor of the approximately 2,700 French nationals recognized as "Righteous" by Yad Vashem (out of a total of 22,000 from all countries), credited with saving about 30,000 Jews. Some 76,000, about a quarter of those in France at the time, died during the Holocaust. Chirac spoke after Simone Veil, a former European Parliament president and French cabinet minister and herself an Auschwitz survivor, praised Chirac, saying: "To have recognized the responsibility of the French [Vichy] state in the anti-Jewish persecutions and to now indelibly mark the memory of the Righteous allows one reasons for hope." Parallel ceremonies took place around France.

France's Shoah Memorial opened an exhibit on June 20 whose subject was the killing of 1.5 million Jews in Ukraine by Nazi firing squads *(Einsatzgruppen)*. The exhibit, originally scheduled to close November 30 but prolonged to January 6, 2008, due to huge public interest, was based on the work of French Catholic priest Patrick Desbois and his Yahad-In Unum foundation for Christian-Jewish understanding. Dubois, head of the Commission for Relations with Judaism of the French Bishops' Conference, had scoured Ukraine since 2004, returning several times each year for an average of 15 weeks annually, to locate "killing fields" that held the remains of Jews massacred by the Nazis.

In what was believed to be the first-ever ceremony where a president of France decorated both a mother and her son together, Nicolas Sarkozy honored Beate Klarsfeld and her son Arno at the Élysée presidential palace on November 23. Beate was promoted to the rank of officer in the national order of the Legion of Honor, while Arno was made a chevalier (knight) of the Order of Merit. Beate, a German-born Protestant, had devoted her life to hunting Nazis and honoring the Shoah dead, together with her husband, Serge, who was already an officer of the Legion of Honor. A lawyer like his father, Arno was honored for his role in human rights causes. He had taken a year off from his practice at the height of the Palestinian intifada to serve as a volunteer with the Israeli Border Police in the Jerusalem area.

The 2007 Shoah Memorial Prize went to painter Alain Kleinmann for his life's work, and to Shlomo Venezia for his autobiography *Son-derKommando—In the Hell of the Gas Chambers,* written with Béatrice Prasquier.

JEWISH COMMUNITY

Demography

In November, Fonds Social Juif Unifié, the social welfare arm of France's Jewish community, presented the results of a study it had sponsored of French Jewry that was conducted by Israeli sociologist Erik Cohen, who had been born and educated in France. The study, based largely on telephone interviews with sample groups of French Jews, was entitled *Happy as Jews in France,* a play on the Yiddish expression, "Happy as God in France." The data showed that 91 percent of the Jewish heads of households questioned said they were "happy" or "very happy" with their everyday lives (68 percent "happy," 23 percent "very happy"), as compared to 7 percent who were unhappy and 2 percent who were very unhappy. Another interesting finding was that the number of Jewish children attending Jewish day schools had shot up from 400 in 1950, to nearly 8,000 in 1978, and to more than 30,000 in 2007, a third of all Jewish children of school age. A major reason for the most recent rise was parents' assumption that their children would be safer in Jewish schools.

The March 1 issue of the Catholic weekly *La Vie* published the results of a survey it conducted among a representative group of 1,000 people to measure religious influence in France. It showed that 64 percent of the French declared themselves "close" to Roman Catholicism, 3 percent said they were close to Islam, and only 0.6 percent professed closeness to Judaism. Some 27 percent said they were atheists. The same poll said that of those polled, the highest number of those close to Judaism were in the Paris area, where the figure was 3.7 percent. About half of France's estimated 600,000 Jews lived in the capital.

Communal Developments

Dr. Richard Prasquier, a 62-year-old cardiologist, was elected president of CRIF on May 13. The Polish-born Prasquier, who arrived in France as a small child, succeeded Roger Cukierman, who served since 2001. Prasquier edged out three other candidates, Arieh Bensemhoun, president of CRIF in the southwest city of Toulouse; Henri Hajdenberg, a past CRIF president; and Jo Zrihen, the CRIF vice president. Bensemhoun and Zrihen were Sephardim from North Africa, and many had expected that one of them would win since Sephardim now outnumbered Ashkenazim in France by 70 percent to 30, and the overwhelming majority of young community activists were Sephardim. CRIF officials explained that Prasquier's victory demonstrated the absence in France of the kind of ethnic Jewish antagonisms sometimes found in Israel, and that Prasquier was elected on the basis of his considerable work on behalf of the community.

Prasquier was the longtime president of the French Committee for Yad Vashem and had also served as adviser to outgoing CRIF president Cukierman. His previous CRIF responsibilities were head of international affairs and point man for relations with the Catholic Church. His excellent contacts in Franch society were underlined soon after his election, when it became known that President Sarkozy would be guest of honor at the next annual CRIF dinner, scheduled for February 13, 2008. Sarkozy would thus be first French head of state to attend the event, which was the highlight of the French Jewish calendar.

Prasquier, a personal friend of Sarkozy, was formally received by him on July 24 to discuss French Jewish affairs. He told reporters afterward that the French leader assured him he would do everything possible to have Israel admitted to the Francophonie, the International Organization of French-speaking countries (including countries like Israel, where French, although not an official language, was spoken by many), a move long opposed by Lebanon, another member state. Sarkozy also told Prasquier that he had invited Israeli president Shimon Peres to visit France. Sarkozy invited Prasquier to accompany him as a member of the official delegation when the French president paid an official visit to the U.S. in November. Prasquier's presence in the group was criticized by pro-Palestinian groups in France.

The Reform movement in France, called *judaïsme libérale,* celebrated its centennial during the week of December 4–11, with much attention focused on the Union Libérale Israélite de France (ULIF), the first Reform organization in the country. While it was extremely active in France, Reform had the allegiance of only about 20 percent of French Jews, predominantly from the middle and upper classes. The majority of religiously affiliated French Jews, who attended Orthodox synagogues where the liturgy was usually based on the North African tradition, were generally of lower-middle-class and blue-collar background.

French Jews and Israel

There were 2,717 immigrants from France to Israel in 2007, a slight drop from 2006, when there were 2,838, and 2005, when there were 3,005, the highest annual figure since 1968. The overall figure for immigration to Israel from all countries for 2007 was about 19,700, the lowest in 20 years.

In 2007 there were also 382 "returnees," French Jews coming back home after having left to settle in Israel. The equivalent figure for 2006 was 429. Although no details were available, most of the returnees were believed to have gone back because of disappointment with Israel or because they found the going too tough—a frequent phenomenon with "immigrants of choice," Jews from Western countries who had the alternative of changing their minds. Israeli officials in Paris privately said that 25–30 percent of immigrants from France left Israel to return home within five years. Another reason for return may have emerged in 2007, a sense that the election results might make France friendlier to Jews. David Roche, head of the Jewish Agency in France, told the weekly newspaper *Actualité Juive,* in an interview published December 13, "I suppose that the election of Nicolas Sarkozy had its effect on the French Jewish community [in bringing aliyah figures down] even though the decision to make aliyah is a personal and intimate one . . . ."

Israeli authorities and French Jewish groups had programs in Israel to aid the immigrants during the first difficult years, particularly in settling them in towns where there were already numerous French speakers, such as Netanya and Ashdod. Roche said that a new Website would be launched in February 2008 to make it easier for potential immigrants from France to find jobs in Israel.

The attachment of many French Jews to Israel was again demonstrated by tourism figures. In 2007 about 250,000 French tourists visited Israel, and approximately 85 percent of them were Jewish. France was the second largest contributor of tourists to Israel for the year, after the U.S. (542,000 visitors). The Israel government tourism office in Paris calculated that some 95 percent of the visitors from France had been in Israel at least once before.

Culture

The Museum of Jewish Art and History in Paris held an exhibition from March 28 through July 1 on "Rembrandt and the New Jerusalem: Jews and Christians in Amsterdam in the Golden Century." Featuring a number of Rembrandt masterpieces, it drew some 56,000 visitors and received exceptional reviews from the media. The exhibit was accompanied by lectures about the history of the period and Jewish life in Amsterdam.

The Paris-based UN Educational, Scientific and Cultural Organization (UNESCO) decided on November 7 to add the name of Eliezer Ben-Yehuda, the father of modern Hebrew, to the list of those personalities who most influenced world culture. Born Eliezer Perlman in Lithuania in 1855, Ben-Yehuda came to Paris for medical studies but then decided to devote his life to the renaissance of Hebrew, and settled in Ottoman-ruled Palestine in 1881. Founder of the Hebrew-language weekly *Hatszvi,* he published the first modern Hebrew dictionary in 1909.

Organizers of the annual Paris Book Fair (Le Salon du Livre), one of the largest events of its kind in Europe, announced in December that the 2008 event, to be held March 14–19, would honor Hebrew literature, and that Israel would be the fair's guest of honor. The focus on Israel was in recognition of Israel's impending 60th anniversary. Some 40 Israeli authors, including Amos Oz, A.B. Yehoshua, and David Grossman, were expected to attend and discuss their works.

A good number of original works of Jewish interest were published in France during the year.

Novels: Serge Koster's *Ces choses qui blessent le coeur* (These Things that Wound the Heart); Yves-Victor Kamani's *Le onzième Templier* (The Eleventh Templar); Myriam Anissimov's *Vie et de mort de Samuel Rozowski* (The Life and Death of Samuel Rozowski); Alain Suied's *Laisser partir* (To Let Go); Yaël König's *Cinq sous et un miracle* (Five Pennies and a Miracle); Joëlle Perelberg's *Oncle Isak* (Uncle Isak); Liliane Atlas's *Le Mâitre des eaux amères* (The Master of the Bitter Waters); and Cyrille Fleischmann's *Riverains rêveurs du metro Bastille* (Dreaming Neighbors of the Bastille Metro Station).

Judaism: Linda Toros's *La Lettre Sépharade* (The Sephardi Letter); Betty Rojtman's *Moïse, prophète des nostalgies* (Moses, Prophet of Nostalgias); Théo Klein's *Une manière d'etre Juif* (A Way of Being Jewish); Mireille Hadas-Lebel's *Philon d'Alexandrie* (Philo of Alexandria); Shmuel Trigano's *Le Monde sépharade* (The Sephardi World); Marie Vidal's *Les sept prophetesses* (The Seven Women Prophets); Johann Sfar's cartoon book *Le chat du Rabbin—Jérusalem d'Afrique* (The Rabbi's Cat—Jerusalem of Africa); Hélène Hadas-Lebel's *Rites et fêtes du Judaisme* (Rites and Holidays of Judaism); Michel de Saint-Chéron's *Sur le chemin de Jérusalem* (On the Path towards Jerusalem); Rafael Draï's *Abraham ou la recreation du monde* (Abraham or the Recreation of the World); Jacquot Gunwald's *Le bonheur de vivre à Jérusalem* (The Joy of Living in Jerusalem); Claude Bochurberg's *Levinas ou la brisure de la coque* (Levinas or the Shattering of the Shell); and Sébastien Tank-Storper's *Juifs d'election: se convertir au Judaïsme* (Jews by Choice: Conversion to Judaism).

Ideas and current events: Johann Sfar's *Pascin;* Pascal Ory's *Goscinny;* Noam Ohana's *Journal de guerre* (War Diary); Benôit Rayski's *Là où vont les cigognes* (Where the Storks Go); Élie Barnavi's *Les religions meurtrières* (The Murderous Religions); Ernest Gugenheim's *Lettres de Mir* (Letters from Mir); Alain Finkielkraut's *Ce que peut la literature* (What Literature Can Do); Rovert Redeckers' *Il faut tenter de vivre* (One Must Try to Live); Christiane Lecerf's *L'entretien* (The Interview); Marie-Christine Weiner's *Les sorbier de Transylvanie* (The Sorb from Transylvania); Bruno Durocher's *Ni idoles, ni étoiles* (Neither Idols Nor Stars); Frantz Vaillant's *Roland Topor ou le rire étranglé* (Roland Topor or the Strangled Laugh); Georges Bensoussan's *Europe, Une passion génocidaire* (Europe, a Genocidal Passion); Jeanne Favret-Saada's *Comment produire une crise mondiale avec douze petits dessins* (How to Provoke a World Crisis with 12 Little Drawings); Line Meller-Saïd's *Blida et des poussières* (Blida and a Few Specks); Henri Raczymow's *Dix jours "polonais"* (Ten "Polish" Days); Jean Cayrol's *Oeuvres lazaréennes* (The Works of Lazarus); Jacques Semelin's *Purifier et détruire: Usages politiques des massacres et genocides* (Purify and Destroy: The Political Use of Massacres and Genocides); Claude Mouchard's *Qui si je criais* (Who If I Shouted); and Anny Dayan Rosenmann's *Les Alphabets de la Shoah* (Alphabets of the Shoah).

History and biography: Claudine Drame's *Reflets de la Shoah au Cinéma 1945–1985* (The Shoah as Reflected in the Movies, 1945–1985); Simone Veil's autobiography, *Une Vie* (A Life); Olivier Guez's *L'Impossible retour* (The Impossible Return); Viviane Teitlebaum-Hirsch's *Enfants cachés, Les larmes sous le masque* (Hidden Children—The Tears under the Mask); David Shapira's *Jacob Kaplan—un rabbin du XXe siècle* (Jacob Kaplan—A Rabbi of the Twentieth Century); Shlomo Venezia and Béatrice Prasquier's *Sonderkommando—Dans l'enfer des chambers à gaz* (Sonderkommando—In the Hell of the Gas Chambers); Alain

Michel's *Jules Braunschvig, Juif humanist, L'homme et l'Alliance* (Jules Braunschvig, Humanist Jew—The Man and the Alliance); Berthe Burko-Falcmann's *Un prénom républicain* (A Republican First Name); Catherine Poujol and Fabien Lacaf's *Les enfants cachés, l'affaire Finaly* (Hidden Children—The Finaly Case); and Pascal Vandier's *Anatole France et l'anti-Sémitisme—Un témoin engagé dans l'Affaire Dreyfus* (Anatole France and anti-Semitism—A Witness Engaged in the Dreyfus Case).

Among the outstanding films of Jewish interest were Marco Carmel's *Comme ton père* (Like Your Father), about an Israeli family settling in France; Ariel Zeitoun's *Le dernier gang* (The Last Gang), about a real gang of mostly Jewish bank robbers that operated in France in the early 1980s; Néomie Lvovsky's *Faut que ça danse* (There Has To Be Dancing), a comedy about an aging Shoah survivor's search for love; Claude Miller's *Le secret* (The Secret), a film adaptation of author Philippe Grimbert's book about his family's wartime tribulations in occupied France; and Idit Cebula's *Deux vies plus une* (Two Lives Plus One), a bittersweet Jewish family drama.

Necrology

The body of David Dahan, 54, head of the Israeli Defense Ministry's purchasing mission in Europe, was found floating in the Seine River near the Normandy city of Rouen on February 21. Dahan disappeared from his home in Paris on January 21 leaving a note that suggested he was contemplating suicide and asked forgiveness from his family. Investigators initially kept all options open, including foul play, but they later said it appeared that Dahan had become depressed because his wife would not move with him to Paris, and subsequently, from their home in Israel, asked for a divorce. Israeli defense minister Amir Peretz paid a quick visit to Paris on January 31 that was believed connected to the disappearance. Peretz presumably met with French officials investigating the case.

Catholic priest Henri Groués died on January 22, aged 94. Better known as "l'Abbé Pierre," he saved Jewish children during World War II but provoked intense controversy by making anti-Semitic statements toward the end of his life. Groués became one of France's most popular personalities in the early 1950s, when he led campaigns to help the homeless at a time when France had yet to emerge from postwar poverty. Since then he supported many other social causes, each time bringing his prestige to bear on government ministers. Long an honorary board member of LICRA, a group that campaigned against anti-Semitism and racism,

Groués caused pained astonishment in 1996 when he defended Roger Garaudy, a former communist intellectual who converted to Islam and became a leading Holocaust denier. Stung by the criticism directed against him, Groués lashed out, saying that Jews in Israel had gone "from being victims to being executioners," and that his opponents were "inspired by the international Zionist lobby." At his death, however, Patrick Gaubert, the Jewish president of LICRA, which had expelled Groués from its board, said: "He was a giant of a man. We were angered against him at one time for extremely justifiable reasons. But nonetheless, overall, he was a giant of a man."

Baron Guy de Rothschild, retired banker, Jewish communal activist, and former senior figure of the French branch of his celebrated family, died on June 12 at the age of 98. He was a former president of the Rothschild Bank and a leading figure both in French aristocratic circles and among horse-breeders. He left France for the U.S. after Germany occupied the country in 1940, but joined the Free French forces, and returned with them to Europe as an officer shortly after D-Day. His bank, taken from him by Vichy authorities during the war, was again nationalized in 1981, this time by Socialist president François Mitterrand. Guy de Rothschild left France the following year, saying: "I was a Jew under Pétain and now I'm a pariah under Mitterrand. Enough is enough." He returned nevertheless in 1984. Rothschild created the FSJU, the social welfare arm of French Jewry, in 1949, and served as its president until 1982. During the June 1967 Six-Day War he was president of the coordinating committee that mobilized French Jewry and its non-Jewish friends in favor of Israel. His son, David, a prominent business leader, was serving as president of the French Shoah Memorial Foundation.

Cardinal Jean-Marie Lustiger died on August 5, aged 80. He had been born a Jew, Aron Lustiger, in 1926, the grandson of a Polish rabbi and the son of recent immigrants to France. Hidden by his parents in a Catholic boarding school during World War II, he decided to convert to Catholicism at the age of 14. His mother was killed at Auschwitz, but his father and sister survived the war and remained Jewish. Lustiger was ordained as a priest in 1954 and was long the very popular chaplain of Catholic students at Paris University. He was appointed bishop of Orleans before becoming archbishop of Paris, and then cardinal in 1983.

Lustiger always insisted that he remained a Jew even after becoming a Catholic, which long caused unease among the French rabbinate, which feared he had a hidden agenda of converting Jews. In fact, Jewish leaders later acknowledged that Lustiger turned out to be the best friend

French Jewry ever had in the French Catholic hierarchy. He played a key role in obtaining the removal of a Carmelite convent from the grounds of the former Auschwitz camp; initiated the ceremony of public repentance by France's bishops for the Church's failure to speak more forcefully against anti-Jewish persecutions during World War II; and played a major role in organizing Pope John Paul II's visit to Israel in 2000. In 2005, he was the pope's personal representative at the 60th anniversary ceremonies of the freeing of the last inmates of Auschwitz.

His funeral service, in the presence of President Sarkozy, former Polish president Lech Walesa, and many top figures in the French government, was a stunning demonstration of Catholic-Jewish reconciliation. Before the coffin was brought into Nôtre Dame Cathedral for a Catholic service attended by leading churchmen, it was laid on trestles just outside the cathedral for a brief Jewish religious tribute that had been conceived by Lustiger himself and outlined in his will. A cousin recited the kaddish prayer over the coffin, onto which earth gathered in Jerusalem had been placed.

Celebrated mime Marcel Marceau died in Montauban, southwest France, on September 22—Yom Kippur—aged 84. Born Marcel Mangel in Strasbourg, capital of the province of Alsace, he was the son of a kosher butcher who was deported and killed at Auschwitz. Marceau was a member of the French Resistance during the war, and afterwards studied theater. His best known character was a sad-faced clown with dark eyes and a reddish mouth. He was an internationally recognized star, and tributes poured in from all over the world at his death. At Marceau's request, the only speaker at his funeral was René-Samuel Sirat, the former chief rabbi of France.

BERNARD EDINGER

Belgium

National Affairs

THE JUNE 10 FEDERAL ELECTIONS and their aftermath suggested that the delicate bonds holding the Belgian nation together might be fraying.

In Flanders, the Dutch-speaking part of the country, the Christian Democratic and Flemish Party (CD&V), allied with the New-Flemish Alliance (N-VA)—a Flemish nationalist grouping—posted a resounding victory, ousting Prime Minister Guy Verhofstadt's "purple coalition" made up of his own Flemish Liberal Democrats (VLD, a free-market party) and the Socialists (SPA). Vlaams Belang (Flemish Interest), a separatist and anti-immigrant party, increased its vote total over the previous election but lost one parliamentary seat. In the French-speaking (Walloon) area, the VLD's sister party, Mouvement Réformateur (MR), defeated the Socialists, while the environmentalist party Ecolo made striking gains.

Immediately after the election King Albert II appointed MR leader Didier Reynders *formateur,* the person designated to organize the new government and then assume the position of prime minister. But conflict between the French-speaking parties and their Dutch-speaking counterparts frustrated his efforts, and the king turned to CD&V leader Yves Leterme, but his efforts proved equally ineffective.

The major roadblock to the creation of a governing coalition was whether to change the electoral system in the district of Brussels-Halle-Vilvoorde (BHV), a question that evoked Flemish-Walloon ethnic tensions and symbolized the fragility of Belgium's national identity.

The problem arose some years earlier, when electoral districts were mapped out so as to correspond to provincial borders, meaning that there would be Dutch- and French-speaking districts. This was done, however, for only nine of the ten provinces. The tenth, Flemish Brabant, suffered the "amputation" of Halle and Vilvoorde, which were joined to the Brussels-Capital Region to form a separate election district. This hybrid entity ensured that residents of Brussels's outskirts (in Flemish territory) had access to both the French- and Dutch-speaking courts and could vote, if they chose, for French-speaking Brussels candidates in both Belgian and European elections. A court ruling in May 2003, however, invalidated this arrangement since it was incompatible with the principle of division of electoral constituencies by province, and gave the government until the next election to remedy the situation. But no remedy had been found by election day 2007.

The Flemish parties submitted a bill aimed at splitting the BHV electoral district so that Halle and Vilvoorde would be attached to the Flemish district of Leuven to the east. This would impact negatively on the French speakers there, however, putting an end to their right to vote for Brussels candidates or have recourse to French-speaking courts (the proposal itself mentioned only districting for electoral purposes, but judicial redistricting would be the next step), and so the Francophone parties opposed the bill and argued for other solutions, such as returning to the previous system of electoral districts unrelated to provincial borders or possibly retaining the old prerogatives of the French-speakers even after moving Halle and Vilvoorde into a Flemish district. But the Home Affairs Committee of the Chamber of Deputies, in charge of examining the matter, was predominantly Dutch-speaking, and therefore unlikely to show sympathy for the Francophone position.

That this struggle was far more a matter of symbolism than of substance, especially for the Dutch-speaking parties, was evident from the fact that the Dutch-speakers would actually lose one or more parliamentary seats if the BHV district were divided, and the Dutch-speaking residents of Brussels would become a tiny minority there. Nevertheless, the Flemish parties wanted to make the point that their region should be monolingual and that the French speakers desiring to live there had to assimilate.

On November 7, more than five months after the elections, negotiations for a new government were still stalled, and the Flemish parties took matters into their own hands. Using their majority in the Chamber of Deputies, they voted to split BHV. This came as a shock to much of the country, since both language groups had traditionally maintained the principle of government by consensus, with respect for minority rights. The action was widely viewed as the imposition of the will of six million Flemings upon four million French-speakers. The Francophone parties responded by breaking off coalition negotiations. Guy Verhofstadt's outgoing government remained in place and ran the country's business in a caretaker capacity, but was not empowered to adopt a budget or make important decisions.

This ongoing political crisis triggered a grass-roots response. In August, a simple Belgian citizen—a woman from Liège—launched an Internet petition for Belgian unity that quickly collected close to 142,000 signatures. On Sunday, November 18, an impressive procession of 35,000–40,000 people walked from Brussels's North Station to Jubilee Park calling for Belgium to remain united. The demonstrators included Walloons, Flemings, and Brussels residents. As they passed the Senate, the petition was presented to its president.

Just a few days before this rally, however, a new obstacle to amicable relations between the linguistic groups emerged. On November 14, the Flemish government refused to confirm the appointments of mayors in three predominantly French-speaking BHV municipalities—Linkebeek, Kraainhem, and Wezembeek-Oppem. The reason given was that these mayors had sent out voting information in French rather than Dutch, and this was deemed a violation of the law.

In early December the king entrusted Verhofstadt with the task of finding a solution. He managed to create an interim government to manage urgent business, including a number of serious economic problems, and also set up a committee to find solutions to the differences between the language groups. This government would remain in place until March 23, 2008.

Israel and the Middle East

As in the past, Belgium—which housed the headquarters of the European Union—espoused the EU (and thus the Quartet) position on Middle East issues. It favored a two-state solution, praised the Saudi-Arab League plan for Arab recognition of Israel in return for an Israeli return to the 1967 borders, and expressed support for the resumption of talks between Prime Minister Olmert of Israel and President Abbas of the PA. While calling for an end to rocket attacks from Gaza into Israel, Belgium also wanted Israel to ease restrictions on the movement of Palestinians in the West Bank and to halt settlement expansion.

Foreign Minister Karel De Gucht visited Israel on March 21–22 as part of a weeklong trip to the Middle East. He met with Prime Minister Olmert, Foreign Minister Livni, and other key figures, and also spent time with the parents of the three abducted Israeli soldiers.

The Anti-Defamation League (ADL) examined Belgian attitudes toward Israel and other Middle Eastern issues as part of its survey of opinion in six European countries. Belgians tended to be pro-Palestinian: 41 percent of respondents had a favorable view of the Palestinians and 24 percent viewed them unfavorably, as compared to 35 percent who were favorable to Israel and 32 percent who were unfavorable. Asked with whom they sympathized more in the present conflict, 31 percent named the Palestinians and 16 percent the Israelis. Forty-nine percent agreed with the view that Israeli treatment of the Palestinians was similar to South African apartheid, 44 percent believed that "American Jews control U.S. Middle East policy," and of those who felt that media coverage of the Middle East was biased, those identifying the bias as pro-Israel outnumbered those seeing it as pro-Palestinian by two to one.

The survey uncovered considerable uneasiness about the prospect of Iran developing a nuclear capacity, with 79 percent of respondents saying they were "concerned" or "somewhat concerned." Sixty-three percent believed that Iran was working to acquire nuclear weapons and 56 percent favored the imposition of economic sanctions.

An important source of information about and analysis of Middle East issues in Belgium was the Brussels-based Transatlantic Institute, an arm of the American Jewish Committee. Throughout the year it hosted programs and issued publications on the Israeli-Palestinian conflict, the threat posed by Iran, and other matters of concern.

Anti-Semitism and Extremism

A total of 69 anti-Semitic incidents were reported in Belgium during the year, the highest number since 2001. The cities most affected were the two largest, Brussels (17 incidents) and Antwerp (16). Some "incidents" were national and even international, involving the media and the Internet. In only one case was physical violence involved, as compared to four such cases in 2006. But the 50 "ideological" incidents—such as slurs and insults—were up from 45 in 2006 and 30 in 2005. A sample of these anti-Semitic manifestations follows.

On January 25, during a routine inspection of travelers' tickets on a De Lijn tram in Antwerp, a noticeably Orthodox Jewish woman who was six months pregnant was asked to show her ticket and ID card. A native English speaker, she did not understand his instructions, and the inspector became angry, saying, "You [people] never pay." He then confiscated her multitrip ticket, which had not been used up. Her husband, demanding a refund, an apology, and the assurance that she would not be fined, contacted the Forum der Joodse Organisaties (FJO), the umbrella body of Jewish groups in Flanders. It brought the matter to the attention of the

Center for Equal Opportunity, which contacted the tram company on February 2 and requested an explanation. None was ever received.

On February 3, a rabbi visiting from abroad got off a train at Brussels's South Station. Identifiably Jewish, as in the previous case, by his clothing, the rabbi was set upon by a group of youths, who spit on him. He did not notify the police, and casually mentioned the incident in a talk he gave that evening at the conference to which he had been invited. He said he was shocked, but that he was mostly sorry for the unfortunate young people who had attacked him.

After receiving information, on February 22, that the Skynet Internet site had a link to the text of the *Protocols of the Elders of Zion* with no accompanying explanation, the Equal Opportunity Center filed a complaint with the company. On March 6 the link was removed and replaced by another that provided the text along with commentary that situated the anti-Semitic work in its historical context, stating explicitly that it was a forgery.

Notified that a Brussels bookstore was selling a CD of the Koran that also included two Arabic sermons with anti-Semitic content, the Center for Equal Opportunity verified the translation and, on August 2, sent a letter to the store manager requesting a halt to the sale of this product. A reply was received on September 19 from the management of the bookstore chain explaining that it had previously been unaware of the content of the CD and had now removed it from the shelves of its stores.

The ADL survey of attitudes in six European nations contained data about Belgian views of Jews. Fifty-four percent—the highest figure among the six countries—said it was "probably true" that Jews were more loyal to Israel than to their country of residence. That same "probably true" response was registered by 36 percent when asked whether Jews had "too much" power in the business world, 40 percent when asked about "too much" Jewish power in international financial markets, and 43 percent when asked whether Jews talked "too much" about the Holocaust. Queried about the source of anti-Jewish incidents in the country, 35 percent cited hostility to Jews and 37 percent anti-Israel feeling. Twenty percent of Belgians blamed the Jews for the death of Christ.

Attention to anti-Semitism should not obscure the fact that the large Muslim minority was a much more inviting target for xenophobia. As Brussels—whose Muslim inhabitants constituted between 17 and 20 percent of the population—was the "capital" of the EU, broader European-wide anxiety about Islam focused on that Belgian city. In late August,

Brussels mayor Freddy Thielemans refused permission for a rally against "Islamization" to mark the sixth anniversary of 9/11, citing a threat to law and order and charging that the organizing group, Stop the Islamization of Europe (SIOE), was racist. SIOE appealed the decision, but it was upheld by an appeals court.

The rally nevertheless took place, illegally, on September 11, attracting about 200 people, many of them far-right members of the European Parliament from several countries (the organizers had hoped for a turnout of 20,000). Police removed the demonstrators by force, arresting most of them and keeping them in custody for several hours. The Website of Vlaams Belang, the separatist, anti-immigrant Flemish party, sarcastically proclaimed, "Today the foreign media has again seen a fine image of how democracy works in Belgium," and denounced Mayor Thielemans as an "Islamosocialist."

Holocaust-Related Matters

On February 3, the Brussels-based Center for Historical Research and Documentation on War and Contemporary Society (CEGES) issued *Docile Belgium,* its 1,114-page final report on the role of Belgian authorities in the destruction of the country's Jewish community in World War II. It had been commissioned by the government in 2003.

The team of historians that carried out the project presented ample proof that "the Belgian state adopted a docile and cooperative attitude in some very diverse but crucial domains, providing collaboration unworthy of a democracy, with a policy that was disastrous for Belgian and foreign Jews," while also pointing out that individual Belgians risked their lives to help Jews. Prime Minister Verhofstadt expressed the hope that the findings would be incorporated in history text books. As a follow-up, CEGES held a conference, hosted by the Coordinating Committee of Belgian Jewish Organizations (CCLJ), to publicize the report.

On October 28, FJO, the Dutch-speaking federation of Jewish organizations, held a forum in Antwerp on "Children of the Holocaust." No one could have predicted that this innocent event would trigger an explosive controversy.

About 1,200 people from all over the world came to hear 33 speakers, including several high-ranking politicians, psychiatrists, historians, survivors, and special guest Arno Lustiger, cousin of the late cardinal of Paris who died in August (see above, pp. 397–98). There was a ceremony honoring the Belgian Righteous among the Nations and Jewish soldiers who served in the Allied armies, as well as exhibitions of books on the Holocaust and photographs that had been taken of Jews being deported. The Museum of Deportation and Resistance had an exhibit with a touch-screen function enabling visitors to view and possibly identify pictures of lost Jewish family members. A number of films were screened as well.

The highlight of forum was the presentation of Antwerp mayor Patrick Janssens, who apologized to the Jewish community on behalf of his city for the involvement of municipal authorities and the police force in the three 1942 roundups that culminated in the deportation of 1,200 Jewish residents of the city to Auschwitz. This was the first time any Antwerp official had ever issued such an apology, and the Jewish community was extremely appreciative.

The next day, however, Bart De Wever, who was chairman of the New Flemish Alliance (N-VA) party and also an Antwerp town councilor, declared that the mayor's apology was uncalled for and had been made for the sole purpose of delivering a political swipe at the separatist Vlaams Belang. According to De Wever, "Antwerp did not organize the deportation of the Jews; [the city] was a victim of the Nazi occupation. Antwerp's officials had to make decisions. In my view, attacking them does not seem very courageous." And he went on to suggest to the Jewish community that remembrance of the Holocaust should not obscure Israel's occupation of Palestinian territories.

There were immediate denunciations of De Wever's remarks from across the political spectrum, and some charged him with anti-Semitism. Perhaps the most anguished complaints came from the Flemish Christian Democrats (CD&V), the party that had allied with the N-VA for the elections and was now seeking to set up a government coalition with it. Michael Freilich, editor-in-chief of the Jewish monthly *Joods Actueel,* called De Wever's statement "scandalous," adding that if he were to become mayor of Antwerp its Jewish citizens would have reason to worry.

So quick and sharp were the expressions of criticism that De Wever backtracked the following morning, October 30. He now said that his words had been misinterpreted: he had not meant that the mayor's apology for the role of local Antwerp officials should not have been made, rather, that it had been made too late. And he apologized if his comments had had the effect of injuring the feelings of the Jews of Antwerp. The Jewish community did not accept the apology.

Another event that focused on children during the Holocaust took place in Jerusalem, an international conference on "Children Hidden in Belgium during the Shoah," held April 15–19. It was conceived by Shaul

Harel, a professor at Tel Aviv University who was himself hidden as a child in Belgium, and was sponsored by the Belgian Foreign Ministry. The nearly 300 participants attended seminars and workshops on the influence of the experience of being "hidden" on the children and their families. Andreé Geulen, a Belgian who helped save as many as 300 Jewish children and had already been recognized as "Righteous among the Nations," was made an honorary citizen of the State of Israel in a ceremony at Yad Vashem. The Institute of Jewish Audiovisual Memory (IMAJ) filmed the entire conference.

The Jewish Museum of Deportation and Resistance (JMDR) in Mechelen—whose name was to be changed to *Kazerne Dossin* [Dossin Barracks] Museum, Memorial and Documentation Center on Holocaust and Human Rights—was planning to expand. With the aid of the Flemish government, a new structure would be built to house the museum, the design to be chosen through an international architectural contest. It would feature a permanent historical exhibition on the racial persecution of Jews and Gypsies in Belgium and northern France during the Nazi era, and also host temporary exhibitions on human-rights issues related to Belgium. The Dossin Barracks project itself would triple the current permanent exhibition space.

Some 35,000–37,000 people visited the museum during 2007, about 40 percent of them French-speaking (since admission was free and there was no ticketing system, the exact number was not available). The great majority of visitors were secondary-school students, and they were given a special 100-minute guided tour in French, Dutch, or German. In addition, the museum chairman appeared at 25 schools in Flanders to relate his personal wartime experiences. The museum was currently located in what had been an SS barracks. For two months the JMDR hosted an exhibit on the famous 20th transport from Mechelen, featuring portraits of 1,200 of the 1,600 deportees. It was also shown in Antwerp and Cologne, Germany.

The JMDR was the moving force behind the creation of the Belgium Museum in Auschwitz, which opened in May 2006. During 2007 steps were taken to install a touch screen on the premises so as to make available the portraits of deportees from Mechelen to Auschwitz.

A plaque paying tribute to the Belgian citizens who provided assistance and helped save the lives of Jews during the Nazi occupation was unveiled on the façade of the Jewish Museum of Belgium, in Brussels, on September 25. The ceremony also recalled the exploits of Captain (later Baron) Jean Bloch, who participated in the liberation of Brussels at the head of a detachment of the Piron Brigade, and was the first liberator to enter the town hall on September 3, 1944.

Sister Francia de Linarès of the order of Our Lady of Zion was posthumously given the title Righteous among the Nations by Yad Vashem, the ceremony taking place on February 1 in Paris. She was the fifth nun of Our Lady of Zion to receive this honor.

JEWISH COMMUNITY

Communal Affairs

The Consistoire Central Israélite de Belgique (Belgian Jewish Central Consistory)—the representative body of the Jewish religion in the country, created, like its French counterpart, by Napoleonic decree in 1808—made preparations for celebrating its bicentennial in 2008. Three high-profile events were planned that, it was hoped, would generate media coverage and educate Belgians, as well as other Europeans, about the Belgian Jewish community: a gala dinner, a pair of colloquia (one in Brussels and the other in Antwerp), and a solemn service in the Grand Synagogue of Brussels.

The Comité de Coordination des Organisations Juives de Belgique (Coordinating Committee of Jewish Organizations of Belgium, CCOJB), the umbrella organization of some 40 secular Jewish groups, mostly in Brussels, had considerable difficulty electing a new chairman. Prior to leaving office at the end of his term, incumbent Philippe Markiewicz organized elections for December 14, 2006, to choose his successor. However, a two-thirds vote of the electoral board was necessary for election, and neither that ballot nor others taken early in 2007 produced a winner. This was the case even in June, after the field had been winnowed down to two candidates: Joel Rubinfeld received 65 votes, a majority but not two-thirds of the 113 total, while Norbert Cigé got 47, and one abstained.

Markiewicz made little secret of his preference for Cigé, who was, like the incumbent, a moderate who favored emphasis on improving intergroup relations. Rubinfeld, a critic of Markiewicz, argued for greater Jewish assertiveness in fighting anti-Semitism and more energetic support of Israel. His supporters went to court, charging Markiewicz with seeking to deprive some of them of their right to vote. As 2007 came to an end the two sides remained deadlocked.

The parallel Antwerp-based organization, Forum der Joodse Organisaties van België (Forum of Jewish Organizations of Belgium, FJO), devoted considerable energy to fighting manifestations of anti-Semitism, as noted above (p. 000) in the case of Bart de Wever's offensive remarks in Antwerp. The FJO also sought to counter calls to boycott Israel by organizing "Support Israel, buy Israeli products!" campaigns in local supermarkets twice during 2007; conducted the annual Holocaust Remembrance Day commemoration on May 8; hosted residents of Sderot and gave them the opportunity to brief the media about the relentless Palestinian rocket attacks on their town; and filed an official complaint against six people with Belgian/European links who participated in the Holocaust denial conference in Tehran in December 2006.

Service Social Juïf (Jewish Social Service) dealt with the welfare needs of the Brussels Jewish community and also provided cultural activities for its volunteers. La Centrale d'Œuvres sociales Juives de Bruxelles (Central Administration of Jewish Welfare Organizations of Brussels), which discreetly collected funds for the community's social institutions, also produced a quarterly bulletin containing articles about Jewish and general cultural matters.

Interfaith Relations

The Sisters of Zion community in Brussels continued its efforts to improve Christian-Jewish relations. In the educational area, it brought together Christians of all ages throughout the year for classes in Biblical Hebrew at four levels of difficulty, with the use of rabbinical sources. There were also Biblical Hebrew weekends in Strasbourg and Evry, near Paris, and the theme was animals in the Bible.

The Sisters of Zion helped organize two interfaith meetings in Brussels, each of them attended by more than 150 people. One was a festive "getting-to-know-each-other" day held in a high school, under the banner, "Jews, Christians, Muslims, Hindus, and Secularists: Let's Build Bridges Together." The other activity was an interfaith walk through Brussels in which the participants were welcomed in various houses of worship, including the Orthodox synagogue in Rue de la Clinique/Kliniekstraat. These large events in turn triggered numerous activities on a smaller scale.

The Sisters of Zion participated in the international colloquium on "Religion(s) and Modernity" that was held at the Museum of Europe in Brussels on May 5. They also created a Website, www.sion.org/bruxelles.htm, to keep people abreast of the calendar of activities of the Jewish community and of joint Jewish-Christian events.

Education

There were two Jewish schools in Brussels that provided primary and secondary education and were recognized by the state: Maimonides Atheneum, which was Orthodox, and Ganenou Atheneum, which was Zionist and also enjoyed recognition from Israel's Ministry of Education.

Maimonides celebrated its 60th anniversary in 2007. To mark the occasion pupils participated in several humanitarian projects to develop their civic spirit, including the collection of money for charitable causes in Belgium, Israel, and Africa. The theme of the 2006/07 school year was "A healthy mind in a healthy body"; every grade was involved in activities related to this theme, culminating in a family rally on foot in the woods (Forêt de Soignes/Zonienwoud) under a clear blue sky. After six years of a successful Dutch-immersion program in the primary grades, the program was extended to the first year of secondary school.

The heavily Orthodox Jewish population of Antwerp created a different educational picture, as some 90 percent of the children attended Jewish schools. The two major ones were Tachkemoni, run by the Shomre Hadass community, and Yesode HaTorah, which serviced the more strictly Orthodox Machsike Hadass. There were also many smaller Hasidic institutions, some not recognized by the state.

Adult Jewish education was available at the Institute of Jewish Studies, the only university-level school in the country that offered degree programs exclusively in Jewish fields. Many of its students were also enrolled at Brussels Free University (ULB), which gave credit for its courses. In fact, a new ULB master's program in the Study of Religion and Secularism included institute courses in the history of the Jews of Belgium; Israeli society; Biblical Hebrew; and Aramaic. In addition to the wide variety of courses offered, the institute also hosted a number of public lectures, perhaps the most unusual being a presentation, in English, on "Jews in China" by Prof. Guang Pan, director of the Shanghai Jewish Studies Center, on October 2.

A long-term project of the institute was *Dictionnaire sur les signes précurseurs du nazisme et les persécutions des Juifs (1918-1945)*, a dictionary of the warning signs of Nazism and persecution of the Jews from 1918 through 1945, which was due to be published soon.

Culture

The Jewish Museum of Belgium, approaching its 25th anniversary, featured a major exhibit entitled "Sarah and Her Brothers" that opened October 11. It was about the Kaliski family—two brothers, René and Chaim, and their sister Sarah—whose works were deeply influenced by the Holocaust. René Kaliski was one of the most outstanding playwrights of the contemporary Belgian theater; Chaim composed a stunning hallucinatory fresco fed by history and his own Jewishness; and Sarah's paintings—as well as her notebooks that were included in the exhibit—were clearly haunted by the memory of the dead.

The Centre Communautaire Laïc Juif (Jewish Secular Community Center, CCLJ), sponsored a number of Jewish cultural activities including lectures, book launches, and symposia. On November 22 the CCLJ had an extraordinary gala at the Royal Conservatory of Brussels in honor of Israel's 60th anniversary. The theme was "Israel in Music: 1947–2007," and several renowned musicians participated.

The women's Zionist group WIZO, which raised money for a number of welfare projects in Israel, held its 21st Book and Art Day in Brussels on March 11, including book signings by authors. It also ran a weekly Monday lecture series.

Zionist cultural programming was provided by the Ben-Gurion Circle. Each month there was an Israel movie night, and, in conjunction with the House of Jewish Culture, the circle sponsored regular lectures. It organized an evening featuring Israeli entertainers, karaoke, dancing, and food to mark the 60th anniversary of the Jewish state.

The Brussels-based Contemporary Memory Foundation was created in 1994 to study and teach the history of Belgian Jews in the twentieth century, and in 2007 it became a "privileged partner" of Brussels Free University's Interdisciplinary Center for the Study of Religion and Secularism. Its research projects during 2007 included an investigation of marginality in Jewish society between the wars, an exploration of painter Arno Stern's career in Belgium, the Brussels Jewish community's reconstruction in the aftermath of the Holocaust, illegal immigration from Belgium to Palestine during the British mandate, and the fate and current status of Yiddish in Belgium.

The Liège Jewish Cultural Center, created in the aftermath of World War II by a battered, decimated community, had become the main driving force behind secular Jewish life in Liège. On May 16 it celebrated the 50th anniversary of its founding. Its annual commemoration of Holocaust Memorial Day in April featured a talk on the influx of Jews from Eastern Europe into that region of Belgium between the wars.

IMAJ, the Institute of Jewish Audiovisual Memory, screened previously unreleased documentaries about Jewish life, and sponsored an Israel film festival June 3–5 with the support of the Israeli embassy. IMAJ also began work on an ambitious project, in cooperation with other institutions, to archive the audio and visual heritage specific to the history of Belgium's Jewish community. This would include religious and secular music, international conferences held in Belgium, debates, and broadcasts, all of which were currently conserved in their original media. Several foundations, some of them outside Belgium, were approached for grant money to carry out the plan.

GEORGES SCHNEK

Netherlands

National Affairs

Immigration and Demography

At year's end the population of the Netherlands was about 16.4 million, with a national average of over 483 inhabitants per km^2. The population grew by 46,000 during 2007, twice as much as in 2006, mostly due to a 15-percent rise in immigration and a decrease in emigration.

To be sure, tough immigration policies aimed mostly at Muslim immigrants had greatly influenced Dutch society and politics since 2001. The results continued to be visible in 2007 and at times affected the Jewish community as well, not intentionally, but because the Jewish community was such a small minority that its circumstances were simply overlooked.

Although total immigration was up, it was down from so-called "non-Western" countries such as Morocco (by nearly 2,000) and Turkey (by nearly 3,000), largely because non-Western would-be immigrants had to pass a Dutch language and culture exam in their original country before they could apply for a visa, as required by a law passed in March 2006. Israel was designated a non-Western country, and in January 2007 the Dutch immigration authorities published its first statistics about Israel. Between March 15 and September 30, 2006, more than 1,500 persons sat for the exam in Israel, but the number of those who passed it was not yet available.

Another example of anti-Muslim sentiments "accidentally" affecting the Jewish community had to do with food. On February 16, Albert Heijn (AH), one of the country's largest supermarket chains, discontinued the sale of kosher meat. For years AH had kept a freezer with kosher meat in just one of its Amsterdam shops. In October 2006, when it began to introduce halal meat in its stores, the chain bowed to pressure to stop selling meat from animals that had been ritually slaughtered without prior stunning, and so anti-Muslim sentiment affected observant Jews. The market for kosher meat in the Netherlands was almost negligible: in 2007 there was just one kosher butcher shop in the whole of the Netherlands, and one or two kosher groceries that sold meat. There were no kosher outlets at all outside Amsterdam.

Politics and Society

In February 2007 the fourth Dutch cabinet led by Jan Peter Balkenende of the Christian Democrats (CDA) was sworn in after four months of negotiations. The coalition also included the Social Democrats (PvdA) led by Wouter Bos and the smaller Christen Unie led by André Rouvoet.

The new government was to include Ahmed Aboutaleb, originally from Morocco, and Nebahat Albayrak, from Turkey, as assistant secretaries of state. On February 15 the Freedom Party (PVV), an anti-Muslim group led by Geert Wilders, raised the issue of "dual loyalties" and demanded that the two either relinquish their original citizenships or step down. The next day former integration minister Rita Verdonk, a hardliner herself, proposed to make dual citizenship illegal for all Dutch citizens. In May Wilders called for closing down all Islamic schools, and in August for a ban on the Koran, which he called the "Islamic *Mein Kampf*." "If you removed all violent and unacceptable passages," Wilders wrote in the national daily *de Volkskrant*, "you would be left with a booklet the size of a Donald Duck comic."

Contrary statements by left-wing politicians on Muslim issues proved equally provocative. On July 14, for example, Minister of Integration Ella Vogelaar (PvdA) likened Muslim immigrants to their Jewish predecessors. Speaking of the Jews she said: "Centuries ago, they too came to the Netherlands and now we say: the Netherlands have been shaped by Jewish-Christian traditions. I can see a similar process with Islam." Historians and other scholars, including several Jews, publicly protested in the newspapers that so-called "Jewish-Christian traditions" were not the result of Jewish influences, but rather reflected shared values influenced by the Greek philosophers that Muslims did not share. "It isn't as if the Dutch had just been hanging out in bearskins being pagans until the Jews arrived with horah, Talmud, fine cooking and the Bible, after which the Dutch suddenly thought: 'Hey, the Old Testament! Cool book!'" said Robbert Baruch, a member of the Council of Rotterdam for Vogelaar's own PvdA.

Dutch political apathy was reflected in the low 46.3-percent turnout in the March provincial elections. Another indication of the same phenomenon occurred earlier, on February 1, the day that environmental organizations called upon the Dutch to switch off the lights for five minutes at 8 p.m. to symbolize the threat of global warming. The manager of the national energy network feared that a breakdown of services would result, but it turned out that so few people turned off their lights that no measurable effects were experienced.

Internationally, public opinion strongly objected to Dutch involvement in the U.S.-led "war on terror." In April, bumper stickers propagating the withdrawal of "our boys and girls" from Afghanistan appeared following the death of a 21-year-old soldier, Cor Strik, who had stepped on a bomb while on patrol. Discussions heated up again in June after a Dutch television crew happened to record a bloody attack, and in July, following another Dutch casualty. In September, a Dutch student was murdered with an axe in Roosendaal Station by a disturbed American looking to take revenge on a Dutch soldier for the country's participation in the Iraq war. While there were strong calls for a parliamentary investigation into Dutch participation in Iraq, the ruling PvdA managed to avert it.

Anti-American demonstrations caused an interesting shift in political alliances. A demonstration "against U.S. imperialism and Zionism" and in favor of Iran by the extreme right Nederlandse Volksunie and the even more extreme splinter groups Blood & Honor and Youth Storm, planned for July 14 in The Hague, was canceled after the not very U.S.-loving, left-wing Anti Fascistische Aktie (AFA) received permission to demonstrate a mere 100 yards from the spot chosen by the extreme right demonstrators, effectively blocking the latter from marching past the American embassy. Some 300 AFA demonstrators showed up anyway, accompanied by a large police contingent.

The rising level of violence in Dutch society caused considerable concern. In March some 150 inhabitants of the Ondiep neighborhood in Utrecht attacked police after an officer shot and killed 54-year-old Rinie Mulder. The policeman had felt threatened, thinking Mulder was brandishing a knife. On October 15 some 30 Moroccan youngsters rioted after policemen killed a 22-year-old man who had stabbed and critically wounded two policemen.

Starting with a knifing on March 20, Dutch high schools experienced many violent incidents. Over the course of the year ten students and one staff member were killed or severely wounded, and an unknown number slightly wounded. In most cases students attacked each other over seemingly unimportant matters, such as the ownership of a pen. While many of the cases involved Muslim aggressors, contrary to popular belief this was not always so, as in one case where a group of skinheads attacked a Moroccan boy.

In November, a national high school students' strike over the obligatory number of periods per year got out of hand in several cities, and students smashed windows, damaged cars, vandalized lampposts, ignited fireworks, and pelted passersby with eggs. In the town of Leiden rioting students chanted, "Hamas, Hamas, Jews to the gas," and 200 students were arrested. At the end of the year some 20 schools, mostly elementary schools, were set afire with fireworks (the year before, seven schools had been treated this way). A police spokesman said that fistfighting and rioting that went on New Year's Eve, ushering in the year 2008, surpassed what went on in previous years, particularly in Amsterdam.

Anti-Semitism and Extremism

Extreme-Right Groups

The organized extreme right showed no real signs of growth. The Nederlandse Volks Unie, a neo-Nazi party founded in 1971, failed to win any local council seats in 2006 even though its overall vote total was up. By going through the official procedure for obtaining permits, the party was able to mount several legal demonstrations. The Nationale Alliantie, which imploded in 2006 due to internal strife, increased police surveillance, and loss of membership, showed hardly any activity in 2007. New Right, an extremist party with a somewhat more politically correct veneer, seemed to be headed in the same direction. In January 2007, after John Middleman, a prominent party member, said "Jews have too much power and New Right is going to remedy that," and that Jews "have to adjust or get lost," a New Right council member in the town of Ridderkerk resigned his membership and started his own party. This left New Right with just one seat on a local council in the whole of the Netherlands.

Meanwhile, the influence of less formally organized extreme rightists appeared to grow. The so-called "'Lonsdale youths"—extreme-right fans of "gabber music"—increased their activity in 2006 and 2007. They participated in violent, racist confrontations with other groups, mostly Moroccans, and joined neo-Nazi factions such as Blood & Honor, Racial Volunteer Force, Youth Storm, and Aktiefront Nederland.

Incidents

CIDI, Holland's anti-Semitism watchdog, documented a sharp increase in anti-Semitic incidents, from 159 reported in 2005 to 261 in 2006, a rise of 64 percent. The number of incidents involving physical violence was down, however, and the steep rise was mostly due to anti-Semitic e-mails linked to Israel's war in Lebanon during the summer of 2006. This was so even though, as usual, only "purely anti-Jewish" incidents were registered and not criticism of Israel, however severe. Also, an anti-Semitic e-mail sent to a great number of addresses was counted as one single incident, as were large numbers of (different) anti-Semitic mails sent by one single person.

One positive development was the decrease of anti-Semitic incidents in schools. According to the CIDI data, only seven occurred in 2006, half of the 2005 total.

There was an increase in the incidence of vandalism at war monuments, peaking around Dutch commemoration days. The phenomenon was undoubtedly due to the rise of extreme-right activity in the streets.

Judicial Response

The Netherlands continued to be one of few EU countries where Holocaust denial and denial of genocide were not forbidden, except when used to insult specific groups, and even in such cases only survivors and their direct descendants could initiate cases. However new EU legislation adopted on April 19 stated that incitement to violence and/or the white-washing of "genocide, crimes against humanity and war crimes on racist or xenophobic grounds" was to be forbidden, and that racist and xenophobic motives would constitute aggravating circumstances for "ordinary" crimes. A period of two years was allowed for updating national legislation to reflect the new EU standard.

According to *Monitor Racism & Extremism 2006,* published in August 2007 by the Anne Frank Stichting and the University of Leiden, the number of discrimination cases tried by the courts was up in 2006, and racism, comprising 55 percent of such cases, was still the most common ground for prosecution. In 2006, one-third of all discrimination cases entailed anti-Semitism, a marked increase from previous years. A growing number of perpetrators were Dutch natives with an extreme-right background; a smaller number were of North African background. While the total number of violent incidents prosecuted went down by some 10 percent in 2006, extreme-right participation in these grew significantly, from 38 in 2005 to 67 in 2006. A particularly worrying tendency was the increase, over the previous decade, in the percentage of perpetrators who were minors: for boys the figure went up from 5 percent to 14 percent in 2006, and for girls from 1 percent to 4 percent.

Attitudes

In July 2007 the Anti-Defamation League (ADL) released a EU-wide survey of attitudes toward Jews. Forty-six percent of the Dutch sample thought it was "probably true" that Jews were more loyal to Israel than to their country of residence. This was a lower rate than that found in Austria, Belgium, Hungary, and the UK, where a majority thought it was "probably true." Of the Dutch respondents, 11 percent believed "Jews have too much power" and 14 percent believed this was true in the realm of international finance. Thirty-one percent thought Jews "talk too much" about their suffering in the Holocaust. Nearly half the Dutch respondents, 45 percent, compared Israeli treatment of Palestinians and apartheid in South Africa. Yet 60 percent believed Hamas was out to destroy Israel, as compared to about a third of the sample that felt that Israel was seeking to destroy the Palestinians. Overall, Dutch attitudes on Israel-related questions were slightly more sympathetic to the Jewish state than had been the case in a similar ADL survey in 2005.

Holocaust-Related Matters

Restitution

Since 2004, restitution of Jewish wartime assets had been an ongoing process. The total amount available was 47.3 million euros, and it was distributed by an independent allocation board appointed by the Jewish community to projects under the categories of culture, media, education, religion, social work, youth, external relations, and remembrance. Despite a set of rules aimed at preventing the bulk of the monies from going to large, established organizations, that purpose proved difficult to fulfill. For one thing, the planning and paperwork involved in applying for money strongly favored large organizations. And for another, projects started with restitution funds were ineligible for further subsidies; established bodies had their own sources of funding to keep these projects going, but smaller and newer ones did not.

By 2007, 17 million euros had been allocated. Roughly a third (6.25 million) had gone to the "religion" category—rather strange considering that in 2000 72 percent of Dutch Jews said they were unaffiliated with any religious organization. Over 7.5 million euros went to building projects, 3 million of that sum to constructing new synagogues, including a splendid new Liberal synagogue and an equally ambitious Orthodox one, both for the Amsterdam community. Large amounts also went to the infrastructure costs of large Jewish organizations.

Priority was supposed to be given to projects that would "ensure the continuity of Jewish life in the Netherlands," but views differed not only over how to ensure this but also over what kind of Jewish life was to be stimulated. Three main groups competed to demonstrate they were the appropriate recipients. Two of them were religious, the Orthodox and the Liberal Jewish communities. The third was JMW, the Jewish Social Work organization, often called "the third, secular Jewish denomination." All three applied for and received large sums for projects involving their membership or clientele.

In September, the Claims Conference announced that more survivors than expected would be eligible for monthly pensions from the Article 2 Fund. Pensions were supposed to be paid to survivors who qualified and had a low yearly income; whereas earlier a spouse's income would be counted, beginning October 1 only the applicant's income would count. In November, 30 Dutch Jewish organizations petitioned German chancellor Angela Merkel to do something about the fact that over 85 percent of the approximately 3,000 Dutch Jewish applicants for restitution in the Netherlands and Israel had been turned down because they had received one-time payments in the 1960s.

Fifteen museums in the Netherlands and abroad were asked to inspect their collections for looted artworks, particularly for 500 paintings that had belonged to art dealer Jacques Goudstikker and were still missing. In 2006 the Dutch state had committed itself to returning 202 works of art to Marei von Saher, the main Goudstikker heir; 170 of these were subsequently auctioned. On February 16 a court in The Hague awarded 9.8 million euros to one of Von Saher's former lawyers.

An exhibition of 50 works of art presumably taken from unknown Holocaust victims, held at the Hollandse Schouwburg in Amsterdam, ended in March. The purpose had been to publicize the existence of these items and possibly locate the owners or their heirs. Three claims were entered by people who recognized their family's property. A symposium was held on March 13 in Amsterdam on the topic "Looted, But from Whom?" It concluded that little more could be discovered about the original owners of this art. Of some 4,500 paintings and other objects believed to have been taken from Jews, some 400 had been restituted over a period of nine years, most of these to the Goudstikker heirs. Some members of the Jewish community wanted to extend the exhibition in the hope that more owners' heirs might come forward.

COMMEMORATION

The passage of time made it difficult to maintain the memory of World War II and the Holocaust as unique phenomena, and the younger generation came increasingly to view the events of those years as just some of many "terrible things" that happened in world history. Also, the growing number of second- and third-generation immigrants from Morocco had little empathy for the fate of Dutch Jews. In an effort to make Holocaust commemoration relevant, well-meaning organizers linked Holocaust memorial events to "other genocides," such as that in Darfur. Those who had other agendas, however, used the broader framework to identify the government of Israel as a Nazi-like perpetrator of genocide against Palestinians.

In January, discussion was still raging about the speech of Max Wieselmann, chairman of Another Jewish Voice, at a yearly Christian commemoration on Christmas 2006. Speaking at the site of the Westerbork concentration camp on the theme of human rights, he drew a parallel between the Shoah and the situation of Palestinians in the occupied territories. This speech, taped by members of the youth organization of CIDI, incensed Jewish organizations and individual survivors (see AJYB 2007, pp. 396–97).

On the May 5, the day the Dutch commemorated their national liberation from Nazi occupation, a Palestinian-European conference on the Palestinian "right of return" was planned for Rotterdam. The date had been chosen to identify Israel's control of the territories with the Nazi occupation of Europe. Although Hamas prime minister Ismail Haniyeh and another cabinet minister were invited to speak, Foreign Minister Maxime Verhagen announced that they would be refused visas, whereupon another scheduled speaker, Ikrima Sabri, withdrew. He was the extremist mufti of Jerusalem known to have called for violence against the U.S., the destruction of Israel, and the expulsion of all Jews, but was not a member of Hamas.

Former Dutch prime minister Dries van Agt, however, did speak at the conference; this was only one of several occasions during 2007 that he voiced vehemently anti-Israel opinions not just at conferences, but on national radio, television, and in the newspapers. In December van Agt launched a Website on Human Rights Day that opened with an article entitled "Name Israel's Atrocities," which claimed that Foreign Minister Verhagen did "not pay attention to Palestinian human rights." The article voiced "deep admiration" for "Dutch peace activists, including many Jewish Dutchmen."

On Friday, November 9, the yearly Kristallnacht commemoration began in Camp Westerbork starting at 7 p.m.—Shabbat had already begun—with Darfur as the main theme. Jewish organizations had earlier objected both to the theme and the timing, which prevented Jews from taking part, but the organizers refused to change anything. In the end, only about 100 people showed up. This contrasted sharply with another commemoration earlier in the year, also in Westerbork but on a Sunday. On July 15, hundreds of people gathered to commemorate the date on which the first deportation train left the camp with the staggering number of 1,750 Jews, only one of whom survived.

In March, the owner of the "Anne Frank tree" received permission from the city of Amsterdam to cut it down. Its historical significance was that Anne Frank could see this tree, part of a neighboring garden, from the window in her Amsterdam hiding place. The tree was severely ill and cutting it down appeared the only option, but the announcement of the decision triggered opposition, and people living nearby took the city to court in November, claiming it was possible to save the tree. Amid much media hype the judge decided the tree could stay pending more study of its condition.

Amoetat Akevoth, a group dedicated to Dutch Jewish genealogical research, joined forces with the Orthodox umbrella body NIK on a project of publishing on-line photographs and translations of gravestones earlier than 1940 in Jewish cemeteries. The database expanded continuously, with translations in Dutch and English.

JEWISH COMMUNITY

Demography

The Jewish community in the Netherlands, estimated at about 44,000 people in 2000, had probably decreased since then due to late marriage, intermarriage, and a low birthrate. Even assuming no decline in their numbers, Dutch Jews constituted about 0.275 percent of the total population of 16.4 million in 2007. Jews, historically "the" minority group in the Netherlands, were almost negligible in comparison to the much more numerous Muslim minority.

Communal Affairs

Like their non-Jewish Dutch counterparts, younger Jews were not "joiners," and therefore membership in synagogues and Jewish organizations had been declining for years; according to the 2000 data, only 54 percent of Jews identified as Jewish and just 28 percent belonged to any Jewish association. As older people died off, the average age of members went up and the organizations struggled to attract enough new ones to make up for the losses. The community was so small that their efforts could be characterized as "fishing in the same small pond."

The core membership of the Jewish community, especially in Amsterdam, consisted of a small number of interrelated families. Parents who had attended the same schools and youth movements sent their children to the same institutions where "everyone knew everyone." The number of Jewish organizations still reflected the much larger prewar communities. Each institution had its own board, and male baby boomers often simultaneously held positions on several boards. When there were openings they were filled by cooptation. The same was true of the boards of the Jewish communities themselves, even though these were elected positions. By 2007 many of the baby boomers were ready to retire from such responsibilities but there were few younger people to replace them.

The Orthodox Jewish community of Amsterdam, the only one large enough for party politics, mirrored the Dutch political system in miniature, with many factions that had to form coalitions in order to govern. The council, which was the policy-making body, consisted of 30 men, the same size as before World War II. Women were barred, a position reaffirmed on June 21, 2007, when that body rejected a package of proposed reforms that would have included women on the board. Several years earlier the board ruled that fathers and sons could not sit on the same board, and some fathers had stepped down so that their sons could be seamlessly elected in their places. Women did serve on the boards of some nonreligious organizations, often replacing their fathers. Many Dutch Jews active in communal life spoke of the need to attract more members, but the Jewish establishment did not seem prepared to make the cultural changes necessary, much less relinquish influence to newcomers.

Everyone agreed that activities for Jews under age 35 were a priority, if only to combat intermarriage. But the fragmentation of the community prevented a coordinated strategy. The Orthodox community did not recognize Liberal conversions, and both of these religious streams deemed a large part of the secular clientele associated with Jewish Social Work (JMW) to be not Jewish. All three had their own youth organizations and did not want to subsidize programs that included members of the others. Such events were considered successful if 20 people showed up. Thus Jewhoo!, a series of evenings organized by JMW for singles, attracting ten people each in Utrecht and in Groningen; in Rotterdam not a single person came.

More successful were parties and other fun events organized outside the framework of the existing youth organizations. In February, for instance, 290 young Jewish adults participated in a party organized by two Jewish students in Amsterdam's fashionable and exclusive club Jimmy Woo. And in December, some 450 students from several European countries attended a weekend organized with the help of the European Center for Jewish Students (ECJS). While the Dutch Orthodox community subsidized the costs of attendance for its members, other Jewish organizations refused to do so for their young people on the grounds that the charges were too high. Thus non-Orthodox participants had to pay a higher cost per person out of their own pockets.

There were an estimated 7,000 Israelis living in Holland in 2000. They and their families constituted another group that had trouble securing funding for their activities. Many had married non-Jewish spouses, and a large number were much less affluent—and hence less socially acceptable—than the Dutch Jewish families that influenced decisions on allocations. The Israelis organized and paid for their own events on an informal basis, outside the existing communal framework.

The three sectors of the organized community—Orthodox, Liberal, and Jewish Social Work—subsidized and controlled their own publications, which were sent out to members or clients. But something of a crisis developed during the year for the independent Dutch Jewish media. *Joods Journaal,* a glossy quarterly funded entirely out of subscriptions and advertising income, folded, and in January 2007 it was announced that its replacement would be an annual, *Joods Jaarboek,* that would make its first appearance in December. However it was later postponed to 2008

Joods.nl, the independent Dutch Jewish Internet site, ceased to exist in May, after the failure of many rescue attempts. The site, which employed two editors, had been financed almost exclusively out of restitution funds. According to founder Naftali Herschler, Dutch Jewish organizations demanded high quality services but were not prepared to help pay for them. The site was unable to generate sufficient money from advertisers.

Joodse Omroep, the Jewish Broadcasting Organization, also faced serious problems. It was financed by public money, and Dutch broadcasting rules demanded pluralistic programming to reflect all streams within Judaism. However it had started out in 1973 as the broadcasting arm of the Orthodox umbrella body NIK, which still owned the broadcasting li-

A number of important Jewish social and cultural events occurred in the Netherlands during the year. On February 4 a gala art auction organized by B'nai Brith Amsterdam raised 50,000 euros for the children's village Neve Michael in Israel. The fifth annual Mimoena, the traditional Moroccan Jewish after-Pesach party, drew 500 visitors from all over Amsterdam. In June, Jom Havoetbal, the Jewish soccer tournament with teams from the Netherlands and several other European countries, brought together some 3,000 Jews from all walks of life. About 250 people participated in the conference for baby-boomers organized by JMW on October 14. In November, the tenth anual Yiddish Music Festival in Enschede drew 500 Jewish and non-Jewish spectators. Skijar, a skiing holiday in France organized by Dutch Jewish students, attracted 75 young adults from 16 European countries. And in December, over 500 children—more than in previous years—spent time at the winter camps of the Dutch Jewish youth movements Bne Akiwa, Hasjalsjelet, Haboniem, and Tikwatenoe.

A Dutch delegation attended the first international Young Hadassah Conference in Rome, July 5–8. That same week another Dutch delegation, made up of 75 Jewish athletes and trainers, flew to Rome for the 12th European Maccabia. They won the gold medal for karate, and silver and bronze for karate, golf, tennis, and chess.

Publications

A large number of accounts by and biographies of Holocaust survivors appeared during the year, especially in the run-up to the annual Dutch commemoration of World War II on May 4. Among them was *Gered uit het vuur, de wonderbaarlijke oorlogsgeschiedenis van een Rotterdams-Joods gezin* (Saved from the Fire: The Miraculous History of a Rotterdam Jewish Family), in which Zwi Laufer described how his parents survived the horrors of the Shoah with their three daughters. *De Zoektocht* (The Search) was a different kind of Holocaust book, telling the story in cartoons. Published by the Anne Frank Foundation in cooperation with the Hollandsche Schouwburg, it came with educational material for 13- and 14-year-old students. The book was later translated in other European languages.

There were many other significant works released. *In de Tenten van Jaäkov, impressies van 75 jaar Progressief Jodendom in Nederland 1931–2006* (In Jacob's Tents: Impressions of 25 Years of Progressive Judaism in the Netherlands) by Chaya Brasz was published by Progressive Judaism to mark its 75th anniversary and given free to all its members. René Süss, a former convert to Christianity and Protestant minister, returned to Judaism and wrote a controversial book, *Luthers theologisch testament: over de Joden en hun leugens* (Luther's Theological Testament: About the Jews and their Lies), which linked Luther's anti-Semitism to the Shoah. In *Nieuwe Nederlanders* (New Dutchmen), historian Bart Wallet documented the integration of Jews in the Netherlands between 1814 and 1851. *Joden in Nederland in de twintigste eeuw* contained short biographies of 506 prominent Jews who lived in the Netherlands in the twentieth century. Many more were available on a Website, including clickable links to relatives of the subjects.

The first copy of *Minhagee Amsterdam,* a Dutch translation by Rabbi R. Evers of the original Hebrew book by Rabbi Jehoeda Brilleman about typically Amsterdam customs, was presented to Mayor Job Cohen in October. *Een kleine kehilla met de jeroesje van een grote* (A Small Jewish Community with a Large Inheritance) was Paul van Trigt's history of the Dutch Jewish community after 1945, using archives and interviews. *Tanach, Hebreeuws/Nederlands* was a Liberal Jewish variation on the new Dutch Bible translation published in 2004, with the Hebrew on the right-hand page and the somewhat adapted Dutch text on the left. CIDI published *Hamas, portret en achtergronden* (Hamas, Portrait and Backgrounds) by researcher Wim Kortenhoeven.

Only 700 copies were printed of *Het Zotte Vleesch* (The Mad Flesh), the first and only reprint after 82 years of Jacob Hiegentlich's novel about his native town of Roermond. Four hundred of them were sold even before publication. The original first edition, published in 1925, was almost completely bought up by Jacob's father, Sallie Hiegentlich, to avoid a scandal. The novel painted a very unflattering picture of important people in Roermond, including many of Sallie's friends. The reprint was presented on May 1 at the unveiling of a monument opposite the synagogue bearing the names of Roermond's 133 Shoah victims.

On May 7, *Tirza,* the latest novel by Arnon Grunberg, received the Libris Literature Award. The novel, published in September 2006, had already won the Gouden Uil for Dutch-language literature in Belgium.

Cefina, the central organization responsible for subsidizing Jewish social organizations in the Netherlands, celebrated its 60th anniversary with the publication *Springlevend,* a book about Dutch Jewish literature.

Personalia

A symposium was held in honor of Hadassa Hirschfeld, who resigned her post as vice chairman of CIDI; Willem Koster resigned as chairman of Cefina, succeeded by Eddy Sajet, and became chairman of the Dutch Union of Progressive Judaism; Rabbi Dov Salzmann left the Jewish community of Enschede and was replaced by Rabbi Elijahoe Philipson; and Dayan Pinchas Toledano, formerly head of the Sephardi Bet Din in London, was appointed part-time rabbi of the Portuguese Jewish community of Amsterdam, which had not had its own rabbi since 1998.

Frans Weisglas, a former speaker of parliament, was appointed Dutch ambassador to Switzerland in May; he was due to move to Bern in 2008. Ed van Thijn retired from Dutch politics after 45 years. Van Thijn, who started his political career on the city council of Amsterdam, later became the city's mayor, and moved on to a parliamentary seat in 1967. He published several autobiographical works, including one on his experiences in hiding during World War II.

Dutch Jews received a number of awards during the year. Jaap Meijers was given the Yakir Award for his communal work; historian Salvador Bloemgarten received the Dr. Henriette Boas Award for his book *Hartog de Hartog Lémon, 1755–1823,* a biography of one of the first Jewish members of the Dutch parliament: author Harry Mulisch received an honorary doctorate from the University of Amsterdam, and his novel *De Ontdekking van de Hemel* (The Discovery of Heaven) was voted "best Dutch book of all time"; Hilde Pach was awarded the Oranje Translators' Award for her Hebrew-to-Dutch translations of Israeli works; and Raoul Rosenthal, a student at the Jewish high school Maimonides, won the 28th National Chemistry Olympiad and later won third prize at the International Chemistry Olympiad in Moscow.

The yearly royal decorations announced in May included several Jews: Dave Verdooner; Sami Kaspi; Leon Heilbron; Benno Troostwijk; Dr. Abraham Baumgarten; Samu de Leeuw; Willem Koster; Harry en Siny Cohen-Kattenburg; Jaap van Velzen; Lenny Kuhr; Appie Drielsma; and Jules Schelvis, one of very few surviving Dutch Jews who spent time in Sobibor, who was also awarded an honorary doctorate by the University of Amsterdam. Rabbi Avraham Soetendorp received the Peace through Dialogue Award from the International Council for Christians and Jews.

In sports, Israeli basketball player Roye Berkowitz was signed by the Dutch champion Eiffel-Towers Den Bosch. Soccer player Haim Magralashvili of Maccabi Haifa received a three-year contract from the Arnhem soccer club Vitesse, and missed one match that was played on Yom Kippur. Israeli basketball coach Arik Shivek returned to the Netherlands to coach the Amsterdam Astronauts. Boxer Barry Groenteman won the national amateur welterweight championship.

Prominent Jews who died in 2007 included former resistance fighter and member of parliament Joop Wolff, 79; Dave Aronson, considered among the world top antiques dealers, 61; the oldest member of the Liberal Jewish community of Twente, Frits Menno Kan, 90; actor Yakov Lind, who authored two books on how he survived World War II under an assumed identity, 80; Betsy Spijer-Nieuweg, who did much for the Jewish community in The Hague, 81; historian and honorary member of the Nederlands Auschwitz Comité Eva Tas, 91; Dick Bruinsma, deputy secretary general of the UN Conference for Trade and Development, 56; Louise (Loes) Adelaar, senior social worker with JMW, 86; poet Hanny Michaelis, 85; Trudel van Reemst-de Vries, who fought in the Spanish Civil War and the resistance, and later worked as a nurse in Westerbork, 93; Rabbi Nardus (Nachum) Groen, 88; Erich S. Grünewald, former chairman of the Jewish community of Groningen, 95; Jaap Loonstein, former secretary of the PUR (the body responsible for survivors pensions) and board member of the Amsterdam Jewish community, 75; Wim Vleeschhouwer, board member of Maccabi Tennis Amsterdam, 86; Joop Boas, chairman of the Jewish students' home Beth Stoedentiem in Delft, leading Zionist, and board member of the Liberal Jewish community of Rotterdam, 77.

ELISE FRIEDMANN

Italy and the Vatican

National Affairs

EARLY IN THE YEAR the center-left government of Prime Minister Romano Prodi fought off a challenge from the center-right, led by former prime minister Silvio Berlusconi. Although Prodi resigned in February, he won votes of confidence in both the Senate and Chamber of Deputies, and remained in office.

In November, the hard-line right formed a new party called simply The Right. Its leader, Francesco Storace, drew sharp criticism from Jews and others for a statement he made at the party's founding session harking back—proudly—to the fascist roots of the Italian right. Berlusconi spoke there as well.

Some Jews, especially on the left, expressed concern about what they saw as Vatican meddling in Italian politics and a growing alliance between the Church and the political right wing. The most blatant example was so-called Family Day, a rally held in Rome in May that was promoted by Catholic groups and backed unofficially by the Vatican. Its purpose was to rally opposition to a proposed law giving more rights to gay couples and other families consisting of unmarried partners. Hundreds of thousands of people turned out. Rome's chief rabbi, Riccardo Di Segni, disappointed many in the Jewish community by declaring, in an article in the Rome Jewish monthly *Shalom,* that he opposed legal recognition of homosexual couples.

Israel and the Middle East

ITALY

Italy—which headed the UNIFIL peacekeeping force in southern Lebanon put in place after Israel's war with Hezballah in 2006—maintained close relations with the Jewish state.

Throughout the year Italy had many political, cultural, and economic exchanges with Israel and other Middle Eastern countries, including high-level meetings. Prime Minister Prodi made a three-day official visit to Israel and the Palestinian territories in July. Around the same time, Foreign Minister Massimo D'Alema was one of ten EU foreign ministers to sign an open letter to Tony Blair, the new EU Middle East envoy, urging "dialogue" with Hamas in the hope of restoring unity in the Palestinian Authority. In August Prodi sparked some controversy by also appearing to call for dialogue with Hamas, saying that this could help the militant faction "evolve." He later backtracked, stating that Italy's policy had not changed: it would not have contacts with Hamas until the latter recognized Israel, accepted past Israeli-Palestinian agreements, and foreswore terrorism. In September, Prodi spent time in Jordan and D'Alema visited Israel, Egypt, and the West Bank.

Israeli, Lebanese, Syrian, and other Middle East officials came to Rome for meetings during 2007. The new Israeli president, Shimon Peres, visited in September, the first foreign trip since his election. After a session with President Giorgio Napolitano and Prime Minister Prodi, Peres—a frequent visitor to Italy in his private capacity—told a news conference that Italy and Israel enjoyed "true friendship" and that bilateral relations were better than ever.

During a three-day September visit to Rome by an American Jewish Committee delegation, AJC executive director David Harris described Italy as a "critically important nation" as regards the Middle East. "With two thousand troops in Lebanon and command of the UNIFIL force, longstanding relations with Iran and Syria, friendly ties with Israel, an interest in encouraging conflict resolution, and membership in key UN bodies, Italy plays a very significant role in the region," he said.

Italy's left wing was generally pro-Palestinian, often vocally so. Criticism of Israeli policies and outright anti-Zionism were frequently heard from politicians and intellectuals as well as in the Italian blogosphere, which included some virulently anti-Israel sites.

Italian Jews since World War II had been generally leftist in their political outlook, but some had begun shifting to the right in recent years as the mainstream left appeared increasingly unsympathetic to Israel. (The Jewish community per se did not adopt political positions.) As noted above, the views of Foreign Minister D'Alema appeared pro-Palestinian, and in an interview in May, Rome Jewish community spokesman Riccardo Pacifici described him as "still prisoner of a distorted vision of the conflict in the Middle East in which Israel is always guilty." In November, D'Alema, taking part in an international day of solidarity with the Palestinian people, described himself as a "long-time friend" of that cause. D'Alema welcomed the outcome of the Middle East summit in Annapolis, stating that the Israelis had to freeze settlements and the Palestinians had to reign in extremists.

Leftist Italian Jews were themselves often highly critical of Israel's policies, but they also worried at how one-sidedly Israel was treated. Gadi Luzzatto Voghera published a book about this in 2007 called *Antisemitismo a sinistra* (Anti-Semitism on the Left). A group calling itself Sinistra per Israele (Left for Israel), which sponsored occasional events and maintained an active on-line forum, supported the Israeli political left while striving to counter anti-Israeli, anti-Zionist, and "even anti-Semitic prejudices" found "in a substantial part of the Italian left."

The issue of possible media bias against Israel was addressed in May at a three-day conference in Rome attended by high-profile journalists from the national press. An ADL survey of Italian opinion released around the same time indeed showed that 45 percent of respondents believed that media coverage had been biased, but of those with this opinion, 53 percent said the bias was in favor of Israel and only 29 percent believed it favored the Arabs.

In September, Turin was the site of a meeting of representatives from Turin University, Hebrew University, and Jerusalem's Al-Quds Palestinian University about how the three institutions might cooperate. Far different was another event that took place in the city the next month, a roundtable organized by a Turin University professor called "Ethnos and Religion: The Case of Israel." It was part of a series of programs, Festivalstoria, which presented Israel as a racist state that wished to annihilate the Palestinians. Pamphlets calling for a cultural and academic boycott of Israel were distributed outside the hall where the roundtable was held.

In Milan there was a concert under the title "Jewish and World Music: Sounds, Words and Poetry in Support of Israeli Soldiers Jailed for Opposing the Occupation of Palestine." Among the performers was the prominent Jewish singer and actor Moni Ovadia, a leftist who had long expressed opposition to Israeli policies toward the Palestinians. Organizers said the proceeds would go to "organizations that support Israeli military conscientious objectors." In a letter to the leftist newspaper *L'Unita*, reprinted in the Turin Jewish paper *Ha Keillah*, one critic of the event asked why the concert and its organizers did not also support "the struggle of Palestinian objectors" who were "tortured and killed as collaborators, traitors and enemies of the [Palestinian] cause."

Egyptian-born journalist Magdi Allam, who had lived in Italy since 1972, made headlines in 2007 with his provocative, best-selling memoir

Viva Israele (Long Live Israel). Allam, deputy editor of the Milan daily *Corriere della Sera,* had been raised as a Muslim but was now an outspoken opponent of radical Islam, and had to employ bodyguards because of threats to his life. He told the Israeli daily *Ha'aretz,* "Those who don't like me and condemn me for my opinions see this [book] as additional proof that I am a traitor to the Arab cause and an enemy of Islam, have sold myself to Israel and work for the Mossad. But for me, *Viva Israele* is a song of praise to Israel's life and to everyone's life." More than 200 intellectuals signed a letter of support for Allam, while around 100, overwhelmingly leftists, signed on to a highly critical letter. Gad Lerner, a leftist Italian Jewish journalist who had been born in Lebanon, drew fire when he published a critical review of the book, as did Moni Ovadia, whose review called the book too one-sidedly supportive of Israeli policy.

There was continuing concern throughout the year about potential terrorism. In July, three North African immigrants, including an imam, were arrested in Perugia on suspicion of having links with Al Qaeda and possibly preparing attacks in Italy.

THE VATICAN

Pope Benedict XVI issued frequent calls for peace in the Middle East and for Israeli-Palestinian reconciliation, as well as several specific appeals for an end to bloodshed in Gaza and a return to negotiations. Also, throughout the year he called for better conditions for Christians in the Middle East. "Christian minorities find it difficult to survive in the midst of such a volatile geopolitical panorama and are often tempted to emigrate," he told representatives of Eastern Oriental Orthodox Churches in February. "In these circumstances, Christians of all traditions and communities in the Middle East are called to be courageous and steadfast."

At a Vatican audience in February, relatives of Ehud Goldwasser and Eldad Regev, two Israeli soldiers abducted by Hezballah in 2006 and still held captive, met with the pope and appealed for his help in gaining their release. Benedict had already called for the Lebanese militia to release the two soldiers or at least to show that they were alive.

Throughout the year the Vatican and Israel held fitful and fruitless negotiations on outstanding questions that clouded their relationship. When Israel and the Holy See established full diplomatic relations at the end of 1993, several key issues were left to joint commissions for resolution. These primarily concerned the Church's financial and legal status in

Israel—including taxation and property rights—as well as restrictions on Arab Christian clergy traveling in the West Bank. One minor agreement was in August, when the Israeli Tourism Ministry and the Vatican reached agreed on the implementation of charter-flight service for Catholic pilgrims to the Holy Land.

Benedict raised the key matters under dispute during a "cordial" audience with President Peres when the latter visited Italy in September. A Vatican statement describing the meeting said, "The hope was expressed for a rapid conclusion to the important negotiations currently underway, and for the creation of constant dialogue between the Israeli authorities and the local Christian communities with a view to the full participation of those communities in constructing the common good." Peres, for his part, reiterated a longstanding invitation to the pope to visit Israel.

Pietro Sambi, the papal envoy to the U.S., addressed the subject of Vatican-Israel ties in a November interview posted on terrasanta.net, the Website of the Franciscan Order, saying that relations had been "better" before the establishment of formal links.

Anti-Semitism and Racism

Racism, xenophobia, and anti-Semitism remained high-profile issues in Italy. An Interior Ministry report published in June described a "galaxy" of small right-wing extremist groups around the country, including skinhead soccer hooligans. Some neofascist groups, it said, were so anti-Zionist that they aligned themselves with radical Islamists. The Vatican spoke out against anti-Semitism on several occasions, and in April announced that the topic would be on the agenda of a synod of bishops called for October 2008. According to a survey published in May by the ADL, 18 percent of Italians polled believed that the Jews were responsible for the death of Jesus. Furthermore, 32 percent believed in the "probable" truth of at least three out of four anti-Semitic stereotypes (the complete results were posted on the ADL Website).

At the beginning of the year, ahead of the January 27 Holocaust Memorial Day, Justice Minister Clemente Mastella proposed a bill on combating racism and anti-Semitism that would also criminalize Holocaust denial. But many intellectuals and historians criticized that part of the bill, citing free speech concerns and opposing criminalization of opinion. Among the critics was Renzo Gattegna, president of the Union of Italian Jewish Communities. Italian Jews, he said, knew the importance of "freedom of thought, and thus of manifesting thought." In the end, the Council of Ministers approved a bill mandating up to three years in jail for "anyone publicizing theories of racial superiority" and up to four years for "anyone committing or inciting to commit discriminatory acts for racial, ethnic, national, religious, sexual or gender motives," but did not criminalize Holocaust denial.

A number of episodes of racism and anti-Semitism made headlines during 2007. In January, for example, vandals scrawled anti-Semitic slogans near the home of Barbara Aiello, an American-born Reform rabbi who lived in the town of Lamezie Terme in southern Italy (see below, p. 438). About 100 neo-Nazis gathered near Varese in April to celebrate Hitler's birthday, triggering reports that dozens of right-wing extremists in northern Italy were attempting to organize a Nazi-style party. The government launched an investigation.

In November, Rome Jewish community spokesman Riccardo Pacifici warned that xenophobia was mounting in Italy and that Jews could not remain silent. His comment came in the wake of attacks against Gypsy (Roma) immigrants from Romania that followed the arrest of one of them for the murder of a woman in northern Italy. Pacifici declared the solidarity of Roman Jews with the Romanians, who were the "object of attacks by xenophobic and racist groups." Also in November, a bookstore at Rome's main train station took copies of Hitler's *Mein Kampf* off the shelves following an appeal by the Rome Jewish community.

Holocaust-Related Developments

On January 16, President Giorgio Napolitano joined Milan's mayor and other dignitaries at a ceremony at Milan's central train station for the formal establishment a new national memorial to the Shoah. Scheduled to open in 2009, it would be housed in a large underground area donated by the Italian state railway near the platform from which more than 8,000 Italian and other Jews were deported to death camps in 1943–44.

The ceremony took place less than two weeks before Holocaust Memorial Day, January 27, which was observed with the usual educational, cultural, and commemorative programs both on the day itself and in the days before and after. These included wreath-layings, lectures, book presentations, exhibitions, concerts, school projects, youth programs, symposia, theatrical performances, recitals, and concerts. Television and radio featured special broadcasts, and newspapers and magazines published articles and special supplements. One theme running through these events was the role and function of Holocaust memory as the actual events receded into history. As part of the observances, some 500 high school students from Tuscany traveled by train from Florence to Auschwitz to learn about the Holocaust in a program sponsored by regional authorities.

President Napolitano addressed political and Jewish dignitaries at the Quirinale presidential palace on Holocaust Memorial Day, saying "all forms of racism, starting with anti-Semitism" had to be fought even when, "disguised as anti-Zionism, it aims at denying Israel's right to exist." As part of observances in Rome, several people were posthumously honored as Righteous among the Nations, and Greek-born Holocaust survivor Sami Modiano, 77, celebrated his bar mitzvah at a ceremony in the city's main synagogue. An inmate of Auschwitz on his 13th birthday, he had never marked this rite of passage.

On the occasion of Holocaust Memorial Day, the town of Maccagno unveiled a plaque and named a piazza in honor of the late Enrico Sibona, a wartime police officer there who was arrested and sent to concentration camps for rescuing Jews. Sibona was named Righteous among the Nations in 1992. In March, on what would have been his 100th birthday, Italian Catholic writer Odoardo Focherini was honored by a union of Catholic journalists. Focherini was arrested for helping save more than 100 Jews during the Holocaust and died in Hersburck, a German concentration camp, in 1944, aged 37.

Justice Minister Mastella came to New York in October to attend an ADL event where the first Giovanni Palatucci Courageous Leadership Award was presented to New York deputy police commissioner David Cohen. The award was named for an Italian police chief who defied the Nazis and saved thousands of Jews during the Holocaust. The ADL created the award to recognize Italian and American police officers who demonstrated "extraordinary leadership in the fight against extremism, bigotry and terrorism." Mastella used the occasion to denounce anti-Semitism and pledge that his government would implement the tough new laws against it. In Rome, meanwhile, prizes in Palatucci's memory were, for the fourth year, presented to police employees or their children who had written university theses on themes related to the Shoah, racism, interfaith dialogue or multiethnic society.

In November, Rome mayor Walter Veltroni accompanied nearly 240 high school students to Auschwitz, an annual project he had begun years before. Israeli ambassador Gideon Meir also went with the group. Veltroni told reporters he wanted to establish a permanent base at the former death camp for visiting Italian students, which could become a branch of the future Holocaust museum in Rome. The city also inaugurated a new program whereby high school students who had already traveled to Auschwitz with Veltroni would spend time during the year effacing anti-Semitic slogans and scrawled swastikas from walls.

In October, neo-Nazi skinheads from the Alto Adige/South Tyrol region came under investigation for visiting Holocaust sites. Photographs were published in the media showing seven young skinheads at Dachau giving the Nazi salute and displaying Nazi symbols.

Citing security fears, the University of Teramo closed its law, political sciences, and communications departments in May to prevent a scheduled talk by convicted French Holocaust denier Robert Faurisson. He had been invited by Professor Claudio Moffa in the face of opposition from the dean, who said Faurisson's qualifications were "absolutely inadequate and don't deserve academic legitimization." About 100 protesters shouted at Faurisson and Moffa outside a café on campus where they held a news conference. Moffa was a well-known leftist who used Holocaust denial to question the legitimacy of Israel. Earlier in the year he had invited Serge Thion, another French Holocaust denier, to lecture, and in April organized a conference on "The Middle East and the Holocaust: Gagged History" that concluded with a taped interview of Faurisson.

In January, a military court in La Spezia sentenced ten former members of the Nazi SS in absentia for their role in the massacre of some 560 civilians in the Italian village of Marzabotto, near Bologna, in 1944.

Erich Priebke, the 93-year-old former SS officer serving a life sentence in Rome for war crimes, was in the news in May, when he won a work-release permit, ostensibly to work for his lawyer as a translator. Priebke was convicted in 1997 of taking part in a 1944 massacre of 335 civilians at the Ardeatine Caves outside Rome and had been serving his time under house arrest. The decision to allow him out drew fierce criticism from Jewish groups, Mayor Veltroni, and others, including U.S. Representative Tom Lantos. In June, when Priebke arrived at his lawyer's office on the back of a motorbike, about 100 protestors demonstrated on the street outside. A judge later ordered Priebke's work-release permit withdrawn.

For the first time, the record of the British Army's 5,000-member Jewish Brigade that fought in Italy during World War II was commemorated. This took place during the April 25 ceremonies marking Italy's liberation from German occupation in 1945. At the event, attended by many delegations of resistance fighters, Jewish leaders carried a banner dedicated to the Jewish Brigade.

A traditional torch-lit march through Rome was held October 14 to mark the anniversary two days later of the deportation of Jews from the capital in 1943. Coinciding with the anniversary, the Italian publisher Einaudi released a boxed set of French director Claude Lanzmann's landmark 1985 Holocaust documentary *Shoah,* comprising four DVDs and a book.

At the end of the year, the Council of Ministers responded to numerous complaints by ruling that annuity checks paid to about 700 Jews as compensation for damage suffered under Italy's World War II racist laws did not constitute taxable income.

Roma Tre University instituted a graduate program in the teaching of Holocaust studies.

JEWISH COMMUNITY

Communal Affairs

As many as 35,000 Jews were believed to live in Italy. About two-thirds of them were formally affiliated with Jewish communities, but their number dwindled from year to year. Rome, with about 15,000 Jews (12,000 formally affiliated), and Milan, with about 10,000 (6,000 formally affiliated), were the largest communities. Outside these two main centers Jews were scattered in a score of other towns and cities, mostly in northern and central Italy.

Several communities experienced sharp internal discord between leaders and between factions, sometimes linked to broader left-right Italian or Israeli politics. In Turin, a bitter clash between the lay leadership and the chief rabbi led to the resignation in January of community president Tullio Levi. He and others had criticized the rabbi for being too rigidly and inflexibly Orthodox, and had called for his dismissal. Another divisive issue, particularly in Milan but by no means absent elsewhere, was whether the children of non-Jewish mothers might attend the Jewish school.

All established communities were Orthodox in orientation and linked under an umbrella organization, the Union of Italian Jewish Communities (UCEI), whose leadership constituted the official political representation of Italian Jewry. This year marked the 20th anniversary of a landmark accord between the UCEI and the Italian state that recognized this status, one of a series of agreements regulating the position of non-

Catholic religions in Italy. In November, the Rome Jewish community celebrated the installation of a new Torah scroll, believed to be the first copied out in Rome in 150 years.

Chabad was very active in several cities, most notably Rome, Milan, and Venice. Early in the year Chabad marked 30 years of activity in Rome with a gala evening attended by the Israeli ambassador and leading Chabad rabbis. Guest of honor was Rabbi Berel Lazar, one of the chief rabbis of Russia, who was born in Milan to parents who were among the first Chabad emissaries sent to Italy. At Hanukkah, Chabad-sponsored public menorahs were lit in at least half a dozen cities around the country. The lighting in Rome marked the 20th anniversary of the first public menorah. Dignitaries including Rome's chief rabbi, Riccardo Di Segni, and the president of the Lazio region attended the Rome ceremony.

Small Progressive (Reform) congregations or groups were active in several cities, two of them in Milan. None were recognized by the UCEI, but the ones in Milan and Florence affiliated with the World Union for Progressive Judaism and were broadening the scope of their services. The Lev Chadash congregation in Milan, for example, claimed 200 members, weekly services, bar and bat mitzvah classes, and other cultural and educational programs. It also had a permanent rabbi and carried out conversions.

Meanwhile, an American Reform rabbi, Barbara Aiello, who had served for a time in Milan, headed a congregation in Calabria, Ner Tamid del Sud (Eternal Light of the South), as well as a study center there focusing on Jewish historical roots in Sicily and Calabria. Her congregation shared a Torah scroll with another small Reform group in Turin. Aiello conducted Reform and interfaith weddings in various parts of Italy, sometimes for foreigners. In July an American boy had his bar mitzvah at her synagogue, and that same month she conducted what she said was the first Reform bar mitzvah ever in the city of Perugia.

A tiny, newly formed Jewish community functioned in Trani, Apulia, where Jews had been expelled 500 years earlier. The group, which operated as a branch of the Naples Jewish community, held services in the medieval Scolanova synagogue that had long been used as a church and reverted to Jewish use in 2005. In May the Trani congregation held a ceremony marking the acquisition of its first Torah scroll.

In March, the Milan Jewish monthly *Il Bollettino* triggered public discussion with a cover story on what it called an "identity crisis" afflicting Italian Jewry. "Something is changing profoundly in our community," wrote *Il Bollettino* editor Annie Sacerdoti. "It seems almost as if the malaise that ever more pervades modern society has also entered our institutions, undermining their former spirit." She noted generational, ideological, religious, and political conflicts. At their heart, Sacerdoti wrote, were "different concepts and different modes" of how to live as a Jew and how to confront social change.

Two developments in particular were changing the face of Italian Jewry, she argued, the passing of the generation that remembered the World War II antifacist resistance and the growing influence of the thousands of Jewish refugees from Arab countries who began arriving in 1956. "So," Sacerdoti wrote, the community was now "divided between present and past, between varying degrees of religiosity and observance, between Jews who want a rigorous observance of Judaism and those who live it 'Italian-style'—at the synagogue only for Pesach, Rosh Hashanah, and Yom Kippur, but often with the desire to transmit a Jewish education to their children, at the community's Jewish school, even if they are in a mixed marriage." The only thing Jews had in common any longer, she believed, was concern for Israel. Over the next several months *Il Bollettino* printed numerous responses from both well-known and ordinary Jews. Some echoed Sacerdoti's pessimism but others suggested that internal conflict was a sign of vitality.

The future of Italian Jewry also formed the topic of the annual national "Moked" conference that took place April 29–30 in Senigallia. The official theme of the event was "Looking Ahead," and discussions focused on the same issues raised by Sacerdoti and others in *Il Bollettino.*

The largest recent group of immigrant Jews in Italy consisted of the families of the thousands of Jews who fled Libya in 1967 in the wake of anti-Semitic violence. Some of Italy's leading Jewish figures, including Milan's chief rabbi, Alfonso Arbib, were either immigrants themselves or were born into such families. Ceremonies were held this year in Milan and Rome to mark the 40th anniversary of the Libyan exodus. Libyan Jews in Italy also launched Memoria (Memory), a project aimed at creating an archive of Libyan Jewry through interviews and collections of documents and photographs, as well as the creation of an online museum of Libyan Jewry.

In addition to religious services, Jewish communities offered a wide variety of other programs and events. At the end of May, the Jewish school in Milan hosted its first intergenerational reunion, encompassing former pupils who had attended from 1938 to 2006. About 1,300 people attended, including former teachers. One aim was to fund-raise for the school, which, organizers said, had a deficit of 1.2 million euros.

Kosher food was experiencing a boom in Italy. There were a growing number of kosher restaurants and shops. This was especially the case in Rome, which featured at least five kosher restaurants as well as snack bars, butchers, groceries, and bakeries. A new store opened there in the spring called the Kosher Bakery Café. Kosher restaurateurs in Rome estimated that about half their clients were not Jewish. In any case, the Rome Jewish community had to more than double the size of its kashrut office from two people to five. In October Rome hosted an international exhibit of kosher wines. Nevertheless, the Jewish press carried repeated complaints about the high cost of kosher products and about confusion over kosher standards and certification.

In the spring, in conjunction with the Simcha Layeled organization, the Trieste Jewish community hosted a group of 25 ailing children from Israel, including Jews, Palestinians, Israeli Arabs, and Druse. Rome hosted the 12th quadrennial European Maccabiah Games in July, where more than 2,000 Jewish athletes from some 38 countries competed in 16 different sports. Hadassah International's youth organization also met in Rome in July. In October, the Rome Jewish community marked the 25th anniversary of a Palestinian terrorist attack on the main synagogue that left a young child killed and dozens injured. As part of the ceremony, Mayor Veltroni laid a wreath.

In the fall, conferences in Milan and Florence discussed the performance of the Italian Jewish media. Jewish magazines were published in Milan, Rome, Turin, and Florence, and smaller newsletters and information sheets were published by independent groups or communal organizations. State-run television carried a regular Jewish program, and in recent years Italian Jewish Websites had proliferated. At the conference in Florence, editors of the magazines *Shalom* (Rome), *Il Bollettino* (Milan), *Ha Keillah* (Turin), *Firenze Ebraica* (Florence), and the Sorgente di Vita TV program discussed possible cooperative strategies.

Interfaith Relations

There were ups and downs in Jewish-Catholic relations during the year. On the one hand, cordial and productive meetings and conferences continued to take place between Jewish and Catholic leaders, including some involving Pope Benedict and other Vatican officials. On the other, lingering controversy over the wartime record of Pope Pius XII, who was placed on the road to sainthood in 2007, and other questions about several of the present pope's actions prompted Jewish concern.

In January, Israel's chief Ashkenazi rabbi, Yonah Metzger, and other Jewish leaders met with Vatican officials in Rome at a conference on Christian-Jewish relations organized by the lay Catholic Sant'Egidio organization. Metzger described relations with the Church in very positive terms and repeated Israel's invitation to Pope Benedict to visit.

The Vatican's Commission for Religions Relations with the Jews and the Israeli Chief Rabbinate issued a joint statement in Jerusalem in March that called "moral relativism" a "serious threat to humanity." It claimed that "secular society still requires religious foundations to sustain lasting moral values" such as the sanctity and dignity of human life. While affirming the principle of freedom of religion, the statement made an exception "wherever and whenever a threat is posed by the promotion, teaching or exercise of violence and specifically terrorism and psychological manipulation in the name of religion." In addition, it said, "it is legitimate for a society with a predominant religious identity to preserve its character, as long as this does not limit the freedom of minority communities and individuals to profess their alternative religious commitments . . . ."

In October, during ceremonies commemorating the 42nd anniversary of the Nostra Aetate document that opened the way to Catholic-Jewish dialogue, the first Lay Catholic-Jewish Conference was held at the Vatican. Also that month the pope visited Naples to participate for one day in the three-day annual interfaith World Peace Meeting, which encompassed leaders of various faiths, including Rabbi Metzger.

The issue of Pope Pius XII's role during the Holocaust years continued to sour Jewish-Catholic relations. Critics accused Pius of having turned a blind eye to the suffering of the Jews; the Vatican, still keeping its wartime-era archives closed to scholars, maintained that he helped save Jews. In March, an Italian newspaper reported that documents had turned up in the archives of the Stasi, the East German secret police, showing Pius to have been an enemy of the Third Reich. Based on this, one Catholic commentator, Sister Margherita Marchione, theorized that Moscow had been behind efforts to criticize Pius's actions so as to weaken support for the Catholic Church in Soviet-dominated postwar Eastern Europe. A new biography of Pius by Italian journalist Andrea Tornielli, published in May, also defended Pius, saying he helped the family of a Jewish school friend escape to Switzerland.

The papal envoy in Jerusalem, Archbishop Antonio Franco, threatened to boycott the annual Yom Hashoah ceremony at Yad Vashem in April because of a caption in one exhibit critical of Pius XII. The caption described Pius as having "abstained from signing the Allied declaration condemning the extermination of the Jews" and said he "maintained his neutral position throughout the war." In the end, Franco attended the ceremony. Yad Vashem said it would review the caption, but urged the Vatican to open its archives from the period to clarify the matter.

In May, Pius was formally placed on the path to sainthood when the Vatican's Congregation for the Causes of Saints approved his beatification. Before actual beatification could take place, however, two miracles would have to be attributed to Pius, and Pope Benedict would have to approve. A number of Jewish organizations sharply criticized the process and urged the Vatican to put beatification on hold until Pius's role during the Holocaust was clarified through opening the archives.

Another Vatican move that alarmed Jews was the decision during the summer to revive a Good Friday prayer in Latin calling for the conversion of the Jews. ADL national director Abraham Foxman went so far as to call it a "body blow to Catholic-Jewish relations." Foxman, who met with Vatican officials in Rome, said his group was "extremely disappointed and deeply offended that nearly 40 years after the Vatican rightly removed insulting anti-Jewish language from the Good Friday Mass, that it would now permit Catholics to utter such hurtful and insulting words by praying for Jews to be converted."

In August, Pope Benedict upset Jews by meeting with controversial Polish priest Tadeusz Rydzyk, director of Poland's Radio Maryja, a station that had broadcast considerable anti-Semitic content. Jewish groups sharply criticized the meeting, during which Rydzyk kissed the pope's hand. Jews were particularly puzzled about the audience because Rydzyk had previously been reprimanded by the Vatican for his remarks about Jews. A statement the Vatican issued after the meeting said it "did not imply any change in the Holy See's well-known position regarding relations between Catholics and Jews."

During the year there were also efforts at dialogue, or rather trialogue, among Jews, Christians and Muslims, as the pope made Vatican outreach to Muslims a priority. In October, Tuscan schoolchildren from the three religions met together in Florence.

Culture

Numerous Jewish and Jewish-themed cultural events took place around the country. These were organized by Jewish communities and institutions, private organizations and promoters, civic and state bodies, or a combination of these, and took place in Jewish community centers, museums, theaters, civic spaces, and other venues.

Exhibitions during the year included one on the experience of Holocaust survivors who transited Italy en route to Israel after World War II, which opened in March at the Museum of Contemporary History in Milan. A large show of contemporary Israeli art opened in Turin in June. In the spring and summer Rome hosted an exhibition on Bauhaus architecture in Tel Aviv.

Among Jewish cultural events were the annual OyOyOy festival in Casale Monferrato in May and the Nessiah Jewish culture festival, held in Pisa, Livorno, and other towns in September, which drew a record crowd of more than 3,000 people. The annual Pitifest Jewish film and culture festival took place in Pitigliano in December. Italy was an enthusiastic participant in the annual European Day of Jewish Culture, held this year on September 2. Events took place in more than 50 cities and towns around the country and drew tens of thousands of people. In November, Rome's first gallery devoted to Jewish and Israel art opened in the old Jewish ghetto.

There were many cultural exchanges between Italy and Israel. Israeli literature had a dedicated following, and a number of Israeli writers, artists and performers presented their work in Italy. In March, for example, Israeli novelist Amos Oz was the focus of the "Dedica" festival in Pordenone and writer Uri Orlev was featured at the Minimondi festival in Parma; Oz would return in October to receive a literary prize in Cosenza. David Grossman took part in the OyOyOy festival as well as in the big Festivaletteratura in Mantova in September, and A. B. Yehoshua gave readings in October. The Habima Israel National Theater performed in Turin in April. Israeli artists took part in "White Night"—a nightlong event in Rome during September when museums, galleries, and other spaces remained open. In December, a major exhibition on Jewish Italy opened at the Israel Museum in Tel Aviv.

As usual, numerous books on Jewish themes or by Jewish authors were published, and there were many book launches, readings, roundtables, and other literary happenings. Significant nonfiction books included *Gli Ebrei di New York* (The Jews of New York) by Maurizio Monilari, a journalist for the *La Stampa* newspaper. Mayor Veltroni took part in a book launch for it cosponsored by the American Academy in Rome and the Rome Jewish community. Tullia Zevi, journalist and former UCEI president, recounted her long and colorful life to her granddaughter, Nathania, in *Ti Racconto la mia Storia: Dialogo fra nonna e nipote sull'ebraismo*

(I'll Tell You My Story: Dialogue about Judaism between Grandmother and Granddaughter).

One book that sparked intense controversy was *Bloody Passover: European Jews and Ritual Murder* by Ariel Toaff, a professor at Bar Ilan University and the son of Rome's former chief rabbi. The book, written in Italian, appeared to accept as true that some medieval Jews may indeed have used Christian blood when making matzos, possibly in revenge for persecution. When it appeared in February there was a torrent of criticism not only from Italians but also from foreign Jewish organizations. "A Jewish tradition of this kind has never existed, nor has any indication or custom that allows the ritual use of human blood," was the reaction of Rome's current chief rabbi, Riccardo Di Segni. The book quickly sold out its first printing, but given the uproar, Toaff asked the publisher to halt further distribution so he could amend the text.

In November, John Mearsheimer and Stephen Walt came to Milan for the official launch of the Italian edition of their controversial book *The Israel Lobby,* sparking heated debate with the authors over their thesis that Israel's American supporters had undue influence over American policies in the Middle East (see above, p. 125).

The annual WIZO Jewish literary awards, presented in October, went to *Una Tromba nello Uadi* (A Trumpet in the Wadi) by Israeli author Sami Michael for best novel, and to *Dieci Bottiglie Verdi* (Ten Green Bottles) by Vivian Jeannette Kaplan for best children's book.

Israeli and Jewish-themed films were shown at a number of festivals and in cinemas. Several were presented at the Venice Film Festival, including *Disengagement* by Israeli director Amos Gitai—his 12th appearance at the festival. In November, the sixth edition of the Roma Kolno'a Jewish and Israeli film festival took place in Rome.

Personalia

In January, Gary Krupp, who headed the New York-based nonsectarian Pave the Way interfaith dialogue group, was named to the Pontifical Order of St. Gregory the Great. He thus became the first Jewish man to be knighted by two popes. In August, the pope knighted Rabbi Leon Klenicki, the ADL's interfaith affairs director emeritus, for his contributions in creating positive relationships between Catholics and Jews around the world. Klenicki was inducted into the Order of St. Gregory the Great at a ceremony at the Vatican's UN mission, presided over by Sean Cardinal O'Malley of Boston.

At a ceremony at Rome's Campidoglio (City Hall) in May, 98-year-old scientist Rita Levi Montalcini, the oldest living Nobel laureate and a life member of the Italian Senate, received a special award from the Technion of Haifa, with President Napolitano in attendance. In November, at a ceremony at the Great Synagogue, Rome's Jewish community awarded her honorary membership. Levi Montalcini, who was on the political left, had recently been insulted by right-wing leader Francesco Storace. Mayor Veltroni, who was at the ceremony in Rome, called Storace's attack "a manifestation of political barbarity like few seen in our recent history."

In November, Yossi Harel, commander of the *Exodus,* the ship that took Jews to Palestine in 1947, was awarded the Exodus Prize in La Spezia, the port from which the ship sailed. The award ceremony took place during a three-day festival featuring Jewish artists and musicians. Also in November, Anna Foa, a leading Jewish historian, became a bylined columnist for the Vatican newspaper *Osservatore Romano,* the first Jew to hold such a post.

The noted Jewish artist, animator, and set and stage designer Emanuele Luzzati died in January at his home in Genoa. He was 85. Luzzati, who was nominated for Academy Awards for his work on two animated films, frequently used Jewish themes. He illustrated a Haggadah and also created the painting that decorates the Jewish archives in Rome (see www.museumluzzati.it).

In September, Alberto Aron Nirenstein, a survivor of the Warsaw Ghetto who wrote a noted book about his wartime experiences, died in Florence. He was the father of Fiamma Nirenstein, one of Italy's best-known Jewish journalists.

RUTH ELLEN GRUBER

Switzerland

National Affairs

UNDER THE presidency of Micheline Calmy-Rey, a Social Democrat from Geneva who also served as foreign minister, Switzerland pursued a policy of "active neutrality" on the international stage. "Switzerland is not a political dwarf," she explained, and claimed that the country used its neutrality to promote peace as well as safeguard its own interests. This statement, along with four federal reports about Swiss foreign policy, was released to counter criticism of Calmy-Rey's clear antipathy toward Israeli actions during the 2006 Lebanon war. "Switzerland does not have a secret agenda; rather, it builds bridges," she said.

While Switzerland was engaged on various diplomatic fronts, the internal political situation became unexpectedly agitated. The campaign that preceded the October parliamentary elections was marked by an aggressive tone and fierce anti-immigrant slogans. Rallies and counter-rallies of left- and right-wing militants sometimes culminated in violent clashes, and police had to intervene.

The largest political party, the Swiss People's Party (SPP), appealed to patriotic sentiment through the use of xenophobic rhetoric suggesting that foreigners, who comprised a quarter of the country's 7.5 million people, threatened the security of Switzerland. One of the SPP posters, for example, showed three white sheep standing on the Swiss flag as one of them kicked a single black sheep away, "to create security," the caption read. One of the party's television ads, "Heaven or Hell," showed negative images of Muslims and young foreigners. The ad was withdrawn by court order.

Despite the street violence for which it was largely responsible, the SPP won the election with a plurality of 29 percent against a divided opposition; this was its fifth consecutive victory. The result was generally attributed to the SPP's formidable financial resources and to its charismatic leader, Justice Minister Christoph Blocher. Nevertheless, Blocher was in for a surprise when parliament convened in December to elect a new seven-member cabinet, according to a prearranged party ratio. Even though all seven of the incumbents wanted to stay in office, which would have made the election a formality, mainstream conservatives joined forces with the left to oust Blocher from the cabinet and in his stead elect a more moderate SPP representative, Eveline Widmer-Schlumpf, minister of justice. Although not a declared candidate, she accepted the post.

Another sign that the Swiss were less than enthusiastic about xenophobic policies was a decision by parliament to end the practice of granting naturalization by popular vote of the residents of the locality the foreigner lived in, a procedure supported by the SPP. There had been many complaints that basing citizenship on such votes bred arbitrariness and discrimination.

If the number of foreigners living in Switzerland was on the rise, so was the number of Swiss living abroad. In 2007, 645,000 Swiss nationals were living outside the country, an 11-percent increase since 2000. They resided mostly in the European Union, the U.S., Canada, Australia, Brazil, Israel, and South Africa. At the same time, about 500 foreign firms and independent billionaires settled in Switzerland, drawn by the flat-rate taxation system and the banking secrecy laws. But Swiss banking institutions were hard hit by the U.S. sub-prime mortgage crisis. UBS and Credit Suisse both reported major losses in the fourth quarter, and were considering significant layoffs.

Israel and the Middle East

Switzerland increased its involvement in the Middle East, both unilaterally and through international organizations. In February 2007 the Swiss government adopted UN Security Council Resolution 1737, passed the previous December, imposing sanctions on Iran, blocking the import or export of sensitive nuclear materiel and equipment, and freezing the financial assets of persons or entities supporting its nuclear programs.

The Swiss government authorized the export of 100 Tommy guns and ammunition to Saudi Arabia for use by the royal family's "national VIP protection team." This arms relationship had started in 2006, when Switzerland exported assault rifles and antiaircraft systems to that country. Switzerland also signed an agreement with Syria for reciprocal promotion and protection of investments; it already had this type of agreement with 120 other countries.

Switzerland was not invited to the Annapolis conference on the Middle East in November, despite the country's sponsorship of the Geneva Initiative, designed to facilitate a deal between Israel and the Palestinian Authority. Among the reasons given were that Switzerland was less generous to the Palestinians than other donor countries, pledging only $80 million for 2008–10, and that it maintained a relationship with Hamas, which the U.S. and the EU were seeking to isolate.

Switzerland supported the reappointment of Jean Ziegler as UN special rapporteur on the right to food, even though he had repeatedly expressed anti-Israel bias. At the same time Switzerland was involved in mediation efforts with Iran on behalf of the U.S., and secretly brokered negotiations between Israel and Syria. Switzerland acted as an unofficial mediator between Lebanese factions, hosting two meetings of Lebanese politicians and intellectuals representing all the parties. Soon after Israel's war in Lebanon ended, the Swiss government provided Lebanon with $18 million in aid.

Only months after its foundation, a new Geneva-based UN agency, the Human Rights Council, proved to be a caricature of itself, hardly better than its predecessor, the Human Rights Commission. With the Islamic bloc controlling 17 of the 47 seats as well as two of the five vice presidencies, it focused mainly on targeting Israel, to which it devoted three special sessions and against which it adopted nine resolutions. In its first year of existence the council condemned only one country, Israel. Not only did it leave the human-rights abuses of China, Cuba, Zimbabwe, Muslim countries, and others unexamined, but also, on the strength of solid Muslim opposition, it canceled a Western-sponsored item on violations in Iran and Uzbekistan. Switzerland, which was a member, abstained.

The Swiss-based International Committee of the Red Cross adopted a new emblem in 2007, a red crystal. Ultimately it would replace the red cross and red crescent to protect humanitarian workers, but the new symbol would have to be introduced gradually since it was not yet well known enough to serve the purpose of protecting those working in conflict zones. The red crystal was adopted so that the Israeli rescue society Magen David Adom could join the international organization without using the Christian or Muslim icons.

Anti-Semitism and Extremism

An opinion survey conducted by the Bern-based GFS Institute showed that 10 percent of the Swiss could be classified as anti-Semites and that another 30 percent expressed such feelings occasionally. These numbers were in line with earlier surveys conducted over the previous ten years. Reponses to specific questions showed that old stereotypes were still alive, such as vastly overestimating the Jewish population and the influence of Jews in international finance. Twelve years after the national debate over Switzerland's attitude during World War II took place, 43 percent of Swiss thought Jews maintained Holocaust memory for their own profit, and 25 percent believed that Switzerland was being blackmailed by Jewish organizations. The survey also demonstrated strongly negative views of Israel, with 50 percent of respondents agreeing that "Israel is waging a war of extermination against the Palestinians" and that the state was led by religious fanatics, and 58 percent convinced that Israel was an arm of the U.S. in the Middle East. Two out of every five people asserted that Israel had too much influence in the world and bore a responsibility for global terrorism. A similar survey was sponsored by the Anti-Defamation League in six European countries, including Switzerland, and its Swiss data were similar to the GFS findings.

The year saw a considerable increase in extremist violence. According to the Federal Police, there was, on average, one violent incident a day involving right-wing extremists. The far right, which had been actively recruiting for some time, counted about 1,800 members in the country, ten times more than in the early 1990s. In 2007, five people were the targets of booby-trapped packages prepared by neo-Nazis.

As had been the case for several years, the neo-Nazis were most visible and active on August 1, when the country annually celebrated Swiss National Day on Grütli meadow, considered the birthplace of Switzerland. In light of the incidents that had taken place there in the past, the government and the cantons bordering the site were reluctant to hold official commemorations there this year. Nevertheless, President Calmy-Rey insisted that the event take place, with a discrete but efficient police presence and a screening of ticket-holders. Since the federal and canton governments refused to fund additional security forces, two private sponsors stepped forward, Nicolas Hayek, founder and CEO of Swatch, and Johann Schneider Ammann, a member of parliament and CEO of a family-owned construction and machinery business. Despite the presence of a handful of nationalist militants, the commemoration attracted a larger audience and received a warmer reception than in previous years. No major incidents were reported except for a fire cracker buried a few feet from the stage that, remotely controlled, went off shortly after the ceremony without causing any harm.

Soccer hooliganism was a major problem. While this was the case in many European countries, it presented a particular challenge in Switzerland since the European soccer championship was to be contested there in 2008. In preparation, the Federal Police centralized information about known hooligans in an electronic database. Beginning in 2007, they had the authority to do a number of things: forbid such people from coming close to soccer stadiums; ban them from entering the country; or force them to check in with a police precinct, which, in turn, could keep them in custody for 24 hours. But the police were instructed to begin by engaging in dialogue and to resort to coercive measures only as a last resort.

Far-right militants attempted to infiltrate into mainstream institutions, and succeeded doing so in the army. For the first time in its history, the Swiss army in 2007 denied promotion to one if its members because he was a defendant in a case of racial discrimination. This reflected the application of a new "zero tolerance" policy toward extremism in the military, under which four soldiers had already been convicted for racial slurs or for giving the Nazi salute while on active duty.

Neo-Nazi parties struggled to maintain themselves. Five members of the Party of the Nationalist Swiss (PNOS) were fined for racist comments in their publications. A new women's group, the Combat Association of Female Nationalist Activists, associated with the PNOS, was founded in 2007 in the Solothurn canton. Its self-described purpose was to "fight against rotting society, radical feminism, and gender egalitarianism." According to police, who closely monitored its activities, the organization had 100–200 members. The increased visibility and violent activity of far-right groups worried not only the police but the government as well. President Calmy-Rey said that Switzerland's traditional image of generating dialogue and building bridges had been tarnished internationally by public violence. She expressed concern for the country's security, especially during the upcoming 2008 soccer championship.

Federal Police continued to treat Islamic fundamentalism as a serious threat. The first trial against people accused of ties to Al Qaeda opened in the Ticino canton. The seven defendants had been arrested in connection with terror attacks in Riyadh, Saudi Arabia, in 2003; they were also accused of belonging to a criminal organization, as well as forgery, fraud, corruption, concealment, and illegal residence. After a two-month trial, all seven were acquitted.

In another case, the Federal Criminal Court declared a couple guilty of supporting radical Islamic organizations via the Internet. The accused stood trial in Bellinzona for allegedly letting groups linked to Al Qaeda promote racially motivated crimes, publicize claims of responsibility for attacks and threats against Western countries, and broadcast images of Islamist attacks and executions. The man, a Tunisian, was sentenced to six months in prison plus an additional 18 months suspended, while his Belgian wife was given a six-month suspended sentence for aiding and abetting him. This was the first time a Swiss court had convicted anyone for supporting an Islamic terror group.

The Department of Foreign Affairs denied entry into Switzerland to a Saudi sheikh. An Al Qaeda supporter, he wanted to participate in a meeting of Swiss Muslims.

The Swiss People's Party filed a motion in the Bern canton requiring that the building of any new minaret, temple, or other religious building be submitted to popular vote. The government of Bern rejected the motion, arguing that refusal of permission to build a house of worship had to be justified by some consideration, and this would be absent in the case of a popular vote. Bern was the third canton to reject this SPP proposal. The party, determined to curb the number of mosques and minarets in Switzerland, also launched a national initiative "forbidding minarets in Switzerland." Its promoters had until November 2008 to collect 100,000 signatures of Swiss citizens so that the matter could be put to popular referendum. There were, at the time, two minarets in the country, one in Zurich and the other in Geneva.

Tariq Ramadan, the Swiss scholar of Islamic law, lost his lawsuit against the U.S. government after he was denied a work visa to teach at Notre Dame University. The Federal District Court in Manhattan ruled that the visa denial was not based on provisions of the Patriot Act, but rather on Ramadan's donation of $1,336 to a Swiss charity later designated by the U.S. as a terrorist group supporting Hamas. During the year Ramadan was also declared persona non grata by the Free University of Brussels. He had been invited to a conference there sponsored by an organization of European Arab students, but was denied the opportunity to speak.

Of all the minorities living in Switzerland, Jews were the group most likely to make use of the antiracism law, according to a study by the Federal Commission against Racism. Between its introduction in 1995 and 2004, 277 lawsuits were filed under the law, about half of them leading to court rulings. In these cases, 81 percent of defendants were found guilty of racism, and a majority of these involved anti-Semitism. The law also contained a provision outlawing the denial of any genocide, and in 2007 the first suit was filed against someone denying a genocide other than the Holocaust: a Turkish political leader, Dogu Perinçek, was convicted after he claimed at a public rally that the Armenian genocide was "an international lie."

Nationalist parties had repeatedly attempted to amend the antiracism law or annul it altogether. Cristoph Blocher, the former justice minister, made another try in 2007 to limit the implementation of the law in relation to genocide denial, but the government rejected his proposal. Two small right-wing parties, the Swiss Democrats and the Freedom Party, filed an initiative "for freedom of speech—no to muzzles!" that aimed at repealing the law entirely. They had until February 2009 to collect 100,000 signatures of Swiss citizens to bring the matter to a national referendum.

Holocaust-Related Matters

The parliamentary commission for the rehabilitation of persons who had been convicted of helping refugees—mostly Jewish—enter Switzerland illegally during World War II finished its work. Beginning in 2004, it rehabilitated 119 people. In dissolving itself, the commission recommended that the individual cantons continue to pursue the task on a regional basis.

The International Committee of the Red Cross admitted that it had been misled in issuing a traveling document to Nazi war criminal Adolf Eichmann on June 1, 1950, which enabled him to escape from Europe and immigrate to Argentina. The document, which bore Eichmann's pseudonym, Ricardo Klement, was recently discovered in the archive of a Buenos Aires tribunal.

JEWISH COMMUNITY

The Swiss Federation of Jewish Communities and the American Jewish Committee signed a cooperation agreement to develop joint projects in the areas of Jewish identity, defense of the Jewish people, and research and analysis.

The Swiss Federation of Jewish Communities requested a financial audit of the World Jewish Congress, of which it was a European affiliate. The audit revealed an undocumented sum of $5 million, including $1.2 million transferred to a Swiss bank account for Israel Singer, the WJC's secretary general. The investigation also raised questions about payments for Singer's expenses, which suggested that the organization's finances were inadequately controlled. Singer was dismissed from his WJC position, which was what the Swiss Federation had requested when the scandal first broke (see above, p. 148).

A fire gravely damaged two Geneva synagogues, the Sephardi synagogue and Hekhal Haness, the largest in the city, during the night of Shavuot. A police investigation could not determined if the cause was arson or a short circuit, and, if the former, whether there was an anti-Semitic motive. The structures were rebuilt.

A new stage in the recognition of Jewish culture in Switzerland was reached with the creation of a chair in Jewish studies at the University of Bern. Several new publications on Jews in Switzerland appeared: Anne Vaïa Fouradoulas's *La Communauté juive de Fribourg et son environnement cantonal (1895–2000),* about the Fribourg community; Stefan Mächler's *Le Grand Déchirement,* about the Swiss Federation of Jewish Communities and the Holocaust; Brigitte Sion's *L'Aventure du judaïsme liberal à Genève,* a history of Reform Judaism in Geneva; and *Suvivre et Temoigner. Rescapés de la Shoah en Suisse,* Holocaust testimonies published by the Geneva School of Social Work.

Philippe Schwed, one of the most knowledgeable historians of Swiss Jewry, died in 2007. He wrote a number of seminal works on Swiss anti-Semitism in the nineteenth and twentieth centuries.

BRIGITTE SION

Central and Eastern Europe

Germany

National Affairs

SINCE 2005 GERMANY HAD BEEN governed by a center-right coalition pairing Chancellor Angela Merkel's Christian Democratic Union (CDU) with Foreign Minister Frank-Walter Steinmeier's Social Democrats (SPD). Merkel's international standing enjoyed a boost in 2007 due in part to her presidency of the 27-member European Union from January to June and of the G-8 industrialized nations throughout the year. On the domestic front, an improving economy and falling unemployment helped win popular support for the government.

In May, in her role as EU president, Merkel cohosted an interreligious conference in Brussels. Afterwards, she said she no longer planned to include a reference to "Christian values" in a new draft of the proposed European constitution, due to objections from Muslims and Jews.

Germany maintained and extended its presence in northern Afghanistan in 2007, despite popular opposition. About 3,200 German troops and six Tornado reconnaissance jets with up to 500 soldiers were part of the NATO-led International Security Assistance Force. In October, the Bundestag approved a one-year extension, with only the Left Party opposed. The next month the Bundestag also approved another year of support for Operation Enduring Freedom, which deployed up to 1,400 German troops in the Horn of Africa and up to 100 special-force personnel in Afghanistan.

A number of tragic incidents fueled public criticism of such commitments. Three German soldiers were killed in May in a suicide bombing. In July, a Taliban group kidnapped two German engineers. One of them was shot and killed, and the other was then shown on Al Jazeera television. Merkel said she would not bow to the kidnappers' demand for the removal of German troops from Afghanistan in return for the engineer's freedom. The hostage was later released. In August, three German policemen were killed in a bomb attack in Kabul.

Germany remained the second largest contributor to the UN-mandated, 34-nation Kosovo Force, with nearly 2,400 soldiers. In 2007, German diplomat Wolfgang Ischinger led a failed attempt to negotiate a settlement of the status of Kosovo.

With Al Qaeda demanding a withdrawal of German troops from Afghanistan and an end to German support of the U.S.-led "war on terror," the country was considered a potential target for terrorism. In November, a videotaped Islamist diatribe against Germany and Austria called the two countries "friends of Jews and Christians about whom Allah warned us . . . ."

In September, police arrested three men in North Rhine-Westphalia on suspicion of planning terrorist attacks on behalf of an Al Qaeda branch. They were reportedly preparing to make a powerful car bomb, and were suspected of having spent time in terrorist training camps inside Pakistan. Because two of them were German Christian converts to Islam (the third was born in Turkey), the arrests prompted talk of increasing surveillance of German converts.

Late in the year, Jihad Hamada, a Lebanese citizen, was sentenced to 12 years in jail in Lebanon for his part in an attempted attack on Germany. He and Yousef al-Hajdib had planted suitcase bombs on German trains in July 2006, but they failed to explode. Al-Hajdib was to stand trial in Düsseldorf for attempted murder.

Interior Minister Wolfgang Schäuble (CDU) argued for greater powers to conduct Internet surveillance. With support from Merkel, he also pushed for German participation in an EU program to record data about airline passengers, and advocated shooting down commercial jets if it appeared that hijackers would use them as bombs.

There were about three million Muslims living in Germany, most of them of Turkish origin. In December, a report commissioned by the Interior Ministry and carried out by professors from the Institute for Criminology at the University of Hamburg suggested that the Muslim community could become radicalized because Muslims felt excluded from mainstream society. Of the 1,750 Muslims contacted by the researchers, 92 percent rejected violence in the name of Islam, considering it sinful and an insult to Allah. But Schäuble said that the other 6 percent were cause for concern. In addition, another 14 percent tended to hold "anti-democratic" views.

In September, a regional appeals court in Frankfurt am Main found that the circumcision of an 11-year-old Muslim boy without his approval was an unlawful personal injury, since subjecting one's child to teasing by other children for looking different was a punishable offense. The court opened the way for financial compensation for the boy, now 14, who reportedly planned to sue his father for 10,000 euros (about $14,000). Observers feared the case might have repercussions for the practice of ritual circumcision in Germany by Muslims and Jews.

Germany's Protestant synod, meeting in Dresden in November, turned down a request by Muslim leaders to expand its Christian-Jewish dialogue to include Muslims. Wolfgang Huber, the top Protestant bishop in Berlin, explained that the postwar Jewish-Christian relationship in Germany was unique and therefore not open to new members.

Germany's top foreign-policy concern in 2007 remained the question of whether Iran's nuclear ambitions were related to energy needs or military objectives, and given Germany's twentieth-century experience and its perceived special relationship with the Jewish people, Iranian president Ahmadinejad's threats to destroy Israel made this issue very sensitive for Germans. Iran reportedly relied heavily on German technology, and critics said Germany should use this dependence to influence Iranian policy. The government itself was divided, Merkel leaning in the direction of tougher sanctions and Steinmeier concerned about protecting German industry.

Merkel consistently took a zero-tolerance position on Iran's combination of anti-Israel taunts and vagueness on its nuclear ambitions. She reiterated this in private meetings with Jewish leaders while in New York for the UN General Assembly in September, when Ahmadinejad was also due to visit the UN. Concerns about Iran and also about rising anti-Semitism in Europe topped the agenda for Merkel's discussions on October 1 with leaders of the World Jewish Congress and the European Jewish Congress. This was Ronald S. Lauder's first official meeting with Merkel since being elected WJC president in June. Also at the meeting were Foreign Minister Steinmeier; EJC president Moshe Kantor; Central Council of Jews in Germany (CCJG) president Charlotte Knobloch; and the new WJC secretary general, Michael Schneider.

A month later, however, Steinmeier warned against the use of force to cope with Iran. Speaking in Hamburg at the annual SPD meeting, he said that "military adventures" were no solution, and that Germany would continue seeking a diplomatic resolution in concert with the U.S., Russia, and China. These remarks followed Steinmeier's talks with Iranian nuclear negotiators on October 25, where he reportedly urged the Iranians to cooperate with the EU, the UN, and the International Atomic Energy Agency.

As if to underscore the differences between herself and Steinmeier, Merkel told German Jewish leaders in November that her government was ready to back tougher sanctions. Receiving the Jewish community's Leo Baeck Prize, Merkel said she saw her three main tasks as combating xenophobia and anti-Semitism; helping support the growth of Jewish life in Germany; and standing up for Israel's right to exist within secure borders. Regarding Iran, she insisted that "my government is following its words with deeds," meaning sharper sanctions. On a visit to President Bush in November at his ranch in Texas, Merkel urged all members of the Security Council to remain engaged on the Iranian issue.

Also in November, the German engineering firm Siemens announced it would withdraw from all new business deals with Iran. Reportedly, less than 1 percent of the firm's business was in the Islamic Republic, and 80 percent of that was related to non-nuclear-power generation. The Siemens announcement followed decisions in the summer by four major German banks—Deutsche, Commerzbank, Hypovereinsbank, and Dresdner—to cut back on dealings with Iran, after U.S. vice president Dick Cheney warned them that they would have trouble doing business in the U.S. Nevertheless, there were reports indicating that trade continued through other banks. Similarly, some small businesses continued to deal with Iran, often through third parties. It was pointed out, however, that a number of American companies did the same, working through Dubai.

Germany's economic ties with Iran ran deep. In 1984, West Germany was the first Western country to send a foreign minister to Iran after its 1979 Islamic revolution. Although Germany had reportedly been Iran's second biggest trading partner in 2006 (the biggest was the United Arab Emirates), trade volume dropped 25 percent through November 2007. In addition, government-backed Hermes export-loan guarantees fell by more than 50 percent from 2006 to 2007, according to figures from the German Ministry of Economics cited by the *Financial Times.* Deutsche Bahn and E.on-Ruhrgas also canceled major projects with Iran. Some feared that China, Russia, and others would fill the trade gap, and there was in fact a growth in Chinese-Iranian trade. But others argued it would take years for those countries to produce the kinds of products that Germany offered, years that might be critical for halting Iran's nuclear program.

There was also ongoing cultural exchange between Iran and Germany. The Frankfurt International Book Fair sent a delegation to Tehran's annual literary event. In the summer, a German orchestra—its female musicians wearing headscarves as required by Iranian law—performed classical works there. Organizers called it the first performance by a Western orchestra in Iran since the Islamic revolution.

December 2007 marked the end of the prison terms of Iranians who had assassinated four Iranian-Kurdish opposition figures in a Berlin restaurant in 1992, an act that had threatened diplomatic relations between the two countries. In October, Israel appealed to Chancellor Merkel not to release the men until Iran gave out information about missing Israeli fighter pilot Ron Arad.

The release of the U.S. National Intelligence Estimate (NIE) report in December, which found that Iran had halted its nuclear-weapons development program in 2003, fueled suspicions in Germany that the U.S. had all along been less interested in stopping nuclear proliferation than in regime change. Critics called on Merkel to divorce her policy from the American line, and some businesses saw the report as a green light to resume trade with Iran. But even the NIE report suggested that Iran could develop a nuclear weapon by 2015. The chairman of the Bundestag Foreign Affairs Committee, Ruprecht Polenz (CDU), said negotiations should be resumed with the aim of getting Iran to stop uranium enrichment. He urged the U.S. to negotiate directly with Tehran.

Popular opinion tended to be critical of Iran. A poll released in May by the Anti-Defamation League showed that Germans and other Europeans saw Iran's going nuclear as a significant threat, and also regarded Hamas as a terrorist organization. Other studies, including a comparative survey of the views of Israelis, Germans, and American Jews by the Bertelsmann Foundation/TNS Emnid, showed much German support for sanctions against Iran.

The spokesman for the Israeli embassy in Berlin told the JTA that "the lesson from history is that we should take people by their word and act accordingly. If Ahmadinejad and others in Iran talk about wiping out Israel from the map while aspiring to acquire nuclear weapons, we should take it seriously."

Germany and Israel

Germany remained one of Israel's strongest supporters in Europe, and Chancellor Merkel was dedicated to promoting bilateral relations in the year leading up to the 60th anniversary of Israel's founding.

Nevertheless, a conference held in Berlin in September on "Perceptions and Perspectives: The Future of the German-American-Israeli Relationship," sponsored by AJC's Berlin office and the Friedrich Ebert Foundation, found a communication gap between the two countries. As one speaker put it, when Germans said "Never again" they meant no more war, but when Israelis said the same words they meant "we will never be victims again," and the difference had serious political implications. "The Holocaust will no longer be sufficient to carry the relationship into the future," said Israeli ambassador Shimon Stein, and he advocated the cultivation of shared values, economic ties, and cultural dialogue.

The 2007 Pew Global Attitudes Survey indicated that 80 percent of Germans believed that a two-state solution was possible for Israel and the Palestinians. Thirty-four percent sympathized with Israel, 21 percent with the Palestinians, and 34 percent were neutral. Thirty-seven percent of Germans considered Israel responsible for the plight of the Palestinians while 29 percent blamed the Palestinians themselves.

Chancellor Merkel continued to insist that there could be no dialogue with Hamas until it met the three requirements set by the "Quartet" (U.S., EU, UN, and Russia): recognizing Israel's right to exist, renouncing violence against Israel, and accepting preexisting agreements. She met in February with Palestinian president Mahmoud Abbas and asked him to help obtain the release of captured Israeli soldier Gilad Shalit. In March, the European Union Council, under Merkel's leadership, announced that it would only release funds to the Palestinian Authority that were dedicated to social projects. Any money beyond those sums would be held back until the new unity government agreed to the three requirements. At the same time, the EU demanded that Israel release taxes and customs duties owed to the Palestinians.

Merkel visited Jordan, Israel, and the Palestinian territories in April for talks on the resumption of peace negotiations. She called the Arab League's initiative to recognize Israel in exchange for the latter's withdrawal from occupied land a "big opportunity." And in June, Germany criticized a proposal by the foreign ministers of ten European countries—France, Slovenia, Spain, Portugal, Cyprus, Bulgaria, Romania, Italy, Greece, and Malta—to redefine EU objectives in the Middle East and resume talks with Hamas while pressing Israel to concede to Palestinian demands.

Foreign Minister Steinmeier attended the Annapolis conference on the Mideast peace process in November 2007. He announced that Germany was prepared to advise the Palestinian Authority, particularly on improving its police and security forces.

A tiff erupted in early March, when members of the German Catholic Bishops' Conference, on their first official trip to the Middle East, compared Israel with the Nazis. Gregor Maria Franz Hanke of Eichstätt, for example, said Ramallah was like the infamous Warsaw Ghetto. Hanke said that while Israel had the right to exist, "this right cannot be realized in such a brutal manner." He said he would include his impressions in his

Easter sermons. Shimon Stein, the Israeli ambassador, reacted with "horror and disgust," and CCJG president Knobloch condemned the remarks as "appalling and completely unacceptable." But Johannes Gerster, president of the German-Israeli Society, noted "that the Catholic bishops have corrected their comparisons and their positions, which were justifiably attacked." Their second thoughts, he suggested, "should be accepted, and not constantly reheated."

After six years of service, Shimon Stein was succeeded as Israeli ambassador by Yoram Ben-Zeev, 63, who officially took office in December, when ceremonies were held at the embassy in Berlin. Ben-Zeev also placed a wreath at a Holocaust memorial at the Grunewald train station, from which tens of thousands of Berlin Jews were deported to Auschwitz. He had previously been coordinator for the peace process under Yitzhak Rabin, consul general in Los Angeles, and senior director general for North America.

Movements to boycott Israeli products, which gained considerable support in other countries, did not get off the ground in Germany. In September, the German Confederation of Trade Unions (DGB) issued a categorical rejection of boycotts "targeted one-sidedly at Israeli citizens, institutions and products." Such boycotts, it said, "weaken the position of the majority on both sides who are ready for peace and will play into the hands of radical and fundamentalist forces." The statement was issued largely as a show of support for the the new Caucus of Jewish Social Democrats (see below, p. 473).

In August, the Kaufhof department-store chain featured Israeli products for a full week. This "Israel Week" sale, the first for a major German chain, was sponsored by the Israeli Institute for Export and Cooperation.

It was announced in October that a soccer player who had refused to take part in a qualifying game in Israel would nevertheless remain on the national team. Ashkan Dejagah, a 21-year-old German athlete of Iranian background, played on the Bundesliga club VfL Wolfsburg. Dejagah, born in Tehran, originally told German Football Association president Theo Zwanziger that he feared for the well-being of his relatives in Iran should he set foot in Israel. He apologized and agreed to play against the Israeli team when it came to Germany in 2008.

Anti-Semitism and Extremism

Anti-Semitic trends in the general public were of concern to Jewish groups, nongovernmental organizations, and the German government.

Left Party legislator Petra Pau, vice president of Parliament and an expert on right-wing extremism and anti-Semitism, submitted a report to Parliament on the matter. It noted another decline in the number of reported anti-Semitic crimes: there were 951 incidents registered in 2007, down from 1,024 in 2006 and 1,193 in 2005. Among these were 23 cases involving injuries and 216 "propaganda" crimes—the use of banned Nazi symbols, texts, or gestures—up from 191 in 2006.

Pau expressed special concern about the desecration of Jewish cemeteries. The Federal Criminal Police Office reported to Pau that there were 30 such vandalisms in 2007, making a total of 267 over the last five years. The perpetrators were apprehended in only four of the 2007 incidents, and Pau wanted the government to explain why so few had been caught. One case she cited exemplified the problem. The historic Ihringen/Kaiserstuhl cemetery had been vandalized twice in recent years and the perpetrators were never apprehended. In August 2007 it happened a third time, and only after a local citizens group pressed the authorities did police arrest four young suspects, all of whom had right-wing extremist connections. The State Criminal Department said it was committed to clearing up the unsolved cases.

In November, Marion Neiss, a historian with the Berlin-based Center for Research on Anti-Semitism, raised the issue again, announcing that the center was preparing to carry out a study about how government authorities handled cemetery desecrations. Only some 10 percent of perpetrators were caught nowadays, she noted, as compared to over 52 percent apprehended during the 1950s.

Several sensational xenophobic attacks during the summer highlighted the threat posed by right-wing extremists. In August, for example, in the state of Saxony, a gang of about 50 beat up several people of Indian background, who were rushed to the hospital with serious injuries. Later that month an Iraqi man was badly beaten by a suspected right-wing extremist in the state of Saxony-Anhalt, and police in the state of Hessen arrested a suspect in an attack on two Africans in the town of Gunterblum.

Demonstrations of civil courage were rare and noteworthy. In late November, four young right-wingers in Mittweida, in Saxony, harassed a six-year-old child, whose foreign family, of German ethnic origin, had recently returned to the country. A 17-year-old girl came to assist the child, and the perpetrators carved a swastika into her hip. Many people reportedly witnessed the incident from their apartments, but none called the police.

The federal government appropriated an additional 5 million euros (about $7 million) to the fight against right-wing violence in 2007, making the total federal expenditure for this purpose 24 million euros (about $37 million). The state of Saxony more than tripled the amount it spent on such projects, raising the sum to 1.7 million euros (about $2.5 million) for the fiscal year. In August, the state of Thuringia committed $620,000 over three years for a program, "Changing Perspectives: Educational Initiatives against Anti-Semitism and Xenophobia," developed by the Central Welfare Council of Jews in Germany.

One specific anti-Semitic crime generated widespread interest in tightening up the laws. On February 5, when school was not in session, there was an arson attempt at the Chabad-run kindergarten in Berlin. While the smoke bomb did not detonate, Nazi graffiti were found scrawled on the school and on toys left outside. An outpouring of support for the school came from politicians and other minority-group leaders.

The government responded in March with an announcement of new measures to combat anti-Semitism and xenophobia, including mandatory jail sentences for Holocaust denial and incitement to hate, that resembled the hate-crime laws in the U.S. The Justice Ministry committed funds to programs such as "Youth for Tolerance and Democracy," and set about building international cooperation in investigating far-right activities across Europe. The ministers of justice in two former East German states, Saxony-Anhalt and Brandenburg, proposed harsh mandatory sentences for all forms of extremist violence. They said these criminals viewed the usual suspended sentences as a kind of victory. In August, the CCJG announced its support.

Other states, however, did not believe that such changes were necessary, arguing that existing laws were sufficient. But another push for the proposed legislation came in September, after another incident, the near-fatal stabbing of Rabbi Zalman Gurevitch in Frankfort, which caused the European Jewish Congress to call for creation of a pan-European bias-crime law. Police ultimately tracked down the perpetrator in that attack thanks to a detailed description of the incident posted on the Internet. The suspect, a 22-year-old German citizen of Afghani background, was charged with attempted murder and causing life-threatening injury. He admitted attacking the rabbi, but denied any intent to kill him.

That same month, a synagogue in Paderborn in North Rhine-Westphalia was vandalized with swastikas and right-wing extremist slogans—daubed in chocolate, presumably to symbolize the brown Nazi uniforms. At this point Petra Pau called on Germany to create a new position in the government that would be in charge of promoting democracy and tolerance. In November, legislators from the center-right Free Democratic Party suggested the creation of a multiparty commission to investigate anti-Semitism in Germany.

Far-right political parties, particularly the National Democratic Party (NPD) and the German People's Union (DVU), enjoyed minor electoral success in some former East German states, passing the 5-percent threshold necessary to place representatives in local parliaments and to become eligible for federal campaign funding. The NPD—whose membership had grown by 200 to 7,200 in the course of a year, according to the Ministry of the Interior—had parliamentary seats in the states of Saxony and Mecklenburg-Western Pomerania, and in four district parliaments in Berlin. The DVU, whose membership had dropped from 8,500 to 7,000 in the same period, had representation only in the state of Brandenburg.

The NPD in particular aroused concern among mainstream politicians and Jewish leaders. Berlin authorities expressed alarm in July at news—later confirmed by the party—that it was planning to open a training school on a seven-square-mile, abandoned property. At the same time, strangely, the NPD was reportedly facing bankruptcy and selling off properties to meet debts.

NPD leaders continued to get into trouble with the law. In August, the party chief in the state of Hessen, Marcel Wöll, was sentenced to four months in jail for Holocaust denial and for beating up antifascist activists outside a meeting of the local council in the district of Wettau. Wöll said he would appeal. The AP reported that Wöll and another party member had said during a council meeting in March that there should be no further subsidies for class trips to Holocaust memorials such as the former death camp at Auschwitz, which he termed "so-called sites of National Socialist terror." A local politician filed suit against him for these statements. Earlier in the year, Wöll was kicked out of a council meeting after he physically accosted youths who were handing out leaflets calling for banning the NPD. They had received official permission to hand out the leaflets.

The research firm Emnid produced a poll for the broadcasting company N24, released in August, showing that 66 percent of Germans agreed that the NPD should be banned. Politicians and Jewish leaders renewed calls for such a ban. German courts had dropped their last attempt in 2003, after it was revealed that some testimony about the party came from informants who may have instigated illegal activities.

Ban or no, other Germans made their feelings about the NPD clear.

In August, the party was barred from holding a memorial marking the 20th anniversary of the death of Rudolf Hess, Hitler's deputy and a convicted war criminal, in Wunsiedel, where Hess was buried. In October, the party had to cancel its annual conference when its chosen venue, the Weser Ems Hall in Oldenburg, Lower Saxony, refused to host it. NPD leaders sued, but the courts agreed that the site's tenant could legally refuse access. And in a story that delighted opponents of the far right, a Dresden hotelier, Johannes Lohmeyer, devised an ingenious way to keep neo-Nazis off his premises. In an open letter, he informed the party that if it did not accept his cancellation of their online reservation, he would donate all their fees to the Dresden synagogue. The reservation was withdrawn and Lohmeyer received a prize from the German-Israeli Society of Aachen for his "courageous act against right-wing extremism."

Far-left extremism found expression primarily through antiglobalization activism. Criticism of Israel was also common, often comparing Israel to Nazi Germany and disseminating conspiracy theories about supposed Jewish influence on world events. According to the Ministry of the Interior, the number of left-wing extremists in Germany had risen by only about 100 people from the previous year, to 30,800 in 2007. In addition, experts noted a rise in anti-Semitic views among Germans of Arab or Muslim background.

The ADL's 2007 survey of European opinion found that 20 percent of Germans answered "probably true" to three of four anti-Semitic stereotypes. About 51 percent of the German sample thought it "probably true that Jews were more loyal to Israel than to their their own countries," and 21 percent thought the same about whether Jews had too much power in business and finance.

Another study, conducted by the Forsa Institute for *Stern* magazine, showed that 25 percent of Germans thought there was a positive side to National Socialism. Released in October, this survey of more than 1,000 citizens followed soon after the firing of TV talk-show host Eva Hermann for commenting positively on the Nazis' support for traditional families. The answers tended to correlate with age: the older one was, the more likely it was that he or she would see a positive aspect to Nazism.

However another survey that focused on teenagers showed that young people were hardly immune to group prejudice. In talks with youth around Germany, the Berlin-based Amadeu-Antonio Foundation against Racism and Xenophobia found that many believed that Jews must have done something to deserve the persecution they suffered during the Third Reich. The study by sociologist Barbara Schäuble, called "I Have Nothing against Jews, but . . . ," was released in November.

Another particular cause of concern was the anti-Semitism and xenophobia shown by some sports fans, particularly people who followed the fortunes of smaller, regional teams. In November it was reported that the authorities had the names of 9,728 people who had participated in violent sport-related incidents, and about 9.8 percent were known to belong to right-wing extremist groups.

Underscoring the presence of anti-Semitism in the mainstream population, a Holocaust survivor who frequently gave presentations to students at the Berlin Police Academy as part of a class in the National Socialist period reported that, in a discussion about xenophobia and anti-Semitism, the trainees "didn't want to be constantly reminded of the Holocaust," and expressed the view that all Jews were rich. Berlin police president Dieter Glietsch confirmed that such comments had been made. In August, a 33-year-old member of Berlin's police force was suspended after investigators found right-wing extremist CDs, DVDs, and T-shirts in his apartment. A police spokesperson said the man was suspected of assisting in the production of some of the material.

In May, the right-conservative Christian Social Union (CSU), the Bavarian sister party of the CDU, suspended six officers—including top youth leaders—for suspected extremist activities. A state investigation was launched on charges of incitement to hate, coercion, and the use of symbols of unconstitutional organizations.

A trial began in Magdeburg, in February, of seven men aged 24–29—all members of a far-right group—accused of burning *The Diary of Anne Frank* at a summer solstice party in 2006 in the village of Pretzien. One of them said he committed the act to symbolically free himself from the evil Nazi period, but prosecutors found the statement disingenuous. A conviction would bring a sentence of up to five years in jail.

Hate spread over the Internet remained a major concern in 2007. According to the Ministry of the Interior, there were about 1,000 Internet sites operated by German right-wing extremists. In August, the CCJG lent its support to calls for the Internet video-sharing portal YouTube to be prosecuted for failing to bar neo-Nazi hate material that was illegal in Germany. Although YouTube, owned by Google, was based in California and thus beyond Germany's legal jurisdiction, German officials could come down hard on its branches in Germany. German-based Website companies were required to remove illegal material as soon as they were informed about it. YouTube's German edition went online in November, and observers said the site was rife with neo-Nazi videos. The CCJG urged the firm to use filters.

In August, a traveling exhibit about anti-Semitism in Germany and elsewhere opened in the atrium of the Foreign Ministry in Berlin. The exhibit, a project by Yad Vashem and the Berlin-based Center for Research on Anti-Semitism, focused on the question of when criticism of Israel crossed the border of legitimacy.

Holocaust-Related Issues

In January, after the UN General Assembly passed a resolution condemning Holocaust denial, German justice minister Brigitte Zypries proposed an EU-wide ban on denial. Prime Chancellor Merkel was EU president at the time. Nine member states had already criminalized Holocaust denial: Austria, Germany, France, Romania, Poland, Slovakia, Belgium, the Czech Republic, and Lithuania. Germany's Supreme Court exempted Holocaust denial from the protections of freedom of expression in 1994.

In March, Holocaust denier Germar Rudolf was sentenced to two-and-a-half years in jail for incitement and Holocaust denial. Rudolf, a chemist, used the Internet and wrote a pseudoscientific book trying to deny and relativize Nazi anti-Jewish policies. At the start of his trial in November 2006 he called the Holocaust a "gigantic con." In September, the Federal High Court upheld a five-year prison term for Holocaust denier Ernst Zündel, rejecting a 600-page proposal to reduce it.

Members of the SPD in the state of Lower Saxony suggested in March that Hitler, born in Austria, should be posthumously stripped of the German citizenship he adopted in 1932. However the CDU, Chancellor Merkel's party, opposed the move. Uwe Schünemann, the state's interior minister, said it was generally illegal to annul the citizenship of a deceased person, and furthermore, such action "could be taken the wrong way by Jewish communities in Germany or abroad," that is, it might be seen as an effort to disassociate Germany from the Hitler era.

When Hans Filbiger, the former governor of Baden-Württemberg, died on April 1 at the age of 93, the current governor, Günther Oettinger (CDU), praised him as an opponent of the Nazis. In fact, as Charlotte Knobloch, head of the CCJG, indignantly noted, Filbinger was forced to resign from his position in 1978 after his World War II actions—including his role as a navy lawyer and judge—were highlighted in a play by Rolf Hochhuth. Oettinger apologized.

An interview with Horst Mahler, one of Germany's most notorious neo-Nazis, in its November 1 issue landed *Vanity Fair* magazine in deep trouble. Among other things, Mahler said that "Hitler was the liberator of the German people." Jewish historian and Holocaust survivor Arno Lustiger started proceedings to sue the magazine's German edition. His attorneys charged that Mahler had denied and belittled the Holocaust, which was illegal in Germany. The publisher said he ran the interview to make Germans aware of the poisonous ideas in their midst, but Lustiger's attorneys denied the relevance of its motivation. Michel Friedman, a former vice president of the CCJG, also filed suit as a private individual against Mahler.

When he gave the interview Mahler had just been released from jail after serving nine months for incitement to hate. In November he was jailed again, this time for raising his arm in the "Hitler greeting" to his jailers when he was put in the slammer in the former East German city of Cottbus. He was now sentenced to another six months behind bars.

NPD head Udo Voigt told Iranian journalists in December that "it's not possible" that the Nazis killed six million Jews, and that Germany should get back the lands taken away from it after the war. Also, his representative, Sascha Rossmüller, asked Iran to assist the NPD, expressing the hope that President Ahmadinejad could be a "partner for a new Germany." Sebastian Edathy (SPD), who headed the Bundestag Committee for Domestic Affairs, filed a lawsuit against Voigt for Holocaust denial.

That same month Germany came under EU pressure to explain why it failed to extradite Sören Kam, a former SS member, for trial in Denmark. Kam, about 85 years old, was living in Kempten. Number eight on the Simon Wiesenthal Center's list of ten most wanted Nazi war criminals, Kam was suspected of having used a stolen population register to identify 500 Danish Jews for deportation. He also was involved in the 1943 murder of anti-Nazi Danish newspaper editor Carl Henrik Clemmensen.

The long-awaited opening of the archives of the International Tracing Service (ITS), set up in Bonn in 1955, came a little bit closer in May, with an agreement between most of the International Commission's 11 member countries on rules governing access to the millions of documents at its facility in Bad Arolsen. The countries had different laws about protecting the privacy of individuals, and this had held up release of the documents for some time. The documents, which contained information about people who were persecuted under National Socialism, were useful primarily to help establish eligibility for compensation or reparations. The ITS also announced plans to transfer digital copies of the archives to each member country. At that point, 12 million documents had been digitized, roughly a third of the total.

The issue of how to fund the upkeep of Holocaust-related historical sites stirred controversy during 2007. At the May 13 ceremonies marking the anniversary of the liberation of Dachau, Pieter J. Ph. Dietz de Loos, head of the International Dachau Committee and a Dutch survivor, angered many of those present by calling for an entrance fee to the site, saying that a contribution from each of the 800,000 annual visitors would help pay for educational programs and additional staff. No sites of this kind in Germany charged an admission fee.

The suggestion was firmly rejected by Dachau Memorial director Barbara Distel. She argued that the country responsible for the crimes of the Holocaust must never charge admission. Another suggestion, proferred in July by Bernd Neumann, Germany's minister of state for culture, to cut government funding to these sites, was also roundly condemned. Salomon Korn, a vice president of the CCJG, said it was important to increase funding both for symbolic memorials and for authentic historical sites, especially as the number of eyewitnesses declined every year.

In June, a new concentration camp memorial was opened at Flossenburg. The ceremonies were attended by Holocaust survivors, Foreign Minister Steinmeier, and Ukrainian president Viktor Yushchenko, whose father had been a prisoner there. The event marked 62 years since the liberation of the camp by U.S. troops.

It was revealed in August that Germany's national Holocaust Memorial, opened in 2005 in Berlin (see AJYB 2006, p. 436), was already in need of repair. About a sixth of the 2,700 cement steles that made up the memorial had deep cracks, which would have to be closed with injections of plastic filler. The memorial had been designed by American architect Peter Eisenman.

Also in August, Germany's Federal Criminal Police Agency held a series of seminars focusing on the fact that former Nazis continued working for the police force after World War II. Although the agency, created in 1951, had insisted for years that it had no connection to the Nazi period, a 2001 book by former member Dieter Schenk related that the agency was actually created and staffed by ex-Nazis. As late as 1959, they held 45 of the 47 top positions, and 33 of the 45 men had been SS leaders. According to Schenk, the makeup of the agency probably influenced the way the force dealt with right-wing extremists, anti-Semitism, and xenophobia.

Der Spiegel magazine reported in August that a box of Hitler's LP records included music by Jewish composers or played by Jewish musicians. Hidden for 62 years in the attic of a summer resort home near Moscow, the records had been taken from Hitler's Wilhelmstrasse bunker in Berlin by a Red Army reconnaissance officer.

In October, the Quandt family, which owned nearly 50 percent of BMW, agreed to support research into the family's use of forced labor during World War II, and opened its archives to an independent historian. What convinced the family to take this step was the public outcry that followed the airing of a TV documentary, "The Silence of the Quandt Family." It included testimony from former forced laborers, some of whom reported that they had asked for financial support from the Quandts after the war and were turned away.

The Holocaust memorial at the former Bergen-Belsen concentration camp in Germany opened a new documentation center in October, featuring recorded testimony from survivors. The camp's entire history was covered, starting with its use by the Nazis and ending with its role as the largest postwar displaced-persons camp for Jewish survivors. Liberated on April 15, 1945, Bergen-Belsen was the first such camp that the SS did not manage to dismantle before fleeing.

Also in October, Dieter Graumann, a vice president of the CCJG, called on the German Association for Expellees to stop its inappropriate comparisons of German suffering with that of victims of Nazi Germany. As the association marked its 50th anniversary, Graumann said it was time the group healed rifts with Poland and the Czech Republic, wiped its slate clean of nationalistic slogans, and stopped its "unfortunate tradition of drawing parallels between the Holocaust and the expulsion of ethnic Germans . . . ." A similar problem existed with regard to the memorial foundation set up by the former East German state of Saxony: Jewish and survivor groups refused to work with it on the grounds that it drew parallels between Nazi crimes and the injustices of communist totalitarianism.

In November, a new memorial to the victims of Nazi Germany's so-called euthanasia program was dedicated near the Berlin Philharmonic. Information about "Action T4"—which gassed to death more than 70,000 mentally handicapped people in 1940–41—was displayed near the spot at Berlin's Tiergarten park where the headquarters of this program were located.

A bold new exhibit opened at the former Neuengamme concentration camp near Hamburg in November, telling the story of women whom the Nazis forced to become sex workers. The exhibit, "Sex-Slave Labor in the Nazi Concentration Camps," was curated by researchers at the memorial at Ravensbrück, the former concentration camp for women. About 220 women were forced to do this work in ten concentration camps. Many survivors had never spoken of the experience before.

The Berlin Philharmonic opened up its Nazi past to the public in November, as part of events marking the orchestra's 125th anniversary. Misha Aster produced a book and documentary film, *The Berlin Philharmonic and the Third Reich.* There also was an exhibit, based on one designed by the Nazis in 1938, about music that the Nazis considered "degenerate," including jazz, works by Jewish composers, and music deemed politically unacceptable.

Also in November, Germany pledged 5 million euros (about $7 million) to the planned Warsaw museum on the history of Jews in Poland. The AP reported that the German ambassador to Poland, Michael Gerdts, said Germany wanted "to make another contribution to the reparations for the terrible suffering perpetrated against the Jews and thus against Poland in the name of Germany." The museum, to be built on the former site of the Warsaw Ghetto, was expected to open in 2010.

COMPENSATION

In March, the Conference for Material Claims against Germany raised pressure on Germany to accept more cases under a law enacted in 1997 to compensate survivors who were not paid for their work during internment in Nazi ghettos. The law was expanded in 2002, but the Claims Conference said Germany had rejected 61,000 out of 70,000 applications either on the grounds that the particular ghetto did not exist at the time claimed, or that certain categories of labor were excluded. In September, Germany announced the creation of a $137-million fund to pay many who had been rejected in the past.

Following its annual negotiations with the conference, Germany agreed in June to raise pension payments for Holocaust survivors to match the higher cost of living in Eastern Europe. Negotiators also secured additional pensions under Article 2 for survivors who still were, or had been, citizens of certain Western European countries. In addition, Germany enacted a new Law for Support of Victims of the Socialist German Dictatorship that granted Article 2 pensions to victims of the German communist regime. This was the third post-reunification law aimed at compensating these victims. Also, the German Ministry of Finance pledged to increase monthly payments to EU residents and to those in non-EU countries such as Ukraine, Moldova, and Belarus. These payments would reach 14,500 Holocaust survivors who met the same eligibility criteria as those for the Article 2 Fund.

Germany also lifted some eligibility requirements, allowing more low-income people to receive Article 2 payments. The agreement added a quarter of a billion dollars to the pension fund over ten years, and the conference launched an ad campaign to reach people who might qualify. Most of the newly eligible had slightly more than the $16,000 maximum annual income. For some, what made them ineligible was the fact that other reparations payments had been counted toward the income total. That would no longer be the case. The funds would be distributed for ten years starting October 1, the same day that a cost-of-living increase was to take effect.

In November, the *Washington Post* reported that more than 76,000 claims filed by Nazi-era victims who had owned property in former East Germany remained unresolved. One of the more sensational cases was that of American lawyer Peter Sonnenthal, a former attorney for the Securities and Exchange Commission. He and his sister had been trying since 1991 to reclaim hundreds of properties they said their ancestors had been forced to sell during the Nazi era.

Germany's Ministry of Finance announced in February that it would return an 1857 painting by Carl Spitzweg to the heirs of Leo Bendel, a German Jewish collector who died in 1940 in Buchenwald. Bendel had been pressured to sell the painting, *Fiat Justitia,* to a dealer, and used the proceeds to help his family flee to Austria. The painting was purchased a few months later on Hitler's orders for a museum he planned, according to *Der Spiegel* magazine.

In March, the heirs of the German Jewish Wertheim family received one of the largest compensation payments ever reported, negotiated during months of secret meetings. The KarstadtQuelle corporation agreed to pay the Claims Conference $117 million for the last remaining major pieces of property that formerly belonged to the family, and would withdraw claims on 50 other Wertheim properties. Some of the funds would go toward Claims Conference programs for Holocaust survivors and the rest to the Wertheim heirs. When they opened their first small shop in 1875, Ida and Abraham Wertheim planted the seed for the foundation of one of Germany's largest department store chains, but their children lost their property when they fled Nazi persecution in 1939. Much of that property ended up within what became East Germany.

In July, Germany's Social Security Tribunal in Kassel ruled that two Holocaust survivors were entitled to German state pensions, in decisions that appeared likely to set precedents. At issue was how to interpret the requirement that "persecution" had to last at least six months to merit a pension. One plaintiff was able to prove that his persecution had started at the point he was forced to wear a yellow Star of David when German troops occupied his town in Poland. The other won recognition for time spent in a ghetto under pro-Nazi Romanian occupation. He had originally been told that Holocaust pensions were only for people living in places under German occupation.

The Dresden State Art Collections announced in June that, in cooperation with Yad Vashem, it would present artwork by Holocaust victims and survivors, alongside relevant pieces from its permanent collection. No museum in the former East Germany had ever done this before. Martin Roth, director of the Dresden Collections, said the exhibit, scheduled for 2009, would show the power of art in times of suffering and barbarism.

The CCJG criticized plans for a Holocaust museum in Leipzig. In August, CCJG vice president Korn said such a museum could distract people from visiting authentic historical locations in former East Germany, including memorials at the former concentration camps of Buchenwald and Sachsenhausen. The current plan was to house the museum in the former Soviet pavilion at the Leipzig fair grounds.

That same month, the city of Lübeck installed its first brass "stumbling block" memorials in the sidewalks in front of several apartment buildings. The blocks, level with the pavement, were engraved with names of people who had lived in the buildings and were deported in 1941. Artist Günter Demnig, who initiated the project as a protest action in 1996 in Berlin and his hometown of Cologne, installed the first 26 of a total of 40 brass blocks in Lübeck. Some 90 Jews still living there in 1941 were deported to Riga, and only three survived.

These memorials were financed by private donations. There were now some 9,000 "stumbling blocks" in Germany. Some cities, including Munich—home of CCJG president Knobloch—refused to allow them. Knobloch herself, who survived the war by hiding with a Christian family, opposed the stumbling blocks as disrespectful, since one could walk on them.

JEWISH COMMUNITY

Demography

About 120,000 people were registered members of German Jewish communities, but estimates of the country's Jewish population, including the unaffiliated, were as high as 200,000. The registered Jewish population had more than quadrupled since 1990 due to the influx of former

Soviet Jews, but this immigration slowed after Germany introduced a tough new immigration law in 2005. According to statistics cited by the U.S. State Department, the number of Jewish immigrants decreased from 3,124 in 2005 to to 1,971 in 2006.

The Central Council of Jews in Germany (CCJG) included 23 regional associations and 104 communities. There were more than 80 synagogues but only about 30 rabbis. Berlin remained the largest community, with about 12,000 members. Charlotte Knobloch was president of the CCJG, Dieter Graumann and Salomon Korn were vice presidents, and Stephan Kramer was general secretary.

In July, figures were released showing a sharp rise in the number of Israelis seeking to live in Germany. Of the 124,830 people who became citizens of Germany in 2006, 4,313 of them were former Israelis, a figure that marked a 50-percent increase over 2005.

Communal Affairs

A major political development occurred in April, when Jewish members of Germany's SPD announced the formation of a Caucus of Jewish Social Democrats. It was led by Peter Feldmann, a Frankfurt city councilor, and Sergey Lagodinsky, a Berlin lawyer. "The SPD greeted us with open arms," Feldmann said in a press release. Lagodinsky said the new group would stand up for "integration of immigrants of Jewish and non-Jewish background, support activities to combat right-wing extremism," and fight for the rights of Holocaust survivors. The caucus saw itself as ideologically close to the Israeli Labor Party and Meretz, and favored a "realistic" evaluation of Israeli policies.

In June, Gesa Ederberg became the first female rabbi appointed to a pulpit in Berlin. In ceremonies at the Centrum Judaicum, Ederberg—ordained by the Jewish Theological Seminary in New York—was formally installed as rabbi of the Beit Ohr congregation, better known as the Oranienburgerstrasse synagogue, in former East Berlin. Her initial contract was for two years. Berlin's senior Orthodox rabbi, Yitzchak Ehrenberg, objected to the installation and said he would not attend any communal events to which Ederberg was invited. (The first woman ever ordained as a rabbi was Regina Jonas of Berlin, who never held a pulpit. She was murdered in 1943 in Auschwitz.)

In August, the CCJG and the Central Welfare Union of Jews in Germany expressed concern about plans by Nativ, an Israeli government agency, to set up operations in Germany, with a new mandate and money from Israel's minister of strategic affairs, Avigdor Lieberman. Nativ had been created in the 1950s to help Soviet Jews come to Israel, and with the fall of communism Nativ's purpose was called into question. Some saw the decision to send emissaries to Germany as an attempt to breathe new life into Nativ by having it encourage German Jews to come to Israel, and feared this could deepen splits in the German Jewish community. In December, an agreement was reached whereby new Israeli cultural centers would open in 2008 to be run jointly by Nativ and the Jewish Agency, but the arrangement was put on hold with the threatened resignation of Lieberman from the Israeli government.

Jewish communal elections were held in Berlin in November. They brought to power a "unity" party that included members of the old, established community and FSU immigrants. Lala Süsskind, 61, became the first female head of Berlin's Jewish community. Born in Poland, she was a past chair of the WIZO women's Zionist organization in Germany. Although Stephan Kramer, the CCJG general secretary, had announced his intention of running for a seat on the board, CCJG officials said it was inappropriate for a top appointed official to do so, and he withdrew. In the past Kramer had expressed interest in ultimately becoming president of the Berlin community.

In August, the magnificent Rykestrasse Synagogue—Berlin's only major synagogue to survive the Holocaust—was rededicated following a two-year renovation. The building, in former East Berlin, had room for up to 2,000 worshipers. Among the guests was Rita Rubinstein, 85, whose parents were married there in 1905, one year after the synagogue opened. Under communism the sanctuary was used by the vestigial Jewish community, but services were seldom held in the years since German reunification.

Chabad opened its Szloma Albam House—Rohr Chabad Center in September. The official ceremony dedicating the sanctuary and study rooms concluded a multiyear building project that cost about $7 million, virtually all of it raised through private donations. A street fair followed, featuring a performance by Avraham Fried, a noted Chabad singer from Brooklyn.

The city of Bochum dedicated a new synagogue in December, nearly 70 years after Nazis destroyed the town's original synagogue. The Jewish community had 1,200 members in 2007, as many as it had before the Nazi period. The new, cube-shaped synagogue cost about $10 million and was financed by the Jewish community, the state of North-Rhine Westphalia, and the federal government. New synagogues were also planned for Schwerin and Potsdam.

In May, two leaders of the U.S.-based Jewish Renewal movement, Rabbi Marcia Prager and Cantor Jack Kessler, held an event called "Ohel Hachidush," a weekend teach-in and Shabbaton, in Berlin. It was the brainchild of Cantor Yalda Rebling.

Construction workers digging in Mainz in September found 20 Jewish gravestones, probably dating to the twelfth century. These were among the oldest Jewish tombstones ever found in the Rheinland-Pfalz region, experts said. Some of the stones included names of famous rabbis.

In November, a Torah scroll that a priest, Gustav Meinertz, had rescued from Cologne's burning synagogue 69 years before was rededicated. The Cologne Jewish Congregation commemorated the anniversary of Kristallnacht with the placement of the repaired scroll in the ark. The synagogue that was the scroll's original home had not been rebuilt. Meinertz returned the Torah to the Jewish community shortly after the end of the war in 1945. The cost of repair was covered by the archbishop of Cologne, Joachim Cardinal Meisner.

Germany announced in November that it would use $1.6 million in Marshall Fund moneys to strengthen relations between German and American Jewish groups through weeklong guided visits by the Americans to Germany. The one-year trial program was called "Germany Close Up: Young Jewish Americans Meet Modern Germany." The funds would be administered by the New Synagogue Berlin-Centrum Judaicum Foundation.

In December, Berlin's Jewish community marked 60 years since the reopening of city's liberal synagogue. Three Berlin cantors took part in the ceremony, led by Rabbi Chaim Rozwaski in the Pestalozzistrasse Synagogue in former West Berlin. When it reopened in 1947, its cantor was Estrongo Nachama, a Greek Jewish survivor of Auschwitz, who learned the German liturgical melodies of Louis Lewandowski and served the Berlin congregation until his death in 2000.

The Potsdam-based Abraham Geiger College, which housed Germany's Reform rabbinical seminary, announced in May that its rabbinical students would spend their first year of study in Israel, in accordance with a new agreement with Hebrew Union College in Jerusalem. The college later advertised plans to open a Jewish Institute of Cantorial Arts, sponsored by the Leo Baeck Foundation Potsdam, the Breslauer-Soref Foundation of California, and the Soref-Breslauer Texas Foundation.

Also in May, Brandenburg governor Matthias Platzeck signed an agreement linking the Potsdam-based Einstein Forum with the Hebrew University in Jerusalem for the development of an educational forum at the former summer home of Albert Einstein in Caputh, in Brandenburg.

Hebrew University had inherited the home from Einstein, who was on the university's first board of governors.

Culture

The Jewish Museum Munich, financed by the city, opened to the public in March. It was part of a larger complex at St. Jakobs-Platz that also encompassed a Jewish community center, a synagogue, a café, and schoolrooms. The new museum sought to educate visitors about local Jewish life, culture, history, and religion.

In July, a former Hamburg hostel for Jews opened as a museum. The Ballin Stadt Museum, located on the city's waterfront, featured a database with the names of five million emigrants who left Europe via Hamburg between 1850 and 1934. The hostel—which offered kosher food—had been built by Jewish businessman Albert Ballin, chief executive of the Hamburg-America Line, for the many Eastern European Jews who passed through the city on their way to the U.S.

Barbra Streisand performed in Germany for the first time in her career in July. Although the 65-year-old singer had reportedly never wanted to set foot in the country, she stood onstage at the Nazi-era open-air Waldbühne Theater and told some 18,000 fans that she was "very happy to be here in Berlin." Before leaving the city, Streisand and her husband, James Brolin, paid a private visit to the city's Jewish Museum.

In June, *Five Days,* a film about the 2005 evacuation of Jewish settlers from Gaza, won the prize for best Israeli film of 2007 at Berlin's annual Jewish Film Festival. The overall favorite film, as voted by the viewers, was *The Galilee Eskimos,* about a kibbutz on the brink of bankruptcy. Sponsors of the festival included the City of Berlin, the Jewish School of Continuing Education in Berlin, Friends of the German Cinema, and private donors.

In December, the World Congress of Russian-Speaking Jews and the CCJG cosponsored the fifth annual Golden Chanukea, a competition for Jewish performers and musicians.

Circumcision was the theme of the fourth issue of the European-Jewish literary magazine *GOLEM,* published in May, which contained essays, fiction, poetry, and artwork. That same theme was addressed again in September in the first issue of *Familienmentsch,* Germany's first Jewish magazine about parenting. It was financed by private donations and a grant from the American Jewish Joint Distribution Committee.

Personalia

In January, American Jewish businessman Arthur Obermayer presented the seventh Obermayer German Jewish History Awards in Berlin. Each year these awards, which included a small stipend, honored non-Jewish Germans who contributed toward recording or preserving the Jewish history of their communities. Cosponsoring the project were the German Jewish Community History Council, the Office of the President of the Berlin Parliament, and the German Jewish Special Interest Group of JewishGen (an international Internet Jewish genealogy organization).

The 2007 winners were Lars Menk, a letter carrier who compiled an 800-page published volume on the etymology and geographical origin of 13,000 German Jewish names; Ernst Schaell, who, over the course of 20 years, restored tombstones in the Jewish cemetery of Laupheim, in Baden-Württemberg, together with other volunteers; Johannes Bruno of Speyer, a former teacher in Rheinland-Pfalz, who devoted his retirement to researching the Jewish history of that town, writing three books and numerous articles; historian Wilfried Weinke of Hamburg, who created exhibits on Jewish history that were on display at the Jewish Museum of Frankfurt and other venues; and Inga Franken of Berlin, cofounder of the One-by-One contact group for children of survivors and perpetrators.

In October, Holocaust historian Saul Friedländer received the Peace Prize of the German Book Trade, in an emotional ceremony at the Paulskirche in Frankfurt. The Israeli historian, 75, was honored for giving voices and names to Holocaust victims. The international prize, presented annually at the Frankfurt Book Fair, carried an award of 25,000 euros. In his acceptance speech, Friedländer read aloud from unpublished letters his family members wrote in 1942, before they were deported to Auschwitz.

The CCJG presented its annual Leo Baeck Prize to Chancellor Merkel for her commitment to good relations between Jews and non-Jews in Germany, her support for Israel, and her engagement on behalf of Germany's Jewish community.

The Jewish Museum in Berlin presented its annual prize for understanding and tolerance to former chancellor Helmut Kohl and German-born historian Fritz Stern, whose family fled the Nazis and came to the U.S. in 1938.

The annual Buber-Rosenzweig medal was presented in November to journalists Esther Schapira and Georg M. Hafner in recognition of their reports on the Middle East conflict. The prize had been given annually since 1968.

Heinz Berggruen, the eminent Berlin-born art collector, died in Paris in February at the age of 93. News of his death prompted the German media to reflect on the generosity he showed in donating his huge collection, "Picasso and His Era," to the country from which he had fled to the U.S. in 1936. Berggruen had been a friend of Picasso and a specialist on Van Gogh, Cézanne, Matisse, and Paul Klee. The art he brought to Berlin after the war helped fill a gap created when the Nazis confiscated what they considered "degenerate" art.

Author and theater director George Tabori died in July at age 93 in Berlin. Tabori was known as an incisive critic of German society who challenged anti-Semitism and underscored what he considered the absurdity of Hitler and Nazism. His father was murdered in Auschwitz but his mother escaped deportation, and her story became the subject of Tabori's 1979 book *My Mother's Courage,* later made into a film. Tabori lived in 17 countries in all, and in Berlin since 1999.

In September, Julius Kurt Goldstein, who fled Nazi Germany in 1933, fought in the International Brigades in Spain against Franco, and survived 30 months in Nazi concentration camps, died at age 93 in Berlin. After his liberation from Buchenwald in 1945 he settled in communist East Germany, where he worked as a journalist and radio director until 1976. Goldstein, honorary president of the Berlin-based International Auschwitz Committee since 2003, long advocated a united front against neo-Nazism. He received Germany's highest honor, the Federal Cross of Merit, in 2005.

Ernst Ehrlich, a Jewish historian, theologian and author, died in October at age 86. Born in Berlin, Ehrlich studied with the famous liberal rabbi Leo Baeck. He survived the war by hiding with a German family, and then fled to Switzerland, where he remained as a permanent resident. After the war he devoted himself to reconciliation between Jews and Roman Catholics. He was active in B'nai Brith, serving as European director from 1966 to 1991 and then becoming honorary vice president.

TOBY AXELROD

Austria

National Affairs

In the national elections of October 2006 the Social Democrats (SPÖ) eked out a slim victory over the ruling conservative People's Party (ÖVP), 35.3 percent to 33.5 percent. In January 2007, after protracted negotiations, the two large parties formed a grand coalition. There was no other choice, since the Socialists ruled out a coalition with the two small far-right parties, the Freedom Party (FPÖ) and the Alliance for the Future of Austria (BZÖ), and an alliance with the Greens would not have provided the necessary majority in Parliament. This teaming of the two major parties had previously occurred in the 1980s and 1990s.

Social Democrat Alfred Gusenbauer replaced Wolfgang Schüssel of the People's Party as chancellor. Schüssel resigned the chairmanship of his party and was not named to a ministerial post in the new government. Instead, Wilhelm Molterer, a trusted political friend of Schüssel, became vice chancellor. Political observers noted that the election had produced little change, since even though a Social Democrat was now chancellor, the allocation of ministerial posts seemed to continue the dominance of the ÖVP. Not only was Vice Chancellor Molterer named finance minister and Martin Bartenstein stayed on as minister of economic affairs, but also the key Interior, Foreign Affairs, and Health ministries went to politicians aligned with the ÖVP. Furthermore, even though the Ministry of Social Affairs was headed by a Social Democrat, its most important departments were relocated to the ÖVP-led Ministry of Economic Affairs. The Social Democratic ministers and state secretaries, all hand-picked by the new chancellor, belonged to the so-called "new leadership generation" whose political careers began while Gusenbauer had headed the Young Socialists.

The conservative bent of the new government was evident in the strict austerity measures it proposed. University fees introduced by the previous government, which Gusenbauer, during the election campaign, had promised to abolish, remained. The new ÖVP health minister, Andrea Kdolsky, announced cuts in government spending on health as well as increases in health-insurance premiums. Privatization of state-owned enterprises was to continue: in a press interview, Finance Minister Molterer announced that the OMV oil company and Telekon Austria might be privatized. Despite SPÖ campaign promises to cancel the previous government's purchase of the Eurofighter combat aircraft, the new coalition said it would go through with the deal. The immigration and asylum policies of the previous government—largely shaped by FPÖ leader Jörg Haider and heavily criticized at the time by the Social Democrats—would remain in place. And the so-called "wealth tax" that the Social Democrats had pledged to enact was no longer mentioned.

Fierce opposition to the new government and its programs came from youth and student organizations, and some of the trade unions. In Salzburg, members of the Federation of Socialist Students barricaded the entrance to the SPÖ headquarters in protest against retention of the student fees. When the new government was sworn in, there were strong protests in Vienna's Heldenplatz, similar to those that greeted the swearing-in of the ÖVP-FPÖ government in 2000 (see AJYB 2001, p. 397). Only a massive police presence enabled Gusenbauer to avoid the embarrassment of entering the Hofburg Imperial Palace, the official residence of the Austrian president, by an underground passage, as his predecessor, Schüssel, had been forced to do seven years earlier.

Whereas the 2000 protests were directed against the entry of xenophobic extremists into the government, this time the target was the SPÖ's willingness to adopt the outgoing conservative government's policies as its own. Indeed, former chancellor Schüssel reported that Gusenbauer, his successor, had "not had to be persuaded of anything." Some argued that the formation of the new coalition would further accelerate the decline of the Austrian Social Democrats, whose numbers had already dropped from about 700,000 members in the mid-1970s to 300,000. Some regional party leaders expressed strong opposition to the coalition agreement, fearing that the policies about to be pursued at the federal level would have dire consequences in the forthcoming provincial elections.

Israel and the Middle East

Chancellor Gusenbauer paid a two-day official visit to Israel in August, where he met with Prime Minister Ehud Olmert, President Shimon Peres, and Foreign Minister Tzipi Livni. Their discussions focused on prospects for a settlement between Israel and the Palestinians. The chancellor said that Austria, which maintained good relations with Syria, was prepared to assist in promoting peace between Israel and Syria. Speaking at the Interdisciplinary Center in Herzliya, Gusenbauer characterized Austrian-

Israeli relations as "excellent" and stressed the importance of combating racism and anti-Semitism. One area of friction between the two countries surfaced during the visit: Prime Minister Olmert expressed strong opposition to an agreement between Austria's state-owned oil company OMV and the Iranian government for the development of Iran's natural gas reserves. Under the terms of the deal, signed in April, OMV would develop Iran's giant Pars gas field, build a liquefied natural gas terminal (LNG), and export the fuel. The U.S. government also expressed strong opposition. Iranian media estimated the value of the project at 30 billion over 25 years.

An international conference entitled "Women Leaders—Networking for Peace and Security in the Middle East" met May 30–31 at Vienna's Hoffburg Palace, organized by Foreign Minister Ursula Plassnik. Some 80 women holding leading positions in politics, economics, the media, and nongovernmental organizations attended. In the course of the conference, Israeli foreign minister Livni spoke with a number of women from Arab and Muslim countries, including Samira Malik, Pakistan's minister for women's affairs, and held a private meeting with Hanan Ashrawi, a well-known moderate member of the Palestinian Parliament. Livni also served on a panel with Hiri Talabani, wife of the Iraqi president. In her public remarks, the Israeli foreign minister praised the "comprehensive" Saudi peace initiative, but warned that it could only achieve its objective if Arab countries normalized relations with Israel.

Barbara Prammer, president of the Austrian Parliament, made an official visit to Israel in July. After being received by President Peres, she met with Prime Minister Olmert and other members of the government. In a session with Holocaust survivors Prammer expressed regret that Austria had waited until 1991 to initiate restitution payments. She stated it was her "personal obligation" to see to it that Austrians were educated in a spirit of tolerance and democracy so as never to repeat the mistakes of the past. On a visit to Yad Vashem in Jerusalem, Prammer wrote in the guestbook that Israel must remain the eternal homeland of the Jewish people.

Bilateral trade relations between Israel and Austria moved sharply higher in 2006 and well into 2007, according to the president of the Economic Chamber of Austria, Christoph Leitl. He made these remarks at a ceremony in honor of Uriel Linn, president of the Israeli Chambers of Commerce, who received the Grand Golden Badge of Honor for Meritorious Service to the Republic of Austria. The principal Austrian exports to Israel were industrial equipment, car components, pharmaceutical products, chemicals, and food, while Israel exported primarily communication equipment, electrical appliances, measuring and control devices, and vegetables and fruits to Austria. Leitl foresaw increased opportunities for Austrian exports with the expansion of Israel's infrastructure, notably roads and railways, and the enlargement of its seaports and airports.

Israel and the province of Upper Austria agreed to engage in joint cultural and scientific projects. An agreement signed in Jerusalem in March committed the two parties to cooperate in research on alternative energies and nanotechnology. Major joint research projects were also planned by the Johannes Kepler University in Linz and the technical universities of Upper Austria with Israeli research centers, including the Weizmann Institute.

Anti-Semitism

The European Court of Human Rights in Strasbourg, France, ruled in favor of Austrian Jewish journalist Karl Pfeiffer, who had been accused of "causing the suicide" of a German professor, Dr. Werner Pfeifenberger. The case originated in 1995, when Pfeifenberger published an article about a so-called "Jewish connection" that had existed since the French Revolution of 1789. When Hitler came to power, according to the article, it was the Jews who declared war on Germany, not the other way around. Pfeiffer, who was then serving as editor of the monthly publication of the Vienna Jewish community, wrote a response asserting that Pfeifenberger was out to diminish the criminality of the Nazi regime. Pfeifenberger sued Pfeiffer for libel, but two Austrian courts, in 1997 and 1998, rejected his suit and held that Pfeiffer's article was based on solid historical facts. Pfeifenberg committed suicide in 2000 after the Justice Ministry sought an indictment against him for violating the Austrian law outlawing support for Nazi activities.

In June of that year, *Zur Zeit,* an Austrian right-wing weekly that received subsidies amounting to hundreds of thousands of euros from the Austrian government, published an article holding Pfeiffer responsible for conducting "a manhunt" against Pfeiffenberger that drove "the Catholic lecturer" to kill himself. The editor of the weekly, Andreas Moltzer, added that an "antifascist" group was conducting a scurrilous campaign against his newspaper. At the time, Moltzer was a member of the European Parliament and active in its neofascist faction.

Pfeiffer then sued *Zur Zeit* and its editor for slander and defamation of character, and a Viennese court ruled in his favor in 2002. But a higher court, on appeal, found against Pfeiffer on the grounds that the latter was indeed "morally guilty" for Pfeifenberger's suicide. Pfeiffer challenged that finding before the European Court of Human Rights. In its 2007 decision the latter held that the Austrian court had violated Pfeiffer's freedom of expression and had failed to protect his good name and professional reputation, and ordered the Austrian government to pay Pfeiffer 5,000 euros for what he endured, plus 10,000 euros to cover his legal expenses.

In a newspaper interview after his exoneration Pfeiffer said it was important to refute the absurd claim that it was the Jews who declared war against Nazi Germany. As for the charge of responsibility for Pfeifenberger's suicide, he asked, "How could I have 'hunted' a man to his death five years after a review I published in 1995? I am happy that I am not at the mercy of Austrian justice. The fact remains that the anti-Semitic rag *Zur Zeit* is subsidized by the Austrian government and the subsidy continues."

In February, a court in Vienna imposed a 15-month sentence on a Croatian man for vandalizing a Jewish school in November 2006 and causing substantial material damage. The man had told reporters after his arrest, "There are too many Jews in this country." Jewish groups criticized the sentence as too light, especially since the perpetrator did not apologize or express regret for the crime.

Holocaust-Related Matters

Compensation and Restitution

The Holocaust Victims' Information and Support Center (HVISC), or Anlaufstelle, established by the Israëlitische Kultusgemeinde (IKG) in July 1999, continued its work of promoting and protecting the interests of Austrian Jewish Holocaust victims and their heirs. Anlaufstelle personnel helped them find documentation necessary for filing compensation claims, apply to social security agencies for pensions, secure payments for nursing care, and regain lapsed Austrian citizenship.

The deadline for submitting applications for in rem restitution (restitution in kind) of publicly owned real estate was extended by one year to December 2007. Ariel Muzicant, head of the IKG, had been working with federal authorities to extend the deadline to the end of 2008. The Anlaufstelle approached a number of cities and communities through the Federation of Austrian Cities (Österreichischer Städtebund) and the Federation of Austrian Communities (Österreichischer Gemindebund) to take action under terms of the law governing the restitution of public property. Only a few had yet heeded the call.

After two disappointing decisions in 2006 by the arbitration panel responsible for in rem restitution, the Anlaufstelle initiated discussions, both public and private, on interpreting the law governing restitution. Law professors expert in the field were asked to provide the Anlaufstelle their views both on the law and on procedures used by the panel in making decisions. This led to a major conference in April on the subject at the law faculty of the University of Vienna in which several of the country's leading legal scholars participated. Following the conference, one of the arbitration panel's controversial decisions was reversed and the other made subject to further review.

The Anlaufstelle also administered the joint project for the establishment of the Vienna Wiesenthal Institute for Holocaust Studies (VWI), which united under one roof the files of the Wiesenthal Documentation Center and the records of Vienna Jewish community, and served as a research institute for visiting scholars and as a showcase for themed exhibitions. In this capacity the Anlaufstelle launched and hosted a VWI Website and assisted in the preparation and organization of events undertaken by the institute.

Among these was a series of Simon Wiesenthal Lectures, the first of which was delivered in March by the American scholar Omer Bartov, who spoke about "The Last Days of Buczacz." Bartov focused on the different ways in which Ukrainians, Poles, and Jews remembered the Holocaust in this formerly multiethnic town, now part of western Ukraine, where Simon Wiesenthal was born. In June the institute sponsored an international conference on "Labor and Extermination," and, in October, a presentation by French filmmaker Claude Lanzmann that included previously unreleased footage taken during the filming of *Shoah,* now available at www.vwi.ac.at. The federal government, in November, announced a decision to support the VWI, although it did not indicate the amount it would contribute.

The task of identifying looted artworks was carried out by the Commission for Provenance Research, on which the Anlaufstelle was represented. The findings were then passed on to an Art Restitution Council, whose new chairman, Clemens Jabloner, president of the Austrian Administrative Court, had chaired the Austrian Historical Commission that had created the original framework for the country's restitution efforts (see AJYB 1999, pp. 361–62). The council's recommendations would go to the appropriate government ministry, which ruled on final disposition of the cases.

In order to make the council's activities more transparent, the Anlaufstelle set up a Website for the dissemination of its recommendations. The Anlaufstelle also reviewed dossiers of possible restitution cases involving federal museums before their submission to the council, often in cooperation with the Dorotheum, Vienna's leading auction house, using a digitalized form of about 18,000 index cards that had the names of persons who did business with public auction houses during the Nazi era and lists of the movable property they conveyed to those houses.

The art restitution law adopted by the Austrian Parliament in December 1998 covered only artworks in federal museums, not those under the jurisdiction of the individual provinces. Eight of the nine provinces (except Tyrol) had restitution laws, but only the museums in Styria (Landesmuseum Joanneum) and the City of Vienna (Wien Museum and Wien Bibliothek) had returned looted artworks in their possession to the legal heirs.

In May, Ingo Zechner, head of the Anlaufstelle, participated in a conference in Vienna on art restitution that was organized by Sotheby's. Zechner's presentation dealt with the due diligence required of auction houses when confronted with artworks of uncertain provenance. He also gave a presentation in July at the annual conference of the International Association of Jewish Genealogical Societies (IAJGS), held in Salt Lake City, Utah, describing the archives of the Jewish community of Vienna

The National Fund (Nationalfond), established in 1995 to handle payments to Austrian survivors of the National Socialist era, also played a major role in the restitution of artworks. In October it made available to the public its database of artworks held in Austrian museums and collections that, according to the most recent provenance research, may have been expropriated during the Nazi era. The English-language version was posted on the Internet on July 3. Speaking at the Sotheby's restitution symposium, Hannah Lessing, secretary general of the National Fund, said that the database contained approximately 8,000 objects, about half from federal museums and the other half from holdings of the City of Vienna. Records of an additional 1,000 objects were being processed.

At a symposium on "Art Looting and Restitution" in January at Vienna's Urania theater, several experts discussed the daunting hurdles facing the restitution of artworks located in Austria. Speakers noted that the provenance of 420 items now housed in Vienna's Museum of Applied

Arts—20 percent of its acquisitions during the Nazi period—was being investigated; the status of 600 paintings and sculptures at the Österreichische Galerie was still unclear; and 40,000 objects in the possession of Vienna libraries, as well as 24,300 acquisitions by museums, had to be classified of "dubious" provenance simply on the basis of their dates of acquisition.

In February, historians Robert Streibel and Robert Holzbauer recommended the return to Dr. Richard Neumann's heirs of two paintings by Martin Johann (Kremser) Schmidt, a famous eighteenth-century Austrian painter. These had been seized by the Nazis in 1938, and when Neumann sought to reclaim them in 1952, Austrian authorities prevailed upon him to take others of lesser value in their stead. It remained unclear whether an out-of-court settlement might now be reached with the heirs so that the works could remain in Austria.

Georges Jorisch, a grandson of a Viennese woman murdered in the Holocaust, filed suit in Manhattan Federal District Court in October demanding the return of a Gustav Klimt painting from the private collection of Leonard A. Lauder, the New York cosmetics magnate. Jorisch claimed that the signed painting, *Blooming Meadow* (1906), now had a value of $10–$20 million. Lauder, who had purchased the painting in 1983 from a dealer, denied that it had ever belonged to Amalie Redlich, Jorisch's grandmother. Ironically, Lauder's younger brother, Ronald, now president of the World Jewish Congress, had played a leading role in advocating the return of stolen art.

The Vienna Chamber of Labor, together with the Vienna Wiesenthal Institute, organized an international conference, held June 27–29, on "Work and Extermination." Held under the auspices of Austrian president Heinz Fischer, the event was opened by Chancellor Gusenbauer. Also taking a hand in planning the conference were the University of Vienna's Institute for Contemporary History and the Jewish community of Vienna. The speakers focused on the connection between economic exploitation and racially motivated mass extermination. The conference took place in a building that had housed important elements of the Nazi bureaucracy that planned and implemented these policies.

The Austrian Reconciliation Fund, which completed its work at the end of 2005, had set up the Future Fund to support research on the Holocaust and on threats to peace posed by totalitarian regimes, promote international humanitarian cooperation and respect for human rights, and process restitution claims that had not yet been settled (see AJYB 2007, p. 475). Waltraud Klasnic, chairperson of its board, reported that in its first year of operation the fund had processed 120 project applications, 80 of which had been approved, amounting to 2.5 million euros.

Remembrance and Commemoration

An exhibition of newly discovered archival records of the Vienna Jewish community, covering the period from the 1938 Anschluss through the Holocaust years, was officially opened at the U.S. Holocaust Memorial Museum in Washington on June 7, followed by another exhibition, starting July 3, at the Vienna Jewish Museum. Workmen found this material by chance, stored in 800 dusty boxes stacked floor to ceiling in a vacant building that community leaders had decided to sell. The boxes were estimated to contain about half a million pages, including index cards produced by the communal emigration office with the names of 118,000 Jews who sought help in leaving the country in 1938 and 1939, and lists of Jews deported from Vienna in 1941 and 1942. The two exhibitions marked the culmination of seven years of work reordering, preserving, and microfilming the archives, a joint project of the Vienna Jewish community and the U.S. Holocaust Museum.

This archival trove, combined with previously known records now located in Israel, made up one of the largest Holocaust archives of any Jewish community—some two million pages. Not only could it be used by families to discover what happened to their relatives and to file restitution claims, but it also provided historians a clearer picture of the daily lives of Vienna's Jews during the Nazi era.

At the start of a three-day visit to Vienna in September, Pope Benedict XVI paid tribute to the Austrian Jewish victims of the Holocaust. Accompanied by Austria's chief rabbi, Paul Chaim Eisenberg, the pope stood in silence for several moments in the Judenplatz before the stone memorial to 65,000 Austrian Jews who perished in Nazi death camps or died in earlier actions. In a brief ceremony, he described the visit as a gesture of "sadness, repentance and friendship towards the Jewish people." Jewish leaders viewed the use of the word "repentance," connoting the acceptance of guilt and responsibility, as highly significant. Since the onset of his papacy, Benedict—who, as a young man, served briefly in Hitler's army—had to confront the legacy of the Holocaust and the often problematic relations between the Catholic Church and the Jews.

The main purpose of the papal visit to Austria was to bolster the Church there, which had been hard hit by plummeting attendance, low birthrates, declining influence, and a series of sex scandals. One demographer predicted that if current trends continued, the Catholic share of the population, 74 percent in 2001, could drop to only 50 percent by 2051, with Muslims constituting 30 percent. Some 15,000 people assembled outside Vienna's St. Stephen's Cathedral for Sunday's papal mass, a low turnout considering that 200,000 Viennese identified as Catholic.

The contemporary history project "A Letter to the Stars" entered its fifth year. The first activity of the group took place in 2003, when schoolchildren released 80,000 balloons at Vienna's Heldenplatz to commemorate the victims of National Socialism. Since then 40,000 young people participated in remembrance programs. In May 2006, 80,000 white roses were placed at the doorsteps of former residences of Holocaust victims. Two groups, each consisting of 30 people, visited with Holocaust survivors abroad, in New York in April and in London in the fall. Also, about 15,000 students, calling themselves "ambassadors of remembrance," contacted Holocaust survivors living abroad for documentation of their life stories, using a database of 2,500 "last witnesses." Approximately 150 people participated in "Remembrance at Kreuzstadl," a ceremony held annually in March to honor the memory of the victims of the South Eastern Defensive Wall construction project (Sudostwallbau). The wall, intended to halt or slow the advance of the Soviet army approaching Vienna, was built by Hungarian Jewish slave laborers under inhumane conditions, resulting in the death of many. Those still alive were murdered in the last months of World War II at Kreuzstadl, near the border with Hungary. In evoking the memory of this tragic event, Austrian writer Robert Menasse spoke of society's responsibility to remain vigilant against threats to freedom.

Foreign Minister Plassnik lauded the resolution adopted in January by the UN General Assembly establishing International Holocaust Day and condemning the denial or belittling of the Holocaust. Plassnik used the occasion to condemn the Tehran conference in late 2006 that featured Holocaust denial as well as the statements along the same lines uttered by Iranian president Ahmadinejad. She noted the longstanding cooperation between Austria and the Yad Vashem Holocaust Memorial in Jerusalem as well as Austria's membership in the International Holocaust Task Force, which develops educational, commemorative, and research programs.

On May 5, Chancellor Gusenbauer and Vice Chancellor Molterer were among the numerous members of Parliament to attend the annual ceremony marking the liberation of the Mauthausen concentration camp, where almost half of the 200,000 inmates were killed or died of disease and hunger. With the strains of klezmer music sounding in the background, Parliament president Barbara Prammer and others delivered speeches honoring the memory of resistance fighters and warning the country's youth against "seducers" who idealized this dark period in Austrian history.

A commemorative plaque was unveiled at the Mauthausen site on November 27, the first such public recognition in the nearly 70 years since the liberation of the camp. Support to erect the commemorative plaque came from the local Mauthausen community and the Austrian Federal Railway Company, which also arranged for engraving, on the 51 stretches of railroad track connecting the station to the camp three kilometers away, the names of the victims.

The project Linz 2009 European Capital of Culture announced in November its plan for an international conference to commemorate the victims of Nazi euthanasia practices. Scheduled for 2009 in Castle Hartheim in Upper Austria, its preliminary title was "Eugenics and Human Genetics."

An unusual program that, since 1992, had allowed 25 young Austrians annually to serve as volunteers at U.S. Holocaust-related institutions in lieu of army service came to a halt in 2007 when, for reasons probably related to security, the U.S. government did not grant visas to would-be participants. In previous years these young men and women performed such work as translating documents, leading tours, and meeting with Austrian and other Holocaust survivors.

Confronting the Past

Minister of Justice Maria Berger announced that rewards of up to 50,000 euros would be given to private persons for information leading to the arrest of Nazi criminals still at large. She mentioned two men as particular targets: concentration camp doctor Aribert Heim, last seen in South America, and SS officer Alois Brunner. Bringing them to justice, she said—if they were still alive—was an important objective of her ministry. She also let it be known that her ministry would update relevant information concerning the arrest of Nazi war criminals and Holocaust deniers, in line with European Union standards.

Four Austrian soldiers faced criminal charges during the year for exchanging Hitler salutes in two videos that appeared on the Internet. Any display of Nazi symbols or propaganda was a crime in Austria. After an investigation, Defense Minister Norbert Darabos, a Social Democrat, said that the four conscripts would be dismissed from the military and charged by state prosecutors, explaining, "There will be absolutely no tolerance for expressions of support for the National Socialist system. We can make no compromises here." Ironically, the matter came to light during Chancellor Gusenbauer's visit to Israel.

Kurt Waldheim, who, hiding his past service with the German army during World War II, served as UN secretary general from 1972 to 1982 and then as president of Austria, died in June at the age of 88. Although he was never convicted of war crimes, Waldheim was a lieutenant in army intelligence, attached to units of the Wehrmacht that executed thousands of Yugoslav partisans and civilians, and deported thousands of Greek Jews to death camps. Despite persistent rumors about his wartime misdeeds, Waldheim claimed that he had left the army after being wounded on the Russian front in 1942.

It was when he announced his candidacy for the Austrian presidency in 1986 that that the truth finally came out, as investigative journalists, historians, and the World Jewish Congress uncovered incontrovertible evidence. These revelations, however, evoked a nationalist and anti-Semitic backlash in Austria that helped bring Waldheim victory. The People's Party, which supported his candidacy, apparently convinced a majority of voters that the accusations constituted an intolerable interference by foreigners in Austria's internal affairs. Many Austrians evidently viewed Waldheim's life as a parable of their own: they understood his denial of complicity with the Nazis and saw him simply as a fellow-citizen of a country occupied by Nazi invaders and forced to serve in their army. Waldheim stressed this point during the election campaign, insisting over and over that, like hundreds of thousands of other Austrians, he just did his duty.

A year after his election, the American Justice Department barred him from entering the U.S., having determined that he had assisted or participated in "the deportation, mistreatment and execution of civilians and Allied soldiers in World War II." At Waldheim's request, the Austrian government appointed a commission of historians from a number of countries, including Israel, to investigate the accusations. In February 1988 the panel reported that he had to have been aware of the atrocities, and, by doing nothing about them, had facilitated them. Specifically, the panel found it hard to believe that Waldheim had not known of the deportation of the Jews of the Greek city of Salonika between 1942 and 1944. Of the city's 60,000 Jews, only 10,000 survived.

Waldheim did not seek a second six-year term when his presidency ended in 1992, largely because no Western country would receive him, and thus he had become an embarrassment to Austria. He continued to insist on his innocence, and, in a 1996 autobiography, contended that his exclusion from the U.S. was engineered by American Jews who, he said, pressured the Reagan administration, which, in turn, felt it had to send a "useful signal" to Jewish voters in anticipation of the 1988 U.S. presidential election.

JEWISH COMMUNITY

Demography

The number of Jews registered with the IKG (as defined by Orthodox Jewish law) stood at the 7,012, a slight increase over the previous year's 6,935. New registrants may have joined for personal reasons, for example to qualify for burial in a Jewish cemetery, or may have been brought in through the community's outreach program, which encouraged unaffiliated Jews to become members. Knowledgeable observers estimated the actual number of Jews in Austria at 12,000–15,000. In a wide-ranging interview with the daily newspaper *Die Presse* shortly before the communal elections, IKG president Ariel Muzicant stated that the community had the potential to double its numbers over the next ten years by attracting Jews from other European Union countries. Apart from a tiny number of exceptions, immigration from non-EU countries remained frozen.

As had been true for generations, the overwhelming majority of the country's Jewish population lived in Vienna. An estimated 40 percent of the Vienna Jewish community was now Sephardi, as was a majority of the population under age 25. The Sephardi Center, located in the city's second district, housed two congregations, one of Bukharan Jews and the other of Jews from the former Soviet republic of Georgia.

Only some 300–400 made their homes outside Vienna, primarily in the large provincial cities of Graz, Salzburg, Innsbruck, and Linz. In some of the provinces, local governments had sought to redress the horrors of the past by creating Jewish centers or museums as reminders that Jewish life, culture, and religious institutions once thrived in these places. An example was the Jewish Museum of Hohenems, a regional museum that recalled the town's Jewish community and its contribution to the development of the province of Voralberg and the surrounding region. The museum also maintained a relationship with the descendants of Jewish families from Hohenems wherever they now lived.

Communal Affairs

In the same *Die Presse* interview mentioned above, Muzicant noted a significant improvement in the community's financial situation. Two-thirds of its debts had been repaid, and the IKG had balanced its budget each year since 2003. Muzicant suggested that if the community continued along its present financial path it would soon be debt-free.

Construction continued apace on the IKG campus located in Vienna's second district, which included the new Zvi Peretz Chayes School, the Hakoah Sports and Recreation Center, and the Maimonides Center, a new nursing facility whose foundation stone was laid in May. Placement of the three facilities in close proximity to one another was expected to promote intergenerational cohesiveness.

President Muzicant and his Atid (Future) list swept to victory in the communal elections held in November. Atid won 41.2 percent of the vote and ten seats on the new executive board that would take office on January 8, 2008, twice the number achieved by the Sephardi runner-up party, Sephardim-Bucharische Juden, which got 19.7 percent of the vote and five seats. Trailing far behind was the left-of-center Bund Sozialdemokratischer Juden—Avoda, which won only two seats. The remaining seven places were garnered by five other factions that contested the election. One of these was Gesher, a ticket backed by younger Jews that won two mandates. One of its platform planks was a call to judge Israeli policies more critically than the community had done in the past.

The Atid victory assured Muzicant of his third five-year term as IKG president. He immediately let it be known that he would meet with representatives of Sephardi party to discuss policy issues. Over the years he had worked closely with that faction and with others represented on the council.

The significance of the election was somewhat marred by a drop in voter turnout from 62.6 percent in the previous election of 2002 to 54.7 percent. But Muzicant downplayed its significance, noting that unlike 2002, when Jews were alarmed by the national coalition between the People's Party and the far-right Freedom Party, there was, in 2007, no similar mobilizing issue to stimulate Jews to go to the communal polls.

Cultural Matters

A new institution, Future House, opened its doors in February for the Jewish community of Vienna. Located in the city's Leopoldstadt district, its five stories had facilities for cultural and recreational activities as well as a library and a café for seniors. Johannes Hahn, the Austrian minister of science, addressed the opening ceremony, as did former mayor Helmut Zilk. Other Austrian dignitaries attended as did President Muzicant of the IKG. Financial support for Future House came from the Republic of Austria, the City of Vienna, and industrial magnate Lev Leviev.

In March, the Department of Contemporary History of the Faculty of Historical and Cultural Studies at the University of Vienna organized a conference on the history of the Jews of Vienna in the early twentieth century. Scholars and artists as well as members of the general public attended the three-day event entitled "Vienna and the Jewish Experience from 1900 to 1938: Acculturation, Anti-Semitism, Zionism." One speaker, Prof. Steven Beller, pointed out that the 200,000 Jews noted in the 1923 Vienna census were 11 percent of the population and constituted the second largest Jewish community in Europe, exceeded only by Warsaw. Prof. Frank Stern underscored the extent to which Viennese Jews were an integral part of the city's society before World War II, and suggested that the interwar period was actually more productive in terms of Jewish contributions to the arts and sciences than the better known fin-de-siècle (1890–1914).

Among the exhibitions mounted by the Vienna Jewish Museum during 2007 was one devoted to the work of architect Oskar Strnad, which ran from March 28 through June 4. Together with Joseph Frank, Strnad founded the Vienna School of Architecture. Strnad's main interest was in designing housing. He said his aim was to "shape without form" and to build "not prisons but open worlds." The exhibition displayed his designs for a villa for the writer Jakob Wasserman, a two-family house in the Vienna Werkbundsiedlung, as well as several communal tenement buildings. Apart from aquarelles and ceramics, the exhibition also featured furniture Strnad designed for Hugo von Hofmannsthal, and a series of Mousseline drinking glasses. Also on display were examples of Strnad's theatrical set designs.

Another exhibition presented at the museum's annex, Museum Judenplatz, from May 15 through August 26, was "Tribute to Paul Goldman, Press Photographer 1943–1965." Goldman, born in 1900 in Budapest, emigrated to Palestine in 1940, and, together with his wife, was initially interned as an illegal immigrant before joining the British Army. After his discharge Goldman earned a living as a press photographer, and though he died almost unnoticed in Israel in 1986, Goldman was one of the most important press photographers of his time. The pictures, most of them taken for international press agencies, focused on everyday life in Israel from the time of its establishment to the mid-1960s. Some of his pictures, notably the one showing Israeli prime minister David Ben-Gurion standing on his head on the Herzliya beach, enjoyed iconic status in Israel. Particularly touching were pictures of the arrival of Holocaust survivors in Palestine, the War of Independence, and operation "Magic Carpet" that brought the Jews of Yemen to Israel.

Queen Silvia of Sweden and Margit Fischer, wife of the Austrian president, joined with dignitaries from the government and the Jewish community for the opening of an exhibition at Museum Judenplatz titled "Joseph Frank: Architect and Outsider" that ran from November 22, 2007 to January 20, 2008. Frank (1885–1967) was one of the most important architects and designers of his time and his household items and textiles, classics of European design, were still popular. Born in Baden, Frank came to Vienna to study architecture, and came under the influence of the Modernist movement. Frank designed his first houses in 1913, and 12 years later founded the household furnishing company Haus und Garten, together with Oskar Wlach. In 1933, facing mounting anti-Semitism in Austria, Frank emigrated with his Swedish wife to Stockholm, and in 1940 came to the U.S. They returned to Sweden in 1946.

The exhibition "Best of All Women" opened at the Jewish Museum, focusing on the changing religious, economic, social, and cultural roles of Jewish women through the ages.

Personalia

Esther Fritsch, president of the Israëlite Kultusgemeinde of Tyrol and Voralberg, was awarded the highest medal of the province of Tyrol in February. The governors of Tyrol and South Tyrol presented the medal and lauded Dr. Fritsch for the exceptional contributions she made to the province during the 20 years she served as president of Tyrolean Jewry.

Raul Hilberg, the eminent Holocaust historian, died in August in Vermont at the age of 81 (see below, p. 715). The Vienna-born Hilberg and his family fled Austria shortly after the Nazi takeover in 1938. After finding temporary haven in Cuba, the family gained entry to the U.S. and settled in Brooklyn, New York. He enrolled in Brooklyn College, but shortly afterward joined the U.S. Army and served in a combat unit in the European theater. After the war he finished his B.A. and earned a Ph.D. at Columbia University. His advisor, Prof. Franz Neumann, recommended Hilberg for a job at the Alexandria Documentation Center, where he reviewed captured Nazi documents. This gave him an unsurpassed knowledge of the German war documents, which he utilized for the monumental work that laid the foundation for all subsequent Holocaust research, *The Destruction of European Jewry,* first published in 1961, translated into many languages, and reissued in revised formats in 1985 and 2004. He taught at the University of Vermont for 35 years.

Hilberg had great difficulty returning to his native Austria. It was not until June 2006 that he set foot in Vienna again, for the purpose of aiding the establishment of the Vienna Wiesenthal Institute for Holocaust Studies. Months later he was named honorary chairman of its International Scientific Advisory Board (see AJYB 2007, p. 477).

Robert Adler, a renowned physicist and inventor born in Vienna in 1913, died in February in Boise, Idaho, at age 93 (see below, p. 712). Adler received his doctorate in physics from the University of Vienna in 1937. He fled the country in 1939, arriving in the U.S. in 1941, where he was hired by Zenith Electronics. The holder of nearly 200 U.S. patents, Adler was best known as co-inventor of the television remote-control device. In 1958 he received the Outstanding Technical Achievement Award of the Institute of Radio Engineers.

Gerhard Bronner—cabaret artist, composer, and writer—died in January at age 84. Born in Vienna's working-class district in 1922, he fled to Palestine in 1938 and returned to his home city in 1948, worked as an entertainer and pianist in Marietta Bar in Vienna, which he bought in 1955. Bronner recorded more than 60 LP records, wrote scores for more than 120 TV shows and 2,000 radio programs, and brought Broadway to the Viennese theater by translating hit musicals into German. The City of Vienna awarded him the Austrian Cross of Honor for Science and Art and the Nestroy Ring. Many people from the worlds of journalism and politics attended his funeral. President Heinz Fischer delivered a eulogy, and Chancellor Gusenbauer described him as the "artistic conscience of Austria." He was buried in the City of Vienna's tomb of honor.

Leon Zelman, head of the Jewish Welcome Service Vienna, died in July at the age of 79. A survivor of the Auschwitz and Mauthausen-Ebensee concentration camps, Zelman later studied journalism at the University of Vienna, where he was active in the Jewish student movement. The highly respected journal *Das Judische Echo,* which Zelman edited from its beginning in 1951 until shortly before his death, had its beginning as a university newsletter for Jewish students. In 1963 he was named head of Reiseburo City of the Austrian Office of Tourism for the purpose of developing tourism with Israel. As cofounder of the Jewish Welcome Service Vienna, he made it possible for thousands of Jews who were forced to flee Austria to renew their ties with their former homeland. In 1984 he initiated the Vienna exhibition "Der Versunkunen Welt" (Sunken World), which displayed the shtetl he remembered from childhood.

Kurt Schubert, who founded Austria's first Jewish museum after World War II, died in February at age 82. The museum first opened in Eisenstadt in 1972, relocated to Vienna in 1991, and is housed in Palais Eskeles in the city's first district. A noted scholar as well, Schubert founded the Institute of Jewish Studies at the University of Vienna in 1966.

MURRAY GORDON SILBERMAN

East-Central Europe and the Balkans

MARKING A MAJOR MILESTONE in the development of post-communist Europe, Romania and Bulgaria joined the European Union on New Year's Day. In December, Poland, Slovakia, Hungary, and the Czech Republic entered the EU's Schengen zone, meaning that citizens could travel freely across these countries' borders.

Jewish communities continued to consolidate their presence and some expanded their operations. Israel had strong political and even stronger economic relations in the region, and thousands of Israelis took up at least temporary residence in East-Central Europe. Reflecting new conditions, the American Jewish Joint Distribution Committee (JDC), long a key resource for Jewish communities, reorganized some of its operation along regional rather than national lines.

Not only the JDC, but also other international Jewish aid organizations such as the Ronald S. Lauder Foundation and the Jewish Agency relied primarily on American philanthropy, and so were vulnerable to the falling dollar, which dropped more than 12 percent in value over the year. The ensuing budget shortfalls forced belt-tightening changes in programming and staff. "Ultimately we provide less service if the dollar doesn't go as far," the JDC's chief financial officer, Eugene Phillips, told the JTA in November. "People are getting hurt."

Bosnia-Herzegovina

Bosnia continued its slow recovery from the three-year war ended by the Dayton Accord of 1995. While in February the number of EU peacekeepers, the so-called EUFOR, was cut from 6,500 to about 2,500, the international community decided to maintain the office of high representative in Bosnia an extra year, until at least June 2008.

In conformity with the constitution implemented under the Dayton Accord, Bosnia was divided ethnically into two separate entities, the Bosnian Serbian Republic and the Bosniak-Croat Federation of Bosnia and Herzegovina. Its federal presidency rotated every eight months among a Bosniak (Muslim), a Croat (generally Catholic), and a Serb (generally Orthodox), in effect barring Jews and other minorities from the office. Early in the year Jakob Finci, president of the Bosnian Jewish community, petitioned the European Court of Human Rights to act against this discriminatory system.

A Jew, Sven Alkalaj, was appointed Bosnian foreign minister in February. He had previously served for ten years as ambassador to the U.S. and also as ambassador to NATO. His first official visit to Israel took place in October. Prime Minister Nikola Spiric, a Bosnian Serb, resigned to protest attempts by the EU's special representative to introduce EU-backed reforms, but returned as prime minister in December.

Racist and neo-Nazi behavior among soccer fans, a problem in many countries, plagued Bosnia as well. In August, fans of the Siroki Brijeg team gave Nazi salutes and chanted "Sieg Heil" during a match with visiting Hapoel Tel Aviv, angering Israeli fans. The game was halted temporarily after firecrackers were thrown from the Israeli stands, setting off a blaze. Referees ejected Israeli fans from the stadium and arrested two of them. At least one was injured in the fracas. (Hapoel won the match 3-0.)

In December, the Jewish community launched an appeal to locate Bosnians who aided Jews during World War II. The purpose was to record their stories as part of a project, undertaken in cooperation with the Bosnian Institute for the Research of Crimes against Humanity, to document Jewish and Muslim life in the country, focusing in part on how the two communities coexisted over the centuries.

Bulgaria

One negative consequence of Bulgarian EU membership was sharply increased inflation, which hit pensioners and others on fixed incomes especially hard. Corruption remained a major problem despite EU monitoring. Israel had widespread investments in Bulgaria, particularly in real estate, construction, and high-tech industry. About 100,000 Israeli tourists visited Bulgaria during the year.

One of Bulgaria's first members of the European Parliament was Dmitar Stoyanov, 23, from the far-right, xenophobic Attack party. Within days of Bulgaria's entry into the EU Stoyanov drew criticism—even from other rightists—for claiming that Jews had too much power. Stoyanov was quoted by a British newspaper as saying, "There are a lot of powerful Jews, with a lot of money, who are paying the media to form the social awareness of the people. They are also playing with economic crises in countries like Bulgaria and getting rich. These are the concrete realities." In response, Emil Kalo, who chaired the Bulgarian Jewish organization Shalom, said he would fully finance Attack if Stoyanov could prove his allegations.

In March, government officials, Jewish leaders, and others marked the 64th anniversary of the rescue of Bulgarian Jews from Nazi deportation. In July, under a deal brokered by French negotiators, Libya freed six medical workers—five Bulgarians and a Palestinian—who had been held for eight years and convicted of involvement in a plot to infect Libyan children with the AIDS virus.

Bulgaria had an active Jewish community of about 5,000 people, some 3,000 of them in the capital city of Sofia. Jewish communities around the country were linked under the umbrella Shalom organization. In July, its board elected Maxim Benvenisti to replace longtime chair Emil Kalo, who left the post ten months before the end of his term.

There were many Jewish groups, organizations, and institutions. A resident rabbi was based in Sofia. Chabad had an increasingly visible presence, which some community members attributed to squabbles within Shalom. An active B'nai Brith lodge played a particular role in combating local anti-Semitism, including initiating action to close down several anti-Semitic Websites. Representatives from Bulgaria took part in international Jewish meetings, such as B'nai Brith Europe's first Young Adults Forum held in Frankfurt at the end of November.

Croatia

In the November general elections, Prime Minister Ivo Sanader's rightist Croatian Democratic Union (HDZ) won the most parliamentary seats but failed to obtain a clear majority. Sanader was given a new mandate to form a coalition.

Concern was expressed during the year over continuing nostalgia in ultra-nationalist circles for Croatia's World War II homegrown fascist Ustashe regime, which ruled the country as a Nazi client state. Nationalist rock singer Marko Perkovic, known as Thompson, came under particular scrutiny. In June, the Simon Wiesenthal Center directed attention to a Thompson stadium concert in Zagreb attended by 60,000 people, including government officials, where many concertgoers wore Ustashe dress or bore Ustashe symbols, and thousands gave the Ustashe salute. Efraim Zuroff, the Wiesenthal Center's Israel director, called on the government to ban such concerts, calling them part of "an ugly wave of revived fascism" and an "extremely dangerous new trend."

The next month Zuroff condemned the live broadcast of a Thompson concert on state television. An official at Croatian TV, Jadranka Kolerevic, was reported to have dismissed the criticism, saying, "Many people die daily in Palestine and he wants to comment on the situation in Croatia." Israeli ambassador Shmuel Meirom termed the remarks anti-Semitic and called for her dismissal, but her supervisors at Croatian TV rebuffed the criticism and dismissed Meirom's protest as inappropriate interference in internal Croatian affairs. Despite protests by the ADL, B'nai Brith, and others, Thompson played concerts in several European, American, Canadian, and Australian cities on a tour to promote a CD released at the end of 2006. No controversial incidents or nationalist symbolism were reported on the tour.

In January, Croatian educators participated in a three-day seminar on teaching the Holocaust. President Stipe Mesic attended a commemoration in April at the former Jasenovac concentration camp south of Zagreb where tens of thousands of Jews, Serbs, Roma, and antifascist Croatian political prisoners were killed. It was now a memorial site. Ivo Rojnica, a wartime Ustashe commander, died in Argentina in December, aged 93.

Relations between Croatia and Israel were generally good, and tens of thousands of Israeli tourists visited Croatia annually. Shimon Peres paid a visit to Zagreb in April. Three months later, congratulating Peres on his election as Israeli president, Mesic said Croatia wanted to develop friendly relations with the Jewish state and pledged to oppose "any manifestation" of anti-Semitism or intolerance.

In February, a 24-year-old Croatian man was jailed for 15 months for having seriously damaged a Jewish school in Vienna in November 2006; the attack was found to have been motivated by anti-Semitism.

About 2,500 Jews lived in Croatia. Most were in the capital, Zagreb, but there were also nine other organized Jewish communities. In the aftermath of a bitter split in 2005–06 (see AJYB 2007, p. 485), two separate Jewish communities functioned in Zagreb, both officially recognized by the government: the longstanding Jewish Community of Zagreb, or ZOZ, which claimed about 1,500 members, and Bet Israel Zagreb, formed by supporters of Rabbi Kotel Dadon, who broke away after the ZOZ refused to renew his contract in 2005. Both communities sponsored cultural, educational, and social programs. The ZOZ also ran a Holocaust research and documentation center and an old age home. The Lauder Foundation had a school affiliated with Bet Israel. In December, the ZOZ appointed Luciano Moshe Prelevic as its rabbi. The community had sent Prelevic to study at a yeshiva in Israel in 2002.

Chabad also had a presence in Zagreb. This year, at Hanukkah, Chabad and city authorities sponsored Zagreb's first public menorah lighting. Rabbi Yisrael Meir Lau, chief rabbi of Tel Aviv and a former Ashkenazi chief rabbi of Israel, attended, as did Zagreb's mayor. The event drew about 1,000 people, and organizers reported that representatives of both feuding congregations were there.

At the end of August the annual "Beyahad" Jewish culture festival and social gathering, which drew Jews from all parts of the former Yugoslavia, took place in Opatija, on the Adriatic.

Czech Republic

Seven months after inconclusive elections (see AJYB 2007, p. 486), a new government headed by Prime Minister Mirek Topolanek took office in January 2007. The ruling coalition, which included Topolanek's center-right Civic Democrats, the centrist Christian Democrats, and the Greens, held only 100 seats in the 200-seat Parliament.

The Czech Republic was a key ally of Israel and the two countries enjoyed strong bilateral relations. At a meeting that took place in Munich in February with Czech foreign minister Karel Schwarzenberg, Israeli foreign minister Tzipi Livni thanked Prague for its support. Livni, Schwarzenberg told reporters, "knows that we are reliable friends."

Israel had many investments in the Czech Republic, including a prominent brewery that began producing kosher beer for the Israeli market during 2007. In the summer, 80-year-old Chanan Rozen, who helped found the Israel-Czechoslovak Friendship League in Israel in 1948, received an award from the Czech Foreign Ministry. Born in Ostrava, Rozen immigrated illegally to Palestine in 1939.

International Jewish leaders praised the Czech Republic on several occasions. In January, Pierre Besnainou, president of the European Jewish Congress (EJC), said he was pleased with the status of Jews in the country and with the attitude of mainstream society and political figures toward them. After leading an EJC delegation that met with President Vaclav Klaus and other senior officials, he reportedly said he would be satisfied if the situation everywhere else would be as good as it was in the Czech Republic. A delegation from the Conference of Presidents of Major American Jewish Organizations visited Prague in February and also met with senior government officials. Among other agenda items, they thanked Czech leaders for their support of Israel.

In January, the educational and cultural center of the Jewish Museum in Prague sponsored a monthlong Holocaust awareness campaign. It featured a display of posters around the city bearing slogans that arbitrarily discriminated against various groups.

High-profile neo-Nazi activity prompted concern during the year even though there were only an estimated 1,000 hardcore neo-Nazis in the country. Anti-Semitic chanting at soccer matches was a problem. In August, Czech Jewish leaders protested to the AC Sparta team after its fans chanted "Jude" at the British team Arsenal during a match in Prague. An AC Sparta spokesman promised the matter would be investigated. "The club's position on the problem has been absolutely clear for a long time. We do not want racists and anti-Semites at stadiums," he said. But the chants continued. At a televised match with rival Slavia in October, Sparta fans chanted "Jude" and unfurled a banner referring to Slavia as "Jude." Czech television cut the audio of the broadcast and said it would not air any more Sparta matches if such behavior continued. In a related incident, a Sparta team member was fined in September for apparently giving the Nazi salute to fans. He claimed afterward that the gesture had only been an attempt to calm them.

In Brno, vandals scrawled swastikas and anti-Semitic slogans around the city to mark Hitler's birthday in April, and the next month police there broke up a neo-Nazi rally by about 600 people. In November, police used tear gas to break up a concert by neo-Nazi bands held at a hotel in Nove Hamry. There were scuffles with some of the 120 extremists in attendance.

Right-wing extremists tried to stage a march through Prague's Jewish Quarter on the anniversary of the 1938 Nazi Kristallnacht pogrom in November. Czech authorities had banned the march by the extremist Young National Democrats group, and some 1,400 police, some in riot gear, prevented marchers from entering the Jewish neighborhood. In some cases, antifascist anarchists clashed violently with small groups of neo-Nazis. Police detained nearly 400 people.

In a remarkable show of solidarity with the Jewish community, thousands of Czechs rallied to protest the march. Many wore yellow Stars of David and some waved Israeli flags. A prayer service took place in front of the historic Old-New Synagogue and there were also other events, including musical performances. Chief Rabbi Karol Sidon, the mayor of Prague, Archbishop Miroslav Vlk, and other prominent personalities addressed the crowds.

There were several episodes of vandalism against Jewish sites. In January, for example, thieves stole bronze parts used on a tomb at the National Memorial Cemetery in the former Terezin concentration camp, and during the summer vandals damaged tombstones in Jewish cemeteries in Bohumin and Pisek.

About 3,000 Jews were affiliated with Jewish organizations, communities or institutions in the Czech Republic, though Jewish leaders believed that thousands more Jews might be living in the country. Prague had the largest community, about 1,500 affiliated members. There was also a sizable population of Israeli expatriates, many of whom did not affiliate. Orthodox, Reform, and Conservative congregations held services, but only a small minority of Prague Jews attended any. In November, the Federation of Jewish Communities for the first time recognized Reform as one of its streams. Prague was one of the stops on a ten-day trip to Eastern Europe by more than 20 American Reform rabbis, the first such European tour for U.S. rabbis sponsored by the World Union for Progressive Judaism.

Chabad, which had a strong presence in the country, marked its tenth year of putting up a public menorah on Hanukkah. The first deputy mayor of Prague lit the first candle.

The Lauder School in Prague, the only Jewish school in the Czech Republic, also marked its tenth anniversary. It now had 120 students, three-quarters of whom had Jewish roots of some sort. Community leaders said the school had recovered from the scandal that beset it in 2003–04, when pornography found on its Internet server led to a community dispute and brought about the resignation of 17 teachers and the withdrawal of about a third of the student body (see AJYB 2005, p. 465).

Many performances, exhibitions, and other Jewish-themed cultural events took place around the country during the year. April saw the launch of a privately sponsored International Music Center in Terezin. In collaboration with the state-run Terezin Memorial, it was to host concerts of music composed by Jewish musicians killed in the Holocaust and would also support various tolerance-education projects.

There were several developments regarding Holocaust-era property restitution, compensation, and looted art. The most newsworthy was the city of Brno's decision not to return the famous Tugendhat Villa, a UNESCO World Heritage Site, to the heirs of its Jewish former owners. The villa, administered by the Brno City Museum, was designed by famed German architect Ludwig Mies van der Rohe and built in 1930 for Fritz and Grete Tugendhat. The couple fled the Nazis in 1938. Their surviving children filed to reclaim the villa at the end of 2006. Even though the statute of limitations on reclaiming real estate had already expired, they claimed the villa as a work of art, not real estate.

In November, the Czech Supreme Court upheld the claim of descendants of Oskar Federer, a Czech Jewish businessman who fled the Nazis in 1939, to 21 paintings once owned by Federer and currently held by art galleries in Ostrava and Pardubice. A new book, *Navraty pameti* (Bringing Back Memory), described the hundreds of objects that had belonged to Jews before World War II and were now in the collections of the Prague Museum of Applied Arts.

Greece

In elections held in September, the ruling New Democrat party retained a narrow majority. But a far-right party, Popular Orthodox Alarm (LAOS), won 3.8 percent of the vote and ten seats in Parliament, thus becoming the first extreme-right party to enter Parliament since the military dictatorship ended in 1974. A 2005 report by the U.S. State Department said the party, headed by Giorgos Karatzaferis, supported "virulent nationalism, anti-Semitism, racism and xenophobia." LAOS's strong showing worried some Greek Jews, but many observers considered the election result nothing more than a backlash against the government's ineffectual response to huge forest fires that swept the country during the summer, killing dozens of people.

In the mainstream media, criticism of Israel and Israeli policy sometimes crossed the line into anti-Semitism, but the problem was much more serious in the extremist press. The Central Board of Jewish Communities and the Greek Helsinki Monitor sued the tiny, extreme-right newspaper *Eleftheros Kosmos* and former LAOS party candidate Kostas Plevris for racism and anti-Semitism. *Eleftheros Kosmos* was acquitted, but not Plevris. In his book *Jews: The Whole Truth,* issued May 2006, Plevris praised Hitler and called for the extermination of the Jews. He declared himself "a Nazi, a fascist, a racist, an antidemocrat, an anti-Semite." In December, Plevris was convicted of inciting racial hatred and racial violence, and given a 14-month suspended sentence. It was the first conviction in Greece under the laws against incitement.

A few instances of vandalism against Jewish sites took place: for example, swastikas were scrawled on a former synagogue in Veria in February and in a cemetery in Ioannina in March. In October, an Israeli on vacation in Greece was hospitalized after a group of young Albanians beat him up while shouting anti-Semitic and anti-Israel slogans.

Greece and Israel were expanding relations. Economic ties were particularly strong. In January, when the Israeli ambassador presented awards to 20 Greek businessmen for promoting bilateral trade, figures were released showing that trade between the two countries had jumped 28 percent in 2006. In March, the U.S. Congress passed a resolution praising Greece for maintaining "excellent relations with Muslim nations and Israel." The next month, at a meeting in Washington launching B'nai Brith International programs on Greek Jewry, the Greek ambassador to the U.S. said relations between Greece and Israel were better than ever. In August, Israel sent dozens of firefighters to join other international teams battling the devastating forest fires.

Holocaust Memorial Day, January 27, was marked with ceremonies in Athens and Thessalonika. In Athens, a plaque was unveiled honoring Archbishop Damskinos, who helped save hundreds of Jews by giving them false documents during World War II. In June, the bust of Col. Mordechai Frizis, a Greek Jewish World War II military hero killed in December 1940, was unveiled in Thessaloniki. Frizis was one of nearly 13,000 Greek Jews who served in his country's armed forces during the war and the first high-ranking Greek officer killed in action on the Albanian front.

The American Jewish Committee signed an association agreement with Greece's Jewish community in May. About 5,000 Jews live in the country. The major communities were those in Athens and Thessaloniki, but smaller communities existed in several other towns. Jewish communities were linked under the umbrella of the Central Board of Jewish Communities. There were a Chabad house and other Chabad facilities in Athens. Both Athens and Thessaloniki had Jewish museums. WIZO and B'nai Brith had functioning organizations in the country.

Hungary

The Hungarian political scene was tumultuous throughout the year as divisions between left and right became increasingly bitter. Young right-wing extremists who took to the streets to protest the leftist government frequently carried the red-and-white striped Arpad flag, an ancient Hungarian banner that was adapted and used by the World War II Hungarian Arrow Cross fascists.

At the official celebration of National Day, March 15, Prime Minister Ferenc Gyurcsany was booed by rightist protesters. There were three rallies that day: one by leftist supporters of the government; a peaceful antigovernment mass rally that drew tens of thousands of supporters of FIDESZ, the main opposition party; and a far-right rally at which one of the speakers was Holocaust denier David Irving, who had served 13 months of a three-year jail sentence in Austria and was now in Hungary to promote a new book. That evening Gyorgy Budahazy, a nationalist leader wanted for his involvement in violent street fights in September 2006, was arrested, setting off clashes between police and far-right protesters. Police used tear gas and water cannon to disperse the demonstrators, some of whom built barricades and set them on fire.

In May, dozens of right-wing extremists, some of them waving the Arpad flag, threw eggs and heckled Gyrucsany with antigovernment and anti-Semitic slogans when he spoke at a Holocaust commemoration and antiracism rally attended by about 10,000 people. It was held at a Holocaust memorial on the bank of the Danube dedicated to the memory of the thousands of Jews shot and thrown into the river by Arrow Cross fascists in 1944.

In August, in the face of condemnation by the government and protests from Jewish and Roma groups, 56 right-wing extremists formed a paramilitary "Hungarian Guard" under the sponsorship of the far-right Jobbik party. The uniform adopted included the red and white Arpad stripes of the Arrow Cross. At a rally of about 1,000 supporters outside Buda castle, Jobbik's leader, Gabor Vana, said the guard had been organized "to carry out the real change of regime and to rescue Hungarians."

Not only Jews and other Hungarians expressed alarm, but protests poured in from abroad. Leaders of the World Jewish Congress and the European Jewish Congress wrote to Gyurcsany, calling the guard an "extremely alarming development" and a danger to democracy. Gyurcsany said he had asked Hungary's chief prosecutor to monitor the group's activities for any violation of the constitution. In October, 600 new members were sworn in.

In this highly charged political atmosphere Jews maintained vigilance against anti-Semitism. The extremists used anti-Semitic rhetoric and at times shouted anti-Semitic slogans during their protests, but physical attacks directed at Jews were rare. In June, a radio broadcaster in Debrecen was beaten up and told to "go back to Israel," and in December three rightists were detained after disrupting the annual Chabad menorah lighting. There were also several instances of vandalism of Jewish sites, including anti-Semitic slogans scrawled on a traveling Holocaust memorial exhibit in the town of Godollo near Budapest.

In an interview in March with the *London Times,* Gyurcsany warned that anti-Semitism in Hungary was on the rise and accused FIDESZ, the main opposition party, of allying itself with it. In the interview he noted that his wife, a law professor, was "of Jewish descent" and had recently been handed a "very clear and unambiguous" anti-Semitic pamphlet outside her university.

Given this background, an attempt at Purim humor by the head of the central Jewish organization only added to the tension. Purim this year fell just before the March 15 national holiday. Jewish Federation president Peter Feldmajer created a sensation when, in a Jewish newspaper, he advised Jews to leave Budapest or stay indoors and lie low over the holiday for fear of anti-Semitic attacks. This "joke" was taken seriously and picked up by the international media, raising a ruckus among Hungarian politicians and diplomats.

An ADL survey released in July presented a worrying picture. Out of six countries surveyed, respondents in Hungary held the highest degree of anti-Semitic views. Half of the Hungarian respondents believed at least three out of four anti-Semitic stereotypes. Furthermore, the percentages were notably higher than those recorded in a previous survey in 2005: 50 percent, up from 38 percent, responded "probably true" to the statement that "Jews are more loyal to Israel than their own country"; about 60 percent, up from 55 percent, responded "probably true" to the statement, "Jews have too much power in the business world"; some 61 percent, up from 55 percent, responded "probably true" to the statement, "Jews have too much power in international financial markets"; and 58 percent, up from 46 percent, responded "probably true" to the statement, "Jews still talk too much about what happened to them in the Holocaust."

In an article in the *Budapest Times,* however, the Budapest-based British author Adam Le Bor denied that the situation was a dire as either Gyurcsany or the ADL survey claimed. He said there was "hysteria" about anti-Semitism that did not square with facts on the ground. "Hungary is home to mainland Europe's second largest Jewish community . . . and Jewish life is thriving," he wrote. "There are Jewish schools, a dozen or so working synagogues in Budapest and an ever-growing number of community centers. The far-right parties have no seats in parliament and, unlike in Poland, for example, open anti-Semitism is not part of mainstream political discourse. The synagogues are not burning. The cemeteries are not being desecrated. In Manchester, England, Orthodox rabbis need a police escort to synagogue to protect them from being attacked. Rabbis in Budapest do not."

There were Holocaust commemorations and similar convocations throughout the year. A week of such events took place around April 16, Hungary's Holocaust Memorial Day. Ceremonies began with a torch-lit

"March for Life" from Budapest's Holocaust Memorial Museum to the main Dohany Street Synagogue, where a large crowd attended a ceremony with Prime Minister Gyurcsany and other dignitaries taking part. In a speech the next day to a special session of the National Assembly, the nation's parliament, Gyurcsany called for "zero tolerance" for hate speech, anti-Semitism, and Holocaust denial. That body refused, however, to allow a Jewish member to recite the Kaddish prayer for the dead at the end of the session, citing rules that barred prayers during parliamentary proceedings.

A month of memorial services commemorating the 1944 deportation of Jews from the Hungarian provinces began in June. That month a bust of Italian businessman Giorgio Perlasca, who saved Jews in Budapest during the Holocaust by posing as a Spanish diplomat, was unveiled. It was commissioned by the Italian embassy and the Italian Institute in Budapest. In October, a plaque was dedicated at the site of a former boarding school where nuns saved dozens of Jewish children and their parents. The sculptural gravestone of wartime heroine Hannah Szenes was moved from Budapest to Israel in May, and a new memorial took its place. A member of the Haganah, Szenes, 23, was parachuted into Nazi-occupied Yugoslavia in 1944 on a mission to help European Jews. Caught trying to cross the border into her native Hungary, she was taken to Budapest and executed by firing squad. Her remains had been moved to Israel in 1950 and reburied on Mt. Herzl in Jerusalem, where the original monument brought from Budapest would be placed.

In the spring, military historian Krisztian Ungvary published a book, *The Hungarian Army in the Second World War,* that detailed atrocities committed by the Hungarian army against Jews and other civilians in territories they occupied. In March, Hungary reopened a war-crimes investigation of 93-year-old Sandor Kepiro, accused of killing more than 1,200 people in Novi Sad, Serbia, during World War II.

Relations between Hungary and Israel were close. In January, ahead of a visit to Israel by Hungarian foreign minister Kinga Goncz, the Israeli foreign minister called those relations "excellent," characterized by regular high-level visits. Israel was one of Hungary's leading economic partners. At the beginning of the year Israeli investments in Hungary topped $4.5 billion and bilateral trade exceeded $500 million.

Pride in Israel's economic performance led President Peres to make an unwise statement in October that touched off a furor in Hungary. In a speech at an economic forum in Israel, he noted that Israeli businessmen had "unparalleled success" around the world to the point where they were "buying up" Hungary—as well as Manhattan, Poland, and Romania. The Hungarian media reacted with dismay, and far-right extremists protested in front of the Israeli embassy in Budapest.

A delegation of 174 Israeli soldiers visited Holocaust memorials during a three-day trip to Hungary in March. In August, the Israeli media reported that police had launched a bribery investigation against the ambassador to Hungary, David Admon, whose term was to end in September. He was suspected, among other things, of using his position to launch private business ventures in Hungary and to receive kickbacks from Israeli businessmen. He was allegedly also being investigated for attempting to arrange commission payments to his son in connection with the privatization of the former Jewish hospital. Both Admon and his son denied the allegations.

At least 100,000 Jews lived in Hungary, the overwhelming majority in Budapest. The main Jewish stream was Neolog, which was similar to what is called Conservative Judaism in the U.S. Reform and Modern Orthodox congregations also functioned, as did Chabad centers. Most Hungarian Jews, however, were secular or unaffiliated.

MAZSIHISZ, the Alliance of Jewish Communities, was the officially recognized representative of mainstream Jewry in Hungary. Nevertheless, there were alternative Jewish groups gaining increased visibility that often criticized MAZSIHISZ for taking a "monopolistic" attitude. Particularly attractive to young people, these nonestablishment entities included the on-line community judapest.org and the downtown café Siraly, co-managed by Marom, a Masorti (Conservative) Jewish youth group, which ran programs throughout the year.

In December, leaders of MAZSIHISZ boycotted the annual year-end luncheon for religious leaders with Hungarian president Laszlo Solyom to protest Solyom's veto of a law that would have allowed members of minority groups to sue people who made statements deemed to be hate speech. Solyom, saying this would stifle free speech and discriminate against members of the majority population, sent the bill to the Constitutional Court for further review. Following the announcement of the MAZSIHISZ boycott, judapest.org sent a platter of traditional Jewish pastry, Flodni, to Solyom, who served it as dessert at the boycotted luncheon. Judapest said it had made the gesture to protest the MAZSIHISZ "monopoly," and asserted that while "Jews in Hungary form a versatile and complex community, their official, political representation doesn't stand on the base of pluralism."

This year, the Reform congregation Sim Shalom—which was not recognized by the established Jewish community—signed a contract for a state-owned building and began fund-raising to convert it into a permanent synagogue and community center. Sim Shalom was founded in 1992 and legally registered as a religious congregation in 2006, making it eligible to receive the 1 percent of income tax that Hungarians may direct to religious organizations. It was served by a female rabbi, Katalin Kelemen, who was ordained at the Leo Baeck College in London and took up her post in 1999.

During the year a new Reform congregation, Bet Orim, was established, and for the time being held services at the Balint Haz Jewish Community Center. The new congregation's rabbi was Ferenc Raj, the younger brother of a prominent Budapest rabbi, Tamás Raj.

There were many cultural and educational events throughout the year. Among them was a training seminar in January on addressing the needs of Jewish children. Israel's Habima Theater performed in Budapest in April as part of an Israeli Spring Festival that saw concerts, films, and exhibitions by Israeli artists over the course of more than two months. In May, Israel was the guest of honor at the sixth Contemporary Drama Festival in Budapest. Central European University again staged a series of regular lectures in Jewish studies. The Kraków-based Austeria publishing house and bookstore opened a branch in Budapest in November.

The sculptor and ceramicist Levente Thury, whose work centered on representations of the Golem, died in May. In November, filmmaker Peter Forgacs was awarded the 150,000-euro Erasmus Prize in Holland. His films often dealt with Holocaust themes or prewar Hungarian Jewish life. The award was presented each year to individuals who made an "exceptional contribution" to European culture, society or social science.

Macedonia and Slovenia

Macedonia and Slovenia had Jewish populations numbering several hundred at most, but each had a small synagogue and an active organized Jewish community. Their members took part in regional and international Jewish conferences and other get-togethers. Both countries staged events for the September 2 European Day of Jewish Culture. Slovenia's Jewish community was served by Chief Rabbi Ariel Haddad, a Chabad rabbi who was also the director of the Jewish museum in nearby Trieste, Italy.

In March, Macedonian Jews held their annual commemoration of the World War II deportation of almost the entire prewar Jewish community. In May, the town of Struga, Macedonia, was the scene of a four-day

"Gesher" meeting of Jewish students from the JDC's Danube and Black Sea region. Some 300 young people from Romania, Bulgaria, Greece, Ukraine, Turkey, Israel, Serbia, Macedonia, Bosnia, and Croatia took part.

Poland

In November, following a hard-fought election campaign, voters ousted the rightist government of Prime Minister Jaroslaw Kaczynski. Kaczynski (whose twin brother Lech remained Polish president) had headed a government composed of his Law and Justice party in coalition with two ultra-nationalist groups, the League of Polish Families and Peasants' Self Defense. In this election neither of the latter two won enough votes to enter the new parliament.

Centrist Donald Tusk, whose Civic Platform party was pro-business and pro-European Union, became the new prime minister. Wladyslaw Bartoszewski, a non-Jewish Auschwitz survivor and "righteous gentile," was named secretary of state in charge of Poland's relations with Russia, Germany, and Israel. Bartoszewski, 85, had served twice as foreign minister in previous postcommunist governments and was considered a respected moral symbol of Poland.

Jews were generally pleased with the election results. The Israeli embassy expressed "satisfaction" that the League of Polish Families had not entered parliament. Jewish groups in Poland had protested a TV campaign ad for the party as anti-Semitic. Even earlier, in February, there was a storm of protest over what was described as a "blatantly anti-Semitic" and "hateful" pamphlet, *Civilization at War in Europe,* published by Maciej Giertych, a Polish member of the European Parliament representing the League of Polish Families and father of Roman Giertych, who at the time was minister of education. The pamphlet asserted that "Jewish Civilization" had no place in Europe. President Kaczynski and other Polish political figures condemned Giertych's views, and the president of the European Parliament officially reprimanded him.

Relations between Poland and Israel were close. There were numerous back-and-forth visits by political figures. Israeli businessmen invested billions of dollars in Poland. They were particularly involved in the construction industry, building everything from homes to shopping malls to hotels. President Kaczynski's wife took part in the dedication of a new Polish Culture Center in Tel Aviv in October. In July, Polish Radio began broadcasting a daily, half-hour show in Hebrew throughout Israel.

As had been the case for some years, about 30,000 young Israelis visited Poland, most of them on organized trips to Holocaust sites, including the annual March of the Living. Incidents of inappropriate behavior by some of the Israelis, however, prompted complaints. A Polish newspaper in May, for example, blasted Israeli teens for, among other acts of vandalism, trashing hotel rooms. On another occasion a group of 35 young, strictly Orthodox men ripped out the gates of the Majdanek camp near Lublin to gain access to the site after it had closed for the day. In July about 60 Israeli students demanded to be allowed into the Auschwitz camp at 11 p.m. To avoid confrontation, guards allowed them in, and they stayed all night. The Israeli embassy denounced the actions of all such visitors.

In May, the government complained about how Poles were depicted in a cartoon in the Israeli daily *Ha'aretz* newspaper that showed Polish passengers on a train drinking liquor and harassing a Jewish woman. A spokesman for the Polish embassy in Tel Aviv said it stereotyped Poles "as vicious drunks and in a negative way. They look very ugly and not nice. This is a very difficult issue."

Israeli director Uri Barbash worked in Poland during the year on *Spring 1941,* the first film co-produced by Israel and Poland. A joint project of the Israeli film company Traxis and Poland's Opus Film, it starred British actor Joseph Fiennes and was based on stories by Holocaust survivor Ida Fink.

There were many Holocaust commemorations and related events throughout the year. In August, the city of Kielce unveiled a menorah-shaped monument to honor the 20,000 local Jews killed in the Holocaust. In the summer, at Poland's request, UNESCO changed the official name of the Auschwitz camp memorial to "Auschwitz-Birkenau. German Nazi Concentration and Extermination Camp (1940–1945)." This would make clear that the camp had been established and run by the occupying German Nazis, not by Poland.

A number of ceremonies during the year honored non-Jewish Poles who saved Jews during World War II. One, which took place at Auschwitz on January 27, the 62d anniversary of the liberation of the former death camp, specifically honored residents of the town of Oświęcim, outside of which the Auschwitz camp was built, who tried to help inmates. A representative of President Kaczynski gave medals to about 40 people and read aloud a letter from him praising their efforts.

In February, the Claims Conference, which was holding its first executive board meeting in Poland, organized a luncheon in Warsaw honoring some 60 Poles recognized as Righteous among the Nations. The next month, at a special session, the Polish Senate passed a unanimous resolution honoring Irena Sendler, now 97, and the Polish underground Council for Assisting Jews. Sendler had helped save some 2,500 Jewish children during World War II. And at a high-profile ceremony in October, President Kaczysnki honored 50 Catholic Poles, many of whom had already been recognized by Yad Vashem, who risked their lives to save Jews.

In November, a statue of Jan Karski was unveiled in front of the Polish consulate in New York. The Polish World War II resistance hero, who died in 2000, was the first to bring eyewitness reports of conditions in the Nazi ghettos to Allied leaders.

At an international book fair held in May in Warsaw, convicted British Holocaust denier David Irving sought to display his books, but was prevented from doing so and escorted off the premises.

Many initiatives were taken during the year to combat anti-Semitism and promote dialogue. In January, the Roman Catholic Church in Poland celebrated its tenth annual "Day of Judaism." Stanislaw Krajewski, the American Jewish Committee representative in Warsaw, told Polish Radio, "This is a significant event by itself because it is perhaps the only national day which is supposed to be observed by all churches all over the country devoted to Judaism. I think it shows two things: The universal dimension of the importance of Jews and Jewish religion for the Church, for Christianity in general; and the specific Polish dimension, the importance of Jews in the history of Poland."

The powerful Catholic broadcasting station Radio Maryja and its director, Father Tadeuz Rydzyk, were subjects of great controversy. In the summer, the magazine *Wprost* released a tape on which Rydzyk accused Jews of using restitution claims to extort millions from the state, and criticized President Kaczynski for supporting the construction of a Jewish museum in Warsaw. These comments drew sharp condemnation from political, intellectual, and cultural figures as well as from Jews. Some 700 Poles, including prominent personalities, signed an open letter condemning Rydzyk and calling for him to be disciplined. Rydzyk rejected the criticism, saying that his statements had been twisted out of context and that he had not meant to offend anyone.

Jewish groups expressed disappointment when Pope Benedict XVI received Rydzyk in an audience in August (see above, p. 442). Around the same time Cardinal Stanislaw Dziwisz of Kraków told Polish bishops that Rydzyk had to be stopped. There was a "threat that the Church in Poland is being identified solely with the position of Radio Maryja," he warned. "More and more, Radio Maryja is not contributing to unity in the Church but is becoming an element of . . . political and social jockeying." The EU denied an application for a grant of 15 million euros for Radio Maryja to establish a school of media studies.

Anti-Semitic graffiti were widespread and other isolated instances of anti-Semitism were also reported. In Łódź, which had a particularly severe graffiti problem, annual clean-up week occurred in March. After the 60 teenage volunteers staged a demonstration against anti-Semitism in their city, they spent the rest of the week painting over the offending scrawls.

About 200 right-wing extremists staged an anti-Semitic, anti-Israel demonstration in Kraków in April, during the annual March of the Living, but they were reportedly outnumbered by antiracism counter-protestors. In September, a Warsaw court sentenced a 29-year-old man to a year and a half in prison for directing anti-Semitic threats at his neighbors, saying such things as, "We'll finish what Hitler didn't," and "Jewess, you will die like your ancestors."

Several Jewish cemeteries were desecrated during the year, including the one recently restored in Czéstochowa, where 100 graves were scrawled with graffiti. President Kaczynski denounced the desecration. Among other episodes of vandalism, the windows of the partially renovated synagogue in Rymanow were broken into in April, and in June the Lublin grave of the nineteenth-century Hasidic rabbi known as the Seer of Lublin was desecrated.

Monika Krawczyk, CEO of the Foundation for the Preservation of Jewish Heritage in Poland, said that cemetery desecrations and the appearance of anti-Jewish graffiti were increasing in those areas that were also experiencing a growing far-right presence. But she also noted the large number of human rights groups and other NGOs opposing such manifestations, as well as programs, in part sponsored by the foundation, that saw thousands of Polish high school students taking part in efforts to clean up and preserve Jewish cemeteries. These programs existed in more than 130 high schools. In the summer, the foundation opened a new Website, www.polin.org.pl.

In September, remains of a Jewish cemetery dating back to 1811 were discovered during a construction project for a new tram line in Łódź. In November, workers discovered about 200 Jewish tombstones at the bottom of a reservoir in Kepno. Experts believed the Nazis had uprooted them from the Jewish cemetery and used them to line the reservoir.

Jewish Community

It was difficult to gauge the number of Jews in Poland. About 5,000 people were formally affiliated with Jewish institutions or organizations, but estimates of Jews living in the country ran as high as 20,000, and the number of those with Jewish roots of some sort was far higher. The umbrella Union of Jewish Religious Communities encompassed eight Orthodox communities around the country; Warsaw, with 500 members, was the largest. Foreign individuals, foundations, and organizations helped support Jewish life in Poland. Especially notable in this regard were three Holocaust survivors from Poland, Tad Taube, Severyn Ashkenazy, and Sigmund Rolat. Jewish religious, cultural, and educational activities continued to expand. In fact the healthy development of Jewish life in postcommunist Poland and the government's strong ties with Israel led a number of Jewish commentators, both in Poland and abroad, to suggest—in the formulation of the Los Angeles *Jewish Journal*—that it was "time to stop hating Poland."

There were Orthodox rabbis in Warsaw, Wrocław (where a new kosher dining hall opened), and Kraków, and rabbis from other countries were frequent visitors. The secular Cultural and Social Association of Jews had a number of branches around the country.

Both Chabad and Reform Judaism were becoming increasingly visible. Chabad had synagogues in Warsaw and Kraków, where it had taken over the historic Izaak Synagogue in the heart of Kazimierz, the old Jewish quarter. Chabad organized a Hanukkah menorah lighting outside the Polish parliament building in December. Beit Warszawa, the Reform congregation in Warsaw, had about 200 members and a full-time rabbi. It ran classes, religious services, a Sunday school, and, among other activities, a conversion course. In December Beit Warszawa took on a second rabbi, Tanya Segal, a Russian-born Israeli woman. In June, the American singer and actor Theodore Bikel, a supporter of the group, conducted Shabbat services at Beit Warszawa. In the summer, a discussion group was formed to investigate the possibility of establishing a Conservative congregation in Warsaw.

At the beginning of the year, an English language on-line newsletter, *Warsaw Jewish Grapevine,* began operation, publishing news about all streams of Polish Jewry. It listed classes, courses, commemorations, social and cultural events, and lifecycle milestones, such as weddings, circumcisions, and b'nai and b'not mitzvah.

In February, a three-day celebration marked the dedication of the synagogue in the building that had housed the Chachmei Lublin Yeshiva, once a renowned center of Jewish life and learning. Only a few dozen Jews now lived in Lublin, and after the war the building had became part of a medical school before its return to Jewish communal ownership in 2004. The ceremony also marked the completion of the structure's partial renovation, although it was not yet decided how to use the building.

The list of Jewish organizations operating in Poland expanded in September when B'nai Brith International established its first lodge in Poland since 1938, when the group's operations in the country were shut down. Numerous Jewish-themed conferences, concerts, performances, and other cultural events took place during the year. The tenth Jewish book fair was held in Warsaw in May. In June, a Jewish cultural center opened in Czéstochowa with a gala ceremony. That same month the cornerstone was laid for the planned Museum of Polish Jewish History in Warsaw, in the presence of a U.S. delegation headed by Tevi Troy, President Bush's deputy assistant for domestic policy. Germany announced in November a donation of five million euros to the project. On the site of the planned new museum organizers set up a permanent tent installation called "Ohel" ("tent" in Hebrew), which showcased information about the museum. Various cultural events were programmed in and around the area, including a festival of contemporary Jewish music in September.

Also in June, Yad Vashem released the text of a diary kept in the ghetto of Bédzin in 1943 by 14-year-old Rutka Laskier. The 60-page diary, which chronicled the horrors of the ghetto in the months before Laskier was deported to Auschwitz and killed, was compared to the Holocaust diary kept by Anne Frank.

The annual Jewish Culture Festival in Kraków in late June and early July drew its usual big crowds. Other Jewish festivals included the fourth annual Singer's Warsaw Festival of Jewish Culture in September and, around the same time, the sixth annual Festival of Dialogue of Four Cultures in Łódź, which spotlighted the Jewish, Polish, Russia, and German cultural streams that historically characterized the city. There was also a summer Jewish culture festival in Wrocław. In October, about 100 people attended a three-day seminar in Kraków on "Rediscovering Judaism in Poland," and a three-day Israeli dance marathon took place near Warsaw.

Polish author and critic Leszek Kolakowski received the prestigious Jerusalem Prize, a literary award presented at the annual Jerusalem International Book Fair. In April, the American Jewish Committee honored Zuzanna Radzik for her work in combating anti-Semitism and promoting Catholic-Jewish dialogue. In 2006 she had been instrumental in obtaining the closure of a bookstore located in a church that sold anti-Semitic literature. As in years past, non-Jewish Poles were honored for their work in preserving Jewish heritage at a ceremony in July, during the Kraków Festival of Jewish Culture; this year, the Israeli ambassador presented awards to 11 people.

In October, the Polish Council of Christians and Jews awarded Rabbi Irving "Yitz" Greenberg its "Man of Reconciliation 2007" award. Greenberg gave several lectures while in Poland. Also in October, at a ceremony at the Jewish Historical Institute in Warsaw, YIVO Institute in New York presented the Jan Karski and Pola Nirenska Prize for 2007 to university lecturer Joanna Tokarska-Bakir for her achievements in popularizing Jewish contributions to Polish culture. In December, Janusz Makuch, director of the annual Kraków Festival of Jewish Culture, was awarded the 2007 ODYS Award, presented by civic and tourist bodies in the Kraków region, and the Kraków Judaica Foundation presented its annual "Felek" award to Wladyslaw Bartoszewski.

British photographer Chris Schwarz, founding director of the Galicia Jewish Museum in Kraków, died in that city in August, aged 59. Schwarz's photographs documenting Jewish heritage sites in southern Poland formed the permanent exhibit of the museum, which opened in 2004.

Romania

Romania entered the European Union as the year began. Parliament suspended President Traian Basescu from office in April for what it termed "grave infringements of the constitution." But in a referendum held the next month, voters rejected Parliament's attempt to impeach him.

The annual Holocaust Memorial Day, instituted in 2004, was observed in October. To mark the occasion a survey was presented showing that some 65 percent of the sample had heard of the Holocaust and only 6 percent declared themselves "interested" or "very interested" in the topic. The data showed ambivalent attitudes toward Jews. More than 50 percent of respondents said that Jews had a good relationship with the mainstream population. Four percent perceived Jews as a "threat" to Romania; 5 percent said they were a "problem"; and 33 percent felt that Jews were "neither a threat nor an advantage."

At a Holocaust Memorial Day ceremony, President Basescu honored a dozen Jewish Holocaust survivors, awarding them national decorations. (Later in the month he similarly decorated three Roma survivors and took the unprecedented step of apologizing for the World War II deportation of thousands of Roma.) In addition, a library was inaugurated for the National Institute for the Study of the Holocaust in Romania. In June, the U.S. embassy and the Institute held a one-day conference in Bucharest on "Holocaust in Romania: Unsolved Problems." Speakers focused on anti-Semitism in public discourse, the need for better education about the Shoah, and the anti-Jewish attitudes of some political figures.

In August, Yad Vashem posthumously named Theodor Criveanu as Righteous among the Nations for having saved Jews while serving as a Romanian reserve officer in Cernauti, then part of Romania. Criveanu, who died in 1988, married the daughter of one of the Jews he saved. The umbrella Federation of Jewish Communities in Romania (FEDROM) and the Association of Romanian Jewish Victims of the Holocaust filed a criminal complaint in January against Ion Coja, a university professor, for denying the Shoah.

In May, Aurel Vlaicu University and the Jewish community in Arad reached an agreement whereby the city's former Orthodox synagogue would be taken over by the university and become the premises of the Shalom Institute for Ecumenical Studies. The university took out a 20-year lease on the building and agreed to renovate it. About 400 Jews lived in Arad.

Romania's Jewish communities included some 10,000–12,000 people, about half of them living in Bucharest. In addition, about 10,000 Israelis were believed to live in the country, most of them in Bucharest. They included students and Israelis who moved to Romania for economic reasons, as well as Romanian-born Israelis returning to their homeland (the nation's new membership in the EU was a strong magnet). One of the more controversial Israelis in Romania was Nati Meir, a native of Afula whose parents were from Romania, who returned to that country in the 1990s and became a citizen. Meir, convicted of fraud in Israel, was elected to the Romanian Parliament in 2004 as part of extreme nationalist Corneliu Vadim Tudor's Greater Romania Party.

Gala ceremonies on September 30 marked two major communal events in Bucharest. Romanian-born Shlomo (Sorin) Rosen, 28, who received his rabbinical ordination from New York's Yeshivat Chovevei Torah, was installed as Romania's new chief rabbi. At the same time, Bucharest's modern new Jewish community center was officially opened.

Chabad in Romania was expanding, catering largely to the expatriate Israeli population. Chabad emissary Rabbi Naftali Deutsch, who moved to Bucharest eight years earlier with his wife and children, ran a kindergarten for 40 pupils. In February a recently renovated synagogue, Yeshua Tova, was inaugurated for use as a Chabad center, with classrooms, a kitchen, a library, and function rooms. As part of the dedication ceremony, the final letters of two Torahs destined for use in the synagogue were completed. Among the guests were Rabbi Shlomo Amar, Israel's Sephardi chief rabbi, and the American ambassador. Amar also paid a visit to the main synagogue.

One of the most active Jewish communities outside Bucharest was in Oradea, on the border with Hungary. In January, a rabbinical student from New York arrived for a six-month stay. The community launched a modern, full-service Jewish community center in September.

In January, FEDROM hosted a gala party to mark the birthday of its president, Aurel Vainer. Vainer spelled out some of the chief policy concerns of the FEDROM leadership a few months later. They included the restoration and care of Jewish heritage sites; the promotion of Jewish cultural and educational activities; closer collaboration with public authorities and NGOs; the development and expansion of FEDROM's relations with international Jewish organizations and Jewish communities in other countries; fighting anti-Semitism and Holocaust denial; promotion of interfaith relations; and bettering the living standards of Romanian Jews through social assistance.

Figures released by FEDROM in December said there were 94 synagogues in Romania, 41 of them still in use. There were also 809 Jewish cemeteries scattered around the country in 724 locations, and only 148 of those places still had Jews living in the vicinity. It estimated that the "rehabilitation and preservation" of this patrimony would require 50 million euros. In 2007, it said, FEDROM had allotted funding for urgent repairs to six synagogues and eight cemeteries.

FEDROM also issued a public denial of charges by a man living in New York, recently repeated in the Israeli newspaper *Ma'ariv,* that FEDROM was engaged in a "profitable racket" of selling off cemetery land. "There is no case of land selling from cemeteries with human remains," it said. The outgoing chief rabbi, Menachem Hacohen, told *Ha'aretz* that land from some cemeteries, where no remains were buried, had been sold, but that "all the works in cemeteries were carried out under strict supervision by teams of ultra-Orthodox rabbis from Israel."

Anti-Semitic trends and incidents during the year sparked concern. There were continuing attempts at rehabilitating wartime fascist leader Ion Antonescu, a Nazi ally. In February, a Bucharest appeals court issued a ruling that exonerated Antonescu from responsibility for attacking the Soviet Union in 1941 in alliance with Germany. It ruled that the attack had been in "self-defense," as the Soviets had occupied parts of Romania in 1940. FEDROM and the Association of Romanian Jewish Victims of the Holocaust expressed "deep astonishment and bitterness" at the court's decision since it "justifies military actions with undisputable aggressive character." They expressed the fear that this ruling could strengthen right-wing extremism in the country.

Work began during the year on the reorganization and modernization of the Rosen Jewish nursing home in Bucharest. Also, several FEDROM-owned properties in small towns were being renovated to serve as holiday accommodations and rest houses.

There were many Jewish-themed cultural events and publications during the year. A large Jewish cultural festival, "Eurojudaica" took place in Sibiu (the 2007 European cultural capital) at the end of June. Celebrations held June 29–July 1 marked the 200th anniversary of the Jewish community in Brasov. In October, during ceremonies marking the 350th anniversary of the Jewish community in Dorohoi (now consisting of fewer than 30 members), a Museum of the History of Northern Moldavian Jews opened. During the year the Great Synagogue in Bucharest and the synagogues in Botosani and Ploesti were reconsecrated after their renovation.

In April, the academic and Jewish communities in Romania mourned the death of 76-year-old Liviu Librescu, the Romanian-born Holocaust survivor who was shot trying to protect his students from a gunman who managed to kill more than 30 people at Virginia Tech University. Tania Grinberg, secretary of the Jewish community in Radauti, died suddenly in October, on the very day she had organized a big Holocaust Memorial Day commemoration in the town. Also in October, Prof. Moshe Carmilly Weinberger traveled from his home in New York to Cluj, in Transylvania, to celebrate his 100th birthday. Carmilly, who had been chief rabbi in Cluj before the Holocaust, helped establish a Jewish research institute at the Babes Bolyai University in Cluj in 1990, which was named in his honor.

Serbia

Nationalism was on the rise in Serbia throughout the year as concern over the fate of Kosovo province dominated the news. Israel had its own concerns about the potential impact of independence for Kosovo, an area that was mostly ethnic Albanian and Muslim, and could conceivably provide a foothold for radical Islam. After the expiration of a December 10 UN deadline for an agreement with Serbia on its status, the province prepared to declare unilateral independence. Kosovo leader Hashim Thaci told the JTA, "I love Israel. What a great country. Kosovo is a friend of Israel."

Various Holocaust commemorations took place during the year. On the January 27 Holocaust Memorial Day, a commemorative ceremony took place in Belgrade organized jointly by the Federation of Jewish Communities and the Serbian government.

Anti-Semitism was a continuing concern. In October, neo-Nazi skinheads attempted to stage a rally in Novi Sad to mark the birthday of SS commander Heinrich Himmler, despite a police ban. Local citizens, Jews included, staged a large counterdemonstration and clashed briefly with the neo-Nazis, who attacked them with bottles and stones. Several dozen members of the pro-fascist National Front were arrested and a Serbian court sentenced three of them to up to 25 days in jail.

Also in October, the Jewish Federation protested the sale of anti-Semitic books such as the *Protocols of the Elders of Zion* at the annual Belgrade Book Fair. Its director had promised to remove them, but the Federation said that the pledge was not kept. The book fair this year was dedicated to the memory of Italian Holocaust survivor and author Primo Levi.

Again in October, organizers canceled a rock concert by a British band that was to have been held at the site of a former Nazi concentration camp in Belgrade, Sajmiste, where 48,000 Jews, Serbs, and Roma were murdered. The Jewish Federation had long called for the neglected camp to be preserved as a memorial site.

At an event at the Belgrade synagogue in October, five Serbs (only one of them still living) were honored as Righteous among the Nations. Serbian president Boris Tadic addressed the ceremony. An International Day against Fascism and Anti-Semitism was marked in November. There were ceremonies, lectures, exhibitions, and a roundtable discussion on Holocaust denial.

Relations with Israel were good, particularly in the economic arena. Israeli investors were behind the $173-million Airport City business park, which opened in 2007 near Belgrade. Israeli ambassador Yaffa Ben-Ari left in August after four years and was replaced by Arthur Kohl. In February, former Jewish Agency for Israel official Arie Livine was honored in Belgrade by the Serbian government for strengthening ties between Serbia and Israel. Livine, the World Jewish Congress's special adviser for the former Yugoslav countries, emigrated from what was then Yugoslavia to Israel in 1956 and worked at the Jewish Agency for 40 years.

About 3,000 Jews lived in Serbia, at least 800 of them in Belgrade. The ten local communities were linked through their membership in the Jewish Federation of Serbia. Most Serbian Jews were secular, but Jewish religious and cultural life flourished. Chief Rabbi Yitzhak Asiel said about 100 people came each week for Friday night dinner in the newly refurbished hall of Belgrade's only synagogue.

Organizational and legal concerns, including the relationship between the federation and local communities, were the focus of debate and discussion during the year. Aleksander Necak was elected president of the federation in March, replacing the ailing and elderly Aca Singer, who was named honorary president. A new statute for the federation was approved at the end of June that, among other things, removed the old description of local Jewish communities as "associated" into the federation and declaring them instead to be its "founders," with community presidents automatically holding seats on the federation executive board. Purim, the High Holy Days, and other holiday celebrations were held in all local communities. According to the federation monthly, "great numbers" attended at Rosh Hashanah. Two Chabad rabbis from the U.S. took part in Rosh Hashanah ceremonies in Novi Sad. For the first time in nearly 70 years, large public celebrations marked Hanukkah. A 2.5-meter-high menorah was set up in the courtyard of the synagogue, and candle-lighting and other festive events were held each night of the holiday. The new Israeli ambassador, Arthur Kohl, lit the candle on the first night.

There were many cultural and educational events. In March, tribute was paid to concert pianist Andrej Preger on his 95th birthday. Belgrade's Braca Baruch Choir gave many concerts and also performed at the Zimria choral festival in Jerusalem. Serbia took part in the annual European Day of Jewish Culture, held on September 2, with events in Belgrade, Novi Sad, Subotica, Nis, and Zemun.

In November, the first regional Limmud Keshet study gathering was held for the former Yugoslavia region, attracting more than 100 people from 13 Jewish communities in Macedonia, Bosnia-Herzegovina, Croatia, and Serbia, as well as from Austria, Sweden, Bulgaria, and Israel. The program included 30 lectures, exhibitions, workshops, film showings, concerts, dance performances, and other events. Sixty participants from 17 countries met in Belgrade from November 30 through December 5 for a seminar on religion and sexuality organized by the European Union of Jewish Students. In December, the Cinema Museum in Belgrade organized a two-day festival of Israeli films. Gordana Kuic, the author of best-selling novels about Sephardi Jews in the Balkans, received the Zensko Pero Award for 2007.

Controversy erupted in the northern town of Subotica after the outside of the Art Nouveau synagogue was painted green during ongoing restoration work. In the fall, the temple's big chandelier was stolen. In November, the Jewish community in Subotica hosted a meeting of small Jewish communities from Serbia, Romania, Croatia, and Hungary.

Like other countries in the region, Serbia was affected by the JDC organizational changes noted above. These included the departure of Yechiel Bar Chaim, who had been JDC director for the former Yugoslavia over nearly two decades. Bar Chaim was reassigned to head JDC nonsectarian activities from Paris, and he was replaced in the Balkans by Robert Djerassi, based in Sofia.

Slovakia

The World War II role of Slovakia's Roman Catholic Church was a matter of controversy during the year. In January, the archbishop of Bratislava and Trnava, Jan Sokol, spoke fondly of the wartime period as "a time of well-being" when Slovaks had "everything we wanted." The country had been a Nazi client state at the time headed by profascist priest Jozef Tiso, whose government deported more than 70,000 Slovakian Jews to their deaths. Tiso was executed as a war criminal in 1947.

Sokol's statement naturally outraged Jews, Roma, and others. The Central Union of Jewish Communities in Slovakia described it as "unacceptable" and declared that Jews felt "offended by Sokol's open admiration of that racist state." Prime Minister Robert Fico also condemned Sokol's statement, as did Roma leaders. In the wake of this controversy, the Slovak Bishops' Conference organized a council to review the Church's wartime and communist-era role, which, according to the head of the Conference, had been "intentionally misinterpreted here . . . under the influence of communist ideology."

In October, the umbrella Central Union of Jewish Communities protested a bill before parliament that would honor another nationalist priest, Andrej Hlinka, who, until his death in 1938, led the nationalist, pro-fascist Slovak People's Party. "The Jewish community in Slovakia considers the name of Andrej Hlinka a symbol of Slovak fascism in the years of 1939–45," it said in a statement. Parliament passed the bill nonetheless.

There were a number of Holocaust commemorations. On March 22, the 65th anniversary of the beginning of the deportation of Slovak Jews, a train pulling two wartime freight cars left Poprad and started a six-month journey around the country. They contained two exhibitions: the first car told of the deportations, and the second reproduced the harsh conditions of the crowded car as they were at that time. The first train, which left on March 25, 1942, carried 1,000 Slovak Jewish women to Auschwitz, and only 20 survived. Prime Minister Fico took part in the ceremony inaugurating the exhibition train.

In June, nine Slovaks were honored as Righteous among the Nations at a ceremony in Bratislava. Slovakia marked its Day of the Victims of the Holocaust and Racial Violence on September 9, the date in 1941 that the government issued its "Jewish Code," a package of harsh anti-Jewish measures modeled on Nazi regulations. President Ivan Gasparovic, Prime Minister Fico, and other officials took part in commemorative ceremonies in Bratislava.

About 3,000 Jews were known to live in Slovakia, in a dozen Jewish communities. The two largest were in Bratislava, the capital, and Košice, in eastern Slovakia, each with several hundred members. Jewish communities around the country were linked under the umbrella Central Union of Jewish Religious Communities, based in Bratislava. All recognized congregations were Orthodox, although an informal liberal group met in Bratislava.

An American-born Chabad rabbi, Baruch Myers, served in Bratislava, and a Slovak-born Israeli, Yossi Steiner, in Košice. In October, Chabad rabbi Ze'ev Stiefel and his family moved from Bratislava to the spa town of Piestany to establish the Chabad Center of Central Slovakia. Stiefel estimated that as many as 5,000 Jews visited the Piestany spa each year (some of the hotels there were run by Israelis). Stiefel also worked with the small Jewish communities of Nitra, Nove Zamky, and others. He traveled regularly to Košice, where he was involved with the sizable group of Israeli expatriates, many of them students at the local veterinary school.

In January, three apparently inebriated men hurled insults at Rabbi Myers and one of his sons as they left the synagogue in Bratislava. Myers, who had been physically assaulted by skinheads twice in the 1990s, reported the incident to police, who arrested two of the men and charged them with expressing sympathy for a movement that denied human rights. Myers told reporters that such incidents were very rare in Slovakia.

The Central Union, Jewish communities, and other institutions hosted a number of cultural and educational programs. Several Jewish periodicals were published in the country and some of the local communities had Websites. There was a B'nai Brith lodge in Bratislava. Despite having only about 70 members, the Jewish community in Komarno had numerous programs, a library, a Website, and a blog, and strove to maintain regional contacts with other small Jewish communities in Slovakia and Hungary. In February, the Jewish community in Banska Bystrica hosted the annual Slovak Maccabi Winter Games.

The scholar Maros Borsky ran the Slovak Jewish Heritage Center in Bratislava, which cared for and preserved Jewish heritage sites. He published a book in September on synagogue architecture in Slovakia that was officially launched as part of the European Day of Jewish Culture, which also included a photographic exhibition and the unveiling of commemorative plaques at Jewish sites.

RUTH ELLEN GRUBER

Former Soviet Union

National Affairs

Russia

In 2007, the Russian Federation maintained a precarious balance between two identities: one, as a semi-authoritarian state with designs on reacquiring regional hegemony and great-power status, the other as a cooperative element within the democratic world community and a reliable trading partner.

What enabled Russia to maintain this duality was the record-breaking rise in energy prices, the backbone of the Russian economy. As the world's largest oil and gas exporter, Russia, under President Vladimir Putin, who was in the eighth and last year of his presidency, confidently advanced its foreign- and domestic-policy agenda. Since 2000, when Putin was first elected president, Russia's economy had expanded about 7 percent annually, with average wages rising six-fold during that period. In 2007 alone, Russia's GDP went up 8.1 percent to reach approximately $1.35 trillion, according to the Russian Federal State Statistics Service. (*Time* magazine named Putin its "man of the year" for 2007.)

Russia's ability to influence world energy prices and virtually dominate European energy markets enabled Moscow to support some of the world's most outspoken anti-Western regimes—such as Venezuela, North Korea, and Iran—without provoking retaliation from the West. And meanwhile, unmoved by criticism of its backsliding on democracy and press freedom, the Kremlin continued to develop its own model of "managed democracy," which was reminiscent of the Soviet epoch although void of superpower status and communist ideology.

The year was marked by a number of diplomatic rows that became trademark signs of Putin's foreign policy. Russia started a heated dispute with Estonia in April, accusing its leadership of rewriting history and even of pro-Nazi sympathies. What provoked this Russian response was the relocation of a Soviet World War II monument in the capital city of Tallinn, an act that precipitated popular unrest there that observers speculated might have been orchestrated by Moscow (see below, p. 536). In May, Russia test-fired a long-range missile and President Putin spoke of a new arms race after the U.S. announced an upcoming expansion of its missile-defense system into Eastern Europe. In July, president Putin personally presided over a diplomatic row between London and Moscow over Britain's bid for the extradition of an ex-KGB agent accused of the murder in London of Alexander Litvinenko, a former KGB agent turned political exile and critic of the Kremlin. And in line with his anti-NATO rhetoric that became especially fierce in 2007, Putin, in November, signed a law suspending Russia's participation in the 1990 Conventional Armed Forces in Europe (CFE) treaty that limited the deployment of heavy military equipment across Europe.

Domestically, the crackdown on political dissent was unparalleled even for Putin's Russia. There was wide-scale harassment of opposition figures and even of ordinary participants in pro-democracy rallies, as anti-Putin forces attempted to pull together a mass protest movement ahead of the parliamentary elections of December 2, 2007, and the presidential contest scheduled for the spring of 2008. In March, for example, dozens were detained after riot police broke up a St. Petersburg protest accusing Putin of stifling democracy. In April, police in central Moscow prevent opposition activists from holding a banned rally against the president.

In the December election, the pro-Kremlin United Russia party took 64 percent of the vote. None of the pro-democracy parties received a single seat in the Russian parliament, the second time in a row this had happened during Putin's presidency. Many observers described the election as neither free nor democratic, not only because of the stifling of opposition activity but also because tight government control over the airwaves, preventing the broadcasting of opposition views.

Former president Boris Yeltsin died in April, mourned by few. Most Russians blamed Yeltsin, Russia's first postcommunist leader, for policies that led to the economic woes of the 1990s, including the soaring cost of living, that many believed were reversed by his hand-picked successor, Putin.

UKRAINE

In Ukraine, the second largest republic of the FSU, 2007 was marked by a protracted political crisis revolving around a power struggle between pro-Western President Viktor Yushchenko and the opposition-controlled parliament.

In the spring, culminating an eight-month standoff, the opposition parties boycotted the parliament's plenary sessions, precipitating a paralyzing government deadlock. Yushchenko responded by dissolving parliament and announcing new elections. They were held on September 30, and yielded mixed results. Yushchenko's party received only 14 percent of the vote, lagging far behind the pro-Russian Party of Regions and the pro-reform Yulia Timoshenko Bloc. Timoshenko had played a key role in rallying support for the Orange Revolution that swept Yushchenko to power in 2004, but the alliance between Yuschenko and Timoshenko broke down soon afterward. Yet the two pro-Western parties together narrowly beat out the Party of Regions led by former prime minister Viktor Yanukovich, and its allies. After ten weeks of political wrangling, parliament appointed Timoshenko prime minister by a tiny margin.

The optimism that followed the Orange Revolution had faded for many Ukrainians as the country's economic growth slowed and prices rose. Nevertheless, Ukrainian democracy appeared strong, and President Yushchenko pledged to continue the quest for membership in NATO and European Union, even though that goal did not appear to be shared by most Ukrainians.

Other Republics

In the Republic of Georgia, President Mikhail Saakashvili surprised many of his supporters and Western allies by imposing a state of emergency and closing television stations critical of his rule, after Tbilisi, the capital city, saw a weeklong massive protest against him late in the year. The U.S.-educated Saakashvili had previously enjoyed a reputation as a pro-Western reformer. The president called early presidential elections, and immediately after they took place on January 5, 2008, he claimed victory. Despite the damage his actions of late 2007 did to his reputation as a democrat, Saakashvili reiterated his intention of bringing his small republic in the Caucasus into the European Union and NATO.

The European Union and the U.S. continued to engage with Kazakhstan, an oil-and gas-rich former Soviet state, despite its spotty record on democratic freedoms and human rights. In the spring, the Central Asian nation's parliament approved a constitutional amendment effectively giving President Nursultan Nazrabayev, the country's leader for 18 years, the right to remain in office for life. In parliamentary elections held August 18, Nazrabayev's party, Nur Otan, won all contested seats in the parliament's lower house, leaving the nation with a single-party system for the first time since the breakup of the Soviet Union. None of the opposition parties could clear the required 7-percent election threshold.

The sudden death in December 2006 of Saparmurat Niyazov, Turkmenistan's president-for-life, marked an end to the authoritarian rule that made him notorious as the most oppressive leader in the region. He had allowed neither basic freedoms nor political and economic reform. Niyazov's successor, Gurbaguly Berdymukhammedov, easily sailed thorough a government-staged election in February 2007. Upon taking control of the gas-rich Central Asian nation, Berdymukhammedov introduced some programs, including a pension system and compulsory secondary education, which had been abolished by Niyazov, but refused to open up a country that remained the worst example of tyranny among the former Soviet republics.

In neighboring Uzbekistan, President Islam Karimov, in power for almost two decades, had little trouble extending his tenure by another seven years through an election in December that international observers refused to recognize as free or fair. The regime continued to suppress civil liberties and human rights, while strengthening ties to Russia and China through long-term oil and gas contracts as part of an apparent attempt to build a bloc of anti-Western regimes that would counterbalance the U.S. military presence in the region.

Israel and the Middle East

As part of its long-term foreign-policy objectives, Russia sought to reestablish its former prominence in the Arab and Muslim world, if not as a power broker, than as an arms and technology supplier.

During 2007 Russia intensified its engagement with Syria and Iran. In the summer, Russia delivered to Syria its MiG-31E interceptors as part of an agreement reached earlier in the year. Moscow also announced plans to sell Damascus its MiG-29M/M2 dual-role fighters, and Syria approved a multimillion contract to purchase 50 Pantsyr-S1E advanced antiaircraft systems from Russia. Iran was suspected of having financed part of the deal, and in return Damascus would Tehran with at least ten of the systems. Since the UN Security Council had imposed sanctions on Iran, the only way Russia could sell it weapons was through such subterfuge.

Russia continued to provide technical assistance to Iran's nuclear program, centered on the nuclear power facility in Bushehr that Russian companies had been developing since 1993, and responded to complaints by repeatedly quoting provisions of international law permitting such deals. Russia insisted that the reactors would comply with all safeguards required by International Atomic Energy Agency. In 2007, Russia announced its commitment to transport spent nuclear fuel from Iran to Russian territory for storage and recycling.

Nevertheless, with the Iranian president threatening Israel with annihilation and Israeli intelligence suggesting a possible military conflict with Syria, these Russian policies were perceived in Israel as extremely dangerous. Already in January 2007Israeli officials voiced extreme concern over Russia's sale of the advanced antiaircraft missiles to Syria, with some destined for Iran. Russia's plans to restore a permanent naval presence in Syrian ports were also cause for concern. The Israelis suspected that the Russians would turn the Syrian ports into electronic-surveillance and air-defense centers and thereby threaten Israeli security. However some experts felt that any such plan was unlikely to materialize due to lack of funds and technical capacity.

Russian-Israeli relations retained a considerable level of ambiguity. On the one hand, the Kremlin's friendliness to Syria and Iran suggested hostility toward Israel and the U.S. Russian engagement in the Middle East peace process which was mostly nominal. Following the conclusion of the U.S.-sponsored Annapolis conference held in November 2007, Moscow said it would host a follow-up summit with the goal of attaining a "comprehensive" Middle East peace.

But at the same time Israel and Russia accomplished a diplomatic breakthrough, agreeing to abolish, as of June 2008, the visa requirement for traveling between the two countries. This was probably the most important positive development in relations between Moscow and Jerusalem since the reestablishment of diplomatic ties in 1991. The new visa-free regime was expected to draw hundreds of thousands of Russians to Israel for business and tourism; Israel predicted it would create 10,000 new jobs in the country. The agreement was despite concern on both sides about potential negative effects: Israelis feared an influx of illegal workers and prostitutes from Russia, while Russians worried about Israeli attempts to obtain sensitive and classified information in Russia.

Ukrainian president Yushchenko paid his first state visit to Israel on November 14–15. At least three times over the previous three years planned visits by Yushchenko had been postponed due to "scheduling conflicts." Some Jewish leaders had said the delays were actually due to Ukrainian concern about upsetting Arab allies, notably Iran and Syria. Discussions were begun between Israel and Ukraine about possibly ending the visa requirement for travel between the two countries, as had already been done in the case of Russia.

Iranian president Mahmoud Ahmadinejad paid a surprise visit to the Belarusian capital of Minsk in May for talks with his Belarusian counterpart, Alexander Lukashenko. Lukashenko had already been in Iran twice. Jewish leaders in Minsk expressed outrage over the visit to their country by the notoriously anti-Israel Iranian leader. Belarus was known to be involved in selling Russian arms to Tehran and other buyers, on a commission basis, and the Belarus military industry was believed to be aiding in the development of the Iranian Shahab 3 and Shahab 4 ballistic missiles.

Anti-Semitism and Extremism

Since the breakup of the Soviet Union none of its successor republics had instituted official anti-Semitic policies, with the exception of Turkmenistan, where only Islam and Orthodox Christianity were recognized as "legitimate" faiths. Nevertheless, in some of the countries government officials occasionally exhibited anti-Jewish attitudes; books and pamphlets expressing hostility to Jews were published and distributed, sometimes in bookstores run by Russian Orthodox diocceses; anti-Semitic views were found on Internet sites; and physical attacks on Jews and Jewish property were not infrequent.

Russia

Human-rights and Jewish activists expressed apprehension about the level of xenophobia and anti-Semitism in Russia, noting that such attitudes in the general population were exacerbated by the absence of an effective and independent judicial system and the prevalence of widespread corruption that hampered prosecution of racist crimes.

According to a report issued by the Moscow Bureau on Human Rights (MBHR) late in the year, there were some 200 attacks on individuals during 2007 motivated by race, creed or ethnicity, in which 60 people were killed and at least 280 injured. These figures were very similar to those published for 2006. Most of the victims, as in previous years, were people from the Caucasus, Africans, and Asians.

According to the Sova Information and Analytical Center, Russian courts, during 2007, convicted 23 people of hate crimes and another 27 of violating hate-speech laws. Both these figures were believed to be the highest annual numbers recorded to date. Indeed, human-rights monitors insisted the number of convictions was nowhere near the number of crimes committed, since the country's courts had a long way to go before they could cope satisfactorily either with hate crimes or with hate literature being published and openly distributed.

Physical attacks on Jews were rare in the Russian Federation. On February 18, three yeshiva students were assaulted near Moscow, and one of them was lightly injured. On June 11, in the city of Ivanovo in central Russia, a group of youths, apparently members of a neo-Nazi gang, attacked a local rabbi and two other Jewish community leaders. There were no serious injuries.

But numerous incidents of vandalism against synagogues and other Jewish institutions were reported. Most commonly this took the form of anti-Semitic graffiti, which were found on Jewish centers in Murmansk and Volzhsky (January) and in Izhevsk (November), and synagogues in Vladivostok and Voronezh (March), Tomsk (April), and Ulyanovsk (November). In the spring, crude anti-Semitic posters were glued to the walls of the offices of the Jewish community in Ivanovo, blaming Jews for the region's economic problems. On May 6, in Saratov in the Volga region, a homemade explosive device went off near the local synagogue, inflicting minor damage. Vandals threw stones and a Molotov cocktail at the synagogue in the southern city Astrakhan on September 22, causing a fire that was quickly put out. On December 24, windows were shattered in the synagogue in Makhachkala, the capital city of Dagestan, an autonomous republic in the Caucasus, and a window was broken in the house of a local rabbi two days later.

Of these incidents, only the Voronezh synagogue desecration resulted in the arrest of the suspected perpetrator, a 20-year-old man who was apprehended shortly after the crime.

Ukraine

The incidence of hate crimes targeting Jews was higher in Ukraine than in Russia even though the latter's population, both Jewish and non-Jewish, was far larger. One theory seeking to explain this was the relatively higher number and hence greater visibility of dark-skinned immigrants in Russia: the comparative absence of this element, the most frequent target of racism, in Ukraine, left Jews as the most recognizable ethnic minority. But Jewish officials placed the blame on Ukrainian officials for not doing enough to discourage anti-Semitism, complaining that police routinely classified what appeared to be anti-Semitic attacks as cases of hooliganism, a lesser offense.

Most anti-Semitic acts committed in Ukraine during 2007 were against Orthodox Jews, who were easily recognizable by their clothing, and against Jewish cemeteries and Holocaust-memorial sites.

The largest numbers of violent attacks took place in the city of Zhitomir, about 90 miles west of Kiev: on March 10, an Israeli yeshiva student wearing Orthodox garb was attacked by assailants who appeared to be members of neo-Nazi skinhead gang; on July 9, a group of youths chanting anti-Semitic slogans attempted an attack on Zhitomir's chief rabbi, Shlomo Wilhelm, inside the synagogue yard, but were held off by guards and community members; the same day, another young gang tried to break into the girls' dormitory at a local Chabad-run Jewish school, hurling verbal insults at the students; on August 6, a Jewish couple was attacked for no apparent reason, both suffering minor injuries; and on September 27, Mendel Lichstein, an Orthodox Jew visiting from Israel, was attacked near the synagogue. Elsewhere in the country, a rabbi was beaten on September 28 in Odessa, suffering a concussion and minor injuries, and the next day a Chabad emissary and two yeshiva students visiting from Israel to celebrate Sukkot were attacked in the city of Cherkassy, in northern Ukraine. In none of these cases were the culprits apprehended.

Vandalism of Jewish sites was a problem throughout Ukraine. On January 2, a swastika was painted on the façade of the Jewish charitable center Beit Dan in Kharkov, the country's second largest city, and a week later vandals damaged a memorial plaque commemorating victims of the Holocaust in the same city, and painted swastikas next to it. Mariupol, in southern Ukraine, was the site of the next incident, where, on January 14, swastikas and the words "Die Yid" and "Death to Yids" were discovered on the façade and fence of a former synagogue. On February 17 a memorial to victims of the Holocaust in Babi Yar, near Kiev, was damaged, as were 41 headstones at a nearby military cemetery that the vandals mistook for a Jewish cemetery. Police apprehended two suspects. The next day swastikas were daubed on the Holocaust memorial in Odessa, about 500 headstones were marred with swastikas or toppled down in a Jewish cemetery there, and "Happy Holocaust" and a swastika were spray-painted on the memorial plaque commemorating Leon Pinsker, a pioneer of the Zionist movement.

Holocaust monuments were desecrated in two separate incidents in the towns of Berdichev and Aleksandria on March 7. On March 16, windows were shattered in a synagogue in Chernovtsy. On March 20, a memorial to the victims of the Holocaust was desecrated and damaged in a Jewish cemetery in the town of Kalush, western Ukraine. Another Holocaust memorial, in Lutsk, on the site of a Nazi wartime massacre of 2,500 local Jews, was desecrated on March 27; vandals destroyed fencing around the memorial and dug out some human remains from the mass grave. On April 12, some 70 headstones were toppled in an old Jewish cemetery in Chernovtsy. A Holocaust memorial was reported damaged on August 27 in Khmelnitsky, in western Ukraine, and three days later Jewish graves were desecrated in a cemetery in Mariupol, southern Ukraine. On May 3, an unidentified person set fire to an exhibit in Kharkov organized by the Jewish Agency for Israel; that same day the Golden Rose Synagogue in Dnepropetrovsk was smeared with black paint.

On May 22, unidentified persons threw eggs at a synagogue in Kolomya, western Ukraine. The next day 19 nineteen headstones were damaged in a Jewish cemetery in Chernigov, north of Kiev. An unidentified individual threw a stone in the window of a synagogue in Zhitomir on August 16. On September 10, anti-Semitic graffiti were discovered on the walls of a Jewish day school in Zaporozhye, eastern Ukraine, and two days later a Holocaust memorial in Aleksandria was desecrated for the second time in four months. On October 5, unknown vandals broke into the Chabad center in the western Ukrainian city of Uzhgorod and set fire to the home of the local rabbi, who was celebrating the holiday of Simchat Torah in a nearby town. The intruders stole money, passports and some official documents.

On October 9, a memorial to the victims of the Holocaust was desecrated in a Jewish cemetery in Ivano-Frankovsk, western Ukraine. A teenager set fire to the front door of a Jewish day school in Kiev on November 1. Around the same time a leading Jewish newspaper in Kiev received e-mail threats, and the Website of the office of the chief rabbi of Ukraine was disabled by hackers. The same thing happened to the Website of a Jewish newspaper in Odessa in mid-December. On November 7 anti-Semitic graffiti were painted on the entrance to the apartment block in Zhitomir where a Hasidic rabbi and his family lived. A Hanukkah menorah displayed in a public square was desecrated in the city of Cherkassy on December 8, just days after a local Cossack leader publicly spoke out against any public celebration of that Jewish holiday.

The spate of anti-Semitic outrages in Ukraine triggered Jewish outrage. The targeting of Orthodox Jews precipitated a meeting of the countries rabbis, who issued a statement calling on the authorities to provide adequate protection and to prosecute the guilty parties. To protest the government's silence in the wake of several attacks, the president of the

European Jewish Congress canceled a planned trip to Ukraine. President Yushchenko finally met with the country's Jewish leaders on October 22 and sought to assuage their concerns. He criticized the law-enforcement agencies for their lackluster response to recent attacks, not only against Jews but also against blacks, Asians, and Arabs. As a result of the meeting the Ukrainian Security Service set up a special task force on hate crime, although considerable skepticism remained about whether it would alter Ukraine's troubling record.

Belarus

Belarus president Alexander Lukashenko generated headlines and drew international condemnation when, during an October 12 news conference broadcast live, he lashed out at Jews for their alleged inimical influence on the town of Bobruisk. Lukashenko described Bobruisk as "a Jewish city" and claimed that "Jews do not care for the place they live in; look at Israel, I have been there."

Rebukes came from the U.S., Israel, and the Council of Europe. Some commentators attributed the remarks, especially the Israel reference, to Lukashenko's desire to please Iran, Belarus's new strategic ally. Lukashenko, clearly concerned by the impact of his remarks, had his ambassador to Israel, Igor Leshchenya, publish a piece in the *Jerusalem Post* explaining that Belarus was not an anti-Semitic country and that Jews fared so well there that many who had left for Israel were now opting to return to Belarus.

Five days after Lukashenko's controversial remarks, 15 gravestones were vandalized in a Jewish cemetery in Bobruisk. A local Jewish leader cautioned that this might not have been an anti-Semitic act, as a Christian cemetery had also been recently vandalized in the vicinity. But anti-Jewish graffiti were found on the gates of the Jewish cemetery as well as a swastika, casting some doubt on his benign assessment.

Other Republics

A rare case of anti-Semitism took place in Armenia, home of a tiny Jewish community, in December. Vandals defaced a memorial to the victims of the Holocaust in the capital city of Erevan, scrawling a swastika and splattering it with black paint.

In Moldova, five youths were detained in March in connection with the vandalism of a Jewish cemetery in Kishinev. This cemetery, which had around 24,000 graves, was one of largest in the former Soviet Union, and had been vandalized numerous times in the past. The Jewish community had not found an effective way to protect it.

In the Baltic States, Lithuania saw a surge in the number of hate-speech investigations in 2007, according to local media. Thirteen cases were initiated by prosecutors in the first half of the year alone. Twenty such cases had been opened in 2006, as compared to just one in 2005, five in 2004, and one in 2003. More then half the 2007 cases involved incitement of hatred against Jews.

In Latvia, a court in Riga reached a decision in the two-year-old case of Aivars Garda, publisher of the newspaper *DDD,* and two of his employees charged with fomenting ethnic hatred for articles that appeared in the paper calling Jews "kikes" and making derogatory references to Russians. The judges acquitted the defendants. *DDD* had a long record of publishing such material with impunity.

Holocaust-Related Developments

Issues related to the Holocaust remained quite sensitive in the Baltic nations, particularly Estonia and Latvia, which had fought alongside the Nazis in World War II. Estonia was a focus of attention in 2007. In the spring, Russia accused Estonian authorities of "rewriting" the results of World War II by moving a memorial to Red Army soldiers who liberated Estonian capital from the Nazis in 1944 away from its original location in central Tallinn. While this dispute seemed likely to strain relations between the two countries, Estonia downplayed the issue and said it was an internal matter. Then, during the summer, Jewish groups outside Estonia expressed dismay that the defense minister and a member of parliament attended a celebration marking the anniversary of the fighting between pro-Nazi Estonian forces and the Soviet Army during World War II.

In May, workers preparing to lay gas pipelines in Gvozdavka, a village in south Ukraine about 100 miles from Odessa, came upon a mass grave. It was believed to contain the remains of thousands of Ukrainian Jews killed by the Nazis. Some Jewish leaders expressed outrage that local citizens, many of whom must have known about these massacres, had kept quiet about them and that it took an unrelated dig to reveal what had happened. They urged that the grisly discovery be used to educate Ukrainians about the extermination of approximately 1.5 million Jews on their soil and teach young people the importance of tolerance.

Soon afterward another mass grave was revealed by workers digging on the site of a planned office complex near Netishin, a town in the Khmelnitzky region of western Ukraine. It contained the remains of at least 60 Jews killed by the Nazis as well as what appeared to be fragments of Torah scrolls.

The Ukrainian government created other Holocaust-related controversies. Early in 2007, President Yushchenko signed a decree recognizing the Ukrainian soldiers who fought alongside the Nazis in World War II as wartime veterans, thus raising their status to that enjoyed in Ukraine by Red Army veterans, which came with substantial social security and healthcare benefits.

And in October, the government awarded the prestigious Hero of Ukraine medal, posthumously, to Gen. Roman Shukhevich, a wartime Ukrainian nationalist who fought alongside the Nazis. Presenting the award, President Yushchenko cited Shukhevich's role in fighting for his country's independence and noted that 2007 was the 100th anniversary of his birth. But Holocaust researchers and Jewish groups claimed that not only were the Ukrainian nationalists of that time allies of the Nazis, but that a force under the general's command was responsible for killing some 4,000 Jews in pogroms in 1941. Ukrainian government officials, however, insisted that the Ukrainian Insurgent Army (UPA), which Shukhevich led until he was killed in combat, did not collaborate with the Nazis and that such stories were misinformation spread by communist and pro-Soviet propaganda. President Yushchenko did acknowledge that some of the recent celebrations honoring Shukhevich had anti-Semitic overtones.

JEWISH COMMUNITY

Demography

The number of Jews in Russia and the other FSU countries continued to decline due to unfavorable demographic processes: an aging Jewish population, high rates of intermarriage, and continuing—although dramatically decelerated—emigration. The largest Jewish communities remained those in the Russian Federation (conservatively estimated at about 250,000), Ukraine (about 80,000) and Belarus (about 20,000).

Aliyah continued to decline. According to the Jewish Agency for Israel, in calendar year 2007, 6,502 Jewish immigrants from the FSU came to

Israel, a 13-percent decrease from the 2006 figure of 7,470. Even though the FSU remained the largest source of aliyah, providing roughly a third of the 19,700 immigrants who came to Israel in 2007, FSU aliyah was declining at a faster pace than aliyah in general, which dropped 6 percent compared to 2006.

The number of immigrants to Israel who returned to their native FSU countries, primarily Russia and Ukraine, remained at a high level in 2007. Although official statistics on returnees were not available, in some republics the statistics for return were probably close to those for aliyah. This was quite likely the case in Ukraine, where 1,450 Jews emigrated to Israel in 2007 and, according to the Va'ad, a Jewish community organization, about the same number returned to Ukraine from Israel.

Communal Affairs

Jewish communal life in Russia was dominated by the Chabad-led Federation of Jewish Communities of Russia (FJC), which far outpaced rival groups in terms of financial resources, political clout, number of affiliated congregations, and scope and variety of programs. An indication of the FJC's prestige in government circle was the highly visible role it had at the ceremony in December marking Putin's "person of the year" award from *Time* magazine, which took place in the Kremlin Palace of Congresses and was nationally televised the following month. Complementing the political backing it received from President Putin and other federal and regional officials was the extensive funding the FJC continued to get from abroad, particularly from its primary donor, Israeli diamond merchant Lev Leviev.

By 2007, the FJC had expanded its network to some 200 communities across Russia. The group's chief rabbi was the Italian-born Rabbi Berel Lazar, who has been a Russian resident for 15 years. Most of the rabbis currently working in the FSU belonged to the FJC network, which paid salaries to over 300 rabbinical emissaries, about half of them working in the Russian Federation and the other half elsewhere in the FSU. While most of the emissaries in the larger communities were foreign nationals, a growing number of FSU-born young men were holding positions as well.

A second national organization of Russian Jews was the Congress of Jewish Religious Organizations and Communities of Russia (KEROOR), which lagged far behink the FJC. It served as an umbrella body for non-Hasidic Orthodox congregations, and its spiritual leader was the Russian-born Rabbi Adolf Shayevich, who also claimed the title of chief rabbi of Russia. KEROOR's president and major financial backer was the Russian-Israeli entrepreneur Arkady Gaydamak.

The Union of Religious Congregations of Modern Judaism in Russia (OROSIR), the central body of the Reform movement, operated a number of congregations in Russia, Ukraine, and Belarus. Its scope of operation was limited by financial constraints and its plans for expansion remained largely unfulfilled. While Reform Judaism appeared to be a popular option among young Jewish professionals in the large cities, it did not have a local financial base and drew its budget almost exclusively from foreign sources. In 2007, OROSIR dedicated a new synagogue in St. Petersburg on a site purchased with the help of a London Reform congregation. This St. Petersburg synagogue was the first new Reform congregation to open in Russia since the fall of communism.

The Russian Jewish Congress (RJC), founded in 1996, was mainly a charitable foundation, and continued to support a few selected community projects. Vyacheslav "Moshe" Kantor, RJC president since 2005, was an industrialist who enjoyed good relations with some key Kremlin officials. He was elected president of the European Jewish Congress in the summer of 2007.

In Ukraine, a number of Kiev-based Jewish umbrella organizations represented community interests. The oldest group, the Ukrainian Va'ad, dealt with communal, charitable, and political issues, relying largely on the authority of its leader, longtime Jewish activist Josef Zissels. Also dealing with such matters was the All-Ukrainian Jewish Congress—United Jewish Community of Ukraine, created and led by businessman Vadim Rabinovich, which claimed to unite some 120 organizations under its aegis. Other organizations in Ukraine included the Jewish Council of Ukraine and the Jewish Foundation of Ukraine.

There were two major rabbinical authorities in Ukraine, each laying claim to the title of chief rabbi of the country: Rabbi Ya'akov Dov Bleich, an American who had been chief rabbi of Kiev since 1992, and Rabbi Azriel Haikin, who was elected chief rabbi in 2003 by Chabad rabbis, who were the majority of all rabbis working in Ukraine. Chabad operated in Ukraine through the Federation of Jewish Communities of Ukraine, which, unlike most other national Jewish groups, was headquartered not in Kiev but in central Ukrainian city of Dneporpetrovsk.

In December, *Focus,* a Russian-language weekly published in Kiev, named Aleksandr Feldman, a Jewish member of the Ukrainian parliament and head of the Jewish Foundation of Ukraine and the International Center for Tolerance, "national philanthropist of the year" and his Aleksandr Feldman Charitable Foundation "national foundation of the year." The paper's list of 200 most influential Ukrainians included at least ten Jews, Feldman among them.

A number of foreign Jewish organizations had extensive operations in the FSU. The American Jewish Joint Distribution Committee (JDC) was the primary provider of welfare and charitable services for the Jewish community. The Jewish Agency for Israel dealt with issues of aliyah and Jewish and Zionist education. Hillel operated off-campus programs for Jewish student students in the larger communities.

On October 18, Russia instituted new and complex visa rules that were clearly designed to make it harder for Western-based groups to send personnel into the country. While this was not directed specifically at Jewish organizations, the FJC and other Russian Jewish groups, which relied on foreign manpower, feared that the new system would make it much harder for them to operate.

On November, 13 Chabad yeshiva students were deported from Russia following a visa incident that prompted a rare case of direct intervention by the U.S. State Department. The young men, who were studying in the provincial city of Rostov, about 1,000 miles south of Moscow, were detained for violating immigration regulations, allegedly having failed to register properly with the authorities upon their arrival. The students were imprisoned overnight and allowed to leave Russia the next day after the U.S. embassy in Moscow made its displeasure known.

There were more than 100 Jewish day schools across the FSU, 75 of them affiliated with the Chabad-run Or Avner network, 15 schools operated by World ORT, and another 15 that belonged to the Shma Israel network, a loose grouping funded by the Canada-based Reichmann Foundation. Or Avner and Shma Israel schools provided Orthodox education; ORT schools were pluralistic, focusing on technology and computer training.

In October, more than 700 Jews attended the Limmud weekend educational marathon held near Moscow. In a rare show of unity, both claimants to the title of chief rabbi of Russia, Berel Lazar of FJC and Adolf Shayevich of KEROOR, attended.

Ukrainian president Yushchenko signed an order in November to return to the Jewish community an estimated 1,000 Torah scrolls that the old communist regime had confiscated and were now held in state archives and museums. The decision was seen as a reversal of a widely criticized move by local authorities in the city of Zhitomir who, in February, ordered that a number of Torah scrolls on loan to the Jewish community be returned to the local archives. Yushchenko also ordered the return of the historic Chernovtsy synagogue to the Jewish community. It had been confiscated from Jews decades earlier by the communists.

On May 16, the first synagogue in Estonia since World War II was dedicated in the country's capital, Tallinn.

In July, some 100 Jews held a prayer meeting and protest outside the European Commission in Brussels, protesting construction being conducted on what experts believed was a 600-year-old cemetery in Vilnius, Lithuania. The city had sold an area that included part of the former Snipiskes Cemetery to developers for construction of a residential and commercial complex. Although local officials said that their research indicated there were no graves there, experts from the London-based Committee for the Preservation of Jewish Cemeteries in Europe (CPJCE) argued that bodies had been found under the ground in question. The group said that as many as 10,000 Jews might be buried in what had been one of the region's largest Jewish cemeteries.

A synagogue in Dushanbe, Tajikistan's capital—the only synagogue in the country—remained under threat of demolition. The work had begun in February 2006 to make way for a new presidential palace, and the mikveh (ritual bath), classroom, and kosher butchery at the century-old synagogue were destroyed before an outcry brought the project to a halt. The question of completing the demolition still remained unresolved at the end of 2007.

In Moldova, protests from local residents, environmentalists, and Jewish activists halted a construction project on the site of a former Jewish cemetery in Kishinev. In the fall of 2006, excavation work in the Alunelul amusement park, located on the grounds of a former Jewish cemetery, unearthed human remains. The outcry that ensued convinced the Kishinev mayor's office to cancel the construction plans in early 2007.

LEV KRICHEVSKY

Australia

National Affairs

AUSTRALIA ENTERED 2007 ENJOYING unprecedented economic prosperity fueled by booming demand for its natural resources. Yet change was the buzzword—from climate change and changing the industrial-relations laws to a possible change of government. With a national election looming late in the year, political debate was framed around the inevitable electoral showdown between long-serving Prime Minister John Howard and the confident leader of the opposition, Kevin Rudd.

Australia's military involvement in Iraq and Afghanistan continued, although the debate over scale and duration of these deployments had given way to concerns over the inherent dangers faced by Australian military personnel. Three Australian soldiers—Trooper David Pearce, Sgt. Matthew Locke, and Pvt. Luke Worsley—were killed in skirmishes in Afghanistan, and two Australians working for U.S. security companies were killed in Iraq.

After five years detention in Guantánamo Bay, Al Qaeda trainee David Hicks returned home to Australia in May after pleading guilty to terrorism charges in a controversial plea bargain. He then served nine months in Adelaide's Yatala prison and was released on December 29 under an interim-control order. Hicks's lawyer read a statement to the media on his behalf in which the convicted supporter of terrorism said he recognized "the huge debt of gratitude that I owe the Australian public for getting me home."

In the wake of the foiled terror attack in Glasgow in June (see above, p. 352), federal police acted on intelligence linking the British terror cell to a Gold Coast-based doctor living in Australia, Mohammed Haneef, and Immigration Minister Kevin Andrews moved to cancel Haneef's work visa. But the case collapsed under legal challenges and the charges were dropped.

In domestic politics, the government's efforts to enact bold policy proposals and boost its sagging poll ratings met with controversy and resistance. In January, Prime Minister Howard sought to initiate a massive $10-billion rescue plan for the Murray-Darling river system, spanning four states. But the plan had to be abandoned when the state of Victoria refused to give up control of its part of the waterway. An inquiry in June found shocking child sex abuse rampant in many indigenous communities in the Northern Territory, prompting the federal government to launch a controversial emergency intervention along military lines. Treasurer Peter Costello's budget became a microcosm of the wider political climate: even though huge sums were allocated for higher education and payments to the elderly, and more tax cuts were proposed, the polls indicated trouble for the government.

Similarly, efforts to sully the reputation of opposition leader Rudd largely backfired. True, Rudd had been involved with disgraced lobbyist Brian Burke, but so had Environment Minister Ian Campbell, who was forced to resign. And then Minister for the Aging Santo Santoro was caught in a conflict-of-interest scandal relating to his stock portfolio, and had to resign as well.

Nevertheless, all year Prime Minister Howard defied the opinion polls and pushed on toward election day. But as he strode the world stage, behind the scenes some of his senior colleagues were advising him to resign, and once the formal election campaign got underway it was clear that the voters felt that eleven-and-a-half years in power were enough.

On November 24 Kevin Rudd—a Mandarin-speaking former diplomat and senior bureaucrat—secured a decisive victory for the Australian Labor Party (ALP) and became the country's 26th prime minister. It was a dramatic fall for Howard, once a dominant figure who now lost not only the position of prime minister but also his own parliamentary seat, after 33 years of public life. The Liberal and National parties that had constituted his coalition would have to rebuild.

Five Jewish parliamentarians were elected, two on the federal level and three in state elections. MP Michael Danby, previously the only Jew in the Federal Parliament, was now joined in the House of Representatives by his ALP colleague Mark Dreyfus. Eric Roozendaal, for Labor, and Ian Cohen and John Kaye, for the Greens, were elected to the New South Wales Legislative Council, the state's upper house.

Israel and the Middle East

The year 2007 marked a high point in Australian political support for Israel. The pro-Israel spirit characterized both the Liberal-National coalition government and the Labor opposition.

Early in the year the National Archives released 1976 cabinet documents previously restricted under the 30-year secrecy rule. They revealed that several Australian Jewish leaders, as well as future prime minister Bob Hawke, then president of the Australian Council of Trade Unions, were targeted for assassination by Fatah and PFLP terrorists in 1975.

In his first address to the Jewish community since assuming the ALP leadership in December 2006, Kevin Rudd told a Yeshiva Centre fund-raising dinner in Sydney on February 20 that he was "an unapologetic and lifelong friend" of Israel and the Jewish people.

The government continued to support the boycott of the Palestinian unity government and made clear that aid to the Palestinians would be conditional on Hamas meeting the three conditions laid down by the international community: recognition of Israel's right to exist, renunciation of violence, and respect for past agreements between Israel and the PA. Foreign Minister Alexander Downer welcomed the reindorsement of the Saudi-sponsored Arab peace initiative at the Arab League Summit in Riyadh in March, which proposed recognizing Israel if it returned to the 1967 borders.

Following the Hamas takeover of Gaza in June, Downer pledged AUS$4 million to PA president Mahmoud Abbas's new government in the West Bank, and a further AUS$3 million in humanitarian funding for Palestinian refugees in Gaza and Lebanon. On a Middle East visit in late June, Downer said he hoped the emergency government would provide an opportunity to revive the peace process with Israel. And in December, Australia pledged AUS$45 million over three years to the PA at the international donors meeting that raised US$7.4 billion to prop up Abbas.

Arab diplomats from 12 countries called on the Australian government in June to adopt a more impartial role in the Middle East. Syria's ambassador to Australia, Tammam Sulaiman, complained that Syria was so neglected that it "strived to get a glance from Mr. Downer." Downer responded: "I would like Syria to play a truly constructive role in constraining extremism. . . . For Syria to constrain the activities of Hezballah in southern Lebanon and in Lebanon more generally, and for Syria to exercise constraint over the activities of Hamas—that will help."

Prime Minister Howard was awarded the Jerusalem Prize by the Zionist Federation of Australia, the State Zionist Council of Australia, and the World Zionist Organization at a Jewish National Fund function in May that was attended by 1,200 people. The honor recognized Howard's many years of support for Israel and the Jewish community. The JNF also announced that a forest would be planted in Israel in his name.

On May 24 Attorney General Philip Ruddock extended for another two years the listing of Hezballah's external security organization as a terrorist group. In September he also re-listed Hamas's Izz a-Din al-Qassam Brigades, Palestinian Islamic Jihad, and Lashkar-e-Tayyiba.

Both the government and the opposition staked out strong positions against the Iranian nuclear-weapons program. Labor, with an eye to the upcoming elections, sought to portray itself to Jews as more anti-Iranian than the government. Robert McClelland, the ALP foreign-affairs spokesperson, told a meeting of the Australia/Israel and Jewish Affairs Council (AIJAC) on March 5 that Australia should lead a campaign to have the UN Security Council refer Iranian president Mahmoud Ahmadinejad to the International Court of Justice for threatening to "wipe Israel off the map." Defense Minister Brendan Nelson attacked the proposal for "cruelly" raising the hopes of Australian Jews, since only countries, not individuals, could be prosecuted before the ICJ. Foreign Minister Downer called the plan "a domestic stunt [that] would embarrass Australia" and added that Australia would not participate in any U.S.-led military operation in Iran.

In an October 26 debate with Downer on ABC TV, the opposition spokesperson on immigration, Tony Burke, supported "in the strongest terms, economic and political sanctions being taken against Iran. We've expressed very deep concern about some of the comments that have come from the Iranian leadership, in particular the comments about wiping Israel off the face of the earth."

On November 7, the Howard government endorsed an earlier Interpol decision to issue arrest warrants for five Iranians and a Hezballah operative suspected of involvement in the 1994 terrorist attack on the Argentine Jewish Mutual Association (AMIA) in Buenos Aires. Later that month Australia was one of only seven countries to challenge the UN Human Rights Council's selective obsession with Israel's human-rights record.

In a wide-ranging preelection interview with AIJAC's *Australia/Israel Review*, both Howard and Rudd outlined their parties' respective positions on the Middle East. The two men spoke of the values shared by Australia and Israel and the importance of the bilateral relationship. Committing themselves to supporting a safe and secure Israel, they reaffirmed that there would be no negotiations with Hamas until it accepted the three international requirements. The main difference that emerged in the interview concerned the Iraq war, as Howard stressed that Australia's 1,500 troops would remain stationed there, while Rudd said he would implement a staged withdrawal of the 520 combat troops in southern Iraq but maintain Australia's naval presence in the Gulf to stop oil smuggling, continue overflights to provide intelligence, and retain the troops protecting the Australian embassy in Baghdad.

Jews and other supporters of Israel sympathized with Howard upon his defeat on November 24, but took solace in the strong support that incoming Prime Minister Rudd and his ALP had demonstrated for Israel.

Prime Minister Rudd and the new Defense Minister, Joel Fitzgibbon, visited Australian troops in Iraq and met government officials there on December 22. In the last week of December, Australia's UN ambassador voted against funding for the UN's follow-up to the 2001 Durban Conference against Racism, scheduled for 2009. Since the original conference had been marred by anti-Semitism, Jews were reassured by this vote that the new government was sensitive to Jewish concerns.

Parliamentary opposition to Israeli policies was vocal but insignificant, more or less confined to members of small parties such as the Democrats and the Greens. Even the latter shifted position in April, deleting from their platform calls for Israel to remove its security barrier and settlers from Palestinian territories.

The fate of the three abducted Israeli soldiers—Ehud Goldwasser, Eldad Regev, and Gilad Shalit—drew considerable attention in Australia. Rallies in support of their release drew more than 500 demonstrators in Melbourne on June 25, the first anniversary of Shalit's capture by Hamas, and 300 in Sydney on July 29. Shlomo Goldwasser, the father of Ehud, spoke before Australian audiences and met with Foreign Minister Downer and opposition leader Rudd in September, hoping to gather support in the fight for his son's release. As he looked on, Parliament unanimously approved a resolution calling for the release of all three of the Israelis. And in November, 700 students on Australian university campuses participated in an international solidarity day for them.

Sydney's Bankstown Council canceled a conference planned for January 27 by the extreme Islamist Hizb ut-Tahrir group. It was to have included an address by the radical Palestinian preacher Sheikh Issam Amira.

In April, Immigration Minister Kevin Andrews called on Sheikh Taj a-Din al-Hilaly, the controversial Egyptian-born imam of Sydney's Lakemba Mosque, to consider leaving Australia permanently. Hilaly had questioned the Holocaust, made inflammatory remarks about Jews, and urged Muslims worldwide to support Iranian president Ahmadinejad. The next month, police dropped an investigation into whether Hilaly distributed $10,000 raised by a charity to Hezballah. But in June, the Australian National Imams Council removed Hilaly as spiritual leader of Australia's 300,000-plus Muslims and elected Sheikh Fehmi Naji El-Imam to a two-year term. Although less controversial than Hilaly, Fehmi had spoken at a pro-Hezballah rally in 2006 and described the organization's members as "freedom fighters."

Jack Roche, a convert to Islam who was jailed in 2004 after confessing to involvement in an Al Qaeda plot to bomb the Israeli embassy in Canberra in 2000, was released from prison in 2007.

In July, four Australian citizens were arrested in Lebanon on terrorism-related charges. Two of them were quickly released and the others were accused of supplying weapons to terrorists.

In December, the *Australian* newspaper reported that police in Victoria were investigating more than 50 men who had attended pro-Hezballah rallies during 2006 for suspected ties to that group. Investigations were also being conducted into a Melbourne-based Hezballah cell believed to be disseminating political propaganda and raising funds for Hezballah in Lebanon.

Dr. Victor Batarseh, the mayor of Bethlehem, arrived in Australia in August to sign a sister-city partnership with the Sydney municipality of Marrickville. He told a rally at the University of Sydney that his city was dying. "Bethlehem is being strangled," he charged, because of Israel's security barrier. Marrickville also had a sister-city relationship with the Syrian town of Safita. After representations from the New South Wales Jewish Board of Deputies in June, Sydney's Leichhardt City Council declined to twin with the city of Hebron, and instead offered support for NGO projects that included both Palestinians and Israelis.

The year saw a flurry of visits between Australia and Israel by politicians, academics, clergy, and businesspeople. Justice Elyakim Rubinstein of the Israeli Supreme Court delivered the AIJAC Hans Bachrach Oration in February. The next month Israel's national infrastructure minister, Binyamin Ben-Eliezer, arrived to sign a memorandum of understanding with Federal Environment and Water Minister Malcolm Turnbull on joint research and development in water technology. This was followed up in October, when a delegation of three state ministers, one shadow minister, and 50 senior executives from the water industry attended Israel's International Water Technologies and Environmental Control Exhibition and Conference. Israeli historian Michael Oren, MK Ephraim Sneh, Middle East expert Professor Barry Rubin, and Israeli Arab Supreme Court Justice Salim Joubran visited Australia in August.

In a groundbreaking event, AIJAC's Rambam Program together with

AJC's Project Interchange sponsored a visit to Israel by seven Indonesian journalists in October. Former IDF spokesperson Nachman Shai visited Australia to address United Israel Appeal functions in November. While in Israel as part of a Christian delegation, Archbishop Philip Aspinall, head of the Australian Anglican Church, criticized Israel's security barrier on ABC Radio in December, and the deputy chief of mission at the Israeli embassy in Canberra responded that the Christian delegation was biased, having originally not even planned to visit Israel, but only the Palestinian territories.

A record number of Australian Jewish students—more than 750—enrolled for Zionist Federation of Australia tours to Israel in the summer of 2007–08. And the New South Wales Board of Jewish Education, which ran outreach services to Jewish students in non-Jewish schools, sent 12 tenth graders for its inaugural six-week tour of Israel in November.

As media reports circulated in June that Australia had initiated discussions with Israel about negotiating a free-trade agreement, Australia's second largest investment firm, Babcock and Brown, announced plans to open a branch in Israel, reflecting the impressive recent success of the Israeli economy. A joint Australia-Israel biotech company, KarmelSonix, announced in November the commercial release of a product developed by Haifa's Technion to measure the severity of asthma attacks.

Israel's new ambassador to Australia and New Zealand, Yuval Rotem, took up his position in Canberra in August, replacing Naftali Tamir.

The Media

Not much changed in the Australian media's coverage of Israel.

The public electronic broadcasters, the Australian Broadcasting Corporation (ABC) and the multiculturally focused Special Broadcasting Service (SBS), were often problematic, if not quite as bad as in previous years. Both often emphasised alleged Israeli breaches of peace agreements while underplaying or ignoring Palestinian breaches. Similarly, coverage of the Annapolis Conference often emphasised the justice and reasonableness of Palestinian positions while subordinating Israeli demands for security and recognition.

SBS featured many documentaries about the Middle East, and this year the choice was far more even-handed than in the past. Nevertheless, "Dateline," SBS's main public-affairs program, continued to exhibit an anti-Western and anti-Israel slant. In May it carried a report on Iran's

Jews that largely glossed over the difficulties they faced, and the following week it aired a show that stressed the hardships that Israeli Arabs suffered. The combined effect was to depict Israeli Arabs as worse off than Iranian Jews.

A disturbing incident occurred on ABC Radio National's "Religion Report." Host Stephen Crittenden interviewed an American professor, Alvin Rosenfeld, about Jewish groups that opposed Israel. Rosenfeld took exception to Crittenden's use of the term "blood and soil Zionism" and his suggestion that revisionist Zionism had been influenced by fascist ideas about race. Crittenden then set out to "prove" his point by interviewing leftist Lenni Brenner, who was notorious for alleging Zionist ties with Nazis. After receiving criticism, Crittenden interviewed mainstream historian Walter Laqueur on the subject.

Among the print media, the *Canberra Times* was, as usual, the most critical of Israel, featuring scathing pieces reprinted from the notoriously anti-Israel *Independent,* published in Great Britain. The Fairfax-owned broadsheets, the Melbourne *Age* and Sydney *Morning Herald,* still had Ed O'Loughlin as their Israel correspondent, and he had a way of slanting his reporting through selective use of facts or subtle phrasing so that Israel was shown in a negative light. The *Age* ran a piece by a Palestinian writer virtually denying Israel's right to exist. AIJAC executive director Colin Rubenstein provided a response, but it appeared on the *Age* Website, not in the paper. The Fairfax-owned *Australian Financial Review* had Tony Walker as its U.S. correspondent, and his articles were often critical of U.S. Middle East policy.

Coverage in the News Ltd. tabloids was generally less comprehensive but fairer, while Greg Sheridan, foreign editor of the *Australian,* the national broadsheet also owned by News Ltd., stood out for his incisive and expert analysis of the Middle East and international affairs in general.

One disappointing feature of the media was the prominence given to a tiny minority of very vocal, anti-Israel Jews led by Antony Loewenstein, who were given substantial column space to express the view that debate on Israel was suppressed, even though the ample coverage they received suggested the very opposite.

Israel's release of the preliminary report of the Winograd Commission led many news outlets to recapitulate the 2006 war against Hezballah. Many of the accounts were inaccurate, tending to explain Israeli actions as an impulsive response to the kidnapping of two soldiers and describing all or most of the Lebanese killed as "civilians." Similarly, the 40th anniversary of the Six-Day War triggered stories of Israel as the aggressor. The release of *The Israel Lobby* by the American scholars John Mearsheimer and Stephen Walt prompted more media criticism of U.S. Middle East policy.

Anti-Semitism and Extremism

Anti-Semitism remained a marginal phenomenon in Australia. No one with aspirations to public credibility would admit to holding anti-Semitic views or associate with openly anti-Semitic organizations. Thus the nativist party One Nation, which gained adherents during the 1990s, virtually disappeared in the 2007 elections, polling 0.3 percent of the vote for the House of Representatives and 0.4 percent for the Senate.

Nevertheless there were an alarming number of anti-Semitic incidents, extreme right-wing groups continued to preach xenophobia and Jew-hatred, and virulent criticism of Zionism and/or Israel, usually but not always by the extreme left, sometimes crossed the line into anti-Semitism.

During 2007 there were 638 reports of "racist violence" against Jewish Australians. These included physical assaults, vandalism, threatening telephone calls, hate mail, graffiti, leaflets, posters, and abusive and intimidating electronic mail. The total was the highest on record, twice the previous annual average and exceeding by 8 percent the previous high, recorded in 2002. Indeed, the combined number of incidents involving physical assault, property damage, and direct face-to-face harassment was more than three times the previous average, and cases of harassment that did not include assault were recorded at a rate close to five times the previous average and two-and-a half times the previous annual high.

Far-right groups in Australia generally combined anti-Jewish propaganda with white supremacy ideology, opposition to immigration, and advocacy of a return to policies that disadvantaged Indigenous Australians. Even so they sometimes found allies among conspiracy theorists elsewhere on the political spectrum who were inspired by quasi-New Age ideas, the Libyan-inspired "Third Way," and political Islam, all of which promoted anti-Semitism while rejecting white racism.

The Australian League of Rights was the oldest and probably best financed extreme-right organization in the country. Its membership now was overwhelmingly elderly, but it continued to hold meetings, conduct action campaigns, and publicize its positions. The league published the weeklies *On Target* and *On Target Bulletin,* the monthly magazines *In-*

telligence Service, New Times, and *Social Creditor,* and a quarterly journal, *Heritage.* It also maintained a Website.

In 2007 the league gave considerable publicity to the self-styled "independent Jews" who criticized Israel. It promoted their leader, Antony Loewenstein, as "an Australian Jewish intellectual," even advertising his book, *My Israel Question.* Also addressed in league publications were the allegedly unbridgeable gap between Jewish and Gentile "morals" and the case for Holocaust denial even against the "Jewish hold on discourse." A full report of the Tehran Holocaust-denial conference in December 2006 was made available on its Website.

The Adelaide Institute consisted of the followers of self-styled Holocaust revisionist Frederick Toben, whose views were so extreme that even revisionist historian David Irving viewed them as a liability to the cause. Despite several legal findings against the content of his Website, Toben continued to participate in international gatherings of Holocaust deniers including the one in Tehran, where he echoed the Iranian president's call for the dismantling of Israel. As the year ended, the Federal Court was preparing new contempt proceedings against Toben for continuing to carry illegal content on his Website.

The Citizens' Electoral Councils (CECs) engaged in mass mailings of literature reflecting the views of Lyndon LaRouche, including bizarre anti-Semitic conspiracy theories targeting antiracist and Jewish groups. Despite spending huge sums on the 2007 election campaign, the LaRouche organization won an embarrassingly small number of votes. Serious allegations were made during the year that the CECs were seeking to infiltrate the national network of the conservative National Civic Council. A number of Australian Jewish communities complained that LaRouche propagandists were distributing material on college campuses and outside venues hosting Jewish community functions.

In most cities there were small groups of violent skinheads who were not necessarily aligned with any formal organization. Their main targets for harassment were Asian and left-wing students. The most important organized group was Australian National Action, which staged rallies in Melbourne and Adelaide and published a newsletter.

There were a number of anti-Semitic Websites that made claims to represent the views of organizations with impressive-sounding names, such as the World Church of the Creator and the White Pride Coalition of Australia. They were believed to be the work of no more than a handful of cranks.

JEWISH COMMUNITY

Demography

According to the most recent census figures, Australia's Jewish community was continuing to grow. In 2006 the census counted some 89,000 Jews in the country, constituting about 0.43 percent of the total population of 21 million. This figure was nearly 5,000 higher than in 2001. The actual number of Jews was probably higher, since religion was an optional question on the census form and about 11 percent of the Australian population did not answer it. Jewish leaders, believing that many Holocaust survivors were especially averse to disclosing their religion, estimated the size of the Jewish community to be around 120,000.

Melbourne had the nation's largest Jewish population, 40,000, followed by Sydney at 35,000 and Perth with 5,000. According to the census, Hebrew was the preferred language at home for some 7,500 Australians.

Communal Affairs

The most important change in communal leadership during 2007 was the election of Robert Goot to succeed Graeme Leonard as president of the Executive Council of Australian Jewry (ECAJ), the Jewish communal representative body. Philip Chester continued as president of the Zionist Federation of Australia and Mark Leibler remained national chairman of AIJAC, as did Jack Smorgon as federal president of the United Israel Appeal and Ron Ferster as head of the Jewish National Fund.

Education

More than half of all Jewish children aged 4–18, including almost 70 percent of those aged 4–12, received full-time Jewish education in the 19 Jewish day schools in Australia. Spanning the religious spectrum, these schools continued to rank at the highest level for academic achievement. This reflected the community's major investment in the schools as a means of preserving Jewish continuity. Day-school enrollment continued to grow despite ongoing concerns over high costs and the challenge to the community to find new sources of funding.

Adult Jewish education in the country was largely under the influence of the Melton Program, which attracted nearly 500 students in Sydney and Melbourne. Short-term courses utilizing guest lecturers also proved popular. Top priorities for the future, according to Australian Jewish educators, were expanded Jewish studies on the university level and teacher education to provide quality faculty for the day schools.

The Australasian Union of Jewish Students (AUJS) continued to play an active and effective role on campus, particularly in combating anti-Zionist and racist manifestations and in promoting Israel-visitor programs for Jewish students.

Interfaith Relations

Cooperation between different religious communities was evident in 2007 with a number of joint actions aimed at building interfaith harmony and understanding. The Executive Council of Australian Jewry (ECAJ), the National Council of Churches in Australia, and the Australian Federation of Islamic Councils repeated their previous calls for tolerance. The Australian Partnership of Religious Organizations (formerly the Australian Partnership of Ethnic and Religious Organizations) hosted the Inaugural Australian Religious Leaders Forum, where AIJAC's director of international and community affairs, Jeremy Jones, spoke at the opening plenary.

Other interreligious groups, such as the World Conference of Religions for Peace and the Griffith University Multi-Faith Centre, also provided the Jewish community platforms for contact and cooperation with other significant religious bodies. The Australian delegation to the Asia/Pacific Regional Interfaith Dialogue, hosted by the governments of Australia, Indonesia, Philippines, and New Zealand, included Jeremy Jones, who chaired the plenary session on education against intolerance.

Churches were important proponents of diversity and tolerance, often in concert with the Jewish community. The Uniting Church in Australia, continuing to explore ways of taking joint action with the Jewish community to combat prejudice, once again held two national dialogues with ECAJ during the year. The Catholic Church also sought to promote understanding: the Australian Catholic Bishops' Committee convened an international Forum on Religion and Peace in the Middle East, with keynote speakers Father Elias Chacour (Israel), Mohammad Sammak (Lebanon), and Jeremy Jones. And after several years of preparation, the Anglican Jewish Australian Dialogue had its third and fourth formal sessions in 2007.

These Christian groups, along with a number of service organizations, asserted moral leadership against anti-Semitism by refusing to allow racist and anti-Jewish groups to hire their premises and by making sure that their representatives did not share public platforms with known extremists.

Culture

The Jewish Museum of Australia and the Holocaust Museum, both in Melbourne, and the Sydney Jewish Museum were world-class institutions that maintained extensive permanent collections of Judaica and Holocaust memorabilia. They received visitors in ever increasing numbers, particularly school groups, and hosted numerous cultural events, such as literary evenings, book launches, and musical and dramatic presentations. Adelaide's Jewish community maintained a virtual museum, the Adelaide Jewish Museum (www.adelaidejmuseum.org).

The annual Jewish film festival, which attracted large and enthusiastic audiences, continued to be held in Sydney and Melbourne.

The Australia Israel Cultural Exchange (AICE), founded in 2002, made a significant contribution to the exchange of culture between the two countries. The third AICE Israeli Film Festival, held in Melbourne in August, was opened by visiting Israeli Film Fund director Katriel Schory. AICE also sponsored exhibitions of Australian Aboriginal art and an Australian film festival in Israel.

Personalia

The prestigious Australian Human Rights Medal for 2007 was won by Jeremy Jones, the AIJAC director of international and community affairs. This was the first time a Jewish Australian had won this honor, which was given for outstanding contributions to reconciliation, interfaith understanding, and fighting racism.

Novelist and poet Jacob Rosenberg was awarded the 2007 National Biography Award for his memoir *East of Time*. The book was chosen from a record 59 entries and was also short-listed for the 2007 Australian Gold Medal for Literature.

Two Australian Jews were named Companions of the Order of Australia, the nation's highest civilian honor. They were Victor Smorgon and David Gonski, philanthropic patrons of the arts.

Jews designated as Members of the Order of Australia were Prof.

Michelle Haber; Justice Stephen Rothman; businessman Peter Ivany; Dr. Murray Esler; former Jewish Care (Victoria) president Alan Schwartz; the late Roslyn Smorgon; Prof. (emer.) Ben Selinger; former federal minister Barry Cohen; Dr. David Rosenberg; lawyer Michael Frankel; and neuropsychologist Prof. Gina Geffen.

Jews receiving medals in the Order of Australia were Samuel Ginsberg; Vicki Vidor; Stan Marks; Joel Solomon, Bernard Freedman; Ernie Friedlander; Harry Atlas; Hanni Chalmers; Robert Simons; Dr. Paul and Zina Conway, Dr. Howard Freeman; David Ganon; Penny Hurst; Peter Kolliner; Henry Krug; Esta Levy; Aleck Miller; Kurt Rathner; Albert Selig; Marcelle Tanner; Dr. John Zalcberg; and Karoline Zolshan.

The Australian Jewish community mourned the passing of Major-General Paul Cullen, Australia's oldest Jewish ex-soldier and only the second Jewish person to hold the rank of major-general; Morris Zion Forbes OAM, NSW deputy crown solicitor and former president of the Australian Jewish Historical Society; Severyn Pejsachowicz, who fought for the Jewish community to be part of the Ethnic Community Council and was active with the NSW Jewish Board of Deputies and B'nai Brith; Walter Jona a former member of the Parliament of Victoria; Lily Adonis OAM, who worked for WIZO in Western Australia since 1935; Hilda Hines, former South Australian Liberal Party MP and former WIZO South Australia president; Agi Shelly, Holocaust writer; Prof. Josef Lederer, former chairman of the Optical Dispensers Licensing Board and renowned optometrist; Michael Hershon, a businessman who ran both the Hestia and Berlei companies; and Gordon Samuels AC, CVO, the NSW Supreme Court judge and president of the NSW Bar Association.

COLIN L. RUBENSTEIN

South Africa

National Affairs

THE YEAR WAS DOMINATED politically by a power struggle between President Thabo Mbeki and the controversial Jacob Zuma, a former deputy president and likely contender for the presidency in the 2009 election.

Early in the year Mbeki made it clear that although the constitution precluded his running for a third term, he was willing to continue serving as president of the country's predominant party, the African National Congress (ANC). Many observers saw this as an attempt to hold on to real power. Zuma emerged as Mbeki's key challenger. A populist with an impressive record in the struggle for a democratic South Africa, Zuma appealed in particular to the disaffected: those concerned with the growing gap between rich and poor, the state's inability to deliver public goods, and Mbeki's style and policies—his centralization of power, his alleged use of state agencies for political purposes, and his business-friendly agenda.

The battle between Mbeki and Zuma for the party leadership was decided at the ANC's national conference, which was held at Polokwane, a town in the Limpopo Province, in December. Zuma won by a wide margin, and in a "night of the long knives" his supporters more or less replaced the old order on the ANC's National Executive Committee, which was responsible for policy formulation. Some interpreted Zuma's triumph as a demonstration of grassroots democracy, others as a harbinger of radical populist innovation. In particular, the business establishment looked askance at the prospect of two uncoordinated centers of power operating until the 2009 general election: the ANC led by Zuma in Luthuli House, its Johannesburg headquarters, and the government led by Mbeki.

To add further uncertainly, the National Prosecuting Authority announced it was going ahead with the prosecution of Zuma, who was accused of accepting bribes related to a multimillion-rand arms deal, tax evasion, and money laundering. The charges emerged from the trial and conviction in 2005 of Schabir Shaik, a one-time financial advisor to Zuma (see AJYB 2006, p. 544).

The newly elected national chairman of the South African Jewish Board of Deputies (SAJBOD), Zev Krengel, was a guest observer at the Polokwane conference, and afterward he urged the Jewish community not to panic. Krengel praised the transparent manner in which the proceedings were conducted and congratulated the winners. "No matter which side one might have supported, it could not be denied that what one saw at all times was a vibrant democracy in action," noted Krengel. He wanted South African Jewry to maintain perspective and give the new leadership "a chance to find its feet and prove itself."

There were indications that the new leadership would focus on strengthening what was called the "developmental state," a term meaning more direct government intervention and coordination of economic policy in an attempt to narrow the gap between rich and poor, and, as part of that, to deal with a massive skills shortage. To be sure, such ideas had been spoken about for years, but would now be treated with greater urgency. At the same time the government indicated that it would not alter its prudent fiscal policies, which were bearing fruit. Growth reached 5 percent, spurred by massive infrastructure projects, and the currency remained strong. But unemployment stayed at well over 20 percent, and labor showed signs of restiveness amid rising inflation, which was estimated at about 7 percent.

Crime remained a major problem. There were 19,000 murders in 2007, 52,000 rapes or attempted rapes, 218,000 serious assaults, and 126,000 robberies with aggravating circumstances. The population was galvanized by the murder of a celebrity, the well-known popular historian David Rattray, whose death provoked an outburst of concern across the country. The fight against crime suffered a setback when the national police commissioner, Jackie Selebi, was served with criminal charges at the end of the year for allegedly maintaining a corrupt relationship with the underworld.

HIV/AIDS continued to wreak havoc. Although the government had finally moved to promote an antiretroviral program, the task was daunting. Over five million people were infected with the virus, and there was little confidence in Minister of Health Manto Tsabalalo-Msimang, who had long insisted that HIV did not cause AIDS and that the disease could be cured by dietary means. She herself underwent a liver transplant during the year that was reportedly the result of heavy drinking.

In May, Tony Leon stepped down as leader of the opposition Democratic Alliance. He was the longest-serving Jewish MP and South Africa's first Jewish opposition leader. At a retirement party hosted by the Cape

Committee of the SAJBOD, Leon spoke of always being conscious "of what it is to be a Jew in public life."

Israel and the Middle East

South Africa's maintained friendly relations with nondemocratic regimes. Its courting of Iran and a number of Arab oil-producing countries, its continued inability to deal effectively with Robert Mugabe's Zimbabwe, and its refusal to support a UN resolution against the military junta in Burma indicated a non-Western foreign policy orientation that included sympathy for the Palestinians in their conflict with Israel.

According to the Islamic Republic News Agency, South Africa's minister of intelligence, Ronnie Kasrils (who was Jewish), praised Iran's nuclear program while on a visit to the country, indicating that Iran should "make use of all the existing potentials to develop peaceful nuclear technology." Kasrils subsequently claimed he was misquoted. Approached for comment on the matter, Michael Bagraim, national chairman of the SAJBOD, said that the Jewish community "strongly supports the international call for the condemnation of Iran building up nuclear capability and believes that any support by our government for its rogue development is both wrong and out of place."

South Africa's voting record in the UN came in for strong criticism from the *SA Jewish Report,* which editorialized (May 4), "When the Security Council discussed sanctions against Iran—a country threatening world stability which has called for Israel's annihilation—South Africa opposed it; during the UN vote condemning Holocaust denial after Iran's infamous 'conference' denying the Holocaust, South Africa's ambassador was absent from the chamber; the Minister of Intelligence Ronnie Kasrils' recent visit to Iran served further to alienate Israel from this country."

In May it was reported that Kasrils had issued an invitation to Ismail Haniyeh, the Hamas leader, to visit South Africa. Jewish leaders expressed grave concern, Michael Bagraim describing the invitation as a sign of South African solidarity with an organization holding a "racist ideology" and "an openly genocidal agenda against the Jewish people." He said, "We condemn in the strongest possible terms Kasrils's invitation to the Hamas movement to visit South Africa, and we call on the government to rethink its position." Bagraim nonetheless praised the South African ambassador to Israel, Major-General Fumanekile Gqiba, for his strong condemnation of terrorism.

Writing in the *SA Jewish Report* (Aug. 8), Joel Pollak, a former speechwriter for Tony Leon, suggested that quiet diplomacy on the part of Jewish leaders had failed and the time had come to "take a stand against the foreign policies of the African National Congress government—not just on Israel, but Zimbabwe, Darfur, and other issues." Pollak was particularly concerned about South Africa's alliance with Iran and the trade contacts between the two countries. He expressed his perplexity about South Africa's voting patterns at the UN Security Council, "where it had opposed or abstained from action against Myanmar, North Korea, Zimbabwe, Sudan and other such regimes."

The *SA Jewish Report,* however, was not quite as sure. In an editorial (May 3), it reflected upon past Jewish political behavior—always clouded by ambivalence during the apartheid years—and considered current options. "The truth is that while Jews in South Africa are grateful for the new democratic dispensation, they nevertheless still feel unsafe, as do many other minority communities. As long as they feel this way, they will always want to tread a fine balance between different approaches." Michael Bagraim captured the nature of this awkward balance and the ongoing need for quiet diplomacy, saying, "The Board needs to tread a delicate line, not out of fear but in order that it remains in a position where it is best equipped to promote the interests of its constituents."

In June, the ANC called on all South Africans to join in a day of mass action against the occupation of Palestinian territory. "Jewish South Africans," responded the *SA Jewish Report* (June 15), "are justifiably furious that the ruling party should officially take so partisan a stance on so complex an issue that affects them deeply." A joint SAJBOD and South African Zionist Federation (SAZF) delegation met with Minister of Foreign Affairs Nkosazana Dlamini Zuma to discuss the government's position on the Israeli-Palestinian conflict. The minister assured the delegation that South Africa was committed to a two-state solution and wished to maintain diplomatic and military ties with Israel. She also indicated that she had been unaware that South Africa had voted against the inclusion of Magen David Adom in the International Red Cross and Red Crescent Society. At the same time, the ANC took out a full-page advertisement in the *SA Jewish Report* committing the party to a two-state solution.

The 2007 Pew Global Project Attitudes Survey indicated that 28 percent of South Africans sided with Israel in the conflict while 19 percent sided with the Palestinians and another 19 percent sympathized with both equally. However the survey was conducted in urban areas only.

Jewish leaders had long been concerned about anti-Israel bias shown by the South African Broadcasting Corporation (SABC). A storm had erupted in 2006 after the chief of news and current affairs, Dr. Snuki Zikalala, had prohibited Paula Slier—whom Zikalala called "that white Jewish girl"—from reporting on the Israeli-Palestinian conflict (see AJYB 2007, pp. 542–43). The SAJBOD had a constructive meeting with the SABC in August 2007 and it was agreed that an independent monitoring group would evaluate SABC reportage on the Middle East for a year. This agreement enraged Paula Slier, who charged the Board of cutting "a deal with Zikalala" that did not include any redress of her grievances. The SAJBOD acknowledged that it should have communicated the details of the meeting to Slier as a courtesy, but claimed that Slier herself had indicated she did not wish them to bring up her case. This was denied by Slier.

With comparisons regularly being made between apartheid South Africa and Israel, it was hardly surprising that Jimmy Carter's new book, *Palestine: Peace Not Apartheid,* attracted considerable attention. Ronnie Kasrils upset the community further by comparing Israel's behavior to that of the Nazis, leading the *SA Jewish Report* (June 5) to condemn the analogy: "In the complex and interminable Israeli-Palestinian conflict, wrongs have been committed by all sides. There is plenty of blame to go around. But resorting to the Nazi analogy by government ministers is something else. It suggests a more sinister motive than objective comment."

There was much hostile print and electronic coverage of the 40th anniversary of the Six-Day War. Thus a cartoon by prize-winning cartoonist Zapiro (Jonathan Shapiro) in the *Mail & Guardian* (June 6) depicted the war as a planned land grab, and the SAZF lodged a complaint against the weekly. But the press ombudsman turned it down, saying, "Your Federation may not like it, but there are other opinions on the subject and there is no reason they should be suppressed."

Despite South Africa's clear pro-Palestinian tilt, President Mbeki saw fit to pay an unexpected visit to the Israel Independence Day celebrations in Durban. Greg Bass, chairman of the KwaZulu Zionist Council, praised the visit and suggested it indicated the president's "commitment to minority rights in general and the Jewish community in particular." Mbeki had not planned the visit in advance. He had been at an unrelated meeting at the Durban Jewish Club where the event was taking place, and decided to drop in.

A number of prominent Israelis visited South Africa. One was Dr. Eli

Opper, chief scientist at the Israeli Ministry of Industry, Trade and Labor. Opper came as the guest of South Africa's Department of Trade and Industry, which invited him with a view toward helping the building of small- and medium-sized businesses in South Africa. Opper was optimistic that exchanges with Israel in the area of technology could aid South African agriculture and farming.

Benjamin Pogrund, director of the Yakar Center in Jerusalem, and Bassam Eid, executive director of the Palestinian Human Rights Monitoring Group, arrived in South Africa together on a visit sponsored by Yakar and the Centre for International Political Studies at the University of Pretoria. Pogrund, a prize-winning journalist born in South Africa, and Eid addressed multifaith gatherings and NGOs.

Issie Kirsh, a South African businessman and founder of Radio 702, established a twenty-four-hour-a-day English-language radio station, 96.6 Ram FM, in Ramallah and Jerusalem. The station was licensed by the Palestinian Authority.

Industrialist, philanthropist, and Jewish leader Mendel Kaplan was an unsuccessful candidate for the presidency of the World Jewish Congress.

Anti-Semitism

After a record year in 2006, the number of reported anti-Semitic incidents declined in 2007, but was still above the average annual figure since records began to be kept. The incidents were not violent in character and usually involved verbal abuse or intimidation often linked with hostility to Israel and Zionism. There was one cemetery desecration, vandals smashing Jewish tombstones at a cemetery in Nigel, near Johannesburg. Also, during the year, a member of the city council of Cape Town, Badih Chabaan of the African Muslim Party, made racist and anti-Semitic comments. He was removed from office on unrelated charges.

Professor Hussein Solomon, a scholar of Islam in Africa at the University of Pretoria, expressed concern at the type of Islam that was so prevalent in the country. Speaking to the Union of Jewish Women (UJW), he referred to South African Islam as "reactionary, anti-Semitic, insular, emotional, stupidly militant, and bereft of all reason." He noted that South African Muslims refused to see the "connection between the vitriolic sermons and publications, the resultant ideologies of hatred that emanate from it and the murderous actions that could arise from this hatred" (*SA Jewish Report,* Mar. 30).

A prominent Muslim business leader, Solly Noor, called on Muslims worldwide to follow the Jewish example and emulate their world domination program, along the lines of the *Protocols of the Elders of Zion,* and "wrest control of South Africa" from the Jews. Noor was speaking at the launch of the second annual First National Bank (FNB) Islamic Finance Business Awards for 2007.

In a panel discussion in Johannesburg exploring relations between Jews and Muslims, the chief rabbi, Dr. Warren Goldstein, and Ebrahim Rasool, the Western Cape premier, stressed the need for dialogue between the two groups. "Both Muslims and Jews understand displays of both fundamentalism and certitude that have often been occasioned by positions taken on Palestine and Israel," explained Rasool. "We have the democratic space to deal with problems without one faith demonizing the other . . . . It is a common set of values that holds us together—justice, peace, and humanity." Rasool's comments were endorsed by the *SA Jewish Report* (Dec. 17), which added its voice to the call for dialogue. An editorial declared: "Both Muslims and Jews are minority groups in this country. Both carry feelings of insecurity deriving from their status. It is essential if we are to live successfully together as South Africans that we always continue to search for and consolidate common ground between us, which is more extensive than what divides us. We must not allow the extremists to negate this."

The Broadcasting Complaint Commission of South Africa dismissed a charge by the Muslim Judicial Council (MJC) against Dr. Jud Newborn, an American cultural anthropologist and guest of the Cape Town Cultural Centre. The MJC charged that during a talk-show interview Newborn had compared Islam and Nazism, and thus was guilty of race hatred and incitement.

The Islamic Unity Convention (IUC), owners of the Muslim station Radio 786, challenged the constitutionality of certain provisions of the Broadcasting Code of Conduct relating to the hearing of complaints. While ostensibly seeking to overturn restrictions on free speech, the challenge, if successful, would have negated a ruling by the Independent Communications Authority of South Africa (ICASA) upholding the SAJBOD's complaint against Radio 786 for anti-Semitic broadcasting. The case, which went back to 1998, was finally adjudicated in 2006 (see AJYB 2007, p. 543). The Ministry of Telecommunications opposed the challenge. In December, the Constitutional Court dismissed it on all counts.

Holocaust-Related Matters

The Cape Town Holocaust Centre presented a multimedia exhibition titled "Witnessing Darfur." It included screenings of *Darfur Diaries: A Message from Home,* which featured recorded testimonies of refugees who fled the conflict. In his speech opening the exhibition, Jody Kollapen, chairman of the South African Human Rights Commission, claimed that "we have the responsibility as Africans to take an interest in what is happening in Darfur. We have to engage civil society and the faith-based community about the political and humanitarian interventions that must happen."

The Holocaust Centre also hosted another exhibition, "German Resistance: The White Rose Movement," brought to South Africa by the Centre and the Friedrich Ebert Stiftung. Franz Josef Mueller, an 82-year-old veteran of the movement that had defied Hitler, and honorary president of the White Rose Foundation, participated in the opening ceremony.

A chair in Holocaust and genocide studies was established at the University of South Africa by the Prime Media Foundation. Tony Blair, the British prime minister, gave the opening address.

In November it was announced that a new Johannesburg Holocaust Centre was to open, directed by Tali Nates. It would be part of the newly established South African Holocaust Foundation, which would include within it the flagship Cape Town Holocaust Centre.

South Africa hosted an event posthumously honoring Theodor Criveanu as Righteous among the Nations. Criveanu blocked the deportation of a number of Romanian Jews to Nazi death camps (see above, p. 518). The certificate and medal were presented to his son, Willie Criveanu, who lived in Johannesburg. Israeli ambassador Ilan Baruch attended the function.

JEWISH COMMUNITY

Communal Affairs

There was some public discussion during the year about forming the equivalent of AIPAC in South Africa. "Ultimately," wrote David Saks, a SAJBOD senior researcher, "the setting up of such a proactive lobby may well depend on the political will of our community to embark on an even more bold approach to public affairs than hitherto, allowing the established representative organizations to get on with their normal work in aid of Israel" (*SA Jewish Report*, May 11).

The SAJBOD maintained interfaith dialogue with the South African Council of Churches, Cape Town's Turkish Muslim community, and representatives of the Baha'i faith. In August, a Western Cape Religious Leaders' Forum was launched to address the many social ills facing Cape society.

In December, Anglican archbishop Njongonkulu Ndungame visited the Habonim Dror Jewish summer camp to speak to participants. He called on the youths to share in addressing the challenges faced by South Africans, saying, "You should ask yourselves: What is it that I can do?"

The Jewish leadership of Gauteng Province met with a delegation from the UJA-Federation of New York. In welcoming the group, Zev Krengel, Gauteng Council chairman, praised the powerful ties of kinship that united the Jewish world. In addition to meeting with Jewish leaders, the delegation met with the outgoing head of the Democratic Alliance, Tony Leon, and with former president F.W. de Klerk.

The SAJBOD published *Reach—Jewish Helping Hands in South Africa,* a record of what Jewish organizations were doing on behalf of the wider South African society. Among the many initiatives, ORT South Africa and MaAfrika Tikkun were particularly noteworthy. ORT teamed up with Bidvest, the international services, trading, and distribution group, to improve the quality of math, science, and technology teaching in underfinanced schools. Bidvest committed 3.7 million rand over four years for skills training. MaAfrika Tikkun began construction of three new community centers in Diepsloot, near Johannesburg.

The Jewish community also received assistance. Helping Hands, launched in 2006, both raised funds and connected young adults to the welfare needs of the community. It raised 3.6 million rand for use by the *hevrah kadishah* (Jewish burial society). Kosher Mobile Meals funded meals for 150 recipients.

The Union of Jewish Women (UJW) celebrated 75 years. Leah Aharanov, president of the International Council of Jewish Women (ICJW), visited South Africa for discussions with the UJW in preparation for the ICJW's proposed quadrennial convention, to be held in Cape Town in 2010.

At its biennial conference, the SAJBOD expressed an upbeat mood.

David Harris, executive director of the American Jewish Committee, was the guest of honor and keynote speaker. Harris spoke about the threat Iran posed to Israel and about the danger that Jews might succumb to fear. Speaking at the same conference, Minister of Safety and Security Charles Nquakula urged the Jewish community to help in the fight against crime.

Zev Krengel was elected national chairman of the SAJBOD, taking over from Michael Bagraim who was elected president. Krengel stressed the Jewish community's commitment to South Africa. He noted that the country had one of the lowest levels of anti-Semitism in the world and that Jews were protected by the constitution. "We are proudly South African and we are proudly Jews," he told the conference.

The SAJBOD hosted an exhibition in December on 120 years of Johannesburg Jewry. The *SA Jewish Report* (Dec. 14) editorialized that despite all the difficulties, "this community in the city of Johannesburg will endure and prosper for another 120 years. There are so many opportunities for creative minds. Who better than the Jews to identify them and make something out of them through passion and hard work?"

Religion

Chief Rabbi Goldstein, working with the National Religious Leaders Forum (NRLF) and the Department of Education, spearheaded the creation of a Bill of Responsibilities, with the aim of building a culture of responsibility in schools. Goldstein, an executive member of the NRLF, presented the idea to President Mbeki and senior cabinet members, explaining that the concept was "very much based on Judaism."

In May the South African Union for Progressive Judaism (SAUPJ) approved the Jewish validity of marriages between same-sex Jewish couples. "This is a matter of justice and principle and we believe it is what Judaism requires of us in this day and age," said Steve Lurie, SAUPJ chairman. "The SAUPJ honors the divine within all human beings, and their right to live with dignity."

Jews for Judaism, a division of the Union of Orthodox Synagogues (UOS), submitted a formal complaint to the Advertising Standards Authority of South Africa (ASASA) about an ad for a Christian missionary group that portrayed a surgeon in a mask, with the caption, "Ten out of ten Jewish doctors recommend Jesus." The ASASA upheld the complaint, accepting the argument that the ad was misleading.

There was controversy from time to time in the columns of the *SA Jewish Report* on various aspects of Judaism and over whether the community was indeed open enough to tolerate full debate. One frequent subject of comment was the Jewish attitude toward homosexuality. Another was the proliferation of small congregations, often located in homes. Martin Sacks, who chaired the Israel-United Appeal, complained that these congregations caused financial problems for the traditional large synagogues.

Rabbi Azriel Goldfein, who headed the Johannesburg yeshiva, passed away in November. Coming to South Africa from the U.S. in 1972, he established the yeshiva together with Rabbi Moshe Kurtstag. In a special tribute, Chief Rabbi Goldstein spoke of Rabbi Goldfein's "revolutionary and dramatic impact on South African Jews." He said that Goldfein's "self-evident burning sense of mission and dedication to building a yeshiva here primarily for the training of South African rabbis for South Africa has literally changed the face of South African Jewry."

Education

The Yeshiva College of Cape Town was renamed the Phyllis Jowell Jewish Day School in honor of the late writer, who specialized in books about the Jewish heritage. The school was largely funded by Mendel Kaplan, who insisted that even though it educated the sons of rabbis, it was "not going to be *haredi* and disrupt the unity of the community."

The new state curriculum, which stressed the development of verbal skills, accepted Hebrew but not Jewish studies to fulfil certain requirements. Students following the new syllabus would matriculate in 2008.

South Africa held its first Limmud gatherings in Johannesburg and Cape Town. These educational retreats proved a great success, with 400 attending in Johannesburg and 200 in Cape Town. Modeled on the Limmud program founded in England in 1980, the retreats attracted a mix of participants who enjoyed open discussion within a tolerant and pluralistic context. "There was an electric feeling that we were all embarking on an incredible journey of magical proportions, the destination not quite clear, other than a commitment to adventure, promising arguments for the sake of heaven," commented Vivienne Anstey, the Limmud chair.

A memorial fund was established in the name of Cyril Harris, the late chief rabbi. The Chief Rabbi C. K. Harris Memorial Fund would award scholarships to both Jewish and non-Jewish South Africans.

Culture

A celebration of Jewish culinary styles, "In our Mother's Kitchen—Jewish Food," was exhibited at the South African Jewish Museum in Cape Town. The museum director, Shea Albert, explained that the aim was "to show people where our Jewish culinary roots came from and how they evolved." Two other exhibitions were hosted by the museum during 2007. One was "The Moving Spirit," photographs taken by the acclaimed Paul Weinberg of religious rituals and spiritual practices. The other was "Between Hearth, Heim and Home: Three Jewish Women's Encounters with the New World," which explored the identities of immigrant and second-generation South African Jews. Two further exhibitions were mounted in Johannesburg. An exhibition of photographs by Marion Davis, "Absence and Loss," looked at memorials in Berlin. "What Will Come" featured works by artist William Kentridge.

Publications of interest included Charles van Onselen, *The Fox and the Flies: The World of Joseph Silver, Racketeer & Psychopath;* Harold Serebro and Jacques Sellschop, *Beyond Redemption;* Aubrey N. Newman, Nicholas J. Evans, J. Graham Smith, and Saul W. Issroff, *Jewish Migration to South Africa: The Records of the Poor Jews Temporary Shelter, 1885-1914;* Andrew Feinstein, *After the Party;* and Colin Tatz, Peter Arnold, and Gillian Heller, *Worlds Apart: The Re-Migration of South African Jews.*

Personalia

Dr. Brian Romberg was elected president of the World Small Animal Veterinary Association; Professor Phillip Tobias, a paleontologist, received the Walter Sisulu Special Contribution Award from the city of Johannesburg; and Justice Arthur Chaskalson, first president of South Africa's Constitutional Court, was honored by the Jewish National Fund.

Among prominent South African Jews who died in 2007 were Aida Geffin, doyenne of South African real estate; Benjamin Eisenberg, distinguished agriculturalist; Bennie Resnick, devoted communal worker in Cape Town; Ruby Caplan, stalwart of the South African Union of Progressive Judaism; Dick Friedlander, former mayor of Cape Town; Maximillian Mendel (Max) Borkum, founding member of the Progressive Party and well-known stockbroker; Isaac Richards, rabbi emeritus of Temple David, Durban; Moïse Israel, founding member of the Sephardi Hebrew Congregation of Cape Town; Richard Lurie, former president of the South African Stock Exchange; Arthur Ginsberg, long-serving member of the Union of Orthodox Synagogues; Nathan Vogelman, highly decorated World War II veteran; David Kuper, chairman of Investec Property Group; Reuben Sher, expert on AIDS; Mannie Feldman, acclaimed architect; Professor Ellison Kahn, legal scholar; Rabbi Azriel Goldfein, yeshiva head; and Violette Fintz, prominent survivor of the Holocaust.

MILTON SHAIN

World Jewish Population, 2008

At the beginning of 2008 the world's Jewish population was estimated at 13.232 million—an increase of about 71,000 over the previous year's revised estimate.[1] While world total population grew by 1.2 percent in 2007,[2] world Jewish population grew by less than half of that, 0.5 percent. Israel's Jewish population grew by 1.6 percent and the rest of world Jewry diminished, on aggregate, by –0.2 percent.

Israel's Jewish population (not including over 315,000 non-Jewish immigrants in the framework of the Law of Return) approached 5.5 million in 2008, over 41 percent of world Jewry. This represented a population increase of nearly 85,000 over 2007. After critically reviewing all available evidence on Jewish demographic trends, it is plausible to claim that in the first decade of the twenty-first century Israel hosts the largest Jewish community worldwide, although there are some who disagree (see below). Demography has produced a transition of singular relevance for Jewish history and destiny—the return of the Jews to a geographical distribution significantly rooted on their ancestral homeland. This has occurred through daily, minor, slow, and diverse changes affecting human birth and death, geographical mobility, and the willingness of individuals to identify with a Jewish collective. This holds true regarding the *core* Jewish population—not including non-Jewish members of Jewish households, other non-Jews of Jewish ancestry, and still other non-Jews who may be interested in or involved with Jewish matters. If the *enlarged* Jewish household composition is considered, including such non-Jewish members, the U.S. holds a significantly larger population aggregate than Israel.

Israel's Jewish population growth—even if slower than during the 1990s—reflects the continuing substantial natural increase generated by a combination of relatively high fertility (2.8 children on average in 2007)

[1]The previous estimates, as of January 1, 2007, were published in AJYB 2007, vol. 107, pp. 551–600. See also Sergio DellaPergola, Uzi Rebhun, and Mark Tolts, "Prospecting the Jewish Future: Population Projections 2000–2080," AJYB 2000, vol. 100, pp. 103–46; and previous AJYB volumes for further details on earlier estimates.

[2]Population Reference Bureau, *2008 World Population Data Sheet* (Washington, D.C., 2008), prepared by Carl Haub and Mary Mederios Kent.

and young age composition (about 25 percent below 15). Neither of these two factors boosting population growth exists in any other country worldwide, where instead, besides possible growth due to international migration, Jewish populations tend to decrease at variable paces. The causes are low Jewish birth rates, an increasingly elderly age composition, and a dubious balance of those who join Judaism and those who lose their Jewish identity.

Determinants of Jewish Population Change

Since the end of the 1980s, major geopolitical and socioeconomic changes on the world scene have significantly affected Jewish population trends. The leading factors were the political breakup of the Soviet Union; Germany's reunion; the European Union's gradual expansion to 27 states with the addition of ten new members in 2004 and of Romania and Bulgaria in 2007; South Africa's transition to a new regime; political and economic instability in several Latin American countries; and the volatile situation in Israel and the Middle East.

Large-scale emigration from the former Soviet Union (FSU) and rapid population growth in Israel were the most visible effects, accompanied by other significant Jewish population transfers and changes in identification. Reflecting these global trends, over 80 percent of world Jewry live in two countries, the United States and Israel, and 95 percent are concentrated in the ten largest country communities. Six of the G8 countries[3] (the U.S., France, Canada, the UK, the Russian Republic, and Germany) comprise 87 percent of the total Jewish population outside of Israel. The aggregate of these major Jewish population centers virtually determines the assessment of world Jewry's total size and demographic trends. The continuing realignment of world Jewish population geography toward the major centers of economic development and political power provides a robust yardstick for explanation and prediction.[4]

Population size and composition reflect the continuous interplay of three major determinants. Two of these are shared by all populations: (a) the balance of vital events (births and deaths); and (b) the balance of international migration (immigration and emigration). Both of these

---

[3]The eight leading world economies, also including Japan and Italy.

[4]See Sergio DellaPergola, Uzi Rebhun, and Mark Tolts, "Contemporary Jewish Diaspora in Global Context: Human Development Correlates of Population Trends," *Israel Studies* 11, 1, 2005, pp. 61–95.

factors affect increases or decreases in the physical presence of individuals in a given place. The third determinant consists of identificational changes (accessions and secessions), and applies only to populations—usually referred to as sub-populations—that are defined by some cultural, symbolic or other specific peculiarity, as in the case of Jews. The latter type of change does not affect people's physical presence, but rather their willingness or ability to identify with a particular religious, ethnic or otherwise culturally defined group. Some, though not all, of these passages receive formal sanction through ritual ceremonies of one sort or another. The quantitative impact of passages that, outside of any ceremonial, occur in either direction involving individual perceptions of and emotional attachments to group identities must not be undervalued.

The country figures presented here for 2008 were updated from those for 2007 in accordance with the known or estimated changes in the interval—vital events, migrations, and identificational changes. In our updating procedure, whether or not exact data on intervening changes were available, we applied empirically ascertained or assumed directions of change, and consistently added to or subtracted from previous Jewish population estimates. If the evidence was that intervening changes balanced each other off, Jewish population remained unchanged. This procedure proved highly efficient in the past. Most of the time, when improved Jewish population figures became available reflecting a new census or survey, our annually updated estimates generally proved on target.

The more recent new research findings basically confirm the estimates we had reported in previous AJYB volumes and, perhaps more importantly, our interpretation of the trends now prevailing in the demography of world Jewry.[5] Concisely stated, we see a positive balance of Jewish vital events (births and deaths) in Israel and a negative one in nearly all other countries; a positive migration balance for Israel, the U.S., Germany, Canada, Australia, and a few other Western countries, and a negative one in Latin America, South Africa, Eastern Europe, Muslim countries, and some countries in Western Europe; a positive balance of

[5]For historical background, see Roberto Bachi, *Population Trends of World Jewry* (Jerusalem, 1976); U.O. Schmelz, "Jewish Survival: The Demographic Factors," AJYB 1981, vol. 81, pp. 61–117; U.O. Schmelz, *Aging of World Jewry* (Jerusalem, 1984); Sergio DellaPergola, "Changing Cores and Peripheries: Fifty Years in Socio-demographic Perspective," in Robert S. Wistrich, ed., *Terms of Survival: The Jewish World since 1945* (London, 1995) pp. 13–43; Sergio DellaPergola, *World Jewry beyond 2000: Demographic Prospects* (Oxford, 1999).

accessions to Judaism over secessions in Israel, and an often negative, or at best uncertain balance elsewhere. While allowing for improvements and corrections, the 2008 population estimates highlight the increasing complexity of the sociodemographic and identificational processes underlying the definition of Jewish populations, and hence the estimates of their sizes. This complexity is magnified at a time of pervasive migration between and within countries, often implying bi-local residences and double counts of people on the move or permanently sharing their time between different places. Some of these errors can be corrected at a later stage. Consequently, the analyst has to come to terms with the paradox of the *permanently provisional* nature of Jewish population estimates.

Sources of Data

Figures on population size, characteristics, and trends are a primary tool in the evaluation of Jewish community needs and prospects at the local level and internationally. The estimates for major regions and individual countries reported in this overview reflect a prolonged and ongoing effort to study scientifically the demography of contemporary world Jewry. Data collection and comparative research have benefited from the collaboration of scholars and institutions in many countries, including replies to direct inquiries regarding current estimates.[6] It should be emphasized, however, that the elaboration of a worldwide set of estimates for the Jewish populations of the various countries is beset with difficul-

---

[6]Many of these activities are carried out by, or in coordination with, the Division of Jewish Demography and Statistics at the A. Harman Institute of Contemporary Jewry (ICJ), the Hebrew University of Jerusalem. Thanks are due to our team members Benjamin Anderman, Judith Even, Uzi Rebhun, Dalia Sagi and Mark Tolts. We gratefully acknowledge the collaboration of many institutions and individuals in the different countries who supplied information or otherwise helped for this update. We thank in particular Chris Kooyman (Amsterdam), Ralph Weill (Basel), Simon Cohn and Claude Kandyoti (Brussels), András Kovács (Budapest), Ezequiel Erdei and Yaacov Rubel (Buenos Aires), Tally Frankental (Cape Town), Salomon Benzaquen and Tony Beker de Weinraub (Caracas), Frank Mott (Columbus, Ohio), Barry R. Chiswick and Carmel U. Chiswick (Chicago), Heike von Bassewitz and Ellen Rubinstein (Frankfurt a. M.), Frans van Poppel (The Hague), Lina Filiba (Istanbul), Oren Cytto, Norma Gurovich, Israel Pupko, Marina Sheps, and Emma Trahtenberg (Jerusalem), David Saks (Johannesburg), David Graham and Marlena Schmool (London), Mauricio Lulka (Mexico City), Rafael Porzecanski (Montevideo), Evgueni Andreev and Eugeni Soroko (Moscow), David Bass (Neveh Daniel), Laurence Kotler-Berkowitz (New York), René Decol (São Paulo), Ira Sheskin (Miami), Allen Glicksman (Philadelphia), Erik H. Cohen (Ramat Gan), Arnold Dashefsky (Storrs, Ct.), Gary Eckstein (Sydney), Gustave Goldman (Toronto), Sylvia Barack Fishman, Leonard Saxe, Charles Kadushin, and Benjamin Phillips (Waltham, Mass.), and Hania Zlotnik (the UN).

ties and uncertainties.[7] Users of Jewish population estimates should be aware of these difficulties and of the inherent limitations of our estimates.

The more recent figures on Israel, the U.S. and the rest of world Jewry reflect updated information on Jewish population that became available following the major round of national censuses and Jewish population surveys in countries with large Jewish populations over the period 1999–2006. This new evidence generally confirmed our previous estimates, but sometimes suggested upward or downward revisions.

Over the last decades the database available for a critical assessment of the worldwide Jewish demographic picture has significantly expanded. Some of this ongoing research is part of a coordinated effort aimed at updating the profile of world Jewry.[8] However, the amount and quality of documentation on Jewish population size and characteristics is still far from satisfactory. In recent years important new data and estimates were released for several countries through official population censuses and Jewish-sponsored sociodemographic surveys.

National censuses yielded results on Jewish populations in Ireland, the Czech Republic, and India (1991); Romania and Bulgaria (1992); the Russian Republic and Macedonia (1994); Israel (1995); Canada, South Africa, Australia, and New Zealand (1996 and 2001); Belarus, Azerbaijan, Kazakhstan, and Kyrgyzstan (1999); Brazil, Mexico, Switzerland, Estonia, Latvia, and Tajikistan (2000); the UK, Hungary, Croatia, Lithuania, and Ukraine (2001); the Russian Republic, Georgia, and

---

[7]For overviews of subject matter and technical issues see Paul Ritterband, Barry A. Kosmin, and Jeffrey Scheckner, "Counting Jewish Populations: Methods and Problems," AJYB 1988, vol. 88, pp. 204–21; and Sergio DellaPergola, "Demography," in Martin Goodman, ed., *The Oxford Handbook of Jewish Studies* (Oxford, 2002), pp. 797–823.

[8]Following an International Conference on Jewish Population Problems held in Jerusalem in 1987, initiated by the late Roberto Bachi of the Hebrew University and sponsored by major Jewish organizations worldwide, an International Scientific Advisory Committee (ISAC) was established under the chairmanship of Sidney Goldstein. See Sergio DellaPergola and Leah Cohen, eds., *World Jewish Population: Trends and Policies* (Jerusalem, 1992). An Initiative on Jewish Demography, sponsored by the Jewish Agency under then Chairman Sallai Meridor, led to an international conference in Jerusalem in 2002 and to data collection and analysis implemented over the years 2003–05. Since 2003, the Jewish People Policy Planning Institute (JPPPI), founded by Yehezkel Dror and chaired by Ambassador Dennis Ross, has provided a framework for policy analysis and suggestions on Jewish population issues. See Sergio DellaPergola, *Jewish Demography: Facts, Outlook, Challenges*, JPPPI Alert Paper 2 (Jerusalem, 2003); *The Jewish People Policy Planning Institute Annual Assessment 2004–2005, Between Thriving and Decline* (Jerusalem, 2005); The Jewish People Policy Planning Institute, *The Conference on the Future of the Jewish People 2007, Background Policy Documents* (Jerusalem, 2007); The Jewish People Policy Planning Institute, *Tomorrow* (Jerusalem, 2008).

Poland (2002); Moldova (2004); and again Canada, Australia, and New Zealand (2006). Population censuses in the U.S. do not provide information on religion, but they have furnished relevant data on countries of birth, spoken languages, and ancestry. Permanent national population registers, including information on the Jewish religious, ethnic or national group, exist in several European countries (Switzerland, Norway, Finland, Estonia, Latvia, and Lithuania), and in Israel.

In addition, independent sociodemographic studies have provided valuable information on Jewish demography and socioeconomic stratification, as well as on Jewish identification. Surveys were conducted over the last several years in South Africa (1991 and 1998); Mexico (1991 and 2000); Lithuania (1993); the UK and Chile (1995); Venezuela (1998–99); Israel, Hungary, the Netherlands, and Guatemala (1999); Moldova and Sweden (2000); France and Turkey (2002); and Argentina (2003 and 2004). In the U.S. important new insights were provided by three large surveys, the National Jewish Population Survey (NJPS 2000–01), the American Jewish Identity Survey (AJIS 2001), and the Heritage, Ancestry, and Religious Identity Survey (HARI 2003). Several other smaller Jewish samples can be obtained from the General Social Survey and similar national studies. Moreover, Jewish population studies were separately conducted in major U.S. cities (notably New York City in 2002 and Boston in 2005—the fifth decennial study in that metropolitan area) and in other countries. Additional evidence on Jewish population trends comes from the systematic monitoring of membership registers, vital statistics, and migration records available from Jewish communities and other Jewish organizations in many countries or cities, notably the UK, Germany, Italy, Buenos Aires, and São Paulo. Detailed data on Jewish immigration routinely collected in Israel help in the assessment Jewish population changes in other countries.

It is quite evident that the cross-matching of more than one type of sources about the same Jewish population, although not frequently feasible, can provide either mutual reinforcement or important critical insights to the available data.

Definitions

A major problem with the Jewish population estimates periodically circulated by individual scholars or Jewish organizations is a lack of coherence and uniformity in the definitional criteria followed—when the issue of defining the Jewish population is addressed at all. The study of a Jewish population (or, for that matter, of any other group that is part of a broader population) requires solving three main problems: (a) *defining* the target group on the basis of conceptual or normative criteria aimed at providing the best possible description of that group—which in the case of Jewry is no minor task; (b) *identifying* the group thus defined based on tools that operationally allow for distinguishing and selecting it from the rest of the population—through membership lists, types of surnames, areas of residence, or otherwise; (c) *covering* the target group through appropriate field work—face to face, by telephone, or otherwise.

Most often in the actual experience of social research, the definitional task is performed at the stage of identification, and the task of identification is performed at the stage of actual fieldwork. It thus clearly appears that the quantitative study of Jewish populations relies only on operational, not normative, definitional criteria, while its conceptual aspects, far from pure theory, heavily depend on practical and logistical feasibility. Moreover, the ultimate technical step—obtaining relevant data from the relevant persons—crucially reflects the readiness of people to collaborate in the data collection effort. In recent years, participation readiness has tended to become a cardinal component of the amount, contents, and validity of information that can be gathered. Such variable readiness reflects the identification outlook of the individuals who are part of the target population, which in turn is an integral part of what should be investigated.

There is virtually no way to break this vicious circle, and therefore research findings reflect, with varying degrees of sophistication, only what can be uncovered. What cannot be uncovered directly can sometimes be adjudicated through various estimation or imputation techniques. Beyond that, we enter the virtual world of myths, hopes, fears, and corporate interests. There is no way to demonstrate the actual validity of some of these claims—at least not within the limits of a nonfiction work.

Keeping this in mind, three major definitional concepts should be considered to provide serious comparative foundations for the study of Jewish demography.

In most countries outside of Israel, the concept of *core Jewish population*[9] includes all persons who, when asked, identify themselves as Jews;

[9]The term was initially suggested in Barry A. Kosmin, Sidney Goldstein, Joseph Waksberg, Nava Lerer, Ariela Keysar, and Jeffrey Scheckner, *Highlights of the CJF 1990 National Jewish Population Survey* (New York, 1991).

or, if the respondent is a different person in the same household, are identified by him/her as Jews. Such a definition of a person as a Jew, reflecting *subjective* feelings, broadly overlaps but does not necessarily coincide with Halakhah (rabbinic law) or other normatively binding definitions. Inclusion does *not* depend on any measure of that person's Jewish commitment or behavior in terms of religiosity, beliefs, knowledge, communal affiliation, or otherwise. The *core* Jewish population includes all converts to Judaism by any procedure, as well as other people who declare they are Jewish. It is also customary to include persons of Jewish parentage who claim no current religious or ethnic identity. Persons of Jewish parentage who adopted another religion are usually excluded, as are other individuals who, in censuses or surveys, explicitly identify with a non-Jewish group without having converted out. In the State of Israel, personal status is subject to the rulings of the Ministry of the Interior, which relies on criteria established by rabbinical authorities. In Israel, therefore, the *core* Jewish population does not simply express subjective identification but reflects definite legal rules, those of Halakhah. This entails a matrilineal Jewish origin, or a conversion to Judaism. Documentation to prove a person's Jewish status may include non-Jewish sources.

The *core* concept offers an intentionally comprehensive and pragmatic approach reflecting the nature of most available sources of data on Jewish population. In countries other than Israel, such data often derive from population censuses or social surveys where interviewees have the option to decide how to answer relevant questions on religious or ethnic preferences.

The question whether Jewish identification according to this *core* definition can or should be mutually exclusive with other religious corporate identities emerged on a major scale in the course of the NJPS 2000–01. The solution chosen—after much debate—was to allow for Jews with multiple religious identities to be included, under certain circumstances, in the standard definition of Jewish population.[10] A category of

[10]In the NJPS version initially processed and circulated by UJC, "a Jew is defined as a person whose religion is Judaism, OR whose religion is Jewish and something else, OR who has no religion and has at least one Jewish parent or a Jewish upbringing, OR who has a non-monotheistic religion and has at least one Jewish parent or a Jewish upbringing." See Laurence Kotler-Berkowitz, Steven M. Cohen, Jonathon Ament, Vivian Klaff, Frank Mott, and Danyelle Peckerman-Neuman, with Lorraine Blass, Debbie Bursztyn, and David Marker, *The National Jewish Population Survey 2000–01: Strength, Challenge, and Diversity in the American Jewish Population* (New York, 2003). *Contemporary Jewry* (the scholarly journal of the Association for the Scientific Study of Jewry, edited by Samuel Heilman), vol. 25, 2005, is devoted to critical essays and analyses of NJPS methods and findings.

Persons of Jewish Background (PJBs) was introduced: some of these were included in the Jewish population count and others were not, based on a more thorough evaluation of their ancestry and childhood. By the same token, persons with multiple ethnic identities including a Jewish one are included in the standard Jewish population count in Canada. The adoption of such extended criteria by the research community tends to stretch Jewish population definitions, with an expansive effect on Jewish population size beyond usual practices in the past and beyond the typical *core* definition. These procedures also tend to limit the comparability of the same Jewish population over time, and of different Jewish populations at the same time.

The *enlarged Jewish population*[11] includes the sum of (a) the *core* Jewish population; (b) all other persons of Jewish parentage who—by *core* Jewish population criteria—are *not* Jewish currently (or at the date of reference of investigation); and (c) all of the respective further non-Jewish household members (spouses, children, etc.). Non-Jews with Jewish background, as far as they can be ascertained, include: (a) persons who have themselves adopted another religion, even though they may claim to be also Jewish by ethnicity or preference—with the caveat just mentioned for recent U.S. and Canadian data; and (b) other persons with Jewish parentage who disclaim being Jewish.

As noted, most PJBs who do not pertain to the *core* Jewish population naturally belong under the *enlarged* definition.[12] It is customary in sociodemographic surveys to consider the religio-ethnic identification of parents. Some censuses, however, do ask about more distant ancestry. For both conceptual and practical reasons, the *enlarged* definition usually does not include other non-Jewish relatives who lack a Jewish background and live in exclusively non-Jewish households. While historians might wish to engage in the study of how many Jews ever lived on earth, and how many individuals today descend from those Jews of the past, such speculation is beyond the purpose of the present article.

The *Law of Return,* Israel's distinctive legal framework for the acceptance and absorption of new immigrants, awards Jewish new immigrants immediate citizenship and other civil rights. According to the current,

---

[11]The term *enlarged Jewish population* was initially suggested by Sergio DellaPergola, "The Italian Jewish Population Study: Demographic Characteristics and Trends," in U.O. Schmelz, P. Glikson, and S.J. Gould, eds., *Studies in Jewish Demography: Survey for 1969–1971* (Jerusalem-London, 1975), pp. 60–97.

[12]Kotler-Berkowitz et al., *National Jewish Population Survey 2000–01.*

amended version of the Law of Return, a Jew is any person born to a Jewish mother or converted to Judaism (regardless of denomination—Orthodox, Conservative, or Reform), who does not have another religious identity. By ruling of Israel's Supreme Court, conversion from Judaism, as in the case of some ethnic Jews who currently identify with another religion, entails loss of eligibility for Law of Return purposes. The Falashmora—a group of Ethiopian non-Jews of Jewish ancestry—must undergo conversion to be eligible for the Law of Return. The law as such does not affect a person's Jewish status—which, as noted, is adjudicated by Israel's Ministry of Interior and rabbinical authorities—but only the specific benefits available under the Law of Return. The law extends its provisions to all current Jews, their children, and grandchildren, as well as to the respective Jewish or non-Jewish spouses. As a result of its three-generation and lateral extension, the Law of Return applies to a large population—the so called aliyah eligible—whose scope is significantly wider than the *core* and *enlarged* Jewish populations defined above.[13] It is actually quite difficult to estimate the size of the *Law of Return* population. The higher estimates to be derived by using this criterion are not discussed below systematically, but some notion of their possible extent is given for the major countries.

Some major Jewish organizations in Israel and the U.S.—such as the Jewish Agency for Israel, the American Jewish Joint Distribution Committee, and United Jewish Communities (UJC)—are significantly involved in sponsoring data collection and tend to influence the rules of research, rendering them more complex. Organizations are motivated by their missions and toward their respective constituencies, rather than by pure analytic criteria. In turn, the understandable interest of organizations in maintaining their functions and securing budgetary resources inclines them to see the Jewish populations under their care increasingly in terms of the *enlarged* and *Law of Return* definitions, rather than the *core*. Thus some surveys, by investigating people who were born or were raised or currently are Jewish, reach a population that *ever* was Jewish, regardless of its present identification.

The following estimates of Jewish population distribution worldwide and in each continent (Tables 1–2 below), country (Tables 3–10), and major metropolitan areas (Table 11) consistently aim at the concept of

---

[13]For a concise review of the rules of attribution of Jewish personal status in rabbinic and Israeli law, including reference to Jewish sects, isolated communities, and apostates, see Michael Corinaldi, "Jewish Identity," chap. 2 in his *Jewish Identity: The Case of Ethiopian Jewry* (Jerusalem, 1998).

core Jewish population. The *core* is indeed the necessary starting point for any admittedly relevant elaboration about the *enlarged*.

Presentation and Quality of Data

Since 2000, our estimates have referred to January 1 of the current year of publication of the AJYB. Efforts to provide the most recent possible picture entail a short span of time for evaluation and correction of available information, hence a somewhat greater margin of inaccuracy. Indeed, where appropriate, we revised our previous estimates in the light of newly accrued information on Jewish populations (Tables 1 and 2). Corrections were also applied retrospectively to the 2007 figures for major geographical regions so as to ensure a better base for comparisons with the 2008 estimates. Corrections of the latest estimates, if needed, will be presented in future volumes of the AJYB.

We provide separate figures for each country with approximately 100 or more resident *core* Jews. Residual estimates of Jews living in other smaller communities supplement some of the continental totals. For each reported country in each continent, the four columns in Tables 4 8 provide an estimate of midyear 2007 total population,[14] the estimated 1/1/2008 Jewish population, the proportion of Jews per 1,000 of total population, and an accuracy rating of the Jewish population estimate.

There is wide variation in the quality of the Jewish population estimates for different countries. For many Diaspora countries it would be best to indicate a range (minimum–maximum) rather than a definite figure for the number of Jews. It would be confusing, however, for the reader to be confronted with a long list of ranges; this would also complicate the regional and world totals. The figures indicated for most of the Diaspora communities should be understood as being the central value of the plausible range of the respective core Jewish populations. The relative magnitude of this range varies inversely to the accuracy of the estimate.

The three main elements that affect the accuracy of each estimate are (a) the nature and quality of the base data; (b) how recent the base data are; and (c) the updating method. A simple code combines these elements to provide a general evaluation of the reliability of the Jewish population figures reported in the detailed tables below.

The code indicates different quality levels of the reported estimates: (A)

---

[14]Data and estimates derived from Population Reference Bureau, *2008 World Population Data Sheet*.

Base figure derived from countrywide census or reliable Jewish population survey; updated on the basis of full or partial information on Jewish population movements in the respective country during the intervening period. (B) Base figure derived from less accurate but recent countrywide Jewish population data; partial information on population movements in the intervening period. (C) Base figure derived from less recent sources, and/or unsatisfactory or partial coverage of a country's Jewish population; updating according to demographic information illustrative of regional demographic trends. (D) Base figure essentially speculative; no reliable updating procedure. In categories (A), (B), and (C), the year in which the country's base figure or important partial updates were obtained is also stated. For countries whose Jewish population estimate for 2008 was not only updated but also revised in the light of improved information, the sign "X" is appended to the rating.

One additional tool for updating Jewish population estimates is provided by several sets of demographic projections developed at the Institute of Contemporary Jewry of the Hebrew University of Jerusalem.[15] Such projections, based on available data on Jewish population composition by age and sex groups, extrapolate the most likely observed or expected Jewish population trends over the first decades of the twenty-first century. Even where reliable information on the dynamics of Jewish population change is not immediately available, the powerful connection that generally exists between age composition of a population and the respective frequencies of births and deaths and migration movements helps provide plausible scenarios of the developments bound to occur in the short term. Where better data were lacking, we used indications from these projections to refine the 2008 estimates as against previous years. On the other hand, projections are clearly shaped by a comparatively limited set of assumptions, and need to be periodically updated in the light of actual demographic developments.

World Jewish Population Size

The size of world Jewry at the beginning of 2008 was assessed at 13,231,700. World Jewry constituted 1.97 per 1,000 of the world's total population of 6,705 million. One in about 508 people in the world is a

[15]See DellaPergola, Rebhun, and Tolts, "Prospecting the Jewish Future," and unpublished tabulations. A new round of population projections currently undertaken in the light of the latest data helped in the current assessment.

Jew. According to the revised figures, between January 1, 2007 and January 1, 2008, the Jewish population grew by an estimated 71,000 people, or about 0.5 percent. This compares with a total world population growth rate of 1.2 percent (0.1 percent in more developed countries, 1.5 percent in less developed countries). Allowing for imperfections in the estimates, world Jewry continued to be close to zero population growth, with increase in Israel (1.6 percent) outweighing decline in the Diaspora (–0.2 percent).

Table 1 gives an overall picture of Jewish population for the beginning of 2008 as compared to 2007. For 2007 the originally published estimates are presented along with somewhat revised figures that take into account, retrospectively, the corrections made in certain country estimates in the light of improved information. These corrections resulted in a net increase of 5,500 in the 2007 world Jewry estimate. Explanations are given below of the reasons for these minor corrections.

The number of Jews in Israel rose from 5,393,400 in 2007 to 5,478,200 at the beginning of 2008, an increase of 84,800 people, or 1.6 percent. In contrast, the estimated Jewish population in the Diaspora diminished from 7,767,300 (according to the revised figures) to 7,753,500—a decrease of 13,800 people, or –0.2 percent. These changes reflect continuing Jewish emigration from the FSU and other countries, but also the internal decrease typical of the aggregate of Diaspora Jewry. In 2007, the estimated Israel-Diaspora net migratory balance (immigration minus emigration) amounted to a minor gain of 6,700 core Jews for Israel.[16] This figure includes Israeli citizens born abroad who entered Israel for the first time. Therefore, internal demographic evolution (including vital events and conversions) produced nearly 90 percent of the recorded growth among the Jewish population in Israel, and most of the estimated decline in the Diaspora. Israel gained a further net migration balance of 8,700 non-Jews under the comprehensive provisions of the Israeli Law of Return and Law of Entrance.[17]

Recently, more frequent instances of conversion, accession or "return" to Judaism can be observed in connection with the absorption in Israel of immigrants from Eastern Europe, Ethiopia, and, to a lesser extent, other countries such as Peru and India. The return or first-time access to

---

[16]Israel Central Bureau of Statistics, *Statistical Abstract of Israel* 59 (Jerusalem, 2008), also available at http//www.cbs.gov.il

[17]As noted, the Law of Return applies to Jews and their extended families. The Law of Entrance applies to all others, some of whom ask for Israeli citizenship.

TABLE 1. ESTIMATED CORE JEWISH POPULATION, BY CONTINENTS AND MAJOR GEOGRAPHICAL REGIONS, 2007 AND 2008[a]

Region	2007 Original Abs. N.	2007 Revised[b] Abs. N.	2007 Revised[b] Percent[c]	2008 Abs. N.	2008 Percent[c]	Yearly % Change 2007–2008	Jews/1000 Total Population
World	13,155,200	13,160,700	100.0	13,231,700	100.0	0.5	2.0
Diaspora	7,761,800	7,767,300	59.0	7,753,500	58.6	–0.2	1.2
Israel	5,393,400	5,393,400	41.0	5,478,200	41.4	1.6	756.3
America, Total	6,041,300	6,044,300	45.9	6,041,900	45.7	0.0	6.7
North[d]	5,649,000	5,649,000	42.9	5,650,000	42.2	0.0	16.9
Central	51,600	54,600	0.4	54,800	0.4	–0.5	0.3
South	340,700	340,700	2.6	337,100	2.5	–1.1	0.9
Europe, Total	1,492,700	1,492,700	11.3	1,481,100	11.2	–0.8	1.8
European Union[b]	1,129,800	1,129,800	8.6	1,127,300	8.5	–0.2	2.3
Other West	19,500	19,500	0.1	19,500	0.1	0.0	1.5
Former USSR[e]	322,000	322,000	2.4	312,800	2.4	–2.9	1.5
Other East and Balkans[e]	21,400	21,400	0.2	21,500	0.2	–0.0	0.2
Asia, Total	5,432,900	5,432,900	41.3	5,517,200	41.7	1.6	1.4
Israel	5,393,400	5,393,400	41.0	5,478,200	41.4	1.6	756.3
Former USSR[e]	20,000	20,000	0.2	19,600	0.1	–2.0	0.3
Other	19,500	19,500	0.1	19,400	0.1	–0.5	0.0
Africa, Total	77,200	77,200	0.6	76,900	0.6	–0.4	0.1
North[f]	4,200	4,200	0.0	4,100	0.0	–2.4	0.0
South[g]	73,000	73,000	0.6	72,800	0.6	–0.3	0.1
Oceania[h]	111,100	113,600	0.9	114,600	0.9	0.9	3.9

[a]January 1.
[b]Including European Union's new entries.
[c]Minor discrepancies due to rounding.
[d]U.S.A. and Canada.
[e]Asian regions of Russia and Turkey included in Europe. Baltic countries included in European Union.
[f]Including Ethiopia.
[g]South Africa, Zimbabwe, and other sub-Saharan countries.
[h]Australia, New Zealand.

Judaism of some of those previously not included or unidentified individuals contributed to slowing down the pace of decline of the relevant Diaspora Jewish populations, and some gains for the Jewish population in Israel.

As noted, corrections were introduced in previously published Jewish population estimates in the light of new information that has become available. Table 2 provides a synopsis of the world Jewish population estimates for the period 1945–2008, as first published each year in the *American Jewish Year Book* and as corrected retroactively, incorporating all subsequent revisions. These revised data correct, sometimes significantly, the figures published until 1980 by other authors and since 1981 by ourselves. Thanks to the development over the years of an improved database, these new revisions are not necessarily the same revised estimates that appeared year by year in the AJYB based on the information

TABLE 2. WORLD JEWISH POPULATION, ORIGINAL AND CORRECTED ESTIMATES, AND TOTAL POPULATION, 1945–2008

Year	Jewish Population			World Population		Jews per 1000 of Total Pop.
	Original Estimate[a]	Corrected Estimate[b]	Yearly % Change[c]	Total (Millions)[d]	Yearly % Change	
1945, May 1	11,000,000	11,000,000		2,315		4.75
1950, Jan. 1	11,303,400	11,297,000	0.57	2,524	1.87	4.48
1960, Jan. 1	12,792,800	12,079,000	0.67	3,027	1.83	3.99
1970, Jan. 1	13,950,900	12,585,000	0.41	3,702	2.03	3.40
1980, Jan. 1	14,527,100	12,819,000	0.18	4,447	1.85	2.88
1990, Jan. 1	12,810,300	12,868,000	0.04	5,282	1.74	2.44
2000, Jan. 1	13,191,500	12,900,000	0.02	6,000	1.30	2.15
2005, Jan. 1	13,034,100	13,032,600	0.20	6,396	1.29	2.04
2006, Jan. 1	13,089,800	13,092,100	0.46	6,477	1.27	2.02
2007, Jan. 1	13,155,000	13,160,700	0.48	6,625[e]	1.14	1.99
2008, Jan. 1	13,231,700		0.54	6,705	1.21	1.97

[a]As published in *American Jewish Year Book*, various years. Some of the estimates reported here as of Jan. 1 were originally published as of Dec. 31 of previous year.
[b]Based on updated, corrected, or otherwise improved information. Original estimates for 1990 and after, and all revised estimates: Division of Jewish Demography and Statistics, The A. Harman Institute of Contemporary Jewry, The Hebrew University of Jerusalem.
[c]Based on revised estimates, besides last year.
[d]Midyear estimate of preceding year. Source: Population Reference Bureau.
[e]Midyear estimate of current year. Source: Population Reference Bureau.

that was available at each date. It is likely that further retrospective revisions may become necessary reflecting ongoing and future research.

The revised figures in Table 2 clearly portray the slowing down of Jewish population growth globally since World War II. Based on a post-Shoah world Jewish population estimate of 11,000,000, a growth of 1,079,000 occurred between 1945 and 1960, followed by growths of 506,000 in the 1960s, 234,000 in the 1970s, 49,000 in the 1980s, and 32,000 in the 1990s. While it took 13 years to add one million to world Jewry's postwar size, over 46 years were needed to add another million. Since 2000, the slow rhythm of Jewish population growth has somewhat recovered, with an increase of 332,000 through 2008, mostly reflecting the robust trends in Israel and its growing share of the world total. Table 2 also outlines the slower Jewish population growth rate as compared to global growth, and the declining Jewish share of world population. In 2008 the Jewish share of world population (1.97 per 1,000) was less than half of what it was in 1945 (4.75 per 1,000).

Distribution by Major Regions and Countries

About 46 percent of the world's Jews reside in the Americas, with over 43 percent in North America. Over 41 percent live in Asia, most of them in Israel, a figure that includes the Asian republics of the former USSR but not the Asian parts of the Russian Republic and Turkey. Europe, including the Asian territories of the Russian Republic and Turkey, accounts for 11 percent of the total. Fewer than 2 percent of the world's Jews live in Africa and Oceania. Among the major geographical regions listed in Table 1, the number of Jews in Israel—and, consequently, in total Asia—increased in 2007. Moderate Jewish population gains were also estimated in Canada and Oceania (Australia and New Zealand). We estimate that Jewish population size diminished to variable extents in South America, Europe, the former Soviet republics (both European and Asian), and Africa. We did not change our estimate of the number of Jews in the U.S. (see below). These regional changes reflect the trends apparent in the Jewish population in each of the major countries. We now turn to a review of recent trends in the largest Jewish communities.

THE AMERICAS

Jewish population in the Americas (Table 3) is predominantly concentrated in the U.S. (5,275,000, or 87 percent of the continental total), followed by Canada (375,000, 6 percent), South America (337,000, 5.5 percent), and Central America (55,000, 1.5 percent).

The United States

Jewish population in the U.S. approached 4.5 million in 1945 and, according to available sources, it grew by about one million until around 1990.[18] Two competing major surveys independently conducted in 2000–2001—the National Jewish Population Survey (NJPS)[19] and the American Jewish Identity Survey (AJIS)[20]—indicated a *core* Jewish population of 5,200,000 and 5,340,000, respectively, in 2001, as against 5,515,000 in 1990. Population projections had long predicted an eventual decrease in *core* Jewish population in the U.S.,[21] reflecting a slowing down of international immigration, postponed Jewish marriages and growing singlehood, rising frequencies of out-marriage (over 50 percent of Jews currently marrying), low Jewish fertility (less than 2 children per woman), attribution to the Jewish side of a minority of the children of intermarriages (up to a third, according to the highest projection), and noticeable aging (nearly 20 percent of the Jewish population above 65).

The NJPS was sponsored the United Jewish Communities (UJC), the roof coordinating body of Jewish federations in the U.S., and advised by a National Technical Advisory Committee (NTAC) chaired the late Vivian Klaff and by Frank Mott. The NTAC included several leading experts on Jewish population studies and senior Jewish community planners. A national random-digit-dialing (RDD) sample covered the entire U.S., subdivided into seven geographical strata based on pre-survey estimates of Jewish population density. Sampling probabilities were proportional to Jewish density in each stratum. Over 175,000 households were screened for possible inclusion based on four questions: (1) What is

---

[18]Sources and findings are reviewed in Sergio DellaPergola, "Was It the Demography? A Reassessment of U.S. Jewish Population Estimates, 1945–2001," *Contemporary Jewry* 25, 2005, pp. 85–131. See also Ira Rosenwaike, "A Synthetic Estimate of American Jewish Population Movement over the Last Three Decades," in U.O. Schmelz and Sergio DellaPergola, eds., *Papers in Jewish Demography 1977* (Jerusalem, 1980) pp. 83–102.

[19]Kotler-Berkowitz et al., *National Jewish Population Survey 2000–01*.

[20]Egon Mayer, Barry Kosmin, and Ariela Keysar, *American Jewish Identity Survey 2001—AJIS Report—An Exploration in the Demography and Outlook of a People* (New York, 2002). See also Barry A. Kosmin, Egon Mayer, and Ariela Keysar, *American Religious Identification Survey 2001* (New York, 2001).

[21]U.O. Schmelz and Sergio DellaPergola, "The Demographic Consequences of U.S. Jewish Population Trends," AJYB 1983, vol. 83, pp. 141–87; U.O. Schmelz and Sergio DellaPergola, *Basic Trends in American Jewish Demography* (New York, 1988).

TABLE 3. ESTIMATED CORE JEWISH POPULATION DISTRIBUTION IN THE AMERICAS, 1/1/2008

Country	Total Population	Jewish Population	Jews per 1,000 Population	Accuracy Rating
Canada	33,600,000	375,000	11.4	B 2006
United States	304,500,000	5,275,000	17.5	B 2001
Total North America[a]	337,927,000	5,650,000	16.9	
Bahamas	300,000	300	1.0	D
Costa Rica	4,500,000	2,500	0.6	C 1993
Cuba	11,200,000	500	0.0	C 1990
Dominican Republic	9,900,000	100	0.0	D
El Salvador	7,200,000	100	0.0	C 1993
Guatemala	13,700,000	900	0.1	B 1999
Jamaica	2,700,000	300	0.1	B 1995
Mexico	107,700,000	39,600	0.4	B 2001
Netherlands Antilles	215,000	200	0.9	B 1998
Panama	3,400,000	8,000	2.4	C 1990 X
Puerto Rico	4,000,000	1,500	0.4	C 1990
Virgin Islands	115,000	500	4.4	C 2006 X
Other	26,070,000	300	0.0	D
Total Central America	101,000,000	54,800	0.3	
Argentina	39,700,000	183,000	4.6	B 2003
Bolivia	10,000,000	500	0.1	C 1999
Brazil	195,100,000	96,000	0.5	B 2001
Chile	16,800,000	20,600	1.2	C 1991
Colombia	44,400,000	2,800	0.1	C 1996
Ecuador	13,800,000	900	0.1	C 1985
Paraguay	6,200,000	900	0.1	B 1997
Peru	27,900,000	2,000	0.1	C 1993
Suriname	500,000	200	0.4	C 1986
Uruguay	3,300,000	17,700	5.4	B 2006
Venezuela	27,900,000	12,500	0.5	B 1999
Total South America[a]	386,600,000	337,100	0.9	
Total	915,527,000	6,041,900	6.7	

[a]Including countries not listed separately.

your religion (or that of other adults in the household), if any? (2) Do you or does any other adult in the household have a Jewish mother or a Jewish father? (3) Were you or any other adult in the household raised Jewish? (4) Do you, or does any other adult in the household, consider your/him/herself Jewish for any reasons? Answers to these questions included options other than yes or no, thus allowing for a nondichotomous resolution of Jewish population definition. Such screening criteria were designed to produce results reflecting UJC planning needs, but were not strictly comparable with the 1990 NJPS.

The final unweighted sample included 4,220 Jewish respondents and 303 people of Jewish background (PJB), for a total of 4,523 Jewish households; 625 non-Jews of Jewish background; and 4,027 non-Jews, for a total of 9,175 respondent households. The 4,027 non-Jewish households, interviewed for a National Survey of Religion and Ethnicity (NSRE), supplied data needed to weight and estimate Jewish population size, and to provide comparative sociodemographic background. The response rate to the screening interview was 28 percent. Weights were directly or indirectly estimated and applied to adjust for the number of telephone lines in the household, and to match sample household and respondent data to the U.S. Census totals for sampling strata, age, gender, and region.[22] Following claims of excessively low respondent rates, selective population undercounts, and other inappropriate procedures during and following fieldwork, the NJPS was submitted to independent professional scrutiny, which concluded that the study—while handicapped by methodological shortcomings such as low response rates, inconsistent survey coverage of relevant subpopulations, and loss of documentation—stood within the range of professionally acceptable research standards.[23]

The total Jewish population was estimated at 5.2 million, including 4.3 million with a clearly Jewish identification, 800,000 persons of Jewish background with no religion and whose Jewish identification was less explicit, and over 100,000 persons either in institutions or who did not report their age. Respondents from the first group, the 4.3 million, were administered a long-form questionnaire, while most respondents from the second, the 800,000, were administered a short-form questionnaire that

[22]Kotler-Berkowitz et al., *National Jewish Population Survey 2000–01*. See also Charles Kadushin, Leonard Saxe, and Benjamin Phillips, "More Nevuchim (A Guide for the Perplexed) for NJPS 2000–01" (Waltham, Mass., 2004).

[23]Mark Schulman, "National Jewish Population Survey 2000–01: Study Review Memo," prepared for the United Jewish Communities, 2003.

covered a limited selection of the survey's variables, very little of them dealing with Jewish identification. The total number of Jews plus non-Jews of Jewish background was estimated at 6.7 million. The 2.9 million households with at least one Jewish member were estimated to include 8.7 million individuals, including a significantly larger non-Jewish component than in 1990.

The 2001 AJIS, directed by the late Egon Mayer, and by Barry Kosmin and Ariela Keysar, was privately sponsored, testifying to substantive disagreements within the Jewish community and among its researchers about the relationship between social scientific research and community planning. AJIS was based on a national RDD sample that replicated the methodology of the 1990 NJPS. Out of all successful contacts, a total of 50,238 respondents agreed to be interviewed. Through screening questions, 1,668 of them qualified for a survey of American Jewish households, at a response rate of 18 percent.[24] The estimated core Jewish population, including Jews with no religion and Jews by choice, as well as Jews in institutions, was 5,340,000. Of these, 3,460,000 were born Jews whose religion was Judaism; 170,000 were converts to Judaism/Jews by choice; and 1,710,000 were born Jews with no religion. The total household membership, including Jews and others of Jewish origin, was assessed at 7,690,000. The total of individuals in surveyed households, including those without any current core Jew but excluding persons in institutions, was 9,740,000. The AJIS data conceptually match the 1990 NJPS figures.

Another national study of American Jews, the Heritage and Religious Identification Survey (HARI), was conducted in two phases in 2001–02 for the Institute for Jewish & Community Research.[25] A total of 10,204 individuals were interviewed using random-digit dialing procedures at a response rate of 29 percent. This sample being considerably smaller than those in the previously mentioned two surveys, the corresponding margin of statistical error is much larger. The HARI study yielded an estimate of 6.0 million Jews, defined as those who say Judaism is their religion or who had a Jewish background (parent or upbringing). Since this definition does not specify the current identificational status of adults and children, it is conceptually closer to an *enlarged* Jewish population than

[24]Mayer, Kosmin, and Keysar, *American Jewish Identity Survey;* and Barry A. Kosmin, personal communication.

[25]Gary Tobin and Sid Groenman, *Surveying the Jewish Population in the United States* (San Francisco, 2003). It was published in two parts, *Population Estimate* and *Methodological Issues and Challenges*.

to a *core* Jewish population, as defined above. Another 4.2 million individuals were defined as of "Jewish heritage," and a further 2.5 million were "connected non-Jewish adults." The grand total of 12,735,000 tends toward—and beyond—even the extensive criteria of the Law of Return.

Combined reading of the two major surveys, NJPS and AJIS, suggests a core Jewish population in the range of 5.20–5.35 million in 2001. Even the higher estimate is about 300,000–400,000 short of the 5.7 million we had projected based on the 1990 NJPS estimate of 5.515 million.[26] During the 1990s there was an influx of at least 200,000 Jewish immigrants from the former Soviet Union, Israel, Latin America, South Africa, Iran, and Western Europe. However, Jewish fertility continued to be low, population composition became significantly more aged, intermarriage rates continued to increase, and propensities to identify with Judaism among younger adults of mixed Jewish–non-Jewish ancestry remained low. These were sufficient reasons for a shrinking core population size. In the historical perspective of Jewish population research in the U.S. over the last 50 years, the new findings were consistent with figures and projections based on earlier sources, such as the 1957 Current Population Survey, the 1970 NJPS, and the 1990 NJPS. The apparent population decline was more likely to be the product of actual demographic trends than an artifact of insufficient data.[27]

As against these data and interpretations, other scholars have suggested that the number of Jews in the U.S. has been underestimated, and in fact might be one million higher than indicated by NJPS and AJIS. One study, published in the 2006 AJYB, compiled many dozens of local Jewish community studies, plus other local estimates, to suggest a U.S. Jewish population of possibly 6.0 to 6.4 million.[28]

As a first observation facing this contention, it should be noted that since 1790 the U.S. Census Bureau has conducted a decennial national population count. Not relying on the sum of population statistics from local authorities or on population updates of older databases, every ten years the census aims at assessing anew the current population. The operation is costly but essential to provide fresh and independent information needed for planning. The same rationale should plausibly apply to Jewish population studies. In this case, dozens of local Jewish commu-

---

[26]See Kosmin et al., *Highlights of the CJF 1990 National Jewish Population Survey*.
[27]DellaPergola, "Was It the Demography?"
[28]Ira M. Sheskin and Arnold Dashefsky, "Jewish Population in the United States, 2007," AJYB 2007, vol. 107, pp. 133–205.

nity studies were carried out by different authors with different sponsors, different purposes, different Jewish population definitions, and different data-collection methods, over a span of more than 20 years. This lack of consistency constitutes one serious flaw in this approach.

Another critical weakness of summing up local studies is tied to the very high geographical mobility of American Jews[29]—mainly from the Northeast to the South and the West—and the diffusion of double residences with the inherent risk of double counts. In the not-too-distant past, migration was generally from smaller to larger population centers, but today the contrary is often true.

Furthermore, most local studies rely partially but significantly on local community lists, and these tend to portray the more identified portion of the population and overestimate the total. In the several studies that combine Jewish lists and random sampling, there is dispute over the methodology for merging and weighting returns from the different sampling frameworks in order to achieve an overall population estimate. Also, several local surveys did not adequately distinguish between *core* and *enlarged* Jewish populations, thus inflating numbers.

And on the top of this, about 20 percent of the national Jewish population estimate comes from places for which no studies exist but only unverifiable estimates provided by local informants. In no way can the results for the 80 percent of the Jewish population covered by local studies be considered representative of the remaining 20 percent. Without detracting from the importance of local studies, the combined product of summing up and inferring is highly problematic, and in no way can seriously match large national studies based on comprehensive and consistent survey criteria.

A different methodology has been attempted through an ambitious and innovative project in progress at the Steinhardt Social Research Institute (SSRI) of Brandeis University. A large number of general social surveys, each including a Jewish sub-sample, were gathered. The number of Jewish cases in such national surveys is usually small, but combining many of them allows for a meta-analysis of a much larger Jewish sample in the context of the total U.S. population.[30]

---

[29]Uzi Rebhun and Sidney Goldstein, "Changes in the Geographical Dispersion and Mobility of American Jews, 1990–2001," *Jewish Journal of Sociology* 48, 1, 2006, pp. 5–33.

[30]The project is directed by Leonard Saxe. See Elizabeth Tighe, Leonard Saxe, Darren Brown, Jennifer Dilinger, Aron Klein, and Ashley Hill, *Research Synthesis of National Survey Estimates of the U.S. Jewish Population; Project Summary, Method and Analysis Plan* (Waltham, Mass., 2005).

At first sight, this new effort seemed to confirm rather than contradict existing notions about Jewish population size. Based on an initial review of 74 studies over the period 1990–2005, the median share of Jews among total respondents was 1.94 percent. Because of the observed lower share of Jews under age 20, the percentage of Jews among total U.S. population, including adults and children, should be downwardly corrected by a factor of 0.935, to 1.814 percent. The 2000 U.S. population census gave a total U.S. population of 281,421,906. A median of 1.814 percent Jews would correspond to 5,104,993 individuals. The average survey response rate on religion was 95 percent. Adjusting upwardly the Jewish population for non-response or no reporting of religion, the Jewish population estimate would become 5,373,677. This estimate, besides being nearly identical to the already mentioned AJIS, is spread over more than 15 years, whose midterm point would correspond to a date in the late 1990s. As noted, in 2001 both NJPS and AJIS indicated an ongoing Jewish population decline. Projecting the SSRI data to 2008, the likely outcome would be lower that the original calculation.

In a later report, the SSRI group suggested a much higher U.S. Jewish population estimate.[31] It did so by relying on 31 surveys selected out of a much broader pool; comparing a few cohorts of the estimates from the new merged database with NJPS (the AJIS was ignored); and evaluating Jewish school enrollment according to various available sources. There are strengths in the SSRI approach but also weaknesses:

- First, the SSRI researchers' decision to narrow their analysis to a selection of surveys they deem fittest out of the many more that are available seriously detracts from the randomness of the data. It is, in fact, the unbiased collection of as many sources as possible—each with its own strengths, weaknesses, and idiosyncrasies—that constitutes the main advantage of the SSRI meta-analysis.
- Second, the SSRI analysis can only consider those explicitly identified by religion, and then seek to extrapolate the number of the religiously identified to a total estimate of American Jews. One important SSRI finding is an existing correlation between survey-sponsoring agencies, survey response rates, and percent of Jews among the total sample. The more broadly representative the agency (such as the U.S. government, as compared to the patron of a narrowly defined special constituency),

[31]Leonard Saxe, Elizabeth Tighe, and Benjamin Phillips, with Ariel Libhaber, Daniel Parmer, Jessica Simon, and Graham Wright, *Understanding Contemporary American Jewry* (Waltham, Mass., 2006).

the higher the response rate; and the higher the response rate, the higher the share of Jews in the sample. Since NJPS and AJIS were studies with a narrowly defined sponsorship (Jewish community agencies), they had low response rates, and their ability to uncover a Jewish population was admittedly on the low side of the range. On the other hand, NJPS and AJIS investigators made special efforts to unveil hidden Jews among the total respondents, which they could do thanks to the detailed range of questions on personal identity they could rely on. Following this effort, the total (or core) Jewish population estimate turned out significantly higher than the number of Jews initially identified by religion. Given these basic differences in survey penetration and administration, it would be quite inappropriate to apply the low NJPS/AJIS ratio of Jews by religion to total Jews to the case of other general surveys with a much better response rate. But this seems to be the logic of the SSRI group when projecting the original survey figures based on religion to total Jewish population estimates, resulting in exaggerated Jewish population totals.

- Third, social surveys typically cover adult respondents and do not collect detailed information on each individual in the household, namely children under 18, which NJPS/AJIS did. One should not assume that the percent of Jews among total *respondents* applies to the percent of Jews among the total *population.* Indeed, each Jewish respondent brings in not only fewer children because of the lower Jewish fertility rate, but also fewer other adults, because of the group's older age composition and the higher prevalence of smaller households, including many more people living alone. Moreover, while a generic respondent brings in other generic members of the household and thereby determines a certain multiplier, a *Jewish* respondent brings in other members not all of whom are *Jewish,* thus determining a lower multiplier. These differences should be weighted into population estimates, but they seem to have been overlooked.
- Fourth, the main thrust of the age-cohort comparisons between the meta-analysis and the NJPS is that they are significantly consistent, which would support and not contradict the basic reliability of NJPS. There is, however, the important exception of one cohort, and perhaps two. The inconsistency concerns Jewish adults aged 35–44 and 45–54 in 2001—born, respectively, in 1957–66 and in 1947–56—all part of the so called baby-boomer generation. Indeed, an apparent phenomenon of cohort erosion had already been noted in comparing NJPS 2001 with NJPS 1990, but similar erosion among the same cohorts is found

in comparing NJPS 1970 with NJPS 1990.[32] More than pertaining to data quality, the crucial question seems to relate to the cultural-ideational patterns of the American baby-boomers. Part of the explanation may be the steady transition among younger adults of Jewish identification from religion to ethnicity, culture, or being "just Jewish." Again, an analysis that relies primarily on the religion category, as in the SSRI, is likely to miss people who feel Jewish through other cultural avenues, whom NJPS/AJIS did include.

- Fifth, whenever a figure provided by NJPS can be matched against a similar figure from another source, the comparison usually holds. Examples of such matches are estimated numbers of children enrolled in Jewish day schools compared with actual school enrollment statistics,[33] and estimates of documented immigrants compared with actual institutional data.[34] In the case of Jewish education, the comparison of enrolled pupils and the total number of children results in an enrollment ratio of slightly over 25 percent. While such an augmented enrollment in Jewish schools defies the intuition of some observers, it actually looks compatible with the emerging higher percent of the Orthodox among younger cohorts of U.S. Jews, in turn reflecting that group's higher birthrates and fewer losses due to assimilation.
- Sixth, the format of general social surveys relies heavily on individual respondents, while only few make available a full roster of the characteristics of all members in a household. Religion is seldom the main focus of investigation and is usually confined to one background question. Direct knowledge of household size and composition cannot go beyond certain limits, leaving its final determination to inference. The SSRI suggestions that U.S. Jewry might comprise 6.5 and perhaps even 7.5 million individuals, or that the yearly birth cohort might exceed 70,000 newborns become plausible only if the reference category is the *enlarged* concept of total population in households, and not under the *core* concept of individually identified Jewish population.

These considerations support the general plausibility of NJPS/AJIS and of the population estimates that can be derived from them. In addi-

---

[32]DellaPergola, "Was it the Demography?"
[33]Marvin Schick, *A Census of Jewish Day Schools in the United States 2003–2004* (Jerusalem, 2005).
[34]HIAS. *Statistical Report* (New York, annual publication).

tion, the approaches that oppose or present alternatives to NJPS and AJIS share two critical weaknesses:

- The first is the inability by either to provide an integrated age-composition of the U.S. Jewish population inclusive of Jewish adults and Jewish children. Age composition is a basic analytic referent, which both synthesizes past changes and functions as an agent of future changes. Current age is an intermediary between the demography of two successive generations, in the absence of which discourse about population trends becomes nearly void of content.
- The second, even more crucial, shared weakness of the two critical approaches is their complete lack of historical perspective. If it is true that today there are more than six million Jews in the U.S., we expect to be told how many were there in 1990, and at previous dates back to the end of World War II. A population, as we have argued, grows or shrinks as a consequence of a limited set of factors whose impact must be assessed along with the overall figure. A much higher figure in 2001 and later implies either that U.S. Jewry recently experienced a growth spurt—against all existing evidence—or that all previous estimates should be significantly raised, which implies over 50 years of gross mistakes in Jewish population studies. What the new higher estimates are suggesting, instead, is that the current assessment of U.S. Jewry can be severed from its past, a discovery of a new entity without historical continuity. While there surely is ample space for a discussion of contemporary U.S. Jewry as a cultural phenomenon not necessarily stemming from its own past or from other strands of Jewish history, this is not appropriate in the realm of population studies.

In the light of this abundant and intriguing evidence, our U.S. Jewish population estimate reflects a well-documented pattern of end of growth, and, in fact, incipient population decrease. As noted, U.S. Jewry is characterized by an aging population composition, and its effectively Jewish fertility levels are significantly below generational replacement due, in part, to a very incomplete inclusion of the children of out-marriage—admittedly a feature that might change in the future, as suggested by the 2005 Boston study.[35]

The number of immigrants has diminished, especially from the FSU.

[35]See Leonard Saxe, Charles Kadushin, and Graham Wright, *2005 Boston Jewish Community Study* (Waltham, Mass., 2006).

Current emigration from Israel is limited to a few thousand a year. A reading of the current age composition of U.S. Jewry and other current evidence suggests that about 50,000 Jewish births occur annually in the U.S. versus nearly 60,000 Jewish deaths, and 5,000 net immigrants. In 2007, 2,094 people migrated from the U.S. to Israel. Following these data and assumptions, the 2001 estimate was adjusted to 5,275,000 in 2006, and the same was retained for 2007 and 2008.

Admittedly, the quality of U.S. Jewish population estimates cannot be compared to the more rigorous sources in Israel and a few other countries. In the absence of better data, comparisons tend to be speculative. Even more significantly, Jewish identification tends to reflect the very different constraints and opportunities of the relatively open environment of the U.S., where a multiplicity of overlapping identities can be legitimately held under the general American panoply, as against a closed society still surrounded by a hostile environment, as in Israel. Our estimate of 5,275,000 core Jews in the U.S. at the beginning of 2008 is a cautious compromise between the two major 2001 Jewish surveys, the NJPS and the AJIS, also accounting for the findings of many other American social surveys and other institutional data, as well as population extrapolations produced under different assumptions.

While by the *core* concept the number of Jews in the U.S. today probably falls behind that in Israel, it is beyond dispute that the U.S. has far larger *enlarged* and *Law of Return* populations. The former comprises at least 6.7 million individuals with some recent Jewish ancestry, and 7.7–8.7 million individuals in households with at least one Jew. Since the Israeli Law of Return would grant Israeli citizenship not only to the Jews, should they move to Israel, but also to their non-Jewish children, grandchildren, and respective spouses, the *Law of Return* category covers in the U.S. a virtual aggregate of 10–12 million individuals, as against 5.8 million in Israel.

In the U.S. the debate about numbers has been invested with an importance and symbolic meaning that far transcends the social scientific discipline. In public debate, Jewish population size has become a proxy for honor, legitimacy, relative visibility in the Jewish world, and probably predominance in the community's politics and resource allocation. This is, in the end, the gist of the numerical competition between population figures for the U.S. and Israel.

One way to get out of this conundrum would be a continuation of the routine of periodical data collection that UJC established with the 1970, 1990, and 2001 NJPSs. A new study would signal recognition of the importance that research plays in national community planning, and might allow for new comparisons, evaluations of any changes in the observed trends, deepened insights, and improved projections for the future. But in 2007, UJC decided not to sponsor a new NJPS in 2010, while at the same time copyrighting the NJPS logo for itself. It can be hoped that research on U.S. Jewish population and community will continue through other avenues. What is certain is that the dispute about Jewish population estimates in the U.S. is bound to continue.

Canada

In Canada the situation is significantly different in terms both of available databases and substantive population trends. An important new piece of evidence became available through the release of the 2006 census results, which included a question on ethnic ancestry (see Table 4).[36] Figures on Jewish ethnicity, released every five years, can be compared with figures on religion, released every ten years. Both types of information concur in providing an estimate of Canada's *core* Jewish population. Ethnic Jews in Canada include persons who hold a non-Jewish religion, hence are not included in the *core* concept. On the other hand, persons without religion may declare a Jewish ethnicity, and are included in the *core*.

Since 1981, people have been able to declare either a single or a multiple ethnic ancestry citing up to four categories. In our case, people can be ethnically Jewish only, or Jewish and something else (perhaps being the descendants of intermarriages), or express multiple cultural identities. Following Jewish ethnicity throughout the last 25 years, an initial total figure of 293,000 in 1981 grew to a peak of 370,000 in 1991, and has since decreased to 349,000 in 2001 and 315,000 in 2006—a decline of 9.6 percent in five years.

More striking changes affected the distribution of Canadians and of the Jews among them between single and multiple ethnicities. Among Canada's total population in 2006, 5.7 million (31 percent) out of the 18.3 million who gave a single ethnic response declared they were Canadian,

---

[36]Detailed information on Canadian census returns is available online from Statistics Canada at http://www.statcan.ca. For the 2006 census, see, among other links, http://www12.statcan.ca/english/census06/data/highlights/ethnic/pages/Page.cfm?Lang=E&Geo=PR&Code=01&Data=Count&Table=2&StartRec=1&Sort=3&Display=All&CSDFilter=5000 (Ethnic origins, 2006 counts for Canada, provinces and territories—20% sample data).

TABLE 4 JEWISH POPULATION IN CANADA, BY DIFFERENT DEFINITIONS, 1981–2006

Year	Jewish Ethnicity			Jewish	Core Jewish
	Total	Single	Multiple	Religion	Population
1981	293,175	264,025	29,150	296,425	312,060
1986	343,505	245,855	97,650		
1991	369,565	245,580	123,725	318,070	356,315
1996	351,705	195,810	155,900		
2001	348,605	186,475	162,130	329,995	370,520
2006	315,120	134,045	181,070		375,000[a]

[a]2008 estimate.
Source: Statistics Canada.

as did 4.3 million (33 percent) out of the 12.9 million who gave a multiple response. All in all, over ten million Canadians out of a total population of over 31 million reported a Canadian ethnicity—what in other epochs used to be called an inexistent construct. Most likely, the rapid growth of "Canadian" as a primary or additional ethnic category affects identification perceptions among Jews. In 1981, 90 percent of total ethnic Jews declared a single ethnicity, but this share has declined to 66 percent in 1991, 53 percent in 2001, and 43 percent in 2006. In 2006, for the first time, the Canadian census shows that fewer than half of those who claim a Jewish ethnic ancestry do not mention an additional ancestry referent. The proportion of Jews with multiple ethnicity is today much higher than among the total population.

The sharp decline in Jewish ethnic identification does not necessarily provide evidence for a decline in Jewish population size, although it clearly points to a powerful process of acculturation. The number of Canada's Jews according to religion increased from 296,000 in 1981 to 318,000 in 1991 (+7.3 percent) and to 330,000 in 2001 (+3.7 percent). As noted, the figure is not available in the 2006 census. It should be stressed, though, that between 1991 and 2001, 22,365 Jews settled in the country, at a time when the Jewish population increased by 11,925. Consequently, the Jewish population defined by religion would have decreased by 10,440 (–3.3 percent) if not for this immigration.

Keeping in mind that some ethnic Jews are not Jewish by religion and that an even greater number of Jews by religion do not declare a Jewish ethnicity, a combined estimate of 312,000 obtained for Canada's Jewish population in 1981, growing to 356,000 in 1991, and 371,000 in 2001.[37] Assuming continuing immigration to Canada but also some internal attrition, we estimate the Jewish population to have grown to 375,000 in 2008, the world's fourth largest. This figure is not strictly comparable with the concept of *core* Jewish population, as it includes a fast-growing number of individuals for whom "Jewish" is only one among multiple ethnic identities, and some of whom may not readily identify as Jewish if asked. Some of these would probably better be included among the non-Jewish component of the *enlarged* Jewish population. Taking into account all ethnic Jews who profess a non-Jewish religion, and other non-Jewish household members, an *enlarged* Jewish population of above 450,000 would probably obtain.

Latin America

In Latin America, the Jewish population was generally in decline, reflecting recurring economic and local security concerns. Nearly 6,000 Jews emigrated from Argentina to Israel in 2002—the highest figure ever in a single year from that country—due to dire economic conditions and special incentives offered on the Israeli side. In 2003 the economic situation eased somewhat and Israel suspended its incentives. About 1,500 Jews emigrated from Argentina to Israel in 2003, declining to 458 in 2004, 397 in 2005, 293 in 2006, and 319 in 2007.[38] Based on the experience of previous years, approximately 20 percent of these migrants were non-Jewish household members in the *enlarged* population. Partial evidence from various sources indicated that less than half of total Jewish emigration from Argentina went to Israel. Permanence in Israel of the new immigrants was high, with only about 10 percent leaving within the first three years.[39] Argentina's Jewish population is assessed at 183,000 in 2008, the world's seventh largest.

In 2004 and 2005 two new Jewish population surveys were undertaken in the Buenos Aires metropolitan area (AMBA). Initial claims of a Jewish population of 244,000[40] were founded on significantly extended def-

---

[37]Charles Shahar, *The Jewish Community of Canada* (Toronto, 2004).

[38]See Israel Central Bureau of Statistics at http://www.cbs.gov.il

[39]Shmuel Adler, *Emigration among Immigrants from Argentina that Arrived During the Period 1.1.89–31.12.02* (Jerusalem, 2004).

[40]Adrian Jmelnizky and Ezequiel Erdei, *Estudio de Población Judía en Ciudad de Buenos Aires y Gran Buenos Aires (AMBA)* (Buenos Aires, 2005).

initional criteria. Of the 244,000, 64,000 reported to be Christians by religion, and another about 20,000 reported some Jewish ancestry but did not consider themselves Jewish. Overall, 161,000 people in the AMBA considered themselves to be totally or partly Jewish—consistent with our own estimate of 165,000. This figure for this major urban concentration appeared coherent with our countrywide *core* estimate. The 244,000 figure would be a good estimate of the *enlarged* Jewish population in Greater Buenos Aires, while the same survey identified over 300,000 persons who were in some way of Jewish origin or attached to a person of Jewish origin. Another survey limited to the city of Buenos Aires pointed to significant aging of the core Jewish population, reflecting the emigration of younger households over recent years.[41] The current situation implies a yearly loss of 500–1,000 through a negative balance of Jewish births and deaths, and emigration.

In Brazil, the 2000 census indicated a rather stable Jewish population of 86,828, up from 86,416 in 1991.[42] Considering the possible omission of individuals who did not answer the census question on religion, we assessed Brazil's Jewish population at 97,000 in 2003 and, allowing for moderate emigration (286 went to Israel in 2005, 232 in 2006, and 261 in 2007), 96,000 in 2008—the world's tenth largest. The census data were consistent with systematic documentation efforts undertaken by the Jewish Federation of São Paulo that found a total of 47,286 Jews,[43] and an assumption that about half of Brazil's Jews live in that city. Brazil's *enlarged* Jewish population (including non-Jewish members of Jewish households) was assessed at 132,191 in 1980 and 117,296 in 1991,[44] and presumably exceeded 120,000 in 2000.

In Mexico, the 2000 census indicated a Jewish population of 45,260 aged 5 and over.[45] Of these, 32,464 lived in the metropolitan area of the capital, Mexico City, while a most unlikely 12,796 were reported in states other than the Federal District and Mexico State—consistent with erratic figures in past censuses. Allocation of the 0–4 age group based on a 2000

---

[41]Yaacov Rubel, *La Población Judía de la Ciudad de Buenos Aires, Perfil Socio-Demográfico* (Buenos Aires, 2005).

[42]See http://wwwibge.br; René D. Decol, "Brazilian Jews: a Demographic Profile," unpublished paper delivered at the International Conference on Jewish Demography, Jerusalem, 2002.

[43]FISESP (Federação Israelita do Estado de São Paulo), *Recadastramento comunitário 2000–01* (São Paulo, 2002).

[44]René Decol, "Imigraçoes urbanas para o Brasil: o caso dos Judeus," unpublished Ph.D. dissertation, Universidade Estadual, 1999.

[45]See Instituto Nacional de Estadistica, Geografia e Informatica, *XII Censo General de Poblacion y Vivienda 2000* (Mexico City, 2002).

Jewish survey suggested an estimate of about 35,000 Jews in Greater Mexico City and 40,000 nationwide. A Jewish population survey undertaken in 2000 provided a countrywide estimate of 39,870 Jews, of whom 37,350 were in Mexico City,[46] confirming the results of a 1991 survey.[47] In 2008, allowing for some emigration to the U.S. and Israel, we estimated the Jewish population at 39,600, the world's 14th largest.

The fourth largest Jewish community in Latin America is in Chile,[48] whose relatively stable Jewish population of over 20,000 is now larger than those of Uruguay[49] and Venezuela.[50] Both of the latter countries experienced significant Jewish emigration in recent years. Around 2000, about 20 percent of the former pupils of Jewish schools in Uruguay and over a third of the adult children of Caracas Jews lived in a different country. Based on recent evidence, the Jewish population estimate for Uruguay was downwardly revised to 17,700 in 2008. The estimate for Venezuela was reduced to 12,500, reflecting emigration tied to the political situation in that country (see the article on Venezuela earlier in this volume).

In Central America, we revised upwardly the estimate for Panama from 5,000 to 8,000 to account for Jewish immigration from other Latin American countries over the years.

EUROPE

Jewish population in Europe tended to be increasingly concentrated in the western part of the continent, and within the European Union (Table 5). The EU encompassed an estimated 1,127,300 Jews in 2008, 76 percent

---

[46]Comunidad Judía de México, *Estudio socio-demográfico 2000* (Mexico City, unpublished tables, 2000).

[47]Sergio DellaPergola and Susana Lerner, *La población judía de México: Perfil demográfico, social y cultural* (México City-Jerusalén, 1995). The project, conducted cooperatively between the Centro de Estudios Urbanos y de Desarrollo Urbano (CEDDU), El Colegio de Mexico, and the Division of Jewish Demography and Statistics of the A. Harman Institute of Contemporary Jewry, The Hebrew University, was sponsored by the Asociación Mexicana de Amigos de la Universidad Hebrea de Jerusalén.

[48]Gabriel Berger et al., *Estudio Socio-Demográfico de la Comunidad Julia de Chile* (Santiago-Buenos Aires, 1995).

[49]Nicole Berenstein and Rafael Porzecanski, *Perfil de los egresados de la Red Formal de Educación Judía Urguaya* (Montevideo, 2001).

[50]Sergio DellaPergola, Salomon Benzaquen, and Tony Beker de Weinraub, *Perfil sociodemográfico y cultural de la comunidad judía de Caracas* (Caracas, 2000). The survey was sponsored by the Asociación Israelita de Venezuela, the Union Israelita de Caracas, and the Asociación de Amigos de la Universidad Hebrea de Jerusalén.

of the continent's total Jewish population. The former Soviet republics in Europe outside the EU comprised 312,800 Jews (21 percent). All other European countries comprised 41,000 Jews (3 percent).

The European Union

On May 1, 2004, the EU expanded from 15 to 25 countries, incorporating the three Baltic countries that had been part of the Soviet Union (Estonia, Latvia, and Lithuania), another five that had been part of the Soviet area of influence in Eastern Europe (the Czech Republic, Hungary, Poland, Slovakia, and Slovenia), and two southern European insular countries (Cyprus and Malta). In 2007 two more countries that had been part of the East European sphere of influence, Romania and Bulgaria, were admitted. The EU's expanded format symbolized an important historical landmark: the virtual boundary between Western and Eastern Europe was erased, with Croatia and Macedonia becoming the next candidates for EU membership. Ongoing disagreements about the future membership of Turkey reflect a dilemma in the definition of Europe's own cultural and geopolitical boundaries facing an Islamic country.

The largest Jewish community in Europe was in France, where a countrywide survey undertaken in 2002 suggested 500,000 *core* Jews plus an additional 75,000 non-Jewish members of Jewish households.[51] Jewish population is slowly diminishing primarily because of emigration, not only to Israel but also to Canada, the U.S., and other countries. Migration to Israel amounted to 2,545 in 2005, 2,408 in 2006, and 2,335 in 2007. Jewish emigration reflected a sense of uneasiness in the face of anti-Jewish acts, including physical violence (see the article on France earlier in this volume). A 2004 survey of Jewish tourists from France to Israel came up with a remarkable estimate of 125,000, or more than 30 percent of all French Jews age 15 and over.[52] Of these, 23 percent (about 29,000) affirmed their intention to move to Israel in the near future. A distant second candidate for possible emigration was the U.S. Of course stated migration intentions are not a proxy for actual migration decisions, but a rising sense of insecurity among French Jewry is undisputable. Our 2008 estimate for French Jews therefore shrinks to 488,000, still the third largest in the world.

---

[51]See Erik H. Cohen with Maurice Ifergan, *Les Juifs de France: Valeurs et identité* (Paris, 2002).

[52]Erik H. Cohen, *Les touristes de France en Israël 2004* (Jerusalem, 2005).

TABLE 5. ESTIMATED CORE JEWISH POPULATION DISTRIBUTION IN EUROPE, 1/1/2008

Country	Total Population	Jewish Population	Jews per 1,000 Population	Accuracy Rating
Austria	8,400,000	9,000	1.1	B 2001
Belgium	10,700,000	30,500	2.9	C 2002
Bulgaria	7,600,000	2,000	0.3	C 2001
Czech Republic	10,300,000	3,900	0.4	C 2001
Denmark	5,500,000	6,400	1.2	C 2001
Estonia	1,300,000	1,900	1.5	B 2006
Finland	5,300,000	1,100	0.2	B 1999
France[a]	62,000,000	488,000	7.9	B 2002
Germany	82,200,000	120,000	1.5	B 2004
Greece	11,200,000	4,500	0.4	B 1995
Hungary	10,000,000	48,800	4.8	C 2001
Ireland	4,500,000	1,200	0.3	B 2001
Italy	59,900,000	28,500	0.5	B 2002
Latvia	2,300,000	10,100	4.3	B 2008 X
Lithuania	3,400,000	3,500	1.1	B 2008 X
Luxembourg	500,000	600	1.2	B 2000
Netherlands	16,400,000	30,000	1.8	B 2000
Poland	38,100,000	3,200	0.1	C 2001
Portugal	10,600,000	500	0.0	C 1999
Romania	21,500,000	9,800	0.5	B 2001
Slovakia	5,400,000	2,600	0.5	C 2001
Slovenia	2,000,000	100	0.1	C 1996
Spain	46,500,000	12,000	0.3	D
Sweden	9,200,000	15,000	1.6	C 1999
United Kingdom	61,500,000	294,000	4.8	B 2001
Other[b]	1,500,000	100	0.1	D
Total European Union 27	479,900,000	1,127,300	2.3	
Gibraltar	28,000	600	21.4	B 2001
Norway	4,800,000	1,200	0.3	B 1995
Switzerland	7,600,000	17,700	2.4	B 2000
Total other West Europe[c]	12,898,000	19,500	1.5	

TABLE 5.—*(Continued)*

Country	Total Population	Jewish Population	Jews per 1,000 Population	Accuracy Rating
Belarus	9,700,000	17,000	1.8	B 1999
Moldova	4,100,000	4,300	1.1	B 2004 X
Russia[d]	141,900,000	215,000	1.5	B 2002
Ukraine	46,200,000	76,500	1.6	B 2001
Total FSU Republics	201,900,000	312,800	1.5	
[Total FSU in Europe][e]	208,900,000	328,300	1.6	
Bosnia-Herzegovina	3,800,000	500	0.1	C 2001
Croatia	4,400,000	1,700	0.4	C 2001
Macedonia	2,000,000	100	0.1	C 1996
Serbia	7,400,000	1,400	0.1	C 2001
Turkey[d]	74,800,000	17,700	0.2	B 2002
Total other East Europe and Balkans[c]	98,400,000	21,500	0.2	
Total	811,098,000	1,481,100	1.8	

[a]Including Monaco.
[b]Cyprus and Malta.
[c]Including countries not listed separately.
[d]Including Asian regions.
[e]Including Baltic countries.

In the United Kingdom, the 2001 national population census included a voluntary question on religion for the first time since the nineteenth century.[53] The total Jewish population of 266,741 for England, Wales, Scotland, and Northern Ireland closely approximated our 273,500 estimate for 2002. One interesting census finding was that the Jewish population is more diffused over the national territory than previously believed. This would also indicate a lower degree of affiliation than had been assumed.

[53]See Barry Kosmin and Stanley Waterman, *Commentary on Census Religion Question* (London, 2002), a publication of the JPR (Institute for Jewish Policy Research). The census is available at http://www.ons.uk.

The age composition of British Jewry is quite old, with 16 percent below 15 versus 22 percent above 65. More detailed data for Scotland (where some census questions were asked differently) indicated 6,448 people currently reporting Jewish religion, as compared to 7,446 who said they were raised as Jews—a net lifetime loss of 13 percent.[54]

About 23 percent of the UK total population indicated they had no religion and another 7 percent did not answer the question—at a time when much of the organized Jewish community publicly supported participation in the census. In the meantime, detailed census tabulations were obtained by the Institute for Jewish Policy Research and the Board of Deputies of British Jews from the Office for National Statistics. An in-depth profile of the sociodemographic profile of British Jewry thus emerged, along with a better evaluation of the quality of Jewish population estimates.[55] Analyses of detailed geographical precincts allowed for estimates of the amount of non-response in areas with higher or lower Jewish densities among the total population. There was a significant correlation between the known Jewish religiosity of the ward and non-response to the religion question. On the other hand, post-census surveys of Jews in London and Leeds did not unveil high percentages declaring they had not answered "Jewish" to the question on religion.

Vital statistics routinely collected by the Board of Deputies Community Research Unit on the annual number of Jewish births are consistent with the census returns. Comparing the uncorrected census returns for the age group 0–9 with the recorded number of Jewish births over the ten years preceding the census, the discrepancy was only 2.5 percent. This confirms that there was an undercount, but it could not have had a very significant impact on Jewish population estimates. The same vital statistics indicated a continuing excess of Jewish deaths (3,672 in 2002, 3,592 in 2003, and 3,257 in 2004) over Jewish births (2,748 in 2002, 2,648 in 2003, 3,076 in 2004).[56] Since 2005, however, the trends apparently re-

---

[54]Also see *JPR/News*, Spring 2003, p. 6.

[55]David Graham, Marlena Schmool, and Stanley Waterman, *Jews in Britain: A Snapshot from the 2001 Census* (London, 2007), JPR Report No. 1; David Graham and Stanley Waterman, "Underenumeration of the Jewish Population in the UK 2001 Census," *Population, Space and Place* 11, 2005, pp. 89–102; David Voas, "Estimating the Jewish Undercount in the 2001 Census: A Comment on Graham and Waterman (2005)," *Population, Space and Place* 13, 2007, pp. 401–07; David J. Graham and Stanley Waterman, "Locating Jews by Ethnicity: A Reply to David Voas (2007)," *Population, Space and Place* 13, 2007, pp. 409–14.

[56]The Board of Deputies of British Jews, Community Research Unit, *Report on Community Vital Statistics 2004* (London, 2005). See also Stephen Miller, Marlena Schmool, and Antony Lerman, *Social and Political Attitudes of British Jews: Some Key Findings of the JPR Survey* (London, 1996).

versed (3,221 deaths in 2005 and 3,107 in 2006, versus 3,339 births in 2005 and 3,314 in 2006).[57] The diminishing number of deaths is an obvious symptom of a shrinking population that loses several hundred people yearly through a negative vital balance. Shrinking synagogue membership is another indicator: household membership declined by 17.8 percent between 1990 and 2005, and by 4.5 percent (nearly 1 percent per year) between 2001 and 2005.[58] At the same time, the internal denominational balance within the community shifted to the strictly Orthodox.[59] This may plausibly explain the apparent increase in the birth rate. But the diminishing number of recorded burials defies explanation, unless a growing number of families do not choose to use Jewish burial societies.

We raised the UK Jewish population estimate from the original census count of 266,741 to 300,000 for 2001, or about 12 percent above the original returns, assuming a lower rate of non-response among Jews than in the general population. The updating must take into account the negative balance of births and deaths, as well as a moderate increase in emigration (594 went to Israel in 2006, and 562 in 2007). We estimated the UK's total Jewish population at 294,000 in 2008, the world's fifth largest.

In Germany, Jewish immigration, which brought into the country over 200,000 Jews and non-Jewish family members between 1989 and 2007, significantly diminished. The German government, under pressure because of high unemployment and a crumbling welfare system, limited Jewish immigration from the FSU in 2005. On January 1, 2005, the previous special immigration law *(Kontingentsflüchtlingsgesetz)* was replaced by a new more restrictive law *(Zuwanderungsgesetz)* that deprived Jews of their privileged status as *Kontingentflüchtlinge*. The new law put integration into German society and good economic prospects before other considerations. Jews aspiring to immigrate to Germany now had to first prove that a Jewish community would accept them, demonstrate that they already knew German, and prove that they would not be dependent on welfare and would integrate into the German labor market.[60]

---

[57]David Graham and Daiel Vulkan, *Britain's Jewish Community Statistics* (London, 2007).

[58]Rona Hart and Edward Kafka, *Trends in British Synagogue Membership, 1990–2005/6* (London, 2006).

[59]Daniel Vulkan and David Graham, *Population Trends among Britain's Strictly Orthodox* (London, 2008).

[60]Jewish People Policy Planning Institute, *Annual Assessment 2006, Deltas Creating Opportunities and Threats,* Executive Report 3 (Jerusalem, 2006).

In 2007, 1,296 immigrants from the former Soviet Union were recorded as new members of German Jewish communities, as compared to 1,971 in 2006, 3,124 in 2005, 4,757 in 2004, 6,224 in 2003, and 6,597 in 2002.[61] Criteria for admission to Jewish communities followed Jewish rabbinical rules. The total number of *core* Jews registered with the central Jewish community, 107,330 on January 1, 2008, marked the first decrease since 1989. A peak of 107,794 had been reached in 2007, as compared to 107,677 in 2006, 105,733 in 2005, and 102,472 in 2004. Of the current total, only 6,363 remained out of the initial pool of 28,081 members that existed at the end of 1990, the rest being recent immigrants. Between 2002 and 2004, the *enlarged* total of Jews and non-Jewish family members who came to Germany from the FSU was larger than the respective number of FSU migrants to Israel, but this ceased to be true beginning in 2005. The age composition of Jewish old-timers—and even more so of newcomers—was extremely skewed toward older ages. In 2007 there were 168 Jewish births and 1,051 Jewish deaths recorded by Jewish communities in Germany. This explains why the Jewish population marginally decreased in spite of immigration.

Allowing for delays in joining the organized community and a preference on the part of some members of a minority not to identify officially with its institutions, we assess Germany's *core* Jewish population at 120,000 in 2008, the world's eighth largest. The *enlarged* Jewish population, inclusive of the non-Jewish relatives of immigrants, is above 220,000, creating a new framework and new opportunities for Jewish religious, social, and cultural life in Germany, but also significant dependence on welfare and senior-citizen services.[62]

In Hungary, our core estimate of fewer than 50,000 Jews (the world's 13th largest Jewish community) reflects the unavoidably negative balance of Jewish births and deaths in a country where the total population's vital balance is notoriously negative. A Jewish survey conducted in 1999 indicated a conspicuously larger *enlarged* Jewish population.[63] However, a demographic extrapolation based on the usually accepted number of post-Holocaust Jewish survivors and accounting for the known or esti-

---

[61]Zentralwohlfahrtsstelle der Juden in Deutschland (ZWJD), *Mitgliederstatistik; Der Einzelnen Jüdischen Gemeinden und Landesverbände in Deutschland* (Frankfurt a.M., 2008).

[62]Julius H. Schoeps, Willy Jasper, and Bernard Vogt, eds., *Ein neues Judentum in Deutschland. Fremd und Eigenbilder der russisch-jüdischen Einwanderer* (Potsdam, 1999).

[63]András Kovács, ed., *Jews and Jewry in Contemporary Hungary: Results of a Sociological Survey* (London, 2004), JPR Report No. 1, 2004. The report significantly underestimates emigration over time.

mated numbers of births, deaths, and emigrants to Israel and to other countries since 1945 closely matches our assessment. In the 2001 Hungarian census only 13,000 people reported themselves Jewish by religion.

Belgium's Jewish population was estimated at above 30,000, the 15th largest worldwide. Stable numbers reflected the presence of a traditional Orthodox community in Antwerp and the growth of the large European administrative center in Brussels. In 2006, 91 people went to Israel, followed by 84 in 2007, reflecting concerns not unlike those experienced in France. Local Jewish population estimates were quite obsolete in comparison with most other EU countries, but the reported order of magnitude was supported by indirect evidence, such as the number of votes collected by Jewish candidates at the 2003 legislative elections.

The next two largest Jewish communities in the EU, and also globally, were those in the Netherlands and Italy. In the Netherlands, a 2000 survey estimated a Halakhic Jewish population of 30,072, of which perhaps as many as a third were immigrants from Israel, and an *enlarged* Jewish population of 43,305.[64] In Italy, total Jewish community membership—which historically comprised the overwhelming majority of the country's Jewish population—declined from 26,706 in 1995 to 25,143 in 2001.[65] Our estimate, below 29,000, adequately allocates for non-members.

Next in Jewish population size are Sweden, estimated at 15,000, and Spain, possibly around 12,000.

The Former Soviet Union

Jewish population decrease continued in the former Soviet Union, reflecting an overwhelming surplus of Jewish deaths over births, high rates of out-marriage and low rates of Jewish identification of the children, and conspicuous though diminishing emigration. Our 2008 assessment of the total *core* Jewish population in the aggregate of the 15 former Soviet republics, including the Baltic states, was 347,900, of which 328,300

---

[64]Hanna van Solinge and Marlene de Vries, eds., *De Joden in Nederland Anno 2000: Demografisch profiel en binding aan het joodendom* (Amsterdam, 2001). The survey was undertaken as a collaborative effort between the Stichting Joods Maatschappelijk Werk and NIDI (Netherlands Interdisciplinary Demographic Institute). See also C. Kooyman and J. Almagor, *Israelis in Holland: A Sociodemographic Study of Israelis and Former Israelis in Holland* (Amsterdam, 1996).

[65]Unione delle Comunità Ebraiche Italiane, *IV Congresso, Relazione del consiglio* (Roma, 2002); Yaakov Andrea Lattes, *Sull'assimilazione in Italia e i metodi per affrontarla* (Ramat Gan, 2005).

lived in Europe and 19,600 in Asia. At least as many non-Jewish family members were part of the respective households, creating an *enlarged* Jewish population twice as large as the *core*.[66] The ongoing process of demographic decline was compensated for to some extent by the revival of Jewish cultural and religious activities, including Jewish education.[67]

In the Russian Republic, the October 2002 census indicated 233,600 Jews, as against our *core* Jewish population estimate of 252,000 for the beginning of 2003 (derived from the February 1994 Russian Microcensus estimate of 409,000 Jews).[68] Allowing for some census undercounts after the compulsory item on ethnicity *(natsyonalnost)* on identification documents was canceled, the fact that the option not to state an ethnicity was allowed for the first time, and a slight upward revision versus our previous estimate, we evaluate the Jewish population at 215,000 in 2008, the sixth largest in the world.

Jewish population size was clearly more stable and resilient in Russia than in the other former Soviet republics. This partly reflected Jewish migrations between the various republics and also lower emigration propensities from Moscow and some of the other main urban areas.[69] Nevertheless, the striking imbalance of Jewish births and deaths, and continuing emigration (3,249 to Israel in 2007) meant ongoing population decline and an elderly age composition. The decline in the number of births to at least one Jewish parent could be estimated at 8,006 in 1988 and 2,177 in 1998. Recorded Jewish deaths were 13,826 in 1988 and 9,103 in 1998. As a result, the estimated negative balance of these vital events was –5,820 in 1988 and –6,926 in 1998.[70] These changes occurred in the

---

[66]Mark Tolts, "Contemporary Trends in Family Formation among the Jews in Russia," *Jews in Russia and Eastern Europe* 2 (57), 2006, pp. 5–23; Tolts, "Post-Soviet Jewish Demography, 1989–2004," in Zvi Gitelman and Yaacov Ro'i, eds., *Revolution, Repression, and Revival: The Soviet Jewish Experience* (Lanham, Md., 2007), pp. 283–311.

[67]Zvi Gitelman, "Becoming Jewish in Russia and Ukraine" in Gitelman, Barry Kosmin, and András Kovács, eds., *New Jewish Identities: Contemporary Europe and Beyond* (Budapest/New York, 2003) pp. 105–37.

[68]Mark Tolts, "Demographic Trends among the Jews of the Former Soviet Union," paper presented at the International Conference in Honor of Professor Mordechai Altshuler on Soviet and Post-Soviet Jewry, Jerusalem, 2003. For a German translation see *Menora: Jahrbuch für deutsch-jüdische Geshichte 2004*, 15 (Berlin/Wien, 2005), pp. 15–44; Tolts, "The Post-Soviet Jewish Population in Russia and the World," *Jews in Russia and Eastern Europe* 1 (52), 2004, pp. 37–63.

[69]Mark Tolts, "Mass *Aliyah* and Jewish Emigration from Russia: Dynamics and Factors," *East European Jewish Affairs* 33, 2003, pp. 71–96.

[70]Tolts, "Demographic Trends among the Jews of the Former Soviet Union"; Tolts, "Demographic Trends among the Jews in the Three Post-Soviet Slavic Republics," paper presented at the 14th World Congress of Jewish Studies, Jerusalem, 2005.

context of the steady net population decrease experienced by the Russian Republic in general, as well as by other European republics of the FSU.

In Ukraine, the population census undertaken on December 5, 2001, yielded 104,300 Jews, whereas we had projected 100,000 on January 1, 2002. Considering that our baseline for the latter estimate was the figure of 487,300 Jews counted in the previous census of January 1989, the fit between expected and actual results was quite remarkable.[71] Taking into account the dramatic pace of emigration since 1989, the other major intervening changes among Ukraine's Jews, and the continuing emigration at the end of 2001, the census fully confirmed our previous assessment of ongoing demographic trends. Adding continuing emigration (1,450 to Israel in 2007), we assess the 2008 *core* Jewish population at 76,500, the 11th largest in the world.

Of the other former Soviet republics in Europe, the main Jewish population was in Belarus, now downwardly reassessed at 17,000 (363 migrants to Israel in 2007). After the accession to the EU of the three Baltic states of Estonia, Latvia, and Lithuania, Jewish population has been fairly stable and is overall assessed, after some adjustments, at 15,500 in 2008. A survey in Moldova found an *enlarged* Jewish population of 9,240 in 2000.[72] According to the results of the Moldova census of October 2004, which did not cover Moldovan territory east of the Dniester River, there were 3,628 Jews. According to the unofficial results of the separate census of that region conducted in November 2004, there were about 1,200 Jews there. We assess the *core* Jewish population at 4,300 in 2008.

Rest of Europe

After Hungary joined the EU together with Poland (where the 2002 census indicated a Jewish population of 1,100), the Czech Republic, Slovakia, Slovenia, Bulgaria, and Romania, only 41,000 Jews in Europe were living outside the EU or the FSU. Of these, 19,500 were in Western Europe, primarily Switzerland (17,700),[73] and 21,500 were in Eastern Europe and the Balkans, primarily Turkey. A survey of Istanbul pointed to an

---

[71]Ukrainian Ministry of Statistics, *Population Census 2001* (Kiyev, 2002); Mark Tolts, *Main Demographic Trends of the Jews in Russia and the FSU* (Jerusalem, 2002).

[72]Malka Korazim and Esther Katz, "Patterns of Jewish Identity in Moldova: The Behavioral Dimension," in Gitelman, Kosmin, and Kovács, eds., *New Jewish Identities*, pp. 159–70.

[73]Bundesamt für Statistik, *Wohnbevölkerung nach Religion 2000* (Neuchatel, 2005).

aging community that has experienced significant past emigration (108 went to Israel in 2007). In that city, 14 percent of the Jewish population was under age 18, versus 18 percent above 65.[74]

ASIA

Israel

Jewish population in Asia is mostly affected by the trends in Israel (Table 6). After World War II, Israel (then Palestine) had a Jewish population of over half a million, which grew nearly tenfold over the next 60 years due to mass immigration and fairly high and uniquely stable reproduction patterns. Information about Israel's population is regularly supplied by the Central Bureau of Statistics, whose yearly data derive from periodical censuses and detailed annual accountancy of intervening events (births, deaths, immigrants, emigrants, and converts). The last census was in 1995 and the next was expected in December 2008.

At the beginning of 2008, Israel's *core* Jewish population reached 5,478,200, forming an *enlarged* Jewish population of 5,793,600 when combined with 315,400 non-Jewish members of Jewish households.[75] For several years now, the main factor driving Jewish population growth in Israel has been the natural increase of births over deaths. In 2004, for the first time, more than 100,000 Jewish babies were born in Israel. In 2007, 107,986 Jewish births and 34,630 deaths produced a net Jewish natural increase of 73,356. Israel's Jewish fertility rate rose slightly to 2.8 children per woman, higher than in any other developed country and twice or more the effective Jewish fertility level of most Diaspora Jewish communities.

In 2007, 22,800 new immigrants, including immigrant citizens, arrived in Israel, of whom 14,500 were Jewish.[76] Current emigration reduced this to a net migration balance of 15,400, of which 6,700 was Jewish. The number of non-Jewish immigrants who subsequently undergo conversion

---

[74]Data provided through the courtesy of the Istanbul Jewish Community Council.

[75]Central Bureau of Statistics, *Statistical Abstract of Israel,* http://www.cbs.gov.il

[76]These data include over 4,600 immigrant citizens, the foreign-born children of Israelis on their first-time entrance to the country. Not included are foreign workers and illegal residents. In 2006, 22,400 Israelis left the country for more than one year, and 9,600 returned to Israel after staying abroad more than one year.

TABLE 6. ESTIMATED CORE JEWISH POPULATION DISTRIBUTION IN ASIA, 1/1/2008

Country	Total Population	Jewish Population	Jews per 1,000 Population	Accuracy Rating
Israel[a]	6,968,400	5,209,200	747.5	A 2008
West Bank and Gaza[b]	3,775,200	269,000	71.3	A 2008
Total Israel and Palestine	10,743,600	5,478,200	509.9	
Azerbaijan	8,700,000	6,600	0.8	C 1999
Georgia	4,600,000	3,500	0.8	B 2002
Kazakhstan	15,700,000	3,700	0.2	B 1999
Kyrgyzstan	5,200,000	800	0.2	B 1999
Turkmenistan	5,200,000	200	0.0	D 1989
Uzbekistan	27,200,000	4,800	0.2	D 1989
Total former USSR in Asia[c]	77,000,000	19,600	0.3	
China[d]	1,332,300,000	1,500	0.0	D
India	1,149,300,000	5,000	0.0	B 1996
Iran	72,200,000	10,600	0.1	C 1986
Japan	127,700,000	1,000	0.0	C 1993
Korea, South	48,600,000	100	0.0	C 1998
Philippines	90,500,000	100	0.0	D
Singapore	4,800,000	300	0.1	C 1990
Syria	19,900,000	100	0.0	C 1995
Taiwan	23,000,000	100	0.0	D
Thailand	65,700,000	200	0.0	C 1998
Yemen	22,200,000	200	0.0	C 1995
Other	932,156,400	200	0.0	D
Total other Asia	3,888,356,400	19,400	0.0	
Total	3,976,100,000	5,517,200	1.4	

[a]Total population of Israel, including Jews in West Bank and Gaza, 1/1/2008: 7,243,600.
[b]Total Palestinian population in West Bank and Gaza: 1/1/2008: 3,500,000 (our revised estimate).
[c]Including Armenia and Tajikistan. Not including Asian regions of Russian Republic.
[d]Including Hong Kong and Macao.

to Judaism is quite low, but new evidence from Israel's rabbinical courts indicates a steady increase. Overall, between 1999 and 2007, over 40,000 people were converted by these courts, some of whom were not permanent residents of the country. The total number of converts in 2007 was 7,881, as compared to 3,811 in 2006 and 5,279 in 2005. Of the 2007 converts, 3,527 were new immigrants of the Ethiopian Falashmora community; 1,197 immigrated from the FSU; 556 immigrated from other countries; and 601 had their conversions processed through the rabbinate of the Israel Defense Forces.[77]

Of the 5,478,200 *core* Jews in 2008, 5,209,200 lived within the pre-1967 borders plus East Jerusalem and the Golan Heights, and about 269,000 lived in the West Bank, where they formed over 10 percent of the total population. Jews represented 75.6 percent of a total population of 7,243,600 in the State of Israel, including East Jerusalem, the Golan Heights, and the Israeli but not the Palestinian population in the West Bank. Considering the total Jewish and Palestinian legal population of 10,743,600 in the State of Israel and under the Palestinian Authority, Jews represented 51.0 percent, or slightly more than half the total between the Mediterranean Sea and the Jordan River.

All the figures in the preceding paragraph relate to the *core* Jewish population. If the 315,000 non-Jewish members of Jewish households are added to the Jewish side, the *enlarged* Jewish population of 5,793,600 thus obtained represented 80.0 percent of Israel's population (as defined above), and 53.9 percent of the total population of Israel and the Palestinian territories. With the addition of about 200,000 non-Jewish foreign workers residing in Israel, *core* and *enlarged* Jewish populations represented, respectively, 50.1 and 52.9 percent of the total population present in Israel and the Palestinian territories, estimated at 10,943,600 in 2008. The extant Jewish majority is constantly declining over the whole territory between the Mediterranean Sea and the Jordan River, and more particularly within the State of Israel.[78]

These estimates significantly reflect an assessment of total Palestinian

[77]Personal communication from Rabbi David Bass, head of tribunal, Israel Special Rabbinical Conversion Courts.

[78]An extensive discussion of the background, thrust, and implications of past and current population changes is provided in Sergio DellaPergola, "Demographic Trends in Israel and Palestine: Prospects and Policy Implications," AJYB 2003, vol. 103, pp. 3–68; and DellaPergola, "Correspondence," in *Azure,* Winter 2007, pp. 3–23. See also Arnon Sofer and Yevguenia Bistrow, *Israel Demography 2004–2020 in the Light of Disengagement* (Haifa, 2004; in Hebrew).

population of the West Bank and Gaza. Following a census held in the West Bank and Gaza in 1997, the Palestinian Central Bureau of Statistics (PCBS) indicated a population of 2,890,000, including East Jerusalem, and used this figure to make population projections based on assumptions about fertility and migration.[79] The projected estimate of 4,081,000 for end 2007, including East Jerusalem, looked too high, since it assumed a level of continuing immigration of Palestinians that did not materialize and in fact was outweighed by some out-migration. The latter figures were, in turn, challenged by a group of American and Israeli investigators, who maintained that current population estimates from Palestinian sources were inflated by one-and-a-half million.[80] In November 2007, the Palestinian Authority undertook a new population census that found 3,760,000 people, including East Jerusalem, 321,000 lower than the previous PCBS estimate. Our own independent assessment—after subtracting East Jerusalem allocated to the Israeli side, accounting for a negative migration balance of Palestinians, and making further corrections—was 3,500,000 on January 1, 2008. Of that total, about 2.1 million lived in the West Bank and 1.4 million in Gaza. The overall decennial growth rate of the Palestinian population was 2.6 percent, quite similar to Israeli Arabs.

Rest of Asia

In the rest of Asia, the Jewish population consisted mainly of the rapidly declining communities in the FSU's eight Asian republics, the largest of which was Azerbaijan with 6,800 Jews, followed by Uzbekistan (4,800), Kazakhstan (3,700), and Georgia (3,500).[81] The largest Jewish population in a single country in Asia besides Israel was in Iran. Our estimate there reflects an effort to monitor intensive emigration since the Islamic revolution of the late 1970s. Small Jewish populations, partly of temporary sojourners, exist in various South and East Asian countries. Rapid economic development and growing relations with Israel render these countries receptive to a small but growing Jewish presence.

---

[79]See www.pcbs.org

[80]Bennett Zimmerman, Roberta Seid, Michael Wise, Yoram Ettinger, David Shahaf, Ezra Sohar, David Passig, and Avraham Shvout, *Arab Population In the West Bank & Gaza: The Million-and-a-Half Person Gap* (Washington, D.C., 2005); Bennett Zimmerman, Roberta Seid, and Michael L. Wise, *The Million-Persons Gap: The Arab Population in the West Bank and Gaza* (Ramat Gan, 2005).

[81]Tolts, "Demographic Trends among the Jews of the Former Soviet Union."

AFRICA

Jewish population in Africa was mostly concentrated in South Africa (Table 7). According to the 2001 census,[82] the white Jewish population amounted to 61,675. After factoring in the national non-response rate of 14 percent, a corrected estimate of 72,000 obtained. Allowing for a certain proportion of actual Jews reported among South African non-whites who reported that they were Jews (11,979 blacks, 1,287 coloreds, and 615 Indians, many of whom practice other religions), we assessed the total size of the Jewish community at 75,000 in 2001. Following a moderate continuation of emigration (137 to Israel in 2007), we estimate South Africa's Jewish population at 71,300 in 2008, the world's 12th largest.

Our revised estimates for North Africa acknowledge the ongoing reduction of the small Jewish populations remaining in Morocco and Tunisia, now assessed at 3,900 overall. Virtually the whole Jewish population is estimated to have emigrated from Ethiopia, but the question remained open regarding the Falashmora—a Christian community of Jewish ancestry that undergoes conversion in the process of migration to and absorption in Israel. In 2007, 3,589 arrived in Israel as discussions took place in the Israeli government about stopping the migration program. Several thousands members of the community still waited to emigrate from Ethiopia, but it was difficult to ascertain how many more might apply.

OCEANIA

Continuing immigration produced some increase in the size of Jewish populations in Oceania (Table 8). Australia's 2006 census indicated a Jewish population of 88,831, up about 5,000 from 2001.[83] Taking into ac-

[82]David Saks, "Community Stable, Ageing—Census," *South African Jewish Report* (Johannesburg, 2003). See also Barry A. Kosmin, Jaqueline Goldberg, Milton Shain, and Shirley Bruk, *Jews of the New South Africa: Highlights of the 1998 National Survey of South African Jews* (London, 1999); and Shirley Bruk, *The Jews of South Africa 2005—Report on a Research Study* (Cape Town, 2006)

[83]Australian Bureau of Statistics, *Population Census 2006* (Canberra, 2007); Australian Bureau of Statistics, *Population Census 2001* (Canberra, 2002). See also Gary Eckstein, *Demography of the Sydney Jewish Community 2001* (Sydney, 2003).

TABLE 7. ESTIMATED CORE JEWISH POPULATION DISTRIBUTION IN AFRICA, 1/1/2008

Country	Total Population	Jewish Population	Jews per 1,000 Population	Accuracy Rating
Egypt	74,900,000	100	0.0	C 1998
Ethiopia	79,100,000	100	0.0	C 2008
Morocco	31,200,000	2,900	0.1	C 2006
Tunisia	10,300,000	1,000	0.1	C 2003
Total North Africa[a]	276,400,000	4,100	0.0	
Botswana	1,800,000	100	0.1	C 1993
Congo D.R.	66,500,000	100	0.0	C 1993
Kenya	38,000,000	400	0.0	C 1990
Namibia	2,100,000	100	0.0	C 1993
Nigeria	148,100,000	100	0.0	D
South Africa	48,300,000	71,300	1.5	B 2001
Zimbabwe	13,300,000	400	0.0	B 2001
Other	372,500,000	300	0.0	D
Total other Africa	690,600,000	72,800	0.1	
Total	967,000,000	76,900	0.1	

[a]Including countries not listed separately.

TABLE 8 ESTIMATED CORE JEWISH POPULATION DISTRIBUTION IN OCEANIA, 1/1/2008

Country	Total Population	Jewish Population	Jews per 1,000 Population	Accuracy Rating
Australia	21,300,000	107,000	5.1	B 2006 X
New Zealand	4,300,000	7,500	1.8	A 2006
Other	9,400,000	100	0.0	D
Total	35,000,000	114,600	3.3	

count several factors—such as continuing immigration and non-response to the question on religion, but also the community's rather old age composition—we upwardly corrected the *core* Jewish population estimate to 107,000 in 2008, the ninth largest in the world. The 2006 census of New Zealand also pointed to some Jewish population increase, to 6,858.[84] We assess the total at 7,500.

Dispersion and Concentration

SIZE AND DENSITY

Reflecting global Jewish population stagnation along with growing concentration in a few countries, 97.5 percent of world Jewry lives in the largest 15 communities, and, excluding Israel from the count, 98.3 percent lives in the 14 largest communities of the Diaspora, of which 70.7 percent lives in the U.S. (Table 9).

In 2008, there were at least 100 Jews in 93 different countries (Table 10). Two countries had Jewish populations above 5 million each (Israel and the U.S.); another seven had more than 100,000 Jews; three had 50,000–100,000; five had 25,000–50,000; ten had 10,000–25,000; eight had 5,000–10,000; and 58 countries had fewer than 5,000. The 66 communities with fewer than 10,000 Jews together accounted for 1 percent of world Jewry. In only six communities outside of Israel did Jews constitute at least about 5 per 1,000 (0.5 percent) of their country's total population. In descending order by the relative weight (not size) of their Jewish population they were Gibraltar (21.4 Jews per 1,000 inhabitants); the U.S. (17.5); Canada (11.4); France (7.9); Uruguay (5.4); and Australia (5.1).

By combining the two criteria of Jewish population size and density, we obtain the following taxonomy of the 26 Jewish communities with populations over 10,000 (excluding Israel). There are four countries with over 100,000 Jews and at least 5 Jews per 1,000 of total population: the U.S., France, Canada, and Australia; another four countries with over 100,000 Jews and at least 1 per 1,000 of total population: the UK, Argentina, Russia, and Germany; one country with 10,000–100,000 Jews

[84]Statistics New Zealand, 2006 Census of Population and Dwelling (Auckland, 2007).

TABLE 9. COUNTRIES WITH LARGEST CORE JEWISH POPULATIONS, 1/1/2008

Rank	Country	Jewish Population	% of Total Jewish Population: In the World %	In the World Cumulative %	In the Diaspora %	In the Diaspora Cumulative %
1	Israel	5,478,200	41.4	41.4	=	=
2	United States	5,275,000	39.1	81.3	70.7	70.7
3	France	488,000	3.7	85.0	6.3	76.9
4	Canada	375,000	2.8	87.8	4.8	81.8
5	United Kingdom	294,000	2.2	90.0	3.8	85.6
6	Russia	215,000	1.6	91.6	2.8	88.3
7	Argentina	183,000	1.4	93.0	2.4	90.7
8	Germany	120,000	0.9	93.9	1.5	92.3
9	Australia	107,000	0.8	94.7	1.4	93.6
10	Brazil	96,000	0.7	95.5	1.2	94.9
11	Ukraine	76,500	0.6	96.0	1.0	95.9
12	South Africa	71,300	0.5	96.6	0.9	96.8
13	Hungary	48,800	0.4	96.9	0.6	97.4
14	Mexico	39,600	0.3	97.2	0.5	97.9
15	Belgium	30,500	0.2	97.5	0.4	98.3

and at least 5 per 1,000 of total population: Uruguay; ten more countries with 10,000–100,000 Jews and at least 1 per 1,000 of total population: Latvia, Ukraine, South Africa, Hungary, Belgium, the Netherlands, Chile, Belarus, Switzerland, and Sweden; and seven countries with 10,000–100,000 Jews and less than 1 per 1,000 of total population: Brazil, Mexico, Italy, Turkey, Venezuela, Spain, and Iran.

JEWS IN MAJOR CITIES

The overwhelmingly urban concentration of Jewish populations globally is evinced by the fact that in 2008 more than half (52.2 percent) of world Jewry live in only five metropolitan areas—Tel Aviv, New York, Jerusalem, Los Angeles, and Haifa. Over two-thirds (67.8 percent) live in those five areas plus Southeast Florida, Be'er Sheva, Paris, Chicago, Washington, D.C., Boston, and San Francisco. The largest 20 Jewish population concentrations encompass 77 percent of all Jews worldwide

TABLE 10. DISTRIBUTION OF THE WORLD'S JEWS, BY NUMBER, AND PROPORTION (PER 1,000 POPULATION) IN EACH COUNTRY, 1/1/2008

Number of Jews in Country	Total	Jews per 1,000 Population: 0.0-0.9	1.0-4.9	5.0-9.9	10.0-24.9	25.0+
	Number of Countries					
Total[a]	93	63	23	3	3	1
100–900	35	31	3	-	1	-
1,000–4,900	23	21	2	-	-	-
5,000–9,900	8	4	4	-	-	-
10,000–24,900	10	4	5	1	-	-
25,000–49,900	5	2	3	-	-	-
50,000–99,900	3	1	2	-	-	-
100,000–999,900	7	-	4	2	1	-
1,000,000 or more	2	-	-	-	1	1
	Jewish Population Distribution—Absolute Numbers					
Total[a]	13,231,700	301,100	1,188,000	612,700	5,650,600	5,478,200
100–900	11,300	9,300	1,400	-	600	-
1,000–4,900	54,900	48,700	6,200	-	-	-
5,000–9,900	57,100	26,200	30,900	-	-	-
10,000–24,900	150,900	52,800	80,400	17,700	-	-
25,000–49,900	177,400	68,100	109,300	-	-	-
50,000–99,900	243,800	96,000	147,800	-	-	-
100,000–999,900	1,782,000	-	812,000	595,000	375,000	-
1,000,000 or more	10,753,200	-	-	-	5,275,000	5,478,200
	Jewish Population Distribution—Percent of World's Jews					
Total[a]	100.0	2.3	9.0	4.6	42.7	41.4
100–900	0.1	0.1	0.0	0.0	0.0	0.0
1,000–4,900	0.4	0.4	0.0	0.0	0.0	0.0
5,000–9,900	0.5	0.2	0.3	0.0	0.0	0.0
10,000–24,900	1.1	0.4	0.5	0.1	0.0	0.0
25,000–49,900	1.3	0.5	0.8	0.0	0.0	0.0
50,000–99,900	1.8	0.7	1.1	0.0	0.0	0.0
100,000–999,900	13.5	0.0	6.1	4.5	2.8	0.0
1,000,000 or more	81.3	0.0	0.0	0.0	39.9	41.4

[a]Grand total includes countries with fewer than 100 Jews, for a total of 1,100 Jews. Minor discrepancies due to rounding. Israel includes West Bank.

TABLE 11. METROPOLITAN AREAS WITH LARGEST CORE JEWISH POPULATIONS, 1/1/2008

Rank	Metro Area[a]	Country	Jewish Population	Share of World's Jews	
				%	Cumulative %
1	Tel Aviv[b,c]	Israel	2,848,700	21.5	21.5
2	New York[d]	U.S.	2,051,000	15.5	37.0
3	Jerusalem[e]	Israel	675,000	5.1	42.1
4	Los Angeles[d]	U.S.	668,000	5.0	47.2
5	Haifa[b]	Israel	658,700	5.0	52.2
6	Southeast Florida [d, f]	U.S.	527,500	4.0	56.1
7	Be'er Sheva[b]	Israel	353,000	2.7	58.8
8	Paris[g]	France	284,000	2.1	61.0
9	Chicago[d]	U.S.	270,500	2.0	63.0
10	Washington[h]	U.S.	215,600	1.6	64.6
11	Boston[d]	U.S.	210,500	1.6	66.2
12	San Francisco[d]	U.S.	208,600	1.6	67.8
13	Philadelphia[d]	U.S.	206,100	1.6	69.4
14	London[i]	United Kingdom	195,000	1.5	70.8
15	Toronto[j]	Canada	180,000	1.4	72.2
16	Buenos Aires[k]	Argentina	165,000	1.2	73.4
17	Atlanta[h]	U.S.	119,800	0.9	74.3
18	Moscow[l]	Russia	95,000	0.7	75.1
19	Baltimore[h]	U.S.	91,400	0.7	75.8
20	San Diego[i]	U.S.	89,000	0.7	76.4

[a]Most metropolitan areas include extended inhabited territory and several municipal authorities around central city. Definitions vary by country. Some of the estimates may include non-core Jews.
[b]As newly defined in the 1995 Israeli Census.
[c]Includes Ramat Gan, Bene Beraq, Petach Tikvah, Bat Yam, Holon, Rishon Lezion, Netanya, and Ashdod, each with a Jewish population above 100,000.
[d]Consolidated Metropolitan Statistical Area (CMSA).
[e]Includes the whole Jerusalem District and parts of Judea and Samaria District.
[f]Miami-Ft. Lauderdale and West Palm Beach-Boca Raton CMSA.
[g]Departments 75, 77, 78, 91, 92, 93, 94, 95.
[h]Metropolitan Statistical Area (MSA).
[i]Greater London and contiguous postcode areas.
[j]Census Metropolitan Area.
[k]Capital Federal and Gran Buenos Aires Partidos (AMBA).
[l]Territory administered by city council.

(Table 11).[85] In 2008, Montreal was excluded from the list of 20 and San Diego was included. The Jewish population in the Tel Aviv urban conurbation extending from Netanya to Ashdod now exceeds by far that in the New York Standard Metropolitan Area, extending from southern New York State to parts of Connecticut, New Jersey, and Pennsylvania. Of the 20 largest metropolitan areas of Jewish residence, 11 are located in the U.S., four in Israel, and one each in Canada, France, the UK, Argentina, and Russia.

Outlook

Beyond the many problems related to Jewish population definitions and data accuracy, it is important to recognize the powerful and persistent trends that daily reshape the demographic profile of world Jewry. Reading current data in historical and comparative context, the recent momentum of Jewish population change in the U.S.—tending to zero growth, at best—lags far behind that of Israel, which is characterized by significant natural increase. While the emergence of Israel as the home of the largest Jewish population in the world is grounded on solid empirical foundations, the U.S. remains a very large, culturally and socioeconomically powerful, and resilient center of Jewish life. The aggregate weight of other Jewish communities around the world, however, is fast diminishing.

SERGIO DELLAPERGOLA

[85]For Israel estimates see Israel Central Bureau of Statistics, *Statistical Abstract of Israel* 59, Table 2-15. For U.S. estimates see Sheskin and Dashefsky, "Jewish Population in the United States, 2007." Some of the figures in the latter are rather outdated and and are based on definitions and methods that are sometimes inconsistent with each other.

National Jewish Organizations

UNITED STATES

Organizations are listed according to functions as follows:

Note also cross-references under these headings:

COMMUNITY RELATIONS

AMERICAN COUNCIL FOR JUDAISM (1943). PO Box 2836, Ponte Vedra Beach, FL 32004-2836. (877)-282-3131. E-mail: acjsln@aol.com. Pres. Stephen L. Naman; Exec. Dir. Rabbi Howard A. Berman. Seeks to advance the universal principles of a Judaism free of nationalism, and the national, civic, cultural, and social integration into American institutions of Americans of Jewish faith. *Issues of the American Council for Judaism; Special Interest Report.* (WWW.ACJNA.ORG)

AMERICAN JEWISH COMMITTEE (1906). The Jacob Blaustein Building, 165 E. 56 St., NYC 10022. (212)751-4000. FAX: (212)750-0326. E-mail: info@ajc.org. Pres. Richard Sideman; Exec. Dir. David A. Harris. Protects the rights and freedoms of Jews the world over; combats bigotry and anti-Semitism and promotes democracy and human rights for all; works for the security of Israel and deepened understanding between Americans and Israelis; advocates public-policy positions rooted in American democratic values and the perspectives of Jewish heritage; and enhances the creative vitality of the Jewish people. Includes Jacob and Hilda Blaustein Center for Human Relations, Project Interchange, William Petschek National Jewish Family Center, Jacob Blaustein Institute for the Advancement of Human Rights, Koppelman Institute on American Jewish-Israeli Relations. *American Jewish Year Book; Commentary; AJC Journal.* (WWW.AJC.ORG)

AMERICAN JEWISH CONGRESS (1918). 825 Third Ave., Ste. 1800, NYC 10022. (212)879-4500. FAX: (212)249-3672. E-mail: pr@ajcongress.org. Pres. Richard Gordon; Exec. Dir. Neil B. Goldstein. Works to foster the creative survival of the Jewish people; to help Israel develop in peace, freedom, and security; to eliminate all forms of racial and religious bigotry; to advance civil rights, protect civil liberties, defend religious freedom, and safeguard the separation of church and state; "The Attorney General for the Jewish Community." *Congress Monthly; Judaism; Inside Israel; Radical Islamic Fundamentalism Update.* (WWW.AJCONGRESS.ORG)

AMERICAN JEWISH PUBLIC RELATIONS SOCIETY (1957). 575 Lexington Ave., Suite 600, NYC 10022. (212)644-2663. FAX: (212)644-3887. Pres. Diane J. Ehrlich; V-Pres., membership, Lauren R. Marcus. Advances professional status of public-relations practitioners employed by Jewish organizations and institutions or who represent Jewish-related clients, services, or products; upholds a professional code of ethics and standards; provides continuing education and networking opportunities at monthly meetings; serves as a clearinghouse for employment opportunities. *AJPRS Reporter; AJPRS Membership Directory.*

ANTI-DEFAMATION LEAGUE OF B'NAI B'RITH (1913). 823 United Nations Plaza, NYC 10017. (212)885-7700. FAX: (212)867-0779. E-mail: webmaster@adl.org. Natl. Chmn. Glen Lewy; Natl. Dir. Abraham H. Foxman. Seeks to combat anti-Semitism and to secure justice and fair treatment for all citizens through law, education, and community relations. *ADL on the Frontline; Law Enforcement Bulletin; Dimensions: A Journal of Holocaust Studies; Hidden Child Newsletter; International Reports; Civil Rights Reports.* (WWW.ADL.ORG)

ASSOCIATION OF JEWISH COMMUNITY RELATIONS WORKERS (1950). 7800 Northaven Road, Dallas, TX 75230. (214)615-5229. FAX: (214)373-3186. Pres. Marlene Gorin. Aims to stimulate higher standards of professional practice in Jewish community relations; encourages research and training toward that end; conducts educational programs and seminars; aims to encourage cooperation between community-relations workers and those working in other areas of Jewish communal service.

CANFEI NESHARIM (2002). 111 Eighth Ave., 11th Floor, NYC 10011. (212)284-6745. E-mail: info@canfeinesharim.org. Exec. Dir. Evonne Marzouk. Educates about protecting the environment, from the perspective of Torah and Jewish law; encourages actions to protect the environment. *Compendium of Sources in Torah and Halacha* (biennial); *Newsletter* (monthly e-mail). (WWW.CANFEINESHARIM.ORG)

CENTER FOR JEWISH COMMUNITY STUDIES (1970). Beit Milken, 13 Tel Hai St., Jerusalem 92107, Israel. 972-2-5619281. FAX: 972-25619112. E-mail: jcpa@netvision.net.il or cjcs@worldnet.att.net. Jerusalem office: Jerusalem Center for Public Affairs. Pres. Amb. Dore Gold; Dir. Gen. Zvi Marom; Chmn. Bd. of Overseers Michael Rukin. Worldwide policy-studies institute devoted to the study of Jewish community organization, political thought, and public affairs, past and present, in Israel and throughout the world. Publishes original articles, essays, and monographs; maintains library, archives, and reprint series. *Jerusalem Letter/Viewpoints; Jewish Political Studies Review.* (WWW.JCPA.ORG).

CENTER FOR RUSSIAN JEWRY WITH STUDENT STRUGGLE FOR SOVIET JEWRY/SSSJ (1964). 240 Cabrini Blvd., #5B, NYC 10033. (212)928-7451. FAX: (212)795-8867. Dir./Founder Jacob Birnbaum; Chmn. Dr. Ernest Bloch. Campaigns for the human rights of the Jews of the former USSR, with emphasis on emigration and Jewish identity; supports programs for needy Jews there and for newcomers in Israel and USA, stressing employment and Jewish education. As the originator of the grassroots movement for Soviet Jewry in the early 1960s, possesses unique archives.

COALITION ON THE ENVIRONMENT & JEWISH LIFE (1993). 116 East 27th Street, 10th floor, New York, NY 10016. (212)532-7436. FAX: (212)686-1353. E-mail:

info@coejl.org. Exec. Dir. Barbara Lerman-Golomb. Promotes environmental education, advocacy, and action in the American Jewish community. Sponsored by a broad coalition of Jewish organizations; member of the National Religious Partnership for the Environment. *Bi-annual newsletter.* (WWW.COEJL.ORG)

COMMISSION ON SOCIAL ACTION OF REFORM JUDAISM (1953, joint instrumentality of the Union for Reform Judaism and the Central Conference of American Rabbis). 633 Third Ave., 7th fl., NYC 10017. (212)650-4160. FAX: (212)650-4229. E-mail: csarj@urj.org. Wash. Office: 2027 Massachusetts Ave., NW, Washington, DC 20036. Chmn. Robert Heller; Dir. Rabbi Daniel Polish; Dir. Religious Action Center of Reform Judaism, Rabbi David Saperstein. Policy-making body that relates ethical and spiritual principles of Judaism to social-justice issues; implements resolutions through the Religious Action Center in Washington, DC, via advocacy, development of educational materials, and congregational programs. *Tzedek V'Shalom (social action newsletter); Chai Impact (legislative update).*

CONFERENCE OF PRESIDENTS OF MAJOR AMERICAN JEWISH ORGANIZATIONS (1955). 633 Third Ave., NYC 10017. (212)318-6111. FAX: (212)644-4135. E-mail: info@prescon.org. Exec. V.-Chmn. Malcolm Hoenlein. Seeks to strengthen the U.S.-Israel alliance and to protect and enhance the security and dignity of Jews abroad. Toward this end, the Conference of Presidents speaks and acts on the basis of consensus of its 54 member agencies on issues of national and international Jewish concern.

CONSULTATIVE COUNCIL OF JEWISH ORGANIZATIONS-CCJO (1946). 420 Lexington Ave., Suite 1731, NYC 10170. (212)808-5437. Chmn. Ady Steg & Clemens N. Nathan. A nongovernmental organization in consultative status with the UN, UNESCO, ILO, UNICEF, and the Council of Europe; cooperates and consults with, advises, and renders assistance to the Economic and Social Council of the UN on all problems relating to human rights and economic, social, cultural, educational, and related matters pertaining to Jews.

COORDINATING BOARD OF JEWISH ORGANIZATIONS (1947). 2020 K Street, NW, 7th Floor, Washington, D.C. 20006. (202)857-6540. FAX: (202)857-6689. Exec. V. Pres. Daniel S. Mariaschin. To promote the purposes and principles for which the UN was created.

COUNCIL OF JEWISH ORGANIZATIONS IN CIVIL SERVICE, INC. (1948). 45 E. 33 St., Rm. 601, NYC 10016. (212)689-2015. FAX: (212)447-1633. Pres. Louis Weiser; 1st V.-Pres. Melvyn Birnbaum. Supports merit system; encourages recruitment of Jewish youth to government service; member of Coalition to Free Soviet Jews, NY Jewish Community Relations Council, NY Metropolitan Coordinating Council on Jewish Poverty, Jewish Labor Committee, America-Israel Friendship League. *Council Digest.*

INTERNATIONAL LEAGUE FOR THE REPATRIATION OF RUSSIAN JEWS, INC. (1963). 2 Fountain Lane, Suite 2J, Scarsdale, NY 10583. (914)683-3225. FAX: (914)683-3221. Pres. Morris Brafman; Chmn. James H. Rapp. Helped to bring the situation of Soviet Jews to world attention; catalyst for advocacy efforts, educational projects, and programs on behalf of Russian Jews in the former USSR, Israel, and U.S. Provides funds to help Russian Jewry in Israel and the former Soviet Union.

JEWISH COUNCIL FOR PUBLIC AFFAIRS (formerly NATIONAL JEWISH COMMUNITY RELATIONS ADVISORY COUNCIL) (1944). 116 E. 27 St., 10th fl., NYC 10016. (212)684-6950. FAX: (212)686-1353. E-mail: contactus@thejcpa.org. Chair Andrea Weinstein; Exec. Dir. Rabbi Steve Gutow. National coordinating body for the field of Jewish community relations, comprising 13 national and 122 local Jewish community-relations agencies. Promotes understanding of Israel and the Middle East; supports Jewish communities around the world; advocates for equality and pluralism, and against discrimination, in American society. Through the Council's work, its constituent organizations seek agreement on policies, strategies, and programs for effective utilization of their resources for common ends. *Insider (Weekly).* (WWW.JEWISHPUBLICAFFAIRS.ORG)

JEWISH LABOR COMMITTEE (1934). Atran Center for Jewish Culture, 25 E. 21 St.,

NYC 10010. (212)477-0707. FAX: (212) 477-1918. E-mail: JLCExec@aol.org. Pres. Stuart Appelbaum; Acting Dir. Rosalind Spigel. Serves as liaison between the Jewish community and the trade union movement; works with the U.S. and international labor movement to combat anti-Semitism, promote intergroup relations, and engender support for the State of Israel and Jews in and from the former Soviet Union; promotes teaching in public schools about the Holocaust and Jewish resistance; strengthens support within the Jewish community for the social goals and programs of the labor movement; supports Yiddish-language and cultural institutions. *Jewish Labor Committee Review; Issues Alert; Alumni Newsletter.* (WWW.JEWISHLABOR.ORG)

JEWISH PEACE FELLOWSHIP (1941). Box 271, Nyack, NY 10960. (914)358-4601. FAX: (914)358-4924. E-mail: jpf@forusa.org. Hon. Pres. Rabbi Philip Bentley; Ch. Murray Polner. Unites those who believe that Jewish ideals and experience provide inspiration for a nonviolent philosophy and way of life; offers draft counseling, especially for conscientious objection based on Jewish "religious training and belief"; encourages Jewish community to become more knowledgeable, concerned, and active in regard to the war/peace problem. *Shalom/Jewish Peace Letter.* (WWW.JEWISHPEACEFELLOWSHIP.ORG)

JEWISH WAR VETERANS OF THE UNITED STATES OF AMERICA (1896). 1811 R St., NW, Washington, DC 20009. (202)265-6280. FAX: (202)234-5662. E-mail: jwv@jwv.org. Natl. Exec. Dir. Herb Rosenbleeth; Natl. Commander Lawrence Shulman. Seeks to foster true allegiance to the United States; to combat bigotry and prevent defamation of Jews; to encourage the doctrine of universal liberty, equal rights, and full justice for all; to cooperate with and support existing educational institutions and establish new ones; to foster the education of ex-servicemen, ex-servicewomen, and members in the ideals and principles of Americanism. *Jewish Veteran.*

———, NATIONAL MUSEUM OF AMERICAN JEWISH MILITARY HISTORY (1958). 1811 R St., NW, Washington, DC 20009. E-mail: nmajmh@nmajmh.org. (202)265-6280. FAX: (202)234-5662. Pres. Edwin Goldwasser; Archivist Tom Wildenberg. Documents and preserves the contributions of Jewish Americans to the peace and freedom of the United States; educates the public concerning the courage, heroism, and sacrifices made by Jewish Americans who served in the armed forces; and works to combat anti-Semitism. *The Jewish War Veteran).*

NATIONAL ASSOCIATION OF JEWISH LEGISLATORS (1976). 65 Oakwood St., Albany, NY 12208. (518)527-3353. FAX: (518) 458-8512. E-mail: najl01@aol.com. Exec. Dir. Marc Hiller; Pres. Sen. Richard Cohen, Minn. state senator. A nonpartisan Jewish state legislative network focusing on domestic issues and publishing newsletters. Maintains close ties with the Knesset and Israeli leaders.

NCSJ: ADVOCATES ON BEHALF OF JEWS IN RUSSIA, UKRAINE, THE BALTIC STATES AND EURASIA (formerly AMERICAN JEWISH CONFERENCE ON SOVIET JEWRY) (1964; reorg. 1971). 2020 K. Street NW, Suite 7800, Washington, DC 200006. (202)898-2500. FAX: (202)898-0822. E-mail: ncsj@ncsj.org. N.Y. office: 823 United Nations Plaza, NYC 10017. (212)808-0295. Chmn. Edward Robin; Pres. Lesley Israel; Exec. Dir. Mark B. Levin. Coordinating agency for major national Jewish organizations and local community groups in the U.S., acting on behalf of Jews in the former Soviet Union (FSU); provides information about Jews in the FSU through public education and social action; reports and special pamphlets, special programs and projects, public meetings and forums. *Newswatch; annual report; action and program kits; Tekuma.* (WWW.NCSJ.ORG)

———, SOVIET JEWRY RESEARCH BUREAU. Chmn. Denis C. Braham; Pres. Howard E. Sachs. Organized by NCSJ to monitor emigration trends. Primary task is the accumulation, evaluation, and processing of information regarding Jews in the FSU, especially those who apply for emigration.

NATIONAL JEWISH DEMOCRATIC COUNCIL (1990). PO BOX 75308 Washington, DC 20013-5308. (202)216-9060. FAX: (202)216-9061. E-mail: info@njdc.org. Chmn. Michael Adler; Exec. Dir. Ira N. Forman. An independent organization committed to strengthening Jewish participation in the Democratic party primarily through grassroots activism. The national voice of Jewish Democrats, NJDC is dedicated to fighting the radical right and promoting Jewish values and interests in the Democratic party. (WWW.NJDC.ORG)

REPUBLICAN JEWISH COALITION (1985). 50 F Street, NW Suite 100, Washington, DC 20001. (202) 638-6688. FAX: (202)638-6694. E-mail: rjc@rjchq.org. Natl. Chmn. David M. Flaum; Exec. Dir. Matthew Brooks. Promotes involvement in Republican politics among its members; sensitizes Republican leaders to the concerns of the American Jewish community; promotes principles of free enterprise, a strong national defense, and an internationalist foreign policy. *RJC Bulletin.* (WWW.RJCHQ.ORG)

SECURE COMMUNITY NETWORK (2004). (212)284-6940. FAX: (212)284-6949. E-mail: scandesk@scnus.org. Chmn. Mark Broxmeyer; Chmn. Law Enforcement Advisory Comm.: Steven Pomerantz. A national body created by the Conference of Presidents, United Jewish Communities, and American Jewish Committee to inform and educate Jewish organizations so they can adopt and institute intelligent and fiscally prudent security policies, procedures, and tactics in the fight against terrorism. (WWW.SCNUS.ORG)

SHALEM CENTER (1994). 881 High Street, Suite 206. Worthington, OH 43085. (877)298-7300. FAX: (888)766-1506. E-mail: shalem@shalem.org.il. Pres. Yoram Hazony (Israel); Academic Director, Daniel Polisar (Israel). The purposes and activities of the Shalem Center are to increase public understanding and conduct educational and research activities on the improvement of Jewish national public life, and to develop a community of intellectual leaders to shape the state of Israel into a secure, free, and prosperous society. *Azure.* (WWW.SHALEM.ORG.IL/HEBREW)

SHALOM CENTER (1983). 6711 Lincoln Dr., Philadelphia, PA 19119. (215)844-8494. E-mail: office@shalomctr.org. (Part of Aleph Alliance for Jewish Renewal.) Pres. Rabbi Mordechai Liebling; Exec. Dir. Rabbi Arthur Waskow. National resource and organizing center for Jewish perspectives on dealing with overwork in American society, environmental dangers, unrestrained technology, militarism, and corporate irresponsibility. Initiated A.J. Heschel 25th Yahrzeit observance. Trains next generation of *tikkun olam* activists. Holds colloquia on issues like environmental causes of cancer. *New Menorah.* (WWW.SHALOMCTR.ORG)

UN WATCH (1993). 1, rue de Varembé, PO Box 191, 1211 Geneva 20, Switzerland. (41-22)734.14.72. FAX: (41-22)734.16.13. E-mail: office@unwatch.org. Exec. Dir. Hillel Neuer; Chm. Amb. Alfred H. Moses. An affiliate of AJC, UN Watch measures UN performance by the yardstick of the UN's Charter; advocates the non-discriminatory application of the Charter; opposes the use of UN fora to attack Israel and promote anti-Semitism; and seeks to institutionalize at the UN the fight against worldwide anti-Semitism. *UN Watch.Briefing* (WWW.UNWATCH.ORG)

UCSJ: UNION OF COUNCILS FOR JEWS IN THE FORMER SOVIET UNION (formerly UNION OF COUNCILS FOR SOVIET JEWS) (1970). 1819 H St., NW, Suite 230, Washington, DC 20005. (202)775-9770. FAX: (202)775-9776. E-mail: ucsj@ucsj.com. Pres. Yosef I. Abramowitz; Natl. Dir. Micah H. Naftalin. Devoted to promoting religious liberty, freedom of emigration, and security for Jews in the FSU (former Soviet Union) through advocacy and monitoring of anti-Semitism, neo-facism, human rights, rule of law, and democracy. Offers educational, cultural, medical, and humanitarian aid through the Yad L'Yad partnership program pairing Jewish communities in the US and the FSU; advocates for refuseniks and political prisoner. (WWW.FSUMONITOR.COM)

WORLD CONGRESS OF GAY, LESBIAN, BISEXUAL & TRANSGENDER JEWS (1980). 8 Letitia St., Philadelphia, PA 19106-3050. (609)396-1972. FAX: (215)873-0108. E-mail: president@wcgljo.org. Pres. David Gellman (San Francisco, CA); V.-Pres Luis Perelman (Mexico City, Mexico). Supports, strengthens, and represents over 67 Jewish gay and lesbian organizations across the globe and the needs of gay and lesbian Jews generally. Challenges homophobia and sexism within the Jewish community and responds to anti-Semitism at large. Sponsors regional and international conferences. *The Digest.* (WWW.GLBTJEWS.ORG)

WORLD JEWISH CONGRESS (1936; org. in U.S. 1939). PO Box 90400, Washington DC, 20090. (212) 755-5770. FAX: (212) 755-5883. Pres. Ronald S. Lauder; Bd. Chmn. Matthew Bronfman. Seeks to intensify bonds of world Jewry with Israel; to strengthen solidarity among Jews everywhere and secure their rights, status, and interests as individuals and communities; to encourage Jewish social, religious, and cultural life throughout the world and coordinate efforts by Jewish communities and organizations to cope with any Jewish problem; to work for human rights generally. Represents its affiliated organizations-most representative bodies of Jewish communities in more than 80 countries and 35 national organizations in American section-at UN, OAS, UNESCO, Council of Europe, ILO, UNICEF, and other governmental, intergovernmental, and international authorities. *WJC Report; Boletin Informativo OJI; Dialogues; Dateline: World Jewry; Coloquio; Batfutsot; Gesher.* (WWW.WORLDJEWISHCONGRESS.ORG)

CULTURAL

AMERICAN ACADEMY FOR JEWISH RESEARCH (1929). 420 Walnut Street, Philadelphia, PA 19106. (215)238-1290. FAX: (215)238-1540. Pres. Robert Chazan. Encourages Jewish learning and research; holds annual or semiannual meeting; awards grants for the publication of scholarly works.

AMERICAN GATHERING OF JEWISH HOLOCAUST SURVIVORS. 122 W. 30 St., #205. NYC 10001. (212)239-4230. FAX: (212) 279-2926. E-mail: mail@americangathering.org. Pres. Sam E. Bloch. Dedicated to documenting the past and passing on a legacy of remembrance. Compiles the National Registry of Jewish Holocaust Survivors-to date, the records of more than 165,000 survivors and their families-housed at the U.S. Holocaust Memorial Museum in Washington, DC; holds an annual Yom Hashoah commemoration and occasional international gatherings; sponsors an intensive summer program for U.S. teachers in Poland and Israel to prepare them to teach about the Holocaust. *Together (newspaper).*

AMERICAN GUILD OF JUDAIC ART (1991). 15 Greenspring Valley Rd., Owings Mills, MD 21117. (410)902-0411. FAX: (410)581-0108. E-mail: office@jewishart.org. Pres. David Klass; 1st V.-Pres. Richard McBee. A not-for-profit membership organization for those with interests in the Judaic arts, including artists, galleries, collectors & retailers of Judaica, writers, educators, appraisers, museum curators, conservators, lecturers, and others personally or professionally involved in the field. Helps to promote members' art. *Hiddur (quarterly); Update (members' networking newsletter).* (WWW.JEWISHART.ORG)

AMERICAN JEWISH HISTORICAL SOCIETY (1892). 15 W. 16 St., NYC 10011. (212)294-6160. FAX: (212)294-6161. E-mail: ajhs@ajhs.cjh.org. Chmn. David Solomon; Pres./CEO Sidney Lapidus. Collects, catalogues, publishes, and displays material on the history of the Jews in America; serves as an information center for inquiries on American Jewish history; maintains archives of original source material on American Jewish history; sponsors lectures and exhibitions; makes available audiovisual material. *American Jewish History; Heritage.* (WWW.AJHS.ORG)

AMERICAN JEWISH PRESS ASSOCIATION (1944). Natl. Admin. Off.: 1828 L St. NW, Suite 720, Washington, DC 20036. (202)785-2282. FAX: (202)785-2307. E-mail: toby@ajpa.org. Pres. Aaron Cohen; Exec. Dir. Toby Dershowitz. Seeks the advancement of Jewish journalism and the maintenance of a strong Jewish press in the U.S. and Canada; encourages the attainment of the highest editorial and business standards; sponsors workshops, services for members; sponsors annual competition for Simon Rockower Awards for excellence in Jewish journalism. *Membership bulletin newsletter.*

AMERICAN SEPHARDI FEDERATION (1973). 15 W. 16 St., 6th Floor, NYC 10011. (212)294-8350. FAX: (212)294-8348. E-mail: asf@cjh.org. Pres. David E.R. Dangoor; Exec. Dir. Lynne M. Winters. The central voice of the American Sephardic community, representing a broad spectrum of Sephardic organizations, congregations, and educational institutions. Seeks to strengthen and unify the community through education, communication, advocacy, and leadership development, creating greater awareness and appreciation of its rich and unique history and culture.

Sephardic Today. (WWW.AMERICANSE-FARDIFEDERATION.ORG)

AMERICAN SOCIETY FOR JEWISH MUSIC (1974). c/o The Center for Jewish History, 15 W. 16 St., NYC 10011. (212)294-8328. FAX: (212)294-6161. Pres. Michael Leavitt; V.-Pres. Judith Tischler & Martha Novick; Sec. Fortuna Calvo Roth; Bd. Chmn. Rabbi Henry D. Michelman; Treas. Cantor Nathaniel Benjamin. Promotes the knowledge, appreciation, and development of Jewish music, past and present, for professional and lay audiences; seeks to raise the standards of composition and performance in Jewish music, to encourage research, and to sponsor performances of new and rarely heard works. *Musica Judaica Journal.*

ASSOCIATION OF JEWISH BOOK PUBLISHERS (1962). c/o Jewish Book Council, 15 East 26th Street, 10th Floor, New York, NY 10010. (212)532-4949. FAX: (212)481-4174. Email: arjhill@jewishbooks.com. Pres. Ellen Frankel. As a nonprofit group, provides a forum for discussion of mutual areas of interest among Jewish publishers, and promotes cooperative exhibits and promotional opportunities for members. Membership fee is $85 annually per publishing house.

ASSOCIATION OF JEWISH LIBRARIES (1965). 15 E. 26 St.,10th fl, NYC 10010. (212)725-5359. FAX: (212)481-4174. E-mail: ajl@jewishbooks.org. Pres. Pearl Berger; V.-Pres. Ronda Rose. Seeks to promote and improve services and professional standards in Jewish libraries; disseminates Jewish library information and guidance; promotes publication of literature in the field; encourages the establishment of Jewish libraries and collections of Judaica and the choice of Judaica librarianship as a profession; cocertifies Jewish libraries. *AJL Newsletter; Judaica Librarianship.*

B'NAI B'RITH KLUTZNICK NATIONAL JEWISH MUSEUM (1957). 1640 Rhode Island Ave., NW, Washington, DC 20036. (202)857-6583. FAX: (202)857-1099. A center of Jewish art and history in the nation's capital, maintains temporary and permanent exhibition galleries, permanent collection of Jewish ceremonial objects, folk art, and contemporary fine art, outdoor sculpture garden and museum shop, as well as the American Jewish Sports Hall of Fame. Provides exhibitions, tours, educational programs, research assistance, and tourist information. *Permanent collection catalogue; temporary exhibit catalogues.*

CENTRAL YIDDISH CULTURE ORGANIZATION (CYCO), INC. (1943 incorporated) (1948-non profit status). 25 E. 21 St., 3rd fl., NYC 10010. (212) 505-8305. FAX: (212)505-8044. E-mail: cycobooks@earthlink.net. Pres. Dr. Barnett Zumoff; Exec. Officer Hy Wolfe. To promote the Yiddish word that is Cyco's purpose. We do this through the promotion, publication and distribution of Yiddish books, music books, CDs, tapes and albums. All in Yiddish!

CONFERENCE ON JEWISH SOCIAL STUDIES, INC. (formerly CONFERENCE ON JEWISH RELATIONS, INC.) (1939). Bldg. 240, Rm. 103. Program in Jewish Studies, Stanford University, Stanford, CA 94305-2190. (650)725-0829. FAX:(650)725-2920. E-mail: jss@leland.stanford.edu. Pres. Steven J. Zipperstein; V.-Pres. Aron Rodrigue. *Jewish Social Studies.*

CONGREGATION BINA (1981). 600 W. End Ave., Suite 1-C, NYC 10024. (212)873-4261. E-mail: samueldivekar@hotmail .com. Pres. Joseph Moses; Exec. V.-Pres. Moses Samson; Hon. Pres. Samuel M. Daniel; Sec. Gen. Elijah E. Jhirad. Serves the religious, cultural, charitable, and philanthropic needs of the Children of Israel who originated in India and now reside in the U.S. Works to foster and preserve the ancient traditions, customs, liturgy, music, and folklore of Indian Jewry and to maintain needed institutions. *Kol Bina.*

CONGRESS FOR JEWISH CULTURE (1948). 25 E. 21 St., NYC 10010. (212)505-8040. FAX: (212)505-8044. E-mail: kongres@earthlink.net. Exec. Dir. Shane Baker. Congress for Jewish Culture administers the book store CYCO and publishes the world's oldest Yiddish journal, *The Zukunft*. Currently producing a two volume anthology of Yiddish literature in America. Activities include yearly memorials for the Warsaw ghetto uprising and the murdered Soviet Yiddish writers, also readings and literary afternoons. *The Zukunft; Bulletin: In the World of Yiddish.*

ELAINE KAUFMAN CULTURAL CENTER (1952). 129 W. 67 St., NYC 10023.

(212)501-3303. FAX: (212)874-7865. Email: lhard@ekcc.org. Hon. Chmn. Leonard Goodman; Chmn. Phyllis Feder; Pres. Bethany Millard; Exec. Dir. Lydia Kontos. Offers instruction in its Lucy Moses School for Music and Dance in music, dance, art, and theater to children and adults, in Western culture and Jewish traditions. Presents frequent performances of Jewish and general music by leading artists and ensembles in its Merkin Concert Hall and Ann Goodman Recital Hall. The Birnbaum Music Library houses Jewish music scores and reference books. *In Harmony (quarterly newsletter); EKCC Events (bimonthly calendar); Bimonthly concert calendars; catalogues and brochures.* (WWW.EKCC.ORG)

FOUNDATION FOR JEWISH CULTURE (1960). 330 Seventh Ave., 21st fl., NYC 10001. (212)629-0500. FAX: (212)629-0508. E-mail: nfjc@jewishculture.org. Pres. Carol B. Spinner; Exec. Dir. Elise Bernhardt. The leading Jewish organization devoted to promoting Jewish culture in the U.S. Manages the Jewish Endowment for the Arts and Humanities; administers the Council of American Jewish Museums and Council of Archives and Research Libraries in Jewish Studies; offers doctoral dissertation fellowships, new play commissions, and grants for documentary films, recording of Jewish music, contemporary choregraphy, fiction and nonfiction writing, and cultural preservation; coordinates community cultural residencies, local cultural councils, and national cultural consortia; sponsors conferences, symposia, and festivals in the arts and humanities. *Jewish Culture News; Culture Currents (electronic).*

HOLOCAUST CENTER OF THE UNITED JEWISH FEDERATION OF GREATER PITTSBURGH (1980). 5738 Darlington Rd., Pittsburgh, PA 15217. (412)421-1500. FAX: (412)422-1996. E-mail: lhurwitz@ujf.net. Pres. Holocaust Comm. Chair Dr. Barbara Burstin; UJF. Ch. James A. Rudolph; Dir. Linda F. Hurwitz. Develops programs and provides resources to further understanding of the Holocaust and its impact on civilization. Maintains a library, archive; provides speakers, educational materials; organizes community programs. Published collection of survivor and liberator stories. (WWW.UJFHC.NET)

HOLOCAUST MEMORIAL CENTER (1984). 28123 Orchard Lake Rd., Farmington Hills, MI 48334. (248)553-2400. FAX: (248)553-2433. E-mail: info@holocaust-center.org. Founder & Dir. Rabbi Charles Rosenzveig. America's first free-standing Holocaust center comprising a museum, library-archive, oral history collection, garden of the righteous, research institute and academic advisory committee. Provides tours, lecture series, teacher training, Yom Hashoah commemorations, exhibits, educational outreach programs, speakers' bureau, computer database on 1,200 destroyed Jewish communities, guided travel tours to concentration camps and Israel, and museum shop. Published *World Reacts to the Holocaust; Survey of U.S. Federal, U.S. State and Canadian Provincial Support forHolocaust Education, Newsletter.*

HOLOCAUST MEMORIAL RESOURCE & EDUCATION CENTER OF CENTRAL FLORIDA (1982). 851 N. Maitland Ave., Maitland, FL 32751. (407)628-0555. FAX: (407)628-1079. E-mail: execdir@holocaustedu.org. Pres. Stan Sujka, MD; Bd. Chmn. Tess Wise. An interfaith educational center devoted to teaching the lessons of the Holocaust. Houses permanent multimedia educational exhibit; maintains library of books, videotapes, films, and other visuals to serve the entire educational establishment; offers lectures, teacher training, and other activities. *Newsletter; Bibliography; "Holocaust-Lessons for Tomorrow"; elementary and middle school curriculum.*

HOLOCAUST MUSEUM AND LEARNING CENTER IN MEMORY OF GLORIA GOLDSTEIN (1995) (formerly ST. LOUIS CENTER FOR HOLOCAUST STUDIES) (1977). 12 Millstone Campus Dr., St. Louis, MO 63146. (314)432-0020. FAX: (314)432-1277. E-mail: dreich@jfedstl.org. Chmn. Richard W. Stein; Curator/Dir. Of Ed. Dan A. Reich; Exec. Dir. Barbara Raznick; Dir. Of Admin. & Dev. Brian Bray. Develops programs and provides resources and educational materials to further an understanding of the Holocaust and its impact on civilization; has a 5,000 sq. ft. museum containing photographs, artifacts, and audiovisual displays. *Newsletter.*

INTERNATIONAL ASSOCIATION OF JEWISH GENEALOGICAL SOCIETIES (1988). 4430 Mt. Paran Pkwy NW, Atlanta, GA

30327-3747. (404)261-8662. Fax: (404)228-7125. E-mail: homargol@aol.com. Pres. Anne Feder Lee. Umbrella organization of more than 70 Jewish Genealogical Societies (JGS) worldwide. Represents organized Jewish genealogy, encourages Jews to research their family history, promotes new JGSs, supports existing societies, implements projects of interest to individuals researching their Jewish family histories. Holds annual conference where members learn and exchange ideas. (WWW.IAJGS.ORG)

INTERNATIONAL JEWISH MEDIA ASSOCIATION (1987). U.S.: c/o St. Louis Jewish Light, 12 Millstone Campus Dr., St. Louis, MO 63146. (314)432-3353. FAX: (314)432-0515. E-mail: stlouislgt@aol.com and ajpamr@aol.com. Israel: PO Box 92, Jerusalem 91920. 02-202-222. FAX: 02-513-642. Pres. Robert A. Cohn (c/o St. Louis Jewish Light); Exec. Dir. Toby Dershowitz. 1828 L St. NW, Suite 402, Washington, DC 20036. (202)785-2282. FAX: (202)785-2307. E-mail: toby@dershowitz.com. Israel Liaisons Jacob Gispan & Lifsha Ben-Shach, WZO Dept. of Info. A worldwide network of Jewish journalists, publications and other media in the Jewish and general media, which seeks to provide a forum for the exchange of materials and ideas and to enhance the status of Jewish media and journalists throughout the world. *IJMA Newsletter; Proceedings of the International Conference on Jewish Media.*

INTERNATIONAL NETWORK OF CHILDREN OF JEWISH HOLOCAUST SURVIVORS, INC. (1981). 13899 Biscayne Blvd. Suite 404, N. Miami, FL 33181. (305)919-5690. FAX: (305)919-5691. E-mail: info@hdec.org. Pres. Rositta E. Kenigsberg; Founding Chmn. Menachem Z. Rosensaft. Links Second Generation groups and individuals throughout the world. Represents the shared interests of children of Holocaust survivors; aims to perpetuate the authentic memory of the Holocaust and prevent its recurrence, to strengthen and preserve the Jewish spiritual, ideological, and cultural heritage, to fight anti-Semitism and all forms of discrimination, persecution, and oppression anywhere in the world.

JACOB RADER MARCUS CENTER OF THE AMERICAN JEWISH ARCHIVES (1947). 3101 Clifton Ave., Cincinnati, OH 45220. (513)221-1875 ext. 403. FAX: (513)221-7812. E-mail: aja@cn.huc.edu. Exec. Dir. Dr. Gary P. Zola. Promotes the study and preservation of the Western Hemisphere Jewish experience through research, publications, collection of important source materials, and a vigorous public-outreach program. *American Jewish Archives Journal, Monographs, Pamphlets, booklets, educational materials and posters.*

JEWISH AMERICAN SOCIETY FOR HISTORIC PRESERVATION (1997). 16405 Equestrian Lane, Rockville, MD 20855. (301)977-3637. FAX: (301)977-3888. E-mail: jashp1@msn.com. Pres. Jerry Klinger. Identifies and publicizes sites of American Jewish historical interest; in cooperation with local historical societies and houses of worship, promotes programs to stress the commonality of the American experience. (WWW.JASHP.ORG)

JEWISH BOOK COUNCIL (1946; reorg. 1993). 520 8th Avenue, 4th Floor New York, NY10018. (212)201-2920. E-mail: jbc@jewishbooks.org. Pres. Lawrence J. Krule; Bd. Chmn. Henry Everett; Exec. Dir. Carolyn Starman Hessel. Serves as literary arm of the American Jewish community and clearinghouse for Jewish-content literature; assists readers, writers, publishers, and those who market and sell products. Provides bibliographies, list of publishers, bookstores, book fairs. Sponsors National Jewish Book Awards, Jewish Book Month, Jewish Book Fair Network. *Jewish Book Annual; Jewish Book World.* (WWW.JEWISHBOOKCOUNCIL.ORG)

JEWISH FEDERATION'S LOS ANGELES MUSEUM OF THE HOLOCAUST (MARTYRS MEMORIAL) (org. mid-1960s; opened 1978). 6006 Wilshire Blvd., Los Angeles, CA 90036. (323)761-8170. FAX: (323)761-8174. E-mail: museumiemp@jewishla.org. Chmn. Gary John Schiller; Director Rachel L. Jayoela. A photo-narrative museum and resource center dedicated to Holocaust history, issues of genocide and prejudice, curriculum development, teacher training, research and exhibitions. *PAGES, a newslettr; Those Who Dared; Rescuers and Rescued; Guide to Schindler's List; Anne Frank: A Teaching.*

JEWISH HERITAGE PROJECT (1981). 150 Franklin St., #1W, NYC 10013. (212)925-9067. E-mail: jhpffh@jps.net. Exec. Dir.

Alan Adelson. Strives to bring to the broadest possible audience authentic works of literary and historical value relating to Jewish history and culture. With funding from the National Endowment of the Arts, Jewish Heritage runs the National Initiative in the Literature of the Holocaust. Not a grant giving organization. Distributor of the film *Lodz Ghetto,* which it developed, as well as its companion volume *Lodz Ghetto: Inside a Community Under Siege; Better Than Gold: An Immigrant Family's First Years in Brooklyn.*

JEWISH MUSEUM (1904, under auspices of Jewish Theological Seminary). 1109 Fifth Ave., NYC 10128. (212)423-3200. FAX: (212)423-3232. Dir. Joan H. Rosenbaum; Bd. Chmn. Robert J. Hurst. Expanded museum features permanent exhibition on the Jewish experience. Repository of the largest collection of Jewish related paintings, prints, photographs, sculpture, coins, medals, antiquities, textiles, and other decorative arts-in the Western Hemisphere. Includes the National Jewish Archive of Broadcasting. Tours, lectures, film showings, and concerts; special programs for children; cafe; shop. *Special exhibition catalogues; annual report.* (WWW.THEJEWISHMUSEUM.ORG)

JEWISH PUBLICATION SOCIETY (1888). 2100 Arch St., 2nd fl., Philadelphia, PA 19103. (215)832-0600. FAX: (215)568-2017. E-mail: jewishbook@jewishpub.org. Pres. Allan R. Frank; CEO/Ed.-in-Chief Dr. Ellen Frankel. Publishes and disseminates books of Jewish interest for adults and children; titles include TANAKH, religious studies and practices, life cycle, folklore, classics, art, history. *Booklink JPS Catalogue.* (WWW.JEWISHPUB.ORG)

JUDAH L. MAGNES MUSEUM-JEWISH MUSEUM OF THE WEST (1962). 2911 Russell St., Berkeley, CA 94705. (510)549-6950. FAX: (510)849-3673. E-mail: pfpr@magnesmuseum.org. Pres. Fred Weiss; Dir. Susan Morris. Collects, preserves, and makes available Jewish art, culture, history, and literature from throughout the world. Permanent collections of fine and ceremonial art; rare Judaica library, Western Jewish History Center (archives), Jewish-American Hall of Fame. Changing exhibits, traveling exhibits, docent tours, lectures, numismatics series, poetry and video awards, museum shop. *Magnes News; special exhibition catalogues; scholarly books.*

JUDAICA CAPTIONED FILM CENTER, INC. (1983). PO Box 21439, Baltimore, MD 21282-1439. Voice Relay Service (1-800)735-2258; TDD (410)655-6767. E-mail: lweiner@jhucep.org. Pres. Lois Lilienfeld Weiner. Developing a comprehensive library of captioned and subtitled films and tapes on Jewish subjects; distributes them to organizations serving the hearing-impaired, including mainstream classes and senior adult groups, on a free-loan, handling/shipping-charge-only basis. *Newsletter.*

JUDAICA INSTITUTE OF AMERICA (2007). 3907 Fordham Dr., Baltimore, MD 21215. (443)621-3584. FAX: (925)892-7381. E-mail: info@judin.org. Pres Ronald J. Schwartz. A nondenominational arts-education initiative that promotes Jewish heritage, literature, identity, and visual culture; supports scholarly research in Judaica. (WWW.JUDIN.ORG)

LEAGUE FOR YIDDISH, INC. (1979). 200 W. 72 St., Suite 40, NYC 10023. (212)787-6675. E-mail: mschaecht@aol.com. Pres. Dr. Zuni Zelitch. Encourages the development and use of Yiddish as a living language; promotes its modernization and standardization; publisher of Yiddish textbooks and English-Yiddish dictionaries; most recent book *The Standardized Yiddish Orthography; Afn Shvel (quarterly).* (WWW.METALAB.UNC.EDU/YIDDISH/YIDLEAGUE)

LEO BAECK INSTITUTE, INC. (1955). 15 W. 16 St., NYC 10011-6301. (212)744-6400. FAX: (212)988-1305. E-mail: lbaeck@lbi.cjh.org. Pres. Ismar Schorsch; Exec. Dir. Carol Kahn Strauss. A research, study, and lecture center, museum, library, and archive relating to the history of German-speaking Jewry. Offers lectures, exhibits, faculty seminars; publishes a series of monographs, yearbooks, and journals. *LBI News; LBI Yearbook; LBI Memorial Lecture; occasional papers.* (WWW.LBI.ORG)

LIVING TRADITIONS (1994), (c/o WORKMAN'S CIRCLE) 45 East 33rd Street, New York, NY 10016. (212)532-8202. E-mail: info@livingtraditions.org. Pres. Henry Sapoznik; V.-Pres. Sherry Mayrent. Nonprofit membership organization dedicated to the study, preservation, and innovative continuity of traditional folk and popular culture through workshops, concerts, recordings, radio and film documentaries; clearinghouse for research in klezmer and other traditional music; sponsors yearly weeklong international cultural event, "Yiddish Folk Arts Program/'KlezKamp.'" *Living Traditions* (newsletter). (WWW.LIVINGTRADITIONS.ORG)

MARTIN BUBER INSTITUTE (1990), 203 Rocking Stone Ave., Larchmont, NY 10538. (914)833-7731. E-mail: HM64@columbia.edu. Hon. Chmn. Prof. Maurice Friedman; Pres. Dr. Hune Margulies. Sponsors seminars, workshops, conferences, and publications to encourage the exchange of ideas about the life and thought of Buber. *Martin Buber Review (annual).*

MEMORIAL FOUNDATION FOR JEWISH CULTURE, INC. (1964). 50 West Broadway, 34th Floor, NYC 10004. (212)425-6606. FAX: (212)425-6602. Pres. Prof. Anita Shapira; Exec. V.-Pres. Jerry Hochbaum. Through the grants that it awards, encourages Jewish scholarship, culture, and education; supports communities that are struggling to maintain Jewish life; assists professional training for careers in communal service in Jewishly deprived communities; and stimulates the documentation, commemoration, and teaching of the Holocaust. (WWW.MFJC.ORG)

MUSEUM OF JEWISH HERITAGE—A LIVING MEMORIAL TO THE HOLOCAUST (1984). 36 Battery Park Plaza, NYC 10004-1484. (212)968-1800. FAX: (212)968-1368. Bd. Chmn. Robert M. Morgenthau; Museum Pres. Dr. Alfred Gottschalk; Museum Dir. David Marwell. New York tri-state's principal institution for educating people of all ages and backgrounds about 20th-century Jewish history and the Holocaust. Repository of Steven Spielberg's Survivors of the Shoah Visual History Foundation videotaped testimonies. Core and special exhibitions. *18 First Place (newsletter); Holocaust bibliography; educational materials.* (WWW.MJHNYC.ORG)

MUSEUM OF TOLERANCE OF THE SIMON WIESENTHAL CENTER (1993). 9786 W. Pico Blvd., Los Angeles, CA 90035-4792. (310)553-8403. FAX: (310)553-4521. E-mail: avra@wiesenthal.com. Dean-Founder Rabbi Marvin Hier; Assoc. Dean Rabbi Abraham Cooper; Exec. Dir. Rabbi Meyer May. A unique experiential museum focusing on personal prejudice, group intolerance, struggle for civil rights, and 20th-century genocides, culminating in a major exhibition on the Holocaust. Archives, Multimedia Learning Center designed for individualized research, 6,700-square-foot temporary exhibit space, 324-seat theater, 150-seat auditorium, and outdoor memorial plaza. (WWW.WIESENTHAL.COM)

NATIONAL MUSEUM OF AMERICAN JEWISH HISTORY (1976). Independence Mall E. 55 N. Fifth St. Philadelphia, PA 19106-2197. (215) 923-3811. FAX: (215) 923-0763. E-mail: nmajh@nmajh.org. Dir./CEO Gwen Goodman. The only museum in the nation to offer education, exhibits, and programs dedicated to preserving the history and culture of the Jewish people in America; located across from the Liberty Bell. (WWW.NMAJH.ORG)

NATIONAL MUSEUM OF AMERICAN JEWISH MILITARY HISTORY (*see* JEWISH WAR VETERANS OF THE U.S.A.)

NATIONAL YIDDISH BOOK CENTER (1980). 1021 West St., Amherst, MA 01002. (413)256-4900. FAX: (413)256-4700. E-mail: yiddish@bikher.org. Pres. Aaron Lansky; V.-Pres. Nancy Sherman. Since 1980 the center has collected 1.5 million Yiddish books for distribution to readers and libraries worldwide; digitized more than 12,000 Yiddish titles, offered a range of educational programs in Yiddish and modern culture, and published *Pakn Treger,* an award-winning English-language magazine. (WWW.YIDDISHBOOKCENTER.ORG)

ORTHODOX JEWISH ARCHIVES (1978). 42 Broadway, New York, NY 10004. (212)797-9000, ext. 73. FAX: (212)269-2843. Exec. V-Pres. Rabbi Shmuel Bloom & Shlomo Gertzullin; Dir. Rabbi Moshe Kolodny. Founded by Agudath Israel of America; houses historical documents, photographs, periodicals, and other publications relating to the growth of Orthodox Jewry in the U.S. and related communities in Europe, Israel, and elsewhere. Particularly noteworthy are its holdings relating to rescue activities organized during the Holocaust and its traveling exhibits available to schools and other institutions.

RESEARCH FOUNDATION FOR JEWISH IMMIGRATION, INC. (1971). 570 Seventh Ave., NYC 10018. (212)921-3871. FAX:

(212)575-1918. Sec./Coord. of Research Herbert A. Strauss; Archivist Dennis E. Rohrbaugh. Studies and records the history of the migration and acculturation of Central European German-speaking Jewish and non-Jewish Nazi persecutees in various resettlement countries worldwide, with special emphasis on the American experience. *International Biographical Dictionary of Central European Emigrés, 1933-1945; Jewish Immigrants of the Nazi Period in the USA.*

SEPHARDIC EDUCATIONAL CENTER (1979). 10808 Santa Monica Blvd., Los Angeles, CA 90025. (310)441-9361. FAX: (310)441-9561. E-mail: newyork@secjerusalem.org. Founder & Chmn. Jose A. Nessim, M.D. Has chapters in the U.S., North, Central, and South America, Europe, and Asia, a spiritual and educational center in the Old City of Jerusalem, and executive office in Los Angeles. Serves as a meeting ground for Sephardim from many nations; sponsors the first worldwide movement for Sephardic youth and young adults. Disseminates information about Sephardic Jewry in the form of motion pictures, pamphlets, and books, which it produces. *Hamerkaz (quarterly bulletin in English).* (WWW.SECJERUSALEM.ORG)

SEPHARDIC HOUSE-THE CULTURAL DIVISION OF ASF (1978). 15 West 16th Street, NYC 10011. (212)294-6170. FAX: (212)294-6149. E-mail: sephardichouse@cjh.org. Pres. Morrie R.Yohai; Dir. Dr. Janice E. Ovadiah. A cultural organization dedicated to fostering Sephardic history and culture; sponsors a wide variety of classes and public programs, film festivals, publication program disseminates materials of Sephardic value; outreach program to communities outside of the New York area; program bureau provides program ideas, speakers, and entertainers; International Sephardic Film Festival every year. *Sephardic House Newsletter; Publication Catalogue.* (WWW. SEPHARDICHOUSE.ORG)

SIMON WIESENTHAL CENTER (1977). 1399 South Roxbury Drive., Los Angeles, CA 90035-4701. (310)553-9036. FAX: (310)553-4521. Email: avra@wiesenthal.com. Dean-Founder Rabbi Marvin Hier; Assoc. Dean Rabbi Abraham Cooper; Exec. Dir. Rabbi Meyer May. Regional offices in New York, Miami, Toronto, Paris, Jerusalem, Buenos Aires. The largest institution of its kind in N. America dedicated to the study of the Holocaust, its contemporary implications, and related human-rights issues through education and awareness. Incorporates 185,000-sq.-ft. Museum of Tolerance, library, media department, archives, "Testimony to the Truth" oral histories, educational outreach, research department, international social action. *Response Magazine.* (WWW.WIESENTHAL.COM)

SKIRBALL CULTURAL CENTER (1996), an affiliate of Hebrew Union College. 2701 N. Sepulveda Blvd., Los Angeles, CA 90049. (310)440-4500. FAX: (310)440-4595. Pres. & CEO Uri D. Herscher; Bd. Chmn. Howard Friedman. Dedicated to exploring the connections between four thousand years of Jewish heritage and the vitality of American democratic ideals. It welcomes and seeks to inspire people of every ethnic and cultural identity. Guided by our respective memories and experiences, together we aspire to build a society in which all of us can feel at home. Skirball Cultural Center achieves its mission through pubic programs that explore literary, visual, and performing arts from around the world; through the display and interpretation of its permanent collections and changing exhibitions; through scholarship in American Jewish history and related publications; and through outreach to the community.. (WWW.SKIRBALL.ORG)

SOCIETY FOR THE HISTORY OF CZECHOSLOVAK JEWS, INC. (1961). 760 Pompton Ave., Cedar Grove, NJ 07009. (973)239-2333. FAX: (973)239-7935. Pres. Rabbi Norman Patz; V.-Pres. Prof. Fred Hahn; Sec. Anita Grosz. Studies the history of Czechoslovak Jews; collects material and disseminates information through the publication of books and pamphlets; conducts annual memorial service for Czech Holocaust victims. *The Jews of Czechoslovakia (3 vols.); Review I-VI.*

SOCIETY OF FRIENDS OF TOURO SYNAGOGUE NATIONAL HISTORIC SITE, INC. (1948). 85 Touro St., Newport, RI 02840. (401)847-4794. FAX: (401)845-6790. E-mail: info@tourosynagogue.org. Pres. M. Bernard Aidinoff; Exec. Dir. Michael L. Balaban. Helps maintain Touro Synagogue as a national historic site, opening and interpreting it for visitors; promotes public awareness of its preeminent role in the tradition of American religious liberty; annually commemorates George Washington's letter of 1790 to the Hebrew Congregation of Newport. *Society Update.*

———, TOURO NATIONAL HERITAGE TRUST (1984). 85 Touro St., Newport, RI 02840. (401)847-0810. FAX (401)847-8121. Pres. Bernard Bell; Chmn. Benjamin D. Holloway. Works to establish national education center within Touro compound; sponsors Touro Fellow through John Carter Brown Library; presents seminars and other educational programs; promotes knowledge of the early Jewish experience in this country.

SPERTUS MUSEUM, SPERTUS INSTITUTE OF JEWISH STUDIES (1968). 618 S. Michigan Ave., Chicago, IL 60605. (312)322-1747. FAX: (312)922-6406. Pres. Spertus Institute of Jewish Studies, Dr. Howard A. Sulkin. The largest, most comprehensive Judaic museum in the Midwest with 12,000 square feet of exhibit space and a permanent collection of some 10,000 works reflecting 5,000 years of Jewish history and culture. Also includes the redesigned Zell Holocaust Memorial, permanent collection, changing visual arts and special exhibits, and the children's ARTIFACT Center for a hands-on archaeological adventure. Plus, traveling exhibits for Jewish educators, life-cycle workshops, ADA accessible. *Exhibition catalogues; educational pamphlets.*

______, ASHER LIBRARY, SPERTUS INSTITUTE OF JEWISH STUDIES (approx. 1930), 618 S. Michigan Ave., Chicago, IL 60605. (312) 322-1749, FAX (312) 922-6406. Pres. Spertus Institute of Jewish Studeis, Dr. Howard A. Sulkin; Director, Asher Library, Glenn Ferdman. Asher Library is the largest public Jewish Library in the Midwest, with over 100, 000 books and 550 periodicals; extensive collections of music, art, rare books, maps and electronic resources; nearly 1,000 feature and documentary films available on video cassette. Online catalogue access available. Also, the Chicago Jewish Archives collects historical material of Chicago individuals, families, synagogues and organizations. *ADA accessible.*

SURVIVORS OF THE SHOAH VISUAL HISTORY FOUNDATION (1994). PO Box 3168, Los Angeles, CA 90078-3168. (818)777-7802. FAX: (818)866-0312. Exec. Dir. Ari C. Zev. A nonprofit organization, founded and chaired by Steven Spielberg, dedicated to videotaping and preserving interviews with Holocaust survivors throughout the world. The archive of testimonies will be used as a tool for global education about the Holocaust and to teach racial, ethnic, and cultural tolerance.

UNITED STATES HOLOCAUST MEMORIAL MUSEUM (1980; opened Apr. 1993). 100 Raoul Wallenberg Place, SW, Washington, DC 20024. (202)488-0400. FAX: (202)488-2690. Chmn. Fred S. Zeidman; Dir. Sara J. Bloomfeld. Federally chartered and privately built, its mission is to teach about the Nazi persecution and murder of six million Jews and millions of others from 1933 to 1945 and to inspire visitors to contemplate their moral responsibilities as citizens of a democratic nation. Opened in April 1993 near the national Mall in Washington, DC, the museum's permanent exhibition tells the story of the Holocaust through authentic artifacts, videotaped oral testimonies, documentary film, and historical photographs. Offers educational programs for students and adults, an interactive computerized learning center, and special exhibitions and community programs. *United States Holocaust Memorial Museum Update (bimonthly); Directory of Holocaust Institutions; Journal of Holocaust and Genocide Studies (quarterly).* (WWW.USHMM.ORG)

YESHIVA UNIVERSITY MUSEUM (1973). Center for Jewish History, 15 W. 16 St.., NYC 10011-6301. (212)294-8335. E-mail: dgoldman@yum.cjh.org. Dir. Sylvia A. Herskowitz. Collects, preserves, and interprets Jewish life and culture through changing exhibitions of ceremonial objects, paintings, rare books and documents, synagogue architecture, textiles, contemporary art, and photographs. Oral history archive. Special events, holiday workshops, live performances, lectures, etc. for adults and children. Guided tours and workshops are offered. Exhibitions and children's art education programs also at branch galleries on Yeshiva University's Main Campus, 2520 Amsterdam Ave., NYC 10033-3201. *Seasonal calendars; special exhibition catalogues; newsletters.*

YIDDISHER KULTUR FARBAND-YKUF (1937). 1133 Broadway, Rm. 820, NYC 10010. (212)243-1304. FAX: (212)243-1305. E-mail: mahosu@amc.one. Pres./Ed. Publishes a bimonthly magazine and books by contemporary and classical Jewish writers; conducts cultural forums; exhibits works by contemporary Jewish artists and materials of Jewish historical value; organizes reading circles. *Yiddishe Kultur.*

YIVO INSTITUTE FOR JEWISH RESEARCH (1925). 15 W. 16 St., NYC 10011. (212)246-6080. FAX: (212)292-1892. E-mail: yivomail@yivo.cjh.org. Chmn. Bruce Slovin; Exec. Dir. Dr. Carl J. Rheins. Engages in historical research and education pertaining to East European Jewish life; maintains library and archives which provide a major international, national and New York resource used by institutions, individual scholars, and the public; provides graduate fellowships in East European and American Jewish studies; offers Yiddish language classes at all levels, exhibits, conferences, public programs; publishes books. *Yedies-YIVO News; YIVO Bleter.* (WWW.YIVOINSTITUTE.ORG)

———, MAX WEINREICH CENTER FOR ADVANCED JEWISH STUDIES/YIVO INSTITUTE (1968). 15 W. 16 St., NYC 10011. (212)246-6080. FAX: (212)292-1892. E-mail: mweinreich@yivo.cjh.org. Provides advanced-level training in Yiddish language and literature, ethnography, folklore, linguistics, and history; offers guidance on dissertation or independent research; postdoctoral fellowships available.

YUGNTRUF-YOUTH FOR YIDDISH (1964). 200 W. 72 St., Suite 40, NYC 10023. (212)787-6675. FAX: (212)799-1517. E-mail: ruvn@aol.com. Chmn. Dr. Paul Glasser; V.-Chmn. Marc Caplan; Coord. Menachem Ejdelman. A worldwide, nonpolitical organization for young people with a knowledge of, or interest in, Yiddish; fosters Yiddish as a living language and culture. Sponsors all activities in Yiddish: reading, conversation, and creative writing groups; annual weeklong retreat in Berkshires; children's Yiddish play group; sale of shirts. *Yugntruf Journal.*

ISRAEL-RELATED

ABRAHAM FUND (1989). 477 Madison Ave., 4th fl., NYC 10022. (212)303-9421. FAX: (212)935-1834. E-mail: info@AbrahamFund.org. Chmn. Alan B. Slifka, Exec. V.P. Dan Pattir. The Abraham Fund Initiatives (TAFI) seeks to enhance relations between Israel's Jewish and Arab citizens by promoting increased dialogue, understanding, and democracy. Founded in 1989, TAFI has contributed more than $8 million to community-based coexistence projects. TAFI also develops regional and national coexistence programs in partnership with other major institutions in Israel and orchestrates public advocacy campaigns to implement change.

AMEINU (formerly LABOR ZIONIST ALLIANCE, FARBAND LABOR ZIONIST ORDER) (1913). 114 W. 26 St., Suite 1006, NYC 10001. (212)366-1194. FAX: (212)675-7685. E-mail: executive@ameinu.net. Pres. Kenneth Bob; Exec. Dir. Doni Remba. Seeks to enhance Jewish life, culture, and education in U.S.; aids in building State of Israel as a cooperative commonwealth and its Labor movement organized in the Histadrut; supports efforts toward a more democratic society throughout the world; furthers the democratization of the Jewish community in America and the welfare of Jews everywhere; works with labor and liberal forces in America; sponsors Habonim-Dror labor Zionist youth movement. *Jewish Frontier.* (WWW.JEWISHFRONTIER.ORG)

AMERICA-ISRAEL CULTURAL FOUNDATION, INC. (1939). 51 E. 42nd St., Suite 400, NYC 10017. (212)557-1600. FAX: (212)557-1611. E-mail: info@aicf.org. Chmn. Vera Stern; Pres. William Schwartz. Supports and encourages the growth of cultural excellence in Israel through grants to cultural institutions; scholarships to gifted young artists and musicians. *Newsletter.* (WWW.AICF.ORG)

AMERICA-ISRAEL FRIENDSHIP LEAGUE, INC. (1971). 134 E. 39 St., NYC 10016. (212)213-8630. FAX: (212)683-3475. E-mail: aifl@aifl.org. Pres. and Chmn. Bd. Kenneth J. Bialkin; CEO William H. Behrer III. A non-sectarian, non-partisan, not-for-profit organization which seeks to broaden the base of support for Israel among Americans of all faiths and backgrounds. Activities include educational exchanges, missions to Israel for American leadership groups, symposia and public-education activities, and the dissemination of multi media information. *Newsletter.* (WWW.AIFL.ORG)

AMERICAN ASSOCIATES, BEN-GURION UNIVERSITY OF THE NEGEV (1972). 1430 Broadway, 8th Floor, New York, NY 10018. (212)687-7721, (800)-AABGU. FAX: (212)302-6443. E-mail: info@aabgu.org. Pres. Zvi Alov; Exec. V-Pres. Doron Krakow. Since 1972, the American Assoicates, Ben–Gurion University of the Negev has played a vital role in building a world-class center for research and education in the desert. A nonprofit cooperation with ten regional offices throughout the United States, AABGU prides itself on its efficiency and effectiveness in raising funds to help Ben-Gurion University bring knowledge to the Negev and to the world. AABGU plays a vital role in helping BGU fulfill its unique responsisbility to develop the Negev, the focus of the future of Israel. (WWW.AABGU.ORG)

AMERICAN COMMITTEE FOR SHAARE ZEDEK MEDICAL CENTER IN JERUSALEM (1949). 49 W. 45 St., Suite 1100, NYC 10036. (212)354-8801. FAX: (212)391-2674. E-mail: pr@szmc.org.il. Natl. Pres. & Chmn. Intl. Bd. of Gov. Menno Ratzker; Chair Erica Jesselson. Increases awareness and raises funds for the various needs of this 100-year old hospital, including new medical centers of excellence, equipment, medical supplies, school of nursing and research; supports exchange program between Shaare Zedek Jerusalem Medical Center and Albert Einstein College of Medicine, NY. *Heartbeat Magazine.*

AMERICAN COMMITTEE FOR SHENKAR COLLEGE IN ISRAEL, INC. (1971). 855 Ave. of the Americas, #531, NYC 10001. (212) 947-1597. FAX: (212)643-9887. E-mail: acfsc@worldnet.att.net. Pres. Nahum G. (Sonny) Shar; Exec. Dir. Charlotte A. Fainblatt. Raises funds and coordinates projects and research with Shenkar College of Engineering and Design, Israel. A unique government academic institute in Israel dedicated to education and reaseach in areas impacting Israel's industries and its artistic and scientific development. Textile, Fashion, Interior and Product design courses are offered with Scientific courses: Plastics, Chemistry, Software and Industrial Management and Marketing. Certified by Israel's Council of Higher Education, it offers continuing education and complete testing facilities for the textile/apparel industry and plastics engineering. *Shenkar News.*

AMERICAN COMMITTEE FOR THE BEER-SHEVA FOUNDATION (1988). PO Box 179, NYC 10028. (212)534-3715. FAX: (973)992-8651. Pres. Ronald Slevin; Sr. V.-Pres. Joanna Slevin; Bd. Chmn. Sidney Cooperman. U.S. fundraising arm of the Beer-Sheva Foundation, which funds vital projects to improve the quality of life in the city of Beer-Sheva: nursery schools for pre-K toddlers, residential and day centers for needy seniors, educational programs, facilities and scholarships (especially for new olim, the physically and mentally challenged), parks, playgrounds, and other important projects. Also offers special services for immigrants—such as heaters, blankets, clothing, school supplies, etc. *Brochures.*

AMERICAN COMMITTEE FOR THE WEIZMANN INSTITUTE OF SCIENCE (1944). 633 3rd Ave, New York, NY 10017. (212)895-7900. FAX: (212)895-7999. E-mail: info@acwis.org. Chmn. Robert Asher; Pres. Pennie Abramson; Exec. V.-Pres. and CEO Marshall S. Levin. Through 13 regional offices in the U.S. raises funds, disseminates information, and does American purchasing for the Weizmann Institute in Rehovot, Israel, a world-renowned center of scientific research and graduate study. The institute conducts research in disease, energy, the environment, and other areas; runs an international summer science program for gifted high-school students. *Interface; Weizmann Now; annual report.* (WWW.WEIZMANN-USA.ORG)

AMERICAN FRIENDS OF ALYN HOSPITAL (1932). 51 East 42nd Street., Suite 3088, NYC 10017. (212)869-8085. FAX: (212)768-0979. E-mail: friends@alynus.org. Pres. Minette Halpern Brown; Exec. Dir. Cathy M. Lanyard. Supports the Alyn Hospital (Woldenberg Family Hospital/Pediatric and Adolescent Rehabilitation Center) in Jerusalem. Treats children suffering from birth defects (such as muscular dystrophy and spina bifida) and traumas (terrorism, car accidents, cancer, and fire), enables patients and their families to achieve independence and a better quality of life. (WWW.ALYNUS.ORG)

AMERICAN FRIENDS OF ASSAF HAROFEH MEDICAL CENTER (1975). PO Box 21051, NYC 10129. (212)481-5653. FAX: (212)481-5672. Chmn. Kenneth Kronen; Exec. Dir. Rhoda Levental; Treas. Robert Kastin. Support group for Assaf Harofeh, Israel's third-largest government hospital, serving a poor population of over 400,000 in the area between Tel Aviv and Jerusalem. Raises funds for medical equipment, medical training for immigrants, hospital expansion, school of nursing, and school of physiotherapy. *Newsletter.*

AMERICAN FRIENDS OF BAR-ILAN UNIVERSITY (1955). 235 Park Ave. So., NYC 10003. (212)673-3460. FAX: (212)673-4856. Email: nationaladmin@biuny.com, beverlyf@biuny.com. Pres. Melvin Stein; Exec. V.-Pres. Mark Medin. Supports Bar-Ilan University, an institution that integrates the highest standards of contemporary scholarship in liberal arts and sciences with a Judaic studies program as a requirement. Located in Ramat-Gan, Israel, and chartered by the Board of Regents of the State of NY. *Bar-Ilan News; Bar-Ilan University Scholar; Heritage Newsletter.*.

AMERICAN FRIENDS OF BETH HATEFUTSOTH (1976). 633 Third Ave., 21st fl., NYC 10017. (212)339-6034. FAX: (212)318-6176. E-mail: afbhusa@aol.com. Pres. Stephen Greenberg; Chmn. Sam E. Bloch; Exec. Dir. Gloria Golan. Supports the maintenance and development of Beth Hatefutsoth, the Nahum Goldmann Museum of the Jewish Diaspora in Tel Aviv, and its cultural and educational programs for youth and adults. Circulates its traveling exhibitions and provides various cultural programs to local Jewish communities. Includes Jewish genealogy center (DOROT), the center for Jewish music, and photodocumentation center. *Beth Hatefutsoth* (quarterly newsletter).

AMERICAN FRIENDS OF HAIFA UNIVERSITY (*see* AMERICAN SOCIETY OF THE UNIVERSITY OF HAIFA)

AMERICAN FRIENDS OF HERZOG HOSPITAL/EZRATH NASHIM-JERUSALEM (1895). 800 Second Ave., 8th fl., NYC 10017. (212)499-9092. FAX:(212)499-9085. E-mail: herzogpr@hotmail.com. Co-Pres. Dr. Joy Zagoren , Amir Sternhell; Exec. Dir. Stephen Schwartz. Herzog Hospital is the foremost geriatric and psychiatric health care facility in Israel, and a leading research center in genetics, Alzheimer's and schizophrenia, with expertise in neurogeriatrics, physical rehabilitation, and long-term respiratory care. Its Israel Center for the Treatment of Psychotrauma provides therapy and seminars to help Israelis cope with the ongoing violence. (WWW.HERZOGHOSPITAL.ORG)

AMERICAN FRIENDS OF LIKUD. P.O.Box 8711, JAF Station, NYC 10116. (212)308-5595. FAX: (212)688-1327. E-mail: Thelikud@aol.com. Natl. Chmn. J. Phillip Rosen, Esq; Pres. Julio Messer,M.D; Natl. V. Pres. Jacques Torczyner; Natl. Treasurer Milton S. Shapiro, Esq.; Exec. Dir. Salomon L. Vaz Dias. promotes public education on the situation in the Middle East, particularly in Israel, as well as advancing a general awareness of Zionism; provides a solid partnership of public support for the State of Israel, its citizens and its democratically-elected governments.

AMERICAN FRIENDS OF MAGEN DAVID ADOM, ARMDI (1940). 888 Seventh Ave., Suite 403, NYC 10106. (212)757-1627. FAX: (212)757-4662. E-mail: info@afmda.org. Pres. Mark D. Lebow; Exec. V.-Pres. Daniel R. Allen. An authorized tax-exempt organization; the sole support arm in the U.S. of Magen David Adom (MDA), Israel's equivalent to a Red Cross Society; raises funds for the MDA emergency medical, ambulance, blood, and disaster services which help Israel's defense forces and civilian population. Helps to supply and equip ambulances, bloodmobiles, and cardiac rescue ambulances as well as 45 pre-hospital MDA Emergency Medical Clinics and the MDA National Blood Service Center and MDA Fractionation Institute in Ramat Gan, Israel. *The Shield.* (WWW.AFMDA.ORG)

AMERICAN FRIENDS OF NEVE SHALOM/WAHAT AL-SALAM (1988). 4201 Church Road, Suite 4, NYC 10013. (856) 235-3667. FAX: (856) 235-4674. E-mail: afnswas@oasisofpeace.com. Pres. Deborah First; V.-Pres. Adeeb Fadil; Exec. Dir. Deanna Armbruster. Supports and publicizes the projects of the community of Neve Shalom/Wahat Al-Salam, the "Oasis of Peace." For more than twenty years, Jewish and Palestinian citizens of Israel have lived and worked together as equals. The community teaches tolerance, understanding and mutual respect well beyond its own borders by being a model for peace and reaching out through its educational institutions. A bilingual, bicultural Primary School serves the village and the surrounding communities.

AMERICAN FRIENDS OF RABIN MEDICAL CENTER (1994). 220 Fifth Avenue, Suite 1301, NYC 10001-7708. (212) 279-2522. Fax: (212)279-0179. E-mail: afrmc826@aol.com. Bd. Chmn. Abraham E. "Barry" Cohen; Exec. Dir. Burton Lazarow. Supports the maintenance and development of this medical, research, and teaching institution in central Israel, which unites the Golda and Beilinson hospitals, providing 12% of all hospitalization in Israel. Department of Organ Transplantation performs 80% of all kidney and 60% of all liver transplants in Israel. Affiliated with Tel Aviv University's Sackler School of Medicine. *New Directions Quarterly.*

AMERICAN FRIENDS OF RAMBAM MEDICAL CENTER (1969). 226 West 26th Street, NYC 10001. (212)644-1049. FAX: (775)562-5399. E-mail: michaelstoler@princetoncommercial.com. Pres/CEO. Michael R. Stoler. Represents and raises funds for Rambam Medical Center (Haifa), an 887-bed hospital serving approx. one-third of Israel's population, incl. the entire population of northern Israel (and south Lebanon), the U.S. Sixth Fleet, and the UN Peacekeeping Forces in the region. Rambam is the teaching hospital for the Technion's medical school.

AMERICAN FRIENDS OF THE HEBREW UNIVERSITY (1925; inc. 1931). 11 E. 69 St., NYC 10021. (212)472-9800. FAX: (212)744-2324. E-mail: info@afhu.org. Pres. George A. Schieren; Exec. Dir. Peter Willner. Fosters the growth, development, and maintenance of the Hebrew University of Jerusalem; collects funds and conducts informational programs throughout the U.S., highlighting the university's achievements and its significance. *Wisdom; Scopus Magazine.* (WWW.AFHU.ORG)

AMERICAN FRIENDS OF THE ISRAEL MUSEUM (1972). 500 Fifth Ave., Suite 2540, NYC 10110. (212)997-5611. FAX: (212) 997-5536. Pres. Barbara Lane; Exec. Dir. Carolyn Cohen. Raises funds for special projects of the Israel Museum in Jerusalem; solicits works of art for permanent collection, exhibitions, and educational purposes. *Newsletter.*

AMERICAN FRIENDS OF THE ISRAEL PHILHARMONIC ORCHESTRA (AFIPO) (1972). 122 E. 42 St., Suite 4507, NYC 10168. (212)697-2949. FAX: (212)697-2943. Interim Pres. Lynn Syms; Exec. Dir. Suzanne K. Ponsot. Works to secure the financial future of the orchestra so that it may continue to travel throughout the world bringing its message of peace and cultural understanding through music. Supports the orchestra's international touring program, educational projects, and a wide array of musical activities in Israel. *Passport to Music (newsletter).*

AMERICAN FRIENDS OF THE OPEN UNIVERSITY OF ISRAEL. 180 W. 80 St., NYC 10024. (212)712-1800. FAX: (212)496-3296. E-mail: afoui@aol.com. Natl. Chmn. Irving M. Rosenbaum; Exec.V.-Pres. Eric G. Heffler. *Open Letter.* (WWW.OPENU.AC.IL)

AMERICAN FRIENDS OF THE SHALOM HARTMAN INSTITUTE (1976). One Penn Plaza, Suite 1606, New York, NY 10119. (212) 268-0300. FAX: (212)239-4550. E-mail: afshi@afshi.org. Pres. Robert P. Kogod; Exec. Dir. Hana Gilat. Supports the Shalom Hartman Institute in Jerusalem, an international center for pluralist Jewish education and research, serving Israel and world Jewry. Founded in 1976 by David Hartman, the Institute includes: the Institute for Advanced Judaic Studies, with research centers for contemporary halakha, religious pluralism, political thought and peace and reconciliation; the Institute for Teacher and Leadership Training, educating Israeli principals, teachers, graduate students and leaders; and the Institute for Diaspora Education, which offers seminars and sabbaticals to rabbis, educators and lay leaders of diverse ideological commitments. (WWW.HARTMANINSTITUTE.COM)

AMERICAN FRIENDS OF THE TEL AVIV MUSEUM OF ART (1974). 545 Madison Ave., 8th Floor (55 St.), NYC 10022. (212)319-0555. FAX: (212)754-2987. Email: dnaftam@aol.com. Chmn. Steven P. Schwartz; Exec. Dir. Dorey Neilinger. Raises funds for the Tel Aviv Museum of Art for special projects, art acquisitions, and exhibitions; seeks contributions of art to expand the museum's collection; encourages art loans and traveling exhibitions; creates an awareness of the museum in the USA; makes available exhibition catalogues, monthly calendars, and posters published by the museum.

AMERICAN-ISRAEL ENVIRONMENTAL COUNCIL (formerly COUNCIL FOR A BEAUTIFUL ISRAEL ENVIRONMENTAL EDUCATION FOUNDATION) (1973). c/o Perry Davis Assoc., 25 W. 45 St., Suite 1405, NYC 10036. (212)840-1166. Fax: (212)840-1514. Pres. Alan Silberstein. A support group for the Israeli body, whose activities include education, town planning, lobbying for legislation to protect and enhance the environment, preservation of historical sites, the improvement and beautification of industrial and commercial areas, and sponsoring the CBI Center for Environmental Studies located in Yarkon Park, Tel Aviv. *Yearly newsletter; yearly theme oriented calendars in color.*

AMERICAN ISRAEL PUBLIC AFFAIRS COMMITTEE (AIPAC) (1954). 440 First St., NW, Washington, DC 20001. (202)639-5200. FAX: (202)347-4889. Pres. Howard Friedman; Exec. Dir. Howard A. Kohr. Registered to lobby on behalf of legislation affecting U.S.-Israel relations; represents Americans who believe support for a secure Israel is in U.S. interest. Works for a strong U.S.-Israel relationship. *Near East Report.* (WWW.AIPAC.ORG)

AMERICAN-ISRAELI LIGHTHOUSE, INC. (1928; reorg. 1955). 276 Fifth Ave., Suite 713, NYC 10001. (212)686-7110. Pres. Mrs. Leonard F. Dank; Sec. Mrs. Ida Rhein. Provides a vast network for blind and physically handicapped persons throughout Israel, to effect their social and vocational integration into the mainstream of their communities. Center of Services for the blind; built and maintains Rehabilitation Center for blind and handicapped persons (Migdal Or) in Haifa.

AMERICAN JEWISH LEAGUE FOR ISRAEL (1957). 450 7th Avenue, Suite 808, NYC 10123. (212)371-1583. FAX: (646)497-0093. E-mail: ajlims@aol.com. Pres. Dr. Martin L. Kalmanson; Exec. Dir. Jeffrey Scheckner. Seeks to unite all those who, notwithstanding differing philosophies of Jewish life, are committed to the historical ideals of Zionism; works independently of class, party, or religious affiliation for the welfare of Israel as a whole. Not identified with any political parties in Israel. Member of World Jewish Congress, World Zionist Organization. *Newsletter.* (WWW.AMERICANJEWISHLEAGUE.ORG)

AMERICAN PHYSICIANS FELLOWSHIP FOR MEDICINE IN ISRAEL (1950). 2001 Beacon St., Suite 210, Boston, MA 02135-7771. (617)232-5382. FAX: (617) 739-2616. E-mail: apf@apfmed.org. Pres. Sherwood L. Gorbach, M.D.; Exec. Dir. Ellen-Ann Lacey. Supports projects that advance medical education, research, and care in Israel and builds links between the medical communities of Israel and N. Amer.; provides fellowships for Israeli physicians training in N. Amer. and arranges lectureships in Israel by prominent N. Amer. physicians; sponsors CME seminars in Israel and N. Amer.; coordinates U.S./Canadian medical emergency volunteers for Israel. *APF News.*

AMERICAN SOCIETY FOR TECHNION-ISRAEL INSTITUTE OF TECHNOLOGY (1940). 55 East 59th Street NYC 10022. (212)407-6300. FAX: (212)753-2925 E-mail: info@ats.org. Pres. Evelyn Berger; Chmn. Larry Jackier; Exec. V.-Pres. Melvyn H. Bloom. The American Technion Society (ATS) raises funds for the Technion-Israel Institute of Technology. Based in New York City, it is the leading American organization with more than 20,000 supporters and 197 satellite offices around the country, the ATS is driven by the belief that the economic future of Israel is in high technology and the future of high technology in Israel is at the Technion.. *Technion USA.* (WWW.ATS.ORG)

AMERICAN SOCIETY FOR THE PROTECTION OF NATURE IN ISRAEL, INC. (1986). 28 Arrandale Ave., Great Neck, NY 11024. (212) 398-6750. FAX: (212) 398-1665. E-mail: aspni@aol.com. Co-Chmn. Edward I. Geffner & Russell Rothman. A non-profit organization supporting the work of SPNI, an Israeli organization devoted to environmental protection and nature education. SPNI runs 26 Field Study Centers and has 45 municipal offices throughout Israel; offers education programs, organized hikes, and other activities; seeks ways to address the needs of an expanding society while preserving precious natural resources. *SPNI News.*

AMERICAN SOCIETY FOR YAD VASHEM (1981). 500 Fifth Ave., 42nd Floor, NYC 10110-4299. (212)220-4304. FAX: (212) 220-4308. E-mail: info@yadvashemusa.org. Chmn. Eli Zborowski. Development and educational arm of Yad Vashem, Jerusalem, the central international authority created by the Knesset in 1953 for the purposes of commemoration and education in connection with the Holocaust. *Martyrdom and Resistance* (newsletter). (WWW.YADVASHEM.ORG)

AMERICAN SOCIETY OF THE UNIVERSITY OF HAIFA (formerly AMERICAN FRIENDS OF HAIFA UNIVERSITY) (1972). 220 Fifth Ave., Suite 1301, NYC 10001. (212) 685-7880. FAX: (212)685-7883. E-mail: asuhtr@att.net. Pres.Paul Amir; Sec./Treas. Robert Jay Benowitz. Promotes, encourages, and aids higher and secondary education, research, and training in all branches of knowledge in Israel and elsewhere; aids in the maintenance and development of University of Haifa; raises and allocates funds for the above purposes; provides scholarships; promotes exchanges of teachers and students.

AMERICAN ZIONIST MOVEMENT (formerly AMERICAN ZIONIST FEDERATION) (1939; reorg. 1949, 1970, 1993). 633 Third Avenue., NYC 10017. (212)318-6100. FAX: (212)935-3578. E-mail: info@azm.com. Pres. James Schiller; Exec. Dir. Karen J. Rubinstein. Umbrella organization for 20 American Zionist organizations and the voice of unified Zionism in the U.S. Conducts advocacy for Israel; strengthens Jewish identity; promotes the Israel experience; prepares the next generation of Zionist leadership. Regional offices in Chicago and Dallas. Groups in Detroit, Pittsburgh, Washington, DC. *The Zionist Advocate.* (WWW.AZM.ORG)

AMERICANS FOR A SAFE ISRAEL (AFSI) (1971). 1751 Second Ave, NYC 10128. 1-800-235-3658. FAX: (212)828-1717. E-mail: afsi@rcn.com. Chmn. Herbert Zweibon; Exec. Dir. Barry Freedman. Seeks to educate Americans in Congress, the media, and the public about Israel's role as a strategic asset for the West; through meetings with legislators and the media, in press releases and publications AFSI promotes Jewish rights to Judea and Samaria, the Golan, Gaza, an indivisible Jerusalem, and to all of Israel. AFSI believes in the concept of "peace for peace" and rejects the concept of "territory for peace." *The Outpost* (monthly). (WWW.AFSI.ORG)

AMERICANS FOR PEACE NOW (1984). 1101 14th Street, NW, Sixth Floor, Washington, DC 20005. (202)728-1893. FAX: (202)728-1895. E-mail: apndc@peacenow.org. Pres. & CEO Debra DeLee; Chmn. Franklin M. Fisher. Conducts educational programs and raises funds to support the Israeli peace movement, Shalom Achshav (Peace Now), and coordinates U.S. advocacy efforts through APN's Washington-based Center for Israeli Peace and Security. *Jerusalem Watch; Peace Now News; Settlement Watch; Fax Facts; Middle East Update (on-line); Benefits of Peace.* (WWW.PEACENOW.ORG)

AMIT (1925). 817 Broadway, NYC 10003. (212)477-4720. FAX: (212)353-2312. E-mail: info@amitchildren.org. Pres. Jan Schechter; Exec. Dir. Arnold Gerson. The State of Israel's official reshet (network) for religious secondary technological education; maintains innovative children's homes and youth villages in Israel in an environment of traditional Judaism; promotes cultural activities for the purpose of disseminating Zionist ideals and strengthening traditional Judaism in America. *AMIT Magazine.*

AMPAL-AMERICAN ISRAEL CORPORATION (1942). 1177 Avenue of the Americas, NYC 10036. (212)782-2100. FAX: (212) 782-2114. E-mail: ampal@aol.com. Bd. Chmn. Daniel Steinmetz; CEO Shuki Gleitman. Acquires interests in businesses located in the State of Israel or that are Israel-related. Interests include leisure-time, real estate, finance, energy distribution, basic industry, high technology, and communications. *Annual report; quarterly reports.*

ARZA/WORLD UNION, NORTH AMERICA (1977). 633 Third Ave., 6th fl., NYC 10017-6778. (212)650-4280. FAX: (212)650-4289. E-mail: arza/wupjna@urj.org. Pres.Rabbi Stanley M. Davids; Exec. Dir. Rabbi Andrew Davids. Membership organization dedicated to furthering the development of Progressive Judaism in Israel, the FSU, and throughout the world. Encourages Jewish solidarity, promoting religious pluralism and furthering Zionism. Works to strengthen the relationship of N. American Reform Jews with Progressive Jewish communities worldwide and to educate and inform them on relevant issues. *Quarterly newsletter*. (WWW.ARZAWUNA.ORG)

BETAR EDUCATIONAL YOUTH ORGANIZATION (1935). 4 East 34th Street, NYC, 10016. (646)742-9364. FAX: (646)742-9666. E-mail: newyork@betar.org. Pres. Dany Danon; Exec. Officer Itzik Simhon. Betar is a Zionist active college students' movement, which dedicates itself to promoting Israeli issues in the American media. Betar was founded in 1923 by Zeev Jabotinsky, among its' famous alumni are Nenachem Begin and Itzhak Shamir. Betar's goal is the gathering of all Jewish people in their ancient land.

BOYS TOWN JERUSALEM FOUNDATION OF AMERICA INC. (1948). 12 W. 31 St., Suite 300, NYC 10001. (212)244-2766. (800) 469-2697. FAX: (212)244-2052. E-mail: btjny@compuserve.com. Raphael Benaroya, Pres. Michael J. Scharf; Hon. Chmn. Josh S. Weston; Chmn. Raphael Benaroya; Exec. V.-Pres. Rabbi Ronald L. Gray. Raises funds for Boys Town Jerusalem, which was established in 1948 to offer a comprehensive academic, religious, and technological education to disadvantaged Israeli and immigrant boys from over 45 different countries, including Ethiopia, the former Soviet Union, and Iran. Enrollment: over 1,000 students in jr. high school, academic and technical high school, and a college of applied engineering. Boys Town was recently designated as the "CISCO Regional Academy," the first center in Jerusalem for the instruction of the CISCO Networking Management Program. *BTJ Newsbrief*

BRIT TZEDEK V'SHALOM—JEWISH ALLIANCE FOR JUSTICE AND PEACE (2002). 11 E. Adams St., Suite 707, Chicago, IL 60603. (312)341-1205. FAX: (312)341-1206. E-mail: info@btvshalom.org. Pres. Steven Masters; Exec. Dir. Elliot Figman. Works for the achievement of a negotiated settlement of the Israeli-Palestinian conflict guided by the traditional Jewish obligation to pursue peace and justice, in the conviction that security for Israel can only be attained through the establishment of an economically and politicvally viable Palestinian state, necessitating an end to Israel's occupation of land acquired in the 1967 war and an end to Palestinian violence; its national office and 30 chapters around the country engage in grassroots political advocacy and public education. *Action Alerts*. (WWW.BTVSHALOM.ORG)

CAMERA-COMMITTEE FOR ACCURACY IN MIDDLE EAST REPORTING IN AMERICA (1983). PO Box 35040, Boston, MA 02135. (617)789-3672. FAX: (617)787-7853. E-mail: media@camera.org. Pres./Exec. Dir. Andrea Levin; Chmn. Joshua Katzen. CAMERA monitors media coverage of Israel, responds to error, omissions, and distortion, promotes factual information and works to educate the media and public about key issues related to conflict in the Middle East. CAMERA encourages members to participate in fostering full and fair coverage through communication with the media. *CAMERA Media Report (quarterly); CAMERA on Campus; CAMERA Media Directory, CAMERA Monographs, Action Alerts, Backgrounders*. (WWW.CAMERA.ORG)

DEVELOPMENT CORPORATION FOR ISRAEL (formerly STATE OF ISRAEL BONDS) (1951). 575 Lexington Ave., 11th Floor, NYC 10022. (212)644-2663. FAX: (212)644-3887. E-mail: raphael.rothstein@israelbonds.com. Bd. Chmn. Michael Siegal; Pres./CEO Joshua Matza. An international organization offering securities issued by the government of Israel. Since its inception in 1951 has secured $25 billion in investment capital for the development of every aspect of Israel's economic infrastructure, including agriculture, commerce, and industry, and for absorption of immigrants. *Israel Hadashot-News*. (WWW.ISRAELBONDS.COM)

DOR CHADASH (2003). 165 E. 56 St., NYC 10016. (212)696-2151. FAX (212)684-6327. E-mail: info@dorchadashusa.org. Founder/Chmn. David Borowich; Exec. Dir. Scott Richman. A community of more than 10,000 Israeli and American Jews living in New York brought together by love of Israel; develops educational, social, and cultural programs related to Israeli themes. (WWW.DORCHADASHUSA.ORG)

EMUNAH OF AMERICA (formerly HAPOEL HAMIZRACHI WOMEN'S ORGANIZATION) (1948). 7 Penn Plaza, NYC 10001.

(212)564-9045, (800)368-6440. FAX: (212)643-9731. E-mail: info@emunah.org. Natl. Pres. Mindy Stein; Exec. V.-Pres. Shirley Singer. Maintains and supports 200 educational and social-welfare institutions in Israel within a religious framework, including day-care centers, kindergartens, children's residential homes, vocational schools for the underprivileged, senior-citizen centers, a college complex, and Holocaust study center. Also involved in absorption of Soviet and Ethiopian immigrants (recognized by Israeli government as an official absorption agency). *Emunah Magazine; Lest We Forget.* (WWW.EMUNAH.ORG)

FEDERATED COUNCIL OF ISRAEL INSTITUTIONS—FCII (1940). 4702 15th Ave., Brooklyn, NY 11219. (718)972-5530. Bd. Chmn. Z. Shapiro; Exec. V.-Pres. Rabbi Julius Novack. Central fund-raising organization for over 100 affiliated institutions; handles and executes estates, wills, and bequests for the traditional institutions in Israel; clearinghouse for information on budget, size, functions, etc. of traditional educational, welfare, and philanthropic institutions in Israel, working cooperatively with the Israeli government and the overseas department of the Council of Jewish Federations. *Annual financial reports and statistics on affiliates.*

FRIENDS OF ISRAEL DISABLED VETERANS—BEIT HALOCHEM (1987). 1133 Broadway, Ste. 232, NYC 10010. (212)689-3220. FAX: (212)253-4143. E-mail: info@FIDV.org. Bd. Chmn. Richard L. Golden; Exec. Dir. Linda E. Frankel. Raises funds to assist disabled Israeli war victims, including civilian victims of terrorism; maintains four centers in Israel providing physical and emotional rehabilitation for them. (WWW.FIDV.ORG)

FRIENDS OF THE ISRAEL DEFENSE FORCES (1981). 350 5th Avenue, Suite 2011 NYC 10118. (212)244-3118. FAX: (212)244-3119. E-mail: fidf@fidf.com. Chmn. Marvin Josephson; Pres. Jay Zises; Natl. Dir. Brig. Gen. Eliezer Hemeli. Supports the Agudah Lema'an Hahayal, Israel's Assoc. for the Well-Being of Soldiers, founded in the early 1940s, which provides social, recreational, and educational programs for soldiers, special services for the sick and wounded, and summer programs for widows and children of fallen soldiers. (WWW.FIDF.COM)

GESHER FOUNDATION (1969). 25 W. 45 St. Suite 1405, NYC 10036. (212)840-1166. FAX: (212)840-1514. E-mail: gesherfoundation@aol.com. Pres./Founder Daniel Tropper; Chmn. Philip Schatten. Seeks to bridge the gap between Jews of various backgrounds in Israel by stressing the interdependence of all Jews. Runs encounter seminars for Israeli youth; distributes curricular materials in public schools; offers Jewish identity classes for Russian youth, and a video series in Russian and English on famous Jewish personalities.

GIVAT HAVIVA EDUCATIONAL FOUNDATION, INC. (1966). 114 W. 26 St., Suite 1001, NYC 10001. (212)989-9272. FAX: (212) 989-9840. E-mail: mail@givathaviva.org. Chmn. Yvonne Baum Silverman; Exec. Dir. Robert Levy. Supports programs at the Givat Haviva Institute, Israel's leading organization dedicated to promoting coexistence between Arabs and Jews, with 40,000 people participating each year in programs teaching conflict resolution, Middle East studies and languages, and Holocaust studies. Publishes research papers on Arab-Jewish relations, Holocaust studies, kibbutz life. In the U.S., GHEF sponsors public-education programs and lectures by Israeli speakers. *Givat Haviva News; special reports.*(WWW.DIALOGATE.ORG.IL)

HABONIM-DROR NORTH AMERICA (1935). 114 W. 26 St., Suite 1004, NYC 10001-6812. (212)255-1796. FAX: (212)929-3459. E-mail: programs@habonimdror.org. (Mazkir Tnua) Jamie Levin; Shliach Onri Welmer. Fosters identification with progressive, cooperative living in Israel; stimulates study of Jewish and Zionist culture, history, and contemporary society. Sponsors summer and year programs in Israel and on kibbutz, 7 summer camps in N. America modeled after kibbutzim, and *aliyah* frameworks. *B'Tnua (on-line and print newsletter).* (WWW.HABONIMDROR.ORG)

HADASSAH, THE WOMEN'S ZIONIST ORGANIZATION OF AMERICA, INC. (1912). 50 W. 58 St., NYC 10019. (212)355-7900. FAX: (212)303-8282. Pres. Nancy Falchuk; Exec. Dir. Morlie Hammer Levin. Largest women's, largest Jewish, and largest Zionist membership organization in U.S. In Israel: Founded and funds Hadassah Medical Organization, Hadassah College of Jerusalem, Hadassah Career Counseling Institute, Young Judaea summer and year-course programs, as well as providing support for Youth Aliyah and JNF. U.S. programs: Jewish and women's health education; advocacy on Israel, Zionism and women's issues; Young Judaea youth movement, including six camps; Hadassah Leadership Academy; Hadassah-Brandeis Institute for International Research on Jewish Women; Hadassah Foundation. *Hadassah Magazine; Update; Hadassah International Newsletter; Medical Update; American Scene.* (WWW.HADASSAH.ORG)

___________ ,YOUNG JUDAEA (1909; reorg. 1967). 50 W. 58 St., NYC 10019. (212)303-8014. FAX: (212)303-4572. E-mail: info@youngjudaea.org. Natl. Dir. Seth Finkelstein. Religiously pluralistic, politically nonpartisan Zionist youth movement sponsored by Hadassah; seeks to educate Jewish youth aged 8-25 toward Jewish and Zionist values, active commitment to and participation in the American and Israeli Jewish communities; maintains six summer camps in the U.S.; runs both summer and year programs in Israel, and a jr. year program in connection with both Hebrew University in Jerusalem and Ben Gurion University of the Negev. College-age arm, Hamagshimim, supports Zionist activity on campuses. *Kol Hat'nua; The Young Judaean; Ad Kahn.* (WWW.YOUNGJUDAEA.ORG)

HASHOMER HATZAIR, SOCIALIST ZIONIST YOUTH MOVEMENT (1923). 114 W. 26 St., Suite 1001, NYC 10001. (212)627-2830. FAX: (212)989-9840. E-mail: mail@hashomerhatzair.org. Dir. Guy Tsfoni; Natl. Sec. Moran Banai. Seeks to educate Jewish youth to an understanding of Zionism as the national liberation movement of the Jewish people. Promotes aliyah to kibbutzim. Affiliated with Kibbutz Artzi Federation. Espouses socialist-Zionist ideals of peace, justice, democracy, and intergroup harmony. *Young Guard.* (WWW.HASHOMERHATZAIR.ORG)

INTERNS FOR PEACE INTERNATIONAL (1976). 475 Riverside Dr., Room 240., NYC 10115. (212)870-2226. FAX: (914)686-8896. E-mail: ifpus@mindspring.com. Intl. Dir. Rabbi Bruce M. Cohen; Intl. Coord. Karen Wald Cohen. An independent, nonprofit, nonpolitical educational program training professional community peace workers. In Israel, initiated and operated jointly by Jews and Arabs; over 250 interns trained in 35 cities; over 80,000 Israeli citizens participating in joint programs in education, sports, culture, business, women's affairs, and community development; since the peace accord, Palestinians from West Bank and Gaza training as interns. Martin Luther King Project for Black/Jewish relations. *IFP Reports Quarterly; Guidebooks for Ethnic Conflict Resolution.* (WWW.INTERNSFORPEACE.ORG)

ISRAEL CANCER RESEARCH FUND (1975). 1290 Avenue of the Americas, NYC 10104. (212)969-9800. FAX: (212)969-9822. E-mail: mail@icrfny.org. Pres. Yashar Hirshaut, M.D.; Chmn. Leah Susskind; Exec. V.P. Donald Adelman. The largest single source of private funds for cancer research in Israel. Has a three-fold mission: To encourage innovative cancer research by Israeli scientists; to harness Israel's vast intellectual and creative resources to establish a world-class center for cancer study; to broaden research opportunities within Israel to stop the exodus of talented Israeli cancer researchers. *Annual Report; Research Awards; ICRF Brochure; Newsletter.*

ISRAEL HUMANITARIAN FOUNDATION (IHF) (1960). 276 Fifth Ave., Suite 901, NYC 10001. (212)683-5676, (800)434-5IHF. FAX: (212)213-9233. E-mail: info@ihf.net. Pres. Marvin M. Sirota; Exec.V.-Pres. Stanley J. Abrams. Since 1960, Israel Humanitarian Foundation (IHF) has funded more than 130 social service projects in Israel that provide funds and programs in a diverse range of areas. IHF strives to improve the standard of living of the Israeli population through its support for education, youth in need, elder care, the disables, and medical care & research projects that directly benefit thousands of people in need.

ISRAEL POLICY FORUM (1993). 165 East 56th Street, 2nd Floor, NYC 10022. (212)245-4227. FAX: (212)245-0517. E-mail: ipf@ipforum.org. 1030 15 St., NW, Suite 850, Washington, DC 20005. (202)842-1700. FAX:(202)842-1722. E-mail: ipf@ipforum.org. Pres. Seymour Reich. An independent leadership institution whose mission is to encourage an active U.S. role in resolving the Arab-Israeli conflict. IPF generates this support by involving leaders from the business, political, entertainment, academic, and philanthropic communitites in the peace effort, and by fostering a deeper understanding of the peace process among the American public. *Forum Fax, Washington Bulletin, Security Watch.* (WWW.IPFORUM.ORG)

THE JERUSALEM FOUNDATION, INC. (1966). 60 E. 42 St., Suite 1936, NYC 10165. (212) 697-4188. FAX: (212) 697-4022. E-mail: info@jfoundation.com. Chmn. Kenneth J. Bialkin; Exec. Dir. Dorothy Kauffman. A nonprofit organization devoted to improving the quality of life for all Jerusalemites, regardless of ethnic, religious, or socioeconomic background; has initiated and implemented more than 1,500 projects that span education, culture, community services, beautification, and preservation of the city's historic heritage and religious sites.

JEWISH INSTITUTE FOR NATIONAL SECURITY AFFAIRS (JINSA) (1976). (202)667-3900. E-mail: info@jinsa.org. Pres. Norman Hascoe; Exec. Dir. Mark Broxmeyer. A nonprofit, nonpartisan educational organization working within the American Jewish community to explain the link between American defense policy and the security of the State of Israel; and within the national security establishment to explain the key role Israel plays in bolstering American interests. (WWW.JINSA.ORG)

JEWISH INSTITUTE FOR THE BLIND-JERUSALEM, INC. (1902, Jerusalem). 15 E. 26 St., NYC 10010. (212) 532-4155. FAX: (212) 447-7683. Pres. Rabbi David E. Lapp; Admin. Eric L. Loeb. Supports a dormitory and school for the Israeli blind and handicapped in Jerusalem. *INsight.*

JEWISH NATIONAL FUND OF AMERICA (1901). 42 E. 69 St., NYC 10021. (212)879-9300. (1-800-542-TREE). FAX: (212)570-1673. E-mail: communications@jnf.org. Pres. Stanley M. Chesley; CEO Russell F. Robinson. Jewish National Fund is the American fund-raising arm of Keren Kayemeth LeIsrael, the official land agency in Israel and is celebrating its 100th Anniversary this year. JNF works in the following areas: water resource development, afforestation and ecology, eduction, tourism and recreation, community development and research. (WWW.JNF.ORG)

JEWISH PEACE LOBBY (1989). 8604 Second Avnue, PMB 317, Silver Spring, MD 20910. (301)589-8764. FAX: (301)589-2722. Email: peacelobby@msn.com. Pres. Jerome M. Segal. A legally registered lobby promoting changes in U.S. policy vis-a-vis the Israeli-Palestinian conflict. Supports Israel's right to peace within secure borders; a political settlement based on mutual recognition of the right of self-determination of both peoples; a two-state solution as the most likely means to a stable peace. *Annual Report.*

KEREN OR, INC. JERUSALEM CENTER FOR MULTI-HANDICAPPED BLIND CHILDREN (1956). 350 Seventh Ave., Suite 200, NYC 10001. (212)279-4070. FAX: (212)279-4043. E-mail: kerenorinc@aol.com. Chmn. Dr. Edward L. Steinberg; Pres. Dr. Albert Hornblass; Exec. Dir. Rochelle B. Silberman. Funds the Keren-Or Center for Multi-Handicapped Blind Children at 3 Abba Hillel Silver St., Ramot, Jerusalem, housing and caring for over 70 resident and day students who in addition to blindness or very low vision suffer from other severe physical and/or mental disabilities. Students range in age from 1 1/2 through young adulthood. Provides training in daily living skills, as well as therapy, rehabilitation, and education to the optimum level of the individual. *Insights Newsletter.*

MACCABI USA/SPORTS FOR ISRAEL (formerly UNITED STATES COMMITTEE SPORTS FOR ISRAEL) (1948). 1926 Arch St., 4R, Philadelphia, PA 19103. (215)561-6900. Fax: (215)561-5470. E-mail: maccabi@maccabiusa.com. Pres. Toni Worhman. Sponsors U.S. team for World Maccabiah Games in Israel every four years; seeks to enrich the lives of Jewish youth in the U.S., Israel, and the Diaspora through athletic, cultural, and educational programs; develops, promotes, and supports international, national, and regional athletic-based activities and facilities. *Sportscene Newsletter; Commemorative Maccabiah Games Journal; financial report.* (WWW.MACCABIUSA.COM)

MERCAZ USA (1979). 155 Fifth Ave., NYC 10010. (212)533-7800, ext. 2016. FAX: (212)533-2601. E-mail: info@mercazusa.org. Pres. Rabbi Steven S. Wolnek; Exec. Dir. Rabbi Robert R. Golub. The U.S. Zionist organization for Conservative/Masorti Judaism; works for religious pluralism in Israel, defending and promoting Conservative/Masorti institutions and individuals; fosters Zionist education and *aliyah* and develops young leadership. *Mercaz USA Quarterly Newsletter.* (WWW.MERCAZUSA.ORG)

MERETZ USA FOR ISRAELI CIVIL RIGHTS AND PEACE (1991). 114 W. 26 St., Suite 1002, NYC 10001. (212)242-4500. FAX: (212)242-5718. E-mail: mail@meretzusa.org. Pres. Lawrence I. Lerner; Exec. Dir. Ron Skolnik. A forum for addressing the issues of social justice and peace in Israel. Educates about issues related to democracy, human and civil rights, religious pluralism, and equality for women and ethnic minorities; promotes the resolution of Israel's conflict with the Palestinians on the basis of mutual recognition, self-determination, and peaceful coexistence. *Israel Horizons.* (WWW.MERETZUSA.ORG)

NA'AMAT USA, THE WOMEN'S LABOR ZIONIST ORGANIZATION OF AMERICA, INC. (1925). 350 Fifth Ave., Suite 4700, NYC 10118-4799. (212)563-5222. FAX: (212) 563-5710. E-mail: naamat@naamat.org. Natl. Pres. Alice Howard. Part of the World Movement of Na'amat (Movement of Working Women and Volunteers), the largest Jewish women's organization in the world, it helps provide social, educational, and legal services for women, teenagers, and children in Israel. It also advocates legislation for women's rights and child welfare in Israel and the U.S., furthers Jewish education, and supports Habonim Dror, the Labor Zionist youth movement. *Na'amat Woman magazine.* (WWW.NAAMAT.ORG)

NATIONAL COMMITTEE FOR LABOR ISRAEL (1923). 275 Seventh Ave., NYC 10001. (212)647-0300. FAX: (212)647-0308. E-mail: ncli@laborisrael.org. Pres. Jay Mazur; Exec. Dir. Jerry Goodman; Chmn. Trade Union Council Morton Bahr. Serves as a bridge among Israel's labor sector, including its General Federation of Labor, Histadrut, the American labor movement, the Jewish community and the general public. Brings together Jews and non-Jews to build support for Israel and advance closer Israel-Arab ties. Cooperates with Israels labor sector. National in scope, it conducts education in the Jewish community and among labor groups to promote better relations with labor Israel. Raises funds for youth, educational, health, social and cultural projects in Israel from a constituency which includes labor unions, foundations, government agencies and individual donors and supporters. *Occasional background papers* (WWW.LABORISRAEL.ORG)

NEW ISRAEL FUND (1979). 1101 14th St., NW, 6th fl., Washington, DC 20005-5639. (202)842-0900. FAX: (202)842-0991. E-mail: info@nif.org. New York office: 165 E. 56 St., NYC 10022. (212)750-2333. FAX: (212)750-8043. Pres. Larry Garber; Exec. Dir. Norman S. Rosenberg. A partnership of Israelis and North Americans dedicated to promoting social justice, coexistence, and pluralism in Israel, the New Israel Fund helps strengthen Israeli democracy by providing grants and technical assistance to the public-interest sector, cultivating a new generation of social activists, and educating citizens in Israel and the Diaspora about the challenges to Israeli democracy. *Quarterly newsletter; annual report; other reports..* (WWW.NIF.ORG)

PEF ISRAEL ENDOWMENT FUNDS, INC. (1922). 317 Madison Ave., Suite 607, NYC 10017. (212)599-1260. Chmn. Sidney A. Luria; Pres. B. Harrison Frankel; Sec. Mark Bane. A totally volunteer organization that makes grants to educational, scientific, social, religious, health, and other philanthropic institutions in Israel. *Annual report.*

POALE AGUDATH ISRAEL OF AMERICA, INC. (1948). 2920 Avenue J, Brooklyn, NY 11210. (718)258-2228. FAX: (718)258-2288. Pres. Rabbi Fabian Schonfeld. Aims to educate American Jews to the values of Orthodoxy and aliyah; supports kibbutzim, trade schools, yeshivot, moshavim, kollelim, research centers, and children's homes in Israel. *PAI News; She'arim; Hamayan.*

PRO ISRAEL (1990). 1328 Broadway, Suite 435, NYC. (212)594-8996. FAX: (212)594-8986. E-mail: proisrael@aol.com. Pres. Dr. Ernest Bloch; Exec. Dir. Rabbi Julian M. White. Educates the public about Israel and the Middle East; provides support for community development throughout the Land of Israel, particularly in Judea, Samaria, Gaza, and the Golan Heights. Projects include the Ariel Center for Policy Research and Professors for a Strong Israel.

RELIGIOUS ZIONISTS OF AMERICA (1909). 7 Penn Plaza, Suite 205, NYC 10001. (212)465-9234. FAX: (212)465-9246. Email: mizrachi@rza.org. Pres. Rabbi Yosef Blau; Exec. Dir. Alan Mond. Disseminates ideals of religious Zionism; conducts cultural work, educational program, public relations; raises funds for religious educational institutions in Israel, including yeshivot hesder and Bnei Akiva. *Voice of Religious Zionism.* (WWW.RZA.ORG)

———, BNEI AKIVA OF THE U.S. & CANADA (1934). 7 Penn Plaza, Suite 205, NYC 10001. (212)465-9536. FAX: (212)465-2155. Shaliah, Rabbi Shaul Feldman; Natl. Dir. Steve Frankel. The only religious Zionist Youth movement in North America, Educating thousands of youths from grade school throughout the US and Canada. We have five summer camps in North America and a summer program in Israel. We educate towards the values of the Religious Zionist Movement which sees the place of all Jews, in Israel, involved in social action, and committed to Orthodox Torah values. *Akivon; Pinkas Lamadrich; Daf Rayonot; Me'Ohalai Torah; Zraim.*(WWW.BNEIAKIVA.ORG)

———, NATIONAL COUNCIL FOR TORAH EDUCATION (1939). 7 Penn Plaza, Suite 205, NYC 10001. (212)465-9234. FAX: (212)465-9246. E-mail: mizrachi@rza.org. Pres. Aaron S. Tirschwell; Chmn. Rabbi Mark Dratch. Organizes and supervises yeshivot and Talmud Torahs; prepares and trains teachers; publishes textbooks and educational materials; organizes summer seminars for Hebrew educators in cooperation with Torah Department of Jewish Agency; conducts ulpan. *Ohr HaMizrach, Torat Yisrael (weekly).* (WWW.RZA.ORG)

SCHNEIDER CHILDREN'S MEDICAL CENTER OF ISRAEL (1982). 130 E. 59 St., Suite 1203, NYC 10022. (212)759-3370. FAX: (212)759-0120. E-mail: mdiscmci@aol.com. Bd. Chmn. H. Irwin Levy; Exec. Dir. Shlomit Manson. Its primary goal is to provide the best medical care to children in the Middle East. *UPDATE Newsletter*

SOCIETY OF ISRAEL PHILATELISTS (1949). 24355 Tunbridge Lane, Beachwood, OH 44122. (216)292-3843. Pres. Robert B. Pildes. MD; Exec. Secry. Howard S. Chapman; Journal Ed. Dr. Oscar Stadtler. Promotes interest in, and knowledge of, all phases of Israel philately through sponsorship of chapters and research groups, maintenance of a philatelic library, and support of public and private exhibitions. *The Israel Philatelist; monographs; books.*

TEL AVIV UNIVERSITY: AMERICAN COUNCIL (FORMERLY AMERICAN FRIENDS OF TEL AVIV UNIVERSITY, INC.) (1955). 39 Broadway, 15th Floor., NYC 10006. (212)742-9070. FAX: (212)742-9071. E-mail: info@tauac.org. Pres. Sam Witkin; Natl. Chmn. Joel Tauber. Promotes higher education at Tel Aviv University, Israel's largest and most comprehensive institution of higher learning. Included in its nine faculties are the Sackler School of Medicine with its fully accredited NY State English-language program, the Rubin Academy of Music, and 70 research institutes, including the Moshe Dayan Center for Middle East & African Studies and the Jaffe Center for Strategic Studies. *Tel Aviv University News; FAX Flash, Connections Newsletter (quarterly).*

THEODOR HERZL FOUNDATION (1954). 633 Third Ave., 21st fl., NYC 10017. (212)339-6040. FAX: (212)318-6176. E-mail: info@midstream.org. Chmn. Kalman Sultanik; Sec. Sam E. Bloch. Offers cultural activities, lectures, conferences, courses in modern Hebrew and Jewish subjects, Israel, Zionism, and Jewish history..

———, HERZL PRESS. Chmn. Kalman Sultanik; Dir. of Pub. Sam E. Bloch. Serves as "the Zionist Press of record," publishing books that are important for the light they shed on Zionist philosophy, Israeli history, contemporary Israel and the Diaspora and the relationship between them. They are important as contributions to Zionist letters and history. *Midstream.*

TO SAVE A LIFE (2003). 16405 Equestrian Lane, Rockville, MD 20855. (301)977-3637. FAX: (301)977-3888. E-mail: tosavealife@hotmail.com. Pres. Jerry Klinger. Provides an opportunity to give directly, efficiently, and personally to help needy Israelis; identifies small charities that are below the radar screen. (WWW.TSAL.ORG)

TSOMET-TECHIYA USA (1978). 185 Montague St., 3rd fl., Brooklyn, NY 11201.

(718)596-2119. FAX: (718)858-4074. E-mail: eliahu@aol.com. Chmn. Howard B. Weber. Supports the activities of the Israeli Tsomet party, which advocates Israeli control over the entire Land of Israel.

UNITED CHARITY INSTITUTIONS OF JERUSALEM, INC. (1903). 1467 48 St., Brooklyn, NY 11219. (718)633-8469. FAX: (718)633-8478. Chmn. Rabbi Charlop; Exec. Dir. Rabbi Pollak. Raises funds for the maintenance of schools, kitchens, clinics, and dispensaries in Israel; free loan foundations in Israel.

US/ISRAEL WOMEN TO WOMEN (1979). 45 West 36th Street, 10th Floor, NYC 10018. (917) 351-0920. FAX: (917) 351-0921. E-mail: info@usisraelwomen.org. Ch. Nina Kaufman, esq.; Exec. Dir. Joan Gordon. Provides critical seed money for grassroots efforts advocating equal status and fair treatment for women in all spheres of Israeli life; targets small, innovative, Israeli-run programs that seek to bring about social change in health, education, civil rights, domestic violence, family planning, and other spheres of Israeli life. *Newsletters.* (WWW.USISRAELWOMEN.ORG)

VOLUNTEERS FOR ISRAEL (1982). 330 W. 42 St., Suite 1618, NYC 10036-6902. (212)643-4848. FAX: (212)643-4855. E-mail: vol4israel@aol.com. Pres. Jeanne S. Schachter; Vice Pres. Carol Stein. Provides aid to Israel through volunteer work, building lasting relationships between Israelis and Americans. Affords persons aged 18 and over the opportunity to participate in various duties currently performed by overburdened Israelis on IDF bases and in other settings, enabling them to meet and work closely with Israelis and to gain an inside view of Israeli life and culture.

WOMEN'S LEAGUE FOR ISRAEL, INC. (1928). 160 E. 56 St., NYC 10022. (212)838-1997. FAX: (212)888-5972. E-mail: wliny@aol.com. Pres. Harriet Lainer; Exec. Dir. Dorothy Leffler. Maintains centers in Haifa, Tel Aviv, Jerusalem, Natanya. Projects include Family Therapy and Training, Centers for the Prevention of Domestic Violence, Meeting Places (supervised centers for noncustodial parents and their children), DROR (supporting families at risk), Yachdav-"Together" (long-term therapy for parents and children), the National Library for Social Work, and the Hebrew University Blind Students' Unit.

WORLD CONFEDERATION OF UNITED ZIONISTS (1946; reorg.1958). 130 E. 59 St., NYC 10022. (212)371-1452. FAX: (212)371-3265. Co-Pres. Marlene Post & Kalman Sultanik. Promotes Zionist education, sponsors nonparty youth movements in the Diaspora, and strives for an Israel-oriented creative Jewish survival in the Diaspora. *Zionist Information Views* (in English and Spanish).

WORLD ZIONIST ORGANIZATION-AMERICAN SECTION (1971). 633 Third Ave., 21st fl., NYC 10017. (212)688-3197. Chmn. Kalman Sultanik. As the American section of the overall Zionist body throughout the world, it operates primarily in the field of aliyah from the free countries, education in the Diaspora, youth and Hechalutz, organization and information, cultural institutions, publications; conducts a worldwide Hebrew cultural program including special seminars and pedagogic manuals; disperses information and assists in research projects concerning Israel; promotes, publishes, and distributes books, periodicals, and pamphlets concerning developments in Israel, Zionism, and Jewish history. *Midstream.*

———, DEPARTMENT OF EDUCATION AND CULTURE (1948). 633 Third Ave., 21st fl., NYC 10017. (212)339-6001. FAX: (212)826-8959. Renders educational services to boards and schools: study programs, books, AV aids, instruction, teacher-in-training service. Judaic and Hebrew subjects. Annual National Bible Contest; Israel summer and winter programs for teachers and students.

———, ISRAEL ALIYAH CENTER (1993). 633 Third Ave., 21st fl., NYC 10017. (212)339-6060. FAX: (212)832-2597. Exec. Dir. N. Amer. Aliyah Delegation, Kalman Grossman. Through 26 offices throughout N. Amer., staffed by *shlichim* (emissaries), works with potential immigrants to plan their future in Israel and processes immigration documents. Through Israel Aliyah Program Center provides support, information, and programming for olim and their families; promotes long-term programs and fact-finding trips to Israel. Cooperates with Tnuat Aliyah in

Jerusalem and serves as American contact with Association of Americans and Canadians in Israel.

YOUTH RENEWAL FUND. 250 W. 57th Street, Suite 632., NYC 10107. (212)207-3195. FAX: (212)207-8379. E-mail: info@youthrenewalfund.org. Pres. Samuel L. Katz; Exec. Dir. Karen L. Berman. The Youth Renewal Fund was established in 1989 to provide supplemental education to disadvantaged youth in Israel. Since inception, YRF has implemented over $10 million in programs that have benefited over 19,500 Israeli children. (WWW.YOUTHRENEWALFUND.ORG)

ZIONIST ORGANIZATION OF AMERICA (1897). ZOA House, 4 E. 34 St., NYC 10016. (212)481-1500. FAX: (212)481-1515. E-mail: info@zoa.org. Natl. Pres. Morton A. Klein. Strengthens the relationship between Israel and the U.S. through Zionist educational activities that explain Israel's importance to the U.S. and the dangers that Israel faces. Works on behalf of pro-Israel legislation; combats anti-Israel bias in the media, textbooks, travel guides, and on campuses; promotes *aliyah*. Maintains the ZOA House in Tel Aviv, a cultural center, and the Kfar Silver Agricultural and Technical High School in Ashkelon, which provides vocational training for new immigrants. *ZOA Report; Israel and the Middle East: Behind the Headlines*.(WWW.ZOA.ORG)

OVERSEAS AID

AMERICAN FRIENDS OF THE ALLIANCE ISRAÉLITE UNIVERSELLE, INC. (1946). 420 Lexington Ave., Suite 1731, NYC 10170. (212)808-5437. FAX: (212)983-0094. E-mail: afaiu@onsiteaccess.com. Pres. Albert Sibony; Asst. Batya Minkowitz. Participates in educational and human-rights activities of the AIU and supports the Alliance system of Jewish schools, teachers' colleges, and remedial programs in Israel, North Africa, the Middle East, Europe, and Canada. *Alliance Review*.

AMERICAN JEWISH JOINT DISTRIBUTION COMMITTEE, INC.—JDC (1914). 711 Third Ave., NYC 10017-4014. (212)687-6200. FAX: (212)370-5467. E-mail: newyork@jdcny.org. Pres. Ellen Heller; Exec. V.-Pres. Steven Schwager. Provides assistance to Jewish communities in Europe, Asia, Africa, and the Mideast, including welfare programs for Jews in need. Current concerns include: Rescuing Jews from areas of distress, facilitating community development in the former Soviet Union; helping to meet Israel's social service needs by developing innovative programs that create new opportunities for the country's most vulnerable populations; youth activities in Eastern Europe and nonsectarian development and disaster assistance. *Annual Report; Snapshots: JDC's Activities in the Former Soviet Union; JDC: One People, One Heart*. (WWW.JDC.ORG).

AMERICAN JEWISH PHILANTHROPIC FUND (1955). 122 E. 42 St., 12th fl., NYC 10168-1289. (212)755-5640. FAX: (212)644-0979. Pres. Charles J. Tanenbaum. Provides college scholarship assistance to Jewish refugees through pilot programs being administered by the Jewish Family Service in Los Angeles and NYANA in New York.

AMERICAN JEWISH WORLD SERVICE (1985). 45 West 36th Street., NYC 10018. (212)736-2597. FAX: (212)736-3463. E-mail:jws@ajws.org. Chmn. Marty Friedman; Pres. Ruth W. Messinger. Provides nonsectarian, humanitarian assistance and emergency relief to people in need in Africa, Asia, Latin America, Russia, Ukraine, and the Middle East; works in partnership with local nongovernmental organizations to support and implement self-sustaining grassroots development projects; serves as a vehicle through which the Jewish community can act as global citizens. *AJWS Reports (newsletter)*. (WWW.AJWS.ORG)

AMERICAN ORT (1922, reorg. 2006). 75 Maiden Lane, 10th fl., NYC 10038. (212)505-7700. FAX: (212)674-3057. E-mail: www.americanort.org; www.waort.org. Pres. Doreen Hermelin; Exec. Dir. Hope Kessler. Consolidation of American ORT and Women's American ORT that coordinates all ORT operations in the U.S., promotes and raises funds for ORT, a nonpolitical organization and the largest nongovernmental global education and training organization in the world. With past and present activities in over 100 countries, ORT has educated nearly 4 million people in a global network of high schools, colleges, apprenticeship programs and teacher training institutes. ORT's global network enables its 300,000 students in more than 60 countries to pursue fruitful careers and live lives of hope. Students at ORT schools everywhere around the world rely on funds raised by American ORT to help them meet tuition costs, build the most up-to-date learning facilities and furnish them with cutting-edge learning tools, computers, laboratories and other equipment. In Israel, 100,000 students attend 145 schools and training centers; there are 47 ORT schools and centers in the CIS (the former Soviet Union) and in the Baltic States; and in the U.S., over 15,000 students are served by ORT's Technical Institutes in Chicago, Los Angeles, and New York, and in Jewish day school programs in Atlanta, Chicago, Cleveland, Detroit, Florida, Los Angeles, and the National Capital Area (Washington, D.C.). Jewish day school students are served by ORT compute technology programs in Atlanta, Cleveland and Miami. (WWW.ORTAMERICA.ORG)

CONFERENCE ON JEWISH MATERIAL CLAIMS AGAINST GERMANY, INC. (1951). 15 E. 26 St., Rm. 906, NYC 10010. (212)696-4944. FAX: (212)679-2126. E-mail: info@claimscon.org. Chairman Julius Berman; Exec. V.-Pres. Gideon Taylor. Represents Jewish survivors in negotiations for compensation from the German government and other entities once controlled by the Nazis. Also an operating agency that administers compensation funds, recovers Jewish property and allocates funds to institutions that serve Holocaust survivors. The Claims Conference—made up of the conference on Jewish Material Claims Against Germany and the Committee for Jewish Claims on Austria—is one of the founders of the World Jewish Restitution Organization, Memorial Foundation for Jewish Culture and the United Restitution Organization. *Newsletter; Annual Report; Guide to Restitution and Compensation; Special Update.* (WWW.CLAIMSCON.ORG)

HIAS, INC. (HEBREW IMMIGRANT AID SOCIETY) (1880; reorg. 1954). 333 Seventh Ave., NYC 10001-5004. (212)967-4100. FAX: (212)967-4483. E-mail:public@hias.org. Chair Michael Rukin; Pres. & CEO Gideon Aranoff. The oldest international migration and refugee resettlement agency in the United States, dedicated to assisting persecuted and oppressed people worldwide and delivering them to countries of safe haven. As the migration arm of the American Jewish community, it also advocates for fair and just policies affecting refugees and immigrants. Since its founding in 1881, the agency has rescued more than four and a half million people. *Bi-Annual report.*

JEWISH FOUNDATION FOR THE RIGHTEOUS (1986). 305 Seventh Ave., 19th fl., NYC 10001. (212)727-9955. FAX: (212)727-9956. E-mail: jfr@jfr.org. Pres. Melvin L. Merians; Exec. V.P. Stanlee J. Stahl. Provides monthly support to 1,700 aged and needy Righteous Gentiles living in 30 countries who risked their lives to save Jews during the Holocaust. The Foundation's education program focuses on educating teachers and their students about the history of the Holocaust and the significance of altruistic behavior for our society. *Newsletter* (3 times a year). (WWW.JFR.ORG)

NORTH AMERICAN CONFERENCE ON ETHIOPIAN JEWRY (NACOEJ) (1982). 132 Nassau St., Suite 412, NYC 10038. (212)233-5200. FAX: (212)233-5243. E-mail: nacoej@aol.com. Pres. Judith L. Wolf; Exec. Dir. Barbara Ribakove Gordon. Provides programming for Ethiopian Jews in Israel in the areas of education (elementary school, high school and college) and cultural preservation. Assists Ethiopian Jews remaining in Ethiopia. National speakers bureau offers programs to synagogues, schools, and Jewish and non-Jewish organizations. Exhibits of Ethiopian Jewish artifacts, photos, handicrafts, etc. available. *Lifeline (newsletter).* (WWW.NACOEJ.ORG)

RE'UTH WOMEN'S SOCIAL SERVICE, INC. (1937). 130 E. 59 St., Suite 1200, NYC 10022. (212)836-1570. FAX: (212)836-1114. Chmn. Ursula Merkin; Pres. Rosa Strygler. Maintains, in Israel, subsidized housing for self-reliant elderly; old-age homes for more dependent elderly; Lichtenstadter Hospital for chronically ill and young accident victims not accepted by other hospitals; subsidized meals; Golden Age clubs. Recently opened a wing for chronically ill children. *Annual dinner journal.*

THANKS TO SCANDINAVIA, INC. (1963). American Jewish Committee, 165 East 56th Street, 8th Fl., NYC 10022. (212)891-1403. FAX: (212)838-2120. Email:

tts@ajc.org. Pres. Richard Netter; Exec. Dir. Rebecca Neuwirth. Provides scholarships and fellowships at U.S. universities and medical centers and Israeli educational institutions to students/teachers/medical professionals from Bulgaria, Denmark, Finland, Norway, and Sweden in lasting appreciation of the rescue of Jews during World War II and to build friendships based on those examples of courage and humanity in history. (WWW.THANKSTOSCANDNAVIA.ORG)

UNITED JEWISH COMMUNITIES (1999). 111 Eighth Ave., 11th fl., NYC 10011-5201. (212)284-6500. FAX: (212)284-6822. Chmn. Joseph Kanfer; Pres./CEO Howard Rieger. Formed from the merger of the United Jewish Appeal, the Council of Jewish Federations and United Israel Appeal, is the dominant fundraising arm for North American Jewry, and represents 189 Jewish Federations and 400 independent communities across the continent. It reflects the values and traditions of education, leadership, advocacy and social justice, and continuity of community that define the Jewish people.

RELIGIOUS AND EDUCATIONAL ORGANIZATIONS

AGUDATH ISRAEL OF AMERICA (1922). 42 Broadway, NYC, 10004. (212)797-9000. FAX: (646)254-1600. E-mail: shafran@agudathisrael.org. Exec. V.-Pres. Rabbi Shmuel Bloom. Mobilizes Orthodox Jews to cope with Jewish problems in the spirit of the Torah; speaks out on contemporary issues from an Orthodox viewpoint; sponsors a broad range of projects aimed at enhancing religious living, education, children's welfare, protection of Jewish religious rights, outreach to the assimilated and to arrivals from the former Soviet Union, and social services. *Jewish Observer; Dos Yiddishe Vort; Coalition.*

———, AGUDAH WOMEN OF AMERICA-N'SHEI AGUDATH ISRAEL (1940). 42 Broadway, NYC 10004. (212)363-8940. FAX: (212)747-8763. Presidium Aliza Grund & Rose Isbee; Dir. Hannah Kalish, Esq. Organizes Jewish women for philanthropic work in the U.S. and Israel and for intensive Torah education. Its new division, N'shei C.A.R.E.S., (Community, Awareness, Responsibility, Education, & Support), conducts seminars and support groups promoting the health and well-being of Jewish women and their families.

———, BOYS' DIVISION-PIRCHEI AGUDATH ISRAEL (1925) 42 Broadway, NYC 10004 (212)797-9000. Natl. Coord. Rabbi Shimon Grama. Educates Orthodox Jewish children in Torah; encourages sense of communal responsibility. Branches sponsor weekly youth groups and Jewish welfare projects. National Mishnah contests, rallies, and conventions foster unity on a national level. *Leaders Guides.*

———, GIRLS' DIVISION—BNOS AGUDATH ISRAEL (1921). 42 Broadway, NYC 10004. (646)254-1600. Natl. Dir. Leah Zagelbaum. Sponsors regular weekly programs on the local level and unites girls from throughout the Torah world with extensive regional and national activities. *Kol Bnos.*

———, YOUNG MEN'S DIVISION—ZEIREI AGUDATH ISRAEL (1921). 42 Broadway, NYC 10004. (212)797-9000, ext. 57. Dir. Rabbi Labish Becker. Educates youth to see Torah as source of guidance for all issues facing Jews as individuals and as a people. Inculcates a spirit of activism through projects in religious, Torah-educational, and community-welfare fields. *Am Hatorah; Daf Chizuk.*

AGUDATH ISRAEL WORLD ORGANIZATION (1912) 42 Broadway, 14th Floor, NYC 10004. (212)797-9000. FAX: (212)254-1650. UN Rep. Prof. Harry Reicher, Esq. Represents the interests of Orthodox Jewry on the national and international scenes. Sponsors projects to strengthen Torah life worldwide.

ALEPH: ALLIANCE FOR JEWISH RENEWAL (1963; reorg. 1993). 7000 Lincoln Drive, #B2, Philadelphia, PA 19119-3046. (215)247-9700. FAX: (215)247-9703. E-mail: alephajr@aol.com. Bd. Chmn. Linda Jo Doctor; Exec. Dir. Debra Kolodny. Serving the worldwide grassroots movement for Jewish spiritual renewal, ALEPH organizes and nurtures communities, trains lay and rabbinic leaders, creates new liturgy and adult learning resources, sponsors conferences, retreats and seminars and works for social and environmental justice. *New Menorah online journal and KolAleph/Or Hador combined quarterly newsletter of the Aleph and the Network of Jewish Renewal Communities (NJRC).* (WWW.ALEPH.ORG)

AM KOLEL JUDAIC RESOURCE CENTER (1990). 15 W. Montgomery Ave., Rockville, MD 20850. (301)309-2310. FAX: (301)309-2328. E-mail: amkolel@aol.com. Pres. David Shneyer. An independent Jewish resource center, providing a progressive Jewish voice in the community. Activities include: religion, educational and cultural programs; classes, workshops and seminars; interfaith workshops and programs; tikkun olam (social action) opportunities. The staff provides training and resources to emerging and independent communities throughout N. America. Am Kolel sponsors Jews United for Justice, the Center for Inclusiveness in Jewish Life (CIJL) and Yedid DC. *Directory of Independent Jewish Communities and Havurot in Maryland, DC and Virginia; Rock Creek Haggadah.*

AMERICAN ASSOCIATION OF RABBIS (1978). 350 Fifth Ave., Suite 3304, NYC 10118. (212)244-3350, (516)244-7113. FAX: (516)344-0779. E-mail: tefu@aol.com. Pres. Rabbi Jeffrey Wartenberg; Exec. Dir. Rabbi David L. Dunn. An organization of rabbis serving in pulpits, in areas of education, and in social work. *Quarterly bulletin; monthly newsletter.*

AMERICAN STUDENTS TO ACTIVATE PRIDE (ASAP/OU College Affairs) (1993). 11 Broadway, 14th fl., NYC 10004. (212)563-4000. FAX: (212)564-9058. E-mail: davidfel@ix.netcom.com. Pres. Zelda Goldsmith; Natl. Dir. Rabbi David Felsenthal; Chmn. Bernard Falk. A spiritual fitness movement of Jewish college students promoting Torah learning and discussion. Supports 100 learning groups at over 65 campuses as well as regional and national seminars and shabbatonim. *Good Shabbos (weekly); Rimon Discussion Guide (monthly); Jewish Student College Survival Guide (yearly).*

ASSOCIATION FOR JEWISH STUDIES (1969). Center for Jewish History, 15 W. 16 St., NYC 10011. (917)606-8249. FAX: (917)606-8222. E-mail: ajs@ajs.cjh.org. Pres. Sara Horowitz; Exec. Dir. Rona Sheramy. Seeks to promote, maintain, and improve the teaching of Jewish studies in colleges and universities by sponsoring meetings and conferences, publishing a newsletter and other scholarly materials, aiding in the placement of teachers, coordinating research, and cooperating with other scholarly organizations. *AJS Review; AJS Perspectives.* (WWW.BRANDEIS.EDU/AJS)

ASSOCIATION FOR THE SOCIAL SCIENTIFIC STUDY OF JEWRY (1971). c/o Prof. Carmel U. Chiswick, Department of Economics (m/c 144), University of Illinois at Chicago, 601 S. Morgan Street, Chicago, Il 60607-7121. (312)996-2683. FAX: (312)996-3344. E-mail: exec@assj.org. Pres. Sherry Israel; V.-Pres. Riv-Ellen Prell; Sec.-Treas. Carmel Chiswick. Journal Ed. Samuel Heilman; Mng. Ed. Uriel Heilman. Arranges academic sessions and facilitates communication among social scientists studying Jewry through meetings, journal, newsletter and related materials and activities. *Contemporary Jewry; Newsletter (electronic).*

ASSOCIATION OF ORTHODOX JEWISH SCIENTISTS (1948). 25 W. 45tSt.·Suite 1405, NYC 10036. (212)840-1166. FAX: (212) 840-1514. E-mail: aojs@jerusalemail.com. Pres. Allen J. Bennett, M.D.; Bd. Chmn. Rabbi Nachman Cohen. Seeks to contribute to the development of science within the framework of Orthodox Jewish tradition; to obtain and disseminate information relating to the interaction between the Jewish traditional way of life and scientific developments—on both an ideological and practical level; to assist in the solution of problems pertaining to Orthodox Jews engaged in scientific teaching or research. Two main conventions are held each year. *Intercom; Proceedings; Halacha Bulletin; newsletter.*

B'NAI B'RITH YOUTH ORGANIZATION (1924, became independent in 2002). 2020 K Street, NW, 7th Floor, Washington, DC 20006. (202)857-6633. FAX: (212)857-6568. Chmn. Howard Wohl; Exec. Dir. Matthew Grossman. Organized in local chapters, BBYO is a youth led international organization offering leadership opportunities and Jewish programming, which helps Jewish teenagers achieve self-fulfillment and contribute to the community. Assists members acquire a greater knowledge and appreciation for the Jewish religion, culture and the State of Israel. (WWW.BBYO.ORG)

CANTORS ASSEMBLY (1947). 3080 Broadway, Suite 613, NYC 10027. (212)678-8834.

FAX: (212)662-8989. E-mail: caoffice @aol.com. Pres. Joseph Gole; Exec. V.-Pres. David Propis. Seeks to unite all cantors who adhere to traditional Judaism and who serve as full-time cantors in bona fide congregations to conserve and promote the musical traditions of the Jews and to elevate the status of the cantorial profession. *Annual Proceedings; Journal of Synagogue Music.* (WWW.CANTORS.ORG)

CENTER FOR CHRISTIAN-JEWISH UNDERSTANDING OF SACRED HEART UNIVERSITY (1992). 5151 Park Ave., Fairfield, CT 06825. (203)365-7592. FAX: (203)365-4815. E-mail: jhe@sacredheart.edu. Pres. Dr. Anthony J. Cernera; Exec. Dir. Rabbi Joseph H. Ehrenkranz. An educational and research division of Sacred Heart University; brings together clergy, laity, scholars, theologians, and educators with the purpose of promoting interreligious research, education, and dialogue, with particular focus on current religious thinking within Christianity and Judaism. *CCJU Perspective.*

CENTRAL CONFERENCE OF AMERICAN RABBIS (1889). 355 Lexington Ave., NYC 10017. (212)972-3636. FAX: (212)692-0819. E-mail: info@ccarnet.org. Pres. Peter S. Knobel; Exec. V.-Pres. Rabbi Steven Fox. Seeks to conserve and promote Judaism and to disseminate its teachings in a liberal spirit. The CCAR Press provides liturgy and prayerbooks to the worldwide Reform Jewish community. *CCAR Journal: A Reform Jewish Quarterly; CCAR Yearbook.* (WWW.CCARNET.ORG)

CLAL—NATIONAL JEWISH CENTER FOR LEARNING AND LEADERSHIP (1974). 440 Park Ave. S., 4th fl., NYC 10016-8012. (212)779-3300. FAX: (212)779-1009. E-mail: info@clal.org. Pres. Rabbi Irwin Kula, Rabbi Brad Hirschfeld; Chmn. Larry Gellman; Exec. V.-Chmn. Donna M. Rosenthal. Provides leadership training for lay leaders, rabbis, educators, and communal professionals. A faculty of rabbis and scholars representing all the denominations of Judaism make Judaism come alive, applying the wisdom of the Jewish heritage to help shape tomorrow's Jewish communities. Offers seminars and courses, retreats, symposia and conferences, lecture bureau and the latest on-line information through CLAL web site. *Sacred Days calendar; monographs; holiday brochures; CLAL Update.* (WWW.CLAL.ORG)

COALITION FOR THE ADVANCEMENT OF JEWISH EDUCATION (CAJE) (1977). 261 W. 35 St., #12A, NYC 10001. (212)268-4210. FAX: (212)268-4214. E-mail: cajeny@caje.org. Pres. Iris Petroff; Exec. Dir. Jeffrey Lasday. The Coalition for the Advancement of Jewish Education (CAJE), the largest membership organization of Jewish educators in North America, hosts annual conferences and offers outreach programming, teacher recruitment, and mentoring, a Job Bank, and a Curriculum Response Service. CAJE has established an Early Childhood Department. Though its Hanukat CAJE Committee, CAJE advocates on behalf of Jewish educators. *Jewish Education News; CAJE Page; timely curricular publications; Hanukat CAJE series.* (WWW.CAJE.ORG)

CONGRESS OF SECULAR JEWISH ORGANIZATIONS (1970). 19657 Villa Dr. N., Southfield, MI 48076. (248)569-8127. FAX: (248)569-5222. E-mail: csjd@csjd.org.. An umbrella organization of schools and adult clubs; facilitates exchange of curricula and educational programs for children and adults stressing the Jewish historical and cultural heritage and the continuity of the Jewish people. *New Yorkish (Yiddish literature translations); Haggadah; The Hanuka Festival; Mame-Loshn.*

CONVERSION TO JUDAISM RESOURCE CENTER (1997). 74 Hauppauge Rd., Rm. 53, Commack, NY 11725. (631) 462-5826. E-mail: inform@convert.org. Pres. Dr. Lawrence J. Epstein; Exec. Dir. Susan Lustig. Provides information and advice for people who wish to convert to Judaism or who have converted. Puts potential converts in touch with rabbis from all branches of Judaism.

COUNCIL FOR JEWISH EDUCATION (1926) 11 Olympia Lane, Monsey, NY 10952-2829. (845)368-8657, Fax (845)369-6583. E-mail: mjscje@aol.com. Pres. Dr. Morton J. Summer; Editor Rabbi Irwin E. Witty. Fellowship of Jewish education professionals-administrators, supervisors, and teachers in Hebrew high schools and Jewish teachers colleges-of all ideological groupings; conducts national and regional conferences; represents the Jewish education profession before the Jewish community; cooperates with Jewish Agency Department of Education in promoting Hebrew culture and studies. *Journal of Jewish Education.*

FEDERATION OF JEWISH MEN'S CLUBS (1929). 475 Riverside Dr., Suite 832, NYC 10115. (212)749-8100; (800)288-FJMC. FAX: (212)316-4271. E-mail: international@fjmc.org. Intl. Pres. Dr. Robert Braitman; Exec. Dir. Rabbi Charles E. Simon. Promotes principles of Conservative Judaism; develops family education and leadership training programs; offers the Art of Jewish Living series and Yom HaShoah Home Commemoration; sponsors Hebrew literacy adult-education program; presents awards for service to American Jewry. Latest innovation-"The Ties that Bind," a motivational and instructional video about Tefillin. *Torchlight; Hearing Men's Voices.* (WWW.FJMC.ORG)

HILLEL: THE FOUNDATION FOR JEWISH CAMPUS LIFE (formerly B'NAI B'RITH HILLEL FOUNDATIONS) (1923). Charles and Lynn Schusterman International Center, Arthur and Rochelle Belfer Building, 800 Eight Street, NW, Washington, DC 20001-3724. (202)449-6500. FAX: (202)449-6600. E-mail: info@hillel.org. Chmn. Edgar M. Bronfman; Pres. Wayne Firestone. The largest Jewish campus organization in the world, Hillel: The Foundation for Jewish Campus Life, is committed to creatively empowering and engaging Jewish students through its network of over 500 regional centers, campus-based foundations, program centers and affiliates. *The Hillel Annual Report; Shavua Tov. Israel Update.* (WWW.HILLEL.ORG)

INSTITUTE FOR COMPUTERS IN JEWISH LIFE (1978). 7074 N. Western Ave., Chicago, IL 60645. (773)262-9200. FAX: (773)262-9298. E-mail: rosirv@aol.com. Pres. Thomas Klutznick; Exec. V.-Pres. Dr. Irving J. Rosenbaum. Explores, develops, and disseminates applications of computer technology to appropriate areas of Jewish life, with special emphasis on Jewish education; creates educational software for use in Jewish schools; provides consulting service and assistance for national Jewish organizations, seminaries, and synagogues.

INTERNATIONAL FEDERATION OF SECULAR HUMANISTIC JEWS (1983). 224 West 35th Street, Suite 410, NYC 10024. (212)564-6711. FAX: (212)564-6721. E-mail: info@ifshj.org. Co-Ch. Felix Posen (Europe), Yair Tzaban (Israel). The International Federation of Secular Humanistic Jews provides a voice for secular Jews worldwide in their common goal to foster Secular Humanistic Judaism as an option for modern Jewish identity. The IFSHJ develops awareness of Secular and Humanistic Judaism by serving as a resource and for general information, and developing literature, conferences, and communications that promote philosophy of Secular and Humanistic Judaism in the world community. *Newsletter (Hofesh); Contemplate: International Journal of Secular Jewish Thought.*

INTERNATIONAL INSTITUTE FOR SECULAR HUMANISTIC JUDAISM (1985). 28611 West Twelve Mile Rd., Farmington Hills, MI 48334. (248)476-9532. FAX: (248)476-8509. E-mail: iishj@iishj.org. Established in 1985 in Jerusalem to serve the needs of a growing movement, its two primary purposes are to commission and publish educational materials and to train rabbis, leaders, teachers, and spokespersons for the movement. The Institute has two offices-one in Israel (Jerusalem) and one in N. America and offers educational and training programs in Israel, N. America, and the countries of the former Soviet Union. The N. American office, located in a suburb of Detroit, offers the Rabbinic Program, the Leadership Program, and the Adult Education Program. *Brochure, educational papers, and projects.*

JEWISH CHAUTAUQUA SOCIETY, INC. (sponsored by NORTH AMERICAN FEDERATION OF TEMPLE BROTHERHOODS) (1893). 633 Third Ave., NYC 10017. (212)650-4100/(800)765-6200. FAX: (212)650-4189. E-mail: jcs@urj.org. Pres. Irving B. Shnaider; Chancellor Stuart J. Aaronson; Exec. Dir. Doug Barden. Works to promote interfaith understanding by sponsoring accredited college courses and one-day lectures on Judaic topics, providing book grants to educational institutions, producing educational videotapes on interfaith topics, and convening interfaith institutes. A founding sponsor of the National Black/Jewish Relations Center at Dillard University. *ACHIM Magazine.*

JEWISH EDUCATION IN MEDIA (1978). PO Box 180, Riverdale Sta., NYC 10471. (212)362-7633. FAX: (203)359-1381. Pres. Ken Asher; Exec. Dir. Rabbi Mark S. Golub. Devoted to producing television, film, and video-cassettes for a popular Jewish audience, in order to inform, entertain, and inspire a greater sense of Jewish identity and Jewish commitment. "L'Chayim," JEM's weekly half-hour program, which is seen nationally on NJT/National Jewish Television, features outstanding figures in the Jewish world addressing issues and events of importance to the Jewish community. (WWW.LCHAYIM.COM)

JEWISH EDUCATION SERVICE OF NORTH AMERICA (JESNA) (1981). 111 Eighth Ave., 11th fl., NYC 10011. (212)284-6950. FAX: (212)284-6951. E-mail: info@jesna.org. Pres. Donald Sylvan, Ph.D.; Bd. Ch. Diane Troderman. The Jewish Federation system's educational coordinating, planning, and development agency. Promotes excellence in Jewish education by initiating exchange of ideas, programs, and materials; providing information, consultation, educational resources, and policy guidance; and collaborating with partners in N. America and Israel to develop educational programs. *Agenda: Jewish Education; planning guides on Jewish Renaissance; research reports; Jewish Educators Electronic Toolkit.* (WWW.JESNA.ORG)

JEWISH ORTHODOX FEMINIST ALLIANCE (JOFA) (1997). 520 Eighth Ave., 4th fl.., NYC 10018. (212)679-8500. FAX: (212)679-7428. E-mail: jofa@jofa.org. Pres. Carol Kauffman Newman; Exec. Dir. Robin Bodner. Dedicated to expand the spiritual, ritual, intellectual, and political opportunities for women within the framework of *Halakhah* through meangful participation and equality in family life, synagogues, houses of learning, and Jewish communial organizations. *JOFA Journal, Quarterly Newsletter.* (WWW.JOFA.ORG)

JEWISH OUTREACH INSTITUTE (1987). 1270 Broadway, Ste. 609, NYC 10001. (212)760-1440. FAX: (212)760-1569. E-mail: info@joi.org. Pres. Terrence A. Elkes; Exec. Dir. Rabbi Kerry Olitzky. An independent national organization that conducts programs and services to empower and assist the Jewish community in welcoming and fully embracing all members of interfaith families—and anyone else looking to explore connections to the Jewish heritage—into Jewish life. *The Inclusive, The Inclusive Professional.* (WWW.JOI.ORG)

JEWISH RECONSTRUCTIONIST FEDERATION (formerly FEDERATION OF RECONSTRUCTIONIST CONGREGATIONS AND HAVUROT) (1954). 7804 Montgomery Ave., Suite 9, Elkins Park, PA 19027-2649. (215)782-8500. Fax: (215)782-8805. E-mail: info@jrf.org. Pres. Daniel Cedarbaum; Exec. V.-Pres. Carl Sheingold. Provides educational and consulting services to affiliated congregations and havurot; fosters the establishment of new Reconstructionist communities. Publishes *Kol Haneshamah*, an innovative series of prayer books, including a new mahzor and haggadah; provides programmatic materials. Regional offices in NewYork, Los Angeles, Chicago, Philadelphia, and Washington DC. *Reconstructionism Today.* (WWW.JRF.ORG)

———, RECONSTRUCTIONIST RABBINICAL ASSOCIATION (1974). 1299 Church Rd., Wyncote, PA 19095. (215)576-5210. FAX: (215)576-8051. E-mail: info@therra.org. Pres. Rabbi Brant Rosen; Exec. Dir. Rabbi Richard Hirsh. Professional organization for graduates of the Reconstructionist Rabbinical College and other rabbis who identify with Reconstructionist Judaism; cooperates with Jewish Reconstructionist Federation in furthering Reconstructionism in the world. *Newsletters; position papers.* (WWW.THERRA.ORG)

———, RECONSTRUCTIONIST RABBINICAL COLLEGE (*see* p. 668)

JEWISH TEACHERS ASSOCIATION—MORIM (1931). 45 E. 33 St., Suite 310, NYC 10016-5336. (212)684-0556. Pres. Phyllis L. Pullman; V.-Pres. Ronni David; Sec. Helen Parnes; Treas. Mildred Safar. Protects teachers from abuse of seniority rights; fights the encroachment of anti-Semitism in education; offers scholarships to qualified students; encourages teachers to assume active roles in Jewish communal and religious affairs. *Morim JTA Newsletter.*

KULANU, INC. (formerly AMISHAV USA) (1993). 11603 Gilsan St., Silver Spring, MD 20902. (301)681-5679. FAX: (301)681-1587. Email: jdzeller@umich.edu. Pres. Jack Zeller; Sec. Karen Primack. Engages in outreach to dispersed Jewish communities around the world who wish to return to their Jewish roots. Current projects include the formal conversion of Shinlung-Menashe tribesmen in India currently practicing Judaism, and supplying materials and rabbis for conversos/marranos in Mexico and Brazil. *Newsletter.*

NATIONAL COMMITTEE FOR FURTHERANCE OF JEWISH EDUCATION (1941). 824 Eastern Pkwy., Brooklyn, NY 11213. (718)735-0200; (800)33-NCFJE. FAX: (718)735-4455. Pres. Dr. Steven Rubel; Bd. Chmn. Rabbi Shea Hecht; Chmn. Exec. Com. Rabbi Sholem Ber Hecht. Seeks to disseminate the ideals of Torah-true education among the youth of America; provides education and compassionate care for the poor, sick, and needy in U.S. and Israel; provides aid to Iranian Jewish youth; sponsors camps and educational functions, family and vocational counseling services, family and early intervention, after-school and preschool programs, drug and alcohol education and prevention; maintains schools in Brooklyn and Queens. Every year distributes 25,000 toys/gifts through Toys for Hospitalized children; runs the Release-time program of Greater NY, offers classes FT/PT through Hadar Hatorah Rabbinal Seminary. *Panorama; Cultbusters; Intermarriage; Brimstone & Fire; Focus; A Life Full of Giving.*

NATIONAL COUNCIL OF YOUNG ISRAEL (1912). 3 W. 16 St., NYC 10011. (212)929-1525. FAX: (212)727-9526. E-mail: ncyi@youngisrael.org. Pres. Shlomo Mostofsky; Exec. V.-Pres. Rabbi Pesach Lerner. Through its network of member synagogues in N. America and Israel maintains a program of spiritual, cultural, social, and communal activity aimed at the advancement and perpetuation of traditional, Torah-true Judaism; seeks to instill in American youth an understanding and appreciation of the ethical and spiritual values of Judaism. Sponsors rabbinic and lay leadership conferences, synagogue services, rabbinic services, rabbinic and lay leader training, rabbinic placement, women's division, kosher dining clubs, and youth programs. *Viewpoint Magazine; Divrei Torah Bulletin; NCYI Suggestion Box; The Rabbi's Letter.* (WWW.YOUNGISRAEL.ORG)

———, AMERICAN FRIENDS OF YOUNG ISRAEL IN ISRAEL—YISRAEL HATZA'IR (1926). 3 W. 16 St., NYC 10011. (212)929-1525. FAX: (212)727-9526. E-mail: ncyi@youngisrael.org. Pres. Meir Mishkoff. Promotes Young Israel synagogues and youth work in Israel; works to help absorb Russian and Ethiopian immigrants.

———, YOUNG ISRAEL DEPARTMENT OF YOUTH AND YOUNG ADULTS ACTIVITIES (reorg. 1981). 3 W. 16 St, NYC 10011. (212)929-1525. FAX: (212)727-9526. E-mail: ncy:@youngisrael.org. Pres. Shlomo Z. Mostofsky. Fosters varied program of activities for the advancement and perpetuation of traditional Torah-true Judaism; instills ethical and spiritual values and appreciation for compatibility of ancient faith of Israel with good Americanism. Runs leadership training programs and youth shabbatonim; support programs for synagogue youth programs; annual national conference of youth directors; ACHVA summer programs for teens IN Israel and U.S.; Nachala summer program in Israel for Yeshiva H.S. girls and Natzach summer program for Yeshiva H.S. boys. *Torah Kidbits; Shabbat Youth Manual; Y.I. Can Assist You; Synagogue Youth Director Handbook.* (WWW.YOUNGISRAEL.ORG)

NATIONAL HAVURAH COMMITTEE (1979). 7135 Germantown Ave., Philadelphia, PA 19119-1720. (215)248-1335. FAX: (215)248-9760. E-mail: institute@havurah.org. Ch. Sherry Israel. A center for Jewish renewal devoted to spreading Jewish ideas, ethics, and religious practices through havurot, participatory and inclusive religious mini-communities. Maintains a directory of N. American havurot and sponsors a weeklong summer institute, regional weekend retreats. *Havurah! (newsletter).* (WWW.HAVURAH.ORG)

NATIONAL JEWISH COMMITTEE ON SCOUTING (Boy Scouts of America) (1926). 1325 West Walnut Hill Lane, PO Box 152079, Irving, TX 75015-2079. (972)580-2000. FAX: (972)580-7870. Chmn. Rabbi Peter Hyman. Assists Jewish institutions in meeting their needs and concerns through use of the resources of scouting. Works through local Jewish committees on scouting to establish Tiger Cub groups (1st grade), Cub Scout packs, Boy Scout troops, and coed venturer crews in synagogues, Jewish community centers, day schools, and other Jewish organizations wishing to draw Jewish youth. Support materials and resources on request.

NATIONAL JEWISH GIRL SCOUT COMMITTEE (1972). 33 Central Dr., Bronxville, NY 10708. (914)738-3986, (718)252-6072. FAX: (914)738-6752. E-mail: njgsc@aol.com. Chmn. Rabbi Herbert W. Bomzer; Field Chmn. Adele Wasko. Serves to further Jewish education by promoting Jewish award programs, encouraging religious services, promoting cultural exchanges with the Israel Boy and Girl Scouts Federation, and extending membership in the Jewish community by assisting councils in organizing Girl Scout troops and local Jewish Girl Scout committees. *Newsletter.*

NATIONAL JEWISH HOSPITALITY COMMITTEE (1973; reorg. 1993). PO Box 53691, Philadelphia, PA 19105. (800)745-0301. Pres. Rabbi Allen S. Maller; Exec. Dir. Steven S. Jacobs. Assists persons interested in Judaism-for intermarriage, conversion, general information, or to respond to missionaries. *Special reports.*

NORTH AMERICAN ALLIANCE FOR JEWISH YOUTH (199650 West 58th Street, NYC, NY, 10019 (212)494-1023. FAX: (212)906-9371. E-mail: info@naajewishyouth.org. Chmn. Joseph E. Brenan; Dir. Heather Kibel. Serves the cause of informal Jewish and Zionist education in America; provides a forum for the professional leaders of the major N. American youth movements, camps, Israel programs, and university programs to address common issues and concerns, and to represent those issues with a single voice to the wider Jewish and Zionist community. Sponsors annual Conference on Informal Jewish Education for Jewish youth professionals from across the continent.

OZAR HATORAH, INC. (1946). 625 Broadway, 11th Fl. NYC, 10012. (212)253-7245. FAX: (212) 437-4773. Email: agutman@ozarhatorah.org. Pres. Henry Shalom; Sec. Sam Sutton; Exec. Dir. Rabbi Jean Paul Amoyelle. An international educational network which builds Sephardic communities worldwide through Jewish education.

PANIM: THE INSTITUTE FOR JEWISH LEADERSHIP AND VALUES (FORMERLY WASHINGTON INSTITUTE FOR JEWISH LEADERSHIP & VALUES) (1988). 6101 Montrose Road, Suite 200, Rockville, MD 20852. (301) 770-5070. FAX: (301) 770-6365. E-mail: info@panim.org. Founder/Pres. Rabbi Sidney Schwarz; Bd. Chmn. Mark Levitt. Institute for Jewish Leadership and Values is a non-profit educational organization dedicated to the renewal of American Jewish life through the integration of Jewish learning, values and social responsibility. Our flagship program, *Panim el Panim*: High School in Washington, each year brings over 1,000 Jewish teens from across the country to Washington, D.C. to learn about political and social activism in the context of Jewish learning and values. We also sponsor the Jewish Civics Initiative, the largest national Jewish service/learning program for teens. The Institute also sponsors a Synagogue Transformation Project, and conducts leadership training. *Jewish Civics: A Tikkun Olam/World Repair Manual; Jews, Judaism and Civic Responsibility.*

PARDES PROGRESSIVE ASSOCIATION OF REFORM DAY SCHOOLS (1990). 633 Third Ave., NYC 10017-6778. (212)650-4000. FAX: (480)951-0829. E-mail: educate@urj.org. Pres. Zita Gardner; Chmn. Carol Nemo. An affiliate of the Union for Reform Judaism; brings together day schools and professional and lay leaders committed to advancing the cause of full-time Reform Jewish education; advocates for the continuing development of day schools within the Reform movement as a means to foster Jewish identity, literacy, and continuity; promotes cooperation among our member schools and with other Jewish organizations that share similar goals. *Visions of Excellence (manual).*

P'EYLIM-LEV L'ACHIM (1951). 1034 E. 12 St. Brooklyn, NY 11230. (718)258-7760. FAX: (718)258-4672. E-mail: joskarmel@aol.com. Natl. Dir. Rabbi Joseph C. Karmel; Exec. V.-Pres. Rabbi Nachum Barnetsky. Seeks to bring irreligious Jews in Israel back to their heritage. Conducts outreach through 12 major divisions consisting of thousands of volunteers and hundreds of professionals across the country; conducts anti-missionary and assimilation programs; operates shelters for abused women and children; recruits children for Torah schools.

RABBINICAL ALLIANCE OF AMERICA (Igud Harabonim) (1942). 3 W. 16 St., 4th fl., NYC 10011. (212)242-6420. FAX: (212)255-8313. Pres. Rabbi Abraham B.

Hecht. Seeks to promulgate the cause of Torah-true Judaism through an organized rabbinate that is consistently Orthodox; seeks to elevate the position of Orthodox rabbis nationally and to defend the welfare of Jews the world over. Also has Beth Din Rabbinical Court for Jewish divorces, litigation, marriage counseling, and family problems. *Perspective; Nahalim; Torah Message of the Week; Registry.*

RABBINICAL ASSEMBLY (1901). 3080 Broadway, NYC 10027. (212)280-6000. FAX: (212)749-9166. Pres. Rabbi Jeffrey Wohlberg; Exec. V.-Pres. Rabbi Joel H. Meyers. The international association of Conservative rabbis; actively promotes the cause of Conservative Judaism and works to benefit *klal yisrael*; publishes learned texts, prayer books, and works of Jewish interest; administers the work of the Committee on Jewish Law and Standards for the Conservative movement; serves the professional and personal needs of its members through publications, conferences, and benefit programs and administers the movement's Joint Placement Commission. *Conservative Judaism; Proceedings of the Rabbinical Assembly; Rabbinical Assembly Newsletter.*

RABBINICAL COUNCIL OF AMERICA, INC. (1923; reorg. 1935). 305 Seventh Ave., Suite 1200, NYC 10001. (212)807-7888. FAX: (212)727-8452. Pres. Rabbi Shlomo Hochberg; Exec. V.-Pres. Rabbi Basil Herring. Promotes Orthodox Judaism in the community; supports institutions for study of Torah; stimulates creation of new traditional agencies. *Hadorom; Tradition.* (WWW.RABBIS.ORG)

SOCIETY FOR HUMANISTIC JUDAISM (1969). 28611 W. Twelve Mile Rd., Farmington Hills, MI 48334. (248)478-7610. FAX: (248)478-3159. E-mail: info@shj.org. Pres. Miriam Jerris; Exec. Dir. M. Bonnie Cousens. Serves as a voice for Jews who value their Jewish identity and who seek an alternative to conventional Judaism, who reject supernatural authority and affirm the right of individuals to be the masters of their own lives. Publishes educational and ceremonial materials; organizes congregations and groups. *Humanistic Judaism (quarterly journal); Humanorah (quarterly newsletter).* (WWW.SHJ.ORG)

TEKIAH: ASSOCIATION OF HILLEL/JEWISH CAMPUS PROFESSIONALS (1949). c/o Hillel Foundation of New Orleans, 912 Broadway, New Orleans, LA 70118. (504)866-7060. FAX: (504)861-8909. E-mail: president@tekiah.org. Pres. Rabbi Jeffrey Kurtz-Lendner. Seeks to promote professional relationships and exchanges of experience, develop personnel standards and qualifications, safeguard integrity of Hillel profession; represents and advocates before the Foundation for Jewish Campus Life, Council of Jewish Federations. *Handbook for Hillel Professionals; Guide to Hillel Personnel Practices.* (WWW.TEKIAH.ORG)

TEVA LEARNING CENTER/SHOMREI ADAMAH (1988). 307 Seventh Ave., #900, NYC 10001. (212)807-6376. FAX: (212)924-5112. E-mail: teva@tevacenter.org. Co-Dir. Nili Simhai; Asst. Dir., Noam Dolgin Exists to renew the ecological wisdom inherent in Judaism. Runs Jewish environmental education programs for Jewish day schools, synagogues, community centers, camps, university groups and other organized groups. *Let the Earth Teach You Torah, Ecology and the Jewish Spirit.* (WWW.TEVACENTER.ORG)

TORAH SCHOOLS FOR ISRAEL–CHINUCH ATZMAI (1953). 40 Exchange Pl., NYC 10005. (212)248-6200. FAX: (212)248-6202. Exec. Dir. Rabbi Henach Cohen. Conducts information programs for the American Jewish community on activities of the independent Torah schools educational network in Israel; coordinates role of American members of international board of governors; funds special programs of Mercaz Hachinuch Ha-Atzmai B'Eretz Yisroel; funds religous education programs in America and abroad.

TORAH UMESORAH–NATIONAL SOCIETY FOR HEBREW DAY SCHOOLS (1944). 160 Broadway, NYC 10038. (212)227-1000. FAX: (212)406-6934. E-mail: umesorah@aol.com. Exec. V.-Pres. Rabbi Joshua Fishman. Establishes Hebrew day schools and Yeshivas in U.S. and Canada and provides a full gamut of services, including placement, curriculum guidance, and teacher training. Parent Enrichment Program provides enhanced educational experience for students from less Jewishly educated and marginally affiliated homes through parent-education programs and

Partners in Torah, a one-on-one learning program. Publishes textbooks; runs shabbatonim, extracurricular activities; national PTA groups; national and regional teacher conventions. *Olomeinu-Our World.*

———, NATIONAL ASSOCIATION OF HEBREW DAY SCHOOL PARENT-TEACHER ASSOCIATIONS (1948). 160 Broadway, NYC 10038. (212)227-1000. FAX: (212)406-6934. Natl. PTA Coord. Bernice Brand. Acts as a clearinghouse and service agency to PTAs of Hebrew day schools; organizes parent education courses and sets up programs for individual PTAs. *Fundraising with a Flair; PTA with a Purpose for the Hebrew Day School.*

———, NATIONAL CONFERENCE OF YESHIVA PRINCIPALS (1956). 160 Broadway, NYC 10038. (212)227-1000. FAX: (212)406-6934. E-mail: umesorah@aol.com. Pres. Rabbi Rabbi Schneur Aisenstark; Exec. V.-Pres. Rabbi Joshua Fishman. Professional organization of elementary and secondary yeshivah/day school principals providing yeshivah/day schools with school evaluation and guidance, teacher and principal conferences-including a Mid-Winter Conference and a National Educators Convention; offers placement service for principals and teachers in yeshivah/day schools. *Directory of Elementary Schools and High Schools.*

———, NATIONAL YESHIVA TEACHERS BOARD OF LICENSE (1953). 160 Broadway, NYC 10038. (212)227-1000. Exec. V.-Pres. Rabbi Joshua Fishman; Dir. Rabbi Yitzchock Merkin. Issues licenses to qualified instructors for all grades of the Hebrew day school and the general field of Torah education.

UNION FOR REFORM JUDAISM (formerly UNION OF AMERICAN HEBREW CONGREGATIONS) (1873). 633 Third Ave., NYC 10017-6778. (212)650-4000. FAX: (212) 650-4169. E-mail: urj@urj.org. Pres. Rabbi Eric H. Yoffie; V.-Pres. Rabbi Lennard R. Thal; Bd. Chmn. Russell Silverman. Serves as the central congregational body of Reform Judaism in the Western Hemisphere; serves its approximately 900 affiliated temples and membership with religious, educational, cultural, and administrative programs. *Reform Judaism.* (WWW.URJ.ORG)

———, AMERICAN CONFERENCE OF CANTORS (1953). 5591 Chamblee Dunwoody Rd. Bldg. 1360, Ste. 200, Atlanta, GA 30338. (770)390-0006. FAX: (770)390-0020. E-mail: accantors@aol.com. Pres. Richard Cohen, Exec. V.-Pres. Scott E. Colbert Exec. VP; Dir. of Placement Barbara Ostfeld; Admin. Asst. Deborah Barber. Members are invested or certified by accredited seminaries, i.e., Hebrew Union College-Jewish Insitute of Religion School of Sacred Music. Through the Joint Cantorial Placement Commission, the ACC serves Reform congregations seeking cantors. Dedicated to creative Judaism, preserving the past, and encouraging new and vital approaches to religious ritual, liturgical music and ceremony. *Koleinu* (monthly).

———, COMMISSION ON SOCIAL ACTION OF REFORM JUDAISM (see p. 623)

———, COMMISSION ON SYNAGOGUE MANAGEMENT (URJ-CCAR) (1962). 633 Third Ave., NYC 10017-6778. (212)650-4040. FAX: (212)650-4239. Chmn. Marshall Krolick; Dir. Dale A. Glasser. Assists congregations in management, finance, building maintenance, design, construction, and art aspects of synagogues; maintains the Synagogue Architectural Library.

———, NATA (NATIONAL ASSOCIATION OF TEMPLE ADMINISTRATORS) (1941). 6114 La Salle Ave., Box 731, Oakland, CA 94611. (800)966-6282. FAX: (925)283-7713. E-mail: nataorg@hotmail.com. FTA Elizabeth L. Hirsh. Professional organization for URJ synagogue administrators. Sponsors graduate training in synagogue management with Hebrew Union College; offers in-service training, workshops, and conferences leading to certification; provides NATA Consulting Service, NATA Placement Service for synagogues seeking advice or professional administrators; establishes professional standards. *NATA Journal.*

———, NATE (NATIONAL ASSOCIATION OF TEMPLE EDUCATORS) (1955). 633 Third Ave., 7th fl., NYC 10017-6778. (212)452-6510. FAX: (212)452-6512. E-mail: nateoff@aol.com. Pres. Lori Sagarin; Exec. Dir. Rabbi Stanley T. Schickler. Represents educators within the general body of Reform Judaism; fosters the full-time profession of the Jewish educator; encourages the growth and development of Jewish religious education consistent with the aims of Reform Judaism; stimulates communal interest in and responsibility for Jewish religious education. *NATE NEWS.* (WWW.RJ.ORG/NATE)

———, NORTH AMERICAN FEDERATION OF TEMPLE BROTHERHOODS (1923). 633 Third Ave., NYC 10017. (212)650-4100. FAX: (212)650-4189. E-mail contact@nftb.org Pres. Aaron Bloom; JCS Chancellor Stuart J. Aaronson; Exec. Dir. Douglas Barden. Dedicated to enhancing the world through the ideal of brotherhood, NFTB and its 300 affiliated clubs are actively involved in education, social action, youth activities, and other programs that contribute to temple and community life. Supports the Jewish Chautauqua Society, an interfaith educational project. *ACHIM (formerly Brotherhood magazine)* (WWW.RJ.ORG/NFTB)

———, URJ DEPARTMENT OF JEWISH EDUCATION (1923). 633 Third Ave., 7th fl., NYC 10017. (212)650-4112. FAX: (212)650-4229. E-mail: jkatzew@urj.org. Chmn. Dr. Rabbi Jan Katzew, Robert Heller; Dir. Dr. Rabbi Jan Katzew. Long-range planning and policy development for congregational programs of lifelong education; materials concerning Reform Jewish Outreach, Teacher Development and Reform Day Schools; activities administered by the URJ Department of Education. *V'Shinantam; Torah at the Center, Family Shabbat Table Talk, Galilee Diary, Jewish Parent Page.*

———, WOMEN OF REFORM JUDAISM—THE FEDERATION OF TEMPLE SISTERHOODS (1913). 633 Third Ave., NYC 10017. (212)650-4050. FAX: (212)650-4059. E-mail: wrj@urj.org. Pres. Rosanne Selfon; Exec. Dir. Shelley Lindauer. Serves more than 600 sisterhoods of Reform Judaism; promotes interreligious understanding and social justice; provides funding for scholarships for rabbinic students; founded the Jewish Braille Institute, which provides braille and large-type Judaic materials for Jewish blind; supports projects for Israel; is the women's agency of Reform Judaism, an affiliate of the URJ; works in behalf of the Hebrew Union College-Jewish Institute of Religion and the World Union for Progressive Judaism. *Notes for Now; Art Calendar; Windows on WRJ.* (WWW.RJ.ORG/WRJ)

———, YOUTH DIVISION AND NORTH AMERICAN FEDERATION OF TEMPLE YOUTH (1939). 633 Third Ave, NYC 10017-6778. (212)650-4070. FAX: (212)650-4199. E-mail: youthdivision@urj.org. Dir. Rabbi Michael Mellen. Dedicated to Jewishly enhancing the lives of the young people of North America's Reform congregations through a program of informal education carried out in URJ Camp-Institutes (11 camps for grades 2 and up), URJ/NFTY Israel Programs (summer and semester), European and domestic teen travel, NFTY/Junior & Senior High School Programs (youth groups), and Kesher/College Education Department (Reform havurot on campuses).

UNION FOR TRADITIONAL JUDAISM (1984). 241 Cedar Lane, Teaneck, NJ 07666. (201)801-0707. FAX: (201)801-0449. Pres. Burton G. Greenblatt; Exec. V.-Pres. Rabbi Ronald D. Price. Through innovative outreach programs, seeks to bring the greatest possible number of Jews closer to an open-minded observant Jewish lifestyle. Activities include Kashrut Initiative, Operation Pesah, the Panel of Halakhic Inquiry, Speakers Bureau, adult and youth conferences, and congregational services. Includes, since 1992, the Morashah rabbinic fellowship. *Hagahelet* (quarterly newsletter);*Cornerstone* (journal); *Tomeikh Kahalakhah* (Jewish legal responsa).

UNION OF ORTHODOX JEWISH CONGREGATIONS OF AMERICA (1898). 11 Broadway, 14th fl., NYC 10004. (212)563-4000. FAX: (212)564-9058. E-mail: ou@ou.org. Pres. Stephen J. Savitsky; Exec. V.-Pres. Rabbi Dr. Tzvi Hersh Weinreb. Serves as the national central body of Orthodox synagogues; national OU kashrut supervision and certification service; sponsors Institute for Public Affairs; National Conference of Synagogue Youth; National Jewish Council for the Disabled; Israel Center in Jerusalem; Torah Center in the Ukraine; New Young Leadership Division; Pardes; provides educational, religious, and organization programs, events, and guidance to synagogues and groups; represents the Orthodox Jewish community to governmental and civic bodies and the general Jewish community. *Jewish Action magazine; OU Kosher Directory; OU Guide to Kosher for Passover Foods; Keeping Posted (NCSY); Synagogue Trends; Our Way magazine; Yachad magazine; Luach & Limud Personal Torah Study, Leadership Briefing, Behind the Union Symbol*.(WWW.OU.ORG)

———, INSTITUTE FOR PUBLIC AFFAIRS (1989). 11 Broadway, 14th fl., NYC 10004. (212)613-8124. FAX: (212)613-0724. E-mail: ipa@ou.org. Pres. Stephen J. Savitsky; Chmn. Mark Bane; Dir. Nathan Diament. Serves as the policy analysis, advocacy, mobilization, and programming department responsible for representing Orthodox/traditional American Jewry. *IPA Currents (quarterly newsletter).*

———, NATIONAL CONFERENCE OF SYNAGOGUE YOUTH (1954). 11 Broadway, 14th fl., NYC 10004. (212)563-4000. E-mail: ncsy@ou.org. Dir. Rabbi Steven Burg. Central body for youth groups of Orthodox congregations; provides educational guidance, Torah study groups, community service, program consultation, Torah library, Torah fund scholarships, Ben Zakkai Honor Society, Friends of NCSY, weeklong seminars, Israel Summer Experience for teens and Camp NCSY East Summer Kollel & Michlelet, Teen Torah Center. Divisions include Senior NCSY, Junior NCSY for preteens, Our Way for the Jewish deaf, Yachad for the developmentally disabled, Israel Center in Jerusalem, and NCSY in Israel. *Keeping Posted with NCSY; Darchei Da'at.*

———, WOMEN'S BRANCH (1923). 156 Fifth Ave., NYC 10010. (212)929-8857. Pres. Sophie Ebert. Umbrella organization of Orthodox sisterhoods in U.S. and Canada, educating women in Jewish learning and observance; provides programming, leadership, and organizational guidance, conferences, conventions, Marriage Committee and projects concerning mikvah, Shalom Task Force, and Welcoming Guests. Works with Orthodox Union Commissions and outreach; supports Stern and Touro College scholarships and Jewish braille publications; supplies Shabbat candelabra for hospital patients; NGO representative at UN. *Hachodesh; Hakol.*

UNION OF ORTHODOX RABBIS OF THE UNITED STATES AND CANADA (1902). 235 E. Broadway, NYC 10002. (212)964-6337(8). Dir. Rabbi Hersh M. Ginsberg. Seeks to foster and promote Torah-true Judaism in the U.S. and Canada; assists in the establishment and maintenance of yeshivot in the U.S.; maintains committee on marriage and divorce and aids individuals with marital difficulties; disseminates knowledge of traditional Jewish rites and practices and publishes regulations on synagogal structure; maintains rabbinical court for resolving individual and communal conflicts. *HaPardes.*

UNION OF SEPHARDIC CONGREGATIONS, INC. (1929). 8 W. 70 St., NYC 10023. (212)873-0300. FAX: (212)724-6165. Pres. Rabbi Marc D. Angel; Bd. Chmn. Edward Misrahi. Promotes the religious interests of Sephardic Jews; prints and distributes Sephardic prayer books. *Annual International Directory of Sephardic Congregations.*

UNITED LUBAVITCHER YESHIVOTH (1940). 841-853 Ocean Pkwy., Brooklyn, NY 11230. (718)859-7600. FAX: (718)434-1519. Supports and organizes Jewish day schools and rabbinical seminaries in the U.S. and abroad.

UNITED SYNAGOGUE OF CONSERVATIVE JUDAISM (1913). 155 Fifth Ave., NYC 10010-6802. (212)533-7800. FAX: (212) 353-9439. E-mail: info@uscj.org. Pres. Dr. Raymond B. Goldstein; Exec. V.-Pres. Rabbi Jerome M. Epstein. International organization of 760 Conservative congregations. Maintains 17 departments and 15 regional offices to assist its affiliates with religious, educational, youth, community, and administrative programming and guidance; aims to enhance the cause of Conservative Judaism, further religious observance, encourage establishment of Jewish religious schools, draw youth closer to Jewish tradition. Extensive Israel programs. *United Synagogue Review; Art/Engagement Calendar; Program Suggestions; Directory & Resource Guide; Book Service Catalogue of Publications.* (WWW.USCJ.ORG)

———, COMMISSION ON JEWISH EDUCATION (1930). 155 Fifth Ave., NYC 10010. (212)533-7800. FAX: (212)353-9439. E-mail: education@uscj.org. Chmn. Temma

Kingsley; Dir. Rabbi Robert Abramson. Develops educational policy for the United Synagogue of Conservative Judaism and sets the educational direction for Conservative congregations, their schools, and the Solomon Schechter Day Schools. Seeks to enhance the educational effectiveness of congregations through the publication of materials and in-service programs. *Tov L'Horot; Your Child; Shiboley Schechter; Advisories.*

———, COMMISSION ON SOCIAL ACTION AND PUBLIC POLICY (1958). 155 Fifth Ave., NYC 10010. (212)533-7800. FAX: (212)353-9439. Chmn. Hon. Jerry Wagner; Dir. Sarrae G. Crane. Develops and implements positions and programs on issues of social action and public policy for the United Synagogue of Conservative Judaism; represents these positions to other Jewish and civic organizations, the media, and government; and provides guidance, both informational and programmatic, to its affiliated congregations in these areas. *HaMa'aseh.*

———, JEWISH EDUCATORS ASSEMBLY (1951). 426 W. 58 St., NYC 10019. (212)765-3303. FAX: (212)765-3310. Pres. Dr. Mark S. Silk; Exec. Dir. Susan Mitrani Knapp. The Jewish Educators Assembly is the professional organization for the Jewish educators within the Conservative movement. The JEA provides a forum to discuss the trends and challenges within Conservative Jewish education as well as provides professional development and a sense of community for educational directors. Services offered: annual conference, placement service, career services, research grants, personal benefits and *V'Aleh Ha-Chadashot* newsletter.

———, KADIMA (reorg. 1968). 155 Fifth Ave., NYC 10010-6802. (212)533-7800. FAX: (212)353-9439. E-mail: kadima@uscj.org. Dir. Karen L. Stein; Dir. of Youth Activities Jules A Gutin. Involves Jewish preteens in a meaningful religious, educational, and social environment; fosters a sense of identity and commitment to the Jewish community and the Conservative movement; conducts synagogue-based chapter programs and regional Kadima days and weekends. *Mitzvah of the Month; Kadima Kesher; Chagim; Advisors Aid; Games; quarterly Kol Kadima magazine.*

———, NORTH AMERICAN ASSOCIATION OF SYNAGOGUE EXECUTIVES (1948). 155 Fifth Ave., NYC 10010. (212)533-7800, ext 2609. FAX: (631)732-9461. E-mail: office@naase.org. Pres. Judith Kranz, FSA, ATz; Hon. Pres. Amir Pilch, FSA; Exec. Dir. Harry Hauser. Aids congregations affiliated with the United Synagogue of Conservative Judaism to further the aims of Conservative Judaism through more effective administration (Program for Assistance by Liaisons to Synagogues—PALS); advances professional standards and promotes new methods in administration; cooperates in United Synagogue placement services and administrative surveys. *NAASE Connections Newsletter; NAASE Journal..*

———, UNITED SYNAGOGUE YOUTH (1951). 155 Fifth Ave., NYC 10010. (212)533-7800. FAX: (212)353-9439. E-mail: youth@uscj.org. Pres. Jesse Olitzky; Exec. Dir. Jules A. Gutin. Seeks to strengthen identification with Conservative Judaism, based on the personality, development, needs, and interests of the adolescent, in a mitzvah framework. *Achshav; Tikun Olam; A.J. Heschel Honor Society Newsletter; SATO Newsletter; USY Program Bank; Hakesher Newsletter for Advisors.*

VAAD MISHMERETH STAM (1976). 4907 16th Ave., Brooklyn, NYC 11204. (718)438-4980. FAX: (718)438-9343. Pres. Rabbi David L. Greenfield. A nonprofit consumer-protection agency dedicated to preserving and protecting the halakhic integrity of Torah scrolls, tefillin, phylacteries, and mezuzoth. Publishes material for laymen and scholars in the field of scribal arts; makes presentations and conducts examination campaigns in schools and synagogues; created an optical software system to detect possible textual errors in stam. Teaching and certifying sofrim worldwide. Offices in Israel, Strasbourg, Chicago, London, Manchester, Montreal, and Zurich. Publishes *Guide to Mezuzah* and *Encyclopedia of the Secret Aleph Beth. The Jewish Quill; and many other publications.*

WOMEN'S LEAGUE FOR CONSERVATIVE JUDAISM (1918). 475 Riverside Dr., NYC 10115. (212)870-1260. FAX: (212)772-3507. Email: womensleague@wlcj.org Pres. Gloria Cohen; Exec. Dir. Bernice Balter. Parent body of Conservative (Masorti) women's synagogue groups in U.S., Canada, Puerto Rico, Mexico, and Israel; provides programs and resources in Jewish education, social action, Israel affairs, American and Canadian public affairs, leadership training, community service programs for persons with disabilities, conferences on world affairs, study institutes, publicity techniques; publishes books of Jewish interest; contributes to support of Jewish Theological Seminary of America. *Women's League Outlook magazine; Ba'Olam world affairs newsletter.*

WORLD COUNCIL OF CONSERVATIVE/MASORTI SYNAGOGUES (1957). 155 Fifth Ave., NYC 10010. (212)533-7800, ext. 2014, 2018. FAX: (212)533-9439. E-mail: worldcouncil@compuserve.com. Pres. Rabbi Alan Silverstein; Rabbi of Council, Rabbi Benjamin Z. Kreitman. Organize and support Conservative/Masorti congregations in Latin America, Europe, Australia and South Africa. *World Spectrum.*

WORLD UNION FOR PROGRESSIVE JUDAISM (1926). 633 Third Ave. NYC 10017. (212)650-4280. FAX: (212)650-4289. E-mail: arzawupjna@urj.org. Chair Steven M. Bauman; Exec. Dir. Rabbi Uri Regev. International umbrella organization of Liberal Judaism; promotes and coordinates efforts of Liberal congregations throughout the world; starts new congregations, recruits rabbis and rabbinical students for all countries; organizes international conferences of Liberal Jews. *World News.* (WWW.WUPJ.ORG)

SCHOOLS, INSTITUTIONS

ACADEMY FOR JEWISH RELIGION (1956). 6301 Riverdale Avenue, Riverdale, NY 10471. (718)543-9360. FAX: (718)543-1038. E-mail: admin@ajrsem.org. Acting Pres. Rabbi David Greenstein; Dean Rabbi Dr. Ora Horn Prouser. The pluralistic rabbinic and cantorial seminary uniting teachers and students from all streams of Judaism, passionately committed to their own paths, yet respectful and supportive of the paths of others. Emphasis on integrating learning, practice, and spirt through traditional and contemporary approaches. Training for congregations, chaplaincy, education, community work. (WWW.AJRSEM.ORG)

AMERICAN JEWISH UNIVERSITY (1947, reorg. 2007). Familian Campus: 15600 Mulholland Dr., Bel-Air, CA 90077. (310)476-9777. FAX: (310)476-0347. E-mail: gleuenthal@uj.edu. Brandeis-Bardin Campus: 1101 Peppertree Lane, Brandeis, CA 93064. (805)582-4450. FAX: (805)526-1398. E-mail: info@thebbi.org. Pres. Dr. Robert D. Wexler. The College of Arts and Sciences is an accredited liberal arts college for undergraduates offering a core curriculum of Jewish, Western, and non-Western studies, with majors including bioethics (a premedical track in partnership with Cedars-Sinai Medical Center), business, English, Jewish studies, journalism, literature & politics, political science, psychology, and U.S. public policy. Accredited graduate programs in nonprofit business administration (MBA), and Jewish education. The Ziegler School of Rabbinic Studies provides an intensive four-year program with Conservative ordination. The Whizin Center for Continuing Education offers non-credit courses to some 8,000 students annually, the largest Jewish adult-education provider in the U.S., as well as cultural-arts programming and outreach services for West Coast Jewish communities. There are three think tanks: the Center for Israel Studies, the Sigi Ziering Institute, and the Whizin Center for the Jewish Future. The Brandeis-Bardin Institute, founded in 1941 and now merged with the university, is a Jewish pluralistic, nondenominational educational institution providing programs for people of all ages: BCI (Brandeis Collegiate Institute), a summer leadership program for college-age adults from around the world; Camp Alonim, a summer Jewish experience for children 8-16; Gan Alonim Day Camp for children in kindergarten to 6th grade; weekend retreats for adults with leading contemporary Jewish scholars-in-residence; Jewish music concerts; Family Days and Weekends, Grandparents Weekends, Elderhostel, Young Adult programs, dance weekends, institute for newly marrieds. *American Jewish University E-zine.* (WWW.AJULA.EDU)

BALTIMORE HEBREW UNIVERSITY (1919). 5800 Park Heights Ave., Baltimore, MD 21215. (410)578-6900; (888)248-7420. FAX: (410)578-6940. E-mail: bhu@bhu.edu. Bd. Chmn. Erika Schon. Offers

PhD and MA degrees in Jewish studies (MAJS); MA in Jewish education (MAJE), and Jewish communal service (MAJCS). Concentrations in biblical and ancient Near Eastern civilization, contemporary Jewish studies, Jewish thought and mysticism, literature, history, and rabbinics. Dual master's degree opportunities available as well as certificate programs in nonprofit management and education. Lifelong learning programs; Joseph Meyerhoff Library; distinguished lecture series. (WWW.BHU.EDU)

———, BERNARD MANEKIN SCHOOL OF UNDERGRADUATE STUDIES. Dean Dr. Barbara G. Zirkin. BA upper division Jewish studies; *LaDa'at* program for high school juniors and seniors.

———, PEGGY MEYERHOFF PEARLSTONE SCHOOL OF GRADUATE STUDIES. Dean Dr. Barbara G. Zirkin. PhD and MA programs: MA in Jewish studies; MAJE in Jewish education; PhD in Jewish studies; dual master's degrees, some jointly with the University of Maryland.

———, LEONARD AND HELEN R. STULMAN SCHOOL OF CONTINUING EDUCATION. Director of lifelong learning Elaine Eckstein. Noncredit programs open to the community, including Jewish studies and Hebrew language courses, trips, retreats, and seminars; *Me'ah,* an intensive group study program.

BRAMSON ORT COLLEGE (1977). 69-30 Austin St., Forest Hills, NY 11375. (718)261-5800. Dean of Academic Services Barry Glotzer. A two-year Jewish technical college offering certificates and associate degrees in technology and business fields, including accounting, computer programming, electronics technology, business management, office technology. Additional locations in Brooklyn.

BRANDEIS UNIVERSITY (1948). 415 South St., Waltham, MA 02454. (781)736-2000. Pres. Jehuda Reinharz; Provost Irving Epstein; Exec. V.-Pres./CEO Peter B. French; Sr. V.-Pres. of Devel. Nancy Winship. Founded in 1948 by the American Jewish community, Brandeis University is a private, coeducational, and nonsectarian institution of higher learning and research located in Waltham, Massachusetts, enrolling approximately 3,100 undergraduate students and 1,200 graduate students. While Brandeis maintains a special relationship with the Jewish community, it welcomes students and faculty of all backgrounds and beliefs. The University's principal components are the undergraduate College of Arts and Sciences, the Graduate School of Arts and Sciences, The Heller School for Social Policy and Management, the Graduate School of International Economics and Finance, and the Rabb School of Summer and Continuing Studies. *Various newsletters, scholarly publications.*

———, NATIONAL WOMEN'S COMMITTEE (1948). MS 132, Waltham, MA 02454-9110. (781) 736-4160. FAX: (781)736-4183. E-mail: bunwc@brandeis.edu. Pres. Marcia F. Levy; Exec. Dir. Joan C. Bowen. Provides support for Brandeis University and its Libraries. It connects Brandeis, a non-sectarian university founded by the American Jewish community, to its members and their communities through programs that reflect the ideals of social justice and academic excellence. In addition to its fundraising activities, NWC offers its members opportunity for intellectual pursuit, continuing education, community service, social interaction, personal enrichment and leadership development. Open to all, regardless of race, religion, nationality or gender. *Connecting.*

CENTER FOR JUDAIC STUDIES, School of Arts and Sciences, University of Pennsylvania. 420 Walnut St., Philadelphia, PA 19106. (215)238-1290. FAX: (215) 238-1540. Dir. David B. Ruderman. *Jewish Quarterly Review.*

CLEVELAND COLLEGE OF JEWISH STUDIES (1964). 26500 Shaker Blvd., Beachwood, OH 44122. (216)464-4050. FAX: (216) 464-5827. Pres. David S. Ariel; Dir. of Student Services Diane M. Kleinman. Provides courses in all areas of Judaic and Hebrew studies to adults and college-age students; offers continuing education for Jewish educators and administrators; serves as a center for Jewish life and culture; expands the availability of courses in Judaic studies by exchanging faculty, students, and credits with neighboring academic institutions; grants bachelor's and master's degrees.

GRATZ COLLEGE (1895). 7605 Old York Rd., Melrose Park, PA 19027. (215)635-7300. FAX: (215)635-7320. Bd. Chmn. Dr.

Matti K. Gershenfeld.; Pres. Dr. Jonathan Rosenbaum. Offers a wide variety of undergraduate and graduate degrees and continuing education programs in Judaic, Hebraic, and Middle Eastern studies. Grants BA and MA in Jewish studies, MA in Jewish education (joint program in special needs education with La Salle U.), MA in Jewish music, MA in Jewish liberal studies, MA in Jewish communal studies, certificates in Jewish communal studies (joint program with U. of Penna. School of Social Work and Temple U), Jewish education, Israel studies, Judaica librarianship (joint program with Drexel U.), and Jewish music. Joint graduate program with Reconstructionist Rabbinical College in Jewish education and Jewish music. Netzky Division of Continuing Education and Jewish Community High School. *Various newsletters, annual academic bulletin, scholarly publications, centennial volume, Gratz newsletter and occasional papers.*

HEBREW COLLEGE (1921). 160 Herrick Road, Newton Centre, MA 02459. (617)559-8600. FAX: (617)559-8601. Pres. Dr. David M. Gordis; Ch. Bd. Dir. Mickey Cail; Hon. Ch. Bd. Trustees Ted Benard-Cutler. Through training in Jewish texts, history, literature, ethics, and Hebrew language, prepares students to become literate participants in the global Jewish community. Offers graduate and undergraduate degrees and certificates in all aspects of Jewish education, Jewish studies, and Jewish music; serves students of all ages through its Prozdor High School, Camp Yavneh, Ulpan Center for Adult Jewish Learning, and *Me'ah*–One Hundred Hours of Adult Jewish Learning. *Hebrew College Today; Likut.* (WWW.HEBREWCOLLEGE.EDU)

———, NATIONAL CENTER FOR JEWISH POLICY STUDIES (1998). 160 Herrick Road, Newton Centre, MA 02459. (617)559-8790. FAX: (617)559-8791. E-mail: jewishpolicy@hebrewcollege.edu. Dir. Dr. David M. Gordis; Assoc. Dir. Rabbi Zachary I. Heller; Chmn. Howard I. Friedman. An international research and development resource for American Jewry that bridges the gap between academics, community leaders, professionals, and the organizations and institutions of Jewish life. *Bulletins, various newsletters, monographs, research reports, and books.*

HEBREW SEMINARY OF THE DEAF (1992). 4435 W. Oakton, Skokie, IL 60076. (847) 677-3330. FAX: (847)677-7945. E-mail: hebrewsemdeaf@juno.com. Pres. Rabbi Douglas Goldhamer; Bd. Chmn. Alan Crane. Trains deaf and hearing men and women to become rabbis and teachers for Jewish deaf communities across America. All classes in the 5-year program are interpreted in Sign Language. Rabbis teaching in the seminary are Reform, Conservative, and Reconstructionist.

HEBREW THEOLOGICAL COLLEGE (1922). 7135 N. Carpenter Rd., Skokie, IL 60077. (847)982-2500. FAX: (847)674-6381. E-mail: htc@htcnet.edu. Chancellor Rabbi Dr. Jerold Isenberg; Rosh Hayeshiva Rabbi Shlomo Morgenstern. Hebrew Theological College, a fully accredited insitution, includes the Bet Midrash for Men, Blitstein Institute for Women, Kanter School of Liberal Arts and Sciences, Fasman Yeshiva High School, Community Service Devision, Silber Memorial Library, Bellows Kollel, Israel Experience Program and Yeshivas HaKayitz summer camp. *Likutei Pshatim, Or Shmuel, Academic Journal.* (WWW.HTCNET.EDU)

HEBREW UNION COLLEGE–JEWISH INSTITUTE OF RELIGION (1875). 3101 Clifton Ave., Cincinnati, OH 45220. (513)221-1875. FAX: (513)221-1847. Pres. Rabbi David Ellenson; Chancellor Emer. Dr. Alfred Gottschalk; V.-Pres. Devel. Erica S. Frederick; Chmn. Bd. Govs. Barbara Friedman; Provost Dr. Norman J. Cohen. Academic centers: 3101 Clifton Ave., Cincinnati, OH 45220 (1875), Dean Rabbi Kenneth Ehrlich. 1 W. 4 St., NYC 10012 (1922), Dean Rabbi Shirley Idelson. FAX: (212) 388-1720. 3077 University Ave., Los Angeles, CA 90007 (1954), Dean Rabbi Lewis Barth; FAX: (213)747-6128. 13 King David St., Jerusalem, Israel 94101 (1963), Dean Rabbi Michael Marmur; FAX: (972-2)6251478. Prepares students for Reform rabbinate, cantorate, Jewish education and educational administration, communal service, academic careers; promotes Jewish studies; maintains libraries, archives, and museums; offers master's and doctoral degrees; engages in archaeological excavations; publishes scholarly works through Hebrew Union College Press. *American Jewish Archives; Bibliographica Judaica; HUC-JIR Catalogue; Hebrew Union College Annual;*

Studies in Bibliography and Booklore; The Chronicle; Kesher. (WWW.HUC.EDU)

———, AMERICAN JEWISH PERIODICAL CENTER (1957). 3101 Clifton Ave., Cincinnati, OH 45220. (513)221-1875, ext. 396. FAX: (513)221-0519. Dir. Herbert C. Zafren. Maintains microfilms of all American Jewish periodicals 1823-1925, selected periodicals since 1925. *Jewish Periodicals and Newspapers on Microfilm (1957); First Supplement (1960); Augmented Edition (1984).*

———, BLAUSTEIN CENTER FOR PASTORAL COUNSELING. 1 West 4th Street, NYC, 10012. (212)824-2238. FAX: (212)388-1720. Email: nwiener@huc.edu. Dir. Nancy Wiener. In partnership with CCAR, prepares spiritual leaderss to sensitively and capably help congregants to deal with the critical issues they face throughout their lives; enables rabbinical students to complete a variety of supervised clinical experiences, including a year of congregational workd as well as pastoral counseling internships, and an academic grounding in psychodynamics and pastoral counseling; and develops new approaches to teaching counseling skills, grounding reflections on practical field work experiences in the teachings of Jewish texts.

———, CENTER FOR HOLOCAUST AND HUMANITY EDUCATION. 3101 Clifton Ave., Cincinnati, OH 45220. (513)221-1875, ext. 355. FAX: (513)221-1842. Email: holocaustandhumanity@huc.edu. Dir. Dr. Racelle R. Weiman. Co-sponsored by Hebrew Union College-Jewish Institute of Religion and Combined Generations of the Holocaust of Greater Cincinnati; offers graduate level courses for educational professionals and clergy; surveys and assesses Holocaust education needs in public and private sectors; innovates curriculum development and evaluation; provides teacher training, pedgogic resources, and programming for general public of all ages and faiths; convenes conferences and symposia; cooperates with university consortium on outreach initiatives; creates traveling exhibits; fosters tolerance education and prejudice reduction in the school system.

———, EDGAR F. MAGNIN SCHOOL OF GRADUATE STUDIES (1956). 3077 University Ave., Los Angeles, CA 90007. (213)749-3424. FAX: (213)747-6128. E-mail: magnin@huc.edu. Dir. Dr. Reuven Firestone. Supervises programs leading to DHS, DHL, and MA degrees; participates in cooperative PhD programs with U. of S. Calif.

———, GRADUATE STUDIES PROGRAM. 1 W. 4 St. NYC 10012. (212)824-2252. FAX: (212)388-1720. E-mail: nysgrad@huc.edu. Dir. Dr. Carol Ochs. Offers the DHL (doctor of Hebrew letters) degree in a variety of fields; the MAJS (master of arts in Judaic studies), a multidisciplinary degree; and is the only Jewish seminary to offer the DMin (doctor of ministry) degree in pastoral care and counseling.

———, HUC-UC CENTER FOR THE STUDY OF ETHICS AND CONTEMPORARY MORAL PROBLEMS (1986). 3101 Clifton Ave., Cincinnati, OH 45220. (513)221-1875, EXT. 367. FAX: (5130221-1842. Email: ethics@huc.edu. Dir. Dr. Jonathan Cohen. Co-sponsored by Hebrew Union College-Jewish Institute of Religion and the University of Cincinnati; dedicated to the study of contemporary moral problems on the basis of values that are at the heart of Judeo-Christian and secular ethical traditions; provides forum for open discussion and reflection on important moral dilemmas that arise in modern life; promotes the incorporation of ethical values in personal life, professional practice, and community development; lauching MA and PhD programs in Jewish and Comparative Law and Applied Ethics; offering development programs for legal, medical, and social work professionals; promoting cooperative research among academic institutions, social service, and not-for-profit organizations in Greater Cincinnati.

———, IRWIN DANIELS SCHOOL OF JEWISH COMMUNAL SERVICE (1968). 3077 University Ave., Los Angeles, CA 90007. (800)899-0925. FAX: (213)747-6128. E-mail: swindmueller@huc.edu. Dir. Dr. Steven F. Windmueller. Offers certificate and master's degree to those employed in Jewish communal services, or preparing for such work; offers joint MA in Jewish education and communal service with Rhea Hirsch School; offers dual degrees with the School of Social Work, the School of Public Administration, the Annenberg School for Communication, Marshall School of Business and the

School of Gerontology of the U. of S. Calif. and with other institutions. Single master's degrees can be completed in 15 months and certificates are awarded for the completion of two full-time summer sessions. (WWW.HUC.EDU)

———, JACOB RADER MARCUS CENTER OF THE AMERICAN JEWISH ARCHIVES (*see* p. 629)

———, JEROME H. LOUCHHEIM SCHOOL OF JUDAIC STUDIES (1969). 3077 University Ave., Los Angeles, CA 90007. (213)749-3424. FAX: (213)747-6128. Dir. Dr. Reuven Firestone. Offers programs leading to MA, BS, BA, and AA degrees; offers courses as part of the undergraduate program of the U. of S. Calif.

———, NELSON GLUECK SCHOOL OF BIBLICAL ARCHAEOLOGY (1963). 13 King David St., Jerusalem, Israel 94101. (972)2-6203333. FAX: (972)2-6251478. Dir. Avraham Biran. Offers graduate-level research programs in Bible and archaeology. Summer excavations are carried out by scholars and students. University credit may be earned by participants in excavations. Consortium of colleges, universities, and seminaries is affiliated with the school. Skirball Museum of Biblical Archaeology (artifacts from Tel Dan, Tel Gezer, and Aroer).

———, RHEA HIRSCH SCHOOL OF EDUCATION (1967). 3077 University Ave., Los Angeles, CA 90007. (213)749-3424. FAX: (213)747-6128. Dir. Sara Lee. Offers PhD and MA programs in Jewish and Hebrew education; conducts joint degree programs with U. of S. Calif.; offers courses for Jewish teachers, librarians, and early educators on a nonmatriculating basis; conducts summer institutes for professional Jewish educators.

———, SCHOOL OF EDUCATION (1947). 1 W. 4 St., NYC 10012. (212)824-2213. FAX: (212)388-1720. E-mail: nysed@huc.edu. Dir. Jo Kay. Trains teachers and principals for Reform religious schools; offers MA degree with specialization in religious education.

———, SCHOOL OF GRADUATE STUDIES (1949). 3101 Clifton Ave., Cincinnati, OH 45220. (513)221-1875, ext. 230. FAX: (513)221-0321. E-mail: gradschool@huc.edu. Dir. Dr. Adam Kamesar. Offers programs leading to MA and PhD degrees; offers program leading to DHL degree for rabbinic graduates of the college.

———, SCHOOL OF JEWISH STUDIES (1963). 13 King David St., Jerusalem, Israel 94101. (972)2-6203333. FAX: (972)2-6251478. E-mail: jerusalem@huc.edu. Acting Pres. Dr. Norman J. Cohen; Dean Rabbi Michael Marmur; Assoc. Dean Rabbi Shaul R. Feinberg. Offers first year of graduate rabbinic, cantorial, and Jewish education studies (required) for North American students; graduate program leading to ordination for Israeli rabbinic students; non-degree Beit Midrash/Liberal Yeshivah program of Jewish studies (English language); in-service educational programming for teachers and educators (Hebrew language); Hebrew Ulpan for immigrants and visitors; Abramov Library of Judaica, Hebraica, Ancient Near East and American Jewish Experience; Skirball Museum of Biblical Archaeology; public outreach programs (lectures, courses, concerts, exhibits).

———, SCHOOL OF SACRED MUSIC (1947). 1 W. 4 St., NYC 10012. (212)824-2225. FAX: (212)388-1720. Dir. Cantor Israel Goldstein. Trains cantors for congregations; offers MSM degree. *Sacred Music Press.*

———, SKIRBALL CULTURAL CENTER (*see* p. 632)

INSTITUTE OF TRADITIONAL JUDAISM (1990). 811 Palisade Ave., Teaneck, NJ 07666. (201)801-0707. FAX: (201)801-0449. Rector (Reish Metivta) Rabbi David Weiss Halivni; Dean Rabbi Ronald D. Price. A nondenominational halakhic rabbinical school dedicated to genuine faith combined with intellectual honesty and the love of Israel. Graduates receive "yoreh yoreh" smikhah.

JEWISH THEOLOGICAL SEMINARY (1886; reorg. 1902). 3080 Broadway, NYC 10027-4649. (212)678-8000. FAX: (212)678-8947. Chancellor Dr. Arnold Eisen; Bd. Chmn. Gershon Kekst. Operates undergraduate and graduate programs in Judaic studies; professional schools for training Conservative rabbis, educators and cantors; the JTS Library; the Ratner Center for the Study of Conservative Judaism; Melton Research Center for Jewish Education; the Jewish Museum; Ramah Camps and the Ivry Prozdor high-school honors program.

Other outreach activities include the Distance Learning Project, the Finkelstein Institute for Religious and Social Studies, and the Wagner Institute lay leadership program. *Academic Bulletin; JTS Magazine; Gleanings; JTS News.* (WWW.JTSA.EDU)

———, ALBERT A. LIST COLLEGE OF JEWISH STUDIES (formerly SEMINARY COLLEGE OF JEWISH STUDIES—TEACHERS INSTITUTE) (1909). 3080 Broadway, NYC 10027. (212)678-8826. Dean Dr. Shuly Rubin Schwartz. Offers complete undergraduate program in Judaica leading to BA degree; conducts joint programs with Columbia University and Barnard College enabling students to receive two BA degrees.

———, GRADUATE SCHOOL OF JTS (formerly INSTITUTE FOR ADVANCED STUDY IN THE HUMANITIES) (1968). 3080 Broadway, NYC 10027-4649. (212)678-8024. FAX: (212)678-8947. E-mail: gradschool@jtsa.edu. Dean Dr. Stephen P. Garfinkel; Asst. Dean Dr. Bruce E. Nielsen. Programs leading to MA, DHL, and PhD degrees in Judaic studies; specializations include Ancient Judaism, Bible and Ancient Semitic Languages, Interdepartmental Studies, Jewish Art and Material Culture, Jewish Education, Jewish History, Jewish Literature, Jewish Philosophy, Jewish Women's Studies, Liturgy, Medieval Jewish Studies, Midrash, Modern Jewish Studies, Talmud and Rabbinics, and Dual Degree Program with Columbia University School of Social Work.

———, H.L. MILLER CANTORIAL SCHOOL AND COLLEGE OF JEWISH MUSIC (1952). 3080 Broadway, NYC 10027. (212)678-8036. FAX: (212)678-8947. Dean Cantor Henry Rosenblum. Trains cantors, music teachers, and choral directors for congregations. Offers full-time programs in sacred music leading to degree of MSM, and diploma of *Hazzan.*

———, JEWISH MUSEUM (*see* p. 630)

———, LIBRARY OF THE JEWISH THEOLOGICAL SEMINARY. 3080 Broadway, NYC 10027. (212)678-8075. FAX: (212)678-8998. E-mail: library@jtsa.edu. Librarian Dr. Mayer E. Rabinowitz. Contains one of the largest collections of Hebraica and Judaica in the world, including manuscripts, incunabula, rare books, and Cairo Geniza material. The 320,000-item collection includes books, manuscripts, periodicals, sound recordings, prints, broadsides, photographs, postcards, microform, videos and CD-ROM. Exhibition of items from the collection are ongoing. Exhibition catalogs are available for sale. The Library is open to the public for on-site use (photo identification required). *Between the Lines.* (WWW.JTSA.EDU/LIBRARY)

———, LOUIS FINKELSTEIN INSTITUTE FOR RELIGIOUS AND SOCIAL STUDIES (1938). 3080 Broadway, NYC 10027. (212)870-3180. FAX: (212)678-8947. E-mail: finkelstein@jtsa.edu. Dir. Dr. Alan Mittleman. Since 1938 has maintained an innovative interfaith and intergroup relations program, pioneering new approaches to dialogue across religious lines. Through scholarly and practical fellowship, highlights the relevance of Judaism and other contemporary religions to current theological, ethical, and scientific issues, including the emerging challenge of bioethics.

———, MELTON RESEARCH CENTER FOR JEWISH EDUCATION (1960). 3080 Broadway, NYC 10027. (212)678-8031. E-mail: stbrown@jtsa.edu. Dir. Dr. Steven M. Brown; Admin. Lisa Siberstein-Weber. Develops new curricula and materials for Jewish education; prepares educators through seminars and in-service programs; maintains consultant and supervisory relationships with a limited number of pilot schools; develops and implements research initiatives; sponsors "renewal" retreats. *Gleanings; Courtyard: A Journal of Research and Reflection on Jewish Education.*

———, NATIONAL RAMAH COMMISSION (1947). 3080 Broadway, NYC 10027. (212)678-8881. FAX: (212)749-8251. Pres. Alan H. Silberman; Natl. Dir. Mitchell Cohen. Sponsors an international network of 16 summer camps located in the US, Canada, S. America, Russia, and Israel, emphasizing Jewish education, living, and culture; offers opportunities for qualified college students and older to serve as counselors, administrators, specialists, etc., and programs for children with special needs (Tikvah program); offers special programs in U.S. and Israel, including National Ramah Staff Training Institute, Ramah Israel Seminar, Ulpan Ramah Plus, and Tichon Ramah

Yerushalayim. Family and synagogue tours to Israel and summer day camp in Israel for Americans.

———, PROJECT JUDAICA (1992). 3080 Broadway, NYC 10027. (212)678-8983. Dir. Dr. David Fishman. Students in this intensive, five year program sponsored with YIVO and the Russian State University for the Humanities in Moscow pursue the university's general curriculum while majoring in Jewish history and culture taught by JTS faculty and advanced students. Graduates receive a diploma (the equivalent of an MA) or a candidate of sciences degree (the equivalent of a PhD) from RSUH.

———, RABBINICAL SCHOOL (1886). 3080 Broadway, NYC 10027. (212)678-8817. Dean Rabbi Daniel Nevins. Offers a program of graduate and professional studies leading to the degree of Master of Arts and ordination; includes one year of study in Jerusalem and an extensive field-work program.

———, RADIO AND TELEVISION (1944). 3080 Broadway, NYC 10027. (212)678-8020. Produces radio and TV programs expressing the Jewish tradition in its broadest sense, including hour-long documentaries on NBC and ABC. Distributes cassettes of programs at minimum charge.

———, REBECCA AND ISRAEL IVRY PROZDOR (1951). 3080 Broadway, NYC 10027. (212)678-8824. E-mail: prozdor@jtsa.edu. Principal Rhonda Rosenheck; Community Advisory Board Chmn. Michael Katz. The Hebrew high school of JTS, offers a program of Jewish studies for day school and congregational school graduates in classical texts, Hebrew, interdisciplinary seminars, training in educational leadership, and classes for college credit. Classes meet one evening a week and on Sundays in Manhattan and at affiliated programs. *High School Curricula.*

———, SAUL LIEBERMAN INSTITUTE FOR TALMUDIC RESEARCH (1985). 3080 Broadway, NYC 10027. (212)678-8994. FAX: (212)678D8947. E-mail: liebinst@jtsa.edu. Dir. Shamma Friedman; Coord. Jonathan Milgram. Engaged in preparing for publication a series of scholarly editions of selected chapters of the Talmud. The following projects support and help disseminate the research: Talmud Text Database; Bibliography of Talmudic Literature; Catalogue of Geniza Fragments.

———, SCHOCKEN INSTITUTE FOR JEWISH RESEARCH (1961). 6 Balfour St., Jerusalem, Israel 92102. (972)2-5631288. FAX: (972)2-5636857. E-mail: sjssg@vms.huji.ac.il. Dir. Dr. Shmuel Glick. Comprises the Schocken collection of rare books and manuscripts and a research institute dedicated to the exploration of Hebrew religious poetry (*piyyut*). *Schocken Institute Yearbook (P'raqim).*

———, WILLIAM DAVIDSON GRADUATE SCHOOL OF JEWISH EDUCATION (1996). 3080 Broadway, NYC 10027. (212) 678-8030. E-mail: edschool@jtsa.edu. Dean Dr. Aryeh Davidson. Offers master's and doctoral degrees in Jewish education; continuing education courses for Jewish educators and Jewish communal professionals; and programs that take advantage of the latest technology, including distance learning and interactive video classrooms.

MAALOT–A SEMINARY FOR CANTORS AND JUDAISTS (1987). 15 W. Montgomery Ave., Suite 204, Rockville, MD 20850. (301)309-2310. FAX: (301)309-2328. Pres./Exec. Off. David Shneyer. An educational program established to train individuals in Jewish music, the liturgical arts, and the use, design, and application of Jewish customs and ceremonies. Offers classes, seminars, and an independent study program.

MESIVTA YESHIVA RABBI CHAIM BERLIN RABBINICAL ACADEMY (1905). 1605 Coney Island Ave., Brooklyn, NY 11230. (718)377-0777. Exec. Dir. Y. Mayer Lasker. Maintains fully accredited elementary and high schools; collegiate and postgraduate school for advanced Jewish studies, both in America and Israel; Camp Morris, a summer study retreat; Prof. Nathan Isaacs Memorial Library; Gur Aryeh Publications.

NER ISRAEL RABBINICAL COLLEGE (1933). 400 Mt. Wilson Lane, Baltimore, MD 21208. (410)484-7200. FAX: (410)484-3060. Rosh Hayeshiva, Rabbi Aharon Feldman; Pres. Rabbi Sheftel Neuberger. Trains rabbis and educators for Jewish communities in America and worldwide. Offers bachelor's, master's, and doctoral degrees in talmudic law, as well as teacher's diploma. College has four divisions: Israel Henry Beren High School, Rabbinical College, Teachers Training Institute, Graduate School. Maintains an active community-service division. Operates special programs for Iranian and Russian Jewish students. *Ner Israel Update; Alumni Bulletin; Ohr Hanair Talmudic Journal; Iranian B'nei Torah Bulletin.*

RABBINICAL COLLEGE OF TELSHE, INC. (1941). 28400 Euclid Ave., Wickliffe, OH 44092. (216)943-5300. Roshei Hayeshiva and Pres. Rabbi Zalman Gifter and Rabbi Yitzchok Sorotzkin; V.-Pres. Rabbi Abba Zalka Gewirtz. College for higher Jewish learning specializing in talmudic studies and rabbinics; maintains a preparatory academy including a secular high school, postgraduate department, teacher-training school, and teachers' seminary for women. *Pri Etz Chaim; Peer Mordechai; Alumni Bulletin.*

RECONSTRUCTIONIST RABBINICAL COLLEGE (1968). 1299 Church Rd., Wyncote, PA 19095. (215)576-0800. FAX: (215)576-6143. E-mail: rrcinfo@rrc.edu. Pres. Dan Ehrenkranz; Bd. Chmn. Donald L. Shapiro; Genl. Chmn. Aaron Ziegelman. Coeducational. Trains rabbis and cantors for all areas of Jewish communal life: synagogues, academic and educational positions, Hillel centers, federation agencies, and chaplaincy for hospitals, hospices, and geriatric centers; confers title of rabbi and cantor and grants degrees of Master and Doctor of Hebrew Letters and Master of Arts in Jewish Studies. *RRC Report; Reconstructionist.* (WWW.RRC.EDU)

SPERTUS INSTITUTE OF JEWISH STUDIES (1924). 618 S. Michigan Ave., Chicago, IL 60605. (312)922-9012. FAX: (312)922-6406. Pres. Howard A. Sulkin; Dean Dr. Dean Bell; Museum Dir. Rhoda Rosen; Lib. Dir. Glenn Ferdman. An accredited institution of higher learning offering one doctor of Jewish studies degree; master's degree programs in Jewish studies, Jewish education, Jewish communal service, and human-services administration; plus an extensive program of continuing education. Major resources of the college encompass Spertus Museum, Asher Library, Chicago Jewish Archives, and Spertus College of Judaica Press.

———, SPERTUS MUSEUM (*see* p. 633)

TOURO COLLEGE (1970). Executive Offices: 27 West 23rd Street., NYC 10010. (212)4630400. FAX: (212)627-9049. Pres. Dr. Bernard Lander; Bd. Chmn. Mark Hasten. Non-profit comprehensive college with Judaic Studies, Liberal Arts and professional programs leading to BA, BS, MA, MS and JD degrees at campuses in NYC and Long Island; emphasizes relevance of Jewish heritage to Western civilization. Undergraduate and graduate degree programs in Moscow and Jerusalem. California campuses offer DO degree and distance learning BS, MS, MBA and PhD degrees.

———, COLLEGE OF LIBERAL ARTS AND SCIENCES. 27-33 W. 23 St., NYC 10010. (212)463-0400. FAX: (212)627-9144. Exec. Dean Stanley Boylan. Offers comprehensive Jewish studies along with studies in the arts, sciences, humanities, and preprofessional studies in health sciences, law, accounting, business, computer science, education, and finance. Women's Division, 160 Lexington Ave., NYC 10016. (212)213-2230. FAX: (212)683-3281. Dean Sara E. Freifeld.

———, INSTITUTE OF JEWISH LAW. (631) 421-2244, ext. 335. A constituent of Touro College Jacob D. Fuchsberg Law Center, the Institute of Jewish Law provides an intellectual framework for the study and teaching of Jewish law. Coedits *Dinei Israel* (Jewish Law Journal) with Tel Aviv University Law School.

———, JACOB D. FUCHSBERG LAW CENTER (1980). Long Island Campus, 300 Nassau Rd., Huntington, NY 11743. (516) 421-2244. Dean Howard A. Glickstein. Offers studies leading to JD degree.

———, MOSCOW BRANCH. Oztozhenka #38, Moscow, Russia 119837. Offers BS program in business and BA program in Jewish studies.

———, SCHOOL OF GENERAL STUDIES. Midtown Main Campus, 27 W. 23 St., NYC 10010. (212)463-0400; Harlem Main Campus, 240 E. 123 St., NYC 10035; Sunset Park extension, 475 53rd St., Brooklyn, NY 11220; Flushing Extension, 133-35 Roosevelt Ave., Queens, NY 11374. Dean Stephen Adolphus. Associate and bachelor degree programs in human services, education N-6, computing, business and liberal arts; special emphasis on service to non-traditional students.

———, TOURO COLLEGE FLATBUSH CENTER (1979). 1602 Ave. J, Brooklyn, NY 11230. (718)252-7800. Dean Robert Goldschmidt. A division of the College of Liberal Arts and Sciences; options offered in accounting and business, education, mathematics, political science, psychology, special education and speech. Classes are given on weeknights and during the day on Sunday.

———, TOURO COLLEGE ISRAEL. 20 Pierre Koenig St., Jerusalem, Israel. (02)6796666. FAX: (02)6796688. V-Pres., Israel, Matityahu Adler; Dean of Faculty, Israel, Prof. Moshe Lieberman. Touro College Israel offers both undergraduate and graduate degrees in management, marketing, economics, finance, and accounting. Touro College also offers a graduate degree in Jewish Studies. Courses in both these programs are given in Hebrew. In addition undergraduate courses in our one year program are offered in English. (WWW.TOURO.EDU)

———, TOURO COLLEGE SCHOOL OF HEALTH SCIENCES (1986). 1700 Union Blvd, Bay Shore, NY 11706. (516)665-1600. FAX: (516)665-6902. E-mail: edwarda@touro.edu. Pres. Dr. Bernard Lander; Dean Dr. Joseph Weisberg. Offers the following programs: MS/MD with Faculty of Medicine, Technion Institute, Israel; BS/MS Occupational Therapy; BS/MS Physical Therapy; MS Public Health; Advanced MS Orthopedic Physical Therapy; MS Forensic Examination; MS Clinical Engineering; MS Early Intervention; MS Gerontology; BS Physician Assistant; AAS Occupational Therapy Assistant; AAS Physical Therapists Assistant.

———, TOURO GRADUATE SCHOOL OF JEWISH STUDIES (1981). 160 Lexington Ave., NYC 10016. (212)213-2230. FAX: (212)683-3281. E-mail: moshesh@touro.edu. Pres. Bernard Lander; Dean Michael A. Shmidman. Offers courses leading to an MA in Jewish studies, with concentrations in Jewish history or Jewish education. Students may complete part of their program in Israel through MA courses offered by Touro faculty at Touro's Jerusalem center.

UNIVERSITY OF JUDAISM (*see* AMERICAN JEWISH UNIVERSITY)

WEST COAST TALMUDICAL SEMINARY (Yeshiva Ohr Elchonon Chabad) (1953). 7215 Waring Ave., Los Angeles, CA 90046. (323)937-3763. FAX: (323)937-9456. Dean Rabbi Ezra Schochet. Provides facilities for intensive Torah education as well as Orthodox rabbinical training on the West Coast; conducts an accredited college preparatory high school combined with a full program of Torah-talmudic training and a graduate talmudical division on the college level. *Torah Quiz; Kovetz Migdal Ohr; Kovetz Ohr HaMigdal.*

YESHIVA TORAH VODAATH AND MESIVTA TORAH VODAATH RABBINICAL SEMINARY (1918). 425 E. 9 St., Brooklyn, NY 11218. (718)941-8000. Bd. Chmn. Chaim Leshkowitz. Offers Hebrew and secular education from elementary level through rabbinical ordination and postgraduate work; maintains a teachers institute and community-service bureau; maintains a dormitory and a nonprofit camp program for boys. *Chronicle; Mesivta Vanguard; Thought of the Week; Torah Vodaath News; Ha'Mesifta.*

———, YESHIVA TORAH VODAATH ALUMNI ASSOCIATION (1941). 425 E. 9 St., Brooklyn, NY 11218. (718)941-8000. Pres. George Weinberger. Promotes social and cultural ties between the alumni and the schools through classes and lectures and fund-raising; offers vocational guidance to students; operates Camp Ohr Shraga; sponsors research fellowship program for boys. *Annual Journal; Hamesivta Torah periodical.*

YESHIVA UNIVERSITY (1886). Wilf Campus, 500 W. 185 St., NYC 10033-3201. (212)960-5400. FAX: (212)960-0055. Chancellor Dr. Norman Lamm; Pres. Richard Joel; Chmn. Bd. of Trustees Morry J. Weiss. The nation's oldest and most comprehensive independent university founded under Jewish auspices, with 18 undergraduate and graduate schools, divisions, and affiliates; widespread programs of research and community outreach; publications; and a museum. A broad range of curricula lead to bachelor's, master's, doctoral, and professional degrees. Undergraduate schools provide general studies curricula supplemented by courses in Jewish learning; graduate schools prepare for careers in medicine, law, social work, Jewish education, psychology, Jewish studies, and other fields. It has seven undergraduate schools, seven graduate and professional schools, and four affiliates. *Yeshiva University Review; Yeshiva University Today.* (WWW.YU.EDU)

Yeshiva University has four campuses in Manhattan and the Bronx: Wilf Campus, 500 W. 185 St., NYC 10033-3201; Midtown Campus, 245 Lexington Ave., NYC 10016-4699; Brookdale Center, 55 Fifth Ave., NYC 10003-4391; Jack and Pearl Resnick Campus, Eastchester Rd. & Morris Pk. Ave., Bronx, NY 10461-1602.

Undergraduate schools for men at Wilf Campus: Yeshiva College (Dean Dr. David Srulowitz) provides liberal arts and sciences curricula; grants BA degree. Isaac Breuer College of Hebraic Studies awards Hebrew teacher's diploma, AA, BA, and BS. Yeshiva Program/Mazer School of Talmudic Studies offers advanced course of study in Talmudic texts and commentaries. Irving I. Stone Beit Midrash Program offers diversified curriculum combining Talmud with Jewish studies.

Undergraduate school for women at Midtown Campus: Stern College for Women (Dean Dr. Karen Bacon) offers liberal arts and sciences curricula supplemented by Jewish studies programs; awards BA, AA, and Hebrew teacher's diploma.

Sy Syms School of Business at Wilf Campus and Midtown Campus offers undergraduate business curricula in conjunction with study at Yeshiva College or Stern College; grants BS degree.

———, ALBERT EINSTEIN COLLEGE OF MEDICINE (1955). Eastchester Rd. & Morris Pk. Ave., Bronx, NY 10461-1602. (718)430-2000. Chmn. Bd. Robert A. Belfer; Marilyn and Stanley M. Katz Dean Dr. Allen M. Siegel. Prepares physicians and conducts research in the health sciences; awards MD degree; includes Sue Golding Graduate Division of Medical Sciences (Dir. Dr. Anne M. Etgen), which grants PhD degree. Einstein's clinical facilities and affiliates encompass Jack D. Weiler Hospital of Albert Einstein College of Medicine, Jacobi Medical Center, Montefiore Medical Center, Long Island Jewish Medical Center, Beth Israel Medical Center, Bronx-Lebanon Hospital Center, and Rose F. Kennedy Center for Research in Mental Retardation and Developmental Disabilities. *Einstein; Einstein Today; Einstein Quarterly Journal of Biology and Medicine.*

———, AZRIELI GRADUATE SCHOOL OF JEWISH EDUCATION AND ADMINISTRATION (1945). 245 Lexington Ave., NYC 10016-4699. (212)340-7705. FAX: (212)340-7787. Chmn. Bd. Moshael J. Straus; Dir. Dr. Yitzchak S. Handel. Offers MS degree in Jewish elementary and secondary education; specialist's certificate and EdD in administration and supervision of Jewish education. Block Education Program, subsidized by a grant from the Jewish Agency's Joint Program for Jewish Education, provides summer course work to complement year-round field instruction in local communities.

———, BELFER INSTITUTE FOR ADVANCED BIOMEDICAL STUDIES (1978). Eastchester Rd. & Morris Pk. Ave., Bronx, NY 10461-1602. (718)430-2801. Dir. Dr. Dennis Shields. Integrates and coordinates the Albert Einstein College of Medicine's postdoctoral research and training-grant programs in the basic and clinical biomedical sciences. Awards certificate as research fellow or research associate on completion of training.

———, BENJAMIN N. CARDOZO SCHOOL OF LAW (1976). 55 Fifth Ave., NYC 10003-4391. (212)790-0200. E-mail:lawinfo@ymail.yu.edu. Chmn. Bd. Of Directors Earle I. Mack; Dean Paul R. Verkuil. Offers a rigorous and enriched legal education leading to juris doctor (JD) degree and two LLM programs—in intellectual property and in general law. Programs and services include Jacob Burns Institute for Advanced Legal Studies; Jacob Burns Center for Ethics in the Practice of Law; Bet Tzedek Legal Services Clinic, including the Herman J. Stich Program for the Aged and Disabled; Cardozo International Institute/Uri and Caroline Bauer Israel Program; Leonard and Bea Diener Institute of Jewish Law; Floersheimer Center for Constitutional Democracy; Ford Foundation Program in International Law and Human Rights; Samuel and Ronnie Heyman Center on Corporate Governance; Kukin Program for Conflict Resolution; Romie Shapiro

Program in International Law and Human Rights; Stephen B. Siegel Program in Real Estate Law; Sol S. Singer Research Program in Real Property Law; Howard M. Squadron Program in Law, Media, and Society; Center for Professional Development. *Cardozo Life; Cardozo Law Review; Cardozo Arts and Entertainment Law Journal; Cardozo Women's Law Journal; Cardozo Journal of International and Comparative Law; Cardozo Studies in Law and Literature; Post-Soviet Media Law and Policy Newsletter; New York Real Estate Reporter.*

———, BERNARD REVEL GRADUATE SCHOOL OF JEWISH STUDIES (1935). 500 W. 185 St., NYC 10033-3201. (212)960-5253. Pres. Chmn. Bd. Mordecai D. Katz; Dean Dr. David Berger. Offers graduate programs in Bible, Talmudic studies, Jewish history, and Jewish philosophy; confers MA and PhD degrees. Harry Fischel Summer Program offers the Revel program during the summer.

———, FERKAUF GRADUATE SCHOOL OF PSYCHOLOGY (1957). Eastchester Rd. & Morris Pk. Ave., Bronx, NY 10461-1602. (718)430-3941. FAX: (718)430-3960. E-mail: gill@aecom.yu.edu. Chair Bd. Dr. Jayne G. Beker; Dean Dr. Lawrence J. Siegel. Offers MA in applied psychology; PsyD in clinical and school-clinical child psychology; and PhD in developmental and clinical health psychology. Programs and services include the Leonard and Muriel Marcus Family Project for the Study of the Disturbed Adolescent; Max and Celia Parnes Family Psychological and Psychoeducational Services Clinic.

———, (affiliate) PHILIP AND SARAH BELZ SCHOOL OF JEWISH MUSIC (1954). 560 W. 185 St., NYC 10033-3201. (212)960-5353. FAX: (212)960-5359. Dir. Cantor Bernard Beer. Provides professional training of cantors and courses in Jewish liturgical music; conducts outreach; publishes *Journal of Jewish Music and Literature;* awards associate cantor's certificate and cantorial diploma.

———, (affiliate) RABBI ISAAC ELCHANAN THEOLOGICAL SEMINARY (1896). 2540 Amsterdam Ave., NYC 10033-9986. (212)960-5344. FAX: (212)960-0061. Chmn. Bd. Julius Berman; Dean Rabbi Yona Reiss. Leading center in the Western Hemisphere for Torah study and rabbinic training. RIETS complex encompasses 15 educational entities and a major service and outreach center with some 20 programs. Grants semikhah (ordination) and the degrees of master of religious education, master of Hebrew literature, doctor of religious education, and doctor of Hebrew literature. Includes Marcos and Adina Katz Kollel (Institute for Advanced Research in Rabbinics); Kollel l'Horaah (Yadin Yadin) and External Yadin Yadin; Israel Henry Beren Institute for Higher Talmudic Studies (HaMachon HaGavohah L'Talmud); Bella and Harry Wexner Kollel Elyon and Semikhah Honors Program; Ludwig Jesselson Kollel Chaverim; Caroline and Joseph S. Gruss Institute in Jerusalem.

RIETS sponsors one high school for boys (Manhattan) and one for girls (Queens).

The Center for the Jewish Future (Dir. Rabbi Kenneth Brander) provides personal and professional service to the rabbinate and related fields, as well as educational, consultative, organizational, and placement services to congregations, schools, and communal organizations around the world; coordinates a broad spectrum of outreach programs, including Association of Modern Orthodox Day Schools and Yeshiva High Schools, Stone-Sapirstein Center for Jewish Education, Gertrude and Morris Bienenfeld Department of Rabbinic Services, Gindi Program for the Enhancement of Professional Rabbinics, Continuing Rabbinic Education Initiatives, Leadership Education and Development Program (LEAD), Kiruv College Outreach Program, Community Kollel and Beit Midrash and Boardroom Learning Programs, Project Kehillah, Myer and Pauline Senders Off-Campus Lecture Series, Jewish Medical Ethics Consultation Service, National Commission on Torah Education.The Torah U-Madda Project, supported by the Joseph J. and Bertha K. Green Memorial Fund, includes the Orthodox Forum and publishes the *The Torah U-Madda Journal* and *Ten Da'at.*

Sephardic components are Jacob E. Safra Institute of Sephardic Studies and the Institute of Yemenite Studies; Sephardic Community Program; Dr. Joseph and Rachel Ades Sephardic Outreach Program; Maybaum Sephardic Fellowship Program.

———, WOMEN'S ORGANIZATION (1928). 500 W. 185 St., NYC 10033-3201. (212) 960-0855. Chmn. Natl. Bd. Dinah Pinczower. Supports Yeshiva University's national scholarship program for students training in education, community service, law, medicine, and other professions. Its Torah Chesed Fund provides monthly stipends to needy undergraduate students.

———, WURZWEILER SCHOOL OF SOCIAL WORK (1957). 500 W. 185 St., NYC 10033-3201. (212)960-0800. FAX: (212)960-0822. Chair Bd. David I. Schachne; Dorothy and David I. Schachne Dean Dr. Sheldon R. Gelman. Offers graduate programs in social work and Jewish communal service; grants MSW and PhD degrees and certificate in Jewish communal service. MSW programs are: Concurrent Plan, 2-year, full-time track, combining classroom study and supervised field instruction; Plan for Employed Persons (PEP), for people working in social agencies; Block Education Plan (Dir. Dr. Adele Weiner), which combines summer course work with regular-year field placement in local agencies; Clergy Plan, training in counseling for clergy of all denominations; Silvia and Irwin Leiferman Center for Professional Training in the Care of the Elderly. *Jewish Social Work Forum.*

———, (affiliate) YESHIVA OF LOS ANGELES (1977). 9760 W. Pico Blvd., Los Angeles, CA 90035-4701. (310)772-2424. FAX: (310)772-7661. E-mail: mhmay@wiesenthal.com. Dean Rabbi Marvin Hier; Bd. Chmn. Samuel Belzberg; Dir. Academic Programs Rabbi Sholom Tendler. Affiliates are Yeshiva University High Schools of Los Angeles, Jewish Studies Institute and Kollel Torah MiTzion.

———, YESHIVA UNIVERSITY MUSEUM (see p. 633)

YESHIVAT CHOVEVEI TORAH (1999). 475 Riverside Drive, Suite 244., NYC 10015. (212)666-0036. FAX: (212) 666-5633. Dean Rabbi Avi Weiss. Dedicated to the training of open Orthodox rabbis who will lead the Jewish community and shape its spiritual and intellectual character in consonance with modern and open Orthodox values and commitments, emphasizing the encounter with classical Jewish texts not just as an intellectual exercise but as a form of divine service. (WWW.YCTORAH.ORG)

SOCIAL, MUTUAL BENEFIT

ALPHA EPSILON PI FRATERNITY (1913). 8815 Wesleyan Rd., Indianapolis, IN 46268-1171. (317)876-1913. FAX: (317)876-1057. E-mail: office@aepi.org. Internatl. Pres. Dr. Jay Levine; Exec. V.-Pres. Sidney N. Dunn. International Jewish fraternity active on over 100 campuses in the U.S. and Canada; encourages Jewish students to remain loyal to their heritage and to assume leadership roles in the community; active in behalf of the State of Israel and Magen David Adom among other causes. *The Lion of Alpha Epsilon Pi (quarterly magazine).*

AMERICAN ASSOCIATION OF JEWS FROM THE FORMER USSR, INC. (AAJFSU) (1989). 100 Church Street, Suite 1608, NYC 10007. (212) 964-1946. FAX: (212)964-1946. E-mail: GeorgeZilberman@yahoo.com. Pres. Yury Zilberman; Bd. Chmn. Mark Gurevich. National not-for-profit, grassroots mutual assistance and refugee advocacy organization, which unites and represents interests of over 600,000 Russian speaking Jewish refugees and legal immigrants from the former Soviet Union. It has chapters and independent associations in seven states, including New York, Ohio, Colorado, New Jersey, Massachusetts, Wisconsin and Maryland. The national organization is a member of the National Immigration Forum and it is affiliated with the United Jewish Communities, Washington Action Office. It has become a founding member of the Jewish Community Relations Council of New York and the New York Immigration Coalition. Local Chapters work in cooperation with Jewish Federation and New York Chapter works in cooperation with JCRC, NYANA, HIAS and UJA-Federation of New York. The AAJFSU assists newcomers in their resettlement and vocational and cultural adjustment, fosters their Jewish identity and involvement in American civic and social affairs, fights anti-Semitism and violation of human rights in the FSU and the U.S. through cooperation with other human rights organizations and advocacy organizations, supports struggle of Israeli Jews for sustainable peace, collects money for Israeli victims of terror, provides assistance in social safety net and naturalization of the elderly and disabled, provides advocacy in cases of political asylum for victims of anti-Semitism in the FSU. *Chronicles of Anti-Semitism and Nationalism in Republics of the Former USSR (in English, annually); Information Bulletin (in Russian, quarterly).*

AMERICAN FEDERATION OF JEWS FROM CENTRAL EUROPE, INC. (1938). 570 Seventh Ave., NYC 10018. (212)921-3871. FAX: (212) 575-1918. Pres. Fritz Weinschenk; Exec. Asst. Dennis E. Rohrbaugh. Seeks to safeguard the rights and interests of American Jews of German-speaking Central European descent, especially in reference to restitution and indemnification; through its affiliate Research Foundation for Jewish Immigration sponsors research and publications on the history, immigration, and acculturation of Central European émigrés in the U.S. and worldwide; through its affiliate Jewish Philanthropic Fund of 1933 supports social programs for needy Nazi victims in the U.S.; undertakes cultural activities, publications; member, Council of Jews from Germany, London.

AMERICAN VETERANS OF ISRAEL (1951). 136 E. 39 St., NYC 10016. E-mail: spielgelsi@aol.com. Pres. Samuel Z. Klausner; V-Pres. David Kaplan. Maintains contact with American and Canadian volunteers who served in Aliyah Bet and/or Israel's War of Independence; promotes Israel's welfare; holds memorial services at grave of Col. David Marcus; is affiliated with World Mahal. *Newsletter.*

ASSOCIATION OF YUGOSLAV JEWS IN THE UNITED STATES, INC. (1941). 130 E. 59 St., Suite 1202, NYC 10022. (212)371-6891. V.-Pres. & Chmn. Emanuel Salom; Sec. Dr. Joseph Stock. Assistance to all Jews originally from Yugoslavia—Bosnia, Serbia, Croatia—and new settlers in Israel. *Bulletins.*

BNAI ZION–THE AMERICAN FRATERNAL ZIONIST ORGANIZATION (1908). 136 E. 39 St., NYC 10016. (212)725-1211. FAX: (212)684-6327. Pres. Michael J. Lazar; Exec. V.-Pres. Mel Parness. Fosters principles of Americanism, fraternalism, and Zionism. The Bnai Zion Foundation supports various humanitarian projects in Israel and the USA, chiefly the Bnai Zion Medical Center in Haifa and homes for retarded children-Maon Bnai Zion in Rosh Ha'ayin and the Herman Z. Quittman Center in Jerusalem Ahava Project. Also supports building of new central library in Ma'aleh Adumim. In U.S. sponsors program of awards for excellence in Hebrew for high school and college students. Chapters all over U.S. *Bnai Zion Voice (*quarterly*).* (WWW.BNAIZION.COM)

BRITH ABRAHAM (1859; reorg. 1887). 136 E. 39 St., NYC 10016. (212)725-1211. FAX: (212)684-6327. Grand Master Robert Freeman. Protects Jewish rights and combats anti-Semitism; supports Soviet and Ethiopian emigration and the safety and dignity of Jews worldwide; helps to support Bnai Zion Medical Center in Haifa and other Israeli institutions; aids and supports various programs and projects in the U.S.: Hebrew Excellence Program-Gold Medal presentation in high schools and colleges; Camp Loyaltown; Brith Abraham and Bnai Zion Foundations. *Voice.*

BRITH SHOLOM (1905). 3939 Conshohocken Ave., Philadelphia, PA 19131. (215)878-5696. FAX: (215) 878-5699. Pres. Seymour Rose; Exec. Dir. Roy Shenberg; Exec. V. P., Jerome Verlin. Fraternal organization devoted to community welfare, protection of rights of Jewish people, and activities that foster Jewish identity and provide support for Israel. Through its philanthropic arm, the Brith Sholom Foundation (1962), sponsors Brith Sholom House in Philadelphia, nonprofit senior-citizen apartments; and Brith Sholom Beit Halochem in Haifa, Israel, rehabilitation, social, and sports center for disabled Israeli veterans, operated by Zahal. Chmn. Martin Winit; Exec. Dir. Saundra Laub. *Brith Sholom Digest; monthly news bulletin.*

FREE SONS OF ISRAEL (1849). 250 Fifth Ave., Suite 201, NYC 10001. (212)725-3690. FAX: (212)725-5874. Grand Master Arlene Hoberman Kyler; Grand Sec. Ronald J. Laszlo. Oldest Jewish fraternal-benefit society in U.S. Affordable membership men & women (18+). Supports Israel, UJA projects, non-sectarian toy drives/ philanthropies. Social Action fights anti-Semitism, supports human rights. Member benefits-IBM Metro Credit Union, scholarships, cemetery, discounted Long

Term Care Insurance, educational and social functions, Free Model Seder. *Free Sons Reporter.* (WWW.FREESONS.ORG)

JEWISH LABOR BUND (Directed by WORLD COORDINATING COMMITTEE OF THE BUND) (1897; reorg. 1947). 25 E. 21 St., NYC 10010. (212)475-0059. FAX: (212) 473-5102. Acting Pres. Motl Zelmanowics; Sec. Gen. Benjamin Nade. Coordinates activities of Bund organizations throughout the world and represents them in the Socialist International; spreads the ideas of socialism as formulated by the Jewish Labor Bund; publishes books and periodicals on world problems, Jewish life, socialist theory and policy, and on the history, activities, and ideology of the Jewish Labor Bund. *Unser Tsait* (U.S.); *Lebns-Fragn* (Israel); *Unser Gedank* (Australia).

SEPHARDIC JEWISH BROTHERHOOD OF AMERICA, INC. (1915). 97-45 Queens Blvd., Rm. 610, Rego Park, NY 11374. (718)459-1600. Pres. Bernard Ouziel; Sec. Irving Barocas. A benevolent fraternal organization seeking to promote the industrial, social, educational, and religious welfare of its members. *Sephardic Brother.*

SIGMA ALPHA MU FRATERNITY (1909). 9245 No. Meridian St., Ste. 105, Indianapolis, IN 46260. (317)846-0600. FAX: (317)846-9462. E-mail: samhq@sam.org. Sup. Prior Leland P.Manders; Exec. Dir. Aaron M. Girson. Founded at the City College of NY as a fraternity of Jewish men, currently active on 70 campuses across North America. Encourages students to take an active role on campus, offers leadership opportunities and financial aid to members and scholarships to leaders of Jewish youth groups. *Octogonian of Sigma Alpha Mu (quarterly).*

WORKMEN'S CIRCLE/ARBETER RING (1900). 45 E. 33 St., NYC 10016. (212)889-6800. FAX: (212)532-7518. E-mail: member@circle.org. Pres. Martin Krupnick; Exec. Dir. Ann Toback. Fosters Jewish identity and participation in Jewish life through Jewish, especially Yiddish, culture and education, friendship, mutual aid, and the pursuit of social and economic justice. Offices are located throughout the U.S. and Canada. Member services include: Jewish cultural seminars, concerts, theater, Jewish schools, children's camp and adult resort, fraternal and singles activities, a Jewish Book Center, public affairs/social action, health insurance plans, medical/dental/legal services, life insurance plans, cemetery/funeral benefits, social services, geriatric homes and centers, and travel services. *The Call.* (WWW.CIRCLE.ORG)

ZETA BETA TAU FRATERNITY (1898). 3905 Vincennes Rd., Suite 300, Indianapolis, IN 46268. (317)334-1898. FAX: (317)334-1899. E-mail: zbt@zbtnational.org. Pres. Kenneth L. Simon, M.D.; Exec. Dir. Jonathan I. Yulish. Oldest historically Jewish fraternity; promotes intellectual awareness, social responsibility, integrity, and brotherhood among over 5,000 undergrads and 110,000 alumni in the U.S. and Canada. Encourages leadership and diversity through mutual respect of all heritages; nonsectarian since 1954. A brotherhood of Kappa Nu, Phi Alpha, Phi Epsilon Pi, Phi Sigma Delta, Zeta Beta Tau. *The Deltan (quarterly).* (WWW.ZBT.ORG)

SOCIAL WELFARE

AMC CANCER RESEARCH CENTER (formerly JEWISH CONSUMPTIVES' RELIEF SOCIETY, 1904; incorporated as American Medical Center at Denver, 1954). 1600 Pierce St., Denver, CO 80214. (303)233-6501. FAX: (303)239-3400. E-mail: edelmanj@amc.org. Pres./CEO Bob R. Baker; Exec. V-Pres. Research Dr. Tom Slaga. A nationally recognized leader in the fight against cancer; employs a three-pronged, interdisciplinary approach that combines laboratory, clinical, and community cancer-control research to advance the prevention, early detection, diagnosis, and treatment of the disease. The exclusive scientific focus of our work is the prevention and control of cancer and other major diseases. *The Quest for Answers; Annual Report.* (WWW.AMC.ORG)

AMCHA FOR TSEDAKAH (1990). 9800 Cherry Hill Rd., College Park, MD 20740. (301)937-2600. Pres. Rabbi Bruce E. Kahn. Solicits and distributes contributions to Jewish charitable organizations in the U.S. and Israel; accredits organizations which serve an important tsedakah purpose, demonstrate efficiency and fiscal integrity, and also support pluralism. Contributors are encouraged to earmark contributions for specific organizations; all contributions to General Fund are forwarded to the charitable institutions, as operating expenses are covered by a separate fund. *Newspaper supplement.*

AMERICAN JEWISH CORRECTIONAL CHAPLAINS ASSOCIATION, INC. (formerly NATIONAL COUNCIL OF JEWISH PRISON CHAPLAINS) (1937). 10 E. 73 St., NYC 10021-4194. (212)879-8415. FAX: (212) 772-3977. (Cooperates with the New York Board of Rabbis.) Supports spiritual, moral, and social services for Jewish men and women in corrections; stimulates support of correctional chaplaincy; provides spiritual and professional fellowship for Jewish correctional chaplains; promotes sound standards for correctional chaplaincy; schedules workshops and research to aid chaplains in counseling and with religious services for Jewish inmates. Constituent, American Correctional Chaplains Association. *Chaplains Manual.*

AMERICAN JEWISH SOCIETY FOR SERVICE, INC. (1950). 15 E. 26 St., Rm. 1029, NYC 10010. (212)683-6178. Email: aud1750@aol.com. Founder/Chmn. Henry Kohn; Pres. Lawrence G. Green; Exec. Dirs. Carl & Audrey Brenner. Conducts voluntary work-service camps each summer to enable high school juniors and seniors to perform humanitarian service.

ASSOCIATION OF JEWISH AGING SERVICES (formerly NORTH AMERICAN ASSOCIATION OF JEWISH HOMES AND HOUSING FOR THE AGING) (1960). 316 Pennsylvania Ave., SE, Suite 402, Washington, DC 20003. (202) 543-7500. FAX: (202)543-4090. E-mail: ajas@ajas.org. Pres. Jodi L. Lyons; Chmn. Michael Ellentuck. Represents nearly all the not-for-profit charitable homes and housing for the Jewish aging; promotes excellence in performance and quality of service through fostering communication and education and encouraging advocacy for the aging; conducts annual conferences and institutes. *Directory; The Scribe (quarterly newsletter).*

ASSOCIATION OF JEWISH CENTER PROFESSIONALS (1918). 15 E. 26 St., NYC 10010-1579. (212)532-4949. FAX: (212) 481-4174. E-mail: ajcp@jcca.org. Pres. Susan Bender; Exec. Dir. Harvey Rosenzweig. Seeks to enhance the standards, techniques, practices, scope, and public understanding of Jewish community center professionals and kindred agency work. *Kesher.*

ASSOCIATION OF JEWISH COMMUNITY ORGANIZATION PERSONNEL (AJCOP) (1969). 14619 Horseshoe Trace, Wellington, FL 33414. (561)795-4853. FAX: (561)798-0358. E-mail: marlene@ajcop.org. Pres. Rabbi Daniel Allen; Exec. Dir. Louis B. Solomon. An organization of professionals engaged in areas of fund-raising, endowments, budgeting, social planning, financing, administration, and coordination of services. Objectives are to develop and enhance professional practices in Jewish communal work; to maintain and improve standards, practices, scope, and public understanding of the field of community organization, as practiced through local federations, national agencies, other organizations, settings, and private practitioners. *Prolog (quarterly newspaper); Proceedings (annual record of papers and speeches).* (WWW.AJCOP.ORG)

ASSOCIATION OF JEWISH FAMILY AND CHILDREN'S AGENCIES (1972). 620 Cranbury Rd., Suite 102, E. Brunswick, NJ 08816-5419. (800) 634-7346. FAX: (732)432-7127. E-mail: ajfca@ajfca.org. Pres. Bert J. Goldberg; Bd. Chair. Lawrence Abramson. The national service organization for Jewish family and children's agencies in the U.S. and Canada. Reinforces member agencies in their efforts to sustain and enhance the quality of Jewish family and communal life. Operates the Elder Support Network for the national Jewish community. *Tachlis (quarterly); Professional Opportunities Bulletin; Executive Digest (monthly).* (WWW.AJFCA.ORG)

AVODAH: THE JEWISH SERVICE CORPS (1996). 116 East 27th Street, 10th Floor, NYC 10016. (212)545-7759. FAX: (212)686-1353. E-mail: info@avodah.net. Exec. Dir. Rabbi David Rosenn. Combines direct antipoverty work in NYC and Washington D.C. with Jewish study and community-building; corps members live together and work full-time for a year on housing, welfare, and education, and other matters. (WWW.AVODAH.NET)

BARON DE HIRSCH FUND (1891). 130 E. 59 St., 12th fl., NYC 10022. (212)836-1358. FAX: (212)453-6512. Pres. Jenny Morgenthal; Mng. Dir. Lauren Katzowitz. Aids Jewish immigrants in the U.S. and Israel by giving grants to agencies active in resettlement, focusing on educational, community development, and vocational training.

B'NAI B'RITH (1843). 2020 K St., NW, Washington, DC 20006. (202)857-6600. FAX: (202)857-2700. Pres. Moishe Smith; Exec. V.-Pres. Daniel S. Mariaschin. International Jewish organization, with affiliates in 58 countries. Offers programs designed to ensure the preservation of Jewry and Judaism: Jewish education, community volunteer service, expansion of human rights, assistance to Israel, housing for the elderly, leadership training, rights of Jews in all countries to study their heritage. *International Jewish Monthly; B'nai B'rith Today.* (WWW.BNAIBRITH.ORG)

———, ANTI-DEFAMATION LEAGUE OF (see p. 622)

———, HILLEL (see p. 652)

———, KLUTZNICK MUSEUM (see p. 627)

———, YOUTH ORGANIZATION (see p. 650)

CITY OF HOPE NATIONAL MEDICAL CENTER AND BECKMAN RESEARCH INSTITUTE (1913). 1500 E. Duarte Rd., Duarte, CA 91010. (626)359-8111. FAX: (626) 301-8115. E-mail: dhalper@coh.org. Exec. V. P. Krontiris; Medical and Scientific Affairs Theodore. City of Hope is one of the world's leading research and treatment centers for cancer and other life-threatening diseases, including diabetes and HIV/AIDS. A pioneer in the fields of bone marrow transplantation and genetics, City of Hope is a Comprehensive Cancer Center, the highest designation bestowed by the National Cancer Institute, and a founding member of the National Comprehensive Cancer Network. *City of Hope Cancer Research Center Report.*

INTERNATIONAL ASSOCIATION OF JEWISH VOCATIONAL SERVICES (formerly JEWISH OCCUPATIONAL COUNCIL) (1939). 1845 Walnut St., Suite 640, Philadelphia, PA 19103. (215) 854-0233. FAX: (215)854-0212. E-mail: coheng@iajvs.org. Exec. Dir. Genie Cohen; Vivian Seigel, President. Not-for-profit membership association of Jewish-sponsored social service agencies in the U.S., Canada, and Israel. Provides member agencies with technical, informational, and communications support; researches funding opportunities, develops collaborative program models, and represents Jewish vocational network nationally and internationally. Sponsors annual conference for members. Member agencies provide a wide range of educational, vocational, and rehabilitation services to both the Jewish and non-Jewish communities. *Executive quarterly newsletter.* (WWW.IAJVS.ORG)

INTERNATIONAL COUNCIL ON JEWISH SOCIAL AND WELFARE SERVICES (1961). c/o American Jewish Joint Distribution Committee, 711 Third Ave., NYC 10017. (NY liaison office with UN headquarters.) (212)687-6200. FAX: (212)370-5467. E-mail: newyork@jdcny.org. Pres. Eugene J. Ribokoff; Exec. V. P. Steven Schwager. Provides assistance to Jewish communities in Europe, Asia, Africa, and the Mideast, including welfare programs for Jews in need. Current concerns include: Rescuing Jews from areas of distress, facilitating community development in the former Soviet Union; helping to meet Israel's social service needs by developing innovative programs that create new opportunities for the country's most vulnerable populations; youth activities in Eastern Europe and nonsectarian development and disaster assistance. *Annual Report, JDC's Activities in the Former Soviet Union; JDC: One People One Heart, Crisis in Argentina Monthly Update.*

JBI INTERNATIONAL (FOUNDED IN 1931 AS THE JEWISH BRAILLE INSTITUTE OF AMERICA, INC.) (1931). 110 E. 30 St., NYC 10016. (212)889-2525. FAX: (212)689-3692. E-mail: sradinsky@jbilibrary.org. Pres. Dr. Ellen Isler; Exec. V.-Pres. Israel A. Taub. Provides Jewish books for the visually impaired, blind and reading-disabled on tape, in large print, and in Braille. International program serves clients in more than 50 countries; sponsors special programs in Israel and Eastern Europe. Periodical and journals available to our subscribers include *Moment, Tikkun, the Jerusalem Reporter and Commentary.* (WWW.JBILIBRARY.ORG)

JEWISH CHILDREN'S ADOPTION NETWORK (1990). PO Box 147016, Denver, CO 80214-7016. (303)573-8113. FAX: (303) 893-1447. E-mail: jcan@qwest.net. Pres. Stephen Krausz; Exec. Dir. Vicki Krausz. An adoption exchange founded for the primary purpose of locating adoptive families for Jewish infants and children. Works with some 200 children a year, throughout N. Amer., 85-90% of whom have special needs. No fees charged for services, which include birth-parent and adoptive-parent counseling. *Quarterly newsletter.* (WWW.USERS.QWEST.NET/JCAN)

JEWISH COMMUNAL SERVICE ASSOCIATION OF N. AMERICA (1899; formerly CONFERENCE OF JEWISH COMMUNAL SERVICE). 520 Eighth Ave., 4th Floor, NYC 10018. (212)532-0167. FAX: (212)532-1461. E-mail: info@jcsana.org. Pres.Glenn Easton; Exec. Dir. Brenda Gevertz. Serves as forum for all professional philosophies in community service, for testing new experiences, proposing new ideas, and questioning or reaffirming old concepts; umbrella organization for 7 major Jewish communal service groups. Concerned with advancement of professional personnel practices and standards. *Journal of Jewish Communal Service; Concurrents.*

JEWISH COMMUNITY CENTERS ASSOCIATION OF NORTH AMERICA (formerly JWB) (1917). 520 Eighth Avenue., NYC 10018. (212)532-4949. FAX: (212)481-4174. E-mail: info@jcca.org. Chair Edward H. Kaplan; Pres. Allan Finkelstein. The leadership network of, and central agency for, the Jewish Community Center movement, comprising more than 275 JCCs, YM-YWHAs, and camps in the U.S. and Canada, which annually serve more than one million members and an additional million non-member users. JCC Association offers a wide range of services and resources to strengthen the capacity of its affiliates to provide educational, cultural, social, Jewish identity-building, and recreational programs to enhance the lives of North American Jews of all ages and backgrounds. Additionally, the movement fosters and strengthens connections between North American Jews and Israel as well as with world Jewry. JCC Association is also the only U.S. government-accredited agency for serving the religious and social needs of Jewish military personnel, their families, and patients in VA hospitals through JWB Chaplains Council. *JCC Circle; Chaplines; other newsletters for JCC professionals.* (WWW.JCCA.ORG)

———, JEWISH WELFARE BOARD JEWISH CHAPLAINS COUNCIL (formerly COMMISSION ON JEWISH CHAPLAINCY) (1940). 15 E. 26 St., NYC 10010-1579. (212)532-4949. FAX: (212)481-4174. E-mail: nathanlandman@jcca.com. Chmn. Rabbi David S. Goldstein; Dir. Rabbi David Lapp; Dep. Dir. Rabbi Nathan M. Landman. Recruits, endorses, and serves Jewish military and Veterans Administration chaplains on behalf of the American Jewish community and the major rabbinic bodies; trains and assists Jewish lay leaders where there are no chaplains, for service to Jewish military personnel, their families, and hospitalized veterans. *CHAPLINES newsletter.*

JEWISH FUND FOR JUSTICE (1984). 330 7th Avenue, Suite 1902, NYC 10001. (212) 213-2113. FAX: (212)213-2233. E-mail: jfjustice@jfjustice.org. Bd. Chmn. John Levy; Exec. Dir. Marlene Provizer. The Jewish Fund for Justice is the only national Jewish organization solely committed to fighting the injustice of poverty in America. By assisting on a non-denominational basis grassroots organizations struggling for decent housing, schools and jobs, and by helping Jews develop community-based, social justice partnerships, the Jewish Fund for Justice brings to life the core Jewish values of *tikkun olam* (repair of the world) and *tzedakah* (righteous giving). Giving opportunities include general support, family, wedding, and youth endowment funds and planned giving. *Annual report, newsletter.* (WWW.JEWISHJUSTICE.ORG)

JEWISH FUNDERS NETWORK (1990). 15 E. 26 St., Suite 1038, NYC 10010. (212) 726-0177. FAX: (212) 726-0195. E-mail: jfn@jfunders.org. Pres. Mark Charendof; Exec. V.-Pres. Ron Meier. International agency providing leadership, programs and services to help Jewish grantmakers be more effective and strategic in their philanthropy. JFN members collaborate and plan so that their money can be used to effectively change the world. Key initiatives: International Conference, regional programs, publications, strategic partnerships, web site, consultation, resources and referral. *Quarterly Newsletter, Reports on Philanthropy.*

JEWISH SOCIAL SERVICES PROFESSIONALS ASSOCIATION (JSSPA) (1965). c/o AJFCA, 620 Cranbury Rd., Suite 102, E. Brunswick, NJ 08816-0549. (800) 634-7346. FAX: (732)432-7127. E-mail: ajfca@ajfca.org. Chmn. Jaclynn Faffer; Chair Norman Keane. Brings together executives, supervisors, managers, caseworkers, and related professionals in Jewish Family Service and related agencies. Seeks to enhance professional skills, improve personnel standards, further Jewish continuity and identity, and strengthen Jewish family life. Provides a national and regional forum for professional discussion and learning; functions under the auspices of the Association of Jewish Family and Children's Agencies. *Newsletter.* (WWW.AJFCA.ORG)

JEWISH WOMEN INTERNATIONAL (1897). 2000 M. Street, NW Suite 207, Washington, DC 20036. (202)857-1300. FAX: (202)857-1380. E-mail: jwi@jwi.org. Pres. Barbara Rabkin; Exec. Dir. Gail Rubinson. Jewish Women International breaks the cycle of violence by developing emotionally healthy adults, empowering women and strengthening families. Jewish Women International accomplishes its goals through direct service programs, education, advocacy and the promotion of "best practice" models. Offers programs in the United States, Canada, and Israel. *Jewish Woman Magazine (quarterly).* (WWW.JEWISHWOMEN.ORG)

LEVI HOSPITAL (1914). 300 Prospect Ave., Hot Springs, AR 71901. (501)624-1281. FAX: (501) 622-3500. E-mail: levihospital@hsnp.com. Pres. Philip M. Clay; Admin. Patrick G. McCabe. Offers outpatient rehab, including therapy sessions in large thermal heated pool. Other programs: adult/geriatric inpatient and outpatient psychiatric program, child/adolescent psychiatric clinic, hospice care, home health care, osteoporosis clinic, Levi Rehabilitation Unit, a cooperative effort of Levi and St. Joseph's hospitals (inpatient rehab). *The Progress Chart; The Legacy.*

MAZON: A JEWISH RESPONSE TO HUNGER (1985). 1990 S. Bondy Drive, Suite 260, Los Angeles, CA 90025. (310)442-0020. FAX: (310)442-0030. E-mail: mazonmail@mazon.org. Exec. Dir. Eric Schockman, PhD. A grant-making and fund-raising organization that raises funds in the Jewish community and provides grants to nonprofit 501(c)(3) organizations which aim to prevent and alleviate hunger in the United States and abroad. Grantees include food pantries, food banks, multi-service organizations, advocacy, education and research projects, and international relief and development organizations. *Annual Report, 2 newsletters each year.*

NATIONAL ASSOCIATION OF JEWISH CHAPLAINS (1988). 901 Route 10, Whippany, NJ 07981. (973)929-3168. FAX: (973) 736-9193. E-mail: cecille3@juno.com. Pres. Rabbi Stephen Roberts; Natl. Coord. Cecille Allman Asekoff. A professional organization for people functioning as Jewish chaplains in hospitals, nursing homes, geriatric, psychiatric, correctional, and military facilities. Provides collegial support, continuing education, professional certification, and resources for the Jewish community on issues of pastoral and spiritual care. *The Jewish Chaplain.*

NATIONAL COUNCIL OF JEWISH WOMEN (1893). 53 W. 23 St., NYC 10010. (212)645-4048. FAX: (212)645-7466. E-mail: actionline@ncjw.org. Pres. Nancy Ratzan; Exec. Dir. Stacy Kass. Works to improve the lives of women, children, and families in the United States and Israel; strives to insure individual rights and freedoms for all. NCJW volunteers deliver vital services in 500 U.S. communities and carry out NCJW's advocacy agenda through a powerful grassroots network. *NCJW Journal; Washington Newsletter.* (WWW.NCJW.ORG)

NATIONAL INSTITUTE FOR JEWISH HOSPICE (1985). PO Box 48025, Los Angeles, CA 90048. (800)446-4448. 330 Broad Ave., Englewood, NJ 07631. (201)816-7324. FAX: (201)816-7321. Pres. Rabbi Maurice Lamm; Exec. Dir. Shirley Lamm. Serves as a national Jewish hospice resource center. Through conferences, research, publications, referrals, and counseling services offers guidance, training, and information to patients, family members, clergy of all faiths, professional caregivers, and volunteers who work with the Jewish terminally ill. *Jewish Hospice Times.*

NATIONAL JEWISH CHILDREN'S LEUKEMIA FOUNDATION (1990). 7316 Avenue U, Brooklyn NY 11234. (718)-251-1222. FAX: (718)-251-1444. E-mail: info@leukemiafoundatin.org. Pres./Founder Zvi Shor. Dedicated to saving the lives of children. Programs: Bone Marrow Donor Search, Stem Cell Banking-freezing cells from babies' umbilical cords for long-term storage, in case of need for bone marrow; Make-A-Dream-Come True-granting wishes for terminally ill children;

Referral Service; Patient Advocacy. (WWW.LEUKEMIAFOUNDATION.ORG)

NATIONAL JEWISH MEDICAL AND RESEARCH CENTER (formerly NATIONAL JEWISH HOSPITAL/NATIONAL ASTHMA CENTER) (1899). 1400 Jackson St., Denver, CO 80206. (800)222-LUNG. E-mail: lungline@njc.org. Pres./CEO Michael Salem, MD; Bd. Chmn. Steve Arent. The only medical and research center in the United States devoted entirely to respiratory, allergic, and immune system diseases, including asthma, tuberculosis, emphysema, severe allergies, AIDS, and cancer, and autoimmune diseases such as lupus. Dedicated to enhancing prevention, treatment, and cures through research, and to developing and providing innovative clinical programs for treating patients regardless of age, religion, race, or ability to pay. *New Directions*; *Medical Scientific Update*. (WWW.NATIONALJEWISH.ORG)

UNITED JEWISH COMMUNITIES (*see* p. 649)

UNITED ORDER TRUE SISTERS, INC. (UOTS) (1846) Linton International Plaza, 660 Linton Blvd.-Ste. 6, Delray Beach, FL 33444 (561)-265-1557. Pres. Marion Polonsky; Fin. Sec. Betty Peyser; Treas. Rose Goldberg. Charitable, community service, especially home supplies, etc., for indigent cancer victims; supports camps for children with cancer. *Inside UotS*. (WWW.UOTS.ORG)

WORLD COUNCIL OF JEWISH COMMUNAL SERVICE (1966; reorg. 1994). 711 Third Ave., 10th fl., NYC 10017. (212)687-6200. FAX: (212)370-5467. Pres. Howard Charish; Assoc. Pres. Dr. Jack Habib; Exec. V.-Pres. Theodore Comet. Seeks to build Jewish community worldwide by enhancing professional-to-professional connections, improving professional practice through interchange of experience and sharing of expertise, fostering professional training programs, and stimulating research. Conducts quadrennial conferences in Jerusalem and periodic regional meetings. *Proceedings of international conferences; newsletters.*

PROFESSIONAL ASSOCIATIONS*

AMERICAN ASSOCIATION OF RABBIS (Religious, Educational)

AMERICAN CONFERENCE OF CANTORS, UNION FOR REFORM JUDAISM (Religious, Educational)

AMERICAN JEWISH CORRECTIONAL CHAPLAINS ASSOCIATION, INC. (Social Welfare)

AMERICAN JEWISH PRESS ASSOCIATION (Cultural)

AMERICAN JEWISH PUBLIC RELATIONS SOCIETY (Community Relations)

ASSOCIATION OF HILLEL/JEWISH CAMPUS PROFESSIONALS (Religious, Educational)

ASSOCIATION OF JEWISH CENTER PROFESSIONALS (Social Welfare)

ASSOCIATION OF JEWISH COMMUNITY ORGANIZATION PERSONNEL (Social Welfare)

ASSOCIATION OF JEWISH COMMUNITY RELATIONS WORKERS (Community Relations)

CANTORS ASSEMBLY (Religious, Educational)

CENTRAL CONFERENCE OF AMERICAN RABBIS (Religious, Educational)

COUNCIL OF JEWISH ORGANIZATIONS IN CIVIL SERVICE (Community Relations)

INTERNATIONAL JEWISH MEDIA ASSOCIATION (Cultural)

JEWISH CHAPLAINS COUNCIL, JWB (Social Welfare)

JEWISH COMMUNAL SERVICE ASSOCIATION OF N. AMERICA (Social Welfare)

JEWISH EDUCATORS ASSEMBLY, UNITED SYNAGOGUE OF CONSERVATIVE JUDAISM (Religious, Educational)

JEWISH SOCIAL SERVICES PROFESSIONALS ASSOCIATION (Social Welfare)

JEWISH TEACHERS ASSOCIATION–MORIM (Religious, Educational)

NATIONAL ASSOCIATION OF HEBREW DAY SCHOOL ADMINISTRATORS, TORAH UMESORAH (Religious, Educational)

NATIONAL ASSOCIATION OF JEWISH CHAPLAINS (Social Welfare)

NATIONAL ASSOCIATION OF TEMPLE ADMINISTRATORS, UNION FOR REFORM JUDAISM (Religious, Educational)

*For fuller listings see under category in parentheses

NATIONAL ASSOCIATION OF TEMPLE EDUCATORS, UNION FOR REFORM JUDAISM (Religious, Educational)

NATIONAL CONFERENCE OF YESHIVA PRINCIPALS, TORAH UMESORAH (Religious, Educational)

NORTH AMERICAN ASSOCIATION OF SYNAGOGUE EXECUTIVES, UNITED SYNAGOGUE OF CONSERVATIVE JUDAISM (Religious, Educational)

RABBINICAL ALLIANCE OF AMERICA (Religious, Educational)

RABBINICAL ASSEMBLY (Religious, Educational)

RABBINICAL COUNCIL OF AMERICA (Religious, Educational)

RECONSTRUCTIONIST RABBINICAL ASSOCIATION (Religious, Educational)

UNION OF ORTHODOX RABBIS OF THE U.S. AND CANADA (Religious, Educational)

WORLD CONFERENCE OF JEWISH COMMUNAL SERVICE (Community Relations)

WOMEN'S ORGANIZATIONS*

AMIT WOMEN (Israel-Related)

BRANDEIS UNIVERSITY NATIONAL WOMEN'S COMMITTEE (Educational)

EMUNAH WOMEN OF AMERICA (Israel-Related)

HADASSAH, THE WOMEN'S ZIONIST ORGANIZATION OF AMERICA (Israel-Related)

JEWISH WOMEN INTERNATIONAL (Social Welfare)

JEWISH ORTHODOX FEMINIST ALLIANCE (Reliigous, Educational)

NA'AMAT USA, THE WOMEN'S LABOR ZIONIST ORGANIZATION OF AMERICA (Israel-Related)

NATIONAL COUNCIL OF JEWISH WOMEN (Social Welfare)

UOTS (Social Welfare)

WOMEN OF REFORM JUDAISM—FEDERATION OF TEMPLE SISTERHOODS, UNION FOR REFORM JUDAISM (Religious, Educational)

WOMEN'S AMERICAN ORT, ORT AMERICA (Overseas Aid)

WOMEN'S BRANCH OF THE UNION OF ORTHODOX JEWISH CONGREGATIONS OF AMERICA (Religious, Educational)

WOMEN'S DIVISION OF POALE AGUDATH ISRAEL OF AMERICA (Israel-Related)

WOMEN'S LEAGUE FOR CONSERVATIVE JUDAISM (Religious, Educational)

WOMEN'S LEAGUE FOR ISRAEL, INC. (Israel-Related)

WOMEN'S ORGANIZATION, YESHIVA UNIVERSITY (Religious, Educational)

YOUTH AND STUDENT ORGANIZATIONS*

AGUDATH ISRAEL OF AMERICA (Religious, Educational)

B'NAI B'RITH YOUTH ORGANIZATION (Religious, Educational)

BNEI AKIVA OF NORTH AMERICA, RELIGIOUS ZIONISTS OF AMERICA (Israel-Related)

HABONIM—DROR NORTH AMERICA (Israel-Related)

HASHOMER HATZAIR, SOCIALIST ZIONIST YOUTH MOVEMENT (Israel-Related)

HILLEL (Religious, Educational)

KADIMA, UNITED SYNAGOGUE OF CONSERVATIVE JUDAISM (Religious, Educational)

NATIONAL CONFERENCE OF SYNAGOGUE YOUTH, UNION OF ORTHODOX JEWISH CONGREGATIONS OF AMERICA (Religious, Educational)

NATIONAL JEWISH COMMITTEE ON SCOUTING (Religious, Educational)

NATIONAL JEWISH GIRL SCOUT COMMITTEE (Religious, Educational)

NORTH AMERICAN ALLIANCE FOR JEWISH YOUTH (Religious, Educational)

NORTH AMERICAN FEDERATION OF TEMPLE YOUTH, UNION FOR REFORM JUDAISM (Religious, Educational)

STUDENT STRUGGLE FOR SOVIET JEWRY—*see* CENTER FOR RUSSIAN JEWRY (Community Relations)

YOUNG JUDAEA/HASHACHAR, HADASSAH (Israel-Related)

YUGNTRUF–YOUTH FOR YIDDISH (Cultural)

*For fuller listings see under category in parentheses

CANADA

AISH HATORAH (1981). 949 Clark Ave., W., Thornhill, ONT L4J8G6. (905)764-1818. FAX: (905)764-1606. E-mail: www.Aish.com. Edu. Dir. Rabbi Ahron Hoch; Dr. Allan Seidenfeld. An educational center, a community center, and a network of synagogues throughout Toronto; seeks to reawaken Jewish values, ignite Jewish pride and promote Jewish unity through education; reaches out to Jews from all backgrounds in a friendly, warm and nonjudgmental environment. *Shabbat Shalom Fax, Monthly newsletter-Village Shul, Winter, Spring, Summer, Fall Calendars.* (WWW.AISH.EDU)

B'NAI BRITH CANADA (1875). 15 Hove St., Downsview, ONT M3H 4Y8. (416) 633-6224. FAX: (416)630-2159. E-mail: fdimant@bnaibrith.ca. Pres. Rochelle Wilner; Exec. V.-Pres. Frank Dimant. Canadian Jewry's major advocacy and service organization; maintains an office of Government Relations in Ottawa and co-sponsors the Canada Israel Committee; makes representations to all levels of government on matters of Jewish concern; promotes humanitarian causes and educational programs, community projects, adult Jewish education, and leadership development; dedicated to the preservation and unity of the Jewish community in Canada and to human rights. *The Jewish Tribune.*

———, INSTITUTE FOR INTERNATIONAL AFFAIRS (1987). E-mail: institute@bnaibrith.ca. Ch. Rochelle Wilner; Natl. Dir. Ruth Klein. Identifies and protests the abuse of human rights worldwide. Advocates on behalf of Israel and Jewish communities in distress. Monitors national and international legislation dealing with war crimes. Activities include briefs and consultations with governmental and non-governmental organizations, research and public education, advocacy and community mobilization, media monitoring, and international conferences and fact-finding missions. *Ad hoc publications on human rights issues.*

———, LEAGUE FOR HUMAN RIGHTS (1964). Co-Chmn. Marvin Kurz & Dr Harriet Morris. National volunteer association dedicated to combating racism, bigotry, and anti-Semitism. Educational programs include multicultural antiracist workshops, public speakers, Holocaust education, Media Human Rights Awards; legal and legislative activity includes government submissions, court interventions, monitoring hate-group activity, responding to incidents of racism and anti-Semitism; community liaison includes intergroup dialogue and support for aggrieved vulnerable communities and groups. Canadian distributor of ADL material. *Heritage Front Report: 1994; Anti-Semitism on Campus; Skinheads in Canada; Annual Audit of Anti-Semitic Incidents; Holocaust and Hope Educators' Newsletter; Combatting Hate: Guidelines for Community Action.*

———, NATIONAL FIELD SERVICES DEPARTMENT. Natl. Dir. Pearl Gladman. Services community affordable housing projects, sports leagues, food baskets for the needy; coordinates hands-on national volunteer programming, Tel-Aide Distress Line; responsible for lodge membership; direct-mail campaigns, annual convention and foundation dinners.

CANADIAN FRIENDS OF CALI & AMAL (1944). 7005 Kildare Rd., Suite 14, Côte St. Luc, Quebec, H4W 1C1. (514)484-9430. FAX: (514)484-0968. Pres. Harry J.F. Bloomfield, QC; Exec. Dir. Fran Kula. Incorporates Canadian Association for Labour Israel (Histadrut) and Canadian Friends of Amal; supports comprehensive health care and education in Israel. Helps to provide modern medical and surgical facilities and the finest vocational, technical education to the Israeli people of all ages.

CANADIAN FRIENDS OF THE HEBREW UNIVERSITY OF JERUSALEM (1944). 3080 Yonge St., Suite 5024, Toronto, ONT M4N 3N1. (416) 485-8000. FAX: (416)485-8565. E-mail: inquiry@cfhu.org. Pres. Ronald Appleby; Natl. Dir. Charles S. Diamond. Represents the Hebrew University of Jerusalem in Canada; serves as fund-raising arm for the university in Canada; recruits Canadian students and promotes study programs for foreign students at the university; sponsors social and educational events across Canada.

CANADIAN JEWISH CONGRESS (1919; reorg. 1934). 100 Sparks Street, Suite 650, Ottawa, Ontario K1P 5B7. (613)233-8703. FAX: (613)233-8748. E-mail: canadianjewishcongress@cjc.ca. Co-pres. Sylvain

Abitbol & Rabbi Reuven Bulka. The community's national voice on public affairs, Canadian Jewish Congress works with governments, community organizations and other partners to fight antisemitism and racism, to promote positive links to Israel and to other Jewish communities, and to support humanitarian and human rights efforts. *DAIS; National Archives Newsletter; regional newsletters.*

CANADIAN YOUNG JUDAEA (1917). 788 Marlee Ave., Suite 205, Toronto, ONT M6B 3K1. (416)781-5156. FAX: (416) 787-3100. E-mail: cyj@idirect.com. Natl. Exec. Dir. Risa Epstein. Strives to attract Jewish youth to Zionism, with goal of aliyah; educates youth about Jewish history and Zionism; prepares them to provide leadership in Young Judaea camps in Canada and Israel and to be concerned Jews. *Judaean L'Madrich; Young Judaean.*

CANADIAN ZIONIST FEDERATION (1967). 5151 Côte St. Catherine Rd., #206, Montreal, PQ H3W 1M6. (514)739-7300. FAX: (514)739-9412. Pres. Kurt Rothschild; Natl. Sec. Florence Simon. Umbrella organization of distinct constituent member Zionist organizations in Canada; carries on major activities in all areas of Jewish life through its departments of education and culture, aliyah, youth and students, public affairs, and small Jewish communities, for the purpose of strengthening the State of Israel and the Canadian Jewish community. *Canadian Zionist.*

———, BUREAU OF EDUCATION AND CULTURE (1972). Pres. Kurt Rothschild. Provides counseling by pedagogic experts, in-service teacher-training courses and seminars in Canada and Israel; national pedagogic council and research center; distributes educational material and teaching aids; supports annual Bible contest and Hebrew-language courses for adults; awards scholarships to Canadian high-school graduates studying for one year in Israel.

HADASSAH–WIZO ORGANIZATION OF CANADA (1917). 1310 Greene Ave., Suite 900, Montreal, PQ H3Z 2B8. (514)937-9431. FAX: (514)933-6483. E-mail: natoff@canadian-hadassah-wizo.org. Natl. Pres. Rochelle Levinson; Natl. Exec. V.-Pres. Lily Frank. Largest women's volunteer Zionist organization in Canada, located in 43 Canadian cities; dedicated to advancing the quality of life of the women and children in Israel through financial assistance and support of its many projects, day-care centers, schools, institutions, and hospitals. In Canada, the organization promotes Canadian ideals of democracy and is a stalwart advocate of women's issues. *Orah Magazine.*

HASHOMER HATZAIR (1913). 1111 Finch Ave. W., #456, Downsview, ONT M3J 2E5. (416)736-1339. FAX: (416)736-1405. E-mail: mail@givathaviva.ca. Shlicha-Ora Merin; Pres. Sheryl Neshel; Sec. Lipa Roth. A Zionist youth movement established over 80 years ago with centers all over the world. In Toronto, there are weekly meetings during the school year where children get a strong sense of their Jewish identity and connection to Israel, celebrate Jewish holidays together and learn to be contributing members of the community. Hashomer Hatzair runs a 6-day residential winter camp and a 6-week summer camp for youth ranging from 7-16 on Otty Lake.

INTERNATIONAL JEWISH CORRESPONDENCE (IJC) (1978). c/o Canadian Jewish Congress, 1590 Dr. Penfield Ave., Montreal, PQ H3G 1C5.9 (514)931-7531. FAX: (514)931-0548. E-mail: barrys@cjc.ca. Founder/Dir. Barry Simon. Aims to encourage contact between Jews of all ages and backgrounds, in all countries, through pen-pal correspondence. Send autobiographical data and stamped self-addressed envelope or its equivalent (to cover cost of Canadian postage) to receive addresses.

JEWISH IMMIGRANT AID SERVICES OF MONTREAL (JIAS) (1922). 5500 Westbury, 2nd Floor, Montreal, Quebec H3W-2W8. (514)342-9351. FAX: (514)342-0287. E-mail: jiasmail@aol.com. Pres. Joe Kislowicz; Exec. Dir. Shellie Ettinger. JIAS is a national organization assisting the lawful entry of Jews into Canada, as well as their settlement and integration. *JIAS News for Clients.*

JEWISH NATIONAL FUND OF CANADA (Keren Kayemeth Le'Israel, Inc.) (1901). 1980 Sherbrooke St. W., Suite 500, Montreal, PQ H3H 1E8. (514)934-0313. FAX: (514)934-0382. E-mail: mtl@jnf.canada.org. Natl. Pres. Sandra Posluns; Exec. V.-Pres. Joe Rabinovitch. Fund-raising organization affiliated with the World Zionist Organization; involved in afforestation, soil reclamation, and development of the land of Israel, including the construction of roads and preparation of sites for new settlements; provides educational materials and programs to Jewish schools across Canada.

LABOUR ZIONIST ALLIANCE OF CANADA (1909). 272 Codsell Ave., Downsview, ONT M3H 3X2. (416)630-9444. FAX: (416)630-9451. Pres. Josef Krystal; City Committee Chmn. Montreal-Harry Froimovitch. Associated with the World Labor Zionist movement and allied with the Israel Labor party. Provides recreational and cultural programs, mutual aid, and fraternal care to enhance the social welfare of its membership; actively promotes Zionist education, cultural projects, and forums on aspects of Jewish and Canadian concern.

MERETZ CANADA (1950s). 1111 Finch Ave. W., Suite 456, Downsview, ONT M3J 2E5. (416)736-1339. FAX: (416)736-1405. Pres. Joseph Podemski., Vice Pres. Lipa Roth. Acts as a voice of Socialist-Democratic and Zionist points of view within the Jewish community and a focal point for progressive Zionist elements in Canada; affiliated with Hashomer Hatzair and the Givat Haviva Educational Center.

MIZRACHI ORGANIZATION OF CANADA (1941). 296 Wilson Ave., North York, ONT M3H 1S8. (416)630-9266. FAX: (416)630-2305. Pres. Jack Kahn. Promotes religious Zionism, aimed at making Israel a state based on Torah; maintains Bnei Akiva, a summer camp, adult education program, and touring department; supports Mizrachi-Hapoel Hamizrachi and other religious Zionist institutions in Israel which strengthen traditional Judaism. *Mizrachi Newsletter*.

NATIONAL COMMUNITY RELATIONS COMMITTEE OF CANADIAN JEWISH CONGRESS (1936). 4600 Bathurst St., Toronto, ONT M2R 3V2. (416)631-5673. FAX: (416)635-1408. E-mail: mprutschi@ujafed.org. Chmn. Ellen T. Cole; Pres. Keith M. Landy; Dir. Manuel Prutschi. Seeks to safeguard the status, rights, and welfare of Jews in Canada; to combat antisemitism, and promote understanding and goodwill among all ethnic and religious groups.

NATIONAL COUNCIL OF JEWISH WOMEN OF CANADA (1897). 118-1588 Main St., Winnipeg, MAN R2V 1Y3. (204)339-9700. FAX: (204)334-3779. E-mail: info@ncjwc.org. Chmn. Carol Slater; Natl. V.-Pres. Roz Fine & Brenlee Gurvey Gales. Dedicated to furthering human welfare in the Jewish and general communities, locally, nationally, and internationally; through an integrated program of education, service, and social action seeks to fulfill unmet needs and to serve the individual and the community. *National ByLines.*

ORT CANADA (1948). 3101 Bathurst St., Suite 604, Toronto, ONT M6A 2A6. (416)787-0339. FAX: (416) 787-9420. E-mail: info@ort-toronto.org. Pres. Arthur Silber; Exec. Dir. Joel Shapiro. Chapters in 11 Canadian cities raise funds for ORT's nonprofit global network of schools where Jewish students learn a wide range of marketable skills, including the most advanced high-tech professions. *Focus Magazine.*

STATE OF ISRAEL BONDS (CANADA-ISRAEL SECURITIES, LTD.) (1953). 970 Lawrence Ave. W., Suite 502, Toronto, ONT M6A 3B6. (416)789-3351. FAX: (416)789-9436. Pres. Norman Spector; Bd. Chmn. George A. Cohon. An international securities organization offering interest-bearing instruments issued by the government of Israel. Invests in every aspect of Israel's economy, including agriculture, commerce, and industry. Israel Bonds are RRSP-approved.

UIA FEDERATIONS OF CANADA (1998). 4600 Bathurst St., Suite 315, Toronto, ONT M2R 3V3. (416)636-7655. FAX: (416)636-9897. E-mail: info@uiafed.org. Pres. Barbara Farber; Exec. V-Pres. Linda Kislowicz. The national Jewish fund-raising orgnazation and community-planning body for Canada.

Jewish Federations and Welfare Funds

UNITED STATES

ALABAMA

BIRMINGHAM

BIRMINGHAM JEWISH FEDERATION (1936; reorg. 1971); Box 130219 (35213-0219); (205)879-0416. FAX: (205)803-1526. E-mail: federation@bjf.org. Pres. Brenda Weinstein; Exec. Dir. Richard Friedman. (WWW.BJF.ORG)

MOBILE

MOBILE JEWISH WELFARE FUND, INC. (inc. 1966); One Office Park, Suite 219 (36609); (334)343-7197. FAX: (334)343-7197. E-mail: mjwf123@aol.com. Pres. Eileen Susman.

MONTGOMERY

JEWISH FEDERATION OF MONTGOMERY, INC. (1930); 2820 Fairlane Dr. (36120-0058); (334)277-5820. FAX: (334)277-8383. E-mail: jfedmgm@aol.com. Pres. Alan Weil; Admin. Dir. Susan Mayer Bruchis.

ARIZONA

PHOENIX

JEWISH FEDERATION OF GREATER PHOENIX (1940); 12701 N. Scottsdale Rd., Suite 201 (85254); (480)634-4900. FAX: (480)634-4588. E-mail: info@jewishphoenix.org. Pres. Neil Hiller; Exec. Dir. Arthur Paikowsky. (WWW.JEWISHPHOENIX.ORG)

TUCSON

JEWISH FEDERATION OF SOUTHERN ARIZONA (1946); 5546 E. 4 St., Suite 100 (85711); (520)577-9393. FAX: (520)577-0734. E-mail: cbaldwin@jfsa.org. Pres.& CEO Stuart Mellan. (WWW.JEWISHTUCSON.ORG)

ARKANSAS

LITTLE ROCK

JEWISH FEDERATION OF ARKANSAS (1911); 1501 N. Pierce St., Ste. 101 (72207); (501)663-3571. FAX: (501)663-7286. E-mail: jflar@aristotle.net. Pres. Doris Krain; Exec. Dir. Ziva Starr. (WWW.JEWISHARKANSAS.COM)

CALIFORNIA

EAST BAY

JEWISH FEDERATION OF THE GREATER EAST BAY (INCLUDING ALAMEDA & CONTRA COSTA COUNTIES) (1917); 300 Grand Ave., Oakland (94610-5022); (510)839-2900. FAX: (510)839-3996. E-mail: admin@jfed.org. Pres. Rob Ruby (WWW.JFED.ORG)

FRESNO

JEWISH FEDERATION OF FRESNO; 295 W. CROMWELL AVE., SUITE 111 (93711-6161); (559)432-2162. FAX: (559)432-0425.

LONG BEACH

JEWISH FEDERATION OF GREATER LONG BEACH AND W. ORANGE COUNTY (1937; inc. 1946); 3801 E. Willow St. (90815); (562)426-7601. FAX: (562)424-3915. E-mail: webmaster@jewishlongbeach.org. Pres. Richard Lipeles; Exec. Dir. Deborah Goldfarb. (WWW.JEWISHLONGBEACH.ORG)

LOS ANGELES

JEWISH FEDERATION COUNCIL OF GREATER LOS ANGELES (1912; reorg. 1959); 6505 Wilshire Blvd., 8th fl. (90048); (323)761-8000. FAX: (323)761-8235. E-mail: webcoordinator@jewishla.org. Pres. John R. Fishel. (WWW.JEWISHLA.ORG)

ORANGE COUNTY

JEWISH FEDERATION OF ORANGE COUNTY (1964; inc. 1965); 1 Federation Way, Irvine (92603-0174); (949)435-3484. FAX: (949)435-3485. E-mail: info@jfoc.org. Pres. Charles Karp; Exec. Dir. Bunnie Mauldin. (WWW.JFOC.ORG)

PALM SPRINGS

JEWISH FEDERATION OF PALM SPRINGS AND DESERT AREA (1971); 69-930 Highway 111, Suite 204 (92270); (760)324-4737. FAX: (760)324-3154. E-mail: msjfedps@gte.net. Pres. Howard Levy; Exec. Dir. Jim Levitas. (WWW.JEWISHPALMSPRINGS.ORG)

SACRAMENTO

JEWISH FEDERATION OF THE SACRAMENTO REGION (1948); 2351 Wyda Way (95825); (916)486-0906. FAX: (916)486-0816. E-mail: federation@jewishsac.org. Pres. Dana Edelstein; Exec. Dir. Michal Kohane. (WWW.JEWISHSAC.ORG)

SAN DIEGO

UNITED JEWISH FEDERATION OF SAN DIEGO COUNTY (1936); 4950 Murphy Canyon Rd. (92123); (858)571-3444. FAX: (858)571-0701. E-mail: fedujf@ujfsd.org. Chair Andrea Oster; CEO Michael S. Rassler. (WWW.JEWISHINSANDIEGO.ORG)

SAN FRANCISCO

JEWISH COMMUNITY FEDERATION OF SAN FRANCISCO, THE PENINSULA, MARIN, AND SONOMA COUNTIES (1910; reorg. 1955); 121 Steuart St. (94105); (415)777-0411. FAX: (415)495-6635. E-mail: info@sfjcf.org. Pres. John Pritzker; Exec. V-Pres. Daniel Sokatch. (WWW.SFJCF.ORG)

SAN GABRIEL AND POMONA VALLEY

JEWISH FEDERATION OF THE GREATER SAN GABRIEL AND POMONA VALLEYS; 258 W. BADILLO ST. (91723-1906); (626)967-3656. FAX: (626)967-5135. E-MAIL: SGPVFED@AOL.COM. (www.sgpv.org)

SAN JOSE

JEWISH FEDERATION OF SILICON VALLEY (incl. Santa Clara County except Palo Alto and Los Altos) (1930; reorg. 1950); P.O. Box 320070, Los Gatos (95032); (408)358-3033. FAX: (408)356-0733. E-mail: info@jvalley.org. Pres. Steve Greenberg; Exec. Dir. Jyl Jurman. (WWW.JEWISHSILICONVALLEY.ORG)

SANTA BARBARA

SANTA BARBARA JEWISH FEDERATION (1974); 524 Chapala St. (93190); (805)957-1115. FAX: (805)957-9230. E-mail: sbjfed@silcom.com. Exec. Dir. Shelly Katz. (WWW.JEWISHSANTABARBARA.ORG)

VENTURA COUNTY

JEWISH FEDERATION OF VENTURA COUNTY. 7620 Foothill Rd. (93004); (805)647-7800. FAX: (805)647-0482. E-mail: ujavtacty@worldnet.att.net.

COLORADO

DENVER/BOULDER

ALLIED JEWISH FEDERATION OF COLORADO (1936); 300 S. Dahlia St., Denver (80222); (303)321-3399. FAX: (303)322-8328. E-mail: information@ajfcolorado.org. Chmn. Noel Ginsburg; Pres. & CEO: Doug Seserman. (WWW.JEWISHCOLORADO.ORG)

CONNECTICUT

BRIDGEPORT

JEWISH FEDERATION OF EASTERN FAIRFIELD COUNTY. (1936; reorg. 1981); 4200 Park Ave. (06604-1092); (203)372-6567. FAX: (203)374-0770. E-mail: comments@jccs.org. Pres. & CEO Eli Kornreich. (WWW.JCCS.ORG)

DANBURY

THE JEWISH FEDERATION OF GREATER DANBURY, INC. (1945); 69 Kenosia Ave. (06810); (203)792-6353. FAX: (203)748-5099. E-mail: info@thejf.org. Pres. Daniel Wolinsky; Exec. Dir. Norman Greenstein. (WWW.THEJF.ORG)

EASTERN CONNECTICUT

JEWISH FEDERATION OF EASTERN CONNECTICUT, INC. (1950; inc. 1970); P.O. Box 1468, New London (06320); (860)442-8062. FAX: (860)443-4175. E-mail: jfec@worldnet.att.net. Pres. Myron Hendel; Exec. Dir. Jerome E. Fischer.

GREENWICH

GREENWICH JEWISH FEDERATION (1956); One Holly Hill Lane (06830-6080); (203)622-1434. FAX: (203)622-1237. E-mail: pezmom3@aol.com. Pres. Martin J. Flashner; Exec. Dir. Pamela Ehrenkranz.

HARTFORD

JEWISH FEDERATION OF GREATER HARTFORD (1945); 333 Bloomfield Ave., W. Hartford (06117); (860)232-4483. FAX:

(860)232-5221. E-mail: info@jewishhartford.org. Pres. Robert Nabolchek; Exec. Dir. Catherine Fischer Schwartz. (WWW.JEWISHHARTFORD.ORG)

NEW HAVEN

JEWISH FEDERATION OF GREATER NEW HAVEN (1928); 360 Amity Rd., Woodbridge (06525); (203)387-2424. FAX: (203)387-1818. E-mail: marinak@megahits.com Pres. David Schaefer; Exec. Dir. Neil Berro. (WWW.JEWISHNEWHAVEN.ORG)

NORWALK

(See Westport)

STAMFORD

UNITED JEWISH FEDERATION (inc. 1973); 1035 Newfield Ave., Ste. 200 (06905); (203)321-1373. FAX: (203)322-3277. E-mail: office@ujf.org. Pres. Martin Greenberg; Dir. of Dev. Gary Geller. (WWW.UJF.ORG)

WESTERN CONNECTICUT

JEWISH FEDERATION OF WESTERN CONNECTICUT (1938); 444 Maine St. N., Southbury (06488); (203)267-5121. FAX: (203)267-3392. E-mail: jfedwtby@aol.com. Pres. Dan Goodman; Exec. Dir. Rob Zwang. (WWW.JFED.NET)

WESTPORT-WESTON-WILTON-NORWALK

UJA/FEDERATION OF WESTPORT—WESTON—WILTON—NORWALK (inc. 1980); 431 Post Road E., Suite 22, Westport (06880); (203)226-8197. FAX: (203)226-5051. E-mail: rkessler@optonline.net. Pres. Ed Goldstein; Exec. Dir. Robert Kessler. (WWW.UJAFEDERATION.ORG)

DELAWARE

WILMINGTON

JEWISH FEDERATION OF DELAWARE, INC. (1934); 100 W. 10th St., Suite 301 (19801-1628); (302)427-2100. FAX: (302)427-2438. E-mail: jfdinfo@shalomdel.org; Pres. Barry Kayne; Exec. V. Pres. Samuel H. Asher. (WWW.SHALOMDELAWARE.ORG)

DISTRICT OF COLUMBIA

WASHINGTON

THE JEWISH FEDERATION OF GREATER WASHINGTON, INC. (1935); 6101 Montrose Rd., Rockville, MD (20852); (301)230-7200. FAX: (301)230-7265. E-mail: info@jewishfedwash.org. Pres. David Butler; Exec. V.-Pres. Misha Galperin. (WWW.SHALOMDC.ORG)

FLORIDA

BREVARD COUNTY

JEWISH FEDERATION OF BREVARD (1974); 210 E. Hibiscus Blvd., Melbourne (32901); (321)957-1836 FAX: (321)951-1848. E-mail: jfbrevard@aol.com. Pres. Gary Singer; Exec. Dir. Joanne Bishins.

BROWARD COUNTY

JEWISH FEDERATION OF BROWARD COUNTY (1943; 1968); 5890 S. Pine Island Rd., Davie (33351-7319); (954)252-6900. FAX: (954)252-6892. E-mail: info@jewishfedbroward.org. Pres. Eric Stillman. (WWW.JEWISHBROWARD.ORG)

COLLIER COUNTY

JEWISH FEDERATION OF COLLIER COUNTY (1974); 1250 Tamiami Trail N., Suite 202, Naples (33940); (941) 263-4205. FAX: (941)263-3813. E-mail: jfccfl@aol.com. Pres. David Willens. (WWW.JEWISHNAPLES.ORG)

DAYTONA BEACH

(See Volusia & Flagler Counties)

FT. LAUDERDALE

(See Broward County)

GAINESVILLE

JEWISH COUNCIL OF NORTH CENTRAL FLORIDA; 1861 NW 21 St. (32604); (352)371-3846. E-mail: oberger@gnv.fdt.net.

JACKSONVILLE

JACKSONVILLE JEWISH FEDERATION, INC. (1935); 8505 San Jose Blvd. (32217); (904)448-5000. FAX: (904)448-5715. E-mail: jaxjewishfed@jon.cjfny.org. Pres. Guy Benrubi; Exec. V.-Pres. Alan Margolies. (WWW.JEWISHJACKSONVILLE.ORG)

LEE COUNTY

JEWISH FEDERATION OF LEE AND CHARLOTTE COUNTIES (1974); 6237-E Presidential Court, Ft. Myers (33919-3568); (941)481-4449. FAX: (941)481-0139. E-mail: jfedswfl@aol.com. Pres. Herb Freed; Exec. Dir. Annette Goodman. (WWW.JEWISHFEDERATIONSWFL.ORG)

MIAMI

GREATER MIAMI JEWISH FEDERATION, INC. (1938); 4200 Biscayne Blvd. (33137); (305)576-4000. FAX: (305)573-4584. E-mail: info@gmjf.or. Pres. Michael M. Adler;

Exec. V.-Pres. Jacob Solomon. (WWW.JEWISHMIAMI.ORG)

ORLANDO

JEWISH FEDERATION OF GREATER ORLANDO (1949); 851 N. Maitland Ave.; PO Box 941508, Maitland (32794-1508); (407)645-5933. FAX: (407)645-1172. E-mail: slandes@jfgo.org. Pres. James S. Grodin; Exec. Dir. Susan Bodner. (WWW.ORLANDOJEWISHFED.ORG)

PALM BEACH COUNTY

JEWISH FEDERATION OF PALM BEACH COUNTY, INC. (1962); 4601 Community Dr., W. Palm Beach (33417-2760); (561)478-0700. FAX: (561)478-9696. E-mail: info@jfedpbco.org. Pres. Norman P. Goldblum; Exec. V.-Pres. Jeffrey L. Klein. (WWW.JEWISHPALMBEACH.ORG)

JEWISH FEDERATION OF SOUTH PALM BEACH COUNTY, INC. (1979); 9901 Donna Klein Blvd. Boca Raton (33428-1788); (561)852-3100. FAX: (561)852-3136. E-mail: dstern@jewishboca.org. (WWW.JEWISHBOCA.ORG)

PENSACOLA

PENSACOLA JEWISH FEDERATION; 800 No. Palafox (32501); (850)434-7992.

PINELLAS COUNTY

JEWISH FEDERATION OF PINELLAS COUNTY, INC. (incl. Clearwater and St. Petersburg) (1950; reincorp. 1974); 13191 Starkey Rd., #8, Largo (33773-1438); (727) 530-3223. FAX: (727)531-0221. E-mail: pinellas@jfedpinellas.org. Pres. David Abelson; Interim Exec. Dir. Bonnie Friedman. (WWW.JFEDPINELLAS.ORG)

SARASOTA-MANATEE

SARASOTA-MANATEE JEWISH FEDERATION (1959); 580 S. McIntosh Rd. (34232-1959); (941)371-4546. FAX: (941)378-2947. E-mail: info@smjf.org. Pres. Scott Gordon; Exec. Dir. Howard Tevlowitz. (WWW.SMJF.ORG)

TALLAHASSEE

APALACHEE FEDERATION OF JEWISH CHARITIES; PO Box 14825 (32317-4825); (850)877-3989; FAX: (850)877-7989. E-mail: mdlevy@pol.net.

TAMPA

TAMPA JEWISH FEDERATION (1941); 13009 Community Campus Dr. (33625-4000); (813)264-9000. FAX: (813)265-8450. E-mail: info@jewishtampa.com. Pres. Lili Kaufman; Exec. V.-Pres. Gary Gould. (WWW.JEWISHTAMPA.COM)

VOLUSIA & FLAGLER COUNTIES

JEWISH FEDERATION OF VOLUSIA & FLAGLER COUNTIES, INC. (1980); 470 Andalusia Ave., Ormond Beach (32174); (386)672-0294. FAX: (386)673-1316. Pres. Steven I. Unatin; Exec. Dir. Gloria Max.

GEORGIA

ATLANTA

JEWISH FEDERATION OF GREATER ATLANTA, INC. (1905; reorg. 1967); 1440 Spring St., NW (30309-2837); (404)873-1661. FAX: (404) 874-7043. E-mail: webmaster@jfga.org. Pres. Martin Kogon; Exec. Dir. Steven A. Rakitt. (WWW. SHALOMATLANTA.ORG)

AUGUSTA

AUGUSTA JEWISH FEDERATION (1937); 898 Weinberger Way, Evans (30809-3636); (706)228-3636. FAX: (706)868-1660/823-3960. E-mail: augustafed1@knology.net. Exec. Dir. Leah Ronen.

COLUMBUS

JEWISH FEDERATION OF COLUMBUS, INC. (1944); PO Box 6313 (31906); (706)568-6668. Pres. Murray Solomon; Sec. Irene Rainbow.

SAVANNAH

SAVANNAH JEWISH FEDERATION (1943); P.O.Box 23527 (31403); (912)355-8111. FAX: (912)355-8116. E-mail: jeafederationhotline@savj.org. Pres. Merry Bodziner; Exec. Dir. Sharon Paz. (WWW.SAVJ.ORG)

ILLINOIS

CHAMPAIGN-URBANA

CHAMPAIGN-URBANA JEWISH FEDERATION (1929); 503 E. John St., Champaign (61820); (217)367-9872. FAX: (217)344-1540. E-mail: cujf@shalomcu.org. Pres. Anthony E. Novak; Exec. Dir. Lee Melhado. (WWW.SHALOMCU.ORG)

CHICAGO

JEWISH FEDERATION OF METROPOLITAN CHICAGO/JEWISH UNITED FUND OF METROPOLITAN CHICAGO (1900); 30 S. Wells, Ste. 4049 (60606); (312)346-6700. FAX: (312)444-2086. E-mail: webinfo@juf.org. Pres. Steven B. Nasatir. (WWW.JUF.ORG)

JOLIET

JOLIET JEWISH WELFARE CHEST (1938); 250 N. Midland Ave. at Campbell St. (60435); (815)741-4600.

PEORIA

JEWISH FEDERATION OF PEORIA (1933; inc. 1947); 2000 W. Pioneer Pwky., Suite 10B (61615-1835); (309)689-0063. FAX: (309)689-0575. Pres. Larry Seitzman; Exec. Dir. Susan Katz.

QUAD CITIES

JEWISH FEDERATION OF QUAD CITIES (1938; comb. 1973); 1705 2nd Ave., Suite 405, Rock Island (61201); (309)793-1300. FAX: (309)793-1345. E-mail: qcfederation@juno.com. Pres. Paul Light; Exec. Dir. Ida Kramer.

ROCKFORD

JEWISH FEDERATION OF GREATER ROCKFORD (1937); 3730 Guilford Rd. (61107); (815)399-5497. FAX: (815)399-9835. E-mail: rockfordfederation@juno.com. Pres. Sterne Roufa; Exec. Dir. Marilyn Youman.

SOUTHERN ILLINOIS

JEWISH FEDERATION OF SOUTHERN ILLINOIS, SOUTHEASTERN MISSOURI, AND WESTERN KENTUCKY (1941); 3419 W. Main, Belleville (62223); (618)398-6100. FAX: (618)398-0539. E-mail: silfed@simokyfed.com. Co-Pres. Harvey Cohen & Carol Rudman; Exec. Dir. Steven C. Low. (www.SIMOKYFED.COM)

SPRINGFIELD

SPRINGFIELD JEWISH FEDERATION (1941); 1045 Outer Park Dr., Ste. 320 (62704); (217)787-7223. FAX: (217)787-7470. E-mail: sjf@springnet1.com. Pres. Rita Victor; Exec. Dir. Gloria Schwartz.

INDIANA

FORT WAYNE

FORT WAYNE JEWISH FEDERATION (1921); 227 E. Washington Blvd. (46802-3121); (219)422-8566. FAX: (219)422-8567. E-mail: fwjewfed@aol.com. Pres. Larry Adelman. (WWW.JEWISHFORTWAYNE.ORG)

INDIANAPOLIS

JEWISH FEDERATION OF GREATER INDIANAPOLIS, INC. (1905); 6705 Hoover Rd. (46260-4120); (317)726-5450. FAX: (317)205-0307. E-mail: info@jfgi.org. Pres. Richard Leventhal; Exec. V.-Pres. Harry Nadler. (WWW.JFGI.ORG)

LAFAYETTE

JEWISH FEDERATION OF GREATER LAFAYETTE (1924); PO Box 3802, W. Lafayette (47906); (765)426-4724. E-mail: jfgl1@aol.com. Pres.Earl Prohofsky; Admin. Judy Upton.

NORTHWEST INDIANA

JEWISH FEDERATION OF NORTHWEST INDIANA (1941; reorg. 1959); 585 Progress Ave., Munster (46321); (219)922-4024. FAX: (219)922-4034. E-mail: defwej@aol.com. Pres. Carol Karol; Exec. Dir. Michael Steinberg. (WWW.JFEDOFNWI.COM)

ST. JOSEPH VALLEY

JEWISH FEDERATION OF ST. JOSEPH VALLEY (1946); 3202 Shalom Way, South Bend (46615); (219)233-1164. FAX: (219)288-4103. E-mail: receptionist@jewishfed.org. Pres. Alan Brown; Exec. V.-Pres. Deborah Barton Grant. (WWW.JFEDSJV.ORG)

IOWA

DES MOINES

JEWISH FEDERATION OF GREATER DES MOINES (1914); 910 Polk Blvd. (50312); (515)277-6321. FAX: (515)277-4069. E-mail: jcrc@dmjfed.org. Pres. Toni Urban; Exec. Dir. Elaine Steinger. (WWW.DMJFED.ORG)

SIOUX CITY

JEWISH FEDERATION OF SIOUX CITY (1921); 815 38th St. (51104-1417); (712)258-0618. FAX: (712)258-0619. Pres. Michele Ivener; Admin. Dir. Doris Rosenthal.

KANSAS

KANSAS CITY

See listing under Missouri

WICHITA

MID-KANSAS JEWISH FEDERATION, INC. (serving South Central Kansas) (1935); 400 N. Woodlawn, Suite 8 (67208); (316)686-4741. FAX: (316)686-6008. E-mail: jpress@mkjf.org. Pres. Jill S. Docking; Exec. Dir. Sandy Diel. (WWW.MKJF.ORG)

KENTUCKY

CENTRAL KENTUCKY

CENTRAL KENTUCKY JEWISH FEDERATION (1976); 1050 Chinoe Rd., Ste. 302, Lexington (40502-2400); (859)268-0672. FAX: (859)268-0775. E-mail: ckjf@jewishlexington.org. Pres.Martin Barr; Exec. Dir. Daniel Chejfec. (WWW.JEWISHLEXINGTON.ORG)

LOUISVILLE

JEWISH COMMUNITY FEDERATION OF LOUISVILLE, INC. (1934); 3630 Dutchmans Lane (40205); (502)451-8840. FAX: (502)458-0702. E-mail: jfed@iglou.com. Pres. Steven Shapiro; Exec. Dir. Alan S. Engel. (WWW.JEWISHLOUISVILLE.ORG)

LOUISIANA

BATON ROUGE

JEWISH FEDERATION OF GREATER BATON ROUGE (1971); 3354 Kleinert Ave. (70806); (504) 387-9744. FAX: (504)387-9487. E-mail: jfedofbr@postoffice.att.net. Pres. Harvey Hoffman.

NEW ORLEANS

JEWISH FEDERATION OF GREATER NEW ORLEANS (1913; reorg. 1977); 3747 W. Esplanade Ave., Metairie (70002-3524); (504)780-5600. FAX: (504)780-5601. E-mail: shalom@jewishnola.com. Pres. Allan Bissinger; Exec. Dir. Michael Weil. (WWW.JEWISHNOLA.ORG)

SHREVEPORT

NORTHERN LOUISIANA JEWISH FEDERATION (1941; inc. 1967); 4700 Line Ave., Suite 117 (71106-1533); (318)868-1200. FAX: (318)868-1272. E-mail: nljfed@bellsouth.net. Pres. Rick Murov; Exec. Dir. Howard L. Ross. (WWW.NLJFED.ORG)

MAINE

LEWISTON-AUBURN

LEWISTON-AUBURN JEWISH FEDERATION (1947); 74 Bradman St., Auburn (04210); (207)786-4201. FAX: (207)783-1000. Pres. Scott Nussinow.

PORTLAND

JEWISH COMMUNITY ALLIANCE OF SOUTHERN MAINE (1942); 57 Ashmont St. (04103); (207)773-7254. FAX: (207)772-2234. E-mail: info@mainejewish.org. Pres. Emily Sandberg. (WWW.MAINEJEWISH.ORG)

MARYLAND

BALTIMORE

THE ASSOCIATED: JEWISH COMMUNITY FEDERATION OF BALTIMORE (1920; reorg. 1969); 101 W. Mt. Royal Ave. (21201-5728); (410) 727-4828. FAX: (410)752-1327. E-mail: information@associated.org. Chmn. Barbara L. Himmelrich; Pres. Darrell D. Friedman. (WWW.ASSOCIATED.ORG)

COLUMBIA

JEWISH FEDERATION OF HOWARD COUNTY; 8950 Rte. 108, Suite 115, Columbia (21045); (410)730-4976; FAX: (410)730-9393. E-mail: info@jewishhowardcounty.org. Pres. Kenneth Goodman; Exec. Dir. Roberta Greenstein. (WWW.JEWISHHOWARDCOUNTY.ORG)

MASSACHUSETTS

BERKSHIRE COUNTY

JEWISH FEDERATION OF THE BERKSHIRES (1940); 196 South St., Pittsfield (01201); (413)442-4360. FAX: (413)443-6070. E-mail: jreichbaum@berkshire.net. Pres. Stephen Rudin; Exec. Dir. Jaquelynne Reichbaum. (WWW.JEWISHBERKSHIRES.ORG)

BOSTON

COMBINED JEWISH PHILANTHROPIES OF GREATER BOSTON, INC. (1895; inc. 1961); 126 High St. (02110-2700); (617)457-8500. FAX: (617)988-6262. E-mail: info@cjp.org. Chmn. Robert Beal; Pres. Barry Shrage. (WWW.CJP.ORG)

MERRIMACK VALLEY

MERRIMACK VALLEY JEWISH FEDERATION (Serves Andover, Haverhill, Lawrence, Lowell, Newburyport, and 22 surrounding communities) (1988); PO Box 937, Andover (01810-0016); (978)688-0466. FAX: (978)688-1097. E-mail: jan@mvjf.org. Pres. James H. Shainker; Exec. Dir. Jan Steven Brodie. (WWW.MVJF.ORG)

NEW BEDFORD

JEWISH FEDERATION OF GREATER NEW BEDFORD, INC. (1938; inc. 1954); 467 Hawthorn St., N. Dartmouth (02747); (508)997-7471. FAX: (508)997-7730. Co-Pres. Harriet Philips, Patricia Rosenfield; Exec. Dir. Wil Herrup.

NORTH SHORE

JEWISH FEDERATION OF THE NORTH SHORE, INC. (1938); 2 E. India Square, Suite 200 (01970-3707); (978)745-4222. FAX: (978)741-7507. E-mail: mail@jfns.org. Pres. Robert Salter; Exec. Dir. Neil A. Cooper. (WWW.JFNS.ORG)

SPRINGFIELD

JEWISH FEDERATION OF GREATER SPRINGFIELD, INC. (1925); 1160 Dickinson St. (01108); (413)737-4313. FAX: (413)737-4348. E-mail: cfschwartz@jewishspringfield.org. Pres. Harold Berman. (WWW.JEWISH SPRINGFIELD.ORG)

WORCESTER

JEWISH FEDERATION OF CENTRAL MASSACHUSETTS (1947; inc. 1957); 633 Salisbury St. (01609); (508)756-1543. FAX: (508)798-0962. E-mail: bluks@jfcm.org. Pres. Bruce Hertzberg; Exec. Dir. Howard Borer. (WWW.JFCM.ORG)

MICHIGAN

ANN ARBOR

JEWISH FEDERATION OF WASHTENAW COUNTY/UJA (1986); 2939 Birch Hollow Dr. (48108); (734)677-0100. FAX: (734)677-0109. E-mail: info@jewishannarbor.org. Pres. Morley Witus; Exec. Dir. Jess Levin. (WWW.JEWISHANNARBOR.ORG)

DETROIT

JEWISH FEDERATION OF METROPOLITAN DETROIT (1899); 6735 Telegraph Rd., Suite 30, PO Box 2030, Bloomfield Hills (48301-2030); (248)642-4260. FAX: (248)642-4985. E-mail: jfmd@jfmd.org. Pres. Larry Jackier; Exec. V.-Pres. Robert Aronson. (WWW.THISISFEDERATION.ORG)

FLINT

FLINT JEWISH FEDERATION (1936); 619 Wallenberg St. (48502); (810)767-5922. FAX: (810)767-9024. E-mail: fjf@tm.net. Pres. Dr. Steve Burton; Exec. Dir. Joel B. Kaplan. (HTTP://USERS.TM.NET/FLINT)

GRAND RAPIDS

JEWISH COMMUNITY FUND OF GRAND RAPIDS (1930); 4127 Embassy Dr. SE (49546-2418); (616)942-5553. FAX: (616)942-5780. E-mail: jcfgr@iserv.net. Pres. Richard Stevens; Admin. Dir. Rosalie Stein; V.P. Maxine Shapiro. (WWW.JEWISHGRANDRAPIDS.ORG)

MINNESOTA

MINNEAPOLIS

MINNEAPOLIS JEWISH FEDERATION (1929; inc. 1930); 13100 Wayzata Blvd., Suite 200, Minnetonka (55305); (612)593-2600. FAX: (612)593-2544. E-mail: webmaster@ujfc.org. Pres. Michael Horovitz; Exec. Dir. Joshua Fogelson. (WWW.JEWISHMINNESOTA.ORG)

ST. PAUL

UNITED JEWISH FUND AND COUNCIL (1935); 790 S. Cleveland, Suite 227 (55116); (651)690-1707. FAX: (651)690-0228. E-mail: webmaster@ujfc.org. Pres. James Stein; Exec. Dir. Eli Skora. (WWW.JEWISHMINNESOTA.ORG)

MISSOURI

KANSAS CITY

JEWISH FEDERATION OF GREATER KANSAS CITY MO/KS (1933); 5801 W. 115 St., Overland Park, KS (66211-1824); (913)327-8100. FAX: (913)327-8110. E-mail: webmaster@jewishkc.org. Pres. Howard Jacobson; Exec. Dir. Todd Stettner. (WWW.JEWISHKANSASCITY.ORG)

ST. JOSEPH

UNITED JEWISH FUND OF ST. JOSEPH (1915); 1816 Walnut (64503); (816)233-1186. FAX: (816)233-9399. Elliot Zidell; Exec. Sec. Sherri Ott.

ST. LOUIS

JEWISH FEDERATION OF ST. LOUIS (incl. St. Louis County) (1901); 12 Millstone Campus Dr. (63146-9812); (314)432-0020. FAX: (314)432-1277. E-mail: submit@jfedstl.org. Pres. Heschel Raskas; Exec. V.-Pres. Barry Rosenberg. (WWW.JEWISHSTLOUIS.ORG)

NEBRASKA

LINCOLN

JEWISH FEDERATION OF LINCOLN, INC. (1931; inc. 1961); PO Box 67218 (68506); (402)489-1015. FAX: (402)476-8364. Pres. Herb Friedman; Exec. Dir. Karen Sommer.

OMAHA

JEWISH FEDERATION OF OMAHA (1903); 333 S. 132nd St. (68154-2198); (402)334-8200. FAX: (402)334-1330. E-mail: pmonsk@top.net. Pres. Steven Pitlor; Exec. Dir. Jan Goldstein. (WWW.JEWISHOMAHA.ORG)

NEVADA

LAS VEGAS

JEWISH FEDERATION OF LAS VEGAS (1973); 2317 Renaissance Dr. (89119-7520); (702)732-0556. FAX: (702)732-3228. Bd. Chr. Michael Unger; Exec. Dir. Meyer Bodoff. (WWW.JEWISHLASVEGAS.COM)

NEW HAMPSHIRE

MANCHESTER

JEWISH FEDERATION OF GREATER MANCHESTER (1974); 698 Beech St. (03104-3626); (603)627-7679. FAX: (603) 627-7963. E-mail: office@jewishnh.com. Exec. Dir. Adam M. Solender. (WWW.JEWISHNH.ORG)

NEW JERSEY

ATLANTIC AND CAPE MAY COUNTIES

JEWISH FEDERATION OF ATLANTIC AND CAPE MAY COUNTIES (1924); P.O. Box 196, Northfield (08225-0196); (609)822-4404. FAX: (609)822-4426. E-mail: karen@jewishbytheshore.com. Pres. Marc Lowenstein; Exec. V.-Pres. Bernard Cohen. (WWW.JEWISHBYTHESHORE.COM)

BERGEN COUNTY

UJA FEDERATION OF NORTHERN NEW JERSEY (merged 2004); 111 Kinderkamack Rd., River Edge (07661); (201)488-6800. FAX: (201)488-1507. E-mail: contact@jewishbergen.org. Pres. Dr. Leonard Cole; Exec. V.-Pres. Howard E. Charish. (WWW.JEWISH BERGEN.ORG)

CENTRAL NEW JERSEY

JEWISH FEDERATION OF CENTRAL NEW JERSEY (1940; merged 1973); 1391 Martine Ave., Scotch Plains (07076); (908)889-5335. FAX: (908)889-5370. E-mail: azjhai@jfedcnj.org. Pres. Robert Kuchner; Exec. V.-Pres. Stanley Stone. (WWW.JFEDCNJ.ORG)

CLIFTON-PASSAIC

JEWISH FEDERATION OF GREATER CLIFTON-PASSAIC (1933); 199 Scoles Ave., Clifton (07012-1125). (973)777-7031. FAX: (973)777-6701. E-mail: yymuskin@jfedcliftonpassaic.com. Pres. Mark Levenson; Exec. V.-Pres. Yosef Y. Muskin.

CUMBERLAND COUNTY

JEWISH FEDERATION OF CUMBERLAND COUNTY (inc. 1971); 1063 E. Landis Ave. Suite B, Vineland (08360-3752); (856)696-4445. FAX: (856)696-3428. E-mail: questions@jfedcc.org. Pres. Edward Roth; Exec. Dir. Kirk Wisemayer. (WWW.JFEDCC.ORG)

METROWEST NEW JERSEY

UNITED JEWISH COMMUNITIES OF METROWEST (1923); 901 Route 10, Whippany (07981-1156); (973)929-3000. FAX: (973)884-7361. E-mail: webmaster@ujcnj.org. Pres. Kenneth R. Heyman; Exec. V.-Pres. Max L. Kleinman. (WWW.UJFMETROWEST.ORG)

MIDDLESEX COUNTY

JEWISH FEDERATION OF GREATER MIDDLESEX COUNTY (org. 1948; reorg. 1985); 230 Old Bridge Tpk., S. River (08882-2000); (732)432-7711. FAX: (732)432-0292. E-mail: info@jf-gmc.org. Pres. Roy Tanzman; Exec. Dir. Gerrie Bamira. (WWW.JEWISHMIDDLESEX.ORG)

MONMOUTH COUNTY

JEWISH FEDERATION OF GREATER MONMOUTH COUNTY (1971); 100 Grant Ave., PO Box 210, Deal (07723-0210); (732)531-6200-1. FAX: (732)531-9518. E-mail: info@jewishmonmouth.org. Exec. Dir. Howard Gases. (WWW.JEWISHMONMOUTH.ORG)

OCEAN COUNTY

OCEAN COUNTY JEWISH FEDERATION (1977); 301 Madison Ave., Lakewood (08701); (732)363-0530. FAX: (732)363-2097. Pres. Dr. Bernie Grabelle; Exec. Dir. Danny Goldberg.

PRINCETON MERCER BUCKS

UNITED JEWISH FEDERATION OF PRINCETON MERCER BUCKS (merged 1996); 4 Princess Rd., Suite 206, Lawrenceville (08648-2207); (609)530-0400. FAX: (609)219-9040. E-mail: mailbox@ujfpmb.org. Pres. Carol Pollard; Exec. Dir. Andrew Frank. (WWW.UJFPMB.ORG)

SOMERSET COUNTY

JEWISH FEDERATION OF SOMERSET, HUNTERDON & WARREN COUNTIES (1960); 775 Talamini Rd., Bridgewater (08807); (908)725-6994. FAX: (908)725-9753. E-mail: info@jfedshaw.org. Pres. Jo Ann Chase; Exec. Dir. Diane S. Naar. (WWW.JFEDSHAW.ORG)

SOUTHERN NEW JERSEY

JEWISH FEDERATION OF SOUTHERN NEW JERSEY (incl. Camden, Burlington, and Gloucester counties) (1922); 1301 Springdale Rd., Suite 200, Cherry Hill (08003-2769); (856)751-9500. FAX: (856)751-1697. E-mail: imorrow@jfedsnj.org. Pres. Dr. Robert Belafsky; Exec. V.-Pres. Jeff Klein. (WWW.JFEDSNJ.ORG)

NEW MEXICO

ALBUQUERQUE

JEWISH FEDERATION OF GREATER ALBUQUERQUE (1938); 5520 Wyoming Blvd., NE (87109-3167); (505)821-3214. FAX: (505)821-3351. E-mail: infor@jewishnewmexico.org. Pres. Janice Posters; Exec. Dir. Sam Sokolove. (WWW.JEWISHNEWMEXICO.ORG)

NEW YORK

ALBANY

(See Northeastern New York)

BROOME COUNTY

JEWISH FEDERATION OF BROOME COUNTY; 500 Clubhouse Rd., Vestal (13850); (607)724-2332; FAX: (607)724-2311. (WWW.TOER.NET/JFEDERATION)

BUFFALO (INCL. NIAGARA FALLS)

JEWISH FEDERATION OF GREATER BUFFALO, INC. (1903); 787 Delaware Ave. (14209); (716)886-7750. FAX: (716)886-1367. E-mail: info@jfedbflo.com. Exec. Dir. Daniel G. Kantor. (WWW.JFEDBFLO.COM)

DUTCHESS COUNTY

JEWISH FEDERATION OF DUTCHESS COUNTY; 110 Grand Ave., Poughkeepsie (12603); (845)471-9811. FAX: (845) 471-3233. E-mail: director@jewishdutchess.org. Exec. Dir. Bonnie Meadow. (WWW.JEWISHDUTCHESS.ORG)

ELMIRA-CORNING

JEWISH CENTER AND FEDERATION OF THE TWIN TIERS (1942); Grandview Ave. Extension, Elmira (14905-0087); (607)734-8122. FAX: (607)734-8123. Pres. John Spiegler; Admin. Diane Huglies.

NEW YORK

UJA-FEDERATION OF JEWISH PHILANTHROPIES OF NEW YORK, INC. (incl. Greater NY, Westchester, Nassau, and Suffolk counties) (Fed. org. 1917; UJA 1939; merged 1986); 130 E. 59 St. (10022-1302); (212)980-1000. FAX: (212)888-7538. E-mail: contact@ujafedny.org. Pres. John M. Shapiro; Exec. V.-Pres. & CEO John Ruskay. (WWW.UJAFEDNY.ORG)

NORTHEASTERN NEW YORK

UNITED JEWISH FEDERATION OF NORTHEASTERN NEW YORK (1986); The Golub Center, 184 Washington Ave. Ext., Albany (12203); (518)783-7800. FAX: (518)783-1557. E-mail: info@jewishfedny.org. Pres. Dr. Lewis Morrison; Exec. Dir. Rodney Margolis. (WWW.JEWISHFEDNY.ORG)

ORANGE COUNTY

JEWISH FEDERATION OF GREATER ORANGE COUNTY (1977); 68 Stewart Ave., Newburgh (12550); (845)562-7860. FAX: (914)562-5114. E-mail: jfogoc@aol.com. Pres. Mona Rieger; Admin. Dir. Joyce Waschitz.

ROCHESTER

JEWISH COMMUNITY FEDERATION OF GREATER ROCHESTER, NY, INC. (1939); 441 East Ave. (14607-1932); (716)461-0490. FAX: (716)461-0912. E-mail: info@jewishrochester.org. Pres. Dennis Kessler; Exec. Dir. Lawrence W. Fine. (WWW.JEWISHROCHESTER.ORG)

ROCKLAND COUNTY

JEWISH FEDERATION OF ROCKLAND COUNTY (1985); 900 Route 45, Suite 1, New City (10956-1140); (914)362-4200. Fax: (914)362-4282.

SCHENECTADY

(See Northeastern New York)

SYRACUSE

SYRACUSE JEWISH FEDERATION, INC. (1918); 5655 Thompson Rd. So., DeWitt (13214-0511); (315)445-2040. FAX: (315)445-1559. Pres. Gershon Vincow; Exec. V.-Pres. Richard Friedman. (WWW.SJFED.ORG)

TROY

(See Northeastern New York)

ULSTER COUNTY

JEWISH FEDERATION OF ULSTER COUNTY (1951); 159 Green St., Kingston (12401); (845)338-8131. FAX: (845)338-8131. E-mail: infor@ucjf.org. Pres. Michelle Tuchman; Exec. Dir. Joan Plotsky. (WWW.UCJF.ORG)

UTICA

JEWISH COMMUNITY FEDERATION AND CENTER OF UTICA (1950; reorg. 1994); 2310 Oneida St. (13501-6009); (315)733-2343. FAX: (315)733-2346. E-mail: jcc1@borg .com. Pres. Ann Siegel; Exec. Dir. Barbara Ratner-Gantshar.

NORTH CAROLINA

ASHEVILLE

WESTERN NORTH CAROLINA JEWISH FEDERATION (1935); 236 Charlotte St. (28801-1434); (828)253-0701. FAX: (828)254-7666. Pres. Stan Greenberg; Exec. Dir. Marlene Berger-Joyce.

CHARLOTTE

THE JEWISH FEDERATION OF GREATER CHARLOTTE (1938); 5007 Providence Rd. (28226-5849); (704)366-5007. FAX: (704)944-6766. E-mail: jfgc@shalomcharlotte.org. Pres. Bob Abel; Exec. Dir. Sue Worrel. (WWW.JEWISHCHARLOTTE.ORG)

DURHAM-CHAPEL HILL

DURHAM-CHAPEL HILL JEWISH FEDERATION & COMMUNITY COUNCIL (1979); 3700

Lyckan Pkwy., Suite B, Durham (27707-2541); (919)489-5335. FAX: (919)489-5788. E-mail: federation@shalomdch.org. Pres. Lew Margolis; Exec. Dir. Orit Ramler Szulik. (HTTP://SHALOMDCH.ORG)

GREENSBORO

GREENSBORO JEWISH FEDERATION (1940); 5509C W. Friendly Ave. (27410-4211); (336)852-5433. FAX: (336)852-4346. E-mail: info@shalomgreensboro.org. Pres. Nancy Brenner; Exec. Dir. Marilyn Chandler. (WWW.SHALOMGREENSBORO.ORG)

RALEIGH

RALEIGH-CARY JEWISH FEDERATION (1987); 8210 Creedmoor Rd., Suite 104 (27613); (919)676-2200. FAX: (919)676-2122. E-mail: info@rcjf.org. Pres. Jim Maass; Exec. Dir. Judah Segal. (WWW.RCJF.ORG)

OHIO

AKRON

AKRON JEWISH COMMUNITY FEDERATION (1935); 750 White Pond Dr. (44320-1128); (330)869-CHAI (2424). FAX: (330)867-8498. Pres. David Kock; Exec. Dir. Michael Wise. (WWW.JEWISHAKRON.ORG)

CANTON

CANTON JEWISH COMMUNITY FEDERATION (1935; reorg. 1955); 2631 Harvard Ave., NW (44709-3147); (330)452-6444. FAX: (330)452-4487. E-mail: cantonjcf@aol.com. (JEWISHCANTON.ORG)

CINCINNATI

JEWISH FEDERATION OF CINCINNATI (1896; reorg. 1967); 4050 Executive Park Dr. (45241); (513) 985-1500. FAX: (513)985-1503. E-mail: info@jfedcin.org. Pres. Marc Fisher; CEO Shepard Englander. (WWW.JEWISHCINCINNATI.ORG)

CLEVELAND

JEWISH COMMUNITY FEDERATION OF CLEVELAND (1903); 1750 Euclid Ave. (44115-2106); (216)566-9200. FAX: (216)861-1230. E-mail: info@jcfcleve.org. Exec. V.-Pres. & CEO Stephen Hoffman. (WWW.JEWISHCLEVELAND.ORG)

COLUMBUS

COLUMBUS JEWISH FEDERATION (1926); 1175 College Ave. (43209); (614)237-7686. FAX: (614)237-2221. E-mail: webmaster@tcjf.org. Pres. & CEO Marsha Hurwitz. (WWW.JEWISHCOLUMBUS.ORG)

DAYTON

JEWISH FEDERATION OF GREATER DAYTON (1910); 33 W. First Ave., Ste. 100 (45402); (937)610-1555. Pres. Joseph Bettman; Exec. V.-Pres. Peter H. Wells. (WWW.JEWISHDAYTON.ORG)

STEUBENVILLE

JEWISH COMMUNITY COUNCIL (1938); 300 Lovers Lane (43952); (614)264-5514. FAX:: (740)264-7190. Pres. Curtis L. Greenberg; Exec. Sec. Jennie Bernstein.

TOLEDO

JEWISH FEDERATION OF GREATER TOLEDO (1907; reorg. 1960); 6465 Sylvania Ave., Sylvania (43560-3918); (419)885-4461. FAX: (419)885-3207. E-mail: jftoledo@cjfny.org. CEO Joel S. Beren. (WWW.JEWISHTOLEDO.ORG)

YOUNGSTOWN

Youngstown Area Jewish Federation (1935); 505 Gypsy Lane (44504-1314); (330)746-3251. FAX: (330)746-7926. E-mail: samkoopl@juno.com. Pres. Dr. Ronald Roth; Dir. Bonnie Deutsch-Burdman.

OKLAHOMA

OKLAHOMA CITY

JEWISH FEDERATION OF GREATER OKLAHOMA CITY (1941); 710 W. Wilshire, Suite C (73116-7736). (405)848-3132. FAX: (405)848-3180. E-mail: office@jfedokc.org. Pres. Harriet Carson; Exec. Dir. Edie S. Roodman. (WWW.JFEDOKC.ORG)

TULSA

JEWISH FEDERATION OF TULSA (1938); 2021 E. 71 St. (74136); (918)495-1100. FAX: (918)495-1220. E-mail: federation@jewishtulsa.org. Pres. Andrew M. Wolov; Exec. Dir. Barry Abels. (WWW.JEWISHTULSA.ORG)

OREGON

PORTLAND

JEWISH FEDERATION OF PORTLAND (incl. Northwest Oregon and Southwest Washington communities) (1920; reorg. 1956); 6680 SW Capitol Hwy. (97219); (503)245-6219. FAX: (503)245-6603. E-mail: federation@jewishportland.org. Pres. Rob Shlachter; Exec. Dir. Charles Schiffman. (WWW.JEWISHPORTLAND.ORG)

PENNSYLVANIA

BUCKS COUNTY

(See Jewish Federation of Greater Philadelphia)

ERIE

JEWISH COMMUNITY COUNCIL OF ERIE (1946); 1611 Peach St., Suite 405 (16501-2123); (814)455-4474. FAX: (814)455-4475. E-mail: jcceri@erie.net. Pres. Robert Cohen; Admin. Dir. Cynthia Penman; Dir. Barbara Singer. (WWW.JCCERI.ORG)

HARRISBURG

UNITED JEWISH COMMUNITY OF GREATER HARRISBURG (1941); 3301 N. Front St. (17110-1436); (717)236-9555. FAX: (717)236-8104. E-mail: communityreview@desupernet.net. Pres. Raphael Aronson; Exec. Dir. David Weisberg. (WWW.JEWISHHARRISBURG.COM)

LEHIGH VALLEY

JEWISH FEDERATION OF THE LEHIGH VALLEY (1948); 702 N. 22nd St., Allentown (18104); (610)821-5500. FAX: (610)821-8946. E-mail: ivfed@enter.net. Exec. Dir. Mark Goldstein.

PHILADELPHIA

JEWISH FEDERATION OF GREATER PHILADELPHIA (incl. Bucks, Chester, Delaware, Montgomery, and Philadelphia counties) (1901; reorg. 1956); 2100 Arch St. (19103); (215)832-0500. FAX: (215)832-1510. E-mail: webmaster@philafederation.org. Pres. & CEO Ira M. Schwartz. (WWW.JEWISHPHILLY.ORG)

PITTSBURGH

UNITED JEWISH FEDERATION OF GREATER PITTSBURGH (1912; reorg. 1955); 234 McKee Pl. (15213-3916); (412)681-8000. FAX: (412) 681-3980. E-mail: ujfinformation@ujfpittsburgh.org. Pres. & CEO Jeff Finkelstein; Chmn. Daniel H. Shapira. (WWW.UJF.NET)

READING

JEWISH FEDERATION OF READING, PA., INC. (1935; reorg. 1972); 1700 City Line St. (19604); (610)921-2766. FAX: (610)929-0886. E-mail: stanr@epix.net. Pres. Sheila Lattin; Exec. Dir. Jay Steinberg. (WWW.READINGJEWISHCOMMUNITY.ORG)

SCRANTON

JEWISH FEDERATION OF NORTHEASTERN PENNSYLVANIA (1945); 601 Jefferson Ave. (18510); (570)961-2300. FAX: (570)346-6147. E-mail: jfednepa@epix.net. Pres. Louis Nivert; Exec. Dir. Mark Silverberg. (WWW.JFEDNEPA.ORG)

WILKES-BARRE

JEWISH FEDERATION OF GREATER WILKES-BARRE (1950); 60 S. River St. (18702-2493); (570)822-4146. FAX: (570)824-5966. E-mail: wbreport@aol.com. Pres. Murray Ufberg; Exec. Dir. Don Cooper.

RHODE ISLAND

PROVIDENCE

JEWISH FEDERATION OF RHODE ISLAND (1945); 130 Sessions St. (02906); (401)421-4111. FAX: (401)331-7961. E-mail: shalom@jfri.org. Pres. Edward D. Feldstein; Exec. Dir. Steven R. Silverfarb. (WWW.JFRI.ORG)

SOUTH CAROLINA

CHARLESTON

CHARLESTON JEWISH FEDERATION (1949); 1645 Raoul Wallenberg Blvd., PO Box 31298 (29407); (843)571-6565. FAX: (843)852-3547. E-mail: webmaster@jewishcharleston.org. Co-Pres. Wendy Goer and Paul Saltzman; Exec. Dir. Ellen J. Katzman. (WWW.JEWISHCHARLESTON.ORG)

COLUMBIA

COLUMBIA JEWISH FEDERATION (1960); 4540 Trenholm Rd., PO Box 23297 (29206-4462); (803)787-2023. FAX: (803)787-0475. E-mail: ternercjf@hotmail.com. Pres. Stephen Serbin; Exec. Dir. Steven Terner.

SOUTH DAKOTA

SIOUX FALLS

JEWISH WELFARE FUND (1938); 510 S. First Ave. (57102-1003); (605)332-3335. FAX: (605)334-2298. E-mail: asnh94@prodigy.com. Pres. Laurence Bierman; Exec. Sec. Stephen Rosenthal.

TENNESSEE

CHATTANOOGA

JEWISH COMMUNITY FEDERATION OF GREATER CHATTANOOGA (1931); 5461 N. Terrace Rd. (37411); PO Box 8947 (37412); (423)493-0270. FAX: (423)493-9997. E-mail: mdzik@jcfgc.com. Pres. Susan Distefano; Exec. Dir. Michael Dzik. (WWW.JCFGC.COM)

KNOXVILLE

KNOXVILLE JEWISH FEDERATION, INC. (1939); 7800 Deane Hill Dr. (37919); (865)693-5837. FAX: (865)694-4861. E-mail: ajcckjf@aol.com. Pres. Scott B. Hahn; Exec. Dir. Dr. Jeff Gubitz. (WWW.JEWISH-KNOXVILLE.ORG)

MEMPHIS

MEMPHIS JEWISH FEDERATION (incl. Shelby County) (1935); 6560 Poplar Ave. (38138-3614); (901)767-7100. FAX: (901)767-7128. E-mail: jfeld@memjfed.org. Pres. Louise Sklar; Exec. Dir. Jeffrey Feld. (WWW.MEMJFED.ORG/MJF)

NASHVILLE

NASHVILLE JEWISH FEDERATION (1936); 801 Percy Warner Blvd. (37205-4009); (615)356-3242. FAX: (615)352-0056. E-mail: jnashjfed@aol.org. Pres. Fred Zimmerman; Exec. Dir. Steven J. Edelstein. (WWW.NASHVILLEJCC.ORG)

TEXAS

AUSTIN

JEWISH COMMUNTY ASSOCIATION OF AUSTIN (1939; reorg. 1956); 7300 Hart Lane (78731); (512)735-8000. FAX: (512)735-8001. E-mail: austinjfed@jfaustin.org. Pres. Linda Millstone; Exec. Dir. Sandy Sack. (WWW.SHALOMAUSTIN.ORG)

BEAUMONT

BEAUMONT JEWISH FEDERATION; PO Box 1891 (77704-1981); (409)832-2881.

CORPUS CHRISTI

COMBINED JEWISH APPEAL OF CORPUS CHRISTI; 750 Everhart Rd. (78411-1906); (512)855-6239. FAX: (512)853-9040.

DALLAS

JEWISH FEDERATION OF GREATER DALLAS (1911); 7800 Northaven Rd. (75230-3226); (214)369-3313. FAX: (214)369-8943. E-mail: contact@jfgd.org. Pres. Donald Schaffer; Exec. Dir. Gary Weinstein. (WWW.JEWISHDALLAS.ORG)

EL PASO

JEWISH FEDERATION OF EL PASO, INC. (1937); 405 Wallenberg Dr. (79912-5605); (915)584-4437. FAX: (915)584-0243. Pres. Richard Krasne; Exec. Dir. Larry Harris. (WWW.JEWISHELPASO.ORG)

FORT WORTH

JEWISH FEDERATION OF FORT WORTH AND TARRANT COUNTY (1936); 4049 Kingsridge Rd. (76109); (817)569-0892. FAX: (817)569-0895. E-mail: jfed@tarrantfederation.org. Pres. Harold Gernsbacher; Exec. Dir. Naomi Rosenfield.

HOUSTON

JEWISH FEDERATION OF GREATER HOUSTON (1936); 5603 S. Braeswood Blvd. (77096-3907); (713)729-7000. FAX: (713)721-6232. E-mail: lwunsch@houstonjewish.org. Pres. Joe Williams; Exec. V.-Pres. Lee Wunsch. (WWW.HOUSTONJEWISH.ORG)

SAN ANTONIO

JEWISH FEDERATION OF SAN ANTONIO (incl. Bexar County) (1922); 12500 NW Military Hwy., Suite 200 (78231); (210)302-6960. FAX: (210)408-2332. E-mail: markfreedman@jfsatx. Pres. Alan Petlin; Exec. Dir. Mark Freedman. (WWW.JFSATX.ORG)

WACO

JEWISH FEDERATION OF WACO & CENTRAL TEXAS (1949); PO Box 8031 (76714-8031); (817)776-3740. FAX: (817)776-4424. E-mail: debhersh@aol.com. Pres. Harry Smith; Exec. Sec. Deborah Hersh. (WWW.AGUDATH-JACOB.ORG/FED.HTM)

UTAH

SALT LAKE CITY

UNITED JEWISH FEDERATION OF UTAH (1936); 2 North Medical Drive (84113); (801)581-0102. FAX: (801) 581-1334. Pres. Robert Wolff; Exec. Dir. Donald Gartman.

VIRGINIA

RICHMOND

JEWISH COMMUNITY FEDERATION OF RICHMOND (1935); 5403 Monument Ave., PO Box 17128 (23226-7128); (804)288-0045. FAX: (804)282-7507. E-mail: webmaster@jewishrichmond.org. Pres. Stewart Kasen; Exec. Dir. Ellen Chernack. (WWW.JEWISHRICHMOND.ORG)

TIDEWATER

UNITED JEWISH FEDERATION OF TIDEWATER (incl. Norfolk, Portsmouth, and Virginia Beach) (1937); 5000 Corporate Woods Dr., Suite 200, Virginia Beach (23462-4370); (757)965-6100. FAX: (757)965-6102. E-mail: ujft@ujft.org. Pres. David Brand; Exec. V.-Pres. Harry Graber. (WWW.JEWISHVA.ORG)

VIRGINIA PENINSULA

UNITED JEWISH COMMUNITY OF THE VIRGINIA PENINSULA, INC. (1942); 2700 Spring

Rd., Newport News (23606); (757)930-1422. FAX: (757)930-3762. E-mail: unitedjc@ujvp.org. Pres. Roy H. Lasris; Exec. Dir. Robert Kessler. (WWW.UJCVP.ORG)

WASHINGTON

SEATTLE

JEWISH FEDERATION OF GREATER SEATTLE (incl. King County, Everett, and Bremerton) (1926); 2031 Third Ave. (98121); (206)443-5400. FAX: (206)443-0306. E-mail: info@jewishinseattle.org. Pres. & CEO Richard M. Fruchter. (WWW.JEWISHINSEATTLE.ORG)

WEST VIRGINIA

CHARLESTON

FEDERATED JEWISH CHARITIES OF CHARLESTON, INC. (1937); PO Box 1613 (25326); (304)345-2320. FAX: (304)345-2325. E-mail: mzltov@aol.com. Pres. Stuart May; Exec. Sec. Lee Diznoff.

WISCONSIN

MADISON

MADISON JEWISH COMMUNITY COUNCIL, INC. (1940); 6434 Enterprise Lane (53719-1117); (608)278-1808. FAX:(608)278-7814. E-mail: mjcc@mjcc.net. Pres. Diane Seder; Exec. Dir. Steven H. Morrison. (WWW.JEWISHMADISON.ORG)

MILWAUKEE

MILWAUKEE JEWISH FEDERATION, INC. (1902); 1360 N. Prospect Ave. (53202); (414)390-5700. FAX: (414)390-5782. E-mail: info@milwaukeejewish.org. Pres. Bruce A. Arbit; Exec. V.-Pres. Richard H. Meyer. (WWW.MILWAUKEEJEWISH.ORG)

CANADA

ALBERTA

CALGARY

CALGARY JEWISH COMMUNITY COUNCIL (1962); 1607 90th Ave. SW (T2V 4V7); (403)253-8600. FAX: (403)253-7915. E-mail: dpowers@cjcc.ca. Pres. Nate Feldman; Exec. Dir. Myrna Linder. (WWW.CJCC.CA)

EDMONTON

JEWISH FEDERATION OF EDMONTON (1954; reorg. 1982); 7200 156th St. (T5R 1X3); (780)487-5120. FAX: (780)481-1854. E-mail: edjfed@net.com.ca. Pres. Stephen Mandel; Exec. Dir. Lesley A. Jacobson.

BRITISH COLUMBIA

VANCOUVER

JEWISH FEDERATION OF GREATER VANCOUVER (1932; reorg. 1987); 950 W. 41st Ave., Suite 200 (V5Z 2N7); (604)257-5100. FAX: (604)257-5110. E-mail: jfed@jfgv.com. Pres. Sondra Green; Exec. Dir. Mark Gurvis. (WWW.JFGV.COM)

MANITOBA

WINNIPEG

JEWISH FEDERATION OF WINNIPEG/COMBINED JEWISH APPEAL(1938; reorg. 1973); 123 Doncaster St., Suite C300 (R3N 2B2); (204)477-7400. FAX: (204)477-7405. E-mail: bfreedman@aspercampus.mb.ca. Pres. Edward Lyons; Exec. V.-Pres. Jonathan Kroft. (WWW.JEWISHWINNIPEG.ORG)

ONTARIO

HAMILTON

UJA/JEWISH FEDERATION OF HAMILTON/WENTWORTH & AREA (1932; merged 1971); PO Box 7258, 1030 Lower Lions Club Rd., Ancaster (L9G 3N6); (905)648-0605 #305. FAX: (905)648-8350. E-mail: cnuscauja@on.aibn.com. Pres. Bonnie Loewith; Exec. Dir. Gerald Fisher. (WWW.JEWISHHAMILTON.ORG)

LONDON

LONDON JEWISH FEDERATION (1932); 536 Huron St. (N5Y 4J5); (519)673-3310. FAX: (519)673-1161. Pres. Ron Wolf; Off. Mgr. Debra Chatterley. (WWW.JEWISHLONDON.CA)

OTTAWA

UNITED JEWISH APPEAL OF OTTAWA (1934); 21 Nadolny Sachs Private (K2A 1R9); (613)798-4696. FAX: (613)798-4695. E-mail: uja@jccottawa.com. Pres. Mitchell Bellman; Exec. Dir. Jack Silverstein. (WWW.JEWISHOTTAWA.ORG)

TORONTO

UJA FEDERATION OF GREATER TORONTO (1917); 4600 Bathurst St. (M2R 3V2); (416)635-2883. FAX: (416)631-5715. E-mail: info@oujafed.org. Pres. Joseph Steiner; Exec. V.-Pres. Allan Reitzes. (WWW.JEWISHTORONTO.NET)

WINDSOR

JEWISH COMMUNITY FEDERATION (1938); 1641 Ouellette Ave. (N8X 1K9); (519)973-1772. FAX: (519)973-1774. Pres. Jay Armeland; Exec. Dir. Harvey Kessler. (WWW.JEWISHWINDSOR.ORG)

QUEBEC

MONTREAL

FEDERATION CJA (formerly Allied Jewish Community Services) (1965); 1 Carrie Cummings Square (H3W 1M6); (514)735-3541. FAX: (514)735-8972. E-mail: fcja@federationcja.org. Pres. Marc Gold; Exec. V.-Pres. Danyael Cantor. (WWW.FEDERATIONCJA.ORG)

Jewish Periodicals

UNITED STATES

ALABAMA

DEEP SOUTH JEWISH VOICE (1990). PO Box 130052, Birmingham, 35213. (205)322-9002. E-mail: informationr@dsjv.com. Lawrence M. Brook. Monthly. (WWW.DEEPSOUTHJEWISHVOICE.COM)

ARIZONA

ARIZONA JEWISH POST (1946). 2601 N. Campbell Ave., #205, Tucson, 85719. (520)319-1112. FAX: (520) 319-1118. E-mail: pbraun@azjewishpost.com. Phyllis Braun. Fortnightly. Jewish Federation of Southern Arizona.

JEWISH NEWS OF GREATER PHOENIX (1948). 1625 E. Northern Ave., Suite 106, Phoenix, 85020. (602)870-9470. FAX: (602)870-0426. E-mail: editor@jewishaz.com. Deborah Susser. Weekly. (WWW.JEWISHAZ.COM)

CALIFORNIA

AMERICAN RABBI (1968). 22711 Cass Ave., Woodland Hills, 91364. (818)225-9631. E-mail: amrabbi@pacbell.net. Ed.-in-Ch./Pub. David Epstein; Ed. Harry Essrig. Quarterly.

JEWISH NEWS WEEKLY OF NORTHERN CALIFORNIA (1946). 225 Bush St., Suite 1480, San Francisco, 94104-4281. (415)263-7200. FAX: (415)263-7223. E-mail: edit@jweekly.com. Woody Weingarten. Weekly. San Francisco Jewish Community Publications, Inc.

JEWISH COMMUNITY CHRONICLE (1947). 3801 E. Willow St., Long Beach, 90815. (562)426-7601, ext. 1021. FAX: (562)595-5543. E-mail: jchron@surfside.net. Marian Leb Martin. Fortnightly except January, July & August/ once per month 21 issues a year. Jewish Federation of Greater Long Beach & West Orange County.

JEWISH COMMUNITY NEWS (1976). 14855 Oka Rd., Suite 2, Los Gatos, 95030. (408)358-3033. FAX: (408)356-0733. E-mail: jcn@jfgsj.org. Cecily Ruttenberg. Monthly. Jewish Federation of Greater San Jose.

JEWISH JOURNAL OF GREATER LOS ANGELES (1986). 3660 Wilshire Blvd., Suite 204, Los Angeles, 90010. (213)368-1661. FAX: (213)368-1684. E-mail:editor@jewishjournal.com. Susan Freudenheim. Weekly. (WWW.JEWISHJOURNAL.COM)

JEWISH NEWS (1973). 15060 Ventura Blvd., Suite 210, Sherman Oaks, CA 91403. (818)786-4000. FAX: (818)380-9232. Phil Blazer. Monthly. (Also weekly Sunday TV and radio broadcasts in LA, NY, and Miami.)

JEWISH SPORTS REVIEW. 1800 S. Robertson Blvd., #174, Los Angeles, 90035. (800)510-9003. E-mail: shel@jewishsportsreview.com. Shel Wallman/Ephraim Moxson. Bimonthly. (WWW.JEWISHSPORTSREVIEW.COM)

LOS ANGELES JEWISH TIMES (formerly B'NAI B'RITH MESSENGER) (1897). 5455 Wilshire Blvd., Suite 903, Los Angeles, 90036. (323)933-0131. FAX: (323)933-7928. E-mail: lajtart@aol.com. Ed.-in-Chief Joe Bobker; Mng. Ed. Jane Fried. Weekly.

SAN DIEGO JEWISH TIMES (1979). 4731 Palm Ave., La Mesa, 91941. (619)463-5515. FAX: (619) 463-1309. E-mail: msirota@sdjewishtimes.com. Michael Sirota. Fortnightly. (WWW.SDJEWISHTIMES.COM)

SHALOM L.A. (1988). 16027 Ventura Blvd., #400, Encino, 91436. (818)783-3090. FAX: (818)783-1104. E-mail: news@sholomla.net. Gal Shor. Weekly. Hebrew. (WWW.SHALOMLA.COM)

TIKKUN MAGAZINE (1986). 2342 Shattuck Ave., Suite 1200, Berkeley, 94704. (510)644-1200. FAX: (510)644-1255. E-mail: magazine@tikkun.org. Michael Lerner. Bimonthly. Institute for Labor & Mental Health. (WWW.TIKKUN.ORG)

WESTERN STATES JEWISH HISTORY (1968). 22711 Cass Ave., Woodland Hills, 91364. (818)225-9631. E-mail: amrabbi@pacbell.net. Gladys Sturman. Quarterly. Western States Jewish History Association.

COLORADO

INTERMOUNTAIN JEWISH NEWS (1913). 1275 Sherman St., Suite 214, Denver, 80203-2299. (303)861-2234. FAX: (303)832-6942. E-mail: miriam@ijn.com. Miriam Goldberg. Weekly. (WWW.IJN.COM)

CONNECTICUT

CONNECTICUT JEWISH LEDGER (1929). 740 N. Main St., W. Hartford, 06117. (860) 231-2424. FAX: (860)231-2428. E-mail: editorial@jewishledger.com. Lisa Lenkiewicz. Weekly. (WWW.JEWISHLEDGER.COM)

JEWISH LEADER (1974). 28 Channing St., PO Box 1468, New London, 06320. (860)442-7395. FAX: (860)443-4175. E-mail: jfecmim@aol.com. Mimi Perl. Biweekly. Jewish Federation of Eastern Connecticut.

DELAWARE

JEWISH VOICE. 100 W. 10th St., Suite 301, Wilmington, 19801. (302) 427-2100. FAX: (302) 427-2438. E-mail: lynn.edelmam@shalomdel.org. Lynn Edelman. 22 times per year. Jewish Federation of Delaware.

DISTRICT OF COLUMBIA

AZURE (1996). 5505 Connecticut Ave., NW, Suite 1140, Washington, 20015. (877)298-7300. FAX: (888)766-1506. E-mail: patrick@shalemcenter.org. Dan Polisar. Quarterly. Hebrew/English. The Shalem Center. (WWW.AZURE.ORG.IL)

B'NAI B'RITH INTERNATIONAL JEWISH MONTHLY (1886, under the name Menovah). 2020 K Street, NW, 7th Floor, Washington, DC 20006. (202)857-2708. FAX: (202)857-2781. E-mail: ijm@bnaibrith.org. Editor Elana Harris. Quarterly. B'nai B'rith International.

CAPITAL COMMUNIQUÉ (1991). 777 N. Capital St., NE, Suite 305, Washington, 20002. (202)216-9060. FAX: (202)216-9061. Jason Silberberg. Biannually. National Jewish Democratic Council.

JEWISH VETERAN (1896). 1811 R St., NW, Washington, 20009-1659. (202)265-6280. FAX: (202)234-5662. E-mail: jwv@jwv.org. Seymour "Sy" Brody. 5 times per year. Jewish War Veterans of the U.S.A. Quarterly

MOMENT (1975). 4710 41 St., NW, Washington, 20016. (202)364-3300. FAX: (202)364-2636. E-mail: editor@momentmag.com. Hershel Shanks. Bimonthly. Jewish Educational Ventures, Inc.

FSU MONITOR (1990). 1819 H Street, NW, Suite 230, Washington, 20006. (202)775-9770. FAX: (202)775-9776. E-mail: ucsj@ucsj.com. Nickolai Butkevich. Quarterly. Union of Councils for Soviet Jews.

NEAR EAST REPORT (1957). 440 First St., NW, Suite 607, Washington, 20001. (202)639-5254. FAX: (202) 347-4916. Dr. Raphael Danziger. Fortnightly. Near East Research, Inc.

SECURITY AFFAIRS (1976). 1717 K St., NW, Suite 800, Washington, 20006. (202)833-0020. FAX: (202)296-6452. E-mail: info@jinsa.org. Jim Colbert. Quarterly. Jewish Institute for National Security Affairs.

WASHINGTON JEWISH WEEK. *See under* MARYLAND

FLORIDA

CHRONICLE (1971). 580 S. McIntosh Rd., Sarasota, 34232. (941)371-4546. FAX: (941)378-2947. Barry Millman. Biweekly. Sarasota-Manatee Jewish Federation.

FEDERATION STAR (2001). 1250 Taimai Trail, No. Ste. 202, Naples 34102. (941)263-4205. E-mail: jfccfk@aol.com. Susan Frank. Biweekly. Jewish Federation of Collier County.

HERITAGE FLORIDA JEWISH NEWS (1976) 207 O'Brien Road, Ste. 101, Fern Park 32730. (407)834-8787. FAX: (407)834-8277. E-mail: news@orlandoheritage.com. Lyn Payne. Weekly. (WWW.HERITAGE.COM)

JACKSONVILLE JEWISH NEWS (1988). 8505 San Jose Blvd., Jacksonville, 32217. (904) 448-5000. FAX: (904)448-5715. E-mail: srgnews@aol.com. Susan R. Goetz. Monthly. Jacksonville Jewish Federation. (WWW.JEWISHJACKSONVILLE.COM)

JEWISH JOURNAL (1977). 1701 Green Rd., Deerfield Beach, 33064. (954)574-5328. FAX: (954)698-6719. E-mail: speskoff@tribune.com. Stan Peskoff. Weekly. South Florida Newspaper Network.

JEWISH PRESS OF PINELLAS COUNTY (Clearwater-St.Petersburg) (1985). PO Box 6970, Clearwater, 33758-6970; 1101 S. Belcher Road, Suite H, Largo, FL 33771. (727)535-4400. FAX:(727)530-3039. E-mail: jewishpress@aol.com. Karen Wolfson Dawkins. Biweekly. Jewish Press Group of Tampa Bay (FL), Inc. in cooperation with the Jewish Federation of Pinellas County. (WWW.JEWISHPINELLAS.ORG)

JEWISH PRESS OF TAMPA (1987). PO Box 6970, Clearwater 33758-6970. (813)871-2332. FAX: (727)535-4400. E-mail: jewishpress@aol.com. Karen Wolfson Dawkins. Biweekly. Jewish Press Group of Tampa Bay (FL), Inc.

L'CHAYIM (2003). 6237-E Presidential Court, Ft. Myers 33919. (941)481-4449. FAX: (941)481-0139. Deborah Robbins Millman. Biweekly. Jewish Federation of Lee & Charlotte Counties.

THE NEWS (2002). 108-A Barton Ave., Rockledge 32955. (407)636-1824. FAX: (407)636-0614. Ann C. Samuels. Biweekly. Jewish Federation of Brevard County.

SARASOTA-MANATEE JEWISH NEWS (2000). 580 S. McIntosh Rd., Sarasota 34232. (941)371-4546. Howard Trevlowitz. Weekly. Sarasota/Manatee Jewish Federation. (WWW.SMJF.ORG)

SHALOM TODAY-BROWARD (1994). 200 E. Las Olas Blvd., 10th Floor, Ft. Lauderdale 33301. (954)356-4000. FAX: (954) 429-1207. E-mail: shalom@sun-sentinel.com. Bob Gremillion. Weekly. Jewish Federation of Broward County.

SHALOM TODAY-PALM BEACH (1994). 3333 S. Congress Ave., Delray Beach 33445. (561)243-6600. FAX: (561)243-6546. E-mail: shalom@sun-sentinel.com. Michelle Simon & Bruce Warshal. Weekly. Jewish Federation of Palm Beach County.

GEORGIA

ATLANTA JEWISH TIMES (1925).1117 Perimeter Center West, Suite N311, Atlanta, GA 30338. (404)564-4550. FAX: (404)252-1172. E-mail: mjacobs@atlantajewishtimes.com. Michael Jacobs. Weekly. (WWW.ATLJEWISHTIMES.COM)

ILLINOIS

CHICAGO JEWISH NEWS (1994). 5301 W. Dempster, Skokie, Ill 60077. (847)966-0606. FAX: (847)966-1656. E-mail: paulinecjn@attglobal.net. Pauline Yearwood. Weekly. (WWW.CHICAGOJEWISHNEWS.COM)

CHICAGO JEWISH STAR (1991). PO Box 268, Skokie, 60076-0268. (847)674-7827. FAX: (847)674-0014. E-mail: chicagojewishstar@comcast.net. Douglas Wertheimer. Fortnightly.

JEWISH COMMUNITY NEWS (1941). 6464 W. Main, Suite 7A, Belleville, 62223. (618)398-6100. FAX: (618)398-0539. E-mail: silfed@simokyfed.com Steve Low. Quarterly. Jewish Federation of Southern Illinois. (WWW.SIMOKYFED.COM)

JUF NEWS & GUIDE TO JEWISH LIVING IN CHICAGO (1972). One S. Franklin St., Rm. 701G, Chicago, 60606. (312)357-4848. FAX: (312)855-2470. E-mail: sondrafargo@juf.org. Sondra Fargo. Monthly (Guide, annually). Jewish United Fund/Jewish Federation of Metropolitan Chicago.

INDIANA

ALEPH: HISTORICAL STUDIES IN SCIENCE AND JUDAISM (2001). Indiana University Press, 601 N. Morton St., Bloomington, 47404. (812)855-3830. FAX: (812)855-8507. E-mail: kcaras@indiana.edu. Editorial address: Sidney Edelstein Center, Hebrew University of Jerusalem, Givat Ram, Jerusalem 91904, Israel. Gad Freudenthal. Annual.

BRIDGES: A JOURNAL OF JEWISH FEMINISM (1996).4860 Washtenaw Ave, Ann Arbor, MI 48108. (734)395-4438. FAX: (812)855-8507. E-mail: clare@bridgesjournal.org. Editorial address: P.O. Box 1206, Ann Arbor, MI 48106. Clare Kinberg. Semiannual. (WWW.BRIDGESJOURNAL.COM)

HISTORY AND MEMORY (1995). Indiana University Press, 601 N. Morton St., Bloomington 47404. (812)855-3830. FAX:

(812)855-8507. E-mail: kcaras@indiana.edu. Editorial address: School of History, Tel Aviv University, Ramat Aviv, Tel Aviv 69978 Israel. Gadi Algazi. Semi-annual.

INDIANA JEWISH POST AND OPINION (1935). 238 S. Meridian St., #502, Indianapolis, 46225. (317)972-7800. FAX: (317)972-7807. E-mail: ads@indy.rr.com. Jennie Cohen. Weekly.

ISRAEL STUDIES (1996). Indiana University Press, 601 Morton St., Bloomington 47404. (812)855-3830. FAX: (812)855-8507. E-mail: kcaras@indiana.edu. Editorial address: Ben-Gurion Research Center, Sede-Boker Campus, Israel 84990. Three times a year.

JEWISH SOCIAL STUDIES: HISTORY, CULTURE, AND SOCIETY (1939, new series 1995). Indiana University Press, 601 N. Morton St., Bloomington 47404. (812)855-3830. FAX: (812)855-8507. E-mail: kcaras@indiana.edu. Editorial address: Taube Center for Jewish Studies, Bldg. 240, Rm. 203, Stanford University, Stanford, CA 94305-2190. Steven J. Zipperstein, Aron Rodrigue. Three times a year.

NASHIM (2001). Indiana University Press, 601 N. Morton St., Bloomington 47404. (812)855-3830. FAX: (812)855-8507. E-mail: kcaras@indiana.edu. Editorial address: P.O. Box 16080, Jerusalem 91160, Israel. Renée Levine Melammed. Semi-annual.

NATIONAL JEWISH POST AND OPINION (1932). 238 S. Meridian St., Indianapolis, 46225. (317)972-7800. FAX: (317)972-7807. E-mail: jpost@surf.ici.com. Jennie Cohen. Weekly. (WWW.JEWISHPOSTOPINION.COM)

PROOFTEXTS: A JOURNAL OF JEWISH LITERARY HISTORY (1980). Indiana University Press, 601 N. Morton St., Bloomington, 47404. (812)855-8507. FAX: (812)855-8507. E-mail: kcaras@indiana.edu. Editorial address: Dept. of Hebrew Language, Box 46, Jewish Theological Seminary, 3080 Broadway, NY, NY 10027-4649. Jeremy Dauber , Barbara Mann. Three times a year.

KANSAS

KANSAS CITY JEWISH CHRONICLE (1920). 4370 W. 109th Street, Suite 300. Overland Park, KS, 66211. (913)381-1010. FAX: (913)381-9889. E-mail: chronicle@sunpublications.com. Rick Hellman. Weekly. Sun Publications. (WWW.KCJC.COM)

KENTUCKY

COMMUNITY (1975). 3630 Dutchmans Lane, Louisville, 40205-3200. (502) 451-8840. FAX: (502) 458-0702. E-mail: jfed@iglou.com. Sheila Steinman Wallace. Biweekly. Jewish Community Federation of Louisville.

LOUISIANA

JEWISH CIVIC PRESS (1965). 924 Valmont St., New Orleans 70115. (504)875-8784. E-mail: jewishcivicpress@yahoo.com. Claire & Abner Tritt. Monthly.

JEWISH NEWS (1995). 3747 W. Esplanade Avenue, Suite 307, Metairie, LA 70002. (504)780-5614. FAX: (504)780-5601. E-mail: jewishnews@jewishnola.com. Julie Schwartz. Fortnightly. Jewish Federation of Greater New Orleans.

MARYLAND

BALTIMORE JEWISH TIMES (1919). 1040 Park Ave, Suite 200., Baltimore, 21201. (410)752-3504. FAX: (410)752-2375. E-mail: editor@jewishtimes.com. Neil Rubin. Weekly. (WWW.JEWISHTIMES.COM)

WASHINGTON JEWISH WEEK (1930, as the National Jewish Ledger). 11426 Rockville Pike, Suite 236, Rockville 20852. (301)230-2222. FAX: (301)881-6362. E-mail: wjweek@aol.com. Debra Rubin. Weekly. (WWW.WASHINGTONJEWISHWEEK.COM)

MASSACHUSETTS

AMERICAN JEWISH HISTORY (1892). 160 Herrick Road, Newton Centre, MA 02459. (671)559-8880. FAX: (671)559-8881. E-mail: ajhs@ajhs.org. Eli Faber. Quarterly. American Jewish Historical Society.

JEWISH ADVOCATE (1902). 15 School St., Boston, 02108. (617)367-9100. FAX: (617)367-9310. E-mail: kristine@thejewishadvocate.com. Y.A. Korff. Weekly. (WWW.THEJEWISHADVOCATE.COM)

JEWISH CHRONICLE (1927). 131 Lincoln St., Worcester, 01605. (508)752-3400. E-mail: chronicle.editor@verizon.net. Ellen Weingart. Fortnightly.

JEWISH GUIDE TO BOSTON & NEW ENGLAND (1972). 15 School St., Boston, 02108. (617)367-9100. FAX: (617)367-9310.

Rosie Rosenzweig. Irregularly. The Jewish Advocate.

JEWISH JOURNAL/NORTH OF BOSTON (1976). 201 Washington St., PO Box 555, Salem, 01970. (978)745-4111 .FAX: (978)745-5333. E-mail: editorial@jewish journal.org. Bette Keva. Biweekly. Russian section. North Shore Jewish Press Ltd. (WWW.JEWISHJOURNAL.ORG)

JEWISH NEWS OF WESTERN MASSACHUSETTS (*see* Jewish Advocate)

METROWEST JEWISH REPORTER (1970). 76 Salem End Rd., Framingham, 01702. (508)872-4808. FAX: (508)879-5856. Marcia T. Rivin. Monthly. Combined Jewish Philanthropies of Greater Boston.

PAKN-TREGER (1980). 1021 West St., Amherst, 01002. (413)256-4900. FAX: (413)256-4700. E-mail: pt@bikher.org. Nancy Sherman. Three times a year. National Yiddish Book Center.

SH'MA (1970). 90 Oak Street, 4th Floor, Newton MA 02459. (781)449-9894. FAX: (781)449-9825. E-mail: susanb@jflmedia.com. Susan Berrin. Monthly. Jewish Family & Life.

MICHIGAN

DETROIT JEWISH NEWS (1942). 29200 Northwestern Highway, Ste. 110, Southfield, 48034. (248)354-6060. FAX: (248)304-8885. E-mail: rsklar@jnonline.com. Arthur Hurwitz. Weekly. (WWW.JNONLINE.US)

HUMANISTIC JUDAISM (1968). 28611 W. Twelve Mile Rd., Farmington Hills, 48334. (248)478-7610. FAX: (248)478-3159. E-mail: info@shj.org. M. Bonnie Cousens, Ruth D. Feldman. Quarterly. Society for Humanistic Judaism. (WWW.SHJ.ORG)

WASHTENAW JEWISH NEWS (1978). 2935 Birch Hollow Dr., Ann Arbor, 48108. (734)971-1800. FAX: (734)971-1801. E-mail: wjna2@aol.com. Susan Kravitz Ayer. Monthly. (WWW.HVCN.ORG)

MINNESOTA

AMERICAN JEWISH WORLD (1912). 4509 Minnetonka Blvd., Minneapolis, MN 55416. (952)259-5280. FAX: (952)920-6205. E-mail: ajw@bcmn.com. Mordecai Specktor. Weekly.

MISSISSIPPI

DEEP SOUTH JEWISH VOICE (*see* Alabama)

MISSOURI

JEWISH CURRENT EVENTS (1958). P.O. Box 16683, St. Louis, 63105. (314-482-3869. E-mail: lraileanu@jewishcurrentevents.com. Michael S. Raileanu. Semi-monthly, Oct.–May. (WWW.JEWISHCURRENTEVENTS.COM)

KANSAS CITY JEWISH CHRONICLE. *See under* KANSAS

ST. LOUIS JEWISH LIGHT (1947; reorg. 1963). 12 Millstone Campus Dr., St. Louis, 63146. (314)743-3600. FAX: (314)432-0515. E-mail: dbaugher@thejewishlight.com. David Baugher. Weekly. (WWW.STLJEWISHLIGHT.COM)

NEBRASKA

JEWISH PRESS (1920). 333 S. 132 St., Omaha, 68154. (402)334-6450. FAX: (402)334-5422. E-mail: ckatzman@jewishomaha.org. Carol Katzman. Weekly. Jewish Federation of Omaha.

NEVADA

JEWISH REPORTER (1976). 3909 S. Maryland Pkwy., Suite 400, Las Vegas, 89119-7520. (702)948-5129. FAX: (702)967-1082. E-mail: editor@jewishlasvegas.com. Leah Brown. Bimonthly. Jewish Federation of Las Vegas.

LAS VEGAS ISRAELITE (1965). PO Box 14096, Las Vegas, 89114. (702)876-1255. FAX: (702)364-1009. Michael Tell. Bimonthly.

NEW JERSEY

AVOTAYNU (1985). 155 N. Washington Ave., Bergenfield, 07621. (201)387-7200. FAX: (201)387-2855. E-mail: info@avotaynu.com. Sallyann Amdur Sack. Quarterly.

JEWISH CHRONICLE (1982). 1063 East Landis Ave.,Suite B, Vineland, 08360. (856)696-4445. FAX: (856)696-3428. E-mail: kirkw@jfedcc.com. Kirk Weissmeyer. Bimonthly. The Jewish Federation of Cumberland County.

JEWISH COMMUNITY NEWS & JEWISH STANDARD (1931). 1086 Teaneck Rd., Teaneck, 07666. (201) 837-8818. FAX: (201) 833-4959. E-mail: pr@jewishmediagroup.com. Rebecca Kaplan Boroson. Weekly. Jewish Federation of North Jersey and Jewish Federation of Greater Clifton-Passaic.

JEWISH COMMUNITY VOICE (1941). 1301 Springdale Rd., Suite 250, Cherry Hill, 08003-2762. (856)751-9500, ext. 248.

FAX: (856)489-8253. E-mail: bkessler@jfedsnj.org. Harriet Kessler. Biweekly. Jewish Federation of Southern NJ.

JEWISH JOURNAL (OCEAN COUNTY) (1999). 320 Raritan Ave., Suite 203, Highland Park, 08904. (732)393-0023. FAX: (732)393-0026. E-mail: jewish@castle.net. Ron Ostroff. Monthly. Published in cooperation with the Jewish Federation of Ocean County.

JEWISH STAR (1985). 230 Old Bridge Turnpike, South River, 08882-2000. (732)432-7711. FAX: (732)432-0292. E-mail: mfertig@thejewishstar.com. Mayer Fertig. Fortnightly. Jewish Federation of Greater Middlesex County.

JEWISH VOICE & OPINION (1987). 73 Dana Place, Englewood, 07631. (201) 569-2845. FAX: (201)569-1739. Susan L. Rosenbluth. Monthly.

JOURNAL OF JEWISH COMMUNAL SERVICE (1899). 3084 State Hwy. 27, Suite 9, Kendall Pk., 08824-1657. (732)821-1871. FAX: (732)821-5335. E-mail: jcsana@aol.com. Gail Naron Chalew. Quarterly. Jewish Communal Service Association of North America.

NEW JERSEY JEWISH NEWS (1947). 901 Route 10, Whippany, 07981-1157. (973)929-3137. FAX: (973)887-5999. E-mail: mleitzes@njjewishnews.com. Andrew Silow-Carroll. Weekly. United Jewish Federation of MetroWest. (WWW.NJJEWISHNEWS.COM)

SPEAKER (1999). 320 Raritan Ave., Suite 203, Highland Park, 08904. (732)393-0023. FAX: (732)393-0026. E-mail: jewish@castle.net. Ron Ostroff. Monthly. Published in cooperation with the Jewish Federation of Somerset, Hunterdon & Warren Counties.

NEW MEXICO

NEW MEXICO JEWISH LINK (1971). 5520 Wyoming NE, Albuquerque, 87109. (502)821-3214. FAX: (505)821-3351. E-mail: susan@jewishnewmexico.org. Susan Abonyi. Monthly. Jewish Federation of Greater Albuquerque.

NEW YORK

AFN SHVEL (1941). 200 W. 72 St., Suite 40, NYC, 10023. (212)787-6675. E-mail: yid league@aol.com. Quarterly. Yiddish. League for Yiddish, Inc. (WWW.LEAGUEFORYIDDISH.COM)

AGENDA: JEWISH EDUCATION (1949; formerly PEDAGOGIC REPORTER). JESNA, 111 Eighth Ave., Suite 11E, NYC, 10011-5201. (212)284-6950. FAX: (212)284-6951. E-mail: info@jesna.org. Amy Stein. Twice a year. Jewish Education Service of North America, Inc.

ALGEMEINER JOURNAL (1972). 225 E. Broadway, NYC, 10002. (212)267-5561. FAX: (212)267-5624. E-mail: Algemeiner@aol.com. Yosef Y. Jacobson. Weekly. Yiddish-English. (WWW.ALGEMEINER.COM)

AMERICAN JEWISH YEAR BOOK (1899). 165 E. 56 St., NYC, 10022. (212)751-4000. FAX: (212)751-4017. E-mail: research@ajc.org. David Singer, Lawrence Grossman. Annually. American Jewish Committee.

AMIT (1925). 817 Broadway, NYC, 10003. (212)477-4720. FAX: (212)477-5213. E-mail: amitmag@amitchildren.org. Charlotte Schneierson. Quarterly. AMIT (formerly American Mizrachi Women). (WWW.AMITCHILDREN.ORG)

AUFBAU (1934). 2121 Broadway, NYC, 10023. (212)873-7400. Voice mail: (212) 579-6578. FAX: (212)496-5736. E-mail: aufbau2000@aol.com. Monika Ziegler/ Andreas Mink/Irene Armbruster. Fortnightly. German-English. New World Club, Inc.

BUFFALO JEWISH REVIEW (1918). 15 E. Mohawk St., Buffalo, 14203. (716)854-2192. FAX: (716)854-2198. E-mail: buffjewrev@aol.com. Rita Weiss. Weekly. Kahaal Nahalot Israel. (WWW.BUFFALOJEWISHREVIEW.ORG)

CALL (1933). 45 E. 33 St., NYC, 10016. (212)889-6800, ext. 225. FAX: (212)532-7518. E-mail: socolove@circle.org. Emily Socolov. Three times a year. The Workmen's Circle/Arbeter Ring.

CCAR JOURNAL: A REFORM JEWISH QUARTERLY (formerly JOURNAL OF REFORM JUDAISM) (1953). 355 Lexington Ave., NYC, 10017. (212)972-3636. FAX: (212)692-0819. Ed. Stephen Pearce. Mng. Ed. Elliot Stevens. Quarterly. Central Conference of American Rabbis. (WWW.CCARNET.ORG)

CIRCLE (1943). 15 E. 26 St., NYC, 10010-1579. (212)532-4949. FAX: (212)481-4174. E-mail: info@jcca.org. Miriam Rinn. JCC Circle Quarterly. Jewish Community Centers Association of North America (formerly JWB).

COMMENTARY (1945). 165 E. 56 St., NYC, 10022. (212)751-4000. FAX: (212)891-6700. E-mail: mail@commentary-magazine.com. Ed. Neal Kozodoy; Ed.-at-Large Norman Podhoretz. Monthly.

CONGRESS MONTHLY (1933). 825 Third Ave., Ste. 1800, NYC, 10022. (212)879-4500. Rochelle Mancini. Six times a year. American Jewish Congress.

CONSERVATIVE JUDAISM (1945). 3080 Broadway, NYC, 10027. (212)280-6065. FAX: (212)749-9166. E-mail: rapubs@jtsa.edu. Rabbi Martin S. Cohen. Quarterly. Rabbinical Assembly and Jewish Theological Seminary of America.

FORVERTS (Yiddish Forward) (1897). 45 E. 33 St., NYC, 10016. (212)889-8200. FAX: (212)684-3949. Boris Sandler. Weekly. Yiddish. Forward Association, Inc. (WWW.YIDDISH.FOWARD.COM)

FORWARD (1897). 45 E. 33 St., NYC, 10016. (212)889-8200. FAX: (212)447-6406. E-mail: newsdesk@forward.com. Jane Eisner. Weekly. Forward Newspaper, L.L.C.

HADAROM (1957). 305 Seventh Ave., NYC, 10001. (212)807-7888. FAX: (212)727-8452. Rabbi Gedalia Dov Schwartz. Annual. Hebrew. Rabbinical Council of America

HADASSAH MAGAZINE (1914). 50 W. 58 St., NYC, 10019. (212)688-0227. FAX: (212) 446-9521. Alan M. Tigay. Monthly (except for combined issues of June-July and Aug.-Sept.). Hadassah, the Women's Zionist Organization of America.

HEEB MAGAZINE (2002). P.O. Box 687, NYC, 10012. E-mail: info@heeb-magazine.com. Joshua Neuman. Quarterly. (WWW.HEEBMAGAZINE.COM)

I.A.J.E. NEWSLETTER (1999). (718)339-0337. E-mail: sanuav@stjohns.edu. Victor D. Sanua. International Association of Jews from Egypt.

JBI VOICE (1978). 110 E. 30 St., NYC, 10016. (212)889-2525, (800)433-1531, FAX (212) 689-3692. Email: dbarbara@jbilibrary.org. Dena Barbara. Ten times a year in U.S. (audiocassettes). English. Jewish Braille Institute of America. (WWW.JEWISH-BRAILE.ORG)

JEWISH ACTION (1950). 11 Broadway, NYC, 10004. (212)613-8146. FAX: (212)613-0646. E-mail: ja@ou.org. Nechama Carmel. Quarterly. Orthodox Union. (OU.ORG/JEWISH_ACTION)

JEWISH BOOK ANNUAL (1942). 15 E. 26 St., 10th fl., New York, NY 10010. (212)532-4949, ext. 297. E-mail: jbc@jewish-books.org. Dr. Stephen H. Garrin. Hebrew & English with bibliography in Yiddish. Jewish Book Council, Jewish Book Annual published by Jewish Book Council.

JEWISH BOOK WORLD (1945). 15 E. 26 St., NYC, 10010. (212)532-4949, ext. 297. FAX: (212)481-4174. E-mail: jbc@jewishbooks.org. Esther Nussbaum. Three times annually. Jewish Book Council.

JEWISH BRAILLE REVIEW (1931). 110 E. 30 St., NYC, 10016. E-mail:dbarbara@jbilibrary.org. (212)889-2525, (800)433-1531. Dena Barbara. 10 times a year in U.S. (braille). English. Jewish Braille Institute of America.

JEWISH CURRENTS (1946) 45 East 33rd Street, 4th floor, NYC, 10016. (212)924-5740. FAX: (212)414-2227. Bimonthly. Association for Promotion of Jewish Secularism, Inc. (WWW.JEWISHCURRENTS.ORG)

JEWISH EDUCATION NEWS (1980). 261 W. 35 St., Fl. 12A, NYC 10001. (212) 268-4210. FAX: (212)268-4214. E-mail: publications@caje.org. Mng. Ed. Judi Resnick. Triannually. Coalition for the Advancement of Jewish Education.

JEWISH FRONTIER (1934). P.O. Box 4013, Amity Station, New Haven, CT 06525. (203)397-4903. FAX: (212)675-7685. E-mail: jewish-frontier@yahoo.com. Nahum Guttman-Graff. Bimonthly. Labor Zionist Letters, Inc. Managing Editor Bennett Lovett-Graff

JEWISH HERALD (1984). 1689 46 St., Brooklyn, NY 11204. (718)972-4000. E-mail: jewishherald@aol.com. Leon J. Sternheim. Weekly.

JEWISH JOURNAL (1969). 11 Sunrise Plaza, Valley Stream, 11580. (516)561-6900. FAX: (516)561-6971. Paul Rubens. Weekly.

JEWISH OBSERVER (1963). 42 Broadway, NYC, 10004. (212)797-9000. FAX: (646)254-1600. E-mail: nwolpin@aol.com. Rabbi Nisson Wolpin. Monthly (except July and Aug.). Agudath Israel of America. (WWW.SHEMAYISRAEL.COM/JEWISHOBSERVER)

JEWISH OBSERVER OF CENTRAL NEW YORK (1978). 5655 Thompson Road, DeWitt, NY 13214. (315)445-2040 ext. 116. FAX: (315)445-1559. E-mail: jocny@aol.com. Bette Siegel. Biweekly. Syracuse Jewish Federation, Inc.

JEWISH POST OF NY (1993). 262 West 38th St., NYC, 10018. (212)398-1313. FAX: (212)398-3933. E-mail: jpost@nais.com. Ed. Gad Nahshon. Monthly. Link Marketing & Promotion, Inc.

JEWISH PRESS (1950). 338 Third Ave., Brooklyn, 11215. (718)330-1100. FAX: (718)935-1215. E-mail: editor@jewishpress.com. Jerry Greenwald. Weekly. (WWW.THEJEWISHPRESS.COM)

JEWISH TELEGRAPHIC AGENCY (1962). 330 Seventh Ave., 11th fl., NYC, 10001-5010. (212)643-1890. FAX: (212)643-8498. Email: www.jta.org/info@jta.org. Ami Eden. Daily.

JEWISH TRIBUNE. PMB #372, 169 South Main St., New City, 10956; Exec. off. (mailing address): 115 Middle Neck Rd., Great Neck, 11021. (845)352-5151. FAX: (516)829-4776. E-mail: lijeworld@aol .com. Jerome W. Lippman. Weekly. Jewish Tribune; Long Island Jewish World; Manhattan Jewish Sentinel.

JEWISH WEEK (1876; reorg. 1970). 1501 Broadway, NYC, 10036-5503. (212)921-7822. FAX: (212)921-8420. E-mail: editor@jewishweek.org. Gary Rosenblatt. Weekly. (WWW.THEJEWISHWEEK.COM)

JEWISH WORLD (1965). 3 Vatrano Road, Albany, 12205. (518)459-8455. FAX: (518) 459-5289. E-mail: news@jewishworldnews.org. Sam S. Clevenson. Weekly.

JOURNAL OF JEWISH EDUCATION-CJE (formerly JEWISH EDUCATION) (1929). 11 Olympia Lane, Monsey, NY 10952. (845)368-8657. FAX: (845)369-6538. E-mail: mjscje@aol.com. Rabbi Irwin E. Witty. Three times a year. Council for Jewish Education.

JOURNAL OF REFORM JUDAISM. *See* CCAR Journal

JTS PUBLICATIONS (1991). 3080 Broadway, NYC 10027. (212)678-8950. FAX: (212)864-0109. E-mail: jowerner@jtsa .edu. Three times a year. The Jewish Theological Seminary. Asst. Dir. of Pub. Jodi Werner.

JUDAISM (1952). 825 Third Ave., Ste. 1800, NYC, 10022. (212)360-1500. FAX: (212)249-3672. E-mail: judaism@ajcongress.org. Shammai Engelmayer. Quarterly. American Jewish Congress.

KASHRUS MONTHLY-YOUR UPDATE ON KOSHER (1990). PO Box 204, Brooklyn, 11204. (718)336-8544. Rabbi Yosef Wikler. Monthly. Kashrus Institute. (EDITORIAL@KASHRUSMAGAZIN.COM)

KASHRUS MAGAZINE-THE PERIODICAL FOR THE KOSHER CONSUMER (1980). PO Box 204, Brooklyn, 11204. (718)336-8544. E-mail: editorial@kashrusmagazine.com. Rabbi Yosef Wikler. Five times per year (January, March, May, July, October). Kashrus Institute. (WWW.KASHRUSMAGAZINE.COM)

KOL HAT'NUA (Voice of the Movement) (1975). c/o Young Judaea, 50 W. 58 St., NYC, 10019. (212)303-4576. FAX: (212)303-4572. E-mail: info@youngjudaea.org. Dov Wilker. Quarterly. Hadassah Zionist Youth Commission-Young Judaea.

KULTUR UN LEBN-CULTURE AND LIFE (1960). 45 E. 33 St., NYC, 10016. (212) 889-6800. FAX: (212)532-7518. E-mail: wcfriends@aol.com. Joseph Mlotek. Quarterly. Yiddish. The Workmen's Circle.

LIKUTIM (1981). 110 E. 30 St., NYC, 10016. (212)889-2525. Joanne Jahr. Two times a year in Israel (print and audiocassettes). Hebrew. Jewish Braille Institute of America.

LILITH-THE INDEPENDENT JEWISH WOMEN'S MAGAZINE (1976). 250 W. 57 St., #2432, NYC, 10107. (212)757-0818. FAX: (212)757-5705. E-mail: info@lilith.org. Susan Weidman Schneider. Quarterly. (WWW.LILITH.ORG)

LONG ISLAND JEWISH WORLD (1971). 115 Middle Neck Rd., Great Neck, 11021. (516)829-4000. FAX: (516)829-4776. E-mail: lijeworld@aol.com. Jerome W. Lippman. Weekly.

MANHATTAN JEWISH SENTINEL (1993). 115 Middle Neck Rd., Great Neck, 11021. (212)244-4949. FAX: (212)244-2257. E-mail: lijeworld@aol.com. Jerome W. Lippman. Weekly.

MARTYRDOM AND RESISTANCE (1974). 500 Fifth Ave., 42nd Floor, NYC, 10110-4299. (212)220-4304. FAX:(212)220-4308. E-mail: yadvashem@aol.com. Ed. Dr. Harvey Rosenfeld; Ed.-in-Chief Eli Zborowski. Bimonthly. International Society for Yad Vashem.

MEOROT (2007, formerly EDAH JOURNAL). 475 Riverside Dr., Ste. 244, NYC, 10115. (212)666-0036. FAX: (212)666-5633. E-mail: meorotjournal@yctorah.org. Dr. Eugene Korn. Semiannual. Yeshivat Chovevei Torah.

MIDSTREAM (1954). 633 Third Ave., 21st fl., NYC, 10017. (212)339-6020. FAX: (212)318-6176. E-mail: midstreamthf@aol.com. Leo Haber. Eight times a year. Theodor Herzl Foundation, Inc. (WWW.MIDSTREAMTHF.COM)

NA'AMAT WOMAN (1925). 350 Fifth Ave., Suite 4700, NYC, 10118-4799. (212)563-5222. FAX: (212)563-5710. Judith A. Sokoloff. Quarterly. English-Yiddish-Hebrew. NA'AMAT USA, the Women's Labor Zionist Organization of America.

NEW VOICES MAGAZINE (1991). 114 W. 26 St., #1004, NYC 10001. (212)674-1168. FAX: (212)929-33459. E-mail: editor@newvoices.org. Ilana Sichel. Five times per academic year. Jewish Student Press Service. (WWW.NEWVOICES.ORG)

OLOMEINU-OURWORLD (1945). 5723 18th Ave., Brooklyn, 11204. (718)259-1223. FAX: (718)259-1795. Email: mail@tupublications.com. Rabbi Yaakov Fruchter. Monthly. English-Hebrew. Torah Umesorah-National Society for Hebrew Day Schools.

PASSOVER DIRECTORY (1923). 11 Broadway, NYC, 10004. (212)613-8135. FAX: (212)613-0772. Email: lieberd@ou.org Deborah Lieber. Annually. Union of Orthodox Jewish Congregations of America.

PRESENTENSE MAGAZINE (2006). 214 Sullivan St., Ste. 2A, NYC, 10012. E-mail: editor@presentensemagazine.org. Ariel Beery. Semiannual. Independently published by volunteer-based grassroots network.

REFORM JUDAISM (1972; formerly DIMENSIONS IN AMERICAN JUDAISM). 633 Third Ave., 6th fl., NYC, 10017. (212)650-4240. Aron Hirt-Manheimer. Quarterly. Union for Reform Judaism. (URJ.ORG/RJMAG)

REPORTER (1971). 500 Clubhouse Rd., Vestal, 13850. (607)724-2360. FAX: (607)724-2311. E-mail: TReporter@aol.com. Judith S. Huober. Weekly. Jewish Federation of Broome County, Inc.

REPORTER (1966). 315 Park Ave. S., NYC 10010. (212)505-7700. FAX: (212) 674-3057. E-mail; editor@waort.org. Marlene A. Heller. Semi-Annual. Women's American ORT, Inc.

RESPONSE: A CONTEMPORARY JEWISH REVIEW (1967). Columbia University Post Office, PO Box 250892, NYC, 10025. E-mail: response@panix.com. Chanita Baumhaft. Annual.

RUSSIAN FORWARD (1995). 45 E. 33 St., NYC, 10016. (212)889-8200. FAX: (212)448-9124. E-mail: rforward99@yahoo.com. Leonid Shkolnik. Weekly. Russian.

SOJOURN: THE JEWISH AMERICAN SAGA (2006). 80 Broad St., NYC 10004. (800)325-8152. E-mail: rkaplan@SojournSaga.com. Robert Kaplan. Bimonthly.

SYNAGOGUE LIGHT AND KOSHER LIFE (1933). 47 Beekman St., NYC, 10038. (212)227-7800. Rabbi Meyer Hager. Quarterly. The Kosher Food Institute.

TORAH U-MADDAH JOURNAL (1989). Att. Dr. David Shatz, 245 Lexington Ave., NYC 10016. (917)326-4856. FAX: (212)340-7788. E-mail: shatz@yu.edu. Dr. David Shatz. Annual. Center for the Jewish Future, Yeshiva University.

TRADITION (1958). 305 Seventh Ave., NYC, 10001. (212)807-7888. FAX: (212)727-8452. Rabbi Shalom Carmy. Quarterly. Rabbinical Council of America.

UNITED SYNAGOGUE REVIEW (1943). 155 Fifth Ave., NYC, 10010. (212)533-7800. FAX: (212)353-9439. E-mail: info@uscj.org. Lois Goldrich. Semiannually. United Synagogue of Conservative Judaism.

UNSER TSAIT (1941). 25 E. 21 St., 3rd fl., NYC, 10010. (212)475-0059. Bimonthly. Yiddish. Jewish Labor Bund.

VIEWPOINT MAGAZINE (1952). 3 W. 16 St., NYC, 10011. (212)929-1525, ext. 131. E-mail: ncyi@youngisrael.org. Esther Altman. Quarterly. National Council of Young Israel.

VOICE OF THE DUTCHESS JEWISH COMMUNITY (1989). 110 Grand Ave., Poughkeepsie, 12603. (845)471-9811. FAX: (845)471-3233. E-mail: director@jewishdutchess.org. Business off.:500 Clubhouse

Rd., Vestal, 13850. (607)724-2360. FAX: (607)724-2311. Sandy Gardner and Judith Huober. Monthly. Jewish Federation of Dutchess County, Inc.

WOMEN'S LEAGUE OUTLOOK MAGAZINE (1930475 475 Riverside Drive, Suite 820, New York, 10115. (212)870-1260. FAX: (212)870-1261. E-mail: rkahn@wlcj.org. Janet Arnowitz. Quarterly. Women's League for Conservative Judaism. (WWW.WLCJ.ORG)

WORKMEN'S CIRCLE CALL. *See* Call

WYOMING VALLEY JEWISH REPORTER (formerly WE ARE ONE) (1995). 500 Clubhouse Rd., Vestal, 13850. (607)724-2360. FAX: (607)724-2311. E-mail: wbreport@aol.com. Gail Wachtel. Every other week. Wilkes-Barre Jewish Community Board.

YEARBOOK OF THE CENTRAL CONFERENCE OF AMERICAN RABBIS (1890). 355 Lexington Ave., NYC, 10017. (212)972-3636. FAX: (212)692-0819. Rabbi Elliot L. Stevens. Annually. Central Conference of American Rabbis.

YIDDISH (1973). Queens College, NSF 350, 65-30 Kissena Blvd., Flushing, 11367. (718)997-3622. Joseph C. Landis. Quarterly. Queens College Press.

DI YIDDISHE HEIM (1958). 770 Eastern Pkwy., Brooklyn, 11213. (718)735-0458. Rachel Altein, Tema Gurary. Twice a year. English-Yiddish. Neshei Ub'nos Chabad-Lubavitch Women's Organization.

DOS YIDDISHE VORT (1953). 84 William St., NYC, 10038. (212)797-9000. Joseph Friedenson. Bimonthly, (November-December monthly). Yiddish. Agudath Israel of America.

YIDISHE SHPRAKH (1941). 15 W. 16 St., NYC, 10011. (212)246-6080, ext. 6139. FAX: (212) 292-1892. Irregularly. Yiddish. YIVO Institute for Jewish Research.

YIVO BLETER (1931). 15 W. 16 St., NYC, 10011. (212)246-6080. FAX: (212)292-1892.E-mail: yivomail@yivo.cjh.org. Dr. David E. Fishman. Biannually. Yiddish. YIVO Institute for Jewish Research.

YOUNG JUDAEAN (1909). 50 W. 58 St., NYC, 10019. (212)303-4588. FAX: (212)303-4572. Email: ugoldflam@young judaea.org. Uri Goldflam. Quarterly. Young Judaea Zionist Youth Movement/Hadassah.

YUGNTRUF: YIDDISH YOUTH MAGAZINE (1964). 200 W. 72 St., Suite 40, NYC, 10023. (212)787-6675. FAX: (212)799-1517. E-mail: yugntruf@yugntruf.org. Elinor Robinson. Two to four times a year. Yiddish. Yugntruf Youth for Yiddish.

ZUKUNFT (The Future) (1892). 25 E. 21 St., NYC, 10010. (212)505-8040. FAX: (212)505-8044. Chaim Beider & Yonia Fain. Quarterly. Yiddish. Congress for Jewish Culture.

NORTH CAROLINA

CHARLOTTE JEWISH NEWS (1978). 5007 Providence Rd., Charlotte, 28226. (704)944-6765. FAX: (704) 365-4507. E-mail: amontoni@shalomcharlotte.org. Amy Montoni. Monthly (except July). Jewish Federation of Greater Charlotte.

JEWISH FEDERATION NEWS (1986). 8210 Creedmoor Rd., Suite 104, Raleigh, 27613. (919)676-2200. FAX: (919)676-2122. E-mail: beth.nathison@rcjf.org. Beth Nathison. Monthly. Wake County Jewish Federation.

MODERN JUDAISM (1980). Oxford University Press, 2001 Evans Rd., Cary, 27513. (919)677-0977. FAX: (919)677-1714. E-mail: jnlorders@oup-usa.org. (Editorial address: Center for Judaic Studies, Boston University, 745 Commonwealth Ave., Boston, 02215. (617)353-8096. FAX: (617)353-5441.) Steven T. Katz. Three times a year.

OHIO

AKRON JEWISH NEWS (1929). 750 White Pond Drive, Akron, 44320. (330)835-0013, Ext. 313. FAX: (330)867-8498. E-mail: lisahoffman@jewishakron.org. Lisa Hoffman. Fortnightly. Fifteen times a year. Jewish Community Board of Akron. (WWW.AKRONJEWISHNEWS.COM)

AMERICAN ISRAELITE (1854). 18 W. 9th St., Ste. 2, Cincinnati, 45202-1371. (513)621-3145. FAX: (513)621-3744. E-mail: aiarticles@fuse.net. Netanel Deutsch. Weekly. (WWW.AMERICANISRAELITE.COM)

AMERICAN JEWISH ARCHIVES JOURNAL (1948). 3101 Clifton Ave., Cincinnati, 45220-2488. (513)221-1875. FAX: (513) 221-7812. E-mail: aja@cn.huc.edu. Ed. Dr. Gary P. Zola; Mng. Ed. Dr. Frederic

Krome. Twice a year. Jacob Rader Marcus Center, American Jewish Archives, HUC-JIR. (WWW.AMERICANJEWISHARCHIVES.ORG)

CLEVELAND JEWISH NEWS (1964). 23880 Commerce Park, Ste. 1, Cleveland, 44122. (216)991-8300. FAX: (216)991-8200. E-mail: editorial@cjn.org. Cynthia Dettelbach. Weekly. Cleveland Jewish News Publication Co. (WWW.CLEVELANDJEWISHNEWS.COM)

INDEX TO JEWISH PERIODICALS (1963). PO Box 18525, Cleveland Hts., 44118. (216)381-4846. FAX: (216)381-4321. E-mail: index@jewishperiodicals.com. Lenore Pfeffer Koppel. Annually. Available in book and CD-ROM form. (WWW.JEWISHPERIODICALS.COM)

JEWISH JOURNAL (1987). 505 Gypsy Lane, Youngstown, 44504-1314. (330)744-7902. FAX: (330)746-7926. Email: yojjournal@aol.com Sherry Weinblatt. Biweekly (except July/Aug.). Youngstown Area Jewish Federation. (WWW.JEWISHJOURNALPLUS.COM)

OHIO JEWISH CHRONICLE (1922). 2862 Johnstown Rd., Columbus, 43219. (614) 337-2055. FAX: (614)337-2059. E-mail: ojc@insight.rr.com. Kris Galloway. Weekly.

STARK JEWISH NEWS (1920). 2631 Harvard Ave. NW, Canton, 44709. (330)452-6444. FAX: (330)452-4487. E-mail: starkjewishnews@aol.com. Karen Phillippi. Monthly. Canton Jewish Community Federation. (WWW.JEWISHCANTON.ORG)

STUDIES IN BIBLIOGRAPHY AND BOOKLORE (1953). 3101 Clifton Ave., Cincinnati, 45220. (513)221-1875. FAX: (513)221-0519. E-mail: lwolfson@huc.edu. Editor David J. Gilner; Managing Editor Laurel S. Wolfson. Irregularly. English-Hebrew-etc. Library of Hebrew Union College-Jewish Institute of Religion.

TOLEDO JEWISH NEWS (1951). 6505 Sylvania Ave., Sylvania, 43560. (419)724-0363. FAX: (419)724-0423. E-mail: sharon@jewishtoledo.org. Laurie Cohen. Monthly. United Jewish Council of Greater Toledo.

OKLAHOMA

TULSA JEWISH REVIEW (1930). 2021 E. 71 St., Tulsa, 74136. (918)495-1100. FAX: (918)495-1220. Ed Ulrich. Monthly. Jewish Federation of Tulsa. (WWW.JEWISHTULSA.ORG)

OREGON

JEWISH REVIEW (1959). 6680 SW Capitol Highway, Portland, OR 97219. Edit.: (503) 245-4340. FAX: (503) 245-4342. Adv.: (503) 546-9883. FAX: (503) 620-3433. E-mail: news@jewishreview.org. Paul Haist. Regular column in Russian. Fortnightly. Jewish Federation of Portland. (WWW.JEWISHREVIEW.ORG)

PENNSYLVANIA

COMMUNITY REVIEW (1925). 3301 N. Front St. Annex, Harrisburg, 17110. (717)236-9555, ext.3402. FAX:(717)236-2552. E-mail: localnews@jewishfedhbg.org. Carol L. Cohen. Fortnightly. United Jewish Community of Greater Harrisburg.

CONTEMPORARY JEWRY (1974, under the name JEWISH SOCIOLOGY AND SOCIAL RESEARCH). Graduate Center CUNY, Room 6112-13, 365 Fifth Avenue, New York, NY 10016. (212) 817-8772. FAX: (914) 235-6717. E-mail: heilman@qc.edu. Samuel C. Heilman. Annually. Association for the Social Scientific Study of Jewry.

JERUSALEM LETTER/VIEWPOINTS (1978). 1515 Locust St., Suite 703, Philadelphia, 19102. (215)772-0564. FAX: (215)772-0566. Zvi R. Marom. Fortnightly. Jerusalem Center for Public Affairs.

JEWISH CHRONICLE OF PITTSBURGH (1962). 5600 Baum Blvd., Pittsburgh, 15206. (412)687-1000. FAX:(412)687-5119. E-mail: lchottiner@pittchron.com. Lee Chottiner. Weekly. Pittsburgh Jewish Publication and Education Foundation.

JEWISH EXPONENT (1887). 2100 Arch St., Philadelphia, 19103. (215)832-0740. FAX: (215)569-3389. E-mail: csmilk@jewishexponent.com. Jonathan Tobin. Weekly. Jewish Federation of Greater Philadelphia. (WWW.JEWISHEXPONENT.COM)

JEWISH POLITICAL STUDIES REVIEW (1989). 1515 Locust St., Suite 703, Philadelphia, 19102. (215)772-0564. FAX: (215)772-0566. Mark Ami-El. Twice a year. Jerusalem Center for Public Affairs.

JEWISH QUARTERLY REVIEW (1910). 420 Walnut St., Philadelphia, 19106. (215)238-1290. FAX: (215)238-1540. E-mail: jqroffice@sas.upenn.edu. Ed. David M. Goldenberg; Mng. Ed. Bonnie L. Blankenship. Quarterly. Center for Advanced Jewish Studies, University of Pennsylvania.

NEW MENORAH (1978). 7318 Germantown Ave., Philadelphia, 19119-1793. (215)247-9700. FAX: (215)247-9703. Rabbi Arthur Waskow, PhD. Quarterly. Aleph: Alliance for Jewish Renewal.

RECONSTRUCTIONISM TODAY (1993). Beit Devora, 7804 Montgomery Ave., Suite 9, Elkins Park, 19027-2649. (215)782-8500. FAX: (215)782-8805. E-mail: jrfnatl@aol.com. Lisa Kelvin Tuttle. Quarterly. Jewish Reconstructionist Federation.

RECONSTRUCTIONIST (1935). 1299 Church Rd., Wyncote, 19095-1898. (215) 576-5210. FAX: (215)576-8051. E-mail: rhirsh@therra.org. Rabbi Richard Hirsh. Semiannually. Reconstructionist Rabbinical College.

RHODE ISLAND

JEWISH VOICE AND HERALD (under the name JEWISH VOICE OF RHODE ISLAND 1973). 130 Sessions St., Providence, 02906. (401)421-4111. FAX: (401)331-7961. E-mail: jrubin@jfri.org. Jonathan Rubin. Bi-weekly. Jewish Federation of Rhode Island. (WWW.JFRI.ORG)

RHODE ISLAND JEWISH HERALD (1930). 99 Webster St., Pawtucket, 02860. (401)724-0200. FAX: (401)726-5820. Luke O'Neill. Weekly. Herald Press Publishing Company.

RHODE ISLAND JEWISH HISTORICAL NOTES (1951). 130 Sessions St., Providence, 02906. (401)331-1360. FAX: (401)272-6729. E-mail: rjhist@aol.com. Leonard Moss. Annually. Rhode Island Jewish Historical Association.

SOUTH CAROLINA

CHARLESTON JEWISH VOICE (2001). 1645 Wallenberg Blvd., Charleston, 29407. (843)571-6565. FAX: (843)556-6206. E-mail: robyncohen@comcast.net. Robyn Cohen. Monthly. Charleston Jewish Federation.

TENNESSEE

HEBREW WATCHMAN (1925). 4646 Poplar Ave., Suite 232, Memphis, 38117. (901)763-2215. FAX: (901)763-2216. E-mail: hebwat@bellsouth.net. Herman I. Goldberger. Weekly.

OBSERVER (1934). 801 Percy Warner Blvd., Suite 102, Nashville, 37205. (615)354-1637. FAX: (615)352-0056. E-mail: judy@jewishnashville.org. Judith A. Saks. Biweekly (except July). Jewish Federation of Nashville. (WWW.NASHVILLE.UJCFEDWEB.ORG)

SHOFAR. PO Box 8947, Chattanooga, 37414. (423)493-0270, Ext. 12. FAX: (423) 493-9997. E-mail: shofar@jcfgc.com. Rachel Schulson. Ten times a year. Jewish Federation of Greater Chattanooga.

TEXAS

JEWISH HERALD-VOICE (1908). P.O. Box 153, Houston, 77001-0153. (713)630-0391. FAX: (713)630-0404. E-mail: editor@jhvonline.net. Jeanne Samuels. Weekly. Four special issues: Rosh Hashanah; Passover; Wedding Planner; Bar/Bat Mitzvah Planner. (WWW.JHVONLINE.COM)

JEWISH JOURNAL OF SAN ANTONIO (1973). 8434 Ahern, San Antonio, 78213. (210)828-9511. FAX: (210)342-8098. Barbara Richmond. Monthly (11 issues). Jewish Federation of San Antonio.

VIRGINIA

RENEWAL MAGAZINE (1984). 5041 Corporate Woods Drive, Suite 150, Virginia Beach, 23462. (757)671-1600. FAX: (757)671-7613. E-mail: news@ujft.org. Reba Karp. Quarterly. United Jewish Federation of Tidewater.

SOUTHEASTERN VIRGINIA JEWISH NEWS (1959). 5000 Corporate Woods Drive, Suite 200, Virginia Beach, 23462. (757)671-1600. FAX: (757)671-7613. E-mail: news@ujft.org. Terri Denison. 22 issues yearly. United Jewish Federation of Tidewater. (WWW.JEWISHVA.ORG)

WASHINGTON

JEWISH TRANSCRIPT (1924). 2041 Third Ave., Seattle, 98121. (206)441-4553. FAX: (206)441-2736. E-mail: editor@jtnews.net. Joel Magalnick. Fortnightly. Jewish Federation of Greater Seattle. (WWW.JTNEWS.NET)

WISCONSIN

WISCONSIN JEWISH CHRONICLE (1921). 1360 N. Prospect Ave., Milwaukee, 53202. (414)390-5888. FAX: (414)271-0487. E-mail: elana@milwaukeejewish.org. Elana Kahn-Oren. Weekly. Milwaukee Jewish Federation. (WWW.JEWISHCHRONICLE.ORG)

INDEXES

INDEX TO JEWISH PERIODICALS (1963). PO Box 22780, Beachwood, OH 44122.

(216)921-5566. FAX: (603)806-0575. E-mail: index@jewishperiodicals.com. Lenore Pfeffer Koppel. Annually. Available in book and CD-ROM form. (WWW.JEWISHPERIODICALS.COM)

NEWS SYNDICATES

JEWISH TELEGRAPHIC AGENCY, INC. (1917). 330 Seventh Ave., 17th fl., NYC., 10001-5010. (212)643-1890. FAX: (212)643-8498. Ami Eden. Daily.

CANADA

CANADIAN JEWISH HERALD (1977). 17 Anselme Lavigne, Dollard des Ormeaux, PQ H9A 1N3. (514)684-7667. FAX: (514) 684-7667. Ed./Pub. Dan Nimrod. Irregularly. Dawn Publishing Co., Ltd.

CANADIAN JEWISH NEWS (1971). 1500 Don Mills Rd., Suite 205, North York, ONT M3B 3K4. (416)391-1836. FAX: (416)391-0829 (Adv.); (416)391-1836. FAX: (416)391-0829. E-mail: jrosen@cjnews.com. Jeff Rosen. 50 issues a year. Some French. (WWW.CJNEWS.COM)

CANADIAN JEWISH OUTLOOK (1963). #3-6184 Ash St., Vancouver, BC V5Z 3G9. (604)324-5101. FAX:(604)325-2470. E-mail: cjoutlook@telus.net. Carl Rosenberg. Six times per year. Canadian Jewish Outlook Society. (WWW.VCN.BC.CA/OUTLOOK)

DAIS (1985) (formerly INTERCOM). 100 Sparks St., #650, Ottawa, ONT KIP 5B7. (613)233-8703. FAX: (613)233-8748. E-mail: canadianjewishcongress@cjc.ca. Jack Silverstone. Three times a year. Canadian Jewish Congress.

DIRECTIONS (1998) (formerly DIALOGUE (1988)). 1 Carré Cummings, Suite 202, Montreal, Quebec H3W 1M6. (514)345-64111. FAX: (514)345-6412. E-mail: etay@cjc.ca. Eta Yudin. Quarterly. French-English. Canadian Jewish Congress, Quebec Region.

JEWISH FREE PRESS (1990). 8411 Elbow Dr., SW Calgary, AB. T2V 1K8. (403) 252-9423. FAX: (403)255-5640. Judy Shapiro. Fortnightly.

JEWISH INDEPENDENT (formerly WESTERN BULLETIN) (1930). 291 E. Second Ave., Vancouver, BC V5T 1B8. (604)689-1520. FAX: (604)689-1525. E-mail: editor@jewishindependent.ca. Cynthia Ransay. Weekly. Western Sky Communications Ltd. (WWW.JEWISHINDEPENDENT.CA)

JEWISH POST & NEWS (1987). 113 Hutchings St., Winnipeg, MAN R2X 2V4. (204)694-3332. FAX: (204)694-3916. E-mail: jewishp@mts.net. Matt Bellan. Weekly. (WWW.JEWISHPOSTANDNEWS.COM)

JEWISH STANDARD (1928). 1912A Avenue Road, Suite E5, Toronto, ONT M5M 4A1. (416)537-2696. FAX: (416)789-3872. E-mail: thejewishstandardasympatico.ca. Ed./Pub. Michael Hayman. Monthly.

JEWISH STANDARD (1928). 5184, Chemin de la Cote-des-Neiges, Suite 407, Montreal, Quebec H3T 1X8. Email: thejewishstandardasympatico.ca. Ed./Pub. Michael Hayman. Monthly

JEWISH TRIBUNE (1950). 15 Hove St., Toronto, ONT M3H 4Y8. (416)633-6224. FAX: (416)633-6299. E-mail: editor@jewishtribune.ca . Norm Gordner. B'nai Brith Canada, Bimonthly. (WWW.JEWISHTRIBUNE.CA)

JOURNAL OF PSYCHOLOGY AND JUDAISM (1976). 1747 Featherston Dr., Ottawa, ONT K1H 6P4. (613)731-9119. Reuven P. Bulka. Quarterly. Center for the Study of Psychology and Judaism.

OTTAWA JEWISH BULLETIN (1954). 21 Nadolny Sachs Private., Ottawa, ONT K2A 1R9. (613)798-4696. FAX: (613)798-4730. E-mail: bulletin@ottawajewishbulletin.com. Barry Fishman. Nineteen times a year. Ottawa Jewish Bulletin Publishing Co. Ltd. (WWW.OTTAWAJEWISHBULLETIN.COM)

SHALOM (1975). 5670 Spring Garden Rd., Suite 508, Halifax, NS, B3J 1H1. (902)422-7491. FAX: (902)425-3722. E-mail: jgoldberg@theajc.ns.ca. Jon M. Goldberg. Quarterly. Atlantic Jewish Council.

LA VOIX SÉPHARADE (1975). 5151 Chemin de la Cote, St. Catherine, Montreal, PQ H3W 1M6. (514)733-4998, FAX: (514)733-3158. E-mail: elieb@fedcjamtl.org. Ed. James Dahan; Pub. Elie Benchitrit. Bimonthly (five times a year). French and occasional Spanish and English. Communauté Sépharade du Québec.

NEWS AND VIEWS (1942) (formerly WINDSOR JEWISH FEDERATION). 1641 Ouellette Ave., Windsor, ONT N8X 1K9. (519)973-1772. FAX: (519)973-1774. Exec. Dir. Harvey Kessler. Quarterly. Windsor Jewish Federation.

WORLD OF LUBAVITCH (1980). 770 Chabad Gate, Thornhill, ONT L4J 3V9. (905)731-7000. FAX: (905)731-7005. Rabbi Moshe Spalter. Quarterly. English. Chabad Lubavitch of Southern Ont.

Obituaries: United States*

ADLER, ROBERT, electronics engineer, inventor; b. Vienna, Austria, Dec. 4, 1913; d. Boise, Idaho, Feb. 15, 2007; in U.S. since 1941. Educ.: U. Vienna (PhD). Asst. to patent atty., 1937–38; laboratory scientist, Acoustics. Ltd., London, 1940–41; research group, Zenith Radio Corp. (later Zenith Electronics Corp.), Chicago, 1941–52, assoc. dir. research, 1952–63, v.-pres., 1959–77, dir. research, 1963–77, v.-pres. research, 1977–82, technical consultant, 1982–97; consultant, Motorola, 1997–2001, Elo Touch Systems, 2001–. Nearly 200 patents are credited to him, including inventions to improve T.V. reception and for touch-screen technology, but the one with the greatest impact on ordinary people was the T.V. remote control, credited by some with creating "a nation of couch potatoes." Rec.: Inst. of Radio Engineers Outstanding Technical Achievement Award, 1958; Inst. of Electrical and Electronics Engineers Edison Medal, 1980; Natl. Acad. of Television Arts and Sciences "Emmy" for invention of remote-control device, 1997.

BISHOP, JOEY (JOSEPH ABRAHAM GOTTLIEB), comedian; b. NYC, Feb. 3, 1918; d. Newport Beach, Calif., Oct. 17, 2007. Served U.S. Army, 1942–45. Dropped out of high school and performed music and comedy in several cities with two friends as "Bishop Brothers" until drafted; after WWII performed standup comedy in night clubs; appeared on T.V. on "What's My Line?" 1950–67, "Password," 1961–67, "The Tonight Show" (often subbing for host Johnny Carson), 1962–92, "The Hollywood Squares," 1966–81, "The Joey Bishop Show" (late-night talk show), 1967–69, "Celebrity Sweepstakes," 1974–77, others; appeared in films *The Deep Six* (1958), *The Naked and the Dead* (1958), *Onionhead* (1958), *Ocean's Eleven* (1960), *Sergeants 3* (1962), *Johnny Cool* (1963), *Texas Across the River* (1966), *A Guide for the Married Man* (1967), *Who's Minding the Mint?* (1967), *Valley of the Dolls* (1967), *The Delta Force* (1986), *Betsy's Wedding* (1990), *Mad Dog Time* (1996); inaugural ball master of ceremonies, 1961; last surviving mem. of "Rat Pack," entertainer friends of Frank Sinatra popular in 1960s.

BUCHWALD, ART, humorist, newspaper columnist; b. Mt. Vernon, N.Y., Oct. 20, 1925; d. Washington, D.C., Jan. 17, 2007. Educ.: U. Southern Calif.; Alliance Française, Paris. Served U.S. Marines, 1942–45. Paris correspondent, *Variety*, 1948–49; columnist, *N.Y. Herald Tribune* European edition, 1949–62, where, among other journalistic coups, he conducted the only interview with Sgt. Elvis Presley; Tribune Media Services syndicated columnist, 1962–, his three-times-

*Including American Jews who died between January 1 and December 31, 2007.

a week column appearing in over 500 newspapers; frequent guest on radio and T.V. Left a video obituary beginning, "Hi. I'm Art Buchwald, and I just died." Au.: *Paris After Dark* (1950); *I Chose Caviar* (1957); *More Caviar* (1958); *A Gift From the Boys* (1958); *Son of the Great Society* (1961); *Have I Ever Lied to You?* (1968); *Washington Is Leaking* (1976); *Down the Seine and Up the Potomac* (1977); *While Reagan Slept* (1983); *Yasmine Is Very Nice and Happy* (1994); *Leaving Home: A Memoir* (1994); *I'll Always Have Paris* (1996); *I Think I Don't Remember* (1997); *Stella in Heaven* (2000); *Beating Around the Bush* (2005); *Too Soon to Say Goodbye* (2006). Rec.: Pulitzer Prize for Outstanding Commentary, 1982; Lifetime Achievement Award, Natl. Soc. of Newspaper Columnists, 2006; Commandeur, Order of Arts and Letters, France, 2006. Mem.: Amer. Acad. of Arts and Sciences.

DECTER, MOSHE, journalist, communal professional; b. Tarentum, Pa., Oct. 14, 1921; d. NYC, June 28, 2007. Served U.S. Army, WWII. Educ.: U. Pittsburgh; CCNY; Jewish Theol. Sem.; New School for Social Research (BA). Political editor, Voice of Amer., 1950–54; research fellow, Fund for the Republic, 1954–59; managing editor, *New Leader,* 1959–60; dir., Jewish Minorities Research, 1960–63; exec. sec., Conf. on the Status of Soviet Jews; dir. research, Amer. Jewish Cong.; ed., *Near East Report,* 1980s; adviser and consultant to Israeli Embassy in U.S.; project dir., adviser, Israel Bonds, 1990s. Played a major role in initiating the Soviet Jewry movement with publication of "Jews in the Soviet Union" issue of *New Leader* (Sept. 14, 1959), organizing Amer. Conf. on Soviet Jewry, 1963. Au.: *McCarthy and the Communists* (with James Rorty, 1954); *Silence and Yearning: The Status of Soviet Jewry* (1966); *Israel and the Jews in the Soviet Mirror: Soviet Cartoons on the Middle East Crisis* (1967); *A Hero for Our Time* (1970); *To Serve, To Teach, To Leave: The Story of Israel's Development Assistance Program in Black Africa* (1977). Ed., *Redemption! Redemption! Redemption! Jewish Freedom Letters from Russia* (1963); *Myths and Facts: A Concise Record of the Arab-Israel Conflict* (1982).

DE TOLEDANO, RALPH, journalist, author; b. Tangier, Morocco, Aug. 14, 1916; d. Washington, D.C., Feb. 3, 2007; in U.S. since 1921. Educ.: Juilliard School; Columbia U. (BA); Cornell U. Served U.S. Army, 1943–46. Founder, coeditor, *Cross-Town,* 1932–33, *Jazz Info.,* 1938–39; assoc. editor, *New Leader,* 1938–43; managing editor, *Plain Talk,* 1946–47; publicity dir., Internat'l Ladies Garment Workers Union, 1947–48; asst. editor, *Newsweek,* 1948–50, natl. reports editor, 1950–60, asst. chief, Washington Bureau, 1956–60; columnist, music critic, *National Review,* 1955–; syndicated columnist, King Features, 1960–71, Natl. News Research Syndicate, 1971–74, 1998–, Copley News Service, 1974–89, Heritage Features Syndicate, 1989–91, Creators Syndicate, 1991–98. Taking the side of Whittaker Chambers who testified that Alger Hiss had been a communist, forged a lifelong bond with Richard Nixon and emerged as a pioneer of postwar American conservatism. Au.: *Seeds of Treason* (with Victor Lasky, 1950); *Spies, Dupes, and Diplomats* (1952); *Nixon* (1956); *Lament for a Generation* (1960); *The Goldwater Story* (1964); *J. Edgar Hoover* (1973); *Hit and Run: The Ralph Nader Story* (1975); *Notes from the Underground* (1997); *Cry Havoc: The Great American Bring-down and How It Happened* (2006); many others. Ghost writer, *The FBI Pyramid from the Inside* by W. Mark Felt (1979), unaware that Felt was "Deep Throat." Cmdr., Natl. Press Club Amer. Legion Post 20, 2005–. Rec.: Freedoms Foundation Award, 1950, 1961, 1974; Veterans of Foreign Wars Americanism Award, 1953.

FELDMAN, GERALD D., historian; b. NYC, Apr. 24, 1937; d. Berkeley, Calif., Oct. 31, 2007. Educ.: Columbia U. (BA); Harvard U. (PhD). Taught German hist. at U. Calif. Berkeley, 1963–2007, holding Jane K. Sather chair, dir., Center for German and European Studies, 1994–2000, founding dir., Inst. of European Studies, 2000–2006. Adviser to Presidential Comm. on Holocaust Assets in the U.S. Au.: *Army, Industry and Labor in Germany, 1914–18* (1966); *German Business between War and Revolution* (1970); *German Imperialism, 1914–18* (1972); *The Great Disorder: Politics, Economics and Society in the German Inflation, 1914–24* (1993); *Iron and Steel in the German Inflation, 1916–23* (1999); *August Thyssen and Hugo Stinnes* (2002); *Allianz and the*

German Insurance Business, 1933–45 (2002); other books and many articles in both English and German. At time of his death was in the midst of research on German and Austrian banks during the Natl. Socialist period. Rec.: Guggenheim Fellowship; Woodrow Wilson Fellowship; Amer. Historical Assn. Central European Hist. Group Best Book Award, 1995; Berlin Prize Fellow, 1998–99; Federal Republic of Germany Commander's Cross of the Order of Merit, 2000; German Studies Assn. Award, 2001.

FELDMAN, MYER, lawyer, presidential adviser; b. Philadelphia, Pa., June 22, 1914; d. Bethesda, Md., Mar. 1, 2007. Educ.: U. Pa. (BS, LLB). Served U.S. Air Force, 1942–46. Atty. in private practice, 1939–42; lect., U. Pa Law School, 1941–42; special counsel, exec. asst. to chmn., S.E.C., 1946–54; counsel, Senate Banking and Currency Com., 1955–57; legislative asst. to Sen. John F. Kennedy, 1958–61; deputy special counsel to pres., 1961–64 (including the "Jewish" portfolio); counsel to Pres. Lyndon B. Johnson, 1964–65; founder, partner, Ginsburg Feldman & Bress, Washington, D.C., 1965–98; pres., Ardman Broadcasting Corp., 1992–. Exec., bd. mem., numerous corporations; produced Broadway plays. Au.: *Standard Pennsylvania Practice* (4 vols., 1958). Mem., bd. dirs., Weizmann Inst., 1963–84; trustee, Jewish Publ. Soc., 1966–78.

FINE, MORRIS, editor, communal professional, b. Warsaw, Poland, Mar. 3, 1914; d. NYC, Aug. 20, 2007; in U.S. since 1921. Educ.: Drew U. (BA); School of Library Service, Columbia U. (MS); Sorbonne. Served U.S. Army, 1943–46. Clerk, Amer. Smelting and Refining Co., 1936–37; staff mem., AJC, 1937–40, asst. dir., Library of Jewish Info., 1940–43, dir., 1946–55, editor, *American Jewish Year Book,* 1946–79; dir., program reports and materials, 1955–1969, program coord., 1969–73, dir. foreign affairs, 1973–78, program assoc., Inst. on Amer. Jewish-Israeli Relations, 1982–92.

HALBERSTAM, DAVID, journalist, author; b. NYC, Apr. 10, 1934; d. Menlo Park, Calif., Apr. 23, 2007, in car crash. Educ.: Harvard U. (AB). Reporter, West Point (Miss.) *Daily Times Leader,* 1955–56, Nashville *Tennessean,* 1956–60 (covered the early civil rights movement); correspondent, *New York Times,* 1960–67, reporting from Democratic Republic of Congo, 1961–62, Vietnam, 1962–65, Warsaw, 1965–66; contrib. editor, *Harper's* magazine, 1967–71. Widely credited with bringing the reality of the Vietnam War home to the American people. Au.: *The Noblest Roman* (1961); *The Making of a Quagmire* (1965); *One Very Hot Day* (1968); *The Unfinished Odyssey of Robert Kennedy* (1969); *The Best and the Brightest* (1972); *The Powers That Be* (1979); *The Breaks of the Game* (1981); *The Amateurs* (1985); *Summer of '49* (1989); *The Next Century* (1991); *The Fifties* (1993); *War In a Time of Peace* (2001); *Firehouse* (2002); *The Coldest Winter: America and the Korean War* (2007). Rec.: Pulitzer Prize for Internat'l Reporting, 1964; George Polk Memorial Award, 1964; Overseas Press Club Award, 1973; Robert Kennedy Book Award, 1999.

HART, KITTY CARLISLE (CATHERINE CONN), actress; b. New Orleans, La., Sept. 3, 1910; d. NYC, Apr. 17, 2007. Educ.: London School of Economics; Royal Acad. of Dramatic Arts, London. Theater and opera performances in *Champagne, Sec* (1933), *White Horse Inn* (1936), *Three Waltzes* (1937), *Walk With Music* (1940), *The Rape of Lucretia* (1948), *Anniversary Waltz* (1954), *Die Fledermaus* (1967), *On Your Toes* (1983), continued to perform one-woman show "Here's to Life" until a few months before she died; acted in films *Murder at the Vanities* (1934), *She Loves Me Not* (1934), *Here Is My Heart* (1934), *A Night at the Opera* (with Marx Brothers, 1935), *Larceny with Music* (1943), *Hollywood Canteen* (1944), *Radio Days* (1987), *Six Degrees of Separation* (1992); panelist on T.V. shows "To Tell the Truth," 1957–78, "What's My Line," "Password," others. V.-chair, N.Y. State Council for the Arts, 1971–76, chair, 1976–96; bd. mem., Empire State Coll., Center for Arts Educ.; special consultant to gov. of N.Y. on women's opportunities. Au.: *Kitty: An Autobiography* (1988). Rec.: Natl. Medal of Arts (1991).

HELMSLEY, LEONA (LENA MINDY ROSENTHAL), hotel owner, real estate investor; b. Ulster County, N.Y., July 4, 1920; d. Greenwich, Conn., Aug. 20, 2007. V.-pres., Pease & Elliman real estate brokerage, NYC, 1962–69; pres., Sutton & Towne Residential, NYC, 1967–70; sr. v.-pres., Helmsley Spear, NYC, 1970–72,

Brown, Harris Stevens, NYC, 1970–72; pres., CEO, bd. chair, Helmsley Hotels, Inc., NYC, 1980–, which ran 30 hotels, including Helmsley Palace, NYC; accused of not paying sales tax on jewelry, 1986, and, together with her husband, Harry, of evading income and corporate taxes, 1987, one employee testifying that she said, "Only the little people pay taxes"; was convicted and served 18-month prison sentence on the tax charge, 1992–94; forced to give up hotels since convicted felons were barred from possessing liquor licenses; subject of several books and T.V. movie, *Leona Helmsley: The Queen of Mean,* 1990; her will left her dog $12 million, reduced to $2 million by surrogate's court . Major contr. to Leona and Harry B. Helmsley Medical Building, Greenwich, Conn.; Helmsley Medical Tower, N.Y. Presbyterian Hosp., NYC; families of firefighters killed on 9/11. Rec.: NY Council on Civic Affairs Woman of the Year, 1970; Town and Country Condos and Coops Woman of the Year, 1981; ORT School of Engineering Service Award, 1981; Les Dames d'Escoffier Professional Excellence Award, 1981; Sales Execs. Club Achievement Award, 1981; Hotel Industry Woman of the Year Award, 1982; included in *Forbes* richest Americans, 2006.

HILBERG, RAUL, historian, educator; b. Vienna, Austria, June 2, 1926; d. Williston, Vt., Aug. 4, 2007; in U.S. since 1939. Served U.S. Army War Documentation Dept., WWII, in charge of examining German-language archives. Educ.: Brooklyn Coll. (BA); Columbia U. (MA, PhD). Research staff, War Documentation Project, 1951–55; mem., Dept. of Political Science, U. Vermont, 1956–91, prof. emer., 1991–. Au.: *The Destruction of the European Jews* (1961, revised eds. 1985, 2003, German ed. 1982); *The Holocaust Today* (1988); *Perpetrators, Victims, Bystanders: The Jewish Catastrophe, 1933–45* (1992); *The Politics of Memory: The Journey of a Holocaust Historian* (1996); *Sources of Holocaust Research* (2001). Ed.: *Documents of Destruction: Germany and Jewry, 1933–45* (1971); *The Warsaw Diary of Adam Czerniakow: Prelude to Doom* (with others, 1979). *The Destruction of the European Jews,* the first full description of how the Holocaust was carried out, in a sense created the field of Holocaust studies and at the same time aroused controversy over its portrayal of Jewish passivity and even cooperation by Jewish leaders with the perpetrators. Mem.: President's Comm. on the Holocaust; U.S. Holocaust Memorial Council; Amer. Acad. of Arts and Sciences. Rec.: Geschwister-Scholl-Preis, 2002; Federal Republic of Germany Order of Merit, 2006.

KITAJ, R.B. (RONALD BROOKS), artist; b. Chagrin Falls, Ohio, Oct. 29, 1932; d. Los Angeles, Calif., Oct. 21, 2007. Served as artist, U.S. Army, 1956–58. Educ.: Cooper Union; Acad. of Fine Arts, Vienna; Ruskin School of Drawing and Fine Art, Oxford U.; Royal Coll., London. Merchant seaman, 1949–51; teacher of art, Ealing Art Coll., Camberwell School of Art, both in England, 1960s, U. Calif. at Berkeley, 1968; first solo exhibition, "Pictures with commentary, Pictures without commentary," Marlborough Fine Art, London, 1963; among his numerous later exhibitions were at Los Angeles County Museum of Art, 1965, "The Human Clay," Hayward Gallery, London, 1976, "An Artist's Eye," Natl. Gallery, London, 1980, Hirshhorn Museum, Washington, D.C., 1981, retrospective of his work shown at Tate Gallery, London, Metropolitan Museum, NYC, Los Angeles, 1994–95, "Kitaj in the Aura of Cézanne and other Masters," Natl. Gallery, 2001. Proponent of figurative art and Pop Art, with Jewish themes becoming increasingly prominent, as Kitaj himself explained in two books, *The First Diasporist Manifesto* (1989) and *The Second Diasporist Manifesto* (2007). Mem.: Royal Acad., 1991, the first American invited to join since John Singer Sargent. Rec.: Venice Biennale Golden Lion, 1995.

KLAUSNER, ABRAHAM, rabbi, military chaplain; b. Memphis, Tenn., Apr. 27, 1915; d. Santa Fe, N.M., June 28, 2007. Educ.: U. Denver (BA, MA); Hebrew Union Coll. (Ordination, MHL). Served as chaplain, U.S. Army, 1944–48. Provost, Hebrew Union Coll., 1948–49; Rabbi, Temple Israel, Boston, 1949–53, Temple Emanuel, Yonkers, N.Y., 1954–89. Organized and directed central com. of the organization Liberated in Germany, 1945–48. The first Jewish chaplain to enter Dachau concentration camp after liberation, Klausner became a key advocate for survivors and his intervention led to improvement in DP camp conditions. Au.: *A Child's Prayer*

Book (1979); *Weddings: A Complete Guide to All Religious and Interfaith Marriage Services* (1986); *A Letter to My Children: From the Edge of the Holocaust* (2002).

KORNBERG, ARTHUR, biochemist; b. Brooklyn, N.Y., Mar. 3, 1918; d. Stanford, Calif., Oct. 26, 2007. Educ.: CCNY (BSc); U. Rochester (MD). Served as medical officer, U.S. Coast Guard, 1942. Medical intern, Strong Memorial Hosp., Rochester, 1941–42; staff mem., Natl. Insts. of Health, 1942–47, chief, Enzyme and Metabolism Section, 1947–53; guest researcher, NYU, 1946, Washington U., 1947, U. Calif., 1951; prof., dept. head microbiology, Washington U. Medical School, 1953–59; prof. biochemistry, Stanford U. Medical School, 1959–88, dept. chmn., 1959–69, prof. emer., 1988–. Mem.: Scientific advisory bd., Mass. Genl. Hosp., several drug companies. Mem., bd. of govs., Weizmann Inst., Israel. Au.: *For the Love of Enzymes* (1989); many scholarly articles. Rec.: Paul Lewis Award in Enzyme Chemistry, 1951; Nobel Prize in Physiology or Medicine, 1959, for his discovery of DNA polymerase, which proved critical for genetic engineering and led to the development of life-saving drugs; Max Berg Award for prolonging human life, 1968; Natl. Medal of Science, 1979; many others. Kornberg Medical Research Building, U. Rochester, named in his honor, 1999.

KORNREICH, MORTON, insurance exec., communal leader; b. NYC, Dec. 4, 1924; d. Boca Raton, Fla., Mar. 27, 2007. Served U.S. Army Air Corps, 1943–46. Educ.: U. Pa. (BA). Asst. to v.-pres. for sales, Allied Stores, NYC, 1949; S. Kornreich & Sons, Inc., 1950–, v.–pres., 1960–73, bd. chmn., 1973–; pres., Kornreich Life Assn., 1972–, Kornreich Internat'l, 1974–. Dir., N.Y. State Motor Vehicle Accident Indemnity Corp. V.-pres., Westchester Jewish Community Center; pres., Temple Emanu-El, Harrison, N.Y., 1982; pres., United Jewish Appeal of Greater N.Y., 1985–86; chmn., UJA-Fed. of N.Y., 1986 (presiding over the merger of UJA and Fed.); natl. chmn., United Jewish Appeal, 1988–90; bd. mem., hon. v.-pres., AJC, chmn., Koppelman Inst. on Amer. Jewish-Israeli Relations; founder, bd. mem., chmn., *N.Y. Jewish Week*; chmn., bd. mem., CLAL. Rec.: AJC Community Service Award, 2006.

KUGLER, ISRAEL, labor leader; b. Brooklyn, N.Y., June 13, 1917; d. Chevy Chase, Md., Oct. 1, 2007. Educ.: CCNY (BA); NYU (MA, PhD). Served U.S. Navy, WWII. Mem., social science faculty, NYC Coll. of Technology (originally called N.Y. State Inst. of Applied Arts and Sciences), 1947–80; v.-pres., Teachers Guild/United Fed. of Coll. Teachers (UFCT), 1954–63, pres., 1963–72; deputy pres., Professional Staff Cong., 1972–76; arbitrator, Amer. Arbitration Assn., N.Y. State Mediation Bd., Natl. Mediation Bd. While head of UFCT organized faculty unions at several N.Y area colleges; got the national Amer. Fed. of Teachers to expel racially segregated local affiliates; led unsuccessful strike against St. John's U. over firing of faculty who wanted to unionize, 1967; merged UFCT with CUNY Professional Staff Conf., 1972. Au.: *From Ladies to Women: The Organized Struggle for Women's Rights in the Reconstruction Era* (1987). Pres., Workmen's Circle, 1980–84; mem., exec. com., Jewish Labor Com., Forward Assn. Rec.: hon. doctorate in humane letters, CUNY.

LEVIN, IRA, novelist, playwright; b. NYC, Aug. 27, 1929; d. NYC, Nov. 12, 2007. Educ.: Drake U.; NYU (AB). Served U.S. Army, 1953–55. Freelance writer, 1950–. Au.: *A Kiss Before Dying* (1953, film versions 1956, 1991); *Rosemary's Baby* (1967, film version 1968); *The Perfect Day* (1970); *The Stepford Wives* (1972, film versions 1975, 2004); *The Boys from Brazil* (1976, film version 1978); *Sliver* (1991); *Son of Rosemary* (1997). Plays: *No Time for Sergeants* (1955); *Interlock* (1958); *Critic's Choice* (1962); *Drat the Cat!* (1965); *Dr. Cook's Garden* (1967); *Veronica's Room* (1973); *Deathtrap* (1978, film version 1982); *Break a Leg* (1979); *Cantorial* (1989); *Sliver* (1991). Rec.: Mystery Writers of Amer. Edgar Award, 1953, 1980, named "grand master," 2003.

LIBRESCU, LIVIU, engineer, educator; b. Ploieşti, Romania, Aug. 18, 1930; d. Apr. 16, 2007, Blacksburg, Va.; in U.S. since 1985. Educ.: Polytechnic U. Bucharest (BA, MA); Academia de Ştiinţe din România (PhD). Researcher, Bucharest Inst. Applied Mechanics, Inst. Fluid Mechanics of Acad. of Sciences of Romania, 1953–75; fired after requesting permission to emigrate, moved to Israel after direct intervention by Prime Minister Begin, 1978; prof. aeronautical and mechanical engineering, Tel Aviv U., 1979–85; prof., engineering science and mechanics, Virginia Tech U., 1985– . Shot to death as he protected his students by holding the door to his classroom closed as a gunman shot into it, giving students time to get out through the windows; in all, 32 were shot to death in the engineering building, only one of them a student in Librescu's class; his burial took place in Israel. Bd. mem., seven scientific journals; guest editor, special issues of five others; cochmn., Internat'l Organizing Com. of Seventh Internat'l Cong. on Thermal Stress, 2007. Au.: *Elastostatics and Kinetics of Anisotropic and Heterogenous Shell-Type Structures* (1976); *Random Vibrations and Reliability of Composite Structures* (with others, 1992); *Thin-Walled Composite Beams: Theory and Application* (2006); numerous scholarly articles. Rec.: Traian Vuia Prize, Romanian Acad., 1972; Dean's Award for Excellence in Research, Virginia Tech Coll. of Engineering, 1999; fellow, Acad. of Engineering of Armenia, 1999; elected mem., Acad. of Shipbuilding of Ukraine, 2000; Frank J. Maher Award for Excellence in Engineering Educ., 2005; Order of the Star of Romania, 2007 (posthumously).

MAILER, NORMAN, author; b. Long Branch, N.J., Jan. 31, 1923; d. NYC, Nov. 10, 2007. Educ.: Harvard U. (SB); Sorbonne. Served U.S. Army, 1944–46. Co-founder, columnist, *Village Voice*, 1955; columnist, *Commentary*, 1962–63, *Esquire*, 1962–63; contrib. editor, *Dissent*, 1953–69. Au.: *No Percentage* (1941); *The Naked and the Dead* (1948; *Barbary Shore* (1951); *The Deer Park* (1955); *The White Negro* (1957); *Advertisements for Myself* (1959); *The Presidential Papers* (1963); *An American Dream* (1965); *Cannibals and Christians* (1966); *Why Are We in Vietnam?* (1967); *The Bullfight* (1967); *The Armies of the Night* (1968); *Miami and the Siege of Chicago* (1968); *Of a Fire on the Moon* (1970); *The Prisoner of Sex* (1971); *Marilyn* (1973); *The Fight* (1975); *The Executioner's Song* (1979); *Ancient Evenings* (1983); *Tough Guys Don't Dance* (1984); *Harlot's Ghost* (1991); *Oswald's Tale: An American Mystery* (1995); *The Gospel According to the Son* (1997); *The Castle in the Forest* (2007); others. Screenwriter; producer; director; actor; candidate for NYC mayor, 1969. Pres., PEN Amer. Center, 1984–86. Rec.: Natl. Book Award for Nonfiction, 1968; Pulitzer Prize for Nonfiction, 1969; George Polk Award, 1969; Natl. Arts Club Gold Medal, 1976; Pulitzer Prize for Fiction, 1980; Emerson-Thoreau Medal for lifetime literary achievement, 1989; Natl. Book Found. Medal for distinguished contrib. to Amer. letters, 2005; Legion of Honor, France, 2006.

MASLOW, WILL, lawyer, communal professional; b. Kiev, Russia, Sept. 27, 1907; d. NYC, Feb. 23, 2007; in U.S. since 1911. Educ.: Cornell U. (AB); Columbia U. (JD). Reporter, *N.Y. Times,* 1929–31; assoc., Arthur Garfield Hays law firm, 1931–34; assoc. counsel, NYC Dept. of Investigation, 1934–36; trial attorney, trial examiner, Natl. Labor Relations Bd., 1937–43; dir. field operations, President's Fair Employment Practices Com., 1943–45; genl. counsel, Amer. Jewish Cong., 1945–60, 1972–1980s, exec. dir., 1960–72, creating the organization's Comm. on Law and Social Action that initiated lawsuits against racial and religious discrimination in housing, employment, and higher educ., and playing a key role in the civil rights movement and fighting Arab boycott of Israel. Faculty, New School for Social Research, 1948–60, CCNY, 1965–84. Ed., *Boycott Report,* 1977–94; *Radical Islamic Fundamentalism Update,* 1995–99. Trustee, Memorial Found. for Jewish Culture; bd. of dirs., Amer. Civil Liberties Union, Interracial Council for Business Opportunity, A. Philip Randolph Inst. Rec.: N.Y. Bar Assn. Award for Defense of Equal Rights, 1963; Amer. Jewish Cong. Stephen Wise Award, 1972; Jewish Council for Public Affairs Natl. Award, 1998.

MELTON, FLORENCE ZACKS, entrepreneur, philanthropist; b. Philadelphia, Pa., Nov. 6, 1911; d. Boca Raton, Fla., Jan. 8, 2007. Sales clerk, department stores, 1924–29; together with husband Aaron Zacks, opened drapery and slipcover store in Hagerstown, Md., that failed, 1937; patented Shoulda Shams, shoulder pad for women's dresses made out of material used for lining helmets in WWII, 1947; patented foam rubber shoulder pads and then, with husband, created R.G. Barry Corp., Columbus, Ohio, to manufacture foam rubber slippers, 1948, which proved immensely successful under the names Angel Treads and Dearfoams, subsequently holding the position of consultant for product development and design.

Bd. mem., United Way, Red Cross Nutrition Corps, 1940s, Huntington Natl. Bank (first woman on board), 1970s. Founding mem., Coalition for the Advancement of Jewish Educ. (CAJE), 1977; with second husband, Samuel L. Melton, established Melton Center for Jewish Studies, Ohio State U., 1976; developed and chaired Melton Mini-School, pluralistic, interactive, two-year program in Jewish studies for adults, together with Melton Center for Jewish Educ. at Hebrew U., 1986, that now operates in over 70 communities around the world. Rec.: Amer. Friends of the Hebrew U. Scopus Award; Jewish Educ. Services of North Amer. Mesorah Award; hon. doctorates, Hebrew U., Jewish Theol. Sem.; Distinguished Service Award, Ohio State U.; inducted into Ohio Women's Hall of Fame, 1994.

MEYERSON, MARTIN, university pres., urban planner; b. Brooklyn, N.Y., Nov. 14, 1922; d. Philadelphia, Pa., June 2, 2007. Educ.: Columbia U. (BA); Harvard U. (MCP). Staff, Michael Reese Hosp., Chicago, 1945–47; asst. prof. social sciences, U. Chicago, 1948–52; assoc. prof, dept. chmn., city and regional planning, U. Pa., 1952–56; prof., 1956–57; Frank Backus Williams prof. city planning and urban research, Harvard U., 1957–63; founding dir., Joint Center for Urban Studies, MIT and Harvard, 1958–63; dean, prof. urban devel., Coll. of Urban Design, U. Calif. Berkeley, 1963–66, interim chancellor, 1965; pres., prof. public policy, SUNY Buffalo, 1966–70; pres., U. Pa. 1970–81, pres. emer., 1981–. Served on numerous govt. and private-sector advisory bds. At U. Pa. redesigned the campus, helped improve the surrounding neighborhood, instituted affirmative action for minorities, and fully integrated women into the student body. Au.: *Politics, Planning, and the Public Interest* (with E.C. Banfield, 1955); *Housing, People and Cities* (1962); *Face of the Metropolis* (1963); *Boston* (1966); *Gladly Learn and Gladly Teach* (1978). Rec.: Amer. Technion Soc. Einstein Medal, 1976; Columbia U. John Jay Award, 1982; U. Calif. Berkeley Distinguished Achievement Award, 1984; Assn. of Collegiate Schools of Planning Distinguished Educator Award, 1996; many others.

MURAVCHIK, EMMANUEL, labor leader, communal worker; b. NYC, Sept. 23, 1916; d. NYC, Jan. 8, 2007. Served U.S. Army, 1943–46. Educ.: Columbia U. (BS); New School for Social Research; NYU. Staff, Socialist Party, 1940s; union organizer, Internat'l Ladies Garment Workers Union, 1940s; asst. natl. field dir., Jewish Labor Com., 1947–49, natl. field dir., 1949–67, exec. dir., 1967–84. Directed study of the labor movement and race issue sponsored by AFL-CIO and financed by Fund for the Republic, 1958–60; made JLC the advocate of organized labor's views within the Jewish community; brought issue of Soviet Jewry to the attention of labor movement with report to Internat'l Confed. of Free Trade Unions, 1962; helped organize march on Washington for civil rights, 1963; emerged as spokesman for Israel within organized labor; backed teachers union in Ocean Hill-Brownville struggle over community control, 1968; when Socialists split over Vietnam War lined up with prowar Social Democrats USA. Mem. exec. bd., League for Industrial Democracy, Social Democrats USA, A. Philip Randolph Inst., Workers Defense League.

NADICH, JUDAH, rabbi; b. Baltimore, Md., May 13, 1912; d. NYC, Aug. 26, 2007. Educ.: CCNY (BA); Columbia U. (MA); Jewish Theol. Sem. (ordination, MHL, DHL). Served as chaplain, U.S. Army, 1942–46. Rabbi, Temple Beth David, Buffalo, 1936–40, Anshe Emet Synagogue, Chicago, 1940–42; lt. col., sr. Jewish chaplain, European theater, 1942–45, adviser to Gen. Eisenhower on Jewish affairs, 1945; toured U.S. to raise funds for UJA, visited foreign countries for Amer. Jewish Joint Distrib. Com., 1946–47; rabbi, Cong. Kehillath Israel, Boston, 1947–57, Park Ave. Synagogue, NYC, 1957–87. As adviser to Gen. Eisenhower, played a major role in improving conditions for Jewish survivors in DP camps; one of first Conservative rabbis to count women in a minyan and call them to the Torah, and suggested in 1974 that the movement consider ordaining female rabbis. Pres., Jewish Book Council of Amer., 1968–72, Rabbinical Assembly, 1972–74, Assn. of Jewish Chaplains of Armed Forces; special adviser to chmn., U.S. Holocaust Memorial Council; bd. mem., NYC Holocaust Comm., Jewish Theol. Sem., Heschel School, 92d Street Y, JBI Internat'l. Au.: *Eisenhower and the Jews* (1953); *Jewish Legends of the Second Commonwealth* (1982).

NEWMAN, DANIEL (DANNY), music press agent; b. Chicago, Ill., Jan. 24, 1919; d. Lincolnwood, Ill., Dec. 1, 2007. Educ.: Wright Junior Coll. Served U.S. Army, WWII. Press agent and business mgr., Mummers of Chicago, 1930s; owned Chicago movie houses, developing some of the earliest drive-ins, late 1940s, press agent for legitimate theater, including Yiddish troupes, 1940s–50s; coproducer of radio program "Famous Names," 1946–51; public relations dir., Lyric Opera, Chicago, 1954–82, public relations counsel, 1982–2001; consultant on performing arts marketing, Ford Found., Theater Communications Group, 1961–82, N.Y. Philharmonic Orchestra, London Symphony Orchestra, Australian Ministry of Culture, Haifa Municipal Theater, Khan Theater (Jerusalem), many others. Pioneered the marketing of subscription sales to cultural events, a strategy largely responsible for the vast increase in the number of resident professional theater companies. Bd. chmn., Anshe Sholom B'nai Israel Cong.; bd. mem., World Council of Jewish Culture, Zionist Org. (Chicago), Bd. of Jewish Educ. (Chicago), Weizmann Inst. of Science, many other Jewish bodies. Au.: *Subscribe Now!* (1977, ten editions); *Tales of a Theatrical Guru* (2006). Rec.: Gold Baton, Amer. Symphony Orchestra League, 1984; Order of Merit (Italy), 1984; many awards from Jewish orgs. Lyric Opera named its box office "Subscribe Now!" in his honor, 2007.

OLSEN, TILLIE, author; b. near Wahoo, Neb., Jan. 14, 1912; d. Oakland, Calif., Jan. 1, 2007. After dropping out of high school she held a long series of menial, temporary jobs and was active in Young Communist League, going to jail twice for involvement in labor organizing, 1930s; while working and raising children wrote privately without publishing; opposition to "duck and cover" drills in San Francisco public schools got both her and her husband investigated by House Un-Amer. Activities Com., 1950s; her first published work, the short story "As I Stand Here Ironing," won O. Henry Award as best American short story of 1961; fellow, Radcliffe Inst., 1962–64; visiting writer, Amherst Coll., 1969–70; writer in residence, MIT, 1973–74; distinguished visiting prof., U. Mass. Boston, 1974; adviser to Feminist Press, 1970s. Au.: *Tell Me a Riddle* (1961, film version, 1980); *Yonnondio: From the Thirties* (1973); *Silences* (1978). Rec.: Wallace Stegner Fellowship in Creative Writing, Stanford U., 1955; Ford Found. Fellowship, 1959, Guggenheim Fellowship, 1975; Amer. Acad. and Natl. Inst. of Arts and Letters citation for distinguished contrib. to Amer. lit., 1976.

PALEY, GRACE, short-story writer, poet; b. NYC, Dec. 11, 1922; d. Thetford Hill, Vt., Aug. 22, 2007. Educ.: Hunter Coll.; NYU; New School for Social Research. Taught writing at Sarah Lawrence Coll., 1966–89, Columbia U., Syracuse U., CCNY; cofounder, Teachers and Writers Collaborative, NYC, 1967. Protested nuclear proliferation, 1950s, Vietnam War, 1960s; accompanied War Resisters League mission to Hanoi, 1969; attended World Peace Conf., Moscow, 1978, and was arrested on White House lawn for carrying anti-nuclear banner there. Au.: *The Little Disturbances of Man* (1959); *Enormous Changes at the Last Minute* (1974); *Later the Same Day* (1985); *Long Walks and Intimate Talks* (1991); *Collected Stories* (1994); *Just as I Thought* (1998); *Begin Again: Collected Poems* (2000). Rec.: Guggenheim Fellowship, 1961; Natl. Inst. for Arts and Letters Short Story Award, 1970; official New York State Writer (first to hold the title), 1986–88; Edith Wharton Award, 1988–89; Vermont Award for Excellence in the Arts, 1993; Rea Award for the Short Story, 1993; Natl. Found. for Jewish Culture Jewish Cultural Achievement Award for Literary Arts, 1994; poet laureate of Vermont, 2003–07.

SAINER, JANET S., gerontologist; b. NYC, July 4, 1918; d. Denver, Col., June 4, 2007. Educ.: Hunter Coll. (BA); Case Western Reserve U. (MSW). Social worker, sr.-citizens groups at NYC synagogues, 1940s–50s; social worker, dir., programs for the aging, Community Service Soc. of N.Y., 1960s–1978, where she developed pilot for Retired Sr. Volunteer Program (RSVP), enacted as a federal program by U.S. Cong., 1969; commissioner, NYC Dept. for the Aging, 1978–89, introducing Citymeals on Wheels (1981), country's first municipal Alzheimer's unit and annual Mayoral Conf. on Alzheimer's Disease (1984), Aging in N.Y. Fund (1984), Grandparent Resource Center, Stay-Well Exercise Program; consultant on issues related to aging, Brookdale

Found., 1990–, where she introduced the Relatives as Parents Program to aid people raising their grandchildren. Treas., Gerontological Soc. of Amer., 1982–87, chair, social research, policy and practice section, 1977. Rec.: Presidential citation for RSVP program.

SCHAECHTER, MORDKHE, Yiddish scholar, educator; b. Czernowitz, Romania, Dec. 1, 1927; d. NYC, Feb. 15, 2007; in U.S. since 1951. Educ.: U. Bucharest (MA); U. Vienna (PhD). Served U.S. Army military intelligence, 1952–54. Archival collector for YIVO in Austria, 1947–51; instr., Weinreich Program in Yiddish Language, Lit. and Culture, YIVO/Columbia U., 1952–2004; sr. lect., Yiddish studies, Columbia U., 1981–93; visiting prof., Jewish Theol. Sem., Yeshiva U., Jewish Teachers Seminary-Herzliah. Au. (in Yiddish): *Authentic Yiddish* (1986); *Pregnancy, Childbirth, and Early Childhood: An English-Yiddish Dictionary* (1991); *The History of the Standardized Yiddish Spelling* (1999); *Yiddish II: An Intermediate and Advanced Text Book* (2004); *Plant Names in Yiddish* (2005). Exec. dir., League for Yiddish, 1979–2004; editor, *Afn Shvel,* 1957–2004, *Yidishe Shprakh,* 1971–86; assoc. editor, *Great Dictionary of the Yiddish Language, IV,* 1980, *Language and Culture Atlas of Ashkenazic Jewry,* 1961–72; founder, Com. for the Implementation of the Standardized Yiddish Orthography, 1958, Yugntruf-Youth for Yiddish, 1964, Task Force for Yiddish Terminology, 1970. Rec.: Itzik Manger Prize, 1994.

SHELDON, SIDNEY, writer; b. Chicago, Ill., Feb. 11, 1917; d. Rancho Mirage, Calif., Jan. 30, 2007. Educ.: Northwestern U. Served U.S. Army Air Force, WWII. Script reader, Universal, 20th Century Fox studios, Hollywood, late 1930s; wrote for Broadway, 1943–44; wrote film screenplays for *The Bachelor and the Bobby-Soxer* (1947), *Easter Parade* (1948), *The Barkleys of Broadway* (1949), *Annie Get Your Gun* (1950), *Redhead* (1959); produced and wrote for TV shows "Nancy," "The Patty Duke Show," "I Dream of Jeannie," created "Hart to Hart." Au. (all together sold over 3 million copies, some made into feature films, others into TV miniseries): *The Naked Face* (1970); *The Other Side of Midnight* (1974); *A Stranger in the Mirror* (1976); *Bloodline* (1977); *Rage of Angels* (1980); *Master of the Game* (1982); *If Tomorrow Comes* (1985); *Windmills of the Gods* (1987); *The Sands of Time* (1988); *Memories of Midnight* (1990); *The Doomsday Conspiracy* (1991); *The Stars Shine Down* (1992); *Nothing Lasts Forever* (1994); *Morning, Noon, and Night* (1995); *The Best Laid Plans* (1997); *Tell Me Your Dreams* (1998); *The Sky Is Falling* (2000); *Are You Afraid of the Dark?* (2004); *The Other Side of Me* (autobiography, 2005). Rec.: Acad. Award for Screenplay, 1947; Tony Award, 1959; Writers Guild Amer. Screen Awards, 1948, 1950; Edgar Alan Poe Award for best mystery, 1970; entered into Guinness Book of Records as most translated author, 1997; Will Rogers Memorial Award, 2002.

SHULMAN, MARSHALL D., Sovietologist, govt. adviser; b. Jersey City, N.J., Apr. 8, 1916; d. Sherman, Conn., June 21, 2007. Educ.: U. Mich. (AB); U. Chicago; Harvard U.; Columbia U. (MA, cert. Russian Inst., PhD). Served U.S. Army Air Force, WWII. Reporter, *Detroit News,* 1937–38; writer, Natl. Safety Council, 1938–39; v.-pres., Council for Democracy, NYC, 1940–42; info. officer, U.S. Mission to the UN, 1949–50; special asst. to U.S. sec. of state (speechwriter), 1950–53; assoc. dir., Russian Research Center, Harvard U., 1954–62; lect. govt., Harvard U., 1956–60; prof. internat'l politics, Fletcher School of Law and Diplomacy, Tufts U., 1961–67; dir., Russian Inst., Columbia U., 1967–74, 1976–77, 1981–82; founding dir., W. Averell Harriman Inst. for Advanced Study of the Soviet Union, Columbia U., 1982–86; Adlai E. Stevenson prof. internat'l relations, Columbia U., 1974–86; special adviser for Soviet Affairs to U.S. sec. of state, 1977–80. Au.: *Soviet Policy in Western Europe and the French Communist Party* (1959); *Some Implications of Changes in Soviet Policy toward the West* (1961); *Stalin's Foreign Policy Reappraised* (1963); *Beyond the Cold War* (1966); *Origins of U.S.-Soviet Relations* (1978); *The Path of U.S.-Soviet Relations* (1980); *East-West Tensions in the Third World* (1986). Fellow, Amer. Acad. of Arts and Sciences; bd. mem., Amer. Council on Germany, Arms Control Assn., Amer. Political Science Assn., Council on Foreign Relations. Rec.: Rockefeller Public Service Travel Award, 1953–54; visiting research scholar, Carnegie Endowment, 1963–64; Ford

Found. Award, 1966; fellow, Amer. Council of Learned Societies, 1971–72.

SILLS, BEVERLY (BELLE SILVERMAN), opera singer, performing-arts exec.; b. Brooklyn, N.Y., May 25, 1929; d. NYC, July 2, 2007. Educ.: Professional Children's School, NYC; studied voice with Estelle Liebling from age 9. Sang on radio programs, 1932–41; performed with touring opera companies, 1945–55; debut with NYC Opera Co. in *Die Fledermaus,* 1955, subsequently performing all over the world in a wide variety of operatic roles; recognized as "superstar" after singing the role of Cleopatra in Handel's *Giulio Cesare* at inaugural NYC Opera performance at Lincoln Center, 1966, and the title role in Massenet's *Manon,* 1968; La Scala debut, 1969; Covent Garden debut, 1973; Metropolitan Opera (NYC) debut, 1975; genl. dir., NYC Opera, 1979–89, diversifying the repertory and proving herself a prodigious fund-raiser; pres., NYC Opera Bd., 1989–90; managing dir., Metropolitan Opera, NYC, 1991–94; chair, Lincoln Center for the Performing Arts, 1994–2002, Metropolitan Opera, 2002–05. Host, "Live from Lincoln Center" on PBS TV; frequent guest host, "The Tonight Show"; numerous TV specials. Many recordings, including *The Art of Beverly Sills* (2002); *The Great Recordings* (2004); *The Very Best of Beverly Sills* (2005); *Beverly Sills: Made in America* (2006). Au.: *Bubbles: A Self-Portrait* (1976); *Bubbles: An Encore* (1981); *Beverly: An Autobiography* (1987). Mem.: bd. dirs., Apollo Theater Found., 1999–2001; bd. trustees, March of Dimes, 1989–90, v. chair, 1990–91, chair, 1991–94. Rec.: Handel Medallion, 1973; Grammy Award for best classical vocal soloist performance, 1976; Emmy Award for TV specials, 1976, 1978; Presidential Medal of Freedom, 1980; March of Dimes Award, 1994; Lewis Rudin Award for Exemplary Service to NYC, 2006.

SONNABEND, ILEANA, art dealer; b. Bucharest, Romania, Oct. 28, 1914; d. NYC, Oct. 21, 2007; in U.S. since 1940. Educ.: Columbia U. With her first husband, Leo Castelli, became interested in Surrealist painters in Paris beginning 1935, opening a gallery in 1939; after arriving in NYC they were private art dealers, 1940–57, specializing in Abstract Expressionists, then ran a gallery in their home, 1957–59; with second husband, Michael Sonnabend, operated Galerie Ileana Sonnabend, Paris, 1962–80, and Sonnabend Gallery, NYC, 1971–. Introduced the work of postwar American Pop and Minimal artists (Andy Warhol, Roy Lichtenstein, Jasper Johns, Robert Rauschenberg, Claes Oldenburg, and others) to Europe; introduced European Conceptual Art, Neo-Expressionism, to U.S., and brought American Post-Minimalists and Neo-Geo artists, some using unconventional media (photography, performance art) to public attention; beside dealing in their artworks, "queen of the Soho art world" helped support fledgling artists, and her personal collection, never inventoried in her lifetime, was assumed to be worth a huge sum.

VLADECK, JUDITH P., lawyer, women's-rights advocate; b. Norfolk, Va., Aug. 1, 1923; d. NYC, Jan. 8, 2007. Educ.: Hunter Coll. (BA); Columbia U. (JD). Assoc., Conrad & Smith, NYC, 1947–57; partner, Vladeck, Waldman, Elias & Englehard, NYC, 1957–. Specializing in labor law and women's rights in the workplace, she won landmark suits against CUNY (1973) and Pace U. (1975) for discriminating against female faculty, Western Electric for sex discrimination in a class-action suit (1978), and Union Carbide (1983) for age discrimination. Mem.: bd. dirs., N.Y. Civil Liberties Union, Tamiment Inst., AFL-CIO Lawyers Coordinating Com., Nontraditional Employment for Women (NEW), Columbia Law School Alumni Assn. Rec.: Hunter Coll. Professional Achievement Award, 1992; ORT Jurisprudence Award, 1996; Women of Power and Influence Award, 1998; ABA Margaret Brent Award, 2002; Columbia Law School Assn. Medal of Excellence, 2003. NEW named its headquarters Judith Vladeck Center for Women, 1989.

WEBER, EUGEN, historian, educator; b. Bucharest, Romania, Apr. 24, 1925; d. May 17, 2007; in U.S. since 1954. Served British Army, 1943–47. Educ.: Inst. D'Études Politiques, Paris; Emmanuel Coll., Cambridge U. (BA, MA, M.Litt.). Lect. hist., U. Alberta, 1954–55; asst. prof., U. Iowa, 1955–56; asst. prof., assoc. prof., prof., U. Calif. Los Angeles, 1956–84, Joan Palevsky prof. modern European hist., 1984–, dept chmn., 1965–68, UCLA dean social sciences, 1976–77, dean Coll. Letters and Sciences, 1977–82.

Au.: *The Nationalist Revival in France, 1905–14* (1959); *The Western Tradition* (1959); *Paths to the Present* (1960); *Action Française* (1962); *Varieties of Fascism* (1964): *A Modern History of Europe* (1970); *Europe since 1715* (1972); *Peasants into Frenchmen* (1976); *France Fin-De-Siècle* (1986); *My France: Politics, Culture, Myth* (1990); *The Hollow Years: France in the 1930s* (1994); *Apocalypses: Prophecies, Cults and Millennial Beliefs through the Ages* (1999). Conceived and hosted 52-part PBS TV series "The Western Tradition" (1989). Rec.: Fulbright Fellowships, 1952, 1982–83; Guggenheim Fellowship, 1962–63, Natl. Endowment for the Humanities Fellowships, 1973–74, 1982–83; Commonwealth Prize of Calif., 1977, 1987; Prix de la Société des gens de letters, 1984; Prix M. Baumont, 1995; Amer. Historical Assn. Scholarly Distinction Award, 1999; many others.

WINE, SHERWIN T., rabbi; b. Detroit, Mich., Jan. 25, 1928; d. Essaouira, Morocco, July 21, 2007, in car crash. Educ.: U. Mich (AB, AM); Hebrew Union Coll. (ordination, BHL, MHL). Served as chaplain, U.S. Army, 1956–58. Assoc. rabbi, Temple Beth-El, Detroit, 1958–59; rabbi, Temple Beth-El, Windsor, Ontario, 1959–63, Birmingham (Mich.) Temple, 1963–2003, which, under his leadership, removed all references to God and concentrated on Jewish ethics and culture. Founder and dir., Soc. for Humanistic Judaism, 1969–; founder and cochmn., Internat'l Fed. Of Secular Humanistic Jews, 1983–; founder and provost, Internat'l Inst. for Secular Humanistic Judaism, 1985–; founding pres., Assn. of Humanistic Rabbis, 1967; founder, Center for New Thinking, 1977, Voice of Reason, 1981, Americans for Religious Liberty, 1982; pres., North Amer. Com. for Humanism, Humanist Inst., 1982–93; founder, Internat'l Assn. of Humanist Educators, Counselors, and Leaders; dean, Tmura Inst., Israel, 2004–. Au.: *Humanistic Judaism* (1978); *The Humanist Haggadah* (1979); *High Holidays for Humanists* (1979); *Celebration: A Ceremonial and Philosophical Guide for Humanists and Humanistic Jews* (1988); *Judaism Beyond God* (1996); *Staying Sane in a Crazy World* (1995). Rec.: Amer. Humanist Assn. Humanist of the Year Award, 2003.

WYSE, LOIS, advertising exec., writer; b. Cleveland, Ohio, Oct. 30, 1926; d. NYC, July 6, 2007. Educ.: Flora Mather Stone Coll. (Case Western Reserve U.). Reporter, *Cleveland News, Cleveland Press,* late 1940s–1951; Pres., Wyse Advertising, Cleveland, 1951–2007, operated N.Y. office, 1966–2007. Ran ad campaigns for major clients such as Sealy Mattresses, Genl. Dynamics, Clairol, Amer. Express, N.Y. Yankees, *New Woman* magazine; devised name of "Bed, Bath, and Beyond," slogan "With a name like Smucker's it has to be good," gave advertising advice to city of Cleveland. Au.: close to 70 books, including *Love Poems for the Very Married* (1967); *Are You Sure You Love Me?* (1969); *More Love Poems for the Very Married* (1971); *Blonde, Beautiful Blonde: How to Look, Live, Work, and Think Blonde* (1980); *Funny, You Don't Look Like a Grandmother* (1990); *Company Manners: How to Behave in the Workplace in the 90s* (1992); *Grandmother's Treasures* (1993); *Women Make the Best Friends* (1995); *How to Take Your Grandmother to the Museum* (with her granddaughter, 1998); *When a Child Is Born* (1999). Wrote "The Way We Are" column for *Good Housekeeping,* 1983–98, syndicated column "Wyse Words." Bd. mem., Consolidated Natural Gas Co., Higbee Co., Beth Israel Medical Center; founding mem., Com. of 200, Catalyst; founder, City and Co., which published books about N.Y. Rec.: inclusion in Cleveland Advertising Club Hall of Fame; Clio Award.

Calendars

SUMMARY JEWISH CALENDAR, 5768–5772 (Sept. 2007–Aug. 2012)

HOLIDAY	5768			5769			5770			5771			5772		
		2007			2008			2009			2010			2011	
Rosh Ha-shanah, 1st day	Th	Sept.	13	T	Sept.	30	Sa	Sept.	19	Th	Sept.	9	Th	Sept.	29
Rosh Ha-shanah, 2nd day	F	Sept.	14	W	Oct.	1	S	Sept.	20	F	Sept.	10	F	Sept.	30
Fast of Gedaliah	S	Sept.	16	Th	Oct.	2	M	Sept.	21	S	Sept.	12	S	Oct.	2
Yom Kippur	Sa	Sept.	22	Th	Oct.	9	M	Sept.	28	Sa	Sept.	18	Sa	Oct.	8
Sukkot, 1st day	Th	Sept.	27	T	Oct.	14	Sa	Oct.	3	Th	Sept.	23	Th	Oct.	13
Sukkot, 2nd day	F	Sept.	28	W	Oct.	15	S	Oct.	4	F	Sept.	24	F	Oct.	14
Hosha'na' Rabbah	W	Oct.	3	M	Oct.	20	F	Oct.	9	W	Sept.	29	W	Oct.	19
Shemini 'Aẓeret	Th	Oct.	4	T	Oct.	21	Sa	Oct.	10	Th	Sept.	30	Th	Oct.	20
Simḥat Torah	F	Oct.	5	W	Oct.	22	S	Oct.	11	F	Oct.	1	F	Oct.	21
New Moon, Ḥeshwan, 1st day	F	Oct.	12	W	Oct.	29	S	Oct.	18	F	Oct.	8	F	Oct.	28
New Moon, Ḥeshwan, 2nd day	Sa	Oct.	13	Th	Oct.	30	M	Oct.	19	Sa	Oct.	9	Sa	Oct.	29
New Moon, Kislew, 1st day	S	Nov.	11	F	Nov.	28	T	Nov.	17	S	Nov.	7	S	Nov.	27
New Moon, Kislew, 2nd day							W	Nov.	18	M	Nov.	8			
Ḥanukkah, 1st day	W	Dec.	5	M	Dec.	22	Sa	Dec.	12	Th	Dec.	2	W	Dec.	21
New Moon, Ṭevet, 1st day	M	Dec.	10	Sa	Dec.	27	Th	Dec.	17	T	Dec.	7	M	Dec.	26
New Moon, Ṭevet, 2nd day				S	Dec.	28	F	Dec.	18	W	Dec.	8	T	Dec.	27
					2009									2012	
Fast of 10th of Ṭevet	W	Dec.	19	T	Jan.	6	S	Dec.	27	F	Dec.	17	Th	Jan.	5

	2008			2009			2010			2011			2012		
New Moon, Shevaṭ	T	Jan.	8	M	Jan.	26	Sa	Jan.	16	Th	Jan.	6	W	Jan.	25
Ḥamishshah-ʻasar bi-Shevaṭ	T	Jan.	22	M	Feb.	9	Sa	Jan.	30	Th	Jan.	20	W	Feb.	8
New Moon, Adar I, 1st day	W	Feb.	6	T	Feb.	24	S	Feb.	14	F	Feb.	4	Th	Feb.	23
New Moon, Adar I, 2nd day	Th	Feb.	7	W	Feb.	25	M	Feb.	15	Sa	Feb.	5	F	Feb.	24
New Moon, Adar II, 1st day	F	Mar.	7							S	Mar.	6			
New Moon, Adar II, 2nd day	Sa	Mar.	8							M	Mar.	7			
Fast of Esther	Th	Mar.	20	M	Mar.	13	Th	Feb.	25	Th	Mar.	17	W	Mar.	7
Purim	F	Mar.	21	T	Mar.	14	S	Feb.	28	S	Mar.	20	Th	Mar.	8
Shushan Purim	Sa	Mar.	22	W	Mar.	15	M	Mar.	1	M	Mar.	21	F	Mar.	9
New Moon, Nisan	S	Apr.	6	Th	Mar.	26	T	Mar.	16	T	Apr.	5	Sa	Mar.	24
Passover, 1st day	S	Apr.	20	Th	Apr.	9	T	Mar.	30	T	Apr.	19	Sa	Apr.	7
Passover, 2nd day	M	Apr.	21	F	Apr.	10	W	Mar.	31	W	Apr.	20	S	Apr.	8
Passover, 7th day	Sa	Apr.	26	W	Apr.	15	M	Apr.	5	M	Apr.	25	F	Apr.	13
Passover, 8th day	S	Apr.	27	Th	Apr.	16	T	Apr.	6	T	Apr.	26	Sa	Apr.	14
Holocaust Memorial Day	F	May	2*	T	Apr.	21	S	Apr.	11	S	May	1	Th	Apr.	19
New Moon, Iyar, 1st day	M	May	5	F	Apr.	24	W	Apr.	14	W	May	4	S	Apr.	22
New Moon, Iyar, 2nd day	T	May	6	Sa	Apr.	25	Th	Apr.	15	Th	May	5	M	Apr.	23
Israel Independence Day	Th	May	8	W	Apr.	29	M	Apr.	19	M	May	9	F	Apr.	5*
Lag Ba-ʻomer	F	May	23	T	May	12	S	May	2	S	May	22	Th	May	10
Jerusalem Day	M	June	2	F	May	22*	W	May	12	W	June	1	S	May	20
New Moon, Siwan	W	June	4	S	May	24	F	May	14	F	June	3	T	May	22
Shavuʻot, 1st day	M	June	9	F	May	29	W	May	19	W	June	8	S	May	27
Shavuʻot, 2nd day	T	June	10	Sa	May	30	Th	May	20	Th	June	9	M	May	28
New Moon, Tammuz, 1st day	Th	July	3	M	June	22	Sa	June	12	Sa	July	2	W	June	20
New Moon, Tammuz, 2nd day	F	July	4	T	June	23	S	June	13	S	July	3	Th	June	21
Fast of 17th of Tammuz	S	July	20	Th	July	9	T	June	29	T	July	19	S	July	8
New Moon, Av	Sa	Aug.	2	W	July	22	M	July	12	M	Aug.	1	F	July	20
Fast of 9th of Av	S	Aug.	10	Th	July	30	T	July	20	T	Aug.	9	S	July	29
New Moon, Elul, 1st day	S	Aug.	31	Th	Aug.	20	T	Aug.	10	T	Aug.	30	Sa	Aug.	18
New Moon, Elul, 2nd day	M	Sept.	1	F	Aug.	21	W	Aug.	11	W	Aug.	31	S	Aug.	19

*Observed Thursday, a day earlier, to avoid conflict with the Sabbath.

CONDENSED MONTHLY CALENDAR (2007–2010)

2007, Jan. 20–Feb. 18] SHEVAṬ (30 DAYS) [5767

Civil Date	Day of the Week	Jewish Date	SABBATHS, FESTIVALS, FASTS	PENTATEUCHAL READING	PROPHETICAL READING
Jan. 20	Sa	Shevaṭ 1	Wa-'era'; New Moon	Exod. 6:2–9:35 Num. 28:9–15	Isaiah 66: 1–24
27	Sa	8	Bo'	Exod. 10:1–13:16	Jeremiah 46:13–28
Feb. 3	Sa	15	Be-shallaḥ (Shabbat Shirah) Ḥamishar 'Asar bi-Shevaṭ	Exod. 13:17–17:16	Judges 4:4–5:31 *Judges 5:1–31*
10	Sa	22	Yitro	Exod. 18:1–20:23	Isaiah 6:1–7:6; 9:5–6 *Isaiah 6: 1–13*
17	Sa	29	Mishpaṭim (Shabbat Sheḳalim)	Exod. 21:1–24:18 Exod. 30:11–16	II Kings 12: 1–17 *II Kings 11:17–12:17*
18	S	30	New Moon, first day	Num. 28: 1–15	

Italics are for Sephardi Minhag.

2007, Feb. 19–Mar. 19] ADAR (29 DAYS) [5767

Civil Date	Day of the Week	Jewish Date	SABBATHS, FESTIVALS, FASTS	PENTATEUCHAL READING	PROPHETICAL READING
Feb. 19	M	Adar 1	New Moon, second day	Num. 28:1–15	
24	Sa	6	Terumah	Exod. 25:1–27:19	I Kings 5:26–6:13
Mar. 1	Th	11	Fast of Esther	Exod. 32:11–14 Exod. 34:1–10 (morning and afternoon)	Isaiah 55:6–56:8 (afternoon only)
3	Sa	13	Teẓawweh (Shabbat Zakhor)	Exod. 27:20–30:10 Deut. 25:17–19	I Samuel 15:2–34 *I Samuel 15:1–34*
4	S	14	Purim	Exod. 17:8–16	Book of Esther (night before and morning)
5	M	15	Shushan Purim		
10	Sa	20	Ki tissa' (Shabbat Parah)	Exod. 30:11–34:35 Num. 19: 1–20	Ezekiel 36:16–38 *Ezekiel 36:16–36*
17	Sa	27	Wa-yaḳhel, Peḳude (Shabbat Ha-ḥodesh)	Exod. 35:1–40:38 Exod. 12:1–20	Ezekiel 45:16–46:18 *Ezekiel 45:18–46:15*

Italics are for Sephardi Minhag.

2007, Mar. 20–Apr. 18] NISAN (30 DAYS) [5767

Civil Date	Day of the Week	Jewish Date	SABBATHS, FESTIVALS, FASTS	PENTATEUCHAL READING	PROPHETICAL READING
Mar. 20	T	Nisan 1	New Moon	Num. 28:1–15	
24	Sa	5	Wa-yiḳra'	Levit. 1:1–5:26	Isaiah 43:21–44:23
31	Sa	12	Ẓaw (Shabbat Ha-gadol)	Levit. 6:1–8:36	Malachi 3:4–24
Apr. 2	M	14	Fast of Firstborn		
3	T	15	Passover, first day	Exod. 12:21–51 Num. 28:16–25	Joshua 5:2–6:1, 27
4	W	16	Passover, second day	Levit. 22:26–23:44 Num. 28:16–25	II Kings 23:1–9, 21–25
5	Th	17	Ḥol Ha-mo'ed, first day	Exod. 13:1–16 Num. 28:19–25	
6	F	18	Ḥol Ha-mo'ed, second day	Exod. 22:24–23:19 Num. 28:19–25	
7	Sa	19	Shabbat Ḥol Ha-mo'ed, third day	Exod. 33:12–34:26 Num. 28:19–25	Ezekiel 37:1–14
8	S	20	Ḥol Ha-mo'ed, fourth day	Num. 9: 1–14 Num. 28:19–25	
9	M	21	Passover, seventh day	Exod. 13:17–15:26 Num. 28:19–25	II Samuel 22:1–51
10	T	22	Passover, eighth day	Deut. 15:19–16:17 Num. 28:19–25	Isaiah 10:32–12:6
14	Sa	26	Shemini	Levit. 9:1–11:47	II Samuel 6:1–7:17 *II Samuel 6:1–19*
15	S	27	Holocaust Memorial Day		
18	W	30	New Moon, first day	Num. 28:1–15	

Italics are for Sephardi Minhag.

2007, Apr. 19–May 17] IYAR (29 DAYS) [5767

Civil Date	Day of the Week	Jewish Date	SABBATHS, FESTIVALS, FASTS	PENTATEUCHAL READING	PROPHETICAL READING
Apr. 19	Th	Iyar 1	New Moon, second day	Num. 28:9–15	
21	Sa	3	Tazria', Meẓora'	Levit. 12:1–15:33	II Kings 7:3–20
23	M	5	Israel Independence Day		
28	Sa	10	Aḥarei Mot, Ḳedoshim	Levit. 16:1–20:27	Amos 9:7–15 *Ezekiel 20:2–20*
May 5	Sa	17	Emor	Levit. 21:1–24:23	Ezekiel 44:15–31
6	S	18	Lag Ba-'omer		
12	Sa	24	Be-har, Be-ḥuḳḳotai	Levit. 25:1–27:34	Jeremiah 16:19–17:14
16	W	28	Jerusalem Day		

Italics are for Sephardi Minhag.

2007, May 18–June 16] SIWAN (30 DAYS) [5767

Civil Date	Day of the Week	Jewish Date	SABBATHS, FESTIVALS, FASTS	PENTATEUCHAL READING	PROPHETICAL READING
May 18	F	Siwan 1	New Moon	Num. 28:1–15	
19	Sa	2	Be-midbar	Num. 1:1–4:20	Hosea 2:1–22
23	W	6	Shavu'ot, first day	Exod. 19:1–20:23 Num. 28:26–31	Ezekiel 1:1–28; 3:12
24	Th	7	Shavu'ot, second day	Deut. 15:19–16:17 Num. 28:26–31	Habbakuk 3:1–19 *Habbakuk 2:20–3:19*
26	Sa	9	Naso'	Num. 4:21–7:89	Judges 13:2–25
June 2	Sa	16	Be-ha'alotekha	Num. 8:1–12:16	Zechariah 2:14–4:7
9	Sa	23	Shelaḥ lekha	Num. 13:1–15:41	Joshua 2:1–24
16	Sa	30	Ḳoraḥ; New Moon, first day	Num. 16:1–18:32 Num. 28:9–15	Isaiah 66:1–24 *Isaiah 66:1–24* *I Samuel 20:18, 42*

Italics are for Sephardi Minhag.

2007, June 17–July 15] TAMMUZ (29 DAYS) [5767

Civil Date	Day of the Week	Jewish Date	SABBATHS, FESTIVALS, FASTS	PENTATEUCHAL READING	PROPHETICAL READING
June 17	S	Tammuz 1	New Moon, second day	Num. 28:1–15	
23	Sa	7	Ḥuḳḳat	Num. 19:1–22:1	Judges 11:1–33
30	Sa	14	Balaḳ	Num. 22:2–25:9	Micah 5:6–6:8
July 3	T	17	Fast of 17th of Tammuz	Exod. 32:11–14 Exod. 34: 1–10 (morning and afternoon)	Isaiah 55:6–56:8 (afternoon only)
7	Sa	21	Pineḥas	Num. 25:10–30:1	Jeremiah 1:1–2:3
14	Sa	28	Maṭṭot Mas'e	Num. 30:2–36:13	Jeremiah 2:4–28; 3:4 *Jeremiah 2:4–28; 4:1–2*

Italics are for Sephardi Minhag.

2007, July 16–Aug. 14] AV (30 DAYS) [5767

Civil Date	Day of the Week	Jewish Date	SABBATHS, FESTIVALS, FASTS	PENTATEUCHAL READING	PROPHETICAL READING
July 16	M	Av 1	New Moon	Num. 28:1–15	
21	Sa	6	Devarim (Shabbat Ḥazon)	Deut. 1:1–3:22	Isaiah 1:1–27
24	T	9	Fast of 9th of Av	Morning: Deut. 4:25–40 Afternoon: Exod. 32:11–14 Exod. 34:1–10	(Lamentations is read the night before) Jeremiah 8:13–9:23 (morning) Isaiah 55:6–56:8 (afternoon)
28	Sa	13	Wa-etḥannan (Shabbat Naḥamu)	Deut. 3:23–7:11	Isaiah 40:1–26
Aug. 4	Sa	20	‘Eḳev	Deut. 7:12–11:25	Isaiah 49:14–51:3
11	Sa	27	Re’eh	Deut. 11:26–16:17	Isaiah 54:11–55:5
14	T	30	New Moon, first day	Numbers 28:1–15	

Italics are for Sephardi Minhag.

2007, Aug. 15–Sept. 12] ELUL (29 DAYS) [5767

Civil Date	Day of the Week	Jewish Date	SABBATHS, FESTIVALS, FASTS	PENTATEUCHAL READING	PROPHETICAL READING
Aug. 15	W	Elul 1	New Moon, second day	Num. 28:1–15	
18	Sa	4	Shofeṭim	Deut. 16:18–21:9	Isaiah 51:12–52:12
25	Sa	11	Ki teẓe'	Deut. 21:10–25:19	Isaiah 54:1–10
Sept. 1	Sa	18	Ki tavo'	Deut. 26:1–29:8	Isaiah 60:1–22
8	Sa	25	Niẓẓavim, Wa-yelekh	Deut. 29:9–31:30	Isaiah 61:10–63:9

Italics are for Sephardi Minhag.

2007, Sept. 13–Oct. 12] TISHRI (30 DAYS) [5768

Civil Date	Day of the Week	Jewish Date	SABBATHS, FESTIVALS, FASTS	PENTATEUCHAL READING	PROPHETICAL READING
Sept. 13	Th	Tishri 1	Rosh Ha-shanah, first day	Gen. 21:1–34 Num. 29:1–6	I Samuel 1:1–2:10
14	F	2	Rosh Ha-shana, second day	Gen. 22:1–24 Num. 29:1–6	Jeremiah 31:2–20
15	Sa	3	Ha'azinu (Shabbat Shuvah)	Deut. 32:1–52	Hosea 14:2–10 Micah 7:18–20 Joel 2:15–27 *Hosea 14:2–10* *Micah 7:18–20*
16	S	4	Fast of Gedaliah	Exod. 32:11–14 Exod. 34:1–10 (morning and afternoon)	Isaiah 55:6–56:8 (afternoon only)
22	Sa	10	Yom Kippur	Morning: Levit. 16:1–34 Num. 29:7–11 Afternoon: Levit. 18:1–30	Isaiah 57:14–58:14 Afternoon: Jonah 1:1–4:11 Micah 7:18–20
27	Th	15	Sukkot, first day	Levit. 22:26–23:44 Num. 29:12–16	Zechariah 14:1–21
28	F	16	Sukkot, second day	Levit. 22:26–23:44 Num. 29:12–16	I Kings 8:2–21
29	Sa	17	Shabbat Ḥol Ha-mo'ed, first day	Exod. 33:12–34:26 Num. 29:17–22	Ezekiel 38:18–39:16
30–Oct. 2	S-T	18-20	Ḥol Ha-mo'ed, second through fourth days	S: Num. 29:20–28 M: Num. 29:23–31 T: Num. 29:26–34	
3	W	21	Hosha'na' Rabbah	Num. 29:26–34	
4	Th	22	Shemini 'Aẓeret	Deut. 14:22–16:17 Num. 29:35–30:1	I Kings 8:54–66
5	F	23	Simḥat Torah	Deut. 33:1–34:12 Gen. 1:1–2:3 Num. 29:35–30:1	Joshua 1:1–18 *Joshua 1:1–9*
6	Sa	24	Be-re'shit	Gen. 1:1–6:8	Isaiah 42:5–43:10 *Isaiah 42:5–21*
12	F	30	New Moon, first day	Num. 28: 1–15	

Italics are for Sephardi Minhag.

2007, Oct. 13–Nov. 10 ḤESHWAN (29 DAYS) [5768

Civil Date	Day of the Week	Jewish Date	SABBATHS, FESTIVALS, FASTS	PENTATEUCHAL READING	PROPHETICAL READING
Oct. 13	Sa	Ḥeshwan 1	Noaḥ; New Moon, second day	Gen. 6:9–11:32 Num. 28:1–15	Isaiah 66:1–24
20	Sa	8	Lekh lekha	Gen. 12:1–17:27	Isaiah 40:27–41:16
27	Sa	15	Wa-yera'	Gen. 18:1–22:24	II Kings 4:1–37 *II Kings 4:1–23*
Nov. 3	Sa	22	Ḥayye Sarah	Gen. 23:1–25:18	I Kings 1:1–31
10	Sa	29	Toledot	Gen. 25:19–28:9	I Samuel 20:18–42

Italics are for Sephardi Minhag.

2007, Nov. 11–Dec. 9 KISLEW (29 DAYS) [5768

Civil Date	Day of the Week	Jewish Date	SABBATHS, FESTIVALS, FASTS	PENTATEUCHAL READING	PROPHETICAL READING
Nov. 11	S	Kislew 1	New Moon, second day	Num. 28:1–15	
17	Sa	7	Wa-yeẓe'	Gen. 28:10–32:3	Hosea 12:13–14:10
24	Sa	14	Wa-yishlaḥ	Gen. 32:4–36:43	Hosea 11:7–12:12 *Obadiah 1:1–21*
Dec. 1	Sa	21	Wa-yeshev	Gen. 37:1–40:23	Amos 2:6–3:8
5	W	25	Ḥanukkah, first day	Num. 7:1–17	
6–7	Th–F	26–27	Ḥanukkah, second and third days	Th: Num. 7:18–29 F: Num. 7:24–35	
8	Sa	28	Mi-ḳeẓ Ḥanukkah, fourth day	Gen. 41:1–44:17 Num. 7:30–35	Zechariah 2:14–4:7
9	S	29	Ḥanukkah, fifth day	Num. 7:36–47	

Italics are for Sephardi Minhag.

2007, Dec. 10–Jan. 7, 2008] ṬEVET (29 DAYS) [5768

Civil Date	Day of the Week	Jewish Date	SABBATHS, FESTIVALS, FASTS	PENTATEUCHAL READING	PROPHETICAL READING
Dec. 10	M	Ṭevet 1	New Moon; Ḥanukkah, sixth day	Num. 28:1–15 Num. 7:42–47	
11	T	2	Ḥanukkah, seventh day	Num. 7:48–59	
12	W	3	Ḥanukkah, eighth day	Num. 7:54–8:4	
15	Sa	6	Wa-yiggash	Gen. 44:18–47:27	Ezekiel 37:15–28
19	W	10	Fast of 10th of Ṭevet	Exod. 32:11–14 Exod. 34:1–10 (morning and afternoon)	Isaiah 55:6–56:8 (afternoon only)
22	Sa	13	Wa-yeḥi	Gen. 47:28–50:26	I Kings 2:1–12
29	Sa	20	Shemot	Exod. 1:1–6:1	Isaiah 27:6–28:13 Isaiah 29:22–23 *Jeremiah 1:1–2:3*
Jan. 5	Sa	27	Wa-'era'	Exod. 6:2–9:35	Ezekiel 28:25–29:21

Italics are for Sephardi Minhag.

2008, Jan. 8–Feb. 6] SHEVAṬ (30 DAYS) [5768

Civil Date	Day of the Week	Jewish Date	SABBATHS, FESTIVALS, FASTS	PENTATEUCHAL READING	PROPHETICAL READING
Jan. 8	T	Shevaṭ 1	New Moon	Num. 28: 1–15	
12	Sa	5	Bo'	Exod. 10:1–13:16	Jeremiah 46:13–28
19	Sa	12	Be-shallaḥ (Shabbat Shirah)	Exod. 13:17–17:16	Judges 4:4–5:31 *Judges 5:1–31*
22	T	15	Ḥamisha 'Asar bi-Shevaṭ		
26	Sa	19	Yitro	Exod. 18:1–20:23	Isaiah 6:1–7:6; 9:5–6 *Isaiah 6:1–13*
Feb. 2	Sa	26	Mishpaṭim	Exod. 21:1–24:18	Jeremiah 34:8–22; 33:25–26
6	W	30	New Moon, first day	Num. 28:1–15	

Italics are for Sephardi Minhag.

2008, Feb. 7–Mar. 7 ADAR I (30 DAYS) [5768

Civil Date	Day of the Week	Jewish Date	SABBATHS, FESTIVALS, FASTS	PENTATEUCHAL READING	PROPHETICAL READING
Feb. 7	Th	Adar I 1	New Moon, second day	Num. 28:1–15	
9	Sa	3	Terumah	Exod. 25:1–27:19	I Kings 5:26–6:13
16	Sa	10	Teẓawweh	Exod. 27:20–30:10	Ezekiel 43:10–27
23	Sa	17	Ki tissa'	Exod. 30:11–34:35	I Kings 18:1–39 *I Kings 18:20–39*
Mar. 1	Sa	24	Wa-yaḳhel	Exod. 35:1–38:20	I Kings 7:40–50
7	F	30	New Moon, first day	Num. 28:1–15	

Italics are for Sephardi Minhag.

2008, Mar. 8–Apr. 5 ADAR II (29 DAYS) [5768

Civil Date	Day of the Week	Jewish Date	SABBATHS, FESTIVALS, FASTS	PENTATEUCHAL READING	PROPHETICAL READING
Mar. 8	Sa	Adar II 1	Peḳude, New Moon, second day (Shabbat Sheḳalim)	Exod. 38:21–40:38 Num. 28:9–15 Exod. 30:11–16	II Kings 12:1–17 *II Kings 11:17–12:17* *Isaiah 66:1, 23*
15	Sa	8	Wa-yiḳra' (Shabbat Zakhor)	Deut. 25: 17–19	I Samuel 15:2–34 *I Samuel 15:1–34*
20	Th	13	Fast of Esther	Exod. 32:11–14 Exod. 34: 1–10 (morning and afternoon)	Isaiah 55:6–56:8 (afternoon only)
21	F	14	Purim	Exod. 17:8–16	Book of Esther (night before and morning)
22	Sa	15	Ẓaw	Levit. 6:1–8:36	Jeremiah 7:21–8:3; 9:22–23
29	Sa	22	Shemini (Shabbat Parah)	Levit. 9:1–11:47 Num. 19:1–20	Ezekiel 36:16–38 *Ezekiel 36:16–36*
Apr. 5	Sa	29	Tazria' (Shabbat Ha-ḥodesh)	Levit. 12: 1–13:59 Exod. 12:1–20	Ezekiel 45:16–46:1 *Ezekiel 45:18–46:15* *I Sam. 20:18, 42*

Italics are for Sephardi Minhag.

2008 Apr. 6–May 5] NISAN (30 DAYS) [5768

Civil Date	Day of the Week	Jewish Date	SABBATHS, FESTIVALS, FASTS	PENTATEUCHAL READING	PROPHETICAL READING
Apr. 6	S	Nisan 1	New Moon	Num. 28:1–15	
12	Sa	7	Meẓora‘	Lev. 14:1–15:33	II Kings 7:3–20
17	Th	12	Fast of Firstborn		
19	Sa	14	Aḥarei Mot (Shabbat Ha-gadol)	Lev. 16:1–18:30	Malachi 3:4–24
20	S	15	Passover, first day	Exod. 12:21–51 Num. 28:16–25	Joshua 5:2–6:1, 27
21	M	16	Passover, second day	Levit. 22:26–23:44 Num. 28:16–25	II Kings 23:1–9, 21–25
22	T	17	Ḥol Ha-mo‘ed, first day	Exod. 13:1–16 Num. 28:19–25	
23	W	18	Ḥol Ha-mo‘ed, second day	Exod. 22:24–23:19 Num. 28:19–25	
24	Th	19	Ḥol Ha-mo‘ed, third day	Exod. 34:1–26 Num. 28:19–25	
25	F	20	Ḥol Ha-mo‘ed, fourth day	Num. 9:1–14 Num. 28:19–25	
26	Sa	21	Passover, seventh day	Exod. 13:17–15:26 Num. 28:19–25	II Samuel 22:1–51
27	S	22	Passover, eighth day	Deut. 15:19–16:17 Num. 28:19–25	Isaiah 10:32–12:6
May 1	Th	26	Holocaust Memorial Day		
3	Sa	28	Ḳedoshim	Levit. 16:1–20:27	Amos 9:7–15 *Ezekiel 20:2–20*
5	M	30	New Moon, first day	Num. 28: 1–15	

Italics are for Sephardi Minhag.

2008, May 6–June 3] IYAR (29 DAYS) [5768

Civil Date	Day of the Week	Jewish Date	SABBATHS, FESTIVALS, FASTS	PENTATEUCHAL READING	PROPHETICAL READING
May 6	T	Iyar 1	New Moon, second day	Num. 28: 9–15	
8	Th	3	Israel Independence Day		II Kings 7:3–20
10	Sa	5	Emor	Levit. 21:1–24:23	Ezekiel 44:15–31
17	Sa	12	Be-har	Levit. 25:1–26:2	Jeremiah 32:6–27
23	F	18	Lag Ba-'omer		
24	Sa	19	Beḥuḳḳotai	Levit 26:3–27:34	Jeremiah 16:19–17:14
31	Sa	26	Be-midbar	Num. 1:1–4:20	Hosea 2:1–22
June 2	M	28	Jerusalem Day		

Italics are for Sephardi Minhag.

2008, June 4–June 16] SIWAN (30 DAYS) [5768

Civil Date	Day of the Week	Jewish Date	SABBATHS, FESTIVALS, FASTS	PENTATEUCHAL READING	PROPHETICAL READING
June 4	W	Siwan 1	New Moon	Num. 28:1–15	
7	Sa	4	Naso'	Num. 4:21–7:89	Judges 13:2–25
9	M	6	Shavu'ot, first day	Exod. 19:1–20:23 Num. 28:26–31	Ezekiel 1:1–28; 3:12
10	T	7	Shavu'ot, second day	Deut. 15:19–16:17 Num. 28:26–31	Habbakuk 3:1–19 *Habbakuk 2:20–3:19*
14	Sa	11	Be-ha'alotekha	Num. 8:1–12:16	Zechariah 2:14–4:7
21	Sa	18	Shelaḥ lekha	Num. 13:1–15:41	Joshua 2:1–24
28	Sa	25	Ḳoraḥ	Num. 16:1–18:32	I Samuel 11:14–12:22
July 3	Th	30	New Moon, first day	Num. 28:1–15	

Italics are for Sephardi Minhag.

2008, July 4–Aug. 1] TAMMUZ (29 DAYS) [5768

Civil Date	Day of the Week	Jewish Date	SABBATHS, FESTIVALS, FASTS	PENTATEUCHAL READING	PROPHETICAL READING
July 4	F	Tammuz 1	New Moon, second day	Num. 28:1–15	
5	Sa	2	Ḥuḳḳat	Num. 19:1–22:1	Judges 11:1–33
12	Sa	9	Balaḳ	Num. 22:2–25:9	Micah 5:6–6:8
19	Sa	16	Pineḥas	Num. 25:10–30:1	I Kings 18:46–19:21
20	S	17	Fast of 17th of Tammuz	Exod. 32:11–14 Exod. 34:1–10 (morning and afternoon)	Isaiah 55:6–56:8 (afternoon only)
26	Sa	23	Maṭṭot	Num. 30:2–32:42	Jeremiah 1:1–2:3

Italics are for Sephardi Minhag.

2008, Aug. 2–Aug. 31] AV (30 DAYS) [5768

Civil Date	Day of the Week	Jewish Date	SABBATHS, FESTIVALS, FASTS	PENTATEUCHAL READING	PROPHETICAL READING
Aug. 2	Sa	Av 1	Mas'e, New Moon	Num. 33:1–36:13 Num. 28:9–15	Jeremiah 2:4–28; 3:4 *Jeremiah 2:4–28; 4:1–2* *Isaiah 66:1, 23*
9	Sa	8	Devarim (Shabbat Ḥazon)	Deut. 1:1–3:22	Isaiah 1:1–27
10	S	9	Fast of 9th of Av	Morning: Deut. 4:25–40 Afternoon: Exod. 32:11–14 Exod. 34:1–10	(Lamentations is read the night before) Jeremiah 8:13–9:23 (morning) Isaiah 55:6–56:8 (afternoon)
16	Sa	15	Wa-etḥannan (Shabbat Naḥamu)	Deut. 3:23–7:11	Isaiah 40:1–26
23	Sa	22	'Eḳev	Deut. 7:12–11:25	Isaiah 49:14–51:3
30	Sa	29	Re'eh	Deut. 11:26–16:17	Isaiah 54:11–55:5 *Isaiah 54:11–55:5* *I Samuel 20:18, 42*
31	S	30	New Moon, first day	Numbers 28:1–15	

Italics are for Sephardi Minhag.

2008, Sept. 1 – Sept. 29 ELUL (29 DAYS) [5768

Civil Date	Day of the Week	Jewish Date	SABBATHS, FESTIVALS, FASTS	PENTATEUCHAL READING	PROPHETICAL READING
Sept. 1	M	Elul 1	New Moon, second day	Num. 28:1–15	
6	Sa	6	Shofeṭim	Deut. 16:18–21:9	Isaiah 51:12–52:12
13	Sa	13	Ki teẓe'	Deut. 21:10–25:19	Isaiah 54:1–10
20	Sa	20	Ki tavo'	Deut. 26:1–29:8	Isaiah 60:1–22
27	Sa	27	Niẓẓavim	Deut. 29:9–30:20	Isaiah 61:10–63:9

Italics are for Sephardi Minhag.

Civil Date	Day of the Week	Jewish Date	SABBATHS, FESTIVALS, FASTS	PENTATEUCHAL READING	PROPHETICAL READING
Sept. 30	T	Tishri 1	Rosh Ha-shanah, first day	Gen. 21:1–34 Num. 29:1–6	I Samuel 1:1–2:10
Oct. 1	W	2	Rosh Ha-shanah, second day	Gen. 22:1–24 Num. 29:1–6	Jeremiah 31:2–20
2	Th	3	Fast of Gedaliah	Exod. 32:11–14 Exod. 34:1–10 (morning and afternoon)	Isaiah 55:6–56:8 (afternoon only)
4	Sa	5	Wa-yelekh (Shabbat Shuvah)	Deut. 31:1–30	Hosea 14:2–10 Micah 7:18–20 Joel 2:15–27 *Hosea 14:2–10* *Micah 7:18–20*
9	Th	10	Yom Kippur	Morning: Levit. 16:1–34 Num. 29:7–11 Afternoon: Levit. 18:1–30	Isaiah 57:14–58:14 Afternoon: Jonah 1:1–4:11 Micah 7:18–20
11	Sa	12	Ha'azinu	Deut. 32:1–52	II Samuel 22:1–51
14	T	15	Sukkot, first day	Levit. 22:26–23:44 Num. 29:12–16	Zechariah 14:1–21
15	W	16	Sukkot, second day	Levit. 22:26–23:44 Num. 29:12–16	I Kings 8:2–21
16–17	Th–F	17–18	Ḥol Ha-mo'ed, first and second days	Th: Num. 29:17–25 F: Num. 29:20–28	
18	Sa	19	Shabbat Ḥol Ha-mo'ed, third day	Exod. 33:12–34:26 Num. 29:23–28	Ezekiel 38:18–39:16
19	S	20	Ḥol Ha-mo'ed, fourth day	Num. 29:26–31	
20	M	21	Hosha'na' Rabbah	Num. 29:26–34	
21	T	22	Shemini 'Aẓeret	Deut. 14:22–16:17 Num. 29:35–30:1	I Kings 8:54–66
22	W	23	Simḥat Torah	Deut. 33:1–34:12 Gen. 1:1–2:3 Num. 29:35–30:1	Joshua 1:1–18 *Joshua 1:1–9*
25	Sa	26	Be-re'shit	Gen. 1:1–6:8	Isaiah 42:5–43:10 *Isaiah 42:5–21*
29	W	30	New Moon, first day	Num. 28: 1–15	

Italics are for Sephardi Minhag.

2008, Oct. 30–Nov. 27] ḤESHWAN (29 DAYS) [5769

Civil Date	Day of the Week	Jewish Date	SABBATHS, FESTIVALS, FASTS	PENTATEUCHAL READING	PROPHETICAL READING
Oct. 30	Th 1	Ḥeshwan	New Moon, second day	Num. 28:1–15	
Nov. 1	Sa	3	Noaḥ	Gen. 6:9–11:32	Isaiah 54:1–55:5 *Isaiah 54:1–10*
8	Sa	10	Lekh lekha	Gen. 12:1–17:27	Isaiah 40:27–41:16
15	Sa	17	Wa-yera’	Gen. 18:1–22:24	II Kings 4:1–37 *II Kings 4:1–23*
22	Sa	24	Ḥayye Sarah	Gen. 23:1–25:18	I Kings 1:1–31

Italics are for Sephardi Minhag.

2008 Nov. 28–Dec. 27] KISLEW (30 DAYS) [5769

Civil Date	Day of the Week	Jewish Date	SABBATHS, FESTIVALS, FASTS	PENTATEUCHAL READING	PROPHETICAL READING
Nov. 28	F	Kislew 1	New Moon, second day	Num. 28:1–15	
29	Sa	2	Toledot	Gen. 25:19–28:9	Malachi 1:1–2:7
Dec. 6	Sa	9	Wa-yeẓe	Gen. 28:10–32:3	Hosea 12:13–14:10
13	Sa	16	Wa-yishlaḥ	Gen. 32:4–36:43	Hosea 11:7–12:12 *Obadiah 1:1–21*
20	Sa	23	Wa-yeshev	Gen. 37:1–40:23	Amos 2:6–3:8
22	M	25	Ḥanukkah, first day	Num. 7:1–17	
23–26	T–F	26–29	Ḥanukkah, second to fifth days	T: Num. 7:18–29 W: Num 7:24–35 Th: Num. 7:30–41 F: Num. 7:36–47	
27	Sa	30	Mi-ḳeẓ, Ḥanukkah, sixth day, New Moon, first day	Gen. 41:1–44: 17 Num. 28:9–15 Num. 7:48–53	Zechariah 2:14–4:7

Italics are for Sephardi Minhag.

2008, Dec. 28–Jan. 25, 2009] ṬEVET (29 DAYS) [5769

Civil Date	Day of the Week	Jewish Date	SABBATHS, FESTIVALS, FASTS	PENTATEUCHAL READING	PROPHETICAL READING
Dec. 28	S	Ṭevet 1	New Moon, second day, Ḥanukkah, seventh day	Num. 28:1–15 Num. 7:48–53	
29	M	2	Ḥanukkah, eighth day	Num. 7:54–8:4	
Jan. 3	Sa	7	Wa-yiggash	Gen. 44:18–47:27	Ezekiel 37:15–28
6	T	10	Fast of 10th of Ṭevet	Exod. 32:11–14 Exod. 34:1–10 (morning and afternoon)	Isaiah 55:6–56:8 (afternoon only)
10	Sa	14	Wa-yeḥi	Gen. 47:28–50:26	I Kings 2:1–12
17	Sa	21	Shemot	Exod. 1:1–6:1	Isaiah 27:6–28:13 Isaiah 29:22–23 *Jeremiah 1:1–2:3*
24	Sa	28	Wa-'era'	Exod. 6:2–9:35	Ezekiel 28:25–29:21

Italics are for Sephardi Minhag.

2009, Jan. 26–Feb. 24] SHEVAṬ (30 DAYS) [5769

Civil Date	Day of the Week	Jewish Date	SABBATHS, FESTIVALS, FASTS	PENTATEUCHAL READING	PROPHETICAL READING
Jan. 26	M	Shevaṭ 1	New Moon	Num. 28: 1–15	
31	Sa	6	Bo'	Exod. 10:1–13:16	Jeremiah 46:13–28
Feb. 7	Sa	13	Be-shallaḥ (Shabbat Shirah)	Exod. 13:17–17:16	Judges 4:4 –5:31 *Judges 5:1–31*
9	M	15	Ḥamisha 'Asar bi-Shevaṭ		
14	Sa	20	Yitro	Exod. 18:1–20:23	Isaiah 6:1–7:6; 9:5–6 *Isaiah 6:1–13*
21	Sa	27	Mishpaṭim (Shabbat Sheḳalim)	Exod. 21:1–24:18 Exod. 30: 11–16	II Kings 12:1–17 *II Kings 11:17–12:17*
24	T	30	New Moon, first day	Num. 28:1–15	

Italics are for Sephardi Minhag.

2009, Feb. 25–Mar. 25 ADAR (29 DAYS) [5769

Civil Date	Day of the Week	Jewish Date	SABBATHS, FESTIVALS, FASTS	PENTATEUCHAL READING	PROPHETICAL READING
Feb. 25	W	Adar 1	New Moon, second day	Num. 28:1–15	
28	Sa	4	Terumah	Exod. 25:1–27:19	I Kings 5:26–6:13
Mar. 7	Sa	11	Teẓawweh (Shabbat Zakhor)	Exod. 27:20–30:10 Deut. 25:17–19	I Samuel 15:2–34 *I Samuel 15:1–34*
9	M	13	Fast of Esther	Exod. 32:11–14, 34:1–10 (morning and afternoon)	Isaiah 55:6–56:8 (afternoon only)
10	T	14	Purim	Exod. 17:8–16	Book of Esther (night before and morning)
11	W	15	Shushan Purim	Num. 28:1–15	
14	Sa	18	Ki tissa' (Shabbat Parah)	Exod. 30:11–34:35 Num. 19:1–22	Ezekiel 36:16–38 *Ezekiel 36:16–36*
21	Sa	25	Wa-yaḳhel, Peḳude (Shabbat Ha-ḥodesh)	Exod. 35:1–40:38 Exod. 12:1–20	Ezekiel 45:16–46:1 *Ezekiel 45:18–46:15*

Italics are for Sephardi Minhag.

2009, Mar. 26–Apr. 24 NISAN (30 DAYS) [5769

Civil Date	Day of the Week	Jewish Date	SABBATHS, FESTIVALS, FASTS	PENTATEUCHAL READING	PROPHETICAL READING
Mar. 26	Th	Nisan 1	New Moon	Num. 28:1–15	
28	Sa	3	Wa-yiḳra'	Levit. 1:1–5:26	Isaiah 43:21–44:23
Apr. 4	Sa	10	Ẓaw (Shabbat Ha-gadol)	Levit. 6:1–8:36	Malachi 3:4–24
8	W	14	Fast of Firstborn		
9	Th	15	Passover, first day	Exod. 12:21–51 Num. 28:16–25	Joshua 5:2–6:1, 27
10	F	16	Passover, second day	Levit. 22:26–23:44 Num. 28:16–25	II Kings 23:1–9, 21–25
11	Sa	17	Ḥol Ha-mo'ed, first day	Exod. 33:12–34:26 Num. 28:19–25	Ezekiel 37:1–14
12	S	18	Ḥol Ha-mo'ed, second day	Exod. 13:1–16 Num. 28:19–25	
13	M	19	Ḥol Ha-mo'ed, third day	Exod. 22:24–23:19 Num. 28:19–25	
14	T	20	Ḥol Ha-mo'ed, fourth day	Num. 9:1–14 Num. 28:19–25	
15	W	21	Passover, seventh day	Exod. 13:17–15:26 Num. 28:19–25	II Samuel 22:1–51
16	Th	22	Passover, eighth day	Deut. 15:19–16:17 Num. 28:19–25	Isaiah 10:32–12:6
18	Sa	24	Shemini	Levit. 9:1–11:47	II Samuel 6:1–7:17 *II Samuel 6:1–19*
21	T	27	Holocaust Memorial Day		
24	F	30	New Moon, first day	Num. 28:1–15	

Italics are for Sephardi Minhag.

2009 Apr. 25–May 23] IYAR (29 DAYS) [5769

Civil Date	Day of the Week	Jewish Date	SABBATHS, FESTIVALS, FASTS	PENTATEUCHAL READING	PROPHETICAL READING
Apr. 25	Sa	Iyar 1	Tazria', Meẓora'; New Moon, second day	Levit. 12:1–15:33 Num. 28:1–15	Isaiah 66:1–24
29	W	5	Israel Independence Day		
May 2	Sa	8	Aḥarei Mot, Ḳedoshim	Lev. 16:1–20:27	Amos 9:7–15 *Ezekiel 20:2–20*
9	Sa	15	Emor	Levit. 21:1–24:23	Ezekiel 44:15–31
12	T	18	Lag Ba-'omer		
16	Sa	22	Be-har, Beḥuḳḳotai	Levit. 25:1–27:34	Jeremiah 16:19–17:14
21	Th	27	Jerusalem Day		
23	Sa	29	Be-midbar	Num. 1:1–4:20	I Samuel 20:18–42

Italics are for Sephardi Minhag.

2009, May 24–June 22] SIWAN (30 DAYS) [5769

Civil Date	Day of the Week	Jewish Date	SABBATHS, FESTIVALS, FASTS	PENTATEUCHAL READING	PROPHETICAL READING
May 24	S	Siwan 1	New Moon	Num. 28:1–15	
29	F	6	Shavu'ot, first day	Exod. 19:1–20:23 Num. 28:26–31	Ezekiel 1:1–28; 3:12
30	Sa	7	Shavu'ot, second day	Deut. 15:19–16:17 Num. 28:26–31	Habbakuk 3:1–19 *Habbakuk 2:20–3:19*
June 6	Sa	14	Naso'	Num. 4:21–7:89	Judges 13:2–25
13	Sa	21	Be-ha'alotekha	Num. 8:1–12:16	Zechariah 2:14–4:7
20	Sa	28	Shelaḥ lekha	Num. 13:1–15:41	Joshua 2:1–24
22	M	30	New Moon, first day	Num. 28:1–15	

Italics are for Sephardi Minhag.

2009, June 23–July 21] TAMMUZ (29 DAYS) [5769

Civil Date	Day of the Week	Jewish Date	SABBATHS, FESTIVALS, FASTS	PENTATEUCHAL READING	PROPHETICAL READING
June 23	T	Tammuz 1	New Moon, second day	Num. 28:1–15	
27	Sa	5	Ḳoraḥ	Num. 16:1–18:32	I Samuel 11:14–12:22
July 4	Sa	12	Ḥuḳḳat, Balaḳ	Num. 19:1–25:9	Micah 5:6–6:8
9	Th	17	Fast of 17th of Tammuz	Exod. 32:11–14 Exod. 34:1–10 (morning and afternoon)	Isaiah 55:6–56:8 (afternoon only)
11	Sa	19	Pineḥas	Num. 25:10–30:1	Jeremiah 1:1–2:3
18	Sa	26	Maṭṭot, Mas'e	Num. 30:2–36:13	Jeremiah 2:4–28; 3:4 *Jeremiah 2:4–28; 4:1–2*

Italics are for Sephardi Minhag.

2009, July 22–Aug. 20] AV (30 DAYS) [5769

Civil Date	Day of the Week	Jewish Date	SABBATHS, FESTIVALS, FASTS	PENTATEUCHAL READING	PROPHETICAL READING
July 22	W	Av 1	New Moon	Num. 28:1–15	
25	Sa	4	Devarim (Shabbat Ḥazon)	Deut. 1:1–3:22	Isaiah 1:1–27
30	Th	9	Fast of 9th of Av	Morning: Deut. 4:25–40 Afternoon: Exod. 32:11–14 Exod. 34:1–10	(Lamentations is read the night before) Jeremiah 8:13–9:23 (morning) Isaiah 55:6–56:8 (afternoon)
Aug. 1	Sa	11	Wa-etḥannan (Shabbat Naḥamu)	Deut. 3:23–7:11	Isaiah 40:1–26
8	Sa	18	'Eḳev	Deut. 7:12–11:25	Isaiah 49:14–51:3
15	Sa	25	Re'eh	Deut. 11:26–16:17	Isaiah 54:11–55:5
20	Th	30	New Moon, first day	Numbers 28:1–15	

Italics are for Sephardi Minhag.

2009, Aug. 21–Sept. 18] ELUL (29 DAYS) [5769

Civil Date	Day of the Week	Jewish Date	SABBATHS, FESTIVALS, FASTS	PENTATEUCHAL READING	PROPHETICAL READING
Aug. 21	F	Elul 1	New Moon, second day	Num. 28:1–15	
22	Sa	2	Shofeṭim	Deut. 16:18–21:9	Isaiah 51:12–52:12
29	Sa	9	Ki teẓe’	Deut. 21:10–25:19	Isaiah 54:1–10
Sept. 5	Sa	16	Ki tavo’	Deut. 26:1–29:8	Isaiah 60:1–22
12	Sa	23	Niẓẓavim, Wa-yelekh	Deut. 29:9–31:30	Isaiah 61:10–63:9

Italics are for Sephardi Minhag.

2009, Sept. 19–Oct. 18] TISHRI (30 DAYS) [5770

Civil Date	Day of the Week	Jewish Date	SABBATHS, FESTIVALS, FASTS	PENTATEUCHAL READING	PROPHETICAL READING
Sept. 19	Sa	Tishri 1	Rosh Ha-shanah, first day	Gen. 21:1–34 Num. 29:1–6	I Samuel 1:1–2:10
20	S	2	Rosh Ha-shanah, second day	Gen. 22:1–24 Num. 29:1–6	Jeremiah 31:2–20
21	M	3	Fast of Gedaliah	Exod. 32:11–14 Exod. 34:1–10 (morning and afternoon)	Isaiah 55:6–56:8 (afternoon only)
26	Sa	8	Ha'azinu (Shabbat Shuvah)	Deut. 32:1–52	Hosea 14:2–10 Micah 7:18–20 Joel 2:15–27 *Hosea 14:2–10* *Micah 7:18–20*
28	M	10	Yom Kippur	Morning: Levit. 16:1–34 Num. 29:7–11 Afternoon: Levit. 18:1–30	Isaiah 57:14–58:14 Afternoon: Jonah 1:1–4:11 Micah 7:18–20
Oct. 3	Sa	15	Sukkot, first day	Levit. 22:26–23:44 Num. 29:12–16	Zechariah 14:1–21
4	S	16	Sukkot, second day	Levit. 22:26–23:44 Num. 29:12–16	I Kings 8:2–21
5–8	M–Th	17–20	Ḥol Ha-mo'ed, first to fourth days	M: Num. 29:17–25 T: Num. 29:20–28 W: Num. 29:23–31 Th: Num. 29:26–34	
9	F	21	Hosha'na' Rabbah	Num. 29:26–34	
10	Sa	22	Shemini 'Aẓeret	Deut. 14:22–16:17 Num. 29:35–30:1	I Kings 8:54–66
11	S	23	Simḥat Torah	Deut. 33:1–34:12 Gen. 1:1–2:3 Num. 29:35–30:1	Joshua 1:1–18 *Joshua 1:1–9*
17	Sa	29	Be-re'shit	Gen. 1:1–6:8	Isaiah 42:5–43:10 *Isaiah 42:5–21*
18	S	30	New Moon, first day	Num. 28: 1–15	

Italics are for Sephardi Minhag.

2009, Oct. 19–Nov. 17] ḤESHWAN (30 DAYS) [5770

Civil Date	Day of the Week	Jewish Date	SABBATHS, FESTIVALS, FASTS	PENTATEUCHAL READING	PROPHETICAL READING
Oct. 19	M	Ḥeshwan 1	New Moon, second day	Num. 28:1–15	
24	Sa	6	Noaḥ	Gen. 6:9–11:32	Isaiah 54:1–55:5 *Isaiah 54:1–10*
31	Sa	13	Lekh lekha	Gen. 12:1–17:27	Isaiah 40:27–41:16
Dec. 7	Sa	20	Wa-yera'	Gen. 18:1–22:24	II Kings 4:1–37 *II Kings 4:1–23*
14	Sa	27	Ḥayye Sarah	Gen. 23:1–25:18	I Kings 1:1–31
17	T	30	New Moon, first day	Num. 28:1–15	

Italics are for Sephardi Minhag.

2009 Nov. 18–Dec. 17] KISLEW (30 DAYS) [5770

Civil Date	Day of the Week	Jewish Date	SABBATHS, FESTIVALS, FASTS	PENTATEUCHAL READING	PROPHETICAL READING
Nov. 18	W	Kislew 1	New Moon, second day	Num. 28:1–15	
21	Sa	4	Toledot	Gen. 25:19–28:9	Malachi 1:1–2:7
28	Sa	11	Wa-yeẓe	Gen. 28:10–32:3	Hosea 12:13–14:10
Dec. 5	Sa	18	Wa-yishlaḥ	Gen. 32:4–36:43	Hosea 11:7–12:12 *Obadiah 1:1–21*
12	Sa	25	Wa-yeshev, Ḥanukkah, first day	Gen. 37:1–40:23 Num. 7:1–17	Zechariah 2:14–4:7
13–16	S–W	26–29	Ḥanukkah, second to fifth days	S: Num. 7:18–29 M: Num 7:24–35 T: Num. 7:30–41 W: Num. 7:36–47	
17	Th	30	Ḥanukkah, sixth day, New Moon, first day	Num. 28:1–15 Num. 7:42–47	

Italics are for Sephardi Minhag.

2009, Dec. 18–Jan. 15, 2010] ṬEVET (29 DAYS) [5770

Civil Date	Day of the Week	Jewish Date	SABBATHS, FESTIVALS, FASTS	PENTATEUCHAL READING	PROPHETICAL READING
Dec. 18	F	Ṭevet 1	Ḥanukkah, seventh day; New Moon, second day	Num. 28:1–15 Num. 7:48–53	
19	Sa	2	Mi-ḳeẓ; Ḥanukkah, eighth day	Gen. 41:1–44:17 Num. 7:54–8:4	I Kings 7:40–50
26	Sa	9	Wa-yiggash	Gen. 44:18–47:27	Ezekiel 37:15–28
27	S	10	Fast of 10th of Tevet	Exod. 32:11–14 Exod. 34:1–10 (morning and afternoon)	Isaiah 55:6–56:8 (afternoon only)
Jan. 2	Sa	16	Wa-yeḥi	Gen. 47:28–50:26	I Kings 2:1–12
9	Sa	23	Shemot	Exod. 1:1–6:1	Isaiah 27:6–28:13 Isaiah 29:22–23 *Jeremiah 1:1–2:3*

Italics are for Sephardi Minhag.

Index